10

‖‖ ‖‖‖‖‖‖‖‖‖‖‖‖‖‖‖ ‖‖‖
**W9-AEE-371**

# Poetry
# Criticism

# Guide to Gale Literary Criticism Series

| For criticism on | Consult these Gale series |
|---|---|
| Authors now living or who died after December 31, 1999 | **CONTEMPORARY LITERARY CRITICISM (CLC)** |
| Authors who died between 1900 and 1999 | **TWENTIETH-CENTURY LITERARY CRITICISM (TCLC)** |
| Authors who died between 1800 and 1899 | **NINETEENTH-CENTURY LITERATURE CRITICISM (NCLC)** |
| Authors who died between 1400 and 1799 | **LITERATURE CRITICISM FROM 1400 TO 1800 (LC)**<br><br>**SHAKESPEAREAN CRITICISM (SC)** |
| Authors who died before 1400 | **CLASSICAL AND MEDIEVAL LITERATURE CRITICISM (CMLC)** |
| Authors of books for children and young adults | **CHILDREN'S LITERATURE REVIEW (CLR)** |
| Dramatists | **DRAMA CRITICISM (DC)** |
| Poets | **POETRY CRITICISM (PC)** |
| Short story writers | **SHORT STORY CRITICISM (SSC)** |
| Literary topics and movements | **HARLEM RENAISSANCE: A GALE CRITICAL COMPANION (HR)**<br><br>**THE BEAT GENERATION: A GALE CRITICAL COMPANION (BG)**<br><br>**FEMINISM IN LITERATURE: A GALE CRITICAL COMPANION (FL)**<br><br>**GOTHIC LITERATURE: A GALE CRITICAL COMPANION (GL)** |
| Asian American writers of the last two hundred years | **ASIAN AMERICAN LITERATURE (AAL)** |
| Black writers of the past two hundred years | **BLACK LITERATURE CRITICISM (BLC)**<br><br>**BLACK LITERATURE CRITICISM SUPPLEMENT (BLCS)** |
| Hispanic writers of the late nineteenth and twentieth centuries | **HISPANIC LITERATURE CRITICISM (HLC)**<br><br>**HISPANIC LITERATURE CRITICISM SUPPLEMENT (HLCS)** |
| Native North American writers and orators of the eighteenth, nineteenth, and twentieth centuries | **NATIVE NORTH AMERICAN LITERATURE (NNAL)** |
| Major authors from the Renaissance to the present | **WORLD LITERATURE CRITICISM, 1500 TO THE PRESENT (WLC)**<br><br>**WORLD LITERATURE CRITICISM SUPPLEMENT (WLCS)** |

ISSN 1052-4851

# Poetry Criticism

*Excerpts from Criticism of the Works of the Most Significant and Widely Studied Poets of World Literature*

## Volume 103

*Michelle Lee*
Project Editor

GALE
CENGAGE Learning

Detroit • New York • San Francisco • New Haven, Conn • Waterville, Maine • London

GALE
CENGAGE Learning

**Poetry Criticism, Vol. 103**

Project Editor: Michelle Lee

Editorial: Dana Barnes, Kathy D. Darrow, Kristen Dorsch, Jeffrey W. Hunter, Jelena O. Krstović, Thomas J. Schoenberg, Lawrence J. Trudeau

Content Conversion: Katrina D. Coach, Gwen Tucker

Indexing Services: Factiva, Inc.

Rights and Acquisitions: Margaret Abendroth, Jacqueline Flowers, and Sari Gordon

Composition and Electronic Capture: Gary Leach

Manufacturing: Rhonda Dover

Product Manager: Janet Witalec

For product information and technology assistance, contact us at **Gale Customer Support, 1-800-877-4253.**
For permission to use material from this text or product, submit all requests online at **www.cengage.com/permissions.**
Further permissions questions can be emailed to **permissionrequest@cengage.com**

While every effort has been made to ensure the reliability of the information presented in this publication, Gale, a part of Cengage Learning, does not guarantee the accuracy of the data contained herein. Gale accepts no payment for listing; and inclusion in the publication of any organization, agency, institution, publication, service, or individual does not imply endorsement of the editors or publisher. Errors brought to the attention of the publisher and verified to the satisfaction of the publisher will be corrected in future editions.

*Gale*
27500 Drake Rd.
Farmington Hills, MI, 48331-3535

LIBRARY OF CONGRESS CATALOG CARD NUMBER 81-640179

ISBN-13: 978-1-4144-4758-2
ISBN-10: 1-4144-4758-2

ISSN 1052-4851

Printed in the United States of America
1 2 3 4 5 6 7 14 13 12 11 10

# Contents

# Preface

*P*oetry Criticism (PC) presents significant criticism of the world's greatest poets and provides supplementary biographical and bibliographical material to guide the interested reader to a greater understanding of the genre and its creators. Although major poets and literary movements are covered in such Gale Literary Criticism series as *Contemporary Literary Criticism* (CLC), *Twentieth-Century Literary Criticism* (TCLC), *Nineteenth-Century Literature Criticism* (NCLC), *Literature Criticism from 1400 to 1800* (LC), and *Classical and Medieval Literature Criticism* (CMLC), PC offers more focused attention on poetry than is possible in the broader, survey-oriented entries on writers in these Gale series. Students, teachers, librarians, and researchers will find that the generous excerpts and supplementary material provided by *PC* supply them with the vital information needed to write a term paper on poetic technique, to examine a poet's most prominent themes, or to lead a poetry discussion group.

## Scope of the Series

*PC* is designed to serve as an introduction to major poets of all eras and nationalities. Since these authors have inspired a great deal of relevant critical material, *PC* is necessarily selective, and the editors have chosen the most important published criticism to aid readers and students in their research. Each author entry presents a historical survey of the critical response to that author's work. The length of an entry is intended to reflect the amount of critical attention the author has received from critics writing in English and from foreign critics in translation. Every attempt has been made to identify and include the most significant essays on each author's work. In order to provide these important critical pieces, the editors sometimes reprint essays that have appeared elsewhere in Gale's Literary Criticism Series. Such duplication, however, never exceeds twenty percent of a *PC* volume.

## Organization of the Book

Each *PC* entry consists of the following elements:

- The **Author Heading** cites the name under which the author most commonly wrote, followed by birth and death dates. Also located here are any name variations under which an author wrote, including transliterated forms for authors whose native languages use nonroman alphabets. If the author wrote consistently under a pseudonym, the pseudonym will be listed in the author heading and the author's actual name given in parenthesis on the first line of the biographical and critical introduction. Uncertain birth or death dates are indicated by question marks. Single-work entries are preceded by the title of the work and its date of publication.

- The **Introduction** contains background information that introduces the reader to the author and the critical debates surrounding his or her work.

- The list of **Principal Works** is ordered chronologically by date of first publication and lists the most important works by the author. The first section comprises poetry collections and book-length poems. The second section gives information on other major works by the author. For foreign authors, the editors have provided original foreign-language publication information and have selected what are considered the best and most complete English-language editions of their works.

- Reprinted **Criticism** is arranged chronologically in each entry to provide a useful perspective on changes in critical evaluation over time. All individual titles of poems and poetry collections by the author featured in the entry are printed in boldface type. The critic's name and the date of composition or publication of the critical work are given at the beginning of each piece of criticism. Unsigned criticism is preceded by the title of the source in which it appeared. Footnotes are reprinted at the end of each essay or excerpt. In the case of excerpted criticism, only those footnotes that pertain to the excerpted texts are included.

- Critical essays are prefaced by brief **Annotations** explicating each piece.

- A complete **Bibliographical Citation** of the original essay or book precedes each piece of criticism.

- An annotated bibliography of **Further Reading** appears at the end of each entry and suggests resources for additional study. In some cases, significant essays for which the editors could not obtain reprint rights are included here. Boxed material following the further reading list provides references to other biographical and critical sources on the author in series published by Gale.

## Cumulative Indexes

A **Cumulative Author Index** lists all of the authors that appear in a wide variety of reference sources published by Gale, including *PC*. A complete list of these sources is found facing the first page of the Author Index. The index also includes birth and death dates and cross references between pseudonyms and actual names.

A **Cumulative Nationality Index** lists all authors featured in *PC* by nationality, followed by the number of the *PC* volume in which their entry appears.

A **Cumulative Title Index** lists in alphabetical order all individual poems, book-length poems, and collection titles contained in the *PC* series. Titles of poetry collections and separately published poems are printed in italics, while titles of individual poems are printed in roman type with quotation marks. Each title is followed by the author's last name and corresponding volume and page numbers where commentary on the work is located. English-language translations of original foreign-language titles are cross-referenced to the foreign titles so that all references to discussion of a work are combined in one listing.

## Citing *Poetry Criticism*

When citing criticism reprinted in the Literary Criticism Series, students should provide complete bibliographic information so that the cited essay can be located in the original print or electronic source. Students who quote directly from reprinted criticism may use any accepted bibliographic format, such as University of Chicago Press style or Modern Language Association (MLA) style. Both the MLA and the University of Chicago formats are acceptable and recognized as being the current standards for citations. It is important, however, to choose one format for all citations; do not mix the two formats within a list of citations.

The examples below follow recommendations for preparing a bibliography set forth in *The Chicago Manual of Style,* 14th ed. (Chicago: The University of Chicago Press, 1993); the first example pertains to material drawn from periodicals, the second to material reprinted from books:

Linkin, Harriet Kramer. "The Language of Speakers in *Songs of Innocence and of Experience.*" *Romanticism Past and Present* 10, no. 2 (summer 1986): 5-24. Reprinted in *Poetry Criticism.* Vol. 63, edited by Michelle Lee, 79-88. Detroit: Thomson Gale, 2005.

Glen, Heather. "Blake's Criticism of Moral Thinking in *Songs of Innocence and of Experience."* In *Interpreting Blake,* edited by Michael Phillips, 32-69. Cambridge: Cambridge University Press, 1978. Reprinted in *Poetry Criticism.* Vol. 63, edited by Michelle Lee, 34-51. Detroit: Thomson Gale, 2005.

## Suggestions are Welcome

Readers who wish to suggest new features, topics, or authors to appear in future volumes, or who have other suggestions or comments are cordially invited to call, write, or fax the Associate Product Manager:

Product Manager, Literary Criticism Series
Gale
27500 Drake Road
Farmington Hills, MI 48331-3535
1-800-347-4253 (GALE)
Fax: 248-699-8054

# Acknowledgments

The editors wish to thank the copyright holders of the criticism included in this volume and the permissions managers of many book and magazine publishing companies for assisting us in securing reproduction rights. Following is a list of the copyright holders who have granted us permission to reproduce material in this volume of *PC*. Every effort has been made to trace copyright, but if omissions have been made, please let us know.

## COPYRIGHTED MATERIAL IN *PC*, VOLUME 103, WAS REPRODUCED FROM THE FOLLOWING PERIODICALS:

*American Poetry Review*, v. 28, March/April 1999 for "A Certain Slant of Sunlight" by Alice Notley; v. 37, September/October 2008 for "A Complicated Muse" by Aram Saroyan. Copyright © 2008 by World Poetry, Inc. Reproduced by permission of the author.—*Arnoldian*, v. 13, winter, 1985/86. Reproduced by permission.—*Chicago Review*, v. 52, autumn, 2006. Copyright © 2006 by *Chicago Review*. Reproduced by permission.—*Contemporary Literature*, v. 38, winter, 1997. Copyright © 1997 by the Board of Regents of the University of Wisconsin System. Reproduced by permission.—*Durham University Journal*, v. 69, June 1977; v. 84, January 1992. Both reproduced by permission.—*Genders*, no. 2, summer, 1988 for "'A Veil of Ice between My Heart and the Fire': Michelangelo's Sexual Identity and Early Modern Constructs of Homosexuality" by James Saslow. Copyright © 1988 by the University of Texas Press. All rights reserved. Reproduced by permission of the University of Texas Press and the author.—*Harvard Review*, 2006. Copyright © 2006 by *Harvard Review*. Reproduced by permission.—*Italian Quarterly*, v. 40, winter-spring, 2003. Copyright © 2003 by *Italian Quarterly*. Reproduced by permission.—*Italica*, v. 45, June, 1968; v. 74, autumn, 1997. Copyright © 1968, 1997 by the American Association of Teachers of Italian. Both reproduced by permission.—*Kenyon Review*, v. 17, spring, 1995 for "Among Lovers, Among Friends" by Sue Russell. Copyright © 1995 by Kenyon College. All rights reserved. Reproduced by permission of the author.—*Literary Review*, v. 48, summer, 2005 for "The New York School Poets: B Is for Berrigan" by Mark Hillringhouse. Reproduced by permission of the author.—*MLN*, v. 117, January, 2002. Copyright © 2002 by the Johns Hopkins University Press. Reproduced by permission.—*Nation*, January 23, 2006. Copyright © 2006 by The Nation Magazine/The Nation Company, Inc. Reproduced by permission.—*Neophilologus*, v. 67, October, 1983 for "Michelangelo's Revelatory Epitaphs" by Ann H. Hallock. Reproduced by permission of the author.—*New Literary History*, v. 24, summer, 1993. Copyright © 1993 by the Johns Hopkins University Press. Reproduced by permission.—*Nineteenth-Century Literature*, v. 58, March, 2004 for "'A Relation, Oh Bliss! Unto Others': Heterosexuality and the Ordered Liberties of *The Bothie of Toper-Na-Fuosich*" by Christopher Matthews. Copyright © 2004 by the Regents of the University of California. Reproduced by permission of the publisher and the author.—*Parnassus: Poetry in Review*, v. 21, winter, 1995 for "That Awkward Grace" by Eric Murphy Selinger. Copyright © 1995 by Poetry in Review Foundation, NY. Reproduced by permission of the publisher and the author.—*Philological Quarterly*, v. 77, fall, 1998. Copyright © 1998 by the University of Iowa. Reproduced by permission.—*Quaderni D'Italianistica*, v. 19, 1998. Reproduced by permission.—*Romanische Forschungen*, v. 102, 1990. Reproduced by permission.—*Romanticism*, v. 14, 2008. Copyright © by Edinburgh University Press Ltd. 2008. Reproduced by permission.—*South Atlantic Bulletin*, v. 42, November, 1977. Copyright © 1977 by the South Atlantic Modern Language Association. Reproduced by permission.—*Studies in English Literature 1500-1900*, v. 46, autumn, 2006. Copyright © 2006 by the Johns Hopkins University Press. Reproduced by permission.—*Studies in Philology*, v. 62, April, 1965. Copyright © 1965 by the University of North Carolina Press. Used by permission.—*Victorian Newsletter*, spring, 1992 for "New Light on Arthur Hugh Clough's Eight-Year Poetic Silence" by Janice E. Keller. Reproduced by permission of the *Victorian Newsletter*; spring, 1992 for "Waiting for Thou: Resurrecting Clough's 'Seven Sonnets'" by Robert Johnson. Reproduced by permission of the *Victorian Newsletter.*—*Victorian Poetry*, v. 42, winter, 2004. Copyright © by West Virginia University, 2004. Reproduced by permission.—*World Literature Today*, v. 80, November/December, 2006. Copyright © 2006 by *World Literature Today*. Reproduced by permission of the publisher.—*Yearbook of English Studies*, v. 36, 2006. Copyright © by Modern Humanities Research Association, 2006. Reproduced by permission of the publisher.

## COPYRIGHTED MATERIAL IN *PC*, VOLUME 103, WAS REPRODUCED FROM THE FOLLOWING BOOKS:

Cambon, Glauco. From *Michelangelo's Poetry: Fury of Form*. Princeton University Press, 1985. Copyright © 1985 by Princeton University Press. Reproduced by permission.—Clements, Robert J. From *The Poetry of Michelangelo*. New

# Gale Literature Product Advisory Board

The members of the Gale Literature Product Advisory Board—reference librarians from public and academic library systems—represent a cross-section of our customer base and offer a variety of informed perspectives on both the presentation and content of our literature products. Advisory board members assess and define such quality issues as the relevance, currency, and usefulness of the author coverage, critical content, and literary topics included in our series; evaluate the layout, presentation, and general quality of our printed volumes; provide feedback on the criteria used for selecting authors and topics covered in our series; provide suggestions for potential enhancements to our series; identify any gaps in our coverage of authors or literary topics, recommending authors or topics for inclusion; analyze the appropriateness of our content and presentation for various user audiences, such as high school students, undergraduates, graduate students, librarians, and educators; and offer feedback on any proposed changes/enhancements to our series. We wish to thank the following advisors for their advice throughout the year.

# Ted Berrigan
## 1934-1983

(Full name Edmund Joseph Michael Berrigan, Jr.) American poet, playwright, novelist, and critic.

## INTRODUCTION

Berrigan was an experimental poet whose influences include the writers of the Beat Generation as well as the artists of the American Expressionist movement. He is often associated with the New York School of Poetry, and is known for overturning formal conventions and rearranging the lines of earlier poems, both his own and those of other poets.

## BIOGRAPHICAL INFORMATION

The eldest of three children, Berrigan was born in Providence, Rhode Island, on November 15, 1934, into a working class Roman Catholic family. His parents were Margaret Dugan and Edmund Berrigan, an engineer. Berrigan attended the local high school and then spent a year at Providence College, but did poorly and left in 1954 to enlist in the army. He served in a non-combat position in Korea for sixteen months and was then stationed in Tulsa, Oklahoma. When his three-year service commitment ended, Berrigan enrolled at the University of Tulsa on the G.I. Bill, earning a B.A. in 1959 and an M.A. three years later. In 1960 Berrigan, unhappy with what he considered the elitist literary community in Tulsa, moved to New York; two years later he married Sandra Alper, with whom he had two children, David and Kate. Separated from his first wife, he began seeing poet Alice Notley whom he married in 1971; the couple had two sons, Anselm and Edmund. Berrigan lived on the Lower East Side in New York where he was active in the local poetry community and worked at a variety of odd jobs, among them writing papers for undergraduates at Columbia University. He served as editor of "C," a Greenwich Village mimeographed magazine that was devoted to the work of neighborhood artists and writers, and in 1966-67 taught poetry at the St. Mark's Art Project. He served as visiting professor at the University of Iowa in 1968-69 and at Essex University in 1973-74; he also taught at a number of other colleges and universities including Yale, the University of Michigan, and the City College of New York. Berrigan's amphetamine use and poor diet, consisting mostly of Pepsi, Twinkies, and hamburgers, contributed to his overall ill health during the 1960s and 1970s. In 1975 he contracted hepatitis and refused treatment for his condition. His health continued to deteriorate over the years, and he died on July 4, 1983, at the age of forty-eight. He was buried in the military cemetery in Riverhead, Long Island.

## MAJOR WORKS

Berrigan's first publication was *A Lily for My Love: 13 Poems,* which appeared in 1959. His first collection to attract critical attention was *The Sonnets,* published by "C" Press in 1964 and then reprinted by Grove Press two years later. The volume earned Berrigan the Poetry Foundation Award in 1964. The sixty-six poems in the collection are primarily comprised of lines from other sonnets, his own and those of other poets from Shakespeare to Frank O'Hara. It was described by Berrigan as "an homage to myself." His next work, a collaboration with poet Ron Padgett and artist Joe Brainard, was titled *Bean Spasms* (1967) and contains numerous allusions to various literary and mythological sources.

Much of Berrigan's work was privately published by "C" Press and other small presses. His poetry volumes throughout the late sixties and seventies include *Many Happy Returns* (1969), *In the Early Morning Rain* (1970), *Red Wagon: Poems* (1976)—which contains some of his best work according to a number of critics—and *Nothing for You* (1977). In 1980 Berrigan published *So Going Around Cities: New and Selected Poems, 1958-1979.* His last book of poems was *A Certain Slant of Sunlight,* written in 1982, but unpublished until 1988. The work consisted of short poems originally written on blank postcards, which obviously limited the length of each poem. They range from one or two line poems to the longest, at thirty-one lines, and most "tend to be composed of units of information . . . or bits of language suggestive of emotional states, happenstance, philosophy, reflectiveness," according to reviewer Alice Notley. In 1994 Aram Saroyan edited and published *Selected Poems* and in 2005, Notley, along with her two sons by Berrigan, produced *The Collected Poems of Ted Berrigan,* a well-received assemblage that includes numerous poems never before published as well as a number of early poems that had been out of print for many years.

## CRITICAL RECEPTION

Berrigan's poetry from the 1960s, particularly the award-winning *Sonnets,* received mixed reviews. Tony Lopez (see Further Reading) describes the work as an "inventive appropriation of the sonnet sequence" and a "textual collage-recycling of various found materials." Lopez compares Berrigan's poetry to the combinations of high art and pop culture being produced by artists such as Andy Warhol and Robert Rauschenberg. Eric Murphy Selinger calls Berrigan's sonnets "a cut-and-paste collage of new material, earlier work, translations from Rilke, Michaux, and Rimbaud, and lines clipped from Ashbery, O'Hara, and Shakespeare." Other critics, however, were not as kind and considered much of his early work jumbled and overly sentimental. Sue Russell complains that Berrigan's sonnets are characterized by "sonorous repetitions, oddball allusions, and elegiac overtones." Jordan Davis calls Berrigan's process in producing the sonnets "plagiarism-as-homage" and sees the work "as a courtly exercise in personal canon formation." According to Davis, "Berrigan was a nimble thief who found new uses for the lines and processes he stole."

By the time *Selected Poems* appeared in 1994, Berrigan's reputation had faded considerably. Based on her reading of the volume, Russell believes Berrigan's legacy is that of "a poet who could not legitimately be called great but who seldom failed to be interesting, both in his work and life." She is, however, put off by his inclusion of various famous males in his poetry, but notes that "women are either absent or represented as bed partners and dinner-makers." Libbie Rifkin has studied Berrigan's career and concludes that even at its height, Berrigan was a "decidedly minor" poet, although she concedes that "among the more consecrated avant-garde poets of his generation, Berrigan made an early and lasting impression." Among his admirers was his friend Mark Hillringhouse, who explains that Berrigan's "method of constructing a poem was to write down personal memories, take lines from newspapers, quote what other people said in conversation, or to tear apart other poets' poems he admired, to turn the lines around and insert his in between theirs then erase them, leaving his own lines intact." Despite this unconventional method of composition, Berrigan's poems are "very deliberate," according to Notley, his wife and editor. "They have a graven quality as if they were drawn on the page, word by word," she contends; she further praises the "remarkable . . . range of tones of voice" in her late husband's poetry. John Palattella, in his review of *The Collected Poems* reports that Berrigan was able to stay true to his working class background while navigating the sophisticated Manhattan poetry scene headlined by a number of prominent Harvard graduates and praises the poet for "balancing cockiness and composure, grit and grace." William Doreski contends that Berrigan's later work is characterized by fragmentation to the point that at least one poem "simply collects quotations." He finds the late poems "more restless and chameleon-like" than the earlier material, but praises the publication of the 2005 volume of collected works so that "Berrigan can now receive the full reading this imperfect but serious artist deserves."

# PRINCIPAL WORKS

## Poetry

*A Lily for My Love: 13 Poems* 1959
*The Sonnets* 1964
*Bean Spasms* [with Ron Padgett and Joe Brainard] (poetry and art) 1967
*Many Happy Returns* 1969
*In the Early Morning Rain* 1970
*The Drunken Boat* 1974
*A Feeling for Leaving* 1975
*Red Wagon: Poems* 1976
*Nothing for You* 1977
*So Going Around Cities: New and Selected Poems, 1958-1979* 1980
*In a Blue River* 1981
*The Morning Line* 1982
*A Certain Slant of Sunlight* 1988
*Selected Poems* [edited by Aram Saroyan] 1994
*The Collected Poems of Ted Berrigan* [edited by Alice Notley with Anselm Berrigan and Edmund Berrigan] 2005

## Other Major Works

*Galileo: Or Finksville* (play) 1959
*Seventeen* [with Ron Padgett] (plays) 1965
*Clear the Range* (novel) 1977
*On the Level Everyday: Selected Talks on Poetry and the Art of Living* [edited by Joel Lewis] (criticism) 1997

# CRITICISM

### Eric Murphy Selinger (essay date winter 1995)

SOURCE: Selinger, Eric Murphy. "That Awkward Grace." *Parnassus: Poetry in Review* 21, nos. 1 & 2 (winter 1995): 298-324.

[*In the following excerpt, Selinger reviews the poetry from the 1994 collection* Selected Poems, *which covers Berrigan's work from* The Sonnets *through* So Going Around Cities.]

Halfway through Alice Notley's new *Selected Poems*—both in length and in emotional trajectory—lies a wry domestic sequence, "Waltzing Matilda." Its protagonist has her hands full. Her writing isn't going well, she complains engagingly, since "the words aren't jostling each other glitteringly in a certain way & they all have referents I think if that is a trouble." Her little boy, meanwhile, has a fever. Whenever her poem gets into a down and dirty Ovidian groove, he throws up, or begs to be tucked back into bed. ("Real-life juxtapositions are the most tasteless," she sighs.) As for her husband, also a poet—well, he's yelled at her, but nothing that makes sense, which leaves her more puzzled than hurt. "He has always in the past been excessively careful with words," she writes to The Adviser. "We both read L=A=N=G=U=A=G=E magazine." They make up, make love, go to poetry readings, wake up "hungover / & chagrined." "I see little difference between you & your husband," The Adviser shrugs in response. "You're both big and awkward sentimental truthtelling fuck-ups." As for all that referential writing? "Buy yourself a Fischer-Price Activity Center, some glue and scissors etc. & get on with it all."

"Waltzing Matilda" first caught my eye as a snapshot of the Berrigan-Notley household: a lucky, productive *ménage* that lasted from 1971 until Berrigan's death in 1983. I've come to suspect its cheerfully fractured self-portrait. (Both poets are more furtive than they appear.) But The Adviser's comments yield a helpful headnote to their work. On the one hand, Berrigan and Notley love to come across as "big and awkward sentimental truthtelling fuckups," affable, benign, endearing, blithe. So what if The Adviser goes on a word too long, bobbling his crisp, predictable "get on with it"? As in baseball, an error here and there keeps you awake. And yet, as they invite you to dote on their work not *despite* the occasional miscue, but *because* of it, they also insist you treat them as artists, "excessively careful with words." "Ted was ceaselessly interested in what you might call technique," Notley writes in her introduction to the new *Selected* Berrigan; he "probably talked about it more than any poet or academician in America." "Technically, she is impeccable, & / If She is clumsy in places, those are clumsy places," Berrigan returns the compliment. That stumble wasn't just a sign of life; it was a deliberate aesthetic gesture, a quick impasto swipe that calls your attention to the "jostle" of paint on the canvas—and, a moment later, to the hand that held the brush.

The risks of this approach are obvious. You don't have to read far into either Selected to find work that steps on your toes or nudges your elbow, calling you a killjoy if you don't grin back. Such poems can try your patience, whether for the jitter and clutter of their verbal surface or the baldness of their sentiment. (To get the pleasure of these poets you need a sweet tooth, and an

appetite. "I like to use a lot of words," says Berrigan; and Notley calls her muse "that blabbermouth.") At their best, though, the twinborn personae invoked in "Waltzing Matilda" team up in a comic and appealing *pas de deux*. The sentimental truthteller saves the craftsman from pretension—the sort you'd find in (let's be wicked) L=A=N=G=U=A=G=E magazine. The artist bails the fuckup out of bathos. You can wear your heart on your sleeve, they reassure each other, as long as you wear your art there, too. Leaning together for balance, they make their way from line to line, in the dance that Berrigan once called "that awkward grace."

If Berrigan and Notley simply kept asking "Can I do *this* in a poem?" their work would be entertaining, even to a formalist like me. Not a goal to be sniffed at. ("Can entertainment have ceased to be a value in poetry?" Notley wonders in her Introduction to Berrigan—a question worth asking, expecially of "experimental" poets.) But as I acquired a taste for their work—Notley charmed and impressed me more quickly, I'll confess—I was struck by how that "Can I do *this?*" grows out of a more searching, savory root. "Can *I* do this in a poem?" Berrigan wonders: I, a "bumpkin with a master's degree," as he saw himself on his arrival in New York. "Can *I* do this," asks Notley: I, a woman determined to write in the "Mainstream American Tradition" of Williams and O'Hara while still "a slave, well mildly, to a baby." Although I will have less time than I'd like to speak of Notley's recent work—she's turned her back on playfulness, out for epic game—I want to trace the different ways each poet "gets on with it all." Cutting and pasting, Activity Centers writ large, they turn initial worry into awkwardly graceful art.

"To me," said Berrigan in 1970, "it's an incredible achievement that I could write a poem." Born into a working-class Irish Catholic family in Providence, Rhode Island, in the Depression, Berrigan grew up in a world he loved, but felt estranged from. "I never told anyone what I knew," he would recall in **"Cranston Near the City Line,"** "Which was that it wasn't / for anyone else what it was for me." He kept those mixed feelings alive in the varied diction of his work, sometimes delicate, touched by hesitant detail—"one chipped glass Scottie; an eggshell teacup & saucer, tiny, / fragile, but with sturdy handle; a gazelle?"—sometimes brusque and selfconsciously masculine: "The piano was black. My eyes were brown. I had rosy / cheeks, every sonofabitch in the world said. I never saw them" (**"Cranston Near the City Line"**). In **"Last Poem"** he conjures two totemic objects from his earliest memory: "a glass slipper & a helpless blue rose." They peg him as, at heart, a Cinderella, forced to scrap and scrape to get along, waiting for escape and transformation. Hence, perhaps, the dream announced in **"Personal Poem #9"**:

> I think I was thinking
> when I was ahead I'd be somewhere like Perry Street

erudite dazzling slim and badly-loved
contemplating my new book of poetry
to be printed in simple type on old brown paper
feminine marvelous and tough

The poet's O'Hara-like ideal self, "erudite dazzling slim," contrasts with the more sentimental description of his ideal poem, "simple type on old brown paper / feminine marvelous and tough." The latter hits closer to home.

Berrigan attended Providence College briefly, did poorly, dropped out. He joined the army, served in Korea, then went back to school in Tulsa, Oklahoma. In his genial short memoir of love and resistance, *Ted,* Ron Padgett recalls that Berrigan was "somewhat cowed" by the poets and artists he met in Tulsa. They were "scornful, elitist, atheistic, and angst-ridden": hardly the model or community for a man inclined to be exuberant, populist, enthusiastic, and religious in the gentle, sometimes mawkish way of another former altar-boy, Jack Kerouac. The "I" of Berrigan's later work gets "high on poems, or pills" primarily to regain his "simple awe that loveliness exists" (**"Words for Love"**) and to affirm his status as a man "ordained to praise / In ordinary places" (**"Heloise"**). Poems by Frank O'Hara and the Beats gave him an alternative, more temperamentally appropriate model for what it meant to be an artist: not just "Strolling, sassy, dashing, brilliant!" (**"Sandy's Sunday Best"**) but "completely interested" (**"Frank O'Hara"**).

At the end of 1960 Berrigan left Tulsa for New York City "to become this wonderful poet, to become a poet," as he put it twenty years on. This mix of braggadocio ("to become this wonderful poet") and more reflective ambition ("to become a poet") suggests the hope and insecurity that spurs his work from those days—an emotional mix equally evident in the note he sent returning his Tulsa University M.A. diploma, "Dear Sirs: I am the master of no art." "How many times I heard Ted describe himself as a bumpkin, socially inept, unsophisticated," Padgett muses. If he was "cowed" by the coolness of Tulsa poets, he was still more "cowed" by the artists he met in New York, whose "dazzlingly witty conversation," writes Padgett, "made him feel cloddish. A combat boot among ballet slippers." To feel himself a poet, a *real* poet, he needed both to be confirmed by others and to achieve a relationship to art other than that vexed ideal of mastery. Consider **"Hearts,"** an early sonnet sadly cut out of the Penguin *Selected*: "At last I'm a real poet," it begins, excitedly:

I've written a
ballade a sonnet a poem in spontaneous
prose and even a personal poem   I can use
punctuation or not and it doesn't even
matter      I'm obscure when I feel like it
especially in my dream poems which I never even

call   Dream Poem   but from sheer cussedness title
Match Game Etc. (for Dick Gallup) or something like
  that

For example, take this poem, I don't know how
to end it, It needs six lines to make it a sonnet, I
could just forget it and play hearts with Joe and
Pat and Dick, but lately I'm always lethargic,
and I don't even like hearts, or Pat, or Joe, or
Dick or / and especially myself, & this is no help.

Like the singer of the sixties' Motown hit "Do You Love Me (Now that I can Dance)?" Berrigan's "I" shouts "Watch me now!" He wants us to cheer him as he does the Ballade, the Personal Poem, the Mashed Potato, the Twist, a little scared that we'll say "no" when he asks, *Do you like it like this?*

I don't mean naively to equate this speaker with the poet. In the Author's Note to *So Going Around Cities,* a New and Selected collection that Berrigan edited in 1980, he says that his ambition has been to create "a character named *I.*" I believe him. But the systole and diastole of **"Hearts"** capture the extremes that Berrigan's work always pulses between: the love of poetic forms and genres and "tricks" for their own sake, as things to *do,* and the fears of solitude, ineptitude, and lethargy that all this *doing* aims to assuage. Berrigan's "Things to Do" poems enact this movement from lassitude to action, or the reverse. **"Things to Do in Providence"** thus starts out flat, words scattered glumly on the page: "Sit / watch TV / draw blanks / swallow / pepsi / meatballs." It kicks into high gear as the "character named *I*" decides to "give [himself] the needle," and four packed pages of conversation, musings, amusements, and finally peacefulness follow. **"Things to Do in Anne's Room,"** by contrast, starts by strutting a Williams three-step across the page—"Walk right in / sit right down / baby, let your hair hang down"—only to dwindle to a fetal curl: "get into the bed / be alone / suffocate / don't die / / & it's that easy." Writing poems usually breaks the "character named *I*" of his sullen mood, especially when he can turn to the reader, the "you," for reassurance. This turn, straight out of *Calamus,* makes for some of Berrigan's most winning moments. At the end of **"Many Happy Returns"** he finds himself "about to be / born again thinking of you"; and in **"Ann Arbor Song,"** a bantering, burlesqued, and somewhat corny poem listing things that will never happen again, he promises his reader that "you'll find me right here, when you come through, again." Such confessions of a faith in being read certify what's come before as written by a "real poet." The poem's value, and more important, the *poet*'s, are both guaranteed by the exchange.

The poems that earned Berrigan the reading he longed for, both from older New American Poets and from himself, were *The Sonnets.* Written in a flurry, sometimes several a day, these poems are a cut-and-paste collage of new material, earlier work, translations from Rilke, Michaux, and Rimbaud, and lines clipped from Ashbery, O'Hara, and Shakespeare. At times they exhibit Berrigan's earlier anxieties, as at the end of **Sonnet LXXV,** where the "character named *I*" is a boy playing a losing game of pin-the-tail-on-the-modern: "looking for today with tail-pin. I / never place it right, never win." This time, however, he can say that "It / doesn't matter," since "The cooling wind keeps blow- / ing and my poems are coming." That the sonnets kept coming, despite interruptions, freed the poet of his worry over being the master of an art. "I wasn't trying to be the master of that form," Berrigan later recalled, "I was just trying to write my works and the form made itself available to me, in fact it forced itself upon me."

Berrigan credited his interest in collage not only to the usual avant-garde suspects (Cage, Burroughs), but also to T. S. Eliot, whose *Waste Land* he "fell in love" with when he returned to school. When the "he" of *The Sonnets* does the police in different voices, of course, the clash between grand allusion and garrulous demotic does not signal a cultural decline. It's meant, instead, to exorcise the ghosts of aesthetic pretension, as when **Sonnet IV** begins by quoting Rilke ("Lord, it is time. Summer was very great") only to turn simply silly: "All sweetly spoke to her of me / about your feet, so delicate, and yet double E!!" I'm no Tulsa intellectual snob, such lines proclaim—but I'm no Tulsa bumpkin, either. The most telling allusion comes in the final sonnet. Now that the "aery charm" of making *The Sonnets* is finished, he writes, "I'll break / My staff bury it certain fathoms in the earth / And deeper than did ever plummet sound / I'll drown my book. / It is 5:15 a.m. Dear Chris, hello." Unlike the end of **"Hearts,"** where the private game of art proved an inadequate substitute for the communal game of hearts, the **"Final Sonnet"** mounts an allusive, masterful performance by disowning mastery and turning to the presumably smaller accomplishments of the social. Since even that final gesture is accomplished in words familiar from earlier sonnets, the last line seems as much a *da capo* as a coda. It foreshadows Berrigan's later interest in occasional poems, poems on postcards, "personal poems" in the Frank O'Hara style: poems as convivial as they are "constructivist." As soon as it was published in 1964, Berrigan mailed copies of *The Sonnets* to poets he admired: Dear Creeley, hello; Dear Aiken, hello. (Padgett quotes Aiken's urbane response: "Thanks for sending me your book, which is fun, I think, but not quite my cup of Mescal.")

Perhaps to end with that genial "Dear Chris, hello," the Penguin *Selected* saves its selection of *The Sonnets* for last. This is, I think, a mistake. The poet rightly saw these poems as a turning point in his career: his "first and last adolescent work," he agrees when Clark

Coolidge suggests the phrase, but also a substantial achievement, after which he felt "a tremendous desire to be slight." Read in chronological order, many of the poems that follow seem an effort to keep in motion, to see what can be done now that one's "book," as if dictated by magic, has been written and drowned. Can I bring the torque and unpredictability native to the collage of *The Sonnets,* Berrigan asks, into a longer and lighter, not to say "slighter," work? Can I pack the speed and looseness of the longer "field" poems into a single bulky, even balky stanza? Can I build a poem worth rereading out of chewy mouth-music and layered non-sequiturs (**"An Orange Clock"**), or do I need to air it out with rhymes and a cheery address to a dedicatee (**"So Going Around Cities"**)?

"If you're the kind of person who thinks that everything a poet writes should be perfect," Padgett warns, "then yes, Ted wrote too much. But that was his job, to write. And even the lesser works always have some purpose; he liked to experiment, try out new moves, new tones, and new shifts of tone." Is it our "job" to read such works? Should they be included in a *Selected*? Padgett's answer would probably be *yes*. To sift them out is to belie the poet's faith that writing was, in Padgett's words, "something you did when you read the sports page or ate a donut. It was something you did when you sat at your desk and thought about the gods. It was something you did with scissors and Elmer's glue." It is also to mask the formal achievement of the poems where the new moves and tones suddenly seem instinctive, effortless. By the time you've read fifty-some pages into the *Selected Poems,* for example, you've heard Berrigan experiment with the rhyming and clashing "hits between words" that build up a poem's "surface," watched him stretch out on the page in **"Bean Spasms"** and **"Tambourine Life,"** and noted his increasing facility with poems that make themselves up as they go along, enacting the discoveries and shifting moods (often the growing relief) of their composition. Some of these poems, like **"Things to Do in Anne's Room,"** are already accomplished work; others, like **"February Air,"** seem successful labtests, their results yet to be tested on more demanding emotional terrain. Then you reach **"Peace,"** a delicate poem elbowed out of anthologies by the flash and glitter of *The Sonnets*. It starts with the question behind so much of Berrigan's work: *What to do?*

> What to do
>       when the days' heavy heart
>               having risen, late
> in the already darkening East
>         & prepared at any moment, to sink
>              into the West
> surprises suddenly,
>       & settles, for a time,
>          at a lovely place
> where mellow light spreads

evenly
                    from face to face?

When Berrigan chats with Tom Clark about "that awkward grace," this is the poem they have before them. He has his eyes on vowels at first: open *ehs,* various *as,* "settling" eventually into a self-conscious, soothing rhyme. Next he plays with pace, rushing and slowing his lines, tossing in an awkwardly inverted simile, threading his beads first on one set of rhymes, then another, then a third:

> The days' usual aggressive
>                    contrary beat
>                              now softly dropped
> into a regular pace
>                    the head riding gently its personal place
> where pistons feel like legs
>                    on feelings met like lace.
>                                        Why,
> take a walk, then,
>                    across this town. It's a pleasure
> to meet one certain person you've been counting on
>                              to take your measure
> who will smile, & love you, sweetly, at your leisure.
>                                        And if
> she turns your head around
>                    like any other man,
>                              go home
> and make yourself a sandwich
>                    of toasted bread, & ham
>                              with butter,
> lots of it
>                    & have a diet cola
>                              & sit down
> & write this,
>                    because you can.

One of Berrigan's least strenuous and most accomplished poems, **"Peace"** makes a small, believable claim about the pleasures of making and proves it, expertly. The poem makes no bid for broader mastery; indeed, the little stumbles of "the head riding gently its personal place" (as opposed to its impersonal one?) and "she turns your head around / like any other man" (*she*'s like any other man? your head is?) seem designed to lower expectations, keep it all casual. They set up, by contrast, the last lines' quiet faith.

My favorite poems by Berrigan share with **"Peace"** a counterpoint of sentiment and surface. Aram Saroyan seems to agree; or, at least, he finds such poems the best way into Berrigan's work. He opens the Penguin *Selected* with **"Words for Love,"** the poem where Berrigan declares himself "in love with poetry." Love means you tally lists of words and names, and let the "minute detail" that "fills [you] up" fill up your poems, even if the clock is a little off. (Somehow it's 2 o'clock in Houston when it's 12:10 in New York.) Love commands that you scuff the surface of your work through twists of diction, cantilevered rhymes, and spotlit repeti-

tions of sound. "I go my / myriad ways blundering," Berrigan declares, breaking the line so that you say, "my, my, indeed you do." Saroyan follows this with **"Personal Poem #9,"** the "feminine marvelous and tough" poem I quoted a few pages ago, and then the gentle New York pastoral **"For You,"** dedicated to James Schuyler—a poem that wages this tug of war between formal device and emotional appeal to good effect:

> New York's lovely weather hurts my forehead
> here where clean snow is sitting, wetly
> round my ears, as hand-in-glove and
> head-to-head with Joe, I go reeling
> up First Avenue to Klein's. Christmas
> is sexy there. We feel soft sweaters
> and plump ruffled skirts we'd like to try.
> It was gloomy being broke today, and baffled
> in love: Love, why do you always take my heart
>      away?
> But then the soft snow came sweetly falling down
> and head in the clouds, feet soaked in mush
> I rushed hatless into the white and shining air
> glad to find release in heaven's care.

Some readers will find more "mush" here than they'd like, especially in the last five lines. I find the pun of "hand-in-glove," the play between "Klein's" and Christmas, the double-sense of "plump" as adjective and verb, and the mannered, nagging, burlesqued repetitions of sound throughout this almost-sonnet piquant enough to balance the sweetness. And, to be honest, I prefer Berrigan at his more "feminine," trying on the skirt of sentiment, to the giddier, self-interrupting poet who writes so much of *The Sonnets,* **"Bean Spasms,"** and **"Tambourine Life."**

In Berrigan's later work, the question is no longer "what to do" but "how long do I have to do it?" Several of his strongest, most memorable poems were written in his last six years—in *So Going Around Cities,* the earlier New and Selected, you find them in the section entitled "Not Dying." It's odd to read these poems in the Penguin *Selected,* with nearly a third of the book still safely tucked under your right thumb, but it's exhilarating to see the poet's gift for brag, there from his earliest poems, suddenly take root and blossom. "I am 43," he writes in **"Red Shift"**: "When will I die? I will never die. I will live / To be 110 & I will never go away, & you will never escape from me" since "I'm only pronouns, & I am all of them, & I didn't ask for this / You did." Such lines give a newly self-questioning spin to the poet's turns to "you" for reassurance; they make me wish that **"Living with Chris"** had been included, with its earlier tragicomic final question: "For god's sake, is there anyone out there listening?") The Monday morning editor in me wants to slip **"Red Shift"** into a closing cadence, and to close the book with Berrigan's **"Last Poem."**

Measured and assured, **"Last Poem"** glances back to memories of the "glass slipper & helpless blue rose," mulls over how the poet "verbalized [himself] a place / in Society. 101 St. Mark's Place, apt. 12A, NYC 10009." It also includes enough awkwardness to shake you out of any easy elegiac mood. (I can come up with four good reasons why the line "I once had the honor of meeting Beckett & I dug him" isn't a pratfall, starting with the reference, a line before it, to "several new vocabularies," but I'm not sure I believe them.) Unlike the **"Final Sonnet,"** which calls on Shakespeare to stage its farewell, **"Last Poem"** seems an authentically Prosperian moment: a poem where "what strength I have's my own." That Berrigan envisions himself dying while writing, finding his words, sums up his faith in poetic *doing*; that he claims to have died while "next to you in bed" suggests how far he's come from the social and artistic anxieties of **"Hearts."** Of the poems that follow in the *Selected,* at least until you get to *The Sonnets,* one is tender, one is funny, and three are slight, stabs at new moves and new tones. None makes as fitting an ending as this:

> The pills kept me going, until now. Love, & work,
> Were my great happinesses, that other people die the
>         source
> Of my great, terrible, & inarticulate one grief. In my
>         time
> I grew tall & huge of frame, obviously possessed
> Of a disconnected head, I had a perfect heart. The end
> Came quickly & completely without pain, one quiet
>         night as I
> Was sitting, writing, next to you in bed, words chosen
>         randomly
> From a tired brain, it, like them, suitable, & fitting.
> Let none regret my end who called me friend.

## Sue Russell (essay date spring 1995)

SOURCE: Russell, Sue. "Among Lovers, Among Friends." *Kenyon Review* 17, no. 2 (spring 1995): 147-53.

[*In the following review of Berrigan's* Selected Poems, *introduced by the poet's second wife Alice Notley, Russell contends that Berrigan's work is interesting, but not necessarily as great as Notley believed it to be. Russell was especially disappointed in* The Sonnets, *which Notley claimed was "obviously a masterpiece."*]

Who is Ted Berrigan, anyway? More than one poetry-literate friend of mine, on hearing that I was assigned to review Berrigan's **Selected Poems,** said, "Yeah, one of the Berrigan brothers *did* write poetry," to which I responded more than once, "No, that's Daniel. *This* Berrigan is not related."

My only prior knowledge of *this* Berrigan came from the recent biography of Frank O'Hara by Brad Gooch, in which Berrigan appears as an occasional hanger-on and index item, a peripheral player in the New York scene of the sixties. As Gooch recounts, "Ted Berrigan, a young poet from Tulsa, Oklahoma, who sent his first fan letter in the fall of 1961, used to stand on Avenue A staring up patiently at O'Hara's apartment before they ever met" (399).

This new collection, with its cover blurbs by Allen Ginsberg and Robert Creeley and introduction by Berrigan's second wife, the poet Alice Notley, casts him in a more central role. After reading the "selected poems," I was left with an impression of a poet who could not legitimately be called great but who seldom failed to be interesting, both in his work and life. As the editor of the early "zine" *C,* mimeographed on legal-sized paper in a Greenwich Village bookstore, he published the work of his fellow New York poets, along with what Notley refers to as "glorious black and white covers" by the artist, Joe Brainard. Notley remarks as well on Berrigan's sense of irony about being a part of an acclaimed school of poets: "Ted used to tell people that he was in charge of the New York School and that anyone could join it if they paid him five dollars—at some point ten for inflation; no one ever joined this way" (x).

I read Notley's introduction with great interest once before I read the poems and then several times after. Her remarks, subjective as they might be, provided a touchstone against which I could test my own response. For instance, Notley quotes Berrigan as saying, "I like my poems to have a surface the way a painting does," and the poems do have surface, but at times surface seems to be all they have. It is hard to get inside them, to get beyond the veneer of odd connections, names, and lifted quotes. Often it seems that Berrigan is aiming for the spontaneity of O'Hara's "I do this, I do that" poems, but forced spontaneity is a contradiction in terms.

Overall, however, O'Hara's continued importance for Berrigan is not necessarily a sign of weakness, nor should it be taken lightly. O'Hara's influence on Berrigan and others had as much to do with the crystallization of a distinctly urban voice as with the talent of a particular man. Even poets not likely to be grouped with the New York School invoke this voice as a means to establish an openness of diction that might not otherwise be accessible within their range.

O'Hara's influence can also be seen in Berrigan's dedication to poetry as a vocation, although Berrigan lived most of his writerly life without a day job like that of O'Hara with the Museum of Modern Art. He earned a small income as an itinerant poet, giving readings and leading workshops at a far range of places, including Yale, the University of Essex in England, and Naropa Institute. According to Notley, Berrigan liked to say that being a poet was a twenty-four-hour-a-day job. To his way of thinking, a poet's sole occupation should be poetry.

It would seem that a fair portion of his nonwriting time was spent collecting potential material through day-to-day interactions with friends and random acquaintances. Constant references to second generation New York poets like Ron Padgett and Dick Gallup, along with Joe Brainard, suffuse the poems with a spirit of generous collaboration and affection. On the other hand, the insistent use of such references and inside jokes can make the reader feel like an intruder on an unfamiliar scene.

Moreover, it is sometimes difficult to tell from the words on the page when Berrigan is making fun of poetic affectation and when he is simply being affected. I often tried to imagine the poems being read, or more likely *performed,* to get a sense of their impact. Nonetheless, there is an inescapable element of playfulness in Berrigan's writing that can be infectious. As Notley mentions, "Ted worked on . . . being friendly" in his poems, and that friendliness comes through in much of his work, not only through the overlay of allusions but also in their generally social tone. Berrigan appears to have been on friendly terms with "great literature" as well. He quotes Donne and Shakespeare with much the same casual attitude as he does his drinking buddies, which does not mean they are any the less exalted.

Paradoxically, *The Sonnets,* which Notley deems "obviously a masterpiece," are among my least favorite poems in the volume. With their sonorous repetitions, oddball allusions (Ford Madox Ford rubs shoulders with Benedict Arnold), and elegiac overtones, these small poems seem to be aiming for a cumulative effect similar to that of Berryman's *Dream Songs,* but they collapse under the weight of the exercise. What's missing here is a conversational thread to pull the pieces together. The lack of a characterizable voice makes the poems seem oddly inert.

More attractive to me is a poem like **"Things to Do in Providence,"** about a visit to Berrigan's family home, which takes the familiar convention of the list poem and bounces it around the page to great effect:

                              Crash
    Take Valium                    Sleep

              Dream &,

                        forget it.

                    *

    Wake up new & strange

                    displaced,

                              at home.

    Read The Providence Evening Bulletin

        No one you knew
                    got married
                    had children
                    got divorced
                    died

        got born

            tho many familiar names flicker &
                        disappear.

                              (62)

Less attractive, though true to its time, is the tendency toward masculine posturing evidenced within the poems. A lively parade of historically familiar male names (Apollinaire, Tzara, Rimbaud, Nijinsky, Juan Gris . . .) play cameo roles, along with notable friends of the period, but women are either absent or represented as bed partners and dinner-makers. It is not surprising that Notley refers to her husband's characterization of a "heroic age" which occurred before their marriage. She paraphrases Berrigan's sentiment: ". . . surely the giants were gone, and by his definition I wasn't one" (x). It did not escape Berrigan that a large number of his cultural heroes were homosexual. In fact, he displayed an odd tendency to make a point of his own heterosexuality, as if the social mores had reversed themselves. One example of this swaggering gesture occurs in **"Dinner at George & Katie Schneeman's,"** where "heterosexual intercourse" adds to the atmosphere of general debauchery:

    She was pretty swacked by the time she
    Put the spaghetti & meatballs into the orgy pasta
        bowl—There was mixed salt & pepper in the
    "Tittie-tweak" pasta bowl—We drank some dago red
        from glazed girlie demi-tasse cups—after
    which we engaged in heterosexual intercourse . . .

                              (100)

Berrigan died in 1983 of liver disease at the age of forty-eight. Sometime earlier, he provided his own epitaph in **"Last Poem":**

                              . . . Love & work
    Were my great happinesses, that other people die the
        source
    Of my great, terrible & inarticulate one grief. In my
        time
    I grew tall & huge of frame, obviously possessed
    Of a disconnected head, I had a perfect heart. The end
    Came quickly & completely without pain, one quiet
        night as I
    Was sitting, writing, next to you in bed, words chosen
        randomly

From a tired brain, it, like them, suitable & fitting.
Let none regret my end who call me friend.

(95)

But the body of Berrigan's work is a reminder that this "great and terrible" grief was, in fact, articulate, in poem after poem, made perhaps less "terrible" through the machinations of his "perfect heart."

## Libbie Rifkin (essay date winter 1997)

SOURCE: Rifkin, Libbie. "'Worrying about Making It': Ted Berrigan's Social Poetics." *Contemporary Literature* 38, no. 4 (winter 1997): 640-72.

[*In the following essay, Rifkin discusses Berrigan's efforts at promoting, legitimating, and mythologizing his own poetic career in his writings, with particular attention to* The Sonnets *and his work as editor of "C" magazine.*]

From its position of relative obscurity in the hazy canon of 1960s experimental poetry, Ted Berrigan's **The Sonnets** mounts an assault on its scholarly future:

> *"The academy*
> *of the future*
> *is opening its doors"*
>
> —*John Ashbery*

The academy of the future is opening its doors
my dream a crumpled horn
Under the blue sky the big earth is floating into "The
   Poems."
"A fruitful vista, this, our South," laughs Andrew to
   his Pa.
But his rough woe slithers o'er the land.
Ford Madox Ford is not a dream. The farm
was the family farm. On the real farm
I understood "The Poems."
      Red-faced and romping in the wind, I, too,
am reading the technical journals. The only travelled
   sea
that I still dream of
is a cold black pond, where once
on a fragrant evening fraught with sadness
I launched a boat frail as a butterfly.

(*The Sonnets* 62)

**Sonnet LXXIV** appeals simultaneously to two distinct audiences: to the disinterested reader, this poem offers itself as a "ready-made," ideal for consumption within the terms of postmodernism, but undisciplined and probably not very good. Within the first few lines one can say something about citation, repetition, and pastiche, quite efficiently characterize the volume's approach to both literary history and poetic form, and move on. From the avant-garde insider, however, the poem demands a closer reading. If one knows Berrigan's biography, or knew Berrigan, the apparently nonsensical splicings are narratable in personal terms; tracking down the poem's many references is a worthwhile exercise in nostalgia, or at least sociology.[1] But one needn't have been there to get the jokes. The poem produces its own insiders by adhering to the first principle of comedy, repetition-with-a-difference. Reciting the epigraph, the first line takes it literally, inflecting the Ashberian middle voice with an obviously inappropriate declamatory tone. Lines 6-8 function similarly: "The farm / was the family farm. On the real farm / I understood 'The Poems'" begins with a bad imitation of confessionalism and then retrospectively takes itself seriously; the words remain stolidly the same while the poem works through a series of shifts in tonal context. **Sonnet LXXIV** becomes a kind of user's guide to literary parody.

Hailing a variety of professionally invested readerships, Berrigan's work makes visible the contours of the literary field in its contemporary moment and, presciently, in ours. Reading it is an experience in reflexivity, as revealing of the critic as it is of the poet. But does cultural savvy translate into cultural value? Does positing an audience actually produce one? Can a poet do as Frank O'Hara says in "Personism: A Manifesto" and make it on "nerve" (498) alone?

\* \* \*

"I came to New York to become this wonderful poet, . . . and I was to be very serious. Not to become but to be. . . . That only took about a year and a half, then I wrote this major work and there I was" (Pritikin 20). In the scores of interviews and talks he gave between the 1967 publication of his debut book, **The Sonnets,** and his death in 1983, Ted Berrigan recounts the beginnings of his poetic career in this way; he compresses the bildungsroman's developmental narrative until it yields the immediacy of the "star-is-born" story. Berrigan's working-class high artist is a pop persona—part ingenue, part impresario. This essay traces this model of the poetic career through **The Sonnets** and Berrigan's little magazine "C" and into the avant-garde art worlds where he sought to be both an innovator and an institutional force—a producer not only of poetic collages but of poetic coteries. The double positioning readable in these two works emblematizes the predicament of a postwar avant-garde ambitiously laying the institutional groundwork for its own posterity. Like many of the poets in his cohort, Berrigan's formal experiments are best understood through their social aims and effects. In what follows, I analyze the sonnet sequence and the little magazine as, in Pierre Bourdieu's terms, "position-takings" on the cultural field. But I depart from Bourdieu in focusing my analysis on the way cultural value is created and contested by an individual actor—a largely unknown poet playing the field in an attempt to produce a self-legitimating career. Gauging the pressures of the role he lived on the works he made, and showing how the works contributed to fashioning that role, I begin to articulate the intersection of individual ambition and collective production, a space where the chiasmic formulations of literary biography have living, human consequence.

Berrigan claimed that he "used the sonnet sequence to be my big jump into poetry and stardom, as it were" (*Talking* [*Talking in Tranquility: Interviews with Ted Berrigan*] 160). For most readers, the closing qualification rings truer than the initial bravado. Perhaps no other contemporary poet better illustrates the relativity of stardom, the multiple constellations in which poets rise to prominence. Official indicators of reputation—from commercial success to notice by major institutions of consecration—suggest that even at the height of his career, Berrigan's was decidedly minor.[2] Through introductory anthologies like Paul Carroll's *The Young American Poets* (1968), Ron Schreiber's *31 New American Poets* (1969), and a 1969 *Newsweek* article entitled "The Young Poets" (Junker), Berrigan achieved a modicum of mainstream renown in his lifetime, but always and only as a member of a generation, a school, or a scene. "Among O'Hara's followers" preceding his name more often than not, what canonical security Berrigan continues to enjoy is largely appositional; he's famous by association. As editor of *"C"* magazine and publisher of "C" press, he brought O'Hara, Ashbery, and James Schuyler together with Ron Padgett, Richard Gallup, and himself and, he claimed, founded the New York school of poets (*Talking* 90-91). Along with Anne Waldman, he launched the St. Mark's Poetry Project, still an organizing force in the New York poetry community.[3] A chronicler, publicist, and tireless talker, Berrigan lives on as an agent of literary history, rather than as a fixture within it.

And yet among the more consecrated avant-garde poets of his generation, Berrigan made an early and lasting impression. He was one of five "young" poets invited to read at the Berkeley Poetry Conference of 1965, an event of unprecedented size and heightened historical import for the "New American" poets. Virtually unknown, he made his entrance at age thirty-one as, in his words, "rookie of the year" and, with *The Sonnets,* achieved a kind of instant majority. He even spawned parodies: Robert Duncan wrote a poem at the conference entitled "At the Poetry Conference: Berkeley after the New York Style," which he described as "a Black Mountain / Berrigan imitation North Carolina / Lovely needed poem for O'Hara" (12). The timing was perfect for Berrigan's combination of individual bravura and imitative reverence. With its poetic of citation and collage, *The Sonnets* enacted on the level of rhetoric the self-canonizing maneuvers that were taking place at the

conference's readings, panel discussions, and, most of all, cocktail parties. Berrigan wrote himself into the institution of the avant-garde by anticipating the moment when the institutions around poetry fold back into poetry itself.[4]

\* \* \*

In the literary field, the degree to which any individual agent can calculate the terms of her or his own success is limited, extremely limited in Bourdieu's view. Bourdieu argues that sociopoetic acts, or "position-takings," "arise quasi-mechanically . . . from the relationship between positions . . . and being determined relationally, negatively, they may remain virtually empty, amounting to little more than a *parti pris* of refusal, difference, rupture" (59). In Bourdieu's analysis, the history of the field of restricted production emerges from the necessary struggle between artistic generations, the old guard and the new. The shape of the struggle, that is, its aesthetic manifestation, is mediated but not fully determined by the socioeconomic and cultural "dispositions" of the various actors involved. This is a vision of transhistoric artistic community as Newtonian battlefield; skirmishes are continuous and inevitable, but they are motored more by the "logic of action and reaction" than by individual desire or will (58).

Against this strange amalgam of economic determinism and avant-gardist revolutionism, Berrigan's communal model of influence appears benignly stagnant. The crown of "second generation" sat easily on Berrigan's head. Indeed, his poetry is so roomy, so full of other poets' names and lines, that it emerges as a kind of free-love alternative to traditional figurations of literary family as necessarily nuclear, claustrophobic, and oedipal. But Berrigan is also an ambitious poet in the line of Keats, whose wranglings with tradition and his own poethood tended more toward solipsism. In *Keats's Life of Allegory,* Marjorie Levinson calls Keats's poetic "masturbatory"—both passive and active, open and reflexive, somehow perpetually adolescent—and argues that it is a stylistic response to a largely class-based alienation from authority. Though Keats enjoys a secure canonicity in the twentieth century, Levinson reminds us of the harsh and personal criticism he suffered in his own time. Fellow poets found repugnant Keats's fetishistic relation to the props of poethood; Byron, for instance, reviled him for "frigging his *Imagination*" (18). That Keats anticipated such criticism in the sonnets on fame confirms the self-reflexiveness of which he is accused. Sonnet XIV, for instance, purports to sermonize about the dangers of self-promotion, but the baroque, sexually charged imagery with which the octet presents the problem of ambitious self-fashioning ("As if a Naiad, like a meddling elf, / Should darken her pure grot with muddy gloom") overshadows the prim lesson of the sestet. The poem ends inconclusively on a question: "Why then should man, teasing the world for grace, / Spoil his salvation for a fierce miscreed?" (469). For Keats, who began working with the then unpopular Shakespearean sonnet in a "Spirit of Outlawry" against first-generation Romantics, the answer lies in the form itself. The challenge of fully inhabiting the Shakespearean mold—not only rhyme scheme, but also metrical variation, cadence, and even rhetorical device—teases the poet into visions of bardic greatness. Indeed, Keats's experiments with the sonnet led directly to the development of his ode stanza and to a period of heightened productivity unparalleled in his brief career.

In seeking to launch himself into posterity via the sonnet sequence, Berrigan tries on not so much a model of poetic form signed by Shakespeare as a model of poetic career signed—at least for the purposes of twentieth-century poets—by Keats.[5] In typical collagist fashion, however, he cuts out the middleman. In a 1980 interview, Berrigan recalled the original impetus behind *The Sonnets*: "I thought something like, 'What do you do if you are a poet and you are just starting out, and you want to be big?' And, I mean, who was bigger than Shakespeare? . . . And I decided you wrote a sonnet sequence. So I wrote a sonnet sequence" (*Talking* 160). Here, Keats's labor of formal imitation and innovation disappears, leaving only the self-conscious ambition with which it was conducted. Setting out to make his name a "household name" as only a high lyric poet writing in the age of television advertising could, Berrigan stirs up the "pure grot" of tradition with the provocative brittleness of his claims for inclusion (*Sonnets* 69). Without making too much of a canonical mismatch, it seems fruitful to suggest that in his ambition, his fraught relation to poethood, the poetic he crafted, and the ambivalence with which he is received, Berrigan resembles Keats, whom he names "the baiter of bears who died / of lust" in **Sonnet LXXVII** (65). Like the earlier sonneteer, Berrigan's vocational self-fashioning often takes the form of an excessive sexuality; his poems engage the fantasy of both being and having the object of desire, in this case, a fully authorized poetic and social identity. The fact that Berrigan was aware of the Keats analogy and worked it—comedically—into his poetry is itself a Keatsian gesture. Like so many of his poetic identifications, Berrigan's approximation to his model is always only partial, and his failures—often quite conscientious—are as instructive as his successes. In the strong glare of Keats's career, Berrigan's is easily dwarfed. Aligning them throws the local vocational challenges of the 1960s New York scene into historical relief even as it makes the case for the poetic career as an overdetermined, reflexively literary phenomenon.

* * *

In a much-cited interview, William Carlos Williams remarked: "Forcing twentieth-century America into a

sonnet—gosh, how I hate sonnets—is like putting a crab into a square box. You've got to cut his legs off to make him fit. When you get through, you don't have a crab any more" (30). Berrigan began work on *The Sonnets* with Williams's moratorium on the form ringing in his ears. By the late fifties, Williams's influence was widespread, and his stance toward traditional form—as promoted by poets from Charles Olson to Robert Lowell—was becoming a kind of dogma. But the Doctor didn't so much pull the plug on the sonnet as pronounce it dead on arrival. In the first half of the century, committed practitioners of the form were limited to such marginalized modernists as E. E. Cummings, Edna St. Vincent Millay, Elinor Wylie, and Edward Arlington Robinson. After World War II, only Edwin Denby, known more as a dance critic than as a poet, and John Berryman, who withheld his sequence from publication until after *77 Dream Songs* won the Pulitzer Prize, took their places on the field as serious sonneteers. *Notebook,* Lowell's sequence of what he called "fourteen-line blank verse sections," came out several years after *The Sonnets.* Once considered de rigueur for poets with epic ambitions—indeed Williams himself wrote a number of imitation Keats sonnets early in his career—the sonnet had become a somewhat embarrassing place to stake one's poetic claim, more congenial for the already established poet than the initiate.

Williams died on March 4, 1963. Berrigan wrote the majority of his sequence in the three months that followed. Elegiac notes sound throughout the work. Paying tribute to the paterfamilias of one's prospective tradition in the form he most famously disdained would seem like a rebellious, even disrespectful way to enter the literary arena, but Berrigan's animus was not negative. Despite the obvious flouting of all but the most rudimentary of the sonnet's conventions—the numbered, boxed, usually fourteen-lined poems *look* like sonnets, but they don't rhyme; they aren't continuous; they don't conform to traditional argumentative structure—the primary impulse of the sequence is consolidation, not revolution. **Sonnet XV,** for instance, can be unscrambled by reading the lines in the order 1-14, 2-13, 3-12, and so on:[6]

In Joe Brainard's collage its white arrow
He is not in it, the hungry dead doctor
Of Marilyn Monroe, her white teeth white-
I am truly horribly upset because Marilyn
and ate King Korn popcorn," he wrote in his
of glass in Joe Brainard's collage
Doctor, but they say "I LOVE YOU"
and the sonnet is not dead.
takes the eyes away from the gray words,
*Diary.* The black heart beside the fifteen pieces
Monroe died, so I went to a matinee B-movie
washed by Joe's throbbing hands. "Today
What is in it is sixteen ripped pictures
does not point to William Carlos Williams.

(20)

The poem creates a kind of cocoon around the battle cry "and the sonnet is not dead," muffling it a little. For a work that claims not only to resurrect a dying poetic form by approximating a radical visual one, but also to immortalize such diverse cultural figures as Williams, Monroe, Brainard, and, implicitly, Berrigan, **Sonnet XV** is a halting, careful poem. Its workmanlike quality is the source of its affective success. The poet has constructed his shrine with an earnestness that runs counter to the kitschy pop imagery and the mechanistic form. In **Sonnet XV,** experimentalist virtuosity is mostly show, easily deciphered and forgotten; the poem works because in it, the "throbbing hands" of the poet seem almost palpable. Written within a year of the New York debut of Andy Warhol's *Marilyn* series, **Sonnet XV** gestures at pop elegy but resists its reveling in mechanical reproduction. Berrigan's poetic collage reproduces Brainard's visual one with an aching imprecision. Apostrophizing Williams and compelling the reader to repeat the mournful process of assembling a whole from fragments, it is closer to the elegiac tradition than might first appear.

This tension between pathos and procedure characterizes the poetic incongruities of the sequence as a whole. Despite the myriad commentaries on form that Berrigan supplied in interviews after its publication, **The Sonnets** is not primarily an experimentalist work. The compositional process combines elements of proceduralism and seriality: beginning with several imitations of Ashbery, Berrigan automatically excerpted lines into two sestets, then allowed the newly formed poem to generate the final couplet via semantic and acoustic association. Working in this way enabled him to develop the volume's characteristic rhythm; repetition of words and lines within individual poems and across the book as a whole produces a kind of "reverb"—a synthetic echo that interrupts the lyric voice whenever it threatens to extend into song. But Berrigan also maintained, "There's a deliberate parade into it—of the first twelve or so—and there's a deliberate parade out of about the last six or seven," suggesting at least the underlying armature of a linear order (*Talking* 51). Elsewhere, he claimed that the sequence was determined chronologically, a collaged diary of the three months in 1963 when it was composed (*Talking* 160). Pressed by admirers and students to theorize his debut work, Berrigan adduced a wide variety of metaphors for form—from "block" to "room" to "still life" to "field" to "voice" to "story." These figures stand in for a host of poetic agendas, a representative history of conceptions of form more reflective of the professionalized context of interpretation than the compositional process itself. The poems' rhetorical ruse is to already encompass this context, to deploy its formal experiments with the retrospective confidence of the literary interview.[7] The few critical accounts we have of the book take the bait; at least among avant-gardes, Berrigan registers as a formal innovator, a process-poet. But in spite of its internal incoherences, the book is at great pains to present itself as a singular aesthetic statement, and to present its poet as a force to be reckoned with.

Just how carefully wrought Berrigan's debut work is becomes apparent when we compare it to *"C"* magazine, which Berrigan conceived as a periodical workshop for the development of group poetics. **Sonnets I-VI** were originally published in the first number of *"C"*, alongside several other Berrigan poems, including an imitation of Ashbery's "Two Scenes" and an homage to Vladimir Mayakovsky. Unlike *The Sonnets,* which rarely cites its sources, **Sonnet I** here emerges as the culmination of an extended process of imitation and combination; virtually all of its lines appear in three of the five poems (including ones by other hands) that directly precede it in the magazine. The reader is encouraged to retrace the compositional steps from the Ashbery poem, to Berrigan's imitation of that poem, to the collaged sonnet. Ashbery's "Two Scenes" is not included, suggesting that it would (or should) be fresh in the minds of Berrigan's intended audience. Since I cannot assume such familiarity, and since *"C"* magazine is not readily available, I will reproduce the poems here—alternating between the original and the imitation. Ashbery's first stanza reads:

I

We see us as we truly behave:
From every corner comes a distinctive offering.
The train comes bearing joy;
The sparks it strikes illuminate the table.
Destiny guides the water-pilot, and it is destiny.
For long we hadn't heard so much news, such noise.
The day was warm and pleasant.
"We see you in your hair,
Air resting around the tips of mountains."

Berrigan's version proceeds:

I

I see myself upon the steps at night:
From every corner comes my motivation.
My book is architecture:
I cultivate it on the colonnade.
Hands point to a dim frieze, in the dark night.
Such sight has not been mine in many months.
Winds from the sky are piercing, and they pierce me.
I bend to my gaze,
Wind on the strictures like stars.

Ashbery's second stanza:

II

A fine rain anoints the canal machinery.
This is perhaps a day of general honesty
Without example in the world's history
Though the fumes are not of a singular authority

And indeed are dry as poverty.
Terrific units are on an old man
In the blue shadow of some paint cans
As laughing cadets say, "In the evening
Everything has a schedule, if you can find out what it
    is."

And Berrigan's:

II

A fragmentary music clears the room.
This is a night not without precedent
Recorded in journals whose sentiments
Weave among incidents
Colorless, tactile, and frequent.
Structure becomes a picture of poet and daughter
In sudden decline to frontiers
While the orchestra plays for its encore,
"Boris Alone On His Trail."

In his **"Two Scenes,"** Berrigan retains the syntax, punctuation, lineation, off-rhyme, and some of the language of Ashbery's poem, particularly the language of seeing and revealing around which the "scenes" are organized. But Berrigan replaces Ashbery's elusive "we" with his more aggressive "I." In line 2, the disembodied "offering" becomes "my motivation"; Berrigan turns Ashbery's exteriorized world inward, claims it for his own. As the opening poem in *Some Trees,* Ashbery's "Two Scenes" was daringly unmoored from reference, gesturing to various urban and industrial landscapes but rooted in none of them, and wafting instead on "hair" and "air," "fine rain" and "fumes." Berrigan gives his settings a sculptural solidity; "architecture" and "stricture" lend aural and imaginative structure to the winds that would vanish in Ashbery's evanescent universe. Taking up the theatrical register of "Two Scenes," Berrigan stages his version of the poem with set pieces, aesthetic ready-mades, not the least of which is Ashbery's poem itself.

The next two poems in *"C"*, **"Homage to Mayakofsky"** and **"It Is a Big Red House,"** derive most of their language from (Berrigan's) **"Two Scenes."** They thus extend the mechanism through which the source poem is altered and refined—processed—into the final poetic product. Ashbery's "Two Scenes" recedes, passes through imitation Mayakovsky, and finally reemerges in **Sonnet I** in the much diminished form of a tonal echo. "From every corner comes my motivation. / My book is architecture" and "A fragmentary music clears the room" combine to become "In the book of his music the corners have straightened." The two final lines of **Sonnet I,** "Wind giving presence to fragments" and "We are the sleeping fragments of his sky," emerge when "fragmentary music" is added to "Winds from the sky are piercing, and they pierce me" and "This is a night not without precedent." A charged lyric word like "presence," repeated and revamped numerous times

throughout *The Sonnets,* here originates as a derivation of "precedent"—a term closer to the quasi-bureaucratic diction of Ashbery's poem. Berrigan thus mobilizes Ashbery's techniques of verbal transformation—generating words metonymically out of shared sound values—in the service of returning Ashbery's rigorously antipoetic language to its lyrical "roots." In the final product, a few letters suggest an entirely different stance toward poetic subjectivity.

When **Sonnet I** is republished as the opening poem of the sequence, however, it appears without this sourcing machinery. Disjunctive and haunted by a sense of their previous poetic environments, the individual words and lines nevertheless form the opening poem of a sonnet sequence and demand to be read in that saturated literary context:

His piercing pince-nez. Some dim frieze
Hands point to a dim frieze, in the dark night.
In the book of his music the corners have straightened:
Which owe their presence to our sleeping hands.
The ox-blood from the hands which play
For fire for warmth for hands for growth
Is there room in the room that you room in?
Upon his structured tomb:
Still they mean something. For the dance
And the architecture.
Weave among incidents
May be portentous to him
We are the sleeping fragments of his sky,
Wind giving presence to fragments.

Though the opening line appears to refer more to the generative possibilities of the letters *i, e,* and *z* than to a particular subject or scene, the poem's repetitions quickly create a sense of internal consistency; self-reference takes the place of reference. We don't need to know that line 3 first appeared in **"Homage to Mayakofsky"** to deduce that "he" is a poet (if not the Poet), perhaps a dead poet, and certainly a figure of some creative power. The third person here opens the sequence under the sign of intertextuality, suggesting that the work depends on some other poet, that it is, primarily, "his." It thus sets forth the central tension of the sequence in classically literary terms; the problem of individuation, which emerges as a social problem later in *The Sonnets* and in the works that follow it, appears here as an invocation of tradition.

While Berrigan doesn't try with any degree of seriousness to build a future exegetical industry into his work, there is, in this first portentous poem in particular, an invitation to interpret; we can't simply let "sleeping fragments" lie. Heroic monumentality, shadowy indecision, and collage come together in the first line; the "dim frieze" is a vaguely Eliotic image of the literary tradition that may not, its dimness and indeterminacy suggest, be accessible to a poet whose individual talent is so easily obscured by his collaging of other poets' materials. "His piercing pince-nez" points suggestively to Olson's claim that in the *Cantos,* Pound drove through his material "by the beak of his ego," though here the phallic figure is a nose whose potency is undermined by its "pinced" condition (Olson 82). Throughout **The Sonnets,** Berrigan presents his inclusion in this illustrious brotherhood as a claim, a question, a joke, and, more aggressively, a challenge. In this first poem, it's also a kind of plea. "Is there room in the room that you room in" reads like an example from a handbook of English usage, showing the different meanings of the word "room"; it's an anxious demonstration of virtuosity, and an earnest request for inclusion. The insistent hands—inspired by Ashbery and Mayakovsky—point as well to Keats's "living hand," held toward and gladly accepted by the poet embarking on his career-making book. **Sonnet I** figures tradition doubly: it is stony and sepulchral, but also "warm and capable," even playful. "Piercing" gives way to a collaborative caress.

Berrigan claimed that "the first eight lines of each sonnet concern[ed] the notation of sensory data," while the last six were "more 'interior'" and metaphysical, and while this pattern doesn't hold for all of the poems in the sequence, it does provide one account of **Sonnet I**'s relatively tight organization (Lewis 150). Whereas the octave inundates the reader with a variety of semantically unrelated but sonically overlapping images, the sestet adopts a prophetic, universalizing tone. And though "Still they mean something. For the dance / And the architecture. / Weave among incidents" opens more questions than it resolves, it does gesture at the ordering potential of aesthetic activity, the capacity of art to shape fragments into structure. In this context, the final line reads as an invocation of inspiration, the wind that will awaken the "sleeping fragments" of the next eighty-seven poems. In it, we hear a hollowed, somewhat mechanical echo of the "pure serene" that Keats breathes in "On First Looking into Chapman's Homer," or the breath with which Wordsworth opens *The Prelude.*

The last sonnet in the sequence retrospectively reinforces the portentousness of the opening. Though it reverses the order of the octave and the sestet, **Sonnet LXXXVIII** follows a similar pattern; the opening six lines cull a series of disjunct images from the rest of the sequence, while the last eight appear to comment on and, in effect, to transcend them. Not surprisingly, **"A Final Sonnet"** meditates on the question of poetic immortality:

> How strange to be gone in a minute!    A man
> Signs a shovel and so he digs    Everything
> Turns into writing a name for a day
>                                         Someone
> is having a birthday and someone is getting
> married and someone is telling a joke    my dream

> a white tree    I dream of the code of the west
> But this rough magic I here abjure    and
> When I have required some heavenly music    which
>   even
>     now
> I do    to work mine end upon *their* senses
> That this aery charm is for    I'll break
> My staff    bury it certain fathoms in the earth
> And deeper than did ever plummet sound
> I'll drown my book.
> It is 5:15 a.m.                Dear Chris, hello.

Berrigan composed the first eighty-seven poems during a two-month period, and then spent another month casting about for the "door out of the sequence" (*Talking* 160). The kernel of **Sonnet LXXXVIII** occurred to him in rereading *The Tempest* on a bus ride from New York City to Providence, Rhode Island. Unlike the other ready-made texts, which—like the reference to Marcel Duchamp's *In Advance of a Broken Arm* in this poem—find their way into **The Sonnets** in much-fragmented or transmuted forms, the final lines of Prospero's penultimate speech are imported whole cloth into this poem. Most of the sonnets in the final third of the sequence are composed of recycled content from the first two-thirds of the book, creating a structure of anticipation. The citation from *The Tempest,* the only "new" material in **"A Final Sonnet,"** punctures this relatively hermetic environment, opening the sequence out into a broader realm of poetic possibility even as it signals—with one of the most famous swan songs in the language—its conclusion.

Prospero's speech marks the end of a poetic career—his own, and, indirectly, Shakespeare's. Why, then, does Berrigan give it such a prominent place in the volume intended to launch *his* career? In interviews and talks on the subject, Berrigan insisted that **The Sonnets** was "the finish of something, not the beginning," and that, completing it, he "gave up that way of writing" (Pritikin 22; *Talking* 161). A quick perusal of **So Going Around Cities,** the collected poems assembled five years before his death, suggests that this assessment is in many ways accurate. Excepting, most notably, the collaborations with Ron Padgett, Anselm Hollo, and Anne Waldman, the vast majority of the poetry that followed **The Sonnets** eschewed proceduralism and collage for more narrative, epistolary, or diaristic modes.

**"A Final Sonnet"** can be read as anticipating this development and commenting on it. Like many of the sonnets, and much of the work that would follow, **"A Final Sonnet"** is dedicated, though unlike most of Berrigan's works not to a recognizably literary recipient but simply to "Chris." Dedication had been a signature convention of the New York school for several years before O'Hara's "Personism: A Manifesto" half-mockingly founded a movement on the practice of "put[ting] the poem squarely between the poet and the person, Lucky Pierre style" (499). For Berrigan, it was one of many ways of "writing a name for a day," freighting a poem with human as well as verbal material in an effort, it seems, to rescue temporarily poem, recipient, and, by association, poet from oblivion. *The Sonnets* and later work employ different strategies to accomplish this aim: epigraphs by O'Hara and Ashbery, or tag lines that position a poem "after" or in "homage to" a relatively well known poet reveal just how public, impersonal, and frankly strategic "personism" could be. Borrowing strategies from first-generation New York poets, Berrigan explodes the fiction of their naiveté. He recognizes that a poet of experience in the O'Hara mold is first and foremost a Poet; the publicity of that role pervades even the most intimately intersubjective poetic scenarios. Dedicating **"A Final Sonnet"** to the unknown "Chris" is a less reflexive, more ingenuous gesture. Here, naming names keeps the poet immersed in the comedy of the quotidian. "Someone / is having a birthday and someone is getting / married and someone is telling a joke" condenses the subject range of this occasional poetic into its most basic elements.

What's missing from this list, most obviously, in a poem so otherwise elegiac, is "someone is dead." As Berrigan's second wife, the poet Alice Notley, suggests in her introduction to his posthumously published *Selected Poems,* "death as a theme, death and new birth, and the loomingness of his own death" became increasingly central to Berrigan's poetry from the mid-seventies on (x). It is central to *The Sonnets* as well, though often leavened with slapstick humor or patent falsehood: "Bearden is dead Gallup is dead Margie is dead" (66). In the 1969 poem **"People Who Died,"** Berrigan would make a sonnet of sorts out of a list of fourteen such "name[s] for a day," only in this poem, the deaths are real and they are delivered straight: "Frank. . . . Frank O'Hara . . . hit by a car on Fire Island, 1966. / Woody Guthrie . . . dead of Huntington's Chorea in 1968" (*So Going* 230). *The Sonnets* are notable, however, for the fact that the poet's death, conceived specifically in terms of a literary posterity, is already a concern. Dead poets populate the sequence. From Williams, "the hungry dead doctor," to Keats, the "baiter of bears who died / of lust," to Guillaume Apollinaire and Jacques Villon, who are, simply, dead, poets in *The Sonnets* are best known for their mortality. And Berrigan is no exception. As early as **Sonnet II,** his own epitaph emerges out of the collage: "Dear Margie, hello. It is 5:15 a.m. / dear Berrigan. He died / Back to books. I read."

*The Sonnets* thus anticipate a personal as well as a poetic end and, in so doing, make a bid for the ultimate endurance. Saying goodbye not only to the form that enabled him to embark on his first major project but also to the crowded, chaotic world of the living, Berrigan strives for majority in Eliot's sense; he produces his sequence as already a synecdoche for his entire oeu-vre and thus proleptically "implies a significant unity in his whole work" (Eliot 47). This is the double-consciousness of *The Sonnets*: full of dailiness, it is zeitgeist poetry that nevertheless attempts to evade the contemporary by pressing time until only the essential elements of the poetic career remain. It's "strange to be gone in a minute," but also preferable to a life of anonymous poverty, however congenial the company. For the poet impatient to be great, bohemia quickly loses its romance. The air is dank with aspiration:

> There is only off-white mescalin to be had
> Anne is writing poems to me and worrying about
>   "making it"
> and Ron is writing poems and worrying about "mak-
>   ing it"
> and Pat is worrying but not working on anything
> and Gude is worrying about his sex life
> It is 1959 and I am waiting for the mail
>
>                                                   (40)

There's a persistent sense in *The Sonnets* that writing poetry of communal experience is something to do while waiting, for the mail, or—more ominously—for posterity to distinguish the "I" from Anne and Ron and Pat and Gude. It seems worth noting that the experience Berrigan records in these poems is often falsified, or at least puréed by the cut-up procedure until it is no longer organically autobiographical. Treating even his own life as a "ready-made," the poet anticipates an afterlife on the bookshelves and syllabi of secure canonicity.

**Sonnet LXXXVIII** thus pits the occasional against the artifactual in a test of endurance. Prospero drowns his book, but Shakespeare lives on, and so, Berrigan hopes, would he. The last line of the poem, "It is 5:15 a.m. Dear Chris, hello," suggests that this kind of survival comes at the cost of immediacy. Telling the time, an O'Haraism that Berrigan often used to kick start a poem in the urgency of a moment, here concludes the sequence on a somewhat uneasy note. Recycled throughout *The Sonnets,* "it is 5:15 a.m." comes paradoxically to designate timelessness even as it gestures toward a new day and another occasion for poetry. Time, written and reiterated in *The Sonnets,* proves itself to be something that it is not, in two very different senses: it becomes a fragment in the spatialized collage system, and an allegorical sign—a marker of its own passing. In the former, Berrigan takes a kind of experimentalist glee; he has developed a sonnet-machine which, if he keeps the gears oiled, will pump out infinite poetic product. But the mournful note that sounds in each obsessive iteration of the time undercuts triumphant proceduralism. Geoff Ward has suggested that in O'Hara, accumulated names and times form a kind of group symbol, a "humanist refuge against temporality, seeking by the mutual support of its members to stave off the negative impact of time on each individual subject" (61). O'Hara's struggle to beat time at its own game "by ingesting and acknowledging certain of its powers" in his occasional poetic is ironic but also earnest; his playfulness is underwritten by "the-will-to believe, in friendship, in art" (60, 62).

In *The Sonnets,* "writing a name for a day" and then shuffling it through the already heavily populated poetic deck represents one response to this problematic. The mechanistic form generates poems against mutability, but its success has the mildly sour taste of a kind of Faustian bargain: submitting to procedure, the poet simply preempts time's mortifying effects. He gets to define the terms in which, inevitably, "[a] hard core is 'formed'" (66). The irony of this situation is not lost on the poet of *The Sonnets,* but, in the flush of inspiration, it is temporarily ignored. In Berrigan's first work, the fact that "The poem upon the page / will not kneel for everything comes to it" fascinates and excites the poet, who is confident in the capacities of his form to shape and contain, comfortable with the balance of power between his art and his life. "The cooling wind keeps blow- / ing and my poems are coming," Berrigan writes in **Sonnet LXXV,** one of the several poems he composed prior to the conception of the sequence. *The Sonnets* are motivated by the fiction that the poet *chooses* to become, as he put it, "the instrument of the technique"; formal mastery and a certain relinquishing of agency are not mutually exclusive (*Talking* 77). *The Sonnets* entrusts the poet's fate to the fate of his words with great good cheer. Monumental, self-elegizing gestures are often coupled with comedic ones, as in **Sonnet LXXXVII,** in which "These sonnets are a homage to / King Ubu" preemptively undercuts "These sonnets are a homage to myself."

**Sonnet XXXVI,** one of the more narrative poems from the middle of the sequence, brings the conflict between personal, communal, and aesthetic endurance into sharp thematic focus. Berrigan republished this poem as **"Personal Poem #9"** in his 1969 collection *Many Happy Returns*; within *The Sonnets* it prefigures his later mode. When the poem first appeared in the second number of *"C",* the dedication read "Homage to Frank O'Hara." In **"Personal Poem #9,"** the tag line disappears entirely. Here, "after Frank O'Hara" reflects Berrigan's abiding concern in *The Sonnets* with literary historical positioning, the effort to imitate and thus rightfully succeed not only one's master, but also, as the poem suggests, oneself:

> It's 8:54 a.m. in Brooklyn it's the 28th of July and
> it's probably 8:54 in Manhattan but I'm
> in Brooklyn I'm eating English muffins and drinking
> pepsi and I'm thinking of how Brooklyn is New
> York city too how odd I usually think of it as
> something all its own like Bellows Falls like Little
> Chute like Uijongbu
>               I never thought on the Williams-
> burg bridge I'd come so much to Brooklyn

> just to see lawyers and cops who don't even carry
> guns taking my wife away and bringing her back
>               No
> and I never thought Dick would be back at Gude's
> beard shaved off long hair cut and Carol reading
> his books when we were playing cribbage and
> watching the sun come up over the Navy Yard
> across the river
>               I think I was thinking when I was
> ahead I'd be somewhere like Perry street erudite
> dazzling slim and badly loved
> contemplating my new book of poems
> to be printed in simple type on old brown paper
> feminine marvelous and tough

>                                              (32)

A study in verb tense, this poem begins with the present, "I do this, I do that" mode, but—like **"A Final Sonnet"**—quickly leaves it behind for a more contemplative, less immanent verbal register that forms an implicit commentary on the fiction of immediacy. Indeed, "thinking" is the central action of the poem; changes in the form of that verb mark time. This "sonnet" (at twenty-two lines it is one of the longest in the sequence) turns on the fact that poems, like poets, exist in time as well as space; the distance from Brooklyn to Manhattan, like the distance from the first line to the second, is the difference between 8:54 and 8:55, between now and then.

It's also the difference between I and "I." **Sonnet XXXVI** takes as its theme the double positioning of the poetic self in time that, I've been arguing, characterizes the rhetorical strategy of the sequence as a whole. Despite the fact that in Berrigan's personal mythology the West Village replaces Parnassus as the idealized final resting place, fame, in the more intimate sense of being "badly loved," is still the ultimate goal. Or was. This poem figures literary stardom as the fantasy of a somewhat naive earlier self, a self ironized, even playfully disavowed, by the speaker of the poem, who, despite the fact that he's across the river, is implicitly "ahead." The tone is bemused, speculative, not rueful; the humor lies in the realization that Brooklyn, an unglamorous land of professionals, low crime rates, and reformed bohemians, is a strangely comfortable place to be.

The joke, of course, is that the poet is not yet "ahead." Unpublished, he's contemplating his breakfast, not his book of poems, and in composing this one in homage to Frank O'Hara, he's trying to write himself into a modified image of greatness. The humor of **Sonnet XXXVI** masks the gravity with which Berrigan approaches this project of self-making. Within the sequence, poems trip lightly across time zones and poetic postures; the poet of English muffins and sensuous experience can become a textual artifact—a type, a name—and then happily resume his fleshly identity. He has this flexibility because he presides over the process of premature aging that in turn produces him as a legend in his own time. Whether he is instructing a prospective publisher that his "new book" is "to be printed . . . on old brown paper," or republishing his own poems and thus conferring the prestigious aura of a "selected" on his second book, Berrigan is his own best promoter. He doesn't attempt to cheat time so much as to put its ravages to work in his public relations campaign. In this early poem at least, the fiction of control is powerful. When majority is a matter of paper selection, the Dorian Gray-like poet can have his greatness and remain "dazzling slim" too; the sense of disassociation that the poem manifests seems a small price to pay.

O'Hara's own time travels are far less directed; his flirtations with self-difference border more closely on dissolution. Berrigan's optimism results in part from his belatedness; with O'Hara's career as a map, he is free to deviate at will. "How to Get There," first published in the Winter 1962 number of *Locus Solus,* appears to have been one of the O'Hara poems that guided **Sonnet XXXVI**'s composition. A meditation on the lies that poems tell about time, "How to Get There" figures the self's temporal progress as spatial displacement, a series of positionings across the New York cityscape. But unlike **Sonnet XXXVI,** the speaker of this poem isn't contemplating his future from the comfortable domesticity of a Brooklyn breakfast; when the poem begins, he's out in the streets, and it's not clear what time it is:

> White the October air, no snow, easy to breathe
> beneath the sky, lies, lies everywhere writhing and
>      gasping
> clutching and tangling, it is not easy to breathe . . .
>                          I see the fog lunge in
> and hide it
>             where are you?
>                     here I am on the sidewalk
>
>                          (O'Hara 369)

The city is covered in fog and "soft white lies" and so, we soon see, is the poem. Line 3 gives the lie to the opening line's breathy confidence; the speaking voice shifts from first to second person and back; at the beginning, there's "no snow," but midway through the weather turns several times in the course of two lines: "it is snowing now, it is already too late / the snow will go away, but nobody will be there." Whereas Berrigan's poem seems to thrill in the capacity of poetic language to shift time zones and city boroughs, particularly when it enables the poet to indulge the fantasy of being present for his own posterity, "How to Get There" seems caught between times, not even fully present to the present. The poem's concluding confusion brings the point home:

>                     never to be alone again
>                     never to be loved

sailing through space: didn't I have you once for my self?
>                          West Side?
>             for a couple of hours, but I am not that person.

"[N]ever to be alone again / never to be loved"—hell, for the famous coterie poet, is not only other people but the other person whom the poetic self inevitably becomes. In the spectral light of these lines, **Sonnet XXXVI**'s vision of being "badly loved" takes on a slightly sickly hue. It is tempting to read these poems as presaging the tragic fall that, in myths of celebrity, always seems to doom the star too quickly risen. As we've seen in **The Sonnets,** Berrigan works by mobilizing such narratives on his own behalf, pushing self-consciousness to the point where it folds back into naiveté, the pleasant illusion that he has it all under control. O'Hara's poetry is itself full of intimations of mortality consciously linked to the strain of living a public persona. "Getting Up Ahead of Someone (Sun)," a poem set on Fire Island and often cited as a foreshadowing of O'Hara's death there several years later, concludes:

> and the house wakes up and goes
> to get the dog in Sag Harbor I make
> myself a bourbon and commence
> to write one of my "I do this I do that"
> poems in a sketch pad
>
>                          it is tomorrow
> though only six hours have gone by
> each day's light has more significance these days.
>
>                          (341)

Written in 1959, five years before the City Lights Books' publication of *Lunch Poems* brought together a critical mass of so-called "I do this I do that" poems in one volume, "Getting Up" performs the literary historical task of genre definition on itself. The tone is only slightly jaded; there's an unexpected sincerity in the last line's meditation on mutability. But the poem sets up an abyssal structure into which it must fall: writing poetry of experience about writing poetry of experience takes its toll; experience dries up, demanding poetry or bourbon for lubrication. For O'Hara, the "I do this I do that" poem *is* the day, and once it's written, "it is tomorrow."

In **Sonnet XXXVI,** "feminine marvelous and tough" gestures to a future in which a poet is words, and not even necessarily his own. Contemplating his new book of poetry, Berrigan composes his own jacket blurb and, presciently, writes his own epitaph. Berrigan had a special talent for recognizing durability: "Grace to be born and live as variously as possible," the line from O'Hara's "In Memory of My Feelings" used as both the epigraph and opening of **Sonnet LV,** is in fact etched on O'Hara's grave. "Feminine marvelous and tough," while not literally etched in stone, comes to have a similar posthumous value as it is repeated, mantralike, throughout so many of the homages and elegies written for Berrigan. The poet of **The Sonnets** anticipates the irony of this fate, lost on most of his mourning friends. The line seems representative, so very "Ted," be-cause—as Berrigan writes in an elegy for O'Hara—it "will never be less than perfectly frank" (Berkson and LeSueur 11). **"Marvelous,"** in particular, ventriloquizes O'Hara in his campier moments and seems markedly out of place in Berrigan's rigorously macho lexicon. Indeed, it appears three times in "In Favor of One's Time," which O'Hara first published in the May 1960 issue of *Poetry* magazine. Spelled "marvellous," the word puns on Andrew Marvell, with whose "The Garden" the poem mischievously plays. The true subject of "In Favor of One's Time" is the compression of poets into words, how—for the historically conscious poet—all words encrypt the names of the poets who once used them. "When I think of Ted, I think of the fact that one of my favorite putative lines of O'Hara was written by him ('feminine marvelous and tough') in an extraordinary homage," writes David Shapiro in his contribution to Berrigan's funereal volume (226). **The Sonnets** is itself an extraordinary homage, not least because it founds a career on the tenuous ground of a mistaken identity.

* * *

In *From Outlaw to Classic: Canons in American Poetry,* Alan Golding elaborates two competing models of canon formation, the "aesthetic" and the "institutional." Narrowly construed, the aesthetic model maintains that poets produce canons by admiring, imitating, and transforming the work of their precursors—all within the bounds of their poems. Golding cites Helen Vendler as a representative proponent of this school of thought: "It is because Virgil admired Homer, and Milton Virgil, and Keats Milton, and Stevens Keats, that those writers turn up in classrooms and anthologies," she argues (46). Conversely, the institutional model holds that the value of poets, poems, indeed the "literary" itself is deter-mined within institutions and by their functionaries. In the twentieth century, most institutional theorists agree, the academy, with its team of teacher-critics, is the only game in town. Golding takes issue with both of these models: he argues that advocates of the aesthetic model don't acknowledge their own institutional positioning and its shaping effect on the canons they discuss, and that the institutional model has no place for individual agency, robbing poets and critics alike of any hand in their own destinies. In their stead, Golding proposes a synthetic theory of canon formation. Discussing the canonizing efforts of poet-produced little magazines like Cid Corman's *Origin,* he suggests that while poets (especially those in the avant-garde) do engage in such efforts—either in their poems or in other institutions—

the academy remains the site where they "get preserved, perpetuated, and disseminated (or, alternatively, suppressed) by nonpoets" (51). However, while the academy may determine poetry's reception among scholars and students, "It does not therefore define the terms of poetry's practice or its relevance for other poets, its power to generate further poetic production" (141).

I have been arguing that Ted Berrigan works at the intersection of the institutional and the aesthetic, and I have been tracing the effects of his double positioning in poetic, social, and biographical terms. My subject, career building, differs from the issue of canon forma-tion mostly in terms of temporal scope, but the two are also importantly related. In **The Sonnets,** in his profes-sional relations with institutional figures like Lita Hor-nick of *Kulchur,* and in *"C",* Berrigan launched his career—that is, created the conditions for his own persistence as a working poet—by admiring, imitating, and transforming, as well as preserving, perpetuating, and disseminating, the works of other poets. Berrigan was quite literally a "poet's poet"; deriving his poetic material (even his identity) from that of his friends and colleagues, he had a personal stake in facilitating their success. Invoking posterity and positing canonicity were means of generating further production—his own as well as others'—in the hope that someday someone might do the same for him. This dialectical strategy emblematizes the historical situation of an avant-garde so complex and internally evolved that, as Bourdieu puts it, "the very structure of field . . . [is] . . . present in every act of production," and "the irreducibility of the work of cultural production to the artist's own labor" appears more clearly than ever before (108-9). Berrigan played both tradition and the individual talent, as it were. In this last section, I will look briefly at *"C"* and suggest how the little magazine worked as a stage for this acrobatic performance.

In May 1964, one year and eight issues into its publica-tion, Berrigan sold the editorial materials surrounding *"C"* magazine to a local bookseller who then sold them to the Syracuse University library. For a fee of one dol-lar per page, Berrigan also wrote a ten-page journalistic account of a year in the life of the magazine and its editor, to be included in the archive along with dummy issues, correspondence, financial records, and original authors' manuscripts. It was a prescient gesture.[8] The magazine ran for another five issues and became, by the time it was phased out in 1966, one of the dominant organs of the second-generation New York school and a spur to the organizing impulses of the St. Mark's Poetry Project. Establishing *"C"* in the wake of the by-then-defunct first-generation journal *Locus Solus,* Berrigan positioned himself on the cusp of a literary period; he and his peers were to be the heirs to Ashbery, O'Hara, Schuyler, and Koch, and the execution of the estate would take place in the pages of the little magazine.

In an interview a decade later, Berrigan described the combination of chance and design by which he founded *"C"* and became the unofficial historian, ringleader, and bursar of the New York school:

> there were these four people, and when I first came to New York . . . from Oklahoma . . . I was very interested in these four people. . . . There weren't many people that were interested in those four people . . . so I got very interested in them. They seemed to me to open up a lot of possibilities. Then someone asked me if I wanted to edit a magazine. So I said, "Sure!" My plan for that magazine was to publish these four people in conjunction with four or five younger people, myself and people that I knew. . . . And I put them in, too. And then I realized that there was such a thing as New York School, because there was a second generation. So in essence, *we* were the New York School because these guys, although they were the real New York School, weren't doing anything about it, and we were. And that struck me as very funny. . . . I used to tell people they could join for five dollars.
>
> (*Talking* 90-91)

At least in this telling, Berrigan's attraction to Ashbery, Schuyler, Koch, and O'Hara is directly tied to their relative marginality to the publishing and critical industries. Despite the promise of the Allen anthology, these poets had limited critical recognition and only four books in print between them. The "possibilities" they opened for Berrigan were varied. They not only offered Berrigan-the-poet models and materials for his experiments in verse, but they made possible the emergence of Berrigan-the-editor and canon-maker, which in turn paved the way for his own canonization (in a limited sense) as a poet.

Berrigan figures his editorial activity as a chance alchemy. Composing his little magazine, he "put in" a selection of poets, and the brew produced literary historical gold. Editing thus represents one variation on the "collaborative" ethos that Berrigan developed throughout his career: making "works"—poetic or otherwise—is a matter of "changing one thing [in someone else's work] and making it be your work," "put[ting] in" or "slap[ping] on" found material and "mak[ing] the changes demanded by that" (*Talking* 121). In conceiving of collaboration as an encounter between any number of different writings, set in motion but not controlled by a single writer, and in exploring this practice through the medium of the little magazine, Berrigan followed the lead of Ashbery and Koch, who edited a special issue of *Locus Solus* devoted to collaboration. That issue includes selections from such varied collaborative works as the ancient Chinese "A Garland of Roses," Coleridge and Southey's "Joan of

Arc," Breton and Elouard's "Immaculate Conception," and troubadour, metaphysical, and cavalier works, along with more expected contributions from Ashbery and Schuyler's "A Nest of Ninnies" and Koch and Jane Freilicher's "The Car." Koch's brief essay on collaboration and a section of notes and commentary on the individual authors and texts combine to make the case for the historical and scholarly significance of the practice. The second in *Locus Solus*'s five-number run, the collaboration issue followed a debut issue containing extended selections from members of the journal's editorial board and their immediate circle. The second issue makes an appeal to a broader public; didacticism prevails over performance. Having posited a new (collective) agent in the field, the editors take a step back to trace the lineage of their dominant poetic.

The first issue of *"C"* contains no such theorization of its poetic or its positioning. The brief note on the contents page states simply that *"C"* "will print anything the Editor likes, and will appear monthly." In "Some Notes about '*C*'," Berrigan claims that "the first issue of '*C*' was deliberately put together by me to reflect the SIMILARITY of the poetry, since I felt the differences to be obvious, and the NEWNESS of such a point of view as we (I) had." Toward that end, he left out page numbers and names of individual authors from the body of the issue and limited the information in the table of contents to the number of poems included by each of the four contributors. While it is possible to distinguish between the works of Berrigan, Dick Gallup, and Ron Padgett, the formatting choices conspire against it. All of the poems (with the exception of Joe Brainard's "diary" and "play") fill approximately the same amount of space on the legal-sized pages; both Padgett and Berrigan include poems titled "Sonnet" in their selections; lines echo across contributors. Berrigan's "A fragmentary music clears the room" responds as much to Gallup's "endless resoundings fill the room" as it does to the source line from Ashbery's "Two Scenes." Like *The Sonnets,* the magazine stands as one work in conversation with itself.

But if "baffling combustions are everywhere," in *"C"* as in *The Sonnets,* they are nonetheless subject to the editor's control and harnessed to his ends. Berrigan makes this clear in "Some Notes": "I was and am '*C*' magazine. . . . And I intended and intend for '*C*' to exist as a personal aesthetic statement by me." Claims like these are always at least partially ironized in Berrigan's self-mythology. But poetic careers consist of more than their rhetorical performances. In the retrospective light of literary biography, the ends justify the means and demand to be examined empirically as well as read rhetorically. Berrigan sent copies of *"C"* to "names" like Barbara Guest, Jasper Johns, and Edwin Denby, all culled from the New York City phone book. Kenneth Koch, whom he already knew, gave him other "names":

John Ashbery, Joe Ceravolo, and Jane Freilicher. Such assiduous marketing efforts resulted in personal notes, financial contributions, and promises of poetry; names became material realities. Johns sent ten dollars and a request that the painter Frank Stella be included on the *"C"* mailing list. O'Hara, with whom Berrigan had been corresponding at his Museum of Modern Art office, invited him to a cocktail party welcoming Ashbery back from Paris. Of this event, at which he secured Ashbery's permission to publish several poems in issue 5, Berrigan writes, "For me this made *'C'* more real than anything that happened so far" ("Some Notes" 8).

As much as the sonnet sequence, then, Berrigan "used [the little magazine] to be [his] big jump into poetry and stardom, as it were." And as in many of Berrigan's longer poetic works, the relatively fixed procedure on which the little magazine was founded quickly began to generate itself; the collaborative circle widened, guest editors took over, the budget increased, and an institution was born. Berrigan was characteristically ambivalent about the ripple effects of *"C"'s* success—thrilling in the society it enabled him to enter, but wary of the challenges to his creative control. In the fourth issue, as in issue 2 of *Locus Solus,* the hermetic organization of the first three issues gives way to a more public, even academic mode. Devoted to Denby's sonnets, this issue contains an essay on his work by O'Hara (originally printed in *Poetry* magazine), as well as an introduction by John Wieners and a notes section at the end. The front and back covers, designed by Andy Warhol, feature photographs of Denby and Gerard Malanga—elderly and distinguished and darkly handsome, respectively—in various stages of embrace. On the "question of taste" raised by the image of the two men kissing, Berrigan cites O'Hara's cocktail party quip as the "final word": "if poetry can't survive a little faggotism, then I don't know what can!" ("Some Notes" 10).

The homoeroticism of the fourth issue functions on a number of levels: depicting the sexualized spectacle of elder and ephebe, the cover photos help to enact the transmission of cultural capital from one poetic generation to the next, at least on the cocktail circuit. Urbane gayness, however veiled, was a signature of the *Locus Solus* group; in *"C"* it works as a citation, a positioning act. Berrigan and his immediate cohort were as insistently straight as O'Hara's circle was gay, a fact that produced a certain insecurity on the part of the would-be heir, which in turn produced such moments of apparently compensatory poetic excess as these lines from **"Tambourine Life"**: "I have many men friends / I would like to fuck / However, I am unable to do so / because I am not a homosexual / fortunately / this makes my life complex / rather than simple" (*So Going* 111). If New York wasn't the "high-powered homosexual scene in the arts" that Amiri Baraka claims it

was in *The Autobiography of LeRoi Jones,* the City Poet's casting couch did hold a certain apocryphal power (187). And *"C"* did in fact gain Berrigan access to O'Hara's bedroom, where he rummaged through unpublished manuscripts and discovered several gems. But the privileges of editorship came at the cost of authorship. Padgett edited issue 7 and filled it with selections from Kenward Elmslie, Schuyler, Koch, Guest, O'Hara, and Ashbery. With issue 8, Berrigan regained control, resuming his policy of presenting himself and a few largely unknown poets.

Five issues later, Berrigan ceased publication. Little magazines have been described as kamikazes on the literary battlefield; death is part of their function. Avant-gardes fertilize the soil and the culture at large grows. I've been arguing, however, that from the perspective of the struggling poet, the rhythms of literary history are not nearly so organic or inevitable. Anticipating and even performing his own demise is one of the ways in which the ambitious poet attempts to assert control over his career. For a coterie poet like Berrigan, death was a seductive means of individuation.

But the institutional strategy leaves traces which survive, and potentially overshadow, the aesthetic vicissitudes of the individual agent. For Berrigan, whose work so assiduously advanced and internalized the social structures that conditioned its reception, collaboration—increasingly with his own alienated self—was addictive. Starting with **"Tambourine Life,"** the long "open form" poem that Berrigan added to daily, the poetry of experience and the poetry of citation and collage begin to merge in less productive ways. The conceptual aggressiveness and personal investment of *The Sonnets* gives way to what Berrigan called his "machine ability." Having produced himself as "this wonderful poet," "Ted" began to live as the subject of his own gossip column—a condition not conducive to either life or writing. The post-*Sonnets* list poems—**"Things to Do in New York City," "Things to Do in Anne's Room," "Things to Do on Speed"**—manifest the difficulty of living a public persona. In them, the present imperative transforms the private, diaristic mode into a bohemian guide to daily life:

> Wake up high up
>     frame bent & turned on
> Moving slowly
>     & by the numbers
> light cigarette
> Dress in basic black.

>                                    (*So Going* 134)

The implied audience of the list poems is doubled. Written for a public, they make a tourist attraction of the poet's home and an example of his life. Written for Berrigan himself, they stand as, in Charles Bernstein's words, "not . . . a document of a life in writing but, inversely, as an *appropriation* of a life *by* writing" (154). Posterity aside, making lists is necessary for survival; writing compels living:

> Now I'm going to do it
>   deliberately
>
>          . . . . .
>
>   get into the bed
>   be alone
>   suffocate
>   don't die
>
>       & it's that easy.

(*So Going* 196-97)

Berrigan died of liver failure—blamed on excessive alcohol and amphetamine use—in 1983 at the age of forty-eight. Literary history is littered with the figures of poets who have lived fast and died young. For living poets, this is a history not to be reromanticized, but to be used.

### Notes

1. The vast majority of writing on Berrigan takes the form of memoir/homage, and all of it appears in small-press publications. More critical engagements include Joel Lewis's "'Everything Turns into Writing': The Sonnets of Ted Berrigan," Barrett Watten's "After Ted," and Charles Bernstein's "Writing Against the Body," all of which frame textual reading in terms of a personal knowledge of the poet.

2. Except for Penguin's posthumous publication of the *Selected Poems,* Grove was the largest press to publish Berrigan's poetry and—despite his imprecations—never took him on as a house poet. The MLA bibliography indexes only six scholarly articles devoted to Berrigan, and he is certainly not a regular presence on syllabi of postwar American poetry courses. *The Sonnets* received brief, favorable mention by Hayden Carruth and Kenneth Koch in omnibus "new poetry" reviews for *The Hudson Review* and *The New York Times Book Review,* respectively. Nor is Berrigan's work widely anthologized: despite his collegiality with Robert Creeley, Frank O'Hara, and the other core poets in Donald Allen's *New American Poetry* anthology (1961), Berrigan wasn't included in Allen's and George Butterick's revised edition, *The Postmoderns* (1982), nor in M. L. Rosenthal's and Sally M. Gall's *The Modern Poetic Sequence* (1983). *The Norton Anthology of Modern Poetry* (1973), edited by Richard Ellmann, contains three of Berrigan's sonnets, along with a disparaging headnote.

3. St. Mark's, an East Village church with a long cultural history, became a focal institution for poets and other downtown artists in 1966 when Harry Silverstein, a sociologist from the New School for Social Research, got a grant from the Office of Economic Opportunity to administer an arts project for local youth. Anne Waldman was hired to assist in the development of the poetry component of the program, which came to include reading series and several important publications (Waldman, *Out of This World* 1-6).

4. In *Theory of the Avant-Garde,* Peter Bürger advances the now familiar claim that the historical avant-garde exposed the ideal of aesthetic autonomy as an institution with historical and material determinants but failed in its mission to reintegrate art and life (46). At the Berkeley Poetry Conference of 1965, representatives of the avant-garde poetic communities that had been developing throughout the fifties witnessed themselves as an institution with internal power structures, systems of communication and reproduction, protections from the market, et cetera. I'm suggesting that by virtue of his relative belatedness and his poetic of collaged citation, Berrigan was uniquely positioned to "reintegrate art and life" by making the historical predicament of the avant-garde his poetic subject.

5. Lawrence Lipking begins *The Life of the Poet: Beginning and Ending Poetic Careers* with Keats's sonnet "On Looking into Chapman's Homer" and suggests that Keats updated the Virgilian model of genre/career development—from bucolic, to didactic, to epic—for the modern poet (3-11, 76-93).

6. I'm indebted to Bob Perelman's discussion of this poem in *The Marginalization of Poetry* (65-66).

7. Berrigan was fascinated by the interview form and exploited it throughout his career. This interest led, most notoriously, to the fabricated interview with John Cage that won one thousand dollars. Berrigan made up both sides of the dialogue, parodying the interviewer's treatment of his subject as "an object to be used" (*Talking* 100-101).

8. Many poets of Berrigan's cohort played the "archive game." In the late fifties and early sixties, at the bidding of such institutional collectors as Harry Ransom of the Humanities Research Center at the University of Texas in Austin, poets began selling their manuscripts, letters, and assorted papers to libraries prior to developing significant reputations.

### Works Cited

Allen, Donald, ed. *The New American Poetry, 1945-60.* New York: Grove, 1960.

Allen, Donald, and George F. Butterick, eds. *The Postmoderns: The New American Poetry Revised.* New York: Grove, 1982.

Ashbery, John. "Two Scenes." *Selected Poems.* New York: Penguin, 1986. 3.

Baraka, Amiri. *The Autobiography of LeRoi Jones.* New York: Freundlich, 1987.

Berkson, Bill, and Joe LeSueur, eds. *Homage to Frank O'Hara.* Spec. issue of *Big Sky* 11/12 (1978). Bolinas, CA: Big Sky, 1988.

Bernstein, Charles. "Writing Against the Body." Waldman, *Nice to See You* 154-57.

Berrigan, Ted, ed. *"C".* Ted Berrigan Papers. Syracuse University Library, Department of Special Collections.

———. *Many Happy Returns.* New York: Corinth, 1969.

———. *Selected Poems.* New York: Penguin, 1994.

———. *So Going Around Cities: New and Selected Poems, 1958-1979.* Berkeley, CA: Blue Wind, 1980.

———. "Some Notes about 'C'." ts. Ted Berrigan Papers. Syracuse University Library, Department of Special Collections.

———. *The Sonnets.* New York: Grove, 1967.

———. *Talking in Tranquility: Interviews with Ted Berrigan.* Ed. Stephen Ratcliffe and Leslie Scalapino. Bolinas and Oakland, CA: Avenue B / O Books, 1991.

Bourdieu, Pierre. *The Field of Cultural Production: Essays on Art and Literature.* Ed. Randal Johnson. New York: Columbia UP, 1993.

Bürger, Peter. *Theory of the Avant-Garde.* Trans. Michael Shaw. Minneapolis: U of Minnesota P, 1984.

Carroll, Paul, ed. *The Young American Poets.* Chicago: Big Table, 1968.

Carruth, Hayden. "Making It New." *Hudson Review* 21 (1968): 399-412.

Duncan, Robert. "At the Poetry Conference: Berkeley after the New York Style." Waldman, *Nice to See You* 12-14.

Eliot, T. S. "What Is Minor Poetry?" *On Poetry and Poets.* New York: Farrar, 1957.

Ellmann, Richard, ed. *The Norton Anthology of Modern Poetry.* New York: Norton, 1973.

Golding, Alan. *From Outlaw to Classic: Canons in American Poetry.* Madison: U of Wisconsin P, 1995.

Junker, Howard. "The Young Poets." *Newsweek* 3 Mar. 1969: 83-86.

Keats, John. *The Poetical Works of Keats.* Ed. Paul D. Sheats. Boston: Houghton, 1975.

Koch, Kenneth. "Poetry in Paperback." *New York Times Book Review* 28 Apr. 1968: 7.

Levinson, Marjorie. *Keats's Life of Allegory: The Origins of a Style.* Oxford: Blackwell, 1988.

Lewis, Joel. "'Everything Turns into Writing': The Sonnets of Ted Berrigan." *Transfer* 2.1 (1988/89): 129-55.

Lipking, Lawrence. *The Life of the Poet: Beginning and Ending Poetic Careers.* Chicago: U of Chicago P, 1981.

Notley, Alice. Introduction. Berrigan, *Selected Poems* vii-xii.

O'Hara, Frank. *The Collected Poems of Frank O'Hara.* Ed. Donald Allen. Berkeley: U of California P, 1995.

Olson, Charles. "The Mayan Letters." *Selected Writings.* Ed. Robert Creeley. New York: New Directions, 1966. 69-130.

Perelman, Bob. *The Marginalization of Poetry: Language Writing and Literary History.* Princeton, NJ: Princeton UP, 1996.

Pritikin, Renny. "From *Program Report from 80 Langton Street, San Francisco:: Writer in Residence:: Ted Berrigan:: June 24-27, 1981.*" Waldman, *Nice to See You* 19-25.

Rosenthal, M. L., and Sally M. Gall, eds. *The Modern Poetic Sequence: The Genius of Modern Poetry.* New York: Oxford UP, 1983.

Schreiber, Ron, ed. *31 New American Poets.* New York: Hill, 1969.

Shapiro, David. "On a Poet." Waldman, *Nice to See You* 223-27.

Waldman, Anne, ed. *Nice to See You. Homage to Ted Berrigan.* Minneapolis: Coffee House, 1991.

———, ed. *Out of This World: An Anthology of the St. Mark's Poetry Project, 1966-1991.* New York: Crown, 1991.

Ward, Geoff. *Statutes of Liberty: The New York School of Poets.* New York: St. Martin's, 1993.

Watten, Barrett. "After Ted." *Ariel 8.* Ed. Rod Smith. Washington, D.C.: Edge, 1995. 104-6.

Williams, William Carlos. *Interviews with William Carlos Williams: "Speaking Straight Ahead."* Ed. Linda Welshiner Wagner. New York: New Directions, 1976.

## Alice Notley (review date March/April 1999)

SOURCE: Notley, Alice. "A Certain Slant of Sunlight." *American Poetry Review* 28, no. 2 (March/April 1999): 11-14.

*[In the following review of Berrigan's last book of poetry, Notley discusses individual poems from A*

Certain Slant of Sunlight, *among them "The Einstein Intersection," "Joy of Shipwrecks," "Tough Cookies," and "In Morton's Grille."*]

Ted Berrigan's book, *A Certain Slant of Sunlight* (Oakland, Calif.: O Books, 1988), written during 1982 and completed six months before his death in July of 1983, is a sequence of poems originally composed on blank postcards each four and a half inches by seven inches. As I've written in the book's Introductory Note, Ken and Anne Mikolowski of The Alternative Press had an ongoing project of sending a set of five hundred such postcards to select people in the hopes of having the cards returned to them with the "picture" side filled with holograph poems and other materials. Individual cards were then included in packets of printed broadsides, bumper stickers, and so on, sent to the Mikolowskis' "subscribers" (the packets were free). The point is that the cards as a constant size and shape became for Berrigan a form, and the poems written in this form became a sequence. The form provided for a poem that could be only as long as the card's size permitted: if the handwriting was kept very small you could wind up with a poem as long as **"What a Dump, or, Easter"** (31 lines including stanza breaks); however, most of the poems are shorter than that, in the eight- to twenty-line range, say. A few are very much shorter, are only a line or two lines in length, and sometimes suggestive of a postcard "message" (e.g. 'SALUTATION / "Listen, you cheap little liar . . ."'). Is such a form a form? There isn't much of the grid in it, to compare it with Berrigan's *The Sonnets,* which is composed very much to a grid. The form isn't a plan for the deployment of words and lines so much as an approach, an ambiance, maybe a tone. Yet there are qualities in the poems' general method which suggest *The Sonnets* and which suggest a fidelity to the sense of the self presented in *The Sonnets.* But *A Certain Slant of Sunlight* isn't about "art" as *The Sonnets* often seems to be, it's about dying and about community; it's about wreckage and salvage, and about states of consciousness that shouldn't be dealt with according to rules.

The poems in *A Certain Slant of Sunlight* tend to be composed of units of information, or stories which stand for something else, or bits of language suggestive of emotional states, happenstance, philosophy, reflectiveness. They are haunted by other people's lines, lines by dead greats and lines by Berrigan's friends (who were often invited to write a few words on the cards). *The Sonnets* is characterized by the use of lines as units of information and knowledge and by the use of other people's lines, but also by the constant repetition of such lines; there is no such repetition in *A Certain Slant of Sunlight.* Repetition, classically, destroys linear time and establishes a simulacrum of the flow of consciousness. *A Certain Slant* works by creating singular structures; as a sequence it is held together by what

might be called its knowingness (the author of *The Sonnets* didn't know very much, in a way—he was only in his late twenties—and the book's knowledge flows from its strict formalism as if tapped from an unconscious which isn't quite the author's). Doug Oliver once suggested to me that a typical Berrigan poem is a cognition, that is, a piece of knowledge or consciousness, a sort of "clicking in." *The Sonnets* are loose seen in this way, the poems in *A Certain Slant* are tight:

### "Poets Tribute to Philip Guston"

I hear walking in my legs
Aborigines in the pipes
I am the man your father was
Innocence bleats at my last
Black breaths—and tho I was considered
   a royal
pain in the ass by
Shakespeare's father, the high alderman,
All the deadly virtuous plague my death!
I could care less?

This is not pretty, sublime, or classical (though some of the others of the poems could be so described); it's both mysterious and blatant, and by virtue of the poet's proximate death extremely serious.

I've often wondered why people don't seem to notice this book so much, it being one of Berrigan's three major sequences (*Easter Monday* has never been published as the sequence Berrigan intended; almost all of its comprising poems have been published separately). *The Sonnets* is esthetically perfect, being based on an idea, and there has been increasingly a taste for such work recently. Berrigan considered *The Sonnets* to be somewhat self-educational, and it is, but that isn't necessarily a drawback. *The Sonnets,* though, is a book that hasn't been properly understood or at least described, and in that lack of understanding may be found the reasons why *A Certain Slant* is neglected. *The Sonnets* is not, as is sometimes stated, concerned with the rejection of the "psychological I"; the psychological I is right there in the book in all its life-plots and circumstances and all its emotional field but stretched across time, warped in time, twisting and doubling back and pushing on into the future rather like karma. In all of Berrigan's work thereafter, and certainly in *A Certain Slant,* the I of it can be large and contemplative or more ordinarily small or, actually usually, both at once. In Berrigan there is a metaphysical I—the transcendent watcher; a presentational I—the character of the ordinary man who buys the *Post* at Gem's Spa to read the sports page; and an I which is deeply entangled in the stories it participates in with others. At death one might be particularly concerned with the latter, since one's responsibilities to others and theirs to one traditionally loom large then. In *A Certain*

*Slant* a "caught" person is speaking, someone caught in the traps of the psychological I (and really, who isn't?), someone enraged and loving who is about to have to leave.

*A Certain Slant* is an "unpleasant" book, in the Shavian sense. It covers a year in the life of a poet who is soon to die in poverty though close in the arms of family, but in the midst of unpleasant arguments with fellow members of an artistic community, in an increasingly venal decade. It isn't generally recognized that he is dying, and he speaks of it only slantwise as in these poems. He is "on drugs"; he is, as the above poem suggests, past caring what others think but not about the proper way to do his job, the poet's job. This "plot" or line throughout the poems is not explicit but is ever pointed at; it isn't ennobled or aggrandized. The author isn't showing off with language for example, things are too extreme for that, though not for having fun with words sometimes. The title **"Poets Tribute to Philip Guston"** refers to an event during the previous year, a tribute to the recently dead abstract-expressionist painter which was held at The St. Mark's Poetry Project. Many people participated; all were counseled to limit their performances to five minutes. Berrigan thought this ridiculous given Guston's philosophy of art and, especially, his art itself: a tidy package of tribute? So he rambled on and on as if a helpless speed-freak until the audience got mad at him and began booing, at which time he turned his presentation into a "statement" about excess, greatness, proportion, and how long it might take for an abstract expressionist to get to the point (remember all those stories about how long such a painter might agonize before and during painting, and really was it ever finished?). He made a mess and he cleaned it up, deliberately. There are people who attended who still don't believe he did it deliberately; his performance that evening is still a scandal; the transcript of the evening which he hired someone to type from the tape is still unpublished. Can this rather small poem mean all of that? The first two lines suggest a Guston, heaps of tubes and shoes, a can-these-bones-live type of thing, and also a creaky person (Berrigan had a bad back and a bad ankle); I am the man your father was, that is, Guston (a lot of the you's in the book are fellow-poets, younger than Berrigan even if of the same poetry "generation," "youngsters" who are down on him); "innocence bleats at my last black" and then whoever Shakespeare's father is (what tight-ass is that?) is really being put down, possibly by Shakespeare himself . . . all the deadly virtuous, *yes my friends you, and I am dying, and I don't have time for your censure.* There is a lot of weight on the "innocence bleats" line and on the "deadly virtuous" line: the first is full of self-justification and self-torture, the second is quite killing. Yet the poem is also small, and light. Poetry isn't sup-

posed to be like that right now; it's supposed to be monumental. Not epigrammatic, that can't be great—not cutting as if cutting to a real person in a real situation.

The poems are in a fairly chronological order, so part of one's reading of it is as a progress through the seasons and a literal year. There are also themes: the censuring of clerk and book keeper types of poets; the arrivals of visitors; the proximity of beloved and friends and people who no longer seem to be those; The Poetry Project (a layered phrase); the deaths of others; politics outside the community; the past. There's a lot of love in the book but also a constant accusatory element, as if the community at hand is not being loving enough, mirroring too the contemporary world. The untitled second poem in the book has a history of unpleasantness behind it though not in it:

> You'll do good if you play it like you're
>     not getting paid
> But you'll do it better if the motherfuckers pay you

(Motto of THE WHORES & POETS GULD—trans, from The Palatine Anthology by Alice Notley & Ted Berrigan 20 Feb 82)

It was censored out of *The World,* the magazine of The Poetry Project, in 1982, which fact is one of the main reasons it appears second in the book, that and because it is a motto and an unromantic statement that poets are rarely paid for their "services." In contrast the fourth poem in the book is the widely anthologized title poem, a classic and deeply felt "good poem" which is about the illness and imminent death of the poet's mother, though that is never mentioned except indirectly:

> . . . the tall pretty girl in the print dress
> under the fur collar of her cloth coat will be standing
> by the wire fence where the wild flowers grow not too
>     tall
> her eyes will be deep brown and her hair styled 1947
>     American
>                         will be too: but
> I'll be shattered by then

The allusion is to a photograph, but it is called "the picture": what does it mean that "mother and son, 33 & 7. First Communion Day, 1941" will be, literally, "on St. Mark's Place" (where the poet resided) when the poet goes there "tomorrow," though "I'll go out for a drink with one of my demons tonight . . . in Colorado 1980 spring snow"? This poem, like some others in the book, was written earlier than 1982 but in a sense was written again when inscribed on a postcard (its form changed by its becoming a "postcard poem"). Berrigan's mother's lung cancer commenced in 1980, and she was expected to die that year but lasted until July 1982, a year to the month before his own death. The poem states that he will meet himself and his past, meeting her death on St. Mark's Place (he expected to be there when she died) but there is also an eerie suggestion of his own death and of her and his meeting in death in an everlasting First Communion.

I'm tempted to proceed through the book poem by poem discussing each one because they are so different from each other, but there's obviously not space for that here. **"The Einstein Intersection,"** another poem towards the beginning "looks" a little like the title poem but isn't in the least like it:

> This distinguished boat
> Now for oblivion, at sea, a
> Sweet & horrid joke in dubious taste.
> That once, a Super Ego of strength, did both haunt
> Your dreams and also save you much bother, brought
> You to the American Shore: Out of The Dead City
>     carried you,
> Free, Awake, in Fever and in Sleep, to the
> City of A Thousand Suns where, there, in the innocent
>     heart's
> Cry & the Mechanized Roar of one's very own this.
>     The 20th Century, one's
> Own betrayed momentary, fragmented Beauty got
> Forgotten, one Snowy Evening. Near a Woods,
>     because
> The Horse Knows the Way: because of, "The Hat on
>     the Bed," and
> Because of having "Entered the Labyrinth, finding No
>     Exit.", is
> That self-same ship, the "U.S.S. Nature" by name,
>     that D. H. Lawrence
>       wrote one of his very best poems about;
>
> THE SHIP OF DEATH; (a/k/a THE CAT CAME BACK)!

The distinguished boat which becomes the ship of death is a compound of body, soul, and ambition and personality, as striven for and then lost; desire and struggle lead to loss, revealing the collapse of the body and the true identity of the self as the ship of death, an ambiguity of course. The poem is labyrinthine like life, justifying the reference to a sonnet of Petrarch's that Berrigan once translated with George Schneeman: "Entered the Labyrinth, finding no Exit." After the deathy opening lines one meets with a succession of literary references generating each other through associational processes. I'm not sure of all the references; the title, **"The Einstein Intersection,"** and Out of The Dead City and City of A Thousand Suns refer to works by Samuel R. Delany, the science fiction writer and a friend, but there are references also to Frost's poem "Stopping By Woods On A Snowy Evening," to the children's song which begins "Over the river and through the woods to grandmother's house we go," to the Petrarch sonnet, to the Lawrence poem, and to a popular song ("the cat came back"). Lawrence's poem's ending hints of rebirth, the cat coming back? Or is the cat coming back death after all? The language of this poem is strangely thrilling though the tone is ironic; it's composed of the odds-and-ends of thinking, the connections the head often makes when not trying to think about something. Berrigan always asserted that he thought in words and that when he wasn't thinking in words he was reading. I don't particularly believe this assertion refers to what goes on in the mind, I think it refers to a sort of self-training, on his part, in being conscious either of words or of nothing, because thinking is useless, blocks action, stirs up messy unhelpful emotion, etc.—or so he thought. **"The Einstein Intersection"** impels the reader through long lines clotted with capitalized phrases which stop one for split-seconds of recognition, cognition: will the reader make it? and does of course, along and hovering and towards, feeling slightly gotten at in such lines as "the Mechanized Roar of one's very own this, The 20th Century." Yes, we've all held it close.

A poem like **"Joy of Shipwrecks,"** which appears further along in the book in what one might think of as the early spring section, is, like **"The Einstein Intersection,"** starred with phrases and words where layered events, small concatenations of meanings, light up, but these are subtler and certainly not capitalized:

> Stoop where I sit, am crazy
> in sunlight on, brown as stone,
> like me, (stoned, not brown; I
> am white, like writer trash), see
> that stick figure, chalky, also
> white, with tentative grin, walking
> toward us? Feel your blood stirring?
> That's Eileen, as typical as sunlight
> in the morning; typical as the morning
> the morning after a typical Eileen night

If the reader remembers **"The Einstein Intersection"** when approaching **"Joy of Shipwrecks"** it will be wondered if it is the Ship of Death that has been wrecked and if so whether that means death or life. The first phrase is really funny—"Stoop where I sit"—since a stoop is a place, a posture, and a lowering of one's standards; the "I" of the poem—is it the poet or the dedicatee?—is "crazy in sunlight" but is that good or bad? "I / am white, like writer trash" alludes to both "poor white trash" and crumpled paper in a writer's wastepaper basket. The word "white" keeps changing as a "stick figure, chalky, also / white" approaches the stoop: "white" is a race now but is also beginning to mean something like "hungover" or white after a long debauched night. The stick figure becomes "Eileen" and the word "Eileen" becomes "I lean," because of "Stoop where I sit" (and because Berrigan always thought of the name that way). But "Eileen" is as "typical as sunlight / in the morning," "Eileen" is made to seem positive; everything feels crazy and wrecked, poor and wrecked, as well as joyous and wrecked. Berrigan was leaning a lot the last few years of his life; he was running out of time and so was trying to get everything said and taken care of. This involved a lot of leaning on others, leaning in on, pressuring of people to listen, people who didn't know he was dying since he wasn't doing it in the conventional way, that is, with a final diagnosis, a doctor, a hospital. This poem doesn't quite say that, but taken with the other poems it does.

I've been showing how certain poems work and what their background is. These have so far been "poem" poems, by which I mean almost traditional poems in that they look and sound like poems and are written in complete (sometimes obsessively complete and byzantinely claused) sentences. There are also "idea" poems, such as **"People Who Change Their Names,"** which is essentially a list of names with punctuation. Another idea poem is **"Tough Cookies,"** which is a list of simple sentences that might be inserted in fortune cookies, inspired by Frank O'Hara's poem "Lines for the Fortune Cookies," and containing such lines as

> You have strange friends, but
> they are going to be strangers.
>
> Everything is Maya, but
> you will never know it.
>
> Your gaity is not cowardice,
> but it may be hepatitis.

Berrigan, incidentally, died of cirrhosis of the liver, a condition which usually is, and had been preceded by a ghastly session of hepatitis. On the next page after **"Tough Cookies,"** in what is probably the autumn part of the book, is a poem called **"Skeats and the Industrial Revolution,"** written in the peculiar non-syntax of the dictionary definition. The title of course is a play on "Keats and the Industrial Revolution"; beneath the title are the words "(DICK JEROME, 3/4 View) / ink on paper," since the artist Dick Jerome had provided an image for the postcard on which the work was written. The definition from Skeats's *Etymological Dictionary* which the poem takes off from is of *God*:

> *God*: perhaps, The being worshipped. To
> whom sacrifice is offered. Not allied to
> 'good.' (which is an adjective, not a
> 'being,' *Godwit*: a bird, or, more recently,
> a 'twittering-machine', (from the Anglo-Saxon
> *God-wiht*: just possibly meaning, 'worthy creature.'
> Viz. Isle of Wight—isle of Creatures. See, also,
> *Song folk*: Childe Ballad #478: "I've been
> a creature for a thousand years." . . .)

This is a dense, allusive gathering of language about deity, worship, song (poetry), and nature, in a light enough tone, but Berrigan is always also serious and these are serious words being defined. Not all of the words come from Skeats, of course. "Twittering-machine" for example is a phrase used by Peter Schjeldahl, in a book review (it's really a Paul Klee title) to describe certain of my own poems from the

seventies. The word "creature" also has a history of reference to myself: I have an early poem called "Creatures" and often preferred the word, in playful conversation, to words like "people" or "humans." There is in *A Certain Slant,* earlier on in the book, a poem called **"Creature,"** dedicated to me, which is a parodic rewriting of one of my better-known poems, "When I Was Alive." The last reference in the work, "I've been a creature for a thousand years" is a rewrite of a line by the singer/musician/composer Neil Young: "I've been a miner for a thousand years" (The singer is "searching for a heart of gold," gold being another word sounding like god or good or godwit though it's omitted. "Childe" probably suggested "Young," another word not quite included.) The poem implies that there is a god, that god is not the same as good since god is more than a human adjective, and that a bird or poet is possessed by god or godwit, though is also a mere creature whose life seems endless.

Among the poems which might be called stories, descriptions which stand for something else is **"In Morton's Grille,"** a reminiscence of a café in which a machine might play a three-minute movie of a purported episode from the feud between the Hatfields and McCoys:

> & a zany 3 minute movie of the Hatfields
> shooting at the McCoys out a log cabin
> window came on; the McCoys ran out of
> bullets, so they started singing, "Pass the
> Biscuits, Mirandy!" Grandma's biscuits were
> so hard, terrible, but saved the day when thrown
> at the real McCoys.

Those are the last seven lines of the thirteen-line poem; it isn't hard to guess that the poem is meant to be about feuds; as I've indicated before, Berrigan was involved at the time in a handful of, how can one put it, not feuds all of them, but situations involving bad feeling stemming from seemingly small incidents. The poems that deal with them are clean and inscrutable:

### Montezuma's Revenge

> In order to make friends with the natives
> In my home town, I let them cut off my face
> By the shores of Lake Butter, on
> The 7th anniversary of their arrival
> In our Utopia It was the First of May.
> Nose-less, eye-less, speechless, and
> With no ears, I understood their reasoning.
> And will spend the rest of my days
> helping them cover their asses. Free.

In this poem the speaker has been longer in his Utopia than "the natives," a reminder that invaders of new lands often quickly become not only the governors of them but the new definition of what a native or citizen is. Any community can be taken over and redefined;

old-timers are often asked not to be who they are, not to represent anything threatening, not to have force or claim intelligence. In another poem, called **"In Your Fucking Utopias,"** the very idea of a utopia seems to represent exclusion:

> Let the heart of the young
>     exile the heart of the old: Let the heart
>         of the old
> Stand exiled from the heart of the young:
>     Let other people die: Let Death be
>         inaugurated.
> Let there be Plenty Money & Let the
> Darktown Strutters pay their way in
> To the Gandy-Dancers Ball. But Woe unto you, O
>     Ye Lawyers, because I'll be there, and
>         I'll be there.

The opening lines are from Whitman's poem "Respondez!" and a Whitmanic/Ginsbergian voice is used in several of the poems, as if the sound itself were a kind of subject, a comment on generosity and where Berrigan had come to find it lacking. Such poems are played off against the book's several overtly political poems, one being "Mutiny!" about the Falkland Islands War, containing lines by the British poet Tom Pickard:

> they kept rolling over, be-
> neath the tracer bullets and
> the Antarctic moon, beneath the
> daunting missiles and the Prince
> in his helicopter, they were
> steaming toward interesting places,
> to meet interesting people, and
> kill them. They were at sea,
> and it was also beneath them.

"They" sounds chillingly like the new arrivals at the shores of Lake Butter. Colonization in the poetry world takes place frequently, though it's always a small event in the eyes of others, who by treating such events as small would make poetry small. The Falkland Islands War, too, was very small; it was, certainly, beneath the attention of most people. One poem that Berrigan loved to read was "To Sing The Song. That Is fantastic," a reggae influenced by the singer Yellowman, about Caribbeans selling M-16s to French Canadians:

> The soldiers shoot the old woman
>     down
> They shoot the girl-child on
>     the ground: we
> Steal & sell the M-16s, use
> The money to buy the weed
> The sky is blue & the Erie is
>     Clean;
> Come to us with your M-16.

It's possible that the book's very short poems create an illusion that the book is slight. The short poem was a form dear to Berrigan's intellect: his influences in this field had initially been Kerouac and Ungaretti. He came

to see the form as a vehicle for meditation and perfection since every part, every piece of every letter of every word, is apparent. But the haiku has felt banalized lately, the short poem seems often directed towards jokes, and again it is a time that seems to prefer either large-scale, personally ambitious poems whose concerns are very general or that descriptive poem that's really prose which continues to haunt the mainstream.

### Windshield

There is no windshield.

This is funny and bleak; the word "windshield" becomes perfectly opaque and then ridiculous: what on earth could a "windshield" be? One pictures a knight holding it up, though the original drawing by George Schneeman (reproduced on the cover of the book) suggests something as fragile as the fan of a Japanese court lady. The poem is obviously in key with the deathiness of the whole book, but it's also perfectly light.

### Okay, First. . . .

"Truth is that which,
Being so, does do its
work."
(I said That.)

The first thing, the fundamental thing, is truth, a working active beingness; it's much better said in the poem, much clearer, isn't it? "I said That." The capital T changes the emphasis: the said truth became different from its speaker, because it was the truth. Those two positions may be contradictory; on the other hand, there they are in the same poem.

### Jo-Mama

The St. Mark's Poetry Project
is closed for the summer. But
all over the world, poets
are writing poems. Why?

This is a poem directed against the provincialism of poetry communities even in a city like New York. Two important words are "world" and "Why?" One rather faint voice in the poem is saying, why bother to write poems if our all-important poetry center is closed; the dominant answering voice states that poetry is an immense community worldwide and ancient in which one's own group is a tiny speak.

I have been leaving out all of the "nice" poems, warm with friendship feelings, fatherly feelings, and love. There are poems which celebrate visits by Joanne Kyger and by English poet friends (Pickard, and Wendy Mulford, Denise Riley, and Doug Oliver, in New York for a poetry festival); there are poems with and for the children and myself; there are two lovely poems with/

about Allen Ginsberg and Peter Orlovsky; there are funny Christmas messages to Barrett Watten and Carla Harryman, and to Jim and Rosemary Carroll. There is an almost literally warm poem for Anne Waldman and Reed Bye, called **"Dinosaur Love"**:

> Anne Lesley Waldman says, No Fossil Fuels
> The best of the free times are still yet to come
> With all of our running & all of our coming if we
> Couldn't laugh we'd both go insane—with changes
>     of attitudes
> At the Horse Latitudes—if we couldn't laugh, we'd
>     All be insane—
> but right here with you, the living seems true, &
> the gods are not burning us just to keep warm.

I'd like to conclude by invoking the beginning and ending of the book, both of which are quasireligious and complicated. The book was meant to contain, in fact, at its beginning, a copy of a horoscope cast for Ted in 1981; I believe it was omitted because it didn't reproduce very well. It would have been a sort of graphic signifying fatedness, a map or plan for temperament born in the stars: that itself signifying all manner of things that can't be helped, among which I think Berrigan might have included class, talent (even genius), certain deep-seated character traits. As a result of which, the reader might have concluded, it has come to this, this final book. The very first poem, called **"Poem,"** is

> Yea, though I walk
> through the Valley of
> the Shadow of Death, I
> Shall fear no evil—
> for I am a lot more
> insane than
> This Valley.

The poem, a rather tonally blasphemic invocation of the 23rd Psalm, suggests Whitman's characterization of death, in "When Lilacs Last in the Dooryard Bloom'd" as "sane and sacred." The poem does sound slightly insane, at least shaky: Berrigan believed in being overt since that was truthful, and one of his favorite lines of poetry was Roethke's "This shaking keeps me steady." (Berrigan's hands trembled when he read his poems in public.) The last two poems in the book are December poems, Christmas poems. The second-to-last, called **"Christmas Card (for Barry & Carla)"**:

> Take me, third factory of life!
>     But don't put me in the wrong guild.
> So far my heart has borne even
>     the things I haven't described.
>
> Never be born, never be died.

The "right guild," if you'll remember from the beginning, from the previously censored second poem, is the Whores & Poets Guild: Berrigan never wanted to belong to a different one. "Never be born, never be died," a

phrase of Buddhist sentiment (and Berrigan had both a strong Buddhist and strong Christian streak) was remembered by Berrigan for years from a tiny pamphlet by a Japanese artist/poet whose name I don't know. The final poem, called **"Poem,"** gives the book to the general world, its meaning to the body politick:

> The Nature of the Commonwealth
> the whole body of the People
> flexed her toes and
> breathed in pine.
>
> I'm the one that's so
> radical, 'cause all I do is pine. Oh I just
> can't think of anything—
> No politics. No music. Nobody. Nothing but sweet
>
> Romance. Per se. De gustibus non disputandum est.
> Flutters eyelashes. Francis, my house is falling down.
> Repair it. Merry Christmas.

The Whores & Poets Guild is similar to the Franciscan order in that it vows poverty and a certain kind of obedience (to principle, you might say), it is itinerant and begging, its members can seem crazy, indeed what seems to be insane might turn out to be exemplar, as in some of the stories in *The Little Flowers of St. Francis.* The "Whores" part simply has to do with money, the poet's practice of prostitution (who doesn't?)—Berrigan was never a courtesan, he was a whore. The "Whores" part also has to do with the body and one's "use" of it simply to keep going, via speed for example, often for the sake of others. The body, like a whore's body, then breaks down relatively early. Whores and other reprobates and scum were of course the core of early Christianity; they, and soldiers for example, are the *used* people, used and cast off. This poem is flirty and sexy too, like a whore? The Nature of the Commonwealth is calling on Francis, at any rate, to repair Her house. Thus the book ends not with the call of death (which was coming soon) but with the call to the poet's task again.

*A Certain Slant of Sunlight* is an important book because, for one thing, it's the only one like it. It faces death and observes the community through a various kind of poem which is true to the life being led. Also, it's the repository of a number of personal virtues one might care to emulate or be inspired by. And may I ask where such virtues, manifestly existing, fit into a philosophy which disallows the psychological I? The psychological I is that which by making terrible mistakes learns how to live and be generous, out of its very self, its I. But back to the specific virtues of this book. It complains but it isn't selfish or even self-centered; it's thoroughly alive; it's prophetic, low-life, and entertaining. It's very deep if you know how to find depth in poetry; it's courageous, and being that, the reader can take courage from it too. Furthermore, the language, the form (they seem to be simultaneous) of the poems is extraordinary in its ability to negotiate quick dense changes and still maintain transparency and the brevity necessitated by the postcards. These poems suggest a direction in poetry that has yet to be picked up: we've all been too obsessed with being "important." But importance isn't necessarily where you think it is; it's really generated by circumstance and is in the flesh and spirit of the poems, not in a presentation of "importance." *These* are important poems.

I'd like to point out that in the poem **"Interstices,"** which is a flashback to the method of *The Sonnets,* that Berrigan says "call me Berrigan." I've obeyed the request: it's created enough distance for me to see the full worth of the work.

## Mark Hillringhouse (essay date summer 2005)

SOURCE: Hillringhouse, Mark. "The New York School Poets: B Is for Berrigan." *Literary Review* 48, no. 4 (summer 2005): 146-80.

[*In the following essay, Hillringhouse recalls his friendship with Berrigan and describes his unusual method of writing poetry.*]

I first met Ted in 1980 at Stevens Institute of Technology in Hoboken, New Jersey during the semester he was teaching there as poet-in-residence. Ted held court in the classroom. His realm was poetry, being a poet and talking to students about his favorite poets, and inspiring his students with his passion for poetry was what he did best. This is where I first interviewed him, after his class in his office. I did a follow-up interview with him in his apartment months later. By then I was starting to get to know him on a friendly basis and Ted told me that I was welcome to stop by any time.

At his apartment, on the way up or down the three flights of marble stairs of 101 St. Mark's Place, I would bump into other itinerant East Village poets who had come over to visit on Ted's invitation: Steve Carey, John Godfrey, Eileen Myles, Elinor Nauen, Simon Pettit, Tom Savage, Harris Schiff, to name a few. A couple times a week, I would walk over after dinner, and after browsing the St. Mark's Bookstore, to sit by the mattress where Ted lay on the floor in the room behind where the kids (Anselm and Edmund) had their bunk beds. It was a four-room railroad flat filled with oddments of stray furniture and makeshift bookshelves.

Ted once asked me if I could get him a cat. I was living with a friend whose wife had twenty cats and so I said, "No problem." I think one of the boys wanted a cat so I came back with a kitten. Ed Smith (a fellow poet) and I had promised to take his kids to Coney Island for the day—Ted said: "If anything happens to my kids you'd better be dead." We said, "Yeah, right, okay."

When we returned, Ted with a pale, shocked look on his face explained that the cat had fallen out the window. There was a window in the kitchen that opened onto an airshaft and sure enough the cat had fallen. Ted asked: "Could you get me another one?" Since I had an endless supply, I said, "Sure," and brought over a new kitten the following day. He named the cat Wystan after W. H. Auden, one of his favorite poets. I think it had an ulcerated eye and six toes.

One time, we took a trip up-town to go gallery hopping, but before reaching the galleries we took a detour and Ted made the cab driver drop us off at an Upper East Side doctor's office. Ted explained it was for his "diet" pills. I laughed when I saw the name "Dr. Sugar" on the door. There was a crowd of people in the office all waiting for their pills. Ted came out with a brown plastic vial of amphetamines that he slipped into his coat pocket. On the corner in front of the Whitney Museum, we bought hot dogs and two Pepsis from a vendor and Ted offered me a couple of his pills. I felt nothing for the first few minutes, and then I understood. Ted was like this every day.

Walking the city with Ted was an experience. He was constantly running into people on elevators, in galleries, in front of bookstores, who knew him. In the Tibor de Nagy Gallery on 57th Street—made famous by John Myers who ran the gallery back in the 50s, and who brought the poets and the painters together and where the New York School was born—Ted finagled a free Alex Katz catalogue from the receptionist with some verbal magic and an old business card he kept in his wallet. On his home turf in the East Village people came up to shake hands, exchange gossip, swap news. He was like the mayor of St. Mark's Place and he made that part of the city into his own small town.

After looking at several galleries, we decided to walk several blocks. On our way back downtown on Fifth Avenue, Ted pulled me into a huge store without looking at the sign above the window. I couldn't imagine why he wanted to go into a video store since he didn't own a VCR. Inside, he stood still and let out an "OOOH." The Brentano's that was once there had vanished. So we got the hell out and ended up at the Gotham Book Store on 47th Street where Ted was greeted warmly by all the sales help. Frances Steloff, Gotham's founder, in her 90s, was sitting in the back room going through her letters. His mission was to locate an out-of-print copy of Edwin Denby's *Looking at the Dance,* which he found without any trouble.

I remember Ted's fondness for Denby's sonnets, which were in some way an influence on his own. Of all of Ted's books, and quite a few come to mind, *The Sonnets* and *Red Wagon* are my favorites. When he read his poetry he was able to convey this extraordinary level of choked-up emotion; his voice had a quaking tremble, as if the dam holding back the water of his life would suddenly burst through.

One night sitting with Ted in the living room, which was odd enough, since I had never in the three years I had known him seen him move from his mattress, Ted handed me a tin box of postcards with short poems written on back in his own delicate handwriting. He said: "Pick out some you want." When I had picked the ones I wanted and showed them to him he said: "Not those—you picked all the good ones!" I had picked ones like **"A Certain Slant of Sunlight"** and Ted grabbed them back and handed me the ones he wanted me to have. I now have two original postcards one of which uses a Polaroid of Bernadette Mayer in a nightgown at sixteen and underneath Ted had written a short poem entitled **"Saint Bernadette and All That."** I couldn't show the card to anyone and I realized why Ted had wanted to dispose of it. Animosity between the two flared up over some alleged stolen copies of Ted's *The Sonnets* that Bernadette Mayer and Lewis Warsh had published under the United Artists label.

The other card he gave me was a reversed line for line Alice Notley (Ted's wife) poem entitled "Christmas in September." Ted inscribed the card to me and handed it back. He must have known then that he was sick or otherwise why would he be giving things away. He gave Ed Smith a Tom Clark pencil drawing of two Boston Red Sox Hall of Famers that had hung on the wall across from his bed. I think it was Ted Williams and Carl Yazstremski.

I always felt welcome there and would carry over some bottles of Pepsi, which Ted drank as he talked non-stop, and I would get a word or two in when his smoking cough left me an opening, or the phone would ring and without missing a beat Ted would pull that conversation into the room.

I always had my camera and so I took some photos. I had never seen Ted standing up in his own apartment, so I shot him standing and then I wanted a portrait and made him sit up from bed where he had been lying half-undressed. The eyes had a certain sad, soulful look with his black, horn rimmed frames and his ubiquitous Chesterfield that burned down in a pendulous cylindrical ash and which would fall off intermittently burning his chest hair.

That was the last time I saw him after those photos. I was away up in Cape Cod when I got the news he had died. I wrote a poem for him, which used some of the very words he said to me in an interview I had done the year before. I called the poem "Independence Day." Ted had died on the Fourth of July and the Yankees had beaten his beloved Red Sox in a "no-hitter."

I read him now and I go back frequently to poems like **"Red Shift"** or **"Things to Do in Providence"** or **"Frank O'Hara"**—heart-breaking, rhythmic, ample— "heavy with that lightness"—poems. Ted's method of constructing a poem was to write down personal memories, take lines from newspapers, quote what other people said in conversation, or to tear apart other poets' poems he admired, to turn their lines around and insert his in between theirs then erase them, leaving his own lines intact.

He wrote the way he spoke and his poems are full of talk, his and others'. Sometimes ideas would present themselves and he would build around those. His poem **"Whitman in Black"** was constructed this way. He told me he had been thinking about Melville in Manhattan, and in a somber mood, imagined him doing penance for his sins, living in obscurity at the end of his life.

Twenty years after Ted's death, I went to the Whitney Museum at Philip Morris across from Grand Central Station on 42nd Street, and there was a show of Alex Katz paintings. On the wall was a portrait of Ted Berrigan by Alex Katz.

## Alice Notley (essay date 2005)

SOURCE: Notley, Alice. Introduction to *The Collected Poems of Ted Berrigan,* edited by Alice Notley, pp. 1-17. Berkeley: University of California Press, 2005.

[*In the following essay, Notley traces Berrigan's literary career, noting the changes the poet made from his earlier, best-known work of the 1960s through the more varied poems of the 1970s and early 1980s.*]

I heard Ted say more than once that his collected poems should be like a collected books. But he didn't always work in sequences, and he wasn't always consciously in the process of writing a book. He wrote many individual poems, and he sometimes seemed to write purely for fun. As for publication, publishers would approach him for a book without knowing exactly what he had, and sometimes it didn't seem to him as if he had that much. If there was a sequence ready, or a book in a unified style like *Many Happy Returns,* certainly he published that. If he had a stack of dissimilar works or if he didn't even know what he had, he still set about the process of constructing a "book." He loved to make things out of pieces, often ones that didn't fit together conventionally. A book was like a larger poem that could be as much "made" out of what was at hand, as "written" in a continuous way out of a driving idea.

This volume is an attempt to be a collected books, but it can't be that precisely and so isn't called *The Collected Books.* Though Ted wrote sequences and constructed books, he didn't produce a linear succession of discrete, tidy volumes. He perceived time as overlapping and circular; the past was always alive and relevant, and a particular poem might be as repeatable as an individual line or phrase was for him from the time of the composition of **The Sonnets** onward. How were we, the editors, to deal with repetitions of poems from book to book? Most especially what were we to do about the book-length sequence *Easter Monday?*

Ted worked for years on *Easter Monday,* which he didn't call finished until shortly before his death, when he finalized the selection and order. Meanwhile, during his lifetime, every one of the poems was published individually, in two chapbooks, **A Feeling for Leaving** and **Carrying a Torch,** and more significantly in the books **Red Wagon** and **So Going Around Cities: New and Selected Poems 1958-1979.** *Easter Monday* has never been presented as a unified sequence until now; but placing its poems together considerably shortens the book **Red Wagon.** So we have shortened **Red Wagon,** and shorter it is still a book, and a good one. But dealing with *Easter Monday* showed us that we would have to construct this **Collected Poems** a little as if we were Ted and not just editors.

Furthermore, there was a lot of uncollected work, including early poems, "short" poems, out-takes from the sequence **A Certain Slant of Sunlight,** a scattering of individual poems from the 70s and 80s, and a set of poems written during the last six months of his life and kept together in its own folder. We decided to organize most of this work into booklike sections. We've discussed ceaselessly what to omit, what isn't "good enough" in the sense of not really holding up next to the others, because if this *is* a collected books, each poem should fill its own space within its own book or section. We are not Ted, but we tried to think like him; and there's still room in the future for a slim volume of retrieved poems, as in *Poems Retrieved* of Frank O'Hara (a possibility Ted would have loved). In the beginning I held out for every scrap of a poem, while Anselm and Edmund had a more selective sense. I gradually gave up on such works as "The 30 Most Common Names in the Manhattan Telephone Directory, 1979," various small-scale "Things to Do" poems, occasional poems (practically anyone's birthday in the late 60s), and the worst of Ted's rather bad "early poems." I retain tender feelings for all of these poems.

With regard to the reprinting of a poem or two from book to book: it doesn't make economical sense to repeat poems, so we have most often chosen to omit poems that have been printed in other sections. Thus, where there are omissions, I indicate in the notes where and what they are. Also, there existed a handful of poems which seemed to float near specific books, stylistically, but hadn't been included in them. The

relevant books were collections not sequences, and we have taken the liberty of placing these poems in the volumes they point to. Again I signal, in the notes, where this has been done; there are not enough of these poems to merit their own section, and in each case they fit gracefully where inserted. I don't think Ted would mind, though more pristine editors than we are might squirm.

If it sounds as if the rules of organization of this book work through exception, I can only say that Ted's work creates the need for exception. His esthetics were fluid, and he was governed more by the impulse to make art than to be consistent. Thus the books or sections are presented in an order that reflects, mostly but not entirely, chronology of publication. **In a Blue River** is "out of order." Though it was published in 1981, most of its poems were written in the early 70s, and it has been placed with other short poems from that time near books from that time. It was, in fact, in the late 60s and early 70s that Ted was most intensely interested in the short poem as a form.

Finally, we have chosen to present fourteen early poems, which, along with certain poems in **Nothing for You,** help demonstrate where **The Sonnets** came from. These not-so-good poems contain a number of the repeated lines in **The Sonnets**; so the book concludes with the beginning, making a circle. One of Ted's favorite concepts was that of a poem or book creating a circular shape whose ending pushes the reader back up into the work. And he always remained interested in his not-very-good poems, because they, too, reflected who he was. A circle is a unity, and oneself was/is always in process back there.

Having explained our general editorial procedure I would now like to take the reader quickly through this volume's sections, focusing on their contents and marking, as practicable in this space, Ted's esthetic changes from book to book and through the years. I've organized this part of the introduction by decade, since Ted's adult life and career seems to lend itself to this shape. In the 60s Ted was a young man and wrote his best-known work; in the 70s he became a more various poet, he entered a second marriage, and his health began to fail; in the early 80s he wrote his last work. He died young, at the age of forty-eight, on July 4, 1983. These poems span a creative period of roughly twenty years (not counting the earliest work), which isn't a long time. It seems remarkable that there should be so many poems.

### THE SIXTIES

This collection begins with **The Sonnets,** Ted's most famous book. It really is quite close to where Ted began, despite the fact that it is a classic. It is a young man's book, the product of relentless self-education, and being partly constructed out of lines from "early poems," often suggests the awkward intensity of inexperience. But it floats above that place as if observing it from the dead: "dear Berrigan. He died / Back to books. I read."

It is important to say once again that *The Sonnets* was written in New York, that Ted had arrived in New York via Providence and Tulsa; that Ted would leave New York for a while but then return to it; that he was always called a New York School poet, and that he mostly liked the attribution. *The Sonnets,* in fact, could reflect no other setting than that city. In these poems New York bricks and human density have become the interior walls of someone always reading and thinking. Outside-in.

*The Sonnets* was written in the early 60s, most especially in 1963: that is, it seems to have been in 1963 that Ted realized he was generating a long sonnet sequence, though he had written some of the poems as early as 1961. Entries in his journals, dated November 16 and 20, 1962, record the composition of the first six sonnets out of lines from previous poems and from his translation of Rimbaud's "Le Bateau Ivre." But there was a point, early in 1963, when he suddenly knew what he was doing: with Dadaist cut-up and Cageian chance methods, transforming not-so-good poems into an astonishing and original structure.

The reader will come to notice that Ted returned to the strict form of *The Sonnets* several times, in his books, to make points about his life and the passage of time. The form is suited to detached self-scrutiny, using lines and phrases from past and present poems, reading material, and ongoing mind, in an order determined by numbers rather than syntax. The pieces of the self are allowed to separate and reform: one is not chronology but its parts and the real organism they create. Ted liked to say that poetry is numbers, and maybe everything is numbers. The sonnet form is "about" the number fourteen, but Ted's sonnets use fourteen as a frame for the disassemblage of the number, making a real advance in the form and its relation to the psyche. To the extent that Ted broke and remade the form, it became possible to use it for more than argument. One could condense cognition into fourteen or so lines, if each piece, each segment of the fourteen, even each phrase in a line, meant enough.

*The Sonnets* has been through four editions. There were originally eighty-eight sonnets, but in the first two editions (from "C" Press and Grove Press) he allowed only sixty-six; in the third edition (from United Artists) he added six more; and in the fourth edition (Penguin Books) I included seven more that he had authorized before his death in 1983. This collection conforms to the Penguin edition in including seventy-nine sonnets.

After the composition of *The Sonnets,* Ted entered a period of further involvement with aleatory methods, cut-up, collage, and transliteration, overlappingly with the more direct poems of *Many Happy Returns.* We have placed three works written according to a "method" (a word he liked) in a single section called *Great Stories of the Chair.* They are the eight-poem sequence **"The Secret Life of Ford Madox Ford,"** the sequence of prose paragraphs "Great Stories of the Chair," and the long poem **"A Boke."** All of *Many Happy Returns* is included in a separate section.

On the manuscript of **"The Secret Life of Ford Madox Ford"** Ted scrawled "1963? or 4?" The first version of the sequence was published in two issues of Ted's magazine, *"C"* (*A Journal of Poetry*), in 1964. The eight poems are hilarious and ferocious. They are obviously transliterations, that is, translations via sound and thought association of works in a foreign language. The original texts are to be found in Pierre Reverdy's *Quelques Poèmes* (see notes). Ted had previously written several transliterative poems: one example from *The Sonnets* is **"Mess Occupations"** (**Sonnet XXXIX**), with the note *"after Henri Michaux."* There is an especially fluid, automatic quality to the lines of *The Secret Life of Ford Madox Ford,* and an occasional vicious literalness: "Eat a potato she said you sober All-American."

*Great Stories of the Chair* reveals a new influence on Ted's writing, that of the prose of William Burroughs, whom Ted did not read until after the composition of *The Sonnets.* Three of the "stories" were published in the journal *Mother,* in 1965, under the title *Paragraphs.* The entire sequence of twelve prose blocks was published in *Angel Hair* 4 (winter 1967/68). The cut-up methods of Burroughs and Brion Gysin do not seem essentially different from Dadaist procedures. However, applied to prose structures which coaxed plot out of words themselves, Burroughsian cut-up resulted in novels that are full-blown visions generated as much verbally as through the senses. Poetry originating from within words (not from within the poet per se) was already Ted's practice. He always asserted that he thought in words, that he was usually either reading, writing, talking, thinking about/in words, or sleeping. Words were literally his mind in process. And to cut up his own poems, for example, was not to do anything other than to think and feel. *Great Stories of the Chair* is blocks of thought and emotion—what else?

Though **"A Boke"** is dated 1966 in *So Going Around Cities,* it was first published in the journal *Kulchur* in the autumn of 1965. It is a cut-up of an article by the poet James Dickey, first published in *The New Yorker,* about traveling around the United States giving poetry readings. **"A Boke"** is a send-up of mainstream humorlessness, but with an autobiographical air to it, and, as Ted once told me, intentionally drawn out to a point veering toward (not quite arriving at) boredom. Interspersed from time to time throughout **"A Boke"** is the line "Remember the fragrance of Grandma's kitchen?" which Ted lifted from Burroughs. Also included in the mix are references to the folk songs "John Henry" and "Nine-Pound Hammer."

It is the book *Many Happy Returns,* published by Corinth Books in 1969, that is Ted's first major statement after *The Sonnets.* The poems included in the collection span a large part of the 60s, beginning with a poem from 1962, **"Words for Love,"** and ending with **"Resolution,"** written in 1968. The forms used include cut-up and collage but also the "personal poem," as derived from Frank O'Hara's work, the "things to do" poem based on the examples of Gary Snyder and Sei Shonogon, and the long poem, as well as what one might call simply the "poem" poem, Ted's version of the emotionally direct, realistic shorter poem. There is a new open-field style in evidence, characterizing especially the great **"Tambourine Life,"** dated "Oct. 1965-Jan. 1966." **"Tambourine Life,"** divided into seventy sections of varying length, is an opening of Ted's voice; it sounds like him talking, though it also sounds "constructed," in unexpected and witty ways. The poem contains much domestic detail, specific 60s references, philosophy presented lightly, and an undercurrent of tragedy. It is dedicated to Anne Kepler—the Anne of *The Sonnets,* who died in a fire set by an arsonist while Ted was writing the poem; the book itself is dedicated to Anne Kepler and to Frank O'Hara, who died in 1966.

Another larger poem in *Many Happy Returns* is the collaged (and visually collage-like) **"Bean Spasms,"** dated 1966. It was written in conjunction with images by George Schneeman and first published in the book *Bean Spasms,* a collaborative volume involving Ted, the poet Ron Padgett, and the artist Joe Brainard. Ted later incorporated into other books the work from *Bean Spasms* that was uniquely by himself.

## THE SEVENTIES

The late 60s mark Ted's departure from New York, and his work from the early 70s is replete with references from other locales. It is significant that Ted's first book of the 70s, *In the Early Morning Rain,* was published by Cape Goliard, a British publisher.

*In the Early Morning Rain* made lavish use of drawings (now lost) by George Schneeman to create spaciousness and to emphasize groupings. The book is a mix of work in older styles employing found materials, chance methods, transliteration, the form of *The Sonnets,* etc., and poems from the late 60s and 1970 in the new, open style of *Many Happy Returns.* In 1968

Ted had begun leading a migrant poetry teacher's life and was spending time in Midwestern university towns like Iowa City and Ann Arbor. The light was different, he was making new friends, and he had begun to feel fated: to be addicted to drugs (pills, mostly speed) and perhaps to die early. The new poems elegize people who have recently died (Jack Kerouac, Rocky Marciano, Franny Winston, and others), allude to the war in Vietnam, celebrate specific evenings and occasions, and also celebrate the overcoming of emotional shakiness through the writing of poetry and through affection for others.

The long poem *Train Ride,* written in 1971 but not published until 1978, is a lavish example of an affectionate poem for a friend: it is a "love poem" addressed to Joe Brainard, and is about love, sex, and friendship. The poem speaks to Joe throughout, informally, frankly, a little in Joe's own style, and includes mock complaints about Ted's and Joe's mutual friends, about Joe himself, and a projected complaint, too, about Ted. The poem was written on a single day, February 18, during the course of a literal train ride between New York and Providence; it filled a rather large notebook. I remember Ted returning from the trip with the poem, slightly confused by the fact that it really was everything he wanted to say to Joe but also probably really a poem. This ambiguity, an unsure edge between life and art (not like Rauschenberg's "gap" but much more razorlike, something that might hurt you in its reality) kept Ted from publishing it for some years.

**"Memorial Day,"** written around the same time in collaboration with Anne Waldman, is a long poem in a similar voice, though the voice is Ted's and Anne's fused. The voice is open, plain speaking, and flexible. It can take on everything a conversation can; and though the poem has a back-and-forth movement in it, it also feels unified and inspired in the way that two people talking sometimes become one thing, the conversation. The poem was written to be performed at a reading at the Poetry Project (St. Mark's Church-in-the-Bouwerie, New York) on May 5, 1971, and Ted and Anne worked on it for several months. Since Memorial Day falls in May and is potentially rich in its association with death and sacrifice/heroism, it was decided in advance that Memorial Day would be the title and subject of the work. The two poets were living in separate towns on Long Island and wrote separately, in asterisk-headed sections, giving or sending their work to each other from time to time for response, but there was no chronological ordering going on. At some point Ted wrote all of what would be the last section, and then Anne arranged the material. Ted always considered it to be the most successful literary collaboration he had participated in, in view of its seriousness and depth.

Meanwhile, and in deliberate counterpoint to such longer structures, Ted was writing many short poems.

He often cited as formal influences the work of Giuseppe Ungaretti (the sequence **"Life of a Man"** in *In the Early Morning Rain* consists of transliterations of Ungaretti's work), and Aram Saroyan's poems, particularly the one-word poems. The section we have called *Short Poems* is divided into two parts. *In a Blue River* contains most of the chapbook of that name, published in 1981 by Susan Cataldo's Little Light Books. *Uncollected Short Poems* consists of a handful of poems first published in *So Going Around Cities,* as well as many uncollected short poems. Most of the poems included in *Short Poems* were written in the late 60s and, especially, the early 70s.

The short poem obviously involves more thought process than writing/reading process, if one can split the two. A short poem is peculiarly naked, whether it's a weighty short poem or a lighter short poem. It often seemed to take years for Ted to decide that a particular one was good enough to be published. And it's not surprising that *In a Blue River* is a later publication. A successful short poem may be capable of projecting new meanings on successive readings, but in a monolithic way, as if a new room has opened out, rather than in the overall, textured way that a longer poem can light up in a mesh of changeable meanings. For example, it may take the reader some time to connect the title **"Larceny,"** in the poem which reads "The / opposite / of / petty / is GRAND," with the crimes of grand and petty larceny. One may be content with the observation that the opposite of petty *is* grand, a meditation on that. On the other hand a poem like **"Laments,"** which both praises and judges Janis Joplin and Jimi Hendrix, is awesome on the level of judgment: "you did it wrong." The fact of judgment, and also this particular judgment—is it only of their deaths? their lifestyles?—constantly opens up more thoughtful space.

*Red Wagon,* published by the Yellow Press in 1976, is possibly the volume of Ted's that least shows his book-constructor's touch: it is more purely a "collection," assembled while he was ill with hepatitis. The poems, however, are solid, and many are among his best. By the time of the publication of *Red Wagon* Ted had taught at the Writers' Workshop of the University of Iowa, Iowa City; at the University of Michigan at Ann Arbor; at Yale; at Northeastern Illinois University in Chicago; and at the University of Essex in England. In 1976 he moved back to New York, where he would spend his remaining eight years. *Red Wagon* includes work written in many cities and two countries. It contains important shorter poems (such as **"In the Wheel"**), a number of open-field poems (for example, the popular **"Things to Do in Providence"**) and sprawling long-lined poems (**"Something Amazing Just Happened"**).

Partway through *Red Wagon,* variety of form cedes to a denser, more slablike entity, beginning with the poem

**"Frank O'Hara"** and the five poems succeeding it, the remnants of a disbanded sequence called **"Southampton Winter."** In the original *Red Wagon,* poems from *Easter Monday* (still in the process of composition) rounded out the book for the most part, as well as a group of five sonnets. These were, in fact, five of *The Sonnets,* three previously published and two seeing print for the first time. Our version of *Red Wagon* omits the *Easter Monday* poems and the group of sonnets. It ends with **"The Complete Prelude,"** a poem made from words and phrases of Wordsworth's poem. The use of another poet's work as a word source had always been a favorite method of Ted's (see, for example, **"Sonnet VI,"** made from a poem by his friend, the poet Dick Gallup.) This method could result in a kind of book review, or a dialogue with a poet's style, or could be used to delve into Ted's own consciousness. Here it is also a way to employ the now-forbidden language of English Romantic Poetry, which being part of the poet's education is part of himself.

If **"Southampton Winter"** had dissolved as a conception, poems such as **"Chicago Morning"** and **"Newtown,"** written in Chicago in 1972 and resembling the **"Southampton Winter"** poems, became the basis for *Easter Monday.* The sequence was not really conceived until Ted's arrival in England in 1973. At both Northeastern Illinois University and the University of Essex Ted took teaching positions that had been held by Ed Dorn, who, like Ted, had recently entered into a second marriage and fathered two more children. Ted became interested in the concept of the second act, as in F. Scott Fitzgerald's now clichéd statement, "There are no second acts in American life." *Easter Monday,* dedicated to Ed Dorn and named for Willem de Kooning's beautiful painting as well as for the day after the day of rebirth, is meant to address the possibility of the second act. Ted had hoped for fifty poems, inspired by the artist George Schneeman's notion that once he'd started a project, a set of collages, say, he might as well do fifty. Ted ended up with forty-six.

Ted kept *Easter Monday* in a folder on the cover of which is inscribed *EASTER MONDAY / Poems (1972-1977).* The poems were written in Chicago, London, Wivenhoe, New York, and Boulder; many are sonnets, most have an impasto texture—thick abstract expressionistic paint—and many of them are composed of other people's words. **"From the House Journals,"** for example, is made from the first lines index to the *Collected Poems* of Frank O'Hara; **"In Blood"** is a selection of lines from a sequence of mine; and **"The Ancient Art of Wooing"** is made from a poem of mine I'd given up on, which was itself made out of a magazine article. A poem like the latter is a little like a palimpsest and a little like urban erosion. But the poems speak to and with the words of people Ted cared about or was interactive with. A few of the poems, on the other hand, are direct addresses to friends, delivered in an almost courtly manner. The sequence is very much about "not dying," in William Saroyan's phrase, not giving in to deathy forces. Ted didn't declare the sequence finished until shortly before he died in 1983, when he made the final decisions for it. There are a handful of *Easter Monday* out-takes to be found in *Nothing for You* and *So Going Around Cities.*

It should be noted that Ted was always open to chapbook and broadside publication. *In a Blue River* and *The Morning Line* are in fact chapbooks, and, as I've indicated, parts of *Easter Monday* were first published in chapbooks. A mimeographed stapled book with the singularly lovely title *A Feeling for Leaving* (Frontward Books, 1975) contains twenty-two of the poems. Another nine were published in 1980 as *Clown War 22* (edited by Bob Heman) under the title *Carrying a Torch.*

By the time *Nothing for You* was published, in 1977, Ted's and my sons, Anselm and Edmund (my co-editors of this edition), were five and three years old. Ted had two other children, David and Kate, from his marriage to Sandy Alper Berrigan. He had always delighted in being with his kids, and there are references to all of them throughout his work. The title *Nothing for You* comes from a word game Anselm and Edmund had made up, which went something like: "No cookies, no candy, no soda. Nothing, nothing for you." This was a great joke, a chant accompanied by laughter. Ted had been asked by Lewis Warsh for a book for Angel Hair Books, but it was one of those times when he felt he had nothing. So he conjured a manuscript out of piles of rejects and old poems and gleefully named it after our sons' chant.

As he constructed the book, the concept of using rejects, supposedly secondclass works, became interesting to him. A world was being created out of poems that *did* belong together, having been written in the process of discovering forms rather than perfecting them. *Nothing for You* actually has something for everyone and was much appreciated, at least by Ted's circle, when it came out. It begins with some twenty poems from the early to late-ish 60s, mostly very old works which had been tinkered with over the years until exactly right. Then there are a number of poems from the late 60s and early 70s that he was very excited by at the time of composition but abandoned when he got something that seemed superior. I remember how much he loved having written **"In Bed with Joan & Alex"** in 1969; but later it felt as if he'd dropped it in favor of poems like **"Things to Do in Providence."** Finally there are more recent poems, such as the rejects from *Easter Monday*, interspersed with poems about people: Paul Blackburn, Tom Clark, Kirsten Creeley, Sandy Berrigan.

INTO THE EIGHTIES

Ted's first publication in the 80s was *So Going Around Cities: New and Selected Poems, 1958-1979.* Appearing midway through 1980, it was a generous selection of poems, honoring, to some degree, the primacy of Ted's books as artistic shapes. There are scaled-down selections from *The Sonnets* and *Easter Monday,* and a section called *Many Happy Returns,* which is slightly different from the book itself. Collections like *In the Early Morning Rain* and *Red Wagon* are broken up into new kinds of groups, small sections reflecting the chronology of Ted's life.

For this volume, we have created a section called *In the 51st State* corresponding to the period of the late 70s through circa 1981. It is composed of a subsection, also called *In the 51st State,* containing twelve poems first published in *So Going Around Cities*; the chapbook *The Morning Line,* published by Am Here Books in 1981; and uncollected poems of roughly the same time period.

For Ted the "51st State" was New York City; the poem **"In the 51st State,"** dedicated to Ted's daughter Kate, ends with the lines: "Bon voyage, little ones. / Follow me down / Through the locks. There is no key." Thus this is also a new and puzzling "state" that Ted has entered, one of feeling older, irrelevant, and failing in health. And yet, in the same poem, after he writes "Au revoir," he counters with the parenthetical lines "(I wouldn't translate that / as 'Goodbye' if I were you)." Ted is in the process of "not dying," though he's only a few years from his death.

The new element in the poems of this section is a longer line combined with discursiveness and apparent autobiography, though Ted continues to use other people's voices and autobiographical facts as well as his own. In **"Last Poem,"** "I once had the honor of meeting Beckett and I dug him" is a quotation from Robert Creeley and in no way corresponds to anything that happened to Ted, except emotionally. There is always a "Beckett" in one's anecdotes. The practice of incorporating the lives of others into his is evident throughout Ted's previous work: in the use of others' poems and prose in cut-ups, in such "found" works as **"Autobiography in 5 Parts,"** in the weave of voices in *Easter Monday.* These techniques are an assertion that he is part of everything and everyone around him, that his reading and his interaction with others do literally become him, and that all words are free and usable. As Tom Clark once said to him, "Who owns words?"

The poems from *So Going Around Cities*—which make up the first part of *In the 51st State*—include several works that became favorite performance pieces of Ted's near the end of his life: **"Cranston Near the City**

Line," "Last Poem," and especially, **"Red Shift."** So-called Performance Poetry had been in the air for a while, and Ted picked up from it the possibility of extending his performing voice and, consequently, his writing voice. **"Red Shift"** wasn't written to be performed in a splashy way, but over the course of a year or two, he developed a set of vocal changes for it, a deliberate tremolo and a slowing down of the long lines, which seemed to stretch the poem far into time and space, allowing him to express the poem's angry urgency. On the other hand, a slightly later poem like **"After Peire Vidal, & Myself,"** in *The Morning Line,* was written precisely with performance in mind. It was declaimed publicly, in mock-troubadour fashion, to answer his friend Rochelle Kraut, who, briefly mad at him, was reading Catullus-like poems "against" him around the Lower East Side.

*The Morning Line* was a flat, stapled, mimeographed chapbook of twenty-two poems in a number of forms. **"Sonnet: *Homage to Ron*"** is made up of words by Ron Padgett; **"44th Birthday Evening, at Harris's"** is a sentimental birthday poem for Ted himself containing a dream; **"Avec la Mécanique sous les Palmes"** is entirely in French; **"Kerouac / (continued),"** is deft maneuvers with found material; **"D N A"** is like the poems in *Easter Monday*; and so on. The title *The Morning Line* refers to betting on horses—which poem, which style shall we choose?—and to a song from the musical comedy *Guys and Dolls:* "I've got a horse right here / His name is Paul Revere . . ."

The *Uncollected Poems* of this section demonstrate a continuation, even further development, of Ted's preferred and reliable forms. One discerns the arrival of the Language Poets in the poem **"I S O L A T E,"** as Ted uses Bruce Andrews's words to review Andrews's book *Film Noir* for *L=A=N=G=U=A=G=E* magazine. The **"Ten Greatest Books"** form (see the two examples in *In The Early Morning Rain*) reappears in the poem **"My 5 Favorite Records."** For the **"Ten Greatest Books"** poems, Ted had named books he was actually reading or could see in his room (they tended to be the greatest books of that exact moment), but **"My 5 Favorite Records"** was a response to a request for a list (not for a poem) from Dennis Cooper, editor of *Little Caesar* magazine. Ted then asked Art Lange, editor of the jazz magazine *Downbeat* and music critic for the *Chicago Reader,* to make a list of what *ought* to be Ted's five favorite records. The result is quite Byzantine; Ted was extremely amused by this work, but public readings of it produced some bafflement in the audience.

The poem **"Rouge,"** on the other hand, is a particularly successful version of what one might call the "linguistic poem," a form with Creeleyesque overtones that Ted had been working on for some years. In the linguistic poem he defines and works out with small words: *it, this,* and *that* in this case, but also the word *know.* I seem to remember giving him the title of the poem, which serves to negate any pedantry. Finally, one is delighted by certain poems that Ted was unable to publish due to the brevity of his remaining years: **"Compleynt to the Muse"** and **"Thin Breast Doom,"** with their allusions to Phil Whalen's manner, the several autobiographical and pseudo-autobiographical poems, and the list poem **"Memories Are Made of This."**

Ted's final book (though these are not his final poems) was *A Certain Slant of Sunlight,* which occupied him for all of 1982. This sequence of poems was written on individual postcards, 4½ inches by 7 inches, sent to him by Ken and Anne Mikolowski of the Alternative Press. There were five hundred cards to work with, one side left blank for a poem and/or image, and the other side incorporating space for a message and address. *Postcard by Ted Berrigan* was printed at the top of the message space, and running sideways, *The Alternative Press Grindstone City.* Many other artists and writers participated in the Mikolowskis' project, producing original art or text for the blank sides of their own five hundred postcards; the finished cards were always sent out singly, along with other Alternative Press items—broadsides, bumper stickers, etc.—in the Press's standard free packets. Ted, so far as I know, was the only participant who turned the postcards into a full-scale writing project and then a book.

The postcard poem was a form dominated by the size of the card, though a relatively longer poem could be written on a card if Ted shrank his handwriting. Ted immediately used semi-collaboration as a way into the poems, inducing everyone he knew to write a line or draw an image on a postcard. He later eliminated the names of the "facilitators," except for the occasional dedication. The poems are often epigrammatic, but are just as likely to be longer; they chronicle, not so explicitly, a difficult year—in terms of health, finances, relationships with friends. They are about the workings of a community, about poetry quarrels and poetry festivals, about cops on the corner and what music is being listened to, what is going on in the newspapers. Ted produced a couple hundred original poems; there are one hundred exactly in *A Certain Slant of Sunlight,* which I edited after his death, according to his instructions.

We also present here a separate section of the best of the out-takes from *A Certain Slant of Sunlight,* thirty-three more "postcard poems," many of which could easily have been included in the book. One suspects Ted of fetishizing the number one hundred; but approximately that number seems to be how many the mind is capable of considering in relation to one another. These additional thirty-three, hopefully, suggest a book of their own.

Though *A Certain Slant of Sunlight* contains many of Ted's "forms," his voice has changed. The necessity for concision, imposed by the size of the card, pushes tone of voice up against language up against form: "HOLLY- WOOD / paid Lillian Gish $800,000 to / disappear so lovely so pure like milk / seems but isn't because of the fall-out / but it would have only cost me five & didn't, so I did." Many of the poems are monologues for the person who provided the phrase or image, or are in dialogue with him/her. Some work with texts of dead poets, Whitman and Lindsay for example, or with songs. There is a flexibility of tone throughout, which has emerged from the lengthier autobiographical poems of the late 70s and early 80s, but must operate more quickly. This book is extraordinary without appearing to be: it doesn't have "monument" written on it, but it isn't like anything else.

Ted's last poems are the fourteen poems—twenty-one pages—he wrote after the completion of *A Certain Slant of Sunlight* during the final six months of his life. It must be obvious by now that Ted did not slow down as a writer during his last years, and these poems are sharp and fulsome. They were kept together in a folder with a handwritten title page: "Poems/ * /Ted Berri- gan." Some are short in the manner of *A Certain Slant of Sunlight,* and there are several longer poems, includ- ing an abrasive **"Stand-Up Comedy Routine,"** made from a *Mad-Libs* form.[1] But Ted's very last poem is a lovely six-page work, **"This Will Be Her Shining Hour,"** written in dialogue with myself and the voices in a Fred Astaire movie on TV. "'Their lives are as fragile as *The Glass Menagerie.'*" That line near the end of Ted's final poem refers to the people in the movie, the people in the poem, and the two of us as both people in the poem and ourselves, comparing them/us to Tennessee Williams's play, to glass figures, to the enduringness of the play about fragile people. What does *lives* mean then? *Lives* seems to be "art," and so one is left thinking about the strength of poetry.

Ted Berrigan's poems are very *deliberate.* They have a graven quality as if they were drawn on the page, word by word. He often wrote in unlined notebooks with a black felt-tip pen, and one might also say they have a black-felt-tip-pen quality. You feel that no words have been crossed out and replaced.

I'm impressed by this graven-ness in *The Sonnets* and *Many Happy Returns,* in *Easter Monday,* but then, too, in most of the later work. It doesn't go away if the feel- ing in the poem is more autobiographical or intimate, as in *A Certain Slant of Sunlight.* The latter poems read as if written with the black felt-tip pen, on the postcard. They have a primary physical reality.

Two more things from this: first, a continuous interac- tion with art and artists gave Ted an active visual and tactile sense. He is often painting, or collaging, or draw-

ing his way through a poem. On the other hand, he agreed with Jack Spicer's notion of the *other* voice that dictates one's poems, and his poems have a "dictated" quality, even the ones that are made from other peoples's words. These two notions aren't incompat- ible. "Dictation" suggests aurality rather than plastic qualities, but there isn't any reason why all the senses shouldn't be working, and Ted had a very fine ear: "Their lives are as fragile as *The Glass Menagerie.*" Listen.

Ted's poetry is remarkable for its range of tones of voice. He actively studied both "tone of voice" and "stance," the range of attitudinal play in human discourse and the projection of character. Here Ted's professed model was Frank O'Hara, but I often find Ted more mysterious and more intense in both tone and stance. Not having O'Hara's education or "class," Ted therefore couldn't be as traditional. He couldn't call on a tone of voice from another decade or century as if he owned it, even though he knew exactly what Whit- manesque or Johnsonian was. He had to reinvent it for himself, from his working-class background and University of Tulsa education and ceaseless self- education.

Ted is often characterized as "second-generation New York School." That label, with its "second-generation," seems to preclude innovation. Ted's career as a poet, after his earliest, sentimental poems, begins in the in- novation of *The Sonnets.* He invented its form, with its "black heart beside the fifteen pieces" and its "of glass in Joe Brainard's collage," if you take fifteen to be most likely fourteen and understand that his heart really is beside the poem not in it. These poems, designed to contain anything and to expand temporally, can do so because the form's finiteness is emphasized. It could probably be argued that this form is the one he was most informed by afterward, even when he was being transparent and "sentimental"—when he had finally learned the uses and control of sentimentality, since he consistently explored the spaces between lines, and the spaces between phrases, within the poem as frame. He had also learned from his sonnet form how to find the congruences in supposedly random happenstance:

> Can't cut it (night)
> in New York City
> it's alive
> inside my tooth
> on St. Mark's Place
> where exposed nerve
> jangles
>
> ("FEBRUARY AIR")

This is verbal, environmental, and emotional hap- penstance, where the parts of the moment click in.

If you the reader are a poet, Ted's poetry is full of resources: forms, techniques, stylistic practices—manners and mannerisms, ways of sounding like a person, ways of achieving exaltation. If you the reader are a reader (of poetry), Ted's poetry is a gift. He is working hard to amuse—make you enjoy this taking up of your time; to "say," what he knows, reasons, feels; and to be like you, at the same time acknowledging his (anyone's) own secret: "I never told anyone what I knew. Which was that it wasn't / for anyone else what it was for me" (**"Cranston Near the City Line"**).

We have, traditionally, the senses, but words are our sensors. We use them to feel our way across and through, up and down. Ted understood this as well as any poet I can think of. So much of his poetry is about the pleasure of movement across the page. He is saying, "This is what we do. This is living, taking its walk." It is a very gentle message, that of the walk through time, laid alongside the message that all time is simultaneous. But, also,

> No-mind
>
>                     No messages
>      (Inside)
> Thanksgiving        1969
>
>                         (**"In My Room"**)

*Note*

1. *Mad-Libs,* an offshoot of *Mad* magazine, contained fill-in-the-blank and multiple-choice do-it-yourself versions of country songs, comedy routines, anecdotes, and so forth.

## John Palattella (review date 23 January 2006)

SOURCE: Palattella, John. "La Vie de Bohème." *The Nation* (23 January 2006): n. p.

[*In the following review, Palattella assesses the 2005* Collected Poems of Ted Berrigan, *contending that the assembly of so many previously unpublished poems and those long out of print affords the reader the opportunity to study Berrigan's work in a way that separates his poetry from the well-known stories of his excessive lifestyle.*]

Several years after Ted Berrigan's death, in 1983, the poet Ron Padgett spent some time reading his friend's papers at Columbia University. It was an unsettling experience, not least because Berrigan was only 48 years old when he died. The two men had met in 1959. Berrigan was working on a master's degree about George Bernard Shaw at the University of Tulsa; he was also a poet, and he came to know Padgett through a little magazine edited by Padgett and sold in a local bookstore. Berrigan grew to detest Tulsa's literary scene, which he found uptight and elitist, and in 1960,

along with Padgett and a few other young Tulsa writers, he moved to Manhattan. Berrigan lived downtown and eked out an existence by reselling stolen books, sponging off friends and working the occasional odd job. Padgett was a student at Columbia and lived uptown. Berrigan often spent weekends with him there, and before long he was earning a little money by ghostwriting papers for Columbia undergraduates. Twenty years later Padgett couldn't help but find it bizarre that many of the ghostwriter's own papers—letters, journals, notes and drafts of poems from those early years in New York City—had ended up at Columbia as well, enshrined in its library's special collections.

The story of Berrigan's short career as a poet is a remarkable one, but it's a story too often told by focusing on the extravagant circumstances of the poet's life. Berrigan fancied being a poète maudit, fashioning himself as an outcast whose derangement and self-abasement were a protest against the timidity and complacency of bourgeois life. "This year, in this season, I am 'sick' because among other things I scorn their new God of analysis," Berrigan told his first wife, Sandy Alpers Berrigan, in a letter in 1962. If you read about Berrigan, you're bound to learn about his reckless treatment of his body and his ghastly diet (he subsisted mostly on Pepsi, greasy hamburgers and peanut butter sandwiches), or about how he forged prescriptions to buy the many milligrams of speed that fueled his marathon sessions of writing, reading, talking and pontificating. Such snapshots of Berrigan's personal life are meaningful, but they provide little guidance for anyone trying to grasp how the words Berrigan wrote continue to live beyond the life he led, an undertaking made more difficult as only a relatively small amount of Berrigan's poetry has remained in print since his death.

*The Collected Poems of Ted Berrigan* changes all that. Packed with hundreds of poems long out of print as well as dozens more previously unpublished in books or magazines, *The Collected Poems* is not simply a book but a portable archive, one that creates a little space between the poet's career and stories about his life. The volume makes it impossible not to notice that there was always more to Berrigan than the *poète maudit* of the Lower East Side. Padgett once characterized his friend as a "combat boot among ballet slippers," a remark meant to convey how Berrigan, a working-class kid from Providence, Rhode Island, who had been in the Army and went to college in Tulsa on the GI Bill, felt cowed during his early years in Manhattan whenever he found himself among urbane poets like Frank O'Hara, Kenneth Koch and John Ashbery, all of whom had graduated from Harvard. *The Collected Poems* shows that Berrigan was equally adept at wearing both shoes, balancing cockiness and composure, grit and grace. In the second poem of *The Sonnets,* Berrigan writes, "dear Berrigan. He died / Back to books. I read."

With *The Collected Poems* providing an unprecedented opportunity to plunge into Berrigan's work, those lines have never seemed more apt.

## Jordan Davis (review date autumn 2006)

SOURCE: Davis, Jordan. Review of *The Collected Poems of Ted Berrigan*. *Chicago Review* 52, nos. 2-4 (autumn 2006): 353-60.

[*In the following review, Davis discusses the recent collection of Berrigan's work, noting the poet's experimentation with the sonnet form and his borrowing from the poetry of others.*]

This is a story about a man who decided to be a poet. It took him ten years. First he met some other people who had decided to be poets and artists. Then he taught himself how to write by stealing other poets' lines. Then, having learned how to write (and incidentally creating a literary movement) he decided to write a major poem. Having achieved these goals, he started over, seeking a new shapeliness for his poetry. All the while, he sought and found many unexpected answers to his main concern: the problem of how to live.

Ted Berrigan was born on November 15, 1934 in Providence, Rhode Island, a few months after his parents were married. He served briefly in Korea, then studied at the University of Tulsa on the GI Bill. In Tulsa, he fell in with, or, depending on who tells the story, took over, a group of teenagers publishing a literary journal, *The White Dove Review,* which was printing work by Allen Ginsberg, Amiri Baraka, and Jack Kerouac. Within a few years Berrigan and many of his younger friends (including Ron Padgett and Joe Brainard) had moved en masse to New York.

Berrigan believed that becoming a poet was as intense an undertaking as becoming a doctor:

> Survival is the hardest test for a poet [. . .] now, you can do various other things for a living *and* write poetry, but it's very difficult to do anything else much in that six or seven years when you are trying to learn. When you are doing your pre-med and med school, you know, your internship, so to speak. I mean, those people don't work, do they, when they are doing that?

In New York, Berrigan supported himself by writing papers for undergraduates at Columbia. He read everything he could find, stealing books to read and then selling them for food and movie money. He wrote poems and composed a master's thesis on "The Problem of How to Live as Dealt with in Four Plays by George Bernard Shaw." One weekend he went to New Orleans, where he fell in love with and married a young woman named Sandra Alper. Her family disapproved and committed their daughter to a mental institution in Florida. Berrigan rescued her and, fleeing zigzag across the country, returned to New York. In the middle of this, he started writing, or as he put it, building, sonnets.

"I wanted to provide in *The Sonnets* a lot of material for footnotes so that scholars for one thousand years could check everything out," Berrigan once said, echoing Joyce. Scanning the annotations in the present edition, it's clear he was only half-joking. Alice Notley's introduction to the **Collected Poems** provides one of the best accounts of Berrigan's sources and methods (along with Padgett's "On *The Sonnets*" and Berrigan's "Sonnet Workshop"). Beyond Shakespeare, the work had various inspirations: William Carlos Williams's indictment of the form; Berrigan's discovery of Dadaist collage; Pound's *Cantos*; and Alfred North Whitehead's *Process and Reality*. The notes—assembled by Notley and her two sons with Berrigan, Anselm and Edmund—illuminate many of the work's obscurities, from the "piercing pince-nez" (of Ezra Pound) and "dim frieze" (of Columbia's Butler Library) of the first sonnet through the *Tempest* allusion, O'Hara misprision, and private referents in the last of the seventy-nine poems.

While Berrigan's sonnets don't usually present the expected characteristics of the form (most notably rhyme), they do update the traditional expectation that the proposition in the first eight lines will be resolved in the last six. Berrigan's poems move rhetorically from descriptions of external phenomena in the octave to descriptions of internal noumena in the sestet. Throughout the sequence, he uses the volta, the turn from proposition to resolution, to shift momentum by disclosing the poem's autobiographical context at erratic intervals, creating a kind of pulp detective poetry.

*The Sonnets* can be, and certainly have been, read as an attempt to make the *Cantos* cohere, or as the strong precursor of Lyn Hejinian's recursive autobiography. But it's more in keeping with Berrigan's plagiarism-as-homage to see the work as a courtly exercise in personal canon formation. By the second poem in the sequence, he had begun quoting from John Ashbery, and quotations from and allusions to Ashbery, O'Hara, and Kenneth Koch pervade the work. Berrigan was a nimble thief who found new uses for the lines and processes he stole. From Ashbery's title "How Much Longer Shall I Be Able to Inhabit the Divine Sepulcher" he dropped the "Sepulcher" to introduce a kind of billboard in the middle of **Sonnet II.** From Koch's "You Were Wearing," Berrigan chose a **"John Greenleaf Whittier tie-clip,"** and he turned Whittier into the running gag of **Sonnet XXXI.** And in **Sonnet XXXVI,** Berrigan's handily imitated O'Hara's I-do-this-I-do-that style:

> It's 8:54 AM. in Brooklyn it's the 28th of July and
> it's probably 8:54 in Manhattan but I'm

in Brooklyn I'm eating English muffins and drinking
pepsi and I'm thinking of how Brooklyn is New
York city too how odd I usually think of it as
something all its own like Bellows Falls like Little
Chute like Uijongbu
     I never thought on the Williams-
burg bridge I'd come so much to Brooklyn
just to see lawyers and cops who don't even carry
guns taking my wife away and bringing her back
     No
and I never thought Dick would be back at Gude's
beard shaved off long hair cut and Carol reading
his books when we were playing cribbage and
watching the sun come up over the Navy Yard
across the river
     I think I was thinking when I was
ahead I'd be somewhere like Perry street erudite
dazzling slim and badly loved
contemplating my new book of poems
to be printed in simple type on old brown paper
feminine marvelous and tough

In late winter 1963, while Berrigan was writing *The Sonnets,* his work drew the small notoriety of a censorship scandal. Padgett, an editor of Columbia's literary journal, gathered some of his friends' work, including three poems by Berrigan, for publication in the *Review.* Noticing the word *fuck* in the proofs, the publication's business manager alerted the Dean of Students, who, hypersensitive to appearances, passed the issue along to the already gray eminence Jacques Barzun. His pronouncement: the poems were "absolute trash." The administration gave the editors an ultimatum: withdraw the poems or be expelled. In response, Padgett and six others resigned from the journal and published the issue that April, by mimeograph, as *The Censored Review.* The story made the *New York Post,* Padgett appeared on the local TV news, and the 800-copy run of the review "sold out in about five minutes." Not one to let an opportunity pass, Berrigan started a mimeo of his own: *C* was printed monthly at first, on legal-sized paper, and distributed by mail to artists and writers the editors admired.

"FUCK COMMUNISM." Berrigan began **"Tambourine Life"** with yippie Paul Krassner's famous bumper sticker centered between the margins, the most visceral opening of any poem since *Beowulf.* A combination of otherworldly surliness and right-baiting obscenity, the line announces Berrigan's intention to capitalize on the attention he amassed in *The Sonnets.* He writes of "the snatches of virgins" and a character who "gets his gat and plugs his dad."

"What kind of person wrote this poem?" Berrigan asks. "That's really what you mean when you say who is speaking." In **"Tambourine Life,"** Berrigan aims to make the answer as complicated and entertaining as possible. In the sixty-nine sections of **"Tambourine Life,"** Berrigan's comic voice ranges from sarcasm to

mock arrogance to deadpan absurdity, while his sincere plain-spoken voice is given over to adjectives such as *lovely, beautiful, marvelous,* and *great.* Oscillating between irony and sincerity in this way generates energy, a kind of alternating current of personal electromagnetism. The sections connect by an associative logic that is obvious in hindsight and impossible to anticipate. The section after "The Russian Revolution" opens with a line from a Patchen poem: "The apples are red again in Chandler's valley." In case the reader misses the connection, Berrigan riffs on the salient word: "redder for what happened there / / never did know what it was / never did care." And so it goes, as Berrigan develops the persona he hinted at in *The Sonnets.*

Released from the idealized self of *The Sonnets,* Berrigan writes memorably about subjects including love, Band-Aids, the code of the west, animals, children's books, the incipient protest movement, sex, parenthood, poetry, money, more sex, and truth. Then, suddenly, death appears:

> Now
> in the middle of this
> someone I love is dead
>
> and I don't even know
>     "how"
>
> I thought she belonged to me
>
> How she filled my life when I felt empty!
>
> How she fills me now!

Just four sections from the end, these lines transform the poem's giddy romp to an instantly sober, though no less electrified, *carpe diem.* This is the first of Berrigan's many remarkable elegies: **"Ann Arbor Elegy," "Frank O'Hara," "People Who Died," "Memorial Day," "Old-fashioned Air,"** and **"Last Poem."**

While the discoveries of *The Sonnets* influenced later poets mainly on the theoretical level, the technique of **"Tambourine Life"** appears to have had an immediate practical effect. Of the poem, Kenneth Koch wrote, "It seemed in a way ahead of everything—absolutely casual, ordinary, and momentary-seeming [. . .] full of buoyancy, sweetness, and high spirits."

A masterpiece, though, can be a burden. In Berrigan's case, the temptation to repeat the formula must have been constant. *Collected Poems* includes several variations on **"Tambourine Life."** *Memorial Day,* a book-length elegiac poem written in collaboration with Anne Waldman, shares its episodic structure. The long sequence *Train Ride* accumulates its episodes over the course of a trip from New York to Providence, declaring "Out the Window / is / Out to Lunch!!" and "We could / bitch all our mutual / friends!!" The short, often terrific poems in Berrigan's 1970 collection *In the Early Morning Rain* sometimes seem like disconnected sections of another **"Tambourine Life"**:

> Someone who loves me calls me
> & I just sit, listening
> Someone who likes me wires me
> to do something. I'll do it
> Tomorrow.

Like the original, these later poems aim for pleasing shapes and statements, but the magic ratio of surliness to charm sometimes slips out of balance. The energy is off, and I suspect Berrigan knew it. He once said:

> I'm not too interested in a collected works in which every poem is a totally terrific and wonderful masterpiece, 'cause that's inhuman. I like books in which every poem is a masterpiece. It's the John Ashbery way to try and have a book in which every poem is really outstanding and terrific. It's the Allen Ginsberg way not to worry about that, but to get in everything that you have around that time that is related and is above a certain level, that is, however fragmentary, or overdone, alive!

Like many poets then and now, Berrigan did stints teaching writing. (In order, he taught at the Iowa Writers' Workshop—where he divorced Alper and married his student Notley—Michigan; Yale; Buffalo; Northeastern Illinois; Essex; Naropa; and the Stevens Institute of Technology.) Berrigan, however, didn't accept apprentices. As he pointed out in a talk at Naropa, "You can study under teachers, masters, add a little tradition to that word—but every individual has to make their own poems, their own story, make their own songs. You can't make perfect replicas of your master's works, so you flunk." The bodhisattva mode Berrigan embraced as pedagogy doesn't look likely to overturn the anxious correctional system Berrigan decried, at least not anytime soon. But changing the system single-handedly was probably never the goal; along with Krassner's "FUCK COMMUNISM," **"Tambourine Life"** also quotes Damon Runyon's "Get the money."

In her introduction, Notley mentions that the chief textual question she faced while assembling the *Collected Poems* was "what were we to do about the book-length sequence *Easter Monday*?" Written between 1972 and 1977, all the poems in the sequence appeared in print during Berrigan's lifetime, mainly in the collections *Red Wagon* and *Nothing for You*. Other poems appeared in various chapbooks. A series with the same title and bracket dates, but with a substantially different table of contents, is the next-to-last section of *So Going Around Cities* (1980). Berrigan did not settle on the final selection of forty-six poems until shortly before his death in 1983. Their appearance, in the *Collected*

*Poems,* in this final arrangement is, along with the volume's excellent notes and introduction, the main reason readers ought to get their hands on the book immediately.

The *Easter Monday* poems have a character almost entirely different from anything else he wrote. A translation from Leopardi would appear to serve as their summary:

> Your movements are really
> Worth nothing nor is the world
> Worth a sigh. Life is bitterness
> And boredom; and that's all. The world's a mudhole.
> It's about time you shut up.

There is no pull or push in these poems, no attempt to woo the reader or go for the laugh. *Easter Monday* is bleakly pure in its attention to ordinary life and the potential for despair, chaos, and anonymous death. A shot rings out in the third line of the first poem. The third poem ends with "cancer of the spine," the fourth with "And I'm the man who killed him." **"Old-fashioned Air"** ends with "And we are back where we started from, Lee, you & me, alive & well!" The poem was written, the notes reveal, after Berrigan learned of his friend Lee Crabtree's suicide.

If *The Sonnets* and **"Tambourine Life"** are bids for literary posterity and popular appeal, *Easter Monday* is born of spiritual ambition. Berrigan has stopped seeking approval. He has let go of his anxiety about what he expected of his life and his poetry:

> God lies down
> Here. Rattling of a shot, heard
> From the first row. The president of the United States
> And the Director of the FBI stand over
> a dead mule. "Yes, it is nice to hear the fountain
> With the green trees around it, as well as
> People who need me." Quote Lovers of speech
> unquote. It's a nice thought
> & typical of a rat. And, it is far more elaborate
> Than expected. And the thing is, we don't *need that*
> much money.

Berrigan, remarried and a new father again, honored his responsibilities ("People who need me") by setting achievable goals and clearing out the unnecessary—the unnecessary, in this case, being the enormous public persona (equal parts W. C. Fields and W. B. Yeats, as one friend put it) that he spent the previous decade assembling. That persona returns at the end of the sequence, in the anthology piece **"Whitman in Black,"** only after Berrigan has purged all attempts to entertain and impress. In **"Newtown,"** "The Ideal Family awaits distribution on / The Planet." **"Swinburne & Watts-Dunton"** is a semi-opaque account of steering himself back from dissolution, **"Soviet Souvenir"** an anxious reckoning with love. The renunciations culminated in

**"Narragansett Park,"** the first poem in the series written at 101 St. Mark's Place, Berrigan's last residence in New York:

> The major planets are shifting (shivering?) but out of
>     my natural habit,
> Self-kindness,
>                 I play them
> something Nashville something quality
> and there is the too easy knell of the games chapel
> The tempting scornful opposite
> Cathedral virus and goof immunization:
> The curves of the Spirit are not very interested in the
>     conquest of matter.
> Color is the idiot's delight. I'm the curves, what's the
>     matter? or
> I'm the matter, the curves nag:
> Call it Amber, it doesn't ride nor take to rider
> Amber it doesn't make me want to pray, it makes me
>     see color
> as we fail to break through our clasped hands.

The whole is marked by the excitement and frustration of a working mind. Berrigan takes solace in the intimacy of "self-kindness" and "clasped hands," abandoning modernism's preoccupation with ideas and things for something like no feelings but in choices.

For Berrigan, the art of living was not a matter of extending the greatest average happiness over the longest possible lifespan (moral miserism). Rather, it was a matter of living in his feelings and those of everyone around him—of approaching as much and as often as possible a pure excited state in which a thing noticed becomes not a new toy but part of the furniture, equipment for living. What this meant for his poetics was that a line had to maintain a relation to the lines around it, as if the lines themselves were in conversation. A good line could be expected to recur in other conversations, sometimes as a reproach, sometimes as a remembrance, and sometimes just as a sound.

## Michael Leddy (review date November/December 2006)

SOURCE: Leddy, Michael. Review of *The Collected Poems of Ted Berrigan*. World Literature Today 80, no. 6 (November/December 2006): 70-1.

[*In the following review of* The Collected Poems, *Leddy takes issue with those critics who have labeled Berrigan as a second generation New York School poet, insisting that he was "an important and innovative poet" with "a distinctive voice."*]

Labels in poetry are seldom helpful and usually reductive. In recent American poetry, perhaps no label has been as reductive as that of "second-generation New York School," applied to poets as various as Joseph

Ceravolo, Ron Padgett, David Shapiro, and Ted Berrigan. But things change. Robert Creeley, Robert Duncan, and Charles Olson are no longer "the Black Mountain poets" (were they ever?), and the publication of *The Collected Poems* affirms Ted Berrigan's identity, not as a belated follower or would-be member of a "school" but as, simply, an important and innovative American poet. Berrigan's poems present a distinctive voice that is the product of both appropriation and invention; no American poet is as adept at collaging found materials into a voice of his own. His work offers verbal wit, painterly abstraction, and tender pathos in ever-varying proportions.

*The Collected Poems* is the most recent in a series of posthumous publications—previously unpublished poems, interviews, presentations, journal excerpts, a new edition of *The Sonnets,* and a *Selected Poems* (see *WLT* [*World Literature Today*] 69:2, p. 364). *The Collected Poems* brings into focus all the elements of Berrigan's art: the dense bricolages of *The Sonnets,* the serial lyric reportage of **"Tambourine Life"** and **"Things to Do in Providence,"** the domestic comedy of **"Small Role Felicity"** and **"This Will Be Her Shining Hour,"** the eloquent sorrow of **"Red Shift"** and **"A Certain Slant of Sunlight,"** the funny aphorisms and notations of the poems of **"500 American Postcards."** This volume lets one see Berrigan's movement into the possibilities of a poetic community: he begins on his own, reconstructing his early unsatisfactory poems with words lifted from elsewhere to make the rich and strange textures of *The Sonnets.* That landmark work enacts a poetics of poverty, the poet using available leftovers and borrowing whatever else is needed to make his poems. In Berrigan's final poetry project, **"500 American Postcards,"** poems often begin with a phrase or line contributed, at Berrigan's invitation, by another poet (Steve Carey, Allen Ginsberg, Bernadette Mayer, among others), with Berrigan now at home in a community of like-minded, generous peers.

*The Collected Poems,* too, is the work of a community: it has the unusual distinction of being a family affair, edited by the poet Alice Notley (Berrigan's second wife) and their poet-sons Anselm and Edmund Berrigan. Notley's notes illuminate the poems as no one else's could, often revealing the unexpected and unlikely origins of poems. (Who would have thought that **"A Certain Slant of Sunlight"** began with a word list and an assignment to write a poem using one word in each line?)

In *Nice to See You: Homage to Ted Berrigan*, Keith Abbott recalls Ted Berrigan in a conversation about Frank O'Hara and legacies: "I want a Collected Ted Berrigan next, right after Frank's, just like his. I don't want to die but I do want that book." Twenty-three years after Ted Berrigan's death, the range of his poetic accomplishment is finally coming into view.

**William Doreski (review date 2006)**

SOURCE: Doreski, William. Review of *The Collected Poems of Ted Berrigan. Harvard Review,* no. 30 (2006): 164-68.

[*In the following review, Doreski explores Berrigan's sources and "his magpie habit of borrowing, quoting, and stealing from other writers."*]

Ted Berrigan died at forty-eight and left a large body of poetry of mixed quality, now collected in a thick squarish volume as solid as a concrete block. Thus the University of California Press continues its conservation of certain poets (including Robert Creeley, Charles Olson, and Lorine Neidecker) once gathered in Donald Alien's *New American Poetry* or otherwise associated with or descended from the experimental movements of the fifties and sixties. Through a circle of friendship Berrigan belonged to the New York School, an arbitrary designation for poets so loosely associated that not all of them even lived or worked in New York. It was a school in the way the term French School, for instance, in the mind of a curator describes painters entirely different in style, subject matter, and technique.

Many of Berrigan's earlier poems—**"The Secret Life of Ford Madox Ford,"** for instance—illustrate his debt to the Hart Crane of "The River" and "Cutty Sark." The staccato, arbitrary flux of conversation shapes these poems, as they do Crane's, and Berrigan generates a surreal aura through ordinary speech phrases, rhythms, and patterns. The "transliterative" Ford Madox Ford sequence, derived from the sound associations of French poetry, exemplifies the method:

> Open the door let me in
> The orbs say no
> Let's sashay up the scene
> And strangle the beans
> A sick kid passed on a prairie new meat.

This search for the surreal element in ordinary life (along with his magpie habit of borrowing, quoting, and stealing from other writers) became the dominant thrust of Berrigan's work, and links him to Frank O'Hara perhaps more closely than to any of the other New York poets. Like O'Hara, he loved the visual arts and, also like O'Hara, his debt to painters and sculptors has been exaggerated by those who don't fully appreciate the difference between language and visual media. Although Berrigan has little of O'Hara's manic energy and not as distinctive a voice, he is sometimes even more inventive in his leaps of fancy and, in his strongest poems, achieves a comparable imaginative compression of disparate and competing imageries.

In *The Sonnets* (1964, 1967), his first widely circulated collection, Berrigan tempers the colloquial extremities of speech-imitation by flexing his lines through aggressive enjambment, imposing a counter-rhythm on conversational flow:

> Andy Butt was drunk in the Parthenon
> Bar. If only the Greeks were a band
> Aid, he thought. Then my woe would not flow
> O'er the land. He considered his honeydew
> Hand. "O woe, woe!" saith Andrew, "a fruit
> In my hand may suffice to convey me to Greece,
> But I must have envy to live! A grasshopper,
> George, if you please!"

> (**XXVII**)

Form imposes a certain dignity on drunken whimsy and, in the rest of the sonnets and some of Berrigan's other early poems, such as **"A Boke"** (a "cutup" of a James Dickey essay), this determined insistence on enjambment and confined rhythm gives force and focus to material that might otherwise seem the expression of adolescent fancy.

Much of Berrigan's middle work, from *Many Happy Returns* up to *Easter Monday,* seems too Olson-influenced, and hardly distinguishable from the verse produced en masse by Ron Loewinsohn, Larry Eigner, Edward Marshall, Ray Bremser, Paul Blackburn, and others working in the same open-field idiom. The patterning of **"Many Happy Returns"** typifies this approach, in which page layout, rather than rhythm, lineation, syntax, or rhetoric, seems the central poetic strategy:

> It's a great pleasure to
> wake "up"
> mid-afternoon
> 2 o'clock
> and if thy stomach think not
> no matter . . .

To my eye and ear this kind of writing seems as dated as the dactyls and anapests of "Hiawatha," especially since Berrigan has no external controlling subject, as Olson did with the history of Cape Ann, and no internal driving force palpable as the mythic and musical sensibility of Robert Duncan. Furthermore, many of the poems of this period are too whimsical, as though a touch of off-color irony were all a poem needs. However, *Memorial Day,* written with Anne Waldman, is a major work of the period and one of the great twentieth-century American poems. It transcends whimsy and its own poetics to become a moving and forceful testimony to the disillusion and angst of the late Vietnam War era. Unfortunately, no brief quotation can convey the cumulative power of this elegant and complex elegy.

In his work of the late seventies and early eighties, Berrigan's speech patterning fragments so drastically that a late poem like **"This Will Be Her Shining Hour"** simply collects quotations (however fictional) about films, or perhaps from films, but manages to ghost a structure so furtive yet pervasive that by the end the reader feels an actual narrative has unfolded in the background, and the closure enforces itself like the climax of a play:

> "You're making a big mistake,
> writing a poem,
> and not watching this."
> "Shut up. I'm getting the last lines."
> "You are not."

These late poems are even more restless and chameleon-like than Berrigan's earliest work. It's difficult to generalize about his friable style, which seems to imitate every kind of poem he encountered. Sometimes he sounds like Gregory Corso, sometimes like Ron Padgett, and sometimes instead of someone's epigone he sounds like Ted Berrigan in his own skin. Sometimes he sounds most like himself when he's borrowing from others, as in the collage-sequence *Easter Monday,* assembled in its full coherence for the first time by these conscientious editors. Thanks to them, and to the largesse of the University of California, Berrigan can now receive the full reading this imperfect but serious artist deserves.

### Aram Saroyan (review date September/October 2008)

SOURCE: Saroyan, Aram. "A Complicated Muse." *American Poetry Review* 37, no. 5 (September/October 2008): 43-5.

[*In the following review of Berrigan's collected works, Saroyan contends that* The Sonnets *is Berrigan's masterpiece and that none of his later work measures up to that early effort.*]

In the early 1960s in New York City, Ted Berrigan, not yet thirty, wrote his masterwork. ***The Sonnets,*** which leads off this voluminous, definitive collection. Made up of 88 sonnets, the sequence stands as a sort of literary counterpart to another early post-modern masterwork by another New Yorker undertaken at approximately the same time, Andy Warhol's silk screens of various Campbell soup cans. Both the poet and the painter, that is, fortuitously discovered an unlikely "theater" by which to release and elaborate, to illuminate and play changes upon, sensibilities that would seem to be light years beyond such old-fashioned, discardable containers.

In Warhol's case, one sees a colorist as pleasing as Matisse in the iconic grid of the soup can: combinations of mauve and purple and green and vermillion never glimpsed on the shelves of the supermarket except perhaps in a dream or, alternatively, seen on early color television sets circa the same period.

In Berrigan's case, the sonnet becomes the vehicle of a sensibility so eclectically learned that the poet in his later years (he died at 48 in 1983) would periodically denounce the work as too literary. Recycling lines from poets as various as Michaux and Edward Arlington Robinson—and prominently including Frank O'Hara, Shakespeare and Rimbaud—he shuffles and reshuffles a pastiche of his New York young adulthood amidst friends, lovers, Pepsis and pills. **Sonnet LV** begins with a line of O'Hara's:

> Grace to be born and live as variously as possible
> White boats    green banks    black dust    atremble
> Massive as Anne's thighs upon the page
> I rage in a blue shirt at a brown desk in a
> Bright room sustained by a bellyful of pills
> "The Poems" is not a dream    for all things come to
>     them
> Gratuitously    In quick New York we imagine the
>     blue Charles
> Patsy awakens in heat and ready to squabble
> No poems she demands in a blanket command    belly
> To hot belly we have laid    serenely white
> Only my sweating pores are true in the empty night
> Baffling combustions are everywhere!    we hunger
>     and taste
> And go to the movies    then run home drenched in
>     flame
> To the grace of the make-believe bed

In different combinations and permutations, many of the lines recur throughout the sequence. One line:

> feminine marvelous and tough

is so prototypically Frank O'Hara that I assumed Berrigan had appropriated it until told by the poet that it was entirely his. Able to conjure the chattily cosmopolitan tone of his closest progenitor, he also shared with O'Hara an innately musical ear. But if O'Hara will chart extensive narrative peregrinations ("Joe's Jacket," "A True Account of Talking to the Sun at Fire Island"), Berrigan seldom goes beyond a page or two in his high lyric mode. John Ashbery, to take another of Berrigan's enthusiasms, is mostly about tonal composition—sheets of quasi-ratiocination, as it were—and not really much about the play of vowels and consonants, but Berrigan delighted in him too, as he also delighted in Allen Ginsberg. But perhaps the biggest surprise, comprising a New York School quantum leap, is that Berrigan also embraced the less casual music of the Black Mountain poets (Robert Creeley, Charles Olson, Robert Duncan et al.). ***The Sonnets,*** is a milestone, then, in keeping its free-and-easy New York School discursive tone while at the same time advancing a palpable beat that includes incisive musical signatures.

Written several years later, **"Tambourine Life,"** a long poem that appeared in *Mother* magazine in the spring of 1967, comprises a sort of sequel. Berrigan was, as Robert Duncan put it, "a master of pathos," which you see in *The Sonnets,* and in the poem about his mother called **"Things to Do in Providence."** At the same time, he was a comic poet, and **"Tambourine Life"** holds the full flavor and flux of that side. Divided into 70 sections of open field poetry, the poem is a comedy made up of words and phrases. That is, the words and phrases are the subject of the funniness: what words do, and what they don't do. The whole thing is a kind of high-spirited cartoon of the rational process: each section, most of them very brief, seems to set up a premise and then to demolish it, like a linguistic episode of the Road Runner:

> The apples are red again in Chandler's valley
> redder for what happened there
>                             never did know what it was
> never did care
>                                    *
>      Just for the record    I found Mr. Walter Steck
>                                  recently
>                     at five o'clock in the afternoon
>                        on Garcia Lorca's birthday
>                        lying in the gutter
>                             on his button    *shame*

What might be called the extra-rational spirit of this work seems specific to the literary sixties. Yet for all that, the poet remains on friendly terms with the rational, and not just for the sake of playing on its linguistic limits. There is a sturdy, Johnsonian moral-arbiter side to Berrigan, as when he tells us in **"The Great Genius"**:

> The Great Genius is
> A man who can do the
> Ordinary thing
> When everybody
> Else is going crazy.

Or this, from his poem **"I Used to Be But Now I Am"**:

> I used to be sentimental about myself, & therefore
>      ruthless,
> But now I am, I think, a sympathetic person, although
>      easily amused.

Being human, after all, is to use language to rational ends constantly, and to programmatically divest his work of this dimension might have seemed the sort of exclusion that could have been arrived at only by way of strict rationality. Then too, wanting to be read and enjoyed as a poet, Berrigan may have considered the sort of alternative today represented by the Language Poets to be one that would simply discourage the common reader.

Ted Berrigan was born in Providence, Rhode Island in 1934, the oldest of four children in a working-class Irish Catholic family. His father was chief maintenance engineer at the Ward Baking Company, his mother a bookkeeper and cashier in the public school lunch program. After graduating from the Catholic La Salle Academy, he attended Providence College for a year and then joined the army. He spent sixteen months in Korea before being transferred to Tulsa, now a sergeant. In 1955, he began studying at the University of Tulsa on the GI Bill, and eventually completed a Master's thesis there on George Bernard Shaw. In 1959, Berrigan met the future poets Ron Padgett and Dick Gallup, as well as Joe Brainard, the future painter and writer to whom *The Sonnets* is dedicated—all at the time still finishing high school. In 1961, he moved with these friends to New York.

Like Frank O'Hara, whom he already admired and soon knew, Berrigan had a social fluency that could disarm and bring unlikely and disparate parties to his table, and he became the central figure of the second and third generations of poets of the New York School. After the end of his first marriage, having fathered a son and a daughter, he met and married the poet Alice Notley, who, along with their poet sons Anselm and Edmund Berrigan, edited *The Collected Poems.* Almost any of the 759 pages here stands in curious juxtaposition to most of the poetry before us today, a measure of the distance we've kept from the stateside literary sixties.

As both *The Sonnets* and **"Tambourine Life"** suggest, Berrigan was engaged by all manner and species of "tone"—loving the swift turns he found both in O'Hara and Ashbery, for instance—and almost perpetrated a hoax when his **"An Interview with John Cage,"** published in *Mother,* received an award from the National Endowment for the Arts and was slated to appear in the NEA's newly-minted annual, the *American Literary Anthology.* While he took great delight in Cage, the poet was also alert to comedic strains in his persona:

> *Cage*: . . . I think everybody should be a machine. I think everybody should be like everybody.
>
> *Interviewer*: Isn't that like Pop Art?
>
> *Cage*: Yes, that's what Pop Art is, liking things, which incidentally is a pretty boring idea.
>
> *Interviewer*: Does the fact that it comes from a machine diminish its value to you?
>
> *Cage*: Certainly not!

The young hipster readership of *Mother* surely got the joke. The piece is daring in its willingness to poke fun at the sacred cows of avant-guardism and Zen Buddhism as well as at the more obvious targets. As the book's publication neared, however, someone in the publisher's office became aware that the interview was made up, comprising quotes from Cage but also from Warhol and William Burroughs, among others. Eventually Cage himself read it, was bemused, but reassured of Berrigan's admiration allowed it to be reprinted with the added disclaimer that it was made up. Berrigan's no less remarkable *Paris Review* interview with Jack Kerouac was in every respect genuine. In effect, whether real or made up, the interview allowed the poet an alternative genre in which to explore his fascination with shifts of tone.

Indeed, so much in these pages seems to be engaged with a kind of high play, both literally and figuratively, and there are moments when one wonders at the inclusion of slighter ephemera. Berrigan was in poor health for more than a decade at the end of his short life—eventually suffering from cirrhosis brought on by complications from drug use, primarily amphetamines—and nothing after *The Sonnets* has the same heft. But the same could be said of Allen Ginsberg's work after "Howl" and "Kaddish," both written before he was thirty-five. However, in both poets' cases that would miss the generative, well-nigh eucharistic role that seems to be the assigned fate of particular artists.

Berrigan's life combined damaging indulgence with unwavering devotion to poetry, usually at the edge of poverty. After Frank O'Hara's death at 40 in 1966, he was the man everyone wanted to see, and he held court judiciously and with a certain solemnity, albeit increasingly from a prone position on a series of day beds in Iowa City, Ann Arbor, Essex, and finally St. Mark's Place on the Lower East Side again. An itinerate poetry professor without tenure, over the years he'd grown enormous.

Near the end of an early poem, **"Words for Love,"** dedicated to his first wife, Sandy Alper, he takes his own measure with remarkable accuracy and prescience:

> At night, awake, high on poems, or pills
> or simple awe that loveliness exists, my lists
> flow differently. Of words bright red
> and black, and blue.   Bosky.   Oubliette.   Dissevered. And O, alas
>
> Time disturbs me. Always minute detail
> fills me up . . .

Knowing the price to be paid for it by the poet and his family, this attention to minute particulars in tone and texture may eventually give one pause. In effect this poet deconstructed himself—and the more sensible destiny he might have pursued—to follow a complicated muse.

Still, for those of us who came of age in the daunting shadow of Donald M. Allen's benchmark anthology, *The New American Poetry 1945-1960* (Ginsberg,

O'Hara et al.), Berrigan's presence, while ultimately chastening, was a tonic, liberating breath of fresh air. He could respond generously and aptly to so many varieties of poetry—enjoying F. T. Prince one moment and the concrete poems of Ian Hamilton Finlay the next—that he had the rare critical authority of "a mind so fine," as Eliot said of Henry James, "it was unviolated by an idea."

I first met him in the spring of 1964 at the Greenwich Village party given by Frank O'Hara and Joe LeSueur for the aged Giuseppe Ungaretti. A twenty-year-old native New Yorker, I'd apprenticed myself to the more rigorous Black Mountain poets. Ted, red-bearded and still slim, having recently come across some of my poems, surprised me by responding warmly and breaking the ice.

"But my friends and I—" he added a moment later, smiling, "—we like to tell a few lies in our poems. Or a few jokes, you know? I think you'd be good at that too"—remarks I found both baffling and intriguing.

In addition to the longer works cited, there are a dozen or more lyrics here in which he gives us a music as brightly raucous as a composition by Charles Mingus. Every once in a while, too, comes something as sweet-sorrowful as a passage out of Ellington. Here is the beginning of **"Peace"**:

> What to do
>     when the day's heavy heart
>     having risen, late
> in the already darkening East
>     & prepared at any moment, to sink into the West
> surprises suddenly,
>                     & settles, for a time,
>                                 at a lovely place
> where mellow light spreads
>                     evenly
>                         from face to face?

The poem ends:

>                             And if
>     she turns your head around
>                         like any other man,
>                             go home
> and make yourself a sandwich
>                     of toasted bread, & ham with butter
>     lots of it,
>         & have a diet cola,
>             & sit down
> and write this,
>             because you can.

It's good to have this work, lucidly introduced and annotated, at hand in one volume.

# FURTHER READING

## Biography

Clark, Tom. *Late Returns: A Memoir of Ted Berrigan.* Bolinas, Calif.: Tombouctou, 1985, 89 p.

> Recounts Clark's friendship with Berrigan, which began in 1965 with an interest in his poetry and continued until Berrigan's death in 1983.

## Criticism

Lopez, Tony. "'Powder on a Little Table': Ted Berrigan's Sonnets and 1960s Poems." *Journal of American Studies* 36, no. 2 (2002): 281-92.

> Discusses Berrigan's early poetry, describing it as experimental and innovative.

---

**Additional coverage of Berrigan's life and career is contained in the following sources published by Gale:** *Contemporary Authors,* **Vols. 61-64;** *Contemporary Authors-Obituary,* **Vol. 110;** *Contemporary Authors New Revision Series,* **Vols. 14, 102;** *Contemporary Literary Criticism,* **Vol. 37;** *Contemporary Poets,* **Eds. 1, 2, 3;** *Dictionary of Literary Biography,* **Vols. 5, 169;** *Literature Resource Center;* **and** *World Poets.*

# Arthur Hugh Clough
## 1819-1861

English poet, essayist, and translator.

## INTRODUCTION

An accomplished lyric poet and satirist, Clough is known for his poetic explorations of the major religious controversies of the early Victorian age. Clough was well regarded by many of his peers as an intellectual whose thoughts on philosophy and religion contributed greatly to the cultural debates of his time. Although his religious poetry is rarely read today, scholars have been reexamining Clough's longer poems and finding in them the seeds of the modernist aesthetic.

## BIOGRAPHICAL INFORMATION

Clough was born in Liverpool, England, on January 1, 1819, to Anne Perfect, a member of a middle-class Yorkshire family, and James Butler Clough, a cotton merchant descended from the landed gentry of Wales. The family consisted of three sons and one daughter, Anne Jemima, later the first Principal of Newnham College, Cambridge. The Cloughs moved to America in 1822 and made their home in Charleston, South Carolina, spending their summers on Sullivan's Island. In 1828 Clough and his older brother Charles were sent to school in England; a year later they both entered Rugby School, where Clough showed great promise as a student and was mentored by the liberal headmaster, Dr. Thomas Arnold. He also became involved with the school's literary magazine, serving as its editor. In 1837 he began attending Balliol College, Oxford, on a scholarship, and after graduation earned a fellowship and tutorship at Oriel College. The college at the time was embroiled in religious controversy pitting liberals against the members of the conservative Oxford Movement, led by John Henry Newman, an Oriel fellow. At Oriel, Clough became friends with Matthew Arnold, the son of his former mentor at Rugby; it was a friendship that would last for the rest of Clough's life. In 1848 Clough resigned his tutorship, plagued by growing doubts about the Church of England doctrines he was required to teach, and traveled to Paris where he met Ralph Waldo Emerson, who further encouraged his religious skepticism. In 1849, after a trip to Rome, he accepted a position as principal of University Hall in London. Unhappy with the institution's secularism, he resigned in 1851 and began earning a living through his writing and various private tutoring jobs. Three years later, he married Blanche Smith, whom he had been courting for a number of years, and more or less retired as a poet, writing very little for the next eight years. He devoted himself more and more to political causes and to the service of health-care reformer Florence Nightingale, his wife's cousin. By 1859 Clough's health had begun to fail and in 1861 he contracted malaria. He died in Florence, Italy, on November 13, 1861, at the age of forty-two.

## MAJOR WORKS

In 1835 while still a student at Rugby, Clough published his first poem, the prizewinning *The Close of the Eighteenth Century.* Although he was long known for his shorter religious meditations, some of which have been included in hymnals and literary anthologies, more recently scholars have concentrated on his longer works. The first of these, *The Bothie of Toper-na-Fuosich* (1848), written in English hexameter, satirized the climate at Oxford during his time there. It was followed a year later by *Ambarvalia,* a collaboration with his clergyman friend Thomas Burbidge, consisting of poems written by Clough and Burbidge during their years at Oxford. Although the collection was virtually ignored by readers and critics, Clough's contribution to the volume—forty short pieces—was reprinted separately in 1850. In 1858 Clough published *Amours de Voyage,* initially as a serial in *Atlantic Monthly.* The verse dialogue *Dipsychus and the Spirit* was started by Clough sometime in the 1850s, but never completed; it was published after his death in 1865. The work is an extended satirical dialogue, set in Venice, between the character Dipsychus and a character identified as "The Spirit"; its targets are worldliness, moral absolutes, and contemporary aesthetics. Near the end of his life, after a long period of silence, Clough began writing again. He produced a number of verse tales dealing with marriage, titled *Mari magno,* (1862) which was published posthumously, as was most of Clough's poetic output which existed only in manuscript form when he died. Two editions of his collected works appeared in 1862, and in 1869, Clough's widow published an enlarged collection, *The Poems and Prose Remains of Arthur Hugh Clough* in two volumes. A number of collections and volumes of selected poems have been published since Clough's time, most recently *Selected Poems* (1987) edited and introduced by Shirley Chew.

## CRITICAL RECEPTION

Since most of Clough's poetry was unpublished during his lifetime, his popularity was limited. Nonetheless, A. L. P. Norrington reports that Clough was highly regarded by most of his contemporaries, but more as a man of intellectual integrity and distinction than as a poet. The limited amount of poetry that was in circulation would inevitably be compared to that of his more famous peers such as Robert Browning, Matthew Arnold, and Alfred, Lord Tennyson. D. J. Enright (see Further Reading) concurs, contending that Clough's many friends admired him for his "innate goodness" and his intellect but were inevitably disappointed by the product of that intellect. The problem for his contemporaries was that his work never went beyond endless introspection and constant raillery against orthodox philosophy and religion. Yet for Enright, Clough "is a distinctive voice in Victorian literature, in all literature, and his poetry finds its source in those very conflicts which his friends would have had him silence." Wendall V. Harris (see Further Reading) reports that the poems of *Ambarvalia* detail the ideological uncertainties Clough faced during his years at Oxford, but concedes that the poet did not successfully connect with his readers on these issues. "The reaction of most of his friends does not . . . indicate that they were able either to enter sympathetically into Clough's perplexities or to see for what purpose he was using his poetry," according to Harris, who notes that the volume's only two poems earning high praise were "When soft September brings again" and "Light Words," neither of which deal with Clough's intellectual struggles.

Following Clough's death and the publication of his collected works, he "became a much-read poet" throughout the latter part of the nineteenth century. According to Norrington, though, his poetry was often considered "prosaic," and his lyrics "too plain in language, too stiff and intricate in movement, his longer poems too unbuttoned." Although his popularity declined in the twentieth century, Stopford A. Brooke (see Further Reading), writing in 1908, still had high praise for Clough's work, contending that virtually all of his poetry was self-revelatory. According to Brooke, despite the poet's outward reserve, "the unconscious disclosure of his soul" was evident throughout his work—all the more effective for being unintentional.

Recent critics have begun to reevaluate Clough's work, concentrating on his long poems. James R. Locke (see Further Reading) makes a case for Clough's *Amours de Voyage* as the source for T. S. Eliot's "The Love Song of J. Alfred Prufrock," noting "close similarities in theme, style and structure" between the two texts. Michael Timko offers a favorable comparison between *Amours* and Tennyson's *Maud*, reporting that whereas the hero of *Maud* has "taken the easy way out,"
Clough's hero is determined to "face fact and not fall prey to illusion." Janice E. Keller contends that Clough "questioned the validity of all *a priori* givens, except truth itself" and he "was among the few Victorian poets whose sole interest was grappling with the pressing concerns of his era." R. A. Forsyth praises Clough for his poetic response to those concerns, insisting that Clough, unlike most of his fellow poets, achieved a "supreme balancing act, precariously holding in equipoise the despair of intolerable atheism and the hope of an embattled faith."

Some critics find Clough's work far ahead of its time in that it anticipated the work of twentieth-century modernists. Robert Johnson believes that Clough's *Dipsychus* has been underrated by many critics and finds in the work a linkage between Clough and "the thinking of a generation of artists to follow." Johnson contends that the poems of Clough's "Seven Sonnets" "directly anticipate in tone [Samuel] Beckett's modernist point of view" in *Waiting for Godot,* written nearly a century later. Clough's poems, according to Johnson, "offer solid documentation of Clough's insightful movement toward positions we now regard as norms for art of the generation to follow his own." Christopher M. Kierstead also suggests that Clough was out of step with his own times, particularly as regards the Victorian conventions governing travel poetry, which regarded travel as self-affirming, whereas Clough seemed to find it disillusioning. Kierstead cites how the "inconclusive ending" of *Amours de Voyage* "baffled, even annoyed Clough's contemporaries," while "*Dipsychus* shows the potential of travel to displace even the most cherished of self-sustaining myths."

---

# PRINCIPAL WORKS

### Poetry

*The Close of the Eighteenth Century: A Prize Poem* 1835

*The Bothie of Toper-na-Fuosich: A Long-Vacation Pastoral* 1848; revised as *The Bothie of Tober-na-Vuolich* 1862

*Ambarvalia* [with Thomas Burbidge] 1849

*Amours de Voyage* 1858

*Mari Magno; or, Tales on Board* (unfinished) 1862

*Poems* 1862

*Dipsychus and the Spirit* (unfinished) 1865

*Letters and Remains* (poetry, essays, and letters) 1865

*Mystery of the Fall* 1869

*The Poems and Prose Remains of Arthur Hugh Clough* (poetry, essays, and letters) 1869

*Poems* 1951
*The Poems of Arthur Hugh Clough* 1974
*Selected Poems* [edited by Shirley Chew] 1987

**Other Major Works**

*A Consideration of Objections against the Retrench-
ment Association at Oxford during the Irish Famine
in 1847* (essay) 1847
*Plutarch's Lives, the Translations Called Dryden's Cor-
rected from the Greek and Revised.* 5 vols. [transla-
tor] (essays) 1859
*Letters of Matthew Arnold and Arthur Hugh Clough*
(letters) 1932
*Correspondence of Arthur Hugh Clough.* 2 vols. (letters)
1957
*Selected Prose Works* (essays) 1964

---

# CRITICISM

### A. L. P. Norrington (essay date 1968)

SOURCE: Norrington, A. L. P. Introduction to *The
Poems of Arthur Hugh Clough,* edited by A. L. P. Norrington, pp. v-xv. New York: Oxford University Press,
1968.

[*In the following essay, Norrington offers an overview
of Clough's life, career, and literary reputation.*]

I

Arthur Hugh Clough was born on New Year's Day
1819, in the same year as Ruskin, George Eliot, Walt
Whitman, and Queen Victoria. His father, James Butler
Clough, came of a well-to-do family long established in
North Wales; his mother, born Anne Perfect, was the
daughter of a Yorkshire banker. They had three sons, of
whom Arthur was the second, and one daughter, Anne
Jemima, who became the first Principal of Newnham
College, Cambridge.

Clough's father went into business in Liverpool as a
cotton merchant, and in 1823 took his wife and young
family out to Charleston, South Carolina, in order to attend to the American end of the trade, and there he
made his home for the next thirteen years. Arthur and
his elder brother were sent back to England to be
educated, and in 1829 were both entered at Rugby
School, where Dr. Thomas Arnold had just become
headmaster. Arthur won a scholarship to Balliol and
went up to Oxford in 1837. He surprised his friends by
only obtaining a second class in 1841, but was elected

to a Fellowship at Oriel in 1842. Six years later he
resigned his Fellowship, and in 1849 was appointed
Principal of University Hall, London, a new hostel for
students, founded by Presbyterians and Unitarians. At
the end of 1851 he resigned this post too. In the following year he became engaged to Blanche Smith, a cousin
of Florence Nightingale, and he had to find a way of
earning enough to marry on. He set sail for America in
October to seek his fortune, but nothing came of it, and
he returned to England next year to take up a post as
examiner in the Education Office. In 1854 he and
Blanche were married.

Clough's responsibilities and salary were at first moder-
ate, but the family income was augmented by Blanche's
father. Clough had 'settled down' at last, but he was not
to enjoy his marriage long. By 1859 his health began to
fail, and in 1861, after months of sick leave spent
wandering in search of health in Europe, he died in Florence on 13 November, aged 42.

II

Clough was thought by many of his contemporaries,
indeed by most of those who came to know him, to be
a man of uncommon distinction. He had been Arnold's
most brilliant pupil at Rugby. He made a deep impression at Oxford, as undergraduate and as young don. It
was the same later in London and New England. Matthew Arnold, Carlyle, Thackeray, and Tennyson, Emerson, Lowell, and C. E. Norton, and many other leading
men on both sides of the Atlantic, knew and admired
him, and were in no doubt about his character and his
ability. J. A. Symonds was going to a tutorial with
Jowett on the day the news of Clough's death reached
Oxford. 'I cannot hear your essay this evening, Mr.
Symonds,' said Jowett, 'I have just heard that Clough is
dead.'

It was the man himself who so much impressed these
eminent Victorians. It cannot have been his career. He
had resigned from two educational appointments by the
time he was thirty-two, and the post in the Education
Office that he accepted two years later was a minor one.
As for his poetry, there was little for them to judge by
in his lifetime, and there were other poets to hold their
attraction. Between 1837, when Clough went up to
Oxford and Victoria came to the throne, and 1861, when
he died, Browning was producing a new volume almost
every other year. Most of Matthew Arnold's poetry was
published during those twenty-four years, and a great
deal of Longfellow's. Wordsworth's *Prelude* appeared
(posthumously) in 1851, and Tennyson, who succeeded
him as Poet Laureate in 1850, published *The Princess*
in 1847, *In Memoriam* in 1850, *Maud* in 1855, and
*Idylls of the King* in 1859.

Clough made the briefest of appearances on this copi-
ous scene. Just before his thirtieth birthday, in December
1848, he published a long poem of some 1,700 lines,

*The Bothie of Toper-na-Fuosich* (reprinted after his death as *The Bothie of Tober-na-Vuolich*). A few weeks later, in January 1849, appeared *Ambarvalia,* a joint production with a clergyman friend, Thomas Burbidge. The book attracted little attention at the time and was not reprinted, though the sheets of Clough's section—forty short poems—were reissued, bound as a separate volume, in 1850. The rest was silence until, in 1858, another long poem, *Amours de Voyage,* was published serially in the newly founded American *Atlantic Monthly.* The bulk of his mature poetic output—in total almost as large as Matthew Arnold's—was still in manuscript when he died, and was known, if at all, only to his wife and a few friends.

One of these friends, C. E. Norton, had been encouraging him, ever since they had met in Boston in 1853, to publish a volume of poetry in America. The project seems to have been well advanced by the summer of 1855, when Clough, who had been sending material to Norton, wrote (14 September) that he thought the book might be called 'The Bothie, Roman Hexameters, and Other Poems—chiefly reprinted'. But before the work of selection and revision had been completed, the 'Roman Hexameters', which would have formed the bulk of the new material, were published as *Amours de Voyage* in the Atlantic Monthly: 'a great event to me', wrote Clough to Norton, 'this is the first money I ever received for verse-making. . . . I should be very glad if next year a volume of my verse should be published.' That was in 1858. By the end of 1860 all the copy for the volume must have been in Norton's hands, for Clough wrote, in February 1861, assuring him that he was not disappointed by 'the postponement of my republication by Ticknor and Fields' (the Boston publishers). It was almost the last letter he wrote to Norton. He died before the American 'republication' could take place.

It was only after his death, therefore, that the products of his 'verse-making' were made available to the public in a collected volume. Two editions appeared simultaneously in 1862, one in London, published by Macmillan with a memoir by F. T. Palgrave (whose *Golden Treasury* had come out in 1861), the other in Boston, published by Ticknor and Fields with a memoir by Norton. The American edition contained one extra poem, but otherwise the material in the two books was identical, as Mrs. Clough and Norton intended. A second English edition in 1863 contained a few more short poems, and in 1869 Mrs. Clough brought out a much enlarged edition (Vol. II of *The Poems and Prose Remains*), containing 'all such additional matter as, after careful consideration, has been deemed worthy to be given to the public'. This remained the standard collection for many years until the last edition (in Macmillan's 'Globe' series) went out of print in 1932.

A new and fuller edition of the poems appeared in 1951 in the *Oxford English Texts* series. This was based on a re-examination of Clough's own manuscript drafts and fair copies, used by Mrs. Clough a century before and preserved by the family.[1] It restores to the canon several *Ambarvalia* poems omitted, according to Clough's instructions, from the previous posthumous volumes, adds a few poems not previously printed, and presents fuller versions of *Dipsychus* and *Mari Magno* than Mrs. Clough saw fit to print. The present *Oxford Standard Authors* edition is a reprint of the poems in the 1951 edition, omitting *Dipsychus Continued, Mari Magno,* and the groups there called Unfinished Poems and Miscellaneous Poems.

### III

If Clough had, perforce, few readers in his lifetime, he became a much-read poet after his death. There were those who thought him overrated. Swinburne, not unexpectedly, admired him not at all. 'There was a bad poet named Clough', he wrote in 1875, 'whom his friends found it useless to puff; for the public, if dull, has not quite such a skull as belongs to believers in Clough.' But the collected poems were reprinted many times before the end of the century, and selections appeared in due course in such popular series as *The Canterbury Poets* (Walter Scott), *The Muses' Library* (Routledge), and Macmillan's *Golden Treasury Series.* The public, it seems, did believe in Clough. He was among the favourite poets of the last forty years of the Victorian era.

Soon after the turn of the century, however, his popularity began to decline rapidly. The decline was hastened by Lytton Strachey's allusions to him in *Eminent Victorians* (1918), *'vignettes dessinées avec un subtil mélange d'apitoiement et de dérision narquoise',* as M. Paul Veyriras describes them. A new selection of the poems edited by Humphrey Milford (*Oxford Library of Prose and Poetry,* 1910) took some twenty years to sell out. The major edition was last reprinted by Macmillan in 1920. There came a time when, for nearly twenty years, Clough's poetical works could only be bought in second-hand bookshops.

The new edition published by the Clarendon Press in 1951 coincided with a revival of interest and provided the means for a reappraisal. Four recent studies, British, American, and French, are evidence of this renewed attention: Lady Chorley's *Arthur Hugh Clough: The Uncommitted Mind* (Oxford, 1962), Walter E. Houghton's *The Poetry of Clough: An Essay in Revaluation* (Yale, 1963), Paul Veyriras's *Arthur Hugh Clough, 1819-1861* (Paris, Didier, 1964), and Michael Timko's *Innocent Victorian* (Ohio, 1966). An extensive selection of his letters, more than half of them printed for the first time, was provided in the two-volume *Correspondence* edited by Frederick A. Mulhauser (Oxford, 1957), and the *Selected Prose Works* edited by Buckner

B. Trawick (University of Alabama Press, 1964) also contains some hitherto unpublished matter. There is thus ample material now available for the student and the scholar, and it is hoped that the present edition may help to satisfy a wider public.

IV

Clough's first published poem, the ***Bothie,*** is written in hexameters—'Anglo-savage hexameters', as he called them—and he used the same metre in ***Amours de Voyage.*** It was a popular metre in the nineteenth century, Longfellow's *Evangeline* (1847) being perhaps the best-known example, though no other poet used it with such freedom and gusto as Clough. But it is unfamiliar to many modern readers, and some account of Clough's practice may be useful.

The quantitative prosody of Greek and Latin is based on the length of syllables, not on their accent or stress. A long vowel makes a long syllable, a short one a short, except when followed by certain combinations of consonants, which, by the rules, make the preceding syllable long, whatever its vowel. Two short syllables equal one long, as two semiquavers equal one quaver. A hexameter contains six feet and each foot, like a bar of music, has the same length: the first syllable is long, and may be followed by one long syllable (spondee) or two short (dactyl). The sixth foot must have only two syllables (the second of which may, in this case only, be long or short), and the fifth foot is almost invariably a dactyl. 'Happily married' is a typical ending for an English hexameter on classical principles.

Elizabethan poets thought that English verse might be written according to the same rules, but their attempts were not successful. They produced verses which, as Milford says, 'can neither be scanned for their false quantities nor read as verses for their false accents'. Later attempts have proved equally unconvincing, including those by Clough himself, in the short pieces **'Trunks the forest yielded', 'From thy far sources',** and *Actaeon.* It will not do. The rhythm of English verse depends upon accent (among other things), not length of syllable, in the classical sense. Rébel, the noun, cannot have the same metrical value as rebél, the verb, though the length of the syllables is the same, and in a Latin hexameter the two words would be metrically interchangeable.

Clough's two long hexameter poems seem to show that he realized better than any of his contemporaries the difference between classical and English prosody. He let 'longs' and 'shorts' go by the board, and went by accent. Each of his hexameters has its six feet, and in each foot there should be one syllable—almost invariably the first—which has a naturally strong and predominant stress. There are thus six predominantly stressed syllables in each line, and each of these syllables is followed—or very occasionally preceded—by one or two unstressed, or less strongly stressed, syllables. Where there are three syllables in the foot, the two unstressed syllables are normally very light; where there are only two, the second syllable may, and quite often does, have almost as much weight as the first.

But some examples will perhaps make the matter clearer; and we will begin with straightforward examples which can hardly be read wrongly.

1. Ónly a / Líberal / mémber, a / wáy at the / énd of the / táble.
2. Dráwn by / móon and / sún from / Lábra / dór and / Gréenland.
3. Árchi / téctural / Beáuty in / Ápplic / átion to / Wómen.
4. Ráphael's / Jóys and / Gráces, and / thý clear / stárs, Gali / léo!

In 1 every foot but the last has three syllables, in 2 every foot is dissyllabic, while 3 and 4 are mixed. But whereas in 1, 2, and 3 no syllables except the first in each foot have any natural stress, in 4 there are two feet, the first and fourth, in which there is a secondary stress; indeed, the two syllables of the fourth foot should be read with almost equal weight.

But Clough was trying his hand out—'Experimental yet the prosody is of the English', as he wrote in one of his notebooks—and he wrote many lines over which the reader may well stumble at first sight, and some which it is frankly impossible to scan with confidence. The following passage from Section IX of the ***Bothie*** will be found to exhibit almost every conceivable irregularity:

> All the great empty streets are flooded with broadening clearness,
> Which, withal, by inscrutable simultaneous access
> Permeates far and pierces to the very cellars lying in
> Narrow high back-lane, and court, and alley of alleys:—
> He that goes forth to his walks, while speeding to the suburb,
> Sees sights only peaceful and pure; as labourers settling
> Slowly to work, in their limbs the lingering sweetness of slumber;
> Humble market-carts, coming-in, bringing-in, not only
> Flower, fruit, farm-store, but sounds and sights of the country
> Dwelling yet on the sense of the dreamy drivers; soon after
> Half-awake servant-maids unfastening drowsy shutters
> Up at the windows, or down, letting-in the air by the doorway;
> School-boys, school-girls soon, with slate, portfolio, satchel,
> Hampered as they haste, those running, these others maidenly tripping;

Early clerk anon turning out to stroll, or it may be
Meet his sweetheart—waiting behind the garden gate
  there;
Merchant on his grass-plat haply, bare-headed; and
  now by this time
Little child bringing breakfast to 'father' that sits on
  the timber
There by the scaffolding; see, she waits for the can
  beside him;
Meantime above purer air untarnished of new-lit fires:
So that the whole great wicked artificial civilized
  fabric—
All its unfinished houses, lots for sale, and railway
  outworks—
Seems reaccepted, resumed to Primal Nature and
  Beauty:—
—Such—in me, and to me, and on me the love of El-
  spie!

In l. 1 the last four feet are clear, but should the first
two be 'Áll the great / émpty' or 'Áll the / gréat empty'?
or even 'All the gréat / émpty', inverting the stress in
the first foot? The answer is not quite any of these. The
proper way to read it is 'Áll the greàt / émpty', with a
secondary stress on the third syllable of the first foot—
unusual in a trisyllabic foot.

In l. 2 the only difficulty is in the fourth foot, 'símul-',
in which a stress heavier than is natural must be placed
on the first syllable.

In l. 3 there are two departures from the normal. The
third foot has four syllables, 'piérces to the', instead of
three, and the last foot, 'lýing in', has three syllables,
though the first two can be almost compressed into one.

In l. 5 the difficulty lies in the fourth and fifth feet, for
which we have four syllables, 'speeding to the', with
only one natural stress among them. The only way to
mitigate the deficiency is to put a secondary stress on
the second syllable of 'speeding', but it is a bad line.

In l. 9 'Flower' is a whole foot, and is to be read as a
dissyllable.

Line 14 is no doubt intentionally unsteady at the outset.
The first foot has four syllables, and the second and
third feet both contain two natural stresses: 'Hámpered
as they / háste, thòse / rúnning, thèse / óthers / máidenly
/ trípping'. The movement of the line is not ill-suited to
the morning rush to school.

Here is the whole passage with the suggested scansion
marked (the *grave* accents indicate secondary stress):

Áll the greàt / émpty / stréets are / floóded with /
  broádening / cleárness,
Whích, with / ál, by in / scrútable / símul / táneous /
  áccess
Pérmeàtes / fár and / piérces to the / véry / céllars /
  lýing in

Nárrow / hígh bàck / láne, and / coúrt, and / álley of /
  álleys:—
Hé that goes / fórth to his / wálks, while / spéedìng /
  to the / súburb,
Seés sìghts / ónly / peáceful and / púre; as / lábourers
  / séttling
Slówly to / wórk, in their / límbs the / língering /
  sweétness of / slúmber;
Húmble / márket / cárts, còming / ín, brìnging / ín,
  not / ónly
Flówer, / fruít, fàrm / stóre, but / soúnds and / síghts
  of the / coúntry
Dwélling / yét on the / sénse of the / dréamy / drívers;
  soòn / áfter
Hálf-awàke / sérvant / maíds un / fástening / drówsy /
  shútters
Úp at the / wíndows, or / dówn, lètting / ín the / aír
  by the / doórway;
Schoól-bòys, / schoól-gìrls / soón, with / sláte, pòrt /
  fólio, / sátchel,
Hámpered as they / háste, thòse / rúnning, thèse /
  óthers / máidenly / trípping;
Eárly / clérk a / nón tùrning / oút to / stróll, or it /
  máy be
Méet his / sweétheàrt /—waíting be / hínd the / gárden
  / gáte thère;
Mérchant on his / gráss-plat / háply, bàre / heáded;
  and / nów by / thís tìme
Líttle / chíld brìnging / breákfast to / 'fáther' that / síts
  on the / tímber
Thére by the / scáffolding; / seé, she / waíts for the /
  cán be / síde him;
Meántìme a / bóve pùrer / aír un / tárnished of / néw-
  lìt / fíres:
Só that the / whóle greàt / wícked / ártificial / cívi-
  lized / fábric—
Áll its un / fínished / hoúses, / lóts for sàle, and / raíl-
  way / oútworks—
Séems reac / cépted, re / súmed to / Prímal / Náture
  and / Beaúty:—
—Súch /—ín me, and / tó me, and / ón me the / lóve
  of / Élspie!

## V

Walter Bagehot, reviewing the first posthumous collection of Clough's poems in 1862, wrote of him as a man
'who seemed about to do something, but who died
before he did it'. Lowell described him as 'dying before
he had subdued his sensitive temperament to the sterner
requirements of his art'. This view of Clough as a poet
of unfulfilled promise has often been repeated. It is
true, of course, that he left much work, and some of his
best, unfinished. But that is not to say that if he had
lived longer he would have written better. The evidence
points the other way.

He wrote almost all his poetry between 1839 and 1852.
To the period before he resigned his fellowship at Oriel
in 1848 belong the *Ambarvalia* poems and many other
short pieces. In 1848, in a mood of release, he wrote
the *Bothie,* and continued to fill notebook after
notebook with verse during the next two or three years,

to which belong *Amours de Voyage, Dipsychus,* **'Say not the struggle nought availeth'**, *Easter Day,* and much else. But the sequel to *Dipsychus* which he wrote in 1852[2] is very inferior; for the next eight years he wrote nothing; and when he began verse-making again, a few months before his death, the result was justly described by Professor Houghton as 'the most dated and least successful of Clough's longer poems', the unfinished *Mari Magno.* It is hard to avoid the suspicion that Clough would have become, had he lived longer, a poet less worth reading.

Secondly, anybody reading his poetry as a whole may well find it hard to recognize the familiar portrait drawn by Matthew Arnold in *Thyrsis*: the gentle shepherd-poet whose 'rustic flute kept not for long its happy, country tone', the 'too quick despairer' whose 'piping took a troubled sound'. Arnold seems to be saying that Clough showed his true bent as a poet in the *Bothie* and then, overcome by the contentions of the world and faltering in his quest for unattainable truth, began to sing out of tune. Nothing, certainly, could be blither than the 'happy country tone' of the *Bothie,* with its glowing pictures of Highland scenery 'where the great peaks look abroad over Skye to the westernmost islands', and its hilarious reading-party talk:

> 'Every woman is, or ought to be, a Cathedral.'
> 'Philip shall write us a book, a Treatise on *The Laws of*
> *Architectural Beauty in Application to Women.* . . .
> Where shall in specimen seen be the sculliony stumpy-columnar,
> (which to a reverent taste is perhaps the most moving of any,)
> Rising to grace of true woman in English the Early and Later. . . .
> Lost, ere we end, in the Lady-Debased and the Lady-Flamboyant.'

But it was not a feebler note that Clough struck in the poetry that he wrote after the *Bothie,* nor always a more melancholy note. What could be more airily and amusingly conversational than *Amours de Voyage*?

> Rome, believe me, my friend, is like its own Monte Testaceo,
> Merely a marvellous mass of broken and castaway wine-pots. . . .
> No one can cavil, I grant, at the size of the great Coliseum.
> Doubtless the notion of grand and capacious and massive amusement,
> This the old Romans had; but tell me, is this an idea?

What, again, could be more vigorous than the satire of, for example, *The Latest Decalogue,* or the Spirit's mockery of the *parvenu* in *Dipsychus*:

> As I sat at the café, I said to myself,
> They may talk as they please about what they call pelf,

> They may sneer as they like about eating and drinking,
> But help it I cannot, I cannot help thinking
>> How pleasant it is to have money, heigh ho!
>> How pleasant it is to have money.

Poetry like this may lack the 'high seriousness' that Arnold thought appropriate, but it was not the 'too quick despairer' of *Thyrsis* who seemed to be talking to us in such a very contemporary voice when the B.B.C. broadcast readings of *Amours de Voyage* in 1958,[3] a hundred years after it was first published.

Lastly, Clough has been pronounced a prosaic poet. It has been maintained that it would have been better if he had said what he wanted to say in prose, not verse. His lyrics (to call them such) are too plain in language, too stiff and intricate in movement, his longer poems too unbuttoned. He would not don the poet's singing robes. 'Consider whether you attain the *beautiful*', Arnold wrote to him, 'and whether your product gives PLEASURE.' Certainly he is an unusual mid-nineteenth-century poet, sometimes a difficult poet, but a poet he had to be.

*Notes*

1. They were deposited in the Bodleian Library by Clough's grandniece, Miss Katherine Duff, in 1953.

2. Lady Chorley has proved beyond reasonable doubt that *Dipsychus Continued* was written during his visit to America (op. cit. pp. 264 ff.).

3. and again in 1967.

**Jacqueline Johnson and Paul Dean (essay date June 1977)**

SOURCE: Johnson, Jacqueline, and Paul Dean. "'Paradise Come Back': Clough in Search of Eden." *Durham University Journal* 69, no. 2 (June 1977): 249-53.

[*In the following essay, Johnson and Dean explore Clough's use of Eden mythology in several of his works, particularly* The Bothie of Tober-na-Vuolich.]

'We are afraid', wrote an anonymous reviewer of Clough's *Poems* (1862), 'that it is the scepticism of Mr Clough rather than his "poetry" which has been his chief recommendation to some of his principal admirers.'[1] This remained true until the publication of R. K. Biswas' *Arthur Hugh Clough: Towards a Reconsideration* (Oxford, 1972), which, in contrast to the earlier work of Katharine Chorley, emphasised literary criticism rather than biographical/psychological speculation. There were areas in Clough's work, however, which Mr Biswas did not seem fully to appreciate, and this paper is an attempt to discuss one of them, namely the poet's repeated use of the Eden-myth and the related story of Jacob, Rachel and Leah, as mediators for his statements about the human condition.

The story of Jacob provides the basis for the central passage in *The Bothie of Tober-na-Vuolich* (1848), in which an Oxford undergraduate writes to his friend Philip about the latter's projected marriage with the Highland girl Elspie, as follows:

> Go, be the wife in thy house both Rachel and Leah
>     unto thee! . . .
> For this Rachel-and-Leah is marriage; which, I have
>     seen it,
> Lo, and have known it, is always, and must be, bigamy
>     only,
> Even in noblest kind a duality, compound, and
>     complex,
> One part heavenly-ideal, the other vulgar and earthy.
>
> (IX. 157, 167-70)[2]

Every man is confronted with the task of reconciling Rachel to Leah, aspiration to actuality. It is often supposed that the conclusion to the *Bothie,* which presents the emigration of Philip and Elspie to New Zealand as a pilgrimage like that of Adam and Eve, to set up a new creation, vindicates the success with which Philip has made this reconciliation. But the tone is not so optimistic. 'There he hewed, and dug; subdued the earth and his spirit; / There he built him a home; there Elspie bare him his children' (IX. 196 f.). Certainly, Philip, like Adam, has dominion over the earth and subdues it. But he subdues his spirit too; and as for Elspie, she becomes the child-bearer and sharer of his toil. Hard work, and the pains of childbirth, are, according to the Book of Genesis, part of the punishment for the Fall, not a privilege of Paradise.

*The Bothie of Tober-na-Vuolich* uses the Eden-myth as a means of universalising certain aspects of the world it presents, in a way which undercuts the apparently satisfactory conclusion of the events. Clough went on to write **'Jacob'** and **'Jacob's Wives',** in which the symbolic significance of the two women is re-affirmed. In the latter poem, Rachel associates herself with the past, idyllic life which she and Jacob led before Leah interfered: Leah dismisses this as useless sentimentalism, and calls upon Jacob to join her in hard work to make the best of their present circumstances. Thus, an argument about history is being developed, in which Rachel stands not only for the 'heavenly-ideal' but also for the past in which the ideal was realised, and Leah not only for the 'vulgar and earthy' but also for Clough's own time, in which the harmonic view of the universe presented by Christianity seemed to have been exploded, and a disjunctive view substituted for it.

With this widening of interest it was natural for Clough to return to Adam and Eve, typological figures with whom he could make a more general examination of the metaphysical problems which the discrediting of traditional Christian doctrine entailed. So, in **'Adam and Eve',** he brought the problem of history and the problem of metaphysics together.

Eve is the chief adherent of the position adopted by Rachel in **'Jacob's Wives'.** She sees very clearly the consequences of the Fall for future generations, 'The questionings of ages yet to be, / The thinkings and cross-thinkings, self-contempts' (I. 125 f.), and in her horror she seeks to return to prelapsarian Eden, declaring, for example, at the birth of Cain, 'My heart is in the garden as of old, / And Paradise come back' (III. 3 f.). She acknowledges the condition of separation from God in which she lives, and begins to elaborate a theology which will bring her, by law, to the state she once enjoyed by nature. She is even hopeful (or shortsighted) enough to tell Cain, after he has murdered Abel:

> For there are rites and holy means of grace
> Of God ordained for man's eternal weal.
> With these, my son, address thyself to Him,
> And seek atonement from a gracious God,
> With whom is balm for every wounded heart.
>
> (XI. 9-13)

Eve is thus, as it were, a Rachel living in a Leah-world. All her instincts are towards the re-creation of the Golden Age when communication with God was freely given, and all her efforts in that direction fail.

Adam, by contrast, immediately establishes himself as a pragmatist, rejecting the Fall and all its implications.

> What!
> Because I plucked an apple from a twig
> Be damned to death eterne! parted from Good,
> Enchained to Ill! No, by the God of Gods,
> No, by the living will within my breast,
> It cannot be and shall not . . .
>
> (I. 23-28)

The assertion of Self has, in his secular universe, replaced God as the source of morality and ethics. Not only does he know Good and Evil, he proclaims himself, in Nietzschean fashion, 'Superior in a higher Good to both' (II. 45). Man is 'Earthy as well as godlike; bound to strive' (III. 51), and what he strives for is 'consummated consciousness of self' (III. 57). The world of the present is anthropocentric; the order of the universe has been inverted, turned inside out. This produces a problem of authority. Eve hears voices which tell her she has disobeyed God. Adam hears voices which tell him he has done no such thing, 'And to discern the Voice amidst the voices / Is that hard task, my love, that we are born to' (IV. 65 f.). It is not difficult to see, in this opposition of a dogmatic external authority and a reliance on private judgement and the voice of conscience, the conflict between Catholic (or Anglo-Catholic) and Protestant attitudes; but this is not a straightforward allegory, since in the world of the poem neither side can claim a more direct contact with God than the other. The psychology is that of the religious impulse, not of particular denominations.

The appearance of Cain and Abel sets up two 'camps', Cain and Adam against Abel and Eve. In his soliloquy Abel shows, by his exposition of the doctrine of Redemption, that he is his mother's son:

> My mother calls the Fall a Mystery.
> Redemption is so too. But oh, my God,
> Thou wilt bring all things in the end to good.
> Yea, though the whole earth lie in wickedness, I
> Am with Thee, with Thee, with Thee evermore . . .
> Nor life, nor death, things here or things below,
> Cast out the sweet assurance of my soul
> That I am Thine, and Thou art mine, my God.
>
> (VI. 22-26, 46-48)

Unable to share his father's apotheosis of Self, or his mother's sense of desolation, he has adapted Adam's subjectivity and built his own Eden within himself.

Against this certainty that the metaphysical connection has been made is set the Adamic self-assertiveness of Cain in the next scene.

> My father, he is cheerful and content,
> And leads me frankly forward. Yet, indeed,
> His leading—or (more truly) to be led
> At all, by any one, and not myself—
> Is mere dissatisfaction: everymore
> Something I must do, individual,
> To vindicate my nature, to give proof
> I also am, as Adam is, a man.
>
> (VII. 17-24)

When this aggressiveness leads to the murder of Abel, Cain is not only delighted to discover that tiresome persons can be so easily got rid of; he regrets that his brother did not show a little more fight and prolong the fun. And when eventually, like Adam, he realises the enormity of his crime, he will not be persuaded by Eve to seek atonement. His pride is such that he will not humble himself before God, even to be forgiven. Abel will not be brought back by 'prayers to empty heaven' (XIII. 39); Cain subscribes to another religion altogether:

> But welcome Fact, and Fact's best brother, Work;
> Welcome the conflict of the stubborn soil,
> To toil the livelong day . . .
> Welcome this worship, which I feel is mine;
> Welcome this duty . . .
>
> (XIII. 52 ff., 56 f.)

The worship of Duty and Fact is, in the fashion of Gradgrind, the substitution for worship of God.

Thus, the present, in the scheme of history, fares little better than the past. It yields a world cut off from the possibility of metaphysical extension, a world where the individual turns in upon himself, and must strive, and fight, to gain 'consummated consciousness of self', in obedience to the voice within.

But Man, if he is 'earthy', is also 'godlike'; Adam's acknowledgment of this compels him at times to look beyond the present into the future, and stirs his hope for some improvement in the human condition, when the spark of Divinity within Man may 'germinate, burst, and rise into a tree' (II. 87). Anything more ironical for it to rise into could hardly be conceived. The words suggest the truth which their speaker cannot see: the condition of falling from grace is permanent in human nature now, and though what Mr Biswas calls Adam's 'acceptance of the dynamics of living' (*op. cit.* p. 254) impels him to equate the future with progress, it is clear that Eve's conception of an endless accumulation of horror is the more realistic vision. Adam (and Cain) see Work, Toil and the struggle with the earth as the means of achievement, not as part of the punishment for the Fall. Eve sees only 'the questionings of ages yet to be' (I. 125), and Cain himself, in moments of clearsightedness, 'slaughter on slaughter, blood for blood, and death, / For ever, ever, ever, evermore!' (IX. 47 f.). Their awareness of the stretch of time is unrelieved by a belief in a Being who can shape time and give it meaning, being Himself beyond it.

Adam, despairing finally of Cain, puts his hopes in Seth.

> This merest man,
> This unambitious commonplace of life,
> Will after all perhaps mend all . . .
> . . . In him at last,
> And in his seed increased and multiplied,
> Earth shall be blest and peopled and subdued,
> And what was meant to be be brought to pass.
>
> (X. 3-5, 7-10)

The opening words of the description (reminiscent of Tennyson's Ulysses on *his* son Telemachus) do not encourage us to hope for much from Seth, and it is not easy to see him fulfilling the potential which Adam senses in himself.

When Adam comes, at the close of the existing text of the poem,[3] to a vision of the future reconcilement of Cain and Abel, the words he addresses to Cain strike us as extremely odd:

> Abel was gone and you were gone, my son—
> Gone, and yet not gone; yea, I seemed to see
> The decomposing of those coloured lines
> Which we called you, their fusion into one,
> And therewithal their vanishing and end.

. . . I was alone—yet not alone—with her [Eve]
And she with me, and you with us, my sons,
As at the first, and yet not wholly—yea,
And that which I had witnessed thus in you,
This fusion and mutation and return,
Seemed in my substance working too.

(XIV. 16-20, 30-35)

Instead of a vision of fulfilment we have one of dissolution and collapse, so vaguely described that the nature of the experience is quite incomprehensible. There is projected a reconciliation—though perhaps it is more accurate to say a disappearance, a dismissal—of those struggles between the harmonic past and the disjunctive present, which have given tension to the poem; and such a reconciliation as can make Adam declare that 'In despite of much, in lack of more, / Life has been beautiful to me' (XIV. 46 f.). But this sentimental affirmation of the good life is contradicted by everything we have previously seen in the poem. There is no reason why we should put our trust in the future any more than in the past. Earlier in the poem, indeed, Adam has spoken of all time being focussed upon the individual:

> The past is something, but the present more;
> Will not it too be past?—nor fail withal
> To recognise the future in our hopes;
> Unite them in your manhood each and all . . .

(XIII. 71-74)

The meaning of the whole course of history, as well as the meaning of the universe and human existence, is thus embodied in Man. Time and space, natural and supernatural, converge on that frail creature, who works for the exaltation of Self, firmly in the present. The ancient myth is a part of us, something repeated in us, the cause of the modern predicament.

In this way Clough adapted the story of the Fall for his own time, and for his own temperament, in a way which we might profitably compare with Tennyson's use of the story in the *Idylls of the King*. There are two places in that work in which it is introduced; the first parallels Enid's love for Geraint with that of Eve for Adam:

> . . . And never yet, since high in Paradise
> O'er the four rivers the first roses blew,
> Came purer pleasure unto mortal kind
> Than lived through her, who in that perilous hour
> Put hand to hand beneath her husband's heart,
> And felt him hers again: she did not weep,
> But o'er her meek eyes came a happy mist
> Like that which kept the heart of Eden green
> Before the useful trouble of the rain . . .

('Geraint and Enid', 762-70)[4]

Likewise, Eden appears (not explicitly, but the suggestion is so strong as to be inescapable) in this passage on the first days of Guinevere's love for Lancelot: when they,

. . . Rapt in sweet talk or lively, all on love
And sport and tilts and pleasure, (for the time
Was maytime, and as yet no sin was dreamed,)
Rode under groves that looked a paradise
Of blossom . . .

('Guinevere', 383-87)

The exclusive concentration on prelapsarian Eden ironically re-inforces the tragedy of the very different, fallen world in which the Round Table is destroyed. But no-one would wish to erect these touches into a Biblical allegory; the method is, to borrow the useful term of Mr F. E. L. Priestly,[5] parabolic, an occasional extension of the presented world for reverberative effect. Tennyson is far less ambitious than Clough in his use of the Eden myth.

Less ambitious; but perhaps his is the greater success. For, although Clough took on a task worthy of a major poet—that of re-working a myth in terms appropriate to his own time—he lacked the gifts of a major poet, particularly the linguistic gifts. In his poems before **'Adam and Eve'**—in **'Dipsychus'** and (less so) **'Amours de Voyage'**—the presence of Eden (or its absence) is felt, but less pervasively. **'Adam and Eve'** is his last effort to come to terms with the myth on its own. If it is a failed experiment, the reasons are linguistic. Clough's very dependence on the Biblical register and the concepts it expresses, and the associations which familiar words inevitably conjure up, work against his wish to re-examine the old certainties. Eve's anachronistic use of concepts like atonement and redemption, Abel's echoing of St Paul's words ('Nor life, nor death, things here, nor things below . . .'), the efforts to imitate Milton, the numerous lapses into bathos and meaningless repetition ('For ever, ever, ever, evermore'), all cripple the poet's struggle to give the old story a contemporary shape. This poem about a disjunctive universe ironically contains the greatest disjunction—of form from content—within itself. It is Clough's ill-luck that (to adapt T. S. Eliot's phrase) he had not genius enough to bring about a change in expression adequate to articulate his perception of the changes in sensibility that characterised the age in which he lived.

### Notes

1. Review in the *Church and State Review,* reprinted in *Clough: the Critical Heritage*, ed. M. Thorpe (1972), p. 160.

2. All quotations from Clough's poetry are taken from *The Poems of Arthur Hugh Clough,* 2nd edition by F. L. Mulhauser (Oxford, 1974).

3. The notes in Mulhauser, *ed. cit.,* tell us that the last scene is 'very rough and unfinished', and that there are some lines in the 1869 *Poems* which 'are clearly intended for a separate speech by Cain

after Adam's last words, or as the beginning of a new scene' (pp. 666 f.). As, however, it is difficult to see that a poem about Adam and Eve can go on much longer after the evaporation of its central figures, and as we can only criticise what we have got and not what we have not got, the poem is in this discussion assumed to be complete.

4. The quotations from Tennyson follow the edition of the complete *Poems* by C. B. Ricks (1969).

5. In his book *Language and Structure in Tennyson's Poetry* (1973).

## Michael Timko (essay date 1982)

SOURCE: Timko, Michael. "Arthur Hugh Clough: Palpable Things and Celestial Fact." In *The Victorian Experience: The Poets,* edited by Richard A. Levine, pp. 47-66. Athens, Ohio: Ohio University Press, 1982.

[*In the following essay, Timko compares Clough's* Amours de Voyage *with Tennyson's* Maud *and finds that Clough's work is in many ways the more satisfying of the two.*]

While no one up to now has been able to explain, the fact remains that Clough has always claimed attention. Certainly one could make a case for being just a bit puzzled as to why this should be, since nothing in his life and career seems to explain the interest he inspired in his own lifetime and continues to inspire among critics and readers today. Born in Liverpool in 1819, the son of a cotton merchant, Clough lived for a short time in Charleston, South Carolina (1822-28), where business had taken his father; but he returned to England to attend Rugby and Oxford, where he was both student and Fellow from 1837 to 1848. He resigned the Fellowship in 1848 because of his inability to subscribe fully to the various beliefs of the Church of England and spent the next few years teaching, traveling, and writing *The Bothie,* (1848), *Ambarvalia* (1849), *Amours de Voyage* (1850), *Dipsychus* (1850), finally taking on an Examinership in the Education Office, London, in 1853. The next year he married Blanche Smith, a cousin of Florence Nightingale's. The rest of his life was spent quietly enough working at the Education Office, writing (*Mari Magno*), and traveling for his health. He died in Florence on November 13, 1861, and is buried there in the Protestant Cemetery.

How does one, in the light of the apparent "failure" of this not so "eminent" Victorian, account for the attraction he has had in the past and still retains?[1] One might explain it by the people who were attracted to him, contemporaries and those who came after, who found in Clough himself and in his work something that inspired

not only friendship but real affection and admiration. I have much to say about Matthew Arnold and Clough below, but Arnold was both a friend and an admirer of Clough. He wrote to his sister at one time that she and Clough were "the two people I in my heart care most to please by what I write"; and he wrote to Clough himself: "My dear old soul. I find that, au fond, when I compose anything, I care more, still, for your opinion than that of any one else about it." Henry Sidgwick also acknowledged the great influence of Clough: "The truth is," he stated, "if Clough had not lived and written, I should probably be now exactly where he was. . . . I can neither adequately rationalise faith, nor reconcile faith and reason, nor suppress reason. But this is just the benefit of an utterly veracious man like Clough, that it is impossible for any one, however sympathetic, to remain where he was."

Carlyle, Emerson, and Tennyson, personal friends, also had words of praise for Clough. There is, of course, the well-known story of Clough's telling Emerson that Carlyle had led them out of the desert and left them there, at which point Emerson, placing his hand on Clough's head, "consecrated" him "Bishop of all England" to lead the people out of the wilderness to the promised land. Emerson himself, after reading the *Bothie,* wrote to thank him: "I cannot tell you how great a joy to me is your poem. . . . [It] is a high gift from angels that are very rare in our mortal state. It delights and surprises me from beginning to end. I can hardly forgive you for keeping your secret from me so well. I knew you good and wise, . . . but how could I know or guess that you had all this wealth of expression, this wealth of imagery, this joyful heart of youth, this temperate continuity, that belongs only to high masters. It is a noble poem. Tennyson must look to his laurels." Carlyle, too, although Emerson in the same letter complained that Carlyle had never mentioned the poem to him, thought highly of Clough. J. A. Froude, Carlyle's close friend, wrote to tell Clough's widow that Carlyle had often told him that he thought more highly of Clough than of anyone else in his generation. Cecil Woodham-Smith, the biographer of Florence Nightingale, tells us that Florence Nightingale's grief over Clough's death was "second only to her grief for Sidney Herbert." Tennyson, with whom Clough spent some time in 1861, thought that Clough had "great poetic feeling." Perhaps the most appropriate comment, however, is that of Dean Stanley, writing in the *Daily News* shortly after Clough's death. "Those who knew him well," Stanley said, "know that in him a genius and character of no common order has passed away." Then he added these prophetic words: "They will scarcely be able to justify their knowledge to a doubting world."

One might, then, attempt to explain Clough's appeal to a doubting world in terms of pity or sympathy, but the real attraction, I would insist, resides in the work itself:

its concerns and the sources of those concerns. It lies, too, in the poet himself, for there is, without question, a close connection between person and writer, believer and the articles of his belief. This close connection has in recent years caused some misunderstanding about Clough and his work. Different critics have tended to focus on certain aspects of the person or his writings, thus emphasizing far out of proportion one facet or another of his personality, his writing, or his interests. In recent years he has been called a quintessential Victorian or a pre-modern; a Carlylian or a democrat; an empiricist or an idealist. He is, of course, all of these and more, and it is the more that makes Clough the single Victorian writer who deserves our close attention at this time. Clough at the same time both defied and defined his age; he attempted to transform it and at times he succeeded in transcending it. To know more about him and his writing is to come to know more about the age in which he lived. Ultimately, of course, it is to come to know more about our own.

There are a number of characteristics of Clough and his work that account for his particular place in Victorian life and literature. He was always in touch with significant movements and important people. He was always aware of the importance of facts (of palpable things, as he called them), while never losing sight of the "spiritual" or celestial. Most important, perhaps, his chief concern was with human beings, their strengths and weaknesses, their foibles and fetishes. He never resorted to type or caricature. As a result, his writings reflect his own ideas as to exactly what human beings are like and how they act in a world that at times seems to be for them if not alien at least inhospitable. Clough does not write about systems or ideologies or movements or theories. He writes about human beings who have those qualities that we call human, and it is for this reason that we respond to him as artist and person.

Clough still remains elusive, however, particularly in his approach to human nature and to life itself. Part of this puzzlement is reflected, as I have already said, in our inability to "place" Clough, to label him, to categorize him. Part of this puzzlement is reflected in various attempts to classify his poems, especially the long ones, as satiric, lyric, narrative, or what you will. Ultimately, the understanding of Clough, I think, is closely bound with not only appreciating those characteristics I cite above, but also seeing the close connection between Clough's artistic and moral concerns. Here is the heart of the problem, for Clough the artist cannot be separated from Clough the human being.

In a recent essay Barbara Hardy has brought this problem into sharp focus. She mentions Richard Gollin's disagreement with Paul Veyriras about the moral and personal in Clough's work; then she writes: "Richard Gollin's remarks on Clough always command

respect, and in a review . . . he takes Paul Veyriras to task for occasionally mistaking Clough's moral concern for his personal compulsion." She goes on to indicate her own disagreement with Gollin:

> I have to begin by admitting that I find myself unable to feel as confident as Mr. Gollin about distinguishing Clough's detached and controlled criticism from his "self-directed utterances." While acknowledging Clough's variousness and toughness, I see his analytic mode as inextricably bound up with his personal compulsions, and indeed welcome his attachment to the personal as a source of warmth and acceptance even in satire.[2]

We need, then, to be clear about this one important point concerning Clough and his writings, and I should think that to deny Clough his "detached and controlled criticism" is to deny him a great deal of his artistic skill. In this matter I find myself siding with Gollin, for to confuse "personal compulsions" with an artist's "analytic mode" is to create a false impression about that artist's art. Clough's moral concern is found throughout his writings, and it is a concern that is an important part of his critical and artistic stance. To dismiss it as an "attachment to the personal" is to fail to see one of Clough's strongest artistic and critical points. Clough's art is, in fact, one that has a very strong moral basis, a morality that is seen throughout his own critical statements and his poetry.

Professor Hardy's inability to grasp fully, as does Professor Gollin, Clough's "detached and controlled criticism" accounts for her failure, in an otherwise impressive essay on Clough's use of lyric and narrative structure, to perceive Clough's admirable use of "distancing"; she mistakes personal feeling for his keen insight into human nature. Thus she can write: "Clough's poems never give themselves up to feeling, but neither do they distance it. . . . A profound and sober respect for life holds him back from satire, as it held back George Eliot too." (p. 268) I am certain that many readers of George Eliot might want to dispute this point, and I know that many of Clough's readers would want to do the same thing. To fail to see Clough's skillful use of distancing in such poems as **Amours** and **Dipsychus** is a denial of one of the fundamental strengths of Clough's poetry, especially the long poems. I will say more of this later; let me begin with some of Clough's own statements about "fact" and feeling.

These are well enough known by this time, and I need not go into much detail here. I have, too, elsewhere written about the Clough-Arnold relationship and Clough's poetic theory.[3] However, a few points might be worth going over, if only to remind ourselves of several matters that seem consistently to be either ignored or forgotten. In the Clough-Arnold relationship it is worth keeping in mind that there is some evidence to suggest that Clough had a great deal of influence on Arnold's critical ideas, especially those concerning the moral aspects of poetry. This point is especially worth pondering since Arnold's influence on modern critical thought is so often stressed in our time. Clough's strong influence on Arnold's critical thought, and thus on our own, has up to now not been fully recognized; certainly, not so much as it should be.

From Arnold's early statements "condemning" Clough's lack of interest in aesthetics, Arnold gradually changes his position until he and Clough are in virtual agreement. In 1845 Arnold can write to Clough and tell him that, since they believe in "the Universality of Passion as Passion," they "will keep pure our Aesthetics by remembering its one-sidedness as doctrine."[4] He can condemn one of Clough's poems for being too "allegorical," and he can also lecture Clough on what is missing from his poetry; he writes to Clough in February of 1848:

> A growing sense of the deficiency of the *beautiful* in your poems, and of this alone being properly *poetical* as distinguished from rhetorical, devotional or metaphysical, made me speak as I did. But your line is a line: and you have most of the promising English verse-writers with you now: Festus for instance. Still, problem as the production of the beautiful remains still to me, I will die protesting against the world that the other is false and JARRING.
>
> (p. 66)

Arnold's emphasis on the beautiful is a plea for Clough to concern himself less with content and morality and more with form, and he continues this line in still another letter of 1848. He tells Clough in no uncertain terms:

> You know you are a mere d_____d depth hunter in poetry and therefore exclusive furiously. You might write a speech in Phèdre—Phedra loquitur—but you could not write Phèdre. And when you adopt this or that form you must sacrifice much to the ensemble, and that form in return for admirable effects demands immense sacrifices and precisely in that quarter where your nature will not allow you to make them.
>
> (p. 81)

"The greatest wealth and depth of matter," Arnold tells his friend in a letter of early 1849, apparently attempting to drive home his point that form must take precedence over matter, "is merely a superfluity in the Poet *as such*." He tells Clough in some detail:

> If I were to say the real truth as to your poems in general, as they impress me—it would be this—that they are not *natural*.
>
> Many persons with far lower gifts than yours yet seem to find their natural mode of expression in poetry, and tho: the contents may not be very valuable they appeal

with justice from the judgement of the mere thinker to the world's general appreciation of naturalness—i.e.-an absolute proprietry—of form. . . . I often think that even a slight gift of poetical expression which in a common person might have developed itself easily and naturally, is overlaid and crushed in a profound thinker so as to be of no use to him to help him to express himself.—The trying to go into and to the bottom of an object instead of grouping *objects* is as fatal to the sensuousness of poetry as the mere painting, (for, in *Poetry,* this is not grouping) is to its airy and rapidly moving life.

"Consider," Arnold concludes, "whether you attain the *beautiful,* and whether your product gives PLEASURE, . . . not excites curiosity and reflexion." (pp. 98-99)

In spite of this emphasis on formalism, Arnold was really not sure of his own position, and the various statements of Clough (statements we must surmise since Clough's letters were apparently destroyed) seemed to have their effect on the advocate of form and beauty. His shift from an "aesthetic" to a "moralistic" critic may be seen most clearly in his views towards style and in his very firm "moralistic" bias, and in both of these aspects his ideas and words are similar to Clough's. In the former, for instance, the views on style, one need only read some of Clough's comments to see their influence on Arnold's own critical theories. Clough defines style as "that permanent beauty of expression, that harmony between thought and word, which is the condition of '*immortal* verse.'"[5] He also emphasizes the necessity of the poet's keeping the style simple and severe, so that it contributes to the "total impression" of the poem. Since the thematic content (that which the earlier Arnold so much deplored and Professor Hardy has so much difficulty with) is, in Clough's poetic theory, the most important element of any poem, the poet must keep the style subordinate to it. He insists that other elements of the poem—form, metre, imagery, diction—not call attention to themselves, but, instead, contribute to the main drift of "what calls itself a single poem." (pp. 165-166) What Clough is objecting to, in this particular case, is the way Alexander Smith, one of the poets he is reviewing, keeps "perpetually presum-[ing] upon" what should be the "real continuity of poetic purpose." In the light of Arnold's particular interest in the Romantics, it is of some significance that Clough concludes this aspect of his review with these words: "Keats and Shelley, and Coleridge, perhaps . . . with their extravagant love for Elizabethan phraseology, have led to this mischief. Has not Tennyson followed a little too much in their train?" (p. 166)

Whether or not he would agree with Clough as to the causes, Arnold, the "later" Arnold, does emphasize the need for subordinating imagery, metre, and diction to the total impression of the poem. A letter to Clough in

1852 seems a complete turnabout from his earlier position; Arnold writes that

> modern poetry can only subsist by its *contents*: by becoming a complete magister vitae as the poetry of the ancients did: by including, as theirs did, religion with poetry, instead of existing as poetry only, and leaving religious wants to be supplied by the Christian religion, as a power existing independent of the poetical power. But the language, style, and general proceedings of a poetry which has such an immense task to perform, must be very plain direct and severe: and it must not lose itself in parts and episodes and ornamental work, but must press forwards to the whole.
>
> (p. 124)

Of course the insistence on the subordination of style to content reflects the firm belief in the moralistic basis of poetry, that which Gollin calls Clough's "moral concern." Arnold's later criticism reveals a moralistic bias as strong as Clough's, and one that is, as I have suggested, quite different from his earlier aesthetic bias. His rejection of *Empedocles* from the 1853 volume because of its failure to "inspirit and rejoice" the reader is surely a reflection of his later insistence that content be placed over form. Perhaps the clearest indication of the great influence that Clough's belief in the moralistic concern of poetry must have had on Arnold's own thinking is revealed in his essay on Wordsworth. In this essay Arnold is now able to say boldly: "It is important, therefore, to hold fast to this: that poetry is at bottom a criticism of life; that the greatness of a poet lies in his powerful and beautiful application of ideas to life,—to the question: How to live. . . . A poetry of revolt against moral ideas is a poetry of revolt against *life*; a poetry of indifference towards moral ideas is a poetry of indifference towards *life*." And in *The Study of Poetry* Arnold can write: "More and more mankind will discover that we have to turn to poetry to interpret life for us, to console us, to sustain us."

It is of the greatest interest and significance that all of these ideas are found in Clough's statements about poetry and literature. What ultimately makes Clough a significant Victorian figure and one of the "major" writers of that period is his high regard and great respect for poetry. For Clough, as it came to be for Arnold, the greatness of poetry lay in its application to life, and it is the specific way that his own poetry demonstrates this belief that gives it its distinction, that enables it to have some meaning for us today. It explains, in fact, why he can be so many things to so many readers and critics; he can be, at one and the same time, as modern as any contemporary and yet, in the words of Barbara Hardy, remain a Victorian writer "visibly imprisoned in his Victorianism, breathing with difficulty under its glass dome." (p. 253)

Obviously, then, for Clough, poetry is more than the spilling out of emotions, the writing about "personal compulsions." In order to perform its role poetry must not simply reflect one's own feelings; the poet cannot be secluded from the real world. It was, in fact, his rejection of poetry as the revelation merely of feelings that caused Clough to have certain reservations about Wordsworth, whom he admired very much. For Clough, Wordsworth, who did at times seem to rely too heavily on feeling rather than fact, was occasionally guilty of sentimentality as well as of a certain seclusion from and evasion of the world. In his lecture on Wordsworth, after pointing out those positive aspects of the poet's writings that warrant our admiration and praise, Clough comments on what he considers to be the unfavorable ones, some of which are due to what he calls Wordsworth's "premature seclusion." He then explains as follows:

> And I cannot help thinking that there is in Wordsworth's poems something of a spirit of withdrawal and seclusion from, and even evasion of the actual world. In his own quiet rural sphere it is true he did fairly enough look at things as they were, he did not belie his own senses, nor pretend to recognize in outward things what really was not in them. But his sphere was a small one, the objects he lived among unimportant and petty. Retiring early from all conflict and even contact with the busy world, he shut himself out from the elements which it was his business to encounter and to master. This gives to his writings compared with those of Scott and Byron a certain appearance of sterility and unreality. . . .
>
> This also sadly lessens the value which we must put on that high moral tone which we have hitherto been extolling. To live in a quiet village, out of the road of all trouble and temptation, in a pure, elevated, high moral sort of matter is after all no such very great a feat.
>
> (p. 119)

This "arbitrary positiveness" in Wordsworth results in what Clough characterizes as "the triviality in many places of his imagery, and the mawkishness . . . of his sentiment." Clough's comments are indeed revealing, for they demonstrate his own awareness of the dangers of substituting one's personal feelings for one's own "moral concern," and they also show his own ability to distinguish "detached and controlled criticism" from "self-directed utterances." As poet and critic he is able to keep separate objective analysis from personal bias. Wordsworth's mawkishness, this excessive sentimentality, Clough explains, comes from his forgetting the importance of the real world; he elaborates:

> instead of looking directly at an object and considering it as a thing in itself, and allowing it to operate upon him as a fact in itself,—he takes the sentiment produced by it in his own mind as the thing; as the important and really real fact.—The Real things cease to be real; the world no longer exists; all that exists is the feeling somehow generated in the poet's sensibility. This sentimentalizing over sentiment; this sensibility over

sensibility has been carried I grant by the Wordsworthians to far more than Wordsworthian excess. But he has something of it surely.

(p. 121)

It is instructive to view the Arnold-Clough relationship in terms of their attitudes towards Wordsworth's "sentimentalizing," his dependence on sentiment and feeling. While Clough deplores this vein in Wordsworth's poetry—"Instead of looking directly at the object . . . he takes the sentiment produced by it in his own mind as the thing; as the important and only real fact"—Arnold cites it as one of the positive aspects of Wordsworth's writing. He praises, as did John Stuart Mill, the "states of feeling" (the words are Mill's) generated by Wordsworth's poetry. Unlike Clough, who rejects the kind of writing that "sentimentalizes over sentiment" and insists that "feeling" is all, Arnold accepts it wholeheartedly. The difference is crucial, I think, and one that has not yet been wholly accepted in discussions of the Clough-Arnold relationship. In this difference lies Clough's ability to see the object as it really is, to let the object operate upon him as a fact in itself, to be, sympathetically at times, detached and objective. Clough could never write, one can be sure, as Arnold did in "Memorial Voices":

> Wordsworth has gone from us—and ye,
> Ah, may ye feel his voice as we!
>
> . . . . .
>
> He spoke, and loosed our heart in tears.
>
> . . . . .
>
> Others will teach us how to dare,
> And against fear our breast to steel;
> Others will strengthen us to bear—
> But who, ah! who, will make us feel?

Who, indeed? Clough's own poetry, often misunderstood, had a much different goal, one that Arnold himself, as his words in "Thyrsis" make clear, failed to understand. Clough prized not a poetry of feeling, of "sentimentalizing," but one of consolation and interpretation, a poetry of truth, one that, indeed, in Barbara Hardy's words, has a "profound and sober respect for life."

A poet and critic who can speak and write as Clough is not very likely to substitute personal feelings and sentiment for moral concern. What Clough found as a major fault in Wordsworth was the absence of the real world: the fact that real things ceased to be real. For Clough, poetry had to teach the significance of and give purpose to life, and it had to indicate in some way one's relationship to what he called the "purer existence." Fittingly enough, or perhaps ironically enough, his fullest statement concerning the role of poetry is found in his review of poems by Smith and Arnold. After deploring

the kind of "languid collectanea" being published so often in his time, the "pleasing stanzas on the beauties of Nature and fresh air," Clough asks rhetorically why is it that people prefer *Vanity Fair* and *Bleak House*. He then gives his own answer:

> Is it, that to be widely popular, to gain the ear of multitudes, to shake the hearts of men, poetry should deal more than at present it usually does, with general wants, ordinary feelings, the obvious rather than the rare facts of human nature? Could it not attempt to convert into beauty and thankfulness, or at least into some form and shape, some feeling, at any rate, of content—the actual, palpable things with which our every-day life is concerned; introduce into business and weary task-work a character and a soul of purpose and reality; intimate to us relations which, in our unchosen, peremptorily-appointed posts, in our grievously narrow and limited spheres of action, we still, in and through all, retain to some central, celestial fact? Could it not console us with a sense of significance, if not of dignity, in that often dirty, or at least dingy, work which it is the lot of so many of us to have to do, and which some one or other, after all, must do? Might it not divinely condescend to all infirmities; be in all points tempted as we are; exclude nothing, least of all guilt and distress, from its wide fraternization; not content itself merely with talking of what may be better elsewhere, but seek also to deal with what *is* here? . . . Cannot the Divine Song in some way indicate to us our unity, though from a great way off, with those happier things; inform us, and prove to us, that though we are what we are, we may yet, in some way, even in our abasement, even by and through our daily work, be related to the purer existence.

> The modern novel is preferred to the modern poem, because we do here feel an attempt to include those indispensable latest addenda—these phenomena which, if we forget on Sunday, we must remember on Monday—these positive matters of fact, which people, who are not verse-writers, are obliged to have to do with.

(pp. 144-145)

Clough makes a distinction, as do most perceptive critics, between mere verse-writers and poets, and for him poetry has to be both consolatory and interpretive. It must not only provide some understanding of what we do here on earth, but it must also give us some insight as to how we "retain to some central, celestial fact." Poetry, for Clough, as critic and as poet, defines in universal terms those actions and ideas we see only as particulars.

From all of this emerge a number of significant matters concerning Clough's importance as critic and poet. One is his relationship to Arnold, one of the major critical influences in our own day. It is important, in this respect, to remind ourselves (or to learn) that Clough in fact was a crucial influence on Arnold's critical thinking. Arnold's heavy emphasis on poetry as a criticism of life owes much to Clough. It is also important to keep in mind the emphasis that Clough placed on what he saw as the ultimate end of poetry: its moral concern. To recognize this is to keep one from falling into the error of mistaking in Clough's own poetry "personal feeling" or compulsion for detached and controlled observation and criticism. Finally, it is especially important to recognize Clough's deep appreciation of "fact" and "reality" as both critic and poet, especially as it relates to his concept of what constitutes the truth. His great concern to avoid what he considered "false or arbitrary positiveness," a fault of which Wordsworth seemed guilty, is at times mistaken for timidity or indecisiveness. Indeed, Clough's reputation as one who failed comes from this very aspect of his thought, an aspect that, in fact, should be considered as one of his great strengths. It is this position that enables him to retain that supreme objectivity, that firm control of content and form, that withholding of judgment so often mistaken for indecisiveness of purpose. This is the Cloughian mark that deserves much more notice and respect than it has received up to now. It is that which constitutes most clearly his contribution to Victorian literature.

His own clearest statement regarding the need for it in poetry is found in his essay on Wordsworth. "There is," writes Clough, "such a thing in Morals as in all Science, as drawing your conclusion before you have properly got your premises. It is desirable to attain a fixed point: but it is essential that the fixed point be the right one. We ought to hold fast by what is true; but because we hold wilfully fast it does not follow what we hold fast to is true. If you have got the truth, be as positive as you please; but because you choose to be positive, do not therefore be sure you have the truth." (p. 120) It is this spirit that led Clough to praise the age of Dryden for its "austere love of truth," its "rigorous uncompromising rejection of the vague, . . . the merely probable." "Such a spirit," he concluded, "I may say, I think, claims more than our attention,—claims our reverence." (p. 137)

One of the best ways to illustrate these qualities is to compare one of Clough's poems with that of one of his contemporaries. A useful comparison, I think, might be made of **Amours de Voyage** with Tennyson's *Maud.* There is some justification for selecting these two poems. They both are poems that represented for their authors a special kind of poetic venture, reflecting some autobiographical concern and revealing their ideas about the period in which they lived. For Tennyson, the poem dealt with "the blighting influence of a recklessly speculative age," while for Clough the poem took place in a world that, "Whithersoever we turn, still is the same narrow crib." For both poets, too, the work dealt with a subject that suggested several important pos-

sibilities: a hero seeking redemption through a loved one in a world he finds difficult to understand, a world not of his own making. Tennyson described *Maud* in these terms:

> This poem is a little *Hamlet,* the history of a morbid poetic soul, under the blighting influence of a recklessly speculative age. He is the heir of madness, an egotist with the makings of a cynic, raised to sanity by a pure and holy love which elevates his whole nature, passing from the height of triumph to the lowest depth of misery, driven into madness by the loss of her whom he has loved, and, when he has at length passed through the fiery furnace, and has recovered his reason, giving himself up to work for the good of mankind through the unselfishness born of his great passion.[6]

There is reason to think that Clough thought of his own poem in something of the same way. One of the mottos or epigraphs he rejected for the poem stated, "He who despairs of himself is mad," and he, like Tennyson, thought of the ending in a wholly positive way. Disagreeing with his friend, Shairp, who could find nothing to admire about the hero, Clough replied:

> But do you not, in the conception, find any final Strength of Mind in the unfortunate fool of a hero? I have no intention whatever of sticking up for him, but certainly I didn't mean him to go off into mere prostration and defeat. Does the last part seem utterly skeptical to your sweet faithful soul?[7]

Shairp's response to the poem may be said to be the typical one to much of Clough's poetry. He saw the poem as a projection of Clough's own "state of soul"; he found it had too much introspection. It was too "Werterish," even though, as he confessed, he had never read Werter. Clough protested, of course, but he could never convince Shairp of what he considered to be the "rightness" of the ending and of his artistic control over the piece. One of the ways to approach the poem in order to appreciate fully this control is to see exactly how Clough presents the hero, Claude, a character who seems to many to be anything but heroic. One clue to Claude may be found in Clough's description of Walter, the hero of Smith's *Life-Drama,* a character who has, for Clough, some admirable qualities; in his review Clough writes:

> Under the guise of a different story, a story unskilful enough in its construction, we have seemed to recognize the ingenuous, yet passionate, youthful spirit, struggling after something like right and purity amidst the unnumbered difficulties, contradictions, and corruptions of the heated and crowded, busy, vicious, and inhuman town. Eager for action, incapable of action without some support, yet knowing not on what arm to dare to lean; not untainted; hard-pressed; in some sort, at times, overcome,—still we seem to see the young combatant, half combatant, half martyr, resolute to fight it out, and not to quit this for some easier field of battle,—one way or another to make something of it.

(pp. 146-147)

While Claude is not simply another Walter, he does have some of Walter's characteristics, especially in his struggle after something "like right and purity" in the midst of contradictions and corruptions. He is also determined to "fight it out, not to quit this for some easier field of battle," a point that Clough is eager to establish in his poem. It is useful, for instance, to compare the hero of *Maud* with Clough's Claude, for one instantly recognizes the truth of Clough's statement regarding the final "strength of mind" of his hero. The hero of *Maud,* in spite of Tennyson's own description, fails to convince anyone of his unselfishness. Throughout much of the poem he is given to a great deal of sentimentalizing and exaggeration, and there is much of the Spasmodic in him. It is difficult to take him seriously, and it makes little difference about or against what he happens to be railing: love, Maud herself, politics, burial fees, etc. The tone is always the same; the impression is that of one who is, in fact, acting a part rather than living a life. There is no real sense of change, no suggestion of either the resolution of Walter or the strength of mind of Claude; his speeches range from the slightly embarrassing:

> And sleep must lie down armed, for the villainous
> centre-bits,
> Grind on the wakeful ear in the hush of moonless
> nights,
> While another is cheating the sick of a few last gasps,
> as he sits
> To pestle a poisoned poison behind his crimson lights.[8]

to the sentimental:

> Maud, with her venturous climbings and tumbles and
> childish escapes,
> Maud, the delight of the village, the ringing joy of the
> Hall,
> Maud, with her sweet purse-mouth when my father
> dangled the grapes,
> Maud, the beloved of my mother, the moonfaced
> darling of all—

to the outright chauvinistic:

> Though many a light shall darken, and many shall
> weep
> For those that are crushed in the clash of jarring
> claims,
> Yet God's just wrath shall be wreaked on a giant liar,
> And many a darkness into the light shall leap,
> And shine in the sudden making of splendid names,
> And noble thought be freer under the sun,
> And the heart of a people beat with one desire;

It is not just that Tennyson's hero is able to tell exactly how God feels, or that he has no hesitation in identifying himself with "the heart of a people"; it is simply that he never stops posing and shouting.

This is not to deny the lyric quality of *Maud,* of course, the "masterpiece of rhythm" as it has been called. We know that Swinburne, a superb critic, praised it highly.

However, in terms of the effectiveness of the piece, especially as a work the message of which depends on the meaning conveyed chiefly through the protagonist, the contrast with Clough's Claude is striking. Whether or not one agrees with the "message" of Clough's poem, the point remains that Claude as a character effectively conveys the meaning of *Amours.* In this respect Claude is a successful portrayal; his own speeches and the way he is described and seen by others combine to convey Clough's central meaning, convincingly and interestingly. Of that central meaning I shall say more below; let me simply note here that it has to do with Claude's "final strength of mind," his refusal to "go off into mere prostration and defeat," and the ultimate resolution of the poem in terms of Claude's particular experience and its meaning in the context of what Clough calls "some central, celestial fact."

Claude succeeds as a character, then, while the hero of *Maud* does not. In contrast to the strained rhetoric of the speeches in *Maud,* those by Claude seem both appropriate and convincing, especially as commentaries on the age, on places, on people, on the situation of the *Amours* itself. Claude's observations on religion, politics, love, and human nature itself are perceptive and, more important, contain no sense of straining after effect:

> No, the Christian faith, as at any rate I understood it,
> With its humiliations and exaltations combining,
> Exaltations sublime and yet diviner abasements,
> Aspirations from something most shameful here upon
> earth and
> In our poor selves to something most perfect above in
> the heavens,—
> No, the Christian faith, as I, at least, understood it,
> Is not here, O Rome, in any of these thy churches,
> Is not here, but in Freiburg, or Rheims, or Westminster Abbey.

(I, iv)

. . . . .

> It is most curious to see what a power a few calm
> words (in
> Merely a brief proclamation) appear to possess on the
> people.
> Order is perfect, and peace; the City is utterly tranquil;
> And one cannot conceive that this easy and *nonchalant*
> crowd, that
> Flows like a quiet stream through street and marketplace, entering
> Shady recesses and bays of church, osteria, and cafe,
> Could in a moment be changed to a flood as of molten
> lava,
> Boil into deadly wrath and wild homicidal delusion.

(II, ix)

. . . . .

> What with trusting myself and seeking support from
> within me

Almost I could believe I had gained a religious assur-
   ance,
Found in my own poor soul a great moral basis to rest
   on.
Ah, but indeed I see, I feel it factitious entirely:
I refuse, reject, and put it utterly from me;
I will look straight out, see things, not try to evade
   them;
Fact shall be fact for me; and the Truth the Truth as
   ever
Flexible, changeable, vague, and multiform, and
   doubtful—
Off, and depart to the void, thou subtle fanatical
   tempter!

                                      (V, v)

. . . . .

Not as the Scripture says, is, I think, the fact. Ere our
   death-day,
Faith, I think, does pass, and love; but Knowledge
   abideth.
Let us seek Knowledge;—the rest must come and go
   as it happens.
Knowledge is hard to seek, and harder yet to adhere
   to.
Knowledge is painful often; and yet when we know,
   we are happy.
Seek it, and leave mere Faith and Love to come with
   the chances.

                                      (V, x)

Much of the success of the portrayal of Claude is due
to the "execution" of the poem, an artistic matter of
which Clough was very much aware. We know that
Clough did much revision in order to achieve a better
portrait of Claude, one that conveyed a rounded rather
than a flat impression. The flatness is what ultimately
undermines our faith in the hero of *Maud,* for the only
voice we hear is his, shrill, strained, unreal. Clough
made certain that that would not happen in *Amours*;
indeed, Claude's is only one voice among many that
help to convey his character. There is always the balance provided by what amounts to a chorus of voices
telling us about Claude; one does not have only the narrator's word, as in *Maud.* Claude's own speculations,
sometimes almost contradictory about certain subjects,
are balanced by the comments of others, particularly
Georgina and Mary Trevellyn. We hear Georgina saying
at the very beginning: "Who can a Mr. Claude be whom
George has taken to be with? Very stupid, I think, but
George says so *very* clever." (I, iii) Of course, we soon
form our own opinion of Georgina, so that her comments are taken in their own frame of reference, another
indication of Clough's artistic handling of events and
characters in the poem. Mary Trevellyn's first impression of Claude also adds to the portrait: "I do not like
him much, though I do not dislike being with him. / He
is what people call, I suppose, a superior man, and /
Certainly seems so to me, but I think he is frightfully
selfish." (I, xiii) Claude himself, Mary, Georgina, and

even implicitly George and Eustace—all these contribute to our final impression of Claude. In this way
Clough avoids the trap Tennyson fell into, for we are
not limited by the one voice. Arnold sensed this, too,
for in writing to Clough at one point he felt it necessary
to contrast Clough's and Tennyson's manner, although
there were certain stylistic similarities; writing to him
in 1855, after reading *Maud,* Arnold said:

> From the extracts I have seen from Maud, he seems in
> his old age to be coming to your manner in the Bothie
> and the Roman poem [i.e., *Amours*]. That manner, as
> you know, I do not like: but certainly, if it is to be
> used, you use it with far more freedom vigour and
> abundance than he does—Altogether I think this
> volume a lamentable production, and like so much of
> our literature thoroughly and intensely *provincial,* not
> European.

                                    (p. 147)

I have written elsewhere of Arnold's view of Tennyson's provincialism,[9] and he is here writing with a
certain amount of willingness to believe the worst of
Tennyson's writing; however, in this particular case I
think that one must acknowledge the correctness of his
judgement. Clough's *Amours* is in many respects a
poem that stands up well when contrasted with *Maud,*
even if one does not agree with Arnold that the latter is
"lamentable"; and a great deal of the attractiveness of
the poem comes from Clough's manner, which indeed
exhibits the "freedom vigour and abundance" praised
by Arnold.

This manner also helps bring out in a positive way
Clough's purpose, for he was most anxious, as his letters to Shairp and others indicate, that the "conception"
as he called it be understood. There is no doubt that
readers have had trouble understanding fully the meaning of both poems, and the largely unfavorable critical
reaction to both, especially *Maud,* might be traced to
this difficulty. Certainly the chauvinistic ending of *Maud*
failed to satisfy many critics; there was one who insisted
that the title might be better if one dropped either vowel.
Tennyson, we remember, had said that the hero was
giving himself up "to work for the good of mankind,"
but the ending, and the previous actions and words of
the hero, failed to convince many of the readers and
critics. Clough succeeded where Tennyson failed in this
respect, for he was able to make his hero both believable and sympathetic. He was also able, as Tennyson
was not, to make clear the reasons why one should find
that "final strength of mind" in his hero, that strength
which enabled him to avoid prostration and defeat. That
some readers and critics did not understand these
reasons, or chose to ignore them, is another matter, but
they are clearly there, especially for the perceptive
reader who understands the nature of Clough's manner
and the full implications of his poetic theory.

What Clough stresses in *Amours* is the way that the
hero responds to each situation and his final resolve to

know, to face fact and not fall prey to illusion, of which war might very well be the greatest, and to false hope. The hero of *Maud,* it becomes clear, has in fact taken the easy way out, for it is not very difficult to identify one's cause as the right one and go on to use "God's wrath" to fight for it. It may indeed be better to "fight for the good" than "to rail at the ill," but, as Claude keeps reminding himself and others, what exactly is the good and what are the proper motivations for action? "Action will furnish belief,—but will that belief be the true one? / This is the point, you know. However, it doesn't much matter. / What one wants, I suppose, is to predetermine the action, / so as to make it entail, not a chance-belief, but the true one." (V, ii) At another point, Claude tells Eustace, "We are so prone to these things with our terrible notions of duty." (II, xi) For Claude it is indeed tempting to accept the illusion: "Ah, did we really accept with a perfect heart the illusion! / Ah, did we really believe that the Present indeed is the Only! / Or through all transmutation, all shock and convulsion of passion, / Feel we could carry undimmed, unextinguished, the light of our knowledge!" (III,vi) Claude cannot, of course, for he knows that he finally must "look straight out, see things, not try to evade them: / Fact shall be fact for me; and the Truth the Truth as ever." (V, v)

The hero of *Maud* has, one is tempted to say, evaded things, but that is not really the point of the comparison. Clough's idea of poetry, we recall, was one that was concerned with the application of poetry to life. It should, we remember, first, be able to teach us the significance of that life, give some purpose to it, and, second, indicate to us our relationship to the "purer existence," indicate to us our unity with that existence. In *Amours* it seems clear that he is attempting to do these things, and particularly so in terms of tracing the thoughts and actions of Claude, his "unfortunate fool of a hero." With what Arnold called "freedom vigour and abundance" of manner, Clough attempted to demonstrate what he saw as his hero's final strength of mind, a strength that refused to accept illusion and insisted on seeing things clearly. Claude's experiences and comments help bring into sharper focus the meaning of human existence. His own actions and words illustrate and give form and shape and feeling to what Clough calls the "actual, palpable things with which our everyday life is concerned." By having his hero resist the easy way, by having Claude insist on following the truth, Clough demonstrates how poetry can, indeed, confer both consolation and inspiration on human beings, how it can help define in universal terms those ideas and actions we tend to see only as particulars.

One recent writer has, in fact, come very close to stressing the qualities that I have cited as the essential ones in understanding *Amours de Voyage* and Clough himself, and she has done this, appropriately in terms of

the Arnold-Clough relationship. "Although Arnold complained of Clough's fluctuation in the Time Stream," writes Dorothy Deering, "he realized that in his own sense of crisis he was constantly thinking of Clough as one of the 'children of the second birth,' acknowledging his 'still, considerate mind' and an individual power that 'the world could not tame.' . . . Furthermore, these qualities bore directly on the impact of his poetry, for they formed the basis of its sincerity, reality, and lack of self-conscious posturings, qualities Arnold admired in Clough's poetry and judged deficient in his own. . . ." So far, so good, but Professor Deering then goes on to mention the one element that I have implicitly emphasized as being also present in Clough's poetry, one not often noted. I refer to the optimistic note often found in his work. "In contrast to the 'beatific vision' of Arnold's romantic imagination," concludes Deering, "which produced joy from an intensely individualistic isolated moment of reception, Clough's epiphanies are public and communal, yet without despair."[10] Patrick Scott, interestingly enough, has called *Amours* Clough's "long-pondered, if tentative, testament of hope." (p. 14) Perhaps we do have, then, some notions about what makes Clough so fascinating a figure, and it should be of some interest to see how these are developed by future readers and critics.

*Notes*

1. For the fluctuations in Clough's reputation see Michael Thorpe, ed., *Clough: The Critical Heritage* (New York: Barnes and Noble), 1972.

2. Barbara Hardy, "Clough's Self-Consciousness" in *The Major Victorian Poets: Reconsiderations,* ed. Isobel Armstrong (London: Routledge and Kegan Paul), p. 253.

3. "Corydon Had a Rival," *Victorian Newsletter,* No. 19 (Spring, 1961), 5-11; "The Poetic Theory of Arthur Hugh Clough," *English Studies,* 43 (August, 1962), 240-247.

4. *The Letters of Matthew Arnold to Arthur Hugh Clough,* ed. with an intro. by Howard Foster Lowry (Oxford, 1932), p. 59. All subsequent references to Arnold's letters are to this edition.

5. Buckner B. Trawick, ed., *Selected Prose Works of Arthur Hugh Clough* (University, Alabama: University of Alabama Pr., 1964), pp. 113-114. All future page references to Clough's criticism will be to this volume; I have ignored the editor's silent corrections of Clough's text.

6. Hallam Lord Tennyson, *Alfred Tennyson: A Memoir* (London, 1897), I, 396.

7. *The Correspondence of Arthur Hugh Clough,* ed. F. L. Mulhauser (Oxford: Oxford University Press, 1957), I, 278.

8. All quotations from *Maud* are from *The Poems of Tennyson,* ed. Christopher Ricks (London: Longmans, Green and Company Ltd., 1969); all quotations from *Armours de Voyage* are from the volume edited by Patrick Scott (Queensland: University of Queensland Press, 1974).

9. "Arnold, Tennyson, and English Idyl: Ancient Criticism and Modern Poetry," *Texas Studies in Literature and Language,* 16 (Spring, 1974), 135-146.

10. Dorothy Deering, "The Antithetical Poetics of Arnold and Clough," *Victorian Poetry,* 16 (Spring/Summer, 1978), 30.

## Robert Johnson (essay date winter 1985/86)

SOURCE: Johnson, Robert. "Modern Mr. Clough." *Arnoldian* 13, no. 1 (winter 1985/86): 1-9.

[*In the following essay, Johnson contends that Clough's* Dipsychus *is more important than has been acknowledged by most critics of Victorian poetry.*]

Arthur Hugh Clough's long dramatic poem *Dipsychus* has received remarkably mixed reviews from critics of Victorian poetry. Special attention has been given the work, for instance, by biographical critics since the poem's protagonist seems often to mouth the artist's own beliefs. These parallels, coupled with difficulties posed by an uneven quality of text,[1] have led to the poem's being dismissed by others as a jumble of intense yet unresolved scenes—a work quite simply best anthologized in pieces as it most frequently still is.[2]

An argument can be made, however, that *Dipsychus* is a more important work than it is often given credit for being, and that the poem's two speaking voices—one of an aloof, priggish poet; the other, of his worldly, logical instincts—tilt at profound human issues. What *Dipsychus* asks, in fact, is what happens to the personality when essential, accepted beliefs die, when standards by which we have measured our success as humans ring hollow and untrue. As such, the poem mirrors an important intellectual journey, its twisted path reflected in the two voices' nocturnal meanderings through Venice's darkened streets. Moreover, to found this philosophical discussion, Clough offers in the early scenes of his drama an image that dominates the exchanges between his poem's voices and which links Clough to the thinking of a generation of artists to follow.

Central to Clough's setting is one distinctive feature of the Venice horizon. The Campanile, a famous tower standing over the Piazza San Marco, looms overhead as Dipsychus circles the city and its dank canals, providing an axle for his entire evening's journey, which begins and ends on the bare plaza beneath it. The tower does more than just hinge his wanderings, though. In the sky above him, it images the dominant need of his personality: to ascend from everyday existence and lord over the world of less sensitive people. Dipsychus is a character whose arrogance in this respect portrays well the proportions to which romantic aspirations for transcendence can grow. He positively cultivates his haughty pose, and it is precisely this arrogance that Clough's poem challenges since all the while Dipsychus longs for vision and the heavens, the night's experience educates him that his proper sphere of influence is the damp plaza below. But, Clough asks, what happens to this type of romantic when denied access to the transcendent, when he finds himself caught within the sphere of material existence, a prisoner of his own limiting space and time? What happens when he is convinced of his being trapped upon the hard, slick surfaces of the physical world and asked to be sensitive and moral there?

As a result, the poem bears careful rereading. For, with this restriction, it anticipates the narrowed view of reality proposed by artists of the early *modern* era, many of whom come to suspect that human endeavor necessarily must be rooted in the physical world and not the shadowy realm of ideals. A brief review of the drama's first movements will document how Clough's opening images portray the needs of his poet-speaker, needs subsequently denied.

Following a *Prologue,* the first scene of Clough's actual narrative opens with his character on the Piazza, on Sunday evening, evidently in substantial mental turmoil. He is brooding over some of Clough's own lines, from a poem called **"Easter Day."** According to that poem, the moral consequences of Christ's not having risen after his death would be devastating. Reality would become morally flattened, the lines argue, if each life lost its ability to replicate Christ's escape from earthly limitations:

> Ashes to Ashes, Dust to Dust
> As of the Unjust also of the Just—
> Yea, of that Just One too!
> Is He not risen, and shall we not rise?
> O we unwise!

(I, 19-23)

Significantly, while pondering the implications of these lines, Dipsychus senses that he is positioned at an intersection in the geography of Venice which presents him with an image of his own state. Around him sprawls the famous Piazza, home of vendors, tourists, whores, while at the plaza's end, "The Campanile to the silent stars / Goes up, above—its apex lost in air" (I, 48-49). And the festive crowd around the tower's base "do what?" he wonders. Do they—does he—rise like the tower, or fall? Or, could his perch be immobile, hung on the edge of an inescapably flat horizon of life, one represented by the plaza itself?

Determining his state is Dipsychus' major goal in the poem, finding if he rises or falls philosophically, spiritually, even economically. And Dipsychus' initial desires are clear. He would go *up,* leaving the crowd around him to their tawdry coupling and fighting and exchange of goods. Yet, in Clough's hands this yearning for ascension is destined for a crushing defeat, and the artist's agent in hacking his character back down from a smug sense of elevation is that voice labeled the Spirit. An alter ego who constantly threatens and nags Dipsychus to relinquish any lofty view of his own possibilities, the Spirit begins his challenge to the poet's assumptions during the first Piazza scene.

These opening exchanges are crucial. In them, the Spirit initiates his major role, as worldly conscience puncturing Dipsychus' moodiness with sharp, deflating commentary upon the prig's understanding of his stature. The Spirit fairly bristles, for instance, in his reply to Dipsychus' memory of the Easter Poem. However, he reveals as well that the function of his attack is more than to play wise-cracking fail. In response to the poet's fathoming the implications of Christ's passion, the Spirit notes:

> 'Twas well enough once in a way;
> Such things don't fall out every day.
> Having once happened, as we know,
> In Palestine so long ago,
> How should it now at Venice here?
> Where people, true enough, appear
> To appreciate more and understand
> Their ices, and their Austrian band,
> And dark-eyed girls—

> (I, 34-42)

No mere prankster, this Spirit, he cuts directly to the source of Dipsychus' Angst: if history is a process of events, then the *event* of Christ's life, logically, must be accepted as removed from the physical and temporal present. Into the poet's adolescent morbidity the Spirit neatly drops a philosophical grenade, cautioning that Dipsychus misses the import of his own lines—that if he is going to live with any success, he will learn how to do so at *his* own point in time. Like the Venetians, Dipsychus should "Enjoy the minute," the Spirit suggests, and the "substantial blessings in it" (I, 50-51). If Dipsychus must go *up,* the Spirit contends, then he should go up, "Up—to the cafe! Take a chair / And join the wiser idlers there" (I, 57-58).

By placing Dipsychus near the intersection of tower and plaza, Clough has constructed a fitting background for his characters' debate. The tower and the possibility

of a risen Christ join to represent vision from above, elevation, removal from the physical world—access to the transcendent. The Piazza, with its daily crush of bodies, portrays the flattened panorama of physical human events. The whole scene can, therefore, be imagined as taking place at the point where a lone vertical axis intersects a vast horizontal plane. The vertical arm of the image, one figured in the tower, suggests the elevation Dipsychus yearns for. The horizontal plane, figured in the plaza as it stretches across that tower's base, then would represent the realm of material existence and understanding. The point where plane and axis meet figures nicely the intersection of the poet's aspirations and the material circumstances in which he finds himself living, what might be called his *now* point in the diagram.

As a result, Dipsychus' arguments with the Spirit are best read as disputes over where on this figure Dipsychus is equipped to live. Dipsychus is haunted by an event and a time in the past; the Spirit warns him that he can only live at the contemporary crossing point, the present. In spite of his lament that the resurrection may have been lost, Dipsychus would be elevated, like Christ after his ascension following Easter, or as a great inspired poet. The Spirit, though, proposes that he is fit only to live on the level plane, with his fellow limited humankind. In addition, when the Spirit reacts to the Easter poem, his message—while deliberately abrasive—is nonetheless one deduced from the situation. As a physical, measurable event, he argues, Christ's point in space and time is not here. To borrow the language of mathematics, Christ's *coordinates* are "Palestine" and "long ago" (I, 37). Whatever the significance of events occurring then, Dipsychus' responsibility is to live at another point, the coordinates of which are "Venice" and "now."

Even the Spirit's logic undercuts Dipsychus' plea for transcendence. That is, simply by assigning Christ coordinates in space and time, the Spirit labels the event of Christ's having lived and died as being significant only in material, worldly terms. Dipsychus' longing is to maintain Christ as an emblem of the *escape* from the limitations of space and time, as an indication of the existence of knowledge that is un-worldly and eternal and which will allow him a personal sense of integration with that eternal perspective.

Consequently, though brief, this scene in Clough's poem is central, for it introduces a key image of the drama as a whole: Dipsychus caught at the intersection of aspiration and physical reality, while a wakening Spirit voice dogs him to abandon his carefully nurtured haughtiness. Dipsychus, he warns, must learn to experience life in full, instant by fleeting instant, before it is lost to him forever. This demand provides primary dramatic energy in the work as Dipsychus is tested repeatedly by the

Spirit's wit and the needs of his own flesh. Always the challenge is to live consciously *now.*

There is a final sting to the Spirit's message. Under his tutelage, Dipsychus realizes not only that access to transcendent knowledge is denied him—if what the Spirit says is true—but given his own personality and needs, he doesn't really fit on the plane of Venice either. With this knowledge Dipsychus' ultimate sense of alienation is born. Watch the Spirit at work, for example, in the early garden scene, as he moves in to undercut Dipsychus' romantic swoon, reminding the young man that all the while he is gesturing to the firmament, one of the parade of passing women has turned to offer him an inviting look:

> "There was a glance, I saw you spy it—
> So! shall we follow suit and try it?"
>
> (II, 66-67)

Unfortunately for Dipsychus, though, by the time he is prepared to weigh the merits of pursuing the woman's attention, her party has gone, her eyes perhaps to be answered by some "wiser youth."

When Dipsychus breaks into calls for the sky, it doesn't answer; below, his fellow worldly creatures go on with their business without him. Moments then pass and are gone, leaving the poet alone, sputtering in their wake. The poet has, in effect, damned himself. Having forsaken the mundane as a threat to his stature, he now discovers he is too clumsy to fit back into the plaza life which he has fled, and so resorts to dulling his fears in world-weary, adolescent bitterness. Self-consciously, he debates how it is his dreams could have been so cruelly shattered. He looks upon the fallen—material—world and laments:

> Let it be enough
> That in our needful mixture with the world,
> On each new morning with the rising sun
> Our rising heart, fresh from the seas of sleep,
> Scarce o'er the level lifts his purer orb
> Ere lost and sullied with polluting smoke—
> A noonday coppery disk. Lo, scarce come forth,
> Some vagrant miscreant meets, and with a look
> Transmutes me his, and for a whole sick day
> Lepers me.
>
> (IV, 66-75)

Beyond immediate character study, Clough has constructed here a tidy parable, predicting the fate of the romantic pose—as pose—when it is faced with a revolution in sensibilities generated by changing nineteenth century understandings of the human perspective on history and time. For what Dipsychus is being denied, ultimately, is an entire attitude about the nature of his being. That is, if one assumes an access to transcendence, with that assumption (whether garnered from Nature, or God, or even "primary imagination") typically comes the expectation of sensing life's wholeness and integration. Listen, for instance, to Wordsworth in the Wye River Valley ("Lines," above Tintern Abbey). Sufficiently aroused, he claims to peer beyond surfaces and into the "life of things" (49). He is mesmerized by his recognition of the orderly repetition in the natural cycle before him: "again" he sees the rising cliffs, the wreaths of twisted smoke, the little stands of woods that seem to run wildly over the country (1-22). The scene is imbued (in his eyes) with continuity; it appears to have escaped the limitations of change and time.

This is the perspective suggested for Dipsychus by Venice's lonely Campanile: it stands for a journey into some eternal unifying knowledge. Life as seen from the plaza, in contrast, lacks this integration; there, people merely bump and pass. Event falls upon event, apparently without necessary relationship. So, on the level place, one experiences personal history as a journey through small *random* encounters. Life intersects life like reeling balls on some enormous billiard table, each chance meeting becoming impetus for yet another, each moment but a coinciding of events and aspirations to name them. Cause and effect seem less sure: the senses appear to record only raw evidence of encounters as they occur and then fade into memory. Though from the tower life might seem whole, on the plaza it fragments and becomes a collage of incidents. Moments feel more like brief, confined spaces than steps toward some goal. It is precisely this sense of randomness that frightens Dipsychus so intensely. Note his cry to the mountains and horizon in Scene II, his yearning to be lifted off the plane of Venice and into their more orderly realm:

> Ah me, me!
> Clear stars above, thou roseate westward sky,
> Take up my being into yours; assume
> My sense to own you only; steep my brain
> In your essential purity. Or, great Alps,
> That wrapping round your head in solemn clouds
> Seem sternly to sweep past our vanities,
> Lead me with you—take me away; preserve me!
>
> (II, 54-61)

In *Dipsychus,* then, Clough anticipates one of the reasons why the unworldly romantic stance comes eventually to satisfy fewer and fewer artists as his century rolls over the hump of the 1850's and into the modern era. The pose fails to salve a growing claustrophobia born of experiencing the individual moment as an intersection, as an isolated, random event in space and time. The poem also emphasizes the importance of Clough's vision within the context of nineteenth century poetry. One artist with whom Clough is often compared, for example, is of course Arnold, and rightly so. Arnold also writes about the terror of alienation and of mankind's resulting great hunger to feel integrated once more. Given the evidence of a poem like "To Marguerite—Continued," Arnold can conceive of mankind as floating endlessly apart, like lonely islands. Arnold, too realizes isolation's destructiveness, and pictures humans longing to break out of their shells of personal experience and to feel integrated within some living whole community—see "Dover Beach." Even the fragmented islands in the Marguerite poem imagine they were once "parts of a single continent" (13-16).

Yet Arnold as well suggests possible avenues through which to escape this sense of random, isolated existence. Generally speaking, he proposes twin means of salvation: first, a return to less intellectual living—as seen in the Scholar Gypsy's travels—in order to become more alert to supposedly natural integrative impulses; and, second, an involvement in the process of Culture, that endless chain of man's highest thinking and accomplishments. As Robert Langbaum aptly summarizes: "Arnold plays a dialectic between these opposite ideas—that Unity of Being derives from the highest culture and that it is original, natural, unconscious. He resolves the contradiction with the synthesizing idea that culture helps us recapture through the highest consciousness our original and unconscious Unity of Being."[3]

What makes **Dipsychus** important is that, finally, it does *not* propose any escape from the predicament of living with change or the limitations of space and time. Clough says, in essence, this is the way we live: alone, facing a duplicitous, changeful, material reality perhaps no more concerned with our individual aspirations than from the well-being of stones and pavement.

Benefitting from hindsight, and having reconsidered the changes in nineteenth century attitudes about time, novelist John Fowles describes a similar reaction in one of his Victorian characters. Of Charles Smithson, Fowles writes: "Now he had a far more profound and genuine intuition of the great human illusion about time, that its reality is like that of a road—on which one can constantly see where one was and where one probably will be—instead of the truth: that time is a room, a now so close to us that we regularly fail to see it."[4]

Clough anticipates this tight new sense of the *now* in **Dipsychus,** pushing his hero like a stalking horse out onto the plane of modernist thinking and watching him freeze there as his philosophical props are cut away, as he sees how fluid and slippery life has become. Clough's vision is shown, thus, to be especially ironic, for even as life is being proven more random and changeful, his character becomes more frightened and stiff, losing in his reaction any opportunity to find joy even in daily experiences. Some new, post-romantic consciousness will evidently be needed to live successfully in the world Clough has prepared for his hero.

Sent out ahead of his creator, Dipsychus establishes the boundaries and weaknesses of a world view that Clough, perhaps, can no longer himself fully trust. Consequently, while Clough's work may continue to be footnoted as a case study in Victorian "doubt," the depth of his uncertainty, it can be shown, runs beyond the typical mid-century terror of isolation or of finding nature "red in tooth and claw." Clough evidently sees past the vagaries of geological interpretation and the challenge of materialist history and economics to their concomitant message about the meaning of human experience itself. Never again, he senses, will mankind be afforded the luxury of assuming theirs is a special place in the cosmos. As he writes in his short poem **"Epi-strauss-ium,"** mankind's stained glass window upon the universe is gone. We see now through a window plain as crystal, and while our sanctuary will as a result be "more sincerely bright" (14), *Dipsychus* indicates we should expect to find no special pew reserved there for our pleasure.

### Notes

1. For a description of the *Dipsychus* manuscript, see *The Poems of Arthur Hugh Clough,* ed. F. L. Mulhauser, 2nd ed. (Oxford: Clarendon Press, 1974), pp. 681-84. References to Clough's poems will be to the Mulhauser edition.

2. For a sense of the variety in critical attitudes concerning Clough's work, readers might begin by reading through the following: Katharine Chorley, *Arthur Hugh Clough: The Uncommitted Mind* (Oxford: Clarendon Press, 1962); Walter E. Houghton, *The Poetry of Arthur Hugh Clough: An Essay in Revaluation* (New Haven: Yale Univ. Press, 1963); Martha Hale Shackford, "The Clough Centenary: His *Dipsychus,*" *Sewanee Review,* 32 (October 1919); and P. G. Schott, "Arthur Hugh Clough: A Case in Victorian Doubt," in Derek Baker, ed., *Schism, Heresy, and Protest* (Cambridge: Cambridge Univ. Press, 1972).

3. *The Mysteries of Identity* (New York: Oxford Univ. Press, 1977), p. 63.

4. *The French Lieutenant's Woman* (New York: Signet), p. 252.

### Simon Gatrell (essay date 1990)

SOURCE: Gatrell, Simon. *"Histoires de Voyage*: The Italian Poems of Arthur Hugh Clough." In *Creditable Warriors,* edited by Michael Cotsell, pp. 159-72. London: Ashfield Press, 1990.

[*In the following essay, Gatrell examines the poetry inspired by Clough's trips to Rome and Venice in 1849 and 1850, maintaining that the poet's best work emerged from these holidays in Italy.*]

> O land of Empire, art and love!
>   What is it that you show me?
> A sky for gods to tread above
>   A soil for pigs below me!

Italy seems to have released some sort of creative spring in Arthur Clough. He went to Rome in April 1849 and to Venice in the autumn of 1850, and the inventory of poems that derive directly from these Italian holidays is impressive: *Amours de Voyage,* **"Easter Day, Naples, 1849," "Say Not the Struggle Naught Availeth," "O Land of Empire, Art and Love,"** and **"Dipsychus"**; indeed one might go so far as to say that there is very little else besides *The Bothie of Tober-na-Vuolich* that ranks in the highest level of his achievement. It is the purpose of this essay to offer some account of what Italy meant to Clough, and why his best poetry was conceived there.

The poem whose opening also opens this essay is usually known by its first line, but Clough once gave it the title **"Resignation, to Faustus,"**[1] and though the poem provides the most direct statement of his response to Italy, it is apparent that Clough also thought of it as a response to the poem by his friend Matthew Arnold called "Resignation—to Fausta."

In fact, Italy plays a crucial role in Clough's response to Arnold. Arnold's poem, set for the most part in the English Lake District, suggests that ordinary people must be resigned to obscurity because their lives are so short and the world about them so vast and enduring; a quiet mind is the best they can hope for. Clough accepts the need for resignation in our lives, but rejects any scale of reference larger than man. Our duty is to experience the world to the full, and in Italy it becomes clear that to do so we must be resigned to the smell and feel and sight of the filth beneath our feet because it is part of the condition of life that allows us also to experience a sky above us fit for gods to tread. In England this truth is harder to come by, because in the north the whole process of the birth and growth of the pure and beautiful from the richly vile is so slow and struggling; dirt can be kept at a distance more easily because less swiftly and openly decaying and festering. Clough notes that in Italy,

> scarcely bound by space or time,
> The elements in half a day
> Toss off with exquisitest play
> What our cold seasons toil and grieve,
> And never quite at last achieve
>
>                                   (54-58)

Life and death and life follow so swiftly on each other's heels that they are scarcely distinguishable; out of death and decay and corruption comes new life so rapidly that there is scarcely a moment to regret the loss before there is a new beauty to replace it, battening on the remains of the old. A society that strives to be aseptic like the middle and upper classes of England (the tourist classes of Clough's time) may preserve itself clean and cool and healthy, but only at the expense of virtuosity and richness in its response to life.

Clough epitomizes what it is that makes Italy as he experienced it so different from the chilly north, in the punning couplet:

> O richly soiled and richly sunned,
> Exuberant, fervid, and fecund!
>
>                                   (35-36)

Italy is everything that England, that the Lake District, is not. But the same principle applies everywhere, and Clough uses a botanical analogy to broaden the reference of his point:

> In forest-shade in woodland bower
> The stem that bears the ethereal flower . . .
> From mixtures fetid foul and sour
> Draws juices that those petals fill.
>
>                                   (46-50)

What seems self-evident in Italy, is, if you think about it, also part of life farther north.

More significantly, though, Clough goes beyond the vegetative aspects of his subject. It is an easy observation to make that life is swifter to flourish and decay and die in a hot climate; it is less evident that:

> In such a clime, who thinks, forgives;
> Who sees, will understand; who knows,
> In calm of knowledge find repose,
> And thoughtful as of glory gone,
> So too of more to come anon,
> Of permanent existence sure,
> Brief intermediate breaks endure.
>
>                                   (70-76)

For English tourists the sight, day after day, of inescapable combinations and swift successions of such extremes of pureness and filth, beauty and ugliness, life and death, soon provokes thought. Once they begin to reflect upon the significance of what they have seen, they begin to understand what is hard for northern puritan minds to grasp, that dirt does not eliminate fineness, that one death is not universal death. This understanding leads to a general forgiveness of the processes of nature, of the existence of pain, sickness, even death; and this understanding, once accepted as true knowledge, will form a satisfying place of rest from the dislocations, the uncertainties, the anxieties of the modern world. This is Clough's resignation. If, as seems to be the case, this mixture of the fair and the vile, this frantic interchange of death and rebirth, is a fundamental principle of nature, then it cannot be evil:

O Nature, if indeed thy will
Thou ownest it, it is not ill!

(77-78)

At the end of the poem Clough blends the filth of the street, the glory of the sky, and the artistic perfection of the Corinthian column into an acceptance of all as essential parts of what a later poet was to seek as "unity of being":

With resignation fair and meet
The dirt and refuse of thy street
My philosophic foot shall greet,
So leave but perfect to my eye
Thy columns set against thy sky!

(84-88)

It is Nature that Clough addresses here, quite comfortable in accepting the human crafted work of art as a work of hers, distinct from her own beauty, but existing within it.

It seems that Clough found the creative abundance of Italy stimulating to his own creativity, and it seems impossible to escape a comparison with two poets of an earlier generation who also produced their finest work while in Italy—Byron and Shelley. All three men were powerfully drawn to republican ideas, eager for the destruction of social, economic, and religious oppressions; and as Byron and Shelley were in Italy during the abortive Carbonari risings in 1820, so Clough was in Paris in the spring of 1848, and in Rome in 1849, two months after the proclamation of the Roman Republic by Mazzini.

But to draw this comparison is also to mark the chasm that separates the Victorian from the Romantic. Byron in Ravenna was actively involved with the Carbonari in 1820, and though disillusioned with what he considered their feebleness and bad judgment, was later still prepared to commit himself to the cause of Greek independence. Clough remained an observer in Paris as in Rome, and, though sympathetic, was always restrained in his enthusiasm and quick to turn to skepticism. Byron and Shelley were thirty years closer to the revolution of 1789 and found it easier to believe in the fulfillment of nationalist and republican dreams.

A paragraph from a letter to Matthew Arnold's brother, Tom (who was in New Zealand), dated February 24, 1849—just over a month before Clough left England for Rome—gives a rapid insight into his attitudes both to his Paris experience and his forthcoming trip:

Today, my dear brother republican, is the glorious anniversary of the great revolution of 48, whereof what shall we now say? Put not your trust in republics nor in any institution of man. God be praised for the downfall of Louis Philippe. This with a faint feeble echo of that loud last year's scream of *à bas Guizot* seems to be the sum total. Or are we to salute the rising sun with Vive l'Empereur and the green liveries? President for life I think they will make him, and then begin to tire of him. Meantime the Great Powers are to restore the Pope! and crush the renascent (alite lugubri) Roman republic[2] of which Joseph Mazzini has just been declared a citizen. The said J. M. has written two long letters to the Spectator attributing the Italian disaster entirely to the damper of the national enthusiasm caused by the Piedmontese interference—which is possible, yet of course he would say so. I fear his own pets now dominant in Rome and Tuscany are not strong enough for the place. Yet some heroic deeds ought to come of them, if they are worth anything.

Despite the resigned skepticism of "Put not your trust in republics nor in any institution of man," Clough could still think of himself as a republican; and his skepticism about their future is balanced by the temperate anticipation of "some heroic deeds" from the citizens of the new Roman Republic. He must have traveled to Italy with mixed feelings: on the one hand excitement at the thought of visiting the city that was for his class and race the embodiment of civilization, and on the other a deep interest in the future of the fragile republican state.

Clough arrived in Rome as the French prepared to besiege the city, and during his stay began to write **Amours de Voyage,** a poem that centered on a man much like himself, a young, unmarried intellectual, traveling alone, in Rome for the first time at the moment when the Roman Republic is forced to fight for its life. Claude is not Clough, and yet there is a strong autobiographical element in the poem, not so much in terms of what happens to Claude (indeed it seems very probable that part of his experiences were based on those of Matthew Arnold elsewhere in Europe[3]), but in the analysis and speculation that Claude offers concerning the three strands of his life in Rome (and subsequently elsewhere in Italy)—art, war, and love.

Claude was consciously designed by Clough as a representative type of Victorian tourist, just as the Meagleses and the Dorritts (never forgetting Mrs. General) were by Dickens. At first Rome disappoints him. A traveler like Claude would have been led by education and by the reports of earlier writers to expect more obvious splendor and less rubbish. But gradually, with the assistance of John Murray's guidebook, and through the kind of serious study which alone could justify a mid-Victorian man leaving his responsibilities at home, Claude learns to discriminate between rubbish and excellence; and it is reasonable to suggest that most of his views on Roman art and architecture reflect Clough's.

Clough too, as his letters make clear, was a careful observer of the struggle between the French and Neapolitans and the Romans. His sympathies, as has already been observed, would have been with the Republic, but he came only slowly to identify with the defenders of the city. He was at first suspicious of Mazzini and unprepared to become emotionally involved with what his reason told him was bound to be a lost cause; but by 3 June he could write to Tom Arnold: "These blackguard French are attacking us again. May the Lord scatter and confound them."[4]

Claude has no previous record of support for republican causes, as he is careful to point out in Canto 2, letter 1: "I, who . . . never beheld a / New Jerusalem coming down dressed like a bride out of heaven / Right on the Place de la Concorde . . ."[5], but he too becomes emotionally committed to the Romans, so that "Will they fight?" of Canto 2, letter 3 becomes "we are fighting at last" of Canto 2, letter 5.

Neither Clough nor Claude goes beyond emotional involvement, however; the Victorian gentleman abroad is incapable of the heroic romantic (or Romantic) gesture. There can, though, be no certainty that Claude's entertaining debate on whether or not he could lay down his life for the "British female" also reflects one of Clough's own concerns. It is also quite difficult to determine whether or not Clough formed any romantic attachment during his weeks in the city; if he did, no evidence survives. It is, however, Claude's relationship with Mary Trevellyn that emerges as the most significant element in the narrative.

For much of the poem he denies that he is in love with her, maintaining a perpetual cool flirtation of the most unromantic kind, and justifying his behavior with an analysis of the nature of sexual attraction that builds on an earlier poem of Clough's **"Natura Naturans"**. Eventually the Trevellyns (a family group with some similarities to the Dorrits) escape Rome for Florence, and though Claude had intended to go with them, at the last minute some inquiries from a third party about his intentions toward Mary offend his fastidious sensibilities, and he remains in the city. Claude refuses to be "circumscribed into action," and his retreat into contemplation of the Ludovisi collection and Vatican marbles echoes hollowly against the accompanying noise of the Romans acting to the last to try to preserve their republic.

The remainder of the poem chronicles the unlucky attempts of Claude to track down the Trevellyns, once Mary's absence has convinced him that he does indeed love her. Canto 4 is only 83 lines long, but is packed with futile journeying across the face of northern Italy. However, his failure to find Mary Trevellyn leads Claude in the end to an earned resourceful resignation. One among several details that might illustrate the development of this strength in the hitherto vacillating and hypersensitive man has a curious echo in a celebrated travel book of three years earlier. While in Florence, having given up the chase, Claude writes thus to Eustace:

> Moping along the streets, and cursing my day, as I wandered
> All of a sudden my ear met the sound of an English psalm tune.
>
> Comfort me it did, till indeed I was very near crying.
> Ah, there is some great truth, partial very likely, but needful,
>
> Lodged, I am strangely sure, in the tones of the English psalm tune.
>
> (Canto 5, letter 5, 88-92)

In *Notes of a Journey from Cornhill to Grand Cairo* (1846), Thackeray wrote of his feelings on hearing English church music in Jerusalem: "It was affecting to hear the music and language of our country sounding in that distant place . . . it was the music that was the most touching, I thought, the sweet old songs of home."[6] Claude though is tougher, less sentimental than Thackeray, for in the next section of the letter he writes:

> Almost I could believe I had gained a religious assurance,
> Found in my own poor soul a great moral basis to rest on.
> Ah, but indeed I see, I feel it factitious entirely;
> I refuse, reject, and put it utterly from me;
> I will look straight out, see things, not try to evade them:
> Fact shall be fact for me; and the Truth the Truth as ever
> Flexible, changeable, vague, and multiform, and doubtful.
>
> (Canto 5, letter 5.96-102)

At the end of the poem Claude paraphrases the famous passage from St. Paul's first epistle to the Corinthians:

> Not as the Scripture says, is, I think, the fact. Ere our death-day,
> Faith, I think, does pass, and Love; but Knowledge abideth.
> Let us seek knowledge . . .
> Knowledge is hard to seek, and harder yet to adhere to.
> Knowledge is painful often; and yet when we know, we are happy.
>
> (Canto 5, letter 10.197-201)

And the reader of Clough can make the connection between this poem and **"O Land of Empire."** It has taken the combination of all of Claude's experiences in Italy to drive him to this tough conclusion—a conclusion which we may fairly believe also to have been Clough's—one which is not without hope, even though Claude continues the letter almost in parody:

Seek it, and leave mere Faith and Love to come with
the chances.
As for Hope,—tomorrow I hope to be starting for
Naples.

(Canto 5, letter 10.202-3)

Claude's is not the only voice in *Amours de Voyage*.
We hear briefly from two of the Trevellyn sisters; but
more importantly there is an unnamed voice (perhaps
that of a narrator, perhaps that of Clough-in-the-poem)
which offers the reader, in elegiacs that open and close
each canto, a different perspective on Italy.

The poem begins with an invocation that also recalls
elements of **"O Land of Empire"**:

Over the great windy waters, and over the clear
crested summits
Unto the sun and the sky, and unto the perfecter earth,
Come, let us go,—to a land wherein gods of old time
wandered,
Where every breath even now changes to ether divine.

Nowhere in *Amours de Voyage* does Clough make clear
the fetid and sour side of the Roman scene (though in
his first letter from Rome the hero Claude does call
Rome "rubbishy," as Clough himself did in a letter to
his mother soon after his arrival[7]) here the ballast to this
ethereality is a different one. The speaker goes on to
cast doubts upon the value of the whole enterprise:

Come, let us go; though withal a voice whisper, "The
world that we live in,
    Whithersoever we turn, still is the same narrow
crib;
'Tis but to prove limitation, and measure a cord, that
we travel;
    Let who would 'scape and be free go to his chamber
and;
'Tis but to change idle fancies for memories wilfully
falser;
    'Tis but to go and have been."—Come, little bark,
let us go!

"Think" and "know": such important words in Clough's
writing, such important activities in his life. And Claude
proves the accuracy of the whispering voice, though,
like Clough, he had to do the traveling to perceive the
truth, and he discovered many incidental beauties on
the way.

Clough's other great Italian poems, **"Easter Day"** and
**"Dipsychus,"** have a close relationship with *Amours de
Voyage,* closer than appears in their currently available
form. It has always been clear from the opening of
**"Dipsychus"** that Dipsychus himself lays claim in some
sense to authorship of **"Easter Day,"** but what is now
obscured is that Claude too has a circumstantial claim
to "authorship" of **"Easter Day."** The later of the two
manuscripts of **"Easter Day,"** the one from which all
published texts have been taken, was, in fact, headed

**"Naples, August 1849."** From this piece of evidence it
is not unreasonable to deduce that Clough (who did not
himself visit Naples in 1849) had Claude in mind as the
inferred writer of the poem, the Claude whose last
words at the end of *Amours de Voyage* were of journeying to Naples.[8]

It would also follow that there is a close identity
between Dipsychus and Claude; and before considering
the Venetian poem, there are a couple of passages
eventually cancelled (one might say censored) from the
final copy for *Amours de Voyage* that should be taken
into account. It is not hard to see that Claude and Dipsychus have much in common; what these cancelled passages show is that Claude at one time had also a certain
kinship with the Spirit. For instance, there is a cynicism
about the state of England that barely surfaces in the
poem as we have it—or only perhaps in Claude's comments on the Trevellyns. In the first and longest draft of
the whole poem, Canto 2, letter 9 (the letter in which
Claude wishes that the "nice and natural people" of
Rome could be "allowed this chance of redemption" in
Mazzini's republic), ended thus:

When God makes a great Man he intends all others to
crush him:
Pharaoh indeed, it is true, didn't put down Moses, but
then that
Happened in barbarous times ere polity rose to perfection,
Ere the World had known bankers and funds and
representation.
Rise up therefore ye Kings and ye, ye Presidents—Ah
well
What is the use of all this? Let me sing the song of
the shopman
And my last words like his let me shout with the
chorus of journals.
Oh happy Englishmen we! that so truly can quote
from Lucretius
Suave mari magno—how pleasant indeed in a tempest
Safe from the window to watch and behold a great
trouble of others.
O blessed government ours, blessed Empire of Purse
and Policemen,
Fortunate islands of order, Utopia of—breeches
pockets,
O happy England, and oh great glory of self-laudation.[9]

The writer of this passage is evidently kin to the speaker
of "How pleasant it is to have money" in scene 4 of
**"Dipsychus,"** though there is a bitter irony that is far
from the Spirit's comfortably self-satisfied tone. And it
is perhaps worth noting that Clough here latches on to
something that Joseph Conrad later emphasized in *Heart
of Darkness,* the security of an empire based on the
policeman at the corner, and its distance from the fertile
southern worlds.

Nor was Claude particularly convinced of the divine
right of his country to power and influence:

Even though England and France by a Nemesis pos-
sibly righteous
Should in the issue succumb to the terrible cossack
they talk of,
Why, I don't know. For the Czar may indeed be the
Lord's own annointed,
Out of that people that walketh in darkness a great
light issue,
Out of that Galilee come a new Era; or anyway
England
France and the like may be the things the Creator is
sick of; the Planet
Certainly still would revolve on its axis. What does it
matter!
Though England fall and France; Europe turn one
Russia in Europe
Men would live I suppose, the earth would turn on its
axis.
Runagates would still visit Rome, and would stare and
wonder as usual,
And the Pope be retained as Custode of Vatican
marbles.[10]

These examples, which show a side of Claude's
personality that hardly surfaces in the poem as we
nowadays read it, help to resolve the question that is
always raised about the relationship between Dipsychus
and the Spirit. Once it is recognized that—potentially at
least—Claude contains elements of the Spirit's nature
within him, and it is accepted that the link through
**"Easter Day"** identifies Claude and Dipsychus closely,
then it seems clearer that the Spirit is an integral element in Dipsychus's personality, that **"Dipsychus"** really is to be read as an internalized debate between
aspects of the same personality.

Though Dipsychus's hypnotic barcarole in the gondola
could have been sung nowhere else, for the most part
Venice appears to be no more than a slightly exotic
background to his poem. After all, there are prostitutes,
rude foreigners, famous buildings, crowds, and so on in
a hundred cities. Is there anything about Venice that
makes it a particularly appropriate setting for **"Dipsychus"**?

Two English writers whose names are particularly associated with Venice, and who are invoked in the poem,
give the basis for an answer. Scene 5 of the poem begins
with the Spirit's enquiry:

What now? The Lido shall it be?
That none may say we didn't see
The ground which Byron used to ride on,
And do I don't know what beside on.

Byron had by 1850 become a tourist attraction, featured
in Murray's guidebooks, but when he was living in
Venice the city was associated in the literate English
mind with riotous and corrupt excess—a reputation
which the visits of successive waves of Victorians did
nothing to diminish. This is how Shelley saw the city
when he first visited Byron there in 1818:

I had no conception of the excess to which avarice,
cowardice, superstition, ignorance, passionless lust, and
all the inexpressible brutalities which degrade human
nature, could be carried, until I had lived a few days
among the Venetians.[11]

And John Pemble, in his excellent study, *The Mediterranean Passion: Victorians and Edwardians in the
South,* has a series of quotations from subsequent visitors who regarded Venice as the most vivid current
example of the decay of greatness through moral
degeneracy—against which, implicitly at least, they
could hold up their own empire of virtue.[12] Clough
certainly makes use of this reputation, though it is not
clear from the poem how fully he accepted it. The gaiety
of the crowd, for instance, in the Public Garden in scene
2 is more strongly felt than its licentiousness.

Ruskin was as certain as anyone of the degeneracy of
modern Venice, but in *Seven Lamps of Architecture*
(published before Clough visited the city) he began his
systematic glorification of its gothic architecture, of the
medieval craftsmen that produced it, and of its basis in
religious and moral ideals. The Spirit, not surprisingly,
is unimpressed by Ruskin's enthusiasm. In scene 4, immediately after his song about the pleasantness of the
possession of money, he continues:

Come, leave your Gothic, worn-out story,
San Giorgio and the Redemptore;
I from no building, gay or solemn,
Can spare the shapely Grecian column . . .
The Doge's palace though, from hence,
In spite of Ruskin's d———d pretence,
The tide now level to the quay,
Is certainly a thing to see.
We'll turn to the Rialto soon;
One's told to see it by the moon.

(204-29)[13]

The Spirit, though not averse to expressing an opinion
of his own, is (like Claude at times) ever the tourist,
ever the essence of conventional wisdom, doing what
his guidebook tells him to (when he was interesting
himself in the hoofprints of Byron's horse, Dipsychus
was off for a bracing bath in the Adriatic). It is, though,
worth remembering that a Corinthian column was
chosen by Clough to represent beauty in **"O Land of
Empire,"** and what the Spirit presumably finds offensively pretentious in Ruskin is his association of
religious faith and social duty with architecture. Thus
the contrast that the poem proposes between Ruskin the
moral aesthetician and Byron the amoral hedonist might
stand for the extremes Clough found mingled in the
personalities of representative educated Victorian gentle-
men and of their exemplar in the poem, Dipsychus/
Spirit—mingled, too, in his own personality.

The topography of Venice is, of course, unique. The
inversion of the normal state of affairs that is so integral
a part of the Venetian experience—where the main

streets are water and only narrow alleys debouching into sudden piazzas are dry land—can lead to strange responses, of which Dickens's hallucinatory dream-vision in his *Pictures from Italy* (1846) is only the most extreme. In scene 10, Dipsychus sees the maze of Venetian alleyways and bridges as an image for his life:

> Aimless and hopeless in my life I seem
> To thread the winding byways of the town,
> Bewildered, baffled, harried hence and thence,
> All at cross-purpose ever with myself,
> Unknowing whence from whither.
>
> (75-79)

The city is entirely flat, and it is only in the campanile spire or the distant Alps (beloved of Dipsychus, inevitably) that the mind can find a symbol of aspiration; and Dipsychus's self-analysis continues:

> Then, in a moment,
> At a step, I crown the Campanile's top,
> And view all mapped below: islands, lagoon,
> An hundred steeples and a million roofs,
> The fruitful champaign, and the cloud-capt Alps,
> And the broad Adriatic.
>
> (79-84)

But this vision of life mapped out from a position of absolute certainty, of complete knowledge, soon fades, and he finds himself again bearing "the workday burden of dull life / About these footsore flags of a weary world" (88-89).

In the end Dipsychus succumbs to his Spirit's insistence, not through intellectual conviction, but through intellectual and emotional weariness. Claude (who is and is not Clough), whose stoical acceptance of his inadequacies in the face of the world is matched by his determination to seek knowledge, to live to the full the intellectual life, has now, in Dipsychus (who is also Clough and not Clough), capitulated to the worldly wisdom offered by his Spirit. It was believed by the mid-Victorians that Venice was in imminent danger of returning, once and for all, to the Adriatic,[14] and in its approaching disintegration the city provides a fitting emblem of Dipsychus's final collapse before the iron rule of common sense propounded by the Spirit.

It is impossible to ignore the autobiographical elements in the fabric of the Italian poems, and it is hard not to believe that Dipsychus's pact with his Spirit does not also represent the conclusion of years of intellectual and spiritual conflict for Clough. The poetic sequel, at any rate, to the poems written in Italy were the limp **Mari Magno** narratives, and the subsequent pattern of Clough's life was formed by engagement and marriage to a woman who epitomized the conventional Victorian.

Clough needed to travel out from England to be able to understand clearly what it was he wanted to write, and these journeys seem also to have been necessary for him to see himself with any clarity. The public garden in Venice at the feast of the Assumption is as far from Hampstead Heath on August Bank Holiday as can be imagined, and one can see much farther around large questions when one views them from a distance.

The Italian setting of these great poems reveals sharply the peculiarly English nature of the anxieties and problems that are debated in them; and it does seem that it was only Italy that could give Clough this perspective. He was in Paris for five weeks in 1848, and there is nothing to show for it; later he was in America for much longer, and again there is nothing significant to show for it. Italy, to end as I began, is a land of vanished Empire, of art, and of love, and in it Clough found the impulse to speak to a land of growing empire, of little art,[15] and little love—to speak to England of what it is to be young, intelligent, sensitive, and English. Without the god-like sky and the fecund soil, Clough, I think, would never have been able to see or express with such clarity these insights into the dilemmas that confronted him, and those like him.

*Notes*

Quotations from Clough's poems are mostly from *The Poems of A. H. Clough,* eds. H. F. Lowry, A. L. P. Norrington and F. L. Mulhauser (Oxford: 1951). There are several respects in which this edition is not adequate, particularly in its reluctance to print all of Clough's poetry, and to note all of the variants to it; references to the text of *Amours de Voyage* are from the edition of the poem by Patrick Scott (St. Lucia, Queensland: 1974), an edition of superior authority to the Oxford text. Clough's letters are quoted from *Correspondence of Arthur Hugh Clough,* ed. F. Mulhauser, 2 vols. (Oxford: 1957).

1. This is the heading for the second manuscript version of the poem; most commentators have noticed the relationship between the two poems. One wonders in passing, with Richard M. Gollin ("The 1951 Edition of Clough's *Poems,*" *Modern Philology* 60 [1962]: 120-27), why the editors of the standard edition did not adopt this title. Gollin also points out that there are twelve lines in one of the two extant manuscripts of the poem that appear neither in the published text of the Oxford edition (64-66), nor in the notes to it (481).

2. This is an adaptation of a line from the third of Book 3 of Horace's odes, "Troiae renascens alite lugubri" (the renascent Troy, accompanied by disastrous omens), and powerfully reinforces Clough's skepticism. The letter is in *Correspondence* 1.244.

3. Eugene August ("*Amours de Voyage* and Matthew Arnold in Love," *Victorian Newsletter* 60 [1981]: 15-20) suggests that Arnold's unsuccessful as-

signation in 1848 with Mary Claude in a Swiss hotel, well known to the Arnold-Clough circle, may have provided Clough with romantic material for *Amours de Voyage.* The coincidence of names is otherwise certainly very remarkable.

4. *Correspondence* 1.256.

5. The passage ironically echoes part of a letter that Clough wrote to Tom Arnold about his early days in Paris in 1848: "I was in extreme enjoyment—walked about Jerusalem and told the towers thereof with wonderful delight" (*Correspondence* 1.214-5).

6. Chapter 13: "Jerusalem."

7. *Correspondence* 1.252.

8. This connection with Claude also provides the most satisfactory answer to the question: why did Clough see Naples as the appropriate site for "Easter Day"?

9. Scott 53-54.

10. Scott 73.

11. *The Complete Works of Percy Bysshe Shelley,* ed. Roger Ingpen and Walter E. Peck (London and New York: 1926) 9.335.

12. John Pemble, *The Mediterranean Passion: Victorians and Edwardians in the South* (Oxford: 1987) 232-35.

13. It is an interesting sidelight on the editing (by Clough's wife) that when "Dipsychus" was first published in the privately printed *Letters and Remains of Arthur Hugh Clough* (1865), the line "In spite of Ruskin's d———d pretence" was replaced by "In spite of doctrinaire pretence." Whether she was frightened of Ruskin or "d———d" or both is uncertain.

14. Pemble 232.

15. Matthew Arnold, in often quoted summaries in letters addressed to Clough, makes it clear how little he believed England was currently an Empire of art:

> Reflect too, as I cannot but do here more and more, in spite of all the nonsense some people talk, how deeply *unpoetical* the age and all one's surroundings are. Not unprofound, not ungrand, not unmoving:—but *unpoetical.*
>
> My dearest Clough these are damned times—everything is against one—the height to which knowledge is come, the spread of luxury, our physical enervation, the absence of great *natures,* the unavoidable contact with millions of small ones, newspapers, cities, light profligate friends, moral desperadoes like Carlyle, our own selves, and the sickening consciousness of our difficulties: but for God's sake let us neither be fanatics nor yet chaff blown by the wind. . . .
>
> (*The Letters of Matthew Arnold to Arthur Hugh Clough,* ed. H. F. Lowry [1932; Oxford: 1968] 99, 111.)

**R. A. Forsyth (essay date January 1992)**

SOURCE: Forsyth, R. A. "Clough's 'Adam and Eve'—A Debating Tract for the Times." *Durham University Journal* 84, no. 1 (January 1992): 59-78.

[*In the following essay, Forsyth praises Clough's work as a response to the major intellectual and religious dilemma of his time and contends that, unlike many of his contemporaries, Clough was able to formulate "a theology which . . . was alert to the real demands of secularization."*]

. . . feudality is gone for ever.[1]

Dr Thomas Arnold (1839)

Something interesting too, if not striking there might be, could I in following the development of English literature indicate to you it's [sic] connexion with the development of English character; point out correctly why it was natural at particular epochs that particular things should be said; how the times affected the writers, and the writers express the times; and what sequence of changing words and deeds has brought down the England of History to the modern England of our own times in the East and in the West.[2]

Arthur Hugh Clough (1852)

For this Rachel-and-Leah is marriage; which, I have seen it,
Lo, and have known it, is always, and must be, bigamy only,
Even in noblest kind a duality, compound, and complex,
One part heavenly-ideal, the other vulgar and earthy:
For this Rachel-and-Leah is marriage, and Laban their father
Circumstance, chance, the world, our uncle and hard taskmaster.[3]

Arthur Hugh Clough (1848)

That which your soul, in marriage with the world,
Imbreeds in you, accept . . .
O man, behold thy wife, th' hard naked world;
Adam, accept thy Eve.[4]

Arthur Hugh Clough (1850)

I

The history of modern religious thought, and indeed the whole modern history of ideas, may be justly regarded as the history of the progressive collapse of the medieval Christian synthesis. Human affairs had traditionally been guided by religious beliefs, which provided men with divine sanctions for carrying out their creaturely roles on earth. The Renaissance witnessed the decline of these beliefs as a result of the rediscovery of the learning of classical antiquity, which advanced the seemingly hubristic idea of man as not merely a creature who reflected his Creator's divine plan, but a being of value in his own right. And by extension, secularization, as this complex ongoing movement is now called, importantly asserts that the human realm is meaningful in itself and not simply because it contains spiritual aspects that are related mystically to some divine reality. Indeed, it is that very realm, contingent and unstable though it is, which is the only true ground of Man.[5]

This epochal change was described by Oscar Wilde, in his polemical essay significantly entitled 'The Soul of Man under Socialism',[6] as a move from the 'worship of pain' to the ideal of 'joy and beauty'. 'Medievalism', he observed, 'is real Christianity, and the medieval Christ is the real Christ. . . . Medievalism, with its saints and martyrs, its love of self-torture, its wild passion for wounding itself, its gashing with knives, and its whipping with rods'. The passionate understanding and application of the Christian ethos declined, however, Wilde continues, when 'the Renaissance dawned upon the world, and brought with it the new ideals of the beauty of life and the joy of living'. These ideals came to be increasingly reflected in various aspects of modern life, but most clearly perhaps by painters who, in a seemingly endless portraiture during the following centuries, represented Christ in a 'falsely' idealized way as a cherubic smiling infant, for example, or 'as a noble, stately figure moving nobly through the world . . . [and] even when they drew him crucified they drew him as a beautiful God on whom evil men had inflicted suffering'. And with each new humanized idealization the crucial and ironic point was, of course, only driven home further, namely that the real figure of Christ actually 'did not preoccupy (the painters) much'. Indeed, *could* not preoccupy them much at all would be more accurate, because with the steady advance of secularization there came the growing awareness, in Wilde's terms, that 'pain is not the ultimate mode of perfection. It is merely provisional and a protest'. The Biblical perception of the world as a 'vale of tears', that is to say, was coming to be seen as anachronistic. The teleological framework of ideas and terminology that had traditionally defined man's self-image needed to be psychologically and politically reconstructed. It needed now to reflect the movement away from the mythical and metaphysical towards some modern alternative such as the revitalized humanistic Individualism that Wilde was arguing for.

The first major phase of secularization culminated in the convergence at the end of the eighteenth century of the industrial-technological revolution and the social and political ideologies that were stimulated by the French Revolution. That period of emergent democratic individualism saw the gradual establishment of Man's responsible jurisdiction in most areas of private and public life. From a specifically theological viewpoint the situation was depicted figuratively as the disappear-

ance of God. This separation was experienced by many Victorians as a bewildering alienation, with the Sea of Faith receding to leave them stranded culturally as well as spiritually. For, with an uncomfortable self-consciousness, they saw themselves to be as much victims of history as they were casualties of a personal crisis of belief. For others, more under the sway of Romanticism's apotheosizing of the creative imagination as a supremely spiritual faculty, the impact on Christianity was reflected in the question: did God create Man, or Man God? Each, it seemed, needed the other. However, it must be stressed that neither response—the disappearance of God, or His creative role—denied Man's essential spirituality. Certainly secularization has from the outset been concerned with freeing mankind from any belief system which suppressed the free expression of human integrity and autonomy. And certainly many of those systems were religious in one way or another. But the goal of secularization has never been atheistical. The motivating concern of its many agencies and aspects has been, rather, to get people to reinterpret their spirituality in ways better accommodated to modern developments than traditional thought was able to provide. This massive renovation of orthodox belief structures resulted in a turmoil of religious attitudes that characterizes much of the intellectual and spiritual life of Victorian England.

The response of Arthur Clough to that turmoil is of particular interest; for he formulated—though in a somewhat fragmentary and unpolished manner—a theology which, by comparison with the efforts of many fellow poets, was alert to the real demands of secularization. The basic problem they all shared was how to devise a religious position that was not in conflict with modern intellectual convictions. The issue is neatly formulated in personal terms by J. C. Shairp in a letter written in 1846 to Clough regarding his indecision about being ordained. Shairp's difficulties sprang from the disconcerting abruptness he experienced in making 'the transition from positive Christianity to one's everyday feelings'. This led to a 'disadjustment . . . (between) all you know and think about in a common way . . . (and) all you profess to believe'. The end result, so widespread as virtually to define the Victorian sensibility in one fundamental aspect, was an 'inability to pass off from a holding of certain facts . . . which it is necessary to hold to . . . into pure spiritual morality'.[7] And for Clough himself this disadjustment was a central feature of his response to the emergent ethos of urban industrialism. It is commonly presented in his writings as an imbalance between the real and the ideal, or the two 'musics' as he called them in 'Why should I say I see the things I see not', the one of the world and the other of the soul. The former was 'loud and bold and coarse', demanding to be heard; the latter was 'soft and low, / Stealing whence we not know, / Painfully heard, and easily forgot'. His aim was to harmonise these 'musics' and his method was, in his own terms, to Serve the World.

The more usual response to their turbulent times among contemporary poets was to look back nostalgically to a Golden Age or, conversely, to an imagined utopia that would either return cyclically or evolve with historical inevitability. Also important was Wordsworthianism, as we may validly describe the Romantic idealization of Nature that was to prove a central feature in moulding the early Victorian response to encroaching industrialization. Through the creative imagination it aimed to establish an intimate, spiritually enhancing relationship between the individual sensibility and the 'active universe' (*The Prelude*, II. 254) so that the mysteries of Nature could be intuitively read as hieroglyphs of the divine order. The Pedlar may be taken as representative in that, 'In all shapes / He found a secret and mysterious soul / A fragrance and a spirit of strange meaning' ('The Ruined Cottage', ll.83-85). But as the revolutionary age came to be more and more dominated by the cash nexus and the profit motive, that meaning inevitably became even more secret and mysterious. As a result the authority of Wordsworth's prophetic credo declined gradually to become at last simply an anachronistic talisman against what Matthew Arnold was to describe as the 'mental strife' ('The Scholar-Gipsy') of his times.

Arnold, of course, is the classic casualty in this modern 'meadow of calamity' (*Empedocles on Etna*) as we may judge, for example, from his 'Lines written in Kensington Gardens'. There we find him, typically, lying in a 'lone, open glade' in the midst of London, 'the huge world, which roars hard by', bemoaning his frustrated inability to create or discover any symbol of peaceful beauty. His alienation is so complete that, despite the appropriately Edenic environment, even this nostalgic escape has been 'buried' for him under the 'huge world' so that,

> I, on men's impious uproar hurled,
> Think often, as I hear them rave,
> That peace has left the upper world
> And now keeps only in the grave.

He can only plead with Nature, in suitably pseudo-religious terms, to allow him to experience her peace, 'Calm soul of all things', which 'abides' regardless of men and which inevitably passes his own understanding. We have here the empty shadow, not the real substance. Instead of being an abiding and comforting symbol of redemptive peace, the Gardens become a parody of *the* Garden, offering him only brief asylum in an unquiet sanctuary, so restless that it ironically heightens his awareness of the 'din of strife . . . in the world's most crowded streets' ('The Buried Life') from which he is seeking to escape.

Although Clough paid tribute to Wordsworth's success 'in giving a perfect expression to his meaning in making his verse permanently true to his genius and his moral frame',[8] he criticized severely, nevertheless, his evasion, as he saw it, of the everyday 'world of life and action'.[9] And he rejected accordingly Wordsworth's attempts at integration with the external world, seeing them not as some 'great consummation' (*The Prelude*, I.81) but as self-indulgent and escapist. 'The Real Things', he writes, echoing Keats's complaint against the 'egotistical sublime', 'cease to be real; the world no longer exists; all that exists is the feeling somehow generated in the poet's sensibility'.[10] It is out of deep philosophical respect for these 'Real Things' that Clough promotes his idea of Service with its strong socio-political bias, as a modern substitute for such outmoded cultural myths as Utopianism and Wordsworthianism. But in spite of that practical bias, and more particularly his ardent Republicanism, which might lead one to have different expectations, it is important to note that he was not advocating, in Wildean vein, the displacement of the brotherhood of man (together with the implied Fatherhood of God) by universal Socialism. For, in his view, it is 'not Liberty, Equality, Fraternity, nor yet Solidarity . . . but *Service* (that constitutes) the highest political watchword'.[11] We have here a most significant amalgamation between (real) social and political issues and (ideal) moral and spiritual considerations that defines Clough's modernity. For he is not, in a Christian Socialist way, simply transporting the spiritual into the realm of the political. Rather, he is expressing the one, absolutely though undoctrinally, in terms of the other, thereby establishing a quite novel politico-religious ethos. It entails acceptance of the secularized world as the truly human realm, whilst resisting, however, the seductions of mere worldliness. Adam's impassioned advice to his errant son, Cain, is perhaps its most succinct expression: 'That which your soul, in marriage with the world, / Imbreeds in you, accept' (**'Adam and Eve'**, XIII.64-65).

But although Service is essentially religious in nature, we must understand, nevertheless, that its fervent pragmatism is an altogether more complex idea than the conscientious and selfless Duty so dear to the Evangelical heart that it seems to be echoing. Indeed, charitable good works, together with public worship and even prayer itself, were all jettisoned by Clough as being aspects of an extraneous devotionality that would distort what he perceived as God's 'newer will' for himself and his fellow Victorians, namely to 'trudge it' in silence (**'Dipsychus,'** x.1.1, 12). His central conviction was that 'the world is here, however it came here, to be made something of by our hands. Not by prayer, but examination; examination not of ourselves, but of the world, shall we find out what to do, and how to do it'.[12] Being honest to God, then, meant bringing human experience in all its aspects down to earth, for God's disappearance made it a sentimental self-indulgence to continue behaving as though His transcendental Presence was still accessible to Man. By thus taking the disappearance of God to be, as it were, literally true rather than merely a timid foreshadowing of the Nietzschean announcement of His death, Clough was able to avoid what he perceived as the abyss of atheism as well as the temptation of subscribing to the Religion of Humanity.

Christ would of course remain the exemplar, though he was to be regarded, in Unitarian mode, as the son of Man, the supreme human being, rather than the Son of God. Through his compassionate love for mankind he would provide the individual with a model in the dual process of making and discovering what Clough called the 'inmost I' (**'Adam and Eve'**,II.41). In the new exclusively terrestrial dispensation this was to be the human expression of the Divine Spirit which lay dormant as the supreme developmental possibility within each and every person. With an optimism that was perhaps more dogged than joyful or enthusiastic, being 'more than stoical'[13] though not actually a Stoic, Clough looks forward to the final outcome of the human enterprise when each individual would become Man, a culmination enabling Mankind and God to be united in the unapocalyptic establishment of the Kingdom on Earth. In such a self-helping apotheosis of Mankind, Christ and Man and the World ('our uncle and hard taskmaster') become, then, the components of the modern Trinity, with every person assuming full adult responsibility for his or her own spiritual destiny. Despite its staunchly secular contexts and terminology, this crucial self-development towards human Christlikeness, 'a Communion and company of the souls of just men made perfect'[14] as he described it, clearly has a millenarian focus that in effect translates daily experience in the secular city into a 'religious' time frame.

In his construction of the present and future, that is, Clough is building on the foundations of the past, in this case retaining the Christian narrative of history although its eschatological machinery has been modified, with the divine timetable now being supplanted by one dependent solely on human endeavour. The result is religious, though obviously not Religious in the profound 'medieval' sense; but neither is it disguised anthropology in the Feuerbachian mode,[15] and certainly not some merely sentimental gesture of religiosity.

It has a positive assured spirituality that contrasts starkly with the more complete scepticism of Arnold. He too builds on the past, but in a negative way, so that we find in his poetry a persistent note of wistful nostalgia. Rather than seeing the past as the precursor of the present and future, his scepticism leads him to perceive it as the desolate ruins of time beneath which lies 'buried' his 'genuine self'. The imaginative outcome is

a despairing sense of alienation and isolation, a sense that is expressed most memorably perhaps in his grieving perception that the symbolic Carthusian ethos, despite its exemplary 'medieval' devoutness through the ages, has now become outworn and anachronistic, a 'living tomb'. Its demise and the absence of any adequate substitute leaves him in a barren void 'between two worlds', able to speak only with a dispirited retrospective finality about yet another glorious ruin of time:

> Not as their friend, or child, I speak!
> But as, on some far northern strand,
> Thinking of his own Gods, a Greek
> In pity and mournful awe might stand
> Before some fallen Runic stone—
> For both were faiths, and both are gone.

('Stanzas from the Grande Chartreuse')

Clough's intellectual position naturally reflected a temperamental disposition. For if, as Coleridge had speculated, mankind could validly be divided into 'two classes of men', the Aristotelians and the Platonists, then Clough clearly belongs to the former. David Newsome has formulated the division from an epistemological perspective: 'Is knowledge limited to our reasoning over things which we can see and sense, or is there some higher order of abstract truth, beyond the reach of our senses and the limits of observation, which man can yet apprehend by some higher faculty than the reasoning power?'.[16] The search for that truth would provide the essentially spiritual impetus of Romanticism with its visionary confidence in the ability of the poetic imagination to perceive a mystical order and meaning in the mere contingencies of mortal existence. Clough, as we have seen, rejected such a view in favour of the more Aristotelian 'scientific' acknowledgement of the concrete materiality of the objective world. And that world, together with the continuous narrative of human history, constituted for him the twin components of reality.

His Aristotelian bias is further corroborated in another quite different yet related dichotomy that interestingly parallels, though in specifically theological rather than aesthetic terms, Coleridge's psycho-philosophical division of mankind into 'two classes'. This was the fundamental and protracted debate between Alexandria and Antioch that took place in the early centuries of Christianity. The Alexandrians were, in the words of Nathan A. Scott Jr., 'warmly responsive to Greek intellectual tradition, most especially to the Platonic sense of the preeminence of the spiritual world', and being eager to find arcane 'spiritual' meanings in the Scriptures they used the allegorical method in order to replicate their 'mysterious language of parable and metaphor'.[17] This Platonic approach was clearly to provide, in due course, the basis for the Romantic 'reading' of the Book of Nature. Instead of this kind of transcendental hermeneutics, the Antiochenes, by contrast, emphasized 'the historical reality of the biblical revelation', stressing, therefore, 'the human and historical side . . . of the Incarnation' rather than its 'eternal and divine element'.[18] Particularly in regard to the Incarnation, but also more widely, Clough's rejection of Romantic Platonism in favour of a somewhat unpopular commonsensical pragmatism plainly stamped him as an Antiochene by temperament. And this natural bias would doubtless have been further consolidated by the Oxford education of his day, which was strongly, indeed exclusively, Aristotelian, to the point even, in F. D. Maurice's view, of it being a 'great evil'.[19] Maurice was of the opinion that 'all little children are Platonists, and it is their education which makes men Aristotelians'.[20] So Clough may well have been indoctrinated. Either way, when his great friend at Oxford, Matthew Arnold, came to formulate *his* 'two classes of men'—Hebrew and Hellene—we may be quite sure that he felt justified in placing Clough in the former category.

Whilst these various divisions have great historical and psychological interest in themselves, we should be careful not to regard them as absolute determinants of the position that Clough came gradually to establish for himself. For without denying their influence, we need also to be aware that a person as intellectually strenuous and morally scrupulous as he was, almost to a fault, would hardly be satisfied with any simple corroboration of merely personal inclination and prejudice. Quite the opposite, in fact. For Truth, however difficult to arrive at and to retain, was an idea of absolute importance in Clough's moral and intellectual life. His tender conscience always made him intensely aware of its invisible presence 'in the depths' like some 'mystic colonnade (that) unbroken keeps its faithful way', and of its frustratingly erratic appearance to human eyes in daily life where it is 'a golden thread (only) seen here and there / In small bright specks upon the visible side / Of our strange being's party-coloured web' (**'Truth is a golden thread'**). But despite these frustrations, the enduring note repeatedly sounded by Clough is that "It fortifies my soul to know / That, though I perish, Truth is so' (**'It fortifies my soul to know'**). Truth, elusive and obscure yet always present, played, therefore, a parallel role to the Deity in human life. Both had traditionally been more plainly visible. Now both had withdrawn, leaving the individual in an uncertain world where ancient Truths had been undermined by scientific fact and relativism alike. So the onus was placed on him to strive for a balanced intellectual and spiritual wholeness. And this wholeness, the modern version of those displaced Truths, could only be achieved by being courageously open-minded. The new openness was a cardinal principle in the creation of the 'inmost I', a goal of dignified independence that Clough hoped

would serve as a truly individual touchstone of moral integrity in the fragmented modern world.

Clough's thought stems immediately from Strauss and Schlegel, with its deeper roots lying in the secular spirituality of Hegelian historicism. The diverse thought of Spinoza, Comte and Mill also provided important strands that were woven selectively into the complex pattern of his thinking. These elements, combined with Carlyle's ethic of Work and Duty—especially as mediated by Clough's ardent 'father', Dr Arnold—provided the pragmatic basis for his concept of Serving the World. The eclectic result, invigorated by the spiritual optimism of Goethe and Emerson, was a kind of chiliastic Godwinism which, promoted with Clough's courageous honesty, potentially held great appeal for his contemporaries.[21] It offered them a stable, albeit stark, place 'to rest my head' rather than the tormented vacillation between those 'two worlds' which Matthew Arnold had envisaged in 'Stanzas from the Grande Chartreuse', and which, in a variety of forms, reflected the disadjustment Shairp had complained of. Arnold's more complete alienation had led him to demythologize Christianity into culture, and in the process, so to speak, to vapourize semantically the venerable concept of Divinity into a somewhat vacuous abstraction, 'the Eternal Power, not ourselves, by which all things fulfil the law of their being'.[22]

In the light of such attempts at redefinition, the very starkness of Clough's demanding viewpoint was perversely comforting. What he proposed, expressed metaphorically, was that the decline of conventional religious views and practices would be more validly understood by comparing it with the slow diurnal draining of colour from the iconography of stained glass windows. For this gradual ebbing away had resulted, when translated into historical terms, not in God being lost, but rather in His being revealed (at least potentially) to human 'sight' for the first time. For previously, the sumptuous 'windows' of devotionality had in fact *intercepted* His eastern glory, whereas now, 'through (western) windows plainly glassed . . . the Orb is manifest to sight' (**'Epi-Strauss-ion'**). But the responsibility for this 'seeing' is laid exclusively on the human observer who must, furthermore, search for the Orb equally in the (ideal) heart within and the (real) mundane world without. That is why in this revised dispensation God is paradoxically both radiantly omnipotent—by definition Present, that is to say—and yet, being also absent, is utterly dependent on Man to bring Him back into human 'sight'. And conversely, and crucially, the creature is utterly *in*dependent of the Creator in his efforts to get Him to re-appear. For those efforts are the same as the courageously open-minded efforts needed for the creation of his 'inmost I'. 'Seeing' God and making the 'inmost I', that is, are obverse and reverse of a single spiritual enterprise.

## II

The major work through which Clough gives poetic expression to his deo-humanism, as we might accurately describe what he himself called his 'devotional pseudo-religion',[23] is **'Adam and Eve'**. This was written mainly in 1848, though, as Blanche Clough commented when she published it posthumously for the first time in her edition of 1869, 'The poem must have lain long in the author's mind'.[24] Significantly, 1848 was also the year in which, after a lengthy period of growing scepticism, Clough resigned both his tutorship and Oriel Fellow-ship. Indeed, as Walter Houghton has persuasively ar-gued,[25] it was this poem rather than either the entertain-ing **'The Bothie of Tober-na-Vuolich',** which was also written and published in that same year, or some earnest justification of his decision in the likely form of a religious pamphlet, that really constituted his *apologia pro abdicatione sua*. Admittedly, the manuscripts of the poem are 'singularly fragmentary', and the poem was added to over the next few years, sometimes in a rough and unfinished manner. Yet, as Mrs Clough justly observed, 'the perfect coherence of thought is very curi-ously felt in all the scattered pieces', and there 'is hardly ever a doubt possible as to either sense or order'.[26] Despite the fragmentariness of the manuscripts and Clough's failure to publish the poem, the protracted period of gestation and the initial writing of most of the work in the seminal year of 1848 indicate there are grounds here for regarding it as something of a personal manifesto.

The myth's obvious attraction for Clough, and he returned to it frequently,[27] was that it encapsulated the Christian account of the human condition and mankind's destiny. In literary terms this traditional account had been given its supreme expression by Milton, and in **'Adam and Eve'** Clough re-reads the myth, putting forward an alternative interpretation as a counter to that monumental achievement, though without any sense of arrogant competitiveness regarding purely poetical greatness. His central argument, which reflects deeply held convictions about the nature and course of English cultural history, was that Milton's perspective on the human condition was unable to offer insights of any practical value into the day-to-day reality of modern experience.[28] Further, indeed, his view was that this limitation was not merely the result of the vagaries of fashion, but that the falsity of Milton's position was an inherent flaw which sprang from the religious intensity and absolutism of the Puritan ethos itself, 'the profound almost rigid conviction, that this one, and no other of all those many paths is or can be, for the just and upright spirit possible'.[29] Milton suffers, that is to say, from the same limitation of zealous bigotry that Clough in his poem would attribute to the devotional Abel, who was 'self-predestined as it were, of his own will and foreknowledge to a single moral and religious aim'.[30]

Instead of these rather strained 'moral sublimities',[31] Clough promotes the pragmatic balance and openness that he believes comes from an eighteenth-century com-monsensical view of things. This ideal, by contrast with Milton's, he thought was inherently sound and of particular value for his own intellectually and spiritu-ally troubled contemporaries.[32] Its programme comprised an acceptance of 'the facts of [the] living palpable world . . . [a] righteous abhorrence of illusion; [a] rigorous uncompromising rejection of the vague, the untested, the merely probable . . . Such I believe, *is* the strong present feeling of the English nation'.[33] Pre-eminent among 'the vague . . . the merely probable' was conventional religious practice, and Clough was convinced that to live truthfully in their complex age Victorians had to bear the responsibility for their own spiritual destiny rather than rely on the merely illusory support provided by such anachronistic practices. He wished to replace the absolute Puritan conviction that sustained Milton's justification of 'the wayes of God to men' by a modern relativistic perspective more conge-nial both to the growing democratic individualism of the times and to his own Republican leanings. 'The maxim of the time', he wrote, 'appears to be that it is man's duty to sustain himself upon a minimum of moral assumption; in point of faith to strive to solve the problem of habituation to living on nothing'.[34] And by 'nothing' Clough here means precisely the opposite of conventional religious practice. As a potentially danger-ous consequence of this maxim his own poetic task may be seen to parallel that 'hard task' confronting Adam himself—how to distinguish the 'Voice' from the myriad inner 'voices' now that the 'Voice' (**'Adam and Eve'**, IV.65-66) was no longer able to be directly heard, being really only an echoing memory. For the multiplic-ity of 'voices' might well lead him to become a kind of self-deceiving ventriloquist carrying on what was merely a 'dialogue of the mind with itself'.[35]

Many other artists in the generations that followed on Milton, even down to our own day, though few perhaps quite as explicitly as Clough, were to return to the myth of a lost Paradise as a source of creative inspiration.[36] This is despite the general decline in the authority of religion, and, in particular, the impact of the Higher Criticism, which was to discredit the historical validity of the Fall itself. The tradition, as it may justly be described in view of its lengthy duration as well as its extensiveness, has produced a wide variety of re-creations of Eden. These, as Max Schulz has shown in his comprehensive study of the phenomenon during the eighteenth and nineteenth centuries, range from elaborate landscaped aristocratic gardens (which the Romantics later expanded to embrace the whole of sacramental Nature), through the artistically engineered splendour of Paxton's Crystal Palace in mid-century, to the *fin de siècle* palace of art in the form of Whistler's Peacock Room.[37] These three historically sequential examples reflect in miniature the steady aestheticization of the religious sensibility after the seventeenth century. They are presented as glittering symbols of beauty dedicated to the pleasure principle, though many of them have overtones of the tranquil wholeness of life in the Garden. But whatever their guise or period, and despite being temporal and earthly, they all clearly express nevertheless a deep and enduring spiritual need in the human psyche. Indeed, Mircea Eliade has described this 'Nostalgia for Paradise' as one of the most ancient and sustained of all human longings.[38]

However, and this is of central importance, Clough, somewhat surprisingly in view of his explicit approach to the topic, was not part of this widespread and ongoing tradition. Rather, he was directly opposed to it. We have seen how his honest conviction that God had disappeared obliged him to repudiate traditional belief patterns and conventional worship as not speaking to modern man's spiritual condition. And with that repudiation there also came, naturally, a parallel rejection of the thought processes and perspectives allied to the very idea itself of Paradise and a Fall from grace. For that idea embodied a nostalgic Golden Age mythology with all its religious associations of guilt and wishful retrospection neatly counterbalanced by the hope of forgiveness and future reward. This view of the human enterprise, with its Alexandrian focus, Clough regarded as anachronistic and Romantically escapist. His response, by contrast, (adopting here Frank Kermode's useful terminology) was to fictionalise the myth of the Fall rather than to attempt its aesthetic renovation in a series of 'palaces', whether horticultural, architectural or socio-political. For myth, as Kermode explains, 'operates within the diagrams of ritual, which presupposes total and adequate explanations of things as they are and were; it is a sequence of radically unchangeable gestures'. Whereas, 'Fictions', on the other hand, 'are for finding things out, and they change as the needs of sense-making change . . . Myths make sense in terms of a lost order of time . . . fictions, if successful, make sense of the here and now'.[39] Kermode's definitions summarise neatly the distinctive quality of Clough's response to secularization in his day with its great central feature that man now stands alone on the spiritual stage of the 'here and now', and that his endeavours to 'make sense' of the changes taking place about him are to be directed exclusively by his own moral sensibility rather than, as hitherto, by divine sanction.

But it is most important to recognize here again that Clough's theodicy was not merely an ingenious contrivance to camouflage, from himself let alone others, atheism in the guise of broadminded Republican humanism. He enthroned a *Deus in absentia,* so to speak, but it was, nevertheless, a quite traditional Godhead, absolute and aloof. Even during the time of his most turbulent

religious questioning and indecision, in 1848, he never denied the existence of a Deity—'a Presence I acknowledge, I am conscious of a Power, whose name is Panacea'.[40] He was the ground of all being and was, therefore, pervasively Present; yet He was also, paradoxically, inaccessible. And to such an absolute degree that He could be best worshipped by a kind of silent deferential neglect, leaving mankind free to get on with the serious spiritual task of total commitment to the human realm. As Kermode observes, 'Men . . . to make sense of their span . . . need fictive concords with origins and ends, such as give meaning to lives', so it is 'ourselves we are encountering whenever we invent fictions', and this is particularly so 'at a time when the revealed, authenticated account of the beginning was losing its authority'.[41] In these terms what Clough was attempting to achieve was a secular concord of 'past and present and future . . . without falsifying (the Victorian) moment of crisis'.[42]

The radical shift of emphasis Clough wishes to bring about through such a secular concord is reflected in various formal aspects of **'Adam and Eve',** with the 'reduction' of the conventional supremacy of the epic as a genre implying a commensurate decline in the heroic status of the religio-philosophical values it characteristically endorsed. Thus we find, for instance, that **'Adam and Eve'** is both simpler and more informal in style and much briefer in presentation, thereby tending to deflate, perhaps even to parody, the dimensions and status of Milton's epic statement. This tendency is also apparent in the general lack of epic 'machinery'. In particular there is, as we would well expect, an absence of elaborate descriptions of geographical setting. In fact, the setting is largely ignored so that attention can be focused on the spiritual anguish and intellectual dilemmas of the protagonists. After the Fall they inhabit a no-man's-land, geographically speaking, outside Eden but not yet in the mundane world. And their coming to terms with this *human* world, which they themselves, so to speak, are giving birth to through the very process of their own painful self-discovery, constitutes the essential substance of the poem. The setting is featureless, then, not simply because that expresses Clough's rejection of Victorian 'palaces', but mainly because it symbolizes the moral and spiritual Service this 'Newfoundland' demands of its first colonists, no less than of all their human descendants.

This is also why the poem, again contrary to usual epic practice, is presented in a series of dramatized scenes between carefully regulated groupings of the characters. These serve to distance the 'philosophy' from Clough himself, thus heightening its 'objectivity', and also to reduce the magisterial power of Milton's epic stance. And finally, it is significant that, unlike Milton's epic, Clough's poem, even though it was originally entitled **'The Mystery of the Fall'**, is not really concerned with the actual Fall itself or with the events leading up to it. Clough's attention, as we have seen, is concentrated on the postlapsarian situation, the mundane world in which the human pair now discover themselves, and in which they beget the first family. By natural extension this initial social group, living and making history in the everyday world, gradually evolves to become the multi-tudinious society of Victorian England. For Clough's strategy is to imply a parallel between mankind's original loss of God through banishment from the archetypal Garden, and the immediate loss suffered as a result of His current disappearance from 'England's green and pleasant land' (**'And did those feet in ancient time'**). That is to say, Clough's fictionalized reading of the myth constitutes his poetic response to the powerful and disruptive thrust of secularization in his age. It is his imaginative Tract for the Times, dramatically presented through the anguished debate of characters who are intended to be representative contemporary individuals as well as mythical arche-types.

### III

In Clough's poem Adam and Eve give opposite interpretations of the Fall, and their differences remain unresolved to the end. Eve's response throughout is one of intense remorse that springs from her deeply religious sensibility. She is distressed by the realization

> That whereas once in His continual sight
> We lived, in daily communing with Him,
> We are now banished, and behold not Him.

(IV.76-78)

In Adam's view, however, her unremitting grief is nothing more than 'some religious crotchet' (IV.21), a supreme example of devotionality. He is a pragmatist, who though not rebelliously hostile to God could also not be described as innately pious. Man is a rational be-ing, Adam argues, living in a rational universe, and he has, therefore, a natural right—a duty, even—to disobey a prohibition so arbitrary. 'What is it then', he asks derisively of Eve, 'you wish me to subscribe to?':

> That in a garden we were put by God,
> Allowed to eat of all the trees but one;
> Somehow—I don't know how—a serpent tempted,
> And eat we did, and so were doomed to die;
> Whereas before we were meant to live for ever.
> . . . why, all that I can say
> Is, that I can't conceive the thing to be.

(IV.30-35, 42-43)

If free will means anything it must mean a belief in the autonomous exercise of Man's rational intellect, even if this means the loss of Paradise through disobeying some obscure edict he cannot understand. 'What!' Adam explodes with irritation and frustration,

> Because I plucked an apple from a twig
> Be damned to death eterne! parted from Good,
> Enchained to Ill!

(I.24-26)

Adam is unable, or refuses, to read their predicament and the events leading up to it in an allegorical way. His literal, commonsensical interpretation reflects his rational temperament, leading him to see those events as a natural development:

> 'Tis done; it was to be done; if indeed
> Other way than this there was, I cannot say:
> This was one way, and a way was needs to be found.
> That which we were, we could no more remain
> Than in the moist provocative vernal mould
> A seed its suckers close, and rest a seed.
> We were to grow. Necessity on us lay
> This way or that to move; necessity, too,
> Not to be over-careful this or that,
> So only move we should.

(I.10-18)

The image of germinating seed is particularly appropri-ate to their new condition, that of having to contend with the forces of nature as true gardeners rather than being merely inmates of Eden. The image also alludes to Eve's pregnancy. But its main import is that the 'seed' has been planted by God's hand 'in the moist provocative vernal mould' of the human psyche, where it has now, at the pre-ordained season in the evolution-ary sweep of time, duly 'sprouted'. This process and Adam's free will complement each other, both being natural, organic aspects of an ordered universe. This world, not Eden, is Man's proper home. We have, then, not something priceless being lost, but an inestimable potential for self-creation and discovery being gained by mankind. And with the translation of the transcenden-tal into terrestial terms we have also the movement from ideal to real, with the real, however, not simply ousting the ideal but becoming rather the appropriate context for its full discovery and proper functioning in human life. Eve, however, never makes this discovery. She remains imprisoned in her grief, the self-indulgent devotionality that ironically prevents her from rediscov-ering the God whose loss she mourns.

An indirect, yet effective way in which the process of germination may be seen to function is in Eve's dreams. In his attempts to comfort her, Adam describes the ter-rifying dreams as 'thick fancies fond . . . [thou] Draws't from thy teeming womb . . . Big with the first maternity of Man' (I.33-34). In due course Eve is delivered of Cain, the son whose future fratricide will, in retrospect, provide ghastly justification for the extremity of her remorse, and also lend weight to her present conviction that 'I am not dreaming, am not crazed. / Did not yourself confess that we are changed?' (I.83-84). Past and present here merge in a way that is paralleled by the commingling of appearance and reality in the prison of dreams where Eve languishes. Eve's dreaming may, in Keats's famous description of the Imagination, 'be compared to Adam's dream—he awoke and found it truth'.[43] What Adam had desired as he dreamed in preparation for the gratification of that desire, proved to be miraculously present on his awaking, dream and reality being thus interfused. Similarly, Eve's dreams are not as Adam describes them— 'cloudiest of clouds' (I.39)—but are indeed the premonitory 'seed' of real events. She, too, awoke to find her dreams coming true, appearance and reality having flowed naturally into each other in the imagination where that 'seed' had lain dormant.

Significantly, although Adam understands and accepts the Fall as a natural event, this doesn't prevent him from feeling guilty and remorseful about what has been lost. As we might expect, the 'seed' of the Fall lay in him as deeply as it had lain in Eve, and consequently he understands very well the dream that preceded her desolate awakening. When he is alone in the following scene, he castigates himself with the memory of the 'irretrievable act!' (II.5). His state of mind is different to that which led him to explode 'What! / Because I plucked an apple from a twig / Be damned to death eterne!'. And yet that sense of personal outrage is still present—'Irretrievable what, I should like to know? / What act, I wonder? What is it I mean?' (II.6-7). In turn his self-assertiveness fades before the absolute physical sense with which he recollects in terror the awful Presence:

> His tread is in the garden! hither it comes! . . .
> He comes. He calls. The large eye of His truth,
> His full, severe, all-comprehending view
> Fixes itself upon our guiltiness—
> O God, O God, what are we, what shall we be?
>
> (II.15, 22-25)

These vivid recollections establish that Adam knows what Eve is talking about because he has effectively shared her dreams. And this heightens his resolve to understand further his present situation. He does not deny his guilt; rather, he embraces it, just as Cain is later to do, albeit more vehemently, after he has murdered Abel. Guilt and remorse bear the recognisable stamp of fallible humanity, and on that account must, perversely, be cherished. For Adam's concern is to use his grief as a springboard rather than to make of it a prison, as Eve has. Instead of her exclusively religious response, he proposes his own dual position—fearful helplessness complemented by courageous enquiry—a duality neatly encapsulated in the lines that commence his description of his own inner condition:

> E'en in my utmost impotence I find
> A fount of strange persistence in my soul.
>
> (II.31-32)

These lines lead into a passage of central importance in the poem, the 'seed' of Clough's manifesto:

> Also, and that perchance is stranger still,
> A wakeful, changeless touchstone in my brain,
> Receiving, noting, testing all the while
> These passing, curious, new phenomena,
> Painful, and yet not painful unto it.
> Though tortured in the crucible I lie,
> Myself my own experiment, yet still
> I, or a something that is I indeed,
> A living, central, and more inmost I
> Within the scales of mere exterior me's,
> I—seem eternal, O thou God, as Thou;
> Have knowledge of the Evil and the Good,
> Superior in a higher Good to both.
>
> (II.33-45)

The distinctive feature of Adam's response is his intense self-awareness. He recognises the significance of 'the curious seething process', (II.57) obscure though it often is, but he is not absorbed in it to the detriment of its continued operation. He has the courage of his convictions and the confidence—a little self-consciously, perhaps even pompously, expressed—that given time and freedom from Eve's 'imaginings' he could 'resolve the problem on my brain' (II.55). But there is clearly nothing pompous about his actual analysis of his state of mind. The nervous rhythm of the lines, the tone of thoughtful excitement which helps syntactically to sustain the long sentences, the accumulation of provisoes and qualifications which assist in heightening the urgency of what is being said without sacrificing exactness of definition, the aptness of the pivotal image of scientific experimentation which captures accurately the mood of 'these operations' (II.59)—all of these qualities help to give the lines a directness and precision that spring from deep imaginative involvement with the issues in hand. Moreover, the artistic success of the lines is commensurate with the great significance of their content. For here Clough epitomizes the seemingly sacrilegious elements of his deo-humanistic thought by equating himself with his Maker through their shared creativity: on the one hand, He, the Creator of the Universe, whose name is Truth; on the other, Man, the creator and discoverer of his own true self by experimental procedures which give it the stamp of scientific veracity. 'Hypothesis the soul of science is' (**'That there are powers above us I admit'**), Clough had satirically commented on the decline of religious belief in the fact of scientific experiment. In the above passage he is exploiting that decline by making the 'hypothesis' of the 'inmost I' the very 'soul' of his Tract. Furthermore, because of the distinctive experience he has undergone in the Fall, Adam has a knowledge of Good and Evil that is, by definition, outside the experience of One who is pure Good. God's knowledge of Good is, to take over Milton's phrase, a 'cloistered virtue'.[44] He has no choice but Good. By contrast, fallen Man may achieve a 'higher Good' precisely because he has no choice but to choose between Good and Evil. This interplay of choice and action is, in Clough's view, the beating heart of the moral life.

IV

Scene IV concludes with Adam urging Eve not to indoctrinate their children with what he sees as her false interpretation of their own history:

> Put not, when days come on, your own strange whim
> And misconstruction of my idle words
> Into the tender brains of our poor young ones.
>
> (IV.100-2)

The 'idle words' Adam refers to are those he had spoken to Eve at the birth of Cain—'This child is born of us . . . and therefore is not pure' (III.48, 50). What he sees as her guilt-ridden 'misconstruction' of those words has led her to teach their children 'rites and forms . . . Which I nor practise nor can understand' (VIII.2-3). The differences of interpretation that underlie the earlier debate between Adam and Eve have obviously endured. And those same 'rites and forms' will also provide a major area of disagreement in the later debate between Cain and Abel. Of more immediate significance, however, is the fact that Adam's 'command' to Eve is also closely connected to the very brief Scene V in which we find him sternly instructing his adult sons not to add injustice and violence to the 'Terror and toil and pain already here' (V.5). In this way the two scenes flow into each other despite the lengthy time span between them. And the two parts of the poem overall are further connected through the parallel between Adam's warning to Cain not to strike Abel and the original Fatherly prohibition forbidding the parents to eat the fruit.

The tone of Abel's interior monologue (Scene VI) is one of restrained intensity. Restrained in the sense that the formality of liturgical rhythms and Biblical diction and phrasing seem to be the natural medium for his reverential temperament. But restrained in another, more disturbing sense as well. For his moral and spiritual fervour soon reveals itself, in fact, to be so overbearing that the formality may be seen as a necessary constraint on the overreaching zeal of his introspection. This duality is reflected in the tension that exists between the two interweaving elements comprising his monologue. On the one hand there is his critical assessment of his father and brother whose irreligious behaviour he contrasts unfavourably with that of his mother and himself. And on the other hand there are his earnest invocations to God to protect his mother's and his cause in the 'unspiritual and godless house' (VI.8) they find themselves in. Whilst the invocations take the form of a prayer, the assessment is comprised of more strictly interior comments on his own earthly situation. But actually that situation is dominated by his religious sensibilities which lead him—paralleling his mother's response to the Fall—to see all human experience in an exclusively devotional, and therefore, in Cloughian terms, in a virtually obsolete perspective. This is the source of his intensity, and it leads at times to an extremity of self-conscious piety that is so unctuous as to verge on the hubristic:

> . . . But oh, my God,
> Thou wilt bring all things in the end to good.
> Yea, though the whole earth lie in wickedness, I
> Am with Thee, with Thee, with Thee evermore.
>
> (VI.23-26)

Abel's fervour springs from his personal conviction, oft-expressed, that he is one of the Elect. Indeed it is, ironically, the frequency of his claims to Election that brings to our attention the dangerous self-deception inherent in his stance. His claims seem to spring from an assurance deeply rooted in faith. However, their insistence points rather to a need that is in danger of being undermined by the very 'sincerity' on which it is so ardently based. He has 'joy, such joy' in repentance,

> That almost I could sin to seek for it.
> Yea, if I did not hate it and abhor,
> And know that Thou abhorr'st and hatest it,
> And will'st, for an example to the rest,
> That Thine elect should keep themselves from it.
>
> (VI.16-20)

The tenuous casuistry of his argument leads him to protest too much—sinning would be such sweet abhorrent pleasure were it not punishable!

Clough proceeds to make his criticism quite explicit, and in order to heighten the irony of the whole self-revealing portrait, he does so precisely at the point where Abel seems to show some unexpected glimmerings of self-awareness. 'Am I not', he asks rhetorically,

> . . . feeding spiritual pride,
> Rejoicing over sinners, inelect
> And unadmitted to the fellowship
> Which I, unworthy, most unworthy, share?
>
> (VI.28-31)

His answer is an urgent plea for help:

> O God, remove it from my heart—pluck out,
> Whatever pain, whatever [wrench] to me,
> These sinful roots and remnants, which whate'er
> I do, how high so e'er I soar from earth,
> Still, undestroyed, still germinate within.
>
> (VI.33-37)

Once again we have a clear echo of Adam's 'seed' metaphor, but here Abel inverts the key words. Instead of being sources of life through their hold on the vital earth, roots become merely tuberous remnants that can never be eradicated. Nature and natural growth are things to soar away from because their rank flourishing contaminates the spirit. In short, Abel, like Eve, is unable to accept the interacting duality that is the essence of Adam's interpretation of the human condition, where the ideal must perceive and express itself in terms of the real. Instead, Abel is presented as a type of embattled Evangelical fundamentalist in a sinful world, invoking God possessively in earnest pulpiteering rhythms to protect him from whatever may

> Cast out the sweet assurance of my soul
> That I am Thine, and Thou art mine, my God.

> (vi.47-48)

### V

Abel's fervent yet ingratiating piety is sharply contrasted, in the immediately following Scene, with an intensity of a quite different kind—his brother Cain's passionate individualism. Whereas devotional Abel is all obedience and self-negation, Cain epitomizes the wilful arrogance of one whose need for self-expression is overriding:

> . . . for at times
> Ungovernable angers take the waves
> Of my deep soul and sweep them, who knows whither
> And a strange impulse, struggling to the truth,
> Urges me onward to put forth my strength,
> No matter how—Wild curiosity
> Possesses me moreover to essay
> This world of action round me so unknown;
> And to be able to do this or that
> Seems cause enough, without a cause, for doing it.

> (vii.7-16)

But here too, as with Abel, there is ambivalence. Our immediate impression is of an individual overpowered by the wuthering ferocity of his own passions. Yet in the context of his opening question, 'Am I or am I not this which they think me?' (vii.1), Cain's struggling impulses against this wild possession may well be interpreted rather differently. From this viewpoint he may be understood instead as a person of admirable courage and determination whose self-confident exploration of personal experience, uncontaminated by metaphysical considerations or religious scruples, is praiseworthy, even heroic. For his curiosity, though disconcertingly wild, does lead him to a vigorous confrontation with the unknown 'world of action round me' (vii.14). Although he is swayed by ungovernable impulses, he still, however, puts 'forth my strength . . . struggling to the truth' (vii.11,10). Although he acts out of envious dissatisfaction with his subservience to Adam, his arrogance does, however, lead him to personal endeavour, 'evermore / Something I must do, individual, / To vindicate my nature' (vii.21-23).

It is as unsatisfactory, then, to think of Cain as a man of swaggering action as it would be to think of him merely as the melodramatic villain of the piece, a vile counterpart to Abel's devotional intensity. Instead he emerges as a representative individual whose steady growth into full human stature is of cardinal interest in the philosophical development of the poem. He comes to assume this increasingly important role, not just by virtue of Abel's absence and Eve's self-inflicted languishment in her mental prison, but because in his mind and soul—and he is the first true *world-born* human being—that central Cloughian struggle of harmonizing the ideal and the real is being painfully played out. Initially he ignores the ideal entirely. But later, as a result of his terrible crime, there are signs of an emergent spiritual awareness, which he must now learn to graft on to his extreme humanist worldliness. His problem, then, is to modify and mould his passionate consciousness into a moral conscience. This development may be understood as the gradual movement towards resolving the opposition between his ardent heart—which Abel in his infuriatingly patronising way had spurned—and his dormant soul—which Abel in his infuriatingly proprietorial way had commended to his God. Immediately after the fratricide that move has not yet been initiated. Instead we see a bizarre consolidation of those two elements of heart and soul as, drunk with his apparent power to 'right ourselves . . . If we are wronged' (ix.7), Cain's violent desire leads him to mimic divine power in acclaiming his victory:

> Victory! victory! victory! My heaven,
> Methinks from infinite distances borne back
> It comes to me re-born in multitude,
> Echoed, re-echoed, and re-echoed again,
> Victory! victory!—distant yet distant,
> Uncountable times repeated. O ye gods!
> Where am I come, and whither am I borne?

> (ix.12-18)

But the victory is hollow—heaven is not his; and those gods are not God. His triumph is a hysterical rant parodying the victory of Christ over Satan's temptation—'I stand upon the pinnacle of earth' whilst 'all about (I hear) the wild seas laughing' (ix.19, 20). They are really, however, the same violent waves which had always swept his soul. His playing at God (the obverse role to Abel's unctuous devotionality), having power over life and space, leads persuasively to a stark reversal of roles within himself. Thus at the very moment of cruellest gloating and hubris, the divine inner Voice of conscience that persistently questions, 'Am I my brother's keeper?' (ix.37), becomes a furious counterpart to those same 'Ungovernable angers' whose imperious, but lesser, voice had earlier swept 'the waves / Of my deep soul'. The murder had been committed impulsively at the climax of mounting anger and frustration. But Adam is at some pains to assert that it also 'needed' to be done, that it was natural in the same way he had years before explained to Eve that the Fall had been natural. The fratricide, too, had been 'provoked' by the 'vernal mould' of human circumstance: 'My son, 'tis done, it was to be done; some good end / Thereby to come, or else it had not been' (XIII.2-3).

Yet Cain remains as unconvinced and inconsolable as Eve had been, though for quite different reasons. Through penitential prayer she had sought forgiveness of the sin which had led to God's withdrawal; to Cain, of course, this approach is unavailable. But he does not merely become hardened in his views. Instead, far from his individualistic self-assertiveness withering as a result of his acknowledging his culpability, it flourishes to become the unexpected agency for his remorse. Rather than seeking 'atonement from a gracious God . . . (through) rites and holy means of grace' (XI.9, 12) as Eve repeatedly urged him to do, Cain insists,

> I ask not for atonement, mother mine;
> I ask but one thing—never to forget.
>
> (XI.14-15)

To his mind, his position is as incontrovertible, and yet, in a sense, also as incomprehensible as the facts he observes in the natural world about him:

> . . . The dull stone
> Cast from my hand, why comes it not again?
>
> (XIII.20-21)

The cast stone and the murdered brother alike cannot return, and in his remorse he associates them as aspects of a single dispensation. They are parts of a universe of (scientific) Fact, and neither 'prayers to empty heaven', which Eve advocates, nor the 'vegetative kindness of the earth' (XIII.39, 40), which Adam commends, can alleviate its intractability. To Cain, then, to be forgiven is to forget. And the self-delusion of forgetting is a worse crime than the original one:

> . . . to forget is not to be restored;
> To lose with time the sense of what we did
> Cancels not that we did; what's done remains—
> I am my brother's murderer.
>
> (XIII.35-38)

Cain's blunt honesty is also, however, a manifestation of a limitation of his sensibility. God has disappeared; but He has also been excluded by Cain. And he is left, as a result, imprisoned as securely in his own passionate heart as were Eve and Abel in their escapist devotionality. So it is appropriate that, despite their obvious differences, Eve should play an effective role in Cain's progress, exhorting him to repent in a speech made the more powerful by the enduring memory of her own culpability:

> You ask not for atonement! O my son,
> Cain, you are proud and hard of heart e'en now.

Beware!
> Prostrate your soul in penitential prayer,
> Humble your heart beneath the mighty hand
> Of God, whose gracious guidance oft shall lead
> Through sin and crime the changed and melted heart
> To sweet repentance and the sense of Him.
> You ask not for atonement! O my son!
> What, to be banished from the sight of God;
> To dwell with wicked spirits, be a prey
> To them and prey yourself on human souls;
> What, to be lost in wickedness and sink
> Deeper and deeper down;
> What, Cain, do you choose this?
>
> (XI.32-46)

Although Cain does not accept Eve's criteria, nevertheless he grasps better than Adam the cast of her mind and the 'mysteries in your heart', which he nicely opposes to 'my heart's secrets' (XI.47, 50). It is Cain, after all, who suggests the best description of Eve's 'dream' as 'A transcript of an inward spiritual fact . . . Not the less true because it was a dream' (XII.4, 6). For Eve, appearance and reality have merged to become indistinguishable because the 'seed' of disobedience had rested within her soul. Comparably, the 'scarce conscious momentary act' (XI.27) that led to Abel's death, Cain now realizes, had also lain within himself as 'an inward spiritual fact'. Eve and Cain, both intensely spiritual, share the torments of guilt and remorse. In their contrasted struggle to achieve a condition of fully human identity, however, Clough clearly promotes Cain's response, despite its seeming perversity, as the proper model for his own Victorian contemporaries. For whilst Cain fully accepts God's current withdrawal, he still continues the struggle. And rather than simply being grief-stricken and offering ritual sacrifices to an absent Deity, he offers trudging Service to the exclusively human world. His courageous openmindedness prevents him from saying 'prayers to empty heaven' (XII.39) because it *is* for him indeed empty. Therefore punishment, though not in any simplistically retributive sense, is what he seeks, not atonement.

Cain's anguish and inconsolable loss is keenly evoked in a passage that echoes Othello's great mourning speech when, made uncertain about Desdemona's fidelity, he felt that his occupation had been lost and his identity jeopardised:

>               O, now for ever
> Farewell the tranquil mind! Farewell content!
> Farewell the plumed troops, and the big wars
> That makes ambition virtue—O farewell!
> Farewell the neighing steed and the shrill trump,
> The spirit-stirring drum, th'ear-piercing fife,
> The royal banner, and all quality,
> Pride, pomp, and circumstance of glorious war!
> And, O you mortal engines, whose rude throats
> Th'immortal Jove's dread clamours counterfeit,
> Farewell! Othello's occupation's gone.
>
> (III.3.348-58)

Othello and Cain share a nobility that is undeniable, though at times it is stubbornly ponderous and perplexing; and by standing him in Othello's shadow at that grievous moment, Clough is able to endow Cain's spiritual struggles with impressive human grandeur. Othello's splendid rhetoric befits his exotic past. Its military subject matter defines the dignified world of biographical fact on which his reputation and identity rest. But his statuesque public image, built on past achievements, towers over his private image, temperamentally uncertain in the alien world of passion. Their imbalance and disintegration is reflected in the poignant cry, 'Farewell! Othello's occupation's gone!'.

That imbalance has as its counterpart in Cain a disparity between the tranquil peace of mind he has lost and the stern acceptance of the world of Fact and Work, 'the conflict of the stubborn soil' (XIII.53). 'Woe to me!' he cries out to his father,

> Abel is dead. No prayers to empty heaven,
> No vegetative kindness of the earth,
> Will bring back [warmth] into his clay again,
> The gentleness of love into his face.
> Therefore for me farewell,
> Farewell for me the soft,
> The balmy influences of night and sleep,
> The satisfactions of achievement done,
> The restorative pulsing of the blood
> That changes all and changes e'en the soul—
> And natural functions, moving as they should,
> The sweet good-nights, the sweet delusive dreams
> That lull us out of old things into new.
>
> (XIII.39-51)

The tranquility that Cain has lost is spun around the simplicities of daily activities. Their balmy restorative quality is reflected in the mellifluous rhythms and vow-elled cadences. The unlikely spirit of Tennyson breathes through the verse, which is quite different in texture to the burnished fanfare of Othello's rhetoric, and indeed to the passionate vigour of Cain as we had hitherto known him. Those earlier 'Ungovernable angers' have now, in retrospective comparison with the present torment they have led to, been calmed; they have about them the unreality of mere turbulence when contrasted with the harsh reality of remorse and guilt which, at the end of each long day,

> Instead of rest, re-carve into my brow
> The dire memorial mark of what still is.
>
> (XIII.55-56)

Cain's 'occupation's gone!'. But unlike Othello, with him it is not a matter for regret or grief, let alone tragic disintegration. Indeed, paradoxically, it is a matter for gratitude and joy, painful though the present experience of it is. For that occupation, as unreal as every other aspect of their unvarying existence in the Garden, has

now been replaced by the strenuous reality of human life in the realm of the ordinary world. His inconsolable loss has thus proved to be the very medium of his emergent conscience. His (ideal) spirituality burgeons from his acknowledgement of his (real) guilt:

> Welcome this worship, which I feel is mine;
> Welcome this duty—
> —the solidarity of life
> And unity of individual soul.
> That which I did, I did, I who am here.
>
> (XIII.57-60)

His self-confidence springs precisely from an awareness of the growing integrity of his soul and his personal moral responsibility in its making. It is a task that is the opposite of the 'dream' of his earlier life, and though undertaken outside the boundaries of conventional religion, it yet reveals its spiritual dimensions through being described as 'worship' and a 'duty'. Cain, through his dignified and hard-won independence, becomes the prototype of the 'inmost I'.

## VI

It is fitting that the final Scene, which takes the form of a visionary dream about the future, should be presented through Adam. Partly this is so because his courageous optimism about the healing power of time makes persuasive the consolation and encouragement he offers his anguished son; and partly because his role as moderator between the extremism of Eve and Cain is a fitting prelude to the harmonizing balance he dreams will enfold all at the end. Furthermore, his culminating dream brings to mind Eve's dream at the beginning of the poem. The dreams are, of course, different in mood—his, peaceful and conciliatory; hers, terrified and guilt-stricken. More important than this difference, however, is a similarity in function. Eve's dream had not simply been some hysterical delusion, but had proved, rather, to be the imaginative 'seed' of the real Fall. Similarly, Adam's dream may, in turn, become the 'seed' of the real Kingdom on earth. And because the 'sprouting' of this process in the 'mould' of history will not be assisted by the Deity, it is appropriate that the original human being himself, rather than some superhuman emissary, should be responsible for dreaming the 'seed' of that far-off event.

Adam's vision incorporates from the outset all the actors in the drama of Man's emergence into the world from Eden, thus suggesting at once the achievement of a kind of balance. This sense of controlled interrelationship is well conveyed in the image of members of the first earthly family sitting for a group portrait in which all will be forever stable and hierarchically ordered:

> I sat, and you were with me, Cain, and Eve
> (We sat as in a picture people sit,
> Great figures, silent, with their place content).
>
> (XIV.5-7)

The balance of the composition expresses benign peace among its component characters, a peace reflected by Abel's begging forgiveness of Cain for having provoked him and having subsequently caused him such hardship. It was all foolishness, he says, 'Because we knew not both of us were right' (xiv.12). Angelic tact could hardly go further, and the brothers embrace. Clough is not, however, simply being sentimental here. Rather, he is stressing once again the duality which has run through the poem and has provided the basis of its debating structure. As indicated earlier, that duality, together with its corollary—intellectual balance of opposites—was pivotal in Clough's thinking. Although they had been violently opposed, both brothers also needed each other; and in that need they paralleled, so to speak, the need of the ideal for the real. Together they formed the great and distinctively *human* harmony which was the proper, indeed the only, accompaniment to the Voice of God. But without that accompaniment, the Voice would be dumb within the heart of man.

As if to stress this, Adam then observes the strange metamorphosis whereby the brothers' embrace leads to their dissolving into each other and disappearing as individuals, only to reemerge as a new interfused entity. Their fusion is an image of the harmonizing of their conflicting viewpoints. It is also employed to suggest the resolution of the earlier hostility between Adam and Eve about her 'dream'. Thus we find Eve wishing that when 'I fade . . . vanish, sink, and cease to be' (xiv.26) it should be back into Adam from whom she had been created. Her hoped-for return, furthermore, is similar in movement to her original emergence from 'the inexistent void' when God's 'awful whisper . . . [and] sovereign strong compulsion' (xiv.22, 23, 27) urged her to assume an individuality which, like her sons, she is now about to lose. This 'fusion and mutation and return' (xiv.34) is also experienced by Adam, who feels, whilst listening to Eve,

> I was alone—yet not alone—with her
> And she with me, and you with us, my sons,
> As at the first, and yet not wholly.
>
> (xiv.30-32)

Everything sinks back into Adam in the wavering, shifting world of his vision, and it is finally resolved in the tranquil innocence of a dreamless sleep. The mutation and fusing dissolution that characterizes the vision also becomes, therefore, an image of the completion of the turbulent events of history, through which Mankind's harmonious end is seen to rest in its tranquil Edenic origins. Adam 'sees' once again the God who had so mysteriously disappeared. Through their own moral endeavours in the mundane world, human beings have made visible once again the omniscient Deity whose true and only home, however, is, and always has been, 'with us'. The human heart, then, may be said to constitute the entire Creation of the omniscient God. That is His royal seat. Adam speaks with Clough's voice when he talks about human life as an experiment which has clear aims and which must be carried on despite the hampering limitations inherent within each person as well as external difficulties of circumstance:

> In spite of doubt, despondency, and death,
> Though lacking knowledge alway, lacking faith
> Sometimes, and hope; with no sure trust in ought
> Except a kind of impetus within,
> Whose sole credentials were that trust itself.
>
> (xiv.41-45)

These statements echo and comment accurately on Adam's response to his then newly-fallen condition. At that earlier time he had found 'E'en in my utmost impotence . . . A fount of strange persistence in my soul . . . A wakeful, changeless touchstone in my brain'. This discovery led to his becoming 'Myself my own experiment' and to his consequent discovery of 'knowledge of the Evil and the Good, / Superior in a higher Good to both' (ii.31-45). The substance of these statements by Adam lies at the heart of Clough's Victorian manifesto. They reflect the courageous open-mindedness needed in the creation and discovery of the 'inmost I', the 'consummated consciousness of self' (iii.57), as Adam was later to describe it, through which every individual would achieve the dignified independence of a truly human identity, and thus be enabled to 'see' once again the God who had disappeared. This was Clough's supreme balancing act, precariously holding in equipoise the despair of intolerable atheism and the hope of an embattled faith.

### Notes

1. Arthur P. Stanley, *Life of Thomas Arnold, D.D.: Head-Master of Rugby* (London: Murray, 1904), p. 723n.

2. Arthur H. Clough, 'The Development of English Literature' in *Selected Prose Works of Arthur Hugh Clough,* edited by Buckner B. Trawick (Alabama: University of Alabama Press, 1964), p. 124. Subsequently referred to as Trawick.

3. Arthur H. Clough, 'The Bothie of Tober-na-Vuolich' (ix.167-72), in *The Poems of Arthur Hugh Clough,* edited by Frederick L. Mulhauser, second edition (Oxford: Oxford University Press, 1974). All quotations from Clough's poetry are taken from this edition, subsequently referred to as Mulhauser.

4. Arthur H. Clough, 'Adam and Eve' (xiii.64-65) and 'Dipsychus' (xii.68-69).

5. In the course of this article quite frequent use is made of abstractions such as Man and Mankind. No gender bias is intended; rather, these abstractions reflect Victorian usage, not least in religious discourse.

6. *Oscar Wilde: Plays, Prose Writings and Poems,* edited by Isobel Murray (London: Dent, 1983), pp. 255-88. All quotations used here are from pp. 286-87.

7. Quoted in Michael Timko, *Innocent Victorian: The Satiric Poetry of Arthur Hugh Clough* (Columbus: Ohio University Press, 1966) p. 41.

8. Trawick, p. 117.

9. Trawick, p. 121.

10. Trawick, p. 121.

11. Evelyn B. Greenberger, *Arthur Hugh Clough: The Growth of a Poet's Mind* (Cambridge: Harvard University Press, 1970) p. 165.

12. Trawick, p. 285.

13. *The Oxford Diaries of Arthur Hugh Clough,* edited by Anthony Kenny (Oxford: Oxford University Press, 1990), p. 252.

14. *Oxford Diaries,* p. 252.

15. For an argument in favour of such an interpretation, see W. David Shaw, 'The Agnostic Imagination in Victorian Poetry', *Criticism,* 22 (1980), pp. 116-39.

16. David Newsome, *Two Classes of Men: Platonism and English Romantic Thought* (New York: St Martin's Press, 1974), p. 2.

17. Nathan A. Scott Jr., 'The "Conscience" of the New Literature', in *The Shaken Realist, Essays in Modern Literature,* edited by Melvin J. Friedman and John B. Vickery (Baton Rouge: Louisiana State University Press, 1970), p. 267.

18. Scott, p. 268.

19. Newsome, p. 8.

20. Newsome, p. 8.

21. For a fuller treatment of Clough's religious thought, see Robindra K. Biswas, *Arthur Hugh Clough: Towards a Reconsideration* (Oxford: Oxford University Press, 1972), Chapter 3.

22. Matthew Arnold, *Literature and Dogma* in *Dissent and Dogma,* edited by R. H. Super (Ann Arbor: University of Michigan Press, 1968), p. 409.

23. Trawick, p. 286.

24. Mulhauser, p. 663.

25. Walter E. Houghton, *The Poetry of Clough: An Essay in Revaluation* (New Haven: Yale University Press, 1963), p. 80.

26. Mulhauser, p. 663.

27. For effective use of the myth and the related story of Jacob, Rachel and Leah, see, for instance, 'The Bothie Of Tober-na-Vuolich', 'Jacob', 'Jacob's Wives', and also, incidentally but most significantly, 'Dipsychus', where after he has succumbed to the sardonic spirit, Dipsychus addresses himself in the following words, which are used in one epigraph to the present essay: 'O man, behold thy wife, th'hard naked world; / Adam accept thy Eve' (XIII.68-69).

28. The best exposition is the lecture on 'The Development of English Literature' delivered in 1852 at University College, London. See Trawick, pp. 124-42.

29. Trawick, p. 128.

30. Trawick, p. 128.

31. Trawick, p. 137.

32. For an extended treatment of Clough's argument, see R. A. Forsyth, 'The "inmost I"—Clough's Response to Culture and "mental anarchy"', *DUJ* [*Durham University Journal*], 52 (1991), 259-68.

33. Trawick, p. 131, p. 137.

34. Trawick, p. 138.

35. Matthew Arnold, 'Preface to First Edition of *Poems*' (1853), in *The Complete Prose Works of Matthew Arnold,* edited by R. H. Super (Ann Arbor: University of Michigan Press, 1960-1974), I, 1.

36. It is precisely this very considered approach to his undertaking, together with the fact that he was not a major or 'strong' poet (to use Harold Bloom's term from his psychoanalytic theory of literary tradition and its mode of functioning, put forward in *The Anxiety of Influence,* 1973, and *A Map of Misreading,* 1975), which prevented Clough from experiencing disabling 'anxiety' from the 'influence' of any 'precursors'. For if his theory *were* applicable here, Bloom would assert that Clough's 'swerving', like any other 'clinamen', would have been psychologically demanded as a 'victimisation' by the 'precursors' rather than decided on as a conscious manifesto by any potential 'ephebe'.

In connection with Clough's use of the myth the following are of interest: Jacqueline Johnson and Paul Dean, '"Paradise come back": Clough in Search of Eden', *DUJ,* 38 (1977), 249-53; Paul Dean and Jacqueline Moore, '"To Own the Positive and Present": Clough's Historical Dilemma', *DUJ,* 45 (1983), 59-62. See also Anthony Kenny, *God and Two Poets: Arthur Hugh Clough and Gerard Manley Hopkins* (London: Sidgwick and Jackson, 1988).

37. Max F. Schulz, *Paradise Preserved: Recreations of Eden in Eighteenth- and Nineteenth-Century England* (Cambridge: Cambridge University Press, 1985). See also Hilary Fraser, *Beauty and Belief: Aesthetics and Religion in Victorian Literature* (Cambridge: Cambridge University Press, 1986).

38. Schulz, p. 1.

39. Frank Kermode, *The Sense of an Ending, Studies in the Theory of Fiction* (New York: Oxford University Press, 1967), p. 39.

40. Kenny, p. 252.

41. Kermode, pp. 7, 39, 67.

42. Kermode, p. 59.

43. *Letters of John Keats,* edited by Robert Gittings (Oxford: Oxford University Press, 1987), p. 37.

44. John Milton, 'Areopagitica', in *Milton's Prose Writings,* edited by Kathleen M. P. Burton (London: Dent, 1958), p. 158.

## Janice E. Keller (essay date spring 1992)

SOURCE: Keller, Janice E. "New Light on Arthur Hugh Clough's Eight-Year Poetic Silence." *Victorian Newsletter,* no. 81 (spring 1992): 23-29.

[*In the following essay, Keller attempts to account for Clough's failure to produce any poetry from 1853 until the months just before he died in 1861.*]

Frederick L. Mulhauser's *The Correspondence of Arthur Hugh Clough* has been a foundation of Clough scholarship since its publication in 1957. In his introduction Mulhauser cites two stressful periods of Clough's life as those in which most of his major poetry was written, 1839-40 and 1849-51, the first during his undergraduate years at Balliol College, Oxford, the second while he was struggling to find a professional career (1: xvi). However, a third period of stress, which Mulhauser seems to misinterpret, occurred in 1852-53. In that period, in addition to the problem of finding employment, Clough found himself embroiled in a difficult courtship with Blanche Smith, whom he eventually married. Except for some conventional lyrics to Blanche, little poetry resulted from this stressful time, and up to now no satisfactory explanation for this lapse has been put forward.

In his introduction Mulhauser regards Clough's relationship with Blanche Smith as untroubled, and his choice of excerpts from Clough's and Blanche's letters almost fully supports this viewpoint. However, the full correspondence between Clough and Blanche shows a shifting pattern of attraction and retreat between them. Furthermore, an analysis of the manuscript letters, now in the Bodleian Library at Oxford, shows that Mulhauser, perhaps unintentionally, spliced two letters into one in a way that does not reflect the actual relationship of the two at this time. Mulhauser also seemed not to realize, along with other Clough scholars, that an 1853 letter to Blanche, from which Mulhauser gives an excerpt, helps to explain Clough's inability to write poetry during the period from May, 1853, until just before his death in November, 1861.

Clough's eight-year silence lasted more than one-third of his adult life, dating his maturity, as Clough did, from the age of 20. This period of silence, in a poet who had been so prolific that in his 42 years he wrote almost as many lines of poetry as his friend Matthew Arnold did in his 66 years, has intrigued almost all writers on Clough. Lytton Strachey blamed Florence Nightingale, whom Clough helped from 1857 to 1859 to produce her report on improving army medical practices, portraying her as an unmerciful taskmistress (169-82). Robindra Biswas conjectures that Clough's avoidance after 1853 of any intellectual work more demanding than reading newspapers, writing impersonal letters to his friends, and drudgery for Florence Nightingale served to sublimate undesired sexual thoughts (443-61). Chorley attributes Clough's silence to unspecified personal tensions which led to his acting as factotum to Miss Nightingale (318). However, blaming Miss Nightingale does not account for Clough's poetic silence from 1853 to 1857.

Clough's poetry, as we know, explored, often satirically, contemporary religious and social problems, including the role of women and the alienation of the intellectual in a mercantile age. Sometime in 1850 he met Blanche Smith, the eldest child of Samuel Smith, a wealthy Unitarian of Combe Hurst, Surrey.[1] Clough had just published two volumes of poetry, ***The Bothie of Tober-na-Vuolich*** in 1848, and, with Thomas Burbidge, a Rugby friend, ***Ambarvalia*** in 1849.

Eighteen fifty was a low point in Clough's life. He was unhappy with his position as principal of University Hall, a residence for students at University College, London, recently founded by the Unitarians and Presbyterians, finding that the requirement of religious conformity which had caused him to give up his Oxford fellowship had only been metamorphosed from Anglican to dissenting orthodoxy. Further, after eleven years as undergraduate, fellow, and tutor at Oxford, Clough missed the intellectual life and his friends at the older university. While he was expansive and articulate with old friends, he found himself shy, reserved and often lonely in London society. Nevertheless his two years at University Hall were productive of some of Clough's best poetry: ***Amours de Voyage,*** written during his 1849 stay in Rome at the time of the short-lived Mazzini republic, and *Dipsychus,* in which a fastidious young English intellectual in Venice is tempted by a worldly alter ego. Seeking more congenial employment, Clough first vainly tried to obtain a post in a new college proposed for Dublin and then, in late 1851, became a candidate for the positions of principal and classics professor at a college in Sydney. The prospect of putting half the globe between him and his friends and family seemed to have been the catalyst in his relations with Miss Smith. The correspondence between Clough and Blanche starts off at the point when he is waiting to hear from the college in Australia. On Clough's part the correspondence is from the first passionate, headlong, and so uncharacteristically candid that he expresses his hesitancies and hostilities. While initially formal—addressing him for the first few months mostly as "Dear Mr. Clough"—and puzzled by his epistolary barrage, Blanche shortly was equally, and devastatingly, honest.

Blanche Mary Shore Smith came from a family which moved in the highest social circles in England. She was a double first cousin of Florence Nightingale, her mother being Florence Nightingale's redoubtable "Aunt Mai," who accompanied her niece to Turkey during the Crimean War. Blanche herself was more conventional. A traditional upper-middle class Victorian daughter, she dutifully obeyed her parents, travelling with them even after her marriage to Clough. However, Blanche had a firm sense of her own importance. A short "chronology" of her life which she sent Clough in March, 1853, shows that as a child she was spirited and self-willed. The contrast between Blanche's willfulness between the ages of seven and nine and Clough's premature seriousness at the same age is marked. Blanche at that age: "Once stole a gingerbread out of a shop; another time struck a respectable governess . . . Used to enjoy life pretty well on the whole . . ." (Mulhauser 2: 619). Clough, however, under the age of ten refused to remove his shoes and stockings at the beach and join his brothers and sister in paddling in the water.

As an adult Blanche was, behind a facade of traditional female passivity, both strong-willed and competent. While during their courtship Blanche was loath to follow Clough's urging that she practice translating the French historian Guizot, in the years following Clough's death she not only edited his works, arranged for their publication, and wrote a memoir of him, but she also published her translation of Jacob Burckhardt's *The Cicerone.*

By failing to include a representative selection of the letters which show Clough, possibly unconsciously, attempting to extricate himself from his engagement to Blanche, Mulhauser allies himself with the bulk of Clough criticism. Most of the extensive commentary published on Clough since his death has tended to ac-

cept Blanche's rather self-serving account of Clough's relationship with her, based mainly on the memoir she wrote for the 1869 *Poems and Prose Remains of Arthur Hugh Clough,* which she edited with the aid of John Addington Symonds. Only a few critics, such as Dennis Enright, have doubted that Clough unhestitatingly embraced matrimony, and Blanche. But a close look in the Bodleian at the stiff ecru-tinted sheets of the letters which Clough and Blanche wrote in England and the flimsy blue tissue on which Clough, in America, scribbled both horizontally and vertically—"crossing" to save paper—shows Clough as highly ambivalent about marrying Blanche and Blanche as initially cool but ultimately determined to possess her evasive suitor.[2]

In the first letter, on December 30, 1851, Clough tells Blanche: "You must not believe me too much . . . I do talk too pretty when I am sitting by you. . . . I was given to that vice . . . and then took to holding my tongue. . . . You must let me say bad things when with you, to make sure of my not saying them when I leave you—for I have a most terrible reluctance to give pain. . . ." By "bad things" Clough presumably means those words which Blanche regarded as too explicitly sexual. He jokes that it was the "devil" which prompted him during a recent walk to say a word to her from which she recoiled, but, more seriously, he explains that the cause of his offense is their age difference. "At the age of 33 men are to [sic] bad, and at 23 girls are so unprepared for it." He asks Blanche whether she wants him to address her as he had spoken during their walk or in "the sycophantic, wheedling, caressing, self-bepraising tone more familiar to you? It is because you will hate all this that I write it." He adds a postscript, "There my dear Blanche, I have kissed the paper that is to go to you. What other piece of sentimentality could I commit?" The next day he again apologizes for having shocked her and, alluding to the story of the Gadarene swine, assures her he has "exorcised the ill spirit though this kind cometh not out in a hurry and I have been sitting among the tombs and in desert places pretty well two years now," a reference undoubtedly to his two years at University Hall.

In Blanche's first note, dated January 1st, she apologizes for having scolded him. "I may have been too hard in giving you such a bitter return for your honesty." He replies the same day that she *was* "too hard," but insists that even if she or all other womankind together cast him off he does not care.

> I ask no girl to be my friend that we may be a fond foolish couple together all in all each to the other. I will ask no one to put off her individuality for me; nor will I, weak and yielding as I am, if I can help it, put off mine for anyone. We are companions—fellow labourers—to the end of our journey here. . . .

> (qtd. in Mulhauser 2: 301)

Then Clough's honesty is only too revealing: "Don't be frightened, for I am a horrid coward at bottom, and you will be able to hen-peck me in no time." But immediately he reverses field and lashes out at her. He would not have written so "fiercely" if her letter had not upset him. He thinks she denies the doctrine of "fellow service" and prefers sentimental love, which he abhors. "It was the thought, I think, that you denied this doctrine . . . which made me write the other sheets [defending himself and reproaching her for rebuking him]—and made me do much more than that, let me tell you, but what, I will not tell you. . . ." But introspective honesty leads him to all but tell her.

> If you will not look at things in this way . . . I must even go my ways and seal myself up again. Was it this thought do you think or mortified vanity that made me after writing these 2 sheets go up and down the dark walk in St. James Park three-quarters of an hour or more tonight doing what I have hardly done since the year 1837?

While the implication of his soliciting a prostitute is inescapable, what is less clear is whether or not he expected sheltered, highly proper Blanche to catch his meaning. At any rate she seems not to have done so.[3]

The next day Clough admits to Blanche that he doubts as to whether they should marry and insists that every man contemplating marriage has such doubts. "If I have been ashamed to conceal mine from you, is that an insult to you? I think not."

After Clough was rejected for the Sydney post—his Oriel College provost would not recommend him because of his religious skepticism—Clough admits to Blanche that before he had applied for the position he had planned a solitary life in order to achieve "elevated action." But even though his purpose in approaching her has vanished, he still wants a life with her. He starkly explains in his Feb. 7th letter, "There has never been in my whole life . . . *any act* of mine, sealing either friendship or love." A month later he writes her that he fears that, in his anxiety to win her before going to Sydney, he was "somewhat brutal" toward her in his "precipitation and necessity."

However, despite impassioned, almost daily, letters to Blanche, Clough characteristically draws back. On Feb. 19th he suggests she might find someone else and states that: "I, for my part, *look about* but do not, *yet* see anybody . . . who . . . may understand things in me better than. . . ." and he trails off. Unsurprisingly, in her answer to this, Blanche writes flatly: "I don't know why I always feel spiteful when I write to you." Clough is not deterred. He concludes a letter: "When you next dislike me mind and let me know. Ever yours all the same AHC."

In general, though, Blanche seems content to play the role that the early Victorians assigned to unmarried, middle-class young women: naive, pious, passive, childlike, and, paradoxically, seeking guidance from males and acting as their moral guides.[4]

Although Clough is wildly miscast in the part of masterful male, he attempts to fill the role, addressing her as "my dear child" and pretending to chide himself for not preferring her cousin Florence Nightingale, who is "more sensible and practical (and indeed! more generally intelligent) than B. M. S. S." Ironically Florence is the Victorian woman probably most frequently cited as the antithesis of paradigmatic Victorian femininity. Even more ironic is Blanche's attempt to reverse Clough's dislike of Florence—he found her too intellectual and hard—in light of his later selfless, and self-destroying, overwork for Florence's proposals to reform British military medical practices.

Blanche, unlike Florence, observes the conventions assigned to early Victorian women. She writes to Clough:

> I always wanted somebody else to do for me, to teach me and keep me up, and punish me when I do wrong, instead of having to do it wearily oneself. While you do some of that for me, dear—I know it is childish, but there, you know, that is a settled thing . . . I like better to be comfortable than almost anything else is not that selfish . . . I am too lazy even to read, which is one reason why I never know anything. . . .

During an April, 1852, visit to Rugby, Clough first jocularly notes the resemblance between the local geological formations and the appearance of the peasantry and then pedantically remarks that place names ending in -by were of Norse derivation. "Read, my dear child, Yes, and elevate yourself now and then. . . ." Obviously unaware that he has been hectoring, he then asks innocently: "What is it that you sometimes feel spiteful at me about?" Her mocking response is to address him as "My dear old man."

Clough's tendency to quote himself—*Dipsychus* opens with lines from **"Easter Day, Naples 1849"**—appears in his correspondence with Blanche. In response to her questioning whether her "mysticism" repels him—it does not, but it does "pain" him—Clough writes: "It seems His newer will we should not think at all of Him, but [turn?] and of the world that He has given us make what best we may." This is, of course, almost word-for-word the religious philosophy of the eponymous hero of *Dipsychus* in Scene 10. 11-14.

A page later Clough is ironically skeptical and then breaks off as he realizes Blanche cannot follow him. "Good truth, I suppose, must relate to things in heavenly places and have no plain or intelligible reference to fact and reality . . . (no, it is a shame to taunt you with that!)." Soon after, in response to a letter in which Blanche asked what the "objects of life" were, Clough replies: "(a) work for others (b) personal relations and (c) making books, poems, music, etc." His role as a maker of poems seems to have been Clough's major attraction to Blanche. In an early April, 1852, letter in which she discusses a number of his published poems she for the first time calls him "my darling." By mid April Clough, who, up until then, had been unwilling to use the word "love," also has advanced to avowals, writing to her "I love you very much my dear child." (Clough's favorite pet name for Blanche is "dear child," and almost every letter closes with "God bless you, my dear child.")

Perhaps it is Blanche's increased ardor that sparks Clough's immediate retreat, or perhaps his own declaration of love frightened him. Whatever the reason, in mid-May (Mulhauser dates Clough's letter May 14th), Clough wrote Blanche to suggest they separate, citing his inability to find employment. While Mulhauser excerpts this letter, he does not mention its successor of the following day. In it Clough admits that his decision to write the previous day's letter, suggesting they separate, resulted from his discovering that the decision to marry was his and Blanche's—not her parents' as he had thought. "Do you not see too that it was not until I knew that your father and mother would leave it to us, that the question came properly before me?" This letter is followed in the manuscripts by the one Mulhauser dates as May 17th (2: 313). In it Clough asserts that he sought "life-companionship" with Blanche when he expected a "career"—in Sydney—but he no longer has that prospect. He holds out the chill hope that even if they are parted in this world they will be joined in some future existence and adds: "It is no selfish weariness of hoping against hope or prospects of other happiness, surely, that has led me thus far on the track that leads away. . . ." But here Mulhauser prints three sentences from a letter that was written on May 21st, according to a penciled notation, in which Clough announces that he is thinking of going to America. The unwarranted implication of Mulhauser's combining of the two disparate letters is that Clough's "track that leads away" takes him across the Atlantic to find a job so he can marry Blanche, which is not, in fact, the actual case.

The letters between the two conflated sections show Blanche skillfully trying to retain Clough and yet acting within the role of "proper" Victorian female. (The excellent British postal system enabled them to exchange letters two and three times daily.) First, in response to her sending him rhododendrons and scarlet azaleas, Clough self-deprecatingly begs her not to send him flowers as "they are a great deal too beautiful for me." He insists that only by renouncing her will he be able to find profitable work. In her response Blanche hopes that if they separate Clough will "keep generally good." She asks him to meet her the next day in a London park and

concludes by pleading: "Let me stay with you, dear." He declares in his reply, "I must *go away* in order to work." While he concedes the life together she sees is possible, he thinks "it would be best preceded by some interval of absence." He suggests they tell her mother he has no prospect of an income and refuses to meet her in the park because it is raining and his pupil is still with him, the latter a disingenuous reason since he earlier had postponed pupils and cut short their lessons in order to see her. After the appointed meeting time passes he sends Blanche a note defending his refusal to meet her: If he had gone and she had not, she would have been sorry! Furthermore their meeting in the park without her mother's knowledge would have been improper.

Blanche's masterly handling of this temporizing forecasts who will predominate. She had gone to the park, but had not expected him and was sure he had thought of her. It was not raining hard, and the flowers she had bought for him she gave to an old woman. Blanche then shrewdly combines bullying and flattery.

> It is difficult not to feel insulted when you do not respond. . . . If we do go on together I shall . . . be willing to learn strength of you. This is the greatest comfort to me to feel you strong and determined to do the right thing.

To further cajole him, Blanche resorts to standard elements of the myth of female inferiority: that women live for love and that meaningful work is solely the province of men. She argues that their being together would not hinder his working and wishes that she could do great work. "Is work the object of life? . . . Sometimes I am terribly inclined to think that love is the object of life. I am afraid it is the weakness of my sects [sic]." She cannily concludes by proposing that they not enjoy each other but that each help the other to work.

Clough is at a loss to answer this masterly assault, admits his nature is perverse, and rejoices that she calls him "'Dear boy,' which is the appellation dearest to me in the whole world."[5] In his next letter to Blanche he has pulled himself together and announces he will not expect to meet her for a month. Blanche responds by praising the concept of work. "I should think I was cruel and wrong besides if . . . for my sake [you] languish in inactivity instead of doing some good work." Then, using a revealing adverb, she states: "I do love you so much now, dear boy. . . ."

In reply Clough admits he is selfish and in the wrong, but he pleads for "Time, time." It is then that Clough first announces that he may go to America, 70 folio pages later than Mulhauser places Clough's initial mention of his plan to leave England: "It seems to me that at the present the natural course is to take it quietly and patiently. I will wait—perhaps go over to America first—You shall see." He adds:

> [Y]ou might within two or three years see someone you should like more than me. I have felt this all along. I have checked you through my own coldness perhaps. . . . Under such circumstances . . . I do not think we are arrived at the moment for union.

The summer of 1852 finds their correspondence increasingly disjunctive. Traveling in Devon with her family, Blanche writes to Clough: "I do wish you were here my darling—you can't think how I want you—." Clough writes: "Believe me, if you feel me doing you harm . . . I will leave you at your slightest indication of the wish—for whatever length of time you please."

But in July Clough's reluctance to commit himself begins to be interspersed with expressions of physical passion: "I must stop a bit, take you into my arms, as it were, and give you a few, few kisses." A letter from Blanche also shows their relationship is growing warmer.

> I like you so much, my darling. I wish you were here. Do you think you would like me as much afterwards. Indeed I'm afraid not . . . it's only yesterday morning I was sitting on your knees being scolded for being cross but I had to box your ears for it. My own darling.

From the time he embarked in November, 1852, for Boston, Clough wrote voluminously to Blanche. In America although he was lionized by Boston's literary and social leaders, Clough was miserably lonely, recapitulating his boyhood experience of separation by the Atlantic from those he loved. In addition his indecisiveness not only kept him from starting proposed schools in Concord and in a southern Boston suburb, but even prevented him from deciding whether to stay in America or return to England. Financially he was no better off than he had been in London. He tutored a few pupils in Greek, wrote some magazine articles and poems, and started a painstaking revision of Dryden's translation of Plutarch's *Lives*. But from the sheer quantity of his letters to Blanche, Clough must have spent much of his time writing to her.[6]

Pages in each letter are devoted to assertions of love, even lover's babytalk—Clough wants to talk to her a "little-ittle-bit." He shows his characteristic self-deprecation in November when he writes: "I only fear I shall be too happy with you." A few days after Christmas, 1852, he complains to Blanche that his friends have not written to him and encloses the poem "That out of sight is out of mind." In January, 1853, he fears he shall be *"almost unwisely"* fond of her. Constantly he implores her to join him in America, about which he is ambivalent. "I am sometimes a little tired, a little sick, sometimes perhaps of the people, who are good enough, but strange to me and not at bottom quite like English people—." On the other hand, responding to Blanche's question as to why he was eloquent by mail but tongue-tied when he was with her, he writes:

> [H]aving come across the water, which I didn't like the thought of, makes me think myself to have done something—so as to loose my tongue. Another thing is that this country is so much more hopeful *for me,* and the people so much more so than London people—

The emotional firestorm which led Clough to abandon poetry for eight years began to build up shortly after he departed from England, leaving boxes of his manuscripts and letters with Blanche. Mulhauser quotes the pertinent elements of Clough's and Blanche's interchanges. In early December Blanche writes for permission to read *Dipsychus.*

> Will you please to give me leave to read *Dipsychus,* for I want to. I have put some of my books in that box . . . so please write and tell me to read it all. . . .
>
> (Mulhauser 2: 350n)

With justifiable anxiety, Clough replies: "[P]lease don't read *Dipsychus* yet—I wish particularly not. You shall see it sometime—but not now, not, please—dear, I beg not. . . ." Of all Clough's poems the one most likely to offend Blanche was *Dipsychus,* in which a Mephistophelian Spirit tries to seduce a chaste young man with Venetian prostitutes. Then, on January 8, 1853, Blanche assures him:

> I won't read *Dipsychus,* dear Arthur, don't be afraid, you know I will do whatever you tell me; it was mere chance that I stumbled on that one poem, and I only just glanced it over, pray forgive me. . . .
>
> (Mulhauser, 2: 350n)

But like another young woman, Blanche could not resist opening the forbidden box. In early March she wrote that she had dipped into the manuscripts and was appalled by what she found:

> It is strange those peeps and reminders of your old times and thoughts and your other sides always upset me . . . it is horrid—they seem to me full of honest coarse strength and perception . . . but I don't like it. I don't like men in general; I like women—why was not the world made all women. . . . I did hardly know that good men were so rough and coarse.
>
> (Mulhauser, 2: 402-03n)

Blanche's thunderbolt devastated Clough, lonely, in a foreign land, and without means of support. He hysterically both complains and capitulates to Blanche in a 5,300-word letter which he wrote over a six-day period that included Good Friday and Easter Sunday. While much of the letter is excerpted by Mulhauser on pages 402-05, some of Clough's self-flagellation that Mulhauser does not include is worth quoting:

> You are above me—better than me. I am soiled—why should I therefore try and come near you. . . . If I had worked more quietly and diligently at my regular work, the feelings you abhor so would not have come upon me perhaps. . . .

The implication is that if Clough had confined himself to tutoring and not written poetry he would not have felt, much less written about, the horrid, coarse masculine emotions that repelled Blanche.

By Easter Sunday Clough is incoherent and defensive.

> Truly it is possible that without a loss of your own self to pity from afar off those aberrations which indeed it is very very hard for anyone who does not shut himself from the life of men and their words to keep wholly clear of. . . . O my dear Blanche, I hope without taking one step downward you will be able to reach out your hand to me. . . . Cannot you do so, cannot you take me up. . . .

Easter Monday he continues:

> Your letter gave me the feeling that if you knew (as you say) all my ideas you would have nothing to say to me . . . that you should be *revolted* . . . you don't know how horrible such thoughts are to me . . . if a few words sufficed . . . to *take away every feeling of tenderness*. . . . Do you think there is no change in me since I used to write letters to Tom Arnold [Matthew's next youngest brother] or whoever else it might be. . . . Did you ever express any dislike that I did not submit to, at least, and respect and learn to understand?

Clough's panic in response to Blanche's censure is understandable, but now seems both ludicrous and pathetic. Blanche, a product of an era in which Mrs. Grundy and Podsnap were unassailable, was indeed formidable, and Clough himself knew that his poetry was too avant garde in its discussion of sexuality and morality for him to finish, much less publish, *Dipsychus.* It also was Clough's misfortune that in his emotional neediness he was overmatched by someone as implacable as Blanche. Shortly after Clough's outburst of self-abnegation, Blanche continues excoriating him about what she had seen in his boxes of letters and manuscripts, but simultaneously retains her stance of childlike dependence on him.

> I felt very hard and angry at first—with the ideas it put into my head. . . . I could not suppose you did not know about wrong, but to be thinking, speaking . . . of things in any way but the highest it incensed me as if you really thought so. Is it necessary for men to coarsen their imaginations. It is curious how very seldom you read any poems, any book of any kind that does not in any degree offend. . . . I hope you are not angry with me. . . .

Whipsawed between the loving, clinging Blanche and the stern, admonishing Blanche—the split angelic / demonic personality types which Victorians contradictorily expected in their women, according to Auerbach—Clough capitulated. Since he could not, like Browning's character, compartmentalize his life between his lover at night and "a world of men" by day, he gave up the poetry that offended his fiancée, returned to England in July, 1853, for a government job found through Carlyle, and married Blanche the following June. Except for **"O ship, ship, ship,"** which Clough wrote for Blanche on May 6, 1853, and which he described as "a doggerel ballad all about nothing," and possibly three other poems which were published in an American magazine in the summer of 1853, Clough abandoned writing poetry from Easter 1853 until a few months before his death in 1861.

Blanche gives her own explanation of the silent years in the memoir she wrote for *The Poems and Prose Remains of Arthur Hugh Clough.* (Indeed, Blanche was indefatigable in organizing editions of Clough's works posthumously, beginning only two weeks after his death.) Blanche's explanation is both disingenuous and confused. She begins:

> It has often been a subject of surprise, that with such evident powers and even facility of production, Clough should have left so little behind him, even considering the shortness of his life, and that for such long periods he should have been entirely silent.
>
> (1: 40)

Since there had been no previous mention of "such long periods" of silence, Blanche seems to be trying to distract attention from the only actual period of silence. Then she alleges that Clough wrote only during "short intervals" when he was free from "the pressure of constant and hard practical work" (1: 40). But Clough's job as an examiner in the Privy Council Education Office was not demanding. Until he added his unpaid labors for Miss Nightingale to his workday, Clough's hours were from 10 to 4 with eight weeks annual vacation.

When Blanche, as the unacknowledged memoirist, describes Clough's life after marriage, her explanations of his poetic silence becomes defensive.

> [I]n June 1854 he married. For the next seven years he lived quietly at home. . . . No events of any moment marked this period; but it was one of real rest and contentment . . . he was able . . . to devote his great faculties freely to the service of others. Up to this date we may almost say that he had been too free from active and absorbing employment for his own happiness.
>
> (1: 44)

Now Blanche implies that when Clough wrote before his marriage he was too *un*occupied to be happy. To her it was only when he was occupied—and not writing—that he was happy. While a bachelor Clough had time to speculate, but marriage ended vain, solitary philosophizing.

> [T]he want of definite and continuous occupation left his mind free to deal restlessly with the great insoluble problems of the world. . . . After his marriage there was none of this enforced and painful communing with self alone. He had plenty to do; and the close relations . . . with his wife's family kept him actively employed. . . .
>
> (44-45)

According to Blanche marriage for Clough had blunted the irritating aspects of his character and molded him into perfection. His humor, which had tended to "irony and sarcasm," now was "natural and healthy." His home life "made many perplexed questions, both social and religious, clear and simple to his mind" (1: 45). She delicately hints that to her goes the credit for Clough's transformation and that an epiphany was about to occur:

> The close and constant contact with another mind gave him a fresh insight into his own, and developed a new understanding of the wants of other people . . . it is quite certain, from little things which he was in the habit of saying, that, had he been permitted, he would have expressed his mature convictions in works of a more positive and substantial kind.
>
> (1: 45)

While it is simplistic to portray Blanche as a succubus, draining Clough of his poetic power, the record of their correspondence and Blanche's memoir indicate a dialectic between them that resulted in his poetic stasis. Only in the last few months of his life did Clough return to poetry, three short poems and *Mari Magno,* a long poem modelled on *The Canterbury Tales,* in which travelers on a ship bound to Boston from England exchange stories about love and marriage. Probably awareness that his life was ending enabled Clough to drop his self-imposed ban and create tales that extolled natural love and sexuality, defying the restrictive morality of both his wife and his time. The one *Mari Magno* tale which critics find embodies conventional prudery may be read as a fantasy of revenge against Blanche for her and his doctors' having exiled him to the south of Europe for his health. It is to Blanche's credit that she did not try to suppress this tale or the others in *Mari Magno* which she found objectionable, although she did argue against including some of them in his collected works.

Indeed in Clough's last days his revived poetic impulse seems to have been sustained by Blanche's love and care. In Florence, on his deathbed, Blanche aided him as he struggled to write the last *Mari Magno* poem,

"The Lawyer's Second Tale," although later she expressed distaste for the story. The tale endorses the love idyll of Christian, a symbolically named Scots girl, with an Oxford fellow. When the Oxford fellow returns briefly to his college, Christian, pregnant, is taken unwillingly to Australia by her uncle and aunt. Years later, happily married to a wealthy man, Christian returns to England and gives their child to the former Oxford fellow, whose marriage to a barren English aristocrat is also symbolic. This seems to be a further, and most daring, development of a theme that often engaged Clough: love between an unspoiled, sensitive, yet hard-working country girl, usually Scottish, and an Oxford fellow or student. But only in *Mari Magno* does Clough advance far beyond the conventional views of contemporary writers: a woman who by all the rules of Victorian society would be considered "immoral" is, unlike Lady Dedlock, not only *not* punished, but is rewarded. She is truly worthy of her name: loving, nonjudgmental both of her lover's leaving her and her relatives' forcing her to leave him, and self-sacrificingly willing to give her son up to his father.

The social, sexual, and religious concerns of Clough's productive period seemingly had simply lain fallow during his eight-year drought. Clough's probing mind, which questioned the validity of all *a priori* givens, except truth itself, had refused to be quelled. *Mari Magno* is a poignant reminder that Clough, before his inner tensions caused him to surrender to Blanche's prudery and cease writing poetry, was among the few Victorian poets whose sole interest was grappling with the pressing concerns of his era.

*Notes*

1. Clough was introduced to Blanche Smith by Richard Monckton Milnes, author, politician, friend of Tennyson and Thackeray, and, for nine years, a suitor of Florence Nightingale. Ironically, Milnes was also a collector of erotica.

2. Except where noted, the sections of letters excerpted are not included in Mulhauser's *Correspondence.* While most are headed only by the day of the week, some can be dated by internal evidence. The excerpts appear in the chronological order determined by the Bodleian, which received the correspondence in 1959.

3. In his introduction to *The Oxford Diaries of Arthur Hugh Clough,* Anthony Kennedy conjectures that obscure references in the diaries may indicate Clough had sexual relations with perhaps two country women living in towns near Oxford (lxiii).

4. See essays in *Suffer and Be Still: Women in the Victorian Age,* ed. Martha Vicinus, especially the essay by Peter T. Cominos, and Nina Auerbach's *Women and the Demon: The Life of a Victorian*

*Myth* 67-73. Also, in her multifarious writings, Blanche's friend Harriet Martineau frequently expressed the archetypal Victorian view that women were expected to set the pattern of morality and guide men.

5.  Katharine Chorley in her biography theorizes Clough had an unresolved Oedipal complex (352-54). Clough's preference for being considered a "dear boy" might support this view.

6.  For details of Clough's experiences in America in 1852-53 see *Correspondence* 2: 329-453 *passim*, and Levy's chapter 9: 139-162.

### Works Cited

Auerbach, Nina. *Woman and the Demon: The Life of a Victorian Myth.* Cambridge: Harvard UP, 1982.

Biswas, Robindra Kumar. *Arthur Hugh Clough: Towards a Reconsideration.* Oxford: Clarendon, 1972.

Chorley, Katharine. *Arthur Hugh Clough: The Uncommitted Mind.* Oxford: Clarendon, 1962.

Clough, Arthur Hugh. *The Correspondence of Arthur Hugh Clough.* Ed. Frederick L. Mulhauser. 2 vols. Oxford: Clarendon, 1957.

———. *The Poems of Arthur Hugh Clough.* Ed. F. L. Mulhauser. 2nd ed. Oxford: Clarendon, 1974.

———. *The Poems and Prose Remains of Arthur Hugh Clough: With a Selection from his Letters and a Memoir.* Ed. his wife. 2 vols. London: Macmillan, 1869.

Clough, A. H. and Blanche Smith. Eng. lett. ms. e. 77-81. Bodleian Library, Oxford.

Clough, B. S. Eng. lett. ms. d. 179. Bodleian Library, Oxford.

Cominos, Peter T. "Innocent Femina Sensualis in Unconscious Conflict." *Suffer and Be Still: Women in the Victorian Age.* Ed. Martha Vicinus. Bloomington: Indiana UP, 1972.

Enright, Dennis. "A Kidnapped Child of Heaven: The Poetry of Arthur Hugh Clough." Byron Foundation Lectures. Nottingham: U of Nottingham, 1972.

Kenny, Anthony, ed. *The Oxford Diaries of Arthur Hugh Clough.* Oxford: Clarendon, 1990.

Levy, Goldie. *Arthur Hugh Clough: 1819-1861.* London: Sidgwick and Jackson, 1938.

Mulhauser, Frederick L., ed. *The Correspondence of Arthur Hugh Clough.* 2 vols. Oxford: Clarendon, 1957.

Strachey, Lytton. *Eminent Victorians: Cardinal Manning, Dr. Arnold, Florence Nightingale, General Gordon.* New York: Harcourt, 1918.

Vicinus, Martha, ed. *Suffer and Be Still: Women in the Victorian Age.* Bloomington: Indiana UP, 1972.

### Robert Johnson (essay date spring 1992)

SOURCE: Johnson, Robert. "Waiting for *Thou*: Resurrecting Clough's 'Seven Sonnets.'" *Victorian Newsletter,* no. 81 (spring 1992): 59-61.

[*In the following essay, Johnson finds that Clough's thinking anticipates "modernist angst," citing as an example the affinities between his "Seven Sonnets" and Samuel Beckett's* Waiting for Godot.]

"To have lived is not enough for them," explains Vladimir as he and Estragon ponder the need of the deceased to "talk about their lives," in Samuel Beckett's celebrated evocation of modern angst. Waiting for Godot, a primary need, even of the dead, is to say something. "Say anything at all!" Vladimir urges (40-41).[1] According to *Godot,* talking, naming our experiences into meaningful patterns, supplies one of the basic strategies humans use to survive their endless, patient vigil. Meanwhile, they long for the arrival of divine, or logical, affirmation. The mind relentlessly at work, scheming linguistic structures in which to locate human significance becomes an image for life's central struggle.

Such diligence is, after all, a source of human dignity. "We have kept our appointment," Vladimir affirms, "and that's an end to that. We are not saints, but we have kept our appointment" (51). To wit, given the options of embracing a willful death or waiting and talking in hopes of receiving meaning from outside of ourselves, humans may choose to wait, and to talk, and to keep themselves busy. Estragon notes: "We always find something, eh Didi, to give us the impression we exist?"

"Yes, yes," Vladimir agrees, "we're magicians" (44).

Beckett's portrait of human perseverance at the crossroads of aspiration and material limitations was not a model easy for audiences to swallow. Early patrons walked out. They refused to accept Beckett's vision as *theater* or as a picture of their lives. Thus, the reputation of *Godot* for breaking intellectual ground in the arts. (For a good critical / historical overview, see Kenner and Graver.)

Yet, nearly a century before Beckett's work debuted, Arthur Hugh Clough labored over a series of poems collected as the **"Seven Sonnets"** of 1851, which directly anticipate in tone Beckett's modernist point of view.[2] In fact, while the poems were left in manuscript form, the group deserve careful attention from readers of Victorian verse. They offer solid documentation of Clough's insightful movement toward positions we now regard as norms for art of the generation to follow his own. Indeed, they document Clough's importance as a thinker.

What, ask the sonnets, is the basis for human understanding of existence, given the limitations of logic, imagination, spiritual insight? Moreover, the group question, are we not—even as Beckett will demonstrate in *Godot*—caught squarely between "despair" and "hope"? Are we not driven to the deliberate, though absurd, ritual of questioning the very imponderables of our situation, simply as a means of living?

Even the tone of Clough's poems foreshadows *Godot*'s wordy attack on the ability of language to grapple with life's quandaries. The sonnets begin and end as formal disputation: a logical attempt to quantify the nature of human confusion. They replicate, one Clough scholar writes, the "resonant gravity" of the intellect at work upon life's essential questions as the mind "circles on its own sense of mystery" (Biswas 371). This is language *as* ritual, as an act of meaning-making. Even as do Estragon and Vladimir's exchanges under their scrawny tree, Clough's poems document the edgy, determined rhetorical behaviors humans embrace in the place of certainty.

**Sonnet I** opens upon the ultimate human fact: Everything passes away. Children die. Life cannot be trusted to respect "dawning" human beauty (l. 2). Nor, the poem asserts, does it seem unnatural that the efforts of the old should be replaced by those of the young (ll. 4-9). We simply grow accustomed to loss. "But," Clough points out, the fact that a person

> Whose perfectness did not at all consist
> In things towards forming which time could have done
> Anything—whose sole office was to exist—
> Should suddenly dissolve and cease to be. . . .
>
> (ll. 10-13)

is a certainty that tries our deepest understandings. What crime can it be merely to exist, that it merits death? The question daunts human comprehension.

We can accept, at least intellectually, **Sonnet II** continues, that the universe, *N*ature, functions in manners beyond our ken. Nature's only "ordinance" being to continue its own grand movements without regard to individual, flickering human consciousness, we recognize—as theory.

Yet, the sonnet also acknowledges, we like to believe ourselves more than "flowers, beasts." And, if man is to conceive of himself as "a Person and a Soul"—in pos-

session of some continuing or non-material element beyond that which decays—then accepting the limitations of uncertainty and sure loss is powerfully disturbing (ll. 9-14)! It is one thing to embrace Nature as a repository of divine or primary purpose; quite another to level ourselves with all the perishable matter in Nature's closet, to be the equal of an ant or leaf or tree.

Romantic pantheism, it would seem, does not soothe Clough's concerns. The returning smoke lines along Mr. Wordsworth's celebrated woody ridge, with its parade of anonymous loss and return, does not provide Clough assurances of a cosmic home.

Nor, **Sonnet III** continues, is there necessarily to be found relief in some Keatsian song of harvest and autumnal splendor. We may well indulge ourselves in the sensuous wonder of Nature's fullness at the cusp of season's change. Moreover, to "see the rich autumnal tints depart," to witness the glow of winter's sun retreat from fields of snow, may a "strange thankfulness impart" (ll. 1-3, 8). But only because it is easier to lose beauty totally than to watch it in the balance, to long for its continuance before our senses. The "assurance" of loss, the poem counsels, offers pleasure because it conquers "blank dismay" (ll. 11-12). Better to lose beauty, than to agonize over its inescapable potential to fade.

"But," **Sonnet IV** counters, if, as human wisdom and man's heart and narrative story would hold, there *is* some essential bit of identity or existence that is not lost through change, then we must believe, as well, that some *Thou* "still" exists who understands or watches over this process of birth and decay (l. 12). In addition, with the embracing of such belief, the "patient heart" is temporarily satisfied and does not push the issue: "The where and how [of *Thou*'s existence, that heart] doth not desire to hear" (l. 14).

How like the awkward patience of *Godot* is this satisfaction. If we are willing, Clough's sonnets argue, to accept as fact the projections of our own thinking, desires, and fictions, we can be lulled into a contentment out of which we rarely climb to seek ultimate answers.

Clearly, though, this patience is not an absolute confidence, not a faith to move mountains. **Sonnet V** asks of *Thou*: If it is that you are "casual" (ll. 1-2) in creating and removing the individual elements of your handiwork, how many infinite-seeming ages must pass before "hopes dead-slumbering" in human kind may "dare to reawake" (l. 7)? "What worse than dubious chances interpose" between humans and divine light to "recompose / The skiey picture [they] had gazed upon" (ll. 12-14)? The romanticized adjective *skiey* itself labels the lost confidence as belonging to flighty realms of trust no longer accessible by the narrative voice of the poems. What are the odds that a "casual" Maker will come to our collective aid, anyway?

"But," continues **Sonnet VI,** whether our edgy patience be a "self-willed arbitrary creed," a deliberate closed-mindedness in "service of untruth," or merely ignorance—embraced as does a dying man hold to important lies or a hunted bird turn away from an approaching enemy—"who about this shall tell us what to think" (ll. 3, 7-14)? Who can sort out what we are truly to believe?

*Thou* remains distanced; "skiey" beliefs lie scuttled over time. And humankind lacks the ability, the sonnets worry, ever fully to engage the ambiguities of our earthly predicament. Whom *would* we ask for answers?

Just so, Estragon pleads to discover, in all our human thrashing at unresolvables, "what truth will there be?" We will inevitably fall back into our endless speaking and forgetting: "We have time to grow old. The air is full of our cries. . . . But habit is a great deadener" (58). We *have* no one to speak with, ultimately, but ourselves. So, we keep doing it—that is our magic. The noisy self-questioning keeps us alive. Always changing our perspective upon our collective plight, but never reaching bottom in our disputations. We play through all our intellectual habits; then we wait, to ask more questions. The cycle buffers us against encountering the knowledge that our existence is difficult to attach to any surrounding, defining system of values.

Thus wonders Clough's final sonnet, as well: "Shall I decide it [what to believe] by a random shot?" (l. 1). Importantly, by asking such a question, we are not indulging in emotional theatrics. For, our hopes and fears are "not mere idle motions of the blood" (l. 3), but sincerely felt. Humans, at their best, *do* recognize the absurdity of their existences.

That is to say: On the one hand, we must suppose that there is a "seed" notion or impulse behind the universe in which we live (ll. 5-8). Yet, in spite of this urge, we cannot escape asking: "What if despair and hope alike be true" (l. 9)? In that case,

> The heart, 'tis manifest, is free to do
> Whichever Nature and itself suggest . . .
>
> (ll. 10-11)

a choice in which we may initially feel some freedom. However, even this sense of freedom does not remove us from acknowledging our status:

> . . . always 'tis a fact that we are here;
> And with our being here, doth palsy-giving fear,
> Whoe'er can ask, or hope accord the best?
>
> (ll. 12-14)

With which conclusion to the sonnet cycle, readers will recall once more the concerns of *Godot.* There is freedom to be had in being cut free of predetermining identities and allegiances. But. once severed from cosmic moorings, who can say if fear or hope is the appropriate response to our situation? To be constantly questioning the nature of our being *is* a conscious choice. Yet, accompanying that interrogation comes the knowledge that such questioning can never end with a sense of resolution. Questioning becomes a manner of living mirrored in the sonnet series' structure, opening in *given*'s, closing with an interrogative. Arguments over whether Clough's series is complete, therefore, seem moot: The series clearly demonstrates that its logical process cannot be concluded.[3] It ends in a question, and that is where humans have to live—in question.

The only position that we can affirm in all of our knowledge is our still being "here." This status has not changed because of or during the rhetorical maneuvering. All we have to build upon is physical existence. Even a format as clever and demanding as the sonnet offers but counterpoint to the knowledge that such arrangements provide artful elaboration of irreducible complexities.

We *are,* then, magicians: enamored of, devoted to, asking enough trying questions to keep our consciousnesses engaged for a bit, but always circling back to our being "here"—under our tree, on a road to who can say. Waiting. Questioning. Knowing that our choice is binary: remove ourselves physically, or patiently abide. We cobble *Thou* together from our worries, hoping it will respond to queries.

As a result, whatever one labels Clough's sonnet sequence—"early modern" or "pre-existential" or simply "high-water Doubt"—the group should not be overlooked in studies of essential Victorian verse. Arthur Hugh Clough, writing with admirable facility in a demanding poetic form born of Renaissance faith in intellect, has captured the spirit of art for a generation to come, a time when faith in intellect, ironically, will falter. He has peered deeply into concerns that will found twentieth-century Western philosophical discursion. Clough has realized that the modern world will sprout endless perspectives, but very few final explanations.

Additionally, Clough is disarmingly honest, his resolution to the series of poems being *not* to resolve the ambiguity uncovered in the course of their rhetorical progress. This willingness to identify the "here" of existence with an acceptance of the ineluctable nature of the questions he pursues would alone mark the sonnet sequence as sufficiently courageous to merit critical attention . . . and more frequent inclusion in standard anthologies.

Here, the expected mid-century philosophical solutions are never embraced—not romantic absorption into Nature, not leap (or return) to faith, not the continuity of sensuality, not even the hard resoluteness of agnosticism. As will Beckett in *Godot*, Clough leaves his art asking questions for the sake of asking, waiting for answers that the narrative voice apparently knows will not come. Whom *do* we ask? Juggling "hope" and "fear" as equals, we comprehend that all the conceivable ultimate solutions are quite probably projections of our own desires.

This is Arthur Hugh Clough's lonely, remarkable stance in his seven sonnets. They capture the thinking of an artist who has stepped into an intellectual arena that will attract, and stagger, minds from the age of Picasso on.

### Notes

1. All references to *Godot* are made to page numbers in the 1979 Grove edition.

2. Citations from the poems are located by line numbers in the Mulhauser edition, which replicates the text and order of Clough's MS. For a brief description of the original text, see Mulhauser 737-38.

3. Katherine Chorley notes of the sonnets: "the drafts in [Clough's] 1851 notebook, although very carefully worked over even as regards superficially insignificant words, do not always show whether he had made his final decision as to what words or phrase to choose of the various alternatives he is trying out. But it is hard to believe that he would have made any radical alterations, since they are already such accomplished work" (250).

### Works Cited

Beckett, Samuel. *Waiting for Godot.* New York: Grove, 1979.

Biswas, Robindra Kumar. *Arthur Hugh Clough: Towards a Reconsideration.* Oxford: Clarendon, 1972.

Chorley, Katherine. *Arthur Hugh Clough: The Uncommitted Mind.* Oxford: Clarendon, 1962.

Clough, Arthur Hugh. *The Poems of Arthur Hugh Clough.* Ed. F. L. Mulhauser. 2nd ed. Oxford: Clarendon, 1974.

Graver, Lawrence. *Samuel Beckett: Waiting for Godot.* Cambridge: Cambridge UP, 1989.

Kenner, Hugh. *Samuel Beckett: A Critical Study.* New York: Grove, 1961.

## Christopher M. Kierstead (essay date fall 1998)

SOURCE: Kierstead, Christopher M. "Where 'Byron Used to Ride': Locating the Victorian Travel Poet in Clough's *Amours de Voyage* and *Dipsychus*." *Philological Quarterly* 77, no. 4 (fall 1998): 377-95.

[*In the following essay, Kierstead demonstrates how Clough's travel poetry was at odds with the conventions of Victorian travel literature.*]

In the Spring of 1849, Giuseppe Mazzini, leader of the newly-declared Roman Republic, fought off attacks from French troops seeking to restore papal sovereignty over the city. At the same time, he withstood a siege of another sort: an obscure English poet, Arthur Hugh Clough, needed his permission to visit the guarded Vatican art gallery. A letter of introduction from Thomas Carlyle won Clough his pass, but the relative absurdity of the affair was not lost on the poet. To his mother, Clough confessed embarrassment at having to bother the hero of the Risorgimento with "trivial English tourist importunities" (1:257).[1] Clough furthermore must have wondered whether looking at statues was the best occupation for a poet at such a crucial moment in European history. Was this what Byron would do?

The importunate encounter with Mazzini grew out of two conflicting impulses in Clough. The first was the need to complete an obligatory step in the ritual of the Grand Tour, which also demanded visits to the coast and ancient ruins. The second impulse was more urgent. Clough was eager to turn his first-hand observation of events in Rome into poetry. Within the past year, he had achieved some success with a travel poem set in Scotland. *The Bothie of Tober-na-vuolich* (1848), a "long-vacation pastoral," concludes with the elopement of an Oxford undergraduate and a Scottish peasant girl, thus seeming to confirm the Republican sympathies of "Citizen Clough," as his fellow Oxonians sardonically called him.[2] The poem won positive reviews for its experimentation with meter and its perceptive, witty treatment of the social and intellectual controversies then consuming Oxford. Elizabeth Barrett Browning, for example, praised the poem's "vigour and freshness," while doubting, somewhat prophetically, whether Clough would rank among the great poets of the age—whether he was an *"artist."*[3] For a poet seeking to reach that next echelon, however, the continent must have seemed an inviting subject. As in Byron's day, Europe was in the midst of profound political upheaval. Clough in fact had recently witnessed the restoration of Republican government in Paris, although, like most reform-minded Victorians, he soon became disillusioned with Louis Napoleon. The fate of Italy, however, was not settled. Recent uprisings in Lombardy, Tuscany, and Rome still promised the resurgence of a new nation from the grip of old-regime politics—and new life for poetry that engaged contemporary political issues.

Indeed, Clough was not the only poet who had focused his attention on Italy. In Florence, Barrett Browning was working on *Casa Guidi Windows* (1851), a poem that would blend eye-witness description of events in Florence with analysis of the political factors that eventually forestalled any hope of unification in 1849. And before disappearing from the literary map with the demise of the "Spasmodic School," Sydney Dobell gained brief fame with *The Roman* (1850). The poem vigorously champions the cause of Italian independence, closing with a popular uprising and the chant of "Down with the Austrians! Arms! Blood! Charge! Death—death to tyrants. Victory! Freedom!"[4] Mazzini himself later congratulated Dobell: "You have written about Rome as I would, had I been a poet. And what you did write flows from the soul, the all-loving, the all-embracing, the prophet-soul."[5]

Clough, in contrast, was finding it difficult to adopt the role of Hero as Poet—to become Carlyle's assertive voice of the age. While intensely drawn to Rome's plight, he seemed unable to cultivate a public, overtly political persona—to progress beyond the roles of spectator, correspondent, and tourist. This struggle to find a voice, however, would fuel the two long works Clough did write in Italy: the epistolary travelogue *Amours de Voyage* (1849; publ. 1858) and the verse-drama *Dipsychus* (1850; publ. 1865), which Clough set in Venice. Both poems are semi-autobiographical records of the poet's response to the spectacle of modern Italy and to the ever-present "Byron"—in his varying guises as celebrated traveler, champion of nationalistic movements, and overall role model for poets. Clough had the opportunity both to continue a popular tradition of Grand Tour poetry and to promote the Risorgimento, but he instead turned his gaze squarely on himself. In *Amours de Voyage,* the disjointed and perplexing atmosphere of revolutionary Rome serves primarily to highlight the economic and cultural forces that construct the experience of travel and, indirectly, the poetry of travel. In *Dipsychus,* the protagonist's dialogue with his own disembodied "Spirit" dramatizes Clough's ambivalence about the ultimate benefits of travel for both the individual and the places visited. For Clough, the inscription of travel in poetry became a necessary if at times exasperating form of disillusionment—a skeptical avoidance of leaps of faith. As contemporary responses to the poems reveal, however, this mindset was at odds with the prevailing Victorian ideology of travel as self-affirmation. The result was that Clough would remain a tourist—an outsider—in the realm of Victorian poetry as well as in Mazzini's Rome.[6]

Even before the Risorgimento had re-ignited English interest in Italy, the country was, from a poetic point of view, well-worn terrain. The success of *Childe Harold's Pilgrimage* (1812-18) gave rise to a host of travelogues, some of them still widely read in Clough's day, such as Samuel Rogers' *Italy* (1822). William Wordsworth's later works include *Memorials of a Tour on the Conti-nent* (1820) and *Memorials of a Tour in Italy, 1837.* Following suit, Richard Monckton Milnes published his own *Memorials of a Residence on the Continent* in 1838. John Edmund Reade also wrote an *Italy* (1839; rev. 1844), and in the style of *Childe Harold,* divided it into four cantos of Spenserian stanzas. Typically, such poems describe the impressions left on the poet by various well-known destinations. The overall aim was to capture for readers the *genius loci*—a sublime spirit of place that produced moments of insight and self-discovery. Poetry that celebrated the continental *genius loci* was to some extent as much a part of the experience of travel as travel itself. A "beautiful passage" from *Childe Harold* or Rogers punctuates dozens of the landmarks described in John Murray's Italian guidebooks. Additionally, for those who preferred Byron's impressions in their entirety, Murray published a pocket-sized travel edition of his works.[7]

The poetic travelogue was one of the last genres of long poetry that could arguably be called "popular" at a time when, as Clough would remark in an 1853 review of "Recent English Poetry," "people much [preferred] *Vanity Fair* and *Bleak House.*"[8] The challenge facing the Victorian poet was to find a new niche in this crowded but still potentially profitable literary market. It was a challenge, as Clough's poetry reveals, that at times must have appeared overwhelming. "Murray" and "Byron" seem to lurk always just around the corner in the world of the poems. After first encountering the middle-class Trevellyns, Claude, the protagonist of *Amours de Voyage,* informs his correspondent Eustace that the mother "[q]uotes, which I hate, *Childe Harold*" (1.209).[9] For a traveler like Claude who initially professes originality, listening to misappropriated quotations from Byron would be distinctly tiresome. The Byronic pose—the bold but melancholy traveler—was becoming an overused, tarnished form of cultural capital.

Dipsychus seems equally troubled over what to do with Byron. Visiting the Venice Academy, he describes a painting of the poet as hero of Greek nationalism:

> . . . somewhat drest-up, [he] draws
> His sword, impatient long, and speaks
> Unto a tribe of motley Greeks
> His pledge word unto their brave cause.
>
> (9.5-8)

The lines convey a grudging respect for Byron, but they are also clearly ironic; indeed, throughout the poems, Clough seldom regards Byron in any other light. Whatever real political commitment Byron made is consumed in this "drest-up" publicity image, one that embodies the dual literary and "touristic" celebrity of Byron as Traveler. For Clough, this is an uneasy co-existence, one that compels him to consider new ways of constituting poetic authority—to envision a travel poetry that is evocative, insightful, but not Byronic.

Clough attempts to break free of Byron in a way that calls to mind Harold Bloom's principle of the "anxiety of influence" in poetic production. If (taking some liberty) we cast Clough as a "strong poet," he acknowledges Byron as a primary forbear while emphasizing his failure to meet the demands of a new era.[10] Clough's charge is that Byron invites the kind of appropriation perpetrated by the Trevellyns. Moving from one sublime locale to the next, Byron lures followers to a designated *genius loci*, like the following described in *Childe Harold*:

> Clear, placid Leman! thy contrasted lake,
> With the wild world I dwelt in, is a thing
> Which warns me, with its stillness, to forsake
> Earth's troubled waters for a purer spring.
> This quiet sail is a noiseless wing
> To waft me from distraction.
>
> (3.797-802)[11]

Clough's poems call attention to what Byron leaves out at such transcendent moments, or more accurately, what he failed adequately to anticipate—the economic apparatus of tourism. Clough emphasizes that the travel-induced epiphany cannot be celebrated as an untainted, wholly original aesthetic experience.

To some extent, Clough "creatively misreads" Byron here: the pre-touristic era to which Clough has assigned him is largely an invented trope of travel literature. As Jonathan Culler has observed of the genre, "the true age of travel has . . . always already slipped by; other travelers are always tourists."[12] Byron in fact carefully distinguishes himself from the "typical" traveler of his day. For example, the endnotes to *Childe Harold* serve as an on-going critique of Lord Elgin, who becomes a tourist indiscriminately romping over and plundering Greece.[13] But the crucial difference with Byron is that such concerns are mostly relegated to the extensive notes at the end of poem; they are not quite the issue at hand. With Clough, in contrast, the endnotes have invaded the poem. The traveler's landscape seems an entangled matrix of guidebooks, annoying tourists, and native workers alternately exploiting and being exploited by the British. It is an environment that invites constant second-guessing.

Even something as seemingly innocuous as a gondola ride raises problematic class issues for Dipsychus, who, like most travelers to Venice, eventually finds himself in a gondola. Struggling to achieve that moment of travel-inspired peace, Dipsychus recites an ode to the gondola—an obligatory component of any Italian travelogue. The ode also echoes Childe Harold at Leman:

> Could life, as does our gondola,
> Unvexed with quarrels, aims, and cares,
> And moral duties and affairs,
> Unswaying, noiseless, swift, and strong,
> For ever thus—thus glide along!
>
> (5.12-16)

The poem continues in the same vein until Dipsychus recalls that the gondola does not move on its own; partaking of the *genius loci* here seems to involve partaking of the native body in an uncomfortable way. The realization causes a confrontation with Dipsychus's Mephistophelean companion, the Spirit:[14]

DIPSYCHUS:

> How light we move, how softly! Ah
> Were all things like the gondola!
> So live, nor need to call to mind
> Our slaving brother set behind!

SPIRIT:

> Pooh! Nature meant him for no better
> Than our most humble menial debtor;
> Who thanks us for his day's employment,
> As we our purse for our enjoyment.

DIPSYCHUS:

> To make one's fellow-man an instrument—

SPIRIT:

> Is just the thing that makes him most content.
>
> (5.33-42)

For the Spirit, the gondolier exists either "behind the scenes" or as part of a picturesque "idea" of travel. In a canceled passage from an earlier draft, Clough continued to develop the implications of the Spirit's aestheticized image of the gondolier. Following the dialogue quoted above, Clough had written:

> Look, he is wedded to his trade;
> He loves, he all but is, his blade;
> His life is in his function! look,
> How perfectly that turn he took—
> His sum has found without one fraction
> Its integer in this small action.
> A pleasant day—a lovely day
> Come sing your sweet songs and be gay!
>
> (*Poems* 695)

The mathematic analogy underscores the reductive simplicity of the Spirit's outlook. The gondolier, however, seems to possess a dormant rage at the Spirit's willful ignorance of economic reality—a rage subtly conveyed through the dual connotations of "blade."[15] To Dipsychus's concerns, the Spirit offers a rejoinder that mixes his typical blend of cynicism and common sense: "Oh, no more fuss! / What's it to him, or he to us? / Sing, sing away, be glad and gay, / And don't forget that we shall pay" (5.57-60). However, Clough implies that such exclusion and forgetting taints poetry with a disturbing falseness. Such poetry does not authenticate the experience of travel; such poetry merely remains immersed, though more subtly, in the touristic cash nexus.

In *Dipsychus,* consuming the foreign body also takes on the more direct form of prostitution, a popular but generally less acknowledged lure of the tourist. Although not promising the same spiritual awakening as the *genius loci,* sexual gratification, as the Spirit suggests, is one way of relieving the pent-up angst that brought Dipsychus to Italy in the first place. Now adopting the pose of "man of the world," the Spirit encourages Dipsychus to indulge his desire freely: "O yes, you dream of sin and shame—/ Trust me, it leaves one much the same" (3.29-30). These could easily be the lines that prompted Clough's future wife Blanche Smith to lament, after she happened upon the manuscript by mistake, "I did hardly know that good men were so rough and coarse. I mean not that they prefer evil, but they consider of it so much" (*Correspondence* 2:402-3). Smith only confirms our most firmly held stereotype of the Victorian age, and in light of such prudishness it is tempting to valorize the Spirit's apparent sophistication. At the same time, however, we should not forget that the repressed Dipsychus exposes the Spirit's essentially consumptive understanding of sex. Dipsychus refuses to accept that "any child of Eve / Were formed and fashioned, raised and reared for nought / But to be swilled with animal delight / And yield five minutes' pleasure to the male" (3.118-21). On one level, the lines are typical of conservative Victorian sexuality, but they also reveal that prostitution, especially that involving men traveling overseas, reduces the foreign body to a kind of souvenir—an ice or a gondola ride that can be enjoyed guilt-free. As much as it celebrates Italy as the antidote to Victorian reticence about sex, the poem also foregrounds the moral complications of travel as sexual self-discovery.[16]

In response to Dipsychus's feelings of guilt, the Spirit reassures him, "we who've lived out in the world, you know, / Don't see these little things precisely so" (4.10-11). The Spirit thus sets up a dichotomy between naive tourist and "man of the world," both attitudes with which Clough seems uncomfortable. In a passage later deleted, Clough described the "man of the world" as "[h]ardening his heart and suppling still his back / Most proud when most on others preying, and / Than all those others more himself a prey" (*Poems* 712). Clough struggles to find some type of travel that evades the false intellectual comforts of tourism while also avoiding the self-centered, oblivious pose of the cosmopolite, who seems more to colonize than to travel.

At the heart of this struggle is the anti-touristic "ideology of originality"[17] to which Claude, like the Spirit, at times lays claim. As revealed in his earlier dismissal of the Byron-quoting Trevellyns, Claude casts himself as an unattached agent, a "traveler" none too interested and certainly undaunted by the political struggle going on around him. The depoliticized zone that Claude fashions for himself, however, soon collapses. As he encounters a mob dragging the corpse of a murdered priest, he remembers, "I was in black myself, and didn't know what mightn't happen" (2.193). He leaves the scene, but not without catching a glimpse of the exciting but threatening spectacle: "Passing away from the place with Murray under my arm, and / Stooping, I saw through the legs of the people the legs of a body" (2.196-97). This is the second time in this scene that Claude has mentioned Murray at his side, as if he is no longer quite so embarrassed to play the tourist. With guidebook prominently displayed, Claude possesses a diplomatic immunity amidst a sea of others who cannot make such a claim. At moments of pressure, of threat to his own body, when he may be called upon to engage himself, Claude is quick to claim the tourist's ready alibi: this is not my affair. Political forces only dimly apparent or willfully ignored by the traveler under normal "guidebook" circumstances are now cast into broader view. The traveler's authority, ultimately, is grounded in the economy of tourism: it allows him to live to gaze another day—to compose a poem rather than adorn one.[18]

*Amours de Voyage* makes a more direct link between poetic production and the political status of the traveler with a satirical ode to the Tiber. Clough may have had in mind a passage from Samuel Rogers' *Italy* (1822) that celebrates the rejuvenating power of Rome along with the artistic gaze specially gifted to invoke that power. Rogers emphasizes the spontaneous authenticity of his poetic effusion:

> And I am there!
> Ah, little thought I, when in school I sate,
> A school-boy on his bench, at early dawn
> Glowing with Roman story, I should live
> To tread the Appian, once an avenue
> Of monuments most glorious, palaces,
> Their doors sealed up and silent as the night,
> The dwellings of the illustrious dead—to turn
> Toward Tibur, and, beyond the City-gate,
> Pour out my *unpremeditated* verse,
> Where on his mule I might have met so oft
> Horace himself.[19]

In a language and tone that recalls Rogers, Claude blends nostalgia for ancient times with the excitement of an "eye-witness" account:

> Tibur is beautiful, too, and the orchard slopes, and the Anio
> Falling, falling yet, to the ancient lyrical cadence;
> Tibur and Anio's tide; and cool from Lucretilis ever,
> With the Digentian stream, and with the Bandusian fountain,

Folded in Sabine recesses, the valley and villa of
  Horace:—
So not seeing I sung; so seeing and listening say I.

(3.214-19)

Claude does not actually view the area under description, which is off-limits due to the siege. The passage thus calls attention to how the image emerges out of the web of texts that make up the traveler's Italy—that is, just how un-"unpremeditated" such verse is. As with Dipsychus's ode to the gondola, a critical voice introduces an ironic turn to the song that brings the facade crashing down. Claude reminds the reader that he sits "on Montorio's height, with these weary soldiers by me, / Waiting till Oudinot enter to reinstate Pope and Tourist" (3.238-39). The jarring, distinctly unsublime closing saps the life from the previous imagery. The poet is not really there, nor, for that matter is the *genius loci,* and it is this wider awareness that distinguishes Clough from the kind of poetry he critiques here. While composing his beautiful lines. Clough remembers that someone is pushing the gondola, that a larger economic framework exists which conditions the poet's gaze. This new travel poetry may lack the sublimity of the *genius loci,* but it may also save the genre from becoming simply another form of travel advertisement. Clough resists the urge to put himself in command of the foreign setting and instead embraces, if reluctantly, the disruptive potential of travel. Indeed, the role of poet-prophet abroad assumes what Claude would call a "factitious" trust in one's instincts. At one point he wonders, in the manner of Hamlet, "*Action will furnish belief,—but will that belief be the true one?*" (5.20). Clough's voice is not boldly public—a poetic call to arms—but it is still politically charged. The political in the poems is cautious and subtle, but as the gondola scene of *Dipsychus* makes clear, the political is still very much present.

Clough apparently had hoped that *Amours de Voyage,* with its appeal to the perplexed, "modern" traveler, would strike a chord with those who had grown tired of their Rogers. The epistolary form of the poem is part of this appeal. The travel letter was hardly a new phenomenon in 1849, of course, but relatively recent improvements in the European postal service—such as pre-paid delivery and shipment via train and steamship—facilitated voluminous travel correspondence. As suggested by Claude's rapid-fire letters to Eustace, especially those written hastily as he traces Mary Trevellyn's footsteps across Italy, the traveler on the continent was now more than ever a correspondent. The off-hand, self-aware tone of the letters likewise speaks to the "modern" traveler. Dorothy Mermin theorizes that the epistolary form of the poem demands a reader such as Claude's friend Eustace, one who will respond positively to "ironic disavowals of seriousness."[20] Travel correspondence especially lends itself to this sense of

audience: the sheer ubiquity of travelers' journals and letters made them "something of a joke" to many Victorians, as Michael Cotsell suggests.[21] The writer well-read in travel literature inevitably struggles to avoid the clichés and truisms to which the genre is prone. Trying to sound "original" thus becomes comically futile in *Amours de Voyage,* an effect enhanced by the sing-song rhythm of Clough's hexameters.

The poem's initial readers, however, did not find it refreshing. After reading the poem in manuscript. Clough's friend J. C. Shairp complained, "[t]here is no hope, nor strength, nor belief" in the poem, and he advised Clough, "don't publish it—or if it must be published—not in a book—but in some periodical" (*Correspondence* 1:275). The inconclusive ending of the poem, in which Claude eventually abandons his pursuit of Mary, baffled, even annoyed Clough's contemporaries. What was one to make of a travel romance that seemed to collapse out of the protagonist's (and, presumably, the author's) lack of will—and in such an enchanted setting as Italy? In *Amours de Voyage,* Clough of course resists using travel as a means to validate cultural norms; rather, the poem deconstructs the experience of travel, turning it to new ends. Clough asked Shairp, "do you not find any final Strength of Mind in the unfortunate fool of a hero? I have no intention whatever of sticking up for him, but certainly I didn't mean him to go off into mere prostration and defeat" (1:278). While Clough took his friend's criticism in stride, it appears to have convinced him that *Amours de Voyage* would be received hostilely, thus compromising his position as Principal at University Hall in London. He wrote to Shairp, "Your censure of the conception almost provoked me into publishing because it showed how washy the world is in its confidences. . . . But I probably shan't publish for fear of a row with my Sadducees" (1:278). In 1858, nine years after the exchange with his friend, the poem finally was published—safely overseas in the *Atlantic Monthly.* The ending, however, still rankled. Ralph Waldo Emerson asked, "How can you waste such power on a broken dream? Why lead us up the tower to tumble us down?" (*Correspondence* 2:548). The irony of the optimistic-sounding title *Amours de Voyage* may seem readily obvious now, but to Clough's contemporaries, it was like a joke that fell flat.

*Dipsychus* shows the potential of travel to displace even the most cherished of self-sustaining myths—and shows even less deference than *Amours de Voyage* to mid-century Victorian taste in poetry. The poem would not be published until 1865, four years after Clough's death. The protagonist of *Dipsychus,* in fact, seems well aware of the poem's lack of commercial potential. As he gazes upon the "somewhat drest-up" portrait of Byron mentioned earlier, he ponders the contrast between himself and the popular, influential Byron:

Verses! well, they are made, so let them go;
No more if I can help. This is one way
The procreant heat and fervor of our youth
Escapes, in puff, and smoke, and shapeless words
Of mere ejaculation, nothing worth. . . .

                                                        (9.21-25)

From poetry as action we go to poetry as mere bodily function. But contained in this apparently disgusted dismissal of his efforts is a hint of something more positive. Traveling overseas and exploring the experience in poetry still offers insight into the most fundamental, troubling questions of the self and the age. The key to such insight is what at first seems like Dipsychus's greatest nemesis, the Spirit:

> I have scarce spoken yet to this strange follower
> Whom I picked up—ye great gods, tell me where!
> And when! for I remember such long years,
> And yet he seems new come. I commune with myself;
> He speaks, I heat him, and resume to myself;
> Whate'er I think, he adds his comments to.

                                                        (9.28-33)

The Spirit interrupts, problematizes, and impedes on instinct, but he is essential: he is the very "spirit" of the age. Clough made this suggestion directly in an 1846 letter on political economy to *The Balance*. While not about *Dipsychus per se*, the letter implies that the perils of the modern traveler mirrored a number of other cultural issues that Clough would later address in the poem:

> The relation in which the moral and spiritual element stands, in our age, to the business-like and economic, reminds one of a traveller on the continent, who, much to his discontent, and not without continual but futile interference, is yet obliged, by his ignorance of language and customs and character, to surrender the conduct of his journey to an experienced and faithful, but somewhat disreputable and covetous-minded, companion.[22]

Elements which Clough would perhaps keep separate—the spiritual, the economic, the political—have become intermeshed and confused. Clough admits his ignorance and his reluctance to trust in instinct, and, in turn, he is forced to abdicate the authority to which the "original" and "authentic" traveler lays claim. At times tourist, at times cosmopolite, the Spirit is at bottom an agitator—a reminder of the difficulty of determining a fixed, authoritative self.

This function of the Spirit is dramatized when Dipsychus, once more seeking the consummation of the *genius loci*, leaps into the lagoon at Lido. While the Spirit's touristic side worries that Dipsychus's purse and clothes will be stolen, the swimmer "will taste again the old joy / I gloried in so when a boy" (6.210-11). The Spirit mocks this higher tourism and the idea that it could

resolve any spiritual crisis: "But you—with this one bathe, no doubt, / Have solved all questions out and out. / 'Tis Easter Day, and on the Lido / Lo, Christ the Lord is risen indeed, O!" (6.232-35). The spirit undermines the ethos of the pilgrim, proclaiming cynically that the tourist's world is all there is. Hence, the Spirit offers an insight that is always revealing but at times crippling as well. Discourse with the Spirit, like Hardy's "full look at the worst," provides an uneasy catharsis, the kind of exhausted relief Clough gets from the refrain, "Christ is not risen," in his poem **"Easter Day, Naples, 1849"**: "My heart was hot within me; till at last / My brain was lightened, when my tongue had said / Christ is not risen!" (3-5).[23]

Lido is also, as the Spirit makes clear to Dipsychus, "where Murray's faithful guide / informs us Byron used to ride" (6.190-91). Clough seems to have had a particular obsession for this section of the *Handbook for Travellers in Northern Italy,* which he references twice in **Dipsychus.** The passage no doubt captured for Clough the "falseness" of modern travel and the tourist's Byron:

> [T]he *lido,* [is] now associated with the name of Byron, as the spot where he used to take his rides, and where he designed to have been buried . . . and the glow spreads with vast intensity, and yet without bestowing any cheerfulness on the scene.[24]

Murray rigidly structures the tourist's gaze: note where Byron used to ride and do not miss the sublime effect of nature on the scene. The *genius loci* thus "packaged" here removes for Clough any spiritual impact it could have had. With the aid of the derisive Spirit, however, Clough seemingly strikes back at Murray, discrediting the sanctified image of Byron that the guidebook has created:

> What now? The Lido shall it be?
> Then none may say we didn't see
> The ground which Byron used to ride on,
> And do I don't know what beside on.

                                                        (6.1-4)

As the Spirit calls attention to the less heroic side of Byron's exploits in Italy, he simultaneously exposes the limitations of the guidebook's universe, leaving a gap in authority that is filled by the poem. Among the landmarks that compose the world of the tourist, a more troubling side to travel exists that will not be found in the pages of Murray. If travel is to lead to true self-awareness, Clough implies, it must now go beyond Byron, at least beyond the second-hand representation of him in Murray. Clough's poetry offers an insight that originates from fully analyzing the space occupied by the traveler, and—crucially—just how the economic apparatus of tourism seeks to define the traveler as subject. Clough concludes that the solitary, bold gesture of Byron is simply no longer possible in the chartered world of the Victorian traveler:

The age of instinct has, it seems, gone by,
And will not be forced back. And to live now
I must sluice out myself into canals,
And lose all force in ducts. The modern Hotspur
Shrills not his trumpet of 'To Horse, To Horse!'
But consults in a railway guide;
A demigod of figures; an Achilles
Of computation;
A verier Mercury, express come down
To *do* the world with swift arithmetic.

(10.105-14)

This call to horse invokes the several scenes in *Childe Harold* where Harold rides off at moments of spiritual crisis, confident of finding some new locus of insight. Dipsychus longs nostalgically for similar moments when he may "love my love unto myself alone, / And know my knowledge to the world unknown; / No witness to the vision call, / Beholding, unbeheld of all" (5.82-85). However, Clough implies that such visionary moments encode a false center, a specious, delusory cultural authority. The appearance in 1869 of Clough's **Poems and Prose Remains** marked the beginning of a favorable reassessment of the poet's willingness to question his own point of view. In a review of the volume, Henry Sidgwick touched on a quality that has continued to strike readers of Clough up to the present day—a kind of intellectual farsightedness or fortitude:[25]

> His point of view and habit of mind are less singular in England in the year 1869 than they were in 1859, and much less than they were in 1849. We are growing year by year more introspective and self-conscious: the current philosophy leads us to a close, patient, and impartial observation and analysis of our mental processes. . . . We are growing also more sceptical in the proper sense of the word: we suspend our judgement much more than our predecessors, and much more contentedly: we see that there are many sides to many questions. . . . We are losing in faith and confidence . . . and we are gaining in impartiality and comprehensiveness of sympathy.[26]

Sidgwick's re-contextualization of Clough is interesting in itself as an example of late Victorian or Aesthetic self-fashioning. The poet is no longer beholden to inspirit the reader: rather than making conclusions, the poet dissects them. This was the same critical ethos that would embrace another poem of that year, Browning's *The Ring and the Book,* which, like **Amours de Voyage** and **Dipsychus,** features the poet as traveler and embraces the concept of truth as process rather than definitive endpoint. Not surprisingly, then, Browning's epic and Clough's poems have managed to find a comfortable home in deconstructionist analyses of our own time, such as E. Warwick Slinn's *The Discourse of Self in Victorian Poetry* (1991). **Amours de Voyage,** according to Slinn, evidences a "lack of a reliable 'ground' of any sort, including the empirical."[27] As Slinn's own diction in fact reveals, the discourse of authority depends largely on metaphors of place:

"Claude's emotional and intellectual conflicts in the poem arise from his growing confrontation with the groundlessness of experience and belief. The fixity and certainty he desires are not there."[28] To speak with authority or certainty is to be "fixed"—to have a secure, unshifting standpoint from which to observe and test one's vision. Travel, particularly in the disrupted setting where Claude finds himself, mirrors the Hegelian nature of knowledge Slinn detects in the poem. Hegel's understanding of science as a dynamic, continuing process rather than the search for a definitive end-point parallels Clough's rejection of the sublime *genius loci* as the essence of travel.[29] For both Hegel and Clough, self-awareness is characterized by "movement" outside of the self. Travel, and reliving the experience of travel in poetry, casts into broad relief the whole shaping of self: it reveals the "many sides" to one's ostensibly stable point of view.

For Clough, this difficult journey toward self-understanding is the ultimate reward of travel and travel poetry. In the closing "l'envoi" of **Amours de Voyage,** the ever-ironic Clough predicts a kind of stumbling, uncertain future for the poem. At the same time, he proclaims what makes his work distinctive:

> So go forth to the world, to the good report and the evil!
> Go, little book! thy tale, is it not evil and good?
> Go, and if strangers revile, pass quietly by without answer.
> Go, and if curious friends ask of thy rearing and age,
> Say, 'I am flitting about many years from brain unto brain of
> Feeble and restless youths born to inglorious days;
> But,' so finish the word, 'I was writ in a Roman chamber,
> When from Janiculan heights thundered the cannon of France.'

(5.217-224)

Clough figures the poem itself as a kind of time and space traveler. Authority is invested not in the observer, but in the text, which is set free to travel the earth. Clough does not lead the "feeble and restless youth" of England to some new promised land, but he does offer them a poetic landscape where, in some tattered form at least, "Knowledge abideth" (*Amours* 5, 198).

**Dipsychus,** for all its pessimism, also manages to see beyond its own despair, an impression left by the poem's prose frame—a conversation between the poet and a distracted old uncle. While the actual poem itself ends gloomily enough, with Dipsychus abandoning himself to the Spirit in the manner of Faust, the uncle concludes simply,

> I don't very well understand what it's all about. . . . I won't say I didn't drop into a doze while the young man was drivelling through his later soliloquies. But

there was a great deal that was unmeaning, vague, and involved; and what was most plain was least decent and least moral.

(292)

Painful as such comments would be to a writer confident of critical acclaim, they show that Clough was capable of putting his own personal struggles in perspective, that he was resigned to the poem's lack of commercial appeal. The dark-comic absurdity of traveling to Italy for spiritual and artistic rejuvenation and returning instead with *Dipsychus* was not lost on him. Ultimately, *The Bothie* would remain the high-water mark of Clough's popularity during his lifetime, but as explorations of travel as a cultural phenomenon, and of poetic production itself, *Amours de Voyage* and *Dipsychus* are perhaps unparalleled in Victorian poetry.

### Notes

1. All references to Clough's correspondence are to F. L. Mulhauser, ed., *Correspondence of Arthur Hugh Clough,* 2 vols. (Oxford U. Press, 1957).

2. Composed soon after Clough's return from France, *The Bothie* has struck some commentators as one of the most politically engaged poems of the century. According to John Goode, the poem is "a radical critique of society and a vision of the possibilities of historical change" ("1848 and the Strange Disease of Modern Love." *Literature and Politics in the Nineteenth Century,* ed. John Lucas [London: Methuen, 1971], 64). Isobel Armstrong has called *The Bothie* "a remarkable linguistic experiment," one that attempted to dissolve class-restrictive hierarchies of language (*Victorian Poetry: Poetry, Poetics, and Politics* [New York: Routledge, 1993], 202). Most recently, Meg Tasker has drawn connections between the poem's politics and its experiments with genre and narrative ("Time, Tense, and Genre: A Bakhtinian Analysis of Clough's *Bothie,*" *Victorian Poetry* 34 [1996]: 193-211).

3. Meredith B. Raymond and Mary Rose Sullivan, eds., *Letters of Elizabeth Barrett Browning to Mary Russell Mitford* (Winfield, Kansas: Armstrong Browning Library of Baylor University, The Browning Institute, Wedgestone Press, and Wellesley College, 1983), 3:286.

4. John Nichol, ed., *The Poetical Works of Sydney Dobell* (London: Smith, Elder, 1875), 1:185.

5. Quoted in Martha Westwater, *The Spasmodic Career of Sydney Dobell* (U. Press of America, 1992), 62.

6. See Simon Gatrell, "*Histoires de Voyage*: The Italian Poems of Arthur Hugh Clough," in *Creditable Warriors 1830-1876,* English Literature and the

Wider World, vol. 3, ed. Michael Cotsell (London: Ashfield, 1990): 159-72, for further discussion of Clough and travel. Gatrell focuses on how Italy, as a space free of the religious and professional restrictions that were draining Clough back home, afforded the poet a measure of creative freedom: "Clough needed to travel out from England to be able to understand clearly what it was he wanted to write, and these journeys seem also to have been necessary for him to see himself with any clarity" (170). In this essay, I explore more fully how the economy of tourism and the political instability of Rome compelled Clough to reassess the overall cultural value of Grand Tour poetry.

7. The *Hand-Book for Travellers in Central Italy* (London: John Murray, 1843) is especially Byron-laden. As James Buzard reveals in *The Beaten Track: European Tourism, Literature, and the Ways to 'Culture' 1800-1918* (Oxford U. Press, 1993), Byron possessed unrivaled marketability as an icon of travel. Attempts to capitalize on his work and reputation were everywhere: "[I]n the Byron of Victorian tourism we can glimpse the same 'star quality' that distinguishes the *divi* of Hollywood and the recording industry. Tourism's Byron . . . [was] open to emulators yet apparently exclusive; free of ordinary determinants of social class and yet redolent with the ineffable quality of 'class' in our modern colloquial sense of the term" (122).

8. Buckner B. Trawick, ed., *Selected Prose Works of Arthur Hugh Clough* (U. of Alabama Press, 1964), 144.

9. References to Clough's poems are to F. L. Mulhauser, ed., *The Poems of Arthur Hugh Clough,* 2d ed. (Oxford U. Press, 1974). Excised passages and prose segments of *Dipsychus* will be cited by page number.

10. See Harold Bloom, *The Anxiety of Influence: A Theory of Poetry,* 2d ed. (Oxford U. Press, 1997).

11. References to *Childe Harold's Pilgrimage* are to *The Complete Poetical Works,* ed. Jerome J. McGann, Vol. 2 (Oxford U. Press, 1980).

12. Jonathan Culler. "The Semiotics of Tourism," in *Framing the Sign: Criticism and Its Institutions* (U. of Oklahoma Press, 1988), 157.

13. See Timothy Webb, "Byron as a Man of the World," in *L'esilio romantico: Forme di un conflitto,* Biblioteca di Studi Inglesi, vol. 52, ed. Joseph Cheyne and Lilla Maria Crisafulli Jones (Bari: Adriatica, 1990). Webb notes. "Byron was quite clear that his own relationship with Italy was deeper and more significant than that of most English visitors" on the continent (286). His let-

ters contain numerous condemnations of English tourists, revealing "an animosity which is raw and deeply personal" (287).

14. In earlier drafts of the poem, Clough referred to the two speakers as Faustulus and Mephistopheles.

15. In this way, *Dipsychus* anticipates Thomas Mann's *Death in Venice* (1930), which likewise reveals the potentially self-destructive obfuscation at work in the tourist/voyeur's gaze.

16. As John Maynard argues in "From Cloister to 'Great Sinful Streets': Arthur Hugh Clough and the Victorian 'Question of Sex'" in *Victorian Discourses on Sexuality and Religion* (Cambridge U. Press, 1993), Clough's poetry is a complex, relatively forward-looking critique of Victorian sexual mores. Clough, however, appears to have been troubled by the carefree sexual indulgence of many Grand Tourists, whom he generally casts as exploitative in *Dipsychus.*

17. I borrow this phrase from Buzard, who uses it to describe the dialectic opposition between "traveler" and "tourist" that emerged in the nineteenth century: "Where the Grand Tourist had enacted a repetitive ritual of classicism and class solidarity, his nineteenth-century counterpart, self-consciously treading in the Grand Tourist's well-beaten path in the midst of inevitable compatriots, would lay claim to an aristocracy of inner feeling, the projection of an ideology of originality and difference" (121-22). Claude, as was shown, reflects this attitude in his initial response to the merchant-class Trevellyns.

18. In the notes to Canto I of *Childe Harold,* Byron comments on the dangers faced by travelers in politically unstable Portugal during the Napoleonic Wars. Recounting how he and a companion were accosted on the way to a theater, Byron concludes, "had we not fortunately been armed, I have not the least doubt that we should have adorned a tale instead of telling one" (188). What is extra-poetical for Byron—the political status of the travel author's person—is central to the poem for Clough. The contrast of Byron as bold "traveler" to the Victorian "tourist" is also highlighted in their respective weapons: Byron arms himself with a pistol most likely, Claude with a guidebook.

19. Samuel Rogers, *Italy: A Poem* (London: T. Cadell, 1830), 139. My italics.

20. Dorothy Mermin, *The Audience in the Poem: Five Victorian Poets* (Rutgers U. Press, 1983), 115.

21. Michael Cotsell, Introduction to *Creditable Warriors,* 13.

22. Trawick, 217. Walter E. Houghton was the first to detect the "shaping plan of the poem" in the letter (*The Poetry of Clough: An Essay in Revaluation* [Yale U. Press, 1963], 163).

23. Dipsychus paraphrases this passage from "Easter Day" at the outset of the poem (1.7-11); hence the Spirit's recollection of it later.

24. *Hand-book for Travellers in Northern Italy* (London: John Murray, 1843), 374.

25. Praise of Clough's farsightedness is a common refrain in commentary on his work. Houghton, for example, lauds the poet's "contemporary relevance . . . his special capacity, so rare in his own age, for double vision. He could see at least two sides to every question. (He could even see two sides to seeing two sides of every question.)" (226). Maynard notes, "the approach to truth through dialectic and critique, disturbing as it was to Clough's contemporaries, now gives an especially attractive and durable, even contemporary quality to his work" (65-66).

26. Henry Sidgwick, review of *The Poems and Prose Remains of Arthur Hugh Clough* (*Westminster Review* 92 [1869]: 363-97; reprint, *Clough: The Critical Heritage,* ed. Michael Thorpe [New York: Barnes and Noble, 1972]: 268-92), 269.

27. E. Warwick Slinn, *The Discourse of the Self in Victorian Poetry* (London: Macmillan, 1991), 93.

28. Slinn, 91.

29. See "On Scientific Cognition," the preface to *Phenomenology of Spirit,* 1807, trans. A. V. Miller (Oxford U. Press, 1977).

**Charles LaPorte (essay date winter 2004)**

SOURCE: LaPorte, Charles. "Spasmodic Poetics and Clough's Apostasies." *Victorian Poetry* 42, no. 4 (winter 2004): 521-36.

[*In the following essay, LaPorte explores Clough's relationship with the Spasmodic School, which is typically associated with such poets as Philip James Bailey and Alexander Smith.*]

Richard Cronin completes a recent tally of the infamous Spasmodic poets with the unusual addition of Arthur Hugh Clough, a darling of Rugby and Oxford and a bosom-friend of the fervently anti-Spasmodic Matthew Arnold.[1] Surely Cronin means to be provocative, yet he points to a real question concerning the cultural reaches of such critically marginalized literary movements as the Spasmodic one. Although Clough's contemporaries never explicitly identified him as a Spasmodic, his mid-century poetry often probes the sensitive religious topics of more recognizably Spasmodic poets like Philip James Bailey and Alexander Smith, and like them he frequently asks whether poetry performs a specifically religious function. Of course, Clough was painfully ambivalent about Christianity after the Oxford Movement and the English popularizing of the Higher Criticism, and so his affinity for the Spasmodics reveals how badly poets such as he wished to fix the relation between religion and poetry. Eventually, Clough became disillusioned with the poetry of Bailey and Smith (a disillusionment encouraged by Arnold and other friends), but his repudiation of a poetic solution to his religious problems corresponded to a dramatic falling-off in his poetic achievement. If Clough's later poetic infertility is, as I suppose, linked to his rejection of the Spasmodics, then he is the foremost casualty of the great mid-century "critical battle" to which this special issue is devoted.[2]

1

Cronin was not the first to associate Clough with the Spasmodics. As George Saintsbury informed readers of his *History of Nineteenth Century Literature* (1896): "*Amours de Voyage* and *Dipsychus,* though there are fine passages in both, bring [Clough] very close to the Spasmodic school, of which in fact he was an unattached and more cultivated member, with fancies directed rather to religiosity than to strict literature."[3] In light of the mordant class-based critiques that served to ruin the Spasmodics for more than one generation of Victorian readers, this depiction of Clough as "in fact" a "more cultivated member" of the Spasmodic "school" contains a certain paradox.[4] W. E. Aytoun used the term to besmirch the poorly trained and classically ignorant T. Percy Joneses of the world, to imply their riotous carelessness of the formal structures of English poetry. Clough, on the other hand, was conspicuously well trained in the type of classicism prized by Victorian literary conservatives (he once boasted himself to be among the best classicists at Harvard: "better than most Yankee-Grecians") and his hexameters in particular would be praised by many—including Arnold, who recommended them in Oxford lectures as the best English model for future translations of Homer.[5] Saintsbury offers to solve the awkward problem of Clough's superlative education by relating his Spasmodism to his departures from "strict literature," yet this begs the question of whether "strict literature" is a tool by which Clough can fairly be measured, especially if it must be distinguished from religiosity, as Saintsbury implies.

Clough himself would not be surprised to find his poetry classed with that of the Spasmodics on the basis of its religious tenor. Arnold had been telling him this much as early as their correspondence of 1848, in his response to Clough's *Ambarvalia* manuscripts. Arnold remonstrates with him in a well-known letter that also grudgingly acknowledges the successes of Philip James Bailey's *Festus*:

> A growing sense of the deficiency of the *beautiful* in your poems, and of this alone being properly *poetical* as distinguished from rhetorical, devotional, or metaphysical, made me speak as I did. But your line is a line: and you have most of the promising English verse-writers with you now: Festus for instance. Still, problem as the production of the beautiful remains to me, I will die protesting against the world that the other is false & JARRING. (emphases Arnold's)[6]

According to Arnold, Clough's early poems suffer from Bailey's ("Festus's") faults in that they are insufficiently beautiful, and therefore unpoetic. Metaphysics do not create beauty, and the creation of beauty is the poet's exclusive problem. Though Arnold himself has not solved the "problem as the production of the beautiful," yet he "will die protesting against" the Clough-Bailey method and its many adherents. Arnold, we see, anticipates Saintsbury by fifty years, inquiring about a means by which one can distinguish the "properly poetical" from Clough's "rhetorical, devotional, or metaphysical" verses—or "strict literature" from his "fancies" and "religiosity." As I have noted, a great deal of Clough's poetry responds to contemporary religious debates; it is hard to know whether such religious poetry, by Arnold's measure, becomes an oxymoron.

It is also hard to know where in the *Ambarvalia* manuscripts Arnold finds the "false & JARRING" *Festus*. Certainly Clough's early lyrics address metaphysics in ways that are formally irregular. "Why should I say I see the things I see not?" affords a good example of such poetry. This poem, from which the *Ambarvalia* collection derives its name, interrogates the music of poetry as a sort of metaphysical problem:

> Are there not, then, two musics unto men?—
>     One loud and bold and coarse,
>     And overpowering still perforce
>     All tone and tune beside;
>     Yet in despite its pride
> Only of fumes of foolish fancy bred,
> And sounding solely in the sounding head:
>     The other, soft and low,
>     Stealing whence we not know,
> Painfully heard, and easily forgot,
> With pauses oft and many a silence strange,
> (And silent oft it seems, when silent it is not)
> Revivals too of unexpected change:
> Haply thou think'st 'twill never be begun,
> Or that 't has come, and been, and past away;
>     Yet turn to other none,—
>     Turn not, oh, turn not thou!
> But listen, listen, listen,—if haply be heard it may;
> Listen, listen, listen,—is it not sounding now?

(ll. 29-47)[7]

Such fitful meter was meant to give pause (or "pauses oft") to readers like Arnold, and it did.[8] The poem's central metaphor of a rarely heard "music unto men," is played out through irregularity and dissonance. Its jarring alternations of pentameters and trimeters unsettle their own established rhythms and repudiate prediction. Intermittent hexameters similarly spring from "unexpected change," and even their repetitions seem labored, as in the stanza's final couplet: "But listen, listen, listen,—if haply be heard it may; / Listen, listen, listen,—is it not sounding now?" Throughout, the alluring alternative of something "soft and low" remains doubtful—or else it is so soft and so low as to reside in the metrical disasters that surround it: "Stealing whence we not know / Painfully heard, and easily forgot." Such verse is indeed "Painfully heard"; Clough meant it to be so. It looks for an alternative music in grotesque departures from poetic regularity, in "pauses oft and many a silence strange." And it doubts its own capacity to establish such music, as it doubts its readers' capacity to detect it: "Haply thou think'st 'twill never be begun, / Or that 't has come, and been, and past away."

Yet surely it is the religious implications of this ***Ambarvalia*** poetry, rather than its jarring formal structures, that drew Matthew Arnold's mind to Philip James Bailey. As Joseph Phelan notes, the elusiveness of Clough's "other" music mirrors the elusiveness of Victorian religious experience, or the problem of that elusiveness in a world in which religious forms were so widely observed.[9] Significantly, Clough composed most of "Why should I say . . . ?" shortly after reading the Higher Criticism of David Friedrich Strauss, when he was racked by doubts about the historicity of the Gospels and while contemplating the resignation of his position at Oriel College, Oxford. Much of Clough's lyric verse at this time reflects his looming religious crisis, and its formal features suggest his emotional strain. For instance, Clough's most famous lyric, the iconoclastic **"Epi-Strauss-ion,"** was written at about the same time as "Why should I say . . . ?," and uses the same metrical play of pentameter, trimeter, and hexameter lines to still more jarring effect. This is apparent from that poem's opening couplet, where a trimeter line following the opening pentameter is end-rhymed so emphatically as to suggest its unnatural reduction: "Matthew and Mark and Luke and holy John / Evanished all and gone!" Like passages of "Why should I say . . . ?," the second line of **"Epi-Strauss-ion"** becomes a pentameter *manqué,* its final feet disconcertingly "evanished."

Bailey's lines, however idiosyncratic, tend to remain in pentameters. Yet "Why should I say . . . ?," does suggest *Festus* at some points. For instance, as the 1847 manuscript attests, Clough removed such explicitly vatic references as the following lines:

Even so Poets now
With more than priestly vow
Made separate from their birth
Walk the great world and mete the measures of the
 Earth
　　And following on their feet
　　Their acolytes withal
Who catching notes that haply fall
　　From the great prophetic song
Tell them out loudly to the listening throng.

(***Poems,*** p. 579)

Such bold Romantic claims about the "more than priestly" craft of poetry might well remind us, as they reminded Arnold, of *Festus*' claim that "Poetry is itself a thing of God; / He made His prophets poets; and the more / We feel of poesie do we become / Like God in love and power,—undermakers."[10] *Festus* affirms poetic truth everywhere that Clough interrogates its possibility. This does not make Bailey more orthodox than Clough; Bailey merely presents an affirmative heterodoxy, rather than a skeptical one. But this surely helps explain why Bailey was so enormously popular, whereas Clough struggled for an audience. It was likely under Arnold's influence that such self-assured passages were removed from the published version of Clough's poem.

Another element of Bailey's success, perhaps, is his distance from Clough's idea of how poets were "[m]ade separate from their birth," if "birth" is meant to imply station or education. *Festus* insists that such accidents are unnecessary to the poetic task. As Bailey claims of himself:

　　　　　　　　He spake inspired:
　　Night and day, thought came unhelped, undes-
 ired,
Like blood to his heart. The course of study he
Went through was of the soul-rack. The degree
　　He took was high: it was wise wretchedness.
　　He suffered perfectly, and gained no less
A prize than, in his own torn heart, to see
　　A few bright seeds: he sowed them—hoped them
 truth.
The autumn of that seed is in these pages.

(p. 413)

It need hardly be said that Bailey's "soul-rack" school was more accessible to the average Victorian than was Clough's Oxford. But Bailey popularized religious and poetic issues debated there. When his "Proëm," for instance, instructs that "True fiction hath in it a higher end / Than fact; it is the possible compared / With what is merely positive" (p. 7), it takes Aristotle's defense of poetry, translates it for the public, and gives it a religious spin. This spin Bailey saw as his mission. As Herbert Tucker has noted in this collection, *Festus'* astonishing length derives partly from Bailey's determination to reconcile Christian doctrine with Victorian moral sensibilities—all Victorian moral sensibilities. In place of Sidney's famous apology that the poet "never lieth" because "he nothing affirms," Bailey suggests just the contrary: the poet never lieth, for he everything affirms. *Festus* presents an alternative to unpalatable orthodoxies in an "omnist" poetic sensibility that finds beauty everywhere in creation. Like Clough's "other" music, *Festus*' poetry is everywhere, and need only be revealed by the poet: "For the creative spirit which thou seekest / Is in thee, and about thee; yeah, it hath / God's everywhereness" (p. 319).

Bailey's gift was to fire the imaginations of many younger poets, who found solace in his poetry for a sordid and religiously problematic age. Emma Mason demonstrates in this issue how Sydney Dobell devoted his career to a sort of poetic Christianity akin to Bailey's. Smith's *A Life-Drama* also reflects Bailey's religious agenda, as in the famous urban bridge scene, where the hero, Walter, demands of a prostitute,

> Your ear, my Sister. I have that within
> Which urges me to utterance. I could accost
> A pensive angel, singing to himself
> Upon a hill in heaven, and leave his mind
> As dark and turbid as a trampled pool,
> To purify at leisure.
>
> (p. 137)

This idea that Walter's private hell should ruin another's heaven will probably fail to inspire a modern reader, but it clearly resonated in a society in which the Christian doctrine of hell had become uniquely and powerfully unsettling.[11] Such theological metaphors were irresistible to many mid-century Victorians, as *A Life-Drama* and *Festus* show. Reflective Victorians, like "pensive angels," balked at concepts of divine justice that for centuries had seemed unexceptional, and they struggled to reformulate this aspect of their religious heritage.[12] As J. A. Froude argued in his infamous mid-century novel, *The Nemesis of Faith,* "For me, and I should think too for every human being in whose breast a human heart is beating, to know that one single creature is in that dreadful place would make a hell of heaven itself."[13] Smith's widely celebrated poem, in turn, redeems (or purports to redeem) individual misery, rural poverty, and urban pollution en masse with a highly Romantic gospel of love: "Walter! dost thou believe / Love will redeem all errors? O, my friend, / This gospel saves you!" These lines, at the conclusion of Smith's long poem, fairly reproduce the conclusion of Bailey's as well. Presumably, then, the Spasmodics stick in Arnold's mind as the exemplar of poetic apologetics in the mid-century, devoted to the specifically religious power of poetry.

Bailey's commitment to poetic theodicy even explains the quasi-religious agenda of the Reverend George Gilfillan, the Spasmodics' most enthusiastic supporter, who was so committed to the religious view of poetry as to subscribe to the poetical view of religion. While testifying to the inspiration (or at least the potential) of the Spasmodic poets, Gilfillan published his hugely popular Biblical study, *The Bards of the Bible* (1850), that repeatedly asserts this conflation of poetry and religious inspiration:

> As the language of poetry is that into which all earnest natures are insensibly betrayed, so it is the only speech which has in it the power of permanent impression. . . . The language of poetry has, therefore, become the language of the inspired volume. The Bible is a mass of beautiful figures—its words and its thoughts are alike poetical. . . . [I]t is a temple, with one altar and one God, but illuminated by a thousand varied lights, and studded with a thousand ornaments.[14]

As the Spasmodics emerged, Gilfillan promoted a specific religious genealogy for the sort of disparate ("varied") images marking their poetics. Indeed, he locates Spasm at the religious heart of Western culture, for "the Bible," seen in this light, is also chiefly "a mass of beautiful figures." Gilfillan's explanation of the Bible's poetic nature, one may observe, could pass for a pastiche of the Higher Criticism. But far from capitulating to what he calls "the startling objections to the Bible which have arrived from across the German Ocean" (p. xix), Gilfillan embraces the Germans' intimation that "poetry" might be a fit term to describe the non-historical nature of the scriptures. Adopting this prescription wholesale, Gilfillan paradoxically insists that the Bible must be reliable (whether historical or not) because it enjoys the inspiration of poetry: "the language of poetry has, therefore, become the language of the inspired volume." He goes so far as to dismiss Robert Lowth, the English progenitor of the Higher Criticism, because Lowth's seminal *Sacred Poetry of the Hebrews* ignores scriptural texts that "have no metrical structure or poetic style" (p. 62). Gilfillan's Spasmodic model, by contrast, is endlessly accommodating: "metrical structure" is by no means essential to poetry, as the Bible itself shows. This elliptical argument presents an extraordinary departure from the usual Victorian response to the Higher Criticism. As we know, Clough was so unnerved by the German critics as to search for consolation in poetry. Gilfillan instead uses "poetry" to beat the Higher Critics at their own game. Gilfillan's characterization of the Bible authors' having "insensibly betrayed" their religious nature, however, is of a piece with Clough's metrical experiments, in which poetry's relation to vivid emotion cannot always be beaten into conventional meters.

2

Arnold's scorn for the Spasmodic model of poetry was never uniformly held even among Clough's Oxford friends. Many embraced the Spasmodic model, protesting (with Gilfillan) that "all earnest natures are insensibly betrayed" into poetry. J. A. Froude affords a good example of this "earnest" camp. Like Clough, Froude suffered acutely from his disillusionment with the Oxford Movement, as with Christianity in general. His *The Nemesis of Faith* made a strong impression on Clough.[15] So it is fitting that Froude's correspondence with Clough about *The Nemesis* exhibits an explicit antipathy to Arnold's ideas of poetry. These letters claim that Clough's religious subjects (like those of *The Nemesis*) were simply more important than any subject of Arnold's:

> Never mind, if the Puseyites hate it[;] they must fear it and it *will* work in the minds *they* have made sick. I admire Matt—to a very great extent. Only I don't see what business he has to parade his calmness and lecture us on resignation when he has never known what a storm is and doesn't know what he has to resign himself to. I think he only knows the shady side of nature out of books. . . . On the whole he shapes better than *you* I think—but you have marble to cut out—and he has only clay. . . . Palgrave wants to put both you and him above Festus Bailey.

> (*Correspondence*, p. 251, emphases Froude's)

Froude's yoking of "the Puseyites," "Matt," and "Festus Bailey" in a single paragraph might normally appear unlikely, since these figures are rarely considered together. Here, though, their grouping points to an important relationship. Arnold, Froude claims, is immune to the emotional turmoil—or sickness—created by the religious crises of the Oxford Movement, and this means that he cannot be expected to comprehend the sort of apologetic poetry that Clough, like Bailey, was writing. That Froude so wildly mixes his metaphors seems in keeping with his Spasmodic sympathies: Clough's religious crisis—a storm—is marble, while Arnold's bookish studies are "only clay." And Froude's contempt for Arnold's lack of experience is telling, especially in his complaint that "he only knows the shady side of nature out of books." It is amusing to see that he falls into the undergraduate slang of Clough's **Bothie** to express his frustration ("*Shady* in Latin, said Lindsay, but topping in Plays and Aldrich" [I, 24]), since Isobel Armstrong has read that poem as an implicit critique of the Oxford Movement.[16] But it is no less clear that Froude's own work reflects his emotions in formally transgressive ways. *The Nemesis* is a generic monstrosity, beginning as a hybrid between epistolary novels and freethinking sermons, and then breaking off midway to conclude, anticlimactically, as a cautionary third-person narrative about hapless would-be adulterers.

Clough's letters from this period reiterate the terms of Froude's religious anxieties in similarly Spasmodic ways. As Clough recorded for his sister, Anne, in April 1848:

> I heard yesterday that people not infrequently take me for some little time after introduction to be no less than a Puseyite: but all the same time I could sometimes be provoked to send out a flood of lava boiling-hot amidst their flowery ecclesiastical fields and parterres. Very likely living in this state of suppressed volcanic action makes one more exasperated than one should be when any sort of a crater presents itself.

> (*Correspondence*, p. 203)

Here Clough depicts Froude's religious "storm" as one of an internal, rather than external strain, and he laments "living in this state of suppressed volcanic action." Like Markham Sutherland, the hero (or anti-hero) of *The Nemesis,* Clough longs to denounce the conservative religious positions of his clerical and academic peers, and he imagines that such denouncement would present a dramatic form of relief to himself: "to send out a flood of lava boiling-hot amidst their flowery ecclesiastical fields and parterres."

The volcanic image is more than merely curious. As Kirstie Blair discusses in this volume, it quickly became the quintessential metaphor of the Spasmodic movement. Aytoun's parody *Firmilian* (1854) clearly delineates the trope's trajectory from distinctive and provocative to predictable and clichéd.[17] The title character's destruction of the Cathedral of St. Nicholas with dynamite, for instance, implicitly weds Clough's religious iconoclasm with the explosion that he contemplates. As Firmilian describes it:

> 'Twas a grand spectacle! The solid earth
> Seemed from its quaking entrails to eruct
> The gathered lava of a thousand years,
> Like an imposthume bursting up from hell!
> In a red robe of flame, the riven towers,
> Pillars and altar, organ-loft and screen,
> With a singed swarm of mortals intermixed,
> Were whirled in anguish to the shuddering stars,
> And all creation trembled at the din.

> (*Blackwood's*, p. 539)

In the context of Clough's letter, indeed, the best part of Aytoun's pastiche may be that his eruption contains an itemized catalogue of High Church symbols: "towers, / Pillars and altar, organ-loft and screen" consumed (surely not by coincidence) "[i]n a red robe of flame." Perhaps *Firmilian*'s "quaking entrails" also evoke the scatological enthusiasm of Sydney Dobell's *Balder* (1854): "The hot and hideous torrent of his dung / Roared down explosive." The overblown imagery of *Firmilian* and *Balder* may even raise questions about the tastefulness of Clough's lava image.

If Aytoun thought to shame the Spasmodics with their own ejaculations, of course, he was only partly successful. Elizabeth Barrett Browning would boldly return to Spasmodic volcanoes by the end of the decade, instructing that poets must "catch / Upon the burning lava of a song / The full-veined, heaving, double-breasted Age."[18] And, more surprisingly, even subsequent generations of Oxford critics would return to this image in defense of Clough's poetic tendencies. A decade later, John Addington Symonds would record the following of **"Easter Day,"** in which Clough's halting meter and simple rhymes mark the emotive weight of his famous refrain, "Christ is not risen":

> [Clough] pours forth torrid thought and feeling like a lava jet into the adamantine mould of stately and severe expression. **"Easter Day"** is a specimen of this success. The poem owes nothing to its rhythm, or its rhymes, or the beauty of its imagery, or the music of its language. It is plain and natural, and without allurements of any sort. But the emotion is so intense, and so thoroughly expressed—the thought is so vigorous and vital in every line—that the grandest poetry is wrought out of the commonest materials, apparently without effort, and by the mere intensity of the poet's will.[19]

Fifteen years after the Spasmodic controversy had blown over, Symonds might be surprised to find himself identified with the Gilfillan school of Spasmodic poetics, yet he plainly shares Gilfillan's assumption that powerful emotion itself creates "the grandest poetry," and that form counts for nothing: "The poem owes nothing to its rhythm, or its rhymes, or the beauty of its imagery, or the music of its language." In Symonds' view, Clough proves that emotively "torrid" poets may use conventional forms, but these are irrelevant to their beauty.

Another supporter of Clough's Spasmodic inclinations was J. C. Shairp, an Oxford friend who had become as religiously conservative as Froude and Symonds were radical. In the early 1850s, indeed, Froude and Shairp presented an unlikely alliance, for the latter felt that Clough's verses were excessively iconoclastic, rather than felicitously so. Yet Shairp understood Clough's poetic aims, like Smith's, to be on some level devotional. As he wrote to Clough of the *Life-Drama* scene quoted above: "I am glad you like A. Smith, as I did. The story is nothing—I could make nothing of it. But the scene on the bridge would please you" (p. 437). Shairp held with Froude that Arnold's model of poetry was inferior to Clough's, since the former failed to express the intellectual and emotional *Zeitgeist* of the mid-century. "The terrible want of fresh heart spoils Mat. to my taste," he wrote in this letter, and in an earlier letter, "Mat, as I told him, disowns man's natural feelings, and they will disown his poetry" (p. 401). Shairp was delighted to learn that Clough had praised Alexander Smith at Arnold's expense in the *North American Review.* His tastes were simply better tuned to the metaphysical speculations of the Spasmodic poet. "I should like much to see yr review of him and Mat," wrote Shairp, "I think there is no comparison between the two" (p. 437).

### 3

What is pitiable about Shairp's poetic observations is that by the time they reached their addressee, then living in Boston, he had already repudiated Alexander Smith's work, and was on his way to becoming a Spasmodic apostate. Like his more famous loss of faith in Christ, Clough's loss of faith in Smith is documented in his correspondence, especially in letters home to his fiancée, Blanche Smith. We know, then, that when Clough first learns of Alexander Smith, he is as animated as the rest of the critical world—or more so, since he identifies with Smith's project. He first writes Blanche on the subject on April 13, 1853: "Do you know, dear, I am very much taken with Alexander Smith's life-drama—it is really what I have had in my own mind" (p. 414). The next letter follows, two days later: "I will read Ruth for your sake, my dearest—You may read Alexander Smith for mine if you like; the first half isn't good but the last is, I think" (p. 415). Then, four days after that, Clough decides that he is inspired to write the *North American Review* piece on Smith and Arnold: "I am going to write a little article this time upon some recent English poetry, in the N.A.R." (p. 417). (At this point, Shairp was still writing enthusiastically, "You've heard of Alexander Smith, whom the reviews are all hailing as 'our new poet.' I've watched the gradual rise of his star in the Critic" [p. 401].) Yet by the beginning of May—eleven days later—Clough had changed his mind, and felt ashamed of his previous Spasmodic sympathies. Again, he writes to Blanche, "If you haven't read A. S. don't trouble yourself; 'tis hardly worth the while" (p. 424). In other words, in the space of a fortnight, Clough goes from declaring Smith's *Life-Drama* "really what I have had in my own mind" to rejecting it as "hardly worth the while." Clough's apostasy has become complete by May 17, when he again excuses himself to Blanche for his former enthusiasm, with a mocking reference to Smith's social status and a gratuitous dig at Elizabeth Gaskell: "I am rather sorry I recommended Master Alexander Smith to you. It was apropos of your making me read Ruth, you know" (p. 434). As late as June 8, Shairp was still writing, "I should like much to see your review of Alexr Smith, but the American review is not often to be had" (p. 437). But after that the subject is mostly dropped from Clough's correspondence.

The correspondence offers no reason for his critical somersault vis-à-vis "Master Alexander Smith," and, as has often been discussed, his *NAR* review suggests a divided mind. So one must look elsewhere to explain Clough's aesthetic about-face. One sensible place to look is to Clough's friendship with the American James Russell Lowell, who seems to have hated Smith.[20] Clough was then spending significant time with Lowell, in addition to corresponding with Coventry Patmore and, of course, Arnold.[21] Their letters provide circumstantial evidence that Clough's enthusiasm was simply beaten down by their combined disapprobation, and thus make it likely that this was determined by peer pressure as much as anything else. This is not to say that Clough did not have prior reservations about the Spasmodic religious model that I have identified as a critical element of Smith's work and the central element of Bailey's. *Dipsychus,* for instance, already contained an epilogue apologizing for its religious tendencies to an imagined curmudgeonly uncle. As the "poet" there puts it: "The real cause of the evil you complain of, which to a certain extent I admit, was, I take it, the religious movement of the last century, beginning with Wesleyanism, and culminating at last in Puseyism" (Epilogue, pp. 81-84). Here too, we see embarrassment over the link between the "rhetorical, devotional, or metaphysical" poetry that Arnold so disliked, and Froude's and Clough's joint disillusionment with "Puseyism." Or, to use Saintsbury's terms, we see Clough's inability to separate "religiosity" from "strict literature."

Clough was soon to abandon *Dipsychus,* his most Spasmodic poem.[22] He revised it somewhat upon his return to England, but his remarkable critical reversal of April 1853 corresponds to a conspicuous falling-off in Clough's poetic production, both in quality and—more obviously—in quantity. During the Spasmodic mid-century, from the time that he read Strauss in 1847 to his American excursion of 1852-1853, Clough produced an enormous amount of poetry, including all his major poems. In the ensuing years, Clough neither finished *Dipsychus* nor began anything else. As many critics have noted, his poetic motivation seemed to disappear. While this disappearance may have been a consequence of steady employment at the Education Office, or of marital happiness (he married Blanche in June 1854), it seems equally likely that Clough's aesthetic growth had been stunted, and that his rejection of Smith in mid-1853 on some level amounts to a rejection of his own achievement.[23] In 1861, Clough would begin a new poetic project, *Mari Magno,* modeling it upon Chaucer's *Canterbury Tales.* But these poems are formally regular and mostly secular, and no generation of Clough scholars has ever found the *Mari Magno* poems nearly as interesting as the Spasmodic *Ambarvalia, Amours de Voyage,* and *Dipsychus.* Even Clough's widow Blanche hesitated to publish *Mari Magno*—not because the poems were religiously scandalous in the manner of **"Epi-Strauss-ion," "Easter Day,"** or *Dipsychus,* but because she found them simply "terrible." If, as I hypothesize, the efforts of Arnold, Patmore, and Lowell combined to reform Clough from his Spasmodic tendencies, then those poet-critics did their friend a terrible disservice. They seem to have ruined him as a poet.

They may also have ruined Clough as a critic. Clough's Spasmodic apostasy even seems to cost him his faculty for judging the poetry of others, if one is to judge by his antipathy to the emerging voice of Walt Whitman in the mid-1850s. As Clough wrote to Emerson on September 12, 1856:

> Charles Norton just showed me Leaves of Grass, which certainly seems remarkable but is it not rather a Waste of power and observation—The tree is tapped, and not left to bear flower and fruit in perfect form as it should—This standing aside and looking on does not seem to me to be the thing that really produces.

(p. 520)

This letter is remarkable for two reasons. The first is that Clough, in retrospect, is profoundly wrong. By most later accounts, Whitman's poetry is "the thing that really produce[d]," since *Leaves of Grass* contributed as much as any work to the shape of the American poetical tradition over the ensuing hundred and fifty years. But the other salient aspect of Clough's letter is that he views Whitman through the prism of the Spasmodics. He criticizes Whitman as unripe or immature, even applying to Whitman the expressions that Arnold, writing Clough, had applied to Smith.[24] That is, Clough finds Whitman's poetry "remarkable," but unpromising because of its lack of poetic form. Nothing in Clough's work better reflects Arnold's early criticisms than this complaint that Whitman's "tree is tapped, and not left to bear flower and fruit in perfect form as it should." Properly cultivated poetic foliage, by the Arnoldian model, is actually more natural than Whitman's wild excesses; it matures into the flower and fruit of "perfect form."

In this context, Clough is surely right to recognize Whitman as a Spasmodic: indifferent to traditional meters, confident that evil is merely a feature of a divine good, intoxicated by Smith's "Gospel of Love," and endlessly self-promoting upon Bailey's grounds that "Poetry is itself a thing of God" and that "He made His prophets poets." Whitman's provocative and recurring theological teasing in the *Leaves* ("Did you guess the celestial laws are yet to be work'd over and rectified?")[25] both mirrors *Festus'* eschatological trajectory and its perceived indifference to earlier poetic "celestial" laws. Whitman is rarely considered in a Spasmodic light, of course, because he has been embraced as the quintessential American poet (in the context of American contemporaries, he seems more atypical), and because he so famously celebrated himself as an original genius, arising *sui generis* from the population. Yet nothing is more Spasmodic than this model of the original poetic genius. We know that Whitman read Smith; we may safely guess that he read Bailey as well.[26] In retrospect, it only seems odd that Whitman has not been seen as a Spasmodic more often.

Perhaps Whitman has not been so viewed because of his zealous patriotism. As he wrote in the 1888 preface:

> I know very well that my Leaves could not possibly have emerged or been fashion'd or completed, from any other era than the latter half of the Nineteenth Century, nor from any other land than democratic America, and from the absolute triumph of the National Union arms.
>
> (p. 574)

This claim, that the Leaves "could not possibly have emerged" from "any other land than democratic America" if not untrue, is arguably disingenuous. By identifying his poetry as a conspicuously and uniquely American endeavor, Whitman neglects his Spasmodic heritage. Whitman is by all accounts a greater poet than the principal Spasmodics, but this does not preclude their influence. Indeed, he may be argued to improve on Smith and Bailey just as Chaucer, for instance, improves on Boccaccio. Like Whitman, Chaucer never acknowledged the influence of his most significant models. Alternately, if Whitman mostly means here that "democratic America" was uniquely receptive to his style of poetry, then the Spasmodic Clough should be the last to argue. During his lifetime, Clough too was more quickly embraced in New England than in England, whereas most of Clough's British obituaries failed even to recognize that he had published *Amours de Voyage* in the opening numbers of the *Atlantic Monthly* to a more receptive American public.

The final irony of Clough's conversion to Arnold's early aesthetics, of course, is that Arnold's own most memorable and influential criticism in later years would return to a Romantic fusion of religion and poetry (or a replacement of religion by poetry) in a manner that calls to mind the poetic projects of Clough and Bailey. Arnold's 1848 repudiation of Spasmodic poetry belies the extent to which he later conceded Clough's and Bailey's implicit argument—and Gilfillan's explicit one—that poetry was doing the devotional and metaphysical work of religion. In his 1880 introduction to Thomas Humphry Ward's anthology *The English Poets*, for instance, Arnold famously proposes poetry as the exclusive heir to traditional religion:

> There is not a creed which is not shaken, not an accredited dogma which is not shown to be questionable, not a received tradition which does not threaten to dissolve. . . . But for poetry the idea is everything; the rest is a world of illusion, of divine illusion. Poetry attaches its emotion to the idea; the idea *is* the fact. The strongest part of our religion to-day is its unconscious poetry.[27]

As in much of his later criticism, Arnold here puts a small twist on an old Romantic idea. His vision is not just that traditional religion entails "unconscious poetry" (an idea that Gilfillan takes to lunatic extremes), but

that poetry provides a more stable spiritual support than traditional religion, and that it is, in fact, "the future of religion." This neo-Romantic enthusiasm owes much to Clough's spirit, if not to his direct influence. Isobel Armstrong has observed that the young Clough and Arnold each wrote poetry as though the other were looking over his shoulder (p. 172). Perhaps the older Arnold felt Clough's ghost on his shoulder still. This famous distinction between the precariousness of dogmas and the factuality of ideas might have been written by the young Clough as easily as by the older Arnold. So if Arnold stymied Clough's poetic life, perhaps Clough animated Arnold's critical one. As late as the 1880s, a Spasmodic apostate could still inspire devotion.

### Notes

1. Richard Cronin, "The Spasmodics," in *A Companion to Victorian Poetry,* ed. Alison Chapman, Richard Cronin, and Antony Harrison (Oxford: Blackwell, 2002).

2. The battle metaphor comes from: [Sir Edward Bruce Hamley], "Alexander Smith's Poems," *Blackwood's Edinburgh Magazine,* March 1854.

3. George Saintsbury, *A History of Nineteenth Century Literature (1780-1895)* (London, 1896), pp. 308-309.

4. Florence Boos, "'Spasm' and Class: W. E. Aytoun, George Gilfillan, Sydney Dobell and Alexander Smith," *VP* [*Victorian Poetry*] 42, no. 4 (2004): 553-583; Antony Harrison, "Victorian Culture Wars: Alexander Smith, Arthur Hugh Clough, and Matthew Arnold in 1853," *VP* 42, no. 4 (2004): 509-520; Herbert Tucker, "Glandular Omnism and Beyond: The Victorian Spasmodic Epic," *VP* 42, no. 4 (2004): 429-450.

5. From January 22, 1853, Arthur Hugh Clough, *The Correspondence,* ed. F. L. Mulhauser, 2 vols. (Oxford: Clarendon Press, 1957), p. 368. See Yopie Prins for the influence of Clough's classical training on his distinctive use of English meters ("Victorian Meters," in *The Cambridge Companion to Victorian Poetry,* ed. Joseph Bristow [Cambridge: Cambridge Univ. Press, 2000], and Yopie Prins, "Metrical Translation: Nineteenth-Century Homers and the Hexameter Mania," in *Nation, Language and the Ethics of Translation,* ed. Sandra Bermann and Michael Wood [forthcoming; Princeton: Princeton Univ. Press, 2005]). Arnold commends Clough in his 1860-1861 "Lectures on Homer" (*On the Classical Tradition,* ed. R. H. Super, *Complete Prose Works of Matthew Arnold* [Ann Arbor: Univ. of Michigan Press, 1960]).

6. Matthew Arnold, *The Letters of Matthew Arnold,* ed. Cecil Y. Lang (Charlottesville: Univ. Press of Virginia, 1996), 1:82.

7. Arthur Hugh Clough, *The Poems of Arthur Hugh Clough,* ed. F. L. Mulhauser, 2nd ed. (Oxford: Clarendon Press, 1974).

8. As Arnold wrote Clough in December 1847, "And as a metrical curiosity the one about 2 musics does not seem to me happy" (*Letters,* 1:76).

9. Phelan, for instance, compares Clough's religious imagery to Newman's imagery in *Loss and Gain* (Arthur Hugh Clough, *Clough—Selected Poems,* ed. J. P. Phelan [New York: Longman, 1995], p. 40).

10. Philip James Bailey, *Festus, A Poem,* 8th American ed. (Boston, 1849), 3197.

11. Robin Gilmour discusses mid-Victorian moral objections to Christian doctrine in "Religion: Reform, Rejection, Reconstruction" (*The Victorian Period: The Intellectual and Cultural Context of English Literature 1830-1890* [New York: Longman, 1993], pp. 85-94).

12. Florence Boos, for instance, identifies this as George Gilfillan's primary motivation for pursuing a literary career (pp. 558-559).

13. James Anthony Froude, *The Nemesis of Faith,* 2nd ed. (London, 1849), p. 16.

14. George Gilfillan, *The Bards of the Bible* (New York, 1851), p. ix-x.

15. Clough recommended *The Nemesis* to his provost E. Hawkins as "a good deal of what I imagine pervades the young world in general" (*Correspondence,* pp. 248-249).

16. Isobel Armstrong, *Victorian Poetry: Poetics and Politics* (New York: Routledge, 1993), pp. 188-191.

17. This is especially apparent in the shorter version of Aytoun's parody that appeared in *Blackwood's Edinburgh Magazine* (75 [1854]: 533-551).

18. Elizabeth Barrett Browning, *Aurora Leigh,* ed. Margaret Reynolds (Athens: Ohio Univ. Press, 1992), Book V, ll. 214-216.

19. John Addington Symonds, "Arthur Hugh Clough," *The Fortnightly Review* 24 (1868): 615-616.

20. We know this because Clough wrote Lowell upon his return to England. In August, Clough wrote, "I hear little or nothing said of your enemy Alexr Smith. People talk mostly about the Camp at Chobham, and the news from Constantinople" (*Correspondence,* p. 459).

21. F. T. Palgrave wrote Clough from England on April 7, 1853: "A poor [review] by Lewes gives long extracts from the last poetical planet—A.

Smith of Glasgow. He appears to be a 'nature' but it is rather spes [expectation] than res [achievement, matter] and to compare him to Keats or Shakspere (in his Poems of course) seems to me to 'over part' him. But I have not read the book itself" (*Correspondence,* p. 413). Antony Harrison demonstrates how Clough's and Arnold's Smith correspondence took place within a larger conversation upon what Arnold perceived as the deficiencies of Smith's Romantic models (pp. 510-511).

22. J. P. Phelan offers the best textual history of the *Dipsychus* manuscripts.

23. In early 1854, when Charles Eliot Norton urged Clough to publish a collected edition of his poetry, he responded self-effacingly that "I don't think I can set to work to unravel my weaved-up follies at this present moment" (*Poems,* p. xiv).

24. "As to Alexander Smith I have not read him—I shrink from what is so intensely immature—but I think the extracts I have seen most remarkable—and I think at the same time that he will not go far" (*The Letters of Matthew Arnold,* p. 264).

25. Walt Whitman, *The Complete Poems,* ed. Francis Murphy (New York: Penguin, 1975), p. 697.

26. Walt Whitman, *Notebooks and Unpublished Prose Manuscripts,* ed. Edward F. Grier (New York: New York Univ. Press, 1984), 5:1771.

27. Thomas Humphry Ward, *The English Poets* (London: Macmillan, 1923), 1:xvii.

**Christopher Matthews (essay date March 2004)**

SOURCE: Matthews, Christopher. "'A Relation, Oh Bliss! Unto Others': Heterosexuality and the Ordered Liberties of *The Bothie of Toper-Na-Fuosich.*" *Nineteenth-Century Literature* 58, no. 4 (March 2004): 474-505.

[*In the following essay, Matthews offers a reading of Clough's* The Bothie of Toper-Na-Fuosich *that analyzes the work's "methods of thematizing both metrical turbulence and heterosexual passion."*]

Any response to Arthur Hugh Clough's 1848 experiment in English hexameter, ***The Bothie of Toper-Na-Fuosich,*** must to some extent attempt to describe the poem's synthesis of an array of formal, narrative, and thematic elements: its formulations of class politics and explorations of religion and duty; its lively, direct, and cagey approach to sexuality; its tonal mix of playfulness and seriousness, earnestness and satire; its general stylistic heterogeneity of epic, pastoral, and realism; and its organization of all of these elements within a rambunctious and fluid meter. Although for many of Clough's contemporaries it was the least successful of the poem's mischievous efforts, his use of hexameters in *The Bothie* has become key to subsequent scholars' understanding of the poem's overall hybridity and its ability to range so widely and wildly.[1] More recently, a different strain of Clough scholarship has begun to admire the poem's sexual directness, the ways in which it seems to be "bursting with . . . instinctive sexual desire": Rupert Christiansen, for instance, appreciates Clough's verse for its unashamed directness and for the way that this "prosy, anxious, witty, multivalent" poem "delves into matters of sexual instinct with a startling frankness and sensuality unparalleled in 19th-century English literature."[2] Still, despite the concomitant and occasionally overlapping scholarly interest in these two facets of the poem, no studies have sufficiently addressed how Clough's poem synthesizes its meter with its sexual talk, or how this synthesis elucidates the poem's politics. Such integration sets the terms of the present essay: describing the poem's hexameters and its heterosexual narrative as intertwined and mutually informing experiments, I examine *The Bothie*'s metrical form as integral to its representation of sexual forms, and its challenges to sexual conventions as integral to its challenges to metrical conventions.

In *The Bothie* Clough offers competing theories about the relationship between erotic desires and political ideals: through a series of arguments among its characters, the poem attempts to describe an erotic life both untainted by politics and yet, paradoxically, politically engaged. Early in the poem Philip Hewson, a middle-class student-radical and the poem's protagonist, describes his inauguration into an erotics very much aligned with his professed class politics: he finds his greatest arousal in the spectacle of laboring women and, in turn, offers that arousal as a sign of his radical sympathies and progressive ideals. The conjunction of Philip's political and erotic agendas initiates a debate between him and his tutor Adam—in particular, a debate between Philip's youthful theory of radical desire and Adam's theory of considered, and conservative, choice. These debates set the stage for Philip's romantic quest, the main drama of the poem, during which he tests and rejects both theories on his way to discovering a sexual mode that blurs the lines between instinctual desire and moral choice, authentic love and politically serviceable marriage.

Throughout *The Bothie* Clough therefore engages in the process of constructing sexuality—specifically "heterosexuality"—as a nexus of sexual desire, political identity, and sexual-political practice.[3] Organized thus, heterosexuality becomes an experiment in form that is intimately connected with his metrical experiment. Clough's modern hexameter, inherited from Homer but fully anglicized, demonstrates that a form that produces scandalous rhythms may simultaneously generate new kinds of linguistic order; similarly, Clough represents heterosexuality in *The Bothie* as a disruption capable of producing an ideal social order. In other words, through his poem's metrical experimentation, and through its allegorization of that experiment, Clough argues that "ordered liberties"—to adapt George Saintsbury's description of modern English prosody—resolve the contradictions of politically useful passion.[4]

Clough might be said to have created in *The Bothie* a poetic form appropriate for the kind of radicalisms with which he felt sympathy in 1848—the year he refused to sign the Thirty-Nine Articles at Oriel College, Oxford, while new revolutionary conflicts broke out on the Continent and the Chartist petition lost its final vote in the British Parliament.[5] But *The Bothie* is neither an explicitly political allegory of foreign or domestic turbulence nor the kind of theological justification that some critics might have expected after his departure from Oxford. Instead, Clough uses a love story to organize the poem's metrical and political ambitions.[6] Whereas the belated appearance of a shadowy "love" in Matthew Arnold's "Dover Beach" (1867) might suggest a weak attempt to compensate for historical, political, and theological turmoil with private romance, sexual love in *The Bothie* is not a marginal compensation but rather the keystone that joins Clough's metrical and political radicalism.[7] As Stefanie Markovits has demonstrated, Clough's next hexametrical love poem, *Amours de Voyage* (composed in 1849 but not published until 1858), similarly "reverse[s] the standard epic hierarchy" so that "the love story provides the major plot line of the work" while major historical events (the 1849 French siege of Rome) perform only "as counterpoint."[8] While love fails in *Amours* to the extent that—important for the "crisis of action" that Markovits describes—"anticlimax characterizes the poem" ("Arthur Hugh Clough," p. 453), heterosexual desire's usurpation of the epic center in *The Bothie* is playful and provocative but not necessarily ironic. Matthew Reynolds argues that *The Bothie*'s final romantic relationship "is too complex to be understood as the realization of a political commitment," and only confirms that "the realm of love and the realm of politics cannot be mapped onto one another."[9] Yet such "complexity" may be a sign not simply of the incommensurability of love and politics but, more tellingly, of the poem's efforts to align them—to define, in fact, modern heterosexual love as politically emblematic not despite but because of its murky resistance to full public disclosure or easy allegiance. Focusing attention on sexuality's status as formal experiment, then, reveals that *The Bothie* represents heterosexual love as capable of producing new structures of both erotic and social relation.[10]

In the following discussion, I begin by presenting a reading of *The Bothie*'s heterosexual and political narrative, and then address the synergy between the poem's sexual and metrical allegories. I have strategically and temporarily separated narrative from meter in the service of demonstrating, ultimately, the profound connection between these two elements in Clough's remarkable poem.

\* \* \*

In *The Bothie* Clough's narrator details the adventures of a group of Oxford students on a reading vacation in Scotland. After a night of neighborhood festivities, the students talk "of noble ladies and rustic girls," and Philip, "the chartist, the poet, the eloquent speaker," expresses an impassioned preference for these "rustic girls":

> Sick of the very names of your Lady Augustas and
>     Floras
> Am I, as ever I was of the dreary botanical titles
> Of the exotic plants, their antitypes, in the hothouse:
> Roses, violets, lilies for me! the out-of-door beauties.[11]

Philip's radicalism—in the mid-century sense of supporting republican ideals and the rights of labor—determines his ideas about female beauty, male desire, and the politics of both: "Oh, if our high-born girls knew only the grace, the attraction, / Labour, and labour alone, can add to the beauty of women," Philip argues, then the cloth used by dressmakers could be "Saved for purposes truly and widely productive" (II, 26-27, 30). Female "labour" produces female "beauty," igniting middle-class male desire and pointing the way to "purposes truly and widely productive." This is Philip's "novel economy":

> Laugh if you please at my novel economy; listen to
>     this, though;
>                 . . . . .
> Never I properly felt the relation of man to woman,
>                 . . . . .
> Never, believe me, revealed itself to me the sexual
>     glory,
> Till in some village fields in holidays now getting
>     stupid,
> One day sauntering 'long and listless,' as Tennyson
>     has it,
>                 . . . . .
> Chanced it my eye fell aside on a capless, bonnetless
>     maiden,
> Bending with three-pronged fork in a garden uproot-
>     ing potatoes.
> Was it the air? who can say? or herself, or the charm
>     of the labour?
> But a new thing was in me; and longing delicious
>     possessed me,

> Longing to take her and lift her, and put her away
>     from her slaving. . . .

(II, 34-49)

Enthralled by eroticized poverty, Philip embraces the radical potential of cross-class coupling, praises the simple exhilarations of headlong desire, and conflates love with a naively politicized and patronizing "longing to take her and lift her, and put her away from her slaving." (Philip in fact wonders whether it was "embracing or aiding that was most in my mind?" [II, 51].) Because of—rather than despite—this confusion, Philip elevates both desire and politics by identifying desire as the most important tool of political change, and political change as the legitimating end of the mystery of sexual attraction. Disregarding the ribbing of his classmates, Philip calls for a new investment of politics with the intensity of erotic desire—and of desire with the importance and social relevance of political struggle. He confesses his own discovery of an apparently natural desire for the beauty of female labor in order to lobby others to create a more just society by modifying their desires.[12]

Philip's language of "relation"—"Never I properly felt the relation of man to woman"—emphasizes both the specifically heterosexual configuration of his desire and that desire's social import: "relation" comes to signify not only the presumably prearranged compatibilities of male and female bodies but also the social connections produced by hetero-passion. Philip spectacularly continues:

>             . . . a new thing was in me, . . . the
>     secret,
> Yes, amid prurient talk, the unimparted mysterious
>     secret
> Long, the growing distress, and celled-up dishonour
>     of boyhood,
> Recognised now took its place, a relation, oh bliss!
>     unto others.

(II, 58-61)

An awakening from masturbatory practices, Philip's encounter with the bonnetless maiden demonstrates that once his desire (that "unimparted mysterious secret") attaches itself to external objects, it has the power to usher him into a larger world of relation "unto others"—of relation structured by but extending beyond the couple.[13] Philip's encounter thus marks a fundamental transition from isolated and arguably pre-social eroticism to a socially instrumental sexuality, one that will employ and mobilize desire in order to chart status, identity, and practice on a grid of social meaning.

While Philip, especially in the early books of the poem, dwells in a naive and troubling unawareness of his desire's privileged power, his passion becomes and remains the poem's heroic force. Both the naïveté and the heroism of Philip's passions stand in stark relief to his tutor's opposition. Adam (a man who, we are told, is nearing forty and fully removed from the instigations of desire) provides the resistance necessary to force a refinement of Philip's theories, urging Philip to temper his passions and trade his inflammatory cross-class rhetoric for a class-blind conception of "the good":

> You are a boy; when you grow a man, you'll find
> things alter.
> You will learn to seek the good, to scorn the attrac-
> tive,
> Scorn all mere cosmetics, as now of rank and fashion,
> Delicate hands, and wealth, so then of poverty also.
>
>                                             (II, 174-77)

While Adam provides a necessary skepticism in the face of Philip's unsavory condescension toward laboring women, Adam's responses teeter on a toothless moralism if not a stodgy conservatism: "Good, wherever found, you will choose, be it humble or stately, / . . . / Yes, we must seek what is good, it always and it only" (II, 179-81). Adam's proffered wisdom not only corrects the naïveté of Philip's ideas but also robs them of their political force, offering absolutism ("it always and it only") and a bland, coercive universalism ("Good, wherever found, you will choose") as cures for the realities that Philip, however imperfectly, perceives. Put off, it appears, by politics in general, Adam offers a complacent morality that preaches class-blindness as a covert support for a status quo of class-sameness.

The political valences of this debate become most clear when Adam and Philip discuss that dreaded radical ideal, equality. Adam tells Philip that his argument rests "Partly on error" because he "long[s] for equality" (II, 214). One of Philip's fellow students jokes, "That's the sore place, that confounded Egalité," calling Philip "the same as the Chartist who made address in Ireland, / *What, and is not one man, fellow-men, as good as another?*" (II, 215-17). Transferring the problem of egalité from homosocial brotherhood to heterosexuality, Adam asks, "*is not one woman as good as another?*":

> Irrespective of wealth and of poverty, pain and enjoy-
> ment,
> Women all have their duties, the one as well as the
> other;
> Are all duties alike? Do all alike fulfil them?
> It is to these we must look, and in these we are not on
> a level.
>
>                                             (II, 220-26)

Rejecting Philip's belief in equality because—in the realm of fulfilling their duties—they "are not on a level," Adam implies that Philip's attention to class difference misleads him to believe in equality, while an attention to *moral* difference would allow an appreciation of *inequality*. Adam offers an exquisite description of a

pervasive and natural—as opposed to unjust—inequality: "Nowhere equality reigns in God's sublime creations, / Star is not equal to star, nor blossom the same as blossom" (II, 229-30). Meanwhile, Adam argues only for the equalities within strata of the class system, emphasizing the compatibilities of "duty" rather than the differences of class: "We must all do something, and in my judgment do it / In our station; independent of it, but not regardless" (II, 253-54). To be sure, Adam's conclusion—that it is only within equal stations that men and women can relate as equals—seems potentially progressive in terms of gender politics, offering to correct the ways in which Philip's class politics take erotic delight in asymmetrical power. But Adam's position necessitates the maintenance of class difference that looks rather ugly in the face of Philip's naive but determined desire to change the world. The reader cheers for Philip, inspired by his humor (if nothing else), when he responds to Adam:

> Doing our duty in that state of life to which God has
> called us,
> Seems to me always to mean, when the little rich
> boys say it,
> Standing in velvet frock by mama's brocaded flounces,
> Eying her gold-fastened book and the chain and watch
> at her bosom,
> Seems to me always to mean, Eat, drink, and never
> mind others.
>
>                                             (II, 257-61)

Such lines remind us that Philip's passions operate as the heroic force of the poem, despite and to a certain extent because of Adam's conservative wisdom.

It has become something of a common critical assumption that *The Bothie* resolves these debates by nudging Philip toward a realization of the wisdom of Adam's advice. Joseph Patrick Phelan argues that although Philip had earlier "refuse[d] to acknowledge the reality of the distinction between 'the good' and 'the attractive,'" he "now sees the reality of the ethical distinction he had earlier failed to acknowledge" ("Radical Metre," p. 183). But Philip's discovery of a sexual "relation unto others" is not overwritten or even fundamentally affected by Adam's theories or by any final relinquishment of passion. Rather, Philip finds that both his and Adam's theories fail; ultimately, Adam adjudicates only a further formalizing of Philip's instinctual compass, still very much intact. The complexity of this solution likewise confounds a long-standing temptation of critics to explain *The Bothie*'s final resolution of Philip's and Adam's opposed worldviews by aligning Clough—both an ex-tutor at Oxford and a one-time radical student—with either Adam or Philip.[14] Perhaps most intriguing, Philip and Adam's intellectual rivalry resembles Clough's famously antagonistic intimacy with Matthew Arnold and their arguments over radical action and conservative reflectiveness.[15] The most compelling fact of these cross-wired identifications, in the end, is their multiplicity: Clough is Philip, Clough is Adam, Arnold is Adam. The body of Clough's work (especially his later poem *Dipsychus* [1869]) suggests that if Clough might be said to represent himself anywhere in *The Bothie,* it is as the argument itself that fluctuates between Adam and Philip.[16] Neither Adam's nor Philip's perspective prevails: the solution that *The Bothie* offers will be neither a conservative squelching of radical passion nor a lusty disregard of "the good." As many critics have noted regarding the poem's formal combination of Latin and Oxfordian slang, as well as pastoral and farce, the sexual-political-moral resolution that *The Bothie* offers is a hybrid one, akin to the "liberal polity of diction" that Matthew Reynolds identifies in the poem's shifting rhetorics (*Realms of Verse,* p. 36).[17] Between instinctual radicalism and conservative reason, Philip discovers a mode in which fervor, both democratic and erotic, produces rather than corrupts formalized sexuality.

Striking out into the highlands with a few of his fellow-students, Philip leaves Adam behind and immediately falls for a tidy embodiment of his "bonnetless maiden" ideal. Delayed at a farmhouse by inclement weather, Philip becomes "Smitten by golden-haired Katie" (III, 198), and soon enough "was with her away in the shearing, / And the next morning ensuing was found in the ingle beside her / Kneeling, picking the peats from her apron" (III, 207-9). His companions leave him there "drying clothes, making fires, making love" (III, 223). With Katie, Philip's theories of attraction are less tested by experience than dramatized, and one of his classmates (already suspecting that Philip's radical passion is really just run-of-the-mill lust) mocks Katie's neat incarnation of Philip's romantic archetype:

> Did you not say she was seen every day in her beauty and bedgown
> Doing plain household work, as washing, cooking, scouring?
> How could he help but love her? nor lacked there of course the attraction
> That in a blue cotton print tucked up over striped linsey-woolsey,
> Barefoot, barelegged, he beheld her, with arms bare up to the elbows,
> Bending with fork in her hand in a garden uprooting potatoes?

> (III, 232-37)

Katie's very suitability to Philip's prejudices will indeed doom their relationship and expose the limitations of the desire that Philip espouses. Philip mysteriously abandons Katie's farmhouse, and the poem discovers him in the mountains lamenting the physical and social boundaries that prevent him from fulfilling his desires: "Souls of the dead, one fancies, can enter and be with the living; / Would I were dead, I keep saying, that so I

could go and uphold her!" (IV, 41-42). Such astral penetration promises precisely the kind of paternalistic, democratic eroticism that Philip advocates, and he experiences with Katie an inauguration into the kind of "relation" he desires: he "felt folded unto her, united, / Yea, without touch united, essentially, bodily with her, / . . . / Yea, for the first time in life a man complete and perfect" (IV, 134-38). But Clough's narrator has begun to expose the extent to which such mingling is destined to be met with resistance (if not from the flirtatious Katie then from the social world), and he also explores the necessity of separating the fantasy of democratic assimilation from an imperial project of erotic conquest in order to achieve a true "relation unto others." Prescient of the elegiac voice of Tennyson's *In Memoriam* (1850) and its concerns with the ways in which a probable loss of identity in the afterlife undermines any hopes of reuniting with dead loved ones, Philip must seek a middle ground between such longing for mingling and a formal structure of relation that allows for individuality sufficient to make relations meaningful. At this point, Philip's self-involved relation with Katie seems barely removed from the ominous "celled-up dishonour of boyhood."

Experiencing a mysterious change of heart, Philip undertakes a second misapplication of his principles and shifts from republican to imperial erotics. A strange letter informs the Oxford party that he "was staying at Balloch," the home of the stately aunt of one of his fellow students, where he has found new love: "Philip to Balloch had come and was dancing with Lady Maria" (IV, 279-80). Writing to Adam of Lady Maria's "imperial sweetness," Philip finds himself with his "old faith and doctrine abjuring" (V, 45-46). He rejects his old approach in favor, it seems, of Adam's, seeking a "relation unto others" through the compatibility available by playing within rather than against the class system. Adam has just composed a letter that urges Philip to do just this, arguing that lowly maidens like Katie, uneducated and unworldly, are simply too vulnerable before their betters to make a truly equal match:

> To the prestige of the richer the lowly are prone to be yielding,
>  . . . . .
> Ignorant they as they are, they have but to conform and be yielding;
>  . . . . .
> How shall a poor quiet girl self-create the law and commandment?
> How shall a poor silly sheep get endowed with the will of a woman!

> (IV, 251-59)

Still, Adam demonstrates a discomfort with the suddenness of Philip's transformation, and he would be right to balk at the extremes to which Philip has taken his logic. Philip explains that the poor are creatures with very different capacities, meant to work and look up in admiration:

> Often I find myself saying, and know not myself as I
>   say it,
> What of the poor and the weary? their labour and pain
>   is needed.
> Perish the poor and the weary! what can they better
>   than perish,
> Perish in labour for her, who is worth the destruction
>   of empires?
>
> (V, 53-56)

If Katie's embodiment of Philip's radical ideal made his overwhelming desires immaturely imperial, then Maria's embodiment of Adam's conservative theories seems to have made Philip too submissive to another's imperial allure. Philip still needs to discover, via a path uncharted by Adam, a woman endowed with "will" and the ability to "self-create," who will neither dominate nor be dominated.

Philip's submission to Lady Maria is as brief as was his domination of Katie: returning from Lady Maria's estate, an accident brings Philip to a cottage (the "bothie" of Clough's title) where he meets Elspie MacKaye—the woman, we now learn, who caused Philip to flee Katie so mysteriously. As we discover in one of Philip's letters to Adam, Philip left Katie because he passed a woman whose look troubled him:

> . . . it had seemed to regard me with simple superior
>   insight,
> Quietly saying to itself—Yes, there he is still in his
>   fancy,
> Letting drop from him at random as things not worth
>   considering
> All the benefits gathered and put in his hands by
>   fortune,
> Loosing a hold which others, content and unambi-
>   tious,
> Trying down here to keep-up, know the value of bet-
>   ter than he does.
>
> (IV, 149-54)

The passing woman's look exposes to Philip the extent to which his pursuit of Katie and other lasses is only a misguided exercise or misapplication of his own (urban, middle-class) privilege. Responding to Philip's narrative of this encounter, the indefatigable Adam waxes mystically upon the rare power of the moral vision of which Philip has become the object. Adam writes to Philip:

> There are exceptional beings, one finds them distant
>   and rarely,
> Who, endowed with the vision alike and the interpreta-
>   tion,

> See, by their neighbours' eyes, and their own still mo-
>   tions enlightened,
> In the beginning the end, in the acorn the oak of the
>   forest,
>
> . . . . .
>
> There are inheritors, is it? by mystical generation,
> Heiring the wisdom and ripeness of spirits gone-by;
>   without labour
> Owning what others by doing and suffering earn.
>
> . . . . .
>
> Working, an instinct blind, in woman and child and
>   rustic.
>
> (IV, 210-26)

Adam is especially charmed by this power that "without labour" is nonetheless "working," and he anticipates Philip's indulgence of luxury with Lady Maria in this praise for the mystical product of a rustic woman's unseen labor. If this penetrating wisdom becomes Philip's, then it is a reward not "earned" but "heired" to him by Elspie's gaze. In other words, even Philip's new insight into his misguided romance with Katie remains stuck within that system of misplaced value and labor that Elspie's gaze exposes. In order to refine his desire's democratic potential, Philip and Elspie will need to discover both a different model of labor and the relations that labor supports and necessitates: the one-sided bestowal of wisdom and the imperialism of passion will need to be replaced by an intuition both mutual and self-originating.

Elspie arguably functions as a sign of Philip's final embrace of Adam's moral wisdom. Adam, after all, approves when Philip meets her, saying rather paradoxically if not a little backhandedly, "Yes, she is beautiful, Philip, beautiful even as morning: / Yes, it is that which I said, the Good and not the Attractive!" (VI, 85-86). Echoing Adam, Elspie tells Philip that her devastating glance registered her perception of his romance with Katie as "all delusion, / All a mere chance, and accident,—not proper choosing" (VII, 25-26). We might say that Philip, then, in order to join with Elspie, comes over to her (and Adam's) way of thinking, no longer following passion alone but instead exercising "choice."[18] But, in the poem's dialectic, Maria rather than Elspie represents Philip's embrace of Adam's stark theory. Philip writes to Adam from Lady Maria's: "Yes, you have conquered, my friend! . . . / . . . I yield to the laws and arrangements" (V, 126-27). Philip's relation to Elspie is the result of the failures of *both* Adam's and Philip's theories, and thus it importantly brings together the remnants of both. Neither low nor high, Elspie is everything that Philip ever wanted in a laboring, rustic maiden, as well as being intelligent, moral, and refined—to the extent that Adam's belief in same-class relationships and Philip's desire for cross-class coupling can coexist. Elspie represents the reconciliation of Philip's original passion with a fortunate choice of the good, regardless of class-based cosmetics but underwritten by the combination of her rustic charm with her suspiciously unrustic refinement. Solving the problem of class, Elspie correspondingly solves the problem of sex. She promises us that these differences dissolve—as Philip might have argued they would—into a balanced relationship in which the *frisson* of class difference will lead to a romance of equality.[19]

Philip's passion is not, then, disciplined into surrender or transformed in any simple way from desire into choice; it remains, rather, a necessary element of the sexuality under construction in *The Bothie.* Philip demonstrates the necessity of retaining passion throughout the process of its refinement—structuring a new sexual subjectivity upon erotic instinct's ability to operate *as* moral intuition rather than upon the replacement of erotic instinct with moral intuition. Philip, in other words, invents his own form of "proper choosing," the synthesis of which involves less Adam's wisdom than Elspie's "instinct blind" (IV, 226) with a healthy dose of Philip's own "blindfold hurry" (IV, 210). Indeed, Elspie's solution allows, or invites, Philip's ardor to reassert itself in the final books of the poem:

> As at return of tide the total weight of ocean,
>
> . . . . .
>
> Sets-in amain . . .
> Heaving, swelling, spreading, the might of the mighty
>   Atlantic;
>
> . . . . .
>
> So in my soul of souls through its cells and secret
>   recesses,
> Comes back, swelling and spreading, the old demo-
>   cratic fervour.
>
> (IX, 102-10)

Rather than squelching his student-desires, Philip becomes a kind of erotic tutor to Elspie, helping her discover her own tidal passion: seemingly for the first time, Elspie "Felt . . . in myriad springs, her sources, far in the mountains, / Stirring, collecting, rising, upheaving, forth-out-flowing" (VII, 162-63). For both Philip and Elspie a flooding passion-as-democratic-fervor has returned to motivate and guide. In Philip's hands, then, Adam's arguments shed their austerity, and their moral earnestness gives way to Philip's erotic earnestness—which in turn gains an aura of moral choice.

While Philip's passion remains essential, his desire for assimilation has been tamed—and that, perhaps, is the real contribution of Adam's skepticism. Philip's final departure with Elspie to New Zealand echoes his earlier desire to feel "into Eden / Carried anew, . . . to see, like the gardener of earth uncorrupted, / Eve from the hand of her Maker advancing, an help-meet" (II, 97-99). But if Philip—an "Adam" to the extent that he does *not* resemble his tutor—may have wanted Katie to become one of his ribs (to be folded into him or to be himself "folded unto her"), then he has learned to maintain the boundaries necessary to engage with Elspie as separate-but-equal. Such boundaries heighten rather than reduce erotic possibility; the result is a couple that embodies a "relation unto others" that itself generates relations to *other* others, a web of social connection with romantic relation at its center. Thus in *The Bothie* Clough imagines a society founded upon and cemented both by such a couple and by the possibility that every other couple will enact this myth over and over again. Aggressively Edenic, Clough's poem mints a heterosexuality that itself promises to manufacture further couples whose erotic connection is not a hermetically sealed contradiction of social relation, but its very foundation.

The idea that the equality of differently gendered lovers enables a productive relation to the social order seems to have been a principle that Clough himself took seriously, although in a way that eschews Philip's romantic rhetoric. On 1 January 1852, in one of his early letters to Blanche Smith, his future wife, Clough defines "the true apple" that ended paradise as woman's mistaken notion that "Love is everything":

> Love is not everything, Blanche; don't believe it, nor try to make me pretend to believe it. *'Service'* is everything. Let us be fellow-servants. There is no joy nor happiness, nor way nor name by which men may be saved but this. . . .
>
> (*Correspondence,* I, 300)

In another letter to Blanche, written a day later, Clough continues his thoughts:

> . . . I ask no girl to be my friend that we may be a fond foolish couple together all in all each to the other. If one that has dreamt of such unreality will open her eyes and look about her and consent to be what alone in plain fact she can be, a help-mate—that is a different thing. I will ask no one to put off her individuality for me; nor will I, weak and yielding as I am, if I can help it, put off mine for anyone.
>
> (*Correspondence,* I, 301)

Rejecting the self-involved, "yielding," and "foolish" couple, Clough calls for mutual "individuality" as a prerequisite for a real relation between others. And his admonition that "service is everything" calls for that relation unto others to become a broader relation of the couple to the world at large. Clough wants nothing to do with a return to the confused identities of Eden: after a lukewarm lamentation of the Fall, Clough looks ahead to a new Eden defined by labor, where love, properly made, becomes a service to the world.[20]

* * *

Such are *The Bothie*'s romantic thesis, antithesis, and synthesis on the level of story. Formally, Clough's metrical experimentation further allegorizes and materializes a sexual architecture that allows Philip's desire to become social practice. Among Clough's contemporaries the poem's sexual and metrical politics certainly shared—to the point of becoming indistinguishable—an ability to arouse scandal. Geoffrey Tillotson suggests that, whether readers understood the bawdy insinuations of its title or not, they still "must have found [*The Bothie*] offensively grotesque" because of its meter ("Clough's *Bothie*," p. 119). And while supporters such as Charles Kingsley, in his *Fraser's* review, called Clough's hexameters "abnormal" (p. 106), William Whewell found the verse generally "uncouth and licentious."[21] Challenging at least the metrical side of such criticisms with a compelling assertion of Clough's musicality and intentional irregularity, Joseph Patrick Phelan connects *The Bothie*'s metrical experimentation with a radical poetic and political assertion of rhythm: he argues that, given Clough's public support for both metrical experimentation and the recent Revolution in France, "it is . . . unsurprising that his first act on eventually leaving Oxford in 1848 should have been the composition of *The Bothie,* a poem which throws off the shackles of classical decorum in every sense by setting the hexameter of Homer and Virgil to 'jig-time' in the Highlands of Scotland" ("Radical Metre," p. 175). "Jig-time" suggests the rhythmic passion of Clough's hexameters, and Clough, aware of the challenges and thrills of the poem's music, repeatedly discovers in the landscapes it describes figures for the unusual, tripping energy of its liberated, homegrown rhythms. *The Bothie*'s figuring of rhythmic passion, however, illuminates not only the poem's metrical but also its sexual scandals and experiments. In fact, *The Bothie*'s meter itself becomes an allegory of the democratic desire whose passionate equalities and inequalities define the poem's main drama.

In *The Bothie* Clough continually returns to water—in the form of tides, oceans, streams, and other liquid movements—in order to think about its hexameter, the erotic passions of Philip's tale, and the ways that meter might activate and embody the passionate rhythms of both verse and desire. Yopie Prins argues that *The Bothie* projects a "metrical allegory into the landscape, self-consciously naturalizing the formal mechanism of its verse," and she identifies one of the poem's many aqueous scenes as just such an allegory of the poem's "turbulent dactyls" ("Victorian Meters," pp. 104, 105):

> Springing far off from a loch unexplored in the folds
> of great mountains,
> Falling two miles through rowan and stunted alder,
> enveloped

Then for four more in a forest of pine, where broad
and ample
Spreads to convey it the glen with heathery slopes on
both sides:
Broad and fair the stream, with occasional falls and
narrows;
But, where the lateral glen approaches the vale of the
river,
Met and blocked by a huge interposing mass of
granite,
Scarce by a channel deep-cut, raging up, and raging
onward,
Forces its flood through a passage, so narrow, a lady
would step it.

(*The Bothie,* III, 21-29)

Prins argues that, "simultaneously describing and enacting the hexameters in which the story is told," Clough's verse "streams along in one continuous sentence, . . . moving laterally across each line and ever downward, until it is forced along a channel 'deep-cut'" ("Victorian Meters," pp. 106, 104). No mere smooth running, Clough's lines describe as they enact a roughness and irregularity that contribute to their turbulence: "The meter gathers momentum," Prins continues, "by running along in such variable feet, 'with occasional falls and narrows,' and even when 'met and blocked' by interposing caesuras, it continues 'raging up, and raging onward' with greater rapidity" (p. 105). Philip's classmates narrate another encounter with the currents of Scotland that again evokes the commotion generated by freedom opposed:

> How under Linn of Dee, where over rocks, between
> rocks,
> Freed from prison the river comes, pouring, rolling,
> rushing,
> Then at a sudden descent goes sliding, gliding,
> unbroken,
> Falling, sliding, gliding, in narrow space collected,
> Save for a curl at the end where the curve rejoins the
> level,
> Save for a ripple at last, a sheeted descent unbroken,—
> How to the element offering their bodies, down-
> shooting the fall, they
> Mingled themselves with the flood and the force of
> imperious water.

(*The Bothie,* III, 160-67)

The poem itself, with its long lines forming a wide column down the page, resembles "a sheeted descent unbroken."[22] The students identify this sheeted fall as liberation, the river "freed from prison," but it is a liberation complicated, varied, and intensified by caesura-like obstacles. While the river rushes "over" it also rushes "between" the rocks, both overcoming and submitting itself to be shaped by them; eventually the water is "in narrow space collected." Such confinement only increases the force of the final fall and its power to assimilate the bodies of the students.

But Clough's watery images figure not only the turbulence of his meter but also the fervor of those passions that are both Philip's liability and his promise. The river's "imperious water" foretells Lady Maria's "imperial sweetness," and, more important, it conjures Philip's assimilative passions in the early books of the poem, his longing to take and lift and put away from slaving his bonnetless maiden and his desire to "fuse" with Katie.[23] Even after Philip has supposedly learned Adam's lessons and courts Elspie, his passion resembles, from Elspie's point of view, these "raging" hexameters:

> You are too strong, you see, Mr. Philip! you are like
> the sea there,
> Which *will* come, through the straights and all between
> the mountains,
> Forcing its great strong tide into every nook and inlet,
> Getting far in, up the quiet stream of sweet inland
> water,
> Sucking it up, and stopping it, turning it, driving it
> backward.
>
> (VII, 124-28)

Philip's willful tide, "forcing its great strong tide into every nook and inlet," recalls the earlier stream that "forces its flood" through narrow passages. Elspie's cry makes clear that even the tide's submission to be shaped by the landscape operates, under the hydraulics produced by such shaping, as a kind of sexual penetration. But Philip's sea is not qualitatively different from Elspie's own stream and its own latent, dactylic turbulence:

> But a revulsion wrought in the brain and bosom of El-
> spie;
> And the passion she just had compared to the vehe-
> ment ocean,
> Urging in high spring-tide its masterful way through
> the mountains,
> Forcing and flooding the silvery stream, as it runs
> from the inland;
> That great water withdrawn, receding here and pas-
> sive,
> Felt she in myriad springs, her sources, far in the
> mountains,
> Stirring, collecting, rising, upheaving, forth-out-
> flowing,
> Taking and joining, right welcome, that delicate rill in
> the valley,
> Filling it, making it strong, and still descending, seek-
> ing,
> With a blind forefeeling descending, evermore seek-
> ing,
> With a delicious forefeeling, the great still sea before
> it;
> There deep into it, far, to carry, and lose in its bosom,
> Waters that still from their sources exhaustless are
> fain to be added.
>
> (VII, 157-69)

Elspie feels her own "vehement ocean" for the first time "Stirring, collecting, rising, upheaving, forth-out-flowing" in the form of a spring and a stream, striving toward its oceanic destination in Philip "with a deli-

cious forefeeling." Clough's metrical allegories thus operate to "describe and enact" (to adapt Prins's phrase) not only turbulent hexameters but also the liberation of Philip's and Elspie's erotic passion. But while Elspie's language suggests an ongoing threat of passion-as-assimilation (a desire to become lost in the "bosom" of Philip's ocean, equivalent to his desire to force his "great strong tide into every nook and inlet"), this imagery also reminds us that *The Bothie* labors toward a mode of passion and relation defined by the ordering of such liberties.[24]

Neither Clough's themes nor his form advocate any simple liberation of unfettered passion or rhythm, and neither does he lobby for an "imperial" passion without the modifications necessary to make such passion a force for social relation. Even as Clough's hexameters offer outlets to passionate rhythms, they construct an architecture in which those rhythms must function, must make musical and rhetorical meaning: the flood must be forced "through a passage." This goes to the heart of the paradox of the "modern hexameter," its new sounds threatening the classical form (a threat clear to Oxford-trained ears) even as a ghostly classicism structures and channels those rough new rhythms. While, according to Phelan, Clough's *Bothie* demonstrates the liberation of "classical learning . . . from the shackles of deference and servile imitation" ("Radical Metre," p. 182), it takes as one of its objects the ordering of such liberation, providing a subtle architecture for its radical release, following a trend that Prins describes as "the harmonization of order and liberty in English prosody" ("Victorian Meters," p. 94). Isobel Armstrong argues that Clough's hexameter lines "sound casual, yet they demand as much technical skill" and discipline as the forms of his other poems; indeed, their peculiar liberties and "flexible irregularities" might even "make his hexameter a precise instrument."[25] Philip himself could be the source of both order and passion: although Philip rages like a wild horse when arguing with Adam, "Snorting defiance and force, the white foam flecking his quarters, / Rein hanging loose to his neck, and head projected before him" (II, 86-87), his classmates describe him as "Philip who speaks like a book" (II, 158). As Prins notes, "the metrical mediation of voice is most fully developed" in Philip, whose speech, "in contrast to [that of] other students in his cohort, . . . is smoothly modulated in perfect dactylic hexameters" ("Victorian Meters," p. 103). Like those springs, tides, and waterfalls, Philip and Elspie's final sexual synthesis will represent the synergetic codependence of passion and structure.

While both Clough and Matthew Arnold "were left," Joseph Bristow argues, "with suggestive metaphors of fluidity" as "the medium in which their sense of displaced authority impossibly tried to take shape" ("Love, let us be true," p. 46), Clough's *Bothie* mobilizes figures of fluidity as not simply signs of loss, lost shape, or displaced authority but as a foundation for fledgling shapes and an opportunity for discovering new forms. Prins observes: "the poem recounts a time away from formal instruction in classical meters, yet during this interval it is continually marking forms of measurement, duration, calculation, and enumeration: times of day, days of the week, months of the calendar, numbers of people, catalogues of places, lists of names, length and width of objects, dimensions of space, all formalized into abstract quantities" ("Victorian Meters," p. 106). Even the watery liberation of the stream that falls "two miles through rowan and stunted alder, enveloped / Then for four more in a forest of pine" is counted off, both in miles and in the feet of the hexameter with which it seems increasingly synonymous. Clough's embrace of a new musicality in fact allows for, in Prins's words, a foundation of fixed and "interchangeable" "intervals of space and time" that underwrites such turbulent rhythms ("Victorian Meters," p. 106). Phelan identifies *The Bothie*'s "new and essentially musical understanding of the hexameter as a series of 'isochronous intervals' between accents" ("Radical Metre," p. 167). Syllables might take more or less time depending on their relative "stress" as long as that time is "made up for," as Clough described to a friend in the fall of 1848.[26] While notoriously roughing up the classical hexameter, Clough's prosody provides an underlying foundation where there may seem to be none; *isochrony*, as a formal equivalence underwriting Clough's hexameter, offers subtle structural stability to the passionate flux that *The Bothie* describes and enacts.

Elspie offers Philip the perfect combination of passion and structure, water and solid ground—again distinguishing herself from Katie and Lady Maria, who represent, respectively, too little and too much structure. Philip's passion for Katie is entirely liquid—"great floods of feeling" that "heave" toward her "sweet shore" (IV, 53-55)—and after leaving her, as we have seen, Philip desires a total dissolution of boundary: "Spirits escaped from the body can enter and be with the living," bringing "Joy, pure joy, as they mingle and mix inner essence with essence" (IV, 43-45). Lady Maria, in contrast, inhabits a desiccated and overly reified landscape; with her, Philip concedes, "I yield to the laws and arrangements" (V, 127).[27] The announcement that "Philip to Balloch had come and was dancing with Lady Maria" suggests the shocking possibility that Philip dances the polite, overly mannered, and formal dances of the elite—very likely the "dismal quadrille" (II, 38) he so dislikes. But Elspie, always synthesizing and balancing the demands of passion and social order, offers a figure for her relation to Philip that incorporates aqueous passion while providing the architecture necessary in *The Bothie*'s drenched landscape. The idea that such ordered liberty and structured passion speak equally and interchangeably to both Clough's radical

meter and the desires the poem seeks to formalize is tellingly demonstrated by Elspie's striking image of architectural and erotic coupling.

Responding to Philip's fear that she doubts the sincerity of his love, and foreseeing her own concerns about both her and Philip's erotic floods, Elspie compares her relationship with Philip to "the high new bridge" (VII, 59) built in her neighborhood:

> . . . I keep saying in my mind—this long time slowly
>   with trouble
> I have been building myself, up, up, and toilfully rais-
>   ing,
> Just like as if the bridge were to do it itself without
>   masons,
> Painfully getting myself upraised one stone on another,
> All one side I mean; and now I see on the other
> Just such another fabric uprising, better and stronger,
> Close to me, coming to join me: and then I sometimes
>   fancy,—
> Sometimes I find myself dreaming at nights about
>   arches and bridges,—
> Sometimes I dream of a great invisible hand coming
>   down, and
> Dropping the great key stone in the middle: there in
>   my dreaming,
> There I feel the great key stone coming in, and through
>   it
> Feel the other part—all the other stones of the
>   archway,
> Joined into mine with a queer happy sense of com-
>   pleteness, tingling
> All the way up from the other side's basement-stones
>   in the water,
> Through the very grains of mine. . . .
>
> (VII, 61-75)

Elspie's bridge perfectly resolves the accumulated aqueous images into an architectural solution to both Philip's sexual journey and the poem's metrical turbulence. As an arch that joins equal lovers and the ark necessary to survive the poem's metrical and erotic floods, Elspie's bridge provocatively figures the "ordering" of Philip's liberty and demonstrates that, with Elspie, Philip enters a structured erotics through a sufficiently social "relation unto others." Elspie's bridge figures her own self-culture—"slowly and with trouble / I have been building myself, up"—and thus the independent individuality that makes "relation" possible. The bridge remarkably asserts that this relation is fundamentally a passion both erotic and structured, a successful relation between two others and a further relation to the world beyond: though constructed "without masons," the bridge presents Philip and Elspie's love as a public-works project, the product of mutual labor to form a social unit that becomes a structure useful for others traversing a liquid landscape.[28]

The bridge configures a complementarity of individual forms, as one free-standing arch longs for another on the opposite bank, and it becomes in some sense a sign of heterosexual morphology—both the cause and the effect of genital alignment. Certainly, the provocative "key stone" evokes erotic penetration, for lack of a better term, as a ritual of personal and relational completion: Elspie feels "the great key stone coming in, and through it / Feel the other part—all the other stones of the archway, / Joined into mine with a queer happy sense of completeness." But, although it is an architectural sign of consummation, citing a general heteroerotics in which union is accomplished through penetration, the bridge offers no simple equivalence of male-female intercourse (and its ideology of complementarity). The penetrative force is a third party, "a great invisible hand" that drops the stone that pierces Philip and Elspie equally, or not at all, as it finds its place within the incomplete arch.[29] Promising a socially useful architecture as the end of sexual desire, the keystone might even function as a rejection of phallic power: the bridge is, after all, Elspie's dream of Philip not as an invading ocean but as an equal sexual and social partner. Revising Philip's fantasies of domination and submission, the bridge abstracts penetrative power from Philip, placing penetration beyond the action of any individual and making "upholding" appear the proper activity of Elspie herself, who has been "Painfully getting [her]self upraised one stone on another." Recalling the architectural innovations of medieval cathedrals, the keystone will allow each arch to put its weight upon the other and thus create a graceful, dramatically floating vault. The bridge thus models equal partnership and democratic union, offering a fantasy of mutuality and non-phallic desire that attributes the joys of penetration to divine agency and mutual labor. Not only—and yet thoroughly—an erotic allegory, the bridge figures a new kind of social contract, a sexuality that constructs social equality from erotic relation.[30]

The bridge is also another allegory of Clough's "metrical making": constructed of arches mirroring one another as they reach to meet, Elspie's bridge figures the metrical resolution of opposites that Phelan describes as one of the accomplishments of Clough's hexameter. Noting the importance of the caesura in *The Bothie,* Phelan identifies one of Clough's innovations as a mid-line switch from dactylic to "pseudo-anapaestic" feet that "transforms the line into two answering 'halves,' with the second providing a mirror-image rather than a repetition of the first" ("Radical Metre," p. 179). Even somewhat independent of this metrical feat, Clough's and Philip's repetitive syntaxes produce mirroring phrases joined by caesuras, such as Philip's declaration that he would like to see women "feel the sap of existence" (II, 107):

Yes, we should see them delighted, delighted

ourselves in the seeing.

(II, 110)

While an instance of Philip's earlier, dominating erotics—the excitement here lies in men watching women feeling—Clough's hexameter has already, through such a metrical and syntactical palindrome, begun constructing its mirroring arches. Given its essential role in joining mirror halves, the caesura resembles the keystone that Elspie envisions joining her to Philip. Unaware, it would seem, of his metaphor's resonance, Phelan argues that "the caesura is for the partisans of musical prosody the keystone of the metrical arch, a pure interval which is at once the underlying principle and the support of the entire arrangement" ("Radical Metre," p. 177). Prins describes the caesura not as a keystone per se but as an architectural feature that creates "a narrow passage across the water . . . where the turbulent dactyls subside briefly enough for us to cross to the next line" ("Victorian Meters," p. 105). The bridge, allegorizing both sex and meter, suggests that Clough's experimental interlocking syllables figure the sexual solution that Philip and Elspie discover.[31]

Clough's caesura, however, is itself fluid: Phelan notes how fully "*The Bothie* exploits the mobility of the caesura" ("Radical Metre," p. 178), and Prins suggests that "Clough manipulates the caesura within each line . . . to create a sense of continual flow through measured interruption" ("Victorian Meters," p. 105). But the caesura structures the very turbulence it generates. Ultimately, because it shifts, functioning both to instigate and to shape rhythmic passion, the caesura produces a more complex mirroring than half to half: while Elspie dreams of a more stable and equitable mirroring, the force and form of her new relation with Philip resides in a meter that restructures and regenerates its freedoms line by line. My violence to one of Clough's shifting mid-line interruptions further illustrates the point. I have repeatedly simplified Philip's phrase "a relation, oh bliss! unto others" into the handier "relation unto others," but Philip's self-interruption is metrically and otherwise important. While "oh bliss!" seems to disrupt the very connection it celebrates, such disruption intensifies the dramatic revelation of those persons with whom the "relation" exists, extending suspenseful pleasure and introducing "others" with even more syntactic and metrical emphasis. Removing the interruption to cut to the chase, I undo Clough's architecture in seeking out its import: like the mirroring caesura and the keystone of Elspie's bridge, "oh bliss!" joins two metrically identical phrases—"a relation" and "unto others." Removing the iambic "oh bliss!" breaks the regularity of the dactylic line:

a relation, [oh bliss!] unto others.

The phrase "oh bliss," as the keystone of this climactic claim, adds seemingly interruptive syllables that in fact order the line, transforming the two phrases "a relation" and "unto others" from being merely rhythmically identical to being interlocked within a dactylic/anapestic pattern and thus contributors to a metrical system. The turbulence created by the caesura—the coy interruption of Philip's declaration of sexual revelation—orders the line musically and foretells a romantic architecture that preserves, and provokes, erotic desire and pleasure ("oh bliss!") even as it strives for an orderly "relation unto others."

This solution seems peculiarly, spectacularly Victorian—not, of course, because it constrains some presumably asocial erotic energy for the sake of public propriety, but because it imagines the erotic and the social as fundamentally linked, positing both an authentically self-originating eroticism and a radical social role for such eroticism. This act of imagining the cooperation between the inner truth that the erotic is taken to measure and the needs of the social order offers a compelling snapshot of a "sexuality" under construction here in **The Bothie** and elsewhere in the middle of the nineteenth century. Charles Dickens in *David Copperfield* (1849-50), for instance, similarly constructs a kind of sexual subjectivity from its hero's negotiation and combination of erotics and ethics, all the while bringing its novelistic technologies to bear on such a solution, much as **The Bothie** mobilizes its poetics. Emphasizing the modernity of its own Victorian solution, Clough's **Bothie**—which Walter E. Houghton describes as a self-consciously "modern poem" (*Poetry of Clough*, p. 93)—presents the erotic-social intersection in terms both frivolous and epic. The poem deploys its formal and thematic hybridity in order to challenge assumptions that "love," flighty and elusive, is marginal to the march of history, and that history, stoic and immense, could never be altered by something as insubstantial as love between uncelebrated people.

However we might measure its success, Clough's poem does continually "map" (*pace* Reynolds) the realm of love upon the realm of politics. Here heterosexual love, neither blandly hegemonic nor comfortably domestic, must become something of an outlaw—from the marginal Highlands to the remote and nearly penal New Zealand—in order to become a form through which a revolutionary relation unto others can be imagined. This heterosexuality's claim to flooding, self-originating desire, in other words, allows it both to resist (Adam's sober wisdom) and to retreat (from England). And resistance and retreat give it the power of utopian vision in order to make it, in the end, an experiment in imagining new social forms.

## Notes

1. In his reclamation of Clough forty years ago, Walter E. Houghton described *The Bothie* as "a modern poem" striving for "a synthesis of elements hitherto kept apart for reasons of simplicity or decorum" (*The Poetry of Clough: An Essay in Revaluation* [New Haven: Yale Univ. Press, 1963], p. 112). Houghton echoes earlier critics in noting Clough's hexameters' "effective expression of both the familiar realities of daily life or political discussion, and at the same time subjects like autumn landscape and the sentiment of love" (p. 114). Robindra Kumar Biswas describes Clough's hexameter as "beautifully adapted" to the poem's "range and variety" (borrowing a phrase of Houghton's) of "material" and "tone" (*Arthur Hugh Clough: Towards a Reconsideration* [Oxford: Clarendon Press, 1972], p. 268).

2. *The Voice of Victorian Sex: Arthur H. Clough, 1819-1861* (London: Short Books, 2001), pp. 54, 9-10. For a similar view, see John Maynard, *Victorian Discourses on Sexuality and Religion* (Cambridge: Cambridge Univ. Press, 1993).

3. During the past twenty-five years scholars have richly explored the late-nineteenth-century production of the clinical terms—and, à la Michel Foucault, social categories—"homosexuality" and "heterosexuality" and their proliferation in popular vernacular, private imagination, and public self-fashioning. Discussing "heterosexuality" in the mid-century, I mean to examine an extended, and necessarily diffuse, construction of a modern desire defined by gender difference and performed as public identity.

4. Saintsbury discusses Tennyson as "the earliest exponent, and to no small extent the definite master, of this new ordered liberty"—i.e., modern English prosody (George Saintsbury, *A History of English Prosody, from the Twelfth Century to the Present Day,* 2d ed., 3 vols. [London: Macmillan and Co., 1923], III, 296).

5. Signing allegiance to the Thirty-Nine Articles (representing the doctrine of the Anglican Church) was required of dons at Oxford and Cambridge. Clough's resignation laments: "I can have nothing whatever to do with a subscription to the xxxix articles—and deeply repent of having ever submitted to one. I cannot consent to receive any further pecuniary benefit in consideration of such conformity" (Arthur Hugh Clough, letter to E. Hawkins, 11 October 1848, in *The Correspondence of Arthur Hugh Clough,* ed. Frederick L. Mulhauser, 2 vols. [Oxford: Clarendon Press, 1957], I, 219). Chartism, the leading issue in the fight to push parliamentary reform further after the 1832 Bill, was a radically democratic movement associated not only with the "disruptive" working classes of the industrial towns but also, in many minds, with the French Revolution. In 1848 the House of Com-

mons rejected for the third time a popular petition first presented in 1839 in the wake of William Lovett's "People's Charter."

6. Biswas argues that although *The Bothie* "is not the religious apologia that might have been expected," its "advanced social thinking" and "sociological realism" "embod[y] Clough's justification for quitting Oxford" (*Clough: Towards a Reconsideration,* p. 265). See also Houghton, *Poetry of Clough,* p. 92.

7. Joseph Bristow describes the tension between those who identify a voice in "Dover Beach" that "speaks to a form of universal experience where love promises to mend the ruptures of historical change" and those who see the poem as "an unconsummated relationship where the speaker's displays of erudition would appear to be compensating for his sexual inadequacy" ("'Love, let us be true to one another': Matthew Arnold, Arthur Hugh Clough, and 'our Aqueous Ages,'" *Literature and History,* 4, no. 1 [1995], 28, 29). Bristow intriguingly proposes that Clough may be Arnold's "love" (see pp. 30-31).

8. Markovits, "Arthur Hugh Clough, *Amours de Voyage,* and the Crisis of Action," *Nineteenth-Century Literature,* 55 (2001), 453.

9. Reynolds, *The Realms of Verse, 1830-1870: English Poetry in a Time of Nation-Building* (New York: Oxford Univ. Press, 2001), p. 139. Biswas similarly argues: "In *The Bothie* the vehicle to final triumph is love, . . . and that love is simply not sufficiently realized for the imposed task" (*Clough: Towards a Reconsideration,* p. 285).

10. My goal in this essay is partly, then, to understand what Geoffrey Tillotson describes as Philip's belief in "love as part of the social order" rather than to parse the (inevitable) breakdown of any tidy alignment of the sexual and the political (see Geoffrey Tillotson, "Clough's *Bothie,*" in Geoffrey Tillotson and Kathleen Tillotson, *Mid-Victorian Studies* [London: Athlone Press, 1965], p. 144). Another goal is to explore in more detail what John Maynard describes as "a kind of providence . . . that brings together [Philip's] moral, even religious seriousness with sexual fulfillment" (*Victorian Discourses,* p. 55).

11. Arthur Hugh Clough, *The Bothie: The Text of 1848,* ed. Patrick Scott (St. Lucia: Univ. of Queensland Press, 1976), p. 10; sec. II, ll. 18-23 (further references are to this edition and are included in the text by section and line number). I refer throughout to *The Bothie of Toper-Na-Fuosich* of 1848 rather than the later version, *The Bothie of Tober-Na-Vuolich,* which famously loses much of

the earlier poem's sexual and metrical daringness. On these changes, see Joseph Patrick Phelan, "Radical Metre: The English Hexameter in Clough's *Bothie of Toper-Na-Fuosich,*" *Review of English Studies,* 50 (1999), 166-87. Phelan describes Clough's later "excisions" as "almost all in the direction of primness and respectability" (p. 184); the most famous of such revisions is that of the title itself, in order to avoid the risqué implication of the "bearded well" that "Toper-na-Fuosich" suggested to a Gaelic, or otherwise informed, ear. Phelan argues that *The Bothie*'s meter also undergoes a "process of standardization" (p. 185) in which "innovation and experiment are . . . sacrificed to metrical orthodoxy" (p. 186).

12. Philip's fascination with working women presages the infamous relationship between Arthur Munby and maid-of-all-work Hannah Cullwick, who married in 1873. Like Munby, Philip fetishizes the hired labor of women: "Aye, doing household work, as many sweet girls I have looked at, / Needful household work, which some one, after all, must do, / Needful, graceful therefore, as washing, cooking, scouring" (II, 118-20). Philip, however, articulates his desire as a form of progressive politics more so, arguably, than Munby, who largely presents his activities as an indulgence of quirky tastes. On Munby and Cullwick, see Leonore Davidoff, "Class and Gender in Victorian England," in *Sex and Class in Women's History,* ed. Judith L. Newton, Mary P. Ryan, and Judith R. Walkowitz (London: Routledge and Kegan Paul, 1983), pp. 17-71; and Anne McClintock, *Imperial Leather: Race, Gender, and Sexuality in the Colonial Conquest* (New York: Routledge, 1995).

13. Geoffrey Tillotson takes Philip's exclamation as an expression of his basic aspiration "to society" ("Clough's *Bothie,*" p. 144).

14. Scholars have noted a variety of clues that connect Adam with Clough (e.g., the poem's dedication to "My Long Vacation Pupils," similarities between Clough's and Adam's ages), but Clough can be identified just as readily with Philip. Patrick Greig Scott suggests that "the portrait of Adam is partly Clough's self-portrait" (Scott, "Explanatory Notes," in Clough, *The Bothie,* p. 35, n. 198-99). But Stopford A. Brooke, with equal persuasiveness, earlier described Clough as having "sketched his own opinions" in his portrait of "the radical and revolutionist" Philip (see *Four Victorian Poets: A Study of Clough, Arnold, Rossetti, Morris, with an Introduction on the Course of Poetry from 1822 to 1852* [1908; rpt. New York: Russell and Russell, 1964], p. 46). Commentators have also noted the parallels between Philip's and Tom

Arnold's respective departures for New Zealand. See for example Biswas, *Clough: Towards a Reconsideration,* p. 263; and Christiansen, *Voice of Victorian Sex,* p. 53.

15. Without drawing easy parallels between the characters and the men, it is possible to note intriguing resemblances among their respective disagreements. In a 30 November 1853 letter, for instance, Arnold admonishes Clough: "You are too content to *fluctuate*—to be ever learning, never coming to the knowledge of the truth" (*The Letters of Matthew Arnold to Arthur Hugh Clough,* ed. Howard Foster Lowry [Oxford: Clarendon Press, 1932], p. 146). See also Arnold's letter to Clough, 12 February 1853, in *Letters,* p. 130. For an extensive discussion of this rivalry and the poets' fraught allegiances to action and thought, see Isobel Armstrong, *Victorian Poetry: Poetry, Poetics and Politics* (London and New York: Routledge, 1993), pp. 165-77; and Markovits, "Arthur Hugh Clough," pp. 454-55.

16. Isobel Armstrong has argued that "it is possible to regard the language and form of nineteenth-century poetry as a model of the structure of consciousness or being itself" (*Language as Living Form in Nineteenth-Century Poetry* [Brighton, Sussex: Harvester Press, 1982], p. xiii). In addition, she argues that a poem that represents consciousness in this way "has to be long enough to have a past on which it can reflect, long enough to contemplate itself, to interpret itself to itself, to transform and create new experience out of its own elements" (p. 34).

17. Patrick Greig Scott writes that Clough's poems "require such hybrid terms as verse-novel, or satiric-epic-pastoral-idyll" ("The Victorianism of Clough," *Victorian Poetry* 16 [1978], 36). Charles Kingsley described the way that Clough's "playful, mock-heroic key gave scope for all sorts of variations into the bucolic, sentimental, broadfarce, pathetic, Hebrew-prophetic, what not" ([Kingsley], rev. of *The Bothie of Toper-na-Fuosich,* by Arthur Hugh Clough, *Fraser's Magazine for Town and Country,* 39 [1849], 105). Yopie Prins notes how *The Bothie*'s "combination of formal and informal language . . . along with its 'irregular' deployment of metrical rules, produce a . . . hybrid and heterogeneous form" ("Victorian Meters," in *The Cambridge Companion to Victorian Poetry,* ed. Joseph Bristow [Cambridge: Cambridge Univ. Press, 2000], p. 103). See also Meg Tasker, "Time, Tense, and Genre: A Bakhtinian Analysis of Clough's *Bothie*," *Victorian Poetry,* 34 (1996), 193-211.

18. Thomas A. Hayward argues that "a union of . . . two modes of perception"—Elspie's "intuitive insight" and Adam's "intellectual wisdom"—is the resolution that "will eventually save Philip (and, by extension, all of us) from the *malus error* of heedless passion or unreal idealization" ("The Latin Epigraphs in *The Bothie of Tober-Na-Vuolich,*" *Victorian Poetry,* 21 [1983], 155, 151). Hayward also argues for a new synthesis in the poem, though in terms different from mine: Philip's "journey of self-discovery" moves "from the highly wrought bucolic world of Vergil, through the intense personal tone of Catullus, to a new synthesis of pastoral virtue and clear-eyed realism in Horace" ("Latin Epigraphs," p. 155).

19. Biswas has also named Elspie's effect as one of dissolution, to the extent that she is a function of "the Victorian intellectual's need to find in women an embodiment of that potent simplicity of elemental nature which dissolves all contradiction and heals all difference" (*Clough: Towards a Reconsideration,* p. 279).

20. Clough later responds to what seems to have been Blanche's resistance to being considered a "helpmate": "The mere man's idea of a wife as a helpmate in duty is not in my judgement an insult to womankind, though it may require modification and purification and correction" (Clough, letter to Blanche Smith, 21 May 1853, in *Correspondence,* II, 435-36). Stefanie Markovits describes both Clough's concern that marriage may limit action as well as his suspicion that the "single life" might be, in his words, "unchivalrous"; but she goes on to note that "Clough's decision to marry is also couched in terms of its ability to aid him in action" ("Arthur Hugh Clough," p. 450). Philip and Elspie's departure for New Zealand emphasizes the ironies and tensions of the effort to align love with political purpose: Hayward reads the turn to Horace in the epigrams of *The Bothie*'s later books as a conservative "return to the legendary rural past" ("Latin Epigraphs," p. 155), but he concludes that, having revealed the unreality of such a Golden Age, Philip and Elspie become good citizens precisely by fleeing civilization. Hayward describes the poem's final relationship as "a turning from the exclusively personal concerns . . . (the lovers' relation to each other) to some familiar social issues (the role of women in marriage and society—i.e., the lovers' relation to others)" ("Latin Epigraphs," p. 154).

21. [William Whewell], "English Hexameters," *North British Review,* 19 (1853), 143. Clough himself, in his scholarly mode, referred to such verse as "lengthy, straggling, irregular, uncertain slips of *prose mesurée*" (Arthur Hugh Clough, "Letters of Parepidemus, Number Two" [1853], in *Selected Prose Works of Arthur Hugh Clough,* ed. Buckner

B. Trawick [Tuscaloosa: Univ. of Alabama Press, 1964], p. 182).

22. Tillotson appreciates the look of the original publication, but he finds one aspect of it "uninviting": "Being English hexameters, Clough's lines are long . . . so that the appearance of the page, designed to take them, resembles a high broad brick wall with one edge jagged" ("Clough's *Bothie*," p. 120).

23. Reynolds suggests that, "since Clough's most frequent point of reference in the poem is Virgil," we might understand his hexameters "as hinting at the diffuse presence of imperial power": "The hexameters are a formal counterpart to the undergraduates' invasion of the Scottish countryside" (*Realms of Verse*, p. 36).

24. Joseph Bristow has described the ways in which "water saturates the poetry of both Arnold and Clough" as a figure for the multiple sexual and social disruptions of the mid-century (see "Love, let us be true," p. 31). But Bristow notes that Clough's mobilization of such figurative language is often meaningfully different from Arnold's. Describing *The Bothie* as "an uproariously energetic poem," Bristow locates such energy especially in Elspie's own oceanic longing for Philip, citing her "hydraulic force": "The contrast with Arnold's poetry could not be more stark" (p. 36).

25. Armstrong, *Arthur Hugh Clough* (London: Longmans, Green and Co., 1962), p. 36.

26. John Conington reminisces that, "in the autumn of 1848. . . . [Clough's] 'Bothie' was just about to be published, and he gave me some account of it, particularly of the metre. He repeated, in his melodious way, several lines, intended to show me how a verse might be read so that one syllable should take up the time of two, or, conversely, two of one" (Conington, quoted in Arthur Hugh Clough, *Memoir of Arthur Hugh Clough,* in *Prose Remains of Arthur Hugh Clough, with a Selection from His Letters and a Memoir,* ed. [Blanche Clough] [London: Macmillan and Co., 1888], p. 33). As Phelan argues, "the idea of slowing down to compensate for an earlier rapid movement strongly implies the existence of a fixed time interval" ("Radical Metre," p. 176).

27. For one curious suggestion of the similarity of flood and desert in *The Bothie,* see John P. McGrail, who argues that the water motif "concerns personal and societal disorder, disintegration—Carlyle's desert" (McGrail, "Three Image Motifs in Arthur Hugh Clough's *The Bothie of Tober-Na-Vuolich,*" *Victorian Poetry,* 13, no. 1 [1975], 76).

28. Michael Timko describes the bridge's imagistic resolution in terms other than, but relevant to, fluidity and architecture: the bridge is "a climactic finish . . . that combines the natural and the supernatural" (*Innocent Victorian: The Satiric Poetry of Arthur Hugh Clough* [Athens: Ohio Univ. Press, 1963], p. 135).

29. A minor debate has surrounded the keystone, although most commentators accept that "the keystone is phallic" (Biswas, *Clough: Towards a Reconsideration,* p. 280). Houghton argues that it is "plain that the keystone is a phallic image, and that the dream is 'Freudian'" (*Poetry of Clough,* p. 107), in response to which Timko argues that "the significance goes beyond the merely sexual" (*Innocent Victorian,* p. 135n). McGrail, also responding to Houghton, contends that "phalluses neither look nor behave like keystones" ("Three Image Motifs," p. 75). While it may indeed be too simplistic to describe the keystone as purely phallic, it seems equally inaccurate to assume that the question that this extended metaphor raises—of the relation between penetration, union, and power—can be dismissed as "merely sexual" or an inaccurate understanding of the behavior of phalluses.

30. My own vocabulary of architecture recalls Philip's earlier, naively "architectural" interest in women, suggested when one classmate says, "Philip shall write us a book, a Treatise upon *The Laws of / Architectural Beauty in Application to Women*" (*The Bothie,* II, 160-61). While the bridge is Elspie's creation, it suggests that one mark of Philip's maturity is an attention to the architecture of the couple beyond the mere technology of female attractiveness.

31. Clough might also have had in mind the rule of the "bridge" used to regulate rhythm in ancient Greek hexameter by controlling the alignment of word endings with foot endings. I am thankful to Yopie Prins for this observation, and for her referral to James W. Halporn, Martin Ostwald, and Thomas G. Rosenmeyer, *The Meters of Greek and Latin Poetry,* rev. ed. (Norman: Univ. of Oklahoma Press, 1980), pp. 8-9.

**Anthony Kenny (essay date 2005)**

SOURCE: Kenny, Anthony. "The London Years." In *Arthur Hugh Clough: A Poet's Life,* pp. 188-212. London: Continuum, 2005.

[*In the following excerpt, Kenny describes the time Clough spent as Principal of University Hall in London (1849-1851) and the poetry he produced during that unhappy period of his life.*]

From Italy Clough returned to England via Switzerland: it had long been his ambition to 'Stand in the shadow of Mont Blanc'. From Geneva he travelled up the valley of the Arve to Chamouni, and there he was inspired to write a ballade **'Les Vaches'**—eight stanzas of uneven length—placed in the mouth of a cowgirl singing to her cows.

> The skies have sunk and hid the upper snow,
> Home, Rose, and home, Provence and La Palie
> The rainy clouds are filing fast below,
> And wet will be the path, and wet shall we.
> Home, Rose, and home, Provence and La Palie.
>
> (*P[The Poems of Arthur Hugh Clough]*, 207)

So runs the first verse, and in the remainder of the poem the girl meditates on her lover, absent for a year. Will he be faithful to her? Shall she be faithful to him? The poem is a pleasing trifle, in the *Lieder* tradition.

Clough was back in London by the end of August 1849. On the last day of the month he was entertained to dinner by Jane Brookfield, the model for Amelia in W. M. Thackeray's *Vanity Fair*. Mrs Brookfield found him a difficult guest: he simply sat at the foot of her sofa, and scrutinized her face, without saying anything. 'His eyes cut one through and through' she complained in a letter to Thackeray in Paris. In reply, Thackeray described his first meeting with her guest, in 1848. 'I took a very great liking and admiration for Clough. He is a real poet and a simple affectionate creature. Last year we went to Blenheim from Oxford and I liked him for sitting down in the Inn Yard and beginning to teach a child to read off a bit of Punch which was lying on the ground. Subsequently he sent me his poems which were rough but contained the real genuine solid[?] flare, I think.'[1]

The uncomfortable evening with Mrs Brookfield began a dismal period in Clough's life. His time as Principal of University Hall was brief and unhappy, marked by constant friction with the Hall's governing body. Before he had even accepted the post, he had been alerted to likely problems by his old friend Gell, who had now returned to England from running his college in Tasmania in order to marry the daughter of his former superior as Lieutenant Governor of Van Diemens Land, the famous explorer Sir John Franklin. Gell had cast an experienced eye over the statutes of the Hall and had warned that they left the principal with too little power and the governors with too much (B [Correspondence of Arthur and Blanche Clough], 341). After only a few days in post, Clough wrote to Tom Arnold to complain that intolerance 'is not confined to the cloisters of Oxford or the pews of the Establishment, but comes up like the tender herb—partout'. In the end, he predicted 'I shall be kicked out for mine heresies' sake' (*M*, [*The Correspondence of Arthur Hugh Clough*], 273).

Initially, the Governors were pleased enough, and regarded Clough as a catch. One of them, Wordsworth's friend Henry Crabb Robinson, wrote in his diary at the beginning of October 'He is modest and amiable, as well as full of talent, and I have no doubt that we have made a very good choice in him.' Robinson thought Clough was wise not to talk about his own religious opinions; but after a while he found that the new Principal was silent on other topics too, and was generally criticized for taciturnity. As Clough's widow wrote of this period in her posthumous memoir 'he became compressed and reserved to a degree quite unusual with him, both before and afterwards. He shut himself up, and went through his life in silence' (*PPR* [*The Poems and Prose Remains of Arthur Hugh Clough*], 39).

In October 1849 A. C. Tait had resigned the headmastership of Rugby to become Dean of Carlisle. Speculation about his successor was rife. Jane Arnold, in a letter to Tom, listed the candidates ('mostly deplorable'): Lake, Cotton, Simpkinson, Goulburn and Gell. Gell, now a temporary curate at St Martin's in the Fields, was preferred by Clough and all the Arnold family, while Lake was the favourite of the Rugby masters, who thought Gell insufficiently scholarly. Matt wrote to Jane in protest:

> Lake is, like most people who have lived at Oxford all their lives without being born philosophers—a perfect child—if all does not go as he wishes it, he can neither keep his temper, nor conceal that he has lost it. He would be as unfit as possible, I think.
>
> (*L* [*The Letters of Matthew Arnold*], 161)

From Rugby, Shairp wrote to Clough 'If you had not been so erratic a bird we might have had you' (*M*, 277). In December the post was given to E. M. Goulburn, a former dean of Merton, who soon showed himself to have been a disastrous choice.

A brief Christmas vacation did nothing to raise Clough's spirits. 'London generally speaking is lonely' he told Shairp on the second day of the new year, 'A loneliness relieved by evening parties is not delightful' (*M*,, 278). It is not surprising that Clough should miss the common room life of Oriel, even though he had often found it stifling when he was forced to be part of it. Moreover, leaving Oxford put a distance between Clough and friends in other colleges like Jowett, Stanley, Prichard and Congreve.

There is a passage in **Mari Magno** which biographers often take to be a description of Clough's life at this time.

> He has a life small happiness that gives,
> Who friendless in a London lodging lives,
> Dines in a dingy chop-house, and returns
> To a lone room, while all within him yearns

For sympathy, and his whole nature burns
With a fierce thirst for some one—is there none?—
To expend his human tenderness upon.

(*P*, 422)

But though Clough was lonely, his position was not at all as here described. His tied house was ample for entertainment, and he could eat his meals in company in Hall. Several of his old Oxford friends were now themselves in London or nearby. Frederick Temple and F. T. Palgrave were both at Kneller Hall at Twickenham, an experimental training college for teachers in the workhouses. He could entertain friends like these in Hall, where he quite enjoyed eating with the young men. In place of the old Oriel breakfasts with Matt and Tom Arnold, he began to take afternoon walks and dinner with Matt and his younger brother Edward (*M*, 273, 279).

It is possible that during 1849 there had been something of a cooling of relations between Matt and Clough after each had reacted so negatively to the other's published poetry. While in Rome Clough wrote only one letter to Matt, as compared with half a dozen to Palgrave. In September Arnold wrote to Clough from Thun, where in the previous year he had tarried for the sake of Marguerite's blue eyes. The letter begins 'It is long since I have communicated with you', and it continues in self-centred vein. There is no word about Clough's adventures in Rome, even though others of his friends had been worrying that he might get himself killed there (*L*, 156; *M*, 271). In the late summer the two poets were both in Switzerland, but made no attempt to join up with each other.

If there was any estrangement, it did not last long. In a letter to Tom Arnold in October 1849, Clough listed Matt, along with Emerson and Carlyle, as one of the profoundest thinkers of the age. He could hardly have known how he could pay a higher compliment. The compliment, however, might not have been appreciated by Matt, if he ever learnt of it. In the letter just quoted he described Carlyle as a 'moral desperado'.

Carlyle's radicalism was indeed beginning to take strange forms. At the end of 1849, now aged 54, he published the first of his *Latter Day Pamphlets,* 'Occasional discourse on the Nigger question' in which he argued that the emancipation of slaves in the British Empire had been a terrible mistake. It had led to the moral ruin of the blacks who were now rotting away in sensuous idleness amid the wrecks of the plantations (Clubbe 1979: 485) On the other hand, Carlyle's savage denunciations of the contemporary ruling classes did not prevent him from accepting frequent invitations to the London and Hampshire establishments of Lady Harriet Baring, who in 1849 became, on the death of her father-in-law, Lady Ashburton. He attended a series of luxurious house-parties at the Ashburtons' Hampshire home, The Grange. He reconciled this with his conscience by making a terrible nuisance of himself whenever he was there.

Lady Ashburton had the reputation of being the most conspicuous woman in the society of the time. An earl's daughter, she did her best to conceal from herself that her husband's £60,000 a year was derived from banking. Philip Ziegler has written of her 'She was anxious to shine in the high aesthetic line, and turned the Grange into a menagerie where literary lions like Carlyle and Thackeray grazed among politicians and assorted grandees.' Visitors were impressed by the grandeur and splendour of the hospitality, managed by a groom of the chambers, a butler, an under-butler and a vast staff. Introduced by Carlyle, Clough became a member of this glittering socio-literary set, a cub among the elder lions.[2]

As well as a literary menagerie, The Grange was also a cauldron of Platonic loves. Carlyle's worship of Lady Ashburton ('the lamp of my dark path') drove his wife to distraction. With Thackeray came his friends the Brookfields, the husband a clerical school inspector and the wife, Jane, the long-term object of what Thackeray called his 'longing passion unfulfilled'. Sadly, Clough has left us no record of his impressions of either menages or menagerie. However, when, on his engagement, he wrote for his fiancée a year-by-year account of the main events of his life, among the items recalled from 1850 'The Grange' figured on equal terms with 'Italy' and with 'University Hall'.

When Clough was first appointed to University Hall his mother had suggested that she and Annie might move to London and live with him. The Principal's house consisted of eight rooms on two floors: four bedrooms, three sitting rooms and a kitchen: clearly there would have been room for the whole family (B, 363, 365). While he was in Rome, Arthur encouraged the idea: 'Mother would not have much cooking to do in London, for there would be the general kitchen to draw on like a bank.' By the spring of 1850, however, he had come down definitely against the proposal. 'Dull and dismal as Liverpool is' he told his mother 'still London is drearier to those who have no old acquaintance in it; and after 30 as I find, one is not very quick at forming new ones.' His prospects in Gordon Square were uncertain: he might leave, voluntarily or involuntarily, in a year or two, while if he stayed, he would probably marry. In either case, the female Cloughs would have to leave, and would find it difficult to rent a house in a respectable part of London. As for Annie, the devoted schoolmistress, 'she will be going into horrid places here as there: and she will have little or nothing else to do. Spite of fleas and noise and teetotums and all that, I think it is well enough that she confine herself on the whole to seeing the dirty children in the way she does at present' (*M*, 282-3). It is difficult to sort out in this letter how much is honest advice and how much is self-protection, but undoubtedly there is also a grain of snobbery. The people who would call, he told his mother, might be rather fine ladies, and it would take her some time to feel at ease with them. During his visits to the Ashburtons the author of *The Bothie* seems to have caught a certain infection.

Amid the general solitude and gloom, Clough continued to write poetry of high quality. An impressive product of the years 1849-51 is a series of poems based on the narratives of the Book of Genesis. A poetic drama, first published posthumously in 1869 with the title **'The Mystery of the Fall',** was pieced together by Clough's widow from four manuscript notebooks and several separate sheets. The modern standard edition prints it as an unfinished drama of 14 scenes with the title **'Adam and Eve'.** This title is less suitable than Mrs Clough's, because powerful scenes in the sequence concern not just the first parents but also their children, the pious Abel and his murderer Cain. Indeed, it is quite possible that Clough had not one, but two, dramatic poems in mind when he wrote these verses.

The earliest poems in the sequence—which constitute scenes II-IV of the published version—were probably written as early as 1848. We see, first, Adam alone just after the Fall, trying to come to terms with the possibility that he has committed some disastrous, irretrievable act. Pangs of remorse alternate with calmer moments in which he dismisses such spasms as idle fits. First, he cries with limbs convulsed:

> Fool, fool; where am I? O my God! Fool, Fool!
> Why did we do't? Eve, Eve! where are you? quick!
> His tread is in the garden! Hither it comes!
> Hide us, O bushes, and ye thick trees, hide!
> He comes on, on, on. Alack, and all these leaves,
> These petty, quivering and illusive blinds,
> Avail us nought; the light comes in and in,
> Displays us to ourselves; displays, ah, shame,
> Unto the inquisitive day our nakedness.
>
> (*P*, 169)

These lines are then dismissed as a passing, if terrible, possession, a curious new phenomenon. For a while, Adam sees himself as a mental alchemist, seeking the formula to transmute the drossy contents of his mind into something splendid and magnificent.

> Though tortured in the crucible I lie,
> Myself my own experiment, yet still
> I, or a something that is I indeed,
> A living, central, and more inmost I
> Within the scales of mere exterior me's
> I—seem eternal, O thou God, as Thou;
> Have knowledge of the Evil and the Good,
> Superior in a higher Good to both.

The Transcendental Ego haunted much of the philosophy of the nineteenth century, from Kant before its beginning to Wittgenstein after its end. But the alchemist Adam is closer to Faust than to Hegel:

> Really now, had I only time and space,
> And were not troubled with this wife of mine,
> And the necessity of meat and drink,
> I really do believe
> With time and space and proper quietude
> I could resolve this problem on my brain.
> But no, I scarce can stay one moment more
> To watch the curious seething process out.
> If I could only dare to let Eve see
> These operations, it is like enough
> Between us two we two could make it out.
>
> (*P*, 170)

We are all familiar with the scientist who is convinced that with a few years leisure and a sufficiently ample research grant he will be able to give a full and final explanation of the workings of the human mind in terms of his own discipline—whether it is biological genetics, or social Darwinism, or cognitive science, or whatever. It was a remarkable intuition of Clough's to see this kind of Luciferian ambition as the first fruits of original sin.

The focus of the next scene is the birth of Cain. Eve, with her newborn, finds Paradise returned. But Adam looks on the baby Cain with a pessimistic eye: he is beginning to believe in the possibility of inherited sinfulness.

> Hope not too greatly, neither fear for him,
> Feeling on thy breast his small compressing lips
> And glorying in the gift they draw from thee
> Hope not too greatly in thyself and him.
> And hear me, O young mother—I must speak.
> This child is born of us, and therefore like us
> Is born of us, and therefore is as we;
> Is born of us, and therefore is not pure.
>
> (*P*, 172)

By the beginning of the third scene Adam has convinced himself that the story of the Fall is just a feminine fantasy of Eve's.

ADAM:

> What is it then you wish me to subscribe to?
> That in a garden we were put by God,
> Allowed to eat of all the trees but one,
> Somehow—I don't know how—a serpent tempted,
> And eat we did, and so were doomed to die;
> Whereas before we were meant to live for ever.
> Meantime, turned out—

EVE:

> You do not think then, Adam
> We have been disobedient to God?
>
> (*P*, 174)

Adam replies that he cannot conceive that God gave such a command as 'you shall not touch these apples here'—but if he did, then they did no wrong in eating them. Shocked, Eve says that if God said—God being God—'You shall not' that is a commandment his creatures must obey. Adam replies defiantly:

> My child, God does not speak to human minds
> In that unmeaning arbitrary way;
> God were not God, if so, and Good not Good.

He refuses to acknowledge that they have done anything wrong. Eve reminds him that when Cain was born he said 'He's born of us and therefore is not pure'. Adam responds that his remark was rash and foolish—'a first baby is a strange surprise'. He is determined that the story of the Fall shall not be passed on to their children, and commands:

> Put not, when days come on, your own strange whim
> And misconstruction of my idle words
> Into the tender brains of our poor young ones

> (*P*, 176)

These three scenes add up to a self-contained treatment of the story of the Fall. The background assumption of the drama is that the Genesis narrative is true. The theme developed in its scenes appears to be that the effects of sin are successive layers of self-delusion, with the female less deluded than the male. This version of the drama may have been completed as early as July 1848, when Matthew Arnold wrote 'productions like your Adam and Eve are not suited to me at present' (*L*, 114, 116).

During the next year or so, Clough developed the poem in a different direction. He wrote a new scene to be placed in front of the original drama, a scene in which from the start Adam is anxious to demythologize the expulsion from Paradise. At the beginning of the poem Eve, pregnant with Cain, is oppressed with a sense of guilt; as the scene opens she has been rehearsing the story of the serpent and the forbidden fruit. Adam refuses to accept it; the whole story is a fantasy.

> What!
> Because I plucked an apple from a twig
> Be damned to death eternal! parted from Good,
> Enchained to Ill? No, by the God of Gods,
> No, by the living will within my breast,
> It cannot be and shall not; and if this,
> This guilt of your distracted fantasy,
> Be our experiment's sum, thank God for guilt,
> Which makes me free!

> But thou, poor wife, poor mother, shall I say?
> Big with the first maternity of Man
> Draw'st from thy teeming womb thick fancies fond,
> That with confusion mix thy delicate brain;
> Fondest of which, and cloudiest call the dream

> (Yes, my beloved, hear me, it is a dream)
> Of the serpent and the apple and the curse.

> (*P*, 166)

It had all begun with a dream of Eve's on the day when she first encountered death: a lamb had fallen from a rock and broken its neck. That night, a harmless snake gliding by their bed gave her a nightmare. Adam had tried to soothe her to sleep:

> In vain; for soon
> I felt thee gone, and opening widest eyes
> Beheld thee kneeling on the turf; hands now
> Clenched and uplifted high; now vainly outspread
> To hide a burning face and streaming eyes
> And pale small lips that muttered faintly 'Death'.
> And thou woulds't fain depart; thou saidst the place
> Was for the likes of us too good.

> (*P*, 166)

Eve's fantasy forced them to leave their comfortable home for a barren countryside and 'a residence sadly exposed to wind and rain'. But Adam admits that he too, has moments when he half-believes Eve's dream to be true.

> Listen! I too when homeward, weary of toil,
> Through the dark night I have wandered in rain and
>    wind,
> Bewildered, haply, scared,—I too have lost heart,
> And deemed all space with angry power replete,
> Angry, almighty; and panic-stricken have cried,
> 'What have I done? What wilt thou do to me?'
> Or with the coward's 'No I did not, I will not',
> Belied my own soul's self.

> (*P*, 167)

But he urges himself to put away such childish dreams. But Eve cannot put aside the horror that haunts her in her pregnancy:

> The questionings of ages yet to be,
> The thinkings and cross-thinkings, self-contempts,
> Self-horror; all despondencies, despairs,
> Of multitudinous souls on souls to come
> In me imprisoned, fight, complain and cry.

> (*P*, 168)

A reader, taking this scene by itself, may give more credit to the male scepticism than to the female foreboding. But, as we have seen, the other scenes—that in this new version come later in the series—present the male as more adept than the female in the work of self-deception. The composite drama is a balanced whole in which the poet seeks to avoid taking sides with either interpretation.

Critics have complained that it is anachronistic to make Adam and Eve discuss the critical issues raised by the Tübingen school and the ethical problems that concerned philosophers like Kierkegaard. But of course to speak of 'anachronism' here is itself to treat Adam and Eve as historical characters belonging to a particular time and culture. What Clough does here with Genesis is what he did with the Gospels in *Easter Day.* In each case he takes a key doctrine of orthodoxy—the Fall, the Resurrection—and examines it by spelling out the consequences of taking it as literally true or literally false.

According to many centuries of Christian theology, the sin of Adam and Eve not only brought death and grief into the world, but also gravely impaired human intellectual faculties. If that is the case, then not only within critical scepticism, but within dogmatic orthodoxy, the question arises: what, after the Fall, did our first parents think had happened? Could they with any clarity remember the events in Paradise? If so, could they interpret them correctly? Clough's poem takes these issues seriously. The dialogues in *Adam and Eve* may be absurd as actual conversations between primitive human beings, but what Clough is doing here is turning latent nonsense into patent nonsense. The nonsense he expresses may contain important messages about ourselves—in particular, about the perennial topics of self-knowledge and self-delusion.

\* \* \*

In the years between 1849 and 1851 Clough wrote poems of various lengths in various metres about other characters in Genesis: Cain and Abel, Lamech, Isaac and Rebecca, and Jacob with his wives Rachel and Leah. Byron had written a famous poem about Cain: in Rome Clough started his own treatment of the topic. On the back of a manuscript of a piece of *Amours* he wrote a monologue for Cain holding the body of Abel. Cain's first emotion is surprise—nobody, after all, has ever seen a dead human being before; the first death in the Bible is that of the lamb killed in sacrifice by Abel himself.

> What? fallen? so quickly down, so easily felled,
> And so completely? Why, he does not move.
> Will he not stir—will he not breathe again?
> Still as a log, still as his own dead lamb.
> Dead, is it then? O wonderful! O strange!
> Dead! Dead! And we can slay each other then?
> If we are wronged, why, we can right ourselves;
> If we are plagued and pestered with a fool
> That will not let us be, nor leave us room
> To do our will and shape our path in peace,
> We can be rid of him.
>
>                                     (*P,* 179)

To this scene, then or later, Clough added others to precede it. One is a monologue for Abel, a mother's boy, highly devout, who looks down on his brother and father as unspiritual and godless, and is very conscious of his standing as one of God's elect. Another is a

monologue for Cain, riled by his brother's smugness, and anxious to perform some action to assert his own independence—'to give proof I also am, as Adam is, a man'. Other scenes bring Cain before his parents after the murder, and lead (in alternative versions) to a final curse or a final forgiveness.

Clough did not make clear whether he intended to bring together the Adam and Eve scenes and the Cain and Abel scenes to make up, together, a single drama. Blanche Clough was, I believe, well inspired when she did so. The case for uniting them is not just that they were written during the same periods of composition. Rather, it is that the Cain and Abel episodes work out further the characters that are given to Adam and Eve in the earlier scenes. Adam blames Eve for causing Abel's death by encouraging him in superstitious practices like sacrifice. Eve exhorts Cain to repentance and prayer, but in response he asks her to curse him: he seeks not atonement but punishment. It is only when Cain comes to say goodbye to Adam that he hears about the Fall for the first time. Adam, having told the story, recommends that it should be forgotten.

> . . . whether a dream, and, if it were a dream,
> A transcript of an inward spiritual fact
> (As you suggest, and I allow might be)
> Not the less true because it was a dream
> I know not.
>
>                                     (*P,* 182)

In a different version, Adam tries to comfort Cain by speaking of the healing touch of time. But Cain insists that to forget the past is not to undo the past. Nothing will bring back warmth into Abel's clay, or the gentleness of love into his face.

However Clough would have concluded the drama if he had brought it to conclusion, the dramatic impetus of the play as we have it comes to an end with Cain's departure into the wilderness:

> Welcome Fact, and Fact's best brother, Work;
> Welcome the conflict of the stubborn soil,
> To toil the livelong day, and at the end,
> Instead of rest, re-carve into my brow
> The dire memorial mark of what still is.
> Welcome this worship, which I feel is mine;
> Welcome this duty—
>     —the solidarity of life
> And unity of individual soul.
>
>                                     (*P,* 184)

Just as in *Paradise Lost* the most heroic figure is the wicked angel Lucifer, so here, one feels, of all the members of that unhappy family it is the murderer Cain with whom the poet most identifies.

The Bible traces out the posterity of Cain, and tells us that his great-great-great-grandson was called Lamech. The fourth chapter of Genesis tells us that Lamech married two wives, Adah and Zillah, and puts in his mouth a single, puzzling, line 'Hear my voice, ye wives of Lamech, hearken unto my speech: for I have slain a man to my wounding and a young man to my hurt.' Clough turned this into the chorus of a hundred-line piece of blank verse, **'The Song of Lamech'.** The poem is in fact mainly concerned with the story of Cain, as told by Lamech to his wives. It may indeed be an earlier treatment than the dramatic version in *The Mystery of the Fall*; but whether earlier or later, it is a much softer and less powerful treatment of the myth. It has a gentle, lilting rhythm and builds up to a happy ending. Adam, in response to a dream, goes to seek out Cain, eastward of Eden in the Land of Nod.

> And Adam laid upon the head of Cain
> His hand, and Cain bowed down, and slept and died.
> And a deep sleep on Adam also fell,
> And in his slumber's deepest he beheld
> Standing before the gate of Paradise
> With Abel, hand in hand, our father Cain.
>
> (*P,* 190)

Lamech's two wives are not fleshed out in the poem; but the bigamous patriarchs of the Old Testament had a fascination for Clough, still seeking a wife to satisfy both his sensuous and his moral needs. In *The Bothie* Philip's well-wishers utter the prayer 'Go, be the wife in thy house both Rachel and Leah to thee'. The poem **'Jacob's Wives',** written at about the same time as **'The Song of Lamech',** spells out this biblical allusion in an antiphonal characterization of the passionate Rachel and the matronly Leah. Jacob sits in the evening beside the door of his tent:

> And Rachel spake and said, The nightfall comes;
> Night, which all day I wait for, and for thee.
>
> And Leah also spake, The day is done;
> My lord with toil is weary, and would rest.

In six stanzas each wife presses on Jacob her claims for preference. Then, each wife under the veil of a pretended tolerance savages the other.

> And Rachel said, But we will not complain,
> Though all life long an alien unsought third
> She trouble our companionship of love.
>
> And Leah answered, No; complain we not,
> Though year on year she loiter in the tent,
> A fretful, vain, unprofitable wife.
>
> (*P,* 212)

After another eight stanzas of balanced abuse between the wives, at the end of the poem honours are even.

> And Rachel wept and ended, Ah my life!
> Though Leah bear thee sons on sons, methought
> The Child of love, late-born were worth them all.

> And Leah ended, Father of my sons,
> Come, thou shalt dream of Rachel if thou wilt,
> So Leah fold thee in a wife's embrace.
>
> (*P,* 214)

None of these biblical poems were published in Clough's lifetime. He wrote drafts and fair copies in notebooks which survive, mainly in the Bodleian library in Oxford. The notebooks bear titles, given by the Clough family, which indicate their principal contents, such as 'Adam and Eve notebooks I and II', '1849-50 (Lamech) Notebook'.

\* \* \*

In the year 1850 two events marked an epoch in English poetry. On 23 April Wordsworth died. Matthew Arnold travelled to Fox How to attend the funeral, and was asked to write an elegy.

> Goethe in Weimar sleeps, and Greece,
> Long since, saw Byron's struggle cease.
> But one such death remain'd to come;
> The last poetic voice is dumb—
> We stand to-day by Wordsworth's tomb

In May Matt submitted the dirge to Clough for his approval: it appeared in print in June.

On the first day of the same month Alfred Tennyson published *In Memoriam,* the poem which established him as the leading poet of the age. Shortly after, he married his sweetheart of 17 years. He was married from the house of an old Rugby friend of Matthew Arnold, who later in the year brought the two poets together. Tennyson had by now become Poet Laureate in Wordsworth's stead (*L,* 170-2).

In the Arnold family it was a year of change. In January Tom Arnold had moved from New Zealand to Hobart, where he had been appointed Inspector of Schools for Van Diemen's Land. Within a month he had met and fallen in love with Julia Sorrell, the daughter of the registrar of the supreme court: his proposal of marriage was accepted on 20 March. In April Jane became engaged to a Quaker philanthropist, William Edward Foster. Matt, who had no great liking for his prospective brother-in-law, invited Clough one day in May to make his acquaintance at breakfast in London. Finally, by the time the news of Tom's engagement reached England in July, Clough was able to report '[Matt] is himself deep in a flirtation with Miss Wightman, daughter of the Judge. It is thought it will come to something, for he has actually been to Church to meet her' (*M,* 286).

Matt and Clough arranged to spend a vacation together. Clough was to travel to Interlaken in July, and Matt was to join him in Switzerland after attending his sister's marriage. However, Matt's own love-making was not going well. Judge Wightman thought the salary of a mere secretary insufficient to support his daughter in appropriate style, and forbade any meeting of the two lovers. The Wightmans left for a continental tour, and Matt rushed after them incognito. When Jane was married on 15 August he failed to appear, and the bride had to be given away by her younger brother Edward. Matt also failed to keep his rendezvous with Clough. He continued his pursuit of Fanny Lucy Wightman like a latter-day Claude. He stayed in the Rhineland, consoling himself by reading Spinoza and writing poems with titles like 'Longing' and 'Separation'.

Clough, left solitary, went south to Venice. He was there on the feast of the Assumption, the day of Jane's wedding. He visited the public garden, and imagined a voice saying to him:

> This rather stupid place to-day
> It's true, is most extremely gay;
> And rightly—the Assunzione
> Was always a *gran' funzione.*
> What numbers at the landing lying!
> What lots of pretty girls, too, hieing
> Hither and thither—coming, going,
> And with what satisfaction showing,
> To our male eyes unveiled and bare
> Their dark exuberance of hair,
> Black eyes, rich tints, and sundry graces
> Of classic pure Italian faces! . . .
> 'Tis here, I see, the custom too
> For damsels eager to be lovered
> To go about with arms uncovered;
> And doubtless there's a special charm
> In looking at a well-shaped arm.

> *(P,* 222-3)

These lines were later taken up into a dramatic drama, to which Clough gave the name *Dipsychus.* Just as in Rome he jotted down self-standing poems which later became integral parts of *Amours de Voyage,* so while in Venice he sketched a number of vignettes which were later incorporated in *Dipsychus.* Such was, for instance, a barcarolle about a trip on the Grand Canal which begins:

> Afloat; we move. Delicious! Ah,
> What else is like the gondola?
> This level floor of liquid glass
> Begins beneath it swift to pass.
> It goes as though it went alone
> By some impulsion of its own.
> How light it moves, how softly! Ah
> Were all things like the gondola

> *(P,* 237)

From the entries in the Venice notebook we can trace Clough's tourist journeys. In the Academy he compares Titian's painting of the Assumption with a modern depiction of Byron's death at Missolonghi. He takes the

*barchetta* to the Lido and thinks once again of Byron, riding upon the sands of Malmocco. He finds the Piazza San Marco overcrowded, but revels in the view from the bell-tower.

> At a step, I crown the Campanile's top,
> And view all mapped below: islands, lagoon,
> An hundred steeples and a million roofs,
> The fruitful champaign and the cloud-capt Alps
> And the broad Adriatic.

> *(P,* 275)

Most of these self-standing entries found their way eventually into the dramatic structure of *Dipsychus*; but some of the entries in the Venice notebook are already in the form of a dialogue between two characters, at this point named Mephisto and Faustulus. Most remarkable are a series of stories in iambic tetrameters, placed in the mouth of Mephisto, describing encounters with prostitutes. Here are two examples:

> Tiring of cafes, quays and barks
> I turned for shade into St Marks
> I sat a while—studying mosaics
> Which we unauthorised laics
> Have leave to like—a girl slips by
> And gives the signal with her eye
> She takes the door; I follow out:
> Curious, amused, but scarce in doubt
> While street on street she winds about
> Heedful at corners, but *du reste*
> Assured and grandly self-possessed
> Trips up a stairs at last, and lands me
> Up with her petticoats, and hands me
> Much as one might a *pot de chambre*
> The vessel that relieves *le membre*
> No would-be-pretty hesitation
> Most business-like in her vocation
> She but the brief half instant lingers
> That strikes her bargain with five fingers.

> *(P,* 692)

> O yes, that was a rare adventure
> I took the pains to make you enter;
> You saw the lady well undrest,
> And wishing her a good night's rest
> Went off because (you said) twas Sunday
> You'd probably return on Monday

> *(P,* 690)

These notebook entries never found their way into printed versions of *Dipsychus,* whether in the nineteenth or twentieth century; at best they lurked in footnotes and appendices. But in the standard edition of 1974 the following was finally given an honoured place:

> Here's many a lady still waylaying
> And sundry gentlemen purveying.
> And if twere only just to see
> The room of an Italian *fille,*
> Twere worth the trouble and the money.

You'd like to find—I found it funny—
The chamber *où vous faites vôtre affaire*
Stands nicely fitted up for prayer;
While dim you trace along one end
The Sacred Supper's length extend,
The calm Madonna o'er your head
Smiles, *con bambino* on the bed.

(P, 233)

*Dipsychus* is in very rudimentary form in the Venice notebooks, and the story of its development belongs to the next chapter. But many a stanza throws light on Clough's interests and observations during this August visit.

* * *

During the year of revolutions Venice had revolted from Austria, and had been declared a Republic. It was reconquered by the Austrians in the summer of 1849, shortly after the fall of Mazzini's Rome. The Venice notebooks contain a number of references to the Austrian occupation, and one vignette shows the Clough-like Faustulus insulted by a Croatian soldier. He has to resist the suggestion that he challenge the man to a duel. Mephisto teases:

Oh never mind, 'twont come to fighting—
Only some verbal small requiting;
Or give your card—we'll do't by writing.
He'll not stick to it. Soldiers too
Are cowards, just like me or you.
What! not a single word to throw at
This snarling dog of a d———d Croat?

(P, 255)

During this same visit to Italy Clough commemorated the heroes of the Risorgimento in a poem *Peschiera*, named after the fortress captured by the Piedmontese in 1848 and lost a year later to the Austrians under General Radetzky.

The tricolor a trampled rag
Lies, dirt and dust; the lines I track
By sentry-boxes yellow black
Lead up to no Italian flag.
I see the Croat soldier stand
Upon the grass of your redoubts;
The Eagle with his black wing flouts
The breadth and beauty of your land.

The poem's message is that the memory of Lombard gallantry in the defence of Peschiera will give pride and hope to those who now endure Austrian servitude. The poem, written in the metre of *In Memoriam*, was a tribute to Tennyson as well as to the Risorgimento. It ends with an echo of his poem's most famous couplet.

This voice did on my spirit fall
Peschiera, when thy bridge I crost,

''Tis better to have fought and lost
Than never to have fought at all.'

(P, 300)

Retracing his steps through Switzerland in September 1850 Clough consoled himself for the dreary prospect of London by drafting on his Geneva hotel bill a poem in rhyming pentameters celebrating the delight of the summer's escape from the city. Entitled **'July's Farewell'** it addresses the countryside:

I come, I come, upon the heart's wings fly to you
Ye dreary lengths of brick and flag, good-bye to you,
Ambitious hopes and money's mean anxieties.
And worldly-wise decorum's false proprieties
And politics and news and fates of nations too,
And philanthropic sick investigations too,
And company and jests and feeble witticisms,
And talk of talk, and criticism of criticisms
I come, I come, ye banks and bowers, to hide in you,
And once again, ye loves and joys, confide in you
. . .

(P, 302)

Life in London on his return was as frustrating as Clough expected. The Council of University Hall continually interfered with the domestic arrangements, and gave orders to the Principal's staff behind his back, and encouraged them to spy on the students. In an outraged letter at the end of October, heavily blotted and cancelled and probably never sent, Clough complained that he was treated no better than a housekeeper (B, 409). In February he was hauled before the Council and rebuked for being unwilling to expel a student 'because his bill for malt-liquor is large, and because he occasionally plays at cards'. Under the statutes—which Gell had warned him against—he was forced to acquiesce in the expulsion. He pointedly refused to offer the Council any advice on how to refill the vacancy or increase the number of students beyond the existing twelve (M, 288, 294).

There were, however, consolations in the winter of 1850-1. The Chair of English Literature and Language at University College became vacant when the Scottish divine Alexander Scott resigned to become the first principal of the Owens college for working men in Manchester. Clough applied for the chair, with testimonials from Frederick Temple and H. H. Vaughan the Oxford Professor of Modern History. He was appointed, and gave a series of lectures on English literature from Chaucer to Scott. His lecture notes have survived, and some have been published: for the most part they are judicious without being exciting. One of the most interesting, on Wordsworth, was delivered late in his professorship, probably in 1852: it analyses the inter-relationships between the romantic poets.

Out of Wordsworth and Byron came forth Shelley; nor is Keats (there is no such thing) an independent genius. We may remark also, how, as the brief career of Byron encloses within itself the yet briefer life of Shelley and Keats's briefest of all, so is Byron himself included in the larger arc of Scott and the yet larger arc of Wordsworth.

In general popularity, the young Wordsworth was displaced by Scott; Scott as a poet had to yield to Byron; but after Byron died young and Scott in premature age, Wordsworth again came into his own.

The lecture teaches us what elements in a poet Clough most valued. Wordsworth's special virtue, he said, was the infinite toil and labour that he expended on style, on the nice and exquisite felicities of poetic diction. He lacked the vigour and heartiness of Scott, and the sweep and fervour of Byron: but in the pursuit of permanent beauty of expression, in achieving harmony between thought and word, they were mere negligent schoolboys in comparison.

Poetry, like science, has its final precision; and there are expressions of poetic knowledge which can no more be rewritten than could the elements of geometry. There are pieces of poetic language which, try as men will, they will simply have to recur to, and confess that it has been done before them.

There is hardly anything in Byron or Scott, Clough says, that later generations will not think they can say over again quite as well: not so with the best of Wordsworth.

Clough admits, however, that Wordsworth wrote far too much. To find the rich spots of pure beauty, you have to traverse waste acres of dull verse that had better been prose. Moreover, Wordsworth was inclined to place feeling above fact. 'He is apt to wind up his short pieces with reflections upon the way in which, hereafter, he expects to reflect upon his present reflections.' His excessive emphasis on nature palls: Clough admits that he cannot heartily sympathize with repeated poems to the daisy. 'Blue sky and white cold, larks and linnets, daisies and celandines—these it appears are 'the proper subject of mankind'; not, as we used to think, the wrath of Achilles, the guilt and remorse of Macbeth, the love and despair of Othello.'

How does Wordsworth compare, from a moral point of view, with Scott and Byron? His frugal life at Grasmere was certainly more rational and dignified than Byron's hot career of wilfulness, or Scott's active but easy existence amid animal spirits. But 'to live in a quiet village, out of the road of all trouble and temptation, in a pure, elevated, high-moral sort of manner is, after all, no such very great a feat' (**PPR,** 315, 324). He has little to offer the man in the busy city street. The lecture is, of course, more interesting for what it tells us about Clough's own ambitions and discipline as a poet than as an overall critical judgement on Wordsworth.

In 1849 F. W. Newman, the Professor of Latin at University College whose resignation had made the University Hall post available for Clough, had published a book entitled *The Soul: its Sorrows and Aspirations*. Now, in 1850, Clough took the occasion of a review of this book to present the first public statement since leaving Oriel of his own religious position.

The review is written in a spirit of revulsion from the religious institutions Clough had rejected. He speaks of himself as a 'new convalescent' who finds it unpleasant to 'talk of his sick-room phenomena, to re-enter the diseased past, and dwell again among the details of pathology and morbid anatomy'. The object of his polemic, Clough insists, is not religion but 'devotionality'; 'The belief', he says 'that religion is, or in any way requires, devotionality, is, if not the most noxious, at least the most obstinate form of *ir*religion' (**PPR,** I, 299).

'Devotionality' appears to mean any prayerful relationship to God which takes the form of an imagined sense of closeness to a personal individual. 'Is it otherwise than superstitious for a Protestant devotee to recognise the sensuous presence of the Son, or for the Romish to believe in the visits of the Mother, who lived and died in Palestine eighteen centuries ago?' Such spiritual communion may, in abstract theory, be possible; but 'to expect it is perilous; to seek it pernicious; to make it our business here is simply suicidal'.

Clough goes on to attack the 'blind benevolence' fostered by Christianity. In Roman Catholic countries almsgiving leads to beggary and laziness; in England enlightened philanthropy peters out into exhortations to be resigned to one's poverty. He mocks those who claim to have discovered God as the designer of the universe ('Was it nobody, think you, that put salt in the sea for us?'). Prayer is important: but the best form of prayer is silence. If one cannot be content with silence it is best to stay with the prayerbook's daily service—the old Catholic forms have the prestige of antiquity and the superiority of taste over the new-fangled observances of the prayer meeting (**PPR,** 304).

The review is an embarrassing piece of work, bullying and bantering in turns, full of insensitive gibe and clumsy humour. Later in the year Clough redeemed himself by writing the finest of all his religious poems, *Hymnos Aumnos*. The sentiments of the poem are not very different from the review; but in style and sensitivity it is as much superior as the Book of Common Prayer is to an impromptu prayer-meeting. The first stanza begins with an invocation to the incomprehensible Godhead:

> O Thou whose image in the shrine
> Of human spirits dwells divine;

Which from that precinct once conveyed
To be to outer day displayed,
Doth vanish, part, and leave behind
Mere blank and void of empty mind,
Which wilful fancy seeks in vain
With casual shapes to fill again.

The poem starts from the assumption that the place to look for God is in the individual's inmost soul ('The Kingdom of God is within you'). Well and good; but attempts to give public expression to the God encountered in the soul yield only meaningless, self-contradictory utterances ('blank and void') or idle images with no contact with reality ('casual shapes').

After the second stanza of the poem has developed the theme of the impotence of human utterance to embody the divine, the third restates the manifesto of the Newman review that silence—inner as well as outer—is the only response to the ineffable.

O thou, in that mysterious shrine
Enthroned, as we must say, divine!
I will not frame one thought of what
Thou mayest either be or not.
I will not prate of 'thus' and 'so'
And be profane with 'yes' and 'no'.
Enough that in our soul and heart
Thou, whatso'er thou may'st be, art.

Clough's agnosticism, at this point, is radical. The *via negativa* is rejected as firmly as the *via positiva*. Not only can we not say of God what he is, we are equally impotent to say what he is not. The possibility, therefore, cannot be ruled out that one or other of the revelations claimed by others may after all be true.

Unseen, secure in that high shrine
Acknowledged present and divine
I will not ask some upper air,
Some future day, to place thee there;
Nor say, nor yet deny, Such men
Or women saw thee thus and then:
They name was such, and there or here
To him or her thou didst appear.

In the final stanza Clough pushes his agnosticism a stage further. Perhaps there is no way in which God dwells—even ineffably—as an object of the inner vision of the soul. Perhaps we could reconcile ourselves to the idea that God is not to be found at all by human minds. But even that does not take off all possibility of prayer.

But only thou in that dim shrine,
Unknown or known, remain, divine;
There, or if not, at least in eyes
That scan the fact that round them lies.
The hand to sway, the judgement guide,
In sight and sense, thyself divide:
Be thou but there—in soul and heart,
I will not ask to feel thou art.

(*P*, 312)

The soul reconciled to the truth that there can be no analogue of seeing or feeling God, that nothing can be meaningfully said about him, can yet—if Clough is right—address him and pray to be illuminated by his power and be the instrument of this action. To this day there has been no more eloquent attempt to be faithful to a critical agnosticism and yet draw support from the consolations of theism.

For the rest of his life Clough retained, with regard to religion, this stance of an agnosticism that made room for prayer. There is nothing incoherent in such a position: an agnostic's prayer to a God whose existence he doubts is no more unreasonable than the act of a man adrift in the ocean, or stranded on a mountainside, who cries for help though he may never be heard or fires a signal which may never be seen. Perhaps it is a mistake to describe Clough's position as agnostic: he seems always to have retained a belief in some kind of divinity, but undoubtedly the God he worshipped was an unknown God. He also adopted a terrifyingly solitary conception of religion, which finds expression in a poem written at this time, entitled posthumously '**The Hidden Love**':

O let me love my love unto myself alone
And know my knowledge to the world unknown;
No witness to my vision call
Beholding, unbeheld of all;
And worship Thee, with Thee withdrawn apart,
Who'er, Whate'er thou art,
Within the closest veil of mine own most inmost heart.

What is it then to me
If others are inquisitive to see?
Why should I quit my place to go and ask
If other men are working at their task?
Leave my own buried roots to go
And see that other plants shall grow;
And turn away from Thee, O Thou most Holy Light,
To look if other orbs their orbits keep aright,
Around their proper sun,
Deserting Thee, and being undone:

O let me love my love unto myself alone,
And know my knowledge to the world unknown;
And worship Thee, O hid One, O much sought
As but man can or ought
Within the abstracted'st shrine of my least breathed-on
    thought.

(*P*, 240)

The soul's love of God, and knowledge of God, is no concern of others; it needs no witness to its vision of God, dim and secret as that vision is. Equally, the self is not to concern itself with the spiritual welfare of others: each human's course is as separate from each other human's as the orbit of one plant or planet is from its neighbour's. Clough could claim authority for his attitude from a passage in the sermon on the Mount which he quoted in a letter to Tom Arnold early in the year.

'Thou, when thou prayest, enter into thy closet, and when thou has shut thy door, pray to thy Father which is in secret' (Matt. 6, 6,*M,* 279).

On 31 August 1850 a Royal Commission was appointed by Lord John Russell's government to inquire into the discipline, studies and revenue of Oxford University. Since Clough's last years at Oriel University reform had been a major concern of his Oxford friends, especially Jowett and Stanley. In 1848 Clough had written from Paris to Stanley proposing an Oxford revolution to match the French one. The aims of academic 'chartists' should be five: the abolition of subscription to the Thirty-Nine Articles; the reconstitution of college fellowships; a new Hebdomadal Board; the opening of matriculation to non-members of colleges; and a permanent commission of reform (*M,* 211). Now, in 1850, Stanley was made secretary of the Royal Commission, and at the end of the year Clough was able to put his proposals formally in evidence before it.

It took two years for the Commission to report, and two more years for its proposals to work their way through Parliament. But the University Reform Act of 1854 enacted almost everything that Clough wanted. In place of the old Hebdomadal Board, composed of heads of house, there was to be an elected Hebdomadal Board. The Vice-Chancellor was to be empowered to licence private halls in which non-college students could live. Antiquated fellowships were to be suppressed, and the funds used to support professorial chairs. The foremost of Clough's proposals, and the one which would have made most difference to his own Oxford career, namely the abolition of religious tests, was inserted into the Bill at the last minute on the motion of a Unitarian private member.

In some ways the reforms went further than Clough had demanded. The powers of Convocation—a chronically conservative body consisting of all MAs—were largely transferred to Congregation, the assembly of senior members actually studying or teaching in Oxford. Honours examinations, hitherto restricted to classics and law, had in 1850 been thrown open to new subjects such as history, law and natural science. Clough had long complained about the narrowness of the Oxford course and its tendency merely to repeat matter covered in school (**PPR,** 202). But he would have preferred to add to history 'the stronger aliment of Political Economy' (*M,* 248). It was only after his death, in 1872, that economics found a place on the syllabus—and then only in the pass school.[3]

### Notes

1. Gordon N. Ray, *The Letters and Private Papers of William Makepeace Thackeray,* 4 vols, Oxford 1945-6, II, pp. 580-1.

2. Philip Ziegler, *The Sixth Great Power: Barings 1762-1929,* London 1992, p. 159.

3. M. C. Brock & M. C. Curthoys, *The History of the University of Oxford, VII, The Nineteenth Century,* Oxford 1997, pp. 331-62.

### Abbreviations

B: Correspondence of Arthur and Blanche Clough in the Bodleian Library (MSS Eng. Lett. c. 189-90, d. 175-9, c. 74-84). Cited by the number of the letter in the *Catalogue of All Known Letters* appended to Mulhauser's edition of the correspondence (= M below).

*K: The Oxford Diaries of Arthur Hugh Clough,* edited by A. Kenny, Oxford 1990.

*L: The Letters of Matthew Arnold,* edited by Cecil Y. Lang. University Press of Virginia, six volumes 1996-2002.

*M: The Correspondence of Arthur Hugh Clough,* edited by F. L. Mulhauser, Oxford, Clarendon Press 1957 (there are two volumes, but a single page numeration runs through both).

*OA: The Oxford Authors: Matthew Arnold,* edited by Miriam Allott and Robert H. Super, Oxford 1986.

*P: The Poems of Arthur Hugh Clough,* second edition, edited by F. L. Mulhauser, Oxford, Clarendon Press 1974. References to poems are given by page numbers of this edition.

*PPR: The Poems and Prose Remains of Arthur Hugh Clough,* edited by his wife, in two volumes, London, Macmillan & Co. 1869.

RD: Rugby Diaries of Arthur Hugh Clough, in Balliol College, Oxford.

### Bibliography

A comprehensive bibliographical guide to works by and about Clough appeared in 1968: Gollin, Richard M., Houghton, Walter E., and Timko, Michael, *Arthur Hugh Clough: a Descriptive Catalogue,* the New York Public Library. This is annotated and is divided into three parts: Poetry, Prose, Biography and Criticism. The critical section contains 500 items.

I list below works most often used while writing this biography.

Allot, M. and Super, R. H., *The Oxford Authors: Matthew Arnold,* Oxford 1986.

Bergonzi, Bernard, *A Victorian Wanderer: the Life of Thomas Arnold the Younger,* Oxford 2003.

Bertram, Jim (ed.), *New Zealand Letters of Thomas Arnold the Younger,* London and Wellington 1939.

Biswas, R. K., *Arthur Hugh Clough: Towards a Reconsideration,* Oxford 1972.

Brock, M. C. and Curthoys, M. C., *The History of the University of Oxford,* Vol. 7, *The Nineteenth Century,* Oxford 1997.

Chadwick, Owen, *A History of the Popes, 1830-1914,* Oxford 1998.

Chorley, Katherine, *Arthur Hugh Clough: the Uncommitted Mind,* Oxford 1962.

Christiansen, Rupert, *The Voice of Victorian Sex: Arthur Hugh Clough,* London 2001.

Clough, Blanche Athena, *A Memoir of Anne Jemima Clough,* London 1897, 1903.

Clubbe, J. (ed.), *Froude's Life of Carlisle,* Columbus 1979.

Faber, Geoffrey, *Jowett: a Portrait with Background,* London 1957.

Greenberger, E. B., *Arthur Hugh Clough: the Growth of a Poet's Mind,* Harvard University Press 1970.

Honan, Park, *Matthew Arnold: a Life,* London 1981.

Hughes, Thomas, *Tom Brown's Schooldays,* London 1857.

Jenkins, Roy, *Churchill,* London 2001.

Kenny, A., *God and Two Poets,* London 1988.

Ker, Ian, *John Henry Newman: a Biography,* Oxford 1988.

Knight, William, *Principal Shairp and his Friends,* London 1888.

Lake, K. (ed.), *Memorials of William Charles Lake,* London 1901.

Lowell, James, *A Fable of Critics,* Boston 1848.

McCrum, M., *Thomas Arnold, Headmaster,* Oxford 1989.

Monsarrat, Ann, *An Uneasy Victorian: Thackeray the Man,* London 1980.

Murray, Nicholas, *A Life of Matthew Arnold,* London 1996.

Newman, J. H., *Letters and Diaries,* Vols VII-VIII, ed. G. Tracey, Oxford 1995, 1999.

Phelan, J. P., 'The Textual Evolution of Clough's *Dipsychus and the Spirit*', *Notes and Queries,* 2000, pp. 230-9.

Prothero, R. G. and Bradley, G. G., *The Life and Correspondence of Arthur Penrhyn Stanley,* 2 vols, London 1893.

Ray, Gordon N., *The Letters and Private Papers of William Makepeace Thakeray,* 4 vols, Oxford 1956-6.

Risk, Ralph, *The Letters of Ralph Waldo Emerson,* 6 vols, New York 1939.

Rouse, W. H. D., *A History of Rugby School,* London 1898.

Scott, Patrick, *Victorian Texts I: Amours de Voyage by Arthur Hugh Clough,* St Lucia, Queensland 1976.

————*Victorian Texts IV: The Bothie by Arthur Hugh Clough,* St Lucia, Queensland 1976.

Stanley, A. P., *The Life of Thomas Arnold D. D.,* London 1844; 1903.

Strachey, Lytton, *Eminent Victorians,* London 1918.

Thorpe, Michael (ed.), *Clough: the Critical Heritage,* New York 1982.

Veyriras, Paul, *Arthur Hugh Clough (1819-1861)* Paris 1964.

Ward, Maisie, *Young Mr Newman,* London 1948.

Ward, Wilfrid, *William George Ward and the Oxford Movement,* London 1889.

Williams, David, *Too Quick Despairer: the Life and Work of Arthur Hugh Clough,* London 1969.

Ziegler, Philip, *The Sixth Great Power: Barings 1762-1929,* London 1992.

### Francis O'Gorman (essay date 2006)

SOURCE: O'Gorman, Francis. "Clough's Difficulties." *Yearbook of English Studies* 36, no. 2 (2006): 123-38.

[*In the following essay, O'Gorman discusses the difficulty modern readers have with Clough's* The Bothie of Toper-na-Fuosich *and offers a new reading of the work.*]

One of the most peculiar poems of the Victorian period must be Arthur Hugh Clough's ***The Bothie of Toper-na-Fuosich: A Long-Vacation Pastoral*** (1848). Although widely reviewed in its day, it has not travelled well to the present and even the angular curiousness of its title seems an invitation to set it aside. Among those today whose professional life is with Victorian literature, few have read it. Why is this so? ***The Bothie***'s neglect is perhaps partly to do with its alien narrative and setting—a romance between an Oxford undergraduate and a Highland girl during a long-vacation reading party in the 1840s—which now feels culturally remote. Clough's shifting tone—the poem moves in and out of satire—leaves the reader distanced from the characters, unable to form easy sympathetic bonds (Clough would explore the possibilities of *unsympathy* further in **Amours de Voyage,** written in 1849 and published in 1858) and this impedes accessibility too: it is at points, to borrow one of the character's words, hard to '[disengage] jest from earnest' (III. 106).[1] The metrical form of the poem—the so-called English hexameter—though zestily handled, provides unfamiliar rhythms for the ear which, again, produce comic affects that query the poem's seriousness. Certainly, each of these may well be a reason why **The Bothie** does not enjoy many readers now (though it never really did). But there is also the question of what it is about. It is not an unreasonable expectation that a poem of this length, crowded with debate about politics and education, revolution and Chartism, class and gender, should have a thematic coherence, a set of arguments, an intellectual substance that is sustained: Clough was hardly a man without ideas. But, to borrow words from Henry James's famous complaint about the English novel, what **The Bothie** actually amounts to is still not a question easy to answer. A reader's chief feeling today is of regarding a conundrum.

It is a suggestive feature of the early reviewers that they felt similarly. James Anthony Froude was guarded. 'People don't expect philosophy', he wrote to Clough, 'in a thing coming out in the shape and with the *tone* of a sketchy poem; and won't look for it, and won't believe it is there when it seems to be.'[2] Something philosophical, something of thought, *seemed* to be in **The Bothie** but what it was the future biographer of Thomas Carlyle could not say. He was happy to commend the 'depth of thought' as 'quite wonderful' but refrained from suggesting what that thought was about.[3] *The Spectator*'s anonymous reviewer in December 1848 was less impressed and more puzzled. Seeing the poem as poor narrative, he was vexed by its apparent absence of meaning. Was it there or not? 'At first view', he said, '**The Bothie of Toper-na-Fuosich** looked like some Oxford satire; but if it does cover any occult meaning, it is confined to the initiated.'[4] A language of esoteric codes seemed the best resort. Ralph Waldo Emerson—an admirer of Clough—was confident that the poem was a 'bold hypothetical discussion of the most serious questions that bubble up at this very hour in London, Paris, and Boston',[5] but he did not say what he thought those questions were. Perhaps they were obvious enough (class, revolution, Chartism, education?), but how the poem discussed them or what it actually said about them Emerson did not venture. Charles Kingsley, a reader usually impatient with the over-difficult, thought that people were wrong to expect **The Bothie** to resolve into something decisive and unmistakable. Of course, this was a perfectly appropriate point, yet it did not entirely answer the case. Kingsley's defence of Clough—he had written to him asking permission to review the poem[6]—seemed a touch over-defensive as if he was, at some subterranean level, protecting himself against more searching questions as

to what he had understood. At the end of the long unsigned review in *Fraser's Magazine* for January 1849, in which he applauds **The Bothie**'s descriptive power, metrical inventiveness, and Greek spirit, Kingsley allows a hypothetical reader to remark, '"But what, after all, is the purpose of Mr. Clough's poem?"'

Kingsley's reply to his own blunt question gives only to take away again:

> This, at least, is its purpose—*'To make people do their duty in that state of life to which God has called them'*. Whether the author attaches exactly the same meaning to those words as his readers do, remains to be proved. Further, we shall say nothing, for the author has said nothing; and he, doubtless, knows a great deal better than we what effects he intends, and we have no wish, or right either, to interfere with him. He seems to think, as indeed, we do, that it is far better to give facts and opinions on different sides, and let the reader draw his own conclusions from them, than to tack a written moral to the last page of his poem, as you sew a direction-card on a little boy's back when you send him off to school. Let the reader try to crack the nut himself; and not, as is usual in these lazy days, expect reviewers to do it for him. It will be wholesome exercise; and we will warrant the kernel worth the trouble.[7]

Suggesting—not a little flatly—that the reader simply adjudicate between different positions debated in **The Bothie,** Kingsley defends his right not to discuss Clough's central meanings. Offering his scorn of literary works that propose clearer intentions—they are like directions for lost schoolboys, he says—Kingsley is partly making a powerful case for the rightly challenging properties of significant literature. But it is difficult to avoid wondering whether he is not also endeavouring to conceal that he has somewhat failed to crack this particular nut himself.

It would be misleading to suggest that readings of the poem have, throughout all its critical history, concluded with bafflement. But losing that initial sense of puzzlement, forgetting altogether something like *The Spectator*'s view, has not been without cost for the authority of some of those more decided, decisive modern readings. Detailed study of Clough's life has brought force into conceptions of the poem's purposes, spurred partly by Katharine Chorley's *Arthur Hugh Clough*.[8] R. K. Biswas proposed in 1972, for instance, that **The Bothie** was, *pace* Charles Kingsley, 'a poem with a thesis'. It 'supplies and embodies Clough's justification for quitting Oxford',[9] he said, and others have developed the notion that the poem is best regarded as commentary on the unreformed University of Oxford that Clough left (also in 1848) after believing himself unable to sign the Thirty-Nine Articles. Christopher M. Kierstead writes in the same vein of Clough's 'perceptive, witty treatment of the social and intellectual controversies then consuming Oxford' (though without, it is true, saying much about them),[10] and Joseph Patrick Phelan's recent article on the revisionary metrics of *The Bothie* in *Review of English Studies* is the latest exploration of this institutional aspect of the poem.[11] Writing in a classical metre adapted to modern English, Phelan says, was part of Clough's broader intention to suggest how the substance of Oxford's classical education needed to be made more serviceable for the present day. It would be folly to argue that such insights have not been helpful, and Phelan's article is the most illuminating study of the poem's ambitious metre to have appeared so far. But their very convincingness suggests that something of *The Bothie*'s peculiarity has been overlooked. Its difficulties are too much part of it to be so thoroughly accounted for. There is interpretative loss in the efforts to analyse the experience of reading Clough's strange text which, with Biswas, propose the poem primarily as a document with a 'thesis'—his or another's. The first reviewers' doubtfulness is worth remembering.

Preserving a sense of that difficulty is not only about being intellectually faithful to the experience of reading *The Bothie.* Problems, uncertainties, blockages in the communication of meaning are dramatized in the poem itself; it is quietly conscious of its own mode of proceeding and dwells on scenes that figure in displaced ways its own interrupted workings. Clough's poem muses on moments in which communicative contact is not quite made, when something is not entirely expressed. An important focus of this engagement is in the context of teaching, the principal interest of this essay. As a text that has to do at the obvious level of plot with teachers and teaching—the Oxford vacation party—it is a striking feature of *The Bothie*'s imaginative priorities that it should represent in such a sustained manner potential scenes of teaching where the instruction does not fully succeed or where there is some impediment to learning or some problem in the act of guiding. *The Bothie* is remarkably aware of how difficult it is to learn under such circumstances and how unclear are sources of ordinary human instruction. In presenting itself as a puzzling text in its own right, it is—on the one hand—merely affirming the limited usefulness of human words and written texts in the transmission of sense. Yet on the other hand, *The Bothie* is also haunted—the word is not insignificant—by embodiments of what it cannot find in ordinary human exchanges and regular scenes of tuition. Amid its representations of language that does not adequately communicate, arguments that do not fully cohere, and books that do not seem to teach, it imagines, as if radically transforming a Romantic conception of visionaries, figures of exceptional insight who, against this background, offer direction to those adrift. These men and women, and the occasions of remarkable instruction they provide, are either highly improbable or otherwise unaccountable and, in one long passage, they

are hailed potentially as the inheritors of the wisdom of the dead. Discarding education, books, arguments, and official teachers, *The Bothie* turns, it seems to me, to something like the uncanny as the ground of human instruction. One of the reasons, then, that this poem is difficult to understand, difficult to *argue* about, is that, in failing to find much to learn from ordinary human communication, it privileges inexplicable knowledge. That which seems to take its origin from mysterious sources, that which is mystifiable and mystified, which seems even to allow the dead a place among the living, is unexpectedly at the crux of the text's thinking about how human beings might best learn. Perhaps, then, my accomplishment is to make a strange text merely stranger, but I do want to suggest a case for thinking seriously about its difficulties in relation to its peculiar flirtation with the ghostly.

*The Bothie* is, at an obvious level, interested in language which does not fully communicate; it is curious about words which are only partially successful in transmitting intent. In *Amours de Voyage* Clough would narrate a lover's failed efforts to catch up with his beloved by literally travelling after her across northern Italy, following this clue and that in an effort physically to track her down. Connection, at the close, is not made; the meeting fails to occur and the relationship is made impossible as, in the broader political context, the individual states of a fragmented Italy remain ununited.[12] In *The Bothie* Clough posited a more successful narrative of love, but thought beyond that about other forms of broken connections between people (and gave his story an apt political context of fraught connections by placing in the foreground the tension in the union between England and Scotland in the banqueting scene in Canto I). There is a symptomatic occasion of *The Bothie*'s persistent interest in language not adequately working in Canto III which points to the broader engagement. When Lindsay ('the Piper') and Arthur, two of the undergraduates, attempt to recount what they know of the absent Philip's movements in that canto, their narrative is always being amended. Their story is relayed with 'the Piper narrating, and Arthur correcting' (III. 153) or with 'Arthur narrating, the Piper correcting' (III. 168). The first version is always not wholly right and language needs must be supplemented with more language. It is emblematic of the poem's wider consideration of language's insufficiency and the place of revision.

The exchanges between Philip Hewson, the poem's hero, and Adam, the tutor, do not completely work. Stumbling attempts at catching wisdom are offered in this texture of impeded statement as the poem refuses to represent wholly successful debate. Adam's reply to Hewson's celebration of ordinary women in the first long discussion is met with the qualified 'There's truth in what you say, though truly much distorted' (II. 133), and later, after listening to Adam's version of the same theme, Philip will wryly match him with 'There's truth in what you say, though I *don't* quite understand you' (II. 272). The words point to the more general preoccupation: the poem is drawing attention to occasions of verbal insufficiency, the mismatch between words and sense. Adam, midway through a correspondence with the absent Philip, admits that in an earlier letter he had been too 'severe [. . .] and hasty' because he had written before he had 'duly read through' Philip's original letter (IV. 203-04). His original words have to be revised, although he notes, in defence, that there had been an obstruction to understanding Philip's letter in the first place because it was not exactly easy to read, 'written in scraps with crossings and countercrossings | Hard to connect with each other correctly' (IV. 205-06). Words do not make themselves transparent in *The Bothie*. Scenes of reading dwell on problems and obstacles, on the necessity for revision, which, appropriately, is what Clough did for the whole poem in the version published posthumously in 1862, neatly if accidentally emblematizing its preoccupation with language that needs substitution (his new title was chosen because—even more suggestively—it did not mean anything specific). It is this difficulty with the verbal, its need for refinement and replacement, on which Adam remarks when he observes by letter to Philip that they are habitually 'poring at, hammering at, stumbling at [meaning]' and failing. That teaching can happen under such conditions is unlikely indeed.

*The Bothie* is dragged back to confessions of impeded meaning and dramatizes, in the midst of its dubiety, a literal debate between tutor and pupil which exemplifies further problems of how the reliable is (or is not) separated from the mistaken, insight despite obstacle. Of the discussions Adam and Philip have, spoken or by letter, the most unsatisfactory is the long debate about women, work, and class in Canto II. It is a scene—the first and only substantial indication in the poem of the kind of intellectual life enjoyed on the reading party—that with peculiar aptness invites a response of an Emersonian kind: an acknowledgement that important topical questions are being discussed but a disinclination to say precisely what the results are. Here is a sustained attempt to communicate broken on the rocks of human limitation, an odd, difficult-to-read, not wholly satisfactory replacement for a debate. The radical and supposedly 'eloquent' (II. 19) Philip Hewson's argument with his tutor is, in the most general of terms, about the nature of modern women in relation to labour, what constitutes admirable femininity, and how work dignifies. Physically labouring women are, Philip claims, more valuable, attractive, and content than upper-class ladies without occupation. 'Better', as he puts it with a horticultural analogy later to be thrown back at him, 'a daisy in earth than a dahlia cut and gathered, | Better a cowslip with root than a prize carnation without it' (II.

81-82). It is an illiberal view of the primacy of work, an over-played insistence on physical labour as the highest calling of women—though to what extent Philip is behind his views or deliberately provoking is an unanswered question. To this argument, or quasi-argument, Adam takes a disconcertingly long time to compose his response, and while he is slowly 'gathering his thoughts' (II. 136) there takes place a lengthy digression as the undergraduates compare women to architecture, hoping that Philip will write a study of the relationship and become 'the Pugin of women' (II. 153). The episode is meant to be an amusing aside and a muted contemporary joke, but it is also a distraction for those endeavouring to keep track of the Adam-Philip dispute. Adam's eventual response does not, however, reveal the argument to be following lines that can be easily tracked anyway. It meets Philip's statement only obliquely.

To the reader unfamiliar with this poem, it is not easy fully to convey how remarkably disconcerting is this 'debate', with its continual, distracting misalignments of response. When Adam finally commences his reply to Philip, it is as if the reader is hearing a response to a slightly different argument, a reply to a partially different set of propositions. It is almost as if the reader has lost part of the conversation and rejoined it a few minutes later. 'You are young', Adam begins, with what is later realized to be characteristic obliqueness,

> you know, he said, re-
> suming to Philip,
> You are young, he proceeded, with something of fer-
> vour to Hewson
> You are a boy; when you grow a man, you'll find
> things alter.
> You will learn to seek the good, to scorn the attrac-
> tive,
> Scorn all mere cosmetics, as now of rank and fashion,
> Delicate hands, and wealth, so then of poverty also,
> Poverty truly attractive, more truly, I bear you wit-
> ness.
> Good, wherever found, you will choose, be it humble
> or stately,
> Happy if only you find, and finding do not lose it.
>
> (II. 172-80)

This, the beginning of Adam's reply, avoids exact, explicit relevance, for Philip has been offering a version of it himself, proposing that one should indeed 'seek the good [and] scorn the attractive'. By applauding those who take up their 'business and duty' (II. 73) and are not separate from 'work, mother earth, and objects of living' (II. 72), Philip has not been privileging mere attractiveness over virtue as his tutor implies. Adam's response continues in the same emphatic but slightly indirect way. Concluding his lengthy reply-that-is-not-quite-a-reply with 'Partly you rest on truth, old truth, the duty of Duty, | Partly on error, you long for equality' (II. 213-14), Adam is still only half in contact with the opposing (quasi-)argument, for *equality* is not the best word, not the exact descriptor, of Philip's claims that those who work with their hands are more admirable than those who do not.

The perplexing argument of Canto II is not simply parodic and the problem is not that both sides are entirely unsynchronized with each other. The proximity to actual, productive debate is closer. But neither side fully hears the other and rejoinders are only partially in focus. Philip's already quoted remark to Adam that there is 'truth in what you say, though I *don't* quite understand you' (II. 272) exemplifies the troublesome nature of this conversation, its absence of reliable conclusions, and its uneven method of trying to reach them. Clough in *The Bothie* offers himself as possessing little faith in the discursive as a way of reaching reliable knowledge. Letters are no more exemplary in the construction of debate and Clough's text offers a written relationship between tutor and pupil marked also by qualification, withdrawal, apology, and indirectness. Adam, at the centre of the dispute with Philip and his habitual correspondent, is no authoritative teacher; he is allowed under these circumstances no special powers in either role, as debater or letter writer. Amid its doubtfulness about human daily communication, Clough's text declines to hail the figure of the literal pedagogue as an exception and cannot bring itself to propose him as a reliable, clear-sighted guide—a man whose words might be trusted and through whose wisdom maturity obtained—in the middle of the seemingly ubiquitous uncertainties of human perception and thought. The business of Adam's life, indeed, is mundane and unappealing; he appears but a cog in a tedious machine, if not quite one who, in gloomy words from *Ambarvalia* (1849), serves the 'broken cisterns' of 'vain Philosophy'.[13] *The Bothie* has, certainly, little patience with the unreformed Oxford syllabus, and the undergraduates' boredom with the curriculum is an obvious feature of Clough's commentary on the university he had just left. Adam is part of an educational system as tedious as it is unenlightening. Yet it is not the reading required by the Oxford system which fails to provide guidance to the young men alone; the poem is not merely vexed with the specific inadequacy of education through knowledge of the 'dismal classics' (II. 279) in an unreformed university. It is, amid its other hesitations about from where or from whom a man might learn, curiously reticent on how useful any books are in giving men a compass by which to steer.

Ordinary human beings customarily do not fully succeed in their efforts to communicate: guidance from books is also largely unavailable. Those which are read in *The Bothie* as part of the Oxford syllabus are, without doubt, separated from any purposeful connection with the problems of lived life. Hope's chorus about his reading is amusing but describes with particular clarity the gap between the 'classics' of the Oxford curriculum and those books that might be said to speak adequately to the present. 'Fare ye well', Hope happily proclaims, as the undergraduates prepare to take a break from reading,

> forgotten unnamed, undreamt of,
> History, Science, and Poets! Lo, deep in dustiest cupboard,
> Thookydid, Oloros' son, Halimoosian, here lieth buried!

(II. 281-83)

Yet if these ancient books, the logic primers, plays, and histories, are cast by the poem as dispiritingly remote, as those which are so dead that they can come into the present only through exhumation (cf. II. 290), *The Bothie* makes little effort to replace them with anything written which is more connected or living. Philip is supposedly a poet but his work is oddly unrepresented: Clough would eventually become a poet-who-no-longer-wrote-poetry but *The Bothie* does not allow its reader to see that Philip has ever done anything to deserve the name. At the heart of his life as a writer is an absence. Finding little of instruction in others' books, and seemingly without his own, Hewson demands peremptorily that Elspie, when they are married, reads nothing. It is a strange requirement from a *soi-disant* man of letters. 'Weary and sick of our books we come to repose in your eye-sight', he tells her (VIII. 115). Elspie will have none of this depression with texts and claims the right to continue reading despite Philip's meagre assessment of its worth, though what she intends to read she does not say. It is the only moment of enthusiasm for books in the whole poem. To be sure, the 'poet' Hewson, having escaped from dreary Oxford, takes some volumes with him to New Zealand but they form only part of a list of possessions and, in the labours he undertakes there, seem hardly of the first priority:

> They are married, and gone to New Zealand.
> Five hundred pounds in pocket, with books, and two or three pictures,
> Tool-box, plough, and the rest, they rounded the sphere to New Zealand.
> There he hewed, and dug; subdued the earth and his spirit;
> There he built him a home; there Elspie bare him his children,
> David and Bella; perhaps ere this too an Elspie or Adam;
> There hath he farmstead and land, and fields of corn and flax fields;
> And the Antipodes too have a Bothie of Toper-na-fuosich.

(IX. 222-29)

The business of making a home and rearing children marginalizes literature. Seen, at the end, with his farmstead and land, the poetry-less poet is freed from any explicit indication of the place the written word might have in his life. Joseph Phelan argues that *The Bothie* suggested, against the alien texts of the Oxford curriculum, that the literature of the syllabus needed to be brought into better contact with modern life; by adapting a classical metre to the vocabulary and sound patterns of contemporary English, Phelan says, Clough enacted a saving form of renovation which was meant to point to a better future. Phelan is, of course, right to stress the poem's impatience with the deadening effect of Oxford's BA requirements, but in fact *The Bothie* cannot bring itself to say much explicitly about the value of books whether found in Oxford or not. Rather than pointing to literature's renewed role in modern existence, the conclusion, despite what the hexameters may be obliquely hinting, is reluctant to offer a significant place for the written word in the life of its protagonists at all. And echoing behind this, perhaps, is a distant fretful sense not just of the authority of books but of the problematic nature of the Book too—the problem for Clough of how to read Scripture—and of other allegedly authoritative documents in the Protestant life, especially the Thirty-Nine Articles that Clough could not bring himself to sign.

After Philip has left the company of his tutor and friends, he sends to Adam a letter about Katie, the Highland girl with whom he briefly falls in love before meeting Elspie. He struggles to find the words he needs to explain his thoughts—'Something like this', he says, trying to pin down an idea, 'but indeed I cannot the least define it' (IV. 161). The letter prompts another reply from Adam, confessing again the inadequacy of language, the difficulty of 'unfaltering' reading, the 'maimed and hampered' efforts to interpret (IV. 221, 227). It is a wittily appropriate conclusion, and a momentarily comic reflection on the difficulties of communicating altogether in the poem that, having finished his writing, Adam is left with a problem:

> So was the letter completed: a postscript afterward added,
> Telling the tale that was told by the dancers returning from Rannoch.
> So was the letter completed: but query, whither to send it?

> (IV. 269-71)

In an epistle musing in part on the obstructions to human conversation and the troubles of relating to others, the absence of Philip's address crisply articulates the awkwardnesses of communication which I have been discussing here—the difficulties in human exchanges, the troublesome nature of words of which the poem is so conscious. Adam's words in his long debate in Canto II had not quite found their mark; now, literally uncertain where his words should go, he is possessed of an unaddressed and unaddressable letter as if winningly

emblematizing the poem's wider lack of faith in the connections that ordinary human beings can make between each other.

*The Bothie* will not easily ascribe to Adam powers of guidance and allows its reader to see in the tutor figure a man of very ordinary abilities, albeit '*topping* in Plays and Aldrich' (I. 24), caught amid the same struggles with knowledge and language as his youthful pupils. In the memorable satire 'Duty—that's to say complying' from *Ambarvalia*, Clough makes duty, among other things, an impediment to enquiry:

> Duty—'tis to take on trust
> What things are good, and right, and just;
> And whether indeed they be or be not,
> Try not, test not, feel not, see not.[14]

But in *The Bothie* neither traditional wisdom nor individual enquiry is prioritized, neither that which is learnt from tutors nor tested in one's own mind. Secure knowledge is even more fugitive and uncertain of location. Yet within its reflections on the difficulties of finding reliable teaching, *The Bothie* is, in strange ways, preoccupied with fantasies of its opposite, just as, to make a comparison from a different field of thought, Charles Williams's Divine City could exist only by incorporating its counter-state.[15] Gloomy about the possibilities of dependable instruction in the ordinary domain of experience, amid the snares of language and the fractures of communication, Clough's text is not without traces of the very thing it does not see the daily world accommodating. If a text can be said to dream, then this is what *The Bothie* does; and if dreams are, as Freud insisted, wish fulfilments, then Clough's poem certainly dreams of that which it believes most difficult to discern in the wakeful, quotidian world. At one level the poem knows of no dependable and rational source of guidance through which a man might seek to direct his life, but at another it invests in fantasies of (im)possibility. *The Bothie* dreams of those who are freed from earthly bounds and possessed of insight beyond the measure of common living. They are those who stand in contradistinction to the poem's dark meditations on the absence of instruction from human teachers engaged in a permanent struggle with a problematic language. These creatures are touched by the mystical and hear, it may be, the distant echoes of the dead. Their interruptions, in Clough's text, into the daily, the regular, the *homely,* constitute *The Bothie*'s distinctive, unobtrusive, but defining engagement with the supra-normal, its own suggestive version of the *Unheimlich.*

Clough's poem is, in fact, variously intrigued by the possibilities of the otherworldly, aside from its imagining of ideal teachers. If those teachers are marked by the distant presence of the spectral—the possibility that the wisdom of the dead lives through them—then elsewhere *The Bothie* is more explicit about the admirable powers of the ghost. Philip, indeed, longs to be one. In an extended passage while separated from Katie, he craves the freedom that the returning dead possess in words that startlingly revise the familiar lover's trope that makes equivalence between separation from the beloved and the state of death. 'Souls of the dead, one fancies,' Philip says,

> can enter and be
> with the living;
> Would I were dead, I keep saying, that so I could go
> and uphold her!
> Spirits escaped from the body can enter and be with
> the living,
> Entering unseen, and retiring unquestioned, they bring,
> do they feel too?
> Joy, pure joy, as they mingle and mix inner essence
> with essence;
> Would I were dead I keep saying, that so I could go
> and uphold her!
> Joy, pure joy, bringing with them, and when they retire
> leaving after
> No cruel shame, no prostration, despondency; memo-
> ries rather
> Sweet, happy hopes bequeathing. Ah! wherefore not
> thus with the living?
> Would I were dead, I keep saying, that so I could go
> and uphold her!

(IV. 41-50)

The ghost as Philip imagines it is freed from the troubling experience of loving and able to enjoy the beloved in remarkably erotic chasteness. Phantoms possess capacities for which the living yearn; they inhabit a world that answers better to Philip's desires and, even as their personalities remain, are undivided in feeling, possessing their emotions in pure forms without disabling equivocation. This association between the *revenant* and clarity of being, between the ghost and directness of experience, is a clue to what happens in the rest of *The Bothie*'s underground thinking about the spectral and the nature of wisdom beyond Philip's ardent account of what pleasures the spirit might take. His jealous aspirations hint at the poem's consequential meditation on the unhampered knowledge of those possessed of exceptional insight, through whom, it may be, the dead communicate. Philip yearns to be a ghost—and at a curious level, the poem itself looks up for guidance to those gifted beyond the ordinary and, perchance, in touch with the deceased. Indeed, it might also be said that the poem performs a kind of ghostliness—in Philip's sense—itself, flitting in and out of its hero's consciousnesses as its narrative perspective moves from his to one outside and back.

The figures of real instruction, the strange visionaries of *The Bothie,* whose words and even glances are worth obeying, are in contact, always, with an unexplained power. As Philip retires from the barn at the end of the feast in Canto I, he is perceived by a bizarre, out-of-place figure, a 'thin man', improbably 'clad as the Saxon' in the heart of the Highlands, who singles him out (I. 182). Without introduction or explanation, the stranger rests his hand on Philip's shoulder and, looking into his eyes, like a new Ancient Mariner, says: 'Young man, if ye pass through the Braes o'Lochaber, | See by the loch-side ye come to the Bothie of Toper-na-fuosich' (I. 186-87). For the first-time reader of the poem, it is a bewildering moment. Who is this speaker? How does he know Philip? What is the Bothie of Toper-na-fuosich? Why should Philip visit it? The speaker eventually proves to be David Mackie, the father of Elspie, the woman whom Philip will eventually marry, and Mackie's instruction is, in due course, obeyed, though as far as Philip is concerned, he stumbles on the Bothie by chance, by 'accident purely' (VI. 37), rather than in direct response to the mysterious command. Some unanalysed force appears to guide him to the remote hut, a force as unknown as that manifested in the unannounced appearance of Mackie. Elspie's father, it appears, is possessed of inner sight, an intuitive perception that descries in Philip a man who would profit from acquaintance with the simple mode of life of his home. The advice proves prophetic—from it follows Philip and Elspie's marriage and their new life together—but its origin is a riddle.

Clough's text dreams of such moments, its texture broken by the fantasized interruptions of the mysterious. Katharine Chorley, the most biographical of Clough's recent critics, thought the poet a thinker firmly rooted in the material, the observable and demonstrable. 'Clough was naturally an empiricist', she says, and he needed, in all arguments, 'empirical grounds, the manageability of concrete as against metaphysical evidence' (p. 54). Yet *The Bothie,* at the very least among Clough's works, suggests something importantly different, for it is a text that opens up a space for that which is valuable precisely because it escapes the terms of the demonstratively explicable, that which is unashamedly uncontainable by reason. Elspie shares something of her father's power and one momentary glance at Philip in Rannoch is enough to bring him—at least, so he later claims—a new and acute sense of self-knowledge. 'Elspie,' he says to her,

> it was your look that sent me away from Ran-
> noch.
> It was your glance, that, descending, an instant revela-
> tion,
> Showed me, where I was, and whitherward going;
> recalled me,
> Sent me, not to my books, but to wrestlings of thought
> in the mountains.
> Yes, I have carried your glance within me undimmed,
> unaltered,

As a lost boat the compass some passing ship has lent
  her,
Many a weary mile on road, and hill, and moorland.

                                        (VII. 38-44)

Books and ordinary men provide him with no adequate compass, but the 'instant revelation' of this strangely penetrating, incomprehensibly powerful gaze is that which he cannot otherwise come by. Elspie dismisses her Highland home as 'ignorant' (VII. 178) and is fretful about the 'birth and education' (VIII. 2) of her lover, yet she possesses a power that no human agent can teach and through which knowledge of an individual's future appears uniquely knowable. *The Bothie* might have been thought to imagine these unfathomable powers as associated with the natural environment; possessed by the untrained Highlanders Elspie and David, such abilities might seem suggestively connected to a life outside of modern civilization and in closer contact with the soil that Philip so ostentatiously admires. But the most unlikely of transformations in the text reveals this connection to be misleading.

Of all the people to possess exceptional human knowledge, the hesitant tutor Adam is the least probable. But such is *The Bothie*'s sense of the extraordinary nature, the incomprehensible quality of the gifted, that it can break up the expectations of character coherence, upset the reader's assumption that personality will remain broadly consistent, to satisfy its hopes that people of wisdom break into the fabric of the day-to-day. So it is that Adam, the dully dutiful bachelor cleric, familiar with the ways of his university rather than beyond, who is embarrassed by the mere mention of women's 'lily-white legs' (II. 126) early in the poem, becomes at the end, without preparation, the adept counsellor of Elspie as she considers her marriage prospects with Philip. From inexact arguer and tutor of limited mind, Adam is transformed, through the alchemy of the poem's desires, into an authoritative guide in the romantic life of a Highland girl who has never been formally educated. Elspie hears much from him that is 'reassuring' (VIII. 35) and comes to tell him everything about her life and love, 'And he calmly approved, as one that had fully considered' (VIII. 58). Earning the pointed title of 'the teacher' (VIII. 55), ironically barely applicable up to that point, Adam instructs Elspie with unobtrusive, unheard expertise, offering 'impartial accurate statement | What it was to do this or do that, go hither or thither' (VIII. 29-30), so that she understands what a relationship with Philip will mean and the principles of a whole range of social issues, the 'relations of rich and poor', and, pointedly enough, 'true education' (VIII. 43).

The psychologically unthinkable transformation of Adam is the most surprising instantiation of *The Bothie*'s belief in the inexplicable nature of wise guidance, its nature as a gift, not as something learnt, that leaves behind the quotidian in the manifestation of unexplained force. Upon the workings of this force the text cannot lift the veil very far. Adam is 'the teacher' at the end, but *what* he says to Elspie, exactly what he approves, what he advises of her marriage, and what he instructs, more locally, of the relations of rich and poor, to say nothing of 'true education', remain undisclosed. The poem keeps its scene of wisdom mysterious; it mystifies the substance of what it hails as true teaching. But perhaps it is not so unexpected that Adam should take this ideal pedagogic role after all, for it was he who, earlier in the text, was given the task of defining the terms of the poem's greatest hopes about the possibilities of human guidance long before he manifested curious powers himself. Adam's letter to Philip in Canto IV, the physical centre of the poem, obtains a rare clarity of meaning as it seeks to define the absence of clarity in most men's experience. In doing so, it suggests the existence of the super-normal, whose wisdom is not of ordinary men and women, whose powers of mystical insight are of singular veracity and scarcity, and whose essences are, perhaps, in transaction with the knowledge of the ancestral dead. 'There are exceptional beings', Adam solemnly writes to Philip,

                          one finds them distant and
    rarely,
  Who, endowed with the vision alike and the interpreta-
    tion,
  See, by their neighbours' eyes, and their own still mo-
    tions enlightened,
  In the beginning the end, in the acorn the oak of the
    forest,
  In the child of to-day its children to long generations,
  In a thought or a wish a life, a drama, an epos.
  There are inheritors, is it? by mystical generation,
  Heiring the wisdom and ripeness of spirits gone-by;
    without labour
  Owning what others by doing and suffering earn; what
    old men
  After long years of mistake and erasure are proud to
    have come to,
  Sick with mistake and erasure possess when posses-
    sion is idle.
  Yes, there is power upon earth, seen feebly in women
    and children,
  Which can, laying one hand on the cover, read-off,
    unfaltering,
  Leaf after leaf unlifted, the words of the closed book
    under,
  Words which we are poring at, hammering at, stum-
    bling at, spelling.

                                        (IV. 210-24)

Adam's words resonate with Wordsworth's—'endowed with the vision', 'there is a power upon earth'—yet the men and women of whom he writes are not, as they might be for the Romantic, gifted with insight into the nature of the divine, or perceptive of the spiritual possibilities of the landscape. What they own instead is the ability to interpret ordinary human character, to read it like an open (or, more impressively, a closed) book and to act as authentic guides in the confusing experience of living daily in the world. They are neither Carlylean heroes nor Romantic visionaries: their terrain of knowledge is the individual human heart. These 'exceptional beings' are not imagined in theistic, let alone Christian, terms but are perhaps, as Adam suggests, somehow 'mystical'; they are the heirs of the learning of the deceased, the 'spirits gone-by', who paradoxically still obtain a kind of life through them; in their being is gathered, it may be, the accrued wisdom of earlier men and women, and they are fantasized in part as the putative conduits through which the dead may make contribution to the present, untroubled by all the difficulties of earthly communication.

The challenge of reading **The Bothie** stems in part from its conviction about the difficulties of ordinary human communication. Fascinated by the problems that impede verbal exchange, Clough in this text is doubtful about sources of human wisdom in the regular world, and suspicious of forms of instruction that come from the everyday or from the formal institutions of teaching. The poem can find no remedy for this except in a dream of its opposite, leaving the reader with writing oscillating between extended doubtfulness and improbable hope. **The Bothie** ascribes to what it hails as authentic wisdom an aura of the unknown and even the spectral; it mystifies the sources of its best teaching so that guidance about that which is truly valuable is always inexplicable in its origins and figured as even ghostly in its nature. A ghost is what Philip desires to be in his love affair with Katie: in that state he perceives neither division nor confining material limitation. The poem itself, in a more oblique fashion, wonders, I think, about what it silently, distantly understands as a form of haunting. It is engaged with figures whose powers of perception, so radically different from the experience of the quotidian world, may come in part from their strange connection, through 'mystical generation', with the knowledge of the past. Julian Wolfreys in the most recent, and most ample, theorization of hauntings in Victorian literature—drawing heavily on Derrida's late-period writing on phantoms—teases out the idea of spectral presences in nineteenth-century literature so that it becomes a great portmanteau category, seemingly helping to define all narrative, or even all texts, or the Gothic in particular, or modernity in particular, or the political in particular.[16] Wolfreys's expansion of the category of the 'hauntological' fatally erodes it (Derrida is hardly free from this problem), leaving a sense of Victorian literary haunting as merely a metaphor rather than a more specific descriptor of a text that contemplates the possibilities of the *revenant*. Clough's long-vacation pastoral has a subtle sense of the place of haunting but it is a more focused one than Wolfreys's, for in its dreams of the wise it locates the possible pres-

ence of the still-speaking deceased. **The Bothie** is indeed a perplexing text and its first reviewers' sense of its troubles still points to important issues which some modern critics have been tempted to overlook. Its difficulties are implicated with its most serious purposes and its strangest visions. In representing the problems of verbal interaction, **The Bothie** makes of the puzzle a descriptor of ordinary human exchange; in figuring its most estimable teachers as those whose powers are beyond rational comprehension, it prizes mystery. In that which cannot be explained is, in the end, its best hope, and the reader's bewilderment is the most useful clue to the curious heart of its drama.

*Notes*

1. Arthur Hugh Clough, *The Bothie,* 1848 text, ed. by Patrick Scott ([St Lucia]: University of Queensland Press, 1976): all references to the poem are to this edition by canto and line number in the main text.

2. Letter to Clough, 21 January 1849, repr. in *Clough: The Critical Heritage,* ed. by Michael Thorpe (New York: Barnes and Noble, 1972), p. 34 (emphasis original).

3. Ibid., p. 36.

4. Unsigned notice in *The Spectator,* 2 December 1848, repr. in *Critical Heritage,* ed. by Thorpe, p. 31.

5. *Critical Heritage,* ed. by Thorpe, pp. 47-48 (p. 48).

6. On 2 December 1848 (Kingsley needed the permission because he was not sure if Clough wanted the poem to have 'a merely Oxonian or a cosmic, circulation'): Frederick L. Mulhauser, *The Correspondence of Arthur Hugh Clough,* 2 vols (Oxford: Clarendon Press, 1957), I, 193.

7. Charles Kingsley's review in *Fraser's,* repr. in *Critical Heritage,* ed. by Thorpe, pp. 37-47 (pp. 46-47, emphasis original).

8. *Arthur Hugh Clough: The Uncommitted Mind. A Study of his Life and Poetry* (Oxford: Clarendon Press, 1962).

9. Robindra Kumar Biswas, *Arthur Hugh Clough: Towards a Reconsideration* (Oxford: Clarendon Press, 1972), p. 265.

10. 'Where "Byron Used to Ride"; Locating the Victorian Travel Poet in Clough's *Amours de Voyage* and *Dipsychus*', *Philological Quarterly,* 77 (1998), 377-78.

11. 'Radical Metre: The English Hexameter in Clough's *Bothie of Toper-na-Fuosich*', *Review of English Studies,* 50 (1999), 166-87.

12. Matthew Reynolds sensibly discusses the relationship between the romantic and the political in *The Realms of Verse: English Poetry in a Time of Nation-Building* (Oxford: Oxford University Press, 2001), esp. pp. 141-56.

13. 'In a Lecture-Room', in *The Poems of Arthur Hugh Clough,* ed. by F. L. Mulhauser, 2nd edn (Oxford: Clarendon Press, 1974), p. 24.

14. *Poems,* ed. by Mulhauser, p. 27.

15. See Charles Williams, *The Image of the City and Other Essays,* ed. by Anne Ridler (London: Oxford University Press, 1958), p. xxi.

16. See the introduction, where all these claims are made, in Julian Wolfreys, *Victorian Hauntings: Spectrality, Gothic, the Uncanny and Literature* (Basingstoke: Palgrave, 2002), pp. 1-24.


## Joseph Phelan (essay date autumn 2006)

SOURCE: Phelan, Joseph. "Clough, Arnold, Béranger, and the Legacy of 1848." *Studies in English Literature 1500-1900* 46, no. 4 (autumn 2006): 833-48.

[*In the following essay, Phelan explores the relationship between Clough and Matthew Arnold and their respective responses to the Revolution of 1848 in France, as well as the influence of Pierre-Jean de Béranger on the work of both poets.*]

In a letter to his friend J. C. Shairp written in early 1847, Arthur Hugh Clough, then still a Fellow of Oriel College, Oxford, describes Matthew Arnold's return to the college after the latter's visit to Paris: "Matt is full of Parisianism; theatres in general, and Rachel in special: he enters the room with a chanson of Beranger's on his lips—for the sake of French words almost conscious of tune: his carriage shows him in fancy parading the Rue de Rivoli;—and his hair is guiltless of English scissors: he breakfasts at twelve, and never dines in Hall, and in the week or 8 days rather (for 2 Sundays must be included) he has been to Chapel *once.*"[1] Clough's tone is clearly ironic; the "chanson of Beranger's" is, he implies, as much of an affectation as Arnold's fashionably long hair, and the subsequent history of Arnold's involvement with the French poet would seem to support this judgment. For Clough himself, on the other hand, the encounter with Pierre-Jean de Béranger (1780-1857) was a formative poetic experience. The French *chansonnier* is cited and named in Clough's work on a number of occasions, and some of the most distinctive themes and features of Clough's poetry are directly traceable to Béranger's influence. Clough's use of Béranger is not, moreover, merely imitative; he tends to insert references to Béranger into

dramatic settings that contextualize and implicitly question the characteristic attitudes of the French poet. Indeed, one of Clough's most creative uses of Béranger's poetry is as part of his continuing poetic dialogue with Matthew Arnold; for Clough, Arnold's sentimental misunderstanding of Béranger is symptomatic of the shallowness and affectation of many of his attitudes and beliefs. These widely divergent attitudes toward the work of Béranger are indicative of the two poets' very different responses to the French Revolution of 1848 and its aftermath. Béranger came to epitomize for Arnold the immorality and cynicism that plunged France into repeated revolutions and upheavals throughout the nineteenth century. Clough, in contrast, always saw in the French songwriter a valuable alternative to the sexual Puritanism, hypocrisy, and class division of British society.

Arnold became an enthusiast for the work of the French songwriter Béranger during the late 1840s. This was, in itself, a rather belated conversion. The high-water mark of Béranger's English reputation was the early 1830s; by the 1840s he was beginning to be supplanted by Victor Hugo, Alfred de Musset, and the representatives of the Romantic school.[2] Elizabeth Barrett notes in a letter of November 1842 to Mary Russell Mitford that he "scarcely takes rank . . . with 'young France'" and describes the "fierce, wild, passionate, & ghastly character of the present literature" as inimical to the appreciation of his songs.[3] The British reception of Béranger's work was, moreover, always tentative due to his extremely controversial subject matter. During the reign of the Bourbons, his radical, democratic, and anticlerical views commanded some respect, but his frankness—or as the British tended to see it, licentiousness—about sexual matters ensured that his work remained largely untranslated. Arnold seems to have treated Béranger as his own discovery, at least among his circle of close friends. In late 1847 he offered to compensate for sending Clough a "cynical" and "beastly-vile" letter of criticism by buying his friend "the Paris diamond edition of Beranger, like mine."[4] Then in March 1848 he answered a (now unfortunately lost) comment of Clough's with the following exhortation: "Burns is certainly an artist *im*plicitly—fury is not incompatible with artistic form but it becomes *lyric* fury (Eh?) only when combined with the gift for this. And Beranger both in [sic]—and ex. They accuse him by his finisht classicality of having banished the old native French Forms. O, you must like him."[5] By the end of 1848, however, Arnold's enthusiasm was clearly beginning to wane. When he visited Switzerland in the autumn of 1848, he took only two books with him— Epictetus and Béranger—and soon came to regret this minimalist approach to holiday reading. He was, he confessed to Clough, "getting tired" of Béranger, and beginning to suspect that there was "something 'fade' about [his] Epicureanism."[6] And from this point onwards there is, remarkably, no further mention of Béranger in Arnold's work or correspondence.

This short-lived enthusiasm for Béranger seems at first sight to have left little imprint on Arnold's poetry. His first collection, published in 1849 as *The Strayed Reveller and Other Poems,* bears almost no trace of Béranger's influence; Arnold goes in for philosophical meditation rather than the "Epicureanism" for which the French poet was notorious in his own day. There are only two poems that might possibly manifest some indebtedness to Béranger. The first is the sentimental "Memory Picture":

> Marguerite says: 'As last year went,
> So the coming year'll be spent;
> Some day next year, I shall be,
> Entering heedless, kissed by thee.'
> Ah, I hope!—yet, once away,
> What may chain us, who can say?
>      Ere the parting hour go by,
>      Quick, thy tablets, Memory![7]

This poem is almost unique in Arnold's poetry in using a refrain—a device which is, as Charles-Augustin Sainte-Beuve and others pointed out, strongly associated with Béranger's poetry—and gives voice to a worldliness about human relations reminiscent of the French poet's.[8] The other poem in the collection that might bear some trace of Béranger's influence is the "Horatian Echo." The comparison between Béranger and Horace had, like the comparison between Béranger and Robert Burns, become proverbial, not least for the way in which both seemed to prefer retirement and simple pleasures to the bustle of contemporary politics.[9] In the "Horatian Echo" the speaker remains aloof from the great political events of the year of revolutions, reminding himself of his own mortality and the transitory nature of all human social arrangements:

> The day approaches, when we must
> Be crumbling bones and windy dust;
> And scorn us as our mistress may,
> Her beauty will no better be
> Than the poor face she slights in thee,
>      When dawns that day, that day.[10]

Both these poems, however, stop a long way short of Béranger's full-blooded Epicureanism; Arnold's "Eugenia," his mistress in the "Horatian Echo," is a mere cipher compared to the lively and capricious Lisette of the French poet's songs.[11] In spite of their formal similarities to some aspects of Béranger's work, these poems are consistent with the grim Stoicism which is the dominant note of the collection.

How, then, are we to account for Arnold's rapid disillusionment with Béranger? Part of the answer is, I think, suggested in the letter to Clough referred to above in which Arnold confesses his growing disenchantment

with Béranger's songs: "I have with me only Beranger and Epictetus: the latter tho: familiar to me, yet being Greek, when tired I am, is not much read by me: of the former I am getting tired. Horace whom he resembles had to write only for a circle of highly cultivated desillusionés roués, in a sceptical age: we have the sceptical age, but a far different and wider audience: voila pourquoi, with all his genius, there is something 'fade' about Beranger's Epicureanism."[12] Like Horace, Béranger was a highly cultivated, disillusioned, sceptical, and personally amoral character; but unlike Horace, he was not writing for a small circle of initiates but for "a far different and wider audience," the kind of audience that might have difficulty interpreting this "Epicureanism" correctly. In other words, the problem with Béranger's poetry for Arnold is its very popularity.[13] This popularity was, as far as can be judged from surviving testimony, a genuinely astonishing phenomenon; his songs celebrating patriotism, love, and social equality were, according to his contemporaries, known and sung by the poor and illiterate as well as by the rich and powerful.[14] It is the need to appeal to this mass audience that has given Béranger's Epicureanism something of a "fade" (dull, insipid, or conventional) quality; in popularizing the attitude to life of a small *côterie,* he has, Arnold implies, been obliged to resort to bland and formulaic responses to experience. This notion that a set of attitudes or beliefs that can be embraced or at least tolerated by a small, select group might resist easy translation to a "far different and wider" public becomes a *leitmotiv* of Arnold's later work. It is the substance of his objection a decade or so later to Bishop Colenso's attempts to popularize the Higher Criticism of the Bible in England; and it is echoed in his comments on Béranger's German counterpart, Heinrich Heine, in the essay "Pagan and Medieval Religious Sentiment" from *Essays in Criticism*: "[As] a condition of sentiment to be popular,—to be a comfort for the mass of mankind, under the pressure of calamity, to live by,—what a manifest failure is this last word of the religion of pleasure! One man in many millions, a Heine, may console himself, and keep himself erect in suffering, by a colossal irony of this sort, by covering himself and the universe with the red fire of this sinister mockery; but the many millions cannot,—cannot if they would."[15] Such attitudes, tolerable and even valuable when embraced by the educated few, become corrosive if allowed to spread unchecked throughout the population.

Arnold's doubts about the value of Béranger's Epicureanism seem, moreover, to be directly linked to the progress of the Revolution of 1848. Arnold's response to this event moved very quickly from mild enthusiasm through lofty disdain to outright opposition. As early as May 1848, while Clough was in Paris attempting to absorb the atmosphere of the "New Jerusalem," Arnold was pointing out to him how "disheartening" the events must be for "the believers in progress"; while the violent counterrevolution of June produced the following outburst: "What a nice state of things in France. The New Gospel is adjourned for this bout. If one had ever hoped any thing from such a set of d———d grimacing liars as their prophets one would be very sick just now."[16] Béranger was one of these "prophets"—he was credited by some with having helped to prompt the 1830 Revolution and was elected to the National Assembly in the aftermath of the Revolution of 1848—and Arnold acknowledges the effect of "seditious songs" like his in fomenting revolution in a letter to Clough of March 1848: "[A]mongst a *people* of readers the litterature [sic] is a greater engine than the philosophy . . . Seditious songs have nourished the F[renc]h people much more than the Socialist: philosophers: though they may formulize their wants through the mouths of these."[17] His disillusionment with Béranger is, then, intimately linked to his disillusionment with the revolution as a whole. "Seditious songs" such as Béranger's promoted the cynical and hedonistic attitudes that disposed the French people toward revolution; and the disastrous outcome of this event, not least for ordinary French people themselves, seems to have led Arnold to a rapid readjustment of his outlook. The rejection, one might even say repression, of Béranger can, then, be seen as the moment at which the definitively Arnoldian persona first begins to emerge.

There is no such rejection of Béranger in Clough's case. He was still expressing a high degree of admiration for the work of the French poet in 1850, telling William Allingham that "Shakespeare and Milton should meet together as Rousseau and Voltaire have in Goethe and in Beranger."[18] Many of his poems (such as **"Les Vaches"** and **"Dance on, dance on"**) are songlike in form and make unusually frequent use of the refrain.[19] And the narrative poem that Clough began during 1850, *Dipsychus and The Spirit,* contains a number of direct references to and quotations from Béranger's work, as does his last poem *Mari Magno, or Tales on Board.*[20] This continuing dialogue with Béranger constitutes one of the ways in which Clough articulated and developed his personal and poetic differences with Arnold, which steadily widened throughout the 1850s. Where Arnold identified himself with Sainte-Beuve, Ernest Renan, and others who saw in Béranger a symptom of France's moral and spiritual malaise, Clough continued to see his attitude to life as a valuable antidote to the Puritanism and hypocrisy dominant in England.[21] And where Arnold saw only danger in the French poet's popularity, Clough saw in his ability to transcend differences of class the possibility of a new and democratic poetics.

*Dipsychus and The Spirit* is set in Venice and takes the form of an extended dialogue between two characters: Dipsychus (meaning "double-minded") and another identified in successive drafts of the poem as Mephistopheles and then as "The Spirit." The drama begins

with Dipsychus reciting part of Clough's own **"Easter Day"** ode—"Christ is not risen!"—and continues with the hero's attempts to resist various temptations placed in his path by "The Spirit."[22] The first of these is the temptation to acquire sexual knowledge by accepting the solicitations of a prostitute in the Public Gardens at Venice. Dipsychus, as is his practice throughout the poem, wrestles with his conscience over the rights and wrongs of the situation, and The Spirit, to encourage him, quotes some lines from Béranger's song "Ma grand'mère":

> Eh?
> What do those pretty verses say?
> *Ah comme je regrette*
>   *Mon bras si dodu*
>   *Ma jambe bien faite*
>     *Et le temps perdu*
>     *Et le temps perdu.*[23]

(1.2.38-44)

The song is a typical piece of hedonism in which the grandmother of the title laments the loss of her youth and sexual attractiveness. The significance of its appearance here in the second scene is that it helps to place Béranger as a spokesperson for the attitude represented by The Spirit. Like Béranger, The Spirit sees nothing inherently wrong in the indulgence of sexual desire for its own sake; it is "as innocent a thing / As picking strawberries in spring" (1.3.33-4). This identification of The Spirit with Béranger is continued by allusion throughout the poem. In scene 5 Dipsychus and The Spirit take a gondola ride and give their differing views on the legitimacy of employing a fellow human being for one's own comfort and convenience. The Spirit gives his opinion in the form of a rousing song with the refrain "How pleasant it is to have money, high ho / How pleasant it is to have money":

> I sit at my table *en grand seigneur,*
> And when I have done, toss a crust to the poor:
> Not only the pleasure, one self, of good living,
> But also the pleasure of now and then giving.
>   So pleasant it is to have money, high-o,
>   So pleasant it is to have money.

(1.5.130-7)

This is generally reminiscent of Béranger in tone and technique rather than a translation of a French original, although there are similarities to a song called "Éloge de la richesse" [Praise of Wealth]:

> Je souris à la pauvreté,
>   Et j'ignore l'envie:
> Pourquoi perdrai-je ma gaîté,
>   Dans une douce vie?
> Maison, jardin, livres, tableaux,
> Large voiture et bons chevaux,
>   Pourraient-ils me déplaire?
> Quand mes vœux prendraient plus d'essor,

Que dans mes mains pleuve de l'or,
        De l'or,
        De l'or,
Et j'en fais mon affaire![24]

[At poverty I smile, no less,
    And envy is unknown to me;
Why should I lose my happiness
    When the good life is thrown to me?
A house, a garden, pictures, books,
A carriage, horses, the best cooks,
    How could they not please me?
When my wishes would run bold
Then let my hands be full of gold,
        Of gold,
        Of gold,
And what I'll do with it you'll see!][25]

Clough's satire is designed to suggest that greed, arrogance, and insouciance are continuous with sexual licentiousness, and atheism is soon added to this cluster of worldly values. In part 1, scene 7, Dipsychus sings a song inspired by the memory of Byron at the Lido in Venice that laments the meaninglessness of existence in the absence of God and includes the refrain "Dong, there is no God; dong" (1.7.14). For once, Dipsychus meets with The Spirit's approval: "Ah!—Not so bad. You've read, I see, / Your Béranger, and thought of me" (1.7.130-1).[26]

Clough is not, however, simply subscribing to the dominant English view of Béranger as a libertine and atheist. If we place these episodes in the context of the poem as a whole, it soon becomes clear that the situation is altogether more complex. Dipsychus's doubts about the morality of his actions can be seen as the product of a refined and scrupulous conscience, but they can also be seen as the result of his ignorance and inexperience of the world. The "temptations" to which he is subject are, after all, merely the raw material of everyday life: love, sex, employment, and worldly success. Far from being a kind of devil incarnate, The Spirit may actually be a much-needed corrective to the attitudes instilled in Dipsychus by an excessively pious and unworldly education. This is certainly the view put forward by the fictional representative of the author in the epilogue to the poem, in response to his uncle's objection to having to hear the devil speak: "'But, sir,' said I, 'perhaps he wasn't a devil after all. That's the beauty of the poem; nobody can say. You see, dear sir, the thing which it is attempted to represent is the conflict between the tender Conscience and the World—now the overtender conscience will of course exaggerate the wickedness of the world, and the Spirit in my poem may be merely the hypothesis or subjective imagination, formed—.'"[27] At this point the author is interrupted by the impatient uncle, who rejects this attempt to argue him into liking the poem, but the point is made, Clough is not rejecting the attitude represented by The Spirit and Béranger but engaging it in dialogue

with its puritanical, high-minded English opposite in a contest that seems to end in victory for the former over the latter.

This dialogue with Béranger continues in Clough's later work and particularly in the *Mari Magno* tales that he was working on at the time of his death in 1861. This poem uses the traditional format of the story sequence; like Chaucer's pilgrims in the *Canterbury Tales,* a group of passengers traveling by steamer from England to the United States passes the time by telling stories to one another. The passengers in question are, as the poem puts it, representatives of "Old England" and "New England," and their destination is "[t]he Puritan great Mother City" of Boston.[28] Appropriately enough, given this destination, each of their stories concerns the moral and emotional complications caused by the characteristically puritanical Anglo-Saxon attitude to sex. In **"The Lawyer's Second Tale,"** a college tutor falls in love with a young Scottish peasant girl and promises to marry her on finding she is pregnant, only for her disbelieving family to take her to Australia.[29] **"The Clergyman's Second Tale"** concerns a happily married man who commits an indiscretion while recuperating from illness abroad, feels obliged to confess to his wife, separates from her, and inflicts misery on his family as a result. These narratives are counterpointed with glimpses of other and more liberal moral perspectives. An artillery captain, who does not tell a story but comments on those of the others, suggests that Edward, the hero of the Clergyman's story, acts both naively and selfishly:

> The Artillery Captain, as we went below,
> Said to the lawyer, life could not be meant
> To be so altogether innocent.
> What did the atonement show? He, for the rest,
> Could not, he thought, have written and confessed.[30]

Clough's critics have been surprisingly and unanimously reluctant to acknowledge the weight of such moments in *Mari Magno*; Katharine Chorley notes the Lawyer's view that Edward's abandonment of his family was "adding crime to crime" (line 334), calling it "the only sane and balanced assessment of values in the poem," but goes on to suggest that Clough's allegiances really lie with Edward's neurotic self-laceration.[31]

It is, however, more plausible to read the poem as introducing competing moral perspectives precisely in order to question the Anglo-Saxon Puritanism of the travelers, and in **"My Tale"** these alternative perspectives are aligned with France in general, and Béranger in particular. The framing narrator, the youngest member of the party, tells a rambling and inconclusive story about a journey by mail coach through southern France in which the arrival of a priest who has just married a young couple prompts the coach driver into singing some inappropriately Epicurean songs with titles like "La verre en main la mort nous trouvera" and "Ah, je dirai à maman!"[32] We are given one of them, a lengthy farewell to love, in its entirety (this is the second stanza):

> "Once in your school (what good, alas! is once?)
> I took my lessons, and was not the dunce.
> Oh, what a pretty girl was then Juliette!
> Don't you suppose that I remember yet,
> Though thirty years divide me from the day
> When she and I first looked each other's way?
> But now! midwinter to be matched with May!
> Adieu, gay loves, it is too late a day!"
>
> (lines 143-50)

This has strong affinities in language and sentiment with a number of Béranger's songs, most notably "Rosette" and "Cinquante Ans," and indeed an earlier draft of the story has the *conducteur* first apostrophising Béranger's heroine "Lisette" rather than "Juliette," and then following this up with a version of Béranger's best known and most frequently translated song, "Le roi d'Yvetot."[33] Faced with this instance of robust popular Epicureanism, the narrator's courage fails him, and he does not provide the promised "pastorale" (line 219) about a "peasant beauty" he met in the Pyrenees (lines 207-28, 210). He treats the party instead to a lyric reminiscence of a similar occasion, and the story ends with a general discussion between the members of the party about the degraded moral and spiritual condition of France:

> [P]re-insular above the rest,
> My friend [the Lawyer] his ardent politics expressed;
> France was behind us all, he saw in France
> Worst retrogression, and the least advance;
> Her revolutions had but thrown her back,
> Powerful just now, but wholly off the track;
> They in religion were, as I had seen,
> About where we in Chaucer's time had been;
> In Chaucer's time! and yet their Wickliffe where?
> Something they'd kept—the worst part—of Voltaire.
>
> (lines 307-16)

The transition from Béranger's songs to a critique of French licentiousness and irreligion is a familiar one in the history of the British reception of Béranger, but it is difficult not to feel here that it is the representatives of "Old" and "New England" who are being criticized. This comment is, after all, made during a poem modeled on the *Canterbury Tales,* and this very fact should alert us to the possibility of an ironic disparity between the tellers' beliefs about themselves and what we as readers are able to see.[34] Moments like these remind the reader of the contrast between the relaxed and grown-up attitude to human sexuality characteristic of Chaucer's fictional world and the unhealthily repressive moral atmosphere exhibited by these "Tales."[35] The last thing France needs, we might think, is a "Wickliffe" to set it on the route toward Protestantism and Puritanism.

**"My Tale"** also seems, somewhat obliquely, to implicate Arnold in this debate over English and French moral values. The woman mentioned in the third stanza of the coach driver's Béranger-esque song is "Marguerite," the heroine of Arnold's "Switzerland" sequence of lyrics; and the stanza itself reads like a satire on the triteness of some of Arnold's sentimentalizing about his missed opportunity with her:

> "You lovely Marguerite! I shut my eyes,
> And do my very utmost to be wise;
> Yet see you still; and hear, though closed my ears,
> And think I'm young in spite of all my years;
> Shall I forget you, if I go away?
> To leave is painful, but absurd to stay."
>
> (lines 151-6)

Clough was not above using this kind of private allusion in his poetry, as the naming of his leading characters "Claude" and "Mary" in **Amours de Voyage** makes clear.[36] In addition, the narrator's lyric, *"currente calamo,"* reads like a pastiche of one of the lyrics Arnold addressed to "Marguerite," the "Memory Picture" discussed above (line 300). There is an undercurrent of satire in the young poet's enraptured description of a peasant girl leading a donkey along a path in the Pyrenees:

> But while I speak, and point them on,
> Alas, my dearer friends are gone;
> The dark-eyed maiden and the ass
> Have had the time the bridge to pass.
> Vainly beyond it far descried,
> Adieu, and peace with you abide,
> Grey donkey, and your beauteous guide.
>
> (lines 292-8)

The language of this poem is unremittingly banal and sentimental, and it is probably impossible to rhyme "pass" with "ass" without a satirical intention. Moreover, the refrain—"The pictures come, the pictures go, / Quick, quick, *currente calamo*"—recalls the refrain of "A Memory Picture": "Quick, thy tablets, Memory!" (lines 299-300).[37] In attributing this Arnoldian lyric to the youngest and most inexperienced member of the party, Clough seems to be suggesting a connection between the values espoused in Arnold's 1849 collection of poems and the confused and defensive response to France attributed to the narrator in **Mari Magno.** He is happy to pay lip service to Béranger's Epicureanism, but is not prepared himself to go any further than a timid anticonventionalism which objectifies and sentimentalizes the objects of his erotic interest.

This difference of opinion between Clough and Arnold on the subject of Béranger is not only a symptom of the personal and artistic estrangement of the two men between 1848 and Clough's premature death in 1861, but also an indication of some of the cultural shifts and splits caused by the events of 1848 and their aftermath. Arnold responded to these events by promoting a poetics of withdrawal and resignation which had its formal counterpart in a stilted neoclassicism, and by the development in his prose works of a view of culture as the legitimate preserve of an educated minority. Clough, in contrast, continued to experiment with forms of poetry that attempted to question the dominant ideas and morality of his age. Unlike most of his contemporaries, he was prepared to see in the French "licentiousness" epitomized by Béranger an imperfectly articulated but valuable alternative to the stifling respectability of mid-Victorian England. In addition, Béranger's example showed that it was possible to produce a poetry that would cross the divide between the comfortable, educated, prosperous world and the world of the "People." This was something that Clough became increasingly preoccupied with, as his famous "Review" comparing Arnold's 1852 collection with the *Life-Drama* of Alexander Smith illustrates. In comparing the work of this "Glasgow mechanic" with that of his friend, Clough suggests that contemporary poetry should "console us with a sense of significance, if not of dignity, in that often dirty, or at least dingy, work which it is the lot of so many of us to have to do."[38] Poetry, he adds, should "divinely condescend to all infirmities; be in all points tempted as we are; [and] exclude nothing, least of all guilt and distress, from its wide fraternisation."[39] This sounds like a description of much of Clough's own poetry during the last decade of his life. His Béranger-esque lyrics and the deliberately simplified style of **Mari Magno** look like an attempt to find a language in which such "fraternisation" might be possible. But his failure to complete or publish most of this work is perhaps indicative of the lack of any tangible connection between himself and the ordinary working people he would like to have addressed. Deprived of any significant contact with the working-class intellectual life which might have nourished and sustained his experiments, Clough allowed his creative work to be repressed and ultimately stifled by the very middle-class morality it had exposed so brilliantly. The figure of Béranger, the poet who crossed the class divide and provided a language of consoling song for the "People," remained for Clough a tantalizingly elusive ideal.

## Notes

1. Arthur Hugh Clough to J. C. Shairp, 22 February 1847, in Clough, *The Correspondence of Arthur Hugh Clough,* ed. Frederick L. Mulhauser, 2 vols. (Oxford: Clarendon Press, 1957), 1:178-9. Rachel was the great French tragic actress of her day; Arnold saw her act ten times during his few months in Paris, and in 1863 he composed three sonnets in her memory. See headnote to "Rachel" in *The Poems of Matthew Arnold,* ed. Kenneth Allott and Miriam Allott, 2d edn. (London and New York: Longman, 1979), p. 521.

2. Pierre-Jean de Béranger's popularity in the 1830s may be judged from the reviews devoted to his work in the journals of this period; see, for example, [T. P. Thompson], "Art. XIII.—1. *Chansons Inédites de M. P. J. de Béranger.* Paris. Baudouin frères. 1828. 180. pp. 132. 2. *Procès faits aux Chansons de P.-J. de Béranger.* Paris. Baudouin frères. 1828. 320. pp. 281.," *Westminster Review* 10, no. 19 (January 1829): 198-215; [J. W. Croker], "Art. VI.—*Chansons de P. J. Béranger, anciennes, nouvelles, et inédites; suivies des Procès intentés à l'Auteur.* Paris 1831," *Quarterly Review* 46, no. 92 (January 1832): 461-77; "Art. XII.—*Chansons Nouvelles et Dernières, de* P. J. de Beranger. *Dédiées à* M. Lucien Buonaparte. Paris: 1833.," *Edinburgh Review* 57, no. 116 (July 1833): 486-504. On the general question of Béranger's reception, see Joseph Phelan, "The British Reception of Pierre-Jean de Béranger," *RLC* [*Revue de Littérature Comparée*] 79, 1 (January-March 2005): 5-20.

3. Elizabeth Barrett to Mary Russell Mitford, London, 27 November 1842, in *The Brownings' Correspondence,* 15 vols. to date, ed. Philip Kelley, Ronald Hudson, Scott Lewis, and Edward Hagan (Winfield KS: Wedgestone Press, 1984), 6:179-82, 180.

4. Arnold to Clough, London, 6 December 1847, in Arnold, *The Letters of Matthew Arnold to Arthur Hugh Clough,* ed. H. F. Lowry (Oxford: Clarendon Press, 1932), pp. 63-4, 63. According to Arnold's unpublished 1847 diary, he had bought his own edition of the poet's work on 6 February of that year; see Arnold, *The Poems,* p. 58, editorial note.

5. Arnold to Clough, London, 1 March 1848, in Arnold, *The Letters,* pp. 67-70, 69. The comparison between Robert Burns and Béranger was a commonplace; it is invoked by almost every British writer on the French poet throughout the nineteenth century; see, for example, Robert Louis Stevenson's article on Béranger in the *Encyclopaedia Britannica*: "It is by [his] socialism that he becomes truly modern and touches hands with Burns" (*Encyclopaedia Britannica,* 11th edn., s.v. "Béranger, Pierre Jean de").

6. Arnold to Clough, Leuk, 29 September 1848, in Arnold, *The Letters,* pp. 91-4, 92-3.

7. Arnold, "Memory Picture," in Arnold, *The Poems,* pp. 113-5, lines 17-24.

8. C. A. Sainte-Beuve, "Béranger," in *Portraits Contemporains,* 2 vols. (Paris: Didier, 1847), 1:60-100, 75-6.

9. See for example "The Three Lyrists; Horace, Burns and Beranger," *Cornhill Magazine* 17

(February 1868): 150-67. When the comparison was mentioned to Béranger, he replied with typical modesty; "Ah! Qu'en dirait l'autre? [Ah! What would the other one have to say about it?]" (see *Edinburgh Review* 108 [July 1858]: 175-96, 189). Arnold himself makes the comparison explicit in the letter already cited expressing his disillusionment with Béranger; see p. 834.

10. Arnold, "Horatian Echo," in Arnold, *The Poems*, pp. 58-60, lines 31-6.

11. See, for example, Béranger, "Ce n'est plus Lisette," from Béranger, *Oeuvres Complètes de P. J. de Béranger*, 2 vols. (Paris: Perrotin, 1846), 1:183-5.

12. Arnold to Clough, Leuk, 29 September 1848, in Arnold, *The Letters*, pp. 91-4, 92-3.

13. Interestingly Gustave Flaubert seems to have arrived at the same conclusion, suggesting in a letter of 1846 to Louise Colet that Béranger was "immensely unfortunate in the kind of people who admire him . . . Say what you will, popularity, which seems to give genius greater scope, actually vulgarizes it . . . I've heard so many fools, so many narrow-minded bourgeois, sing his songs about beggars and the 'Dieu des bonnes gens' that he must really be a great poet to have kept my esteem despite all the hullabaloo" (*The Letters of Gustave Flaubert, 1830-1857*, trans. and ed. Francis Steegmuller [Cambridge MA: Belknap Press, 1980], p. 80). Flaubert contributed to the decline of Béranger's reputation by associating him with the incomparably stupid Homais in *Madame Bovary*; see, e.g., book ii, chapter i: "Mine is the God of Socrates, of Franklin, of Voltaire, and of Béranger! I am for the profession of faith of the 'Savoyard Vicar,' and the immortal principles of '89!" (*Madame Bovary*, tr. Eleanor Marx Aveling [New York: Modern Library, 1918], p. 89).

14. Sainte-Beuve described him as "the most popular poet there has ever been in France" ("Béranger," *Atlantic Monthly* 1, no. 4 [February 1858]: 469-76, 469). Sainte-Beuve is identified as the author in *Poole's Index to Periodical Literature*.

15. In his critique of Bishop Colenso's efforts, Arnold comments, "The highly-instructed few, and not the scantily-instructed many, will ever be the organ to the human race of knowledge and truth. Knowledge and truth, in the full sense of the words, are not attainable by the great mass of the human race at all. The great mass of the human race have to be softened and humanised through their heart and imagination, before any soil can be found in them where knowledge may strike living roots" (Arnold, "The Bishop and the Philosopher,"

in *The Complete Prose Works of Matthew Arnold*, ed. R. H. Super, 11 vols., *Lectures and Essays in Criticism*, vol. 3 [Ann Arbor: Univ. of Michigan Press, 1960-77], pp. 40-55, 43-4). Arnold, *Essays in Criticism*, 1st ser. (Chicago and London: Univ. of Chicago Press, 1968), pp. 118-34, 132; Heinrich Heine in fact seems to have supplanted Béranger as the type of the radical, freethinking songwriter in British public opinion during the 1850s and 1860s.

16. Arnold to Clough, London, 24 May 1848, in Arnold, *The Letters*, pp. 80-3, 80; Arnold to Clough, London, ca. late June or early July 1848, in Arnold, *The Letters*, pp. 83-5, 84.

17. Typically, Béranger resigned from the National Assembly as soon as he was elected on the grounds that he preferred to retain his independence and impartiality; see Jean Edmond Mansion, introduction to Béranger, *Chansons Choisies de Béranger*, ed. Mansion (Oxford: Clarendon Press, 1908), pp. iii-liii, xxviii. Arnold to Clough, L[ansdowne] House, 8 March 1848, in Arnold, *The Letters*, pp. 74-5, 74.

18. Clough to William Allingham, Gordon Square, 18 December [1850], in Clough, *The Correspondence*, 1:287.

19. Paul Veyriras notes over forty instances of the use of refrains in Clough's poetry and suggests the possible influence of both Burns and Béranger; see Veyriras, *Arthur Hugh Clough: 1819-1861* (Paris: Didier, 1964), pp. 533-4.

20. Clough started writing *Dipsychus and The Spirit* in 1850, but there is textual evidence that much of the current manuscript dates from 1854 at the earliest; see Phelan, "The Textual Evolution of Clough's *Dipsychus and The Spirit*," *RES* [*Review of English Studies*] n.s., 46, no. 182 (May 1995): 230-9.

21. Arnold's indebtedness to both Ernest Renan and Sainte-Beuve is clear in many of his works and fully documented in Super's edition of his prose. For Sainte-Beuve's eventual rejection of Béranger, see his above-mentioned article, "Béranger," in the *Atlantic Monthly*, pp. 469-76, 469; for Renan's more forthright condemnation of Béranger see Arthur Arnould, *Béranger: Ses amis, ses ennemis, et ses critiques*, 2 vols. (Paris: Joel Cherbuliez, 1864), 1:184-212.

22. Clough, *Dipsychus and The Spirit*, in Clough, *Clough: Selected Poems*, ed. Phelan (Harlow: Longman, 1995), pp. 155-234, part 1, scene 1, line 26; Clough, "Easter Day. Naples 1849," Clough, *Clough: Selected Poems*, pp. 256-62, lines 5, 6, 8, 23, 26, 35, 47, 58, 63, 71, 76, 85, 94, 156.

All subsequent references to *Dipsychus and The Spirit* will be to this edition and will be noted parenthetically in the text by part, scene, and line number.

23. This is actually a slight misquotation. The refrain to Béranger's song begins with the line "Combien je regrette," which suggests that Clough is quoting from memory. Béranger, "Ma grand'mère," Béranger, *Œuvres Complètes*, 1:17-9, lines 5-8.

24. Béranger, "Éloge de la richesse," *Œuvres Complètes,* pp. 150-2, lines 13-24.

25. My translation.

26. An earlier version had "Voltaire"; cf. Clough's comment to Allingham cited in note 18 above.

27. Clough, "Epilogue," *Dipsychus and The Spirit,* in Clough, *Clough: Selected Poems,* pp. 231-4, 231.

28. Clough, "The Lawyer's Second Tale," *Mari Magno, or Tales on Board,* in Clough, *The Poems of Arthur Hugh Clough,* ed. F. L. Mulhauser, 2d edn. (Oxford: Clarendon Press, 1974), pp. 426-39, line 516. Subsequent references to this text will appear parenthetically by line number.

29. The Highland romance, exemplified in "The Lawyer's Second Tale," is one of Clough's perennial themes and the subject of his narrative poem *The Bothie of Toper-na-Fuosich* (1848).

30. Clough, "The Clergyman's Second Tale," *Mari Magno, or Tales on Board,* in Clough, *The Poems,* pp. 357-67, lines 329-33.

31. Katharine Chorley, *Arthur Hugh Clough* (Oxford: Clarendon Press, 1962), p. 262.

32. "Death will find us with a glass in our hands" and "Ah! I'll tell mother!" (my translation). Clough, "My Tale," *Mari Magno, or Tales on Board,* in Clough, *The Poems,* pp. 344-53, lines 129-30. All subsequent references to "My Tale" will be to this edition by line number and will appear parenthetically in the text.

33. See, for example, the two versions of "Le roi d'Yvetot," the second entitled "The King of Brentford," in Michael Angelo Titmarsh [W. M. Thackeray], *The Paris Sketch-Book* (London, John Macrone, 1840), 2 vols., 2:323-34.

34. Jeffrey M. Jeske argues that the stories exploit the conflict between the teller and his tale to revisit some of Clough's habitual philosophical conundrums; see "Clough's *Mari Magno*: A Reassessment," *VP* [*Victorian Poetry*] 20, 1 (Spring 1982): 21-32.

35. Albert Morton Turner notes that Chaucer's influence makes itself felt most clearly not in the main tales themselves, but in the other sections: "the prologue, the links, and the third or 'My Tale'" ("A Study of Clough's *Mari Magno,*" *PMLA* 44, 2 [June 1929]: 569-89, 585).

36. A possible allusion to Mary Claude, a Lakeland neighbor of the Arnolds who may well have been the original "Marguerite"; see Eugene R. August, "*Amours de Voyage* and Matthew Arnold in Love: An Inquiry," *VN* [*Victorian Newsletter*] 60 (Fall 1981): 15-20.

37. "Currente calamo" means "with flowing pen."

38. "Recent English Poetry [by Alexander Smith, Matthew Arnold, William Sidney Walker, and William Allingham]," *North American Review* 77, no. 160 (July 1853): 1-30; rprt. as "Review of Some Modern Poems by Alexander Smith and Matthew Arnold," in Clough, *Prose Remains of A. H. Clough,* ed. [Mrs. Clough] (London: Macmillan, 1888), pp. 355-78, 357.

39. Ibid.

## Richard Cronin (essay date 2008)

SOURCE: Cronin, Richard. "Byron, Clough, and the Grounding of Victorian Poetry." *Romanticism* 14, no. 1 (2008): 13-24.

[*In the following essay, Cronin compares the differing approaches to the poetry of travel and tourism taken by Byron and Clough.*]

In Scene VI of **Dipsychus,** the Spirit wonders, as people on holiday often do, what he should do next:

> What now? The Lido shall it be?
> That none may say we didn't see
> The ground which Byron used to ride on,
> And do I don't know what beside on.
>
> (VI. 1-4)[1]

When Byron was living in Venice or nearby, for two years from 1817 to 1819, he had already, as he frequently complained, become one of the objects that English visitors to Venice liked to inspect. But he had only himself to blame, because it was Byron, even more powerfully than Scott, who had established the fashion for literary tourism. The thousands of British visitors who took a boat on Lake Leman or a guided tour of the dungeons of the castle of Chillon did so to honour Rousseau and the Swiss patriot Bonnivard, but also and more directly as witnesses to the fame of the poet of *Childe Harold* and *The Prisoner of Chillon*. It is no wonder that they were drawn in such numbers to the Lido when the poet himself rode on it, and continued to visit it when it summoned into presence not the poet himself but, perhaps still more potently, his memory. 'Murray's faithful guide / Informs us' (**Dipsychus,** V. 190-1) that the 'shore of the Littorale, towards the Adriatic' which 'constitutes the *Lido*,' is 'now associated with the name of Byron, as the spot where he used to take his rides, and where he designed to have been buried.'[2] There is then a double appropriateness in Clough's reference to Byron. Byron himself was, both in his own lifetime and after it, one of the prime tourist sites of Venice, and it was Byron who, more than any other poet, had set the fashion for tourist poetry of the kind that Clough himself wrote,[3] not just in **Dipsychus,** but in **The Bothie of Tober-na-Vuolich** in which an Oxford reading party spends the long vacation in the Scottish Highlands, and in **Amours de Voyage,** in which an Oxford intellectual visits Rome in the Spring of 1849. Clough is, of course, a very different poet from Byron, but I want to begin by suggesting that one clue to their differences may be found in the different ways in which they thought about tourism and tourist poetry.

In 1809 Byron sailed from England as a late exponent of the grand tour, the range of his travels constricted by the European war, but his intent, his serious intent at any rate, in accord with that of his eighteenth-century predecessors. He was completing his education, equipping himself so that on his return he might cut a proper figure when he took his seat in the House of Lords. He set sail again in 1816, in pique at the scandal that had engulfed him, determined to find in Europe a space in which he could preserve his own selfhood from any bourgeois impingements on its autonomy. It was travel as a theatrical kind of self-indulgence. At least that was how it seemed to Clough's closest associate, Matthew Arnold. When he visited Switzerland on his wedding tour, Byron's kind of travelling seemed to him quaintly irrelevant, a long gone fashion now scarcely comprehensible:

> What helps it now that Byron bore,
> With haughty scorn which mocked the smart,
> Through Europe to the Aetolian Shore
> The pageant of his bleeding heart?
> That thousands counted every groan,

And Europe made his woe her own? ('Stanzas from the Grande Chartreuse', 133-8)

Mid-nineteenth-century travellers tended to be members of precisely that bourgeoisie that Byron went to Europe to escape. Since Byron's death a new industry had developed to cater to their needs. In 1836 John Murray III produced his *Handbook for Travellers on the Continent,* the first modern tourist guidebook, Thomas Cook organised his first excursion five years later, in 1841, though it was not until 1855 that he organised a tour to Europe, and in 1847 Bradshaw supplemented his domestic railway timetable with his *Continental Railway Guide.* Byron prepared for his 1816 journey by ordering from his coachmaker a huge carriage modelled on one of Napoleon's. Clough, as his Dipsychus complains, lives in less expansive times:

> The modern Hotspur
> Shrills not his trumpet of 'To Horse,
>   To Horse!'
> But consults columns in a railway guide . . .

> (X. 108-10)

He has become a 'demigod of figures; an Achilles / Of computation,' who conquers the world not by force of arms but with 'swift arithmetic'.

Even in 1816 Byron had come across bourgeois tourists, but they seemed to him people of a different species. He discovered a woman fast asleep at Chillon, 'the most antinarcotic spot in the world', and he remembered, 'at Chamouni, in the very eyes of Mont Blanc, hearing another woman, English also, exclaim to her party 'Did you ever see any thing more *rural*?—as if it was Highgate, or Hampstead, or Brompton, or Hayes . . .'[4] He could not know what had become entirely obvious to Clough, that even as he made these observations he was busy writing the poems that would encourage thousands more cockneys to venture abroad, and, what is more, would provide them with the vocabulary that would enable them to articulate their European experience. By mid-century a woman at Chillon would not be sleeping, but earnestly consulting Murray's *Handbook for Travellers in Switzerland and the Alps of Savoy and Piedmont,* where in Murray's description of the Castle she would have read,

> Lake Leman lies by Chillon's walls:
> A thousand feet in depth below
> Its massy waters meet and flow . . .

Murray adds a note pointing out that in fact the depth of the lake near the castle 'does not exceed 280 ft,'[5] showing himself typically Victorian in his mastery of 'swift arithmetic', but just as typical in his admiring citation of one of Byron's poems. Murray's Handbooks often quote poetry, and Byron's poetry most of all. Murray was after all the son of Byron's publisher, and the firm retained the copyright to the poems. In 1857 he published a pocket-sized edition of the poetry 'so as to enable Travellers to carry it with their other HANDBOOKS'.[6] This was commercially astute, of course, but it was an astuteness founded on Murray's clear-eyed recognition that the aristocratic Byron was precisely the poet most admired by the rapidly expanding group of middle-class tourists on whom the success of his Handbooks depended.

When Byron sighed, Arnold tells us, the whole of Europe 'made his woe her own.' He surveys the Byron phenomenon from a historical distance that seems only a polite disguise for the cultural distance that separates him from those who continue to admire the poems in which Byron makes a theatrical display of his own sensibility. He has in mind people such as Mrs Trevellyn in Clough's *Amours de Voyage,* who

> Quotes, which I hate, Childe Harold; but also appreciates Wordsworth;
> Sometimes adventures on Schiller; and then to religion diverges;
> Questions me much about Oxford; and yet, in her loftiest flights still
> Grates the fastidious ear with the slightly mercantile accent.
>
> (I. 209-12)

The slightly mercantile accent and the habit of quoting Byron seem equivalent and equally decisive class markers.

James Buzard, to whom I am indebted for my understanding of nineteenth-century travel, has usefully distinguished between travellers and tourists; travellers, whose experience is authentic, unmediated, and tourists, who merely consume a product manufactured for them by entrepreneurs such as Thomas Cooke and John Murray. Dipsychus and the Spirit as they walk along the Lido consulting their Murray confess themselves tourists, enjoying an experience that is theirs not as a privilege of rank or even of education but simply because they can afford it. It is a knowledge that Dipsychus suffers. He is wonderfully receptive to the emollient glide of the gondola in its passage along a canal— How light we move, how softly! Ah, / Were all things like the gondola' (V. 17-8)—but cannot put out of his mind that his pleasure is bought at the expense of 'our slaving brother set behind!' (V. 36). The Spirit, on the other hand, is confident that the gondolier is as grateful to them for his 'employment' as they are to their purse for their 'enjoyment.' (V. 39-40) He understands the annual summer holiday as the nineteenth-century's chief festival, because it is the festival that best celebrates commerce:

> As I sat at the café, I said to myself,
> They may talk as they please about what they call pelf,
> They may sneer as they like about eating and drinking,
> But help it I cannot, I cannot help thinking
>> How pleasant it is to have money,
>> heigh ho!
> How pleasant it is to have money.
>
> (V. 130-5)

But in being so frankly and so unapologetically a tourist the Spirit shows himself quite unusually self-aware. More commonly, as Buzard points out, tourists are other people, whose most important function is to maintain the confidence of travellers in their own superiority. To borrow Buzard's title, tourists mark out a beaten track that usefully allows travellers to bolster their self-esteem by diverging from it.

In *Dipsychus* Clough shows that he is already well aware of the distinction that Buzard makes, or something very like it, and he is aware, too, of an analogy between travel and writing. But both distinctions, between kinds of travellers and kinds of writers, are mutable, worryingly vulnerable to change: yesterday's travellers are very apt today to seem today like common tourists. Byron is a key instance. When Byron recorded his arrival in Venice his verse swelled to affirm the unquestionable authenticity of his experience of the city:

> I stood in Venice, on the "Bridge of Sighs;"
> A palace and a prison on each hand:
> I saw from out the wave her structures rise
> As from the stroke of the Enchanter's wand . . .
>
> (*Childe Harold's Pilgrimage,* IV. 1-4)

But the same lines, not so many years later, after they have been recited by a thousand people standing on precisely the same spot, become an unmistakable index not of the proud traveller but of the humble tourist. The cultural icons that Byron celebrates in the fourth canto of *Childe Harold* suggest that he had a remarkable eye for all those tourist sites that were almost immediately to become hackneyed. In Rome, for example, he notes the Coliseum by moonlight, the Dying Gladiator, St Peter's, the Laocoon: he tours the city as though he had a Murray in his hand despite the fact that it was to be twenty-five years before the *Handbook for Travellers in Central Italy* was published. The reason that Clough's Claude so hates it when Mrs Trevellyn quotes *Childe Harold* is precisely because it so clearly identifies her as a tourist. Clough's Claude knows that by 1849 the authentic, the traveller's, response to Rome must be pointedly unByronic. He does not break out into any embarrassing apostrophes immediately after his arrival—'Oh Rome! My country! City of the soul!' (*Childe Harold,* IV. 694)—far from it:

> Rome disappoints me much: I hardly as yet understand, but
> *Rubbishy* seems the word that most exactly would suit it.
>
> (I. 19-20)

Byron's sentiments have become hackneyed, and so, Claude's supple, conversational hexameters suggest, has his style. Byron's Spenserian stanzas stand exposed as vapid, theatrical, and, like Mrs Trevellyn's accent, just a little bit vulgar.

It was, of course, only the price that Byron paid for his unprecedented success. His taste seems so akin to the taste of a popular handbook because popular handbooks derived their taste from Byron. The quotations thickly sprinkled through Murray's pages acknowledge as much. Cockneys quote him as they stand on the Bridge of Sighs not because there is a peculiar affinity between Byron's verse and the Cockney sensibility but because it was so hard for the nineteenth-century traveller looking at Venice not to see the city as Byron had seen it. When Byron sighed, as Arnold put it, 'thousands' all over Europe 'counted every groan.' This was Byron's greatness, and yet—and I think the innuendo is audible in Arnold's lines[7]—when a sentiment is shared by 'thousands' it risks losing its poetic status: it risks becoming just another instance of the 'swift arithmetic' with which commerce consolidates its control over the world.

By mid-century, as Samuel Chew has shown, Byron's reputation was at an all-time low.[8] He had become the poet in their difference from whom Victorian poets could most easily assert the authenticity of their calling. But Clough, I want to suggest, had his doubts:

> What now? The Lido shall it be?
> That none may say we didn't see
> The ground which Byron used to ride on,
> And do I don't know what beside on.
>
> (Scene VI. 1-4)

This is the Spirit, of course, and the Spirit's tastes are conventional, his values masculine and his manners bluff. 'What a set!' exclaimed Arnold (*Essays in Criticism Second Series,* 238), flinching fastidiously from the doings of Byron, the Shelleys and the Godwins, but the Spirit seems to recall Byron's Venetian exploits with a tolerance that hovers easily between amusement and admiration. It is the manner that is revealing, the rhyme of 'ride on' with 'beside on'. The reader is invited to savour the hapless joining of the two prepositions: it becomes a kind of shared joke. It would betray a shameful lack of humour to respond to such a lapse in style with anything other than amused indulgence, and as with the style so with the behaviour that the couplet recalls. The rhyme treats Byron's failings generously, and properly so, because the Spirit has learned to rhyme like this by reading *Don Juan,* a poem that Byron began to write in Venice, in the months when he took his morning ride along the Lido.

Clough's Spirit is a Regency gentleman who has survived into an age in which young men like Dipsychus are rather too much given to scrupulous self-absorption. In the frame with which Clough supplied his poem a poet recites *Dipsychus* to his uncle, and the uncle, who is likely enough of an age with Byron, finds that much of what the Spirit says is 'sensible enough.' The uncle blames Thomas Arnold for producing a younger generation distinguished by over-sensitive consciences, and Dipsychus seems to him their fit representative, 'a sort of hobbadi-hoy cherub, too big to

be innocent, and too simple for anything else,' as his uncle puts it, none too politely. In the person of the poetic nephew, character and author merge, for Clough, who lends his own poems to Dipsychus, was himself Arnold's prize pupil. For that generation a preference for Wordsworth over Byron came close to being a marker of their group identity, which is why in *Amours de Voyage* Mrs Trevellyn, in Claude's eyes, goes some way to redeeming herself for quoting *Childe Harold* by also appreciating Wordsworth.

Almost all its modern readers have agreed with the young poet in Clough's epilogue that in *Dipsychus* 'the thing which it is attempted to represent is the conflict between the tender conscience and the world.' It is, after all, the conflict that Clough portrays in all three of his major poems. In *The Bothie* and *Amours de Voyage* the poem's hero swithers between political and erotic commitments. In *Dipsychus,* no doubt because the poem is unfinished, the hero's dilemmas seem more various. A prostitute propositions Dipsychus and the Spirit encourages him to respond. Even if all that he gains from the experience is the lesson that sex offers no escape from 'the emptiness of things,' (III. 46), it will at least have served to cure him of his penchant for the 'high amatory-poetic.' (III. 37) Dipsychus is tempted and appalled, appalled precisely because he has been tempted: 'O moon and stars forgive! And thou, clear heaven, / Look pureness back into me.' (III. 14-5) Unabashed, the Spirit simply changes tack and offers to introduce him to an eligible young woman—'A virtuous attachment formed judiciously / Would come, one sees, uncommonly propitiously.' (IV, 26-7) But for Dipsychus the prospect of a good match is as distasteful as an encounter with a prostitute. He is insulted by a German officer and resists when the Spirit goads him to issue a challenge. The Spirit's easy Church of Englandism (he takes Communion at Easter and sends his wife the rest of the year) counters Dipsychus's intensely spiritual scepticism:

> Ting, ting, there is no God; ting, ting—
> Dong, there is no God; dong,
> There is no God; dong, dong!
>
> (VI. 13-5)

While the Spirit worries about the thistles and leaving his belongings unattended, Dipsychus bathes ecstatically: 'Ye great winds blow, / And break, thou curly waves, upon my breast.' (VI. 214-5) And at the last he is confronted with the problem of choosing a profession when all seem so distasteful: 'The Law! 'twere honester, if 'twere genteel / To say the dung-cart.' (X. 1-2)

Byron, I think, hovers behind these episodes, but only as a rather shadowy presence. The Spirit's sentiments quite often recall Byron's but it is in style that the affinity is most evident, as when, for example, the same thought is clinched by the same rhyme. The narrator doubts the wisdom of Juan's cloistered education:

> For my part I say nothing—nothing—but
>   *This* I will say—my reasons are my
>     own—
> That if I had an only son to put
>   To school (as God be praised that I have
>     none)
> 'Tis not with Donna Inez I would shut
>   Him up to learn his catechism alone,
> No—no—I'd send him out betimes to college,
> For there it was I pick'd up my own
>     knowledge.
>
>                   (I. 52)

The Spirit has the same doubts about Dipsychus:

> And you still linger—oh, you fool!—
> Because of what you learnt at school.
> You should have gone at least to college,
> And got a little ampler knowledge.
>
>                 (VI. 37-41)

The Spirit rounds on Dipsychus very much as Byron rounds on his hero, or as the couplet may round on the first six lines of a Byronic octave. So, when his meetings with Donna Julia provoke in Juan a Wordsworthian desire to enter into 'self-communion with his own high soul,' the narrator remarks:

> If *you* think 'twas philosophy that this did,
> I can't help thinking puberty assisted.
>
>                (I. 93. 7-8)

This is very like the Spirit's response to Dipsychus's suggestion that he was able to resist the Venetian prostitute's invitation thanks to an inborn purity:

> Cry mercy of his heavenly highness—
> I took him for that cunning shyness.
>
>              (III. 192-3)

It is unsurprising, I suppose, that the Spirit should challenge the Wordsworthian Dipsychus by borrowing the inflections of Byron, the great counter-spirit of Wordsworth's age.[9] Much more remarkable is Dipsychus's own behaviour in the Academia. The first painting in the whole gallery that Murray draws to the visitor's attention is Titian's *Assumption of the Virgin,* quoting the painter Thomas Phillip's admiring appreciation, which ends, 'It is a glorious work, its power of colour is immense; far beyond that even of any other picture of Titian that I have seen'. (*Handbook for Travellers in Northern Italy,* Part 1, 326.) But Dipsychus turns away from it to what he suspects is only a 'modern daub,'

> Where Byron, somewhat drest up, draws
> His sword, impatient long, and speaks
> Unto a tribe of motley Greeks
> His pledge word unto their brave cause.
>
>             (IX. 5-8)[10]

The painting, like the scene it records, has its tawdry aspect—the moment of heroic commitment got up as costume drama—but it means more to Dipsychus than any vision of transcendence no matter how gorgeous. 'God's name,' he concludes, is better celebrated by 'noble deeds' than by contemplating 'the ecstatic Virgin rise,' and Byron's commitment of himself to the Greek cause, embarrassingly theatrical though it may be, is as noble a deed as the history of modern poetry has to offer. Byron drawing his sword and pledging himself to the cause of Greek Independence figures the possibility that haunts ***Dipsychus*** as it haunts all Clough's major poems, the possibility that it might somehow be possible to reconcile the contemplative life of the poet with a heroic life of action, that the man of imagination might also show himself a man of power. The stanzas at once dream of that reconciliation and reveal its improbability, not least through the choice of stanza form. Byron is nominated as his role model by a poet writing in the *In Memoriam* stanza, the stanza in which Tennyson had recently and famously repudiated noble deeds in favour of self-involvement:[11]

> O hollow wraith of dying fame,
> Fade wholly, while the soul exults,
> And self-infolds the large results
> Of force that would have forged a name.
>
>            (LXXIII. 13-6)

Lending one's sword to a noble cause, a species of heroism just, if barely, possible to Byron only thirty years before, had since become, as the painting in the Academia betrays, operatic. For Dipsychus the process of reconciling himself with the world will take the less glamorous form of choosing a profession and choosing a wife, but Byron remains an appropriate model.

When a group of cultivated young men meet in Disraeli's *Vivian Grey,* and the conversation turns to Byron, one of them comments, 'If one thing were more characteristic of Byron's mind than another, it was his strong, shrewd, common sense; his pure, unalloyed sagacity.'[12] This may seem an unexpected compliment, but much later in the century John Morley seems to have had similar qualities in mind when he detected in Byron 'a quality of poetical *worldliness* in its enlarged and generous sense of energetic interest in real transactions.'[13] By 1853, as is evident in his composite review of Matthew Arnold and Alexander Smith, Clough had become concerned by the unworldliness of modern poetry, by its inability to accommodate 'the actual, palpable things with which our every-day life is concerned,' and in particular he was concerned that it had so little to say of relevance to life as it was experienced by most men of the mid-nineteenth century, whose lives were given over to 'business and weary task-work,' whose lot it was to make the most of the 'unchosen, peremptorily appointed posts' that they occupied and that seemed to condemn them to 'grievously narrow and limited spheres of action.' Readers preferred *Vanity Fair* and *Bleak House* to any modern poetry, and Clough thinks the reason plain enough: the novels, unlike the poetry, have shown themselves able to 'include these indispensable latest addenda—these phenomena which, if we forget on Sunday, we must remember on Monday—these positive matters of fact, which people, who are not verse-writers, are obliged to have to do with.'[14] It was the novel, not poetry, that had something to say about the common or garden, weekday world.

The fastidious Claude objects to Rome as 'rubbishy', but it is its rubbishiness, its vast and disorderly accumulation of urban detritus, that best defines the modern city. *The Prelude* can accommodate such material in Book VII, the 'London' book, only to gag at it: Byron, in the London books of *Don Juan*, can find in it the stuff of life. For Byron, the modern epic needs to reach not so much after order as after inclusiveness: it needs to accommodate as many as possible of those 'indispensable latest addenda' that most poems find no space for, and in *Dipsychus* Clough follows Byron's lead. His poem finds room for a *'gramolata persici'* (V. 309), a *'pot de chambre'*,[15] for Sir Sidney Herbert, the Colonial Secretary, (III. 172) and for a song by Béranger:

> Ah comme je regrette
> Mon bras si dodu,
> Ma jambe bien faite
> Et le temps perdu!
>
>                                    (II. 44-8)

But more important to Clough even than these 'latest addenda' is the need for poetry to address itself to what seemed to him the most pressing business of life, the business that confronts one after another Philip Hewson, Claude and Dipsychus, all three of his three leading men. All of them are faced with the need to choose some 'sphere of action', in the knowledge that any choice available to them is bound to seem 'narrow and limited', certainly when compared with the choice so flamboyantly made by the splendidly-uniformed Byron when he stepped ashore on Cephalonia. But to refuse the choice is to remain spectator rather than actor, it is to consign oneself to irrelevance, to share the fate that, Clough feared, had overtaken his friend Arnold, and most of his other poet contemporaries. Dipsychus ends the poem yielding to the Spirit's harsh, sardonic ultimatum:

> 'Tis Common Sense and human wit
> Can find no higher name than it.
> Submit, submit!
>
>                                    (XI. 192-4)

Dipsychus is given to reciting his own poems, and he usually speaks as though submission to the world will involve giving up the habit—both of making poems and of reciting them:

> Verses! well, they are made, so let them go;
> No more if I can help. This is one way
> The procreant heat and fervour of our youth
> Escapes, in puff and smoke, and shapeless words
> Of mere ejaculation, nothing worth
> Unless to make maturer years content
> To slave in base compliance to the world.
>
>                                    (IX. 21-7)

But *Dipsychus,* the poem if not the character, tries to show that making poems might not be just a waste of breath, an investment in shapeless 'puff and smoke,' and it does so most persuasively in its metrics.

Dipsychus records his resolution to write no more poems in the blank verse that he consistently employs in his more reflective moments, and, whether by accident or design, the lines covertly name the poet who had made that choice the natural one: the line that ends by suggesting that poems are made of shapeless 'words' is followed by a line that ends by insisting that they are nothing 'worth'. Dipsychus, like Claude and like Clough and Arnold, is a devoted Wordsworthian. The Byronic Spirit teases him with it:

> The Devil! We've had enough of you,
> Quote us a little Wordsworth, do!
> Those lines that are so just, they say:
> 'A something far more deeply' eh?
> 'Interfused'—what is it they tell us?
> Which and the sunset are bedfellows.
>
>                                    (V. 290-5)

He takes Wordsworth's 'sense sublime' and its 'dwelling' in 'the light of setting suns' and packs them off to bed together, as if they were Juan and Dudu in the harem. The effect is only possible because the Spirit goes in for some metrical cross-dressing, taking the blank verse of 'Tintern Abbey' and re-writing it as an outrageous set of couplets in which 'tell us' rhymes with 'bedfellows' (a rhyme itself borrowed from *Don Juan*, I. 156). Wordsworth, as the recently published *Prelude* only served to underline, had made of blank verse a metre so adept in representing the activity of the reflective mind that the turn of the lines seemed to disappear in the turns of thought that they mapped. Blank verse is Dipsychus's favourite metre because blank verse allows him to live in a world of thought that does no 'violence to [him]self' (XII. 26), and it was just that perfect conformity of self and rhythm that Clough had once offered as the decisive proof of Wordsworth's superiority to Byron and to Byron's principal model, Walter Scott: 'that harmony between thought and word, which is the condition of "*immortal* verse," they did not, I think—and Wordsworth did—take pains to attain.'[16] (317) Clough, when he argues in this vein, denies that any distinction can properly be made between style and content. But the Spirit of *Dipsychus* is as potent a satirist of aesthetic as of moral orthodoxies. Clough may claim that style is not 'the mere put-on dress of the substantial meaning,' but the Spirit suggests that Wordsworth's style is, or at least has become, the costume that poets tend to put on when they affect sincerity:

> But, let me say,
> I too have my *grandes manières* in my way;
> Could speak high sentiment as well as you,
> And out-blank-verse you without much ado.
>
> (XII. 51-4)

But such is his scorn of affectation that, despite the claim, he continues to speak in his preferred heroic couplets.

*Dipsychus*'s predecessors, *The Bothie* and *Amours de Voyage,* especially the latter, are written in hexameters so flexible that the metre shows itself as more consonant with the speaking voice than one had believed possible. But however lightly it obtrudes itself the metre is never forgotten, which is why it is so different from Wordsworthian blank verse. It is the metre that tilts those poems towards the mock-heroic. More than that, the metre works to define the poems' perspective on the world. In the earlier poem, it is the metre that establishes the safe distance from which a group of undergraduates are free to contemplate the life that, nevertheless, at the end of their student days they know that they will have to join.[17] In *Amours de Voyage,* more witheringly, it fixes Claude at an ironic distance from all those commitments that might save him from a life of unattached emptiness. Again here I suspect that the significant model is the Byron of the *ottava rima* poems. Byron was entirely right to insist in a letter to Douglas Kinnaird, 'As to "Don Juan"—confess—confess—you dog—and be candid—that it is the sublime of *that there* sort of writing—it may be bawdy—but is it not good English?'[18] And yet, despite the sterling Englishness of Byron's sentences, his stanza is never quite naturalised, and the effect is to maintain a cosmopolitan detachment from the subject matter no matter how English that subject matter may be. Like Byron's *ottava rima* Clough's hexameters never quite become 'natural'

There are hexameters in *Dipsychus,* too—Clough knew by then that they were his signature tune. Dipsychus falls into them, as we would expect, when he looks at life from a distance, a *spectator ab extra,*[19] and finds:

> Yes, it is beautiful ever, let foolish men rail
>     at it never.
> Yes, it is beautiful truly, my brothers, I grant
>     it you duly.
> Wise are ye others that choose it, and happy
>     ye all that can use it.
>
> (V. 63-5)

The internal rhyme distinguishes these from the hexameters of the earlier poems, but they are distinguished still more sharply when the Spirit comments on their introduction:

> (Hexameters by all that's odious,
> Beshod with rhyme to run melodious!).
>
> (V. 70-1)

Dipsychus responds by removing the rhyme, but he maintains the metre and the distance from which he observes the world around him:

> All as I go on my way I behold them
>     consorting and coupling;
> Faithful, it seemeth, and fond; very fond,
>     very possibly faithful.
>
> (V. 72-3)

The Spirit is not at all appeased:

> (Bravo, bravissimo! this time though
> You rather were run short for rhyme though;
> Not that on that account your verse
> Could be much better or much worse.)
>
> (V. 78-81)

The Spirit at such moments only makes explicit a general truth about hexameters as Clough and perhaps all other English poets use them: their chief difference from blank verse is that they are always so very noticeable.[20]

*Dipsychus* is the most formally various of all Clough's poems: there are couplets, both tetrameter and pentameter, there is blank verse, there are hexameters, quatrains, and a large number of other stanza forms, and the prologue and epilogue are written in prose. But the poem remains consistent in its self-consciousness. Whatever verse form may be used, the form calls attention to itself. So, for example, when Dipsychus expresses his discomfort at being able to afford enjoyments, such as a trip in a gondola, purchased at the expense of other men's poverty and other men's labour, he does so in a quatrain:

> How shall I laugh and sing and dance?
>     My very heart recoils,
> While here to give my mirth a chance
>     A hungry brother toils.
>
> (V. 47-50)

The sentiment seems praiseworthy enough, so why is it that most readers will anticipate the Spirit's response, 'Oh come, come, come!'? The answer surely lies in the choice of stanza. Dipsychus chooses to express himself in a verse form that has already acquired a fixed character, so that it is impossible to hear him without being reminded of writers such as Isaac Watts:

Why should I love my sport so well,
  So constant at my play,
And lose the thought of heaven and hell,
  And then forget to pray![21]

It is the verse form, not the sentiment, that ensures that Dipsychus's remark is defined by its priggishness.

*Dipsychus* is the poem that best displays Clough's brilliance as a metrist, but it remains brilliance of a rather peculiar kind. It does not result in the kind of poetry that Clough admired in Shakespeare and Virgil and Wordsworth, poetry that has attained 'the one form which of all others truly belongs to it.' Wordsworth's poetry sometimes achieves what Clough calls a 'final precision' that is not to be found in Byron, and I do not believe that it is to be found in his own work either. It is this failure in Byron that gives what substance it has to Swinburne's judgement of Byron that 'no poet of equal or inferior rank ever had so bad an ear',[22] and similar charges were brought against Clough. When Arnold complains in 'Thyrsis' that Clough's verse did not sustain its 'music' (221), and when he imagines a revenant Clough cutting for himself 'a smoother reed' (78), he is not, I suspect, indirectly regretting Clough's subject matter but objecting to his lack of proper musicality. It was an objection that Clough was capable of bringing against himself. When Dipsychus recites as his own work Clough's great hymn to unbelief, **'Easter Day. Naples, 1849'**, he comments in one draft on its 'unripe words and rugged verse', and in another he dismisses it as displaying 'poor metre and worse sense.' (684 and 686)

The pressing theme for the mid-Victorian poet, it seemed to Clough, was to offer a kind of consolation by finding 'a sense of significance, if not of dignity, in that often dirty, or at least dingy, work which it is the lot of so many of us to have to do, and which some one or other, after all, must do.' It was the failure to address that issue which made Arnold's poems and the poems of most of his contemporaries seem to him unsatisfying if not irrelevant. At the end of the poem the Spirit insists that Dipsychus submit to the world, which means taking up one of those 'unchosen, peremptorily appointed posts which are the only posts that the world has to offer. But the poet ought to make us feel, Clough writes, that in taking up such a post, we can still retain 'some central, celestial fact':

Cannot the Divine Song in some way indicate
  to us our unity,
though from a great way off, with those
  happier things; inform us,
and prove to us, that though we are what
  we are, we may yet, in some
way, even in our abasement, even by and
  through our daily work, be
related to the purer existence.

          (*Prose Remains of Arthur Hugh Clough,* 357)

Clough can at times sound very like Dipsychus, and when Dipsychus sounds like this the Spirit responds impatiently: 'Come, come, don't maunder any longer.' (XIV. 78) Dipsychus must 'submit, submit', and submit wholly. The Spirit will not settle for a 'moiety', not even for even for 'nine tenths.' The Spirit's is the brutally simple and unyielding arithmetic that rules the age, and in surrendering to it there seems little prospect that Dipsychus will continue to hear the 'Divine Song'. But *Dipsychus* has found room for songs of a very different kind, often not at all divine, 'How light we move, how softly! Ah, / Tra lal la la, the gondola! (V. 61-2). Dipsychus feels his life passing him by:

Twenty-one past, twenty-five coming on;
One third of life departed, nothing done.

          (XIV. 1-2)

But the only way to so something is to agree to fill one of those uncomfortable, ill-fitting posts that are all life has to offer. It seems a glum prospect, and there is nothing in the poem's conclusion to alleviate the glumness. But in the poem's metres and in its stanza forms there is, and it is something, I suspect, that Clough learned from Byron.

In the *ottava rima* poems Byron makes a running joke of the struggle to fit his thought into his stanza. It is as if almost every stanza confronts Byron with an emergency: the poems become a record of the unimaginable number of solutions that Byron contrives to find for his intractable formal problem. It is this, I suspect, that persuades the Clough of *Dipsychus* that he has more to learn from Byron's stanzas than from Wordsworth's blank verse. The stanza and the thought often seem to fit each other no better than, in Clough's analysis, the nineteenth-century soul fits the nineteenth-century world. But Byron shows how that lack of fit can become the ground of a rich and various comedy. The spirit points out to Dipsychus:

The ground which Byron used to ride on,
And do I don't know what beside on.

          (VI. 3-4)

The thought can be shoe-horned into the couplet, the rhyme can be completed, only by placing 'beside' next to 'on'. The couplet invites its reader to groan, but with that special groan with which one welcomes a comfortably bad joke. Clough, like Arnold and like many of his contemporaries, often wrote as though only 'some central, celestial fact' could have the power to console him for the miseries of life, but Byron suggested another possibility to him. *Dipsychus* is a comic poem, and there is much consolation to be found in laughter.

### *Notes*

1. *Dipsychus* is quoted from *The Poems of Arthur Hugh Clough,* ed. F. L. Mulhauser, second edn

(Oxford, 1974). The poem survives in five manuscripts, and all printed versions of it, from the first in *Letters and Remains of Arthur Hugh Clough* (London, 1865), edited by Clough's widow, are conjectural. Mulhauser includes material that he believes to have been omitted by Blanche Clough 'for reasons of propriety', and records all major variants.

2. *Handbook for Travellers in Northern Italy* (2 vols, London, 1854), i. 333.

3. Christopher M. Kierstead points out that Clough detects in poems such as *Childe Harold* 'an overused tarnished form of cultural capital,' but Kierstead, unlike me, believes that despite Clough's 'grudging respect' for Byron, his attitude towards him remains 'ironic'. See Christopher M. Kierstead, 'Where "Byron used to ride": locating the Victorian travel poet in Clough's *Amours de Voyage* and *Dipsychus*', *Philological Quarterly,* 77. 4 (Fall, 1998), 377-95.

4. Thomas Moore, *The Letters and Journals of Lord Byron with Notices of his Life* (London, 1873), 311.

5. *A Handbook for Travellers in Switzerland and the Alps of Savoy and Piedmont* (London, 1846), 167.

6. Quoted in James Buzard, *The Beaten Track: European tourism, literature, and the ways to culture, 1800-1918* (Oxford, 1993), 119.

7. Compare, for example, Arnold on Leopardi's volume of 1824, which 'hardly sold, I suppose, its tens, while the volumes of Byron's poetry were selling their tens of thousands.' The slenderness of the sale confirms that it is the Italian poet who is the 'true artist.' *Essays in Criticism Second Series* (London, 1888), 188.

8. Samuel Chew, *Byron in England* (London, 1924), 220-62.

9. Walter E. Houghton is alert to the Byronic quality of *Dipsychus*. The Spirit's wit, he suggests, works 'to show things "as they are," as Byron said of a similar poem called *Don Juan,*' and he notes that Clough preferred the later to the earlier Byron. See *The Poetry of Clough* (New Haven and London, 1963), 166 and 227. Michael Timko also makes the comparison, *Innocent Victorian: The Satiric Poetry of Arthur Hugh Clough* (Cleveland, 1963), 153-4. Masao Miyoshi indicates that Clough understood Wordsworth and Byron as antitheses each of the other, so that Dipsychus is mocked by the Spirit 'out of his Wordsworth only to hurry along to the "the ground which Byron used to ride on," the Lido, where the mood of a worldly-wise and naughty Byron overtakes him.' See Masao Miyoshi, 'Clough's Poems of Self-Irony', *Studies in English Literature 1500-1900,* 5 (Autumn, 1965), 691-704.

10. This was originally an independent lyric. See *Poems of Arthur Hugh Clough,* 710.

11. The usual assumption is that Clough wrote *Dipsychus* 'during or soon after a journey to Venice in the autumn vacation, 1850' (*Poems,* 65), but J. P. Phelan has suggested allusions in the second revision to a volume of *The Stones of Venice,* not published until 1853, and to a letter sent to Florence Nightingale by Sidney Herbert in October, 1854, identifying her as 'the one person in England . . . capable of organizing and superintending' a scheme to despatch a group of nurses to the Crimea. See J. P. Phelan, 'The Textual Evolution of Clough's *Dipsychus and the Spirit*', *Review of English Studies,* 46 (May, 1993), 230-9.

12. Benjamin Disraeli, *Vivian Grey* (2 vols, London, 1826), ii. 164.

13. John Morley, 'Byron' in *Critical Miscellanies* (3 vols, London, 1886), i. 213.

14. *Prose Remains of Arthur Hugh Clough,* ed. Blanche Clough (London, 1888), 356-7.

15. In the draft in the Venice notebook, quoted in J. P. Phelan, 'The Textual Evolution of Clough's *Dipsychus and the Spirit*'.

16. *Prose Remains,* 317. But even in this lecture on Wordsworth, Clough is aware that the Wordsworthian manner courts a danger:

> It is, I believe, that instead of looking directly at an object, and considering it as a thing in itself, and allowing it to operate upon him as a fact in itself, he takes the sentiment produced by it in his own mind as the thing, as the important and really real fact. The real things cease to be real; the world no longer exists; all that exists is the feeling, somehow generated in the poet's sensibility.
>
> (315)

17. J. P. Phelan argues that in *The Bothie,* Clough 'liberated the English hexameter from servile dependence on its antique prototype,' and hence expressed through his metre his sympathy with Philip Hewson's radical sentiments. See J. P. Phelan, 'Radical Metre: The English hexameter in Clough's *The Bothie of Toper-na-Fuosich, Review of English Studies,* 50 (May, 1999), 166-87. But a radicalism that expresses itself in the Englishing of a classical metre is of an unusually, even comically, academic kind, very far removed from the activities of the Chartists that Hewson claims to admire.

18. *Byron's Letters and Journals,* ed. Leslie A. Marchand (13 vols, London, 1973-94), vi. 232.

19. The title Clough gave to the expanded version of the Spirit's song, 'As I sat at the Café I said to myself.' See *The Poems of Arthur Hugh Clough,* 698.

20. A point well made by Henry Sidgwick: 'Clough has not *naturalised* the metre', 'Clough's line is, and is meant to be, conscious of being a hexameter,' it is accompanied by 'a wink implying that the bard is singing academically to an academical audience, and catering for their artificial tastes in versification.' See *Clough: The Critical Heritage,* ed. Michael Thorpe (London, 1972), 286

21. Isaac Watts, 'The Child's Complaint', 1-4. R. K. Biswas suggests that the Spirit's Song, 'As I sat at the café, I said to myself, / They may talk as they please about what they call pelf' (V. 130-195, parodies Watts's 'The Sluggard': 'I made him a Visit, still hoping to find / He had took better Care for improving his Mind.' See Robindra Kumar Biswas, *Arthur Hugh Clough: Towards a Reconsideration* (Oxford, 1972), 402-3. Patrick Scott had earlier offered evidence of Clough's use of Watts, 'The Text and Structure of Clough's "The Latest Decalogue"', *Notes and Queries,* 212 (Oct., 1967), 378-9.

22. A. C. Swinburne, *Essays and Studies* (London, 1875), 246.

---

# FURTHER READING

## Criticism

Brooke, Stopford A. "Arthur Hugh Clough." In *Clough: The Critical Heritage,* edited by Michael Thorpe, pp. 370-83. London: Routledge and Kegan Paul, 1972.

    Contends that Clough's poetic observations on the spiritual struggles he and many of his countrymen were undergoing were always personal even when he attempted to achieve a certain amount of self-detachment.

Enright, D. J. "'A Kidnapped Child of Heaven'—The Poetry of Arthur Hugh Clough." In *Nottingham Byron Lecture,* pp. 3-23. Nottingham, UK: University of Nottingham, 1972.

    Discusses Clough's literary reputation among his contemporaries, noting that while he had many friends who held his intellect and character in the highest regard, there were few who felt the same way about his poetry.

Greenberger, Evelyn Barish. *Arthur Hugh Clough: The Growth of a Poet's Mind.* Cambridge, Mass.: Harvard University Press, 1970, 270 p.

    Comprehensive study of Clough's intellectual and moral development over the course of his career as a poet.

Harris, Wendell V. "A Mind in Tension: *Ambarvalia.*" In *Arthur Hugh Clough,* pp. 52-65. New York: Twayne, 1970.

    Discusses *Ambarvalia,* containing poems composed during Clough's intellectual struggles at Oxford. Harris notes that the volume's poor reception by reviewers was of little concern to Clough, but he was deeply troubled by the growing distance between his own philosophical and religious beliefs and those of his friends.

Locke, James R. "Clough's *Amours de Voyage*: A Possible Source for 'The Love Song of J. Alfred Prufrock.'" *Western Humanities Review* 29, no. 1 (winter 1975): 55-66.

    Presents evidence suggesting that Clough's *Amours* inspired one of T. S. Eliot's most famous poems, despite Eliot's failure to mention Clough in any of his writings.

Scott, Patrick. "Three Literary Sources for Clough's 'Farewell, My Highland Lassie.'" *English Language Notes* 17, no. 3 (March 1980): 192-95.

    Examines literary, rather than biographical sources for Clough's poem, often believed to have been inspired by a love affair with a Scottish girl.

———. "Clough, Bankruptcy, and Disbelief: The Economic Background to 'Blank Misgivings.'" *Victorian Poetry* 44, no. 2 (summer 2006): 123-34.

    Discusses the economic references and imagery in Clough's poetry, possibly inspired by the commercial activities of Clough's father.

# Michelangelo
## 1475-1564

(Full name Michelangelo di Lodovico Buonarroti Simoni) Italian artist and poet.

## INTRODUCTION

Widely considered an archetypal Renaissance man, Michelangelo was prodigiously talented as a painter, sculptor, architect, engineer, and poet. His voluminous correspondence and notebooks that record his thoughts and activities on an almost daily basis, as well as recollections and biographies by his contemporaries, document his life and work in an unprecedentedly thorough manner. While it was not published until almost sixty years after his death, his only work of poetry, *Rime* (1623), has made an important contribution to the study of his psychology and art, attracting continued interest among literary critics.

## BIOGRAPHICAL INFORMATION

Michelangelo was born in Caprese, in Tuscany, Italy, to Lodovico di Leonardo di Buonarroti di Simoni, a banker and government official, and his wife, Francesca di Neri del Miniato di Siena. The family moved to Florence a few months after his birth. Michelangelo's mother was gravely ill for many years and died when he was seven; at various times over the course of her illness and after her death, the young boy was sent to live with a stonecutter and his family in Settignano, where his father owned a farm and a marble quarry, and where he learned the skill of using a hammer and chisel. His father in time sent Michelangelo to study with the noted scholar Francesco da Urbino in Florence, but he remained uninterested in all but the study of painting, so at the age of thirteen he became apprenticed to Domenico Ghirlandaio, a successful Florentine artist. From 1490 to 1492 Michelangelo studied at the Humanist academy, which was founded by Lorenzo de'Medicihe and which included the most prominent scholars and writers of the time, notably the Neoplatonists Marsilio Ficino and Pico della Mirandola. At that time Michelangelo had already begun sculpting and was awarded with a commission from Lorenzo. When Lorenzo died in 1492, Michelangelo returned to live with his father, continuing his study of painting and sculpture and also striving to improve his knowledge of human anatomy by dissecting corpses at a local church hospital. Because of the political upheaval caused by the fanatical reforming priest Girolamo Savonarola in 1494, Michelangelo moved first to Venice and then to Bologna in search of work, but returned to Florence at the end of that year, when the atmosphere in that city was calmer, undertaking various projects for the Medicis.

Michelangelo travelled to Rome in 1496 and soon began to work on a commission by Cardinal Raffaele Riario—the beginning of what would become a most illustrious career. Between 1497 and 1499 he completed one of his most famous sculptures, the *Pietà*; during that period he also met and apparently fell in love with the poet Vittoria Colonna, marquise of Pescara, to whom many of his sonnets are dedicated. Returning again to Florence, Michelangelo completed his masterwork, the statue of the *David,* in 1504, thus establishing himself as the greatest artist of his era. One monumental work followed another for the remainder of his life as he alternated between Rome and Florence to work on the ceiling of the Sistine Chapel, frescoes, and such architectural projects as the Medici Chapel, the Laurentian Library, and the dome of St. Peter's Basilica. Though often vilified for his prickly personality and extreme individualism, he was also honored in his own time as an artistic genius. In 1532, when he was fifty-seven years old, Michelangelo met twenty-three-year-old Tommaso dei Cavalieri, to whom the longest sequence of the *Rime* is dedicated. His celebration of Cavalieri's physical perfection and his expressions of love for him in the poems led to speculation about Michelangelo's sexuality from his own era onward. While no proof exists either way, most modern scholars acknowledge the homoerotic component of Michelangelo's verse but also point out that he guarded his privacy fiercely and that early biographers like Giorgio Vasari portray him as living an asexual, monkish existence. Michelangelo continued to work on his projects until the end of his life and died in 1564 of natural causes.

## MAJOR WORKS

Michelangelo's only work of poetry is the *Rime*—a collection of three hundred and two pieces, mostly sonnets and madrigals, but also sestinas, epigrams, and *orazione* (prayers)—that he dismissed in his own lifetime as "silly things" and "heavy pastries." The poems are dedicated to Vittoria Colonna, Tomasso dei Cavalieri, and to an unidentified "donna bella e cruella" (beautiful and cruel woman), as well as to friends and patrons. He composed the poems mainly in the 1530s and 1540s, when he was working feverishly on commissioned art projects; Michelangelo apparently did not find the writing process easy, and his verse shows a seriousness of approach, with much self-critical editing and revision. Besides love, the main themes of the poems are faith, old age, death, the role of the artist, and tension between humility and pride. Critics have noted the strong influence of Neoplatonism in the poems, especially in the religious pieces addressed to Vittoria Colonna; for Michelangelo, art was a reflection of divine perfection and an avenue to God. The language of the poems is often dramatic and dense, characterized by extreme imagery and paradox. Yet in some pieces, as scholars have noted, Michelangelo's tone is witty, self-mocking, satirical, and even burlesque. Commentators often divide Michelangelo's poetry into four periods: 1504-32, a formative period, during which he imitated the verse of Francesco Petrarca and experimented with form and style; 1532-36, the period of intense love poems to dei Cavalieri; 1537-46, when he wrote sonnets, often with religious themes, to Vittoria di Colonna; and 1547-64, when he became increasingly preoccupied with the themes of death, redemption, and ambiguity.

Since Michelangelo's own time, critics have noted the homoerotic element in his love poems and they have debated the question of his sexuality. When Michelangelo's grandnephew, Michelangelo Buonarroti *il Giovine* (the younger), published the *Rime* for the first time in 1623, he changed the pronouns in key amorous poems to deflect from what he called the "ignoble element" in his great uncle's work. The original pronouns were not restored until Cesare Guasti's 1863 edition of the *Rime*. While modern critics and readers continue to be fascinated by the homoerotic dimension of Michelangelo's work, the consensus is that the poet was clearly aware of his attraction to men and denigrated the love of women in his verse, but that it likely went unacknowledged and that he probably never acted on his impulses. As James M. Saslow has written, "[h]e may not have thought of himself as a 'homosexual,' but he was aware that there were such people, that many of his passionate declarations were taken as indication that he was one of them, that the objects of his affections required a language that violated gender norms, and that it was both safer and less guilt-inducing to forego actions and conceal emotion."

## CRITICAL RECEPTION

Even though Michelangelo's poetry has been available to readers and critics for centuries, systematic scholarly evaluation of it did not begin until the twentieth century.

Before that, his verse was regarded as another way to approach his life and art and most commentaries remained superficial. Early critics viewed Michelangelo's poetry as obscure and as yet another testament to his overall genius, but they did not study its literary qualities. Scholar Ann H. Hallock has written about the history of criticism of Michelangelo's poetry, emphasizing the key essays of Ugo Foscolo in the nineteenth century. In the late twentieth and early twenty-first centuries there has been a profusion of critical study of the *Rime*. Frederick May, Thomas Mussio, and Gavriel Moses (see Further Reading) have traced the seminal influences of Neoplatonism, Dante, Petrarch, St. Augustine, and the Bible on Michelangelo's poetry. Various aspects of Michelangelo's poetic style have received indepth treatment from Christopher Ryan, Glauco Cambon, Robert J. Clements, Itala Rutter (see Further Reading), and Jean-Pierre Barricelli, while Cambon, Hallock, and Santa Casciani treat Michelangelo's growing preoccupation with death toward the end of his life. Clements and Justin Vitiello study his portrayal of the role of the artist in the artistic process and draw parallels with Michelangelo's painting and sculpture. The issue of Michelangelo's homoeroticism has remained a topic of high interest, with Saslow addressing what can be deduced about this question in the context of Michelangelo's own time; Joseph Francese focusing on Michelangelo's apparent conflict between earthly, physical beauty and divine beauty; and William J. Kennedy suggesting that the diversity of commentaries on Petrarch's poetry had a liberating effect on Michelangelo's verses. In general, commentators now regard Michelangelo's poetry not as a sideline that illuminates his artistic genius, but as a distinct and compelling manifestation of his wide-ranging creativity.

---

# PRINCIPAL WORKS

### Poetry

*Rime de Michelagnolo Buonarroti, racolte de Michelagnolo suo nipote* 1623
*Le rime de Michelagelo Buonarroti* 1863
*The Complete Poems of Michelangelo* 1960
*Michelangelo Buonarroti: Rime* 1960

### Other Major Works

*Le lettere di Michelangelo Buonarroti* (letters) 1875
*The Letters of Michelangelo.* 2 vols. (letters) 1963

# CRITICISM

### Robert J. Clements (essay date June 1946)

SOURCE: Clements, Robert J. "Michelangelo and the Doctrine of Imitation." *Italica* 23, no. 2 (June 1946): 90-9.

[*In the following essay, Clements discusses Michelangelo's ideas regarding imitation as applied to his art and his poetry, calling attention to the religious dimension of his thought and concluding that his ideas were individualistic.*]

Michelangelo's friend and biographer, Giorgio Vasari, gave testimony that the Renaissance painters, no less than their literary contemporaries, viewed the doctrine of imitation as licensing the copying of both nature and older masters. "Perchè io so che l'arte nostra è tutta imitazione della natura principalmente, e poi, perchè da sè non può salir tanto alto, delle cose che da quelli che miglior maestri di sè giudica son condotte."[1] The imitation of nature alluded to here meant to some a literal representation (from photographic to "discreet") of nature: to others an ideal representation advanced by the neo-Platonists.[2] While Michelangelo never carried out his intention of composing a treatise on art, we nevertheless possess scattered written evidence which reveals his feelings about *imitatio*. His remarks will recognise both types of imitation mentioned by Vasari. We shall see that Michelangelo is more reserved than many *Cinquecentisti* about approving literal imitation, that his conception of ideal imitation is tempered by his intense religiosity, and that he entertained definite prejudices about copying other masters.

To what stage had the doctrine of imitation evolved at the beginning of Michelangelo's creative period, the dayspring of the sixteenth century? Giorgio Valla's Latin translation of Aristotle's *Poetics* had already appeared (1498). Its famous prescription about art imitating nature was applied to painting as well as poetry. Of course, the ideal of photographic imitation was as old as art itself; in the Trecento Boccaccio showed that it accounted in large measure for Giotto's reputation: "Ebbe uno ingegno di tanta eccellenzia, che niuna cosa dà la natura . . . che egli con lo stile e con la penna e col pennello non dipignesse sì simile a quella, che non simile, anzi piuttosto dessa paresse, in tanto che molte volte nelle cose da lui fatte si truova che il visivo senso degli uomini vi prese errore, quello credendo esser vero che era dipinto."[3] This literal view, which had its proponents in the sixteenth century as well as the fourteenth, was one which Michelangelo never favored. He never considered art a slavish imitation of nature, even though Montaiglon suggested that his crouching figure of an ape skulking behind one of the *Captive Youths* represented Painting, "la scimmia della natura."

In so far as Leon Battista Alberti extolled literal imitation Michelangelo could only disagree with him. Alberti's mechanism to facilitate the imitation of nature (a net which the painter held against his eye, on which he traced the outlines of the object to be copied, and a table establishing the proportions of the average man) led precisely to the type of mechanical or geometric copying decried by Michelangelo, who held that an artist worthy of the name should measure sufficiently with his naked eye and who condemned Dürer for trying to reduce art to synthetically standardised proportions. Vasari quotes him as asserting "che bisognava avere le seste negli occhi e non in mano."[4] In his *Della pittura* (1436) Alberti opined that since painting imitates nature, the artist's lines and colors should appear in relief and like the object imitated;[5] Alberti preceded Michelangelo in his belief that the artist should imitate the beautiful elements in nature. "Per tanto bisogna porre ogni studio ed industria principalmente in conoscere, imparare, ed esprimere il bello."[6] Like Buonarroti, he claims that "quella idea della bellezza non si lascia conoscere dagli ignoranti, la quale a pena si lascia discernere da quei che sanno."[7]

Leonardo believed that art must imitate, even mirror nature. Nature in this case was nothing Platonic, but merely visible external nature. He advised painters to carry mirrors with them to check their paintings against the reflections of the object painted. He even called these reflections "the true painting." He wrote, "Quella pittura è più laudabile, la quale ha più conformità con la cosa imitata."[8] If Michelangelo could only dissent from such practices and sentiments, especially considering the source, he could not help but agree with Leonardo's section, "Dell'imitare Pittori," in which Da Vinci warned his colleagues not to imitate other painters, lest they then be called grandchildren rather than children of nature.

Curiously enough, the writer whose ideas on *mimesis* coincided on most points with Michelangelo's was Lodovico Dolce, that critic who joined with Aretino to attack the *Giudizio universale* as morally improper. The main point of similarity is their mutual conviction that the painter portraying the human body should make an idealised imitation. Dolce urged making a composite of several models, and we shall see below that this was Michelangelo's frequent practice. A point of dissension was Dolce's inciting the artist to surpass nature, which aim is illogical and impossible in Michelangelo's aesthetics, as we shall learn below. Dolce's doctrine of ideal imitation and Varchi's claim that artists must imitate nature "con alcuna discrezione" make them two outstanding antagonists of the doctrine of literal imitation and ally them with Buonarroti.

These painters were the principal theorists treating of *imitatio* whose ideas might have been known to Michelangelo. If their views are representative of their respective periods, then they will help us understand to what an extent Michelangelo was a nonconformist in his thinking, for his theories differ in varying degree not only from those of these predecessors and contemporaries, but even from those of his survivant Bellori. If any close affinity with Michelangelo is to be sought in the Cinquecento, it is in Lomazzo, whose neo-Platonic view of imitation did not appear until the issuance of his *Idea del tempio della pittura* in 1590.

Given this frame of reference, we turn now to Michelangelo's thoughts on the two major types of imitation stated by Vasari in our initial paragraph. After recording his views on these two issues and pausing over occasional *rapprochements* among writings of his contemporaries, we shall conclude with an examination of his position on the Question of the Ancients and Moderns.

Michelangelo Buonarroti, like his fellow craftsmen, held art to be an imitation, but an imitation of God's forms rather than Plato's natural ones. In the third dialogue of Francisco de Hollanda's *Dialogos em Roma,* Messer Lattanzio elicits the following definition of painting from Michelangelo:

> Sómente a pintura, que eu tanto celebro e louvo, será emitar alguma só cousa das que o imortal Deos fez, com grande cuidado e sapiencia, e que elle inventou e pintou semelhantes ao mestre.[9]

He further explains that painting will be excellent in so far as it resembles and best imitates some work of immortal God, whether man, animal, fish, or fowl. Buonarroti restricts his definition of the works of God to living things. We are a long way from the bed which Plato used in his *Republic* (X) to illustrate how the painter imitates an imitation of a creation of God. The most noble imitations, Michelangelo continues, will be those representing the most noble (living) things with the greatest delicacy and knowledge. In both theory and practice, he is disinterested in the copying of inanimate objects. He adds specifically that a man's foot is a more worthy subject for imitation than his shoes, or a man's flesh than his clothing.

The point is that the artist's function is to select and represent beauty in God's universe. This beauty comes into visible presence from a higher source and is more readily apparent to sensitive artists (*persone accorte* or artists endowed with an *intelletto*) than to others:

> A quel pietoso fonte onde sian tucti
> S'assembra ogni beltà: che qua si uede,
> Piu c' altra cosa alle persone acorte.[10]

Michelangelo effected a compromise between the neo-Platonic ideal (or Idea) of beauty and a Christian recognition that God is the source of all form and art. In this he was closer to Plato than to the neo-Platonists,

by the way. A sentence written by Rensselaer Lee to apply to Lomazzo describes with equal aptness Michelangelo, who "could temporarily divert the theory of imitation entirely from Aristotelian channels by declaring that ideal beauty, the image of which one sees reflected in the mirror of his own mind, has its source in God rather than in nature—a quasi-religious and mystical doctrine in harmony with the serious temper of the Counter Reform, and one that did not empirically find a standard of excellence in selecting the best from concrete and external nature, but discovered it in a Platonic fashion in the subjective contemplation of an inward, immaterial idea."[11] This was, in essence, Michelangelo's theory of art. The "subjective contemplation of an inward idea" comes naturally to an artist whose ideal is

> un choncetto di belleza,
> Immaginata o uista dentro al core.[12]

Among some *Cinquecentisti* the goal of the artist was "non solo d'imitar, ma di superar la natura."[13] In Michelangelo's theory, this would be a logical impossibility, as well as pointless arrogance. God places beauties of form and color in the artist's media themselves—rock or pigment—and the artist's function is to find them and bring them to light.

> E ne' marmi l'inmagin richa e uile
> Secondo che 'l sa trar l'ingegnio nostro.[14]

God grants to a happy few an *intelletto* for reproducing or even imitating these forms:

> et solo à quello arriua
> La man, che ubbidisce all'intelletto.[15]

It follows that since all art is preexistent in nature, placed there by the Sommo Fattore (Dante's title becomes especially accurate here), then no artist could in his imitation surpass nature, that is, improve upon God. The best he can possibly do is to imitate (two verbs are used by Francisco de Hollanda quoting Michelangelo: *emitar* and *terladar*). To be capable of even this much the artist must be a genius.

Buonarroti's disinterest in photographic imitation spared him from the headaches of a court portraitist, an indignity suffered by even the best of painters in an age when their profession made sycophants of them. His insistence upon capturing the inner or spiritual man and abandoning realistic portrayal for "transcending to the universal form" led him to generalise his portraits. When people complained that there was no actual resemblance portrayed in the faces of Giuliano and Lorenzo over the Medici sarcophagi, he countered with "Who will care in a thousand years whether or not these features resemble theirs?"[16] When Catherine des Médicis wrote Michelangelo from Blois, requesting him to do an equestrian statue of her husband, Henri II, she stipulated that she wanted a good likeness; she sent his picture by an agent and gave specific instructions in a covering letter. In view of Michelangelo's intransigent attitude about photographic portraits, one can easily give credence to Vasari's statement that Michelangelo refused to study portraiture.[17] Among those critics who believed in ideal rather than literal imitation, Dolce (and even Alberti) urged painters to follow the plan of Zeuxis in portraying Helen and to choose the best feature from several models. Vasari and Condivi alike record that Michelangelo was partial to this view and adopted this procedure.[18]

The second major conception of imitation, namely plagiarism, was only a shade less acceptable to the artists than to the poets. This type of *mimesis,* which had been identified with Dionysius of Halicarnassus and perpetuated by Quintilian, had its most staunch literary proponent during Michelangelo's lifetime in Vida, who incited fledgling writers to steal repeatedly from the masters who preceded them. In the fine arts, plagiarism of classic artists especially was condoned: "E parte si debbono imitar le belle figure di marmo, o di bronzo de' Mestieri antichi. La mirabil perfettion delle quali chi gusterà e possederà a pieno, potrà sicuramente corregger molti difetti di essa Natura, e far le sue Pitture riguardevoli e grate a ciascuno: perciochè le cose antiche contengono tutta le perfettion dell'arte, e possono essere esemplari di tutto il bello."[19] In a sense, all the *Cinquecentisti* followed this precept, for novice painters and sculptors busily copied from previous models. Sculptors were expected to copy such statuary as the *Laokoon,* newly discovered at the Thermae of Titus. In painting, where no such ancient models existed, the Trecento and Quattrocento artists had to serve in lieu of their ancient predecessors. Giotto and Masaccio had to fill in for Zeuxis and Apelles. Michelangelo, in fact, claimed that Raphael had thus learned from him.

Part of Michelangelo's early fame rested upon his ability to copy ancient drawings. Vasari related pridefully that Michelangelo counterfeited ancient drawings so artfully that they were indistinguishable from the originals.[20] He implied that Michelangelo was not trying to deceive anyone and absolved him of blame by explaining that Michelangelo merely wished to keep the originals as samples of others' art to emulate and surpass. After all, he did give back the imitations. The exculpation is typical of the Renaissance. The story of Michelangelo's sleeping *Cupid,* carved and artificially aged to simulate an ancient statue and sold as such in Rome is familiar to all students of Buonarroti's life. In fact, this forgery was the production which won him his first contract in Rome. Moreover, the work which first drew him to the attention of Lorenzo de' Medici was an imitation of a marble faun which Michelangelo encountered in the Giardino Mediceo. In Renaissance theory,

the gifted writer or artist was expected to rival or surpass the ancients. Michelangelo was one of these: Condivi tells us that in copying the antique faun Buonarroti supplied what the original lacked.

Before quoting Michelangelo directly on the subject of plagiarism or copying from earlier craftsmen, let us examine to what an extent he, like other Cinquecento artists and writers, has been subjected to source studies. At the risk of becoming long-winded, we list a number of charges of plagiarism leveled by generations of fine arts scholars.[21] First, the paintings: Grimm holds that the *Adam, Noah,* and *Goliath* owe their essential idea to the gates of Ghiberti, which Michelangelo claimed were worthy of Paradise. The motiv of the nude figures in the Doni *Madonna* (or *Holy Family*) is said to be derived from Luca Signorelli's *Madonna.* Symonds claims that *Charon's Boat* and *Minos* in the *Giudizio universale* are borrowings from the *Divina Commedia.* It has even been alleged that Michelangelo copied from himself and that the large oil study of *Leda* in the National Gallery resembles in form the *Notte,* which he was executing at about the same period.

Among the sketches, the unfinished nude (rear perspective) in the Casa Buonarroti is said to owe its conception to the Hercules of a sarcophagus in the Lateran. The figure of a sack-laden *putto* on the Louvre drawing of Mercury would originate in a statue on the Fontana Cesi in Rome. Two sketches of a nude woman in the Musée Condé at Chantilly are purported to originate in an antique group of Graces in the Libreria Piccolomini in Siena; a nude study in the Louvre may have derived from the ancient Sidamara Sarcophagus.

Finally, the statuary. The *Brutus,* according to Vasari, was imitated from a Roman cornelian owned by Giuliano Ceserino. It has been noted that the open-handed gesture of the *Madonna della Febbre,* with the limp right arm of Christ, resembles the *Pietà* of Jacopo del Sellaio which had been in the Chiesa San Frediano in Florence. Mackowsky and others have noted that the *St. Matthew* has similarities with the *Laokoon,* which Michelangelo knew from the moment of its discovery, while Grünwald posits that the ancient *Pasquino* was the original model. The head of the *David* was allegedly based upon the type of head on Donatello's *San Giorgio.* De Tolnay even finds that the composition of the *Pietà* "can hardly be explained otherwise than by Michelangelo's fascination with the figure of Christ in Leonardo's *Last Supper.*"[22]

There are many other alleged borrowings, but if only a few of these were valid, they would illustrate that Michelangelo followed the practice of Renaissance writers in culling the best from earlier masters and processing it into their own works. This culling device became a common practice in literature and was endorsed by Minturno, Cammillo, Boiardo, and others.[23] Condivi used this bee image in connection with Michelangelo himself, when recalling how Zeuxis had used many models for his Crotonian Venus. Of Michelangelo's use of nature he wrote: "Così il bello dalla natura scegliendo, come l'api raccolgono il mel da' fiori, servendosene poi nelle loro opere."[24]

Michelangelo, like Leonardo, would grant that apprentice painters should copy from established artists. Each of them, however, ruled against copying by any but novices. We have quoted Leonardo on the subject. Whether or not Michelangelo was guilty of the imitations charged to his account, whether they were conscious or unconscious, he was in principle against either plagiarism or imitation. He scoffed that if one has no real talent, then one cannot even imitate well enough to justify the effort. "Colui che va dietro ad altri non li passa innanzi e chi non sa far bene da sè, non può servirsi bene delle cose d'altri."[25]

We have further testimony. Vasari tells an ironic, revealing anecdote. Buonarroti was shown a story painted by an artist who had appropriated so many parts from other drawings and pictures that there was little original in it. Michelangelo's cutting comment was:

> —Bene ha fatto; ma io non so al dì del Giudizio, che tutti i corpi piglieranno le lor membra, come farà quella storia, chè non ci rimarrà niente.[26]

As for those zealous scholars who would detect imitations within the several works of Michelangelo, claiming that the *Leda* and the *Notte* have the same proportions, we recall the following quotation, recorded by Condivi, which is capital in an understanding of Buonarroti's feelings about imitation:

> È stato di tenacissima memoria, dimanierachè avendo egli dipinte tante migliaia di figure, quante si vedono, non ha fatta mai una, che si somigli l'altra, o faccia quella medesima attitudine; anzi gli ho sentito dire che *non tira mai linea, che non si ricordi, se più mai l'ha tirata; scancellandola, se si ha a vedere in pubblico.*[27]

Michelangelo's views on the doctrine of imitation, both of nature and of established artists, shed light on his stand in the Quarrel of the Ancients and Moderns, which provoked so much sixteenth and seventeenth century debate. One could imitate ancient works, but could one surpass them? As we have seen above, Michelangelo did not agree with his contemporaries who thought artists could surpass nature. But he did agree that one could surpass ancient craftsmen. As a boy, having left the workshop of Ghirlandaio and engaged in copying the ancient statues of the Giardino Mediceo, he had felt certainly that one could only approach the ancients, at best. Yet as life went on, his goal became *aemulatio* rather than *imitatio.* We have already noted his blunt

remark that those who follow after artists can never pass ahead of them, a remark Milanesi believed to be aimed at Bandinelli and the latter's copy of the *Laokoon.* The Renaissance conception of Italy as the third home of classicism (Hellas > Rome > Italy) was obviously entertained by Michelangelo. He came to feel that Italian artists were the natural successors to the ancients and that whereas God theoretically grants to a certain international elect an "intellect for beauty," a second "intellect for form" is necessary, and this is the Hellenic patrimony to the new Greece: Italy. He maintained that a work made in Italy bears a particular classic stamp which no one, not even Albrecht Dürer, can counterfeit. In the *Dialogos em Roma,* Buonarroti asserted,

> o modo do pintar de Italia . . . é o grego antigo[28]

Being a direct descendent implies potentialities of equality with the ascendant. Knowing his Renaissant self-confidence as well as his personal bias, one is entitled to question whether Michelangelo committed a fraction of, or any of, the artistic plagiarism which zealous scholarship has attributed to him. It was conceivable to him that the Ancients not only might be surpassed, but that they might be surpassed by him. When he executed plans of a church for the Florentines in Rome, he claimed that if the design were carried out, "nè Romani nè Greci mai ne' tempi loro feciono una cosa tale."[29] Michelangelo heard himself lauded many times as equal and superior to the Ancients. Cosimo Bartoli credited Michelangelo with the fact that Italy no longer needed be jealous of Rome, and the eulogies at the ceremony of Buonarroti's burial in Florence (his body having been smuggled out of Rome in a packing-case) almost unanimously pictured him as the equal or better of Apelles, Phidias, and Vitruvius. Michelangelo himself could compare his countrymen favorably with the Ancients. Admiring the terra cotta statuary of Antonio Begarelli, which was colored to simulate marble, he exclaimed: "Se questa terra diventassi marmo, guai alle statue antiche."[30] As one studies Buonarroti's enumeration of cities boasting splendid art and architecture contained in the *Dialogos em Roma,* one clearly senses that he considered his fellow Italians as rivaling the ancients, but artists of other lands as lagging behind. Michelangelo, no less than Vasari, knew that there was an artistic *rinascita,* at least in Italy.

Our chief purpose in these pages has been to reproduce and analyze Michelangelo's rare thoughts on the doctrine of imitation, one of the most variously interpreted and misinterpreted concepts which the Renaissance inherited from antiquity. We have attempted to show in what ways Michelangelo's thinking about art was as determined and nonconformist as his practicing of art. Yet there has been a secondary purpose. In a sense, these pages have been an exercise to show that while Michelangelo left no treatise on art and was even unwilling to talk about art, as Fra Ambrosio da Siena once testified, one can find scattered among his poems and letters, among contemporary records and biographies, elements of a possible aesthetic which he never took time to compose. Endeavoring to isolate and analyse these elements, the present writer is discovering that whereas Michelangelo's thinking is individualistic, the issues which preoccupy him (*e.g.,* imitation, glory, decorum, *etc.*) are quite typical of the time and place in which he lived.

### Notes

1. Giorgio Vasari, *Le Vite de' più eccellenti pittori, scultori, ed architettori* (Florence, 1878), I, 222.

2. Three notably competent works should be consulted for an understanding of *imitatio* among the Cinquecento artists: Rensselaer W. Lee, "Ut Pictura Poesis: The Humanistic Theory of Painting." *The Art Bulletin,* December, 1940, pp. 197-269; Anthony Blunt, *Artistic Theory in Italy* (Oxford, 1940); Erwin Panofsky, *Idea* (Leipzig-Berlin, 1924). None of these, however, treats fully the case of Michelangelo.

3. Giovanni Boccaccio, *Decamerone,* VI, V.

4. Giorgio Vasari, *Le Vite* (Florence, 1881), VII, 270.

5. Leon Battista Alberti, *Della pittura* (Milan, 1804), p. 82.

6. *Ibid.,* p. 88.

7. *Ibid.,* p. 89.

8. Leonardo da Vinci, *Trattato della pittura* (Lanciano, 1914), p. 202.

9. Francisco de Hollanda, *Da pintura antigua: Dialogos em Roma* (Porto, 1930), p. 239.

10. Michelagniolo Buonarroti, *Die Dichtungen,* edit. by Frey (Berlin, 1897), p. 53.

11. Rensselaer W. Lee, *op. cit.,* p. 207.

12. *Dichtungen, ed. cit.,* p. 50.

13. Lodovico Dolce, *Dialogo della pittura* (Florence 1735), p. 176.

14. *Dichtungen, ed. cit.,* p. 54.

15. *Ibid.,* p. 89.

16. Giorgio Vasari, *Le Vite,* Blashfield-Hopkins edition (New York, 1901), p. 119, note.

17. See J. A. Symonds, *Life of Michelangelo Buonarroti* (London, 1893), I, 263.

18. Giorgio Vasari, *Le Vite* (Florence, 1881), VII, 270; Ascanio Condivi, *Vita de Michelangelo* (Pisa, 1823), p. 80.

19. Lodovico Dolce, *Dialogo della pittura* (Florence, 1735), p. 190.

20. Giorgio Vasari, *Le Vite, ed. cit.,* VII, p. 141.

21. Several of these items are mentioned in De Tolnay's authoritative *Youth of Michelangelo* (Princeton, 1943), pp. 70-71 and *passim.*

22. *Ibid.,* p. 92.

23. See W. L. Bullock, "Precept of Plagiarism in the Cinquecento," *Modern Philology,* XXV (1928), 307.

24. Ascanio Condivi, *Vita di Michelangelo* (Pisa, 1823), p. 80.

25. See Vincenzo Pascale, *Michelangelo Buonarroti poeta* (Naples, 1902), p. 135.

26. Giorgio Vasari, *Le Vite, ed. cit.,* VII, p. 281.

27. Ascanio Condivi, *Vita di Michelangelo* (Pisa, 1823), p. 83.

28. Francisco de Hollanda, *ed. cit.,* pp. 190-191.

29. Giorgio Vasari, *Le Vite, ed. cit.,* VII, p. 263.

30. *Ibid.,* p. 281.

### Robert J. Clements (essay date March 1954)

SOURCE: Clements, Robert J. "Eye, Mind, and Hand in Michelangelo's Poetry." *PMLA* 69, no. 1 (March 1954): 324-36.

[*In the following essay, Clements focuses on Michelangelo's concept of the relationship between the artist's intellect, his "inner vision," and his hand, cautioning that he "would disagree emphatically with nineteenth-century theories of spontaneous and unguided creativeness."*]

Although Michelangelo was so self-conscious about his poems as to dismiss them as "silly things" and "heavy pastries," the neo-Platonic pieces provide us with avenues to his most intimate thoughts on art. In his *canzoniere* one learns that two little-known guideposts alongside his theoretical approach to painting and sculpture are the special interrelations existing between the eye and the hand and between the intellect and the hand. It is with these relationships which he recognized between, first, vision and manual execution and between, second, poetic conceptualizing and manual execution, that these pages will be concerned.

Referring in one of his sonnets to "that fine art which defeats nature if one bears it down from heaven," Michelangelo acknowledges, like Sappho,[1] that he is one of the elect granted a special perception of beauty and form: "io naqqui a quella ne sordo ne cieco"[2] ('I was born neither deaf nor blind to that art'). The idea that the providentially endowed artist has a visual acuity for the forms or *concetti* in the ideal world, which he then reduces from immateriality to materiality, is neo-Platonic, of course, and reminiscent of Ficino: "Idque munus similiter divinae providentiae nobis est amore concessum."[3] The crucial agent in the entire art process is the eye, for it must glimpse the earthly forms which are reflections from the higher sphere, receive them, and reconvert them into finer and greater images as they pass along to the mind (or soul). The eye must also perceive the preexisting forms implanted by God, the *Sommo Fattore,* in the ὕλη, to be discovered and delivered from the superfluous matter encasing them. So keen was this latter visual faculty in Michelangelo that he could look at certain marbles in the quarries of Seravezza and discern the forms potential within them and order these marked with an "M" (as Vincenzo Danti witnessed) for cutting and transporting. He could perceive the magnificent *David* "growing" within the defective block of marble which Sansovino had rejected as inadequate without supplementary pieces. He could visualise the contours of a mighty colossus in a lofty mountain at Carrara, just as Deinokrates had seen the figure of King Alexander in Mount Athos.

The process by which the eye functions to communicate form and beauty to the mind, which may then charge the hand to "find" or "free" that divinely ordained or implanted beauty, can be put together from several of the poems. Thus, in Michelangelo's sonnet, **"Dimmi di gratia, Amor, se gli ochi mei,"** he asks Love whether the beauty he contemplates on his lady's countenance is the true beauty to which he aspires. Love replies that beauty seen through the eye is indeed true and inherent beauty, but that when it passes through the eye to the soul it becomes (again) something divine. It is this transfigured beauty which constitutes the real attraction and motivation for those who appreciate beauty most: lovers or artists. Michelangelo's question reads:

> Dimmi di gratia, Amor, se gli ochi mei
> Veggon 'l ver della beltà, ch' aspiro,
> O s' io l'o dentro, allor che, dou' io miro,
> Veggio scolpito el uiso di costei . . .
>
> (*Dichtungen,* p. 22)

Tell me as a kindness, Love, if my eyes see the true nature of the beauty for which I long, or if I possess it within me when, gazing on the face of my lady, I see it sculptured.

Love replies:

> La beltà che tu uedi, è ben da quella,
> Ma crescie, poi ch' a miglior loco sale,
> Se per gli ochi mortali all' alma corre.
> Quiui si fa diuina, onesta, e bella

Com' a se simil uuol cosa inmortale.
Questa, e non quella, a gli ochi tuo precorre.

The beauty which you see comes truly from your lady; but this beauty grows, since it ascends to a better place when through mortal eyes it passes on to the soul.

There it is made into something divine, worthy, and fine, since any immortal thing wishes other things similarly immortal. It is this divine beauty, and not the other, which guides your eyes onward.

The process by which this sensual image grows into something finer within the soul was described for Michelangelo by Ficino, who turned out to be an even greater influence on Michelangelo than did Poliziano, the other guest the young apprentice had known through the Medici household. "Nam procedente tempore amatum non in mera eius imagine per sensus accepta perspiciunt, sed in simulacro iam ab anima ad ideae suae similitudinem reformato, quod ipso corpore pulchrius est, intuentur."[4]

When the true artist reaches the point of reproducing some beauty, it is not merely a facsimile of visible beauty which he tries to set down, but rather the image which develops (*crescie*) within him. What must be rendered is a concept of beauty, fancied or seen within the heart:

> un choncetto di belleza,
> Inmaginata o uista dentro al core . . .
>
> (*Dichtungen,* p. 50)

This could make a lyrical answer to those literal-minded critics who found no resemblance to the real-life dukes in the features of the effigies of Lorenzo and Giuliano or no verisimilitude in the proportions of the *Pietà* in St. Peter's. It also explains further Michelangelo's intense dislike of portraiture. The figures which survive the direct attack of his mallet and chisel or his furious brush strokes are not facsimiles of the models before him, but *typoi,* reminding us of Socrates' statement to Kleiton, "The sculptor must represent in his figures the activities of the soul."[5]

Another piece refers to the manner in which the outward image is received into the mind and expands to such an extent that it is transmuted into an inner image, invalidating entirely its former self:

> Mentre c' alla belta, ch' i' uiddi im prima
> Apresso l' alma, che per gli ochi uede,
> l'inmagin dentro crescie, e quella cede
> Quasi uilmente e senza alcuna stima.
>
> (*Dichtungen,* p. 24)

As I draw my soul, which sees through the eyes, closer to beauty as I first saw it, the image therein grows, and the other recedes as though unworthily and without any value.

This sonnet fragment, like the sonnet partially reproduced above, dates from about 1530. The poems with the highest neo-Platonic content were written after Michelangelo had reached his fifties and after the year he met Tommaso Cavalieri. From this period dates a madrigal which holds that the eyes are just as greedy for beauty as the soul is for salvation, sight being the only sense which perceives this beauty, as Ficino made clear: "Si oculus solus agnoscit, solus fruitur" (op. cit., II.ix). Like the soul, the eyes ascend heavenward in their quest:

> Gli ochi mie, uagi delle cose belle,
> E l'alma insieme della suo salute
> Non anno altra uirtute
> C'ascenda al ciel che mirar tucte quelle.

> (*Dichtungen*, p. 201)

My eyes longing for beautiful things together with my soul thirsting for salvation have no other power to ascend to heaven than the contemplation of beautiful things.

The poem borrows for its conclusion the notion in Ficino's *Commentarium in Convivium* (v.iv) that beauty is a splendor which streams down from the highest heavens.

People of perception (*persone accorte*) glimpse through their senses the higher beauty which comes into visible presence from its upper sphere:

> A quel pietoso fonte, onde sian tucti,
> S'assenbra ogni belta, che qua si uede,
> Piu c' altra cosa alle persone accorte,
>    Ne altro saggio abbian ne altri fructi
> Dal cielo in terra; e chi u' ama con fede
> Trascende a Dio e fa dolce la morte.

> (*Dichtungen*, p. 53)

Every beauty which is seen here below by persons of perception resembles more than anything else that celestial source from which we are all come; nor can we on earth have any other foretaste of its beauty or other fruits of heaven; and he who loves you loyally transcends to God and his death is made sweet.

In this sonnet also the Ficinian definition of beauty as a beam from God's visage is thematic.

This unusual visual faculty which is granted to only a happy few (Michelangelo uses such Reformational words as "elect" and "grace" to describe natural artistic endowment)[6] strengthened his proud and personal belief as a craftsman that a gifted artist "has true proportion in his eyes," just as a musician has "true pitch" in his ears ("nè sordo nè cieco"). He takes pride that his eye is so keen that his works, whether architectural elevations or major statues, have been executed without the aid of compasses or rulers or T-squares, an accomplishment of which few can boast. Yet, at the same time he realizes as a Platonist that these geometric measurements which

some like Pacioli have mistakenly called "divine proportion" are not identical with the proportions of divine Ideas, resisting *quadrature* and mathematical tables, which the artist endowed with *intelletto* must "capture" in stone or pigment.

It would seem that a genius capable of discovering preëxistent forms would have little need of the tricks and instruments of the trade. He would scorn the mirrors, plumb lines, and measuring devices of his contemporaries. Dissenting from a Pythagorean tradition and fearful lest it become a manacle or an artistic nostrum, a Michelangelo must deplore the rigid mathematical formulations of the human body established by Vitruvius and continued by Luca Pacioli's *De divina proportione* (1497), Pomponio Gaurico's *De Sculptura* (1504), Vincenzo Poppa's *Trattato della Pittura* (n.d.), and Alberti's thorough tabulation of the exact measurements of the various members of the body. This very precise formulation in *De Statua* was based on the examination of many different models, Alberti admittedly having been inspired by Zeuxis' achieving the proportions of the Crotonian Venus by taking the best features of several virgins. (Actually, Zeuxis was aiming not at striking an average, but at making a composite, as if mindful of the Greek epigram, "Thou hast the eyes of Hera, the hands of Athena, the breasts of the Paphian, the ankles of Thetis.")[7] Michelangelo felt that Dürer's figures lost rather than gained by the German's reliance upon ratios, geometric patterns, reticles, and even lutes.[8] He would renounce quantitative resolutions of form, from the Greeks' *teleon* down to later "golden sections," not because he would disagree that these formulations afforded a pleasing rectangle, but because he felt that the eye unaided might find an equally harmonious ratio. Michelangelo entertained definite convictions about balance, *contrapposto,* and the serpentine line, as Lomazzo tells us, but his only passing interest in numerical ratio was in shaping his bodies as many as eleven *facce* in length, and his pyramidal constructions on a 3:2:1 ratio.[9] He did not use these ratios, however, as guides or checks. Although Michelangelo disapproved of Da Vinci's formulae on proportion, he could only applaud Leonardo's games invented to improve the eyes' ability to judge distances and proportions. In fact, Michelangelo made Piero Soderini the unwilling participant in such an improvised game. The gonfaloniere told the sculptor that the nose of the marble *David* was too long. Concealing some marble dust in his palm, Michelangelo climbed up his ladder and, feigning to work with his hammer and chisel, appeared to reduce the proportions of the offending member. After a while, he solicited another opinion from Soderini, and the latter cried, "I like it much better that way. You have given life to the statue."[10] To Michelangelo, who did not take criticism easily, as we are aware, this proved satisfactorily that still another employer lacked what every person of perception should have: "compasses in the eyes."

At least four texts testify to Michelangelo's belief that a gifted artist carries his compasses in his eyes. In Lomazzo's *Trattato* one reads:

> Onde egli una volta trovandosi a Monte Cavallo in Roma ebbe a dire queste o simili parole: che i pittori e scultori moderni dovrebbero avere la proporzione e le misure negli occhi per poterle mettere in esecuzione: volendo accennare che questa scienza appresso i moderni era perduta rispetto a quelle statue maravigliose degli antichi, come quelle di Fidia e Prassitele collocate ivi in Roma.
>
> (II, 165)

> Whence, finding himself once at Monte Cavallo in Rome, he had more or less the following words to say: that the modern painters and sculptors ought to have proportion and measures right in their eyes, in order to put them into execution: wishing to point out that this science had been lost among the moderns, if compared to those marvelous statues of the classic artists, such as those of Phidias and Praxiteles located there in Rome.

Elsewhere in the *Trattato,* Lomazzo states that Michelangelo measured these statues at Monte Cavallo and learned that "the faces had to be made proportionally larger as the figures were placed higher, so that the work might appear most proportionate to the eye" (I, 45). Such ease in handling foreshortening resulted from the fact that these ancient artists "kept their measures in their eyes."

There is a more succinct quotation in Vasari (VII, 270), who cites Michelangelo as declaring "che bisognava avere le seste negli occhi e non in mano, perchè le mani operano, e l'occhio giudica" ('that it was necessary to keep one's compass in one's eyes and not in the hand, for the hands execute, but the eye judges'). One must depend on the naked eye, even when working in architecture. Thus, Michelangelo is said to have designed his model for the cupola of St. Peter's "sans règles, sans calcul, avec le seul sentiment qui guide un grand artiste."[11] Vasari, so often a mouthpiece of Buonarrotian thought, twice asserts that "the judgment of the eye" is more reliable than compasses or instruments (I, 148, 151).

Lomazzo's *Idea,* echoing Michelangelo's remark about compasses, observes that the Florentine's use of proportions is unusual but admirable: "He gave his figures the proportion of Saturn, making the head and feet small and the hands long, composing the members with great accuracy (*ragione*) and forming them with great breadth; the contours are wondrous, very great due to the depths of the muscles and preserving the order of the design and of the anatomy, regarding which it is

written that he used to say that proportion should be in men's eyes so that they might know directly how to judge what they see."[12] Finally, in Lomazzo's *Trattato,* Michelangelo is quoted as stating that "mathematics, geometry, and perspective are to no avail unless the eye is accurate to begin with and trained in seeing." He adds that however much the eye may practise lengthily with these perspectives, "only when it can see without the aid of angles, lines, or distances any longer can it become apt and cause the hand to execute on the figure all that is desired and leave nothing to be hoped for by way of perspective" (II, 36).

Michelangelo's justifiable reliance on his trained eye is documented by none other than Castelvetro. A few years before there had been excavated the statue of a river god with beard broken and missing, although the tip remained fixed on the chest. No one could imagine how the beard must have looked in its original state. Michelangelo, whose own Fiumi were to be bearded,[13] requested some clay and executed the missing beard, knotting and twisting it so that it fitted exactly onto the remnant tip. All marveled, concludes Castelvetro, at his ability to grasp total basic form without need of instruments to assist him in visualizing the missing portion.[14]

A further evidence of Michelangelo's mistrust of mathematical praxis to guarantee accuracy of proportion is the mere fact that, among the drafts and outlines which have come down to us, there are just two figures whose major proportions are plotted out in *braccia* by two or three horizontal and vertical lines. These are two studies of a river god for the Medici Tombs, now in the British Museum (Berenson, 1491).

It is understandable from all this if an occasional painted or sculptured figure of Michelangelo's is out of proportion. Milton Nahm complains that "Michelangelo actually painted some of the stooping figures in his compositions as much as twelve 'heads' in height."[15] Warren Cheney observes that the *Sibilla Libica*'s right thigh is nearly one-third longer than her left and that the right leg of the *Aurora* is 15 percent longer than the left.[16] In the face of such charges, Michelangelo the Platonist could respond that a work could have a proportion sufficient to itself and its own needs, transcending such instrumental measurements as in Dürer's *Proportionslehre.* This he definitely felt in the case of the *Madonna della Febbre,* for example, where the cadaver of Christ in the Virgin's lap is unnaturally small, yet pleasing to the spectator. Warren Cheney calls this quality "creative proportion" and views it as a characteristic by which Michelangelo anticipates modern sculptors. Whether or not one agrees with Cheney, the proportions of Christ and the Virgin are not those of the models, but, as we have said above, of *typoi* existing in the *intelletto.*

Bellori and Danti echoed the language of Michelangelo. Bellori, defining his "Idea," notes that this Idea "measured by the compass of the *Intelletto* becomes the measure of the hand."[17] Vincenzo Danti lauds the efficacy of "la misura intellettuale" in painting and sculpture, although not in architecture—a timid reservation! In his *Trattato delle perfette proporzioni* he claimed for Michelangelo the discovery of the authentic proportions of the human body, thanks not only to long study of anatomy but equally to this "intellectual vision." He even goes so far as to posit replacement of "material compasses" by "compasses of judgment" as the ultimate purpose of striving for perfect proportions.[18]

Whereas the vision of competent artists is unfailingly accurate, incompetents require gadgets to capture exact proportions. Even with such aids and such experiments in optics as Leonardo's, the accuracy of their vision is not guaranteed. There are, as any neo-Platonist worth his salt could tell you, an inner and an exterior vision. As Ficino among others noted, there is an inner or higher vision which is part of man's *anima prima* and which Plotinus had described as "another vision to be awakened within you, a vision, the birthright of all, which few turn to use" (*Enneads* I.vi.9). One of the faculties of the Lower Soul, the *anima secunda,* is the exterior vision. This very terminology is used by Michelangelo in the *Dialogos em Roma* when he is criticising Flemish painting.[19] It denotes a vision which cannot discern the true Idea through the veil of matter, a vision which cannot perceive unity and form behind the obvious and apparent, even with the help of such externals as mirrors or reticles. And—this was important to Michelangelo—a vision which is satisfied with bright colors. Writing in his *De' veri precetti della Pittura* (Ravenna, 1586), Armenini managed to sound very much like Michelangelo himself instructing a young garzone in the art of painting: "One must not follow merely the judgment of the exterior eye, which judgment can be easily dazzled by the charms of a variety of colors; and it would be all too easy to judge the works of this art if one followed only this judgment; but one must have recourse to the eye of the *intelletto,* which eye, illumined by the requisite rules recognizes the True in all things" (p. 23). Pico and Ficino held that the Intellect sees "with an incorporeal eye" and "calls itself away not only from the body, but also from the senses and the imagination"; it thus transcends and becomes a "tool of the divine."[20]

Is it any wonder that we find such severe condemnations of the senses in Michelangelo's written works (e.g., "Voglia sfrenata el senso è, non amore, che l'alma uccide"),[21] with his neo-Platonic and his Christian principles marshaled against them? Persuaded that *persone accorte* were few and far between, he developed an Horatian scorn for the great majority. He was sure that most of the public admitted to see his paintings in the Sistine Chapel would not understand their excellence or discern their beauty—even those confreres who sat for hours attentively copying his figures until he was moved to sarcasm. As George Santayana once claimed, "There are portentous works, like those of Michelangelo and Tintoretto, to which everyone will assign a high rank in the history of art; but the interest and wonder which they arouse may rarely, and only in some persons, pass into a true glimpse of the beautiful."[22]

Leon Battista Alberti compounded two Platonic images to make of a winged eye his personal emblem. Michelangelo might have done likewise. One of his poems, perhaps an echo of a pseudo-Platonic epigram, dramatizes especially the crucial function of the eye in taking in beauty through an "active contemplation," a beauty which grows (*cresce*) and occupies the entire being:

> fa' del mie corpo tucto un' ochio solo;
> nè fie poi parte in me che non ti goda!
>
> (*Dichtungen,* p. 118)[23]

> Make of my entire body one single eye, nor let there
> be then any part of me not taking pleasure in thee!

Ficino (v.iii) anticipated Michelangelo in recognizing that some beauties are too overpowering to be taken in by "the small pupil of the eye": "quo enim pacto caelum, ut ita loquar, totum parva oculi pupilla caperetur. . . . ?"

The preceding paragraphs treat of the relationship between the eye and the hand, separate and yet interdependent, like the Eye-Principle and Hand-Principle which Plotinus saw included within the Intellect-Principle.[24] Michelangelo held definite ideas also regarding the relationship between the brain (mind) and the hand. One day Benedetto Varchi paid him one of those extravagant compliments to which the academician was addicted, "Signor Buonarroti, you have the brain of a Jove." The sculptor, for so his reply characterized him at the moment, responded, "Si vuole il martello di Vulcano per farne uscire qualche cosa" ('But Vulcan's hammer is required to make something come out of it').[25] This incident serves to introduce us to Michelangelo's conviction that between the conceptions of the mind and the realizations of the hand, there is, as the Italian phrases it, "the whole sea."

The original inspiration comes to the mind (representing nature), and the hand (representing art) may or may not be qualified to execute it. Each has to perform under optimum conditions. In 1542 Michelangelo wrote to an unknown prelate at the court of Paul III, complaining of his difficulties with the Duke of Urbino, "Io rispondo che si dipinge col ciervello et non con le mani" ('I reply that one paints with the brain and not [merely] with the hands').[26] One must have a free mind to work, for *mens agitat molem.* This genius who was prey to constant tribulations, real or imagined, claimed that he could not create when troubled, that pressures were a curb and not a spur. This genius in whose mind thanatophobia dwelled like a leitmotiv asserted in a poem that if he set to thinking upon death, "both art and genius vanish" (hand and mind fail to respond) and he could create nothing.[27] The immediacy of the correlation between hand and mind is stated in a letter to Fattucci: "chè e' non si può lavorare con le mani una cosa, e col ciervello una altra, e massimo di marmo" ('for one cannot shape one thing with one's hands, and another with one's brain, especially in marble').[28]

Michelangelo was scarcely flattered or pleased by the well-intended but ingenuous strophe addressed to him by Fausto Sabeo, with its line, "Fingimus, ingenio namque ego, tuque manu."[29] Not only was the comparison audacious, but revealed a basic misunderstanding of the artist's intellectual independence. Michelangelo would deny that he was a mere hand-worker as vehemently as he denied that he was a shopkeeping artist. He and his confreres were bent intensely upon raising the popular conception of painting and sculpture as a trade identifiable with guilds and shops not only to the level of a profession, but also, as Paolo Pino suggested, to the status of a liberal art and branch of philosophy.[30] For this reason, Leonardo's statement that "painting is a mental thing," which appears at first sight like a trivial little jotting, was a tenet, a program, and a challenge to be taken with high seriousness.

More consonant with Michelangelo's taste and more laudatory than Sabeo's line was the verse addressed to him by his disciple Bronzino, "I consecrated to you my hand and my *intelletto*."[31]

This insistence on the mental phase of painting and sculpturing implied a demand for more freedom of conception and ideation on the part of the artists, the freedom proclaimed in those verses of Horace ("Pictoribus atque poetis, *etc.*,") which Michelangelo quoted from memory to Diego Zapata in the *Dialogos em Roma*.[32]

The loftier the conception of which the *intelletto* is capable, the greater the challenge to the hand. Remembering the Horatian counsel to set a goal commensurate with one's powers ("Sumite materiam vestris aequam viribus"),[33] Michelangelo draws therefrom a distinction between the competent and the incompetent artist. The able painter is timid about essaying even that type of painting which he knows best, whereas an ignorant dauber audaciously loads his canvas with subjects and effects of which his hand has not mastered the technique: "And hereby one recognizes the wisdom of a great man, in the fear with which he does the thing which he understands the best and, conversely, the ignorance of others in the audacious temerity with which they

encumber pictures with what they cannot really learn to do."[34] Michelangelo more than once felt unable to match with technique the tremendous concepts of which his intellect was capable. Such a concept was his colossus to be sculptured from a mountain top at Carrara, a project which remained a velleity. Both Condivi and Vasari admit that he keenly sensed and resented this disparity between mind and hand, about which Horace cautioned, a disparity he felt increasingly tragically during the final lusters of his long life when he kept chiseling even though "he could hardly hold up his head" (Don Miniato Pitti). In a late letter to his nephew Lionardo, he cried, "La mano non mi serve" ('My hand serves me not').

> CONDIVI: He is also endowed with a most forceful imaginative power; the result of this is that he has scarcely ever been satisfied with his creations and has belittled them; it has not seemed to him that his hand has succeeded in executing that Idea which he conceived within himself.[35]
>
> VASARI: He had such a powerful and perfect imaginative faculty that the subjects which presented themselves to his intellect were such that, being unable to express with his hands so great and terrible concepts, he often abandoned his works and even destroyed many of them.
>
> (VII, 270)

These passages show the tragic implications of the famous fourth line in his sonnet **"Non ha l'ottimo artista alcun concetto,"** where Michelangelo stated that there was no unfulfillment between the conceptions of a great artist and his realizations in stone, provided that the hand is really capable of obeying the mind:

> Non ha l'ottimo artista alcun concetto,
> Ch' un marmo solo in se non circoscriua
> Col suo souerchio, et solo à quello arriua
> La man, che ubbidisce all' intelletto.
>
> (*Dichtungen*, p. 89)

> The best artist has no concept which some single marble may not enclose within its mass, but only the hand which obeys the *intelletto* can accomplish that.

In his essay on Corot, Paul Valéry writes that Michelangelo's first two lines describe that happy moment when there is no longer any discrepancy between the intentions and the means of the competent artist. They describe an intimate correspondence between the master's thought and material, "remarquable par une réciprocité dont ceux qui ne l'ont pas éprouvée ne peuvent imaginer l'existence." Vincenzo Danti, who separated sculpture into three components (*intelletto, mano, materia*) regretted that a poor marble could nullify this correspondence,[36] a fact only too familiar to Buonarroti, who complained that his marbles were too often blemished by *peli* (cracks), *rotture* (breaks), and *isforzature* (strains). Valéry further calls these two verses the formula of Michelangelo's sovereign ambition. Sometimes, even despite all his efforts, the conceptions resisted translation by mind and hand into even sketches or models, that stage which Michelangelo called the "first birth of the concept."

Michelangelo supplies us with two further opinions regarding this relationship between intellect and hand, which constitute a "doppio valor." His sonnet, **"Se ben concietto à la diuina parte"** suggested that if the *intelletto* has captured aright the divinely implanted form in the ὕλη, then a lesser effort of art (the hand) is required: "e non è forza d'arte" (*Dichtungen*, p. 228). He observes that poor painters will never be tormented by the failure of their hands to carry out their conceptions. The reason? Poor painters cannot visualize the Idea through their limited exterior vision; imperfect conceptions can easily be rendered by imperfect hands: "o mao pintor não pode nem sabe imaginar nem deseja de fazer boa pintura na sua Idea" ('the poor painter is neither able nor knows how to imagine, nor even desires to do good painting according to its Idea').[37] The poor results will be due alike to a weak hand and a weak *immaginativa*.

If one gives credence to Michelangelo's writings, the artist knew that he was one of the elect granted the grace of *intelletto,* that God was the donor of this faculty, and he knew the manner in which the divine intellect guided the artist's hand:

> Se 'l mie rozzo martello i duri sassi
> Forma d'uman aspecto or questo or quello,
> Dal ministro, che 'l guida iscorgie e tiello
> Prendendo il moto, ua con gli altrui passi.

> (*Dichtungen,* p. 106)

He knew these things as faithfully as he had known his catechism as a child. Both as one of the world's most self-conscious artists and as a Renaissance neo-Platonist, he would disagree emphatically with nineteenth-century theories of spontaneous and unguided creativeness.

To conclude, inner vision and the *intelletto* both set the degree of challenge offered to the hand. Both are the property of a restricted elect of gifted artists. Both are cognitive faculties which attest divinity. Both represent nature in contrast to the hand, which represents art. They could never be in conflict, but neither are they ever identified. True to the Plotinian tradition, Michelangelo keeps the Eye-Principle distinct from the Intellect-Principle.

### Notes

1. Sappho, *Oxyrhynchus Papyri,* xv, 1922, No. 1787.

2. Carl Frey, *Dichtungen des Michelagniolo Buonarroti* (Berlin, 1897), p. 196.

3. *Commentarium in Convivium* v.xiii.

4. *Commentarium in Convivium* vi.vi.

5. Xenophon, *Memorabilia,* Loeb ed., p. 237.

6. Note also the notion of grace in the verses of our second paragraph.

7. *Anthologia Palatina,* 5.94.

8. Ascanio Condivi, *Vita di Michelangelo,* lii.

9. *Trattato della Pittura* (Rome, 1844), I, 34-35; ii, 97.

10. Vasari, *Le Vite de' piu eccellenti pittori, scultori, ed architettori* (Florence, 1878-85), vii, 156.

11. G. K. Loukomski, *Les Sangallo* (Paris, 1934), p. 88.

12. *Idea del tempio della Pittura* (Milan, 1590), p. 44.

13. De Tolnay, *The Medici Chapel* (Princeton, 1948), plate 77.

14. Lodovico Castelvetro, *Poetica* (Basilea, 1576), pp. 214 f.

15. *Aesthetic Experience and its Presuppositions* (New York, 1946), p. 155.

16. "What Sculptors have learned from Michelangelo," *London Studio,* Jan. 1940, pp. 2-5.

17. Reproduced in E. Panofsky, *Idea* (Leipzig, 1924), p. 131.

18. *Primo libro del trattato delle perfette proporzioni* (Perugia, 1830), pp. 44, 52.

19. De Hollanda, *Da Pintura antigua* (Porto, 1930), p. 189.

20. E. Panofsky, *Studies in Iconology* (New York, 1939), p. 140.

21. *Dichtungen,* p. 83.

22. *Philosophical Review,* xxxiv (May 1925), 288.

23. Here the admirer becomes the artist speaking, as noted by Valerio Mariani, *La Poesia di Michelangelo* (Rome, 1941), p. 3.

24. Plotinus, *Enneads* v.ix.6.

25. Vasari, vii, 270.

26. Gaetano Milanesi, *Le Lettere di Michelangelo* (Florence, 1875), p. 489.

27. *Dichtungen,* p. 235.

28. Milanesi, *Lettere,* p. 450.

29. In James Hutton, *The Greek Anthology in Italy* (Ithaca, 1935), p. 213.

30. *Dialogo di Pittura* (Venice, 1946), p. 92.

31. In Giovanni Papini, *Vita di Michelangiolo* (Milan, 1949), p. 583.

32. De Hollanda, *Da Pintura antigua*, p. 232.

33. *Ars poetica*, vv. 38-39.

34. De Hollanda, p. 240.

35. Condivi, *Vita* (Pisa, 1823), p. 83.

36. *Il primo libro del trattato*, p. 87.

37. De Hollanda, p. 234.

## Robert J. Clements (essay date April 1965)

SOURCE: Clements, Robert J. "Prayer and Confession in Michelangelo's Poetry." *Studies in Philology* 62, no. 2 (April 1965): 101-10.

[*In the following essay, Clements notes that Michelangelo often intermingled prayer and confession in his poetry.*]

Michelangelo composed two, and possibly three, prayers which have come down to us. He was a firm believer in prayer, as we know. Echoing a Petrarchan epistle of 1360, he admitted in a letter complaining of his painful gallstones that he had more confidence in prayer than in medicine. When embarked on a new commission he would pray for its successful outcome and even urged that his father pray likewise. Describing the simple husbandman in his idyll on the Golden Age, Michelangelo alleges: "Onora e ama e teme e prega Dio."[1] His artist's creative urge could thus naturally find an outlet in prayer.

A minimal orison in his handwriting is a surprising addition to a pen sketch of torsoes: "Deus in nomine tuo salvum me fac!" (G [Girardi edition] App. 9). The youthful hand would indicate the early age at which Michelangelo feared for his salvation. A jubilant poem-prayer or paean of utter simplicity from 1505-06 reads: "Laudate paruoli / el Signiore nostro, / laudate sempre!" (G App. 15). Quaint and curious—an opportunity missed by those romanticising painters who filled the Casa Buonarotti with their evocations of the master—is the picture of the thirty-year old artist exhorting youngsters to prayer.

Finally there is the longer prayer found among his autographs, not of his handwriting but with some of his jottings accompanying it. Guasti, who reproduced it, did not claim that it was of Michelangelo's composition, but the spirit of this *Orazione* corresponds closely to the religious effusions among his late poetry:

O, padre altissimo, che per tua benignità mi facesti christiano, solo per darmi lo regno tuo; di nulla l'anima mia creasti, e incarcerasti quella nel misero mio corpo; donami gratia, che tutto quanto il tempo che io starò in questa carcere inimica dell'anima mia, nella quale tu solo mi tieni, io ti laudi; perche laudandoti tu mi darai gratia di beneficare i proximi mia, et di fare bene in particolare all'inimica mia, et quelli sempre a te racomandare. Concedami gratia ancora, sanctissimo Dio, che havendo a patire passione corporale, che io conosca che quelle non offendano l'anima mia; rammentandomi del tuo Figlio sanctissimo, che per l'humana salute morì tanto vituperosamente: e per questo mi consolerò, et sempre lauderò il tuo sancto nome. Amen.[2]

This poem is typical not only of Michelangelo's vocabulary and syntax and spelling but of his innermost thoughts: his fixation with the Crucifixion,[3] his fear for his own carnal sins ("Vivo al peccato, a me morendo vivo"),[4] and even his attempts to pardon his enemies, real and imagined ("Un generoso, alter e nobil core / Perdon' e porta a chi l'offend'amore")[5].

One of Michelangelo's incomplete sonnets is a hymn of praise which he tentatively wishes to express as a prayer:

Ben sarien dolce le preghiere mie,
se virtù mi prestassi da pregarte:
nel mio fragil terren non è già parte
da frutto buon, che da sé nato sie.
    Tu sol se' seme d'opre caste e pie,
che là germuglian, dove ne fa' parte;
nessun propio valor può seguitarte,
se non gli mostri le tuo sante vie.

(G 292)

It is difficult to separate the elements of prayer and those of confession in Michelangelo's *Rime,* for avowals of moral inadequacy are then accompanied by requests for salvation. The importance of confession as a sacramental rite is demonstrated by two letters on the deaths respectively of his brothers Giovansimone and Gismondo; he inquired immediately in each case whether the brother had died "confesso." None could dispense with the need of prayer and few with the need for confession. Man is born in sin. So Michelangelo was, as was his father before him (G 66). He retains free will, however. We can assume that as a young man Michelangelo went occasionally to confession, that as an older man he found poetry the medium for his *confiteor.* Even as architect and artist he was constantly providing the means for this sacramental act to be carried out. Whether meditating on floor plans for St. Peter's or the Gesù (which he did not finally execute) or contemplating the decoration of a little chapel in the country,[6] the atmosphere for prayer and the space for confession were on his mind.

In his later years, in fact, he developed a mystical or personal relationship with Christ and God which we have characterized as baroque.[7] This sense of immediate proximity, symbolized by the solicitous nearness of Nicodemus to Christ in the Florentine *Deposizione,* eventually did away with the necessity of intermediaries. Even if priests themselves shrived one another in the confessional, Michelangelo elected to purge himself in his poetry and art. Just as artists begin to feel a familiarity with their models, Michelangelo came to know Christ. Poems, mere *goffagini* when treating of profane topics, became a serious thing when they conveyed his religious passion. Sufficiently serious to become the language of the *culpa.*

We have seen evidence of a fear of the day of wrath already in the brief poem from 1505-6. As early as 1532-33 we encounter the first real confessional outpouring to Christ, written in pale ink on the back of a letter from Figiovanni. The thoughts are anything but pale. The judgement of Christ on the Cross (*legnio*) and his unworthiness occupy his thoughts, a reminder swelling on a crescendo which will become deafening during his long span of life. If the following piece were from late 1533 it could allude to his passion for Febo di Poggio, but if it coincides with his first contacts with Tommaso Cavalieri, Michelangelo's sin was rather that of intention than commission. Although he partakes of the consequences of Original Sin, his own fall from grace causes him great anxiety:

> Forse perché d'altrui pietà mi vegna,
> perché dell'altrui colpe più non rida,
> nel mie propio valor, senz'altra guida,
> caduta è l'alma che fu già sì degna.
> Né so qual militar sott'altra insegna
> non che da vincer, da campar più fida,
> sie che 'l tumulto dell'avverse strida
> non pèra, ove 'l poter tuo non sostegna.
>
> (G 66)

Michelangelo's interest in secondary causes (so obvious in Donato Giannotti's *Dialogi*)[8] leads him to look for indirect justifications even for sin; his sins were necessary to teach him greater humanity and humility:

> O carne, o sangue, o legnio, o doglia strema,
> giusto per vo' si facci el mie peccato,
> di ch'i' pur nacqui e tal fu 'l padre mio.
> Tu sol se' buon; la tuo pietà suprema
> soccorra al mie preditto iniquo stato,
> sì presso a morte e sì lontan da Dio.
>
> (G 66)

Still and always the sense of imminent death, coupled with a feeling of unworthiness.

Late in life he shows gratitude for the succour and guidance which God has granted him, and hopes for its intensified continuance as his need for it is doubled:

> Di giorno in giorno insin da' mie prim'anni,
> Signor, soccorso tu mi fusti e guida,

onde l'anima mia ancor si fida
di doppia aita ne' mie doppi affanni.

> (G 287)

Sometimes Michelangelo's guilt feelings are based on some vague and imprecise offense, which he is unable or unwilling to recall. An example is his confessional poem (ca. 1555) petitioning the Redeemer to forgive a vaguely-remembered sin which must be known to Christ:

> L'alma inquieta e confusa in sé non truova
> altra cagion c'alcun grave peccato
> mal conosciuto, onde non è celato
> all'immensa pietà c'a' miser giova.
>
> I' parlo a te, Signor, c'ogni mie pruova
> fuor del tuo sangue non fa l'uom beato:
> miserere di me, da ch'io son nato
> a la tuo legge; e non fie cosa nuova.
>
> (G 280)

The last four words, which have been variously interpreted and translated, imply "it's the same old story," and are an acknowledgement that the artist has worriedly been petitioning forgiveness for over half a century. Artistically, they are an admission that the old poet has long abused this same motif. This same *Schuldcomplex* disturbs him in a somewhat later poem:

> Penso e ben so c'alcuna colpa preme,
> occulta a me, lo spirto in gran martire;
> privo dal senso e dal suo propio ardire
> il cor di pace, e 'l desir d'ogni speme.
>
> (G 291)

Here the poet turns to Divine Love to save him through its intercession.

The most guilt-ridden verses Michelangelo ever wrote are of a tremendous poignancy, and so meaningful that we have already mentioned the incipit above:

> Vivo al peccato, a me morendo vivo;
> vita già mia non son, ma del peccato:
> mie ben dal ciel, mie mal da me m'è dato,
> dal mie sciolto voler, di ch'io son privo.
>
> (G 32)

At times the confessional poem is so insistent as to become demanding, an imprecation. One of the most pitiful of Michelangelo's sonnets is the later **"Vorrei voler, Signor, quel ch'io non voglio,"** in which he complains bitterly of the veil of ice which God has permitted to intervene between them. The artist, who as iconographer saw Doubt as an allegorical figure "armato e zoppo,"[9] wants no more of it. The two tercets reach a paroxysm of emotion:

> Squarcia 'l vel tu, Signor, rompi quel muro
> che con la suo durezza ne ritarda
> il sol della tuo luce, al mondo spenta!
>
> (G 87)

This piece, as has not been hitherto noted, echoes similar demands for reassurance in the poetry of Vittoria Colonna:

> Deh squarci omai la man piagata il velo
> Che 'n questo cieco error, ecc.

or

> Spezza dell'ignoranza il grosso muro . . . !¹⁰

The poor Marchioness, persecuted for her religious beliefs, had even greater reason for wishing assurances from God that she was in the right. Both poets are longing for the inner peace and assurance of salvation sought also by Juan de Valdés, who influenced the Marchioness during her Neapolitan-Ischian days. Indeed, the French-Romanian scholar Façon found a great spiritual affinity between the **Rime** of Michelangelo and the *Alfabeto Cristiano* of Valdés, a work condemned by the Pope.¹¹ There is also an affinity of course with Petrarch, Michelangelo's idol, who had sought long to renounce the flesh and whose imprecation to the Virgin for divine intercession parallelled Michelangelo's appeals to Christ.

Prayer need not always be confession or petition. It may be thanksgiving. The following two tercets, not to be confused with amorous sentiments expressed to some *beatrics,* attain one of the highest points of the canzoniere:

> In me la morte, in te la vita mia;
> tu distingui e concedi e parti el tempo;
> quante vuo', breve e lungo è 'l viver mio.
>     Felice son nella tuo cortesia.
> Beata l'alma, ove non corre tempo,
> per te s'è fatta a contemplare Dio.

> (G 37)

Throughout the confessional poetry there is, as we have seen, a constant awareness of the error of the poet's ways. "I' conosco e' mie' danni e 'l vero intendo" (G 43). Sometimes, however, his prayers will place some of the responsibilities on God Himself. Such hints of a shrugging despair—and one sampling follows—come during his later years.

> Gl'infiniti pensier mie d'error pieni,
> negli ultim'anni della vita mia,
> ristringer si dovrien 'n un sol che sia
> guida agli etterni suo giorni sereni.
>     Ma che poss'io, Signor, s'a me non vieni
> coll'usata ineffabil cortesia?

> (G 286)

As God the Father was less a subject of Michangelo's art than was Christ, similarly Christ is the recipient of more of these confessional and prayerful poems than was God. The **Rime** show that the image of the *Christus Judex* loomed large in Michelangelo's vision since the turn of the century. There are many hints in the poetry which convince us that the tremendous task of painting the *Last Judgement* was one he knew he must inevitably undertake. The fact that the mature artist painted every inch of the *Judgement,* with the aid of only a paint-mixer, must be accepted as indication perhaps akin to Loyola's flagellation, of a penance and a petition for grace and "cortesia." The largest fresco in Rome centers upon the Christ to whom his poems flow, and he was too scrupulous to paint that Christ as other than austere. Indeed, the anger of his *Christus Judex* is the proof that in 1534 Michelangelo was by no means sure that his poetic petitions would be granted. It was while pausing from the labours of painting his pessimistic fresco of humanity that Michelangelo pondered (1534-36) man's fate and wrote: "allor conosco bene / l'errore e 'l danno dell'umana gente" (G 132). It was at that time that he recognized "'l vecchio e dolce errore, / nel qual chi troppo vive / l'anima 'ncide e nulla al corpo giova" (G 133), then that he meditated on the "etterni danni dell'alma" (G 135), on man's "dura sorte" (G 136). The reclothing of man's soul on Judgement Day was then naturally on his mind:

> Se l'alma al fin ritorna
> nella suo dolce e desïata spoglia,
> o danni o salvi il ciel, come si crede. . . .

> (G 140)

Indeed, the love poetry of the years 1534-39 is balanced by fleeting recollections of the solemn and august theme which was occupying his work days. The Last Judgement and the reclothing of souls is also a principal theme when Michelangelo is obliged a few years later to write fifty epitaphs on the death of Cecchino.

The long-suffering and righteous Christ invades the late "trembling hand" sonnets, of which the most imposing is the "Non fur men lieti che turbati e tristi." Although no poem mentions the act of the *Deposizione,* this powerful sonnet-hymn to the Redeemer probably dating from this stage of his life (1555-1560) seems to reveal to us the feelings of the artist looking down with consummate commiseration upon the Saviour's august face. Of all the poetry which comments directly upon Michelangelo's concern for Christ's shedding his blood for man (G 280, 289, 290, 294, 302), none is a finer verbal expression of the visible *sympatheia* than this piece, three-planed in vision like a baroque composition:

> Non fur men lieti che turbati e tristi
> che tu patissi, e non già lor, la morte,
> gli spirti eletti, onde le chiuse porte
> del ciel, di terra a l'uom col sangue apristi.
>     Lieti, poiché, creato, il redemisti
> dal primo error di suo misera sorte;
> tristi, a sentir c'a la pena aspra e forte,

servo de' servi in croce divenisti.
    Onde a chi fusti, il ciel ne diè tal segno
che scurò gli occhi suoi, la terra aperse,
tremorno i monti e torbide fur l'acque.
    Tolse i gran Padri al tenebroso regno,
gli angeli brutti in più doglia sommerse;
godé sol l'uom, c'al battesmo rinacque.

(G 298)

This piece parallels a sonnet to the Redeemer of Vittoria Colonna: **"Gli angeli eletti al gran bene infinito."**[12]

It also carries Dantean echoes, for when the Trecento poet reflects on the Crucifixion he recalls:

Però d'un atto uscir cose diverse;
che a Dio ed ai Giudei piacque una morte:
per lei tremò la terra e il ciel s'aperse.

The lines are found in *Paradiso,* VII, 46-48.

This magnificent assurance to Christ that his sacrifice will not prove vain is closer to the spirit of Michelangelo-Nicodemo than are the many poems where Michelangelo speaks to the divinity concerning his own salvation. Or, if his own redemption is so everpresent in his mind at this moment of extreme pity, even more compelling is his realisation of the enormity of Christ's mortification and sacrifice to make that salvation possible:

Ma pur par nel tuo sangue si comprenda,
se per noi par non ebbe il tuo martire,
senza misura sien tuo cari doni.

(G 294)

Of this lofty inspiration is another hymn to the wounded and grieving Saviour. Except for one tercet, it is less reminiscent of the *Christus Judex* than of the artist's sketches of the stations of Christ's Passion and the Pietàs:

    Scarco d'un'importuna e greve salma,
Signor mie caro, e dal mondo disciolto,
qual fragil legno a te stanco rivolto
da l'orribil procella in dolce calma.
    Le spine e' chiodi e l'una e l'altra palma
col tuo benigno umil pietoso volto,
promettton grazia di pentirsi molto,
e speme di salute a la trist'alma. . . .
    Tuo sangue sol mie colpe lavi e tocchi,
e più abondi, quant'i' son più vecchio,
di pronta aita e di perdono intero.

(G 290)

This poet, who once objected symptomatically that he was "lapidated every day as though he had crucified Christ," achieved in these lines a closeness to his divine confessor which he could have never achieved through a priest. Here again the crucifixion is recalled, including

the nails which are absent from Haman's crucifixion present on the British Museum drawing of the Crucifixion presented to Vittoria Colonna. In the verses quoted above Michelangelo seems to be thinking of all the Christs he had drawn, painted, or sculptured, except that of the Day of Wrath. However, the first tercet is an intrusive outcry against the upraised arm of the *Christus Judex*:

    Nor mirin co' iustizia i tuo sant'occhi
il mie passato, e 'l gastigato orecchio;
non tenda a quello il tuo braccio severo.

(G 290)

Signor, nell'ore estreme,
stendi ver' me le tuo pietose braccia,
tomm'a me stesso e famm'un che ti piaccia.

(G 161)

In his spiritual drought Michelangelo prays for the "rain" of grace. How impossible it was for Michelangelo's contemporaries—the Aretinos, the Gilio da Fabrianos, the Pope Pauls, and all the others who criticised it at one stage or another—to fathom the deep almost convulsive personal meaning of the *Giudizio*! The *Rime* which held the secret were at that point scattered on random sheets, on folios of sketches and designs. Michelangelo's exclusive interest in religious themes of art was not merely the product of his working as artist-laureate of the Church of Peter, as a Tolstoy would claim, but grew out of his anguished conviction that during his unfortunately prolonged life, greater pains and efforts were necessary to offset the increasing obstacles and deterrents to his own salvation. When Pope Paul complained about the nudities on the *Giudizio,* Michelangelo replied that the Pope's *Last Judgement* could be easily arranged ("si puo facilmente acconciare"). His own personal final judgment, he knew, would not be that easily arranged.

### Notes

1. Michelangiolo Buonarroti, *Le Rime,* edited by Enzo Noè Girardi (Laterza, 1960), p. 36. Hereafter, the letter G will identify the number of the poem assigned to it in the Girardi edition.

2. Included in the Guasti edition of the *Rime* (Florence, 1863), p. xl.

3. This fixation is more apparent from the *Rime,* from the drawings, and from the models than from completed sculpture or painting, of course.

4. *Rime,* Girardi edition, p. 17.

5. *Ibid.,* p. 80.

6. Cardinal Aldiosi of Pavia requested Michelangelo on 3 May, 1510, to undertake a small canvas of John the Baptist for a little chapel at La Magliana. See H. Thode, *Michelangelo* (Berlin, 1912) I, 352.

7. See R. J. Clements, "Michelangelo as a Baroque Poet," *PMLA,* LXXVI (1961), 182-192.

8. Donato Giannotti, *Dialogi* (Florence, 1939), especially, pp. 91 ff.

9. *Rime,* Girardi edition, p. 36.

10. See Vittoria Colonna, *Le Rime* (Rome, 1840) Appendix, pp. 347 and 214.

11. See N. Façon, *Michelangelo Poet* (Budapest, 1939), passim.

12. Vittoria Colonna, *Le Rime, ed. cit.,* p. 227.

## Robert J. Clements (essay date 1965)

SOURCE: Clements, Robert J. "Art as Thematic in the Poetry." In *The Poetry of Michelangelo,* pp. 60-88. New York: New York University Press, 1965.

[*In the following essay from his full-length study of Michelangelo's verse, Clements surveys the major themes of the poems and emphasizes Michelangelo's preoccupation with the depiction of beauty, the role of the artist, and the tension between pride and humbleness.*]

Michelangelo's major work of art was himself. Living in an age when man, as Burckhardt reminds us, tried to make a work of art of everything, including the state itself, our artist tried to shape himself with the same care and discipline he used in giving form to the *hyle* of art. None of his works is more magnificent than his own head, translated into bronze from the death mask by the worthy and faithful Daniele da Volterra. God, as Michelangelo declared, was the master sculptor behind him, guiding his hammer. Buonarroti was aware that the materials present in his own poor body were defective, making it less adaptable to a great work of art. He complained . . . of at least eleven illnesses.[1] Recent scholarship has found him the victim of the "mal francese,"[2] which the French called "la maladie italienne." As he admitted in a letter to Bartolommeo Angiolini as early as 1523, Michelangelo was "in bad shape, for if I work one day I have to rest four days" (CCCLXXVIII). Sometimes he felt that his talents were meager and that he was indeed a poor specimen of art. Berni's *capitolo* serves as *praetextum* for his admission:

> So I am yet in the number of those
> Whom some worthless and clumsy painter
> Has eked out with his brushes and paintpots.
>
> (G 85)

Thus, when he refers to his own *turpissime* paintings (G 79) which he offers to Vittoria Colonna, he could perforce be including himself.

> He will try, however, to make a better creation of himself:
> To make an actual man into a good painting

This concept of Michelangelo himself as a work of art is brilliantly exploited in Rilke's tale "Von Einem der die Steine belaüscht,"[3] as well as in Meyer's "In der Sistina," where Michelangelo cries, "Bildhauer Gott, schlag zu! Ich bin der Stein."

The notion that one depicts himself in one's art is occasionally found in the *Rime.* . . . It was an idea which Michelangelo may have heard or read from Savonarola, or even Leonardo: "It is in one's nature to paint oneself / and in every work make one's mood manifest." His madrigal (G [Girardi edition] 173) to the Marchioness of Pescara bears the thesis that an artist paints himself—his subjective self—even into his portraits of others. If the artist is happy or sad, his subject will share this mood:

> Thus each would benefit thereby,
> To paint her with light heart and dry eyes,
> She would be made beautiful, nor should I be made ugly.
>
> (G 168)

Attempting a synthesis of his two greatest current loves, sculpture and Vittoria Colonna, Michelangelo compares himself to a *concetto,* an art form, which is brought into full realisation through the working of love. The manner in which the lady purges him of his baser nature is analogous to the paring away of the excess of a figure lodged in marble.

> As when, O lady mine,
> With chisell'd touch
> The stone unhewn and cold
> Becomes a living mold,
> The more the marble wastes,
> The more the statue grows;
> So, if the working of my soul be such
> That good is but evolved
> By Time's dread blows,
> The vile shell, day by day,
> Falls like superfluous flesh away.
> Oh! take whatever bonds my spirit knows,
> For will and power inert within me stay.
>
> (G 152) (Mrs. Henry Roscoe)

Thus, as Panofsky has also observed, the katharsis accomplished by a noble love is similar to the creative process of sculpture, in which the inner *sensus visivus* recognises only the ideal and authorises only ideal creation.

In the *Rime* there are evidences of the struggle between pride and modesty which stirred ceaselessly in Michelangelo.[4] In his moments of assurance he could indulge in a burst of vanity:

> To the great peril of my soul
> Sculpting here things divine.
>
>         (G 282)

At other times he would reveal a modesty and even pose a philosophic and Christian basis for his humility. In his **"Stanze in lode della vita rusticale"** he writes as a principle:

> Pride devours itself
>
>        (Frey CLXIII)

Even the poems to Febo and Cavalieri show a tremendous self-abasement, akin to his later appeals to Christ.

Michelangelo's letters and recorded conversations bear out this struggle between *hybris* and modesty. He was capable of writing to the King of France that he would turn out for that patron "una cosa di marmo, una di bronzo, una di pittura" to rival the best of the ancients.[5] He is confident that his Façade of San Lorenzo will be "the mirror of architecture and sculpture for all Italy."[6] His claims and boasts of competence in his three major arts would make a long list. There is at the same time a curious humility to counterbalance them. In Letter CDXXII he admits "I am a poor man and of little worth, going about striving in that art that God has given me," a humble admission which nevertheless reminds his correspondent Martelli that he is one of God's elect! When people praised him he was uncomfortable and asked them to desist: "Leave me alone wrapped in my shroud."[7] He disclaimed the talents people attributed to him, not wishing to be like the "crow in Aesop": "so that if the legitimate owners of the ornaments with which you have clothed me will come for them, I remaining naked shall be the laughing-stock of everyone."[8]

In the contrary pulls of pride and modesty there was always as a deterrent his knowledge that artists were mere executors for God, the *sommo artefice*. True, this knowledge could contribute to his confidence, since he was given an *intelletto* by God to bring out the divinely implanted beauties in the materials. But even more, it contributed to his modesty, since the greatest works of the artist could be viewed as the eventual creations of the "divine hammer" rather than of his own mallet. The *principium et fons* of art, as the **Rime** insist over and over, is God himself. In a sonnet which Frey and Girardi assign to the Cavalieri group, shortly after 1534, Michelangelo acknowledges his debt to heaven:

> In that fine art with which one may defeat nature,
> If he bears it down from heaven with him,
> Even though nature exert herself at every point.
>
>         (G 97)

Nature is viewed equally as an ally or agent in the productions of heaven:

> Nor does it happen otherwise with lofty and novel things,
> That nature produces with effort;
> At the birth of these heaven is liberal with its gifts.
>
>         (G 106)

God is not only the master creator who empowers a select few artists to complete his task for him. He also supplies the lofty subject matter of art, the most noble being the human body itself.

> He who made the whole made every part,
> And then from the whole chose the most beautiful part,
> To exhibit here below his most lofty creations,
> As he has now done with his divine art.
>
>         (G 9)

In examining below several of the **Rime** dedicated to the art of sculpture, we shall find confirmation in Michelangelo's allegedly Platonic piece on the divine hammer of the *Cratylus*: **"Se 'l mie rozzo martello i duri sassi"** (G 46).

The artist's view of God as the fountainhead of art is amply chronicled in the *Diálogos em Roma* of Francisco de Hollanda. Francisco quotes Michelangelo as saying, "This sublime science comes not from any single land, but from heaven."[9] Or again, art is a gift "received from the immortal God."[10] When, in the *Diálogos,* Michelangelo is asked to define great painting, he replies, "That painting which I celebrate and praise will be merely the imitation of some of the creations of immortal God, done with great care and wisdom."[11]

Yet the **Rime** give evidence that Michelangelo cannot remain content with his modest role as apprentice to God. Just as he suddenly changes character and writes at one point that, like Christ's, his sputum can cure blindness,[12] so does he pridefully arrogate to himself powers he usually attributed only to God, such as the power to create life:

> Thus I can give to both of us long life
> Whether in color or in stone.
>
>         (G 239)

He can give beauty:

> Portray her with light heart and dry eyes:
> She would be made beautiful and I not ugly.
>
>         (G 173)

Finally, he even sees himself placing *concetti* within the marble:

> As I do in stone or on candid paper,
> Which had naught within, and now has what I wish.
>
>         (Frey CVII)

Since Christian doctrine held that only God actually creates, this thought is so untypical of Michelangelo that he could have expressed it only in an exalted moment when feeling like unto God himself.

Michelangelo's theory of the *concetto,* the art form contained within marble or other materials, is by now familiar to students of his life. Although it is implicit in his works of art themselves, especially in the *San Matteo* and the *Schiavo detto "Atlante,"* it is explicit only in his poetry. The theory has of course Platonic origins, with the Neo-Platonists believing that every Idea of the Higher Soul has a reflection here on earth, an image actually guarded within the *hyle.* There are, in the words of Vincenzo Danti, three elements in the creation of a work of art: the *intelletto* which conceived of the work originally and implanted it in nature; the *mano* which obeys the *intelletto* and "discovers" the implanted forms; and the *materia* which is the custodian of the form, "gardien du contour pur," as Gautier phrased it.[13] Plato's three categories of divine form—Ideas, Concepts, and Seeds—are all lodged in this material. As Ficino notes: "Eodem ordine a natura in materiam formae descendunt."[14] The most succinct statement of this belief is in one of the love poems, which we have quoted above. **"Sì come per leuar, Donna, si pone."** As this poem illustrates, the work grows out of the rock, the *concetto* is disengaged from its *soverchio,* as the artist's *intelletto* guides his hand. All three of these italicised words are found *passim* in Michelangelo's poems based on the theme of the fine arts.

No poem explains more clearly this basic process of art than the following quatrain, **"Non ha l'ottimo artista,"** of 1538-44.

> Nothing the greatest artist can conceive
> That every marble block doth not confine
> Within itself; and only its design
> The hand that follows intellect achieve.
>
> (G 151) (H. W. Longfellow)

No four lines of Michelangelo's were more famous, not even the quatrain on the *Notte,* written in reply to Strozzi's epigram. Indeed, his contemporaries were quick to seize the seminal importance of these verses. Benedetto Varchi launched Michelangelo's fame as a poet in the Florentine Academy by giving an explication of them in 1546 and calling the full piece "a most lofty sonnet full of that ancient purity and Dantean gravity." (The sonnet was received with greater enthusiasm than Varchi's commentary, which was to be called by Foscolo, in one of his two essays in English on Michelangelo's poetry, "an elaborate dissertation of an alarming length.")[15] Later in the century this had become the only poem of Michelangelo's known to Renaissance France, hungry for theories on art and saturated with plagiarisms of Italian poetry. Although

the *Rime* of Michelangelo were not translated into French until 1860, Philippe Desportes (1546-1606) lost no time in recognising the importance of this sonnet. . . .[16] Danti, Bellori, Lomazzo, and even Galileo knew this quatrain and commented on its underlying theory. In Spain it was known early to Saavedra Faxardo. . . . Bellori redefined Michelangelo's *concetto* as a "perfection of nature, miracle of art, prefiguration of the Intelletto, example of the mind, light of the imagination."[17]

Although the notion corresponds exactly to the Platonic view of art, it reflects also the notion held by some Aristotelians of the Renaissance that (in the words of a contemporary Latin version of the *Metaphysics*): "In lapide est forma Mercurii in potentia." Or, "Actio agentis nihil aliud est quam extrahere rem de potentia ad actum" and "agens extrahens rem de potentia ad actum, non largitur multitudinem sed perfectionem."[18]

Several incidental features of this theory of Michelangelo appear in different poems. The *concetto* within the rock, metal, or pigment is living, a fact which explains the recurrence of the expression *pietra viva* in his writings:

> After many years and many attempts
> The wise man in his quest arrives at the right concept
> Of a living image,
> In Alpine and hard stone—only as he nears death.
>
> (G 241)

> The living image
> Lasts longer in the hard Alpine stone.
>
> (G 239)

> When godlike art has, with superior thought,
> The limbs and motions in idea conceived,
> A simple form, in humble clay achieved,
> Is the first offering into being brought:
> Then stroke on stroke from out the living rock,
> Its promised work the practised chisel brings,
> And into life a form so graceful springs,
> That none can fear for it time's rudest shock.
>
> (G 236 var.) (Fanny Elizabeth Bunnett)

This latter sonnet to Vittoria Colonna is important in explaining the role of preliminary models in the Platonic theory of the artist. The presence of the *concetto* waiting in the rock does not obviate the necessity of practice and training, and indeed the necessity of possessing a God-given *intelletto. Intelletto* (the νουσ of Plato and Platonism) is mentioned as a perceptive power, given sparingly as grace, in a number of poems (G 164, 166, 273) and in the *Diálogos* of Francisco de Hollanda.

It was easy for Michelangelo, who mused over swords in sheathes (G 54) and spirits in bottles (G 267), to mull over figures in stone. Once the artist conceives of the *concetto* living in marble or paint, it is a slight step to suppose that this hidden form has the powers of movement and speech: "if rocks . . . could speak like us" (Letter XXXVI). As we have noted in the sequence of epitaphs to Cecchino de' Bracci (G 212, 216, 195), the headpiece of stone speaks to lament the boy's death and even to regret that it was brought down ("against my will") from its lofty mountaintop (G 275). In some pieces of the Bracci series it is hard to distinguish whether Cecchino or his living headstone or bust is speaking, for now the lad has become a living *concetto* within the stone.

The dating of the poems attesting to Michelangelo's belief in preexisting art forms shows it to be a basic tenet of his philosophy of art until not only 1547, but even 1550. We cannot accept James Ackerman's view that it was a conviction limited to Michelangelo's "Florentine period," whatever is meant by this latter expression. Michelangelo was so haunted by the theory of potential form that he applied it to the art of writing, in the surprising incomplete sonnet already referred to . . . **"Siccome nella penna e nell'inchiostro."** The theory is applied in an unusual way even to the art of the silversmith or the goldsmith. Just as the rocks in the quarry wait for the sculptor to come and liberate their inner form, so does the mold wait expectantly for the smith:

> Not only does the mold, empty of a completed work,
> Wait to be refilled with gold
> And silver melted down by fire,
> Which only in breaking can then yield forth . . .
>
> (G 153)

The tremendous importance of Michelangelo's *Rime* in providing an avenue of understanding to his art is never more clearly demonstrated than here. For this basic belief of his, without the documentation of his poetry, would have passed into his grave with him.

Sculpture, as Michelangelo's preferred art, figures largely in the poetry. Although Michelangelo eventually evolved a conviction that he had achieved excellence in all three major arts, his feelings about sculpture were entrenched during youth, when he had left Ghirlandaio's studio to work with Bertoldo. He admired Ghiberti and Donatello greatly and when he went to Rome he signed his letters "Michelangiolo scultore" consistently until 1526. Indeed, one example of Michelangelo's irony was his *ricordo* of 10 May, 1508, when he acknowledged, "I, Michelangelo Buonarroti *sculptor,* have received 500 ducats on account, for the *paintings* of the Sistine Chapel [italics mine]."[19] He would have been willing to call himself exclusively a sculptor in those late years when he still struggled with the Palestrina and Rondinini Pietàs, except that the world's voice was louder than his own and he now held the coveted post of artist-architect laureate of Christendom.

Let us consider his poems involving sculpture in chronological sequence. One sonnet, written at some time between 1528 and 1546, hails God himself as the master sculptor. A curious mixture of Platonic and Christian sentiments inspired this piece in which he acknowledges God as the force behind his hammer.

> If my rude hammer the unwilling stone
> To human form and attitude doth mold,
> It moves with him, who doth it guide and hold,
> His will and impulse taking for its own.
> But one diviner doth in heaven abide,
> Which shapeth beauty with no hand to aid;
> No hammer is, save by another, made,
> Then doth th' eternal one make all beside.
>
> (G 46) (Elizabeth Hall)

The poet then states that whereas the blow which falls from highest is most forceful, his own inspiration has gone up to heaven. Whether this deceased person is his brother Buonarroto or a friend is not certain. His hammer will falter, unless God, the divine smithy (*divina fabbrica*) will grant that his beloved friend, unique in this world, help him to perfect his instrument. After this sonnet Michelangelo penned the name "Lionardo." In any case, after the sonnet he wrote a rough (and if the friend was Vittoria Colonna, possibly Bernesque) comment: "He/she was alone in exalting virtues in the world with great virtue; nor had he/she anyone to handle the bellows. Now in heaven he/she will have many companions for there are found none but those whom virtues pleased; when I hope that here below my m[allet] will end up up there . . . He/she will have in heaven at least someone to handle the bellows, whereas down here there was no companion at the forge where virtues are exalted." This last phrase could refer to the convent seclusion in which Vittoria passed her last years.

Girardi, after examining the handwriting, conjectures that the sonnet may have been written on the death of Michelangelo's brother Buonarroto in 1528, the prose being a reminder to the nine-year-old Lionardo, his nephew, of Buonarroto's virtues. Not only is the Platonic *Cratylus* vaguely remembered in the reference to the heavenly instrument which has its earthly counterpart, but also, as Girardi reminds us, the Dantean passage:

> Lo moto e la virtu de' santi giri,
> come dal fabbro l'arte del martello,
> da' beati motor convien che spiri, etc.
>
> (*Para.* [*Paradiso*] II, 127-29)

Around 1545-50 Michelangelo leaned on sculpture as a theme for several poems. A sonnet (1545-46) pays tribute to the durability of art, and especially sculpture, hailed as the "prim' arte."

> With deep delight may sound, sane taste behold
> That work of highest art, complete and rare,

Which shows the face with movements apt and fair,
With wax, or clay, or stone, in human mold.

But if injurious time too rough or bold,
Shall shatter or distort those limbs, or tear,
Then not in vain the beauty lingering there
Recalls in thought what was so fair of old.

So does thy own great loveliness allow
To see His work who did the Heavens adorn,
Th' Eternal Artist unto whom we bow.

Time passes, comes old age, and still more thou
Comest as each thought of that fair past is born
Unchanged, unchilled by passing winter now.

(G 237) (G. Grinnell-Milne)

These lines are most typical of Michelangelo's theory of art, except for the assumption that works in wax or clay could stand as equals with works of stone. The only worker in terra cotta whom Michelangelo is known to have praised was Antonio Begarelli, and Michelangelo could only wish that he had worked in stone: "If this earth were to become marble, woe to the statues of old."[20]

Perhaps contemplating a bust he had just executed of Vittoria Colonna, as some conjecture, Michelangelo acknowledges that God is after all the greatest sculptor.

In this mere living stone
Art would have milady's face
Go on living here throughout the years:
How should heaven feel about her,
She being its handiwork, but this being mine,
Not mortal now, but divine,
And not merely so in my eyes?
Yet she must depart, sojourning here a short time.
Her fortune is crippled on its stronger side,
If a stone remains while death hustles her away.

(G 240)

(One is reminded of Berni's indignant observation that great artists like Michelangelo must die "like asses.")

Who will exact vengeance therefrom?

That a death must be "avenged" is apparent also from the threnody of the Night and Day (G 14); that time and death are traitors we know from the allegory on art (G 172).

Nature alone, if only her children's works
Abide here below, while her own time steals away.

(G 240)

Nature must carry out the revenge, since her creation (the model) decays and man's work (the bust) remains.

Michelangelo, who had spent so many years perfecting himself in the disciplines of his profession, writes a madrigal stating his belief that mastery comes late, so late as to be "near death." Certainly sculpture, which had required so many types of study, including those years at anatomy which "ruined his stomach," is the best medium to illustrate his point. Indeed, on his deathbed Michelangelo complained that he was dying before having mastered the "alphabet" of his profession.

That wise man, who through labors manifold
And length of years, toils at the rebel stone
Shall see one form alone
Perfect, in living grace, before he die;
Since to high things untold
Late we attain, and soon must bid goodby.
If nature equally
From age to age devising many a face
Have beauty's absolute created here
In yours most fair, she's old and must decay;
And therefore does your grace
Combine with potent fear
With strangest food my soul to stay
Nor can I deem or say
Beholding you, which most shall harm or bless
Creation's end, or so great happiness.

(G 241) (Nesca Robb)

Underneath is appended a bizarre postscript of Michelangelo to Riccio: "Since you wish some installments, I can send you only what I have on hand. It's your bad luck, and your Michelangelo encloses his respects."

His severe belief that mastery in the arts comes almost on the threshold of death is confirmed by a fragment of the *Rime*:

No one attains full mastery
Before the extreme term
Of art and of life.

(G App. 35)

Since Michelangelo believed this conviction he expressed twice in the *Rime,* it not only furnished him the appetite to work on into his last years but also explained his bitterness at the relatively young craftsmen who gave him so much trouble in the workshop of St. Peter's during the winter of his life.

The notion that the poet paints or sculpts his own moods into the subjects he portrays has been discussed earlier in this chapter. When the artist is picturing someone he loves, the model inevitably provokes the moods which are subsequently placed back into the finished work.

If it is true that one working in hard stone
Makes others' images in his own likeness,
So do I often make it pale and weak
Just as milady makes me.
And it seems that I keep taking myself as model
When my intention is to make her.
I might well add that the stone,
Being so harsh and hard,

Resembles her all the more, and thus me, the model.
In any case, I'd be unable,
While she destroys and shatters me,
To carve aught else but my afflicted limbs.
But if my art commemorates her beauty
Over the years, and makes her endure,
This will cheer me up and I shall make her fair.

(G 242)

Under this madrigal Michelangelo wrote "Da scultori," an unusual admission that for once he is writing as a sculptor for sculptors.

If painting in general is never the central theme of a poem by Michelangelo, . . . there are a few poems which speculate on painting and sculpture together. One of these (**"I' mi son caro assai piu ch'i' non soglio"**) will be mentioned below in our brief discussion of poetic treatments of the rivalry between art and nature.

An interesting sonnet clarifies the role of the sketch or model in the art process. Michelangelo, whose dynamic brush and chisel strokes so often led him to disregard the carefully elaborated *pensiero* (draft) or model, pays lip service (1545-46) to this preparatory phase of art:

Da che concecto à l'arte intera e diua
Le membra e gli acti di alcun, poi di quello
D'umil materia un semplice modello
È il primo parto che da quel deriua.
   Poi nel secondo im pietra alpestra e uiua
S'arrogie le promesse del martello,
E si rinascie tal concecto bello,
Che 'l suo ecterno non è chi 'l preschriua.

(G 236, var.)

Michelangelo, as this poem and its variant testify, insisted then on not merely single sketches or models but on a plurality of them from which the artist might choose the most perfect. This implied advice is also apparent from other counsels, one to the painter Antonio Mini ("Draw, Antonio, draw, Antonio, don't waste time") and one to the young sculptor Giovanni Bologna whose clay model he criticised with the sharp comment: "First learn to sketch out, and then to finish."[21]

The art of the goldsmith or silversmith, if we are to believe Benvenuto Cellini (whom Michelangelo flattered as "il maggior orefice che mai ci sia stato notizia")[22] was a craft "totally unknown" to Michelangelo.[23] Yet, as in the verse of Gasparo Visconti, Tebaldeo, Cei, and Serafino d'Aquila (as Girardi shows), fire was an important theme in Michelangelo's poetry, fire that inflames the heart, fire that calcinates rock, and fire that purifies metal and man alike. Fire refines and cleanses man, just as does a noble love. The image of the phoenix renewed by fire also intrudes several times upon the poet's imagination, since love may be viewed as a rebirth. This is the burden of **"Sol**

**pur col foco il fabbro il ferro stende"** (G 62 . . .). The tremendous heat achieved by the founder's furnace is no more intense than that of the poet's passion, which kindles him until he fairly sparkles:

Never did a furnace or stove burn so hot
That my sighs might not have made it more roaring;
And when it happens that I have (him/her) about for a
   while,
I give off sparks like iron in ardent fire.

(G 54)

The intensity and durability of the fire which bespeaks a great love are as rare as are those of the fire which was needed to cast his *Giulio II,* and just as difficult to achieve.

Michelangelo's **Rime** reflect the debate among the humanistic writers on art and on poetry as to whether nature or art was the greater formative factor of genius. Usually this rivalry was viewed as a competition between native genius and the disciplines of training and practice. In Michelangelo's aesthetics this was an important issue, and his own conclusion was the compromise effected by preceding theorists all the way back to Horace: One might as well renounce art unless one's gifts were God-given ("quell'arte che Dio m' à data"), for even then one had to study and practice for long years.[24]

There are several reflections of this conflict in the **Rime,** some in excerpts already quoted in other contexts. A majority entertain the hopeful thought that art can triumph over nature:

. . . and still it is a great boon to me
If I vanquish nature in making her beautiful

(G 172)

Cause bows and gives in to effect,
Whence by art is nature vanquished.

(G 239)

For nature is made better by art:

As a stone enriched by carving,
Is of more value than its original rock,
Or as a paper with writing or painting
Is regarded more highly than a torn or cut sheet.

(G 90)

The inclusion of the words "scritta carta" in this context of the fine arts shows how Michelangelo the poet like a Procrustes tried to fit his art theories (as he did in the sonnet **"Siccome nella penna e nell'inchiostro"**) into tentative literary theory.

However, looming over the rivalry of art and nature are two forces even more powerful. The first is fear of death in the face of which both competing forces can avail naught:

If in thy name I've conceived some image
It is not without conceiving death at the same time,
At which thought art and genius take flight.

                    (G 284)

The second force is God himself. God surpasses the
normal creative processes of nature and artist alike. The
sepulcher of Cecchino Bracci was to carry the legend:

Buried here is that Braccio, by whose face
God wished to correct nature.

                    (G 213)

The contest between art and nature makes an interesting
appearance in the curious madrigal **"Costei pur si delibra,"** which we shall examine in Chapter VIII, in which
the artist exults that he can defeat nature.

One final time he shows his pleasure that art can outdo
nature. The ability of art to award immortality—Michelangelo cautiously uses sculpture as his first example
but then includes painting as well—assures eternity to
artist and subject alike. Like Pindar, he might have
claimed as much for poetry, as he was elsewhere to hail
the immortal "inchiostri" of Vittoria Colonna and Giorgio Vasari. Yet the following poem (1545-46) was in its
own way to win the artist eventual immortality, for it
was sent not only to the Marchioness of Pescara but
also to Giannotti for inclusion in the printed florilegium
being prepared.

Lady, how can that be, which each discerns,
As slowly passing years the truth make known
That longer lives the image carved in stone,
Than he, the maker, who to dust returns?
To the effect doth yield, surpassed, the cause,
And art of man doth nature's self subdue;
I know, who in fair sculpture prove it true,
Which still of time and death defies the laws.
Thus I to both us twain long life can give,
In paint or marble, as my wish may be
The semblance of thy face and mine to show.
A thousand years hence after we have lived,
How fair thou wert, and I how sad, they'll see;
And that I was no fool to love thee so.

                    (G 239) (Elizabeth Hall)

This poem has been called "one of the most singular
that the prodigious artist wrote, interpreting the
omnipotence of his genius."[25] It is interesting that to
Michelangelo immortality meant a thousand years, not
even the Great Year of Plato. Similarly, when the like-
nesses of his Giuliano, and Lorenzo in the Sagrestia
Nuova were challenged, he countered by asking who
would care a thousand years hence.

There are three versions of this sonnet. In his effort to
match *concetto* and *materia* Michelangelo's first version filled the form more densely. With the same number
of syllables, the variants of the first draft included new

attributes: "in una pietra dura" is enriched to "in pietra
alpestra e dura" and the "quante uo' bella fusti" is added
at the expense of only the adjective "destructo." This
sonnet seems to explain the willingness of Michelangelo to do a portrait of Vittoria Colonna, despite his
intense dislike of portraiture.

This distaste for portraiture, so evident from an
examination of his artistic production, had solid grounding in his Christian and personal, as well as aesthetic,
convictions. Portraits were denials of the humility which
Christ preached to even the mighty. They were an
imposition of the Renaissance Maecenate system, often
offensive to the dignity and inventive license of the artist. Part of Michelangelo's troubles with patrons may
well have resulted from his unwillingness to indulge in
portraiture; conversely, this would be a reason why
Titian, Raphael, and Velásquez ate high on the hog at
princely tables. It is symptomatic that Michelangelo's
most famous rupture with Giulio II was healed only by
his accepting "a noose around his neck" to execute a
bronze statue-portrait of that pontiff. The final major
objection was of course Michelangelo's admitted habit
of viewing subjects with his "inner eye" rather than
outer vision. His Medici dukes were *typoi*, Platonic ideals which troubled those older Florentines who remembered them as bearded men looking different from the
conceptions of Michelangelo. Michelangelo declined to
do portraits, but it was not easy to resist pressures from
the wealthy and powerful patrons who assumed that
portraiture was a fixture of the social system or from
friends who expected it as a natural concomitant of affection.

Here again the poetry exhibits Michelangelo's position
on this dilemma of the ethical artist. There are two
pieces which display his reticence and indeed his ability
to extract himself gracefully from such pressures. Both
come from the early 1540s, when he was sufficiently
established to speak out.

The first pressure was exerted in two sonnets by Gandolfo Porrino of Modena praising Michelangelo and
requesting that the artist do a commemorative portrait
of Faustina Lucia Mancini Attavanti, who died in 1543
and whose tomb existed until recent times in a chapel
of Santa Maria Aracoeli, Rome. This young matron was
greatly admired by Porrino, Molza, Annibal Caro, and
her prestige among the humanists might have swayed a
younger artist. Yet Michelangelo's sonnet responds to
the request with courtesy and firmness:

That new transcendant fair who seems to be
Peerless in heaven as in this world of woe
(The common folk, too blind her worth to know
And worship, called her Left Arm wantonly),
Was made, full well I know, for only thee:
Nor could I carve or paint the glorious show

Of that fair face; to life thou needs must go,
To gain the favour thou dost crave of me.

(G 178) (J. A. Symonds)

In eight verses Michelangelo has praised the young lady, protected her name from vulgar gossip which led Guasti and Frey to assume her a courtesan, indulged in one of his Petrarchan puns (Mancina = left-handed), and turned down the request. Now, a sonnet written for his own amusement or escapism could end here as a *non finito*. But a sonnet for circulation requires six more lines. Michelangelo accordingly fills six more verses with further praise and a second refusal.

. . . Michelangelo declined to undertake a portrait for the sepulcher of young Cecchino Bracci, who was more intimately associated with him than was La Mancina. More intimate, moreover, was Luigi del Riccio, who exerted an even greater pressure than Porrino. Michelangelo again insisted that the dead youth was closer to the petitioner than to himself. Having suggested in the first case that Porrino do a word portrait of La Mancina instead, Michelangelo here objects that Riccio and Cecchino had become one, and thus:

It is fitting that to do him one portray you.

(G 193)

It was the egotistical and wealthy men who wished effigies of themselves who could set up the most irresistible pressures. Michelangelo's belief that an artist cannot work well under pressure, so vividly expressed in his *Lettere,* is adumbrated in a brief note to his quatrain: "His splendor was your life" (G 214). This note also supports his belief that quality is often at odds with quantity. Apologising for the quality of his stanzas, he adds: "Clumsy things, but since you want me to do a thousand of them, there are perforce all sorts."

Other persuasions on the fine arts make less sustained appearances in Michelangelo's **Rime.** This practitioner of the arts who disliked shop talk to the point of avoiding any company where he might have to "lecture" and who never got around to writing a treatise on the arts, as he once expressed the intention of doing, could not help letting his convictions and prejudices about art infiltrate his poetry. We have seen above how images and processes of the fine arts inform the **Rime.** Sometimes the artist stands blatantly before us, as in the sonetto caudato on the painting of the Sistine Vault, with its outright disclaimer that painting for him is the wrong endeavor. Even when Michelangelo is writing exclusively in his capacity as poet, his ideas on art intrude incidentally or accidentally. Sometimes he plunders the fine arts' natural propensities for metaphor. For example, he makes memory itself into a fine art. Writing on the death of old Lodovico, his father, he sighs:

Yet memory paints my brother for me,
And sculpts thee living within my heart,
While filial piety then stains my face even more.

(G 86)

The impression seems to remain that sculpture, his "alma scultura" and his "prim'arte," leaves a deeper impression than painting.

Michelangelo's interest in the nude figure, even to the extent of using it for decoration where other artists would use foliage, emerges at several points, sometimes subtly and even unconsciously.

Nor does God in his grace show himself to me
elsewhere
More clearly than in a graceful and mortal veil:
And that alone do I love because in this he is mirrored.

(G 106)

Here it is fitting that I pause and sleep for a while,
So that I may return my terrestrial veil in all its beauty.

(G 209)

Complementary to Michelangelo's love of the nude figure was his dislike of the clothing so exploited by Venetian, Flemish, and French painters. In a penned annotation to a poem on Cecchino's death he cannot refrain from a sarcasm against "the usual clothes of silk and gold which would beautify a tailor's mannequin" (G 192). This scorn for clothes dummies breaks out again in G 54, "Thou art not made like a mannequin at a tailor's." He admits his disinterest in rich raiment in G 267, noting that his own clothes are of the sort draped on a scarecrow. When he wishes to depict Dame Poverty, so much more worthy than overdressed and overbejeweled Wealth, he dresses this excellent woman "in rough and dull-colored clothing" (G 67). One recalls Michelangelo's scornful answer to Pope Giulio II, who had complained that the apostles intended for the first version of the Sistine Ceiling were not sumptuously dressed. Finally, in the stanzas in praise of rustic life, the allegorical figure of Truth goes about as naked as any of Michelangelo's *Ignudi* or *Dannati* or *Noè* and his sons.

Poor and nude Truth goes about alone.

Whereas Fraud is dressed like a Venetian portrait:

Clad in gold and variegated embroideries
Fraud goes about . . .

(G 67)

If the sonnet **"Veggio nel tuo bel uiso, Signior mio"** embodies Michelangelo's belief that the body is infused with divinity and light and is thus a reflection of God, this is a thought he had probably read in the commentary of his early friend Ficino: "Non enim corpus hoc uel illud desiderat: sed superni luminis splendorem per corpora refulgentem admiratur, affectat, et stupet."[26] Not as a Platonist, but simply as a *membrificatore* who had studied anatomy for years, Michelangelo asks his listeners in the *Diálogos em Roma*: "What judgement will be so barbarous as not to understand that a man's foot is more noble than his shoe? That his flesh is more noble than that of the sheep from which his clothing is made?"[27]

A corollary to Michelangelo's dislike of rich clothing and draperies was his disregard for high colors. He had greater esteem for line than color, as is well known. Vasari records Michelangelo's complaint that poor artists cloak the poverty of their techniques with "the variety of tints and shades of colors."[28] Armenini recalls Michelangelo's scorn for a public which looks at the high colors in a painting rather than the figures which show spirit and movement.[29] Even in this Michelangelo was Platonic, for Ficino had held color to be a minor element in art: "Eadem nos ratio admonet ne formam suspicemur esse colorum suavitatem."[30] In his *capitolo* on Michelangelo supposedly addressed to Sebastiano del Piombo, the discerning Francesco Berni wrote that those who would follow Michelangelo must reject color:

> Whoever wishes to practice your trade,
> Let him quickly sell his colors to the ladies.

An amusing indictment of color is contained in the curious *contr' amour* "Tu ha' 'l uiso piu dolce che la sapa," derived from the amusing praise of Lorenzo's *Nencia* by her country-bumpkin admirer. In this satirical piece, of which two variant versions remain, white seems to be the target of laughter: the white of the maligned lady's hair, teeth ("white as a parsnip"), and even cheeks. The high color of the lady's face is better set off by this white background:

> Thy cheeks are red and white as when thou siftest flour,
> Like poppies against fresh white cheese.
>
> (G 20)

In his note to this piece Ceriello also notes the "whimsical violence of the colors."

Perhaps the most curious marriage of poetry and art in the **Rime** are the *terzine* from the mid-twenties, seemingly an instruction on the painting of the eye. Since two or more lines are missing, it may be that these are part of a longer didactic piece:

> The eyelid, with its shading, does not prevent my seeing
> When it contracts, but the eye is free
> From one end to the other in the socket in which it moves.

The eye, underneath the lid, moves slowly.
The lid uncovers a small part of the large eyeball,
Revealing only a small part of its serene gaze.
The eye, being under the lid which covers it, moves up and down less.
Thus, when not raised up the lids have a shorter arc;
They wrinkle less when extended more over the eye.
The whites of the eyes are white and the black more so than funeral drapes,
If that is possible, and more than leonine
The yellow which crosses from one fiber to the next.
But even if you touch its upper and lower edges,
You'll not surround the yellow and black and white.

> (G 35)

Nothing is known of the intent, extent, or even content of this poem. Michelangelo's didactic moments, like the one which provoked his disputed letter to Pope Paul III on the Vitruvian principles, were few. Frequently love poems open as disguised observations on art and even on technique, but of course never with such long or incompatible *exordia* as this. The poem seems to be an exercise on a passage from the work on optics by Leonardo or Leon Battista Alberti. Typically, Michelangelo is disinterested in the color of the eye and when he reaches this point in his lesson, he halts abruptly. Indeed, *color* in the first line merely means *ombra* (shade).

In Michelangelo's time painting, sculpture, and the kindred arts were not yet known as the "belle arti," this etiquette attaining currency by the eighteenth century, alleged incubator of the "science" of aesthetics, when the Abbé Du Bos and others spoke and wrote of the "beaux-arts." Certainly the current Cinquecento term of *arti del disegno* was one more compatible to Michelangelo, who steadfastly maintained that design was the common denominator of all arts, who counseled, as we observed, to Antonio Mini, "Disegnia, disegnia, disegnia," and who in the dialogues of De Hollanda went so far as to claim that design was the binding principle of all arts, trades, and many disciplines. This is not to conclude that Michelangelo would have denied to art the term "belle arti" through a denial of beauty, nor that he did not speak of "la bell'arte" (G 97), but rather to assume that he and his colleagues preferred a term (*disegno*) explaining *what* art is rather than *how* it is.

Beauty, never easy to define in any age, was no more easily formulated in the Cinquecento. The two competing definitions were the Aristotelian and the Platonic, distinguished without impartiality by Benedetto Varchi in his *Libro della Beltà e Grazia*: "We should then know that beauty is taken in two ways, one according to Aristotle and the rest, who claim that it consists in the proportion of the members, this being called corporeal beauty known and consequently loved only by the crowd and plebeian men—and, as is known, enjoyed with all five senses; those who love this beauty principally are little or no different from brutish beasts. The other beauty consists in the virtue and customs of the soul, whence is born the grace we are discussing; this is called spiritual beauty, which is consequently known by good and speculative men only; so declared Plotinus, the great Platonist, inferring from this beauty that no beautiful person was evil."[31]

Despite the Platonic theorising on beauty at the time, especially in Pico and Bembo, the definition of beauty as physical proportion enjoyed wide circulation, partly resulting from Vitruvius's treatise and such other works as Agnolo Firenzuola's *Dialogo delle bellezze delle donne,* Dürer's *Proportionslehre,* and Luca Pacioli's treatise on "divine" proportions. Even Vasari, whose aesthetics so often coincided with Michelangelo's, departed from him in declaring that "beauty is a rational quality dependent on rules, whereas grace is an indefinable quality dependent upon judgement and therefore on the eye."[32]

Michelangelo, who talked little of grace but much of beauty, followed rather the Platonic tradition in his thinking. Beauty is not an agreeable concordance of lines and proportions. What Vasari called grace just above would serve as a Buonarrotian definition of beauty. He knew very well the Ficinian chapters on beauty in the *Commentarium in Convivium,* such chapters as "Pulchritudo est splendor divini vultus" and "Pulchritudo est aliquid incorporeum." The emphasis on "typical" rather than rational or geometric beauty Michelangelo knew from Plotinus, with whom he was acquainted, as was Varchi. If, as Varchi suggests, Plotinus held that good men perceived beauty more easily, Michelangelo would rather state that those possessed of the *intelletto* recognised beauty. Here, however, Michelangelo did not depart from Plotinus, for Plotinus assumed that the beholder of beauty must be endowed with *nous,* or Intellect Principle, before perceiving beauty. As Michelangelo explicitly simplifies his theory, this perceptive gift is necessary: "Every beauty visible here on earth / Resembles that merciful fount whence we all derive / More than anything else, to men with perception" (G 83). Savonarola, Michelangelo's early idol and a Dominican versed in the Platonism of his antagonists, could express the same view of beauty attributed by Varchi to Platonists. "You won't say that a lady is beautiful just because she has a beautiful nose or beautiful hands, but only when all the proportions are present. . . . This beauty then comes from the soul." Compare Savonarola's archenemy Ficino, "Proportio, illa cuncta includit corporis composita membra, neque est in singulis, sed in cunctis, etc."[33] In a sermon based on Ezekiel, Savonarola, almost like a Platonist, distinguishes Higher beauty and beauty of the senses: "The beauty of man and woman is greater and more perfect in so far as it is similar to the primary beauty."

The true nature of beauty as something transcending the five senses is very clearly set forth in a poetic dialogue in which the poet Michelangelo asks Love to define the exact nature of the beauty to which he aspires:

> Tell me please, Love, if my eyes
> See the true nature of the beauty for which I long
> Or if I possess it within me when, gazing on the face
> Of my lady, I see it sculptured.

Love explains that the true *concetto* progresses from outer to inner vision where it is converted to beauty itself, something divine.

> The beauty which you see comes truly from your lady;
> But this beauty grows, since it ascends to a better place
> When through mortal eyes it passes on to the soul.
> There it is made into something divine, worthy, and fine,
> Since any immortal thing wishes other things similarly immortal.
> This divine beauty, and not the other, guides your eyes onward.
>
> (G 42)

This sonnet, according to Michelangelo the Younger, dates from *ca.* 6 January, 1529. It accompanies the sonnet **"Spirto ben nato, in cu' si spechia e uede"** (G 41), infused with the theme of beauty (*belle membra, bell'opera, in belta, la belta, bell'opera*) and details the interplay of love and beauty. This transfer of the *concetto* through the visual sense to something divine is even more economically expressed in the quatrain (1524-29):

> As I draw my soul, which sees through the eyes,
> Closer to beauty as I first saw it,
> The image grows therein, and the first image
> Recedes as though unworthy and without value.
>
> (G 44)

Michelangelo found a similar conversion of the image of the soul in Ficino's *Commentarium*; "Nam procedente tempore amatum non in mera eius imagine per sensus accepta perspiciunt, sed in simulacro iam ab anima ad ideæ suæ similitudinem reformato, quod ipso corpore pulchrius est, intuentur."[34]

In his *Rime* Michelangelo returns several times to two constants of his theory of beauty. First, the source of beauty is God or Nature. Second, God grants to only a certain elect the power to discern divine beauty. The divine process of creating beauty is endless, if one is to believe the curious sonnet **"Sol perche tuo' bellezze al mondo sieno"** (Frey CIX, 46 var.). Here Michelangelo states that nature bestows beauties on certain individuals, only to take them back when that person declines, and use them to form again another "angelic and serene" beauty. Still another poem posits God as the source of all beauty:

He who made the whole, created every part
And then from all selected the most beautiful,
To exhibit here on earth his lofty creations,
As he has done just now with his divine art.

(G 9)

This early poem (1511-12), which does not correspond closely to any theory of invention of the artist, while vaguely reminiscent of the compounding of the pluri-modellistic Crotonian Venus, was abandoned by the artist. It is not one of those autonomous *non finiti* of his poetry, but seems rather an effort abandoned.

Michelangelo, to whose art posterity has denied the term of grace and allotted stintingly any acknowledgement of beauty, definitely felt that beauty was an objective he was achieving. Describing his art, in a passage partially quoted above, he slips unconsciously into the phrase "bell'arte." Such art was, moreover, a goal to which he was predestined:

If I was born neither deaf nor blind to beautiful art,
Destined to one who burns and steals my heart,
The fault is his who predestined me to fire.

(G 97)

Or even more simply:

As a faithful augury of my vocation
Beauty was given to me at birth,
Which is the lantern and mirror of both the arts.

(G 164)

Here the term "both arts" is usually accepted as meaning painting and sculpture. It could even be construed to mean both categories of art, pictorial and literary. Mariani, in his *Michelangelo,* finds this an echo of the delicate admission of Sappho in a recently discovered fragment: "I cherish elegant beauty; destiny has allotted to me since childhood the love of all beauty." A third passage finds Michelangelo claiming to discern beauty through predestination:

Since by my clear star
My eyes were made capable
Of distinguishing easily one beauty from another.

(G 173)

Granted Michelangelo's special perception for beauty, what are the particular beauties he will seek to render as an artist? Condivi listed the types of natural beauties which attracted the artist: "Not only did he love all human beauty, but universally every beautiful thing, a beautiful horse, a beautiful dog, a beautiful countryside, a beautiful plant, a beautiful mountain, a beautiful wood, and every site and thing beautiful of its kind."[35] Curiously, the natural subjects listed by Condivi offered little interest to Michelangelo. He did not exercise his craft in *lontani.* He felt that the artist's first duty was to capture beauty, terribility, and mansuetude in religious painting and sculpture. In grasping for an example of extreme beauty, Michelangelo almost spontaneously makes an analogy with church art:

Thy beauty appears much more beautiful
Than that of a man painted in church.

(G 20)

As has been suggested, to Michelangelo the finest beauty for an artist is that of the nude male, for it is in the noble human body that divine beauty is most manifest (G 106). The beauty of Tommaso Cavalieri and of Cecchino Bracci is the theme of many of his greatest paeans. True to his dislike for descriptive portraiture, he avoids telling the color of their eyes or hair, the shape of their face, and the like. To Cavalieri he expressed his assurance (*ca.* 1534) that in contemplation of the friend's physical beauty he transcended to something above the senses, something which brought him rather feelings of peace:

No mortal object did these eyes behold
    When first they met the placid light of thine,
    And my Soul felt her destiny divine. . . .
    And hope of endless peace in me grew bold:
Heaven-born, the soul a heavenward course must hold;
    Beyond the visible world she soars to seek
    (For what delights the sense in false and weak)
    Ideal Form, the universal mould.
The wise man, I affirm, can find no rest
    In that which perishes; nor will he lend
    His heart to aught which doth on time depend.
'Tis sense, unbridled will, and not true love,
    That kills the soul; love betters what is best,
    Even here below, but more in heaven above.

(G 105) (William Wordsworth)

Similarly, even a beautiful (*leggiadra*) body can be a mere *spoglia* (corpse) (G 139) when love is impossible.

When the comely young Cecchino Bracci died, Michelangelo found himself in a position requiring him to compose a block of funereal verse. He discovered beauty the most dependable theme and he exploited it in a number of ways. Indeed, the theme (*begli*) occurs in the very first verse of the initial poem in the series and in the last line (*beltà*) of the final poem. To judge from the gentle, regular face probably designed by Michelangelo and carved by Urbino (Francesco Amadori) in the Church of Aracoeli the boy deserved the overworked epithet.

Naturally, the poems on Cecchino return again and again to the struggle of beauty and death:

Death wished to strike, without the heavier blow
Of weary years or overweight of days,
The beauty that lies here, that seen in heavenly rays
We still his earthly countenance might know.

(G 182) (Ednah Dow Cheney)

The beauty which lies here, on earth did win
By far over every other beautiful creature,
That death, ever resentful of nature,
To become friends with her, did kill and extinguish it.

(G 183)

He who controls me cannot through death
Return the beauty . . .

(G 186)

This insistent theme of beauty eventually tires the reader and proves a thinning vein. In any case, the unfairness of a youth dying just at his *Blütezeit* disturbed Michelangelo deeply, for whom Cecchino

Remains creditor of so many years and beauty.

(Frey LXIII, 50)

As we have seen, the sonnet **"Sol perche tuo bellezze al mondo sieno"** held that beauty is deathless, being taken by God from one individual to be reborn in another. Another familiar piece . . . stresses the deathlessness of beauty, which will outlast even the work of art which has given it long existence:

The beauty, which existed at first, is remembered
And keeps vain pleasure for a better place.

(G 237)

The purport is that even if sculpture has its term (certainly the suggested media of wax and terra cotta will reach that term before stone) the work of art still affords a glimpse to be remembered of the God-ideated *concetto*.

There are a few generalities about the power of beauty, as there were about the power of love. For example, beauty scatters a burning fire (G 170). Many are the poems deploring the fact that beauty keeps an old man at war with himself.

Most of the remarks on beauty occur in the context of love. Indeed, love itself can be defined as beauty. Beauty perceived through the eyes becomes converted into love:

Love is a concept of beauty
Imagined or seen within the heart,
Friend to virtue and gentility.

(G 38)

However, if beauty is converted into love, true love survives the passing of external beauty. Of this Michelangelo was ever more certain as he aged. Thus, in 1546 he wrote:

Only fallacious hope is offered by that love that dies
As beauty dies, fading continually from hour to hour,
And subject to the changing of a beautiful face . . .

(G 259)

The love that outlasts the changes of the flesh attains paradise on earth: "e qui caparra il paradiso."

Dealing with the theme of unrequited love, Michelangelo asserts that the more the lover's face is distorted with anguish, the more beautiful does the beloved's face appear (G 123), but he does not mind. How much more beautiful her face would then seem if he were to die, but then her beauty and the analogy would die.

On the relation of beauty to love, the poet asks Love itself to arbitrate his question.

If there is one part in women which is beautiful
Whereas the other parts are ugly,
Must I love them all,
Because of the pleasure I take from the one alone?
The part that appeals,
While the enjoyment saddens us,
To our reason, yet would have us
Excuse and even love our innocent mistake.

The answer is given in indirect discourse:

Love, which recounts to me
The annoying vision,
Says in its wonted angry voice
That its heaven expects or claims none such.
And yet the heaven which I seek
Wishes that kindness toward what displeases be not vain.
For in the eyes habit makes every unsightly feature whole.

(G 256)

Girardi feels that these verses from 1545-46 are not addressed to Vittoria, although that lady's limited beauty might have inspired them. The idea that in the realm of love reason has no place foreshadows the debates on reason versus passion in the following century. The thought that habit eventually blinds the lover to the faults of his mistress or lover anticipates the Stendhalian phenomenon of *crystallisation*.

The madrigal **"Ben uinci ogni durezza"** (G 114) is an ecstatic outpouring of appreciation for beauty combined with infinite grace and kindness, a combination which leaves an old scarred veteran like himself, inured to the fire-ordeals of love, half dead with joy and blinded from the contemplation of it.

Michelangelo, like his master Petrarch, knew that beauty and cruelty often came hand in hand. Nature in her wisdom provided that beauty be accompanied by an equal amount of asperity: "Che l'un contrario l'altro ha temperato" (G 69). However, the beauty more than compensates for the cruelty.

Other minor improvisations on the theme of beauty show a tremendous preoccupation with it on the part of a man who rationalised that his own ugliness served the useful function of accentuating the beauty of his friends and even his art (**"Costei pur si delibra"**). Yet the inability of the beauties surrounding him to bring him peace is interestingly conjectured by Amendola, in the preface to his edition of the *Rime*: "This superb creator of spirituality and beauty wanders through the world like a chilly Eros; he loves more than he is loved, he produces beauty rather than enjoys it; he enriches the world of others, but remains poor and sad in his own soul, which is turned elsewhere."[36]

If the constant stream of poetry composed up until 1560 is a revealing *journal intime* acquainting us with Michelangelo's final relations with his art, so also are the letters a lifelong record of the tribulations brought on by the fine arts. They contain a complete repertory of the hardships of the artist's life: financial distress, dissatisfaction with the Maecenate system, troubles brought on by assistants, technical problems seemingly insoluble, pressures, humiliations, and even enmities. Many times the dissatisfaction boils over, as in the following two letters. The first, to Luigi del Riccio, complains that thirty-six years of loyal service to his profession have left him wondering if he should not have followed a trade:

> Painting and sculpture, fatigue and loyalty have ruined me, and things are still going from bad to worse. It would have been better if in my youth I had hired myself out to make sulphur matches. I should not now be in such a passion.[37]

No glowing picture of the artist's life is drawn for his unappreciative brother Giovan Simone:

> I've knocked about all over Italy leading a wretched life for these twelve years. I've endured every shame, suffered every hardship, racked my body in every task, exposed my very life to a thousand perils. . . .[38] . . .

Throughout, Michelangelo was sustained by the knowledge that he was serving God through his art, perhaps even more fully than was his brother Lionardo in a Dominican cowl. However, late in life, when Michelangelo was turning ever more longingly toward Christ and nursing a very real concern for his salvation, he went through moments when his entire life seemed a *vanitas vanitatum . . . .* At such moments he set down renunciations of the arts which bespeak crises rather than momentary vexations.

There are visible in the *Rime* periods of renunciation and dissatisfaction with the arts, times when his patience simply ran out. Obviously no religious scruples lie behind the outburst in his *capitolo*: **"I' sto rinchiuso come la midolla"** of 1546-50.

Love, the muses, and the flowery grottoes—
My scribblings and drawings now are used
For inns and privies and for brothels.
What avails it to try to create so many childish things
If they've but brought me to this end, like one
Who crosses o'er the sea and then drowns on the
  strand.
Precious art, in which for a while I enjoyed such
  renown,
Has left me in this state:
Poor, old, and a slave in others' power.
I am undone if I do not die soon.

> (G 267)

Two sonnets composed several years later show that grave concern for his salvation was leading Michelangelo to renounce the fine arts. In 1554 Michelangelo knew that the death he had considered imminent for almost five decades would not now be long in coming. Accordingly, he penned his magnificent sonnet of renunciation:

> The course of my long life hath reached at last,
> In fragile bark o'er a tempestuous sea,
> The common harbor where must rendered be
> Account of all the actions of the past.
> The impassioned fantasy, that, vague and vast,
> Made art an idol and a king to me,
> Was an illusion, and but vanity
> Were the dreams that lured me and harassed.
> The dreams of love, that were so sweet of yore—
> What are they now, when two deaths may be mine,
> One sure, and one forecasting its alarms?
> Painting and sculpture satisfy no more
> The soul now turning to the Love Divine,
> That oped, to embrace us, on the cross its arms.

> (G 285) (H. W. Longfellow)

This sonnet was sent on 19 September, 1554 to Vasari, precisely the biographer who had done so much to bring glory and satisfaction to Michelangelo. It forms a curious contrast with the self-confident and assured sonnet which Michelangelo had sent to Giorgio on the first appearance of the Vite (1550). The change of tone was so marked that Giorgio sent him a letter pressing him to come back to Florence, even urging him in the name of Duke Cosimo.

On his autograph manuscript of this poem Michelangelo, as if to reaffirm his renunciation, added the variant verse: "Or ueggio ben com' era d'error carca" ("Now I see clearly how [this fantasy] was laden with error").

Another sonnet (1555) directed to Vasari and to his friend Beccadelli echoes this turning away. Indeed, it strikes the sternly religious and ascetic note which characterised some of Beccadelli's verses:

> Earth's work and toys have occupied, amused
> Years granted me on God to meditate;
> Not only I forgot Him in that state,

But e'en His favors I for sinning used.
And what made others wise in me infused
But folly, making me perceive it late . . .
Grant me to spurn all here of greatest worth,
Those beauties that I honor most and prize;
Ere death give earnest of eternal day.

(G 288) (Warburton Pike)

The sincerity of these verses is incontestable. Angiolo Orvieto has shown the dismay which lay behind them. "Particularly dramatic in these lines is the new aspect, almost of vanity, in which art appears to him . . . Art is vain, no less than love; only death remains. Or what is worse, death with its menace of a thousand punishments."[39] As he so often did on catching himself being "serious," Michelangelo toned down the mood of the poem with a bantering footnote or commentary. To Vasari he wrote, "I send you two sonnets. Although they are silly things, I'm doing it so that you may see where I'm keeping my thoughts. And when you are eighty-one years old, as I am, you'll believe me." Both recipients were, however, sobered by the message of the verses. Beccadelli, off to Austria on one of his missions, took time to reply with a pious sonnet, equally humble, but making no reference to Michelangelo's turning his back on the values which had sustained him during his brilliant career.

There are earlier hints—from the 1530s—which forecast abdication:

False hopes and vain desire

(G 51)

Oh false world, I recognise clearly
The error and damnation of humankind.

(G 132)

Led through many years to the last hours,
Late I recognise, oh world, thy empty pleasures.

(G 133)

These doubts and dissatisfactions eventually focus upon painting, sculpture, and architecture. Yet, even as he was torn by this psychomachy, the old artist resolutely plied his profession, almost to the last day of his life.

Sometimes the fine arts seem to fade in importance as they are set against deep human or ethical values. The "natural man" in the stanzas praising rustic life knows the trivial value of the "crowning achievements of art." This is not to say that Michelangelo's Platonism ever led him to an ethical condemnation of art, comparable to the belittling of art in the *Republic*. Imitative art, however, like genius and memory, gives way before virtue:

And now I well see the error of those who would
  believe
That grace divine which rains from you
Might correspond in worth to my weak and waning
  works of art.
Genius and art and memory give way:
For even in a thousand attempts a gift of heaven
Can never be paid for by mere assets of mortal man.

(G 159)

Whereas mere poetry, the "sister art" of painting (Lomazzo), cannot make art pale in comparison, the deeply spiritual sonnets of Vittoria Colonna are something greater than words and succeed in making Michelangelo's paintings and drawings *turpissime* (G 79). We have seen painting and sculpture cast in the shadow by love of God, fear of death, and the rest, but here it is the *cortesia* of a great lady, raining from her like grace, which invalidates the fine arts.

It is understandable that Michelangelo, beset by failing health, unrequited loves, professional pressures, religious crises, should make dismissal of the arts part of a more general renunciation of life itself. . . . Less understandable is that Michelangelo should revise his basic definition of art, so abundantly characterised in his spoken and written words as "a gift of God," "art from heaven," and so on. It seems in his despair to have become a mere worldly activity. Could this old man, who spent a few of his last hours half-blind, running his hand over the smooth surfaces of the Belvedere Torso, actually have lost his faith in the divinity of art?

*Notes*

1. Cf. R. J. Clements, *Michelangelo's Theory, ed. cit.,* [*Michelangelo's Theory of Art* (New York University Press, 1961)], pp. 360-64.

2. Giovanni Papini, *La vita, ed. cit.,* pp. 497-98.

3. See R. J. Clements, *The Peregrine Muse* (University of North Carolina, 1959), pp. 37-39.

4. Cf. R. J. Clements, *Michelangelo's Theory, ed. cit.,* pp. 410-13.

5. *Lettere,* ed. Milanesi, [*La lettere di Michelangelo Buonarroti, publ coi ricordi ed i contratti artistici per cura di Gaetano Milanesi* (Firenze, Coi tipi dei successori Le Monnier, 1875)] p. 519.

6. *Ibid.,* p. 383.

7. See Valerio Mariani, *La poesia, ed. cit.,* p. 87.

8. Donato Giannotti, *Dialogi, ed. cit.,* p. 43.

9. Francisco de Hollanda, *Diálogos em Roma, ed. cit.,* [*Da pintura antigua: Diálogos em Roma* (Porto, 1930)] p. 191.

10. *Ibid.,* p. 241.

11. *Ibid.,* p. 239.

12. *Rime,* ed. Girardi, p. 53.

13. Vincenzo Danti, *Prime libro delle perfette proporzioni* (Perugia, 1830), p. 87.

14. Marsilio Ficino, *Commentarium in Convitum,* II, iv.

15. Ugo Foscolo, *Opere,* Edizione Nazionale (Florence, 1953), X, 450.

16. Philippe Desportes, *Oeuvres* (Paris, 1858), p. 186.

17. Giovanni Battista Bellori, *Vite dei pittori, scultori ed architettori* (Rome, 1672), p. 13.

18. J. E. Taylor, *Michelangelo Considered as a Philosophic Poet* (London, 1852), pp. 83-85.

19. From Michelangelo's *Ricordi,* 10 May, 1508.

20. Vasari, *Vite, ed. cit.,* [Georgio Vasari, *Le Vite de' più eccellenti pittori, scultori, ed architettori* (Florence, 1878)], VII, p. 281.

21. *Ibid.,* VII, 219; also F. Baldinucci, *Notizie dei professori del disegno* (Florence, 1846), II, 556.

22. *Lettere,* ed. Milanesi, p. 532; Thode, *Michelangelo,* I, 83 ff.

23. Benvenuto Cellini, *Vita,* viii, 41.

24. See R. J. Clements, *Michelangelo's Theory, ed. cit.,* pp. 43-48.

25. *Rime,* ed. Ceriello, p. 256.

26. Ficino, *Commentarium in Convitum,* II, vi.

27. Francisco de Hollanda, *Dialoghi* (Rome, 1953), pp. 141-42.

28. Vasari, *Vite, ed. cit.,* VII, 210.

29. Giovan Battista Armenini, *De' veri precetti della Pittura* (Ravenna, 1586), pp. 226-27.

30. Ficino, *Commentarium in Convitum,* V, iii.

31. *Trattati d'arte del Cinquecento,* ed. P. Barocchi (Bari: Laterza, 1960), p. 89.

32. A. Blunt, *Artistic Theory in Italy, 1450-1600* (Oxford, 1940), p. 93.

33. Ficino, *Commentarium in Convivium.*

34. *Ibid.,* VI, vi.

35. Condivi, *Vita* [Ascanio Condivi, *Vita di Michelangelo* (Pisa, 1823)], lxv.

36. G. Amendola, *Le poesie di Michelangelo* (Lanciano, 1911), p. 19.

37. *Lettere,* ed. Milanesi, p. 488.

38. *Ibid.,* p. 151.

39. Angiolo Orvieto, in *Il marzocco* (17 May, 1931), p. 1.

### Bibliography

#### EDITIONS OF THE POETRY

Michelangiolo Buonarroti, *Rime,* edizione di Enzo Noè Girardi. Bari: Laterza, 1960.

Symonds, John Addington, trans. *The Sonnets of Michel Angelo and Thomas Campanella.* London: 1878.

#### BOOKS AND ESSAYS ON MICHELANGELO'S RIME

Foscolo, Ugo. "Poems of Michel Angelo," *Retrospective Review,* XII (May, 1826). Reprinted in the *Edizione nazionale delle opere di Ugo Foscolo,* X (Florence, 1953) 468-91.

Giannotti, Donato. *Dialogi de' giorni che Dante consumò nel cercare l'Inferno e 'l Purgatorio.* Florence, 1939.

Girardi, Enzo Noè. *Studi sulle Rime di Michelangiolo.* Milan: Eroica, 1964.

Hall, S. Elizabeth. *Sonnets of Michelangelo.* London: Routledge & Kegan Paul, 1905.

Mariani, Valerio. *La poesia di Michelangelo.* Rome, 1941.

Orvieto, Angiolo. "Valutazioni della poesia di Michelangelo," *Il Marzocco,* May 17, 1931.

Papini, Giovanni. *La vita di Michelangiolo nella vita del suo tempo.* Milan, 1949.

Robb, Nesca. *Neoplatinism in the Italian Renaissance.* London: George Allen and Unwin, 1935.

Varchi, Benedetto. *Due lezzioni, nella prima delle quali si dichiara un sonetto di M. Michelangelo Buonarroti.* Florence, 1549.

———. *Orazione funerale nell'essequie di Michelagnolo.* Florence, 1564.

**Richard Fabrizio (essay date June 1968)**

SOURCE: Fabrizio, Richard. "Michelangelo and Music: The Fame of a Poet." *Italica* 45, no. 2 (June 1968): 195-200.

[*In the following essay, Fabrizio discusses how the musical settings of Michelangelo's verse and the musical analogs to his art reflect both the style and themes of their originals.*]

Often in determining the fame of a poet tangible evidence is provided by the number, the quality, and the influence of editions and translations of his work. How profoundly one art has infiltrated its sister might be still another method of showing the extent of that "bubble reputation." Indeed this cross-artistic method has the advantage of yielding fresh insights and odd glances both into the original work and into the history of taste. Reinterpretation of Dante, for instance, through the mirror of music and painting has covered a course from the romanticism of Liszt's *Dante Symphony* to the fragmented images of Rauschenburg's illustrations for the *Commedia.* One is by no means surprised by Dante's immense influence on the other arts. But what if Dante had been primarily a painter or a sculptor who merely dabbled in poetry and the effect of his poetry, *mutatis mutandis,* had been equally as strong? This is precisely the case with Michelangelo's poetry, and one is not a little overwhelmed to find the effect it has had on music and musicians.

More noticeable among scholars than among composers has been the "relative obscurity" of Michelangelo's poetry.[1] All be it, Enrico Bevilacqua's comment that musicians used Michelangelo's poetry only to graft their works to a sure source of success has at least some truth in it.[2] Hugo Wolf no doubt was awed by the fact that the poems he was setting were not merely poems but poems by Michelangelo.[3] But it is no less true that in an era in which artists are less kind to the Renaissance than they were wont to be, leading composers like Dallapiccola in Italy, Nicholas Flagello in the U.S.A., and particularly Benjamin Britten in England, have turned once more to the emotion-loaded poetry of Michelangelo.[4] Composers have responded to the struggle, to the pensive and grim aspects of life which dominate Michelangelo's oeuvre. Titles like Benoit-Méchin's *Le Tombeau* (1931), Flagello's *Contemplazioni* (1960?), Pfitzner's *Das Dunkle Reich* (Op. 38) are indicative of their position. **"Chiunche nasce a morte arriva"** was of especial interest to the composers. This ballade with its grimness and horror was scored by Pfitzner, Trunk, Wolf, Dallapiccola, and Vycpálek.[5]

Michelangelo was the great sculptor to Hugo Wolf. For him the problem of scoring was not only translating poem *qua* opem into music. He felt that the poetry of a sculptor must somehow be sculpturesque: sculpture implying a medium that is ponderous and monumental. Therefore, Wolf concluded that "a sculptor must certainly sing bass;"[6] and so when he came to set Michelangelo's poems, he naturally scored them for bass voice. Whether all sculpture actually demonstrates such heaviness is suspect in the light of the open and geometric work of the constructivists. The decided preference, however, of the composers who have glanced at Michelangelo's poetry seems to indicate such

feeling. Michelangelo's prime regard for sculpture, according to the composers, was in conformity with a basically somber attitude toward life. Thus the scores are replete with markings like "gedämpft," "sehr ruhig," and "più lento." That zestful and ironic debate in poetry between Strozzi and Michelangelo on *La Notte* was put into music by Theodore Streicher.[7] But "night," with its gloomy connotations, clouds the music. Liszt confirmed this disposition when he included the poem as an epigraph above the second of his *Trois odes funèbres.* Nor is the baroque struggle in the poetry ignored: frequently the *lieder* are to be sung or played "etwas zogernd" or "agitato." Spiritual conflict haunts the poems. Broken, photomontage glimpses of such plaguing feeling are attempted in Dallapiccola's dodecaphonic *Tre poemi* (1949).

The whole range of the poetry, from the love to the confessional poems, is represented in music. Approximately 30% of the works are scored. Composers have done their share to bring the poetry a much deserved attention. Recordings of Britten, Flagello, and Wolf have given the poems a larger audience than they might have otherwise enjoyed.[8] More than thirty composers from Norway to Italy, from the U.S.A. to the U.S.S.R. have set the poems.[9] Of these Wolf has been the most influential. He intended to set a complete cycle but completed only three. Yet these three are recalled in the works of Courvoisier, Schoek, and Trunk.[10] Composers have also initiated interest in Michelangelo's poetry. In Czechoslovakia—where no translator has yet produced an edition of the poems—one composer, Ladislav Vycpálek (b. 1882), has set a Czech translation of **"Chiunche nasce a morte arriva"** to music. Tyútchev (1803-1873), the great Russian metaphysical poet, has translated at least one of Michelangelo's sonnets, and this appears in the popular Myaskovsky's *Sonnet,* for voice and piano, Op. 8b.

One of the ironies of the history of the poetry in music is that Michelangelo was flattered but not particularly stirred by the contemporary settings of his poems. The frottolist Tromboncino, the madrigalist Jacob Arcadelt, Costanzo Festa, and Jean de Conseil set various of the poems. Indeed in Tromboncino's *Fioretti di frattole,* Bk. II, 1518, for the first time a poem (G [Michelangelo, *Rime,* ed. E. N. Girardi, Bari, 1960] 12) by Michelangelo appeared in print. In a letter to Sebastiano del Piombo, Michelangelo says of Festa's and Conseil's compositions: "they are considered wonderful things to sing; the words didn't merit such a setting" (Aug., 1533).[11] He repeats these words almost exactly when he writes to Luigi del Riccio about Arcadelt's setting:[12] "it is considered to be beautiful" (May/June 1542). Such diplomacy and humility in these letters contrasts with the sharp irony of his reply to Aretino who had suggested a master plan for *The Last Judgment.* While feeling safe within the bounds of his own media (sculpture, painting, architecture), Michelangelo suffered from insecurity when it came to the arts of sound (poetry and music).

But not only through the poetry has Michelangelo entered into the world of music. Although outside the strict limits of this paper, Michelangelo's stature as the ultimate artist has also inspired composers. Several operas are based on this aspect of Michelangelo. In each of the operas listed below he alone is capable of completing impossibly complex pieces of sculpture or paintings. In a two-act anonymous drama, *Michelangelo e Rolla* (Torino, 1927?), Michelangelo is a judge in a sculpting contest: "Il giudizio di Michelangelo è un ordinato emanato del cielo" (Act II, Sc. 2). Rolla is a sculptor, a genius. He is prevented by social and artistic circumstances from entering his masterpiece in the competition. Michelangelo solves Rolla's artistic problem by being the one man able to fix a fault in Rolla's statue. But Rolla poisons himself unaware that in the meantime Michelangelo has also solved his social problem. In spite of his genius Rolla suffers misfortune. This story seems to have provided the basis for three operas: 1. Federico Ricci's *Michelangelo e Rolla,* with libretto by Commarrano, performed in Florence on 30 March 1841 and revived in Florence on 18 April 1786;[13] 2. Temistocles Solera's *Michelangelo e Rolla* or *Genio e Sventura,* performed at Padua in 1843,[14] and 3. C. Buongiorno's *Michelangelo e Rolla,* performed at Kassel and Piacenza on successive nights in 1903. One opera, Nicolò Isouard's *Michel-Ange* (1802) with text by Etiènne Delrieu, neatly solves two issues in the Michelangelo biography: it gives him a female lover and it brings him to Spain. Fiorina, daughter of the famed painter, Perugino, is in love with Michelangelo, who has been away in Spain for a number of years. A series of comic contrivances typical of the eighteenth-century novel allows Michelangelo, secretly returned from Spain, to surreptitiously complete a painting which, at a contest judged by (among others) Leonardo da Vinci, wins him the hand of Fiorina from the snares of her guardian Scopa. Gérard, to whom the opera is dedicated, is evidently compared to Michelangelo, a symbol for the great artist.

To catalogue the musical analoques to Michelangelo would be an impossible task. Both Felix Witting and Giuseppe Marchiano, for instance, compare him to Beethoven, while Albert Schweitzer compares Bach's *Christ lag in Todesbanden* to a painting by Michelangelo in which we "see a knot of bodies in conflict."[15] After more than four hundred years the musical interest in Michelangelo has not abated.

### Notes

1. Robert J. Clements, *The Poetry of Michelangelo* (New York, 1966), p. 3.

2. Enrico Bevilacqua, "Michelangelo scrittore" (fasc.), Milano-Roma, 1926, p. 642.

3. Ernest Newman, *Hugo Wolf* (New York, 1909), pp. 216-217.

4. See Luigi Dallapiccola, *Tre poemi* (1949), for voice and chamber orchestra; Benjamin Britten, *Seven Sonnets of Michelangelo,* Op. 22, for tenor and piano; Nicholas Flagello, *Contemplazioni di Michelangelo* (1960?), for soprano and orchestra.

5. In the sixth part of Pfitzner, *Das Dunkle Reich,* Op. 38, for chorus, orchestra, and organ; in the second part of Trunk, *Von der Vergänglichkeit,* Op. 16, for male chorus and organ; in the second part of Wolf, *Drei Gedichte von Michelangelo,* 1898, for bass voice and piano; in the second part of Dallapiccola, *Tre poemi,* for voice and chamber orchestra; in the second part of Vycpálek, *In Memoriam,* Op. 18, for unaccompanied chorus.

6. Newman, *Hugo Wolf,* pp. 216-217.

7. See song five in Theodor Streicher, *Zwölf Lieder* (1922?), for voice and piano. Streicher also set (for the poems see Michelangelo, *Rime,* ed. E. N. Girardi, Bari, 1960—hereafter refered to as G followed by the number of each poem as given by Girardi): G 32, G 293, G 274, G 87, G 247, G 8, G 7, G 4, G 288, G 290, G 294, G 298.

8. See Britten, *Seven Sonnets* (G 84, G 98, G 89, G 60, G 95, G 59, G 41) on H.M.V. B 9302 and C 3312, or London Records LL 1204; Flagello, *Contemplazioni* (G 8, G 45, G 100, G 301), Serenus Records, SRE 1005 and SRS 12005; Wolf, *Drei Gedichte* (G 54, ll 65-72; G 21; G 76), Electrola E 91 0002.

9. Those not specifically mentioned in the text are: Denmark: Niels Vilhelm Gade (1817-1890), *Michelangelo,* Op. 39, an overture. England: William Henry Harris (b. 1883), Michelangelo's *Confession of Faith*; William Platt (1867-?), *Six Songs,* 1895?, for voice and piano, contains G 89, France: Jeanne Leleu (b. 1898), *Six Sonnets de Michel-Ange* (Paris, 1925). Germany: Hugo Kaun (1863-1932), "Die Augen stets der Schönheit zugetan" (G 107), for mixed chorus [see Richard Schaal, *Hugo Kaun* (Regenburg, 1946)]; Richard Strauss (1864-1949), *Fünf Lieder,* Op. 15, for middle voice and piano, contains G 138; George Vollerthun (b. 1876), "Beati voi, che su nel ciel godete" (G 134), Op. 11, No. 1. Italy: Ildebrando Pizzetti (b. 1880), *Tre liriche,* 1944, for voice and piano, contains G 87. Lichenstein: Joseph Rheinberger (1839-1901), *Gesänge altitalienischer Dichter,* Op. 129, for voice and piano, contains G 119. Netherlands: Matty Niël (b.?), *Drei Lierden,* 1961?, for voice and piano, contains G 102. Norway: Olav Fartein

Valen (1887-1952), *Sonetto di Michelangelo, Op.* 17, No. 1, for orchestra, contains as an epigraph the first seven lines of G 76. Switzerland: Hans Haug (b. 1900), *Michelangelo* (text by Michelangelo, Bibel, Goethe, Milton, Hölderlin), 1937?, oratorio for soloists, double-chorus, organ, and large orchestra; Erich Schmid (b. 1907), *Michelangelo-Gesänge,* Op. 12, for baritone and piano. U.S.S.R.: Sergey Ivanovich Taneyev (1856-1916), *Terzetti,* Op. 23, contains a sonnet by Michelangelo.

10. For Walter Courvoisier see his *Zwei Sonette von Michelangelo* [G 66, G 290] *und alt-italienisches Sonett* (Dante?), Op. 18, for voice and piano, and see also Theodor Kroyer, *Walter Courvoisier* (Munich, 1929), pp. 40-43; for Othmar Schoeck see his *Zwei Gesänge nach Dante und Michelangelo,* Op. 9, for baritone and piano, his *fünf Liedern* (Michelangelo, Hesse, Anacreon, Goethe), Op. 31, for voice and piano, and also see Hans Corrodi, *Othmar Schoeck* (Fraunenfeld, Switzerland, 1956), pp. 29-30, p. 116, pp. 416-417; for Richard Trunk see his *Von der Vergänglichkeit,* Op. 16, part two is a setting for G 21 for male chorus and organ, and see also Alfons Ott, *Richard Trunk* (Munich, 1964), pp. 36-37.

11. All quotations from Michelangelo's letters refer to the edition of E. H. Ramsden (Stanford, 1963). Festa's composition has not been discovered. For further information on Festa see: Alfred Einstein, *The Italian Madrigal, trans.* Krappe, Session, and Strunk, 3 vols. (Princeton, 1949), I, 157; Herman-Walter Frey, "Michelangelo und die Komponisten seiner Madrigale," *Acta Musicologica,* XXIV (1952), 147-198, and Leto Puliti, "Lettera ad Aurelio," in Aurelio Gotti, *Vita di Michelangelo* (Firenze, 1875), II, 95-96. Jean de Conseil wrote two or more pieces using the *rime,* but they also have not been discovered. On Conseil see Herman-Walter Frey and Leto Puliti.

12. Jacob Arcadelt (c. 1505-c. 1567), *Primo libro de' madrigali a quatro voci* (Venezia, 1543). G 93, G 147 Part I, and G 147 Part II were scored. The music for the first has not been found; the others are found in a modern edition: *Tre madrigali di Michelangelo Buonarroti posti in musica da Bartolommeo Tromboncino e da Giacomo Archadelt* (Firenze, 1875). See also Alfred Einstein, *The Italian Madrigal,* I, 161-162; Herman-Walter Frey, "Michelangelo," in *Acta Musicologica,* XXIV (1952), 147-198; Achille Lauri, "Madrigali di Michelangelo," in *Rivista Musicale Italiana,* Anno 50, Fasc. II (April-June, 1948), 131-134; Achille Lauri, "Nel IV Centenario di Vittoria Colonna," in *Rivista Musicale Italiana,* Anno 50, Fasc. II (April-June, 1948), 124-131 [reprinted in the same magazine, Anno 50, Fasc. I (April-June, 1951), 142-15, under the title, "Poesia e musica nella Roma Rinascimentale"]; Leo Puliti, "Lettera," in Gotti, *Vita di Michelangelo,* II, 92-93. See E. L. Ramsden (II, 255) who believes that G 93 was commissioned for a Florentine festival, the feast of St. John the Baptist, which was celebrated on June 24.

13. For complete information on the cast of the first performance see: F. De Villars, *Notices sur Luigi et Federico Ricci* (Paris, 1886), pp. 61-62.

14. For details of Solera's life see: Raffaello Barbiera, *Figure e figurine del secolo che muore* (Milano, 1899), pp. 313-399.

15. Felix Witting, *Michelangelo und Beethoven* (Strassburg, 1916); Giuseppe Marchiano, *Michelangelo e Beethoven* (Milano, 1955); and Albert Schweitzer, *J. S. Bach,* trans. Ernest Newman (New York, 1952), II, 161.

## Ann H. Hallock (essay date November 1977)

SOURCE: Hallock, Ann H. "Ugo Foscolo and the Criticism of Michelangelo's *Rime.*" *South Atlantic Bulletin* 42, no. 4 (November 1977): 21-30.

[*In the following essay, Hallock charts the various phases of criticism of Michelangelo's verse (focusing especially on the pivotal nineteenth-century essays of Ugo Foscolo) and calls for a reexamination of his work.*]

Throughout the centuries scholars of varying stature have examined and commented upon Michelangelo's poetry. Their remarks have often been perceptive. Yet for the most part they have also been quite general and open to being questioned or even rejected by us because they have historically ignored the fundamental factor necessary to attain a true understanding of this poetry: Michelangelo's own poetics.

This critical oversight is certainly the product of the sublime and powerful image that has been evoked by the name Michelangelo ever since the first half of the sixteenth century. "Che dicendo Michelangelo, solo, mi pare di dire ogni cosa insieme,"[1] concluded Benedetto Varchi in his funeral oration for Michelangelo, whom he felt to be a divine personality, "prodotto in cielo, e mandato in terra da Dio non per huomo semplicemente, ma per altero mostro, e nuovo miracolo degl'huomini."[2] Ariosto exhibited his similar adoration when he wrote: ". . . quel ch' a par sculpe e colora, / Michel più che mortale Angel divino."[3] Completing the dimensions of the awesome image indelibly linked to the name "Michelangelo" since the times of his contemporaries are the titanic drama of his professional life cultivated and vividly depicted in the biographies by Ascanio Condivi and Giorgio Vasari and his fabled, solitary, and *terribile* personality. The fascination of this image has brought unprecedented interest to the verse of one considered a minor poet. Yet, in turn, the true merit of Michelangelo's poetry and of Michelangelo as a poet remains virtually unrecognized because the approach to both has been colored and clouded by the dominance of Michelangelo's legendary fame as an artist. Consequently, studies of his verse have been largely limited to the relatively superficial professional, biographical, and psychological dimensions suggested by the traditional concept of Michelangelo, and the evaluation of the poet has been governed by the image of the artist.

If we read the statements of Michelangelo's contemporaries, we find that they undiscriminatingly transfer their idolization of him as an artist to his work as a poet. Pietro Aretino voiced the enthusiasm of his age for Michelangelo's poems when he wrote that "gli scritti di Michelagnolo meritan d'essere conservati in un'urna di smeraldo," while Vasari eulogized the poet by describing him as no less than a "divinissimo poeta." Though Michelangelo's *Rime* were never published in his lifetime, his poems were avidly sought and diffused by the frottolist Bartolommeo Tromboncino, the madrigalist Jacob Arcadelt, Constanzo Festa, and Jean de Conseil, who set them to music, and in this form they became a vogue within the cultured Italian circles.[4] Enrico Bevilacqua's observation that musicians used Michelangelo's poetry only to graft their works to a sure source of success[5] contains much truth and indicates the uncritical acclaim automatically attributed to the poems of the incomparable artist. Popular enthusiasm for the legend of Michelangelo as an artist of extraordinary genius was intense enough to perpetuate ready acceptance of the unexamined corollary that he was also a great poet.

Consequently, Michelangelo's fame as a poet continued as a "popular tradition" throughout the seventeenth and eighteenth centuries, while his poetry went almost totally unobserved. Interest in the poetry per se was, in fact, so negligible that even though Michelangelo had readied his verse for publication, the *Rime* were not published until 1623[6]—and then only as a result of the interest of his grand-nephew, Michelangelo *il Giovine,* who radically altered the poems as he prepared them for publication, purging them of what he considered to be ignoble elements unbefitting the image of his illustrious ancestor and transforming their style to conform with standard literary tastes.

Although the poems were republished in 1726,[7] they continued to be "talked of more than . . . read" until their appearance in the appendix of Richard Duppa's biography of Michelangelo in 1806.[8] In this work the literary stature of the poems was elevated by the collaboration of Wordsworth and Southey on their translation. Their translations and their consideration as two of England's most distinguished poets that Michelangelo's poetry was worthy of translation did much to arouse new interest in it. Shortly thereafter, in 1821, Duppa's collection appeared with some additions in the first annotated edition of the *Rime,* undertaken by Niccolò G. Biagioli, whose frustrated patriotic and religious fervor found its outlet in exalting a famous compatriot. Biagioli's spellbound admiration for Michelangelo led him to seek no less than the revelation of "gli altissimi intendimenti del Poeta" and the "strettissima parentela di Michelagnolo poeta con quei due primi occhi del poetico cielo dell'universo [Dante e Petrarca], non che d'Italia," as well as to "onorare e magnificare . . . e quel divinissimo ingegno, e per lui l'Italia nostra, immortale e feconda madre d'eroi, di gloria, e di virtù."[9]

The editions of Duppa and Biagioli succeeded in bringing new, critical attention to Michelangelo's poetry. They stimulated the exiled Ugo Foscolo, who was then residing in England, to publish an essay on Michelangelo's *Rime* in the *New-Monthly Magazine* in 1822,[10] which was followed by a second essay in 1826.[11] With these two essays Foscolo became their first true critic. Acknowledging the predisposition of his predecessors, he wryly observed with particular reference to Biagioli: "Whoever is over-anxious to regard as extraordinary all that may proceed from the pen of a distinguished man, pushes his admiration to the extent of superstition, which, while it adds nothing to the glory of the author, greatly diminishes our respect for the critic."[12] He also underscored their wholly unexamined acceptance that the sublime artist was also a great poet:

> The Italians, though constantly repeating, as a popular tradition, that Michel Angelo was a distinguished poet, seem to have never entered into the real character of his verses. In their innumerable metrical collections, of every kind and age, and from authors good, bad, and indifferent, we never hit upon a single extract from Michel Angelo. Even Tiraboschi, the voluminous historian of Italian literature . . . passes very carelessly over his verses, and merely observes "that Nature had also endowed him with a happy turn for poetry."
>
> (450)

Having at last divested the *Rime* of the traditional veneration for Michelangelo that had shielded them from an objective analysis, it is sadly ironic that the man who cautioned his readers against pushing "admiration" into the realm of "superstition" and chided others for having never "entered into the real character of Michelangelo's verses" should himself be no less immune than his predecessors to the temptation to superimpose preconceptions of Michelangelo the super-artist upon Michelangelo the poet. This is a particularly unfortunate event in the history of the *Rime.* Since Foscolo's criticism prepares the major critical approaches subsequently taken toward the *Rime,* as the following discussion will reveal, the critical evaluation of Michelangelo's poetry was to continue to be dominated by the image of Michelangelo the artist.

Foscolo failed to heed his own caveat and spuriously approached the poems with the traditional image of Michelangelo in his mind's eye. He begins his criticism by directly comparing the artist to the poet, who is found inferior, for while "Nature had gifted Michel Angelo, in a supreme degree, with the *imitative* imagination necessary to form a painter, sculptor, and architect . . . she had sparingly accorded to him the *creative* imagination of a poet" (454-455). The preponderant image of Michelangelo the artist leads Foscolo to presume that the poems were for their author little more than a "relaxation and outpouring of his feelings" (454), and he concludes his line of argument in the statement that the *Rime* are a

> compound of thought and sentiment, which always excites to meditation, and sometimes touches the heart; but neither describes, nor paints, nor works powerfully on the imagination . . . he does not express himself, at all times, with that perspicuity which can only be attained from the constant habitude of writing, nor with that poetical diction which imparts warmth and brilliancy even to the coldest reasonings. The versification betrays the same want of exercise in composition. . . . He had not . . . the same right to be an innovator in literature as he had in the fine arts.
>
> (456-457)

As a result of his obvious susceptibility to the influence of Michelangelo as an artist, Foscolo set up a damning criterion of the poetry that was to underly criticism of the *Rime* for the next 150 years: the poems are a dilettante's dabbling in a form of expression in vogue among his contemporaries. Foscolo's acceptance of the ready excuse offered by the prevailing image of Michelangelo to dismiss the *Rime*'s intensely individualistic poetic style as merely the marginal, dilettante activity of an unlettered artist instituted at once the most permanent and damaging direction in the later evaluation of Michelangelo's poetry. Its unconventional poetics is seen as proof of the literary inadequacy of their author, rather than the mark of a bold and imaginative work. Such a conclusion automatically precludes further investigation of the *Rime*'s original style, which seems cacophonous to those finely attuned to classical literary norms. As a result, subsequent critics will easily explain away Michelangelo's unconventional verse, which does not adhere to their own standards.

Foscolo politely excused the discrepancy between Michelangelo's poetry and traditional literature by saying,

> The versification betrays the same want of exercise in composition: there is in it more of ear than of skill. The melody is rarely imperfect in any of his lines; but

we scarcely ever meet with a succession of verses in which the sound of the words, and the variety of the numbers and position of the accents, are so combined as to produce a sustained and general harmony.

> (456)

Subsequent *literati,* subscribing to the ready excuse the image of Michelangelo as an artist offers to dismiss his unorthodox poetic style, have been less condescending. They include G. Passerini, G. Saviotti, T. Parodi, E. Bevilacqua, G. Toffanin, M. Cerini, M. Barbi, G. Ferrero, V. Piccoli, M. Marcazzan, B. Nardini, U. Bosco, M. Fubini, and, alas, the powerfully influential Benedetto Croce. Even though the latter proposed to return to the *Rime* with "pacato senso" in opposition to the spellbound approach of his contemporaries enflamed by the dramatic image of the artist, Croce's conclusions parallel those of Foscolo. He, too, repeats that Michelangelo "le veniva componendo per semplice 'diletto.'"[13] Nor is he any less immune than Foscolo to the temptation to measure Michelangelo's verse against his sublime art: "Quei suoi concetti e sentimenti non sboccavano, messi in versi, nelle visioni titaniche a cui volgeva l'opera dello scalpello e del pennello" (394-395). Croce additionally brushes aside Michelangelo's poetic style as that composed "senza la disciplina e l'abilità del letterato, e perciò con improprietà, zeppe, oscurità, contorsioni, durezze, che non si possono accettare" (395). Thus unburdened of having to treat *Michelangelo*'s expression, Croce accepts only those rare lyrical moments that accord with his own aesthetics, namely, when Michelangelo

> si distrigava dallo straccio e dal viluppo di quelle forme, sorpassava con forte emissione di voce l'impacciato dire e quasi il balbettare a cui di solito lo constringevano, e usciva in versi precisi e vigorosi, benché mai o quasi mai in componimenti armonizzati e compiuti. Ma quei versi stessi, se ben si osservi, sono piuttosto espressivi che poeticamente espressivi.
>
> (395-396)

As a result of the negative critical approach to the *Rime* established by Foscolo, which at once acknowledged Michelangelo as a great artist and virtually discounted him as a poet in his own right, the intrinsic value of Michelangelo's poetry was necessarily reduced to almost solely that of its content. Foscolo prepared the major areas of subsequent investigation of the *Rime*'s content as well in his two essays. He renewed the interest in the study of Michelangelo's poetry as writings representative of the sixteenth-century revival of Platonic philosophy, which had already been underscored by Berni ("Ho visto qualche sua composizione: / Sono ignorante, e pur direi d'averle / Lette tutte nel mezzo di Platone")[14] and by Biagioli. In his essay of 1822, Foscolo emphasizes the "conception of ideal beauty which was always real in Michel Angelo," as well as the Neoplatonic doctrine of love Buonarroti expresses—in particular, that revealed in the poems inspired by Vittoria Colonna. The latter theme predominates in Foscolo's second essay, for he was by then convinced that "if we would form any just notion as to the poetry of Michel Angelo, we must raise the veil which hides the immaculate countenance of that sacred love which was the sole argument of his song."[15] While later studies of the *Rime* rarely omitted consideration of the Platonic philosophy revealed in Michelangelo's verse, J. E. Taylor, Thomas Mann, G. Thomas, L. von Scheffler, N. de Sanctis, R. J. Clements, and A. Bizziccari have made it the sole focus of their criticisms. Thomas, de Sanctis, and Mann continued the investigation of Michelangelo's expression of the Neoplatonic doctrine of love that had aroused Foscolo's keen interest.

Correlating the Platonic doctrine, which he saw to be the basis of Michelangelo's poetry, with that which subtends the Italian literary tradition, Foscolo reiterates Benedetto Varchi's and Biagioli's emphasis on the Platonic kinship existing between Dante, Petrarch, and Michelangelo, whom he proclaims to be "the most true and worthy" follower of Petrarch. "Nor let it be imagined that by following the refined doctrines of Petrarch, Buonarroti departed in any degree from those of his great master, Alighieri, since both these suns of Italy borrowed their light from the sacred fount of the divine Plato" (473), Foscolo admonished. In so doing, he also touched on the affinity of Michelangelo's style with that of Dante (whose *Comedy* the artist knew by heart and on which he was considered an expert by his contemporaries), briefly commenting that Michelangelo's verse manifests the "vigorous conceptions and severe style of Dante" (473). This direction, which had been prepared by Michelangelo's fame as a *dantista* and by Varchi's interpretation of Michelangelo's sonnet **"Non ha l'ottimo artista"** as "pieno di quella antica purezza e dantesca gravità,"[16] was later taken by F. Farinelli and F. Rizzi.

But most importantly, in addition to noting the philosophic and stylistic concurrences existing between Dante and Michelangelo, the Romanticist adds a new dimension to the traditional parallelisms established between the two; namely, the affinity of their sublime spirits:

> And whoever has meditated upon the productions of these two extraordinary minds, will be constrained to confess, that never did two souls agree with so perfect a harmony; whether we look at the awful and terrible nature of their imaginings, or at the perfectness of their representations. The thirst for renown, the consciousness of their own worth, the scorn of the blind vulgar, a constant dissatisfaction with things appertaining to this world, and an incessant panting, and, as it were, striving after the mysterious beatitudes of heaven, may be seen a thousand times in the writings and in the lives of both these illustrious Italians.[17]

In so observing, not only does Foscolo institute a psychic parallel between Dante and Michelangelo that was to find all too fertile a ground—particularly in Germany—during the nineteenth and twentieth centuries, but he also launches the psychological investigations of the *Rime* inspired by the heroic image of Michelangelo. With this psychological approach to the *Rime,* Foscolo inaugurates the second major critical direction taken toward the poems, which was to parallel the importance of that adhering to his estimation of Michelangelo as a great artist and merely a dilettante poet.

Foscolo's probing delineation of Michelangelo's spirit prepares the tenor of the second paramount interpretation of the *Rime.* He emphasizes the "pale light of sadness" and "utter discontent with mortal things" that subtend the *Rime,* and underscores Michelangelo's contempt for the "infamous vulgar [which] always was, and always will be, the scourge of generous minds." Touching first on the nature of "lofty spirits" that "have never known how to support either the scoffs or the restraints of the malignant and ceremonious multitude . . . wherefore, to preserve their independence, they fly, as much as possible, to the stillness of solitude" in order to underscore Michelangelo's quest for "untrodden and lonely ways," Foscolo then considers the question: "But for what cause is it that the most rare and lofty spirits cannot accustom themselves to the tedious business of life, and that it seems as if the sentence of infelicity was always impressed upon their existence?" Turning next to the weary artist's yearning for death, which had "now become his sole desire," and, finally, to his unflagging religious faith, which had "assisted him to overcome the obstacles which blind ignorance, and envy, and malignity, opposed to the perfecting of the monuments which he wished to raise to the immortal glory of God," Foscolo penetrates Michelangelo's inner spirit. As a result of his approach, the *Rime* have been interpreted largely from a psychological point of view, emphasizing the dramatic aspects of Michelangelo's personality suggested by his legendary image.

One hundred years of Romanticists and Decadentists too numerous to mention considered the *Rime* to be the revelation of Michelangelo's titanic personality. Giovanni Amendola voiced this view of Michelangelo's poetry when he proclaimed: "Non è l'opera di Michelangelo, ma è Michelangelo stesso che ci sta dinanzi."[18] Both groups sought in the poems those aspects of Michelangelo's legendary personality that accorded with their own penchants. The Romanticists dwelt on indications of his patriotism, quest for liberty, exceptional spirit, and indomitable will. The Decadentists pursued the *terribile* Michelangelo of suffering, solitude, night, death, psychological trauma, and spiritual anguish, as well as his genius, titanism, and superhumanism. The image of Michelangelo reduced his poetry to a vogue, and again its true merit was obscured by these awed admirers' "virtù non di attirare ma di allontanare dalle cose che avvolgono nel vapore dei loro incensi."[19]

Parallel to these emotional pursuits of the psychological and biographical dimensions of the **Rime** have been those prompted merely by the denial of any other intrinsic value to Buonarroti's poetry. G. Toffanin, T. Parodi, and M. Marcazzan have taken this position, while others, such as Nina Facon, have studied Michelangelo's verse to determine the evolution of the artist's thought. The predominant psychological approach to the **Rime** has also resulted in the correlation of Michelangelo's poetry with his art to determine the *forma mentis* underlying and manifest in both (*cfr.* C. Boito, T. Parodi, and V. Mariani)—in particular, Michelangelo's inherent sense of conflict and struggle, which has been the focus of studies by W. Pater, M. Gengaro, and W. Binni.

The immediate comparison of Michelangelo's art with his poetry—the last dimension of the influence of the image of Michelangelo the artist upon the evaluation of his verse—has included several other directions as well. It has successfully sought to enhance our understanding of Michelangelo's art through the study of his verse and Michelangelo's ideals as an artist expressed in the **Rime**. These areas have been investigated by V. Fazio-Allmayer, U. Bosco, and R. Clements, as well as innumerable art historians.

Literary critics who, like Foscolo, have compared Michelangelo's verse to his art have been similarly disappointed and have also judged the **Rime** to be a relatively impoverished creation. T. Parodi speaks for Toffanin and Croce as well when, as a result of this comparison, he concludes that "la deficienza del poeta di fronte all'artefice dobbiamo soprattutto cercarla nel suo lasciar ogni contemplazione plastica visiva, e nell'impicciolirsi al tempo stesso del suo mondo lirico."[20]

Others, however, have been so influenced by the concept of Michelangelo as an artist that they have arrived at the opposite conclusion. They have seen his poetry to be but a different manifestation of his artistic activity and have interpreted it thereas. Voicing this viewpoint, Francesco Flora states:

> Michelangelo fu nei suoi versi migliori quello stesso che era nelle arti figurative. Adoperò la parola (pur se quest'impressione sembri abusata) come una sostanza di pietra sotto il chiaro e lo scuro; parve squadrarla o scalpellarla traendola dal blocco dell'universo come una figura chiusa nel marmo. . . . È vero insomma che le sue poesie sono in noi interpretate dalle sue statue e pitture e architteture.[21]

While studies of the **Rime** biased by the image of the artist have produced valuable insight into Michelangelo, his plastic expressions, and the themes of his poetry, they have clearly been subject to inevitable limitations. Most importantly, however, the dominance of Michelangelo's image has resulted in the consideration of only the superficies of his poetry and has not encouraged a careful, comprehensive investigation of the **Rime**'s own poetic merits. Notwithstanding accurate and penetrating observations by Flora and Di Pino in the course of their essays, the maximum concessions they make to Michelangelo the poet is that he is merely a sculptor-poet[22] or a poet only in rare moments and fragments.[23]

How often, instead, as a result of superimposing the artist on the poet, that "certain original and unaccustomed air" characterizing Michelangelo's verse noted by Foscolo, that "energia di stile che nasceva dalla sua severa coscienza" (Flora), those "difficoltà che esse oppone all'intelligenza letterale che sono connaturate all'espressione poetica di Michelangelo; e ne costituiscono, per così dire, la forma stessa" (Marcazzan and similarly Toffanin and Ceriello), that "poesia . . . sempre succosa e densa e tutta concentrazione spirituale senza pompa di frasi" (T. Parodi), that "nuda realtà" (Croce) which "ci è apparsa prima come imperfetta e singolare struttura, [e] la sentiamo poi come castità di forma: castità che risponde ad una divina umiltà di spirito" (Amendola) have been similarly recognized, but, due to the pursuit of content, have remained unexplored by those who view the **Rime** merely as an autobiographical expression or by the prejudiced *literati* who cannot consider Michelangelo's poetry as other than the unsuccessful, dilettante activity of an artist.

In conclusion, the predominant influence that the traditional image of Michelangelo the artist has had upon the approach to his poetry is vividly underscored by the fact that while throughout the centuries his **Rime** have been investigated by many and renowned critics, only very recently he has been recognized as a truly creative poet[24] and his verse has been subjected to a vertical study[25]—this notwithstanding Karl Frey's painstaking work,[26] which, since 1897, has at once provided the basis for a substantive and objective critical analysis, and dispelled any doubt as to Michelangelo's serious involvement as a poet. In this year marking the 502nd anniversary of the artist's birth, the time is ripe for an objective reassessment of Michelangelo the poet.

### Notes

1. Benedetto Varchi, "Orazione funebre," in *Michelangelo,* ed. Jacopo Recupero (Roma: De Luca Editore, 1964), p. 297.

2. Ibid., p. 307.

3. Ludovico Ariosto, *Orlando Furioso,* canto XXXIII, 2.

4. For information on the poems of Michelangelo set to music, see Leto Puliti, "Di alcune poesie di Michelangelo musicate dai contemporanei," in Aurelio Gotti, *Vita di Michelangelo Buonarroti* (Firenze: Tipografia della Gazzetta d'Italia, 1875), II, pp. 89-122; and Richard Fabrizio, "Michelangelo and Music: The Fame of a Poet," *Italica*, 45 (1968), pp. 195-200.

5. Enrico Bevilacqua, "Michelangelo scrittore," *Rivista d'Italia* (May 15, 1926), p. 642.

6. *Rime di Michelagnolo Buonarroti. Raccolte da Michelagnolo suo Nipote,* in Firenze appresso i Giunti, 1623.

7. *Rime di Michelagnolo Buonarroti il vecchio con una Lezione di Benedetto Varchi e due di Mario Guiducci sopra di esse* (Firenze: D. M. Manni, 1726).

8. Richard Duppa, *The Life of Michel Angelo Buonarroti, with his Poetry and Letters, and Outlines of Sculpture, Paintings, and Designs* (London: John Murray, 1806).

9. *Rime di Michelagnolo Buonarroti il vecchio, col comento di G. Biagioli* (Parigi: presso l'Editore in via Rameau No. 8, 1821), p. xxx.

10. Ugo Foscolo, "Michel Angelo," *New-Monthly Magazine*, 4 (1822), pp. 339-347, rpt. in Ugo Foscolo, *Opere,* a cura di Cesare Foligno (Firenze: Felice Le Monnier, 1953), 10, pp. 447-459.

11. Ugo Foscolo, "Poems of Michel Angelo Buonarroti," *Retrospective Review,* 13 (1826), pp. 248-265, rpt. in Ugo Foscolo, *Opere,* op. cit., 10, pp. 469-491.

12. Ugo Foscolo, "Michel Angelo," *Opere,* op. cit., p. 453.

13. Benedetto Croce, *Poesia popolare e poesia d'arte,* 4th ed. (1932; rpt. Bari: Laterza, 1957), p. 394.

14. Francesco Berni, "Capitolo a Fra Bastian del Piombo," in *Poesie e prose* criticamente curate da E. Chiòrboli (Firenze: Olschki, 1934), p. 168, vv. 25-27.

15. Ugo Foscolo, *Opere,* op. cit., p. 473.

16. "Lezzione di Benedetto Varchi sopra il sottoscritto sonetto di Michelangelo Buonarroti fatta pubblicamente nella Accademia fiorentina la seconda domenica di quaresima l'anno 1546," first published in *Due lezioni di M. Benedetto Varchi, ecc.* (Fiorenza: Torrentino, 1549).

17. Ugo Foscolo, *Opere,* op. cit., p. 479.

18. Ed. Giovanni Amendola, *Michelangelo Buonarroti, poesie,* con prefazione di G. Amendola (Lanciano: R. Carabba, 1931), p. 10.

19. Benedetto Croce, op. cit., p. 394.

20. Tommaso Parodi, *Poesia e letteratura* (Bari: Laterza, 1916), p. 186.

21. Francesco Flora, *Storia della letteratura italiana,* 15th ed. (1940, Milano: Arnoldo Mondadori Editori, 1965), 3, p. 32. Similarly, A. Foratti, V. Mariani, G. Galassi, and M. Gengaro.

22. Francesco Flora, op. cit.

23. Guido Di Pino, "Le 'rime' di Michelangelo," in *Stile e umanità* (Messina: G. d'Anna, 1957), pp. 101-119.

24. Notably, Luigi Baldacci, "Lineamenti della poesia di Michelangelo," *Paragone,* Anno 6, No. 72 (dicembre, 1955), pp. 27-45; R. Scrivano, *Il manierismo nella letteratura del Cinquecento* (Padova: Liviana, 1959), pp. 85-88; and Natalino Sapegno, "Appunti sul Michelangelo delle Rime," *Rivista di cultura classica e medieovale,* 7, No. 1-3 (1965), pp. 999-1005.

25. Gianfranco Contini, "Il senso delle cose nella poesia di Michelangelo," *Rivista Rosminiana,* 31-IV (aprile, 1936), p. 386 ff, rpt. in G. Contini, *Esercizi di lettura* (Firenze: Felice Le Monnier, 1947), pp. 323-346.

Pier Luigi De Vecchi, "Studi sulla poesia di Michelangelo," *Giornale storico della letteratura italiana,* 140, Anno 80, fasc. 429 (1963), pp. 30-66, and fasc. 431 (1963), pp. 364-402.

Enzo Noè Girardi, *Studi sulle rime di Michelangiolo* (Milano: L'Eroica, 1964).

Hugo Friedrich, "Michelangelo Buonarroti," in *Epochen der italienischen Lyrik* (Frankfurt am Main: Vittorio Klostermann, 1964), pp. 329-412.

Walter Binni, *Michelangelo scrittore* (Roma: Edizioni dell'Ateneo, 1965).

26. Karl Frey, *Die Dichtungen des Michelangiolo Buonarroti* (Berlin: Grote, 1897).

**Frederick May (essay date 1978)**

SOURCE: May, Frederick. "The Poetry of Michelangelo." In *Altro Polo: A Volume of Italian Studies,* edited by Silvio Trambaiolo and Nerida Newbigin, pp. 15-44. Sydney, Australia: Frederick May Foundation for Italian Studies, University of Sydney, 1978.

*[In the following essay, May explores the various themes in Michelangelo's poems, emphasizing connections with the Bible and with the verse of Francesco Petrarca and Dante.]*

Gradually, we have come to recognise how persistently Dante works in stone and air in creating his poetry. So it is with Michelangelo, whose own study of Dante had made him realise how intent the older poet had been on shaping the intellect in stone, by discovering how an immediately communicable energy of passion might be achieved. Simultaneously, and (this is true of both of them) with a rugged profundity, vast masses of air were re-arranged in startling and disconcerting new shapes. Let me give two simple linked antiphonal examples: Dante's clusters of poems to the Donna Pietra and Michelangelo's **"Io crederrei, se tu fussi di sasso":**

1 Io crederrei, se tu fussi di sasso,
   amarti con tal fede, ch'i potrei
   farti meco venir più che di passo;
   se fussi morto, parlar ti farei,
   se fussi in ciel, ti tirerei a basso
   co' pianti, so' sospir, co' prieghi miei.
   Sendo vivo e di carne, e qui tra noi,
   chi t'ama e serve che de' creder poi?

2 I' non posso altro far che seguitarti.
   e della grande impresa non mi pento.
   Tu non se' fatta com'un uom da sarti,
   che si muove di fuor, si muove drento;
   e se dalla ragion tu non ti parti,
   spero c'un dì tu mi fara' contento:
   ché 'l morso il ben servir togli' a' serpenti,
   come l'agresto quand'allega i denti.

3 E'non è forza contr'a l'umilitate,
   né crudeltà può star contr'a l'amore;
   ogni durezza suol vincer pietate,
   sì come l'allegrezza fa 'l dolore;
   una nuova nel mondo alta beltate
   come la tuo non ha 'ltrimenti il core;
   c'una vagina, ch'è dritta a vedella,
   non può dentro tener torte coltella.

4 E non può esser pur che qualche poco
   la mie gran servitù non ti sie cara;
   pensa che non si truova in ogni loco
   la fede negli amici, che è sì rara: . . .

5 Quando un dì sto che veder non ti posso,
   non posso trovar pace in luogo ignuno;
   so po' ti veggo, mi s'appicca addosso,
   come suole il mangiar far al digiuno;
   com'altri il ventre di votar si muore,
   ch'è più 'l conforto, po' che pri' è 'l dolore. . . .

6 E non mi passa tra le mani un giorno
   ch'i' non la vegga o senta con la mente;
   né scaldar me' si può fornace o forno
   c'a' mie sospir non fussi più rovente;
   e quando avvien ch'i' l'abbi un po' dintorno,
   sfavillo come ferro in foco ardente;
   e tanto vorre' dir, s'ella m'aspetta,
   ch'i' dico men quand'i' non ho fretta.

7 S'avvien che la mi rida pure un poco
   o mi saluti in mezzo della via,
   mi levo come polvere dal foco

   o di bombarda o d'altra artiglieria;
   se mi domanda, subito m'affioco,
   perdo la voce e la risposta mia,
   e subito s'arrende il gran desio,
   e la speranza cede al poter mio.

8 I' sento in me non so che grand'amore,
   che quasi arrivere' 'nsino alle stelle;
   e quando alcuna volta il vo trar fore,
   non ho buco sì grande nella pelle
   che nol faccia, a uscirne, assa' minore
   parere, e le mie cose assai men belle:
   c'amore o forza el dirne è grazia sola:
   e men ne dice chi più alto vola.

9 I' vo pensando al mie viver di prima,
   inanzi ch'i' t'amassi, com'egli era:
   di me non fu ma' chi facesse stima,
   perdendo ogni dì il tempo insino a sera;
   forse pensavo di cantare in rima
   o di ritrarmi da ogni altra schiera?
   Or si fa 'l nome, o per tristo o per buono,
   e sassi pure almen che i' ci sono.

10 Tu m'entrasti per gli occhi, ond'io mi spargo,
   come grappol d'agresto in un'ampolla,
   che doppo 'l collo cresce ov'è più largo;
   così l'immagin tua, che fuor m'immolla,
   dentro per gli occhi cresce, ond'io m'allargo
   come pelle ove gonfia la midolla;
   entrando in me per sì stretto viaggio,
   che tu mai n'esca ardir creder non aggio.

11 Come quand'entra in una palla il vento,
   che col medesmo fiato l'animella,
   come l'apre di fuor, la serra drento,
   così l'immagin del tuo volto bella
   per gli occhi dentro all'alma venir sento;
   e come gli apre, poi si serra in quella;
   e come palla pugno al primo balzo,
   percosso da' tu' occhi al ciel po' m'alzo.

12 Perché non basta a una donna bella
   goder le lode d'un amante solo,
   ché suo beltà potre' morir con ella;
   dunche, s'i' t'amo, reverisco e colo,
   al merito 'l poter poco favella;
   c'un zoppo non pareggia un lento volo,
   né gira 'l sol per un sol suo mercede,
   ma per ogni occhio san c'al mondo vede.

13 I' non posso pensar come 'l cor m'ardi,
   passando a quel per gli occhi sempre molli,
   che 'l foco spegnerien non ch'e' tuo sguardi.
   Tutti e' ripari mie son corti e folli:
   se l'acqua il foco accende, ogni altro è tardi
   a camparmi dal mal ch'i' bramo e volli,
   salvo il foco medesmo. O cosa strana,
   se 'l mal del foco spesso il foco sana!

*No. 54 in Girardi's edition*

What is obvious about Michelangelo's poem, from the very first lines, is that two major processes are at work. They are independent, they enjoy asymmetry (in accent as in rhythm), and they lock only in the final paradox-in-chiasmus. One process is topographical (what *is* and what *is potential*), the other, creative, surging, dynamic, seed ejaculated into a womb, biting, ravishing. As Dante had shown, the two may neatly be bound together by the alliteration of *f* with which Michelangelo begins the intertwining of his caducean serpents: *fussi, fede, farti, fussi, farei.* Again as in Dante, the *f* alliteration is a device to tell us that a hesitation step is incorporated into the dance. Courteously, Michelangelo must follow the man he is addressing. The point is conclusively established by the reference to the tailors' dummy, whose puppet-like movements illuminate the quantum-leaps of the poem.

Equally, of course, the dummy is used to posit the inside-outside debate (the poem as sacrament), with its very tough preposing of a rigorous exploration of *through*. Cautiously recalling that swooping iteration of *per l'aere* in *Inferno,* V, 84, 86 and 89, where the air is carved by the purposes of love, we may note how Michelangelo apparently deliberately groups together all the uses of *per* in these octaves. Is it significant that they fall in the stanzas 9-13? Could there be a hint of the five *lineae* of Venus in the assembly? Of the confessional—since even conservative critics see Michelangelo's as severely confessional poetry—in the Augustinian adoption of thirteen?

Let us look at occasions for *per* (with all its reminders of the *Planctus*, and Michelangelo is the great Renaissance master of the *Complaint,* and the ambiguity of the *Pietà*):

> *per tristo e per buono* (9, 7)
> *per gli occhi* (10, 1) *per gli occhi* (10, 5)
> *per sî stretto viaggio* (10, 7)
> *per gli occhi* (11, 5)
> *né gira 'l sol per un sol suo mercede* (12, 7)
> *per ogni occhio* (12, 8)
> *per gli occhi* (13, 2)

Eight occurrences, then, with nine actual repetitions of the word *per.* Four of them, it will be noted, are *per gli occhi,* with a modulation into *per ogni occhio.* As I have said, the stanzas are octaves. The rhyme-scheme is *a, b, a, b, a, b, c, c.* In other words, a sound re-evocation of the mediaeval intertwining of duple and triple. Added, you get five. Or you can cube two to get eight. Or you can square three, and find yourself with nine.

I mention these structural points simply because they matter in a work conceived in such careful detail. It's all very well to see the overwhelming force at play in this poem, but let's also have the patience to recognise that Michelangelo is unendingly inventive in combining rhetorical precision with accuracy in parody, that most reputable of Renaissance arts. It's easy to place a bor-

rowing from Petrarch, the lift of Poliziano, the pragmatic mysticism of Lorenzo de' Medici. How do you fare with unravelling the interplay of *Inferno,* XIII, with *Inferno,* XV?

Further, you can hear the Dantesque punning in the final unity of chiasmus and paradox. You may even think fancifully of T. S. Eliot and his lines from *Little Gidding*:

> Who then devised the torment? Love.
> Love is the unfamiliar Name
> Behind the hands that wove
> The intolerable shirt of flame
> Which human power cannot remove.
> We only live, only suspire
> Consumed by either fire or fire.

—with their Ambrosian conclusion:

> And all shall be well and
> All manner of thing shall be well
> When the tongues of flame are in-folded
> Into the crowned knot of fire
> And the fire and the rose are one.

Eliot's Neo-Platonic contrariety-composition outlines Dante's argument drawn on by Michelangelo. It also tells us that we must go back to the beginning of Michelangelo's poem, since this antiphonal chant has its origin in an exploration of the *I-You* bond and hypothesis. The whole poem is a careful in-folding.

Michelangelo is, in fact, suggesting that man must confront the inevitability of metaphor, and the consequent progress through metamorphosis to myth. In an earlier poem, he had told his reader that, just as the man who rides by night must rest and sleep occasionally, so does he trust that God will restore life and due form to him, after his many afflictions. Ill doesn't last where good doesn't last, but the one is often transformed into the other. One of the simplest ways of looking at mutability.

Now apply it to a suppose, a whimsy, a conceit. Deceive your mind into believing that you're Pygmalion or that necrophily has come in upon you. Or, subtler still, a form of necrophily so exalted that we can only call it hagiophily, has enchanted you. Are these all extremes of narcissism (if it may be conceded that any form of love ever transcends self-love)? Is each of the stanzas an emblem, cast in the form of a looking-glass?

Clearly, no stanza is as simply an emblem as, for instance, those comprising Petrarch's *Standomi un giorno solo a la fenestra,* for there is a thrust towards debate, as there is in the Dantesque emblems that we meet in *Purgatorio,* X. What is noticeable, too, is the extent to which the poet involves popular belief (with slight overtones of magic), as when he refers to the binding power of the grape in the last line of stanza 2. It is difficult, too, to over-estimate the power of the last two lines of the next stanza, where he makes the homely—and erotic and copulative—point that the sheath for the straight-bladed knife cannot hold within itself the knife of curved blade.

Michelangelo is not your Neo-Platonic who refines every symbol, all allegory, and the edifice of emblem, into a bland and stifling pomposity. He never made the mistake of conforming with good taste. This poem is convulsed by the crude and titanic imagery of stanzas 10 and 11. There is the untamed force of the womb-amphora. There is the bridge across to the binding promise of the bitten grape in stanza 2. Like the straight-bladed knife, they burn, each an aspect of this multiple Phoenix, in a purifying, transforming, ecpyrosis. This, perhaps, is a poem of the immanent salamander.

It would be easy to lose sight of the second part of the original equation, the air that is reshaped as the stone is modelled. With deliberate self-mockery—self-deflation, you might say—he uses the air to inflate a ball, which may then be punched into the heavens. Irony of this order needs careful watching, for the air is as contained and kept in loving, transforming captivity as powerfully as the grape dropped into the amphora-belly. Cervical tightness and giddy space.

Let me remind you that the only serenity with which you will emerge after submitting yourself to the scrutiny of a poem or group of poems by Michelangelo, is the peace of one who has survived a battering similar to that prescribed for the would-be pilgrim of eternity at the beginning of Dante's *Inferno*. It is akin to the experience of infinity given us by Leopardi in his image of shipwreck: 'E il naufragar m'è dolce in questo mare'.

Yet there is a resolution in this: Michelangelo has an almost mediaeval sense of his own vileness, his own need to avoid complacency. After all, if you have powers such as his, they must drive you to criticise your own inadequacies, to strive to reach further and further. You can see what might be done, if a word (or a gesture in words) could achieve greater immediacy, greater direction, release more of its ambiguities, find a more fruitful context for those ambiguities. More, you know why words (and the images into which they can be forged) are slipping into banality. You have learned a great deal about the preserving force of rhetoric, of kinds of rhetoric. You can even ignore fashion, and search out continuity.

A poet of this order is trying to live with, for he builds into his poem a vision of what it might be, something well beyond what it is. This vision is uncannily there, busy in the space. It would seem the most natural thing in the world to him: why, isn't it happening in the Bible all the time? And to the most significant, the most essential of the figures embodied there? Michelangelo could comprehend (in the fullest sense of the word) the myth of David, the torment of Moses, the mother-daughter use of space as time in the case of the Virgin Mary, as she takes part in the Passion of Christ, and the centonism and journey and enclosure of Joseph. Above all, Michelangelo is concerned to define and use the space of Jeremiah, partly because Dante had used and determined him so devastatingly in the *Vita nuova,* but mostly because this was a path of unceasing movement and work into the *Planctus.*

I could be being very fanciful—Michelangelo as a poet has the effect of leaving you altogether bewrayed (and very good for you, too)—I could be being most fanciful, but I find superimposed on the poem I've been looking at (as, indeed, on all his poetry) a chiasmus of the random and the traditionally ordered. The random needs all our concentration, however, for it is the intuited randomness of the coded instruction which is in question. Michelangelo has grasped what we must be told to do, and how, and (within awing infinities of speculation) why. Look at the flow, arrest, and counter-dance of stanza 8.

Undoubtedly, Michelangelo is riotously parodying the last line of the *Inferno,* the last line of the *Purgatorio,* the last line of the *Paradiso.* From the rest of the poem, we may deduce the eyes-stars-covenant-love pattern as a good, reassuring piece of bread-and-butter tradition. Let's also recall that we're thoughtfully immersed in the inside-outside debate. At this moment, the poet decides to use the whole stubbornness of the body. (By the way, it is noticeable how seldom he does this in his poetry. Most often, he works by way of metonymy from the face.) I'm reminded of what he does in that poem of old age, where (like Villon's anti-heroine) he enumerates the dissolutions of the flesh. By bluntly telling us that there's no hole in the skin large enough for the proper utterance, not only has Michelangelo brought before us the complex reality of shaping the *logos* in terms of a column of air—and how many people *do* listen carefully to *how,* with what airy colouring, something is offered to them?—but he has also tumbled us into a world of farce, and a kind of farce seen as distasteful, vulgar, improper, by those who would ignore in poetry what they cannot prettify.

Without one superfluous word, Michelangelo has shown us man the colander. Or, if you like, man who goes on the sea of life in a sieve of a body. Michelangelo was as familiar as any of us with the tradition of the talking cunt in the French *fabliau,* of the equally loquacious anus. He knew that one of the most eloquent comments—so dismissive of Dante's claims to be serious as a pilgrim of love, a pursuer of *gentilezza*—is the fart with which *Inferno,* XXI, concludes. Here is invective, the intellect as a disciplined rhetoric of passion, as Beckett is so convincingly (and bitingly) to argue in Molloy's world (with its trenchant appeal to St Augustine).

Naturally, it is to Beckett that we may look for enlightenment on much that's here (as elsewhere) in Michelangelo, but we'll resist many temptations, simply stress a shared preoccupation with certain Belacqua or Sordello analyses of randomness, and turn firmly back to the metaphysical collision in this poem at this point. Let us look at a high-minded image of air: in a sigh, we may express the poetry of the soul's desire for love; or its insight into love; or its grief that life translates love into something less than beauty, truth and goodness—which it should, in fact, exemplify; or that love is pain and loss; or that love is absence, separation, misunderstanding.

In all sublimity, is its own silliness, its own squalor. Love's real shaping of air may be hilariously (and, to some, disgracefully) comic. So I'll use the device of self-denigration. Good rhetoric, of course, the device of *diminutio*. The body has a number of openings, suggests Michelangelo, and all tend to produce extraordinary noises, none of which even remotely does justice to the quality of love you inspire in me. With Donleavy, we might murmur, 'The maddest midsummer of Michelangelo M.'

But he's forced us to pay attention to his masses of air. If you can, in mythology, whisper a secret into a hole in the ground, so here you may puff your love into a ball and punch it into the heavens. Is it altogether unlike the mystery of the sealed jar that is the womb of the Virgin Mary? Or whispering a kiss into Lucy Locket's pocket, before you quickly tie it up with ribbon? Or even whispering into a mother's ear when you're a child? Apparent crudity is often the unbearable beauty of the world of secrets.

Let me go back to an early phase in Michelangelo's art, the *Madonna of the Stairs*. There are some very simple Neo-Platonic devices to latch on to: a Sybilline secret (prophecy of the future, prediction of the *Pietà*, as some have seen it); a vast command of air; a bridge of Innocents and of transformation; steps of reach and contrition. You can see (too) a fiercely rhetorical transferring outwards of an inward, contained, and irresoluble torment. What is happening within him has to be set almost impersonally before the world. You can strip away those kinds of ornament with which the world is familiar; you can discard those modes of thought by which the world will expect you to be disciplined; you can reject those directions in which the world may expect your imagination to travel; you may stand firm against the usual forms of nonconformity. You may do all these because your mind, working on a commonplace thought about

the concept of idea, has seen how to produce continuous revolution by dislocating idea within image, image within metaphor, metaphor within symbol (organised or stilled), symbol within fable, fable within rhetoric. It is worth observing at this point just how *talkative* Michelangelo's sculpture is to become. It unites with speech, telling you that it finds being stone dearer even than sleep, so long as shame and hurt prevail. There's great good fortune in not seeing, not feeling. So, don't wake it up. Keep your voice down.

In other words, Michelangelo never makes things simple for us. He demands that we keep totalities of stone, tumults of inflected speech, and whole universes of air, in fearless play. He imposes freedom upon us, and that is why he is so appallingly *terrible*. Look at stanza 6. You have no licence merely to contemplate it. The poet is using the good, old-fashioned courtesies of recited and received verse, but his ellipses are his own. So much of Michelangelo's poetry, so much of his uniquely shaped space, is in these ellipses. To adapt Beckett's term, Michelangelo's line of *trim* is in this stanza and the next, a line of gentle inclination, gentle asymmetry. We have also noted that there is a dominant *f* pattern running through the poem, embracing the being of man, all that is *copula,* man the maker (with God the Creator beyond, within, or as immanent reason), and the duality of fire.

In elemental—and Biblical—terms, man is forged in the furnace, or there is the possibility that (food for giants, witches, or other man-devouring evils) he ends up in the oven. In these stanzas, then, the *f* arrangement makes and breaks logics as fast as they're assembled, using the dignity of the style in tension with the blunt thrusts, the crude assertions, the disastrous silences of shyness. One glance at stanza 7, and you're at once aware that Michelangelo has mingled disparate characters, events, spiritual realities, artistic values, cadences, and personal searches, from Dante's *Commedia,* evolving, not confusion, but a most deceptive incandescence. Michelangelo is working a kind of irony for which we have little preparation, since we most infrequently reflect on why the *Planctus* and Dante's *Vita nuova* should draw so delicately and so wittily on Jeremiah and his *Lamentations.*

What I'm saying is that there are no comfortable equations, no clear pictures of the kind that you can summarise, if only because Michelangelo has known how to build into his structures the stop-start world of the tongue-tied stammerer, the man who is shy with adoration. What are the sprays of sparks, the prodigal fountains? Michelangelo is patently fusing Dante and the Bible: 'Yet man is born unto trouble, as the sparks fly upward' from the *Book of Job,* with those lines from *Paradiso,* XXXIII, where Dante asks that his tongue shall be granted such power that one single spark of

God's glory may be vouchsafed the future. The metaphysical stretch is not untypical, but its dynamic here is rather overpowering. We have the correctly unrelenting arrogance of humility, as we find it in Dante, a determination, if you like, to tell forth the mind of God, to speak with the voice of God. It's wise, perhaps, at this turn of the revelatory stair, to remember Aldous Huxley:

### Philosophy

'God needs no christening,'
Pantheist mutters,
'Love opens shutters
On Heaven's glistening,
Flesh, key-hole listening,
Hear what God utters' . . .
Yes, but God stutters.

It's wise, too, to remember that in the traditions of the *commedia dell'arte* is the mask of Tartaglia, the stammerer. He is committed in advance neither to good nor evil. His character is decided by the exigencies of the plot.

There is a curious fashion among some critics to see in Michelangelo's poetry a minor world, a world which may be neglected. The reverse is true. The triviality of critics has made them fail in alertness. If among the least demanding of poetry's aims is that of concentrating experience for us by means of never-ending ambiguity interacting with an austere beauty of contemplation, then Michelangelo does it in abundance, frequently with a single concept in a single context. Consider line 6 of stanza 12, where the walk of a lame man is set against flight, however slow. Let it implode, and it's the kind of poetry which haunts you for ever. But it has to explode, as well. It's limping Vulcan, married to beautiful, unfaithful Venus. It's Vulcan, set in the paradigm of the eagle Jupiter. It's Vulcan, creator of the wonderful net, that lattice of a final poetry, the wisdom of irony, the comprehension of shame that is ultimately to be set against that which Jacopone da Todi enjoined upon men and women anxious to follow Christ. Shame is the key to Dante's *gentilezza*.

It's a vehement meditation on the frustrating temporariness of this life, the curse of mortality, the transience of everything. At the same time, it's a sardonic reassertion of the principle of pause and hesitation, the quantum-leap, the presentation of the other kind of space. It's the double of those whose feet were maimed that myths might be fulfilled, that man might be redeemed: Oedipus is an image distinguishing fire from fire in *Inferno,* XXVI, let us remember, and Oedipus joins with Isaac in an Akedah which can only prefigure Christ. Michelangelo is not over-dramatising himself, not abasing himself into self-pity. Simply, like Dante before him, he is reaching into the furthermost parts of delicacy, wit and the shock that informs them.

Add another of poetry's demands: that man shall be enchanted because his necessary structures are laid bare, reclothed, again made naked, and so on, in an endless game, spread backwards and forwards and in every direction that is remotely deemed sideways. All you're called on to be is as precise as Alice, and to wear your sensible shoes.

For you must go in archetypal pursuit. Not for you the wild boar that will slay Adonis and wound with proper sign Odysseus, but the Jabberwock. Michelangelo's poem—and this comment embraces all his poetry, however ecstatic it may on occasion seem—is an essay in multifoliate *Jabberwocky.* You have only to look seriously at stanza 10: at once, the fusion-inversion-reversion of the rose as gryphon, of Christ as Mary, of Mary as Christ, leaps out as a basis for Michelangelo's poetry here. He could be bearing in mind Dante's reminder in *Paradiso,* XXXIII, that Mary is 'Virgin Mother, daughter of your own Son'; he could be stressing Jacopone's cry from the Virgin, that Christ is 'Son, Father, and Husband'; he could be hearking back to Florentine days, when Bernardo Accolti sang his *Hymn to the Madonna,* in which the Virgin is seen as carrying her own Creator within her belly.

You may take the demands of poetry further: poetry is a manifesto for itself, a declaration of aims and objects and achievements. A poem may (with justice) ask the reader to do something new, to accept new canons, to restore contexts, strengths, and possibilities. It may ask him to revise prejudice, to relearn the meanings of words and phrases, and to come alive. All these things can provoke fear, resentment, violence. When the whole art of such new poetry (which is as centonistic as is Eliot's new poetry of *The Waste Land*) is brought to bear unflinchingly on speaking of a love which gives, which responds, which suffers, as opposed to a love which asserts, takes, imposes, dictates, bargains, or (our prevailing form of self-destruction) briskly transacts, then the only thing you can do with the poet is say that he's interesting as a poet, but you'll do better to calculate his genius by his sculpture and his painting.

Not the least part of Michelangelo's genius, as Thomas Mann divined so shrewdly, was that he never loved for the sake of being loved and in fact felt unworthy of it. His was the courage exactly to fulfil the Neo-Platonic conceit: in death was the completing illumination of love. We are not too far from the last lines of Sophocles' *Oedipus Rex.*

Whatever Michelangelo may have taken from Petrarch, he has no hint of the earlier poet's self-indulgence: he awards himself nothing. In fact, it would be easy to mistake what he's talking about for a one-sided, unrequited love. It is, more accurately, the nexus of argument which is comprehended in the single symbol of the one-way pendulum. That, in its turn, is the new universe of poetry offered by Michelangelo, where random ellipses come like the fugitive fables of the *Commedia.* After all, the smile of *Inferno,* V, which is itself re-evoked in the Cheshire Cat, becomes the smile on the fable of the Golden Age in Matelda's telling, when *Purgatorio,* XXVIII, is moving towards its inevitable climax in *viso.*

It is useless to seek the traditional logics of Luther's old goat, Aristotle. Michelangelo is working all the time with the more compelling logics of images, many of them silent, shaping by their silence. As in his painting, Michelangelo is devoted to the secret poem. As with the sculpture, we are at the stage where we have patiently to work out the idiom to which he arrived by ruthless processes of elimination. Reduced idiom is not impoverished idiom. Let me study the example of the use by Michelangelo of the human face. As I have said, some of the more foolish critics have failed to grasp the kind of metonymy involved, preferring to suggest a dotty superficiality in Michelangelo, that he could proclaim that he is inspired to love, to reverence, to passion, to personal grief by beauty of face.

Let us take a late face, one that is possibly the face of Vittoria Colonna:

> Quantunche sie che la beltà divina
> qui manifesti il tuo bel volto umano,
> donna, il piacer lontano
> m'è corto sì, che del tuo non mi parto,
> c'a l'alma pellegrina
> gli è duro ogni altro sentiero erto o arto.
> Ond' il tempo comparto:
> per gli occhi il giorno e per la notte il core,
> senza intervallo alcun c'al cielo aspiri.
> Sì 'l destinato parto
> mi ferm'al tuo splendore,
> c'alzar non lassa i mie ardenti desiri,
> s'altro non è che tiri
> la mente al ciel per grazia o per mercede,
> tardi ama il cor quel che l'occhio non vede.

> (258)

What immediately strikes one about the poem is that its fifteen lines are an indication of how it means to go on. Michelangelo is no fool about the traditional magics associated with fifteen—still commemorated in our giving eight for fifteen when we're playing fives and threes at dominoes—he's recalling the power of the number, both in erotic and in diabolic terms. (It's always wise not to forget that Michelangelo used the parameter of the diabolonian critically, rather as had Dante before him. The limping figure in the poem with which I began this detailed work is, among his many *personae,* the lame devil Asmodeus, whether from literature, folk-lore, or a twisting of *Talmud* or the Persian *Avesta.*) Equally, he's no fool about the rugged square (use of

shape, thrust of air) at the ends of lines 1 and 2, where *volto umano* falls beneath *beltà divina.* Naturally, the *rime equivoche* of *parto* and *parto* are intensified and ramified by the compound *comparto,* itself directly bound to the vowel modulation (and a device which swoops straight back into the first poem, with its street that is strait) of *erto* and *arto.* Once we start looking at this poem as a number of completely cohering visual—or concrete—poems, we begin to see how some of the obliquities work, and we must always work by obliquity with Michelangelo. The focus is in space outside, or away from the apparent body of main action. The face matters—it may be the face of a mother lost when you're six, a mother forever seen as beautiful, tender, gentle, spiritual—but it must finally relate to journey, path, the harshness of self-discovery, self-criticism. This poem has a Dantesque arrow of Dantesque images: *piacer, parto, pellegrina.* Yet the words *parto* and *pellegrina,* though spatially so differenced, are finals: they belong to the right-hand vertical. Compare each of the four sides of the rectangle made by the first six lines, bearing resolutely in mind that, with nine lines to come (that is, two groups of three will be set against three groups of three, however arrived at), the looking-glass line between the clutch of six and the cluster of nine will be a transforming line: the journey must be codified as it was in the earlier poem, with co-ordinates of *occhio* and *core.*

As Lewis Carroll is to make abundantly clear when Alice goes through the looking-glass, the chess-board on which we'll move has ordinary chronological time as one dimension, with mystic, spiritual time as its other dimension. In such a world, as in the world of this rectangle, where the divine hypothesis of line 1 acknowledges the severity of the Way, that is Christ, that is Christ's *gentilezza,* in line 6, and where the stress-pause-stress, as *donna* reaches to *alma,* dances asymmetrically with that daunting construction over on the right, a square dipping through *lontano, parto* and *pellegrina* into *sentiero erto o arto,* in such a world, the latent Christ (your gryphon, your persistent fish in *Alice*) comes from the intersection of time with the timeless.

Michelangelo was most old-fashioned in his love of, his concern for the Bible. The face, let's not deceive ourselves, is the blending of Leah and Rachel (as, in terms of eyes, the Middle Ages rejoiced to do). It is the pre-figuration of the Virgin Mary, and (at once) the duality of the active and contemplative lives. Need we search further than the tomb of Julius II for corroboration? Need we remember more than Dante's re-evocation of the sisters in *Purgatorio,* XXVII, in his antelucan dream? Is it altogether accidental that so many of Michelangelo's words here occur in those lines of Dante's dream? Michelangelo's is a surreal poem, an oneiric poem, the dream of (as he is) another Joseph. For him, Joseph is the very type of the *cento.* Elegantly, chastely, robustly, he fulfils it here. Michelangelo has every right to expect us to seize upon his source of terminology and transferred image. Can we yet see what he's done with them?

Can we, for example, see how he has refashioned what Dante wrought before him, the exquisite interpenetration of Christ and Venus? This is a fishers-of-men poem, where Venus adopts the net in which she herself was trapped by Vulcan. The lattice is markedly one of energy, the kind of energy which can only lead to immeasurable grief and the correct compassion of aloneness. Watch the manner in which he divides time, note the chiasmus of eyes and heart, night and day (with inbuilt that myth which is so important to him, the Phoebus-Phaethon struggle, matching the terrible fate of Marsyas, with which he identified himself so pungently). Set the *com* element of *comparto* together with the *senza* of *senza intervallo,* and you have the irregular carving of the poem restored to the intensity of stone and air.

It has been recorded of Michelangelo that there were long periods of his life when he (apparently) produced no major work, but pottered about, dressing blocks of stone, drafting poems in the manner of Petrarch, or making sketches of relatively little moment. Allowing for romantic myth, we can accept that Michelangelo was indeed elaborating and perfecting structures during these times, and the structures he hands down to us are his own, and governed by a set of cadences which we are only now beginning to glimpse. Michelangelo may have had, in the day-to-day expression of living, all the unapproachability and even irascibility of a man vexed by human frailty (hostile to creation whether it comes from within you or without), he may even have struck his contemporaries as a man who could hate and deserve hating, but he never failed to understand the aloneness that we must all contribute always to everything.

No intimacy can be founded on a pretence of togetherness, only on a shared love of one another's aloneness, one another's agony (that ecstasy which blinds with recognition). We are still moving through the decorated literature and drama of aloneness, for the austerity of Michelangelo is hard to bear. The luxuriousness of Beckett helps to prepare us for a future when we shall be strong enough to attempt the entire structures of Michelangelo, as one day we may get around to being brave enough for Dante.

Let me remind you again of the link through Jeremiah. The Jeremiah of the Sistine Chapel ceiling is a self-portrait. It is unequivocally a moral figure, a figure of debate, perhaps of defeat—that is, not of final defeat, but defeat in an area of argument among many: after all, Plato and Savonarola are to remain a duality in Michelangelo until the end. Duality, indeed, dominates.

Here is earthly anguish, the hint of the diabolonian. Associated with it must be the externalised and grieving soul—Michelangelo again using his air to project an inwardness, to shape the secret, to make visible the invisible.

Altogether, Jeremiah is in challenging company, with the face the key on either side and in him. And all must be taken back to what the *Planctus* borrowed, to what Dante related to himself, principally because it had featured in the *Planctus*:

> O vos omnes qui transitis per viam,
> attendite, et videte
> si est dolor sicut dolor meus!

It is basic within our discussion that the *trans* of *transitis* be carried, and that the full realisation of how both Dante and Michelangelo can (in harmony with the *Planctus*) use the *per viam.* Journey is valueless without its conferring metamorphosis. Such transformation will (in its simplest form) be an interplay (that is, interludes which are woven together in oblique patterns, of which the Knight's move in chess is archetype) of duple and triple. It is a commonplace to accept the Cabbalistic androgyny of Adam in the Sistine Chapel. This, certainly, may be made to work as a dualism in the poetry, in constant interaction with the trine of body, soul and spirit.

Dante freed subsequent poets into the joy of the preposition, if they had the courage to enjoy their freedom. Few men have. Michelangelo takes all prepositions—look at his use of *in,* for example, and his chiselling with it of the linked adverbial areas of *inside* and *outside.* It's pointless to think you're going to concern yourself with the poetry of Michelangelo, unless you realise that poetry can be rhetoric, grammar, technique of any kind. That poetry, in fact, *resides* in the device. But, back to Michelangelo and the preposition: Dante taught us that, of all the prepositions, *per* is final, eschatological, the preposition of man's dawning insight, his stumbling upon the poetry of salvation.

Bearing in mind the never-absent *way,* here are some illuminating insertions of *per* by Michelangelo. In his **"Spirto ben nato,"** the idiom *per tempo,* with its general sense of *speedily,* occurs:

> Spirto ben nato, in cu' si specchia e vede
> nelle tuo belle membra oneste e care
> quante natura e 'l ciel tra no' può fare,
> quand'a null'altra suo bell'opra cede:
> spirto leggiadro, in cui si spera e crede
> dentro, come di fuor nel viso appare,
> amor, pietà, mercè, cose sì rare,
> che ma' furn'in beltà con tanta fede:
> l'amor mi prende e la beltà mi lega;
> la pietà, la mercé con dolci sguardi
> ferma speranz' al cor par che ne doni.

Qual uso o qual governo al mondo niega,
qual crudeltà per tempo o qual più tardi,
c'a sì bell'opra morte non perdoni?

(41)

The poem itself analyses the implications of timelessness, the arrest of mortality, often a major debate when, in classical mythology, mortal loved immortal. But we have to work back from the *speedily* to a rapid dexterity of our own. Swiftly, we must learn to rotate the Petrarch he has borrowed through the Dantesquely Platonic paradigms he is setting out. Even more tumultuously, for there are sonorous dignities slowing the ostensible, while sending the actual hurtling on its way, is the intertwining of the *sp* alliteration with the *per* (inside-outside) group. *Spirto* reaches to *specchio* (a nice ellipsis: Rachel, looking into the *speculum perfectionis,* that is Christ, in *Purgatorio,* XXVII), and finds a simple repetition in the *spirto* of line 5, where the *specchia* position is occupied by *spera*. Impeccably, for this is a world of stately rhetoric, the whole of the end of the line becomes an echo, an image, a rhyme. We only needed two syllables, we receive three. Suddenly, we recall the punning use of the *sdrucciolo* by Poliziano. The echo is fascinating, nothing less than the revelation of Christ's wounds to the doubting Thomas. A quick glance at the rest of the poem shows that there's nothing inherently improbable in such a memory. The latent idea continues, of course, in the complex of relationships making up his *Conversion of St Paul.*

This *spera* modulates to *speranz'* (in line 11). Meanwhile, our run of *per* begins with the buried *per* of *spera,* is a metathesis in *prende* (often found in Dante), is buried again in *speranz',* entirely itself in *per tempo,* and concludes as the first syzygy of *perdoni.* We may also claim the syncopated *per* to be found in the use of *opra* in lines 4 and 14. Now, only the glib and facile can find in the Petrarchan original, *Spirto gentil che quelle membra reggi,* a tidy political *canzone*. There is no possibility that Michelangelo saw it as other than an invitation to select and differentiate a number of its elements, while preserving a number of its preoccupations: the need to look at spiritual discipline in terms of mutability; the sacramental values to be deduced from the apparent; the structures unifying and dividing inside and outside; the nature of gift and its communication to giver and receiver (ours is fast becoming a society in which it is impossible to see gift as Michelangelo refers to it in line 11); the nature and the realm of cruelty (and man's inaccessibility to beauty); the transforming power of mercy, or even elementary goodness of will; the Pauline insistence (for we must understand the triple meaning of *conversion* in his case) that *caritas* makes itself intelligible to men through beauty, truth and goodness.

Exactly where you'd expect to find it, if you're mindful of Michelangelo's trim, is the word *beltà*. But look at where it is repeated; look, too, at where he sets *mercé*. It's a most extraordinary arrow, but it is, I'm sure, the burning arrow of which he talks in the poem for Tommaso dei Cavalieri, **"Se 'l foco fusse alla bellezza equale,"** a poem in which he probably comes closest to telling us how to exercise a genuine curiosity, a true love for his poetry. Only compassion, he says, compassion on the part of Heaven, prevents there being generated a fire equal to the beauty of your eyes. Were there such a fire, then earth would have no part so frozen that it didn't burn like a kindled arrow, the arrow sent burning through the air, the consuming arrow (as I may now gloss).

In **"Spirto ben nato,"** love is mentioned twice, both times in the left-hand vertical. On both occasions, there can be no doubt that *caritas* is implied, with Eros as instigator of contemplation. Is it in any way mysterious? Isn't this the triad of Jacob, Leah and Rachel? Didn't Michelangelo learn to see this as a mystery (in the spiritual sense) working in the flesh, as (ever more surely) he comprehended why Dante's reading of the Bible, as shown in his writings, could give him a why?, a where?, a what? And let him come to see how well he knew the way.

When he first uses *amor,* he carves it as one of three Graces, setting them as the first half of line 7. They state, they invade, theirs is the welcome intrusion. But they are also part of a very formal rhetoric, immaculately developed. Note, too, how the art of memory is drawn on: the three Graces (*amor, pietà, mercè*) are firmly set on one side of the rostrum, while *beltà* is brought into the middle foreground. Then, having inflected everything with the fact of faith (which is, of course, the fact of *poetry*: all that Vico is so overwhelmingly to argue about man, metaphor and myth rather later), he proceeds (with explosive demureness) to tally what happens with his Graces, uniting one (love) with beauty in one of those shuttling copulatives—that is, both sides of the *and* keep moving backwards and forwards across the conjunction, especially when (as here) the two verbs belong to a frequently met idiom 'to seize and bind'. Then the shared essence of *pietà* and *mercè* gives them a singular verb and a sharing of *dolci sguardi.*

All poetry for Michelangelo has to be argument, whether active or contemplative. For a mind of his order, where can statement begin? Only with death. **"Spirto ben nato"** is a tiny fragment of what can only be called the disinterested pursuit of truth. To say as much, is to invite derision, because we are all so infinitely wise, we see much further into what men do than did Michelangelo, that we can reject and mock his silent, hovering concept of truth. We have little taste for his austerity, his disconcertingly correct use of language, for we prefer our words eroded, mitigated. We prefer flight to confrontation.

You can see an impossible conceit in the last three lines of the poem, a grappling with mortality, a making mortality serve the abstract purposes of immortality. This is fair enough: Michelangelo elsewhere displays how pen and ink are neutral tools, capable of producing the good, the bad, the indifferent. They must, for we need a reassuring spectrum, if humanness is to persist. Somewhere in all this is a doctrine of divine compassion. Does it sound a muddle? Indubitably. And that is why poetry is incantational, riddling. Why, out of its magics, we deduce very slowly what we need to know and see. Worldly vanity lacks shape, substance, direction, satisfaction. In criticism (and self-criticism is the most profitable form) is construction. All poetry, then, is criticism.

Again, since the truth of life is the imitation of Christ, that *gentilezza* posited by Dante, then so much poetry may itself be imitation, or modes founded in imitation. We saw how Michelangelo re-works the older poets, and the poets of the Bible. They are not merely sources, they are focus upon focus, icon upon icon, where each meditation will have to be stripped to the simplicity which will serve Michelangelo's ends, not falsify the original, yet drive the honest later reader (or speaker) into a completely personal experience of a kind of poetry hitherto unknown to him, though apparently couched in language, and employing devices so familiar to him that he's lulled into believing he knows all about what's going on. He doesn't.

Even after the hammering we have been given by Luigi Pirandello, with his dissection of the relevance to us of *if* and *if only* . . . even after the Beatles have brought us to view iteration and anaphora as we had never consented to view them when seduction was attempted by Bach or Vivaldi, even after we have been moved by Kipling's *If* (whether to tears or to frivolity), can we honestly say that we're ready for what Michelangelo does with *se* in his **"S'un casto amor, s'una pietà superna"**?

> S'un casto amor, s'una pietà superna,
> s'una fortuna infra dua amanti equale,
> s'un'aspra sorte all'un dell'altro cale,
> s'un spirto, s'un voler duo cor governa;
> s'un'anima in duo corpi è fatta etterna,
> ambo levando al cielo e con pari ale;
> s'amor d'un colpo e d'un dorato strale
> le viscer di duo petti arda e discerna;
> s'amar l'un l'altro e nessun se medesmo,
> d'un gusto e d'un diletto, a tal mercede
> c'a un fin voglia l'uno e l'altro porre:
> se mille e mille, non sarien centesmo
> e tal nodo d'amore, e tanta fede;
> e sol l'isdegno il può rompere e sciorre.

(59)

We're slightly prepared by Petrarch's *S'amor non è, che dunque è quel ch'io sento?*, but only slightly. You can't put this poem aside as an exercise in lover's hyperbole. It's a lover's hyperbole only comprehensible in terms of a meditation on the love known to the Fool for Christ. Man must learn shame, the shame that comes with insight into the image of Christ crucified between two thieves, says Jacopone da Todi. Michelangelo transforms it in his sonnet **"La ragion meco si lamenta e dole"**:

> La ragion meco si lamenta e dole,
> parte ch'i' spero amando esser felice;
> con forti esempli e con vere parole
> la mie vergogna mi rammenta e dice:
> —Che ne riporterà dal vivo sole
> altro che morte? e non come fenice.—
> Ma poco giova, ché chi cader vuole,
> non basta l'altru' man pront' e vittrice.
> I' conosco e' mie danni, e 'l vero intendo;
> dall'altra banda albergo un altro core,
> che più m'uccide dove più m'arrendo.
> In mezzo di duo mort' è 'l mie signore:
> questa non voglio e questa non comprendo:
> così sospeso, el corpo e l'alma muore.

(43)

My Lord—Love, that is, and it's idle to try and distinguish Eros from Caritas here—is between two deaths. That shifts the sense ineluctably to Eros. Equally, it offers a remarkable metaphysical conceit, in which the good thief and the bad thief become moved to a plane of interpretation where one can be seen as the emblem of the death of the body, the other as the emblem of the death of the soul. More, we are told by Michelangelo that one death is undesired by him (death in the flesh), the other he doesn't understand. Finally, he tells, in such a state of suspense, both body and soul die. It's in this state of suspense that (perhaps with acute detail of patience) we must find out what Michelangelo is talking about. Nothing is immediately obvious, save that Michelangelo has somehow got hold of space and taught it tricks it never knew before.

Ungainsayably, we're back to the irresistible force of pause, of those *quanta* with which I began, those instructions to us to involve ourselves in hesitation, so that we might follow the logics of reason, lamentation, grief, part, hope, love, being, happy (happiness), strength, example (and the *exemplum morale*), truth, the word, shame, memory, speech . . . You can continue the list throughout the poem, and then double back. What are the significant orders? Where do the stresses fall? Where are the links? What do you do with an *f* alliteration which drives relentlessly into the phoenix that is Christ? Where that modulates through *vuole* and *vittrice*? Again, what are we to make of that 'treachery' metaphor, 'which kills me the more I yield to it'? Are we wrestling with diabolic forces? Asserting the flimsy barricade of faith (flimsy because we don't know how to make it strong)? Is this an essay in the pathos of the Christian comedy?

I'm drawn back again and again to that phoenix. It's worth juxtaposing it with Shakespeare's *The Phoenix and the Turtle.* It must reflect Petrarch and Lactantius, as well as traditional classical thinking. It also rests in the poem as a kind of brusqueness, a severe dismissal of any softening by foolish hope. Clearly, then, you have to undergo all these forms of love, but they serve always to etch more deeply your lines of grief, to oblige you more precisely to understand why the irony of death. Why, for that matter, irony at all.

It is in the *se* poem that Michelangelo stresses how we have to become skilled in the wisdom of the knot. Tentatively, now, we are re-learning the craft of maze and knot and labyrinth, of mystic spiral and mesh. Michelangelo's aggregated hypothesis, his *se* poem, is a microcosm of the *Hypnerotomachia Poliphili,* itself a summation of mobile structures, for we have to remember (as Dante instructed) that all dreams have as their special mark the flow and anamorphic presentation of time. You may even spin your anamorphic time and so carve space into postulate and argument.

John Osborne, in his play *Luther,* early has Martin Luther enter upon a vital *if*:

'If my flesh would leak and dissolve, and I could live as bone, if I were forged bone, plucked bone and brain, warm hair and a bony heart, if I were all bone, I could brandish myself without terror, without any terror at all—I could be indestructible.'

This is not exactly the position or the game upon position of Michelangelo, yet there's much of the same stripping. Ultimately, we all have to keep ourselves warm with the metaphysic that lies in the whirling spaces of skeletons. Michelangelo is never more a mediaeval man, for all his living when he did, than when he reads afresh the undying message of the dance of death.

It is a counter-dance in which we're transcending our own metaphors, a dance of counterpoint and counter-positioning. It's the process whereby Michelangelo parallels, in his poetry as in his sculpture and painting, the *contrapasso* which Dante enunciates at the end of *Inferno,* XXVIII. From what is, from what is done, from what is thought, must be deduced the correct image or lattice of images. When, in a carving or a picture, Michelangelo has a figure look in one direction, gesture in another, incline in a third, he is filling out the rhetoric of debate as he would with the words and allegories in the poetry. Follow closely the arguments of *The Conversion of St Paul* (and I am deliberately following through myself the implicit punning on stone, which matters so much in all this artist's work); note the way that angles in early sculptures are found again in later work—trim must be emphasised; observe with him his commandments in his lines, **"Non posso altra figura immagi-**

**narmi,"** where the poet investigates the possibility-impossibility of devising simulacra which will outface the ever-creating reality of the love inherent in Tommaso dei Cavalieri:

Non posso altra figura immaginarmi
o di nud'ombra o di terrestre spoglia,
col più alto pensier, tal che mie voglia
contra la tuo beltà di quella s'armi.
Ché da te mosso, tanto scender parmi,
c'Amor d'ogni valor mi priva e spoglia,
ond'a pensar di minuir mie doglia,
duplicando, la morte viene a darmi.
Però non val che più sproni mie fuga,
doppiando 'l corso alla beltà nemica,
ché 'l men dal più veloce non si scosta.
Amor con le sue man gli occhi m'asciuga,
promettendomi cara ogni fatica;
ché vile esser no può chi tanto costa.

(82)

Now, in this poem, Michelangelo is being abundantly tough with us. We are to consider the whole question of doubling, doubles, the magic implicit within the Amphitryon legend. The Renaissance may have been elegant in its treatment of tales of twins, but it wanted to bond such tales to its deeper needs. We have to search no further than Straparola to find naked folk-lore, but one (pure) shining eye, a body of gold, and adamantine heart. He grows amidst woes and becomes a figure of authority, being reborn in a thousand places, if he dies in one. Outwardly, he glows green as an emerald, and he's constant and solid with those who are faithful to him.

There's little need to talk of the sorry brigade of Falsity, Discord, and such adversaries of mankind. Michelangelo sees them in a stark light: the Devil at work. What matters to us is that the poet is modestly (if surely) drawing a self-portrait in Truth, as he had drawn a moral self-portrait in Jeremiah. I rejoice in all the symbols of which he's compounded, but I'm especially fascinated by the green of the emerald. According to the lapidarists, the emerald guaranteed your chastity. Press the greenness home: Here's your Green Man. Is this a mingling of the defiance of the figure of David, a proclamation of a kind equalled in bad taste only by Michelangelo's own crudeness in describing his discomfort on the scaffolding in the Sistine Chapel, in contemplating the holes for utterance to be found in the human body, in offering the *minutiae* of his own decay (including the piles of surrogate shit) at the end of his life, David (then) mingled with Sir Gawain's Green Knight, to whom he will confess kisses but not the girdle? Is he seeing himself as the Wild Man of the Golden Age Woods? Woods in which rediscovery may be made, as Orlando found himself again, or Dante came to his own self-awareness? Vegetation Man, happy in his own androgyny, serene in the rightness of loving both Tommaso dei Cavalieri and Vittoria Colonna?

The wisest thing is to search again and again through the whole of Michelangelo's Golden Age poem, remembering particularly the lame figure of inadequate Doubt, limping and bounding, master of the hesitation, and (ironically) index to the progress of Truth for, whatever may be the formal and rhetorical protests of Michelangelo in the poems, he knows that we men and women build from doubt to flight, from perplexity to pause, from lie to self-deception. Michelangelo fashions a poetry which runs with determination from unquenchable demand to unquenchable demand: it is Mosaic, Christian, Dantesque. Did he, by the way, model Moses on the figure of Cato in the Ante-Purgatory? But, to make Michaelangelo's poetry Michelangelo is doing this: you can take airy nothing (your naked shadow, the form beyond death, the form your necromancer can summon into your service) or you can take a living person, use him (her) as a screen-figure, as Dante makes use of screen-ladies. There is, however, no refuge from the transforming effect of your beauty, the beauty of the one in whom love is revealed.

Assimilation can be the only answer, if the sacramental force of love is to be comprehended. Certainly, any kind of alienation or flight is noxious and self-destructive, not only in the short run, but also when we are reflecting on life at and after death. Death is rebirth, perhaps the only true birth, but birth itself must be set in its place: the mystery of the Incarnation has to be contended with, if there's to be progress to the Crucifixion. Suddenly, Michelangelo compresses the newness of rebirth into the child's tears, Love may dry them, promising you (at the same time) that all your labours of love will be held dear, that you yourself will be able to hold them dear, for (and there's a litotes playing games in the final line of the poem) the loved one who costs you so much is not even potentially unworthy.

A sombre man, Michelangelo is urging entelechy upon us. If we read or recite his poetry, it's inside us, its potential awaiting transformation into the actual. Do we have realities which can do anything about anything? He writes ambushes for us, as he sculpts and paints the most insidious labyrinths. He's doing this no less when he's telling fairy-stories in the guise of complaints against old age, or writing allegories rich in feigning abstractions. We may prepose a Golden Age, aptly pastoral. Poverty is a fairer state than Riches, and the processes of Accountancy cause no stir. There's no place in our ideal landscape (inner and outer) for Doubt, Perhaps, How and Why. Doubt, for example, is a figure in armour, and lame. It goes hopping about. Insecure as any marsh reed. Why is thin, with a multitude of keys at his belt, some of which ill accord with the locks, so that doors suffer. He and his company are night-birds. How and Perhaps are close relatives, sun-challenging giants, gone blind with gazing on his brightness.

So the tale continues, with Truth shown as poor, naked and solitary. He's much prized among humble people, has work, you have to supply the critical space of doubt and evasion which he cut away. And keep an eye on the Green Knight and the severed head of the *contrapasso*.

Perfectly confessional and perfectly indicative is **"Dal ciel discese e col mortal suo, poi,"** where Dante is aptly (and correctly, if only in Jungian terms) seen as his own Beatrice, coming down from Heaven:

> Dal ciel discese, e col mortal suo, poi
> che visto ebbe l'inferno giusto e 'l pio
> ritornò vivo a contemplare Dio,
> per dar di tutto il vero lume a noi.
> Lucente stella, che co' raggi suoi
> fe' chiaro a torto el nido ove nacq'io,
> né sare' 'l premio tutto 'l mondo rio;
> tu sol, che la creasti, esser quel puoi.
> Il Dante dico, che mal conosciute
> fur l'opre suo da quel popolo ingrato
> che solo a' iusti manca di salute.
> Fuss'io pur lui! c'a tal fortuna nato,
> per l'aspro esilio suo, co' la virtute,
> dare' del mondo il più felice stato.

*(248)*

I have no quarrel with Michelangelo's Dante, mischievously inflected with Petrarch though it is in this sonnet. It is sheerly androgynous, *animus* and *anima,* a candid examination of the theory of poetry as *alma*-search. Dante's own metaphors will serve as now Michaelangelo's are to serve, as aspects of the poet himself. They are a new metonymy of a new kind of reality, all adding into a massive figure of an exile so completely desirable, *worshipful.* Suffering has become a cleansing fire that is itself poetry in action.

Michelangelo transfers Dante's image of Beatrice's greeting, which is simultaneously the fount of his well-being, to the possible gift of the ungrateful people, whose most severe lack of recognition is reserved always for the prophets to whom it gives birth. In a highly ironical sense, Michaelangelo lets us see a truth in **"Salus populi, suprema lex"**: in this case, the well-being *bestowable* by the people becomes the supreme law. We are commanded to build our experience—the poem—by way of what is consciously absent. Exile, inward and imposed from without, is the most terrifying compound symbol of how we must construct with void upon void. As I have said, Michelangelo accepts the artistic imperatives of the one-way pendulum, the gift of loving (and not to count the cost, never to seek love in return, always to find yourself unworthy of it), and to know that, within the cold stone of these principles, the vision of Paradise is to be found, and may be shared with all men.

Michelangelo is going to wait a long time for evaluation as a poet. It's easy enough to see the simple A B C and combining ordinary logics. There's no difficulty with his borrowings, though it's none too simple to lay hold on the ways in which he's rotated, mitigated, recast his booty. You can be very poised about his Neo-Platonism, about his movement through the Bible, through prevailing folk-lore and day-by-day magics, and you can riddle out his polished rhetorical constructions, and equally deft use of seeming clumsiness, coarseness, and unavoidable collision. You can see his frustration with the transitory and the corporeal; you can even (at the end) see the rueful translation of the beautiful figure of pause and hesitation into the Lutheran griping of the bowels, a constipation which has to be relieved by a violent purge.

Suspense is all, perhaps, that ironical time which man can spare from ingestion, digestion, excretion, whether it's his body he's feeding and voiding, or his greed. His greed, says Michelangelo, will bring his soul to carrion. The double death can afford a pungent metaphysic of space by decay. No wonder, then, that Michelangelo pleads that those faces which are beautiful and urge men to love and create, shall be exempt from the removal of mortality. Poetry must always push the impossible by way of fantasy so far that it yields all men the freedom to be unafraid of learning who they are. Certainly, Michelangelo does this. Whether he is as great a poet as I think him, this will only be decided if (I submit) men and women accept that they have to start all over again, and to learn the very discipline of thought which will make it possible for them to decry his aims and the paths to their attainment. We are an over-decorated age and we see little, and hear practically nothing. We enjoy the false harmonies of compromise.

Start with Michelangelo's conceit of the game of night. He sets it out forthrightly in his **"Ogni van chiuso, ogni coperto loco."**

> Ogni van chiuso, ogni coperto loco,
> quantunche ogni materia circumscrive,
> serba la notte, quando il giorno vive,
> contro al solar suo luminoso gioco.
> E s'ella è vinta pur da fiamma o foco,
> da lei dal sol son discacciate e prive
> con più vil cosa ancor sue specie dive,
> tal c'ogni verme assai ne rompe o poco.
> Quel che resta scoperto al sol, che ferve
> per mille vari semi e mille piante,
> il fier bifolco con l'aratro assale;
> ma l'ombra sol a piantar l'uomo serve.
> Dunche, le notti più ch'e' dì son sante,
> quanto l'uom più d'ogni altro frutto vale.

(*103*)

Everything that's bounded by the material contains night, even when day prevails, and opposes that night to the play of the light of the sun.

Man, he goes on, plants his seed in the shadows, and night, therefore, is more holy to him than day.

In European folk-lore we still have the game of dark. It is a good game with which to begin the gathering of wisdom. And, as Michelangelo insists, live out exactly the truth that wastefulness is how we must define ingratitude. Central to all is the poet's hint that we should live and relive those final sequences of *Purgatorio,* XXVII. There, if anywhere, is a gently guiding movement in the game of dark. So, in the full comprehension of Leah and Rachel, for a fragment of the time being, we may start to see a Michelangelo poem: 'Fuor sei dell'erte vie, fuor sei dell'arte'—Dante is told.

The moral is very clear: Virgil's truth is true, but limited. Beatrice's admonition is to come, and Beatrice's admonition (says the poetry of Michelangelo) is scattered throughout the later poet's work. Read it. There are the rules for Michelangelo. The summation, as Beatrice says herself, is enticingly simple: the happy man.

**Ann H. Hallock (essay date October 1983)**

SOURCE: Hallock, Ann H. "Michelangelo's Revelatory Epitaphs." *Neophilologus* 67, no. 4 (October 1983): 525-39.

[*In the following essay, Hallock uses Michelangelo's epitaphs for Cecchino de' Bracci as a starting point for a discussion of his handling of the theme of death throughout his poetry.*]

In January, 1544, Francesco ("Cecchino") de' Bracci, the nephew of Michelangelo's secretary and friend Luigi del Riccio, died at the age of fifteen. His death prompted a largely-overlooked, integral part of Michelangelo's poetic expression. His uncle turned to Michelangelo with the request that he sculpt a tombstone for Cecchino's grave. He also asked him to write fifteen epitaphs commemorating Cecchino so that he and Cecchino's parents could choose from this selection a Michelangelo epitaph for the youth's tombstone. Michelangelo responded to Del Riccio's request for the sculpted work with the sonnet

> A pena prima aperti gli vidd'io
> i suo begli occhi in questa fragil vita,
> che, chiusi el dì dell'ultima partita,
> gli aperse in ciel a contemplare Dio.
>     Conosco e piango, e non fu l'error mio,
> col cor sì tardi a lor beltà gradita,
> ma di morte anzi tempo, ond'è sparita
> a voi non già, m'al mie 'rdente desio.
>     Dunche, Luigi, a far l'unica forma
> di Cecchin, di ch'i' parlo, in pietra viva
> etterna, or ch'è già terra qui tra noi,
>     se l'un nell'altro amante si trasforma,
> po' che sanz'essa l'arte non v'arriva,
> convien che per far lui ritragga voi.[1]

While Michelangelo graciously refused to sculpt the youth's tombstone, he generously tripled the requested fifteen epitaphs and wrote forty-eight instead. Although the jesting notes written on several epitaphs indicate that he composed a few in response to the dinners and gifts with which Del Riccio plied him, the reason for his avid interest in this poetic project for the young nephew of a friend is immediately disclosed by the epitaphs themselves. They reveal that Del Riccio's plea offered Michelangelo an incomparable opportunity to express his thought's preeminent *vita/morte* nucleus, now triggered by his direct confrontation with Cecchino's death and the request that he write on this subject. In this nucleus' syncretic antitheses Michelangelo had captured the totality of his existential-religious world-view: life which bears death and (in its mirror-image ideal, *morte/vita*) death which is eternal life. The revelation and elaboration of this quintessential binomial epitomizing his world-view is the primary goal of both his art[2] and his *Rime.* Thus he zealously seized this unique occasion to lay bare the *vita/morte* binomial which orders his artistic creations. Not surprisingly, therefore, in the mini-laboratory offered by the succinctness of the quatrain epitaphs Michelangelo relentlessly experiments with the expression of his *vita/morte* nucleus, exploring and exploiting all possible expressive avenues to enunciate its key words, *vita* and *morte,* and their associated terms *vivo, morto, vive,* and *muore.* As such, the epitaphs present a singular, microscopic view of the nucleus and concommitant poetics which order his *Rime.*

At times he expresses his nucleus in contexts conforming to the contemporary tastes which would maximally appeal to Cecchino's parents and relatives. In the remaining epitaphs, however, he steadfastly presents the *vita/morte* binomial with the highly personal existential-religious connotations revealed in the rest of the *Rime.* Irrespective of context and connotations, in virtually all his epitaphs the poet underscores the *vita* and *morte* terms of his binomial through the stylistic means which he employs throughout the *Rime* as a constant in his presentation of his nucleus. In the following, representative verses from the epitaphs, we find typical examples of antithetical pairing ("Se più che vivo, morto ha degno ospizio"),[3] caesuras ("Or ne son certo che, vivo, ero morto"),[4] rhythmic stress ("Che l'alma viva, i' che qui morto sono"),[5] rime ("I' fu Cecchino mortale e or son divo: . . . / Che molti morti, e me partorì vivo"),[6] and *enjambement* ("Più che vivo non ero, morto sono / Vivo e caro a chi morte oggi m'ha tolto").[7]

Moreover, in these epitaphs he also displays a singular preference for syntactical distortion to underscore the words of his binomial. This technique reveals itself immediately in his blatant abuse of syntax in the exemplary verses

Chiusi ha qui gli occhi e 'l corpo, e l'alma sciolta
di Cecchin Bracci morte, . . .[8]

Chi qui morto mi piange indarno spera,[9]

and

A la terra la terra e l'alma al cielo
qui reso ha morte; . . .[10]

Examining first the content complying with contemporary taste which Michelangelo exploited in order to incorporate and stylistically highlight his *vita/morte* nucleus, we find that he toys with the wide variety of commonplace contexts which lent themselves to his purposes. Among them is the cliché that Cecchino was the life of those who loved him. If this is so, Michelangelo wryly argues in his expression of the *vita/morte* binomial, then his demise has deprived his loved ones of their lives. He elaborates his binomial in this context by means of the constant juxtaposition of *morte* and *vita:*

Era la vita vostra il suo splendore:
di Cecchin Bracci, che qui morto giace.
Chi nol vide nol perde e vive in pace:
la vita perde chi 'l vide e non muore.[11]

In a similarly trivial vein, he exposes the *vita/morte* nucleus within the popular consideration that the deceased lives in the hearts of those who loved him. His manipulation of this cliché around the *vita/morte* binomial appears in two epitaphs:

De' Bracci nacqui, e dopo 'l primo pianto,
picciol tempo il sol vider gli occhi mei.
Qui son per sempre; né per man vorrei,
s'i' resto vivo in quel che m'amò tanto.[12]

and

Qui vuol mie sorte c'anzi tempo i' dorma,
né son già morto; e ben c'albergo cangi,
resto in te vivo, c'or mi vedi e piangi,
s'l'un nell'altro amante si transforma.[13]

Elsewhere, he turns this concept into a more personalized statement by extolling Cecchino's death as a *morir buono,* disclosing his underlying, fundamental tenet that "Chi cresce per mancar, gli è 'l morir buono":

Più che vivo non ero, morto sono
vivo e caro a chi morte oggi m'ha tolto;
se più c'averne copia or m'ama molto,
chi cresce per mancar, gli è 'l morir buono.[14]

Exploring other ramifications of the life the dead retains in his survivors, he contends that pity for Cecchino's eyes lives in those whom he has left behind. He further threads his *vita/morte* binomial contextually and stylistically into this context by adding a corollary twist, namely, that while Cecchino was alive, pity for his eyes was dead:

> Se qui son chiusi i begli occhi e sepolti
> anzi tempo, sol questo ne conforta:
> che pietà di lor vivi era qua morta;
> or che son morti, di lor vive in molti.[15]

In a grim rendition of this cliché, Cecchino requests that the sepulchre sealing his bones and remains not be opened so his beauty will live unaltered in those who admired it. This permutation of the *vita/morte* nucleus appears in the following verses:

> I' fu' de' Bracci, e qui dell'alma privo
> per esser da beltà fatt'ossa e terra:
> prego il sasso non s'apra, che mi serra,
> per restar bello in chi m'amò già vivo.[16]

In these trite, commonplace contexts which Michelangelo exploits and shapes around the words *vita* and *morte,* his nucleus necessarily has little more than the most superficial literal meaning. In less conventional contexts, however, he lays bare the *vita/morte* nucleus' fundamental connotations as his quintessential existential-religious interpretation of life *vis-à-vis* death and life eternal. In this miniature of his poetry, he again portrays terrestrial life as subject to time and to fortune. Cecchino is at last free from time which has borne him to death and is ". . . fuor degli anni e dell'ore / Che m'han qui chiuso . . ."[17] He is also liberated from the vagaries of fortune and admonishes others to save their pity for those who are, instead, still plied by inexorable fate:

> Deh serbi, s'è di me pietate alcuna
> che qui son chiuso e dal mondo disciolto,
> le lacrime a bagnarsi il petto e 'l volto
> per chi resta suggetto alla fortuna.[18]

Michelangelo's irreducible concept of the mortal and immortal natures of man as earth and spirit emerges repeatedly in verses such as

> A la terra la terra e l'alma al cielo
> qui reso ha morte; . . .[19]

> Se 'l mondo il corpo, e l'alma il ciel ne presta[20]

> I' fu' de' Bracci, e qui dell'alma privo
> per esser da beltà fatt'ossa e terra . . .[21]

and

> Chiusi ha qui gli occhi e 'l corpol, e l'alma sciolta
> di Cecchin Bracci morte, . . .[22]

Underscoring his belief in the utter mortality of the body, he constantly refers to the condition to which death has reduced it, namely, *terra, carne, ossa,* and *spoglia,* as seen in the above verses which find their epitome in the following quatrain:

> La carne terra, e qui l'ossa mie, prive
> de' lor begli occhi e del leggiadro aspetto,

> fan fede a quel ch'i' fu' grazia e diletto
> in che carcer quaggiù l'anima vive.[23]

Elsewhere he extols his corollary conviction that death is not just the reduction of the body to its basic mortal elements but also the liberation of the soul from that "carcer quaggiù [in cui] l'anima vive." His ideal perception of death as the joyous moment of the soul's release from its mortal bonds and return to its heavenly origin emerges emphatically in this epitaph:

> Deposto ha qui Cecchin sì nobil salma
> per morte, che 'l sol ma' simil non vide.
> Roma ne piange, e 'l ciel si gloria e ride,
> che scarca del mortal si gode l'alma.[24]

Precisely because he sees death as the moment of the soul's long-awaited reunion with its Maker, Michelangelo disparages those who wish that Cecchino would return to life and thereby rebind his liberated soul to this mortal being. He states his horror at this thought in Cecchino's words:

> Se fussin, perch'i' viva un'altra volta,
> gli altru' pianti a quest'ossa carne e sangue,
> sarie spietato per pietà chi langue
> per rilegar lor l'alma in ciel disciolta.[25]

In these epitaphs, as in his other poems, Michelangelo also discloses the syncretic nature of his *vita/morte-morte/vita* nucleus. He views mortal life as death when compared to immortality:

> Che l'alma viva, i' che qui morto sono
> or ne son certo che, vivo ero morto.
> I' fu' de' Bracci, e se 'l tempo ebbi corto,
> chi manco vive più speri perdono.[26]

Michelangelo welds death and eternal life both conceptually and stylistically with his constant juxtaposition of these terms and insistent rotation of *enjambement,* alliteration and rime around them and their synonyms in the verse "Po' c'allor nacqui ove la morte muore,"[27] and in the following epitaphs:

> I' fui de' Bracci, e qui mie vita è morte.
> Sendo oggi 'l ciel dalla terra diviso,
> toccando i' sol del mondo al paradiso,
> anzi per sempre serri le suo porte.[28]

and

> I' fu' Cecchin mortale e or son divo:
> poco ebbi 'l mondo e per sempre il ciel gode.
> Di sì bel cambio e di morte mi lodo,
> che molti morti, e me partorì vivo.[29]

While revealing his ideal concept of death as eternal life, Michelangelo also proclaims his unbridled exaltation of death as a "gran ventura" which has no equal in life when he asserts

> Gran ventura qui morto esser mi veggio:
> tal dota ebbi dal cielo, anzi che veglio;
> chè, non possendo al mondo darmi meglio,
> ogni altro che la morte era 'l mie peggio.[30]

and

> Qui giace il Braccio, e men non si desia
> sepulcro al corpo, a l'alma il sacro ufizio.
> Se più che vivo, morto ha degno ospizio
> in terra e 'n ciel, morte gli è dolce e pia.[31]

Thus woven as the very woof and warp of the epitaphs, Michelangelo's personal, ideal view of death emerges in its full reality. It is dear

> (I' fu' de' Bracci e se ritratto e privo
> restai dell'alma, or m'è cara la morte,)[32]

because it promises the reduction of his being to its essence,

> A la terra la terra e l'alma al cielo
> qui reso ha morte;[33]

and disintegrates the prison in which the soul is incarcerated:

> La carne terra, e qui l'ossa mie, prive
> de' lor begli occhi e del leggiardo aspetto,
> fan fede a quel ch'i' fu' grazia e diletto
> in che carcer quaggiù l'anima vive.[34]

and promises eternal life for the soul:

> po' c'allor nacqui ove la morte muore[35]

> Che l'alma viva, i' che qui morto sono
> or ne son certo che, vivo, ero morto.[36]

Michelangelo elaborates his *vita/morte* nucleus into its fullest spiritual connotations in the madrigal he wrote to accompany his epitaphs. It may, therefore, be considered his definitive statement on their governing life/death binomial. In this composition he presents death as the soul's moment of liberation from the corporal body, whereupon it becomes *beato*. He expresses this view of the soul's liberation by death, out of the mortality in which it was born, into life eternal *vis-à-vis* the life/death nucleus in the verses

> S'è ver, com'è che dopo il corpo viva,
> da quel disciolta, c'a mal grado regge
> sol per divina legge,
> l'alma e non prima, allor sol è beata;
> po' che per morte diva
> è fatta sì, com'a morte era nata.

The poet then shifts the focus of his madrigal to the immortal life of the soul gained through death, which he views as an occasion for rejoicing rather than sorrow:

> Dunche, sine peccata,
> in riso ogni suo doglia
> preschiver debbe alcun del suo defunto,
> se da fragile spoglia
> fuor di miseria in vera pace è giunto
> de l'ultim'ora o punto.

He concludes his madrigal's philosophical capsulization of the significance of death with the admonishment that the real friend of the deceased should be more concerned about the departed's immortal nature than with his mortal being:

> Tant'esser de' dell'amico 'l desio,
> quante men val fruir terra che Dio.

The entire madrigal containing Michelangelo's essential statement on his vision of death wherein he incorporates virtually all the spiritual ramifications of his syncretic *vita/morte, morte/vita eterna* nucleus reads as follows:

> S'è ver, com'è, che dopo il corpo viva,
> da quel disciolta, c'a mal grado regge
> sol per divina legge,
> l'alma e non prima, allor sol è beata;
> po' che per morte diva
> è fatta sì, com'a morte era nata.
> Dunche, sine peccata,
> in riso ogni suo doglia
> preschiver debbe alcun del suo defunto,
> se da fragile spoglia
> fuor di miseria in vera pace è giunto
> de l'ultim'ora o punto.
> Tant'esser de' dell'amico 'il desio
> quante men val fruir terra che Dio.[37]

In addition to its significance as the full interpretation of the ideal, *morte/vita eterna,* permutation which orders many of the epitaphs, the madrigal is the key to Michelangelo's entire poetic production, for he composed it to epitomize his poetics and his poetic expression. His definitive madrigal was occasioned by the request, "Mostratelo à Michelagnolo come à censore," with which Donato Giannotti accompanied the sonnet he sent to Del Riccio. The poem Michelangelo was to judge reads

> Messer Luigi mio, di noi che sia,
>     Che siam restati senza il nostro sole?
>     Dove udirem' quelle sante parole
>     A cui cedeva vinta ogni armonia?
> Ove vedrem bontate et cortesia
>     Congiunte insieme? Ove l'honeste e sole
>     Bellezze, che facean strada a chi suole
>     Cercar qua giù da gire al ciel la via?
> Il mondo è fatto rio, poiché la scorta
>     Che gli mostrava il dritto et vero calle
>     Morte gli ha tolto col suo mortale gielo.
> Noi, che senza essa siam per la via torta,
>     Che vogliam far più in questa afflitta valle?
>     Deh, presto andiam a ritrovarla in cielo.

> Telos.[38]

Michelangelo complied with Giannotti's demand that he criticize his sonnet by sending Del Riccio the madrigal cited above, which he accompanied with the following postscript:

> A non parlar qualche volta, se ben scorrecto, in grammatica, mi sarebbe vergogna, sendo tanto pratico con voi. Il sonnecto di messer Donato mi par bello quante cosa facta a' tempi nostri; ma perch'io ò cactivo gusto, non posso far manco stima d'un panno, facto di nuovo, benché romagnuolo, che delle veste usate di seta e d'oro che farén parer bello un uom da sarti. Scrivetegniene e ditegniene e dategniene e racommandatemi a llui.[39]

With this closing, Michelangelo pointedly mimics the excessive, artificial style of his contemporaries. By so doing, he seals his decisively negative judgment of their expressive patterns. To their poetic "veste usate di seta e d'oro," epitomized by Giannotti's sonnet, Michelangelo unabashedly upheld a "panno facto di nuovo, benché romagnuolo" of his own *gusto,* which differed so utterly from that of his contemporaries that he defined it as "cactivo." As Michelangelo the *censore* intended, the diametrically-opposing poetics governing his taste in poetry and the precise nature of the ideal "panno facto di nuovo" expressing them are immediately delineated by a comparison of his madrigal with Giannotti's sonnet.

Giannotti's composition strictly conforms to the poetic norms of the *Cinquecento.* It adheres to the form and content extolled by that Bembian age, namely, the Petrarchan sonnet and the Neoplatonic tenets Bembo had popularized. The Neoplatonic fiber of the Italian *Cinquecento* is blatantly woven into both the content and the terminology of the sonnet's quatrains, in which Giannotti at once presents his interpretation of Cecchino's death as the loss of a Neoplatonic ideal and expresses this concept through Neoplatonic clichés. He describes Cecchino as one who was a *sole,* whose words were *armonia,* who was the union of *bontate* and *cortesia,* and, lastly, whose singular *bellezze* achieved Neoplatonism's highest goal, for they provided the way to Heaven ". . . a chi suole / Cercar qua giù da gire al ciel al via." This ultimate, most popular Neoplatonic concept serves as the basis for the grandiloquent conclusion of the sonnet's *terzine.* Therein, Giannotti expands his Neoplatonic interpretation of Cecchino's death to its most dire consequences, whereby its superficiality reaches the point of banality, as he answers the rhetorical question he posed at the outset of his poem, "Messer Luigi mio, di noi che sia, / Che siam restati senza il nostro sole?" In the first *terzina,* he replies that without Cecchino's beauty to lead it along the "dritto e vero calle," the entire world has been "fatto rio." Consequently, he and Del Riccio are "per la via torta." As such, he sees no reason for them to continue on in this Dantean "afflitta valle," and concludes his Neoplatonic line of argument

in the logically-correct, yet unconscionable exhortation that they hasten to rejoin their young guide in Paradise.

Thus borrowing the Neoplatonic concepts and the poetic form popularized by Bembo and his followers, Giannotti composed a harmonious Petrarchan sonnet cloaked in the fashionable garb of Neoplatonism, which he pursued to the most banal conclusions. Clearly, his composition is exactly as Michelangelo defined it with his usual acumen and succinct revelation of truth. The poem is "bello quante cosa facta a' tempi nostri," for it is written in the conventional metrical form of the *Cinquecento* (the Petrarchan sonnet), its rhetoric reflects the elaborate, superficial ideals of the times, and it is also resplendent in its faddish, Neoplatonic trappings. Precisely because Giannotti's conventional sonnet consists entirely of second-hand form, rhetoric, and content (albethey the most prized and elegant of the day!), Michelangelo aptly described it as "veste usate di seta e d'oro." Moreover, he accurately perceived that such *veste usate di seta e d'oro* give the illusory appearance of beauty to something which has virtually no substance, and that these raiments *farén parer bello un uom da sarti.* His analogy is unerringly correct in every detail, for Giannotti's sonnet is exactly like a *uom da sarti* dressed in *veste usate di seta e d'oro,* which make it *parer bello.* Underneath its elegant, second-hand superficiality—which has worn very thin indeed—Giannotti's poem is hollow and virtually without substance.

The madrigal with which Michelangelo deliberately challenged these "veste usate di seta e d'oro" opposes every aspect of the content and form of Giannotti's epitome of the poetry of the times, which views Cecchino's demise in terms of the shallow, traditional concept of death as a loss for the survivors, and elaborates this perspective through elegant, conventional philosophical avenues, rhetoric and form. Michelangelo's *panno facto di nuovo* is an essential, original poetic expression, which presents his own philosophy on death and is structured entirely around the *vita/morte* nucleus of his thought. His madrigal does not view death as a loss for the deceased's survivors and cause for mourning, but, rather, as the gain of eternal life for the demised and reason for rejoicing.[40] He elaborates this expression of his syncretic, ideal *morte/vita* nucleus by means of his emblematic, original *modus operandi,* ordered entirely toward the quintessential elaboration of his inspiration.

To achieve the unequivocal, concise, yet complete formalization of his *morte/vita* nucleus, Michelangelo characteristically structured his madrigal as a syllogism. The first six verses form the premise. They establish his basilar assumption that death releases the soul from the body and signifies eternal life for the soul. Through death the soul becomes *beata* and *viva,* and ". . . per morte diva / E fatta sì, com'a morte era nata." He extends this fundamental assumption into the conclusion. In fact, his premise that the deceased is one who ". . . da fragile spoglia / Fuor di miseria in vera pace è giunto," serves as the basis for his conclusion that death is cause for rejoicing ("Dunche, sine peccata / In riso ogni suo doglia / Preschiver debbe alcun del suo defunto"). He typically completes his syllogistic madrigal with a closing, aphoristic statement capsulizing his consideration. The maxim is a riming distich, which drives home the fundamental perspective which should govern the Christian survivor's attitude toward death:

> Tant'esser de' dell'amico 'l desio,
> Quante men val fruir terra che Dio.

In striking antithesis to the flamboyant, inane content of Giannotti's sonnet and to the artificial rhetorical question around which the sonnet is loosely structured, the rhetorical device and content of Michelangelo's composition comprise a compact unity in which the content presents a soundly-reasoned, fundamental consideration of death and unerringly arrives at death's most profound significance by virtue of the syllogistic structure. Thus interwoven, the content and the syllogistic structure achieve the essential formalization of Michelangelo's ideal *morte/vita* nucleus.

Similarly, the language Michelangelo employs in his madrigal vividly contrasts the ornate, superficial, and conventional language found in Giannotti's poem, which Michelangelo ridiculed in the closing to his critical comments on Giannotti's work with the words, "Scrivetegniene e ditegniene e dategniene e racommandatemi a lui." Giannotti embellished his composition with worn-out Neoplatonic clichés and terminology, has incorporated a Dantean expression and overtones, and concludes with an erudite display of Greek. Michelangelo's expression is characteristically simple, straightforward, and utterly devoid of all elements which do not function toward the most parsimonious realization of his *vita/morte* nucleus. Even his employment of Latin is not a useless embellishment of his composition with a scholarly tone, as is Giannotti's Greek closing. On the contrary, the Latin expression Michelangelo incorporates in his madrigal, *sine peccata,* so immediately evokes all fundamental Christian tenets that it underscores the orthodoxy of his assertion that death must be greeted with joy.

Like its syllogistic structure and language, the madrigal's style and metrical form are also ordered solely toward the essential realization of the *vita/morte* nucleus. In this instance, as in the other poems of the **Rime,** style is strictly related to language, serving to isolate the key words of his argument, and thus articulate the essence of his *vita/morte* consideration. His characteristic stylistic pattern is immediately apparent in the madrigal's first six verses, to which I will limit this study. They state the premise ordering the entire madrigal, *i.e.,* death signifies the soul's release from the body and, therefore, its beatitude and eternal life. Each of the key words of this premise emerges from the madrigal's verbal matrix as a result of the stylistic stress placed on it. Michelangelo underscores *viva,* the last word of the first verse, by means of its terminal position and by a following caesura. He emphasizes *l'alma,* the subject of *viva,* by its position as the first word of the fourth verse and by the preceding caesura. The explanation for the soul's life, namely, its separation from the body, is capsulized in the word isolated by the second verse's caesura: *disciolta.* The nature of the soul's life resulting from its separation from the body is stressed at the end of the fourth verse in the concluding word of the clauses of verses 1-4: *beata.* Through this stylistic emphasis of the key words of his consideration, Michelangelo has pared the premise of verse 1-4 to its schematic quiddity: *viva disciolta l'alma beata.*

The fifth and sixth verses bring to the fore the essence of his premise that death signifies eternal life for the soul. By means of *enjambement* and trochaic rhythm, he isolates the fifth verse's last two words—a binomial epitomizing his premise—*morte/diva.* Ultimately laying bare the *morte/vita* nucleus governing his premise, he expresses the quintessence of his view of death as life in the concluding words of the clause isolated by caesuras at the end of the premise, *a morte era nata.*

Through such skillful employment of caesuras, *enjambement,* positional and rhythmic stress, Michelangelo formalizes a verbal diagram enunciating the essence of his assertion that death signifies the soul's liberation from the body and birth into eternal life. He reserves rime, the remaining stylistic element, to underscore the blessed life into which the soul is born. Masterfully formalizing this two-fold *unicum*—the soul's simultaneous birth and beatitude—he employs rime to fuse the two words representing the concurrent life and beatitude of this event, *viva/diva,* and *nata/beata.*

Thus, through total unity of form and content achieved with his full exploitation of the freedom of rime and versification offered by his preferred metrical scheme, the madrigal, Michelangelo attains the quintessential, yet complete realization of his ideal *morte/vita* nucleus. The content, imagery, rhetorical devices, language, style, rime, and metrical scheme he employs differ drastically from the merely elaborate, randomly-combined elements found in Giannotti's sonnet. Indeed, they are tightly interwoven into an essential unity whose every component functions directly in relation to the quintessential and total realization of the *vita/morte nuce* of Michelangelo's inspiration.

With this "panno facto di nuovo" he unabashedly and definitively upheld to his contemporaries' "veste usate di seta e d'oro" the poet himself substantiates his poetics and resultant poetic expression. He affirms his utter and purposeful rejection of the artificial, superficial, borrowed content and form of the poetry of the *Cinquecento* for an essential, original poetry reflecting his own tastes. He attests that his poetics express themselves, above all, in relation to the *vita/morte* nucleus governing his thought. Moreover, with his own exemplary madrigal he demonstrates the manner in which he realized the diverse, existential-religious connotations the *vita/morte* symbol has as the representation of his personal concept of existence. He arrives at the most concise and precise elaboration of this nucleus by means of the syllogistic structure. At the same time, his style brings out the essence of his content by reducing it to a highlighted verbal schemata forming the total, essential statement of the *vita/morte* nucleus. This epitome of his *panno facto di nuovo* written at the peak of his poetic production thus testifies that Michelangelo's poetic expression is dominated by his quest for the quintessential, complete expression of the *vita/morte* symbol through a content and form wholly ordered toward that goal.

A study of his **Rime** confirms this fact. Michelangelo developed the expression of the *vita/morte* nucleus in the formative period (1504-1531) of his poetic career. Therein he employs it to epitomize not only his existential view ("Chiunche nasce a morte arriva"),[41] but also his spiritual crisis caused by his compromising amorous inclinations. He believed that they caused his life to be one of spiritual death and thereby jeopardized his soul's ideal passage through death into life eternal. As one bound to love, he pours out his anguish and lays bare the *vita/morte* epitome of his damnable state in the writhing, tortured verses

> Vivo al peccato, a me morendo vivo;
> vita già mia non son, ma del peccato:
> mie ben dal ciel, mie mal da m'è dato,
> dal mie sciolto voler, di ch'io son privo.
>   Serva mie libertà, mortal mie divo
> a me s'è fatto.   O infelice stato!
> a che miseria, a che viver son nato![42]

The *morta/vita* nucleus similarly emerges as the quintessence of the poetry inspired by Tommaso de' Cavalieri (1532-1536), as this representative quatrain reveals:

> Vivo della mie morte, e se ben guardo,
> felice vivo d'infelice sorte;
> e chi viver non sa d'angoscia e morte,
> nel foco venga, ov'io mi struggo e ardo.[43]

In the madrigals directed to Vittoria Colonna and the *donna* "bella e crudele" (1537-1546), the *vita/morte* interpretation of his thought manifests its consummate achievement. These compositions are contemporary to the epitaphs and his exemplary madrigal and comprise the majority of the poems he selected for publication. In those inspired by the donna "bella e crudele," *morte* and *vita* become the epitome of the cruel, amorous battle she wages against him:

> Questa mie donna è sì pronta e ardita,
> c'allor che la m'ancide ogni mie bene
> cogli occhi mi promette, e parte tiene
> il crudel ferro dentro a la ferita.
> E così morte e vita,
> contrarie, insieme in un picciol momento
> dentro a l'anima sento;
> ma la grazia il tormento
> da me discaccia per più lunga pruova:
> c'assai più nuoce il mal che 'l ben non giova.[44]

He reveals the life/death essence of this battle even more blatantly in poems such as the following, representative madrigal which also manifests his characteristic employment of concrete metaphors, similes and terminology drawn from military operations to vividly incorporate her warfare:

> Il mio refugio e 'l mio ultimo scampo
> qual più securo è, che non sia men forte
> che 'l pianger e 'l pregar? e non m'aita.
> Amor e crudeltà m'han posto il campo
> l'un s'arma di pietà, l'altro di morte;
> questa n'ancide, e l'altra tien in vita.
> Così l' alma impedita
> del suo morir, che sol poria giovarne,
> più volte per andarne
> s'è mossa là dov'esser sempre spera,
> dov'è beltà sol fuor di donna altiera;
> ma l'imagine vera,
> della qual vivo, allor risorge al core,
> perché da morte non sia vinto amore.[45]

In the compositions inspired by Vittoria Colonna, daring metaphors, similes and vocabulary taken from his artistic experience graphically figure the spiritual metamorphosis Michelangelo undergoes as this virtuous spiritual sculptress of his existence reshapes with love his obstinate being out of death into its virtual spiritual perfection. The words he derives from his artistic experience to express the life/death nucleus in this context are those taken from sculpting, *pone/levare*, *accresce/lima*, and *cresce/scemare*; those borrowed from metal casting, *ristoro/rompa-strazi*; and their parallels in his own life, *crescendo/mancar-morte*, as witnessed in the following madrigal and sonnet:

> Sì come per levar, donna, si pone
> in pietra alpestra e dura
> una viva figura,
> che là più cresce u' più la pietra scema;
> tal alcun'opre buone,
> per l'alma che pur trema,
> cela il superchio della propria carne
> co' l'inculta sua cruda e dura scorza.
> Tu pur dalle mie streme
> parti puo' sol levarne,
> ch'in me non è di, me voler né forza.[46]

and

> Se ben concetto ha la divina parte
> il volto e gli atti d'alcun, po' di quello
> doppio valor con breve e vil modello
> dà vita a' sassi, e non è forza d'arte.
>
> Né altrimenti in più rustiche carte,
> anz'una pronta man prenda 'l pennello,
> fra' dotti ingegni il più accorto e bello
> pruova e rivede, e suo storie comparte.
>
> Simil di me model di poca istima
> mie parto fu, per cosa alta e prefetta
> da voi rinascer po', donna alta e degna.
>
> Se 'l poco accresce, e 'l mie superchio lima
> vostra mercé, qual penitenzia aspetta
> mie fiero ardor, se mi gastiga e 'nsegna?[47]

While the content graphically figures the quintessence of his thought, as in the exemplary madrigal the style of the compositions directed to these two women reduces their content to its essential statement of his *vita/morte* nucleus. At the same time, however, it also transmits *in toto* the tremendous tension accompanying this inner drama. It does so by straining his expression to the breaking point with *enjambements,* caesuras, antithesis, distorted syntax, difficult and harsh rime schemes, and the abolition of all melody and harmony. Through this singular "espressione tormentata, sofferta, la più lontana possibile (nei suoi centri più intensi) dalle vie facili . . . il rifiuto dell'armonia, e più, della melodia e la ricerca di forme in tensione e in contrasto dinamico,"[48] which characterizes his poetic expression until 1547, Michelangelo also communicates the acute tension and conflict inherent to his *vita/morte* struggle.

In his final poetic period (1547-1564), as a result of the belief in faith encouraged by Vittoria Colonna, the conflict of Michelangelo's *vita/morte* interpretation of existence utterly dissolved in the redemptive blood of Christ. To epitomize this heightened spiritual understanding, he submits his life/death binomial to a metaphoric consubstantiation, and it becomes Christ's *sangue.* That *sangue*—the very symbol of life and death in their absolute mortal and spiritual dimensions, and the promise that death will be eternal life—now becomes the consummate expression of Michelangelo's *vita/morte* nucleus and dominates his thought. Abandoning the freest of all metrical forms through which he could so completely realize the terrible drama of his inner being, he replaced the madrigral with the Petrarchan sonnet as his preferred poetic form. The harmonious and serene Petrarchan style transmits the spiritual peace he at last secured at the end of his life, while the imagery of a ship's safe arrival in a calm harbor formalizes the tranquil conclusion to his life's stormy *iter.* Again form and content faithfully merge to present the quintessence of his inspiration:

> Scarco d'un'importuna e greve salma,
> Signor mie caro, e dal mondo disciolto,

> qual fragil legno a te stanco rivolto
> da l'orribil procella in dolce calma.
>
> Le spine e' chiodi e l'una e l'altra palma
> prometton grazia di pentirsi molto,
> e speme di salute a la trist'alma.
>
> Non mirin co' iustizia i tuo sant'occhi
> il mie passato, e 'l gastigato orecchio;
> non tenda a quello il tuo braccio severo.
>
> Tuo sangue sol mie colpe lavi e tocchi,
> e più abondi, quanti'i' son più vecchio,
> di pronta aita e di perdono intero.[49]

Thus, throughout his lyric poetry Michelangelo single-mindedly translates his inner world into the *vita/morte* nucleus, around which he orders all facets of language and versification. The forty-eight epitaphs and their accompanying madrigal in which he incessantly explores stylistically and conceptually the expression of the *vita/morte-morte/vita* nucleus in the core of the **Rime** are, therefore, not egregious elements. They emerge, instead, as Michelangelo's revelation of that thought and poetics which shape his singular *panno facto di nuovo.*[50]

### Notes

1. Ed. Enzo Noè Girardi, *Michelangelo Buonarroti, Rime* (Bari: Gius. Laterza & Figli, 1960), p. 99, poem numbered 193. *N.B.* Michelangelo's poems will subsequently be referred to by the number given to them by Girardi in this book and will appear as G plus the number of the poem.

2. Michelangelo's earliest sculpted creations were conceived and executed as paired, antithetical unicums representing life and death (1491-1503). See Charles de Tolnay, *The Youth of Michelangelo* (Princeton: Princeton University Press, 1947), pp. 75-92. In the *Medici Chapel,* begun in 1524 and completed in 1532, Michelangelo achieved the total syncretic expression of his life/death-death eternal live nucleus. In this work the four rivers of Hades (intended to be placed below the sarcophagi) symbolize eternal fluctuation and the unyielding forces exerting their power over the life of man. The allegories of time—*Day, Night, Dusk* and *Dawn*—whose onward flow has brought man to his death, recline upon the sarcophagi. Yet they are now the vanquished, not the victors. In fact, the sarcophagi are cleft in the middle, and they apotheoses of the *Duchi* sit high above them. These figures fix their gaze eternally on the Virgin and Child, and represent mankind's victory, made possible through Christ, over the inexorable forces of fate, death and time. See Charles de Tolnay, *The Medici Chapel* (Princeton: Princeton University Press, 1948), pp. 29-75.

3. G221, v. 3.

4. G226, v. 2.

5. G226, v. 1.

6. G223, v. 4.

7. G204, vv. 1-2.

8. G224, vv. 1-2.

9. G199, v. 1.

10. G215, vv. 1-2.

11. G214.

12. G203.

13. G194.

14. G204.

15. G179.

16. G225.

17. G201, vv. 1-2. *Cfr.* G14, G17, vv. 5-7; G21, G50, vv. 1-2; and G92.

18. G180. *Cfr.* G1, G104, vv. 1-7; G86, vv. 49-53.

19. G215, vv. 1-2. *Cfr.* G106, vv. 1-2, G264, vv. 4-6, and G274, vv. 9-11.

20. G228, v. 1.

21. G225, vv. 1-2.

22. G224, vv. 1-2.

23. G197.

24. G220. *Cfr.* G86, vv. 49-57; 61-63.

25. G198.

26. G226. Michelangelo again states his view that the shortest mortal life is best for the soul in G133, vv. 11-13, G134, vv. 14-15, G269, vv. 9-11, G294, vv. 10-11, and G295, vv. 10-11.

27. G201, v. 4. *Cfr.* G86, v. 46.

28. G219.

29. G223.

30. G196.

31. G221.

32. G202, vv. 1-2.

33. G215, vv. 1-2.

34. G197.

35. G201, v. 4.

36. G226, vv. 1-2.

37. G192.

38. Ed. Karl Frey, *Die Dichtungen des Michelagniolo Buonarroti* (Berlin: Grote, 1897), p. 269.

39. Girardi, *op. cit.,* p. 371.

40. Michelangelo expresses this view of death also in a letter to Vasari denouncing the celebration Michelangelo's nephew gave for the birth of his first son. Michelangelo states: ". . . mi pare che Lionardo non abbi molto giudicio e massimo per fare tanta festa d'uno che nasce, con quella allegrezza che s'à a serbare alla morte di chi è ben vissuto." *Lettere di Michelangelo Buonarroti pubblicate coi ricordi ed i contratti artistici* per cura di Gaetano Milanesi (Firenze: Le Monnier, 1875), p. 533.

41. G21, v. 1.

42. G32.

43. G56.

44. G124.

45. G112.

46. G152.

47. G236.

48. Walter Binni, *Michelangelo scrittore* (Roma: Edizioni dell'Ateneo, 1965), p. 12.

49. G290.

50. This text is an elaboration of material discussed in Ann H. Hallock, *Michelangelo The Poet* (Palo Alto: Page-Ficklin Publications, 1978).

## Glauco Cambon (essay date 1985)

SOURCE: Cambon, Glauco. "Humor, Transgressions, and Ambivalences." In *Michelangelo's Poetry: Fury of Form*, pp. 3-40. Princeton, N.J.: Princeton University Press, 1985.

[*In the following essay from his full-length study of Michelangelo's verse, Cambon surveys elements of humor, satire, and playfulness in the early pieces, as well as the poet's increasing use of verbal ambiguity and religious themes in his late pieces.*]

In 1898 Heinrich Wölfflin gave this afterthought on the Sistine Chapel ceiling frescoes, which he had just described as a triumph of vitality:

> If the figures painted on the ceiling did not so clearly betray the surging joy of their creator at work, one could say that the artist had vented his bad mood there and endeavored to avenge himself for the unloved task: let the Vatican gentlemen get their ceiling, but they might as well have to strain their necks for it.[1]

Whether Wölfflin thought of it or not when writing that passage, a burlesque poem by Michelangelo himself voices the resentment we could never descry in the hovering giants that sprang from his brush during the years of this Herculean labor (1508-1512). It is a well-known caudate sonnet penned in the same period,[2] apparently never meant for publication (unlike so many others), and it is visually corroborated by a sketch in which the artist caricatures himself in the act of painting a ceiling just above his head. The poem is kept in the Archivio Buonarroti at the Florence Laurenziana Library,[3] but the critical editions of Michelangelo's poetry by Guasti (1863) and Frey (1897)[4] had made it widely known by the time Wölfflin published his book on Italian Renaissance art:

> I'o gia facto un gozo in questo stento
> chome fa l'acqua a' gacti in Lombardia
> o ver d'altro paese che si sia
> ch'a forza 'l ventre apicha socto 'l mento.
>    La barba al cielo ella memoria sento
>    in sullo scrignio e 'l pecto fo d'arpia.
>    e 'l pennel sopra 'l uiso tuctavia
>    mel fa gocciando un ricco pauimento.
> E' lombi entrati mi son nella peccia
> e fo del cul per chontrappeso groppa
> e' passi senza gli ochi muouo inuano.
>    Dinanzi mi s'allunga la chorteccia,
>    e per piegarsi indietro si ragroppa,
>    e tendomi com'archo soriano.
> Però fallace e strano
> surgie el iuditio che la mente porta
> ché mal si tra' per cerboctana storta.
>    La mia pictura morta
> difendi ormai Giovanni e 'l mio onore
> non sendo in loco bon ne io pictore.

> I've developed a goiter on this chore,
> as water does to cats in Lombardy
> or wherever such kind of trouble happens,
> for my belly strains up to touch my chin.
>    My beard rears up, my occiput I feel
>    upon my back, my chest turns harpy-like,
>    and the paintbrush drips all over my face
>    so as to make a gaudy floor of it.
> My loins have pushed up well into the paunch,
> I use my butt for counterweight as crupper,
> my feet I move, unseeing, to little purpose.
>    On the front side my pelt stretches lengthwise,
>    on the back it wrinkles up as I bend,
>    and I tauten much like a Syrian bow.
> Therefore my very faculty of judgment
> has become faulty and odd, for it is hard
> to shoot a dart through an old crooked pipe.
>    My painting, which is dead,
> now please defend, Giovanni, and my honor too,
> for I am out of place, and am no painter.

Since biographical sources and direct evidence tend to date the inception of Michelangelo's verse writing either to the last years of the fifteenth century or to the first years of the sixteenth (mainly 1502),[5] this sonnet belongs to the first phase of his poetry, not to the ripe harvest of those definitively Roman years (the 1530s and 1540s) that saw his involvement with Tommaso Cavalieri and Vittoria Colonna and his sodality with fellow expatriates from Florence like Luigi del Riccio

and Donato Giannotti. The burlesque sonnet might accordingly strike us as marginal to Michelangelo's main body of poetical work, as indeed part and parcel of his literary apprenticeship, considering the dominance of Platonic earnest in theme and style of his mature phase.[6] It is this earnest, with the attendant soarings, sublimations, and convolutions, that first comes to our minds when we think of Michelangelo as poet; we do not primarily consider him an earthy Bernesque writer, regardless of the admiration Berni professed for his style (all things and no words for their own sake),[7] an admiration that was not limited to the burlesque parts of Michelangelo's canzoniere.

Now the relative importance or ratio of comical to "serious" writing in Michelangelo's canon, while drastically lower than is the case with Berni or with Lorenzo de' Medici (Michelangelo's patron and substitute father in the formative years from 1489 to 1492), does bear scrutiny. To begin with, the comical vein does not entirely dry up after Michelangelo's initial phase; it cannot be relegated to mere apprenticeship even though his literary talent for the most part developed in another direction altogether. We only have to recall the striking *capitolo ternario* from the 1540s where the artist lavishes saturnine humor on a caricature of himself in the compounded predicament of isolation, filth, pent-up bile, poor health, and relentless hard work. And then there is the late sonnet written to Giorgio Vasari by way of a thank-you note for some practical gifts (a mule and sundry victuals), though the mood here is jovial, not atrabilious. Earlier work in a comparable mode can also be adduced, notably the three *ottava rima* stanzas (G 20, from 1518-1524) obviously echoing Lorenzo de' Medici's comico-rustical idyll *Nencia da Barberino*,[8] then the similarly attuned and incomplete stanzas G 54 from 1531-1532, and the affable *capitolo ternario* G 85 of 1534 to Francesco Berni.

Statistics and chronology aside, there are further aspects to be taken into account. Michelangelo's ineradicable Tuscan wit is attested by Vasari and Condivi, and it was certainly nurtured in Lorenzo's entourage at the San Marco gardens. There Pico della Mirandola, Cristoforo Landino, and Marsilio Ficino acquainted the apprentice sculptor with the essentials of Plato's thought while Angelo Poliziano and Lorenzo himself administered a good dose of vernacular humor to spice up the diet of literary sophistication to which Michelangelo was treated daily at the Medici table. Lorenzo's and Poliziano's affinity for Tuscan folk taste is well known and amply documented by some of their best poetry; it was also compatible with their humanist erudition. Michelangelo's variations on Laurentian rustic theme and mode in the *strambotto*-like stanzas mentioned above are one result of that rich exposure and a proof of its fruitfulness—for in the transition from G 20 to G 54 a leavening takes place, and certain attitudes of discourse and imagery show consonance with much else in his *canzoniere*. The same can be said of the differently keyed sonnet cited above. It has nothing immature or uncertain about it, and it formulates recurrent motifs of the **Rime.** The racy lexicon and idiomatic phrasing quicken the diction. It is a pungent Florentine voice we hear, straight from the market square, and if it makes the persona its own reflexive target it is because it can laugh at the whole world. The laughter has the savagery of satire without moralizing purposes; it is rage turned inside out, with the result that caricature wreaked on the self-punishing speaker arouses a cathartic hilarity. Realist depiction is pushed by hyperbole to the verge of hallucinatory effect—a process that will peak in the *capitolo* of the 1540s with its similar subject and approach to paint an anti-self-portrait that is also the portrait of Michelangelo's anti-self, his underground voice.

Underground and Florentine with a vengeance, the sonnet cannot be abstracted from its occasion, the protracted work in Pope Julius II's Rome. If we accept Girardi's 1512 dating, the same predicament also elicited a scathing invective from the poet in sonnet G 10.[9] Chafing at Julius's overbearing, unpredictable moods (and see the complaint voiced in sonnet G 6) and resenting the blatant intrigues of the Roman court, Michelangelo could not help feeling a deep loneliness. Thus he would delve into his municipal soil to find relief in the earthy dialect that was himself, his roots, his forsaken city. The savage mirth of those words from the Arno's shore, *gozzo, scrigno, peccia, cul, corteccia*; words to horrify the effete courtiers and Petrarchizing purists; words to be felt, not just heard, in their tactile quality, like clay to be modeled into bizarre shapes or flung at irritating strangers; the bluntness of statement; the liberating outrage—it was all an epistolary conspiracy with the witty fellow Tuscan, Giovanni da Pistoia, who was to receive more such "off the record" missives from Michelangelo.

To view the sonnet as a mere literary exercise in the familiar Florentine tradition that went all the way back to Cecco Angiolieri two centuries before and to Rustico di Filippo, as if the mask had nothing to do with the outraged-amused writer, would do it scant justice.[10] Michelangelo was always the careful craftsman in whatever he did, including literary exercise; yet such exercise was deeply motivated. The confessional stance was intrinsic to his whole writing, even at its most artificial. We can also profitably reflect on the circumstance that, though this poem has generally been seen as a link in the intermittent chain of Michelangelo's "Bernesque" verse, it took shape long before its author could have heard of Berni, who was still in his teens at the time. Michelangelo, who did get some literary education along with the solid training in painting and sculpture, toward the turn of the century immersed himself in the protracted study of vernacular classics,

Dante and Petrarch in particular (as Condivi. reports in his biography). A 1534 lyric (G 84) shows awareness of the "three styles" (the low, the middle, and the lofty) in literature, and we can credit its author with the discrimination needed to comply with the requirements of the art to which he last initiated himself to practice it with almost lifelong fidelity (i.e. until 1560). As with the other arts he mastered, the craftsman's discipline helped to make the medium transparent and pliable to his inner fire. Writing was a challenge, not a hobby.

There can be little doubt that in the "low-style" vernacular chosen for an expressive outlet in sonnet G 5, medium promptly matched motive to make it easier for the underground man in Michelangelo to emerge on the page. The manuscript shows no variant or erasure, and there are no other known drafts. One aspect we have failed to consider so far in this cantankerous persona is the extent to which his rebellion involves the very art he had been practicing rather than just the formidable pope who kept him at it. Michelangelo's final disclaimer of his status as a painter cannot be taken at face value, if we but keep in mind the impressive upshot of his back-breaking toil at the Sistine Chapel's ceiling; not even his epistolary avowals of preference for sculpture over painting will make us forget that he earnestly competed with other artists to secure this task while having to engage in the planning and execution of the project that was to be, for over three decades, his marble albatross: Julius II's monumental tomb. Far from intruding on our interpretive commitment, these biographical facts help us to understand the poem that took shape as a private communication to a friend fully aware of the circumstances. All we can do is eavesdrop on the concentrated exchange. About thirty-five years later the tercets that take up the topic in comparable vein (G 267) will give us less "in-talk" and more direct revelation, since the persona will be explicitly speaking to himself rather than to a conspiratorially addressed correspondent; and in talking to himself he will grimly, if humorously, take stock of everything he is and has done.

Meanwhile, if we listen to the private conversation between Michelangelo and Giovanni da Pistoia during a lull in the painter's relentless work, we get a surprising unofficial picture. The giant turns dwarf, the sublime artist plays "angel of the odd" to make light of the burden he has taken on. It is a liberating game, we guess, for the destructive self-caricature has a hearty overtone and the low-pitched voice evinces a breeziness that undercuts the literal message. Yet the *coda* tercets prevent us from taking the bulk of the sonnet as pure tongue-in-cheek talk, so earnest they are. Or are they? Is not their seriousness actually a new mask, a subtler counterfeit of tone? Our judgment sways in the scales like the writer's own, "fallacious and strange." The self-mockery channels a protest, but the protest in turn fails to stifle the bizarre hilarity of the whole scene.

Michelangelo demystifying himself and his own best work is uproarious, and if in the process he has belittled his figure to offset the majestic images with which he manages to people that murderous ceiling, the laughter is still gigantic. He seems to dismiss the whole endeavor with an annoyed gesture, but the incongruity between that gesture and the permanent outcome of the endeavor so decried can only heighten our wonderment at the pent-up genius who could both release such boundless energy and make merciless fun of the procedure. Try as he may, the underground man cannot convince us of his smallness. He is the genie in the bottle, as poem G 267 will clarify after 1545:

> I' sto rinchiuso come la midolla
> da la sua scorza, qua pover e solo,
> come spirto legato in un'ampolla . . .

> I am enclosed as the fruit's pulp is
> by its own husk, poor and alone as I am here,
> like a genie confined within a bottle. . . .

The related image of pulp and husk already looms in the 1511-1512 sonnet, second tercet:

> Dinanzi mi s'allunga la *chorteccia*,
> e per piegarsi indietro si ragroppa,
> e tendomi chom'arco soriano.

> On the front side my *pelt* stretches lengthwise,
> on the back it wrinkles up as I bend,
> and I tauten much like a Syrian bow.

The Italian word *corteccia* (from Latin *cortex*) is multivalent; in this context it metaphorically denotes the human skin (and that has reminded some scholars, especially Robert Clements,[11] of the skin of St. Bartholomew in the Sistine Last Judgment, of which Michelangelo was to make a bizarre self-portrait). Its primary meaning, however, is vegetal, denoting either a fruit's husk or peel or a tree's bark, and in this sense its synonym *scorza* recurs not only in the burlesque tercets of G 267 but also in some high-pitched madrigals, notably G 152 and G 158, with the same self-disparaging implication:

> tal alcun'opre buone,
> per l'alma che pur trema,
> cela il superchio della propria carne
> co' l'inculta sua cruda e dura *scorza*

> just so some good works,
> for the still trembling soul,
> my own excess flesh hides
> with its uncouth, crude and crusty shell

(G 152)

> Caduto è il frutto e secca è già la *scorza*,
> e quel, già dolce, amaro or par ch'i' senta

> Fallen the fruit and dry is now its *husk*,
> and what was sweet tastes bitter now to me.

(G 158)

Clements connects this recurrent imagery (for which see also G 51) to the salient theme of the potential form hiding in the marble block as it waits for the sculptor's liberating mallet and chisel, with its metaphoric correlative of the redeemed soul waiting to be released from its enveloping shell of flesh and sin, and madrigal 152 makes the connection good.

On a different line of development, in the burlesque tercets of the late 1540s the image ushers in the climactic one of the genie in the bottle, whereas in the caudate sonnet from 1511-1512 it modulates into the likewise significant simile of the Syrian bow. And here we may notice a consonance with the motto-like verse that Michelangelo had jotted down ten years before on a sheet carrying two sketches of a David figure:

> Davicte colla fromba e io coll'arco.

> Michelagnolo.


> David with his sling and I with the bow.

> Michelagnolo.

Even if we accept Girardi's interpretation, according to which the sling stands for strength and the bow for ingeniousness, it is far from inappropriate to descry a similarity of meaning and function in the comical simile of the bow as the sonnet uses it, for it conveys resilience, namely strength and resourcefulness combined on the part of the grotesquely struggling persona. In the very teeth of the unsparing reflexive sarcasm, this makes the difference between total defeat and survival. It also outlines a dynamic pattern that can be said to typify Michelangelo's syntactical rhythms and overall poetic impact: torsion, tension, and sudden release. Nor is this pattern irrelevant to the "serpentine form" that Lomazzo reports as Michelangelo's specific prescription for pictorial or sculptural design[12] and that actually marks so much of his visual art.

Since the caudate sonnet on the Sistine ceiling labors anticipates in significant respects the *capitolo ternario* from the late 1540s, it would seem advisable to analyze the two revealing poems in juxtaposition, chronologically distant though they are; but before spanning that long interval for the sake of specific comparison, I will touch on the other burlesque poems that intervene. I shall leave out of this context the biting sonnet G 6 (a reproach to Pope Julius II that casts additional light on the preceding poem) as well as the better known sonnet

G 10, which—as an outburst against Roman corruption and personal wrongs—has obvious power (thanks to the germane folksy language) but nothing properly humorous about it. Closer to our context is poem G 20, a set of three *ottava rima* stanzas in the manner of Lorenzo the Magnificent's rustic idyll, *Nencia da Barberino*; it shows the eager versatility of Michelangelo in a phase of his literary development (1518-1524) when he was still feeling his way into expressive maturity and eclectically appropriating many a cherished model. It also bespeaks his love for the rich native idiom of the Florentine countryside, a welcome relief from the stylized rarefactions to which Petrarchan mannerism was subjecting literary Tuscan. Michelangelo himself was no stranger to that rarefying trend, since Petrarch (if not Bembo's Petrarchism) was with him from the start, to judge from several pieces of his early season that pale by comparison with the coeval endeavors in the burlesque, satirical, or polemical mode.

Symptomatically enough, a nonburlesque love poem from 1507 (sonnet G 4) had achieved a sensuous grace that is missing from his early attempts at Petrarchan style; and if Clements has rightly indicated in certain verses from Poliziano's *Stanze per la giostra* the lexical and iconic model,[13] that model is so successfully appropriated that the tribute to a vanished master becomes a personal achievement on the part of the pupil. I would not hesitate to place this joyful lyric alongside the humanist sculpture of the Bargello *Bacchus* as evidence of the surviving Quattrocento spirit in an artist bound for bleaker shores. But the folklike stanzas of poem G 54, at the beginning of the 1530s, resume the Nencia-like intonation of G 20 to modulate it into a variegated mimesis of nonrustic plebeian language. Some critics (Barelli, for instance) have defined this language as Bernesque to characterize its comical hyperboles without taking the trouble to add that, if anything, Michelangelo here outdoes his younger friend in stylistic capers and, above all, in emotional fervor. By 1531-1532 (the dating to be gathered from the manuscript itself) Berni was famous, and his maverick work could very well stimulate Michelangelo's offbeat strain; at the same time, if Lorenzo and Berni (and perhaps Angiolieri for the initial cadence) must be reckoned with as compounded models, the experiment goes way beyond literary pastiche to achieve a strange dramatic tone of its own. Berni's burlesque verse, like his literary parodies, has a steadier ring, whereas Michelangelo's voice restlessly ranges through an ample register from low to high and back, and the earthy imagery, which does not shun scatology, can also light up into glowing intensity.

Several images stay with us for their poignant concreteness, sustained as it is by a narrative fluency of Florentine plebeian type that authenticates the whole dramatic monologue:

Io crederrei, se tu fussi di sasso,
amarti con tal fede, ch'i' potrei
farti meco venir più che di passo . . .

(lines 1-3)

I do believe, were you just made of stone,
that I would love you with such faith that I
could make you come to me at a brisk pace . . . ;

Tu non se' fatta com'un uom da sarti,
che si muove di fuor, si muove drento;
e se dalla ragion tu non ti parti,
spero ch'un dì tu mi farai contento:
ché 'l morso il ben servir toglie a' serpenti,
come l'agresto quand'allega i denti . . .

(lines 11-16)

You are not made like a tailor's manikin,
which one can move outside and also inside;
and if you don't part company with reason,
I hope one day you'll make me happy, finally:
for niceness takes away their bite from snakes,
the way sour fruit will tie your teeth and tongue . . . ;

una nuova nel mondo alta beltate
come la tuo non ha 'ltrimenti il core;
c'una vagina, ch'è dritta a vedella,
non può dentro tener torte coltella . . .

(lines 21-24)

a lofty beauty as yours is, which the world
never saw the like of, has no other heart;
for a sheath that is good and straight to see
will never hold a twisted knife inside. . . .

And again, in the incomplete fifth stanza, the joy of seeing his reluctant sweetheart after just one day of absence fills our plebeian Romeo like a good meal after long fasting; in stanza 6 he sighs for her, and his sighs "would make a heated furnace even more redhot"; when she is around, he

sfavill[a] come ferro in foco ardente

sparkle[s] like iron glowing in the fire.

In the following stanza, when she smiles or greets him on the street he "jumps up like a rocket" and, to his chagrin, becomes self-defeatingly speechless; for the great love he feels inside (stanza 8) might lift him up to the stars, but when he wants to express it, there is no suitable outlet, and this immense love once uttered will look and sound too much smaller than it is, such flights of the soul not being amenable to words.

With stanza 10, the platonizing motif of the beloved image entering the lover's soul through his eyes to grow into full mastery of his inner being undergoes an uproarious burlesque metamorphosis, which both parodies genteel Renaissance poetry (as well as two nonburlesque pieces by Michelangelo himself, madrigal G 8 and fragment G 44) and fulfills the dramatic requirements of the jolly monologue as such. This is the tenor of the two poems in question:

> How can it be that I am no longer mine?
> O God, o God, o God,
> who has taken myself away from me
> so as to be closer to me than myself
> and have more power on myself than I?
> O God, o God, o God,
> how can he transfix my heart
> who does not even seem to touch me?
> What is this, Love,
> that enters the heart through the eyes,
> and in such small space seems to grow inside?
> What if it were to overflow?

(G 8)

> While to the beauty that I saw before birth
> my soul draws near, seeing through the eyes,
> the image grows inside, and my own soul
> yields and dwindles to worthless paltriness.
> Love, that busy engineer so apt with tools,
> keeps coming back so I won't cut the thread [of my
>     life].

(G 44)

And this is the tenor of the burlesque monologue at stanza 10:

> You entered through my eyes, from which I pour
>                                         myself out,
> as a cluster of unripe grapes pressed into a bottle
> will regain its full size once past the neck;
> just so your image, which outside makes me drench
> in tears, grows inside thanks to the eyes,
> so that I swell like skin brimming with fat;
> since you entered me through such a narrow path,
> I dare not believe you'll ever find your way out.

The thematic link among the three passages is emphasized, if anything, by the glaring antinomy between the lofty earnest of poems G 8 and G 44 on the one hand and the thick, degrading comicality of poem G 54's stanza 10. The degradation, however, is far from destructive. Pulling down the fantasies of Platonic love from heaven to earth is the same as translating an abstraction into flesh and blood, and in this case to degrade is to revitalize, as the rich vernacular language and the physiological tenor of the imagery show. Laughter here sounds life-enhancing, not nihilist; Rabelaisian, not Swiftian. The intertextual dialectic between "high" and "low" style mirrors a protracted debate in Michelangelo's own spirit between sensuous and sublimated eros, pagan and Christian-Platonic values, a debate reappearing within the scope of many an individual poem and ultimately reflected also in the alternative linguistic choices that we can schematically

polarize as vernacular Florentine versus stylized literary Tuscan, burlesque versus lyrical-elegiac, plebeian versus intellectual. The debate is also between the underground and the sublimated self.

But surely the "low" register of the burlesque stanzas on hand is far from monotonous or one-dimensional, if we listen to its modulations. Already stanza 3, pleading for humility and love against cruelty, had developed on a totally nonparodic level of diction and idea while coming to a sharp close with the knife-and-sheath metaphor quoted above—a conclusion, by the way, that harmonizes with the folksy sententiousness so prominent in Michelangelo's writing. Then the (self-) parody of stanza 10 shades with stanza 11 into the mercurially baroque simile of the ball inflated to full capacity and then tossed around by the Florentine players with their fists, just as the helpless speaker of the poem fills up with the contemplated image of his lover to jump to the sky at the direct impact of her eyes ("percosso da' tu' occhi al ciel po' m'alzo"). With this caper the poem touches the acme of the bizarre (a bizarre nourished by observant realism, to be sure) to modulate with the last two stanzas into rationalizing reflection (stanza 12) and confessional paradox (stanza 13).

The remarkable fact is that although these two conclusive stanzas or *rispetti* do not really jar with the overall intonation, they move away from the mimetic "vulgarity" of the previous ones to come closer and closer to the kind of sophisticated meditation that would have hardly sounded out of tune in the concert of "wellbred" love lyrics (generally Petrarchan) to which Michelangelo himself contributed many a composition. Indeed, the last stanza culminates in an equivalent of the several madrigals on the cherished torment of love for Vittoria Colonna or for the "donna bella e crudele," Michelangelo's dark lady:

> Tutt'e ripari miei son corti e folli:
> se l'acqua il foco accende, ogni altro è tardi
> a camparmi dal mal ch'i' bramo e volli,
> salvo il foco medesmo. O cosa strana,
> se 'l mal del foco spesso il foco sana!

> All my defenses fall short, they are foolish:
> if fire burns water, nothing else will do
> to rescue me from the illness I crave,
> except fire itself. Oh what a strange thing,
> that fire often should heal the pain of fire!

The conceit of fire and water, the concentrated elegant diction mark this conclusion as an utterance of Michelangelo's troubadour persona, as if the jocular impersonation of the plebeian lover had been just self-parody and self-disguise, and as if at the end the speaker, having had his cathartic fun with language and mimicry, were unmasking himself before his internalized audience to reveal the essential identity of comical and sad, plebeian and sophisticated, naive and self-conscious eros. Desire is king—love that moves man and beast, nobleman and serf; love that dictates inside the strangest metaphors, whether in the low or in the lofty style. And in the related interplay between low comedy and what the medieval ancestors, Provençal or Sicilian and Tuscan, had called *fin' amor* (refined love) humor arises, a dawning realization of the irreducible paradox in the human predicament; it will peak, albeit taking a turn for the darker shades, in the self-decrying tercets of the late 1540s.

Concurrently we can detect in the thirteen *rispetti*-like stanzas a movement from expansiveness to concentration, from uninhibited laughter and even fecal imagery (stanza 5) to purified stylization; from—I feel tempted to add—Quattrocento municipal folksiness, as reflected also in the choice of popular meter, to Cinquecento courtliness. Even the years of composition, 1531-1532, point to the incidence of that historical threshold. Republican Florence has just surrendered (1530) after a long struggle against the besieging pro-Medici forces in which Michelangelo had a prominent role as chief engineer of city fortifications, and Duke Alessandro has reimposed autocracy under Spanish and papal protection; an era is at an end, and this poem, beyond its conscious mimetic intentions, covertly commemorates its demise. No Bacchus, no laughing satyr boy will issue now from the hands of the sculptor who will soon have to leave raped Florence behind for unloved Rome, where he will die without ever revisiting his Tuscan homeland.

With the irremediable fall of the Florentine Republic in 1530 and Michelangelo's definitive move to Rome in 1533 (a move prompted by the enmity of Duke Alessandro de' Medici), we may note the disappearance from Michelangelo's verse of that hearty Laurentian laughter whose intermittences had so far brightened his lines—unless we want to include in that vein the light worldly humor of *capitolo* G 85, written in 1534. A detached, sometimes self-derogatory humor will hover around the fifty epitaphs for Cecchino dei Bracci (1544) in the form of short accompanying messages to Cecchino's uncle, Luigi del Riccio, who kept soliciting those verse tributes from an avowedly reluctant or poetically "dried up" author. "This is for the trout; and if you don't like the piece too much, please don't marinate the trout next time . . ."; "This is for the bread and figs . . ."; "You patch this up, please . . ."; "This is what the trout say, not I . . . Urbino [the assistant and servant] ate them . . ."; "The gawky piece! My spring is dry; we must wait for rain, and you are in too much of a hurry . . ."; "Since poetry was becalmed last night, I'm sending you four bare sketches for the three finer pieces of Mr. Constipation. . . ."

The personal note to poem G 197, adding a sexually risqué variant, mockingly asks the correspondent to "take those two lines, which are a moral thing" so as to complete the fifteen first compositions he had solicited from the writer. Another poem, from a different context, carries the postscript "Of things divine one speaks in a blue field" because the sheet on which the poem is written happens to be of blue paper. Occasionally the dry humor invades the compositions themselves, as when the poet (G 184) puns on Cecchino's family name to say that the latter's "arms" (*bracci*) were too feeble to repel death's attack, and it would have been better to be "feet" (*piedi*) and run away from death instead of trying to resist. This could stand, however, as a rare example of Michelangelo's poetic failures in the worst baroque taste; it matches poem G 177 of 1543, where a Dame Mancini is mourned by proxy with this kind of scoffing epitaph: that if she could have defended herself from death with her right hand, she would have survived, but she happened to be "left-handed" (*mancina*)! Michelangelo's protobaroque leanings, strongly emphasized by Clements,[14] do not inevitably result in poetical felicities.

After the deaths of Luigi del Riccio in December 1546 and Vittoria Colonna in 1547, Michelangelo abandoned the selective publication project on which del Riccio had been actively helping him. Stricken by those bereavements and plagued by disease, he gathered enough despair and bile to feel the need for an outlet in the form of self-mockery (poem G 267) that pushes to the limit the similar slant of poem G 5. The self-caricature of that early piece had more sheer fun than bitterness; by comparison, the *capitolo ternario* from the late 1540s has reversed the dosage of those two ingredients to the point where the distillation leaves a bitter taste: unrelieved destructiveness lurks in it, the venom of black humor. And if in the comical folk idyll of poem G 54 the persona had been able to state that "allegrezza" (mirth) conquers "dolore" (sorrow), here his visceral utterance tilts the scales the other way:

> La mia allegrezz'è la maninconia . . .

> My only mirth is melancholy . . . ,

which reminds us that this medical term originally meant black bile.

The poem has come down to us only in one copy by the hand of Donato Giannotti's scribe, in Archivio Buonarroti XIV, Codex Giannotti, and there is no reason to suppose either that it cost its author the fastidious revision process that many other poems underwent, or that he ever penned it with a view to having it published sometime; it sounds rather like a secret confession, a talk to himself from the deep smoldering underground, the "foul rag-and-bone shop of the heart." His closest correspondents had vanished: Giovanni da Pistoia, Sebastiano del Piombo, Luigi del Riccio, Vittoria Colonna—those with whom he could share his laughter or outrage, his intimate concerns, his plans, his spiritual soarings. It is no accident that from now on the overwhelming majority of his letters should be addressed to his nephew Lionardo, a makeshift son with whom he can have only a one-sided, one-way communication on practical matters that concern the younger man's well being; and while the aging artist lavishes on Lionardo his good old Florentine shrewdness, along with his generosity, he shares next to nothing of his inner self; in fact as the years go on he keeps his nephew at arms' length. We see now why, in deepening and expanding the cue of sonnet G 5 on the troubles of his professional toil, Michelangelo suppresses any reference to a listening "Thou" and transforms dialogue into monologue. He has no one to talk to, and he turns inward to nihilist laughter.

He turns to Florence, too; for his voice is never so Florentine as when he wallows in these inner saturnalia. It is the Florence he left behind in space and time, the city he grew up in and fought for, its alleys, squares, and gardens, its churches and palaces, its people who bequeathed their virulent language to him, and their passion for art. Carnival and Lent would blend in the remembered processions through those streets, the acme of communal *allegrezza,* mirth, turning into the skeleton dance, a death's head laughter to crown the ritual.[15] History confirmed that ritual in macabre jollity. *La mia allegrezza è la maninconia*: my *canto carnascialesco* is my acknowledgment that all is vanity, I have no fetishes left, my loves are gone, my body fails, and as to my art, what is the use of making "so many puppets" (*Che giova voler far tanti bambocci*)? The kermess of laughter becomes a carnival of death:

> ch'i' son disfatto, s'i' non muoio presto

> for I am done for if I don't die soon,

the final paradox of the clown persona—clown, and ascetic in thin disguise. The erstwhile admirer of Fra Girolamo Savonarola will avow, in the last years' access of religious soul-searching,

> Né pinger né scolpir fia più che queti
> l'anima, volta a quell'amor divino . . .

> Neither painting nor sculpture will now appease
> my soul that turns toward that love divine. . . .

A thin line separates the fecal and ribald grotesquerie of poem G 267 from the austere *autos da fé* of the terminal phase.

The grotesquerie is the artist persona's concrete experience seen from the backstage viewpoint, hence the reversal of perspective, language, and tone vis-à-vis the prevalent style in Michelangelo's *canzoniere.* The (saturnalian) reversal makes a strange phantasmagoria of everyday reality, which a jaundiced yet amused eye heightens, by sheer acuity of observance, to eerie power:

> I' sto rinchiuso come la midolla
> da la sua scorza, qua pover e solo,
> come spirto legato in un' ampolla:
>    e la mia scura tomba è picciol volo,
>    dov'è Aragn' e mill'opre e lavoranti,
>    e fan di lor filando fusaiuolo.
> D'intorn'a l'uscio ho mete di giganti,
> ché chi mangi'uva o ha presa medicina
> non vanno altrove a cacar tutti quanti.

> I am enclosed just as the fruit's pulp is
> by its own husk, poor and alone as I am here,
> like a genie confined within a bottle:
>    my gloomy tomb affords scant space to flight,
>    where Arachne and her countless works and toilers
>    make bobbins of themselves to their own spinning.
> Around my door I have the dung of giants,
> for nowhere else will always go to shit
> those who ate grapes or took some laxative.

"Picciol volo," scant space for flight: the pent-up genie had once freely soared, on the wings of love, in the skies that Tommaso Cavalieri and Vittoria Colonna had opened to him ("Volo con le vostr'ale senza piume . . . ," I fly with your wings, I featherless . . .), and he had peopled the huge spaces of the Sistine Chapel. Now he has that mutely blared Doomsday of 1541 well behind him. He has crawled back into his nest—den, workshop, and tomb—to cast a detached glance on everything he has been through; his own doomsday is at hand, and the humor is the humor of a survivor, *allegrezza è la maninconia.* Giordano Bruno, a man of a later generation who is going to burn with a comparable inner fire, will likewise say of himself: *In tristitia hilaris, in hilaritate tristis*—merry in sadness, sad in mirth. There is emblematic and stylistic consonance between Bruno's high-strung verse and Michelangelo's.

All in all, the imagery conveys a sense of inexorable closure to offset an erstwhile openness; "I' sto rinchiuso," I am enclosed, is the first syntagm, the keynote, and it triggers a series of cognate similes: the pulp within the fruit husk, the genie in the bottle, the lonely man in his tomb-like house and workshop that in turn seems besieged by mountainous filth, and then (tercets 6 and 7) the soul in his filthy, ailing body. In unsparing degradation to the point of cruel self-ridicule, the soul cannot issue either from the anus (line 20) or from the mouth (line 21), since the poet even has trouble breathing; the crescendo of disgust from tercets 3 through 7 pushes the self-degrading process to an extent undreamed of in the by now remote sonnet (G 5) on the straining work at the Sistine ceiling. The bluntness of language matches anything in Berni (anything except the sexual lexicon, which is conspicuously absent from Michelangelo's writing in general), and the upshot is a stifling sense of being trapped in matter at its densest, in the *carcer terreno,* the earthly jail that the Platonizing poet had been alternately decrying and transfiguring in his love poetry. The beauty of the body shines with God's own glory; the decay of the body is infernal, and there is no exit save death (last line: "I am done for unless I die soon").

This ambiguity (or isotopy, to use Greimas's terminology[16]) permeates Michelangelo's verse with structuring force. Here of course it shrinks to its negative pole, recalling the luminous alternative by default:

> Fiamma d'amor nel cor non m'è rimasa;
> se 'l maggior caccia sempre il minor duolo,
> di penne l'alma ho ben tarpata e rasa.

> No flame of love has remained in my heart;
> if bigger pain drives out the lesser one,
> I have a soul plucked clean of any feathers.

This eleventh tercet resumes the telescoped image of the second one ("e la mia scura tomba è picciol volo," and my gloomy tomb affords scant space to flight) to push it to its negative extreme, for now the impossibility to fly/flee is determined not just by warping enclosure but by the persona's loss of wings, and in this way even the quantum of hope that could have clung to the lingering potential inherent in the "genie confined within a bottle" is dissolved. One has no trouble recognizing the Platonic panoply in those wings, now clipped, that had lifted the autobiographical persona's soul to the heights of (erotic or religious) ecstasy in so many of the earlier poems for which Marsilio Ficino's remembered conversation and carefully read commentary on Plato's *Symposium* had provided their ideological incentive.[17] The main point is the polarization of structural imagery into openness/closure, light/dark, infinity/limitation, sky/earth, spirit/matter, rarefaction/density, energy/inertia, love/disgust. After the losses visited on the aging artist, these poles of experience can be only mutually exclusive instead of complementary, as what Anthony Perry has called the "integrative tradition" of Renaissance Platonism would have postulated in theory and verse.[18]

A split has occurred and the only conceivable way out of the utter destitution voiced by this autobiographical satire will be the ascetic Christianity of the last poems. Meanwhile the disabused poet pokes fun at his own degradation in merciless burlesque:

> Io tengo un calabron in un orciuolo,
> in un sacco di cuoio ossa e capresti,
> tre pillole di pece in un bocciuolo.
> 　Gli occhi di biffa macinati e pesti,
> 　i denti come tasti di stormento
> 　c'al moto lor la voce suoni e resti.
> La faccia mia ha forma di spavento;
> i panni da cacciar, senz'altro telo,

> dal seme senza pioggia i corbi al vento.
> 　Mi cova in un orecchio un ragnatelo,
> 　ne l'altro canta un grillo tutta notte;
> 　né dormo e russ'al catarroso anelo.

> I have a bumblebee within a jug,
> bones and tying strings within a leather sack,
> three pills of pitch inside a little jar.
> 　The bluish stone of my eyes crushed and ground,
> 　my teeth like keys on a musical instrument
> 　to make the voice ring and stop at their motion.
> My face is downright frightening to look at;
> my clothes alone would be enough to scare
> the crows away from the seed into the wind.
> 　A spiderweb is nestling in one ear,
> 　in the other one a cricket chirps all night;
> 　snoring, I catch no sleep at my raspy breath.

The same amused note that had come through at the outset with the transmogrified persona keenly watching the ubiquitous spiders at work rings out again in this pathetic and funny self-portrait. It is actually an anti-self-portrait; the artist literally takes himself apart and reduces his own physical reality to a catalogue of unrelated objects. The reifying estrangement, the obvious work of a *fiorentino spirito bizzarro* turning against himself,[19] takes shape as emblematic riddle: the buzzing "bumblebee" in the skull, the skeleton and nerves in their "leather bag," the kidney stones in their "jar"; the eccentric rebus images are connected only by their absurdity and by the common underlying motif of *closure,* which echoes the iconic series of the first part (tercets 1 through 7).

Thus the regressive motion of withdrawal, already formulated in the introductory section, reverberates on an even smaller scale at this point where the object of destructive analysis (his own body) replaces the earlier one (the house with himself in it); and the metaphoric insects are within him just as he in turn is within the house, with a Chinese box effect. The titan makes himself a dwarf, just as he had in the sonnet on the Sistine ceiling labors: the "genie in the bottle" within the house is besieged by [the dung of] "giants" outside. It is part of the saturnalian inversion of roles, even though the genie in the bottle need not be a self-belittling image but rather a regression to pure potentiality. The potentiality, however, is dissipated, and what is left of the regressively oversheltered genie is bugs and inanimate objects, and finally a scarecrow. As Yeats would say, "An aged man is but a paltry thing, / A tattered coat upon a stick . . ."; and Montale's description of his Muse ("La mia Musa") in his late phase will resort to the same figuration. Yeats and Montale alike were authorities on old age, but Michelangelo in his bitter burlesque vein had pointed the way.

The three conclusive tercets gradually drop the burlesque tone to lay bare the unrelieved anguish of the old man who has only death to look forward to. His poems of love and his drawings are put to paltry, dirty use, and what is the point of sculpting so many "bambocci" (puppets, children's stuff, toys) if they have brought him to this pitiful end, like him who crosses the sea only to "drown in snot"? The very last stanza is totally serious and could figure in any of the unburlesque pieces where our hard-tried artificer unmasks his pain before God:

> L'arte pregiata, ove alcun tempo fui
> di tant'opinion, mi rec'a questo,
> povero, vecchio e servo in forz'altrui,
>     ch'i' son disfatto, s'i' non muoio presto.

> The vaunted art, in which for a while I was
> so highly esteemed, now brings me just to this,
> that I am poor, old and enslaved to others,
>     so that I'm done for if I don't die soon.

Once more Michelangelo Buonarroti bares himself. "Pull down thy vanity / I say pull down"; but unlike Pound, who rescues his commitment to art from the harsh self-judgment, Michelangelo finds no such saving grace in the occupation that was his life and his pride. From saturnalian masquerade to a cry de profundis, his was a ruder jolt.

We have seen that Michelangelo's burlesque compositions, increasingly sporadic though they may be, are marginal only in appearance. They provide a singular counterpoint to the majority of his lyrics, in which he strove to match the mannerist refinement of courtly poetry, and they rehearse the same thematic gamut (love, art, suffering, the pain of aging, death) as the main body of his verse unfolds. At times they function as a distorting mirror of that verse, as is the case with the late 1540s *capitolo* G 267 that we have just discussed. At other times (see the late sonnet G 299) the jolly style of Tuscan camaraderie and courtesy seems to have replaced clownery and black humor alike, not to mention the asceticism of the coeval sonnets that had left mundane vanities behind.

The desultoriness of the comic mode in Michelangelo somehow testifies to the subterranean persistence of that folksy Florentine current that had surfaced much more frequently in the decades before his final departure from the unrenounceable city. Because this mode connected him with a local tradition of long standing that was in itself the alternative to official Petrarchism, it enabled him to channel deep-seated concerns in the homespun language of his vernacular roots, which he could thus keep alive in his exile. This use of folksy language was a recessive phenomenon within his own canon of verse just as it was in the verse production of Italy at large during the century marked by foreign domination, partial resurgence of feudal economy, and Counter-Reformation. But it kept up an inner debate in Michelangelo that prevented his poetical verve from drying up under the formalizing influence of courtly mannerism. We can actually trace to the persistence of this inner source the linguistic vigor that makes itself felt in so much of his nonburlesque writing.

That pervasive ingredient operates in depth to nurture the vocabulary of a poetry increasingly subjected to the pressure of a leaner style. Take for instance sonnet G 94, which deals with Tommaso Cavalieri in the Platonic convention of sublimated love between worthy men that Ficino had certified:

> D'altrui pietoso e sol di sé spietato
> nasce un vil bruto, che con pena e doglia
> l'altrui man veste e la suo scorza spoglia
> e sol per morte si può dir ben nato.
>     Cosí volesse al mie signor mie fato
>     vestir suo viva di mie morta spoglia,
>     che, come serpe al sasso si discoglia,
>     pur per morte potria cangiar mie stato.
> O fussi sol la mie l'irsuta pelle
> che, del suo pel contesta, fa tal gonna
> che con ventura stringe sì bel seno,
>     ch'i' l'arei pure il giorno; o le pianelle
>     che fanno a quel di lor basa e colonna,
>     ch'i' pur ne porterei duo nevi almeno.

> Merciful to others and to itself alone
> merciless, a lowly beast is born that painfully
> clothes the alien hand and sheds its own pelt
> and through death only can be called well born.
>     Would I were fated in such way to clothe
>     my lord's live body with my own dead skin,
>     so that, as a snake sheds its skin on the rock,
>     even by death I could change my condition.
> O how I wish that hairy skin were mine
> which, woven of its fiber, makes a gown
> so fortunate as to clasp his handsome chest,
>     for then I'd have him by day too; or else
>     to be the slippers that sustain that weight
>     for then I'd carry him for two solid winters.

Even if scholars like Edgar Wind and Robert Liebert[20] may be right in tracing the central imagery of this poem to the Marsyas myth, a stock reference in humanist culture and Renaissance iconography, the prime impulse comes from a personal imaginative experience to be soon expressed in the self-portrait Michelangelo was going to sketch in the skin dangling from St. Bartholomew's hand in the *Last Judgment*—an experience already embodied in an early sonnet (G 4) that had no cruel connotations. That sonnet shows, if anything, a touch of erotic fetishism attached to clothes.

In describing a Bolognese beauty (with the artful borrowings from Poliziano that Clements has spotted),[21] the poem achieves an individualized Buonarrotian tone by the unabashed sensual feeling of the sestet, where the speaker envies the woman's ribbon or belt for the privilege to clasp her. And although the poem does not belong to the burlesque type, it is far more significantly remote from the Petrarchan model on account of its rich, suggestive language. This makes it cognate with the burlesque writing that stems from the same Quattrocento source; witness the successful Laurentian impersonation of peasant eros (G 20) that Michelangelo enacts a little later in the three ottava rima stanzas styled on Lorenzo's *Nencia*. The kinship will result even clearer from a collation of G 4 with the comical *ottava rima* poem (G 54) written during Michelangelo's last Florentine years (a poem, incidentally, that was to provide him with the knife and sheath simile for one of the Cecchino Bracci epitaphs of 1544).

What sonnet G 94 for Cavalieri takes over from the early sonnet for the Bolognese girl is more than a governing image, though that alone would be enough. It is also a concrete language (hairy skin, gown, slippers) and a tactile sensibility to suit the frank embodiment of effusive libido—the same that had leavened the marble form of Bacchus, that had rioted in the Centaur battle bas-relief, that had guided the sculptural painter's eye and hand to shape the Sistine ceiling's *Ignudi*.

Undeniably, a morbid element has entered the picture in the later sonnet, which by comparison makes the kindred lyric from 1507 sound detached despite its linguistic, pictorial, and tactile exuberance. The longing for identification with the admired girl's clothes there, while skirting fetishism, expressed an uncomplicated eros; the self-flaying wish to *be* the clothing of beloved Tommaso, the self-debasing desire to *be* his footwear in sonnet G 94 from almost three decades later are of a piece with the ecstasy and torment of obsessive love. At this point nothing would prevent the author from covertly recalling the Marsyas myth as an adjunct vehicle to his fantasy while ostensibly clinging to the emblem-like images of the silkworm and the snake. But the central point is confessional and private, so much so that Michelangelo here is on the verge of undermining the self-imposed Platonic sublimation in the second tercet (the only such instance in the love poems for Cavalieri[22]).

A less intimate ambiguity of note, however, nestles in sonnet G 97:

> Al cor di zolfo, a la carne di stoppa,
> a l'ossa che di secco legno sièno;
> a l'alma senza guida e senza freno
> al desir pronto, a la vaghezza troppa;
>> a la cieca ragion debile e zoppa
>> al vischio, a' lacci di che 'l mondo è pieno;
>> non è gran maraviglia, in un baleno
>> arder nel primo foco che s'intoppa.
> A la bell'arte che, se dal ciel seco
> ciascun la porta, vince la natura,
> quantunche sé ben prema in ogni loco;
>> s'i' nacqui a quella né sordo né cieco,
>> proporzionato a chi 'l cor m'arde e fura,
>> colpa è di chi m'ha destinato al foco.

> With heart of sulphur, with flesh made of tow
> and bones that are but a heap of dry wood;
> with a soul lacking all guide and defense
> against the excesses of a prompt desire;
>> with a blind reason weak enough to stumble
>> and get stuck in the mistletoe and snares
>> the world teems with, it is indeed no wonder
>> that one should blaze at the first fire he meets.
> If art is lovely, and a gift from Heaven
> enabling us to conquer even Nature
> whose stamp is well imprinted on all things;
>> if from birth I'm not deaf or blind to her
>> to match whoever burns and steals my heart,
>> the blame is his/hers who decreed fire my lot.

The sonnet is in dead earnest, poles apart from the experiments in rustic idyll as well as from the unsparing, cathartic black humor we saw at work in the *capitolo* indited around 1547-1549. The vocabulary is far more restrained, it eschews any plebeian, markedly "low" element, to suit the confessional tone aimed at a high level of communication in one version of what Baudelaire would have called "mon coeur mis à nu," my heart laid bare.

Yet the blunt, pithy wording in the two opening lines injects an invigorating keynote into the whole utterance; and they appropriately echo a lusty passage in the rustic idyll stanzas of a decade before (G 20, lines 17-19):

> Quand'io ti ueggo, in su ciascuna poppa
> mi paion duo cocomer in un sacco,
> *ond'io m'accendo tutto come stoppa*

> When I see you, both of your breasts to me
> look like two watermelons in a bag,
> *so that I blaze as if I were made of tow.*

> (emphasis mine)

Other factors of style conspire to set the unmistakable tone; to begin with, the alignment of nouns denoting concrete things, the materials of which body and soul are metaphorically made (but we shall not hear of *soul* per se, "alma," before line 3): sulphur ("zolfo"), tow ("stoppa"), dry wood ("secco legno," a frequent self-definition in the whole *canzoniere*). Concurrently, the metaphoric equations into whose service those concrete nouns are enlisted: they translate heart into sulphur, flesh into tow, bones into dry wood, that is, the whole living body into inanimate objects, kindling, and fuel for the threatening bonfire of love. This procedure—justifying Berni's claim that Buonarroti said "things" while the fashionable Petrarchists said mere "words"—is germane to the one that will be applied in G 267 to dismember and estrange the persona's physical reality into a set of weird or sleazy objects.

In the sonnet at hand, to be sure, the upshot is not self-degradation but self-justification; and the point could not be more convincingly made, whether we take into account the rhetorical maneuver on which the poem builds toward its climax, or the expressive vividness of the material imagery as such. The iterative series that structures the poem makes for cumulative energy, rhetorically as well as lyrically; it sets up a breathless yet suspenseful rhythm—syntax, imagery, and argument pressing against the containing metric mould toward the intense resolution. The suspense effect, twice enacted (first in the octave, then in the sestet), arises from the proleptic withholding of sentence and thought completion each time until the end of the metric subdivision; and the prolepsis works even more strongly because, each time, logical resolution is delayed by a parallelistic array of anticipatory images and/or argumentative clauses. The initial metaphoric equations are already in themselves implicit arguments, and they contain the whole sequence *in nuce*. Because they are so materially vivid and unprecious, they lend concreteness to the ensuing abstract nouns in the octave (soul, reason), which become dramatic agents in their own right—the soul a dazzled creature, reason a bird caught in the mistletoe traps so familiar to Italian bird hunters even today.

The material quality of those keywords in the first two lines ensures that the fire they are called upon to kindle will not remain a conventional abstraction. When the word "fire" recurs in final clinching position at the end of the second tercet (and it had almost concluded the second quatrain too), it has gathered all the energy provided by that realistic fuel; it blazes unforgettably. And yet fire is a commonplace emblematic image in Petrarchist poetry. But here it is also reinforced by the heightening progression that makes the logical, rhetorical, and iconic development of the sonnet so sweepingly compact.

The logic, however, is far from simple or reassuring; it is, if anything, subversive. The line of reasoning along which the octave unfolds seems to prepare us for a very different conclusion from the one that will actually emerge in the sestet: a conclusion, to wit, stressing the opportunity to reform one's ways after the understandable first weakness of the flesh in the face of profuse temptation. Instead of that, the concessive attitude of the premise yields to a dramatically stubborn one vindicating the inevitability of the sensual conflagration that at first sounded forgivable and therefore neither final nor destructive:

> If art is lovely, and a gift from Heaven
> . . . . .
> if from birth I'm not deaf or blind to her
> . . . . .
> the blame is his who decreed fire my lot.

Nor is this all. Rhetorically speaking, the parallel structure and iterative arrangement conceal the logical swerve from the anticipated course, for "A la bell'arte

. . ." in line 9 echoes the similar beginnings of lines 1, 2, 3, 4, 5, and 6 ("Al cor di zolfo . . . a l'ossa . . .; a l'alma . . . al desir pronto . . . a la cieca ragion . . . al vischio, a' lacci . . ."). This iterative, anaphoric pattern is so insistent that it almost persuades us to assimilate "la bell'arte," art the lovely, to the previously decried agents of moral defeat: the sulphurous heart, the susceptible flesh, the unguided soul, the weak reason. But art is placed *apart* from them, whether metrically, syntactically, or logically; they crowd the long sentence that takes up all of the octave's metrical space, whereas it (art) claims for itself the entire sentence that winds through the sestet. Logically, art governs the final argument in favor of self-justification by defining its premise with two mighty "ifs": "if we have it from Heaven" and "if from birth I'm not deaf or blind to her." These "ifs" are not hypothetical; they have causal, conditioning value, making the consequence inescapable:

> colpa è di chi m'ha destinato al foco.

> the blame is his who decreed fire my lot.

Furthermore, art is given an emphatically positive qualifier, "bella," lovely, and the relative clause employed to define its essence makes Heaven its source and victory over nature its power—a far cry from the weakness of body and soul that the octave seemed to deplore. Art's function, then, is antithetical to that of the several agents—body, psyche, reason—that together make up man's vulnerable self. They lead man to defeat; art grants him victory over powerful, ubiquitous nature. With this, it would seem that the previous line of reasoning is neatly inverted by making art the redeeming force that countervails human weakness vis-à-vis insidious nature.

Yet a further element has intervened to complicate matters in the conclusive tercet, where the speaker brings in his own individual reality ("if from birth I am not deaf or blind to her") to sharpen the focus and thereby seal the transition from the general aphoristic considerations of the octave to a testimonial of personal experience. It is the suffering and acting self that verifies (or subverts) the detached vision of part 1, for he alone can put ideas to the test. And once the autobiographical persona introduces himself into the picture, the whole poem is refocused in such a way that an unexpected ambiguity creeps in to match the heightened tone; logic transcends itself; rhetorical scaffoldings melt into vision; defeat and victory are no longer mutually exclusive. Defeat will actually amount to a kind of victory in the next poem (G 98), likewise inspired by Tommaso Cavalieri: "se vint'e preso i' debb'esser beato," if my bliss must lie in my being conquered and caught.

The ambiguity, a not so rare occurrence in Michelangelo's writing, manifests itself semantically and hinges on grammar:

> s'i' nacqui a quella né sordo né cieco,
> proporzionato a chi 'l cor m'arde e fura,
> colpa è di chi m'ha destinato al foco.

> if from birth I'm not deaf or blind to her,
> to match whoever burns and steals my heart,
> the blame is his who decreed fire my lot.

The double pronoun "chi" in the second line of this tercet, in the opinion of readers like Girardi or Barelli, may refer to Michelangelo's beloved friend, Cavalieri, for whom the poem was apparently written between 1534 and 1538, or to art personified as a feminine entity in the previous lines. As in English, the Italian relative pronoun by itself does not mark gender or number, only the personal agent as distinguished from an inanimate or nonhuman one. This means that the enkindler and stealer of the persona's heart is Tommaso himself, or else the personification of art, since art also claims so much of the poet's energy that it ends up consuming him utterly. Above all, art in his view is intimately tied to beauty, on which it depends for inspiration and model, hence it may well attract to itself the erotic charge otherwise more readily aimed at the inspirer in flesh and bone. In fact the artist-lover persona here proclaims himself *neither deaf nor blind* to *art the lovely,* and by implication to loveliness itself, which feeds art and from it is reborn to enduring shape.

Similarly, in madrigal G 164 of the early 1540s, composed for Vittoria Colonna, he will say that from birth ("nel parto") he has been given beauty ("la bellezza") as a trustworthy model ("fido esemplo") to his vocation ("vocazione"), beauty that is "lamp and mirror" to him ("lucerna e specchio") in both his arts (painting and sculpture); and he will go on to deny any possible allegation of low erotic sensualism ("s'altro si pensa, è falsa opinione," if anybody thinks otherwise, he is in the wrong). Of course, along with the conceptual analogy of madrigal G 164 to the sestet of the sonnet under examination (for the close linkage of art to physical beauty, for the definition of art as a vocation given at birth, and for its lofty purpose), we have to heed a conceptual and expressive difference of note. The madrigal for Vittoria Colonna unambiguously sublimates beauty (and the artist's business with it) beyond any sensual implication, whereas the sonnet for Cavalieri counterpoints sublimation with erotic ardor and guilt, thereby achieving deeper resonance in its ambiguity. The madrigal amounts to a univocal statement this side of poetical drama, the sonnet is a strong dramatic monologue on a par with Michelangelo's best writing. One thinks of Yeats's dictum that poetry is born of the writer's quarrel with himself, unlike mere rhetoric, which arises from his quarrel with others.

The inner tensions, the partly unresolved ambiguities of the sonnet for Cavalieri engage more than our interpretive skills; they involve us empathetically with the persona that plays hide-and-seek with the reader, whom he is receiving in his confidence only up to a point and no further, thereby reserving for himself an area of privacy to which only the unnamed, evasively implied partner can be admitted. The mystifying tactic of personal protection balances the crying need for assertive self-revelation. The ambiguity inherent in the expression "chi 'l cor m'arde e fura" can be resolved in the light of our previous considerations on the close nexus between art and its inspiring model of beauty. The one implies the other; they cannot be separated in the persona's consciousness even if we favor Tommaso as the direct referent of the "chi," for reasons of dramatic relevance. Then we may want to dwell on the speaker's denial of being deaf and blind to art and, by irresistible implication now, to the erotic appeal of beauty in the last line but two; that denial offsets the blindness ascribed to "feeble reason" in line 5 of the sonnet, as if to suggest that the shaping-intuitional power of art outreaches by far the range of plodding reason and thus redresses the persona's balance. Art is an inborn gift from Heaven and a conqueror of nature.

The Promethean claim seems about to conclude the sonnet on a triumphant note of uplift, were it not that the last line throws that victory into question again:

> colpa è di chi m'ha destinato al foco.

> the blame is his who decreed fire my lot.

The line memorably climaxes the whole crescendo, and it becomes even more intriguing when we pursue its implications. To begin with, it casts unexpected guilt or blame ("colpa") on the very vocation of art. Has that vocation, or has it not, come from heaven? Perhaps that heaven should be understood Platonically, and astrologically as sometimes happens in Dante, rather than just in the traditionally Christian sense; after all, the most Platonic poems of Michelangelo happen to be those written for Cavalieri. If so, the artistic calling is a matter of astrological determination; and let us remember that in other poems of the same phase Michelangelo does harp on the theme of destiny as determined at birth by the configuration of stars. See, for example, sonnet G 104, doctrinally modeled on Ficino's ideas.

Even more cogently, madrigal 258 of a decade later will semantically equate birth ("parto") with destiny: ". . . il destinato parto / mi ferm'al tuo splendore," the destiny of my birth stops me in the presence of your splendor. In sonnet G 97 (whatever the constellation involved) the destiny of birth has earmarked the autobiographical persona for a calling that is at the same time lofty and dangerous. "Foco," fire, the very last word, summarizes the essence of that calling. Art, connected as it is with beauty and eros, is a consuming fire with infernal as well as heavenly connotations; how else to account for its tormenting, guilt-ridden aspect? Maybe not all the "sulphur" of line 1 has been purified away by the lesser "fire" (foco) of part 1, line 8. One thinks of the Ganymede and Phaethon drawings that Michelangelo donated to Cavalieri.[23] One thinks of the hidden projections of his personal experience into various heavenly or infernal figures of the *Last Judgment,* so provocatively analyzed by De Tolnay[24] and, most recently, by Liebert[25] in his psychoanalytical way.

Our amazement grows when we come to dwell on that other cryptical pronoun, "chi," in the last line. Who is this "chi"? It cannot be Cavalieri this time because he did not preside over Michelangelo's destiny at birth, and it cannot be art itself because what is in question is the prime cause of Michelangelo's artistic vocation. If so, the entity responsible for this fateful predisposition can be identified only with one of the angelic intelligences that move the heavenly spheres and influence nature—a minister of God. His is the blame. An almost Lucifer-like rebelliousness lurks in the lines we are scanning. Ambivalence and transgression can be the demonic fuel of poetry; and for an earnest Christian like Michelangelo, what transgression could be stronger than implicit blasphemy?

The half-veiled accusation indirectly leveled at God in the sonnet at hand finds counterparts in other works by Michelangelo, signally visual. Thus for instance the aggressive expression and irate gesture of St. Bartholomew toward the sun-like Christ of the *Last Judgment* have elicited pointed comments from experienced critics like De Tolnay, who, without entering the kind of psychoanalytical hypothesis that Liebert has now ventured on the basis of Michelangelo's early family predicament, frankly emphasizes the personal semiotics our artist injected into the biblical narrative. The angry Saint brandishes a knife in the direction of Christ and the recoiling Madonna, and it is obviously the knife with which he was skinned, but the pelt carried in St. Bartholomew's other hand is a slightly distorted portrait of Michelangelo himself. A transgression takes place on sacred iconography: Bartholomew should be exhibiting his own pelt, not anybody else's; he should not look as if he were threatening Christ, even if the anger is really aimed at his flayers and he is just pressing his case with Jesus the Judge, neutralizing the traditional intercession of Mary who in fact averts her face. That transgression compounds with a loaded autobiographical symbolism, Michelangelo having shown persistent interest in his own skin (*pelle, scorza, scoglia*), Marsyas-like, throughout his poetry (sonnet 94, for instance). Now his empty skin dangles from the Saint's hand over the infernal abyss into which the damned are being cast; has he slipped out of it altogether to join that hellish

company, or is he identifying with the martyred Saint and appropriating the latter's aggressive protest/plea? We even know that flaying was a household word for Michelangelo and Urbino, his servant in Rome. And we know that the whirling fresco (De Tolnay calls it a new version of Gigantomachia) aroused protests from Counter-Reformational ecclesiastics even before the artist's death; they (but Pietro Aretino of all people had preceded them) saw rampant irreverence in the formidable imagery.[26]

At the same time, we know Michelangelo's prayers, whether formulated in searching verse or in the gripping forms that issued from his mallet and brush. The transgressions, the ambivalence that masked and also counterbalanced them, bespeak a torn spirit yearning for wholeness, a wholeness he was to approach only in his last years. But the suffering, the flaying, the wavering between private martyrdom and damnation was what powered the expressive release of so much of his art, and of his poetry. We find the ambivalence in sonnet G 63, where this infernal suffering is emblematized as the fire that melts rock in the kiln to make it harder and perennial, "like a soul that had been purified in hell to return among the other high and divine ones." Or in the next piece, quatrain G 64, which picks up that theme to develop it in a different way:

> Se 'l foco il sasso rompe e 'l ferro squaglia,
> figlio del lor medesmo e duro interno,
> che farà 'l più ardente dell'inferno
> d'un nimico covon secco di paglia?

> If fire shatters compact stone and melts iron,
> being the very offspring of their hard entrails,
> what will the one that burns harder than hell
> do to an inimical sheaf of dry straw?

This imagery, which may call to mind Hawthorne's "Ethan Brand," brings us back to sonnet 97's trial by fire with its ambivalent mixture of despair and defiance, damnation and triumph. The paradox is far from contrived.

We have found paradox in the comical verse, *allegrezza e maninconia,* and we can see it in the grotesque masks that Michelangelo the painter or sculptor sometimes juxtaposes to his elect figures like Night in the Medici Chapel or the handsome Dreamer in the drawing donated to Cavalieri. The infernal section of the *Last Judgment* has afforded him a chance to place a few such grimacing trolls in the apocalyptic context where—we cannot help noticing—the soaring saved souls just reendowed with their bodies, the heavenly Court, and the downward whirling clusters of the damned eagerly snatched by the waiting demons make one maelstrom between earth and sky, instead of being sharply polarized in two separate zones. In this regard it is not far-fetched to refer to Arnold Hauser who, in his volume on Renaissance, mannerism, and baroque,[27] remarks that humor in the modern sense arose in mannerist Cinquecento, when the two opposite sides of an earnest issue would be seen together, Shakespeare and Cervantes being its greatest formulators. Humor of this kind is covertly transgressive even in its elegant form, and the lusty or eerie kind that Michelangelo sparingly cultivated is no exception. But because it is only the other side of real earnest, its ambiguities and transgressions find a counterpart in the passionate or meditative utterances that make up the greatest part of his verse work.

On close reading, indeed, burlesque verse turns out to share with many of Michelangelo's other poems certain vital elements like concrete language, thematic imagery, and structural complexity. The latter can appear intertextually, rather than just within the body of each text taken by itself, as evidence of the continuing debate our poet carried on within his own soul and mind. It may be the sudden suicidal thought surfacing from the soul's underground, as if the writer were one of the damned he was to paint in the *Last Judgment* (G 52, **"S'alcun se stesso al mondo ancider lice,"** if anybody is allowed to kill himself in this world); or it may be the fictionally entertained hypothesis of the Pythagorean-Platonic myth of metempsychosis (madrigal G 126, "Se l'alma è ver, dal suo corpo disciolta, / che 'n alcun altro torni / a' corti e brevi giorni," if it is true that the soul, once severed from its body, / may in another one return / to the short days of unenduring life). These thoughts, articulated under the protective guise of lyrical divagation, are nonetheless heretically transgressive for the devout Christian that Michelangelo sincerely strove to be. Isolated as they are within the body of his verse, they crucially counterpoint it. To be sure, they cannot be found in other Cinquecento canzonieri.

More extensively, a potentially transgressive ambivalence links certain love sonnets from the early 1530s (G 60, G 88) to a coeval one (G 87) addressed not to Tommaso Cavalieri but to God himself—whom the poet persona invokes with the selfsame appellation as he does Tommaso. The intriguing intertextual ambiguity will extend to the late religious sonnets to Christ, which explains why some editors date G 87 to that late phase before Girardi revised the dating on the strength of the handwriting. . . .

*Notes*

1. Heinrich Wölfflin, *Die klassische Kunst: Eine Einführung in die italienische Renaissance* [1898], 9th ed. (Basel and Stuttgart: Schwabe & Co. Verlag, 1968), pp. 71-72. Translation mine.

2. Numbered 5 by Enzo Noè Girardi in his critical edition of Michelangelo's poems (Bari: Laterza, 1960), and the same numbering is retained by Et-

tore Barelli's edition, with an introduction by Giovanni Testori (Milan: Rizzoli, 1975). Unless specific considerations dictate additional references, henceforth Michelangelo's poems will be indicated according to Girardi's edition, that is, with a G followed by the pertinent number, in this case, G 5.

3. Archivio Buonarroti (AB) XIII folio 6a; facsimile reproduction in Robert J. Clements, *The Poetry of Michelangelo* (New York: New York University Press, 1966), appendix; and in the Barelli-Testori edition of Michelangelo's *Rime,* p. 38.

4. *Le Rime di Michelagnolo Buonarroti . . . cavate dagli autografi e pubblicate da Cesare Guasti, Accademico della Crusca* (Florence: Le Monnier, 1863); *Die Dichtungen des Michelagniolo Buonarroti, herausgegeben und mit kritischem Apparat versehen von Carl Frey* (Berlin: G. Grotesche Verlagsbuchhandlung, 1897); 2d ed., with a foreword by Hugo Friedrich (Berlin: Walter De Gruyter & Co., 1964).

5. Ascanio Condivi, *Vita di Michelangiolo* [1553], modern edition, with an introduction by Antonio Maraini (Florence: Rinascimento del Libro, 1927); Giorgio Vasari, *La vita di Michelangelo nelle redazioni del 1550 e del 1568,* ed. Paola Barocchi (Milan and Naples: Riccardo Ricciardi, 1962). Apropos Condivi's remarks on the beginnings of Michelangelo's poetic activity, see Frey, pp. 305-306, and generally his commentary on the first six poems as ordered in his edition (pp. 301-306).

6. This component of Michelangelo's thought and art, stemming from his contacts with Marsilio Ficino and Pico della Mirandola during the last years of Lorenzo de Medici's life, has been acknowledged by most scholars, from John Addington Symonds, *The Life of Michelangelo Buonarroti,* 2 vols. (London: John C. Nimmo, 1893) to Charles De Tolnay, *Michelangelo,* 5 vols. (Princeton: Princeton University Press, 1943-1960), and *Michelangelo: Sculptor-Painter-Architect* (Princeton: Princeton University Press, 1975). De Tolnay also formulates an underlying neoplatonic pattern of myth and thought for the Sistine Chapel ceiling frescoes. Before him, Erwin Panofsky had stressed certain Platonic aspects or motifs in Michelangelo's art and writing in *"Idea," ein Beitrag zur Begriffsgeschichte der älteren Kunsttheorie* (Leipzig and Berlin: Teubner, 1924), pp. 64-68. Robert Clements has confirmed the importance of the Platonic affinities in *Michelangelo's Theory of Art* (New York: Gramercy, 1961) and in *The Poetry of Michelangelo.* Meanwhile Pier Luigi De Vecchi was pinpointing the specific connections between Michelangelo's poetry and Ficino's treatise *De Amore* in "Studi sulla poesia di Michelangelo,"

*Giornale storico della letteratura italiana* 80, vol. 140, fasc. 431 (3d trimester 1963), pp. 370-402.

7. The famous part of the *capitolo ternario* in which Francesco Berni praises Michelangelo's poetry and sculpture to their common friend, the painter Sebastiano del Piombo, is reproduced by Barelli as a postscript to Michelangelo's poem in the same meter (G 85), which Michelangelo addressed to Berni writing under the name of Sebastiano. Here is the relevant passage (lines 12-23) from Berni:

> Poi voi sapete quanto egli è da bene,
> com'ha giudicio, ingegno e discrezione,
> come conosce il vero, il bello e 'l bene.
> Ho visto qualche sua composizione;
> son ignorante, e pur direi d'avélle
> lette tutte nel mezzo di Platone.
> Sì ch'egli è nuovo Apollo e nuovo Apelle:
> tacete unquanco, pallide viole,
> e liquidi cristalli, e fiere snelle;
> e' dice cose, e voi dite parole:
> così, moderni voi scarpellatori,
> et anche antichi, andate tutti al sole.

> Then you know how honest a man he is,
> how he has judgment, talent and discretion,
> how he knows what is truth, beauty and good.
> I have seen some of his lyrical poetry;
> I'm ignorant, and yet it seems to me
> as if I'd read it all in Plato's best.
> For he is a new Apollo and Apelles:
> so now shut up, you "pallid violets,"
> and "liquid crystals," and "slender animals";
> he speaks out real things, and you speak only words:
> and then you too, stone carvers of our time
> and of antiquity as well, get out of the way.

8. The rustic impersonation does not prevent Michelangelo here from injecting a comical but unmistakable reference to his own profession as sculptor in the two last lines:

> dunche s'i massi aver fussi possibile,
> io fare' oggi qui cose incredibile.

> then if I could get hold of the marble blocks
> today I would accomplish the unbelievable.

This suffices to distinguish the poem from a mere imitation of Lorenzo's masterpiece. In the end Michelangelo parodies and dramatizes himself, whereas Lorenzo—without ever identifying with Vallera—had detached fun with the exuberant peasant that woos the country girl Nencia.

9. In his essay "Spiritualità di Michelangelo: Per una interpretazione della Tomba di Giulio II," *Michelangelo* 9, nos. 38-39 (1982), pp. 29-39, as well as in earlier publications, Alessandro Parronchi argues that this bitter sonnet attacking the mundane depravations and unchristian militarism of Papal Rome is not aimed at Julius II but at Alexander VI, the notorious Borgia pope who, among other things, caused Savonarola to be burned as a heretic in 1498. The expression "quel del manto" (the mantled one) at line 11 would accordingly refer to Cardinal Riario, Michelangelo's controversial patron at the time, and not to Julius II, and the dating of the poem would recede from 1512 to 1497 (i.e. from Michelangelo's second to his first Roman period). If so, Michelangelo's poetical activity began earlier than is generally believed, and Condivi's opinion would have to be accepted over Frey's strictures (1502 being the initial date for him and Girardi). Parronchi's argument cannot be overlooked, especially when he points out that in the second part of sonnet G 10 Michelangelo complains of getting no orders and losing money. This complaint is hardly justifiable if Julius II is the cause, for if anything the Pope kept Michelangelo very busy (even if, on one occasion, he kept Michelangelo waiting for the sum the artist had requested to finance his work on the Tomb).

10. For a concise vindication of the sonnet's expressive vehemence, see Guido Di Pino, *Vocazione e vita di Michelangelo Buonarroti* (Turin: Edizioni RAI, 1965), pp. 63-64.

11. Clements, *The Poetry of Michelangelo,* p. 48.

12. Giovan Paolo Lomazzo, *Trattato dell'arte della Pittura Scultura ed Architettura, in 7 libri,* [Venice, 1584], 3 vols. (Rome: Tipografia Gismondi, 1844):

> Dicesi adunque che Michelangelo diede una volta questo avvertimento a Marco da Siena pittore suo discepolo, che dovesse sempre fare la figura piramidale, serpentinata, e moltiplicata per una, due, e tre. Ed in questo precetto parmi che consista tutto il secreto della pittura, imperocché la maggior grazia, e leggiadria che possa avere una figura è, che mostri di muoversi, il che chiamano i pittori furia della figura. E per rappresentare questo moto, non vi è forma più accomodata, che quella della fiamma del fuoco, la quale secondo che dicono Aristotile, e tutti i filosofi, è elemento più attivo di tutti, e la forma della sua fiamma è più atta al moto di tutte, perché ha il cono, e la punta acuta, con la quale par che voglia romper l'aria, ed ascender alla sua sfera. E questa anco si può servare in duo maniere, una è che 'l cono della piramide, che è la parte più acuta, si collochi di sopra, e la base, che è il più ampio della piramide, si collochi nella parte inferiore come il fuoco; ed allora s'ha da mostrare nella figura ampiezza e larghezza come nelle gambe o panni da basso, e di sopra si ha d'assottigliare a guisa di piramide, mostrando l'una spalla, e facendo che l'altra sfugga, e scorci, che 'l corpo si torca, e l'una spalla s'asconda, e si rilevi, e scopra l'altra. . . . Ma perché sono due sorte di piramidi, l'una retta come è quella che è appresso S. Pietro in Roma, che si chiama la piramide di Giulio Cesare, e l'altra di figura di fiamma di fuoco, e questa chiama Michelangelo serpentinata, ha il pittore d'accompagnare

questa forma piramidale con la forma serpentinata, che rappresenta la tortuosità d'una serpe viva quando cammina, che è la propria forma della fiamma del foco che ondeggia. Il che vuol dire che la figura ha da rappresentare la forma della lettera S retta, o la forma rovescia, come è questa S, perché allora avrà la sua bellezza. E non solamente nel tutto ha da servare questa forma, ma anco in ciascuna delle parti. Diceva più oltre Michelangelo, che la figura ha da essere moltiplicata per uno, due, e tre. Ed in questo consiste tutta la ragione della proporzione, di che tratteremo diffusamente in questo libro.

(Vol. 1, chap. 1, pp. 33-34)

And so they say that Michelangelo once gave this precept to Marco the Sienese painter, a pupil of his: that he should always make the human figure pyramidal, serpentine, and multiplied by one, two, and three. And I do think that in this precept lies the whole secret of painting, for the greatest grace and comeliness a figure can have is that it would seem to move, which painters call "fury of the figure." And to depict this motion there is no better form than that of fire, which according to Aristotle and all the philosophers is the most active element, and the shape of its flame is the most suited to motion because it has a cone and a sharp tip, by which it seems to try and break through the air and rise to its own sphere. And this can be reproduced in two ways. One is to place the pyramid's cone, its sharpest part, in the upper half, and the base, which is the pyramid's broadest part, in the lower half like fire; and then one must show the figure's amplitude and breadth as in the legs or lower draping, while toward the top it must taper off like a pyramid by showing one shoulder fully and letting the other recede into foreshortening; likewise the body as a whole should twist, and one shoulder should hide and protrude and uncover the other one. . . . But because there are two kinds of pyramid, one straight like the monument close to St. Peter's in Rome which is called the pyramid of Julius Caesar, and the other shaped like a fiery flame (and that is what Michelangelo calls serpentine), the painter must match this pyramidal shape with the serpentine form that represents the tortuousness of a live snake in motion, which is the very form of swaying flame. That is to say, the figure must be patterned on the letter S recto or verso, for then it will have its beauty. And not only in the entire composition should this form be retained, but also in each of its parts. Michelangelo besides said, that the figure must be multiplied by one, two, or three. And in this lies the whole rationale of proportion, which we shall treat at length in this book.

For a thoughtful treatment of this and other aspects of Michelangelo's aesthetics see David Summers, *Michelangelo and the Language of Art* (Princeton: Princeton University Press, 1981). Also very useful, because it contains Benedetto Varchi's discussions and Paolo Pino's and Ludovico Dolce's germane approach to art problems, is Paola Barocchi, ed., *Trattati d'arte del Cinquecento fra Manierismo e Controriforma* (Bari: Laterza, 1960).

13. Clements, *The Poetry of Michelangelo,* pp. 202-203.

14. Ibid., pp. 38-59 ("Michelangelo as a Baroque Poet").

15. See the *frottola* lyric G 21 (dated by Girardi to before 1524), a type of macabre composition usually indited for Carnival parades to offset the rambunctious *canti carnascialeschi.* Michelangelo's piece has reminded some critics of Luigi Alamanni's similar poem from 1511.

16. Algirdas Julien Greimas, *Sémantique structurale* (Paris: Larousse, 1966).

17. Marsilio Ficino, *Sopra lo amore overo Convito di Platone,* ed. Giuseppe Rensi (Lanciano: Carabba, 1914).

18. Anthony Perry, *Erotic Spirituality—The Integrative Tradition from Leone Ebreo to John Donne* (University: University of Alabama Press, 1980).

19. This commonplace expression is often used now to mean "bizarre Florentine wit," but it is lifted from Dante's *Inferno* VIII, 62, which stymies the hated sullen spirit Filippo Argenti ("bizzarro" stems from "bizza," anger). I take the liberty of adapting the semantic import of *bizzarro* to modern usage.

20. Edgar Wind, *Pagan Mysteries of the Renaissance* (London: Faber and Faber, Ltd., 1958), chap. 11, "The Flaying of Marsyas," pp. 142-46; chap. 12, "A Bacchic Mystery by Michelangelo," pp. 147-57. Robert S. Liebert, *Michelangelo: A Psychoanalytical Study of His Life and Images* (New Haven: Yale University Press, 1983), 343-60.

21. Clements, *The Poetry of Michelangelo,* pp. 204-205.

22. In his spirited biography, *Michelangelo—His Life, His Times, His Era,* trans. Heinz Norden (New York: Ungar, 1963), p. 340, G. Brandes says of the poems for Tommaso Cavalieri:

> There is in these poems a passion that could scarcely ring stronger and purer—the passion of a lover, surely not of one who is loved in return. We are amazed to see a man of such gruff virility speak like a woman of his love to another man.

Elsewhere in the same chapter ("Poems and Letters," p. 350) Brandes remarks that Michelangelo "wrote from inner necessity," without thinking of publication in the first place, and that he burned all the poetry of his youth only because "it might have afforded an insight into his youthful life he wished to deny to prying eyes."

23. Liebert, *Michelangelo,* chap. 16, "Tommaso de' Cavalieri and Other Young Men," pp. 270-311.

24. De Tolnay, *Michelangelo,* vol. 5, pp. 19-50.

25. Liebert, *Michelangelo,* chap. 18, "The Last Judgment," pp. 331-60. Another sensitive psychoanalytical interpreter of Michelangelo's art work in

general is Leo Steinberg; see for instance his essay "The Metaphors of Love and Birth in Michelangelo's *Pietàs,*" *Studies in Erotic Art,* ed. Theodore Bowie (New York: Basic Books, 1970), pp. 231-85.

26. Symonds, *The Life of Michelangelo Buonarroti,* vol. 2, pp. 45-58; De Tolnay, *Michelangelo,* vol. 5, pp. 45-46. De Tolnay points out that St. Bartholomew (who holds with one hand his own dangling pelt with Michelangelo's face on it, and with the other hand aims the skinning knife toward Christ and the Madonna) closely resembles Pietro Aretino (of whom we have a fine portrait by Titian).

27. Arnold Hauser, *The Social History of Art,* vol. 2: *Renaissance, Mannerism, Baroque* (New York: Vintage Books, 1957), pp. 147-49.

## James M. Saslow (essay date summer 1988)

SOURCE: Saslow, James M. "'A Veil of Ice between My Heart and the Fire': Michelangelo's Sexual Identity and Early Modern Constructs of Homosexuality." *Genders,* no. 2 (summer 1988): 77-90.

[*In the following essay, Saslow examines Michelangelo's art and poetry for evidence of his homosexuality, taking into account his historical context and the general problems inherent in scholarly conjecture about this topic.*]

The painter, sculptor, architect, and poet Michelangelo Buonarroti (1475-1564) presents a tantalizing dilemma of gender and sexual identity, for these issues occupied an important but obscure place in his life and work.[1] A central figure of the Italian Renaissance, Michelangelo is the first creative artist in early modern Europe whose inner and outer life is recorded in almost day-to-day detail and one of the earliest personalities whose emotions toward other men are known in any depth. But the voluminous sources are often frustratingly silent, ambiguous, or misleading about the artist's love life, sexual attitudes, and self-image. Michelangelo's biography illustrates in miniature several historiographical problems inherent in current attempts to resurrect and characterize homosexual behavior and identity in the period before 1700. This essay seeks to outline the issues and obstacles in fifteenth- to seventeenth-century history through the lens of what we know, do not yet know, and may never be able to determine about even an exceptionally well-documented individual.

Although Michelangelo wrote a great deal, all of it must be decoded through multiple layers of ambivalence, confusion, and fear. The difficulties of unraveling his actions, values, and self-concept regarding sex and gender fall into three categories: the shortage of surviving evidence, the strong partisan bias of virtually every outside commentator, and the differences between the conceptual grid through which Renaissance culture classified and interpreted sexual behavior and our own modern constructions of sexuality. Although these obstacles are shared in some degree by all biographers, each is particularly acute for the history of homosexuals and has nuances unique to their changing social and legal position.

This much we do know. As his repeated poetic images of fire, arrows, and slavery reveal, Michelangelo held love to be the highest and most urgent of earthly desires, second only to that love for God to which it formed the terrestrial counterpart.[2] He was painfully aware of his overwhelming attraction to other men and explicitly disparaged the love of women. In painting and sculpture, his lifelong subject was an obsession with the ideal nude male form, to the point of endowing such female subjects as the Doni Madonna and the Sistine Chapel Sibyls with masculine anatomy and proportions.

His immediate and excited attachment in 1532 to the twenty-three-year-old Roman art lover Tommaso de' Cavalieri, though not unlike his other emotionally charged relationships with young men, was the most profound and long-lasting of his life. He presented Cavalieri with numerous impassioned love poems and drawings on erotic allegorical subjects, all of which reveal both his deep love and his ambivalence about that feeling.[3] By most accounts Michelangelo remained celibate, describing his infatuations as "chaste" and insisting on their purely spiritual ecstasy. At the same time, his writings and drawings, especially those given to or inspired by handsome young men, reveal his full knowledge of both historical and contemporary homosexuality, from Plato's *Symposium* to accusations leveled against the artist himself.[4]

The first obstacle to reconstructing the meaning of these experiences to Michelangelo and his contemporaries is the limitations of surviving sources. From the standpoint of modern inquiry, these are deficient in two respects: they are relatively uninterested in recording sexual matters or in relating them to other aspects of personality.

Direct evidence about private sexual activity is, of course, hard to come by for most people of any orientation. But while heterosexuals at least give *prima facie* evidence through their children, for most homosexuals (and, e.g., childless married couples) the first question to be answered is: did they engage in overt genital activity? The question is critical because scholars uncomfortable with homosexuality often attempt to dismiss considerations of orientation in cases where behavior is inconclusive and are quick to interpret lacunae in documentation as evidence that the practice was rare.

So it is unfortunate that chroniclers like Michelangelo's close friend Giorgio Vasari, the first modern art historian and our prime source for many Renaissance artists, were generally not concerned to document sexuality except when behavior was eccentric or publicly scandalous. Vasari mentions homosexuality per se only once—in relation to the painter Sodoma, whose derogatory nickname I will return to later.[5]

In that pre-Freudian era, connections between an individual's sexual psychology and other behavior were not so readily assumed or investigated. In his treatise on painting, *L'Aretino,* Ludovico Dolce observantly contrasted Raphael, whom he praised for properly delineating the appropriate physical qualities of each sex, with his rival Michelangelo, who "does not know or will not observe those differences" since all his figures look like men. But Dolce makes no attempt to relate this stylistic dichotomy to the parallel contrast between Raphael's interest in beautiful model-mistresses and Michelangelo's love of male companionship and male beauty. To give an analogous lesbian example discovered by Judith Brown, when the seventeenth-century nun Benedetta Carlini claimed to have visions that required her cellmate to masturbate her, she was not punished for lesbianism as such but for blasphemy.[6]

The second of our three obstacles—the biases of outside commentators—is sometimes difficult to disentangle from the first: it is not always clear whether a chronicler neglects homosexual implications because they genuinely did not cross his mind or because he knew all too well that such connections were being drawn, to Michelangelo's discredit, and protectively sought to downplay or omit them. Conversely, sources that do mention homosexuality are seldom objective or complete. This problem of partisanship, while universal, is particularly acute for sexual matters: the need to "take sides" in reporting Michelangelo's sexuality is a direct consequence of the sixteenth century's strong civil and ecclesiastical penalties for homosexuality, which increased in severity during his lifetime as the Catholic Counter-Reformation gathered momentum.[7]

Not surprisingly, Michelangelo's enemies were quickest to assert his sexual misbehavior, while friends steadfastly maintained his total chastity. We do not know the identities of the "evil, foolish and invidious mob" whose smutty insinuations Michelangelo protests in poem 83; but many people apparently assumed he was actively homosexual, including such relative strangers as the father of a prospective apprentice who offered as an added incentive the boy's services in bed (which Michelangelo indignantly refused).[8]

One major accuser, the often bawdy writer Pietro Aretino, offers a fascinating case study in ambivalence and unscrupulousness. In a letter of November 1545, Aretino criticized Michelangelo's *Last Judgment* fresco in the Sistine chapel for its lascivious nudity and then threatened blackmail over Michelangelo's delay in responding to a request for some of his drawings: "If you had sent me what you had promised, you would have done only what it was in your best interest to do, since by so doing, you would have silenced all those spiteful tongues, who say that only certain Gherardos and Tommasos can obtain them."[9] The snide insinuation about two of Michelangelo's young *innamorati,* Gherardo Perini and Tommaso de' Cavalieri, shows Aretino willing to exploit fear of public exposure; yet Aretino himself had earlier fled Venice to escape a sodomy charge, and he wrote frankly about his homosexual inclinations to both his patron and, jokingly, to a woman he was courting.[10] We may never be able to resolve the question whether Aretino constitutes an especially reliable witness because of his personal familiarity with the subject, or whether his testimony is tainted by a cynical willingness to employ a double standard for personal gain.

At the opposite extreme from Aretino, but equally suspect for their polemical tone, are records like the worshipful biography written by Michelangelo's disciple Ascanio Condivi in 1553. Condivi's pointed defense of Michelangelo's chastity was virtually dictated by the artist in a thinly veiled attempt to refute his critics. Whereas in his *editio princeps* (1550) Vasari had devoted a full page to Michelangelo's singular love for Cavalieri and his admiration of the youth's "infinite beauty," Condivi mentions Cavalieri only in passing, and his explicit refutation of those who suspect that Michelangelo's love of beauty is "lascivious and indecent" is clearly motivated by the desire to assert Michelangelo's orthodox piety in the face of persistent rumors to the contrary. Apparently sensitized to Michelangelo's touchiness on the subject by the Condivi account, Vasari paraphrased it in his second (1568) edition, adding that the artist loved beauty, "but not with lascivious and disgraceful thoughts, which he proved in his way of life, which was very frugal."[11]

The tendency to obscure or regularize Michelangelo's true feelings persisted after his death. When his poems were first published in 1623, his moralizing grandnephew and editor, Michelangelo the Younger, changed the genders of many passionate poems' addressees from male to female as well as rewriting other passages that seemed to flirt with heretical doctrine. Although this obstacle was effectively removed in the later nineteenth century, when editors consulted the autograph manuscripts, other omissions and misrepresentations were perpetuated much longer by embarrassed or hostile modern scholars.[12]

While these scattered and contradictory bits of evidence are painfully inadequate, the knottiest problems in interpreting such biographical data are ultimately not so much documentary as conceptual. Beyond the issue whether Michelangelo engaged in sexual activity lie several deeper questions as to how he and his contemporaries understood whatever homosexual behavior they did practice. The so-called essentialist school of gay historians, holding that homosexual behavior and identity are fundamentally the same throughout history, seeks to interpret past sexuality in terms of transhistorical constants of inherent personality. The opposing social constructionist school, building on the insights of Michel Foucault about radical breaks in Western epistemology, stresses instead the discontinuities between historical epochs and the influence of larger cultural forces in constructing shifting paradigms for the expression of humankind's implicitly malleable bisexual potentialities.

According to the social constructionists, two crucial factors in defining the modern "gay" identity are a sense of core individual identity as an inherently homosexually oriented person and a sense of group identity based on this shared orientation and participation in collective social institutions. Neither, it is argued, could come into existence prior to the rise of self-aware urban subcultures in the eighteenth century and the invention of the medical-psychological term, hence the social category, of "the homosexual" in the nineteenth.[13]

This school is undoubtedly correct to emphasize the determining role of these social phenomena, and such scholars as Jeffrey Weeks and Alan Bray have outlined several fundamental respects in which the moral and philosophical taxonomies of Michelangelo's time differed from our modern notion of homosexuality as a discrete, all-encompassing psychological identity. There was no single Italian term corresponding to our definition of "a homosexual," indicating that male homosexuality was recognized only vaguely as an intrinsic way of *being,* or what we would now call "orientation." Theologically and legally, *sodomia* was defined as certain physical *acts* that might be engaged in sporadically by a variety of people, and such taboo same-sex behavior was sharply separated from other equally intense same-sex emotions, which were highly valued.

This conceptual framework obviously had a controlling effect on Michelangelo's sexual self-awareness. By his own insistence and that of most other witnesses, he remained celibate (though we are far less informed about his activities prior to age thirty, the period of his first surviving letters and poems). The sharp distinction in Renaissance thought between being and doing, between desire and action, meant that by avoiding any sexual acts, Michelangelo was probably able to maintain a conscious self-image of "not homosexual" despite his avowed passionate feelings for men.

It remains an open question, therefore, whether calling him homosexual as it were "against his will" is an impermissible anachronism. To assert that he was nonetheless homosexual in some fundamental "orientation" requires at least the addition of such Freudian concepts as repression and sublimation. Michelangelo did once suggest an awareness of something of that kind: when a priest friend told him it was a shame that Michelangelo had never taken a wife, his excuse was that his "demanding art" had been his wife, and his works would be his sons.[14]

I would contend that evidence from Michelangelo and his contemporaries should lead us to reconsider whether there was not in fact more continuity between the Renaissance and modern social/conceptual matrices than the established social-constructionist viewpoint can account for. Regarding the sociological underpinnings of "modern" homosexuality, recent research has uncovered recognizable homosexual subcultures as far back as the medieval and early modern periods.[15] When the existence of this substratum is coupled with recorded attitudes by and about individual "deviants," I think we can push back the temporal frontier of an emerging sense of distinctive homosexual identity, at least in embryonic form, to the beginning of the sixteenth century.

I will consider here five factors that imply a somewhat greater degree of protomodern "homosexual consciousness" than has previously been posited in the sixteenth and seventeenth centuries. First, while the construction of thought in terms of polarized opposites (such as would later lead to "heterosexual/homosexual") was not formalized until the seventeenth century, Renaissance theorists were at pains to contrast relationships on the basis of the two genders of object choice. Allied to this development, a complex terminology existed for male homosexual behavior and the individuals who practiced it, terms which suggest some rudimentary notion of an associated personality type. The conceptual separation between love and sex was more fluid in practice than in theory. Some individuals known or suspected of homosexual behavior, Michelangelo among them, articulated their sense of persecution and strategies for evading or resisting it; and Michelangelo's writings also evince sporadic attempts to find an alternative vocabulary for "anomalous" desires and values.

As to the first point, the lack of our modern terms "heterosexual" and "homosexual" did not prevent Renaissance theorists from marking a clear division between two kinds of love differentiated by the gender of one's chosen object. One of Michelangelo's sonnets analyzing his feelings for Tommaso de' Cavalieri takes as its theme precisely this opposition:

> Violent passion for tremendous beauty
> Is not perforce a bitter mortal error,
> If it can leave the heart melted thereafter,

So that a holy dart can pierce it quickly . . .
The love for what I speak of reaches higher;
Woman's too much unlike, no heart by rights
Ought to grow hot for her, if wise and male.

      (Ed. Girardi, no. 260; trans. Gilbert, no. 258)

Of course, we are not yet here at "homosexuality," since this idealized male love is still officially modeled on such classical exemplars as Socrates' chaste love for Alcibiades. In this taxonomy, male-male love is understood in terms of classical *amicitia.* Its goal is fundamentally spiritual—as Michelangelo implies, it is anagogic to the higher love of the (male) godhead. There is, then, a second complicating factor in classifying types of male love besides gender: that is, the presence of lustful desire (toward women) or its absence (toward other men).

Nevertheless, the distinction was made and, slightly later, a more pointedly contrasting vocabulary developed for it. In a gloss on the young character of Colin Clout in Edmund Spenser's *The Shepherd's Calendar* (1579), who rejects the attentions of an older male shepherd and himself pursues the maid Rosalind, "E. K." declared "paederastike much to be preferred before gynerastike, that is the love which enflameth men with lust toward womankind."[16]

If there was a vocabulary for object choice, there was also an extensive terminology for male homosexual activity and individuals who engaged in it, suggesting that some rudimentary notion existed of their distinctive psychological "nature." Unlike modern constructs, however, this conception was not inclusive of both parties: the terms used by Castiglione, Aretino, and other sixteenth-century authors distinguished between an active and passive partner. There is some faint indication that the active partner had a definable variant personality: in a comic tale by Matteo Bandello, the poet Porcellio declares that "to divert myself with boys is more natural to me than eating and drinking." However, to the extent that a predilection for sodomitical acts was seen as implying any distinctive personality traits, these were imputed almost exclusively to the passive partner; most of the nouns referring to him—androgyne, hermaphrodite, ganymede—were derogatory terms misogynistically imputing causality to a degree of effeminacy or gender confusion.

In contrast to the humor or scorn attached to "feminine" passivity, the "masculine" actions of the aggressive/penetrating partner, while legally culpable, were somewhat tolerated socially as not involving any abdication of the prerogatives of adult male dominance, and no special terms evolved for these individuals. In consequence, some phenomena that *we* would consider informed by homosexual experience or sensibility passed conceptually unnoticed. Since Michelangelo was consistently the older and thus presumably dominant "masculine" partner (the objects of his affection were in or barely out of their teens), it would barely have occurred to such contemporaries as Lomazzo to look for any character traits in him different from those of heterosexual men, whose relations with women were constructed on a similar basis of superior age and power.[17]

Perhaps the most suggestive evidence that the Renaissance conception of homosexuality was beginning to approach later conceptions is that the boundary between spiritual and physical passion was more vague and permeable in practice than in theory, a fact not unknown to the theoreticians. Montaigne, Erasmus, and Bacon all wrote in praise of the approved spiritual love between men, but Bacon, at least, understood a further dimension of such affairs, since he also had sex with his servants and followers. The Mantuan humanist Mario Equicola took care to insert in his treatise *On Love* a caveat that "not a word of this work is to be understood as the love of boys or sexual acts against nature."[18]

The problem stems from the ambiguity of Renaissance language about love: the sources use the same words to refer to actions and relationships that appear to have been located at quite different points along the continuum of eroticism from purely emotional affinity to genital expression. In the shortage of unambiguous first-person testimony, one group of scholars, such as Bray, emphasizes the "official" spiritualized content of ideal classical *amicitia*; the extreme of this argument interprets any expression of male-male passion or love as merely a conventional formula of friendship phrased in the high-flown language of Neoplatonic allegory. Others, most recently Joseph Pequigney in his study of Shakespeare's sonnets, read every sexual metaphor, however tenuous or veiled, as an allusion to overt behavior.[19]

Consequently, any remark about Michelangelo's love life is still open to a spectrum of interpretations. Vasari and Benedetto Varchi, for example, both state that he greatly loved Tommaso de' Cavalieri (and the artist's own writings say so repeatedly), but we still do not fully understand what degrees of "love" the term implied for them. When Vasari records that the love between the painters Polidoro da Caravaggio and Maturino Fiorentino grew so great that "they determined like brothers and true companions to live and die together" as well as collaborate professionally all their lives, he says nothing expressly about sexual love; but the relationship bears suggestive parallels with two earlier Venetian boatmen who lived and operated a business together for several years before being arrested for committing sodomy aboard their craft.[20]

The porous boundary between passionate but chaste Neoplatonic language and everyday practice, at least in the popular mind, can be inferred from the frequency with which Michelangelo, on his own or through Condivi, denied rumors and accusations of homosexual activity. Despite his protestations of "chaste love" and "honest desire," other people seem to have presumed that his stated desire to have Cavalieri "in my unworthy ready arms for always" also bespoke a less philosophical interest in handsome young men.

To be sure, this suspicion, which may well derive (in Michelangelo's phrase) from "those who see themselves in others," says little about his actual behavior, but the potential for a spillover into overt eroticism must have seemed plausible (if distasteful) even to Cavalieri, whom he reassuringly admonishes for "giv[ing] heed to such falsehood." Small wonder that Cavalieri did, since virtually every symbol of ideal male relations Michelangelo could have chosen had by this time become hopelessly contaminated or conflated with erotic associations as well. The grafting of elevated, explicitly Christian motives onto classical exempla had always been selective and inherently unstable: his gift to Tommaso of the paired drawings of the *Rape of Ganymede* and the *Punishment of Tityos* is officially interpreted as representing sacred versus profane love, but Plato himself acknowledged the former myth's pederastic content, and the word "ganymede" had denoted a boy used for sexual purposes since the Middle Ages. Even the language of Condivi's rebuttal was readily open to a self-defeating second meaning. He compares the master's love of young men to that of Socrates for Alcibiades, but the (unwillingly) chaste young man of Plato's *Symposium* also figured in bawdy Renaissance literature (though perhaps only somewhat later) as a symbol of a youth's initiation into sodomy.[21]

While these statements were meant to establish publicly that he drew a clear-cut line between passionate *amicitia* and sexual activity, Michelangelo's words also testify that this theoretical cleavage was no clearer or easier to maintain in his mind than it had become in his ambiguously conflated sources. His later poems allude to "my evil, deadly desires" and lament that "my senses and their own fire have bereft / all . . . peace from my heart."[22] There would be no reason to feel guilty about a male love unless it did, contrary to dogma, contain some component of forbidden physical desire; nor would it be necessary to "lose peace" over that desire unless he was conscious of what it meant and the need to struggle against it.

If Michelangelo's understanding of such critical terms as "love" and "desire" still remains obscure, the foregoing analysis should make clear that these words were not, as some have maintained, reserved exclusively for contexts of emotional intimacy, while sexual attraction would have been described primarily in other terms. A more sophisticated linguistic analysis is still called for,

one that would acknowledge that Renaissance language is multifaceted and ambiguous. As Foucault observed, the sixteenth-century system of discourse was based on an epistemology of poetic resemblances; in consequence, everything in Renaissance philosophy is overdetermined, and their thought patterns cannot be conceived as rigidly excluding any level of associative meaning.

The fourth factor suggesting the presence of some protomodern consciousness of homosexuality at this time is that, however much Michelangelo himself praised and idealized his male infatuations, he was acutely aware of some discrepancy between his desires and the moral and legal constraints of his society. He acted out and wrote about the limitations these imposed on his ability to speak frankly and fully about his intimate relationships. His lifelong fearful expectation of hurt from other people, while often justified, suggests a pervasive sense of persecution:

> Often, in the pleasure of tremendous kindness,
> some attack on my life and dignity
> is masked and hidden. . . .
>
> (No. 251; trans. Gilbert, no. 249)

Such feelings imply some rudimentary sense of a gap between himself and the surrounding society—what we today would term "alienation," another significant factor in defining modern gay consciousness.

Michelangelo's strategy for coping with this awareness was to try to prevent, by discretion or ambiguity, even his "chaste wish" and "honest love"[23] from becoming too well known to a public likely to see them in a less elevated light. Vasari observed this tendency toward prudent indirection, writing that Michelangelo "was very masked and ambiguous in his speech, his words having almost two meanings."[24] For example, in a letter to Cavalieri accompanying his gifts of the deeply confessional *Ganymede* and *Tityos* drawings, he avoided identifying their classical erotic subjects. His drafts for this letter strongly imply that he was conscious of something in the drawings that was best left unstated. He wrote: "It would be permissible to name to the one receiving them the things that a man gives, but out of nicety it will not be done here." Whether he meant merely the titles of the drawings or the emotions they symbolized, in the final version Michelangelo omitted even this enigmatic apology. Cardinal Ippolito de' Medici was so taken with the series of presentation drawings that he insisted on borrowing them to be copied; Cavalieri's account notes that "I tried hard to save the Ganymede," as if he too was wary of its public dissemination.[25]

There are scattered examples among Michelangelo's contemporaries of other homosexually oriented men who knew both that their feelings deviated from the norm and that those feelings made their relationship to society problematic. He would have known that his important Florentine artist friends Leonardo da Vinci, Sandro Botticelli, and Benvenuto Cellini were all arrested for sodomy between 1476 and 1552, and that Giovanni Bazzi was publicly ridiculed.[26] Commenting on a painting of Christ as an ideal androgynous youth, Leonardo alluded bitterly to his earlier legal difficulties: "When I painted our Lord as a boy, you put me in jail; if I were now to paint him as a grown man, you would do worse to me."[27] And when Bazzi's horse won the annual Palio race in Siena, he defiantly threw back in the faces of his fellow citizens the mocking nickname they had given him, insisting on being announced to the crowd as "Il Sodoma," the sodomite—arguably the first public "coming-out" statement in European history.[28]

Two qualifications about this sporadic awareness must be acknowledged. First, none of these artists saw himself as a member of a group defined by their common sexuality but perceived his predicament only in individual terms. Michelangelo's stated objection to being accused of sodomy is not that any such condemnation is unjust, but only that in his case it is untrue. Hence, he doubtless felt no commonality with an outspoken nonconformist like his acquaintance Sodoma. It follows that his sense of struggle against the limitations of nonconformity was not consciously articulated as a political or aesthetic theory: Michelangelo could no more speak in modern terms about the gender-crossing implications of his own work than did Lomazzo.

All the same, the final element of his life that suggests to our eyes an emerging new consciousness is the hints in his poetry of a search for an alternative vocabulary to characterize previously inexpressible feelings. Although he could not free himself entirely from the gender assumptions of his own time, he struggled to bend or extend their application to specific persons through self-conscious wordplay.

He described the gender-variant intellect and valor of his spiritual friend Vittoria Colonna as "a man within a woman" and referred to her as *amico,* using the masculine form of the word for "friend." Conversely, he described himself as a bride in relation to God—the customary locution for nuns—and as an archetypally feminine "mold" waiting passively to be filled by Colonna's seminal beauty.[29] More importantly, his habit of drafting verses to a female and then changing the gender of the addressee suggests his strikingly protomodern awareness of the arbitrariness of gender constructs and can be read as a pioneering attempt to subvert the heterosexual conventions of Petrarchan courtly love poetry to the exaltation of a male beloved. Something of the same self-conscious transposition can be seen slightly later in the letters of England's James I to his beloved favorite, the duke of Buckingham, in which he calls Buckingham his "wife" and characterizes himself as a prospective widow.[30]

In sum, I think that what is known about Michelangelo's search for sexual and gender identity supports the hypothesis that, during his lifetime, many important elements of the modern conception of homosexuality—as a distinct psychological construct and social status, requiring its own expressive vocabulary even if it sometimes had to be concealed—were beginning to emerge. He may not have thought of himself as "a homosexual," but he was aware that there were such people, that many of his passionate declarations were taken as indication that he was one of them, that the objects of his affection required a language that violated gender norms, and that it was both safer and less guilt-inducing to forgo action and conceal emotion.

It may still be argued that all the above evidence bespeaks an inner reality far removed from modern constructs. But there are too many ambiguities in the record, too-frequent hints of his interconnected passion, ambivalence, confusion, guilt, and touchiness to be accounted for by the purely practical caution of someone secure in his "nonhomosexual" identity. In sexual terms, as in much else, the Renaissance and Michelangelo as one of its foremost creators represent a transitional phase rather than one wholly different from modernity. If his time was not yet ripe, it produced at least the first buds of a consciousness that would only flower and bear fruit under much different social conditions.

I am well aware of the risk of historical anachronism here, but one senses in Michelangelo's emotional drama many of the dynamics commonly experienced by modern gay individuals in adolescence: stirrings of both intense physical desire and romantic infatuation, the gender of whose object is sometimes unclear, though tending mostly toward male fantasies, and a sense of cognitive dissonance with the antisexual values of the surrounding culture (in his case, strongly internalized from an increasingly Counter-Reformatory Catholicism).[31]

While it is difficult to carry this kind of psychobiographical speculation further, I would suggest that Michelangelo accommodated to this conflict as many adults do today by willfully suppressing his own feelings where they were at variance with received social constructs. While one or two of his contemporaries ventured a bit further into adolescent "acting out" (Leonardo, Sodoma), he took refuge in, and came to believe, his own rationalizations and sublimations. And the pains taken to correct public perception by a man nominally so contemptuous of worldly opinion may easily read as protesting too much, out of the chronic anxiety engendered by self-denial.

If all these layers of repression, denial, and self-concealment forced on Michelangelo complicate our reconstruction of his biography and psychology, they also took their toll on him during his own lifetime. Infatuated with a heterosexual (Cavalieri) who apparently needed reassurance that his intentions were honorable, always alert for another attack on the morality of his acts and his art, and energetically sublimating through his work, Michelangelo wrote often of his frustrated longing and of the inextricability of joy and pain in love. As he put it in lamenting his inability to feel the intense love of God (or Cavalieri) that he yearned for, "A veil of ice hides between my heart and the fire [of love]."[32]

The "ice" that ultimately stunted and froze his full expression of more earthly love was crystallized by both internal and external constraints on his deepest emotions. Perhaps the ultimate reason we cannot fully know him is that he could never fully come to know himself.

### Notes

1. A preliminary version of this essay was presented at a conference on "The New Gender Studies" at the University of Southern California in January 1987. I am grateful to panel chair Professor Joanne Glasgow for her support and interest and to Columbia University for enabling me to attend the conference.

2. The most comprehensive general study of Michelangelo's poetic imagery is Robert Clements, *The Poetry of Michelangelo* (New York: New York University Press, 1965); on love, see especially pp. 89-133, 184-220. Among more recent studies, see Walter Binni, *Michelangelo scrittore* (Turin: Einaudi, 1975); Glauco Cambon, *Michelangelo's Poetry: Fury of Form* (Princeton: Princeton University Press, 1985); and James M. Saslow, *Ganymede in the Renaissance: Homosexuality in Art and Society* (New Haven and London: Yale University Press, 1986), chap. 1. The present essay is an attempt to deal with theoretical and methodological questions about homosexual identity I did not explicitly address in that context; see further my essay, "Homosexuality in the Renaissance: Behavior, Identity, and Artistic Expression," in the forthcoming anthology on gay and lesbian history edited by Martin Duberman, George Chauncey, and Martha Vicinus (New York: New American Library).

3. Primary sources for their relationship are assembled by Christoph L. Frommel, *Michelangelo und Tommaso de' Cavalieri* (Amsterdam: Castrum Peregrini, 1979). Cavalieri and the works he inspired are treated by all major monographs on the artist, from Charles de Tolnay, *Michelangelo,* 5 vols. (Princeton: Princeton University Press,

1943-60), esp. vol. 3, *The Medici Chapel,* to Howard Hibbard, *Michelangelo* (New York: Harper and Row, 1974), pp. 229-36. For a thorough if still controversial psychoanalytic reading of the Cavalieri works, see Robert S. Liebert, *Michelangelo: A Psychoanalytic Study of His Life and Images* (New Haven and London: Yale University Press, 1983), esp. pp. 270-311, to which I owe some of the psychological observations below.

4. Several drawings for Cavalieri are based on Ovid's *Metamorphoses,* which is replete with classical homosexual myths, notably the rape of Ganymede by Jupiter. The reference to Socrates and Alcibiades from the *Symposium* is made in Condivi's biography of Michelangelo, generally held to have been dictated by the artist himself: Ascanio Condivi, *Vita di Michelangiolo* (1553; Florence: Rinascimento del Libro, 1927), pp. 98-99; *Life of Michelangelo,* trans. Alice Sedgwick Wohl, ed. Hellmut Wohl (Baton Rouge: University of Louisiana Press, 1976), p. 105. All poems are cited herein following the numbering in the standard Italian edition: Enzo Noè Girardi, ed., *Michelangelo Buonarroti: Rime* (Bari: Laterza, 1960). For accusations against Michelangelo, see below, esp. n. 8.

5. Giorgio Vasari, *Le vite de' più eccellenti pittori, scultori ed architettori . . .* (1568), ed. Gaetano Milanesi, 9 vols. (Florence, 1865-79), vol. 6, pp. 379-86 (hereafter Vasari/Milanesi). For a typical tendency to argue from silence, see Arno Karlen, *Sexuality and Homosexuality: A New View* (New York: Norton, 1971), p. 109. The urge to declare an ambiguous artist heterosexual has been particularly strong with regard to Leonardo, Freud's frank diagnosis of repressed homosexuality in *Leonardo da Vinci and a Memory of His Childhood* (Harmondsworth: Penguin, 1963) notwithstanding: see Giuseppina Fumagalli, *Eros di Leonardo* (Milan: Garzanti, 1952); Raymond Stites, *The Sublimations of Leonardo da Vinci* (Washington: Smithsonian Institution, 1970).

6. Ludovico Dolce, *Dialogo della pittura intitolato "L'Aretino"* (Venice, 1557), English translation in Robert Klein and Henri Zerner, eds., *Italian Art 1500-1600: Sources and Documents* (Englewood Cliffs: Prentice-Hall, 1966), pp. 61-65. I am indebted for some of the insights here to discussions with my students in a graduate seminar on Michelangelo at Columbia University, 1987, especially Mary Vaccaro. On Carlini see Judith Brown, *Immodest Acts: The Life of a Lesbian Nun in Renaissance Italy* (New York and Oxford:

Oxford University Press, 1986), with a perceptive overview of the problem of lesbian self-concept and identity in this period.

7. For general background on social and legal penalties, see Saslow, *Ganymede,* introduction and chap. 1; Alan Bray, *Homosexuality in Renaissance England* (London: Gay Men's Press, 1982), for England; Vern R. Bullough, *Sexual Variance in Society and History* (Chicago and London: University of Chicago Press, 1976), chaps. 3, 7, 8, 13, 14. The intensification of Christian hostility that began in the Middle Ages is outlined by John Boswell, *Christianity, Social Tolerance, and Homosexuality* (Chicago: University of Chicago Press, 1980).

8. English translation from *Complete Poems and Selected Letters of Michelangelo,* trans. Creighton Gilbert (Princeton: Princeton University Press, 1980), no. 81. For the incident with the apprentice, see *Il carteggio di Michelangelo,* ed. Giovanni Poggi, Paola Barocchi, and Renzo Ristori, 4 vols. (Florence: Sansoni, 1965-79), vol. 1, no. CXIV; E. H. Ransden, ed. and trans., *The Letters of Michelangelo,* 2 vols. (London: Peter Owen, 1963), vol. 1, no. 195.

9. Pietro Aretino, *Lettere sull'arte di Pietro Aretino,* ed. Fidenzio Pertile and Ettore Camesasca, 3 vols. (Milan, 1957-60), vol. 3, p. 177, n. 1, no. CCCLXIV; trans. Thomas Caldecott Chubb, *The Letters of Pietro Aretino* (Hamden, Conn., 1967), p. 224. On Gherardo (Perini), see Vasari/Milanesi, vol. 7, p. 276.

10. On the sodomy charge see Aretino, *Lettere,* vol. 3, pp. 112, 199, n. 266, 150, 235; Patricia Labalme, "Personality and Politics in Venice: Pietro Aretino," in David Rosand, ed., *Titian: His World and His Legacy* (New York: Columbia University Press, 1982). Aretino also wrote a satirical play, *Il marescalco,* based on a homosexual staff member of Federigo's court.

11. Condivi, pp. 98-99, trans. Wohl, pp. 102-05. Vasari/Milanesi, vol. 7, pp. 223, 271-72, trans. G. deVere, 2d ed., 3 vols. (New York: Abrams, 1979), vol. 3, pp. 925-27. The differences between Vasari's earlier and later versions are set forth by Paola Barocchi, *La vita di Michelangelo nelle redazioni del 1550 e del 1568,* 4 vols. (Milan: Ricciardi, 1962); see especially vol. 1, pp. 86, 118.

12. The first modern editor to print the original texts was Cesare Guasti, ed., *Le rime di Michelangelo Buonarroti* (Florence, 1863), but he appended paraphrases that obscured or allegorized the more obvious male references. For a thorough denunciation of past alterations or bowdlerizations, see

John Addington Symonds, *The Life of Michelangelo Buonarroti,* 2 vols. (London and New York, 1899), appendix 5, vol. 2, pp. 381-85, and text, vol. 2, pp. 132-40, 166, n. 1; and further in Saslow, *Ganymede,* pp. 13-15.

13. The bibliography on this overarching controversy in gay studies has proliferated rapidly, beginning with Michel Foucault, *The History of Sexuality,* vol. 1 (London, 1979). The basic theoretical points are made by Robert Padgug, "Sexual Matters: On Conceptualizing Sexuality in History," *Radical History Review* 20 (1979): 3-33; Arthur N. Gilbert, "Conceptions of Homosexuality and Sodomy in Western History," *Journal of Homosexuality* 6, nos. 1-2 (1980-81): 57-68; and in numerous publications by Jeffrey Weeks, notably *Coming Out: Homosexual Politics in Britain from the Nineteenth Century to the Present* (London: Quartet Books, 1977), and most recently, his essay in Pat Caplan, ed., *The Cultural Construction of Sexuality* (London: Tavistock, 1987). The arguments for this viewpoint and the opposing "essentialist" school are carefully analyzed by John Boswell, "Revolutions, Universals, Categories," *Salmagundi* 58-59 (1982-83): 89-113.

14. Vasari, trans. deVere, vol. 3, p. 1931. Compare Freud's application of the concept of sublimation to Leonardo, a similarly repressed homosexual (n. 5 above).

15. Evidence for premodern urban subcultures has been advanced by Boswell, *Christianity, Social Tolerance, and Homosexuality,* for the Middle Ages, and Guido Ruggiero, *The Boundaries of Eros: Sex Crime and Sexuality in Renaissance Venice* (New York and Oxford: Oxford University Press, 1985), for the fourteenth and fifteenth centuries. Bray cites evidence suggesting an active London subculture by the late sixteenth century, though he does not claim it as such.

16. *The Shepherd's Calendar,* January, lines 56-59, and initialed commentary (included in original published text), possibly by Edward Kirke. This reference was brought to my attention in an unpublished lecture by Professor Stephen Orgel.

17. I have discussed the terminology used for homosexual acts and individuals in this period more extensively in my *Ganymede in the Renaissance,* chaps. 2 and 3 (with further bibliography).

18. Equicola, *Libro di natura d'Amore* (Venice, 1525), 112r; Ruggiero, *The Boundaries of Eros,* pp. 115-16. Bacon's life and thought are discussed by Bray, p. 49; on friendship literature see generally Bullough, chap. 15.

19. Joseph Pequigney, *Such Is My Love: A Study of Shakespeare's Sonnets* (Chicago and London:

University of Chicago Press, 1985). The concept of a "sliding scale" of eroticism and the difficulty of determining the physical component of given cases were introduced perceptively in regard to women by Carroll Smith-Rosenberg, "The Female World of Love and Ritual," *Signs: Journal of Women in Culture and Society* 1, no. 1 (1975), reprinted in her *Disorderly Conduct: Visions of Gender in Victorian America* (New York and London: Oxford University Press, 1985); Smith-Rosenberg's analysis is specifically applied to the Renaissance era by Lillian Faderman, *Surpassing the Love of Men: Romantic Friendship and Love between Women from the Renaissance to the Present* (New York: William Morrow, 1981). I am indebted to Joseph Cady for the discussion of these issues in his unpublished paper "'Masculine Love' in Renaissance Writing."

20. Vasari/Milanesi, vol. 5, p. 143, vol. 7, pp. 223, 271-72; Benedetto Varchi, *Due lezzioni* (Florence, 1547, published 1590), p. 183, reprinted in Guasti (see n. 12). For Michelangelo's letters to Febo di Poggio and Cavalieri, see *Carteggio,* nos. CM, CMXIX, CMXVII, CMXVIII, CMXLI; trans. Ramsden, vol. 1, pp. 184, 187, nos. 193, 198.

21. *Rime,* ed. Girardi, nos. 58, 59, 61, 72, 83, 88; Condivi/Wohl, p. 105; Plato, *Symposium,* 215B-20B, and *Laws,* vol. 1, 636D. *Alcibiade, fanciullo a scuola,* first published at Oranges, France in 1652, but attested as early as 1630, has been variously attributed to such sixteenth-century Italian authors as Aretino and Antonio Rocco: see partial trans. by Michael Taylor in Cécile Beurdeley, *L'Amour bleu* (New York: Rizzoli, 1978), pp. 124-26. For general background on the etymology of *ganymede,* see Saslow and Boswell, passim.

22. *Rime,* ed. Girardi, nos. 254, 291; trans. Gilbert, nos. 252, 289 (cf. Girardi nos. 292, 293, 302).

23. Girardi, nos. 58, 59, 72, 83; trans. Gilbert, 56, 57, 70, 81.

24. Barocchi, *La vita di Michelangelo,* vol. 1, p. 125 (passage omitted from 1568 edition).

25. *Carteggio,* vol. 4, nos. DCCCXCIX, CM, CMXXXII (from Cavalieri); trans. Gilbert, p. 253, no. 49 (for a variant translation, see Ramsden, vol. 1, no. 191); Saslow, *Ganymede,* pp. 47-51. This strong sense of persecution is an important theme throughout Liebert, *Michelangelo: A Psychoanalytic Study.*

26. For these various accusations and trial records, see Jacques Mesnil, *Botticelli* (Paris, 1938), pp. 98, 204; Luca Beltrami, *Documenti e memorie riguardanti . . . Leonardo da Vinci* (Milan, 1919); Luigi Greci, *Benvenuto Cellini nei delitti e nei*

*processi fiorentini . . .* (Turin, 1930); Vasari/Milanesi, vol. 6, pp. 379-86; and the discussion of the artists in Saslow, *Ganymede,* passim.

27. Leonardo, *Codex atlanticus,* fol. 252r; see Carlo Pedretti, *Leonardo da Vinci: A Study in Chronology and Style* (Berkeley and Los Angeles: University of California Press, 1973), pp. 161-62.

28. Vasari/Milanesi, vol. 6, pp. 379-86. Somewhat later, a Mr. Plaine of New Haven colony, executed for sodomy in 1646, outraged the authorities because "to some who questioned the lawfulness of such filthy practice, he did insinuate seeds of atheism, questioning whether there was a God": Jonathan Katz, *Gay American History* (New York: Avon, 1976), pp. 34-35. It remains an open question whether the perceived links between homosexuality, heresy, and treason dating back to the Middle Ages (see Boswell) reflect a consciously anti-authoritarian stance among the participants or merely the fears of outside observers.

29. Girardi, nos. 87 (suggesting that the "bride" text might refer to Cavalieri), 152, 153, 235; *Carteggio,* no. MCXLVII; *Letters,* trans. Ramsden, p. 120, no. 347; Cambon, pp. 67, 76-84.

30. For specific examples of shifts in addressee, see most recently Cambon, pp. 137, 150-52, passim (though he does not explore the issue of gender ambiguity as such). *Letters of King James VI and I,* ed. G. P. Akrigg (Berkeley: University of California Press, 1984), e.g., no. 218.

31. Symonds, *Life of Michelangelo,* vol. 2, p. 385, was the first to suggest the possibility that "the tragic accent discernible throughout Michelangelo's love poetry may be due to his sense of discrepancy between his own deepest emotions and the customs of Christian society."

32. Ed. Girardi, no. 87; Gilbert, no. 85. On the possible reference to Cavalieri, see above, n. 29.

**Justin Vitiello (essay date 1990)**

SOURCE: Vitiello, Justin. "Michelangelo's Poetry: 'Enough! Or Too Much.'" *Romanische Forschungen* 102, no. 1 (1990): 1-23.

[*In the following essay, Vitiello discusses Michelangelo's depiction of the role of the artist and the artistic process in a group of his poems known as the "Night Sonnets."*]

The insights of one iconoclastic genius may help us comprehend another. In *Die Geburt der Tragödie* (1871), Nietzsche expounds on a theory of art, life and metaphysics that can, I think, clarify and establish the *inherent* poetic value of Michelangelo's *Rime*:

. . . die Bilder des Lyrikers [sind] nichts als *er* selbst und gleichsam nur verschiedene Objektivationen von ihm, weshalb er als bewegender Mittelpunkt jener Welt "ich" sagen darf: . . . Insofern aber das Subjekt Künstler ist, ist es bereits von seinem individuellen Willen erlöst und gleichsam Medium geworden, durch das hindurch das eine wahrhaft seiende Subjekt seine Erlösung im Scheine feiert. Denn dies muß uns vor allem, zu unserer Erniedrigung *und* Erhöhung, deutlich sein, daß die ganze Kunstkomödie durchaus nicht für uns, etwa unserer Besserung und Bildung wegen, aufgeführt wird, ja daß wir ebensowenig die eigentlichen Schöpfer jener Kunstwelt sind: wohl aber dürfen wir von uns selbst annehmen, daß wir für den wahren Schöpfer derselben schon Bilder und künstlerische Projektionen sind und in der Bedeutung von Kunstwerken unsere höchste Würde haben—denn nur als *ästhetisches Phänomen* ist das Dasein und die Welt ewig *gerechtfertigt*.[1]

In spite of his apparently fragmentary eclecticism of Neoplatonic,[2] Christian,[3] High Renaissance, mannerist, baroque[4] and Aristotelian[5] strains, Michelangelo's "craggy versification, knotted syntax and passionate poetic thinking"[6] can, in my judgment, be explicated, elucidated and "justified" via his artistically achieved unity as an "esthetic phenomenon," i.e., as a poet. Thus, I will analyze some of his *Rime*—especially the Night Sonnets and one of his Bernesque *capitoli*[7]—to demonstrate how their form, imagery and meaning are resolved poetically in terms of the Nietzschean dialectics[8] of "I" and true author as an alchemical "subtle knot, which makes us man."[9]

Enzo Noè Girardi indicates two factors determining interpretations of the *Rime* that have complicated the task of assessing Michelangelo as a poet *per se*: "da un lato la soverchiante, poliedrica personalità umana ed artistica dell'autore; dall'altro, . . . la relativa indisponibilità della nostra tradizione critica, dominata da una . . . serie di arcadie e di classicismi, verso gli scrittori non solamente non 'inquadrati,' ma anche, com'è il caso di Michelangelo, troppo chiusi, difficili, anomali, inameni per vincere l'opposizione del 'buon gusto' dominante."[10] The first feature, so compelling for the Romantics, the Victorians,[11] Croce[12] and his followers and some contemporary scholars,[13] has encouraged an overly biographical interest in Michelangelo's poetry and the development of the stance that his verse must be understood mainly in relation to his letters, painting, sculpture and architecture.[14] The second, emphasized by such prominent cultural figures as Foscolo,[15] Croce[16] and Sapegno,[17] has as its primary focus the *Rime*'s lack of lyrical polish, their rough hewn, conceit-laden, "nonpoetic" nature.[18]

In this last decade,[19] however, considerable attention has been paid in Michelangelo criticism to the uniqueness of his enigmatic *corpus poeticum,* its *petrosità,*[20] now deemed to have aesthetic value, and to what Eugenio

Montale termed its "unicum" for "questo contrasto fra la durezza del mezzo e l'ineffabilità del pensiero."[21] Walter Binni has characterized such a *nescio quid* as "singolare fertilità . . . , fertile ambiguità."[22] It is precisely this quality that strikes me as most worthy of serious study.

If a valid critical interpretation of the *Rime as poetry* is to be developed,[23] it is crucial that we be misled neither by any hesitancy at cracking the hard shell of hermetic verse, nor by any awe we experience upon approaching a titan of Western culture, nor by his own famous confession of inadequacy: «Io esco di proposito, perchè ò perduto la memoria e 'l cervello, e lo scrivere m'è di grande affanno, perchè non è mia arte.»[24] To the contrary, we should depart from relevant critical appraisals like those of Girardi, who evaluates Michelangelo's lyrics vis-à-vis "una bellezza non piacevole, non distesa, non melodica, ma forte, contratta, aspra, conforme a una visione drammatica del mondo e della vita."[25] Such a statement serves as a "door of perception" to the poet's inherently paradoxical vision.[26]

Michelangelo's fundamentally ironic way of seeing through the veils of reality and penetrating the arcana of the universe is even apparent in **"O notte, o dolce tempo",**[27] a sonnet generally acclaimed as his candid paean to night.[28] In fact, the opening, exclamatory anaphora, "o . . . o . . . ," leads the reader to expect a hymn of praise. Yet the interjection of "benchè nero" deflates the laudatory expansiveness (before it has a chance to intensify) and casts the whole mood of the poem in a certain doubt[29] that will persist throughout the Night Sonnets. An oxymoronic pattern is thus present from the beginning and is further developed through the violent image and elision of line 2: "con pace ogn'opra sempr'al fin assalta."[30]

The spiritual restorative granted to the "intelletto intero" that pays homage to night seems adulterated in its sweetness. Furthermore, Michelangelo's glimmerings of intellectual lucidity (where light is air and fire) are abruptly undercut by the coarse (earthy?) and liquid imagery, and the corresponding plosive sound and staccato rhythm of lines 5-6:

> Tu mozzi e tronchi ogni stanco pensiero;
> ché l'umid' ombra ogni quiet' appalta.

"The solace from healing Night"[31] is not realized through a serene effort of will. The meditation takes root as a violation; and the poet is possessed in this therapeutic assault, left in a state of mental exhaustion and melancholia. He is more a sick plant (i.e., subject to water and earth in a stagnant, morose, humor) than an active mind.

But Michelangelo emerges from the "infima parte" of his consciousness, the lowest level of being in the Neoplatonic scheme. In another rapid change of image and mood, the sonnet soars with his "sogno" into realms recollected through nostalgia of the soul that longs to reascend:

> e dall'infima parte alla più alta
> in sogno spesso porti, ov'ire spero.

The release from the ectoplasmic, however, cannot be fully realized in dreams. Perhaps the ascent from earth and water to air is inhibited by the awareness that night, as Plato perceived, attacks the human mind with figments of its corruption. Knowing this Platonic truth or not, the poet vacillates. He yearns for the true moment of freedom: death—when the soul will—in another grand Western dream—depart from the prison of the body:

> O ombra del morir, per cui si ferma
> ogni miseria a l'alma, al cor nemica,
> ultimo delli afflitti e buon rimedio.

Yet he does not reach the realm of the blessed, nor does he even transcend human agony. The tercets describe only the relief from pain and sorrow that night, that earthly specter created in death's image,[32] can bring to a man suffering incurable torment. Such a liberation appears as soothing as a blood-letting, as peaceful as annihilation:[33]

> tu rendi sana nostra carn' inferma,
> rasciughi i pianti e posi ogni fatica,
> e furi a chi ben vive ogn'ira e tedio.

Much like Shakespeare's sonnets about the human conquest of temporality[34] that leave us with a stronger sense of time's ravages than of our immortal being, Michelangelo's poem of nocturnal peace conveys a gnawing fleshly and spiritual anguish. For the process inducing tranquility is as destructive as it is regenerating. The paradoxical language—"afflitti" vs. "rimedio," "rasciughi" vs. "furi"—reveals an ironic view of the conventional meditation of Lorenzo's "O sonno placidissimo, omai vieni" or Bembo's winged reveries.[35] Even the rhyme scheme functions to give this time of *dolcezza* a sulphuric aftertaste: "nero"—"intelletto intero," "assalta"—"esalta," "stanco pensiero"—"spero," "appalta"—"alta," "si ferma"—"inferma," "nemica"—"fatica," "rimedio"—"tedio." The counterposing of light and dark, health and sickness, intellectual clarity and spiritual malaise,[36] reinforces the conflict that seems to have no comforting end. After all is said and done, the poem ends with the words "ira e tedio," dramatizing the poet's search for a precarious, perhaps illusory, "pace," and expiring in a state of unresolved dualism.[37]

Such a "dissociation of sensibility" is brought to the fore even more vividly in **"Perché Febo non torce."** This sonnet has been interpreted as the antithesis of **"O notte, o dolce tempo,"** as the poem "in dispregio"[38] contrasting with the latter "elogio della notte."[39] It is evident that **"Perché Febo non torce"** tips the scales in favor of conceits that debunk and debase night. Yet in the light of the above analysis of **"O notte, o dolce tempo"** and of the generally discordant harmony of "il binomio dì—sole—notte—luna"[40] in Michelangelo's work, this view of praise and blame must be qualified.

The very first quatrain of **"Perché Febo non torce"** establishes a tension between the lucid beauty of the night's creation (the oxymoronic cast of the sonnet impresses us already) and the gloomy violence done by the brazen "vulgo" to this sacred creature called night. The radiance bestowed upon the earth is a kind of corruption (as light, in Neoplatonic terms, is corrupted by its infusion into matter). The sun's embrace ("le braccia sua lucenti"), by its very absence, and the masses' intrusive ignorance, are both sources of personal and universal disquietude. The implied "intelletti" who do understand "quel sol" (the night) as the most hallowed time of illumination are condemned to the "globo freddo e molle." Phrasing the dilemma in the negative (earth and water as hindrance to air and fire), the poet constructs the framework for a micro- and macrocosmic war:

> Perché Febo non torce e non distende
> d'intorn' a questo globo freddo e molle
> le braccia sua lucenti, el vulgo volle
> notte chiamar quel sol che non comprende.

In the second quatrain, Michelangelo develops the agon of light and dark in earthy, humble terms. The structural transition seems abrupt, yet these seemingly unrelated incidents, the creation of night and day and the lighting of a candle or torch, communicate most effectively the concrete sense of the drama:

> E tant'è debol, che s'alcun accende
> un picciol torchio, in quella parte tolle
> la vita dalla notte, e tant'è folle
> che l'esca col fucil la squarcia e fende.[41]

The images, compounded with the elisions, truncations, enjambments, and the "off-set" anaphora ("tant'è"), prepare the stage for the mindless harm done to night. She is victim of the capricious brute force that wrenches forth crude light and violates the sacred.

To the desecration of the octave, the first tercet contrasts a moment of refuge. Michelangelo reflects on the genesis of night:

> E s'egli è pur che qualche cosa sia,
> cert'è figlia del sol e della terra;
> ché l'un tien l'ombra, e l'altro sol la cria.

Darkness, the ultimate creation, rather than bringing all to perfection, comes into being (and becoming) through antithesis.[42] Earth "holds," plants, and protects the shadow by blocking the sun, while the sun fosters, or nourishes, darkness by its absence. The progenitors seem at odds in this strange dance, and the chiaroscuro imagery and rapid juxtaposition of "qualche cosa sia" and "cert'è figlia" make for an immaculately disturbing conception that cannot be redeemed from its original dualism.

Night, then, has divine parents and a nobility revealed to superior intellects. Yet she is not to be worshipped—or even praised. In her vulnerability—"vedova, scura, in tanta gelosia, / c'una lucciola sol gli può far guerra"—she is almost grotesque, as defenseless as Berni's "orinale." Here the dialectical form "gli" is most poignant[43] in contributing to an ambivalent portrait that gives rise to basic questions about Michelangelo's ironic vision: by feigning scorn, is the poet praising the night; by "veiling" admiration, is he debunking her; or is he doing both simultaneously, playing a game in the "Gran Teatro del Mundo" that has no simple winner or loser?[44] Finally we must wonder whether the poem is merely "a versatile exercise in the baroque" or the wrestling of a mind that "breaks up the old tables" and frames a new, powerful, dramaticopoetic statement.[45]

In any event, Binni's comment seems apropos: «Così come l'arduo giuoco concettistico, che può giungere a limiti di più aperto virtuosismo e di eccessiva fiducia nella poetica del mirabile, dell'inatteso, dell'ingegnoso (fino ad anticipi di manierismo e di prebarocco proprio nel senso di più lambiccate e autonome trovate) raramente però resta isolato e slegato da ragioni e possibilità più poetiche» (p. 62). This suggests to us what has finally been stated in a positive way by Glauco Cambon[46]—i.e., that Michelangelo was "an Italian Metaphysical"—and more fully developed in Alma B. Altizer's *Self and Symbolism in the Poetry of Michelangelo, John Donne and Agrippa D'Aubigné.* The latter work establishes that, while Michelangelo could be heavy-handed in his use of "an ingenious or witty imaginative-conceptual figure created by reformulating traditional images or ideas that are brought together to be disparate or contradictory" (x of Introduction), he possessed the gift that T. S. Eliot admired in the English Metaphysicals,[47] namely the capacity to create "an imaginative-intuitive figure that brings together seemingly disparate images or ideas in a unified embodiment of a direct intuition into underlying forms of experience" (Altizer, x-xi of Introduction). In this light, Michelangelo's dualism can be seen as a unified poetic experience.

To substantiate such a view, I would like to examine perhaps the most "seemingly disparate images or ideas" in his work, those found in his Bernesque *capitolo,* **"I' sto rinchiuso come la midolla"** (pp. 127-128).[48] Here we can witness, in the most overt yet hermetic of terms, the violent inter-play of elements and the genuinely magical processes that are unique in Michelangelo's poetry.

In citing this peculiarly brilliant example of what John Freccero has called "literary self-creation,"[49] I appeal to the clinical spirit of Anton Chekov's letter to M. V. Kiselev: "Homer, Shakespeare, Lope de Vega, the ancients generally . . . did not fear to grub in the 'dunghill' . . . (and) were more stable in their moral relations than we . . . The Greeks . . . were not ashamed to sing such love as really is in beautiful nature . . . To a chemist, nothing on earth is unclean. A writer must be as objective as a chemist . . . ; he must know that dungheaps play a very respectable part in a landscape, and that evil passions are as inherent in life as good ones."[50]

One can grant that Michelangelo tended more toward anatomy and alchemy than chemistry and that he longed for Neoplatonic and Christian flight from his own dungheap. But it still seems germane to explore the poetic value of a work that springs from the sewers of the Renaissance mind and goes "beyond the range of Italian art,"[51] doing violence to lyric decorum in the name of a new aesthetic. To do otherwise would be to paint buskins and doublets on the sinewy naked souls of the Last Judgment.

John Addington Symonds found arresting Michelangelo's "steady determination to treat men and women as nudities poised in the void."[52] **"I' sto rinchiuso,"** much more than "a malodorous description of his maladies,"[53] represents the poet's most sardonic vision of his decaying form through a tragico-burlesque self-flagellation,[54] a stripping away of all the layers of visceral agony to the raw nerves[55] of the soul:

> I' sto rinchiuso come la midolla
> da la sua scorza, qua pover e solo,
> come spirto legato in un'ampolla:[56]
> e la mia scura tomba è picciol volo,
> dov'è Aragn' e mill'opre e lavoranti,
> e fan di lor filando fusaiuolo.
>
> D'intorn'a l'uscio ho mete di giganti,
> ché chi mangi'uva o ha presa medicina
> non vanno altrove a cacar tutti quanti.
>
> I' ho 'mparato a conoscer l'orina
> e la cannella ond'esce, per quei fessi
> che 'nanzi dì mi chiamon la mattina . . .
>
> L'anima mia dal corpo ha tal vantaggio,
> che se stasat' allentasse l'odore,
> seco non la terre' 'l pan e 'l formaggio.

The versification is, of course, that of *La "Divina" Commedia.* Furthermore, if we can, like Swift,[57] answer "no" to the rhetorical question, "Should I the Queen of Love refuse, / Because she rose from stinking Ooze?" ("The Lady's Dressing Room"), the thematics of Michelangelo's poem will seem as eschatological as they are scatological. For just as Dante's hilariously gruesome band of squabbling "gargoyles" (*Inferno,* XXI-XXII) configures, naturally with hierarchical reservations, the onward Christian soldiers of the Church Militant, so Michelangelo has "del cul fatto trombetta" and resounded with bitter blasts of his own "Giorno della Vendetta." The *capitolo* is flooded with echoes of the most deeply serious classical and Christian experience. The motifs of the body as prison of the soul, the fates (become solicitous spiders), and the Titans (either piling up the poet's stool or mounting up as the hubristic evacuations themselves), and of *conosce te ipsum* (especially as *terrae limus*), *meditatio mortis, contemptus mundi,* the *via purgativa* (always literal as well as "mystical" in the Dantean sense), and the Eucharist (bread and cheese, in this case, for very personal reasons), pervade this buffoonish self-portrait, which, for all its bizarre and hideous caricature, mirrors the poet's vital concerns: his body's enslavement to temporal vicissitudes, the nostalgia of his soul to transcend flux ("di penne l'alma ho ben tarpata e rasa"), salvation and its relation to his calling: art—which, at the hour of his dissolution, seems flatulent indeed:[58]

> L'arte pregiata, ov'alcun tempo fui
> di tant'opiniön, mi rec' a questo,
> povero, vecchio e servo in forz' altrui,
>
> ch'i' son disfatto, s'i' non muoio presto.

As R. J. Clements has shown,[59] Michelangelo, in dramatizing his "ordeal of art," often has recourse to the phoenix image. In the case of **"I' sto rinchiuso,"** we can, in fact, perceive a kind of archetypal pattern of rebirth emergent from the poet's expiring.[60] There is a foreshadowing of such a *disegno* in the imagery of some of the *terzine*:

> La mia allegrezz' è la maninconia,
> e 'l mio riposo son questi disagi:
> che chi cerca il malanno, Dio gliel dia.

Here we must rely on Erwin Panofsky's exegesis of the mythography and astrology linked to Saturn or the saturnine character.[61] Panofsky demonstrates how this mythological entity symbolizes wisdom in misery, old age, abject poverty, and death ("povero, vecchio e servo"), and, in the Plotinian conception, philosophical and religious contemplation and the melancholy that is the essence of genius. Furthermore, Panofsky associates this genius—whose appearance is transformed "from the fantastic into the terrifying and repulsive" (p. 78)— with cannibalism (is the poet devouring his own children, his "bambocci," his works, and vomiting them forth once again?), castration ("Fiamma d'amor nel cor non m'è rimasa"), and ingestion (which, in the sixth and seventh stanzas, is connected to problems of metempsychosis and digestion, afflatus and flatus). Finally Saturn, as the great art historian argues, becomes the prototype for Father Time, the image of cosmic continuity, and the Great Destroyer or Revealer.

This iconological sketch provides us, I would argue, with a key to Michelangelo's use of the grotesque. Perhaps this technique "was adopted to implement his terribility" with "the Savonarolian aim of purging through dread and arriving at the instillation of virtue."[62] But, more importantly, through the unabashed delight in his own chimerical countenance, ("La faccia mia ha forma di spavento"), the poet presents himself as a "satyr-gargoyle," a hybrid daemon, and thus raises his *capitolo* to the level of myth.[63]

A second *terzina* enriches such a significance:

> Io tengo un calabron in un orciuolo,
> in un sacco di cuoio ossa e capresti,
> tre pilole di pece in un bocciuolo.

The *concetto* is hilarious.[64] Pursuing Panofsky's iconology, we can see the "calabron" as a figure of Silenus's "many misfortunes" (p. 62 ff.). Panofsky recounts how Silenus,[65] follower of Bacchus (discoverer of honey), in an avid quest for a bee-hive, happened upon a hornets' nest and incurred the perfect *contrappasso* punishment. In this context, Michelangelo dons the mask of divinely inspired fool, a parody of Bacchus, a deity linked to rites of spring and ecstatic rebirth.

The final mythical parallel concerns another Dionysian god: Christ:[66]

> Chi mi vedess' a la festa de' Magi
> sarebbe buono; e più, se la mia casa
> vedessi qua fra sì ricchi palagi . . .
>
> Che giova voler far tanti bambocci,
> se m'han condotto al fin, come colui
> che passò 'l mar e poi affogò ne' mocci?

The popular reference to birth in a manger ("sarebbe buono") and the vilifying one to failing to walk on water (which becomes "mocci") help to create the image of a degrading but ultimately exultant *imitatio Christi*[67] (as all re-enactments of the Passion are). Moreover, the poet has fused scatology (where snot is related to diarrhea, pus from hornet stings, the froth of castration, from which Aphrodite is born in one version, blood, and wine—all liquid to remedy the dryness of melancholia and to let the poet flow in eternal sources of joyous inspiration) and eschatology (where the transcendent meaning of the association Saturn—Silenus—Christ is embodied as a cyclical dialectic of mind—body—spirit, suffering—joy—sublime passion, and death—ecstasy—rebirth or resurrection).[68]

Therefore, the virulent confession of the poet's odor of decrepitude, shaped with brilliant linguistic extravagance comparable to Francisco de Quevedo's in the "unquotable" *Poemas satíricos y burlescos,*[69] assumes a mythical dimension where the poet is archetypal divinity of sempiternal Creation. We can read **"I' sto rinchiuso"** as a prelude to what Binni (p. 76) has designated the "debolezza senile" of Michelangelo's late, submissively Christian verse. But it strikes me, as do the capitulations of Donne in the *Holy Sonnets* and of Quevedo in the *Poemas religiosos,* as the senescence of Nietzsche's Silenus, who rises to the occasion when captured by King Midas:

> Als er [Silenus] ihm endlich in die Hände gefallen ist, fragt der König, was für den Menschen das Allerbeste und Allervorzüglichste sei. Starr und unbeweglich schweigt der Dämon; bis er, durch den König gezwungen, endlich unter gellem Lachen in diese Worte ausbricht: "Elendes Eintagsgeschlecht, des Zufalls Kinder und der Mühsal, was zwingst du mich dir zu sagen, was nicht zu hören für dich das Ersprießlichste ist? Das Allerbeste ist für dich gänzlich unerreichbar: nicht geboren zu sein, nicht zu *sein, nichts* zu sein. Das Zweitbeste aber ist für dich—bald zu sterben."

> Wie verhält sich zu dieser Volksweisheit die olympische Götterwelt? Wie die entzückungsreiche Vision des gefolterten Märtyrers zu seinen Peinigungen.

(p. 29)

As Norman O. Brown would say, Silenus's is the ego strong enough to live because it is strong enough to die. And in spite of Michelangelo's apparent "surrender" to orthodoxy in his later work, in **"I' sto rinchiuso"** we are in the presence of Dionysian wisdom and ecstasy, where, in Freccero's terms, the poet has managed "to create an autonomous universe of auto-reflexive signs without reference to an anterior Logos,"[70] and where the prefiguration of Nietzsche's "true author" contributes to the idolatry of the poetic creation of a universal self as its own end.[71]

Thus, regarding the *capitolo,* we must ask questions similar in structure to those posed in our reading of the Night Sonnets. Is this "wild old wicked man"[72]—who is the poetic *persona*—reviling his body, or parading it in a ritual *trionfo*? Is his humiliation a mask for daemonic pride?[73] Is his hand trembling from feebleness, or waggish excitement? Are the bitterness of the comedy and the glee of the tragedy ultimately drowned out in the resonant laughter of Silenus's companions (who, we might imagine, are joined by Silenus himself in the style of a modern tutelary deity, the village idiot)?: ". . . the beehive turns out to be a hornets' nest. Thus he (Silenus) is miserably stung on his bald pate, falls from his donkey, gets kicked, wrenches his knee, yells for help and is finally rescued by his companions who laughingly teach him to treat his stings with mud and mire and finally manage to put him on his feet" (Panofsky, *Studies* . . . , p. 62). If, like Silenus (or Hephaistos,[74] Ares, and Aphrodite in the Homeric scene of Olympian farce), the poet is immortal—and, after all, he has created himself so—then even his self-abasement, floundering, and "bambocci" are aspects of

the divine.[75] The bellowings of derision he aims at himself reverberate, in truth, as exaltation, or even prophecy.[76]

The Michelangelo of "un linguaggio agitato, talvolta impulsivo, incerto o esitante . . . , una stilizzazione violenta, volontaristica e concettuosa," the poet who cannot find "una forma chiara, pacificata in se stessa,"[77] must be re-evaluated as "eternally justified" in his total vision. Even his devotional verse is tinged with Silenian, or Dionysian, ecstasy:

> E se talor, tuo grazia, il cor m'assale,
> Signor mie caro, quell'ardente zelo
> che l'anima conforta e rassicura,
>
> da che 'l proprio valor nulla mi vale,
> subito allor sarie da girne al cielo:
> ché con più tempo il buon voler men dura.

(p. 139)

Violence to grammar fuses with the anticipated violence of rapture as culmination of suffering. This so-called "assoluta incapacità di trovare una misura"[78] is most felicitous, artistically, because, as Blake perceived, without travelling "the road of excess," one does not reach "the palace of wisdom."

Berni, serious for once, seems to divine the uniqueness of Michelangelo's poetry in his attack on the Petrarchists: "e' dice cose e voi dite parole." Even in the realm of abstraction, Michelangelo, like the Metaphysicals, could project the feeling of a "sillogismo"[79] with an individual brand of vigorous language, a sense of cosmic agon, and the intuition of the mythical nature of "le cose":

> Ogni van chiuso, ogni coperto loco,
> quantunche ogni materia circumscrive,
> serba la notte, quando il giorno vive,
> contro al solar suo luminoso gioco.

In the most common of spaces, matter included, a secret meaning of night can be cherished—though only by opposing playfully hostile forces. Once again, Michelangelo appeals to an aristocracy of intelligence, initiated into the mysteries of the dark. Implied in this hermetic vision is a certain Neoplatonism concerning the perception of Ideas through pure intellect and suggesting a scorn for the irreality of the visible world. Nevertheless, this inverted lucidity does not allow for any kind of stability, since the "Farsa Grossolana del Mondo" is the *locus* of experience of the transcendent:

> E s'ella è vinta pur da fiamma o foco,
> da lei dal sol son discacciate e prive
> con più vil cosa ancor sue specie dive,
> tal c'ogni verme assai ne rompe o poco.

The syntactical tension, the staccato effect of "da lei dal sol son . . . ," and the extreme contrast of the images of "specie dive" and "verme," render the concept of night's essence in a most dramatic fashion. The battle rages on multiple levels: in the macrocosm, on earth, and underground. And the verb forms convey the passivity of the sacred and the aggression of the vulgar.

The fundamental dichotomy is amplified in the tercets, where Michelangelo elaborates on the generation of the base and the holy:

> Quel che resta scoperto al sol, che ferve
> per mille vari semi e mille piante,
> il fier bifolco con l'aratro assale;
>
> ma l'ombra sol a piantar l'uomo serve.
> Dunche, le notti più ch'e' dì son sante,
> quanto l'uom più d'ogni altro frutto vale.

A brazen crudity and virtual rape of the sanctified darkness are depicted in this scene of the cultivation of pustulating vegetal matter. Two antithetical series of associations emerge: (1) soulless objects—their reproduction in the open light of day—their brute strength—their consummate profanity in mere existence; (2) man, the creature of intellect and soul—his procreation in the dark of night and womb—his godlike frailty (*Ecce Homo*?)—the sacredness of his essence. The rub is that man must depend on the sexual, or vegetal, function and is plunged into a world where his divinity is forever condemned to precarious becoming and anxiety-riddled being.

Yet the poem takes a radical turn in the last two lines. The travesty of peace has no dénouement. But a certain *modus operandi* is perceptible whereby day partakes of the holiness of night and the other fruits of creation are part of the same order as man. Again dealing with apparently disparate elements, Michelangelo fuses images of earth and fire and forges what Panofsky sees as an Aristotelian "vision": "both reality and Idea had come to be located in the human consciousness . . . within which they could blend into a unity."[80]

I would carry the argument beyond Aristotelian categories, however, for Michelangelo anticipates Giordano Bruno's view that "the wise man is the man who researches not by grasping totality through dead concepts but by capturing the infinitely living unity of the universe, by making himself one with the creative power which is none other than the Creator Himself."[81] Perhaps Michelangelo's sense of man as, in the words of the *Asclepius,* "a great miracle, worthy of honor and veneration,"[82] represents only a momentary glimpse of mythical unity. Nevertheless, in spite of Michelangelo's ambivalence toward the act of "piantar," his Passion draws him toward alchemical faith in the human, "a miraculous being, subject to change, a being capable of uttering all words, transforming all things, and drawing all characters, a being capable of responding to every call and calling every god."[83]

We are really not terribly far from Nietzsche's "dem geheimnisvollen Ur-Einen" (p. 25).[84] In the *disegno* and *operosità* of Michelangelo's poetic art there are melded elements of form and content, sophisticated and popular language, the fleshly and spiritual transfiguration through suppuration of poems as apparently alien as **"I' sto rinchiuso"** and **"Ogni van chiuso,"** ecstasy and conscious literary self-creation, and mythical experiences that seem in opposition but are, on a higher plane of truth, integrated cyclically and archetypally.[85]

The final Night Sonnet, **"Colui che fece,"** is an harmonious recapitulation of and coda to the thematics I have traced throughout. It treats of a Michelangelesque myth of creation, the illusion of dualism in the essentially non-hierarchical cosmic unity, and the reverberations of astrology. At the same time, it personalizes these universals in Bernesque and dialectical manners.

The octave recounts, with characteristic syntax, truncation, and imagery, the simultaneous genesis of time and humankind, night and day, and the poet's destiny:

> Colui che fece, e non di cosa alcuna,
> il tempo, che non era anzi a nessuno,
> ne fe' d'un due e diè 'l sol alto all'uno,
> all'altro assai più presso diè la luna.
>
> Onde 'l caso, la sorte e la fortuna
> in un momento nacquer di ciascuno;
> e a me consegnaro il tempo bruno,
> come a simil nel parto e nella cuna.

In this progression of difficult conceits, a paradoxical *stato d'animo* vitalizes the following abstractions: the Neoplatonic idea of primary creation as an act free of matter (or is it magical creation *ex nihilo*?), time as the "Siamese twin" of the human species, dualism as the *sine qua non* of temporality, and the fatalistic notion of the influence of the stars. Herein, the tortured *persona* is both a bastard of pure caprice and a very special child and *event* in the Grand Design. Influenced by a passage from Ficino, himself more than just a dabbler in magic,[86] Michelangelo sees his poetic self as victim and champion, slave and master of time and fate, buffoon and creator:

> E come quel che contrafà se stesso,
> quando è ben notte, più buio esser suole,
> ond'io di far ben mal m'affliggo e lagno.

The artist, by nature, a self-contradictory being, is subject to flux yet capable of bestowing, or forging, immortality. He dies, and yet he is fecund, shaping matter into creations transcending nature, time, and death. In other words,

> La causa a l'effetto inclina e cede,
> onde dall'arte è vinta la natura.

I' 'l so, che 'l pruovo in la bella scultura,
c'all'opra il tempo e morte non tien fede.

Dunche, posso ambo noi dar lunga vita
in qual sie modo, o di colore o sasso,
di noi sembrando l'uno e l'altro volto;

sì che mill'anni dopo la partita,
quante voi bella fusti e quant'io lasso
si veggia, e com'amarvi i' non fu' stolto.

(p. 113)

The "fattor," as grotesque as a chaste Silenus, lives on in his "immagin viva in pietra alpestra e dura"—or in words, "set to music perhaps." By seeking his opposite, the artful beast of melancholia partakes of the radiance and resilience of the universe.

Similarly, in **"Colui che fece,"** the poet, wallowing in self-pity,[87] suddenly frees himself from his lot in the microcosm[88] and turns contradiction into "die aus Schmerzen geborene Wonne" (Nietzsche, p. 34).

Pur mi consola assai l'esser concesso
far giorno chiar mia oscura notte al sole
che a voi fu dato al nascer per compagno.

His providential mate is god of light, Apollo and Christ merged.[89] The original plan of Creation is fulfilled in this relationship. The poet, Dionysian and, in the excesses of lament, Magdalenian, becomes Apollonian as creator of the dream form of a work of art and Christ-like in his own Passion and self-referential Logos. Finally, as archetypal Hermaphrodite God, he finds "consolation," or justification, in "the infinite and living unity (where) all limitations (are) abolished forever":[90] "So God created man in his *own* image, in the image of God created he him; male and female created he them" (Genesis 1:27).

Through Michelangelo's self-destructive fawning and grovelling before his "Signore" (the conventional ambiguity of this word is now seen as a unity) and his obsession with his double as self-fulfillment, an alchemical transformation of Renaissance categories is realized in the dynamic universe of a poetry created by the infinitely fecund worm.[91] Perhaps, since the limitless possibilities of the human make instability its very condition, there is no lasting peace for Michelangelo. Dante and the Edmund Spenser of the *Mutabilitie Cantos* can resolve such a dilemma in a vision of eternal harmony. But Michelangelo's only "ontological certainty" pullulates "at the center of the human vortex."[92] His instinct for experiencing reality dialectically, never totally repressed by the authority of the Counter-Reformation,[93] takes vital shape in an exploding and imploding poetic vision, where, as Beckett says in *Endgame,* "the bigger a man is the fuller he is . . . And the emptier"—and vice versa.[94]

*Notes*

1. Friedrich Nietzsche, *Werke* I, ed. K. Schlechta (Darmstadt: Wiss. Buchges., 1963): 38-40.

2. The debate as to the extent of Neoplatonic influence in Michelangelo's work is still ongoing between the Panofskian school, which maintains that the artist/poet was essentially Neoplatonic in his metaphysics, and those who would qualify and/or challenge this view. See, for example, Charles De Tolnay, *The Art and Thought of Michelangelo* (New York: Pantheon, Random House, 1964); Umberto Bosco, «Non ha l'ottimo artista,» *Rivista di Cultura Classica e Medievale* VII, 1-3 (1965): 181-86; Edgar Wind, *Pagan Mysteries in the Renaissance* (New York: Norton, 1968); Creighton E. Gilbert, "Michelangelo's Poetry: The Private Art of a Public Person," in R. L. Weaver, et al. eds., *Essays on the Music of J. S. Bach and Other Divers Subjects: A Tribute to Gerhard Herz* (Louisville: University of Louisville Press, 1981): 69-83; Gavriel Moses, "Philosophy and Mimesis in Michelangelo's Poems," *Italianistica: Rivista di Letteratura Italiana* X, 2 (May-August 1981): 162-77; Giancarlo Maiorino, "In Search of True Form: Michelangelo's Power of Expression and the Aesthetic Lure of the *Non-finito*," *Rivista di Studi Italiani* I, 1 (June 1983): 51-81; and Sara Gelber, "Apocalyptic and Demonic Structures in Michelangelo's Love Poetry," *Carte Italiane: A Journal of Italian Studies* VI (1984-85): 34-50.

3. See, for a recent and most useful article, Itala Rutter, "Michelangelo's *Rime*: Form and Meaning," *Canadian Journal of Italian Studies* VIII, 31 (1985): 160-72.

4. Erwin Panofsky has summed up the problem of whether Michelangelo is High Renaissance, mannerist or baroque in *Studies in Iconology* (New York: Harper and Row, 1967). In short, while Michelangelo's style manifested characteristics of all three periods, according to Panofsky, it was ultimately Michelangelesque.

5. See Panofsky, *Idea: a Concept in Art Theory* (Columbia: University of South Carolina Press, 1968), pp. 119-21.

6. D. Carne-Ross, "The Poetry of Michelangelo," *Times Literary Supplement* LXXII, 8 June 1973, p. 439. This succint article focuses on "those poems where Michelangelo is doing something he did not, *and could not,* do in the fine arts" (p. 439).

7. On the influence of Berni on Michelangelo, see Eugenio Montale, *Michelangelo poeta* (Bologna: Boni, 1975), p. 16.

8. See Alma B. Altizer, *Self and Symbolism in the Poetry of Michelangelo, John Donne and Agrippa D'Aubigné* (The Hague: Martinus Nijhoff, 1973),

p. 106: "For Michelangelo the crux is the dialectical relationship between subject and object, inner form and outer form, creator and created."

9. Donne's "The Extasie." See John Freccero, "Donne's 'Valediction: Forbidding Mourning'," *E.L.H.* xxx (1963), p. 362: "There was at least one science in Donne's time . . . which still held to a theoretical continuity between matter and spirit: the science of alchemy." I am indebted to this article for insights applicable to Michelangelo.

10. «La critica letteraria su Michelangelo,» *Aevum* XL (1966), pp. 254-55. See, also, Montale: «La grandezza del Buonarroti scultore, pittore e architetto stingeva . . . sulle rime e le rendeva intoccabili, forse ingiudicabili» (p. 16).

11. For the most emphatic view, see W. P. Kerr, "The Poems of Michael Angelo," *Edinburgh Review* CLXVIII (1888), p. 3: "It would be a daring and foolish thing to say that the poems are as valuable in themselves, apart from all thoughts of the author, as they are when regarded as his confessions—his own personal words."

12. *Poesia popolare e poesia d'arte* (Bari: Laterza, 1946), p. 391: «Dietro di quelle rime, c'è bene Michelangelo, il gran Michelangelo . . . »

13. Most broad-ranging among them is R. J. Clements in *The Poetry of Michelangelo* (New York: NYU Press, 1966): "The value of the *Rime* is not an autonomous one. Beyond the many inherent values which we have attributed to them, their value lies not only in their being identified closely with one of the world's greatest creative spirits, but also in their magnificent potential for explaining that enigmatic man and his work" (pp. 341-42).

14. See, for instance, Panofsky, *Idea . . .* and *Studies . . .* ; Charles De Tolnay, *The Art and Thought of Michelangelo*; Clements, *Michelangelo's Theory of Art* (New York: NYU Press, 1961); and Helen O. Borowitz, "Michelangelo's Harsh Music," *Art Journal* xxix (New York, 1970): 318-25.

15. Foscolo's articles on Michelangelo in British journals are well enough known not to cite. Girardi's discussion of them (p. 262 ff.) is also worthy of attention.

16. Op. cit., p. 391: "ma in esse (le rime) non è veramente, o solo in rari tratti, un Michelangelo poeta ed artista."

17. *Compendio di Storia della Letteratura Italiana* (Florence: La Nuova Italia, 1964), II, 133-34: « . . . a lui (Michelangelo) mancò un'adeguata educazione letteraria e una sufficiente disciplina artistica, e cioè l'attitudine a esprimersi in forme chiare e liberate, senza quelle contorsioni e du-

rezze e improprietà che son proprie degli scrittori nei quali il pensiero lotta faticosamente con la forma e non giunge a trovar la sua via, se non a tratti e non senza stento.» Although Sapegno revises his devaluation with more sympathy in his «Appunti sul Michelangelo delle *Rime,*» *Rivista di Cultura Classica e Medievale* VII (1965): 999-1005, his negative judgment has become a leitmotif of Michelangelo criticism.

18. Another current that deserves mention is the study of Michelangelo as philosopher in poetic form. See J. E. Taylor, *Michael Angelo considered as a philosophic poet* (London: John Murray, 1852); Walter Pater, *The Renaissance* (London: Macmillan, 1912); Nesca A. Robb, *Neoplatonism of the Italian Renaissance* (London: George Allen and Unwin, Ltd., 1935); Thomas Mann, «La concezione dell'amore nella poesia di Michelangelo,» *Letteratura Moderna* I (December, 1950): 427-34; John Arthos, *Dante, Michelangelo, and Milton* (London: Routledge and Kegan Paul, 1963); Alvaro Bizziccari, «L'Idea della bellezza nelle poesie di Michelangelo,» *Italia* XLI (1964): 252-65; and Eugenio Garin, «Il pensiero,» in *Michelangelo: artista, pensatore, scrittore* (Novara: Istituto Geografico De Agostini, 1965), II, 529-41. For a summary of critical judgments of Michelangelo's verse in Italy from the Renaissance to the early 1970's, see Mario Acacia, *Michelangelo's Poetry and Its Fortune in Italian Literary Criticism* (University of Toronto, Ph.D. Dissertation, 1973).

19. As early as 1973, Acacia concluded that "modern scholarship tends toward the acceptance of Michelangelo as a poet worthy of consideration" (*Dissertation Abstracts International* XXXVIII A, 10, 6154A, April 1978).

20. For positive views of this poetic quality, see Montale; Pietro D'Angelo, *La poesia di Michelangelo* (Palermo: Herbita, 1978); Frederick May, "The Poetry of Michelangelo," in S. Trambaiolo and N. Newbigin, eds., *Altro Polo: A Volume of Italian Studies* (Sydney: Frederick May Foundation for Italian Studies, University of Sydney, 1978), 15-44; Rutter; and Glauco Cambon, *Michelangelo's Poetry: Fury of Form* (Princeton: Princeton University Press, 1985).

21. Op. cit., p. 17.

22. In *Michelangelo scrittore* (Rome: Edizioni dell'Ateneo, 1965), p. 63. See, also, F. May, who claims status as a major poet for Michelangelo insofar as he succeeds in "concentrating experience for us by means of never-ending ambiguity interacting with an austere beauty of contemplation" (p. 26).

23. We must attempt to develop in this direction continually in spite of May's reservations: "Mich-

elangelo is going to wait a long time for evaluation as a poet" (p. 43). Cambon's recent book (1985) shows that Michelangelo "is coming at last into his own as a poet" (p. 176).

24. *Lettere,* ed. S. Milanesi (Florence: Le Monnier, 1875), n. 182, p. 544. For commentary, see Clements, *Michelangelo's Theory* . . . , pp. 411-12; and P. L. DeVecchi, «Studi sulla poesia di Michelangelo,» *Giornale Storico della Letteratura Italiana* CXL (1963), pp. 63-64. One wonders, however, if this could not be merely a polite excuse for tardiness in correspondence. At any rate, we should always keep in mind Antonio Machado's most subtle observation: "Cuando un poeta teoriza sobre poesía, puede decir cosas muy verdaderas, pero nunca dirá nada justo de sí mismo" (*Los complementarios* [Buenos Aires: Losada, 1957], p. 16).

25. *Studi sulle rime di Michelangiolo* (Milan: L'Eroica, 1964), pp. 23-24.

26. This vision, it seems, is the essence of Michelangelo's search for "harmony between the ideal and reality, to create a link between the physical and the eternal, to fuse life and spirit *within* the bonds of earth" (Rutter, p. 163). A similar view is expressed in Ann H. Hallock, "The Origins of Michelangelo's Poetic Expression," *Italian Quarterly* LXXXI (Summer 1980): 17-29, and in Gilbert, p. 78. See, also, Hallock, *Michelangelo the Poet: the Man Behind the Myth* (Pacific Grove, CA: Page Ficklin, 1980).

27. For all quotations from the *Rime,* see Girardi's edition (Bari: Laterza, 1960). The Night Sonnets are found on pp. 58-60.

28. See E. Bevilacqua, *Michelangelo scrittore* (Milan-Rome, 1926), p. 649; G. G. Ferrero, *Il petrarchismo del Bembo e le rime di Michelangelo* (Turin: L'Erma, 1935), pp. 79-82; G. Contini, «Il senso delle cose nella poesia di Michelangelo,» *Rivista Rosminiana* XXXI (1937), p. 288; Clements, *The Poetry* . . . , pp. 100-01; and G. R. Sarolli, "Michelangelo: The Poet of Night," *Forum Italicum* I (1967), pp. 138-39. Binni (p. 62) offers a slightly different interpretation: «carico . . . è . . . di un sentimento poetico che si traduce nel ritmo stanco e rotto, malinconico e ricco di conflati di esperienza dolorosa della vita e di aspirazioni ad una dimensione senza pene ed affanni.»

29. To have a more comprehensive view of such a treatment, students of the Renaissance need only recall Shakespeare's ambiguous attitude regarding blackness in his sonnets to the Dark Lady.

30. Rutter clearly understands the seemingly "non-poetic" techniques Michelangelo employs for their basic artistic value: "Michelangelo's poetry confronts the reader with a special quality of tension, contrast and harshness. The language is often . . . replete with paradoxes; thoughts develop through polarity between extreme images and with an elliptic syntax . . . at times truly tortuous" (p. 160).

31. Sarolli, p. 138.

32. In his perceptive study, *Le rime di Michelangelo Buonarroti* (Padua: Liviana, 1965), Sergio Romagnoli calls night "un'immagine, un presentimento della morte" (p. 129).

33. It is difficult to interpret "buon rimedio," with Romagnoli, exclusively "in senso pietoso" (p. 129).

34. See, especially, Sonnets 12 and 60.

35. In her «L'influsso di Giovanni Boccaccio nella lirica di Michelangelo,» in V. Branca *et al.* eds., *Il Rinascimento: Aspetti e problemi attuali* (Florence: Olschki, 1982), Florinda Iannace sees the poet as "più vicino a Bruno . . . che non a Bembo" (p. 462).

36. See Clements, *The Poetry* . . . , pp. 100-01: "Night was the comforting time when moon and stars invited the soul to sink into welcome lethargy, the body to give way to drowsiness . . . Mindful as always of the duality of body and soul, the poet views the healing and restoring of spirit as important as the resting of the senses and body. In this sonnet that horrid marble incubus which threatens the repose of the *Notte* . . . is replaced by lofty dreams." Yet the loftiness, I maintain, is ultimately undercut.

37. See Hans Sckommodau, «Michelangelo, poeta,» in *Atti del Quinto Congresso Internazionale di Lingue e Letterature Moderne* (Florence: Valmartina, 1955), pp. 130-31; and J. Venturini, «Le Dualisme de Michel-Ange,» *La Revue d'Esthétique* XIV (1961): 365-91.

38. U. Bosco, *Il Rinascimento e la lirica di Michelangelo* (Rome, 1960-61), p. 124.

39. Ferrero, pp. 79-82, and Contini, p. 288.

40. Clements, «Unità nel pensiero di Michelangelo: il binomio dì—sole—notte—luna,» in *Atti del Convegno di Studi Michelangioleschi* (Rome, 1966), pp. 427-42.

41. A compelling argument for Michelangelo's liberation from Petrarchism might focus on his use of the image of "l'esca" in contrast to Petrarch's in Sonnet 90 of the *Canzoniere*. Michelangelo explodes where Petrarch is attracted and repulsed. May (p. 27) and Iannace (p. 463) also underscore the ultimately non-Petrarchan nature of Michelangelo's verse.

42. See Hallock's article, pp. 28-29, for an analysis of how Michelangelo thinks poetically via "antithetical approaches."

43. See Borowitz, p. 318.

44. Sckommodau expresses a comparable idea: «Manca un centro fermo a questa poesia . . . Michelangelo è profondamente commosso dal senso di dubbio che avvolge tutto il vivere umano . . . Ricerca le tracce del mistero, che ora riconosce con l'occhio . . . , ora possiede nel sentimento . . . , ma che il suo spirito non può seguire fino all'ultima cagione» (p. 130). However, I hope to demonstrate how this "senso di dubbio" is resolved in a mysterious and all the more radiant vision.

45. Bevilacqua (pp. 649-50) condemns the poem as verging on "marinismo." For more sympathetic views of Michelangelo's "baroquism," see Helmut Hatzfeld, «L'Italia, la Spagna e la Francia nello sviluppo del barocco letterario,» in *La critica stilistica e il barocco letterario* (Florence, 1957); and Clements, *The Poetry* . . . , pp. 38-59. For another positive assessment of Michelangelo's unique, "breathtakingly novel" voice, see Gregory L. Lucente, "Lyric Tradition and the Desires of Absence: Rudel, Dante and Michelangelo ('Vorrei uoler')," *Canadian Review of Comparative Literature* x, 3 (September, 1983), p. 325: "Michelangelo recasts old metals, but the coin he strikes is genuinely new."

46. "Sculptural Form as Metaphysical Conceit in Michelangelo's Verse," *Sewanee Review* LXX (1962), p. 155. See, also, his *Michelangelo's Poetry: Fury of Form.*

47. Altizer disclaims any indebtedness to Eliot (IX, n. 6), but his essay, "The Metaphysical Poets," seems to be omnipresent in spirit throughout her book, above all when she describes how Michelangelo repairs "the split between thought and imagination." For a direct comparison between Michelangelo's *poetry* and that of Eliot, see Max Nänny, "Michelangelo and T. S. Eliot's 'The Love Song of J. Alfred Prufrock'," *Notes on Modern American Literature* VII, I (Spring-Summer 1983): Item 4.

48. This poem has caused some embarrassment among scholars. Clements notes its "disjointed and crude manner" (*Michelangelo's Theory* . . . , p. 363) and its descent "to the level of the vespasian" ("Berni and Michelangelo's Bernesque Verse," *Italica* XLI [1964], p. 275). Chandler B. Beall, in the same issue of *Italica* (commemorating the poet's death) omits the *capitolo* from "The Literary Figure of Michelangelo." To my knowledge,

the only comprehensive reading of "I' sto rinchiuso" is Carne-Ross's. Other insightful comments that help us interpret this poem are found in May (pp. 20-23), Gilbert (p. 73), Moses (p. 171) and Cambon (1985, pp. 9-10 and 21-26). These scholars clearly perceive how Michelangelo mixes and compounds the sublime and commonplace (Moses), the comic and the tragic (Gilbert), the crude and the titanic (May).

49. In "The Fig Tree and the Laurel: Petrarch's Poetics," *Diacritics* v (Spring, 1975), p. 34.

50. In *The Modern Tradition,* eds. R. Ellmann and C. Feidelson, Jr. (New York: Oxford University Press, 1965), pp. 244-45.

51. Carne-Ross, p. 439.

52. *Life of Michelangelo Buonarroti* (London: Macmillan, 1893), I, 172.

53. Clements, "Berni . . . ," p. 266.

54. May (p. 21) characterizes this technique as "deliberate self-mockery—self-deflation."

55. Such "nakedness" may remind us of William Butler Yeats's "A Coat":

> I made my song a coat
> Covered with embroideries
> Out of old mythologies
> From heel to throat;
> But the fools caught it,
> Wore it in the world's eyes
> As though they'd wrought it.
> Song, let them take it,
> For here's more enterprise
> In walking naked.

Iannace's appreciation of Michelangelo's poetry "per la forza delle immagini, per la primitività delle espressioni, per una lingua che rifugge da qualunque facile melodiosa rima e per quell'irrompente sincerità . . . attraverso il quale transpariscono muscoli e nervi e bile e sangue" (p. 463) is also germane in this context.

56. See Moses's observation regarding this stanza's "view of the self, precious liquid trapped in a gross outside container" (p. 166). Here again, according to Moses, Michelangelo transcends traditional Neoplatonism.

57. Significantly, Michelangelo does not suffer from the malady of Swift's Strephon as diagnosed by Norman O. Brown in *Life Against Death* (New York: Vintage, 1959): "sublimation and awareness of the excremental function are mutually exclusive, and the conclusion is drawn that sublimation must be cultivated at all costs, even at the cost of repression" (p. 188).

58. On a sublime, but interrelated note, Maiorino points out: "Hope of conquering the highest beauty could be fulfilled only by sacrificing art to death, which (for Michelangelo), implied a transformation of the artistic into the spiritual" (p. 76).

59. *Michelangelo's Theory* . . . , p. 394.

60. See, also, May, who maps out an "itinerary" for understanding the mythic dimensions of Michelangelo's poetry: "you must go in archetypal pursuit" (p. 27).

61. *Studies* . . . , p. 76 ff.

62. Clements, "Berni . . . ," p. 216.

63. See May, p. 20: "Michelangelo is suggesting that man must confront the inevitability of metaphor, and the consequent progress through metamorphosis to myth."

64. For further comment on this strophe, see Gilbert, pp. 73-74.

65. Moses finds echoes in Michelangelo's poems of the Silenus passage in Plato's *Symposium,* which serves as "an illustration of the theme that beauty is buried deep inside an outer mass (body or marble), which must be removed in order to reach or liberate the precious inside" (p. 176).

66. Mircea Eliade, in his various studies (see, above all, *Patterns in Comparative Religion* [Cleveland: World Publishing Company, 1958]), has shown how the idea of the Christian deity, even though he breaks certain patterns by being born in winter and dying in spring, is rooted in the tradition of the seasonal cycle as symbol of death and rebirth. The methodology of the present analysis, however, is literary, not anthropological, being as it is grounded in Erich Auerbach's *Studi su Dante* (Milan: Feltrinelli, 1971), especially the chapters «Figura» (pp. 174-221) and «Passi della *commedia* dantesca illustrati da testi figurali» (pp. 239-60).

67. May sees "the latent Christ" that "comes from the intersection of time with the timeless" (p. 30) in a number of Michelangelo's works and detects therein "a meditation on the love known to the Fool for Christ" (p. 36). Maiorino makes an even more directly useful comparison for my purposes, linking the Christ of the Rondanini Pietà and the self-portrait of "I' sto rinchiuso": "As (Michelangelo) attacked the body of Christ . . . and broke its limbs . . . , so the cancer of time produced similar effects on him:

> I am broken up, ruptured and cracked and split
> From my labors so far. . . ."

                                                (p. 72)

68. See, again, Maiorino: "While forms have been created and then destroyed, the existence of Christ-Michelangelo is transubstantiated into an uplifting vision of human essence . . . (via) death-resurrection symbolism" (p. 74).

69. See Amédée Mas, *La Caricature de la Femme, du Mariage et de l'Amour dans l'Œuvre de Quevedo* (Paris: Ediciones Hispano-Americanas, 1957), p. 243.

70. "The Fig Tree . . . ," p. 38. See, also, p. 34, where the comment regarding Petrarch's laurel might be re-applied to Michelangelo's monster: "It stands for a poetry whose real subject matter is its own act and whose creation is its own author." De Tolnay's association of God with the creative force of art (p. 48) is further proof.

71. See Maiorino's point as to how Michelangelo, the "proud *creator* and *artifex,*" envisions that "growth and decay incarnate spiritual processes as well. In its ascending phase, physical impenetrability has been shattered by a transcendental thrust that delivers form from the instants of time into a state of eternity" (p. 75).

72. Gilbert (p. 73) is also reminded by Michelangelo of "the old man Yeats."

73. I do not mean to cast Michelangelo's ultimate submission to Christ in any shadow of doubt. But the sincerity of his faith does not necessarily explain his poetics.

74. May (p. 26) also compares the art of Michelangelo to Vulcan's.

75. See, also, Maiorino's excursus on p. 75.

76. See, for another reinforcing argument, May's comparison of Michelangelo and Jeremiah (p. 31).

77. Sckommodau, p. 131.

78. DeVecchi, p. 60.

79. Contini, p. 289.

80. *Idea* . . . , p. 17. Altizer presents a related theory: "Michelangelo's most original vision as poet-artist transcends both Neoplatonic and Christian symbolism: the willful, self-affirming imagination participates dialectically in reality; it gives form and is given form" (p. 102). Both Panofsky and Altizer seem to reflect the Blakean view expressed in the first and second series of "There Is No Natural Religion" and in "All Religions Are One."

81. Eugenio Garin, *Science and the Civic Life in the Italian Renaissance* (Garden City, N.Y.: Anchor Books, 1969 ed.), p. 164. See, also, Maiorino's conclusion *in re* Michelangelo's sculpture: "the

unconquerable form of matter, in Bruno's words, truly 'is all that it can be; and so it has all measure, has all species of figures and dimensions' (*Cause,* 126) in the aesthetic realm of the unfinished" (p. 78).

82. Garin, p. 150.

83. Ibid., p. 150.

84. Cambon (p. 157) also perceives archetypal patterns in Michelangelo's verse: "fiercely destructive masculinity and . . . the creative female principle."

85. Another argument for this viewpoint is Michelangelo's association of night with death and procreation. Freccero's explanation of "the most famous of all 'metaphysical' *double-entendres,* 'to die'" ("Donne's 'Valediction . . .'," p. 365), clarifies its alchemical meaning: "The 'death' of volatilization is like the marriage of man and wife, for from the 'putrefaction' of the 'Hermaphrodite' is generated the seed of a new creature. Like the death of a Christian, this decomposition is also a birth: 'Amen, Amen, I say to you, unless the grain of wheat falling into the ground die, itself remaineth alone. But if it die it bringeth forth much fruit'" (John 12, 24-5). For further elucidation of archetypal marriages, see Blake's *The Marriage of Heaven and Hell.*

86. De Vecchi, pp. 371-72. For further suggestions regarding Michelangelo's interest in the magical sciences, consult Romagnoli, p. 136, and Sarolli, p. 138.

87. See, also, May: "Michelangelo has an almost mediaeval sense of his own vileness" (p. 21).

88. Garin, discussing the importance of magic during the Renaissance (*Medioevo e Rinascimento: studi e ricerche* [Bari: Laterza, 1961], pp. 188-89), points to "una strana mitologia" involving "l'unità essenziale del tutto come natura dinamica" and "la posizione preminente dell'uomo, che attraverso l'azione rovescia il motivo del microcosmo, inteso come formula abbreviata del tutto, in quello dell'uomo signore delle cose . . ."

89. De Tolnay sees such a relationship in Michelangelo's drawings (p. 105). In the poetry, the association of sun, redemption, and Logos makes such an interpretation viable.

90. Garin, *Science and the Civic Life* . . . , p. 164. Closely connected to this view of the Hermaphrodite is May's interpretation of Michelangelo's Dante as "sheerly androgynous, *animus* and *anima,* a candid examination of the theory of poetry as *alma*-search" (p. 42).

91. Garin's description of the "mago-astrologo" (*Medioevo . . .* , p. 161) could fit "Michelangelo poeta": «vedeva orrende forze in agguato di là dal breve giro della ragione; e l'uomo sospeso su un abisso, e con un abisso dentro di sé; e indugiava su sogni e visioni, sulla strana resistenza del corpo, sugli impeti brutali, sulle passioni, le malattie, il dolore e la morte; e trovava strane parentele fra miracoli e mostri, fra santità e follia, fra visioni profetiche e allucinazioni . . . » Garin does not make such a connection himself in "Il pensiero," but does refer to Michelangelo's "tormentoso scontento del mondo e di se stesso" (p. 532) and his "grande raffigurazione poetica della tragedia umana nel mondo" (p. 540).

92. Freccero, "Donne's 'Valediction . . .'," p. 376.

93. For an elaboration on Michelangelo and Reformation ideas, see Lucente, pp. 327-28.

94. (New York: Grove Press, 1958), p. 3. Carne-Ross (p. 139) has envisioned in Michelangelo's poetry (*in re* "I' sto rinchiuso") "a scene of Beckett-like desolation and constriction"; and May comments: "it is to Beckett that we may look for enlightenment on much that's . . . in Michelangelo" (p. 23).

## William J. Kennedy (lecture date March 1990)

SOURCE: Kennedy, William J. "Petrarchan Authority and Gender Revisions in Michelangelo's *Rime.*" In *Interpreting the Italian Renaissance: Literary Perspectives,* edited by Antonio Toscano, pp. 55-66. Stony Brook, N.Y.: Forum Italicum, 1991.

[*In the following essay, originally delivered as a lecture in March 1990, Kennedy focuses on the ways in which Michelangelo was influenced by various commentators on Petrarch and concludes that, "[b]y viewing Petrarch's authority as a contested model, Michelangelo was able to accommodate his own gender variations on Petrarch's theme [of love]."*]

In 1623, fifty-nine years after Michelangelo's death, the artist's grandnephew Michelangelo Buonarroti Jr., "il Giovine," published an edition of 137 poems attributed to his illustrious granduncle. For that slim volume the editor revised the gender markings of nouns and pronouns in eighteen poems that Michelangelo had addressed to a male beloved, Tommaso de' Cavalieri. The profile of Michelangelo as a homosexual poet who appropriated figures and motifs from Petrarchan poetry and boldly reshaped them for the male object of his desire was lost until 1863 when Cesare Guasti, the poet's first dependable modern editor, restored the nouns and pronouns to their original gender. If it is true that sexual attitudes inform a whole civilization, then the gender revisions of Michelangelo's editors tell us a great deal about their respective moments in history. Michelangelo's original gender references tell us even more about his own moment in history, for when he addresses his male beloved in language that Petrarch directs towards a female, he comes to challenge the undisputed authority of Petrarch and a number of commentaries on Petrarch's poetry available at the time.

Like most Italian poetry in the second quarter of the sixteenth century Michelangelo's submits to the authority of Petrarchism, if not always in style and language, at least globally in its generic form and topical matter. Petrarchism itself became a site of contestation and debate as competing interpretations of its claims governed its horizon. The majority of early printed editions of Petrarch's poetry, from the very first in 1471 to Castelvetro's posthumous edition of 1582, appear with commentaries on individual songs and sonnets. In the competitive commercial atmosphere of Renaissance publishing, these commentaries allowed editors to gain a marketable edge over other editors by promoting in their footnotes the most extensive or least intrusive or best informed or least confusing or most edifying explanation of Petrarch's poetry. There are ten major commentaries that compete with one another in this way, and each inscribes a dominant feature of Renaissance ideology. This common feature is the prestige accorded to the antinomies of controversy and authority.

The commentaries include ones by Antonio da Tempo (early fifteenth century, printed 1471), Francesco Filelfo (mid-fifteenth century, printed 1476), and Girolamo Squarciafico (1483) who celebrate Petrarch's years of public service to the Visconti of Milan; by Alessandro Vellutello (1525) who rearranges the order of the *Rime* in order to tell a better story; by Sebastiano Fausto da Longiano (1532), Sylvano da Venafro (1532), and Antonio Brucioli (1548) who represent Petrarch as the model for a sixteenth-century courtier; and by Giovanni Andrea Gesualdo (1533), Bernardino Daniello (1541), and Ludovico Castelvetro (1545?, published 1582) who explore stylistic, rhetorical, and moral features of the poetry. Their commentaries codified norms of reading and writing Petrarchan poetry in the European Renaissance with considerable impact on creative imitations of Petrarch.

These commentators, of course, are male, and they articulate their assumptions about gender and sexuality from a male perspective. Their explicit evaluations of male and female roles in the amatory situation, and especially their moral evaluations, put Michelangelo's sexual identification to the test with sometimes disturbing results. As Michelangelo works to accommodate to his homosexual experience the heterosexual norms of love articulated by Petrarch's commentators, he apprehends his own desire from a new and alien perspective. The *Rime* that Michelangelo addressed at the age

of fifty-seven to Tommaso de' Cavalieri, a handsome Roman aristocrat thirty-four years his junior whom he met at Rome in spring or summer of 1532, trace that perspective.

Sonnet 94 (Girardi ed.) provides a good example not only of Michelangelo's Petrarchan imitation but also of the way in which its transgressive conflicts derive from cultural practices inscribed in the commentaries.

> D'altrui pietoso e sol di sé spietato
> nasce un vil bruto, che con pena e doglia
> l'altrui man veste e la suo scorza spoglia
> e sol per morte si può dir ben nato.
> 　　Così volesse al mie signor mie fato
> vestir suo viva di mie morta spoglia,
> che, come serpe al sasso si discoglia,
> pur per morte potria cangiar mie stato.
> 　　O fussi sol la mie l'irsuta pelle
> cje, del suo pel contesta, fa tal gonna
> che con ventura stringe sì bel seno,
> 　　ch'i'are' pure il giorno; o le pianelle
> che fanno a quel di lor basa e colonna
> ch'i' pur ne porterei duo nevi almeno.

[Kind to others and unkind only to itself, a vile beast is born that with pain and travail clothes another's hand and divests his own skin and only through death can be said to be well born.

So my fate might have wished to clothe my lord's living [flesh] with my own dead spoils that, as a snake sloughs by a rock, so through death could I change my own condition.

O if I were only my own hairy skin / O if only that hairy skin were mine (= belonged to me) that, in contact with his skin, makes such a garment that with luck presses against such a beautiful breast so that I would possess him throughout the day; or the slippers that make of themselves for him a base and column so that I would also carry them for at least two snows (= two years).]

The poem dramatizes what James Mirollo has studied as a topos of envied propinquity (Mirollo 125-59). Its speaker imaginatively wishes to become a piece of clothing that might touch the beloved's body. In Petrarch's *Rime sparse* the topos dominates a group of three sonnets, numbers 199 to 201, that narrate how the speaker finds a glove that covered Laura's hand. The excruciating twist in Michelangelo's sonnet involves not just the speaker's homosexuality nor even his focus on a garment more intimate than a glove, but a train of association leading from turmoil associated with the speaker's gender identification to a perception of the social marginality associated with his role as an artist.

Michelangelo's ambivalence accords with an anxiety that commentators note in Petrarch's sonnets 199-201. Petrarch's speaker responds to the sight of Laura's beautiful hand when she removes a silken glove. In sonnet 199, "O bella man che me destringi 'l core" 'O beautiful hand that grasps my heart,' he envies the glove for its intimacy with the beloved:

Così avess' io del bel velo altrettanto!
O inconstanzia de l'umane cose!
pur questo è furto, et vien chi me ne spoglie.

(Would I had again as much of that lovely veil! Oh the
inconstancy of human life! Even this is a theft, and one
is coming who will deprive me of it.)

In sonnet 200 he complains as the beloved puts the
glove back on her naked hand:

Non pur quell'una bella ignuda mano
che con grave mio danno si riveste,
ma l'altra et le duo braccia accorte et preste
son a stringere il cor timido et pianto.

(Not only that one naked hand, which clothes itself
again to my heavy sorrow, but the other, and those two
arms, are alert and swift to press my timid, humble
heart.)

In sonnet 201 he admits that he pilfered Laura's glove
as a prize, and he expresses shame and anger for not
holding on to his theft,

Né mi riede a la mente mai quel giorno
che mi fe' ricco et povero in un punto
ch' i' non sia d'ira et di dolor compunto
pien di vergogna et d'amoroso scorno.

(Nor does that day, which made me rich and poor at
the same time, ever come to mind without my being
moved with anger and sorrow, full of shame and
amorous scorn.)

Petrarch's commentators understand that reaction as an
instinctual mark of the super-ego. Squarciafico comments that in sonnet 201 the speaker suffers the pangs
of a delicate conscience; he cannot recall the theft
without feeling guilty. "Poscia conclude quello non potere retenere per esser furto: si che di bona conscientia
si mostra qui per il nostro poeta: non pur nel catino suo
volontieri haverie pescato senza haverne conscientia"
'Then he concludes that because it is stolen he cannot
keep it, so that our poet reveals his own good conscience; not even in his own basin would he have will-
ingly fished without having a conscience about it' (75ʳ).
Gesualdo understands the action as a complex narrative
about moral anxiety. The speaker has stolen the glove
and does not wish to believe that Laura misses it; even
after someone else points out his crime, he does not
wish to surrender the talismanic, fetishistic article of
clothing. "Onde il Poeta havendo tolto il guanto di M.
L. caduto peravventura in terra o da lei forse lasciato in
parte, onde tor si potè. Ella non so come avvedutasene,
o per altra persona sapendolo il volse si, che costretto
fu rendergliele a non partire di la benche la conscientia
com' huom da bene il mordesse, essendo elli furto"
'Whence the poet took Laura's glove that opportunely
fell to the ground or that she perhaps left behind. When
she found out about it, I do not know how, perhaps by
learning about it from some other person, he did not

want to let go of it, since he was obliged to return it to
her, even though because of the theft his conscience
gnaws at him as a good person' (HHvᵛ 245ᵛ). When the
speaker's conscience finally prevails, his impulse succumbs to a disturbed reaction.

In the commentaries of Sylvano da Venafro, Bernardino
Daniello, and Antonio Brucioli a murkier sense of being ineffectual undermines the speaker's self-esteem. In
their readings the lover regrets that he has squandered
the opportunity to exploit his own gains. Chance has
awarded him possession of the beloved's glove, but he
foolishly returns it to her when she complains of the
loss. Sylvano construes the theft as a vendetta upon the
beloved for the sorrows that she has caused—"& in-
tenda vendetta la incomodita di che le fusse stato cagione se se havesse ritenuto il guanto" 'the vendetta is
the inconvenience that she would have been put to if he
had held on to her glove' (cxxxxviʳ). Daniello iterates
the speaker's sense of self as an abused, beleagured,
downtrodden lover: "si duole di non haversi ritenuto il
guanto: e non haver saputo usare quel bene, che la
buona sua sorte gli havea posto dinanzi" 'he laments
that he did not know how to capitalize upon the favor
that good fortune had conferred upon him' (124ʳ).
Antonio Brucioli repeats Daniello's comment nearly
verbatim: "e duolsi di non si havere ritenuto esso
guanto, & non havere saputo usare quel bene che la
buona sua sorte gli haveva posta avanti" (137ʳ).

The most eccentric commentator, Alessandro Vellutello,
explains the first of these sonnets as part of an obsessive erotic drama. In his reorganization of the sequence
in order to tell a better, or at least more coherent, story,
Vellutello places "O bella man" and its companions
after Canzone 126, "Chiare fresche et dolci acque"
'Clear, fresh, sweet waters.' He notes that in this canzone the speaker recounts how he had come upon Laura
as she bares her arms for washing in the waters of the
Sorgue, "& forse delle braccia lavare" 'perhaps to wash
her arms' (36ᵛ). By placing the sonnets about Laura's
glove in proximity to this canzone, Vellutello implies
that the speaker cannot resist stealing an item of clothing that Laura has left on the shore. He wishes that he
could steal even more, especially the veil that covers
her face: "desiderando di poter altrettanto haver del
velo ch'ella portava in testa" 'wishing as much to be
able to possess the veil that she wore on her head' (37ᵛ).
Here the emphasis shifts from theft and guilt to pruri-
ence and carnal arousal, and two of Vellutello's successors, both accused of Protestant heterodoxy at various
times in their careers, reaffirm this shift. For Fausto da
Longiano the beloved's hand represents a synecdoche
for the rest of her body that Petrarch covets: "La mano
era una delle principali cose che Petrarcha amasse in
Laura" 'her hand was one of the principal features to
which he was attracted' (75ʳ). For Castelvetro the
dominant object of Petrarch's quest is carnal satisfac-

tion: "Primieramente pone quel bene, che gliene segue, che è di potere vedere la mano ignuda" 'First he posits the benefit that accrued to him, i.e. of being able to see her naked hand' (345). When the speaker recognizes the sinful nature of his carnal obsession, he experiences remorse.

Each of these commentaries explains the narrative as an instance of what Freud in his *History of an Infantile Neurosis ("Wolf Man")* (1918) calls "deferred action." Its pattern affords a model for the structure of trauma that includes, first, an imperfectly comprehended and spontaneously repressed event and, second, a perfected understanding of the event that proves to be traumatic. In the case of Freud's Wolf Man the repressed event concerns a sexual experience at the age of one and a half years to which the subject reacted upon its revival in a dream at the age of four and which he understood under analysis at the age of twenty-five. "This is simply another instance of *deferred action*. At the age of one and a half the child receives an impression to which he is unable to react adequately; he is only able to understand it and to be moved by it when the impression is revived in him at the age of four; and only twenty years later, during the analysis, is he able to grasp with his conscious mental processes what was then going on in him" (17.110). The deferral generates an entirely new set of judgments and meanings whereby three separate events, past and present, interpenetrate. The associative chains that link them pass across a temporal barrier that marks them as different moments of meaning. In Michelangelo's case the first event is his attraction to Tommaso de' Cavalieri; the second is his reading about erotic attraction in Petrarch's poetry; the third is his understanding of that attraction in terms analogous to those of the commentators.

If this later moment of meaning proves to be traumatic because it brings the primal scene to consciousness, it is also powerfully expressive of an ideology that confers meaning upon the scene to begin with. It situates the event with a system of moral, religious, ethical, legal, and philosophical representations that transform the subject's consciousness. In the case of Petrarch's furtive theft, the commentators perceive that Petrarch's speaker all along covets the beloved's naked body; only later does he recognize that the pilfering of Laura's glove masks his own carnal desire. The commentators conclude that this particular subject becomes conscious of a transgressive event—fleshly desire or the theft of property—that evokes his sense of guilt and remorse. Their moral response accords with a sixteenth-century ideological imperative to define and protect private property, to territorialize it, and to articulate legal mechanisms that defend it. Whereas the text of Petrarch's fourteenth-century poetry hardly reflects upon these issues in that manner but locates them instead in a realm of almost ritualized heightened awareness, sixteenth-century interpretations of it locate them in a realm of urgent legislative seriousness. Petrarch's poem registers one ideological concern, but the Renaissance commentaries register another.

These new concerns intervene upon Michelangelo's version of Petrarch's topos in surprising ways. It is not to claim that Michelangelo was an avid reader of the commentaries, but rather that he participated in the same system of representations that they do. Since their assumptions are his, he approaches Petrarch's text as they do, understanding its subject on the threshold of misconduct. He displaces the initial authority of Petrarch's model—where guilt and remorse hardly prevail—with the belated authority of sixteenth-century interpreters. Michelangelo's emphasis on the speaker's guilt and remorse colors his imitation of Petrarch, but his poem develops that emphasis with a new turn. The transgression at stake concerns neither private property nor the possession of so trivial an object as the beloved's glove, but rather the very identities of the lover and the beloved as private persons, identities marked by sexual boundaries and territorial definitions of gender.

Not the least problem is the identification of the silkworm itself, the "baco da seta" left unnamed in the text. To associate the speaker's voice with the author's implies that Michelangelo is imagining himself rather than the beloved to be the silkworm. The opposite may also be true. In several adjacent poems Tommaso de' Cavalieri's name lends itself to a series of plays on the figure of the beloved as a horseman, knight, or cavalier. In the sixteenth-century however, one dialect meaning of *cavaliere* is also 'silkworm.' Thus Nicolo Tommaseo and Bernardo Bellini's 1865 UTET *Dizionario della lingua italiana* identifies *cavaliere* as "baco da seta" in a letter by Torquato Tasso to Scipione Gonzaga: "Con quale artificio il verme, che cavaliero in queste parti è nominato, pascendosi di foglia tessa a se medesimo ricca e vaga prigione di seta." This synonymy appears also in two English-Italian dictionaries of the Renaissance, William Thomas's *Principal Rules of the Italian Grammar*: "cavaliere: a knight, or horseman, or a silke worme" (Fiv$^r$), and John Florio's *Queen Anna's New World of Words*: "cavaglière, a knight or gentleman serving on horsebacke. . . . Also a silke worme or spinner. Also a kind of great Seacrab or lobster" (p. 89). Who, then, is Michelangelo's silk worm, the lover or the beloved, Michelangelo himself or Tommaso de' Cavalieri? The sliding signifier permits, even encourages a crossing of boundaries and blurring of identities between man and boy, lover and beloved.

The issue of crossed boundary and blurred identity dominates the poem in a series of contrasts and antinomies. The sonnet's first quatrain oxymoronically juxtaposes death against life, pain against pleasure, torment against kindness in its figure of a silkworm. The worm consumes its own life as it makes cloth for the use of another.

> D'altrui pietoso e sol di sé spietato
> nasce un vil bruto, che con pena e doglia
> l'altrui man veste e la suo scorza spoglia
> e sol per morte si puó dir ben nato.

> (Kind to others and unkind only to itself, a vile beast is born that with pain and travail clothes another's hand, and divests his own skin and only through death can be said to be well-born.)

Significantly the speaker degrades the silkworm as a *vil bruto*. From Michelangelo's autograph copy of this poem, originally written at the bottom of a letter sent to him by Cardinal Ridolfi in 1535, Enzo Noè Girardi has derived his authoritative reading of *bruto* (Girardi 277-78, cf. Guasti 179), but it is not impossible to imagine the noun sliding perhaps more appropriately into *bruco* 'grub, maggot,' thereby evoking the topos of Psalm 22.6, "But I am a worm, and no man; a reproach of men, and despised of the people." Against that degradation, however, the speaker projects this worm's elevation to a higher form of life through death. It achieves immortality in the cloth it leaves behind. Significantly too the speaker designates a glove as the first article of clothing that its silk will provide. This direct reference to the glove of Petrarch's sonnets summons a literary authority for this poem, but it is an authority that the sestet will challenge by acting out the speaker's homoerotic impulse with alternative and contradictory possibilities of meaning.

The sestet immediately wrenches the speaker's visionary imagination back to reality with the volitive subjunctive, "O fussi sol" 'if only I were,' repeated by implication in line 12. Depending upon the reading that one accords to the ambivalent *fussi* in line 9, one may find that the registers of this erotic fantasy shift from passive to active and vice versa. If one reads the verb as *fossi* in the first person singular form, it would express the speaker's wish to be or become a substance identical with the hairy garment that covers the beloved's body ('If I were only my own hairy skin'), and, by implication in line 12, a substance identical with slippers that the beloved's feet penetrate '(If I were only those slippers'). As the moods and tenses of the verbs shift from the imperfect subjunctive *fussi* to the present indicative *fa* and *stringe* and then to the conditional *are(i)* and from the present indicative *fanno* to the conditional *porterei*, they register fluctuations in the speaker's distance from and proximity to reality. The speaker can only wish to be or become articles of clothing that have a fixed locus and identity lacking to him. If one reads *fussi* as *fosse* in the third person singular form, however, these lines would convey the speaker's wish to possess as a talismanic fetish the

beloved's garment ('If only that hairy skin were mine') and his shoes ('If only those slippers were mine'). The verbal ambiguities that Vellutello, Fausto, and Castelvetro noted in Petrarch's poem here multiply the dimensions of Michelangelo's fantasy.

An antithetical series of evaluations moves yet counter to these possibilities. It concerns the articles of clothing themselves. The first is a *gonna*, a long shirt that could extend downwards to cover the beloved's genitals, his gonads, and hide them from view. As the speaker becomes this *gonna*, dangling beneath the beloved's waist, he would appear to conceal the beloved's phallic identity and replace it with his own transformed identity. As he reduces himself to an "irsuta pelle," a skin, a bark, or a rind around the latter's body, he would appear also to surrender his own phallic identity to the beloved. To the extent that he allows his own hairy skin to make contact with the beloved's skin he fulfills his wish for sexual satisfaction, but no sooner does he experience this satisfaction than he repudiates it because it puts his own maleness in question.

The result is, as in Freud's analysis of the Wolf Man's dream, a distortion that consists in "an interchange of subject and object, of activity and passivity: being looked at instead of looking" (17.104). And as in Freud's interpretation of the Wolf Man's dream it is "from his threatened narcissism that he derived the masculinity with which he defended himself against his passive attitude" (17.110). The fantasy exposes him to a terrifying loss of boundary that blurs ordinary distinctions of time, space, and his own body. If the speaker's unconscious imagination has drawn him to this impasse, his conscious reasoning must reject the abasement and low self-esteem that it implies, abasement and low self-esteem like those that Sylvano, Daniello, and Brucioli discerned in Petrarch's text. The issue concludes with a powerful ambivalence about the erotic union dramatized in Michelangelo's poem.

Part of the ambivalence returns to the fundamental question about whom the silkworm represents as a figure—the lover or the beloved, the speaker who degrades himself as a "vil bruto/bruco" in the beloved's presence, or Tommaso de' Cavalieri, the nobleman whose name means "silkworm." Who is the silkworm and what does it do? Is it the paid artist who clothes the beloved object or the beloved object who clothes the laboring artist? As an emblem of production, the worm's cocoon belongs to both and neither. It is a medium of exchange between them, the one given in recompense for the other, capital investment for artistic investiture, and vice versa. But who invests in whom? The artist competes for the beloved's attention without ever sharing the prerogatives of the latter's aristocratic class. From the artist's point of view the situation proves demeaning and demoralizing when the beloved wields the upper hand. The latter's domination confirms the artist's social marginality. The figure of the silkworm, potent as an expression of sexual conflict, constitutes also a powerful expression of social conflict.

The commentaries, then, both open and close possibilities for Michelangelo's understanding of Petrarch. They open possibilities by suggesting that Petrarch's text is a contested ground for interpretation subject to revision by poets who imitate the text ever afterward. They close possibilities by inscribing in Petrarch's text a social agenda that regulates and controls sexuality. By viewing Petrarch's authority as a contested model, Michelangelo was able to accommodate his own gender variations to Petrarch's theme. By contesting the commentators' authority as moral arbiters of prescribed sexuality, Michelangelo was able to extend the possibilities of representing human desire in poetry. The structure of meanings that we find there, neither inappropriate nor idiosyncratic on Michelangelo's part but already socially and culturally inscribed in the commentaries on Petrarch's *Rime sparse,* represent a charge of energy earned in its engagement with textual history.

### Works Cited

Antonio da Tempo. *Francisci Petrarcae poetae excellentissimi Rerum uulgarium fragmenta.* Venice: Domenicus Siliprandus, 1477.

Brucioli, Antonio. *Sonetti, canzoni, et triomphi di M. Francesco Petrarca con breue dichiaratione, & annotatione di Antonio Brucioli.* Venice: Alessandro Brucioli & i frategli, 1548.

Buonarroti, Michelagnolo. *Rime di Michelagnolo Bvonarroti Raccolte da Michelagnolo suo Nipote.* Florence: Appresso i Giunti, 1623.

Buonarroti, Michelangelo. *Le Rime di Michelangelo Buonarroti cavate dagli autografi e pubblicate da Cesare Guasti.* Florence: Felice le Monnier, 1863.

Buonarroti, Michelangiolo. *Rime.* Ed. Enzo Noé Girardi. Bari: Laterza, 1960.

Castelvetro, Lodovico. *Le rime del Petrarca brevemente sposte per Lodouico Casteluetro.* Basel: P. de Sedabonis, 1582.

Daniello da Lucca, Bernardino. *Sonetti, canzoni, e triomphi di messer Francesco Petrarcha con la spositione di Bernardino Daniello da Lucca.* Venice: Giovanniantonio de Nicolini da Sabio, 1541.

Fausto da Longiano, Sebastiano. *Il Petrarcha col commento di M. Sebastiano Fausto da Longiano.* Venice: Francesco di Alessandro Bindoni e Mapheo Pasini, 1532.

Filelfo, Francesco, *Le canzone & sonecti del Petrarcha.* Bologna: Sigismundi de libris, 1476.

Florio, John. *Queen Anna's New World of Words.* London: Edward Blount and Willam Barret, 1611.

Fowler, Mary, with Morris Bishop. *Catalogue of the Petrarch Collection in Cornell University Library.* 2nd ed. Millwood, NY: Kraus-Thomson, 1974.

Freud, Sigmund. *The Standard Edition of the Complete Psychological Works.* Trans. James Strachey et al. 24 vols. London: Hogarth Press, 1953-74.

Gesualdo, Giovanni Andrea. *Il Petrarcha colla spositione di Misser Giovanni Andrea Gesualdo.* Venice: Giouann' Antonio di Nicolini & fratelli da Sabbio, 1533.

Mirollo, James V. *Mannerism and Renaissance Poetry: Concept Mode, Inner Design.* New Haven: Yale UP, 1984.

Petrarca, Francesco. *Canzoniere.* Ed. Gianfranco Contini. 3rd ed. Turin: Einaudi, 1964.

*Petrarch's Lyric poems.* Trans. Robert M. Durling. Cambridge, Mass.: Harvard UP, 1976.

Squarzafico, Hieronimo. *Li Canzoneti dello Egregio poeta messer Francesco Petrarcha.* Venice: Petrus de Piasiis, 1484.

Sylvano da Venafro. *Il Petrarca col commento di M. Syluano da Venaphro.* Naples: Antonio Iouino & Matthio Canzer, 1533.

Thomas, William. *Principal Rules of the Italian Grammar.* London: H. Wyckes, 1567.

Tommaseo, Nicolo, and Bernardo Bellini, eds. *Dizionario della lingua italiana.* Turin: UTET, 1865.

Vellutello, Alessandro. *Le volgari opere del Petrarcha con la espositione di Alessandro Vellutello da Lucca.* Venice: Giovanniantonio & Fratelli da Sabbio, 1525.

### Jean-Pierre Barricelli (essay date summer 1993)

SOURCE: Barricelli, Jean-Pierre. "Michelangelo's *Finito*: In the Self, the Later Sonnets, and the Last Pietà." *New Literary History* 24, no. 3 (summer 1993): 597-616.

[*In the following essay, Barricelli theorizes about a possible relationship between Michelangelo's unfinished poems and one of his sculptures, the* Rondanini Pietà, *suggesting that both attest to Michelangelo's notion of beauty as openness.*]

Unlike Bernini and Palestrina, whose aesthetic attitudes find easy association with the Counter-Reformation, Michelangelo, whose life and manner of thought stemmed from a worldview as personal and intense as it was anguished, defies classification. From the moment

Ariosto referred to him as "Michel più che mortal Angel divino" (Michael, more than a mortal, Angel divine),[1] the supernaturally inspired artist was claimed by the counterreformers.[2] Yet, without going so far as to identify him with the Reformation, I see a stronger Reformational spirit in him than many of his contemporaries would have admitted.[3] Whether in poetry or painting, sculpture or architecture, he was not, as we know, the mystical contemplator of beauty that romanticized histories tend to make him, but rather one of the most travailed and complex religious minds of the Renaissance, one that saw humanism less as a shift of emphasis away from thoughts of God, sin, divine justice, and punishment, than as an opportunity to focus on problems that concerned him deeply: existential solitude, the working of history, and the supreme experience of death. As one critic notes, to exalt man did not mean, for Michelangelo, to eliminate our distance from God.[4] Michelangelo's worldview evolved over the years, sufficiently to enclose within his long lifetime both the vigorous and pagan optimism of the Sistine Ceiling and the disconsolate and Christian pessimism of the *Last Judgment,* painted almost defiantly in juxtaposition to it in the same chapel. His poetry follows the same evolution. However, I see the *Rondanini Pietà* . . . , the supposedly unfinished sculpture of Mary and Jesus that kept his chisel busy almost to the day of his death in February of 1564, as the culminating piece of his ultimate worldview. Michelangelo's four Pietàs (assuming his authorship of the *Palestrina*) connect like a spiritual autobiography: the youthful and idealized two-figure Vatican piece (late 1490s); the solemn and unfinished Palestrina trio (according to scholars, between 1540 and 1559, possibly 1555), where because of his somewhat erect position Christ is not totally lifeless; the similarly unfinished and disconsolate four-figure ensemble (1547-1555) topped by Nicodemus (the sculptor's self-portrait) formerly in Florence's Duomo, where, because of his body's serpentine limpness, Christ betrays genuine lifelessness; and the last one in Milan, back down to two figures, with Mary propping up Jesus as in the *Palestrina,* but both in afflictive postures, both racked in the final, wordless dialogue between mother and son.

In these four sculptures, one may notice the passage from serenity to dejection to disillusion to agony, dramatically reflecting, particularly in the confrontation of the first and the last creations, the two phases of the Renaissance suggested by Michelangelo's biography: the confident elegance of the Apollonian mode prior to the 1530s and the depressing restiveness of the Dionysian mode that followed. Through their inner coherence, the four statues project a chronological continuity and stand out like inspired translations of the motif of universal sorrow, derived from the parable of the Weeping Mothers, into a language of mystery. The polished Vatican duo shows Christ horizontal on the Virgin's lap at a relaxed distance from her body, unpained, and dead in his flesh as man. This makes him live all the more in his divine essence, and the Virgin, young and beautiful in her blessedness, wears therefore a countenance of serenity. Because of this, a sense of charity, of giving to the world her sacrificed offspring, as indicated by her left arm and hand extended in an act of generosity (compare this with her right hand which clasps what is mortally hers—her son), prevails and is even more evident than love, certainly more than sorrow. In their idealized, Neoplatonic beauty, whatever agitated emotion the figures experience appears, not in their serene countenances, but in the flow of their drapery.

The subsequent Pietàs present vertical Christs, thus allowing greater latitude for the suggestion of gravity. In the Florentine piece, the Savior's body is held up by the three surrounding figures, but its gravity keeps pulling it down lumpishly. In the Palestrina group, the body seems less heavy, as if standing and preparing the same desire for ascension that gives the Rondanini sculpture a more ethereal quality. In a reversal of relationships from the *Vatican Pietà,* Michelangelo's roughly chiseled last sculpture betrays strong gravitational pull, to be sure: the weight of the flesh leans heavily away— almost fearfully—from the soul which struggles to leave in the opposite direction. Pain and fear grip this body which, with a whisper of breath left in its agonized position, clings to an invisible life through resignation. But more significantly, it pleads for release, seeking to free itself from universal sorrow. There is an uncanny antiphysicality about it. And the mother, rather than support her son physically, rests her hand on his shoulder as if in correspondence with his desired ascent to Heaven.[5] The gesture abets her son's aspiration to an abstract existence akin to divinity, and the duo thereby reduces itself to the mystical symbiosis of faith (Christ) and love (Mary). The contrast with the *Vatican Pietà* is clear, for there the reduction stressed different values: beauty (Christ) and charity (Mary). If for no other reason, these two sculptures, in their discrete allegories, present only two figures.

A remarkable feature of the *Rondanini Pietà,* obviously not an integral part of it, is a polished arm of Christ in an advanced state of completion, surviving from a previous and more broadly conceived Pietà which Michelangelo apparently rejected but left on the sculpture as he whittled the block of marble down to create the two closely merged figures we have today.[6] Historians have conjectured what is logical: that Michelangelo probably changed his mind about the composition when he discovered a serious flaw in the block. Such a discovery had disappointed him before, with the *Florentine Pietà.* But the violence in the change of his chisel's direction assumes considerable significance when one compares the vigorous arm of the first version with the limp arms of the second, which lend to the whole an "erschöpfende Ausdruck" (exhausted expression).[7]

If the change is due to Michelangelo's typical *incontentabilità* (dissatisfaction), as Giorgio Vasari describes his restive psyche,[8] its violence is due to the radical and angry world weariness that inspired his *Last Judgment.* Thus Marcel Reymond's labeling Michelangelo one of the shapers of the new Christian style of the Counter-Reformation does not contribute to a psychological understanding of the artist's final period.[9] While a few associations can always be made to illustrate Reymond's premise, I find it more convincing to refer to Reformational rather than to counterreformational tendencies in his later art, stripped as it is down to unadorned form and founded as it was on spiritual, moral concerns reminiscent of Savonarola—"di marca ancora savanaroliana: è la religiosità impegnata, profonda, quasi ascetica che si ritrova negli ideali di molti riformatori italiani e che la Controriforma non realizzò mai" (still bearing a Savanarolan stamp: it is the involved, profound, almost ascetic religiosity one finds in the ideals of many Italian reformers the Counter-Reformation never achieved).[10]

Some scholars are wont to emphasize the relationship between an internalized Savonarolan asceticism and dire self-critical assessments, especially in the context of "old age style" and an appurtenant social isolation that becomes a kind of rugged, reductionist aesthetics.[11] But I find that the notion fits Michelangelo tenuously. The "psycho-stylistic phenomenon"[12] of the so-called *Alterstil,* or, as David Rosand describes it, a "rugged freedom of execution," indeed a *sprezzatura*-like "disregard for externals,"[13] makes sense only if one considers *principally* Michelangelo's long-standing desire for self-expression, whether framed in "the subjectivity of his response to external experience,"[14] or in his susceptibility to what qualified reason and consciously keeps realism at a distance. In this endeavor, as his relative lack of interest in poetic form with polished style and in finished sculpted structures shows, he makes little attempt to conceal effort, and his "unembarrassed reductiveness" relates less to pathological than to spiritual verities.[15] Erwin Panofsky's theory about the final phase of the works of masters—that they go off incomprehensibly on their own[16]—does fit Michelangelo more than tenuously, except that I find his last direction reasonably comprehensible. His "preditto iniquo stato" (predestined state of wickedness) in 1552 stems from his distance from God: "sì presso a morte e sì lontan da Dio" (so near to death and so far from God).[17] If this is true, commentators who underscore his postlapsarian state, his ill health after 1550, and the resulting irritability and cantankerousness which stoked

his pessimism, may be guilty of some overstatement.[18] *Incontentabilità* lay in his nature. Perhaps it was an imperative for creation.

One of the recent translators of his poetry, James Saslow, remarks that while Michelangelo's primary concern was the salvation only God could provide, "his ultimate desire [was] to free his soul from the restraints and failings of the body so that it may in time ascend to heaven."[19] To attain this ascension, he had to cope creatively—as he did—with the primary condition of "depressing isolation"[20] and the ultimate mystery of life. Hence what Kenneth Clark calls his "transcendental pessimism."[21] For Michelangelo's travailed, religious intellect made solitude (which the Counter-Reformation hardly encouraged) and the consciousness of death as a divine and liberating gift to man (which the severe Counter-Reformation made the punishment for our sins) two major principles of his ethics. Indeed, on this philosophical level, a fundamental incompatibility existed between Michelangelo and the Counter-Reformation—which may help to explain in part why among writers of the seventeenth century his reputation waned, though his colleagues had praised him.[22] Solitude, Hegel would have said, nourished his being; only a mind conscious of man's alienation could produce the *Last Judgment* mural, which the counterreformers instinctively misinterpreted as being heretical. Popes, like Paul IV, nearly destroyed it—the very prelates who could not even understand why Michelangelo had made the Virgin's face in the *Vatican Pietà* so young.

Closer in spirit to the Reformation, Michelangelo freely expressed his teleological doubts about life, doubts which for him grew out of humility—the sense behind the indignation of the *Last Judgment* is but one example—rather than out of arrogance, and he did not appreciate the Council of Trent's telling him which Bible to read.[23] The pride of a Counter-Reformation artist had no standing in his eyes, nor did the Counter-Reformation heroes attract his attention, which focused spontaneously on human and not on heroic struggles and concerns. Saints are rare in his artistic production. And the iconographic tradition of martyred blood lacked sincerity for Michelangelo. His art shaped itself around concepts, not conventions and canon. Nudity, for instance, gained symbolic significance as his philosophy evolved. For him, the nudes in the *Last Judgment* (many piously draped subsequently by others) represent existential man alone in the conflict that pits grace against free will; they are not indecent, as the brilliant pornographer Pietro Aretino charged, because they stand for an idea—and this, too, the Counter-Reformation failed to grasp.[24] For this reason, he could not despise the flesh in the Neoplatonic fashion of the Counter-Reformation; whether finished or unfinished, his sculpted human figures all bespeak an ancient *gravitas* that served him on the one hand as a *memento mori* and, on the other, through their reminder of death, as a supreme experience to help make life intelligible. As the poem **"Mentre m'atrista e duol"** (As it saddens me and pains) explains, Christ's is the blood that helps us to understand. Michelangelo did not care to lend his talent to the Church in order to illustrate *its* dogma; in a spirit of introverted aestheticism, he wanted to unveil *his* inspiration, *his* personal vision, as if in direct, uninstitutionalized communion with God. (Would I be wrong if I recalled Dante's *Purgatorio,* at whose end true freedom is attained as the ascending soul acquires the moral wisdom to shed the onus of temporal institutions?)

Art, Michelangelo maintained, expresses an inner judgment, synthesizing objective data inwardly in an act of private ascension. Furthermore, art represents a spiritual contest with the self, forever in a state of incompletion and unfulfillment, and the contest becomes a form of humble atonement before the divine mystery. This attitude was no doubt strengthened by his close friendships with the poet Vittoria Colonna who, despite her fidelity to the Holy See, read Martin Luther avidly and, in the company of Carnesecchi and Bernardino Ochino, felt, with her group of *spirituali,* that the Church needed the moral renewal achievable by embracing a more urgent Christianity. To this group, we must add his friendship with the historian Benedetto Varchi, whose praise of Juan de Valdés's reformational enterprise, as reflected in Valdes's Indexed *Diálogo de doctrina Cristiana* (Dialogue on Christian Doctrine) of 1529 and the movement of the *alumbrados* (illuminati), reached Michelangelo's ears repeatedly. Clear parallels exist between the sculptor's ideas of renewal and the Reformation's "intimistic" notion of penance; between his need to touch divinity and the Reformation's belief in man's linear relationship with God; between his pessimism, not about the human condition, but about man's historically recorded abusive greeds and the Reformation's view of earthly evils caused by man's vanity and self-esteem. As Robert Clements points out, the sonnet **"Di morte certo, ma non già dell'ora"** (Sure of death, though not of its hour) sounds like a jeremiad embracing a near Calvinistic view of man's inevitable perverseness.[25] According to this world optic, we exist in a state of contest and captivity—both themes prevalent in Michelangelo's sculpture—or, say, in a state of churning moral exercise even as we go about our daily duties, both when we live at times the life of faith, in its intimate purity, and when we are obliged to live usually the life of reality, in its complicated sinfulness. Without compassion, history forces man's evolution at the same time that man forces history to evolve.

In his own convoluted way, Michelangelo addressed these issues in his poetry—poetry, however, that in mood and mode underscored the power and primacy of sculpture. More than poetry, Michelangelo made sculpture the aesthetic metaphor of the human condition.[26] Together with philosophical implications, including how God infuses the human spirit with a sublime vision, this artistic creed is expressed in a 1538 sonnet to Vittoria Colonna:

> Non ha l'ottimo artista alcun concetto
> c'un marmo solo in sé non circonscriva
> col suo superchio, e solo a quello arriva
> la man che ubbidisce all'intelletto.
>
> (The best of artists has no idea
> That the rough stone does not include within
> Its superfluous shell, and only the hand that obeys
> Arrives at the figure inside.)

(212)

Michelangelo's "concept"[27] reduced world weariness, disillusion with the vital promises of the earlier Renaissance, concerns over senescence, illness, and the withering of the flesh, over *propinqua morte* (see the poem that begins "Giunto è già 'l corso della vita mia / con tempestoso mar, per fragil barca, / al comun porto" [With fragile skiff through stormy seas / I have covered the course of my life / And reached our common harbor] [323][28]) and the elusiveness of salvation, to the tight "shell" or to that restricted volume that is left for his chisel after the "excess" (*superchio*) has been removed. The reduction exhausts the mortal being and prefigures death. Once again, the process relates to Michelangelo's notion of the self—of *his* self, constantly unfinished because constantly aspiring.

At least thirty years before the *Rondanini Pietà,* his spiritual dejection had already found a medieval, macabre image to express itself. However, the poem that pictures the death of all things, **"Ogni cosa a morte arriva"** (Every thing reaches death), which introduces several speaking cadavers, recalls François Villon and does not impress me especially with originality:

> e le nostre antiche prole
> al sole ombre, al vento un fummo.
> Come voi uomini fummo, . . .
>     . . . . .
>
> e or siàn, come vedete,
> terra al sol, di vita priva.
>
> (Our generations gone by are like shadows
> In the sun or smoke in the wind.
> Like you, we were men.
> Like you, happy and sad.
> And now we are, as you see,
> Lifeless earth under the sun.)

(62)

But in the middle 1560s, the theme of death, associated with his favorite image of the night (see **"O notte, o dolce tempo, benché nero"** [Oh night, oh gentle hour, though black]), reappeared with passionately painful intensity because it had modulated from a matter of speculation, part of it conceitfully literary, to one of existential reality, felt independently of conventions. The "hand" now could no longer "obey the intellect," for the limbs were frail, the marble seemed harder, and the plume moved all too hesitatingly over the paper. What are now identified as Michelangelo's "trembling hand sonnets" form intertextually verbal analogues to the spirit of the *Rondanini Pietà,* an autobiographical contemplation of death in marble whose aspiration for freedom affirms his art's attempt at a direct communion with God.

Renunciation follows from the final, gloomy solitude of the artist, a deluded renunciation of life, art, and love that sees art particularly no longer as a refuge from fears of death: "né pinger né scolpir," he writes, "fie più che quieti / l'anima" (Neither painting nor sculpture will quiet the soul anymore) (285), now that the soul has turned to divine love.[29] This "puritanical" denigration of the arts in favor of religion, observes Clements, made the sonnet **"Giunto è già 'l corso della vita mia"** (Arrived at last the term of my life) a favorite among Protestant Englishmen like Wordsworth and New Englanders like Longfellow.[30] And the final sonnet of the ***Rime*** culminates the spiritual process, as it is dedicated to the Savior whose blood purges the ignominious guilts of mankind through the Crucifixion. It relates intimately to the *Rondanini Pietà*: both unfinished, both implying a cross, and both presenting a slumping image in resignation.[31]

It is significant that Michelangelo emphasized—perhaps even chose, though he had written frequently in this form before—the sonnet form at the end of his life, into whose closed and tightly organized shape, so unsuited to the breadth of his concepts, he strove to hammer vast worldviews, including a psychology of guilt and a philosophy of regeneration and peace. By comparison, Petrarch's conceptual base was simple: a direct expression of love variously experienced; hence, any one sonnet of his can emerge as a polished product. Michelangelo's verses, on the other hand, rough and contorted like the last *Pietà,* announce a voluntary struggle with limitation or condensation, like switching from a larger to a narrower image on the same block of marble, the result leaving more to the imagination than would otherwise be possible. For the later Michelangelo, the agony of creation was more spiritual than technical. The struggle served as a metaphor for existence. Hence the primacy of sculpture, which carves rock, over the "softer" arts of pencil and brush, in the mind of this artist who insisted on identifying himself, not as a painter, poet, or architect, but as a *scultore.* More and more he aimed at simplification, the removal of accessories, in order for the *idea* to be revealed in the nude, as it were, like the figures in the *Last Judgment,* indeed like the

desolate presence of Christ in the *Rondanini* stone. Form that defies spatial needs, that writhes and twists, provided Michelangelo with what amounts to an exaltation of self-punishment, whereby the artist "engages an increasingly dramatic and solitary path toward a sense of religiosity"[32] that Reformers could only welcome. The choice of the sonnet form and its attendant reductionism relates to his anxiety for spiritual renewal and to his humble hope for divine succor. His synthetic verses bind the syntax in order to gain strength, and in the process, in which intuition plays a critical role, his expression becomes, not poetically musical or sentimental, but metaphysical. Language, then, like the marble of the sculpture, becomes denaturalized, powered by associations and ulterior meanings, so that the ears that hear and the eyes that see are freed from the shackles of convention, of "institutional" expectation.

This attitude might well spell Michelangelo's definition of beauty—not in the finished material body rehearsed by fashion but in the aura that emanates from it like a liberated soul, a semblance of divinity (Michelangelo's concession to Neoplatonism). Beauty lies, not exclusively in the idealized figure like the *Vatican Pietà* with its formal regularity and polish akin to a Petrarchan sonnet, but more convincingly in the imperfect shape that exudes moral sorrow and suffering, like the doleful countenance and weighty flesh of the *Rondanini Christ.*

It is here that the much discussed *non finito* assumes special importance. But a surprising number of critics have allowed themselves to wander fancifully afield with specious theories about the *non finito.* Henry Thode, for example, turns Michelangelo's *incontentabilità* into a dissatisfaction born of the incompatibility between pagan form and the mystical, Christian substance of his work—an unconvincing thesis, in my opinion, in that it would make the artist an overt counterreformer, which, I maintain, he was not.[33] Even less convincing appears the thesis of Toesca in *Le Arti* of 1938-39 which holds that Michelangelo liked antique and broken down, decayed statues, hence his own unfinished pieces![34] Benvenuto Cellini's explanation in *La vita* of 1560 sounds more plausible on a technical and realistic basis—that Michelangelo conceived from the frontal viewpoint, and when he viewed his figures from different angels his recognition of their comparative weakness made him abandon them to a state of incompletion.[35] But in the long run even this explanation by a fellow sculptor strikes me as naïve. Better is Aldo Bertini's and Adolfo Venturi's belief which attributes the incompletion to the sculptor's emotional intensity and his figure's form endeavoring to liberate itself from the rock.[36] Better, too, is Baldini's view, though he errs when it comes to the *Rondanini Pietà*:

> To understand the crucial issue of the *non finito* in Michelangelo's work, it is necessary to make a distinction between those works which remained uncompleted

for reasons beyond the artist's control and those which, though "unfinished," have been carried by the artist to a definite and poetic conclusion, satisfactory to himself. Thus . . . we . . . eliminate works like the three *Slaves* or *Prisoners* in the Accademia in Florence, the *St Matthew* in the same gallery, and the *Rondanini Pietà* in Milan. . . . For the *Prisoners* and the *St Matthew* we have historical evidence to show that work was abandoned for external reasons, and in the case of the *Rondanini Pietà* we know that completion was prevented by the artist's death in 1564.[37]

While Baldini recognizes the different figurative effects achieved by the *non finito*—that is, how the appearance of the subjects varies when finished areas alternate with unfinished ones and the resulting variations in the portrayed psychological stresses—he stops short of granting full latitude to the possibility, as Valerio Mariani has it, that Michelangelo was torn by the conflict between spirit and matter, or to what Vasari, further refining the notion of "dissatisfaction" with a given work's progress, ultimately saw as the artist's inner struggle.[38] Certainly he was impatient to see his "concept" take shape, but once, as in the *Rondanini Pietà,* it took shape—thoroughly and unequivocally expressive shape—he left the work, as André Chastel says, "deliberately open."[39]

"Das Vollendete," writes a German critic, "ist immer stabil, in diesem Sinne unlebending" (The *finito* is always stable, and in this sense not alive).[40] Another German critic avoids defining *non finito* with dubious reasoning—"Eine Definition des Nonfinito ist eine logische Unmöglichkeit, ein Widerspruch in sich selbst" (A definition of the *non finito* is a logical impossibility, a contradiction in itself)—but he reacts perceptively to the difference between the completed *Vatican Pietà* and the uncompleted *Rondanini Pietà*:

Wer am gleichen Tage in Rom unmittelbar nach dem Jugendwerke das Alterswerk, nach der früher Pietà die Pietà Rondanini gesehen hat, der steht ohne Fassung vor der ungeheuren Kluft, die von diesem einen Leben überbrückt werden soll. Dort, in St. Peter, das Wunder des Leibes—frei, wie alle klassische Form, von jeder Transzendenz und Symbolik, frei auch von dem Gegensatz des Innen und Aussen; die Ehrfurcht von der sinnlichen Erscheinung und dem organischen Wuchs. Hier eine fast amorphe Säule der Trauer, die allen Gesetzen des Erscheinenden, aller Statik und Schwere enthoben zu sein scheint.

[Who, on the same day in Rome, has seen the older work immediately after the younger work, the Rondanini Pietà after the earlier Pietà, this person is left insecure before the enormous gap which is supposed to bridge a lifetime. There in St. Peter's stands the wonder of the human body—free, like all classical form, of any transcendence or symbolism, free also of the contrast between the inner and the outer; it's the awe we experience before the physical appearance and the organic growth. Here we have an almost amorphous column of grief, which seems exempt from all laws of appearance, statics, and weight.][41]

Hence I must reject out of hand Saslow's opinion that the Rondanini sculpture is "an incomplete testimony to frustration" and that the *non finito* is a visual "miscarriage,"[42] or Howard Hibbard's opinion that the piece is "hardly a potential work of art . . . [a] wreck [that is] unbearably pathetic."[43]

Like the *bozzetti* or unfinished drawings that art lovers and dealers started collecting during Michelangelo's time, claiming that they were indeed finished in the sense that the concept had been satisfactorily translated, the *Rondanini* sculpture impresses with its total effect and refuses to be submitted to analyses of detail. I might adapt Clark's words in *An Artist Grows Old* to my purpose: the *Pietà* represents "a craving for complete unity of treatment, as if [it] were an organism in which every member shared in the life of the whole."[44] It is so powerfully conceived that its roughness makes it no less real as a thing of beauty; even if death had not silenced Michelangelo's chisel, he still would not have finished this particular piece which, like the self, can exist only unfinished. Ultimately, the unfinished aspect is accidental, however—merely a matter of execution. The *Pietà* was completed the moment the sculpture reached the point of revealing the *concept* (Pliny the Elder valued unfinished works because they reveal *lineamenta reliqua* [preliminary drawings] of the original concept "left visible"[45]). And it is its survival in this state that makes its inner pulse beat. Some, like Rodin, would argue with Chastel that Michelangelo deliberately left works unfinished for aesthetic reasons—an argument that surely must apply, if it applies anywhere, to the last *Pietà*.[46] Others, like Moore, who like Canova admired this work immensely (particularly the legs), would insist that a sculptured creation as the expression of the artist's spirit and outlook on life "matters more than a finished or a beautiful or a perfect work of art," and that in a finished state the *Pietà* "would have lost its point."[47] And Ruskin would say that the object of sculpture is, not to extract a form from a stone, but to affix an effect on marble without even realizing the form.[48]

We may observe the phenomenon of the *non finito* from either an Eastern or a Western perspective. An East Asian source expresses well the notion of unfinished beauty. Commenting on Lao Tse, Okakura Kakuzo, the late-nineteenth-century Japanese sage, said in his *The Book of Tea* something that corroborates the theory of the *non finito* that I have been trying to postulate. He was alluding to Lao Tse's favorite metaphor of the vacuum—the only receptacle of the truly essential (for example, the reality of a room lies in the vacant space enclosed by the walls and roof, just as that of a pitcher of water lies in the emptiness into which the liquid may be put). Since the potency of the vacuum stems from its "all-containingness," motion—meaning vitality—exists only here, and in art the principle enhances the value of suggestion: "In leaving something unsaid the beholder is given the chance to complete the idea and thus a great masterpiece irresistibly rivets your attention until you seem to become actually a part of it. A vacuum is there for you to enter and fill up to the full measure of your aesthetic emotion."[49] Read "unsculpted" for "unsaid," and let "the beholder" join Michelangelo, allowing him to "become actually a part" of the *Pietà,* and we have the principle of the finished unfinished in terms of the self.

From a Western perspective, German romantic theory is equally useful: the notion of the "open text" that produced so many fragments—literary *bozzetti,* as it were. Kant established the imagination as the only link between the world of perception and the "real" world, and by giving it free reign, the romantics invited the reader into the text. By extension, if not by sympathy, postmodernist literature prevents textual closure, disdaining mimetic plot and favoring that kind of Russian Formalist "defamiliarization" that goads the reader into creating his own plot from the "open" text. In this sense, what Michelangelo sought could not be retrieved into the sensual or mimetic world, and this is why he kept his text open or fragmentary.

All these sources, in my opinion, have much to say. To repeat, Michelangelo never thought of finishing the Rondanini work in the formal sense—in the sense that would have meant final polishing with rasps, file, pumice stone, and wads of straw that make the surface lustrously smooth; he never would have wanted to finish it, I believe, in the manner of the *Vatican Pietà.* Baldini and especially Clements have pointed out how, during his later years, Michelangelo's poetry abandoned its aggressive hues, becoming more tainted with disillusioned melancholy and detachment from the things of this world, more spiritually concerned and aspiring, more focused on what Reformers called *individual* faith and contrition, more obsessed with the reality of death and more aware of the tie joining religion and art. In the process, he developed a mystical idea of poetry as he did of sculpture. Neither sonnet nor sculpture had to be *finito* to produce its effect or convey its idea. The sonnet **"Molto diletta al gusto intero e sano"** (Much does it expand intact and wholesome taste) is "unfinished," having only two quatrains, but standing as a complete composition since, like the *Pietà,* it is conceptually finished, relating the idea that beauty has value *in itself,* and that this beauty survives intact the deformations stemming from the sculptor's execution. The eight verses need no further elaboration. The concept of beauty, Michelangelo would say, can be imagined, seen in the heart, a suprasensual essence, in fact an abstraction.

Fritz Irwin Baumgart likes to refer to the enchantment of the imperfect.[50] I prefer the lure of the abstract. The *Rondanini Pietà* appears as Michelangelo's ultimate su-

prasensual experience, a final sublimation, as Ettore Sestieri says,[51] felt at the moment of death by a man now quite removed from life, or aspiring to the passage. Hence his constant sculpting away as the last day approached. One may argue that other statues were left unfinished, like *Day* and *Dusk* on the Medici tombs, and, strikingly, like the famous *Prisoners* in Florence's Accademia, who also seem to struggle for final release, and who may have been sculpted in the same period (Tolnay dates them, not 1519, but after 1534). But even if these had not been in a different city at the time, I doubt that they would have invited the repeated bites of his chisel at the end of his years. With the *Rondanini Pietà,* however, there is a pronounced searching for something beyond release that did not obtain for the *Prisoners:* an exploration of the limits of figurative art on the threshold of abstraction. There is more that is nonfigurative or nonrepresentational in this Pietà than mimetic. Such an intent seems to obtain here. For only in abstraction, with its inevitable ambiguity, can spirit become liberated from matter. The Counter-Reformation sought certainties; Michelangelo's ambiguities were bothersome to the movement, and his doubting, sculpted expressionistically in the very mood of the *Pietà,* was irritating. I would surmise, too, that the medieval look the *non finito* gives the sculpture because of its Gothicizing schematization and synthesis, not to mention the violent rejection of the evidently more conventionally conceived original version, gave the Church cause for great uneasiness. To this medieval dimension, a tendency in the late Michelangelo, we should add the possible medieval inspiration from artists like Giovanni da Milano and the Master of Flémalle, together with (as de Tolnay has indicated[52]) the pre-Renaissance pietàs where a standing God holds up Christ's body. No surprise, then, that the Counter-Reformation disliked the *Rondanini Pietà* and distanced itself from it.

Michelangelo's poem describing his sculpture of slumbering Night advises the viewer that, if we awaken him, she will speak to him. The same holds for the mother and son of the *Rondanini Pietà* sculpture which, in more ways than one, has spoken to the twentieth century especially.[53] The two figures have revealed what Michelangelo finally came to realize as an artist: that the mastery of a priori form as an avenue of inquiry and means of expression is inadequate, for eventually there comes a time when the artist struggles to free himself from form in an attempt to deal directly with spirit or the divine. If this can be accomplished, it is not to look for life in what is but in what is becoming—in the process. A sculpture is a moment in time, empirically and mathematically established; yet its *effect* must extend beyond that moment and deal with transformation, growth, decay, flight, movement, and change—with process. The finished piece creates a dilemma; only the *non finito* like the *Rondanini Pietà,* whose meaning emerges from the geometry of its unfinished structure, stands a chance of inviting ulterior deliberations.

With the foregoing in mind, I look again at this *Pietà*. Two disquieting figures, not without fear, groping their way out of stone, suggesting in Christ's upright yet falling pose that death is not a final solution; his feet set outward, in no way sustaining his legs which pull with them a body that clings to the rock as to its sole security. He can neither stand nor fall, breathe nor expire; he shrinks away from his previous vital arm and shows legs that do not seem to belong to his chest, and above these limbs he presents a distorted, unformed face. Here anguish makes no sound, and, except for her eyes, Mary is mute. Her eyes, though, relate a long and painful story; her arm and hand are not poised in an act of giving. Such simplicity breeds complexity. How could Michelangelo not have known that completion of the statue would be undesirable because it would sacrifice the total effect? And the effect avers that mankind has choked itself; hence the absence of space in the composition: no air passes through the bodies' limbs or between the bodies themselves. Indeed, it has been observed, this consubstantiation of a mother's and her son's figures produces a sense of absolute fusion, making "the loved form issue . . . from the diminishing core of the stone," as if enacting, by virtue of this abbreviation, "the Incarnation from Mary's body."[54] A finished product would have impaired such a sense.

But more than mankind chokes in the portrayal; the representation in this psychic autobiography is Michelangelo himself. If the *Florentine Pietà* was created for his own tomb (therefore his portrait in the face of Nicodemus) and the representation of mother and son there bespeaks a desire for a unification of life and death, the *Rondanini Pietà* on the other hand was created for his soul which, like the unfinished self—that endless aspiration to make direct contact with the divine—struggles toward freedom from form and all it implies. The body—imperfect matter—is always unfinished, as is the soul, so long as the body enslaves it. As a sculptor working with "'l . . . rozzo martello i duri sassi," that is, with "rude hammer the unwilling stone," he needs God's assistance, not to bring the statue to completion, but to pass beyond anguish into freedom:

> Onde a me non finito verrà meno
> s'or non gli dà la fabbrica divina
> aiuto a farlo, c'al mondo era solo.
>
> (Wherefore unfinished I must meet my end,
> if the divine maker does not help me do so,
> me who on earth was alone.)
>
> (89)

This is the concept locked captive within the rock that the sculptor tries to liberate. More than any other sculpture, the *Rondanini Pietà* expresses it eloquently.

It makes a philosophical statement that is also expressed in another poem which, like the former, may well be chiseled under the work:

> Negli anni molti e nelle molte pruove
> cercando, il saggio al buon concetto arriva
> d'un'immagine viva
> vicino a morte, in pietra alpestra e dura.
>
> (After many years and many attempts
> The wise man in his quest arrives at the right concept
> Of a living image,
> In Alpine and hard stone—only as he nears death.)
>
> (274)

The notion of *pietra viva* or "living stone" occurs frequently in Michelangelo's writings. The *Rondanini Pietà,* therefore, is a "living image." This being so, it surely exists beyond itself. Because it makes a *complete* statement, it is not unfinished; we ponder its metaphysical message.

At this point, I may conclude. Michelangelo's so-called poetic and sculptural *non finito* addresses questions about the meaning of beauty, about the conceptual transmission of ideal values into supposedly unfulfilled realizations. Too often, Michelangelo's agonized poetic syntax and incompleted statues have been received as just that: unfinished. This reception posits the notion that our mind conceptualizes art in terms of completion. I have argued here that the *Rondanini Pietà* is conceptually completed (the word *concetto* being used by Michelangelo repeatedly, like the idea of a *bozzetto*), an accomplished objectification of an idea whose lyrical and aesthetic intensity would be diminished by further honing—as Lao Tse implied—that is, by further manipulation (which means mutilation) of the poetic fantasy. The viewer must fill the open text. As, given the broad scope of his idea, there is much that must necessarily remain silent—a vacuum—in Michelangelo's poetry, there is much in his sculpture that must remain understood only by suggestion, where suggestion becomes more accurate than the polished expression of a closed text.

To understand Michelangelo's reality, one must look not only at the artwork itself, not only at his travailed life primarily during his later years, but also at his position between Reformation and Counter-Reformation, reflected in his ultimate literary focus on the sonnet as a poetic form that reduces expression to tight and spiritual cogency; it shapes its block of verbal marble to the same conceptually airless and accomplished, "unfinished" expression one finds in the *Rondanini Pietà*. For him, the form related to a mode of strictures, a mode related in spirit to the philosophy of the Counter-Reformation which attempted to countermand the enfranchising impulses of the Reformation with constraining reaffirmations of dogma. Michelangelo struggled for liberation; liberation posits struggle; and the *non finito* came as close to liberation as possible. In many instances, the rigorous sonnet shrank expressively to a few verses: eight, six, four, three. Suggestion was reduced to a hint. If one follows the process closely, using the *Rondanini Pietà* as indicator, a different notion of beauty emerges, one which encompasses the unfinished self no differently from the way it encompasses a fragmentary poem or sculpture, and out of it grows a realization that what remains *non finito* in Michelangelo's self-conscious creation is as *finito* as Schubert's "Unfinished" Symphony.

### Notes

1. Lodovico Ariosto, *Orlando furioso,* ed. Lanfranco Caretti (Milan, 1954), p. 852, Canto 33, verse 12. Here and elsewhere, unless otherwise noted, translations are my own.

2. The noted counterreformer Francesco Bocchi concurred with the interpretation of "divine" as applied to the "perfect" Michelangelo.

3. Or some modern scholars. Leo Steinberg, for example, writes that, judging from the frescoes in the Cappella Paolina (*The Conversion of Paul* and *The Crucifixion of Peter*), Michelangelo "speak[s] from the heart of Catholicism" (Leo Steinberg, *Michelangelo's Last Paintings* [New York, 1975], p. 6).

4. See Rocco Montano, *Lo spirito e le lettere* (Milan, 1970), II, 36.

5. See Giuseppe Zucca, "L'ultima Pietà di Michelangelo," *Capitolium,* 24 (1949), 121, with whom I disagree somewhat in this interpretation. The posture of Christ in this Pietà reminds me of what we read in the poem for the sculpture *Notte* for the Medici tombs: "e perchè dorme ha vita" (and because she sleeps she has life).

6. It is believed that the Rondanini sculpture derived from an ancient Roman column. Michelangelo's original intention was to have Christ leaning forward, held up with difficulty by the Virgin. The surviving arm belongs to this version. The sculptor removed the head and chest when he decided to bring the two figures closer together. The severed head of the Savior has been located recently in Rome.

7. The phrase is from Von Dagobert Frey, "Die Pietà Rondanini und Rembrandts' 'Drei Kreuze,'" in *Kunstgeschichtliche Studien für Hans Kauffmann* (Berlin, 1956), p. 232. Henry Moore sensed the importance of the original arm: "It has nothing to do with the composition. Nevertheless, it was left there" (quoted in Philip James, *Henry Moore on Sculpture* [New York, 1967], p. 93).

8. See Giorgio Vasari, *Le vite de' più eccellenti pittori scultori ed architettori* (1568), 9 vols., ed.

Gaetano Milanesi (Florence, 1865-79), VII, 243. Or see Giorgio Vasari, *The Lives of the Artist,* tr. George Bull (Harmondsworth, 1971), p. 404.

9. Marcel Reymond, "L'Art de la Contre-Réforme: ses caractères généraux," *Revue des Deux Mondes,* n.s. 12, vol. 2 (15 Mar. 1911), 411n, 1.

10. Maria Calì, *Da Michelangelo all'Escorial* (Turin, 1980), p. 101.

11. For a discussion of the theory of isolation, see A. E. Brinckmann, *Spätwerke grosser Meister* (Frankfurt a/M, 1925).

12. Steinberg, *Michelangelo's Last Paintings,* pp. 19 ff.

13. David Rosand, "Style and the Aging Artist," *Art Journal,* 46 (1987), 92.

14. James M. Saslow, *The Poetry of Michelangelo* (New Haven, 1991), p. 5.

15. Rosand, "Style and the Aging Artist," p. 92. While admitting the presence of the spiritual or psychological being, Rosand tends to define the old age issue in terms of pathology, aiming toward what might be a phenomenology or physiology of style: for "we . . . may know . . . [the] mind . . . through the movements of [the] hand" (p. 92).

16. See Erwin Panofsky, lecture on Titian, 27 Sept. 1963, given at New York University's Institute of Fine Arts, quoted in Steinberg, *Michelangelo's Last Paintings,* p. 19.

17. These lines are from the sonnet "Forse perché d'altrui pietà mi vegna" (Perchance pity may reach me from another), in Michelangelo Buonarroti, *Rime* (Milan, 1975), p. 115; all subsequent references to Michelangelo's poetry will be to this edition, hereafter cited in text.

18. Howard Hibbard refers to Michelangelo's testy annoyances at his difficulty urinating or his kidney stones, expressed in letters to his nephew Lionardo. See Howard Hibbard, *Michelangelo* (New York, 1974), p. 280.

19. Saslow, *The Poetry of Michelangelo,* p. 29. In support, Saslow quotes the sonnet "Ben mi dove' con sì felice sorte" (Well it had to, with such happy fate) (c. 1535) and the madrigal "Gli occhi mie vaghi delle cose belle" (My eyes in love with lovely things) (c. 1534-42).

20. Kenneth Clark, *The Artist Grows Old* (Cambridge, 1971), p. 8.

21. Clark, *The Artist Grows Old,* p. 8. I find it questionable, however, to ascribe it squarely to old age.

22. See Romeo De Maio, *Michelangelo e la Controri-forma* (Bari, 1978), pp. 408-32.

23. Michelangelo did not know Latin, and the Council of Trent forbade the Italian Bible, a fact that left him bereft of "the book of humanity" during the last five years of his life.

24. See De Maio, *Michelangelo e la Controriforma,* p. 418.

25. Robert J. Clements, *The Poetry of Michelangelo* (New York, 1966), p. 294.

26. Saslow says that Michelangelo ranked writing over the other arts, quoting the *più degno lavoro,* or "worthier task," the work of "your pencil," alluded to in a 1550 sonnet ("Se con lo stile o coi colori avete" [If you have with pen or colors]) dedicated to a writer, Giorgio Vasari, but the poem represents a courtesy in appreciation of Vasari's having included Michelangelo in his *Le vite,* the lives of the great artists of his day. More significant is the sculptor's letter to Benedetto Varchi, in which he expresses the superiority of sculpture (see *A Documentary History of Art. II. Michelangelo and the Mannerists: The Baroque and the Eighteenth Century,* ed. Elizabeth Gilmore Holt [New York, 1958], pp. 15-16).

27. Saslow defines Michelangelo's *concetto* as "the ideal, preexisting image of an artistic project, which is formulated in the mind of the artist by a process of inspiration that is quasi-divine and which the artist then attempts to 'real-ize' in the less than perfectly tractable medium of the physical world" (*The Poetry of Michelangelo,* p. 34).

28. The madrigal "Si come per levar, Donna, si pone" (As when, O Lady mine, one removes) describes the integument of the body—the rough stone—that contains the pure soul—the figure—infused there by God.

29. Michelangelo writes of the "affettuosa fantasia / che l'arte mi fece idol e monarca" (the affectionate fantasy / that made art my idol and sovereign).

30. See Clements, *The Poetry of Michelangelo,* p. 296.

31. Except for a juvenile effort in wood, Michelangelo never left us a crucified Christ. He did not want to show the Lord become "servo de servi in croce" (slave of slaves on a cross) (see "Non fur men lieti" [They were no less happy]), preferring the depositions, however pitiful, of the *Florentine* and *Rondanini Pietàs.*

32. Calì, *Da Michelangelo all'Escorial,* p. 103.

33. See Henry Thode, *Michelangelo: Kritische Untersuchungen über seine Werke,* 3 vols. (Berlin, 1908-13).

34. See Pietro Toesca, "Un capolavoro di Michelangelo: La Pietà di Palestrina," *Le Arti,* 1 (Dec.-Jan. 1938-39), 105-10.

35. See Benvenuto Cellini, *La vita* (Turin, 1973).

36. See Aldo Bertini, *Michelangelo fino alla Sistina* (Turin, 1942), and Adolfo Venturi, *Storia dell'arte italiana,* 11 vols. (Milan, 1901-40), 9.1, 10.2. See Umberto Baldini, Introduction to *The Complete Sculpture of Michelangelo,* tr. Clare Cooper (London, 1981-82), pp. 12-14.

37. Baldini, *The Complete Sculpture of Michelangelo,* p. 13.

38. See Valerio Mariani, *Michelangelo* (Turin, 1942), and Giorgio Vasari, *La vita di Michelangelo,* ed. Paola Barocchi, 5 vols. (Milan, 1962).

39. See André Chastel, *Art et humanisme à Florence* (Paris, 1954).

40. Georg Kauffmann, *Michelangelo und das Problem der Sekularisation* (Opladen, 1972), p. 35.

41. Werner Körte, "Das Problem des Nonfinito bei Michelangelo," *Römisches Jahrbuch für Kunstgeschichte,* 7 (1955), 297 and 295.

42. Saslow, *The Poetry of Michelangelo,* pp. 22 and 35.

43. Hibbard, *Michelangelo,* p. 289.

44. Clark, *An Artist Grows Old,* p. 8.

45. Pliny the Elder, *Natural History,* Loeb Classical Library, ed. E. H. Warmington, tr. H. Rackham (Cambridge, Mass., 1948), IX, 366-67: bk. 35.145.

46. See Linda Murray, *Michelangelo: His Life, Work, and Times* (New York, 1984), p. 84.

47. James, *Henry Moore on Sculpture,* p. 183.

48. See John Ruskin, *The Seven Lamps of Architecture* (London, 1925), ch. 5. §21, p. 311.

49. Okakura Kakuzo, *The Book of Tea* (Rutland, Vt., 1956), p. 46.

50. See Fritz Irwin Baumgart, "Die Pietà Rondanini," *Jahrbuch der preussischen Kunstsammlungen,* 56 (1935-36), 44-56. Other sources to consult are D. Redig de Campos, "Note sulla Pietà Rondanini," *Ecclesia,* 5 (1950), and Michele De Benedetti, "Il considetto 'non finito' di Michelangelo e la sua 'ultima Pietà,'" *Emporium* (1951), 99-108.

51. See Ettore Sestieri, Introduction, in his *L'ultima Pietà di Michelangelo* (Rome, 1952).

52. See Charles de Tolnay, "Michelangelo's Rondanini Pietà," *Burlington Magazine,* 65 (1934), 146-57.

53. Similarly, Steinberg has given a modern, expressionistic revaluation of the *Conversion of Paul* and the *Crucifixion of Peter,* both painted in the 1540s and, before Expressionism, both regarded much less seriously than his other, more "famous," paintings. The *Rondanini Pietà* sculpture falls in the same category.

54. See Leo Steinberg, "The Metaphors of Love and Birth in Michelangelo's Pietàs," in *Studies in Erotic Art,* ed. Theodore Robert Bowie and Cornelia V. Christenson (New York, 1970), p. 271.

## Thomas E. Mussio (essay date autumn 1997)

SOURCE: Mussio, Thomas E. "The Augustinian Conflict in the Lyrics of Michelangelo: Michelangelo Reading Petrarch." *Italica* 74, no. 3 (autumn 1997): 339-59.

[*In the following essay, Mussio explores the influence of St. Augustine's writings on those of Michelangelo, via the latter's reading of the poetry of Petrarch.*]

Source studies on Michelangelo's *Rime* reveal the great variety of influences under which the artist may have worked, but most of the ideological influences that have been posited can be grouped into two broad categories: the strictly Christian and the neoplatonic. These categories, of course, overlapped to a large degree, especially in the context of fifteenth- and sixteenth-century Italy. Yet they are helpful to the extent to which they indicate different visions of the soul, its conflicts, and its relationship to the deity. There is also a third ideological thread running through the *Rime* which derives mainly from Petrarch. It posits that the loving subject's identity is based not on a model of the soul's purity, as in the neoplatonic model, nor on its infirmity, as in the Pauline model, but rather on the experience of loving. The Petrarchan influence is stronger than either the Christian or the neoplatonic, as it controls Michelangelo's reading of both Biblical and neoplatonic texts.

The Petrarch who is most influential on Michelangelo is not the master of eloquence whose lexicon the *petrarchisti* sought to imitate but rather the careful reader of Augustine's *Confessions.* Augustine's importance for Petrarch is broad and deep, particularly as a model of a suffering soul, divided against itself in numerous ways and for an extended time, chained to its own worldly talent and ambition, and resistant to the grace that was offered him. In turn, Michelangelo finds in Petrarch's *Canzoniere* and in the Francesco of the *Secretum* the same type of model, and his manipulation of Petrarchan conceits and images reveals his sympathy with the penitent and suffering Petrarch. In this way, even though

Michelangelo may not have read the *Confessions,* at least as a whole text, he intuits the concerns of the pre-converted Augustine through his close reading of Petrarch.

The penitent, questioning, and often dramatic tone of Michelangelo's poetry might suggest that behind the major sources of Paul, Dante, and Petrarch lies the more subtle influence of the pre-converted Augustine of the *Confessions.*[1] A careful reader of the *Confessions* and Michelangelo's *Rime* notices in both the importance of the concept of habit as a complicating factor in their portraits of desire and will. In both, there is an exploration of the middle state between grace and "non-grace" in which the speakers find themselves. Also, the pre-converted speaker of the *Confessions* and Michelangelo share a concern about the inscrutability of their consciences and hence, the extreme difficulty in having them healed. Finally, in both works, the speakers' spiritual conflict is exacerbated by a sometimes strong insecurity about God's presence in the world. These parallels are significant. None of the cited Christian, neoplatonist, or other sources, including Paul, Dante, Della Casa, Benivieni, Bembo, Ficino, or Colonna are much concerned with the concept of habit or the fear of God's grace. Nevertheless, certain limits about our knowledge of Michelangelo's familiarity with Latin preclude our ability to read the one against the other strictly as a matter of influence.[2] Also, even though Michelangelo's poetry does not adhere dogmatically to his major sources, the lack of a patterned treatment of Augustine makes any argument for influence in this case still more difficult, since we have neither very strong verbal echoing nor external evidence for any such relation. Further, the similarities may be explained, in part, by Michelangelo's direct contact with people who were very familiar with Augustinian ideas—Colonna and Petrarch, and to a lesser extent, Ochino, Savonarola, and Gilles of Viterbo,[3] as well by Michelangelo's reading of Paul, in whom Augustine also took great interest. This essay will focus on the way in which Michelangelo's verse is influenced by Augustine's *Confessions* through the intermediary of Petrarch. By comparing the lyrics of Michelangelo to the texts of his non-Petrarchan poetic, Biblical and philosophical influences, one sees that Michelangelo's reading of these texts is often refracted through Petrarch and ultimately Augustine.[4]

It is often difficult to distinguish the ideas of Paul from those of Augustine, first because of Paul's dramatic influence on the Church Fathers and second, because Augustine relies so heavily on Paul's writings in the narration of his own conversion. In the first eight books alone of the *Confessions,* up to the conversion scene, there are around forty citations from Paul's *Letters.* It is clear that Paul's life narrative was one of those in which Augustine inserted his own, but more important, the citations show Augustine's reverence for Paul's emphasis on the unworthiness of humanity, the vanity of human wisdom, the need for humility, and the exemplarity of Christ.[5] A third reason for caution in trying to distinguish too finely between the two thinkers is that by the time Michelangelo was writing during the Reformation, the two were often mentioned nearly interchangeably around such controversies as predestination, the role of grace, and the justification through works or faith.[6] Yet while they may not be easily distinguishable on the basis of doctrine, the reader of the *Letters* and the *Confessions* finds that the two works differ greatly in tone and emphasis. It is the Augustine of the *Confessions* with whom Petrarch sympathized, and it is this Augustine that is conveyed to Michelangelo.

In his analysis of Michelangelo's noted sonnet, **"Vorrei voler"** (G [Girardi edition] 87), Gregory Lucente, while noting the differences in tone and complexity, sees Paul as the source of the model of Michelangelo's portrait of the divided soul. Michelangelo begins his poem, "Vorrei voler quel ch'io non voglio," and Lucente links it to Paul's letter to the Romans (Rom. 8.15): "For that which I do I allow not: for what I would, that I do not; but what I hate, that I do" (Lucente 324). Lucente allows the phrasing of Paul's letter to override the more clear verbal echo in Petrarch: "Or qui son, lasso, et voglio esser altrove, / *et vorrei più voler, et più non voglio,* / et per più non poter fo quant'io posso" (*Petrarch's Lyric Poems* 118.9-11). In contrast to the passage in Paul which seems mainly to assert the irrationality of desire and human weakness in controlling it, Petrarch's poem presents a situation which mirrors that of Michelangelo's sonnet: in both the speakers *desire to desire* something. The situation of Petrarch's sonnet is the following: the speaker marks the sixteenth year "de' miei sospiri," and he is aware that now the time of his life is growing short; the speaker laments that he wants to want more, but cannot; this weakness in the face of "antichi desiri" proves to the speaker that his static will is stronger than his new will. This situation is markedly different from the one Paul describes in which he is assailed by sin. In contrast to Paul who basically only comments on the infirmity of his will, despite his knowledge of the good, both Michelangelo and Petrarch go further by portraying a genuine internal conflict and a divided will. While Paul may be said to be in a middle state because of his position between despair at the infirmity of his own will and the hope for God's grace, the other two are poised between two internal wills, one new and the other old, hardened, and habitual. Unlike the two verse passages which are flooded with doubt, Paul's passage is controlled by an introduction whose language rings with a decided point of view: "quod enim operor non intellego." Further,

while Paul locates the disparity between action and desire—his actions cannot reflect his desire—the poets stress the inaction that comes from the internal division in the will.

In contrast to Michelangelo, Colonna's poetry, which is also informed by Paul's writings, reveals virtually no overt statement of the divided will. Instead, her verse follows Paul's emphasis on the infirmity of the will. In "S'io potessi sfrondar," Colonna writes that even though she would like always to keep her eye on the "alta luce prima," her ardent and honest "voglia" is not capable of keeping her eye focused. Also, in "Poi che la vera e invisibile luce," the poet asks why, after the light of mercy has shined through Christ and his "piaghe," does she allow herself to be led off the true path by a "scorta infida"? Scripture calls her, but the "laberinto" of the world fools her "cieco veder" (Colonna 76, 62). Colonna's verse relies on the theme of the weakness of the will or intellect that trusts in itself and is in this way blind to the grace of Christ, through whom one has justification.

The contrast with Colonna's poetry shows clearly that Michelangelo has read Paul in a way which complicates the issue of the infirmity of the will. Although Paul's letter remains an important source for the poem, it cannot be said to be the only, or even the main source. Michelangelo's description of two wills, a weaker and a stronger one, is reminiscent of Augustine's description in Book 8 of the *Confessions*:

> In this warfare I was on both sides, but I took the part of that which I approved rather than the part of that which I disapproved. . . . But while I wanted to follow the first course and was convinced that it was right, I was still slave to the pleasures of the second.
>
> (165-66)

Augustine's passage goes on to explain the suspended state in which the soul finds itself, and despite the lack of clear verbal echoes in Michelangelo's poem, the passage shows a strikingly similar interest in the divided will. At any rate, within the passage there is a phrase which is actually closer in sound to Michelangelo's phrasing than Paul's letter: "sed tamen consuetudo adversus me pugnacior ex me facta erat, *quoniam volens quo nollem perveneram*" [since through wanting I arrived at what I should not want] (translation and emphasis mine).

Leaving aside the possibility that Michelangelo had direct access to at least the content of Book 8, the link between Augustine's divided will and that of Michelangelo is Petrarch. Besides the verbal echo of Petrarch's sonnet, Michelangelo shows that he is capable of reading Paul against the grain, according to the example of Petrarch.[7] In sonnet 76, for instance, he evokes Paul's language in the second letter to the Corinthians. In the final tercet of the sonnet Michelangelo writes: "Questo, signor, m'avvien, po' ch'i' vi vidi, / c'un dolce amaro, un *sì e no* mi muove" (Girardi 76.12-13). The last line clearly echoes Paul's, "Do I make plans like a worldly man, ready to say *Yes and No* at once. As surely as God is faithful, our word to you has not been *Yes and No*" (2 Cor. 1.17-18; emphasis mine). Against Paul's affirmation of himself as a man of God and not a vacillating, "worldly man," Michelangelo sees himself caught in the indecision and stasis of a divided will—he is exactly what Paul claims he is not. In the poem one sees Michelangelo reading Paul through Petrarch, for Petrarch adopts a similar phrase in sonnet 168. Thinking that he is nearing his goal, he writes:

> Io, che talor menzogna e talor vero
> ò ritrovato le parole sue,
> non so s'il creda, et vivomi intra due:
> né sì né no nel cor mi sona intero.

(5-8)

Petrarch's reading of his middle state as a state of "half" wills, in which he neither fully believes nor fully disbelieves contrasts with the integrity espoused by Paul in his letter. Like Petrarch, Michelangelo describes his soul as divided, perhaps even to a greater extent than Petrarch's model for, unlike Petrarch's soul which lives "intra le due," Michelangelo describes his internal division as a doubleness: a "yes" and a "no" move him. The effect of this difference is that Michelangelo's middle state appears even more internalized within his character.

In **"Vorrei voler"** the Petrarchan lens also prevails, in a highly complex way. First, the language of Michelangelo's poem echoes that of several of Petrarch's poems. Besides the verbal resonance of the sonnet 118 to which I have already referred and which portrays a clearly divided will, the opening line of Petrarch's sonnet 235 consists of a cadence similar to that of **"Vorrei voler"**: "Lasso, Amor mi trasporta ov'ir non voglio" (1). The similar passive position of the speakers of the poem and their division against themselves makes the other verbal affinities more convincing as evidence of Michelangelo's purposeful adoption of Petrarch's language and organization. In the first quatrain of both, the poets mention what occupies their "cor." While Michelangelo pictures a veil of hidden ice between his heart and God, Petrarch focuses on his beloved: ". . . nel mio cor siede monarca." The second quatrain of both ends with a comment on pride: Michelangelo beseeches God to chase away "ogni spietato orgoglio," while Petrarch playfully notes that he must be wary of the blows of his lady's "duro orgoglio." Although the earlier parts of these poems are disparate in tone, the final tercets of Petrarch's sonnet bring it close to the dangerous situation described in Michelangelo's poem. Continuing the

extended metaphor comparing his will to "la debile mia barca," Petrarch notes that his ship is driven "nel mio mar orribil" where "a sé doglie e tormenti / porta," conquered by the waves and left thoroughly undone. These similarities allow one to read Michelangelo's **"Vorrei voler"** as a reading of Paul's *Letter,* while it is at the same time a meditation on the idolatry of art and earthly love, and on the divided will. Michelangelo's substitution of "Amor" with a more internalized representation of desire in the syntax of the "vorrei voler" line, "monarca" with the hidden veil of ice, and the pride of his lady with his own "spietato orgoglio" indicates Michelangelo's complication and internalization of the traditional lyric conflict.

Yet Michelangelo retains Petrarch's powerful vision of the will whose weakness and division against itself has left it in a state of need. In his late sonnet, **"Giunto è già,"** Michelangelo adopts Petrarch's image of the will as a "fragil barca" within which he, like Petrarch, had mistakenly worshipped his art, "idol e monarca," and desired "quel c'a mal suo grado ogn'uom desia" (G 285.1-8). Recognizing the stasis to which his will, "carca d'errori," has led him, a stasis which recalls Petrarch's final image in sonnet 235 of a ship without a sail, the speaker turns to the meditation of the crucifixion: ". . . volta a quell'amor divino / c'aperse, a prender noi, 'n croce le braccia" (G 285.14). Now, rather than toward the "braccia" of his beloved the speaker moves toward salvation in the "braccia" of Christ.[8] Yet this apparently Pauline resolution of the Petrarchan conflict is only tentative, for even though the speaker recognizes what he should want, it is far from clear that he wants it fully. His past desire still afflicts him, as he questions himself: "Gli amorosi pensier, già vani e lieti, / che fien or, s'a duo morte m'avvicino? / D'una so 'l certo, e l'altra mi minaccia" (G 285.9-11). While the poet does renounce these things, he does not fully embrace God. Even as the speaker turns to the cross, he recalls his art, even as he renounces it: "Né pinger né scolpir fie più che quieti / l'anima, volta a quell'amor divino / c'aperse, a prender noi, 'n croce le braccia" (12-14). The ambiguity of the tone and language of this tercet, especially the "fie" of the first line, leaves a doubt if the passage amounts to a statement or to a wish to be freed from his inner division, a wish similar to that in **"Vorrei voler."**

Closely related to the theme of the divided will is the theme of imprisonment in desire, and while it is possible that Paul played some role in the creation of **"Vorrei voler,"** Michelangelo's steady return to the concept of habit, an idea not present in writings of Paul, shows that Paul is far from the major controlling source in Michelangelo's portrayal of internal conflict. Indeed, the *Rime* reveals Michelangelo's unceasing experimentation with the expression of habitual conflict in his borrowings from Dante, Petrarch, and the neoplatonists of the Medici circle. Although Michelangelo's poetry reveals his engagement with the neoplatonism of his day and that of Petrarch, he clearly never commits himself fully to its doctrines.[9] Standard images, such as the body as a "mortal velo" or a "carcere" of the soul do figure in the poems, but rather than dominate, they form only a part of the poet's conceits. Even though his series of epitaphs for Cecchino Braccio do reveal a consistent use of the body / soul dichotomy, the soul is not as clearly privileged over the body as in the platonists, for besides the neoplatonic treatment of the imprisonment theme, one finds a strong current running through the *Rime* of desire as the soul's entrapment in its own habits, such that the soul paradoxically wants to escape itself.

In several poems Michelangelo describes the soul's resistance to the grace that would bring conversion by portraying the soul as covered over by the residue of years of wrong choices. This "trista usanza" keeps from the poet "la grazia che 'l ciel piove in ogni loco" (sestina 33.5-6). In madrigal 143, the poet's complaint reflects his doubt that grace is sufficient to overcome the shortness of time left to him and the inveterateness of his wrong desire:

> Quant'ognor fugge il giorno che mi resta
> del viver corto e poco,
> tanto più serra il foco
> in picciol tempo a mie più danno e strazio:
> c'aita il ciel non presta
> *contr' al vecchio uso in così breve spazio.*
>
> (1-6; emphasis mine)

He concludes with the same idea in madrigal 130 in which he reveals the skepticism with which he views the redeeming power of grace: ". . . né danno alcun da tal pietà mi scioglie: / ché l'uso di molt'anni un dì non toglie" (10-11).

The concept of habit figures throughout the Rime,[10] especially in Michelangelo's later poetry. Beseeching God's help, the speaker of sonnet 293 begins: "Carico d'anni e di peccati pieno / e col trist'uso radicato e forte." He later notes that he does not have the "forze" to change his "costume." In the unfinished sonnet 297, Michelangelo reasserts the connection between habit and wrong desire:

> Se lungo spazio del trist'uso e folle
> più temp'il suo contrario a purgar chiede,
> la morte già vicina nol concede,
> né freno il mal voler da quel ch'e' volle.
>
> (1-4)

By itself the last line may appear as a Pauline reading of the weakness of the will against "il mal voler." Yet the first two lines suggest that the "trist'uso" controls the "mal voler" as much as the other way around. In

another unfinished sonnet 301, the speaker locates himself within habit, as if caught, from which he seeks to escape through prayer: "Del mie tristo uso e dagli esempli rei, / fra le tenebre folte, dov'io sono, / spero aita trovar. . . ."

This pessimism about the strength of his bondage in habit clearly recalls Augustine's extended interest in habit throughout the *Confessions,* and in particular, a passage toward the climax of the work, which may ultimately be the controlling text of the theme of habit in Michelangelo's poetry. Augustine writes:

> For my will was perverse and lust had grown from it, and when I gave in to lust habit was born, and when I did not resist the *habit* it became a necessity. . . . But my new will which had come to life in me and made me wish to serve you freely and enjoy you, my God, who are our only joy, was not yet strong enough to overcome the old, hardened as it was by the passage of time.
>
> (164; emphasis mine)

Besides dramatizing a turning point in Augustine's life, this famous passage develops the problem of the simultaneously (or alternatively) repentent and recalcitrant soul described by Paul in his letter to the Romans. Augustine's contribution to this portrait of the divided soul lies in his identification of the process out of which his wrong desire has been formed. Unlike Paul who maintains a sense of the soul's distance from wrong desire by locating this desire only vaguely in his "members," or his body, Augustine clearly traces the origin of his evil will to his free will: "For my will was perverse and lust had grown from it, and when I gave in to lust habit was born." Thus, by positing a complex of wills all traceable to free will, rather than positing separate wills of the soul and the body, Augustine heightens the conflict between these wills, as they all have their source in a single personality, even as this personality has evolved over time. Thus, the conflict no longer hints at a neoplatonic struggle between appetite and reason; now the conflict is between old and new wills whose source is the same and which may become entangled with one another.

The passage from Augustine links the divided will with habit in a way which anticipates Michelangelo's implicit criticism of the overly optimistic neoplatonic model of the soul which held that if it could only be free of the body it would return to its pure state. Michelangelo's resistance to what he feels he should want is linked to his image of his identity, not merely as soul but as an *already formed soul.* Habit's strength lies in its basis in desire that is deeply rooted in the soul. Rather than seeing desire as something that should be intellectualized and sublimated and thus distanced from its immediate source, Michelangelo sees it as that which actually constructs the soul. Luigi Baldacci has observed that

Michelangelo rejects the neoplatonic ladder of love as a theory of the perfection of the soul in favor of his close attention to the soul's formation through the process of loving (36). Baldacci's claims are supported in part by the "fabbro poems" (sonnets 62 and 63) in which the poet is transformed by the shaping power (fire) of his love for his lady. In sonnet 62, the fire which represents desire is intimately tied to the poet's identity—the fire is the force by which the will can be shaped. The last tercet of the poem allows for a kind of ascent through love, but it implicitly disputes the Neoplatonic myth: ". . . s'al ciel ascende [il foco] per natura, / al suo elemento, e ch'io converso in foco/ sie, come fie che seco non mi porti" (62.12-14). The poet, in imagining himself turned into fire, identifies so closely with his desire that it is impossible to distinguish the desire from the self. The "mi" here, the subject, is not the rational power of the soul rising to contemplate heaven; rather, it is the whole poet. If desire is to lift him up, it must lift all of him. The first quatrain of sonnet 63 also stresses the formative role of desire in the construction of the soul:

> Sì amico al freddo sasso è 'l foco interno
> che, di quel tratto, se lo circumscrive,
> che l'arda e spezzi, in qualche modo vive,
> legando con sé gli altri in loco etterno.

Desire, once again as fire, binds within the self ("legando con sé") the other ("gli altri") forever ("in loco etterno"). At its most basic level the poem argues that the experience of desire, once endured, makes the soul stronger or ennobles it. Yet even when the immediate desire is taken away, its effects remain "in etterno loco"—that is, forever within the mold of the soul. The phrasing of the poem even prompts a doubt that the poet could ever be freed from desire: ". . . *se* mi dissolve / il foco" (emphasis mine). Not only is his identity shaped by his past desire, but by his desire that his desire pass away.

Of Michelangelo's major sources it is Petrarch who most influences him in this critique of neoplatonism as well as of the schematic idealism of the scholastics. While the concept of habitual desire as an impediment to salvation does not figure significantly in Colonna's verse and only subtly and tentatively in Dante's, Petrarch's *Canzoniere* charts out an extended period in which the speaker is caught in desire for Laura. In "Il buon Pastor con opre, e voci pronte" Colonna does note the "lungo errore" of humanity which Christ's suffering tried to displace but which persists: "Gran nebbia copre un cor, gran sasso il preme . . . / Non si consuma come cera, o neve." Colonna's poem points to the persistent wrong desire in humanity, but in focusing on humanity in general she remains faithful to the Pauline doctrine of the natural infirmity of all people, and hence, she feels no need to trace wrong desire to the habits, and by extension, the free will of any individual.

While one could point to several passages in Petrarch's *Canzoniere* or *Secretum* which could be said to influence Michelangelo's "augustinian" interest in habit, two texts epitomize Petrarch's thought on this subject: sonnet 67 and canzone 80 of the *Canzoniere*. The whole narrative of the *Canzoniere* reveals how closely the speaker's identity is tied to his experience of loving, and Petrarch defines himself against Amor and Laura. In confronting the problem/Pleasure of the fixity of his desire for Laura the poet struggles with various models and situations that, in the end, present a self capable of a wide range of reactions. This struggle includes vacillations, and Petrarch's organization of his poems within the *Canzoniere* represents the fluctuations in his perception of the important relationships between Amor, himself, and Laura. While this quality of the *Canzoniere* may explain the general importance of habit for Petrarch against more simple models of conflict based on the body/soul dichotomy,[11] the two poems mentioned above focus Petrarch's criticism of the psychology of conversion in Dante. In sonnet 67 Petrarch alludes obliquely to *Inferno V* in order to show that the will that is developed through the experience of love is not so easily rooted out as Dante suggests. In this poem Petrarch describes a scene in which he sees the "altera fronde," which reminds him of his lady's "treccie bionde." He approaches the tree and falls into a hidden river "non già come persona viva." The shame he feels at this fall is accompanied by a pleasure. The rewriting of Dante's description of his fall, apparently out of sympathy with Francesca—"caddi come corpo morto cade"—points to the fact that the "first" fall of Petrarch's first sight of Laura is always potentially repeatable, while Dante's pilgrim's swoon only faintly suggests the strength of the construction of the self through sexual, human love. In the construct of Dante's universe the pilgrim must move on—how easy the pilgrim's one swoon seems compared to the restless reworkings and returns to Laura in Petrarch's *Canzoniere*. Petrarch's return to the moment of his first sight of his beloved constitutes much of the *Canzoniere*.[12]

Michelangelo's madrigal 131 appropriates the language of Dante's pilgrim's conversion, while recalling subtly Petrarch's critique, in order to emphasize the strength of habit:

> Sotto duo belle ciglia
> le forze Amor ripiglia
> nella stagion che sprezza l'arco e l'ale. . . .
> E parte pur m'assale,
> appresso al dolce, *un pensier aspro e forte*
> di vergogna e di morte;
> nè perde Amor per maggior tema o danni:
> *c'un'or non vince l'uso di molt'anni.*

> (1-11; emphasis mine)

Recalling the "selva oscura" of the libidinous wood at which the pilgrim's journey to redemption begins,

Michelangelo sees no "pensier aspro e forte" (8) of death or shame strong enough to conquer habit: ". . . c'un' or non vince l'uso di molt' anni" (11). Like Petrarch, Michelangelo resists the equation of shame and fear with conversion, since both recognize the pleasure that accompanies their pain.[13]

Sestina 80 not only serves as a contrast to Dante in the way the poets view the Ulysses story, but it also places in relief the two main doubts about the self felt throughout the *Canzoniere*—doubt about guidance and doubt about the self's ability to change. The narrative of the poem is the following: the poet begins with an axiomatic warning that in order to avoid death, one should not trust his "picciol legno" to the "onde fallaci" and "scogli"; he has entrusted the ship to "l'aura soave" since entering "l'amorosa vita" and has been led into the rocks repeatedly; he wanders blindly without heeding the sail, until God ("altrui") presents him a port at a distance; this gives the poet hope, yet in a powerful statement about the soul's resilience to change, he says that even if he reaches the port, he will want to go out to sea again, "sì m'è duro a lassar l'usata vita." While in *Inferno* XXVI Ulysses is a reminder of the pilgrim/poet's conversion as the poet distances himself from the Greek, Petrarch anticipates imitating Ulysses. Like Ulysses, for whom even the love of his wife and child could not keep him from his desire for travel, so Petrarch cannot be turned for long from his "amorosa vita." The sign from God, the "lume di notte," is not strong enough to change the poet.

The fixity of the will is often related in Michelangelo's verse to the self's inability to know itself. Surrounding this theme, Michelangelo's manipulation of the images of rock, ice, and the veil reveal his subtle differences from Paul and Colonna's reading of Paul. In **"Vorrei voler"** (87), a veil of ice "s'asconde" representing a third unknowable will that lies hidden between the poet's two differing wills: "tra 'l foco e 'l cor di ghiaccia un vel s'asconde / che 'l foco ammorza, onde non corrisponde / la penna all'opre, e fa bugiardo 'l foglio" (2-4). This veil, whose source is unknown, represents the desire that keeps the poet from wanting what he feels he should want. The oxymoronic image linking the light and flexible veil to the brittle and heavy ice reflects the double bind of Michelangelo's soul—it is as unchangeable as glacial ice (note "spietato orgoglio," 8), but the source of this fixity is as transparent as a veil.[14] Hence, the poet adopts a supplicating posture toward God partially because he feels helpless in correcting his soul, for it has been formed by wrong desire and the origin of this desire is deep and untraceable.

While Colonna's more common image of an inhibiting will is that of "nebbia" which surrounds the heart and which is dispersed with the light of grace, figured as the "gran lume" or "Sole," when she does use the image of

the veil, it is more in line with Paul's letter. In the letter Paul notes that their hardened hearts have placed a veil over the minds of the Jews, so that when they read Moses, they do not truly understand. According to Paul, only "when a man turns to the Lord" is the veil removed. For Colonna, veils usually hide the true image of the deity.[15] Colonna's sonnet, "L'altezza de l'oggetto, onde a me lice." seems to be a source for Michelangelo's images of ice and the veil:

> Da lei mi vien, che la mia lingua al gelo
> Pigro s'egli vi toglie, ad altro sforza,
> Ch'attorno spesso, ò nobil donna, invio.
> Squarciate dunque de l'affetto il velo,
> Che 'l lume in voi del buon giuditio ammorza,
> Io per me son, quasi senz'onda rio.
>
> (9-14)

The last tercet holds the clearest echo of line 9 of Michelangelo's poem: **"Squarcia 'l vel tu, Signor. . . ."** Colonna's image does resemble that of Michelangelo in that both evoke Paul's letter. The echo in the words, "velo, "lingua," and "ammorza" suggests that the poems are in dialogue around their source. However, Colonna's poem is a clearer reading of Paul's letter, for she focuses on the "good judgment" (l. 11), which is hampered by the veil on the affections. This is felt in another poem, "Deh manda Santo Spirto al mio intelletto," in which the poet asks the Holy Spirit, "sgombra / Ben indurato giel." Her eye looks for heaven but is often clouded over, loving itself "più che 'l vero obietto" (Colonna 66). The mixed metaphor of "uncovering" a "hard coldness" intimates that Colonna reads the hardening of the Jews hearts and their intellectual blindness described by Paul as the same thing.

The image of the hidden veil is part of a larger theme developed in Michelangelo's *Rime* of the inscrutability of the will. Indeed, the inability of the poet to locate and define clearly his desire as distinct from the soul is an important source of the pathos felt in his penitential poems. The soul often suffers from an anxiety whose source is lost to the poet. In the incomplete sonnet 280, the soul "inquieta e confusa in sé" suffers from a "grave peccato / mal conosciuto." Yet how this desire shapes the self remains a mystery. In sonnet 63 the poet calls his desire an "occulto gioco" within him, as if he were unaware of exactly how it affected him. The fact that it is described as a "gioco" calls to mind the mischievous Amor of earlier love lyrics, but "gioco" also implies the unpredictable effects of desire's presence.

It would appear that Paul were again the ultimate source for the expression of the mystery of the will, but Colonna's more straightforward reading of Paul makes Michelangelo's exploration seem more unusual. In her "Cibo, del cui meraviglioso effetto," Colonna describes the rebellious will that knows yet perversely rejects God:

"pur da noi s'usa ogn'ingegno / Et ogni poder nostro incontro a noi" (19). This phrasing more clearly recalls Paul's letter in its insistence that the will works against its own good. Colonna implies that the will was infirm from the start, while Michelangelo's model is poised between a neoplatonic vision of the potentially pure soul, which has been corrupted, and a soul whose free will has corrupted itself. The mystery of this original free will is pointed to in the introduction to Michelangelo's sestina 70 when the poet compares this will (*arbitrio*) to the mysterious astrological outside forces: "Crudele stella, anzi crudele arbitrio / che 'l potere e 'l voler mi stringe e lega" (1-2). The replacement of "crudele arbitrio" for "crudele stella" strongly hints that the poet feels no more control over this original will that binds his power and desire than over the mysterious workings of fortune or providence.

This theme in Michelangelo's poetry again resounds in the voice of Augustine. In the *Confessions,* Augustine cites Psalm 19 twice within the first two books, where he searches for the motivations of his life before his conversion. In one instance, Augustine asks himself, "How can I explain my mood? It was certainly a very vile frame of mind and one for which I suffered; but how can I account for it?" (52). He concludes with the citation from Psalm 19: "Who knows his own frailties" (52). Augustine fashions the theme in his own words in a passage in Book 4 when he contrasts God's knowledge of him (citing Matt. 10.30) with his own ignorance of himself: "Can I, then, love in another what I should hate in myself, though both of us are human? *Man is a great mystery, Lord.* You keep count of the hairs on his head . . ." (84; emphasis mine). This passage points to Augustine's failure to explain the state of his will: Not only does one see in these passages the difficulty of rooting out habit but also one reason for it—the strange mystery of the will.

Both the *Canzoniere* and the *Secretum* reflect this Augustinian theme. Besides simply indicating rhetorical play, the Petarchan paradoxes point to the mystery of the will. Sonnet 178 exemplifies how Petrarch acknowledges the spontaneity and force of sudden mysterious thoughts that contradict "friendly," self-preserving thoughts. The poem's first quatrain is a litany of typical paradoxes: "Amor mi sprona in un tempo et affrena, / assecura et spaventa, arde et agghiaccia, / gradisce e sdegna . . ." (1-3). In the second quatrain the speaker begins to feel pleasure become bitter, but he cannot explain why, except to point to an unidentifiable new will in his mind: "d'error sì novo la mia mente è piena" (8). The poet then finds hope in "un amico penser," which would guide him toward happiness, but "poi quasi maggior forza" usurps this thought and leads the speaker's soul "mal suo grado" to its death. The speaker is never able to identify the source of this stumbling block. Such mysterious underminings of the will are discussed also in the *Secretum.* At one point toward the end of Book 1, Francesco asks: "Stando così le cose, che è dunque quel che mi trattiene? quale è il celato ostacolo pel quale fino ad ora codesta meditazione non mi ha profittato nulla . . ." (*Il mio segreto* 89). And again, no source is identified. Thus, Petrarch's general concern for such a "celato ostacolo" in both his works anticipates Michelangelo's formulation in a veil of ice that hides (*s'asconde*) between his heart and God.

The double despair concerning the hardened will of wrong desire that he can identify and the undermining will of a seemingly unknowable desire, both with which Michelangeo identifies, leads to the pessimism concerning spiritual conversion found throughout the *Rime.* It is apparent that on some level Michelangelo does not want the grace offered him, despite his praise of his lady and her beneficial effects, because of the strong resistance to change built into the soul over many years. He expresses his confusion in several ways. The triple negative with which he begins madrigal 149 mirrors his indecisiveness:

> Non posso non mancar d'ingegno e d'arte
> a chi mi to' la vita
> con tal superchia aita,
> che d'assai men mercé più se ne prende.
>
>                                        (1-4)

He needlessly inserts the hackneyed proverb about modesty in madrigal 148 as a way to justify his hesitance in accepting the grace offered him: "Il troppo è vano e folle; / che modesta persona / d'umil fortuna ha più tranquilla pace" (10-12). Further, while the poet acknowledges that grace brings him peace, "superchia pietà mi rasserena," in the next line he complains of having lost his life: ". . . se mi vuol vivo affreni il gran contento, / c'al don superchio debil virtù muore" (sonnet 150.12-14). Again, in madrigal 130 the poet must defend himself against the "volto divino" of grace in order not to die, spiritually: "ond'io m'armo e consiglio / per far da quel difesa anzi ch'i' mora" (5-6).

This resistance to grace is clearly linked to Michelangelo's vision of the force of habit and his doubt and fear in the purifying process of conversion. Centering his fear of grace on the exemplary life story told by Dante, Michelangelo again recalls Petrarch's critique of Dante's representation of conversion. Like Michelangelo, in both the *Convivio* and the *Commedia* Dante describes the overwhelming effect of grace on the viewer, particularly the weak viewer. The pilgrim in the *Paradiso* is only gradually able to endure the light from the sun, and even this sight is a privilege of ascending to heaven: "Molto è licito là, che qui non lece / a le nostre virtu, mercé del loco / fatto per proprio de l'umana spece" (*Paradiso* 1.55-57). The association made repeatedly in the *Convivio* of overwhelming light ("superchio lume") with grace runs throughout the *Commedia*. Blinded by the dazzling light of the angel, the pilgrim shades his eyes to diminish the "soverchio visibile" (*Purgatorio* 15.15). Later Dante compares the angel's appearance to the sun "che nostra vista grava / e per soverchio sua figura vela" (*Purgatorio* 17.52-53). Yet while these visions of divine grace, though difficult for the eye to sustain, have for Dante a cauterizing effect, healing the wound of his spiritual blindness, for Michelangelo, grace threatens to dissolve his soul at the same time in which it dissolves his sin, because his soul and the wrong habitual desire are bound together as tightly as rock within rock.[16] Grace seems to come all at once, and the speaker instinctively resists. In madrigal 148 the poet fears that the "doppia mercè" of his lady's grace might conquer his "picciola virtute" and that such a "superchio piacer" would kill him. In madrigal 149 this "superchia aita" is described as stifling, and it paradoxically cools desire in the poet: "Questa, di grazie piena, / n'abonda e 'nfiamma altrui d'un certo foco, / che 'l troppo con men caldo arde che 'l poco" (12-14). Indeed, in sonnet 150 the poet seems to prefer the state of sadness in which he somehow felt more alive: ". . . con superchia pietà me rasserena, / par, più che 'l pianger, la vita mi toglia . . . c'al don superchio debil virtù muore" (7-14).[17]

Michelangelo's repeated expression of doubt and hesitation concerning conversion recalls Augustine's own resistance to grace in Book VIII of the *Confessions* when he struggles against insidious voices within his memory that inhibit him from turning fully to God (176). Both Augustine and Michelangelo sharply perceive the strength of habit, but importantly here, both present habit as organically connected with the self. Augustine pictures habit as the internalization of the past and the formation of voices. Analogously, Michelangelo sees habit as the crusty exterior that has grown out from the soul and is so much a part of the soul that the two cannot be separated, for if one tries to cut away the habit one is in danger of harming the soul itself. The contraction of the soul with its desire figures also in Augustine and Michelangelo's similar delays in converting. Augustine writes: "Time was passing and I kept delaying my conversion to you, my God. Day after day I postponed living in you, but I never put off the death which I died each day in myself" (*Confessions* 128). In the same way in sonnet 294, Michelangelo recognizes his "superchio indugio" in turning to Christ.

Michelangelo's anxiety about the state of his soul is exacerbated by his sense of God's absence. Although Michelangelo's poetry abounds with the idea that there is a trace of God in natural beauty and a hint of divine love in the love of the beautiful,[18] the poetry also sometimes indicates either the speaker's doubts about or lack of insight into the connection between the present physical world and the absent divine one—an attitude which chafes against the optimism of early sixteenth-century neoplatonism. In sonnet 76 Michelangelo reveals his insecurity about the origin of desire when he probes his memory and implicitly challenges the neoplatonic idea that God inhabits the world in all that is beautiful:

> Non so se s'è la desiata luce
> del suo primo fattor, che l'alma sente,
> o se dalla memoria della gente
> alcun' altra beltà nel cor traluce. . . .
>
> (1-4)

Here the speaker is not sure whether or not physical beauty can be a reassurance of the deity's presence in the world or if worldly desire can be justly rationalized as an intimation of divine love, as Ficino and others held. While Clements sees the last two lines of the quatrain as a continuation of the neoplatonic conceit, this time taking up the principle of anamnesis, the syntactical division of the "or" (*o*) at the beginning of the third line suggests, rather, a contrast between the two thoughts. In addition, instead of translating "memoria della gente" as "racial memory," as Clements does, making "della" a subjective genitive, one could make "della" an objective genitive and render the phrase, "arising from my memory of people." The contrast made in this reading between the two parts of the quatrain is consistent with the uncertainty in the speaker's tone through the first two quatrains: I do not know whether my desire for you is connected to some higher desire for the divine or if I desire you because I am reminded of a previous love, or if some beautiful image, detached from its true object, is the cause of my desire.

The confusion of the poet implicitly calls into question the sufficiency of the neoplatonic model of desire, especially as the poet recalls the uniqueness of his beloved. The poet is torn between the idea that his situation of distance from his beloved enacts a similar distance from God that could be overcome by contemplation of beauty in others—the neoplatonic idea, and the idea that this distance simply cannot be overcome. The "dolce amaro" to which the poet refers at the end of the poem epitomizes this conflict between desire for the absent other and the consolation of philosophy, and in the last two tercets of the poem, Michelangelo indicates that he remains undecided about the beauty of his beloved's relation to the deity, for if this were accepted, any similar beauty would lead to the same sublime object. In the end, the eyes of the beloved control the lover's imagination: ". . . certo saranno stati gli occhi vostri" (14). This control operates in two opposing, unresolved ways: first, in the eyes, as in neoplatonist doctrine, may contain traces of divinity that spark a love that leads back to the "primo fattor" and encourage the lover toward this higher love, disregarding the means; and second, the eyes may inhibit such a movement by reminding the poet of the beloved's uniqueness.

In **"Deh fammiti vedere in ogni loco!"** (274), the beseeching tone, struck from the introductory "deh" makes Michelangelo's anxiousness about the absence of his beloved particularly poignant:

> Deh fammiti vedere in ogni loco!
> Se da mortal bellezza arder mi sento,
> appresso al tuo mi sarà foco ispento,
> e io nel tuo sarò, com'ero, in foco.
>
> (1-4)

As in much of Michelangelo's verse there is an ambiguity about whether the speaker's object is the deity or his earthly beloved (Lucente 324). In any case, the speaker feels the absence of the *divine*, whether the deity itself or a reflection of the deity in the beloved. The feeling expressed in the poem is that the speaker's wrong desire, figured as fire (*foco*) feeding on "mortal bellezza," would be extinguished by contact with a greater fire. Yet this greater fire, while present in the imagination of the speaker, remains only a figure of hope for him, for the "immortal" beauty which the speaker seeks is unseen. Since the object of desire is seen by the poet as a transformative and vivifying power, when it is absent, the poet feels helpless, trapped, and tormented. This sentiment contrasts with the neoplatonic optimism in the power of the intellect to find God through contemplation of the *concept* of beauty. The second stanza of the poem reveals that Michelangelo is focusing his critique of neoplatonism not on the idea that God is present in the world but on the idea that one can perceive the deity through the use of reason:

> Signor mie caro, i' te sol chiamo e 'nvoco
> contr' a l'inutil mie cieco tormento:
> tu sol puo' rinnovarmi fuora e drento
> le voglie e 'l senno e 'l valor lento e poco.
>
> (5-8)

In invoking God's help, the poet partially corrects the accusatory tone of the first line by asking God to free him from his "cieco tormento." This phrase can be read in two ways: first it refers to the complexity of the speaker's conflict which he himself cannot understand; and second, it refers to how the speaker's conflict blinds him to the presence of God in the world.

Michelangelo's poetry recalls the anxiety of the preconverted Augustine of the *Confessions* in which Augustine, caught in worldly desire, wonders why God remains so absent from him:

> I strayed still further from you and you did not restrain me. I was tossed and spilled, floundering in the broiling sea of my fornication, and you said no word. . . . You were silent then, and I went on my way. . . .
>
> (43)

Later, in Book III the speaker asks: "Where were you in those days? How far away from me" (62). Although Augustine's retrospective point of view does influence the tone of these passages—the anxiety conveyed here is tempered by the converted self's hope for salvation—Augustine's rhetoric does recreate partially the anxiety, helplessness, and anger of his past self. The deity's silence and apparent apathy toward the suffering Augustine is cast as a father's neglect of a wayward son. The accusatory tone of the passages above indicates the speaker's resentment at being left without guidance, while the speaker simultaneously recognizes the weakness of his own will to counter the strong force of his other will. If the deity only revealed himself directly or through some clear sign, this conflict in the will would be resolved.

Michelangelo's poetry at times echoes this desire to have his weak will subsumed in the divine will. For instance in sonnet 288, the remorseful speaker asks God blankly to reverse his past earthly, "cieco" desire: "Mettiti in odio quante 'l mondo vale" (5-9). The resolution of moral blindness which is closely connected to habitual wrong desire is sought both by Michelangelo and Augustine in some external sign, some type of guidance, and in Michelangelo's verse one senses an anxiety about finding such help. It must be said here that Michelangelo's scepticism about the neoplatonic doctrine of God's presence in the beauty of the world (a doctrine shared by Augustine himself) forms only a minor part of the theme of God's absence in the *Rime.* Indeed, Michelangelo often finds a guide to heaven in his beloved.[19] Rather, the anxiety about absence is felt in the poetry's tone and the poet's position in relation to God. Augustine's lament, "O God, Hope of my youth, where were you all this time? Where were you hiding from me? . . . I was looking for you outside myself and I did not find the God of my own heart" reminds one of Michelangelo's only late renouncement of the world and its wisdom (*Confessions* 111). The evolution of the artist's poetry indicates a usurpation of such worldly guides by one true guide.

Here again it is Petrarch who links Michelangelo with Augustine, for Michelangelo seems to have been sensitive to Petrarch's criticism of Dante. While Dante places himself in the position of receiving special grace in ascending all the way to the very presence of God, Petrarch situates himself in a world of flux in which guides are unreliable and mortal. Petrarch repeatedly questions the possibility of such a blessed journey and such a privileged means of conversion. In sonnet 189 Petrarch impugns Dante's credibility in giving the pilgrim so constant and able a guide as Virgil. In this poem he describes a journey at sea in which he imagines himself to be, at first, a ship with Amor at the helm and his thoughts ("penser") as eager oarsmen. Suddenly a storm begins to toss the boat. His guides, the stars (Laura's eyes), are mysteriously taken from him, and in an oblique reference to Virgil's guidance of Dante's pilgrim, Petrarch notes that he has lost his reason and art among the waves: "morta fra l'onde è la ragion e l'arte" (13).[20] How, Petrarch seems to ask, does one maintain a stable self within such an unstable world and such inconstant guides? While Dante is always reliving the escape from the "naufragio," Petrarch continues to imagine himself still within it. The *Commedia* has several moments in which the pilgrim/poet symbolically looks back to see the disaster from which he has been saved. In contrast, Petrarch returns repeatedly to the vision of himself at sea or wandering in the wilderness, without a constant or real guide such as Dante's Virgil and Beatrice. Petrarch can only conjure up imaginary and unreliable guides, as in sonnet 277, when at sea, he drifts "senza fidata scorta" (8).

As in the *Commedia* the self at sea is the central image of the self in the *Canzoniere.* But the differences are clear. Dante poet is in firm control of his "little bark" while Petrarch wanders, "chiuso gran tempo in questo cieco legno" (80.13). Sestina 80 reveals how many forces conspire to defeat the will of the self at sea—the menacing rocks, storms, and the ship itself, the "cieco legno," which may represent the poet's body or desire. It is this blindness that is caused by both the mystery of the world and the wrong desire in the will, which turns the speaker at the end of the *Canzoniere* to adopt at last a supplicating gesture toward God.

Despite the lack of external evidence that would make a direct link between Michelangelo and Augustine, enough evidence exists to show that Michelangelo may have intuited many of Augustine's central concerns about his soul and its salvation through the voice of Petrarch. Michelangelo's spiritual struggle, which extended over a long period of time, places him in line with Augustine of the *Confessions* and Petrarch who emphasized their long suspensions in habitual, divided states of will and desire. They truly were neither Aeneas nor Paul.

### Notes

1. Arturo Farinelli suggests the connection concerning tone between the *Psalms,* Augustine, Petrarch, and Michelangelo (25). Robert Clements, however, does not mention any such link in his chapters, "Poetry as Prayer and Confession" and "Sources and Originality" in *The Poetry of Michelangelo.* In "Il petrarchismo di Michelangelo e la tradizione lirica toscana," Enzo Girardi considers the confessional strain in Michelangelo as merely tangential, and he considers Petrarch's greatest influence as a source of words and conceits which Michelangelo used without regard for their original use, though his treatment of Petrarch is superficial compared to his study of Dante's influ-

ence. I would like to thank Robert J. Rodini and Gregory Lucente for their careful reading of early drafts of this essay.

2. The earliest known translation of the *Confessions* into Italian is in 1564, and hence it is impossible that Michelangelo had contact with the fully translated text. The possibility does remain, however, of the existence of a partial translation. For a list of translations, see Augustine's *Le Confessioni di Sant' Agostino,* edited by Giuliano Vigini.

3. Several studies have indicated that Michelangelo was not unaware of Augustine's works. For Michelangelo's relation to the Augustinian reformer, Gilles of Viterbo, see Doston. For the relationship between Michelangelo, Vittoria Colonna, and Occhino see Campi's *Michelangelo e Vittoria Colonna.* Also, Paul Oskar Kristeller, among other scholars, has noted Augustine's importance for Ficino.

4. This method might be challenged by the strong evidence that Petrarch was also a close reader of Paul who patterned his conversion after Paul. Yet, as Bortolo Martinelli's study on the moral patterning of the *Canzoniere* suggests, it is difficult to differentiate between the influences of Paul and Augustine, even if the Petrarchan theme of new life found in old age reflects the conversion of Paul (127-39). Moreover, there is ample evidence that Augustine's *Confessions* was even more influential on Petrarch than Paul's letters. See Albert Rabil's chapter, "Petrarch, Augustine, and the Classical Tradition" (95-114).

5. See especially Augustine's citations of 2 Cor. 2.16 (57); 1 Cor. 1.27-30 (94 and 163); 1 Cor. 8.1 (154); 1 Cor. 3.1 (154); and Romans 5.6 (145).

6. In recounting the debate between two theologians, Seripandi and Flaminio, on predestination, Paolo Simoncelli quotes one of Seripendi: ". . . esclamerò don Paulo apostolo 'O altitudo divitiarum,' o vero dirò con Agostino che questo giudicio è giusto . . ." (80). For a similar passage showing the closeness of Paul and Augustine from a theologian's point of view, see Simoncelli on the question of justification through works (107). Kristeller writes that Augustine himself, as a bishop, "confronted with many moral and social problems and polemic discussions with contemporary heretics," was led "to complete the theological speculation of St. Paul and the earlier Church Fathers" (355-56).

7. It is possible that Petrarch's sonnet 118, like "Vorrie voler," was based on Paul's letter, but this possibility does not contradict the contention that Petrarch was at the same time influenced by Augustine.

8. "Giunto è già" is also a reminiscence of Petrarch's "Giunto m'à Amor fra belle e crude braccia" (sonnet 171), which portrays the speaker's nearing the goal of his desire.

9. Neoplatonic images and ideas surface throughout the *Rime*. Especially prominent is the flight to heaven through love of the divinity which shines through mortal beauty. For passages that epitomize the harmonious relation between virtue and beauty, see poems 41, 72, 147, and 155. The Ficinian idea of God's shining through souls outwardly to their bodies appears in poem 106, among other places: ". . . ne Dio, suo grazia, mi si mostra altrove / più che 'n alcun leggiadro e mortal velo" (12-13).

10. For the importance of habit in the poetry see also 25, 92, 294, and 295.

11. Although Petrarch does occasionally set up divisions in the soul, such as "voglia" against "ragione" (sonnet 101), these philosophical divisions have little to do with poetic effect or the psychological depth of the poetry. Sonnet 178 epitomizes Petrarch's tendency to represent the self as a bundle of equally strong, often contradictory impulses. In this poem he takes care to acknowledge the spontaneity and force of sudden mysterious thoughts that contradict "friendly," self-preserving thoughts.

12. For poems that point specifically to this "return" see 61, 62, 65, 66, 181, 201, 207, 325, and 329.

13. See Petrarch's *Canzoniere* 270, 22.

14. Michelangelo returns to this idea in the unfinished sonnet 291: "Penso e ben so c'alcuna preme, / occulta a me, lo spirito in gran martire."

15. As another example, see Colonna's, "Veggio di mille ornati veli avolto," 14.

16. I would put forth the suggestion that Michelangelo's slave sculptures portray not the neoplatonic soul trying to get free from the body as much as soul is covered with the layers of its own choices. For the neoplatonic interpretation of the slave sculptures, see Tolnay (93).

17. In madrigal 113, Michelangelo sets "l'infinita beltà" in apposition with "'l superchio lume" (7), thus strongly hinting at the connection between the God and the light of beauty emanating from his lady, and further, between "infinita" and "superchio." "Com'esser può dissimile e dispari / l'infinita beltà, 'l superchio lume / da ogni mie costume, / che meco ardendo, non ardin del pari?" (6-9). Grace, here as often in Dante associated with light, proves overwhelming to the poet. For another example of Michelangelo's resistance to grace, see madrigal 252.

18. See Michelangelo's *Rime* 15, 83, 89, and 279.

19. See especially the sonnets for Cavalieri, 105 and 106.

20. In the *Purgatorio,* Virgil tells the pilgrim that he has led him to the earthly paradise "con ingegno e non arte" (27.130).

### Works Cited

Augustine. *Confessions.* Trans. R. S. Pine-Coffin. 1961. Harmondsworth: Penguin, 1984.

———. *Le Confessioni di Sant'Agostino.* Ed. Giuliano Vigini. Milan: Editrice Bibliografica, 1995.

Baldacci, Luigi. "Lineamenti della poesia di Michelangelo." *Paragone* 72 (1955): 27-45.

*Biblia Sacra Vulgata.* Ed. Roger Gryson. Stuggart: Deutsche Bibelgesellschaft, 1969.

Campi, Emidio. *Michelangelo e Vittorio Colonna: un dialogo artistico-teologico ispirato da Bernardino Occhino.* Turin: Claudiana, 1994.

Clements, Robert. *The Poetry of Michelangelo.* New York: New York UP, 1965.

Colonna, Vittoria. *Rime di Vittoria Colonna.* Naples: Bulifon, 1692.

Dante. *Tutte le opere.* Ed. Fallani, Maggi, Zennaro. Rome: Newton, 1993.

Dotson, Esther Gordon. "An Augustinian Interpretation of the Sistine Ceiling." *Art Bulletin* 61 (1979): 223-56.

Farinelli, Arturo. *Michelangelo and Dante: Michelangelo poeta.* Turin: Paravia, 1943.

Girardi, Enzo. *Studi su Michelangelo scrittore.* Florence: Olschki, 1974.

Kristeller, Paul Oskar. "Augustine and the Early Renaissance." *Studies in Renaissance Thought and Letters.* Rome: Edizioni di Storia e Letteratura, 1956.

Lucente, Gregory. "Lyric Tradition and the Desires of Absence: Rudel, Dante, and Michelangelo." *Canadian Review of Comparative Literature* (Sept. 1983): 305-32.

Michelangelo. *Rime.* Ed. Enzo Noè Girardi. Bari: Laterza, 1960.

Martinelli, Bortolo. "L'ordinamento morale del *Canzoniere.*" *Studi petrarcheschi* 8 (1976): 93-167.

Petrarca, Francesco. *Petrarch's Lyric Poems.* Trans. and ed. Robert M. Durling. Cambridge: Harvard UP, 1976.

———. *Il mio secreto.* Ed. and Trans. Ugo Dotti. Milan: Rizzoli, 1981.

Rabil, Albert, ed. *Renaissance Humanism: Foundations, Forms, and Legacy.* Vol. 1. Philadelphia: U of Pennsylvania P, 1988.

Simoncelli, Paolo. *Evangelismo italiano del '500.* Rome: Istituto Storico Italiano per l'età Moderna e Contemporanea, 1979.

Tolnay, Charles de. *Michelangelo: Sculptor, Painter, Architect.* Trans. Gaynor Woodhouse. Princeton: Princeton UP, 1975.

## Santa Casciani (essay date 1998)

SOURCE: Casciani, Santa. "The Iconography of Death in Michelangelo's Lyric Poetry." *Quaderni d'italianistica* 19, no. 2 (1998): 25-39.

[*In the following essay, Casciani charts the evolution of Michelangelo's depiction of the theme of death through progressively more realistic stages in his poems.*]

In a letter to Giorgio Vasari, Michelangelo commented that death was sculpted in his every thought (***Rime*** 628). Throughout his career as sculptor, painter and poet, Michelangelo was fascinated with the notion of death, which existed in a reciprocal affinity with life. Donato Giannotti, in one of his dialogues, describes Michelangelo's thinking as similar to Socrates in the *Phaedo,*[1] searching for self-knowledge through the contemplation of death. Specifically, in an imaginary dialogue with Giannotti, Michelangelo affirms that human pleasure derives more from the contemplation of death than from earthly delights. He argues that death, while by its very nature destroying all things, makes it possible for humans to recognize and perfect themselves (Barolsky 14). Thus death is an appetite protecting us from our passions, it allows us to become complete human beings, and it is the only thought that moves us to recognize our true selves.

In the *Phaedo,* Plato states that the quintessence of true knowledge rests in the search for death, and "that true philosophers make dying their profession" (121). He believes that in order to seek authentic knowledge the soul must flee from the body, which is a hindrance to the very acquisition of knowledge. The soul, when imprisoned by the body, is not "free of all distractions"—distractions that restrain it from pursuing the very essence of true knowledge. Plato states that "the body intrudes . . . into our investigations, interrupting, disturbing, distracting, and preventing us . . . from getting a glimpse of the truth" (119). Thus contemplation of death must be done with the desire "to get rid of the body" (120), so that one may "contemplate things in isolation with the soul" (120). According to Plato, the more one contemplates death the more knowledgeable one becomes about life. Specifically, the more perfectly one is able to visualize death, the more perfect the search for the perfect object becomes: "[because] you are likely to attain more nearly to knowledge of your

object in proportion to the care of accuracy with which you have prepared yourself to understand that object in itself" (119). The realization of true knowledge occurs through a paradoxical process of "two sets of opposites, going round in a sort of cycle" (127). Thus the purpose of life is to contemplate death because it is essential to self-knowledge, for "if there is such a thing as coming to life again . . . it must be a process from death to life" (127). The very process of the contemplation of death as a process of self-knowledge brings the philosopher closer to picturing the true essence of life. (119).

In his artistic production, Michelangelo represents death in a reciprocal affinity with life in much the same manner as Plato.[2] In fact he comes to understand that this symbiosis of apparent opposites comprises a dialectical relationship, which follows Plato's exegesis of the paradoxical process of meaning within which "two sets of opposites" (127) co-exist. In Madrigal 124, Michelangelo states: "E così morte e vita, / contrarie, insieme in un picciol momento / dentro a l'anima sento [And thus, within my soul / I feel both death and life, though opposites, / together for a brief moment.]"[3]

Giorgio Vasari affirmed that Michelangelo often spoke in vague and ambiguous terms, leaving those who spoke to him of two minds about what he had said. This ambiguity extended to Michelangelo's perception of death as an integral part of life:

> Essendogli ragionato de la morte da un suo amico, . . . rispose che tutto era nulla perché se la vita ci piace, essendo anco la morte di mano d'un medesimo maestro quello non ci dovrebbe dispiacere.
>
> (Vasari 912)

> [He was imprecise and ambiguous in his speech, which often was double-edged . . . when a friend spoke to him about death, he answered that it was all one and the same. If we like life, we should not dislike death since both derive from the hand of the same master.][4]

Thus for Michelangelo, in order for the human soul to experience pleasure—pleasure that allows the artist to create—it must acquire a taste for the contemplation of death.

The depiction of death in Michelangelo's lyrical production is a source of self-reflection on his inner life and on his contemplation of his place within the cosmos. Musing on death becomes a transcendent appetite allowing him to meditate continuously on the dialectical relationship between life and death, as he attempts to sculpture and transform his feeble flesh into a touchstone of eternal repose and peace. In his poetry, he relates this inner conflict in relation to Plato's *Phaedo,* the Christian tradition, Petrarch, and the neo-platonic humanists of the Renaissance. Past criticism of Michelangelo's lyric poetry—a body of more than three hundred sonnets, madrigals and other poems—has questioned whether Michelangelo's lyrical production possesses the same quality and depth of artistry as his sculptures and paintings.[5] This tradition of criticism began with Michelangelo himself, who stated in a letter to Giorgio Vasari in 1557 that "lo scrivere m'è di grande affanno, perché non è mia arte [writing is of great difficulty to me because it is not my art]" (Michelangelo, *Rime* 628). However, Michelangelo's poetry is a "significant body of artistic composition and possesses an integrity of its own" (Lucente 306). In order to appreciate fully his poetry, we should examine it from his depiction of the tensions inherent in it, tensions that are built on comparative paradoxes (Michelangelo, *The Poetry* 42). Specifically, we must capture his troubled dialogue with his inner soul, allowing his reflective conversation with himself to unfold the cultural and intellectual realities of his times.

In his poetry, Michelangelo negotiates historical fragments to represent for himself the true essence of death and its capacity for molding his own individuality as an artist, poet and human being. This rich tapestry of his poetic dialogue is built around Plato's sense of the binary opposition between death and life; for Michelangelo it is both true and ironic that in death lies the beauty of creation, which is both individual and universal life. In sonnet 84, **"Sì come nella penna e nell'inchiostro,"** written to Tommaso Cavalieri as his contribution to the Renaissance artistic dispute *ut pictura poesis [as is painting so is poetry]* (Clements 22), Michelangelo states that the search for the perfect word or the perfect artistic gesture resembles the arduous attempt to achieve clarity through the contemplation of the last things, i.e. death:

> Sì come nella penna e nell'inchiostro
> è l'alto e 'l basso e 'l medïocre stile,
> e ne' marmi l'immagin ricca e vile,
> secondo che 'l sa trar l'ingegno nostro;
> così, signor mie car, nel petto vostro,
> quante l'orgoglio è forse ogni atto umile;
> ma io sol quel c'a me proprio è e simile
> ne traggo, come fuor nel viso mostro.
> Chi semina sospir, lacrime e doglie,
> (l'umor dal ciel terreste, schietto e solo,
> a vari semi vario si converte),
> però pianto e dolor ne miete e coglie;
> chi mira alta beltà con sì gran duolo,
> ne ritra' doglie e pene acerbe e certe.

> [Just as within pen and ink there exist
> the lofty and the low and the middling style,
> and within marbles are images rich or worthless,
> depending on what our talents can draw out of them,
> thus, my lord, there may be in your breast
> as much pride as acts of humility;
> but I only draw out of it what's suitable
> and similar to me, as my faces shows.
> As earthly rain from heaven, single and pure,

> is turned into various forms by various seeds,
> one who sows sighs and tears and pains
> harvests and reaps from them sorrow and weeping;
> and one who looks on high beauty from great sadness
> is sure to draw from it harsh pain and suffering.]

With this sonnet, the poet enters into the Renaissance dispute over the aesthetic theory known as *ut pictura poesis*. The dispute concerned the similarities between poetry and painting and the aims of artistic creation. Michelangelo adopts a different approach from many of his contemporaries, who admit that parallels between painting and poetry existed, yet posited that one medium was superior to, or at least in competition with the other.[6] Michelangelo, however, believes that marble and ink are essentially equal in their power. It is the artist's gaze, "chi mira [who looks]" that translates the raw material into creative expression, for it ". . . a vari semi vario si converte [is turned into various forms by various seeds.]"

For Michelangelo, the artistic process begins with the artist's contemplating his raw material with "sì gran duolo [from great sadness.]". This painful process hones the artist's gaze through "doglie e pene acerbe e certe [harsh pain and suffering,"] emptying him out and allowing him to experience a void. The void then provokes the artist to desire the object of contemplation through a paradoxical process of oppositions: desire and its lack of fulfillment. These oppositions create tension between the presence and absence of the highest beauty, "alta beltà [high beauty.]" Although Michelangelo does not mention death as a part of the artistic process, the theme of death prevails through the artist's creation of a void. In **"Sì come nella penna e nell'inchiostro,"** Michelangelo portrays artistic contemplation as an ascetical process. Although "death" is a thought, which allows the artist to recognize himself, "ma io sol quel c'a me proprio è simile / ne traggo, come fuor nel viso mostro [but I only draw out of it what's suitable / and similar to me, as my face shows,] it is also a passage to enlightenment. Furthermore, Michelangelo argues that artistic gratification does not come from the delights and pleasures of life, but from suffering and pain. The suffering caused by the gaze on high beauty creates the void which is both desire and the inability to experience the complete pleasure of high beauty, as an object in itself of contemplation. This contemplation, in platonic terms[7] represents the search for perfect cosmic form and for the Christian the soul's return to God.[8] This unfulfilled desire molds the process that lies behind the ink and marble. The writing, the setting down, the chiseling away, the picturing, and the framing that the artist, the poet, and philosopher discover emerge from the contemplation of the true essence of what the individual "I" can see and create.

Perfection does not lie in the beauty of the final product. Rather it is a transcendent appetite, which induces the artist, poet and philosopher to contemplate eternal ecstasy.

Michelangelo's search for the perfect form recalls that of Lorenzo de' Medici, the Magnificent. In his *Comento sopra alcuni de' suoi sonetti,* Lorenzo states that the search for perfection is nothing but an appetite inducing the artist to contemplate formal perfection (De' Medici 34). Thus an artist is capable of representing this perfection of form only when his or her intellect can comprehend and decipher in Plato's sense, the "object in proportion." It is the artist's appetite/desire, which shapes this search for perfection, as Michelangelo portrays it in sonnet 151:

> Non ha l'ottimo artista alcun concetto
> c'un marmo solo in sé non circonscriva
> col suo superchio, e solo a quello arriva
> la man che ubbidisce all'intelletto.
> Il mal ch'io fuggo, e 'l ben ch'io mi prometto,
> in te, donna leggiadra, altera e diva,
> tal si nasconde; e perch'io più non viva,
> contraria ho l'arte al disïato effetto.
> Amor dunque non ha, né tua beltate
> o durezza o fortuna o gran disdegno,
> del mio mal colpa, o mio destino o sorte;
> se dentro del tuo cor morte e pietate
> porti in un tempo, e che 'l mio basso ingegno
> non sappia, ardendo, trarne altro che morte.

> [Not even the best of artists has any conception
> that a single marble block does not contain
> within its excess, and that is only attained
> by the hand that obeys the intellect.
> The pain I flee from and the joy I hope for
> are similarly hidden in you, lovely lady,
> lofty and divine; but, to my mortal harm,
> my art gives results the reverse of what I wish.
> Love, therefore, cannot be blamed for my pain,
> nor can your beauty, your hardness, or your scorn,
> nor fortune, nor my destiny, nor chance,
> if you hold both death and mercy in your heart
> at the same time, and my lowly wits, though burning,
> cannot draw from it anything but death.]

Michelangelo's appetite leads him to desire perfection of form, but once he realizes that this human appetite/desire is not capable of grasping the perfect essence of the object, the artist experiences imperfection, emptiness, a void. For Michelangelo this void is the very representation of death. This particular sonnet written to Vittoria Colonna[9] between 1538-44 has received ample commentary,[10] beginning in 1546 when Benedetto Varchi (1503-1564) lectured on the sonnet in the first of his *Lezzioni* at the Academy of Florence. Once again, as in the sonnet **"Sì come nella penna,"** Michelangelo ascribes creative power to the artist, saying "solo a quello arriva / la man che ubbidisce all'intelletto [by the hand that obeys the intellect.]" However, his intellect is incapable of grasping fully the very perfection of

Vittoria's beauty, thus his search for the ideal leads him to contemplate imperfection, the void, death itself. He laments that: "contraria ho l'arte al disïato effetto [my art gives results the reverse of what I wish.]" He senses his impotence, his lack of power when faced with the potential perfection hidden within his raw material, in the excess of the marble. Thus the process of creation leads him to experience the void of imperfection, powerlessness, death.

However, like Plato in the *Phaedo,* Michelangelo represents the search for true knowledge by means of a paradoxical process of "two sets of opposites, going round in a sort of cycle" (127). In the last two lines of the sonnet, the poet again laments the failed artistic vision. Michelangelo draws life from death in the arduous process of creation, in the burning intellect in which resides the desire for life. The artist's sense of powerlessness, of the void, moves him forward to understand the final powerlessness of death. Paradoxically this contemplation of death allows the artist to understand life itself.

Michelangelo's concept that the contemplation of death is analogous to reflecting on life itself is particularly notable in his unfinished sonnet 74:

> I' piango, i' ardo, i' mi consumo, e 'l core
> di questo si nutrisce. O dolce sorte!
> chi è che viva sol della sua morte,
> como fo io d'affanni e di dolore?
> Ahi! crudele arcier, tu sai ben l'ore
> da far tranquille l'angosciose e corte
> miserie nostre con la tuo man forte;
> ché chi vive di morte mai non muore.

> [I weep, I burn, I waste away, and my heart
> is fed by all this. O sweet destiny!
> Who else is there who lives only on his death,
> as I do, on suffering and pain?
> Oh, cruel archer, you know just the moment
> in which to put rest, with your powerful hand,
> our brief and anguished misery;
> for one who lives on death never dies.]

In this poem Michelangelo meditates on his own death and considers that this self-reflection helps him determine who he is as a human being. The reflection on his own death jolts him into thinking about the nothingness facing all human beings at the end of their earthly existence. However, the contemplation of the void allows him to measure the distance that separates life from death thus, reinvigorating his desire to live more fully by keeping the image of death before him—an image, which represents an ascetical movement. In Plato's terms, Michelangelo contemplates death as an "object in itself." This meditation illuminates his sense of self, allowing him to glimpse himself *sub specie aeternitatis.* Through this illumination, the poet sublimates the very idea of life and death, reframing his place within the scheme of things when he claims that ". . . chi vive di morte mai non muore [for one who lives on death never dies.]"

Sonnet 74 is also reminiscent of Petrarch's *Canzoniere,* bringing to mind the duality between appearance and reality in Petrarch's lyrical poetry. Giuseppe Mazzotta noted this tension in Petrarch's sonnet "Erano i capei:"

> Erano i capei d'oro a l'aura sparsi
> che 'n mille dolci nodi gli avolgea,
> e 'l vago lume oltra misura ardea
> di quei begli occhi ch'or ne son sì scarsi;
> e 'l viso di pietosi color farsi,
> (non so se vero o falso) mi parea:
> i' che l'esca amorosa al petto avea,
> qual meraviglia se di sùbito arsi?
> Non era l'andar suo cosa mortale
> ma d'angelica forma, e le parole
> sonavan altro che pur voce umana:
> uno spirto celeste, un vivo sole
> fu quel ch' i' vidi; et se non fosse or tale,
> piaga per allentar d'arco non sana.

> [Her golden hair was loosened to the breeze, which
>    turned in a
> thousand sweet knots, and the lovely light burned
>    without mea-
> sure in her eyes, which are now so stingy of it;
> and it seemed to me (I know not whether truly or
>    falsely)
> her face took the color of pity: I, who had the tinder
>    of love
> in my breast, what wonder is it if I suddenly caught
>    fire?
> Her was not that of a mortal thing but of some angelic
> form, and her words sounded different from a merely
>    human
> voice: a celestial spirit, a living sun was what I saw,
>    and if she were not
> such now, a wound is not healed by the loosening of
>    the bow.][11]

Mazzotta states that, although Laura's beauty[12] is the primary object of the poet's contemplation, it becomes "the pretext for raising what is perhaps the fundamental question of the sonnet, the meaning of appearance" (62). Therefore, "the poet's memory in a real sense . . . is the privileged metaphor" (61). Mazzotta continues that the most significant element in Petrarch's lyric poetry is the metamorphosis which occurs within the form of the narcissistic self: "Metamorphosis is for Petrarch the metaphor of spatial and temporal disloca- tion, the hint that no form is ever stable and that every form is always moving toward still other forms" (66). Petrarca professes himself unable to achieve serenity and calm in contemplating Laura's beauty and to arrive at a point of equilibrium within the turbulence of time and meaning surrounding his inspiration. Laura is the means through which the poet tries to achieve balance and serenity. The poet, aware of his own failure to ar- rive at a point of stillness, "by the act of memory . . .

tries to give Laura's apparition a stabilized and fixed presence that may redeem and abolish time; but the im- age cannot be deciphered" (Mazzotta 63). In Petrarch, the self, who exists in the tension between appearance and reality, confronts its own limits because it cannot reconcile itself within its own true form. Thus the es- sence of desire is its existence in perennial tension.

In Petrarch, the elements of appearance and reality are irreconcilable because "the conceptual implication of the story is clear: whatever authentic self-knowledge is possible, it is equivalent to death" (Mazzotta 65). In his poem, **"I' piango,"** Michelangelo, like Petrarch confronts the problem of imagination and reality. However, while Petrarch, in T. S. Eliot's words, cannot find the "still point of the turning world" in the contemplation of Laura's beauty, Michelangelo reaches this point in his contemplation of death. For Michelan- gelo contemplating the end of his earthly existence grants him the transcendental illumination necessary for all self-reflection, since through this is how the poet fully understands himself within a cosmic perspective. Therefore, the transcendence made possible by the meditation on his own death creates the distance neces- sary for achieving eternal life through art.

Michelangelo's poem 21 is a *memento mori,* a grim warning that death is the culmination of the inexorable passage of time; the poet describes time's ravages, which leads inevitable to death:

> Chiunche nasce a morte arriva
> nel fuggir del tempo; e 'l sole
> niuna cosa lascia viva.
> Manca il dolce e quel che dole
> e gl'ingegni e le parole;
> e le nostre antiche prole
> al sole ombre, al vento un fummo.
> Come voi uomini fummo,
> lieti e tristi, come siete;
> e or siàn, come vedete,
> terra al sol, di vita priva.
> Ogni cosa a morte arriva.
> Già fur gli occhi nostri interi
> con la luce in ogni speco;
> or son voti, orrendi e neri,
> e ciò porta il tempo seco.

> [Whoever's born must come to death
> in the course of time, and the sun
> doesn't leave a thing alive.
> Gone are joy and cause of sadness,
> and all thinking and all speech,
> and our ancient pedigrees,
> shadows in the sun, smoke in the wind.
> Once, we too were men like you,
> sad and joyful, just as you are;
> now we are, as you can see,
> dust in the sun, deprived of life.
> Everything must come to death.
> Once our eyes were fully whole,
> with a light within each cavern;

now they're empty, black, and frightful:
that's what time brings in its wake.]

In this poem, Michelangelo appropriates the Petrarchian image of Laura's eyes of "Erano i capei." In Petrarch's sonnet, Laura, the poet's muse and inspiration, is a "vivo sole [living sun]." But the sun has been extinguished and the muse's beauty, the beauty of a young woman, lives only in the poet's memory. Petrarch elegiacally remembers Laura in whom, the "vago lume oltra misura ardea / di quei begli occhi ch'or ne son sì scarsi [lovely light burned without measure in her eyes, which are now so stingy of it]." The poet's desire for Laura, the perfect image, dwells in the tension between the recollection in memory of a young Laura and in her reality as an old woman. In this shimmering tension, he tries, in dialectical terms, to fix in his memory the image of Laura, making her alive only through recollection.

Michelangelo however, reveals in the void. In contrast to Petrarch's living sun, he contemplates the avenging of the ". . . sole / [che] niuna cosa lascia viva [sun [which] doesn't leave a thing alive]". The eyes that in Petrarch's sonnet were once full of light and burned without measure, now become ". . . voti, orrendi e neri [empty, black and frightful.]" In Michelangelo's poem, time plays a role as in Augustine's *Confessions*. Of time's relentless passage, Augustine states that the passage of time does not turn uselessly through our senses, but transcends wondrous effects in our soul (IV.viii.13). Similarly, Michelangelo portrays the same movement of time, but also echoes Plato in describing its "wondrous effects." Time's very relentlessness, its continuous passage, creates a new space for the artist in which he is purified, emptied, and empowered to achieve greater self-knowledge.

In the *Phaedo,* Socrates states that true "philosophers abstain from all bodily desires and withstand them and do not yield to them" (142). Thus a philosopher's soul, in order to be set free by philosophy must follow reason and not "allow pleasure and pain to reduce it [the soul,] once more to bondage, thus condemning itself to an endless task" (143). Unlike Socrates, who in the *Phaedo* takes poison to terminate his life to arrive at the contemplation of the "true and divine and unambiguous" (143) form, Michelangelo chooses not to withdraw from earthly life. He prefers to live in the tension between life and death. In **"Canzone 22,"** the poet states:

> [. . .]
> L'anima mia, che con la morte parla
> e seco di essa stessa si consiglia,
> e di nuovi sospetti ognor s'attrista,
> el corpo di dì in dì spera lasciarla:
> onde l'immaginato cammin piglia,
> di speranza e timor confusa e mista.

(27-32)

[My soul is in conversation with Death,
and is consulting with him about itself,
saddened by new anxieties constantly,
the body hoping to leave it from day to day;
so it sets off down the road it's had in mind,
confused by its compounded hope and fear.]

Although Michelangelo's self-knowledge relies on and resides in the contemplation of life's ultimate end, death becomes sublimated within a never-ending dialectical process.

Furthermore, in poem 52 Michelangelo discusses the temptation to take one's own life in order to arrive at a higher form of existence:

> S'alcun se stesso al mondo ancider lice,
> po' che per morte al ciel tornar si crede,
> sarie ben giusto a chi con tanta fede
> vive servendo miser e 'nfelice.
> Ma perché l'uom non è come fenice,
> c'alla luce del sol resurge e riede,
> la man fo pigra e muovo tardi el piede.

> [If anyone's allowed to kill himself in this world,
> thinking to return to heaven through death,
> it would surely be justified for one who lives
> in such loyal service, wretched and unhappy.
> But, because man is not like the phoenix,
> which rises again and returns to the sun's light,
> I keep my hand slack and move my foot slowly.]

In this sonnet, Michelangelo affirms his belief that since we humans cannot rise like the phoenix from our own ashes, we are wise to refrain from ending our lives. Michelangelo, very much a part of Catholic culture,[13] refrains from taking his own life. Furthermore, in order for the "object" of death to continue to give meaning to his life as a human being and artist he must allow the void that he created by his very contemplation of death to persist so that he may gaze upon it indefinitely. Like Plato, Michelangelo recognizes that the human soul is "inconstant and variable" (137), but unlike the Greek Philosopher, he believes that the soul can become whole only through Christ's redemption, as we can see in his poetry of meditation and prayer written at the end of his life. Michelangelo's supplication in sonnet 293 shows his meditations on the soul; the poet prays:

> Carico d'anni e di peccati pieno
> e col trist'uso radicato e forte,
> vicin mi veggio a l'una e l'altra morte,
> e parte 'l cor nutrisco di veleno.
> Né proprie forze ho, c'al bisogno sièno
> per cangiar vita, amor, costume o sorte,
> senza le tuo divine e chiare scorte,
> d'ogni fallace corso guida e freno.
> Signor mie car, non basta che m'invogli
> c'aspiri al ciel sol perché l'alma sia,
> non come prima, di nulla, creata.
> Anzi che del mortal la privi e spogli,

prego m'ammezzi l'alta e erta via,
e fie più chiara e certa la tornata.

[Loaded down with years and filled with sins
and with bad habits, strong and deeply rooted,
I see that I am close to both of my deaths,
and yet I still nourish my heart with poison.
And I haven't, on my own, the strength that's needed
to change my life, love habits or destiny,
without your divine and shining companionship,
my guide and rein on every treacherous route.
It's not enough, dear Lord, just to make me yearn
for heaven, for my soul to be remade,
and not as it was the first time, out of nothing:
Before you strip it of its mortal flesh,
I pray you, shorten by half the high, steep road,
so my way back may be more clear and certain.]

In this sonnet, Michelangelo echoes Petrarch's idea of the weight of sin as delineated in "Io son sì stanco sotto '1 fascio antico [I am so weary under the ancient bundle.]" However, he also recollects the Christian philosophy of the two deaths seen in Paul's letter to the Corinthians (15:20-23). In this letter, Paul considers two types of death: the death of Adam, which represents the death of man as a sinner, and the death of Christ, which represents that of redemption. Death, for Paul, cannot be the consequence of sin and at the same time death in Christ. Death for the author of the letter to the Corinthians occurs as punishment for Adam's sin, but it is also the occasion through which humans participate in Christ's death. Thus death is both human frailty and the means by which we partake of the divine act of redemption. Although Michelangelo sees himself "vicin . . . a l'un e l'altra morte [close to both deaths,]" he is aware that in order to be redeemed, he must die in God's grace. Furthermore, he recognizes that human transcendence is limited and that it is not sufficient for God to implant in him the will to aspire to heaven. Thus he asks God to strip him of all that is mortal, so that he may participate in Christ's Calvary, the "erta via [steep road.]" This is the road which separates man from God and which was bridged only when Christ died to redeem humankind. In this sonnet, once again we observe sin and redemption, exemplars of Plato's two sets of opposites go around in a sort of cycle. However, this circular movement from God to man and from man to God also recalls Augustine's sense of eternal yearning to be with God. For Michelangelo, the path to eternal happiness is open only to those who die in God's grace.

Michelangelo negotiates in his poetry his way through a wide variety of symbolic discourses and historical signs; he bridges the tensions of these many discourses ranging through the platonic, Christian, neo-platonist, Renaissance humanist traditions to represent the theme of death as a source of life and artistic production. Michelangelo's poetry emerges as a way station in which these historical fragments intercommunicate and unfold, weaving themselves into the rich tapestry of his poetic dialogue. Through his poetry Michelangelo embeds himself in both metaphysical and artistic speculation about the ends of life and the relationship of human life and philosophical speculation. Thus, his poetry possesses a richness of texture that both explicates and gives purpose and life to the cultural reality, which surrounds him.

### Notes

1. For a general discussion of Michelangelo's artistic relationship to Socrates see (Barolsky, *Michelangelo's Nose.*)

2. Ascanio Condivi, Michelangelo's biographer, stated that he heard Michelangelo praise Plato many times and, like Plato, he was in constant pursuit of universal beauty (*Vita di Michelangelo*, 80).

3. All passages from Michelangelo poetry follow Saslow's bilingual translation (Michelangelo, *The Poetry*).

4. Unless otherwise noted, all translations from Italian are mine.

5. For a comprehensive bibliography on the controversy surrounding Michelangelo's poetry, see (Lucente, "Lyrical Tradition.")

6. For a discussion on Michelangelo's *Ut Pictura Poesis*, see (Renssalaer, "*Ut Pictura Poesis*" and Praz, *Mnemosyne.*)

7. For a general discussion on Michelangelo's Platonism see (Clements, *The Poetry of Michelangelo.*)

8. Michelangelo's Christian Platonism comes from Francesco Petrarca. For a discussion of Augustine's influence on Michelangelo's poetry see, (Mussio, "The Augustian Conflict.")

9. For a study delineating Michelangelo's poetry written for Vittoria Colonna, see (Fedi, "L'immagine vera".)

10. For a discussion of neoplatonic influences regarding this particular sonnet, see (Panofsky, "The Neoplatonic Movement" and de Tolnay, *The Art and Thought of Michelangelo*); and for a discussion of this sonnet in relation to Michelangelo's artistic relationship to the *concetto,* see (Altizer, *Self and Symbolism.*)

11. All passages from Francesco Petrarca's poetry follow Durling's bilingual translation (Petrarch, *Petrarch's Lyric Poetry*).

12. The inaccessibility of Laura's beauty can be compared to Michelangelo's concept of "altà beltà [high beauty]" of sonnet 84.

13. Even though Michelangelo was in close contact with the Italian Reformation, he remained a devout Catholic who never abandoned the teachings of the Roman church. In fact, from some of his letters we can see that he believed in the Sacraments of the Church. See the letter written to his nephew Leonardo on January 21, 1548 in which he speaks of Giovan Simone's last rights before his death in Michelangelo (552). For studies on Michelangelo's religious poetry see (Eisenbichler, "The Religious Poetry of Michelangelo" 121-134; de Tolnay (*The Art and Thought of Michelangelo* 100-123; and Francese, *Il 'nicodemismo' di Michelangelo* 143-148).

## Works Cited

Agostino [Santo]. *Confessions*. Vol. 1. A cura di Marta Cristiani, Luigi F. Pizzolano and Paolo Siniscalco. Milano: Fondazione Lorenzo Valla, Arnoldo Mandatori, 1993.

Altizer, Alma B. *Self and Symbolism in the Poetry of Michelangelo, John Donne, and Agrippa d'Aubigné*. The Hague: Martinus Nijhoff, 1973.

Barolsky, Paul. *Michelangelo's Nose: a Myth and its Maker*. University Park: The Pennsylvania State UP, 1990.

Buonarroti, Michelangelo. *The Poetry of Michelangelo*. Tr. James M. Saslow. New Haven and London: Yale UP. 1991

———. *Rime e lettere di Michelangelo*. A cura di Paola Mastrocca. Torino: U.T.E.T., 1992.

Clements, Robert. *The Poetry of Michelangelo*. New York: New York UP, 1964.

Condivi, Ascanio. *Vita di Michelangelo Buonarroti scritta da Ascanio Condivi suo discepolo*. Pisa: Presso Niccolò Capurro, 1823.

De' Medici, Lorenzo, *The Autobiography of Lorenzo de' Medici the Magnificent: A Commentary on My Sonnets*. Tr. James Wyatt Cook, together with *Comento de' Miei Sonetti*. Ed. Tiziano Zanato. Binghamton: Medieval & Renaissance Texts & Studies, 1995.

De Tolnay, Charles. *The Art and Thought of Michelangelo*. New York: Random House, 1964.

Eisenbichler, Konrad. "The Religious Poetry of Michelangelo: The Mystical Sublimation." *Renaissance and Reformation*. 1 (1987): 121-134.

Fedi, Roberto. "L'imagine vera': Vittoria Colonna, Michelangelo, e un'idea di canzoniere." *Modern Language Notes* 107 (1992): 46-73.

Francese, Joseph. "Il 'nicodemismo' di Michelangelo nei 'sonetti sulla notte'." *Quaderni d'italianistica*. 14 (1993): 143-148.

Lucente, Gregory L. "Lyrical Tradition and the Desire of Absence: Rudel, Dante and Michelangelo ('Vorrei uoler')." *Canadian Review of Comparative Literature*. 3 (1983): 305-306.

Mazzotta, Giuseppe. *The Worlds of Petrarch*. Duke UP, 1993.

Mussio, Thomas E. "The Augustinian Conflict in the Lyrics of Michelangelo: Michelangelo Reading Petrarch." *Italica*. 74 (1997): 339-359.

Panofsky, Erwin. "The Neoplatonic Movement and Michelangelo." In *Studies in Iconology: Humanistic Themes in the Art of The Renaissance*. New York: Harper Torchbooks, 1967.

Petrarca, Francesco. *Petrarch's Lyric Poems: The "Rime Sparse" and Other Lyrics*. Tr. and Ed. Robert M. Durling. Cambridge: Harvard UP, 1976.

Plato. *The Last days of Socrates*. Trans. Hugh Tredennick and Harold Tarrant. New York: Penguin Books, 1993.

Praz, Mario. *Mnemosyne: The Parallel between Literature and the Visual Arts*. Princeton: Princeton UP, 1970.

Renssalaer, Lee W. "*Ut Pictura Poesis*: The Humanistic Theory of Painting." *Art Bulletin*. 22 (1940): 197-269.

Vasari, Giorgio. *Le vite de' piú eccellenti architetti, pittori, et scultori italiani, da cimabue, insini a' tempi nostri*. A cura di Luciano Bellosi e Aldo Rossi. Torino: Giulio Enaudi Editore, 1991.

## Christopher Ryan (essay date 1998)

SOURCE: Ryan, Christopher. "Rough Beauty." In *The Poetry of Michelangelo: An Introduction*, pp. 231-55. London: Athlone Press, 1998.

[*In the following essay from his full-length treatment of Michelangelo's verse, Ryan defends his poetry from critical charges of roughness and fragmentation, also noting that the structure of Michelangelo's poems resembles his sculpture in their density.*]

[Elsewhere] I drew attention to a division of opinion regarding the quality of Michelangelo's poetry as a whole.[1] No study, however introductory, would be complete without confronting the problems underlying that division, even if these do not for the most part admit of definitive 'solutions'. [Here] I shall set out the broad lines along which I think the response can best be pursued to three major questions: what was Michelangelo's attitude to his own poetry? How is one to account for the negative assessments made by critics of that poetry? What are the features of Michelangelo's poetry that might lead one to a contrary, basically positive assessment?

Anyone who enjoys and values Michelangelo's poetry may appear to be in the uncomfortable position of esteeming highly a body of poetry held in little regard by its own author. Michelangelo appended brief comments to 44 of his poems, the great majority of which (35 in all) are unflattering to the poems concerned:[2] he several times calls them scribbles (*polizini*)[3] or clumsy things (*cose goffe*),[4] and often implies that they are, at best, worth only as much as the small gifts of food and wine for which they are presented as a form of thanks.[5] Furthermore, the two references Michelangelo makes within his poems to the quality of his poetry are, as we have seen,[6] similarly critical: he confesses to Berni that he blushes as he writes, since his poetry is rough and clumsy, not that of a professional (poem 85:46-8); and late in life he refers scathingly to his scribblings about love, the muses, flowery grottoes, which have met very unromantic fates (267:46-8).[7] However, it becomes clear from closer scrutiny that such negative comments do not in fact remotely amount to a general condemnation by Michelangelo of his own poetry, and indeed that the evidence indicating that he attached considerable importance to his poetry greatly outweighs such negative estimates of it as may be gleaned from those comments.

Let us take first the negative or dismissive comments appended to various poems. The total of 35 drops by almost half if we exclude, as we certainly should, the 17 comments attached to poems lamenting the death of Cecchino Bracci:[8] these poems (all but two of them quatrains) were, as we have seen, . . . laboriously written to fulfil, and in part evade, a personal debt to Luigi del Riccio, and need not be taken as anything other than idiosyncratic jottings from one close friend to another, referring to poems which must be deemed in any case among the slightest and weakest Michelangelo wrote. The remaining 18 comments (discussed immediately below) were again made to del Riccio; these, too, should be read as semi-jocular remarks to this close friend.[9]

The context and tenor of the self-criticisms made by Michelangelo within his own poems likewise preclude their being taken as definitive general comments. Both poems are extended humorous parodies, and we should no more take at face value Michelangelo's poetic self-description to Berni (in poem 85) than, say, his calling Berni's burlesque poetry in the same poem *divin carmi* or *versi belli*; and in poem 267 we cannot accept as straightforward his dismissing his love poetry as 'scribblings' (*scombiccheri*) at line 47, when we rightly regard as outrageous his reference two lines later to his visual works of art as 'so many rag-dolls' (*tanti bambocci*).[10]

Michelangelo's negative remarks certainly do, however, allow us, indeed compel us, to conclude that he was, to some extent, diffident about his own poetic powers, and

that he regarded at least some of his poems as being so rough as to benefit from revision even by such poetic non-professionals as Luigi del Riccio and Donato Giannotti. The latter point is clear from the comments he appended to seven of the poems he sent to del Riccio (Giannotti's judgement is invited, via del Riccio, on three of these occasions).[11] These range from the laconic 'Revise as you see fit' that follows poem 208 (a quatrain), to the somewhat more extended: 'Messer Luigi—You, who have the spirit of poetry—please would you shorten and revise one of these [two] madrigals, whichever seems to you the less lamentable'.[12] None of the 35 negative remarks, however, refers to any poem which the majority of critics would regard as among Michelangelo's best[13] (and indeed in the view of the present writer only a handful of the poems which received such comments are of more than indifferent quality).[14] The only conclusion we are certainly justified in drawing is, then, that as regards a considerable number of his weaker poems, Michelangelo was not averse to being facetious and also, in the case of some of these, recognized that they could benefit from revision. Few even of the greatest admirers of his poetry would dispute Michelangelo's implied judgement on these poems.

The counter-evidence, suggesting that Michelangelo did in fact attach considerable importance to his own poetry, is altogether more persuasive. In the first place, no one, least of all a man of Michelangelo's sensitivity to criticism, would have planned to bring out a substantial selection of his poetry (about a hundred pieces) if he had regarded that poetry as of little worth; yet, as we have seen, this is what he planned to do in the mid 1540s, through the agency of del Riccio (who had the assistance of Giannotti).[15] Furthermore, we know that Michelangelo devoted a great deal of time and energy to this project: he revised the extant poetry he intended to include, and appears to have written a number of poems specifically for the project. It *may* indicate some hesitation on Michelangelo's part regarding the value of his poetry that he did not carry the project to completion after del Riccio died in 1546. However, two other very different considerations may well have weighed equally or more with him, one aesthetic or personal and one practical: for whatever reason, Michelangelo chose not to include in the projected work many of his finest poems,[16] and he may after del Riccio's death have come to wonder about the value of publishing an anthology which did not display the full range of his poetic powers; and for such an impractical man as Michelangelo, who had relied on two close friends (first Angiolini, then, when he died, del Riccio) for much of the management of his affairs, the practical consequences of the latter's death must have been far-reaching, especially since no one else seems to have filled any comparable role after 1546. The fact that the project was aborted, then, does not by any means invalidate its attestation to

Michelangelo's deeming his poetry to be of more than minor interest.

Secondly, Michelangelo's so-called *canzoniere* administers the *coup de grâce* to any proposal that the 18 dismissive or flippant comments on poems outside the Cecchino Bracci series indicate either that his judgement on the poems concerned was totally negative or that those comments signify a dismissive attitude by their author to his poetry as a whole. For the simple fact of the matter is that Michelangelo wished all 18 of these poems to be included in the projected anthology; and the poet cannot have held simultaneously that these poems were devoid of all merit and worthy of publication.

In addition, the considerable energy Michelangelo undoubtedly devoted to revising his poetry as a whole points in the same direction. As Girardi's critical edition makes clear, the great majority of Michelangelo's poems underwent some degree of revision.[17] In the case of 54 poems the eminent editor regards those revisions as having been of sufficient significance to merit their being printed in his critical apparatus as distinct drafts through which the poems progressed to reach their final form;[18] twelve such drafts of poem 81 are given, for instance, and poems that underwent between four and seven such revisions are common.[19] Moreover, major revisions were by no means confined to the poems Michelangelo prepared for the aborted publication: 27 of the 54 poems so revised had no connection with that project.[20] Nor were the reworkings merely something that Michelangelo indulged in to overcome the failings of his early poetic apprenticeship: only six of the 54 poems subjected to such major revision belong to the 55 poems composed before the great central period began in 1532.[21] Moreover, eight of the 36 poems of the final period were substantially reworked,[22] three of these undergoing five or more revisions.[23]

Further confirmation of the fact that Michelangelo did indeed attach importance to his poetry is to be found in such evidence as we have of his response to public recognition of his poetry: his letters expressing gratitude to Arcadelt for setting one of his madrigals to music,[24] and to Varchi for his lecture to the Florentine Academy on his poetry,[25] show understandable pleasure at the poems' being given such acclaim, and no hint of anger or fear that they might be ridiculed.

If, then, there is nothing of weight in Michelangelo's attitude to his own poetry to inhibit us from esteeming it highly, and much to support our so doing, what is to be made of the negative judgement passed on it by a significant number of Italian literary critics, whether explicitly by denying it major importance or, perhaps more damningly still, implicitly by condemning it to the category of meriting scant mention at best?[26] With

the literary tradition before Guasti's epoch-making edition of 1863 had made the poetry available in a relatively comprehensive and accurate form, we need not concern ourselves. Furthermore, there is *some* force in the argument that it is really only since the relatively recent critical edition of Girardi (1960) that Michelangelo's poetry has been readily susceptible of just evaluation, and that literary criticism in general and survey histories of criticism in particular will take some time properly to absorb and accord a place to his poetic achievement. It would, however, be unwise simply to ignore the judgement of such major figures of modern literary criticism as Croce, Toffanin and Fubini, who, while acknowledging some minor merits in Michelangelo's poems, have denied that his corpus as a whole constitutes a significant poetic achievement. The negative criticisms of Michelangelo's poetry may be summed up under two heads: it is too fragmentary, and it is too rough.[27] Each of these criticisms can, I believe, be partly, though only partly, met. Let us consider them in turn.

When the charge of fragmentariness is so fundamental as to amount to the claim that Michelangelo attained notable poetic expression only in occasional lines, or passages of a few lines, then, I would submit, that criticism will not hold. In evidence I would refer to the presentation and analysis of a significant number of poems in the various chapters above, among which I would point principally to the outstanding and very different achievements of the sonnets 5, 10, 41-2, 58-9, 83, 87, 102, 105, 151, 285 and 293; the madrigals 133, 153, 161 and 258; the *capitoli* 85 and 267; the *barzelletta* 21; and the double sestet 164.

A second, less dramatic way in which the charge of fragmentariness can be directed at Michelangelo's poetry is to note that he left a significant number of poems incomplete. As it stands, however, this charge is too broad, and careful distinctions need to be made. The term incomplete or unfinished is often attached to all poems of Michelangelo which do not contain the minimum number of lines required for inclusion in an established genre. This is particularly the case with the sonnet form, in which such incomplete or unfinished instances abound: 37 all told.[28] Although this still leaves a very substantial corpus of 79 complete sonnets,[29] 37 poems is a significant number. However, if one brings into play the distinction I made early in my discussion . . . , restricting the term unfinished to those poems in which words or lines are undoubtedly missing, and designating simply as partial those poems which are grammatically complete and observe the poetic form within the number of lines they do have, then the situation changes dramatically. On this definition there are only nine unfinished sonnets;[30] these undoubtedly are fragmentary in the every sense. The remaining 28 incomplete sonnets, which will here be termed *partial*,[31] are certainly fragmentary, but only in the restricted sense that they could have been fuller; it seems very likely that at least the great majority of them represent attempts at sonnets that were never carried through to completion.[32] Even in their partial state, however, several of these sonnets constitute a satisfying and often interesting piece of poetry in their own right, and may well represent all that Michelangelo wished to say on a given occasion. The principal evidence for such an assessment must be the quality of the partial sonnets themselves; I would suggest consideration of poems 32, 37-9, 257 and 279.[33]

The case of the madrigal is somewhat more complicated in view of the looser definition of its form. . . . Here it is sufficient to say that in the strict definition of an unfinished poem adopted here (one which is grammatically and semantically incomplete because a word, line or lines is missing), only one of Michelangelo's 99 madrigals is unfinished; there are in addition three madrigals which may be judged incomplete or partial in that imperfection in their rhyme-scheme may indicate that the poet intended to complete them at a later date but did not do so.[34] On any account, however, Michelangelo wrote a considerable number of complete madrigals, 95 in all.[35]

Indeed if one looks at Michelangelo's poetry as a whole, a similar conclusion must be drawn to that just made regarding his principal genres. Overall, there are only 15 poems that are unfinished in the strictest sense,[36] a figure which clearly constitutes only a very small proportion of Michelangelo's 302 poems. Even if one adds to these the 33 partial poems (mainly sonnets),[37] the number of poems that may be deemed incomplete in any sense rises only to 48, still a relatively small proportion which leaves a substantial body of 254 complete poems.

There is a third sense in which the charge of fragmentariness may be levelled at Michelangelo's poetry: the vast majority of his poems are confined to the shorter forms, ranging from the occasional isolated couplet or tercet,[38] through the much more frequent quatrain,[39] to the sonnet[40] and madrigal,[41] the two principal genres. Of the 20 poems which do not fall within these shorter categories,[42] only 12 are of more than 20 lines,[43] and of these 12 only six are complete.[44] It is only a partial riposte to this objection that for the most part the themes of which Michelangelo treats are so immense that no poem of any length could hope to do justice to them, for it can equally well be argued that such vast topics demand, at least some of the time, essays in the longer genres. The nub of this objection is that Michelangelo is not, in his own way, either a Dante or a Petrarch. That is both true and regrettable. It would be wrong to conclude from this that there is *no* unity to Michelangelo's corpus, since, as I have tried to show, a basic set of

themes centring on love and religion do recur; but Michelangelo's unwillingness, or, as seems more likely, his inability to explore these themes successfully in anything longer than the sonnet and madrigal forms does constitute an undoubted limitation. Such a limitation, however, cannot of itself condemn a poet totally. To use an analogy from Michelangelo's visual art, we may be sorry that his poetry contains no equivalent of the Sistine Ceiling, the New Sacristy or even the Last Judgement; this still allows us to believe that the poetry we have is akin to Michelangelo's smaller works, perhaps most of all to his drawings, with even some poetic equivalents of his few presentation pieces.[45] It is much to be grateful for. All in all, the fragmentariness present in Michelangelo's poetry is not such as to prevent one from regarding that poetry as a notable, if undoubtedly limited, achievement.

The second principal head under which objections may be made to ascribing high value to Michelangelo's poetry is roughness. My short reply to such an objection is to accept that in many ways the poetry is rough, but to maintain that how greatly that characteristic will constitute an obstacle to valuing the poetry will vary from person to person. More so even than in the case of formal imperfection (with which it is clearly connected), the presence of repeated, and in many cases, poetically unjustifiable roughness of diction and grammar will preclude some from esteeming highly anything other than a small proportion of Michelangelo's poems. If a person finds that fluency and correctness of expression are necessary conditions of good poetry, then he must deem that much of Michelangelo's poetry fails to meet the test.

I shall argue below both that Michelangelo's poems are often not as rough as they seem at first sight, and that, even where roughness is present, this is not always a defect and may even be an intended poetic strength. I fully accept, however, that often in Michelangelo's poetry there is a roughness which is simply unpleasant to the ear, constitutes a barrier to understanding and seems to originate either in Michelangelo's imperfect command of language or in an unwarrantable disregard on his part of the simple proprieties of speech. Such, for instance, are his frequent use of the indicative when a subjunctive or conditional is clearly demanded (see, e.g., *era* at 99:10); his disconcerting substitution of one part of speech for another (e.g., *esse* supplying for *cui* at 167:8, 'l'ali, / con esse mi giugnesti'); his failure fully to complete a phrase when that completion is delayed for poetic effect (e.g., at 135: 8-9, where *timore di morte* comes out thus: 'Fra 'l timore e gl'inganni / d'amore e morte'); the appearance of isolated phrases lacking any form of verb (as at 66:3, '[. . .] perché dell'altrui colpe più non rida, / *nel mie propio valor, senz'altra guida,* / caduta è l'alma che fu già sì degna'); or even at one point his making use of that perennial verbal refuge, the infinitive, when something more complex is called for (204:3: 'se più c'averne copia or m'ama molto'). If to these frequent grammatical errors are added occasional faults in metre and rhyme,[46] then it is clear that roughness must be accepted as a major feature of Michelangelo's poetry, and more than understandable that some should find its pervasive presence an insurmountable barrier to a positive appreciation of Michelangelo's poetry as a whole. I shall now try to articulate why, like many others, I find such defects in Michelangelo's poetry more than outweighed by its merits.[47]

There can be no doubt that for many of us it is awareness of Michelangelo's immense attainments in the visual arts that first stimulates us to approach his poetry, and it seems reasonable to assume that knowledge of greatness in the one realm predisposes us to make a favourable assessment of his attainments in the other. Such a predisposition has its dangers, of course (as negative critics of the poetry have not been slow to point out),[48] but, if linked to a concern for strictly poetic qualities, appreciation of the nature of Michelangelo's greatness in the visual arts can be turned to good account, by making us sensitive to central features of the poetic achievement itself.

In the first place, awareness of certain broad features of Michelangelo's achievements in the visual arts can help to make us alert to some major characteristics of his poetic style. As we have seen, Michelangelo in his poetry refers to sculpture as the *prim'arte*;[49] and further witness to sculpture as his greatest concern is given in his letters.[50] Even without this written testimony, however, we would have little doubt of sculpture's primacy in Michelangelo's achievements in the visual arts: a considerable number of his paintings and drawings evince marked sculptural qualities, most notably perhaps many of the figures on the Sistine Ceiling.

That predilection for sculpture marks his poetry, too, not just in the most obvious sense that Michelangelo in creating poetry evidently found that sculpture much more often supplied him with imagery to express his thoughts than any other form of art,[51] but in the more subtle sense that in its very texture the poetry frequently shows sculptural qualities.[52] Several times in the discussion of individual poems I have had occasion to allude to one such quality: the thudding sound created by the rhythmic beat of strong accents, reminiscent of hammer blows on a chisel. This major feature of Michelangelo's poetry will, I hope, in view of the previous discussion, adequately be evoked in the reader's mind by recalling such lines as 'tomm'a me stesso e famm'un che ti piaccia' (from the central period, 161:17), and 'c'aperse, a prender noi, 'n croce le braccia' (from the final years, 285:14). Here I wish to concentrate on a connected sculptural quality to which attention is less frequently drawn: the sense of mass or density created by Michelangelo's poetry.

Although Michelangelo was, occasionally at least, capable of lines or even entire poems of great clarity, his poetry does not by and large make for easy reading. At times, as we have noted, the difficulty stems from imperfection, notably grammatical inaccuracy. Often, though, the poetry cannot be readily comprehended because of certain stylistic features which together convey a sense of mass or volume (with a corresponding difficulty for intellectual penetration). Odd though it may seem, Michelangelo's words often create not just an aural or visual but also a tactile sensation, as if the poem had the weight and texture of a hard, substantial piece of stone.[53] When allied to a sense that a poem is not just weighty but cleverly crafted, the experience of reading Michelangelo's poetry can be akin to that of being in the presence of sculpture. The total impression is, of course, created by a multiplicity of stylistic qualities operating at once, but I would highlight two recurrent features as being particularly influential in evoking the basic sense of mass: ellipsis, and inversion of word order.

Ellipsis by its very nature creates a sense of density, for the words we have on the page say less than the writer intends to be understood, so that objectively there is more there than at first sight meets the eye; and subjectively the reader, to reach understanding of what is being said, must struggle to evoke what is only suggested, not stated. While any set of grammatically intelligible words has more than two dimensions, in the broad sense that the words 'contain' meaning, the sensation of words' being three dimensional is greatly heightened if the element of within-ness is emphasized by the reader's being forced to recognize that implied in the words is more meaning than they initially seem to bear.

Ellipsis in Michelangelo's poetry[54] is often found in the use of a single word where, strictly, two or more are demanded, as when, in poem 192, he makes the word *suo* convey the sense of the dead person's being dear to the one who is mourning his death: 'in riso ogni suo doglia / preschiver debbe alcun del *suo* defunto' ('everyone must replace with laughter all his weeping for any dead person *dear to him*': 8-9). Sometimes a short phrase is inserted whose meaning becomes clear if we bear in mind the Latin roots of the Italian language: thus, for instance, the economical construction of the Latin ablative absolute is pressed into service at 86:45, 'come *tuo mezzo* qui nascer mi volle' ('here where *by means of you* [heaven] wished me to be born'); and later in the same poem 'Deo gratias' ('thanks [be] to God'), a phrase (itself elliptic in form) that would undoubtedly have been familiar to Michelangelo's readers from the Catholic Mass, appears (in equally elliptic form) in Italian guise, 'dove, *Die gra-za,* ti prosumo e stimo [. . .]' ('where, *through the grace of God,* I presume and believe you are [. . .]': 64).[55]

At other times the meaning of an entire group of lines depends on our being able to discern that a key term needs to be added, explicated from what is stated. Perhaps the most startling, and certainly one of the most difficult, examples of this occurs in poem 293, where the sense of the first tercet turns on our being able to supply a missing word. The lines, already encountered above . . . read:

> Signor mie car, non basta che m'invogli
> c'aspiri al ciel sol perché l'alma sia,
> non come prima, di nulla, creata.

(My dear Lord, it is not enough for you simply to implant in me the will through which one aspires to heaven for my soul to be [recreated, and] not simply, as it was before, created from nothing.)

As they stand, these words fail to make sense, for the verb at the end of line 10, *sia,* lacks a past participle. What seems to be happening here grammatically is that the past participle at the end of line 11 (*creata*) is being made to fulfil the dual role of completing both the sentence 'perché l'alma sia' and the phrase 'non come prima, di nulla'. If this is the case, then the first implicit *creata,* at the end of line 10, has to be distinguished mentally from the second (at the end of line 11) by being understood as referring to a *second* creation (a *re*creation, as I have translated).[56] The supplying of some word such as *ricreata* is both demanded logically and accords fully with the New Testament background against which this poem ought to be read, where salvation is often described as a new creation, a recreating of man through Christ in the image of God after this image has been blurred by sin.[57] This is a particularly dramatic example of ellipsis, but it does, I think, convey well the sense of compactness often experienced when reading Michelangelo's poetry.

A similar sense of words being tightly bound is effected by the inversion of word order, a feature encountered at least as often as ellipsis in Michelangelo's poetry. When the meaning of words does not emerge clearly from the page, does not flow out in accordance with rhythms that have become natural to a language, then the first impression we have of the words concerned is that of an impenetrable mass. When on a second or subsequent reading, after the work of mental reconstruction has revealed that there is indeed meaning giving form to the words, then the first impression is not entirely dispelled: it remains that of a mass, but shaped now rather than formless. If our repeated reading reveals not only that there is a basic shape, because the words can convey meaning when reconstructed according to more normal, natural patterns of the language, but also that the specific shape given by the poet carries a force and a nuance that are lost by any restructuring of them, so that the original poetic structure now stands forth as being not just intelligible but intelligent, finely and uniquely crafted, then the analogy between poetry and sculpture becomes sharper still.

It is true, of course, that inversion of word order is commonly to be found in poetry. It is, however, used with such intensity and frequency by Michelangelo as to be distinctive, immensely reinforcing the sculptural quality of his poems. A passage whose subject matter is itself unity or binding may aptly serve as a first example. In poem 34, a sonnet, Michelangelo is anxious to convey to his beloved that he loves him (or her—the gender is unspecified) with a spiritual love, and that in loving him he loves God. Lines 9-11 are designed to reinforce that claim, made in the octet, by asserting the inseparability of Michelangelo's power of discernment and the divine beauty:

> Come dal foco el caldo, esser diviso
> non può dal bell'etterno ogni mie stima,
> ch'exalta, ond'ella vien, chi più 'l somiglia.

(My discerning power itself can no more be separated from the eternal beauty than can heat from fire; it exalts whoever most resembles him from whom it comes.)

Here Michelangelo begins at the end: so anxious is he to convey the inseparability of his *stima* and eternal beauty that he begins not with the first but with the second term of the comparison he is making, in which second term separation is physically impossible: 'Come dal foco el caldo [. . .]'. Within the immediately following main clause, setting out the first term (which is psychological or spiritual), the normal word order is reversed to bring out the indivisibility being claimed: the key words, containing the verb 'esser diviso non può', are shot out at the beginning of the sentence, even though, of course, this requires delaying the subject to the end, the effect being all the more forcefully obtained by the reversal of verb (*non può*) and predicate (*esser diviso*) and the breaking up of the grammatical unit 'diviso dal bell'etterno'. The transposition of the subject, predicate and verb has the further advantage that, through the resulting proximity of the predicate and verb to the second term of the comparison in the opening line of the sextet, these need not be repeated *vis-à-vis* that second term, but may readily be understood as applying also to it. In the subordinate clause, too, which constitutes the final line of the tercet, transposition is the order of the day. The main thrust of the entire poem is to assert the linking of the human and the divine in Michelangelo's love; when in line 11 the poet wishes to declare that he exalts the Creator in the created, he is so eager to give pride of place to the Creator that he introduces a second subordinate clause highlighting

God's role before completing the first on which the second depends grammatically: *ond'ella vien* qualifies the as yet unmentioned *'l* of the following clause.

Clearly, dramatic anticipation and its opposite, unexpected delay, are crucial to the successful use of the inversion of word order. Michelangelo can deploy either a single word or an entire clause for such purposes. . . . [One] of the revealing moments in poem 86 occurs when Michelangelo speaks of his own sensitivity to pain. The tercet which calls forth from him this, in the context, unusually personal remark begins: 'Nostri intensi dolori e nostri guai / son come più e men ciascun gli sente' (25-6). These two lines are given much of their force by the simple anticipation of *intensi,* the essential adjective, as the second word of the sentence, although it ought not, in strict grammatical terms, to appear until much later; here a combination of anticipation and ellipsis allows Michelangelo to convey in two dense lines what might otherwise have to read (ignoring other demands of the poetic line): 'Nostri dolori e nostri guai son [più e men] intensi come ciascun più e men gli sente.'

Sometimes the anticipation of a single word is much more violent, requiring considerable effort to find the apt place to which it may, mentally, be transposed. Such is the case with *qual* at 66:5: 'Né so qual militar sott'altra insegna / non che da vincer, da campar più fida [. . .]' ('I know no other standard under which to fight that will give greater hope, not of victory but of escape [. . .]'). For most of us, it may take some little time before we realize that *qual* modifies *altra,* and that line 5 needs to be reconstructed in the following order if it is to make sense: 'Né so sott[o] qual altra insegna militar'.[58] Having thus reconstructed, we may admire the boldness of Michelangelo in giving the essential word a more prominent position in the sentence, thereby also enabling him aptly to begin a line expressing hesitation and puzzlement with the halting rhythm of three successive monosyllables: 'Né so qual'. If slowness in finding the meaning of line 5 does occur, the reader of the poem may take comfort from the fact that his or her difficulties are compounded by Michelangelo's delaying a key element for understanding that meaning until the end of the quatrain: for the phrase *più fida* of line 6 only makes sense if we know that with which it is being compared, that which would give greater hope, and this we are not allowed to do until line 8 when Michelangelo adds 'ove 'l poter tuo non sostegna', thus: 'sie che 'l tumulto dell'avverse strida / non pèra, ove 'l poter tuo non sostegna' ('so that the tumult of the hostile shouts may not cause me to perish, where your power does not sustain me'). Had the final phrase (or equivalent) of line 8b occurred at the beginning of the quatrain, then our difficulties would have been, if not removed, at least lightened. That, though, would have been at a price, for the delaying of the

phrase to the end of the quatrain helps the poet achieve two effects: it allows him fully to match and carry forward at the beginning of the second quatrain the uncertainty with which the poem had opened (the hesitancy of 'Né so qual' at line 5 matches rhythmically the express tone of the opening 'Forse perché'); and it enables him to pair and contrast the downfall of his own soul, spoken of at the end of the first quatrain ('caduta è l'alma che fu già sì degna'), with the potential source of its uprightness, mentioned at the end of the second quatrain ('ove 'l poter tuo [. . .] sostegna'). If, on reflection, we would prefer not to have our difficulties lightened, then we should take full cognizance of the implications of the natural occurrence to us of that word 'lightened': here, as often elsewhere, the effect of Michelangelo's words is not one of lightness but of weight and mass, though these are shaped to his purposes.

Awareness of the primacy of sculpture in Michelangelo's visual art may, then, make us more readily appreciate the sculptural quality of his poetry. A second way in which familiarity with basic features of Michelangelo's visual art can help us to recognize or articulate fundamental qualities of his poetry is by focusing our attention on the dramatic interplay in the poetry of boundless energy and bounded form, comparable to that operative in his visual art. It is a feature of Michelangelo's visual art that, although it is marked by forceful, even violent movement,[59] it by and large works within the limits of the forms Michelangelo is depicting. In particular, the almost exclusive subject of that art, the human figure, although it twists and turns in various expressions of an enormous energy animating it, is generally portrayed as observing the parameters of the human body, disregard of which would make the figures unrealistic and the energy both less notable and less credible. More positively, one reason why Michelangelo's portrayal of the human being catches our attention is that when the artist depicts two characteristics that are often in tension, the aspiration towards the infinite and the constraints of finite limits, he creates figures which are at once immensely powerful and believable.[60]

The various chapters of this book will, I hope, already have sufficiently made clear the energy which characterizes much of Michelangelo's poetry, and in particular the central role played by movement in his poetic depiction of the human being: movement *outwards* in human love, towards the ideal of human beauty (both physical and spiritual), and supremely movement *upwards,* towards the absolute perfection of beauty, truth and goodness which, for Michelangelo, really existed in the form of a personal God. We have seen also how in his poetry Michelangelo's descriptions of beauty strain language in a whole variety of ways. What I should now like to do is to draw attention to the fact that in his poetry, too, Michelangelo observes very definite limits.

The attraction of Michelangelo's poetry (for those able to accept its imperfections) is in no small measure due to the fact that immense energy and boundless aspiration express themselves within the severe limits of short poetic forms.[61] One may indeed conclude that in his best poetry those very limitations operate not just as a constraint, but as a means of liberating and directing energies which might otherwise have raged uselessly within. To illustrate this point I shall here concentrate on the rhyme-schemes of the two principal poetic genres within which Michelangelo worked, the sonnet and the madrigal.[62] Both, patently, are short forms, whose very brevity itself imposes tight limits precisely when the content of the poems written in them is of notable interest and range.[63] What merits some comment are the further, particular constraints under which Michelangelo himself chose to operate in what were already genres with closely bounded limits.

From its first appearance in Italy in the thirteenth century, the sonnet had a tightly shaped poetic form.[64] Although that form had changed somewhat by the sixteenth century, the evolution had not been in the direction of making fewer demands. The line-length remained hendecasyllabic throughout, while the structure evolved clearly into two groups of lines, consisting of a double quatrain followed by a double tercet. The rhyme-scheme within both quatrains was the same, almost exclusively ABBA (*rima incrociata*), although with very occasional variations, principally in the scheme that had been favoured by the earliest sonneteers, ABAB (*rima alternata*). The sestet allowed for greater variety in its rhyme-scheme: the clear majority of Italian sonnets of the sixteenth century were of two equally common patterns, CDE CDE (*rima ripetuta*) and CDC DCD (*rima alternata*), but other patterns were often used (particularly CDE EDC, CDC CDC and CDC EDE).

In their rhyme-schemes all of Michelangelo's sonnets conform to these accepted norms. Indeed his sonnets evince a greater tightness of form than that usual in the sonnet *oeuvre* of most of the Italian poets of his time. In his complete sonnets he only once, in poem 43, makes use in the octets of the still admissible scheme ABAB, confining himself otherwise to ABBA. And in the sestets, rather than follow the pattern found in most poets, that of frequent use of the two common sequences (CDE CDE, CDC DCD) with a generous sprinkling of the less usual forms, Michelangelo restricts himself in the sestet of 70 of his 79 complete sonnets to the *rima ripetuta* (CDE CDE), while the other nine all have the *rima alternata* (CDC DCD),[65] with no instance of any of the less common patterns.[66] Moreover, Michelangelo's attachment to the *rima ripetuta* scheme in the sestets appears to have increased with experience. Four of the 13 sonnets written before 1532 do not conform to this pattern,[67] but the proportion drops to four out of

51 in the central period[68] and one out of 15 in the final years.[69] In expressing himself so frequently in the sonnet form, then, and in further imposing his own severe limits within that already strict form, Michelangelo was setting himself a demanding poetic challenge. It seems reasonable to conclude that he felt that the tightness of the sonnet form, enhanced by his own self-imposed limits, enabled him to produce some of his best poetry.[70]

In contrast to the sonnet, the madrigal in early sixteenth-century Italy had a very loose poetic form indeed (within the constraint of overall brevity).[71] Commenting on the madrigals of his time, Pietro Bembo (the most important observer and arbiter of literary practice in early sixteenth-century Italy) exaggerated only slightly when he wrote: 'everyone gives [madrigals] the form that seems most pleasing to him'.[72] Although madrigals occasionally consisted of either only hendecasyllables or only heptasyllables, they were normally a free combination of both of these line-lengths, with the median number of lines being about 12.[73] As regards rhyme-scheme, all that was required by common practice was that no more than three line-endings should be unrhymed; in addition, most (though by no means all) madrigals ended with two hendecasyllablic lines that rhymed with each other (the delightfully named *rima baciata*, 'kissed rhyme', which I shall call coupled rhyme). The rhymes in the body of the poem could be either coupled (e.g., AABB), alternate (e.g., ABAB) or delayed (e.g., ABBCABC).

It is often noted that in writing in the madrigal form Michelangelo was adopting a much looser genre than any of the others he employed, looser by far than the sonnet, to which it compared roughly in length (the median length of Michelangelo's madrigals is in fact 13.5 lines). What is not usually observed is that, in using this looser form, Michelangelo adhered strictly to such 'rules' as there were, and frequently went far beyond them in imposing his own more tightly organized form.

Michelangelo did, of course, adhere to the universal practice of using only hendecasyllables and heptasyllables, and in fact in all of his madrigals without exception he adopted what was simply the more normal custom of mixing the two line-lengths. As for the one strict 'requirement' of rhyme, that no madrigal should contain more than three unrhymed endings, it is striking that in his 95 complete madrigals Michelangelo never makes use of the 'maximum' number of three unrhymed line-endings;[74] indeed 89 of his madrigals have no unrhymed line-endings at all.[75] As regards the frequent tendency in the madrigal writing of his day to end with two rhyming hendecasyllables, 86 of Michelangelo's complete madrigals end in this way; of the other nine, eight have no final *rima baciata*,[76] and one ends with a *rima baciata* but not with two hendecasyllables.[77] It is noteworthy that the eight madrigals which end without a coupled rhyme confirm rather than disprove that Michelangelo worked to a definite plan in composing his madrigals, for it is not the case that these eight poems simply lack a rhyme that the others have. These eight poems differ not just in the matter of rhyme but of line-length: for whereas all the final two lines with coupled rhymes are hendecasyllables (with the one exception noted), the opposite is the case with the two final lines that are unrhymed: only one of these eight couplets consists of two hendecasyllables;[78] it seems evident that where Michelangelo does not end with a rhymed hendecasyllabic couplet, he is attempting to achieve his ends by a different poetic technique, rather than merely failing to measure up to a common though not absolutely necessary standard.

Clearly, the very low number of unrhymed line-endings and the high number of final hendecasyllables in coupled rhyme show Michelangelo's desire to go beyond the strict requirements or common form; it was a desire he showed in several other, less easily noticeable ways. A further look at the 86 madrigals which end with a coupled rhyme in hendecasyllables will reveal that all but three of these (all three of which, moreover, are among Michelangelo's earliest poems) end with not one but two pairs of coupled rhymes.[79] Furthermore, there is a strongly dominant line-length within this penultimate rhymed couplet, for in 66 out of these 83 cases this couplet consists of a hendecasyllable followed by a heptasyllable.[80] Two-thirds of Michelangelo's madrigals, then, show that he had a marked preference for ending with two pairs of coupled rhymes with a pattern in the number of syllables per line: 11 + 7 + 11 + 11. Again the exception to the rule tends to prove rather than disprove the view that Michelangelo worked to a plan in composing his madrigals. Of the 17 rhymed penultimate couplets which do not conform to the line-length scheme of a hendecasyllable followed by a heptasyllable, 16 consist of two lines of the same length: 11 of two heptasyllables,[81] and five of two hendecasyllables.[82] In the case of the first of these groups, the majority of the lines in the body of the poem are heptasyllables in all but one of the 11 poems,[83] and it seems that Michelangelo wished to end by pairing in the final four lines the lightness of the dominant shorter line (in the penultimate couplet) with the weightier hendecasyllables ('required' in the final couplet); in the case of the other five madrigals, the two final couplets of hendecasyllables serve to emphasize the dominance of this longer line in the body of all five poems.[84]

Although the positive stylistic features of Michelangelo's poetry to which I have so far pointed [here]— sculpture-like density, and immense vitality bounded by strict form—are admirable in their own right, they must in the last analysis be linked to a further factor, if that poetry is to be judged of major interest: the quality of thought expressed.[85] Michelangelo's poems for the most part lack the melodiousness which may either compensate for or enhance the particular beauty intrinsic to powerful thought;[86] neither sonority nor rhythmic incantation spares or softens for Michelangelo's poetry as a whole the stark question of whether it warrants serious intellectual attention. It is because I believe that such a question can be answered very much in the affirmative that I would most wish to champion his poetry. Here, as on other matters of poetic evaluation, personal factors undoubtedly play a part, but certain recurrent themes of Michelangelo's poetry can be specified as offering a basis for judgment. Since the poetry has been considered in detail in the course of this book, I need do no more here than recall some salient points from earlier discussions.

Two aspects of Michelangelo's thought stand out as particularly worthy of attention, and each links closely both to his art and to the positive stylistic qualities which consideration of that art can bring to the fore. It is often noted, but bears repetition, that the first and last of what may be considered Michelangelo's truly great works of visual art have the same subject: death, and specifically the poignancy of death, illustrated in quite different ways in the early St Peter's *Pietà* and in the two *Pietà* of Michelangelo's final years. The parallel with his poetry is close: his first, halting poem of any kind (**'Molti anni fassi qual felice, in una'**) is concerned with death, its suddenness and ineluctability; and the first of his poems to merit attention as a major piece in its own right, in no way dependent on autobiographical interest (**'Chiunche nasce a morte arriva'**, poem 21), is likewise solely and unflinchingly concerned with the transience of life and the universality of death. Most of the poems of Michelangelo's late years, too, several of them among the finest of his *oeuvre* (poems 285 and 293, for example, **'Giunto è già 'l corso della vita mia'**, **'Carico d'anni e di peccati pieno'**), are concerned with the same theme. Indeed the thought of death was never far from the poet's mind, not even in the great central period (when perhaps the possibilities of life most fully beckoned him), as in their different ways **'Veggio nel tuo bel viso, signor mio'** (83) and **'Condotto da molt'anni all'ultime'ore'** (133) bear witness. There is, no doubt, a native wisdom in the fact that 'human kind / cannot bear very much reality';[87] equally, though, we condemn ourselves to immaturity if we construe a view of life that ignores or minimizes death. Michelangelo as poet no less than as visual artist would have us not forget.

This grim theme rings the more true because it is set within a poetically more dominant one of a rich appreciation of life; and, as befits an artist, what most fully draws this poet is the encounter with beauty. For Michelangelo the poet as for Michelangelo the artist, it is, as I have remarked before, specifically human beauty that he wishes almost exclusively to celebrate. Unless we are strikingly odd members of the human race, it does not take Michelangelo or any other poet to make us alive to the multiple beauty to be found in our fellow human beings. Few of us, though, will have been able to give voice to our emotions as did Michelangelo, in such poems as **'S'un casto amor, s'una pietà superna'** (59), **'Veggio co' be' vostr'occhi un dolce lume'** (89) and **'La forza d'un bel viso a che mi sprona?'** (279). These poems and their many companions may not only articulate but school our emotions, reminding us that human beauty is a complex interplay of matter and mind, body and soul, physicality and personality.

Most of all, perhaps, Michelangelo's enthralment with human beauty can draw us towards what has been called a second innocence. Central to his celebrations of human beauty is the fact that he found within it a fuller and more permanent beauty, which, in common with the mainstream religious tradition and the most vital philosophical movement of his time (Christianity and Neoplatonism), he was happy to call divine. It is hardly to be expected that merely through contact with Michelangelo's poetry the non- or a-religious reader of today will feel moved to adopt the profoundly religious viewpoint of the poet; and, it may be said, it is as little likely that many of today's religious readers will feel inclined to endorse Michelangelo's particular set of beliefs. But all of us, religious or not, may be brought to *wonder* about the depths in human beauty, and to question ourselves about life's ultimate horizons, when faced with a poet who was, *at least* in the visual arts, inspired to the greatest heights by what he regarded as the infinite beauty to be glimpsed through finite, human beauty. In the oft-quoted line 'l'amor mi prende e la beltà mi lega' (41:9), we sense the degree to which Michelangelo was entranced by human beauty; in **'Per fido esemplo all mia vocazione'** (164) we hear of the artistic dedication with which inspiration by beauty had to be twinned; and recurrently we are brought face to face with the fact that Michelangelo was moved as he was by human beauty because he believed that in it he caught sight of a *transcendent* beauty that urged him to expressive heights. He could thus address a fellow human (Cavalieri) in these words of monumental simplicity: 'La tuo beltà non è cosa mortale' (78:9). For most of us, 'the trivial round, the common task'[88] deaden rather than lift, and risk confining us totally to the all too mundane. The innocence of a Michelangelo writing such poetry in his full maturity and old age may help evoke and quicken the perennial youth within us all.[89]

A. J. Smith remarks: 'Michelangelo's brevity is often the condition of this chiselled weight, language cut down cleanly to the bone as the poet strives for an ultimate condensation of felt thought with so little concern to be easy or smooth.' Turning specifically to the first quatrain of the sonnet **'Deh fammiti vedere in ogni loco!'** (274), he comments: 'However rough hewn, it is certainly not crude; there is a rhetoric at work. [. . .] A very little attention to the arrangement of clauses will show how carefully the syntax has been managed to catch not merely the balances and emphases but the cadences, nuances, pitch of the mood.' This is but one example; the critic adds immediately: 'Such writing does not come by chance, and there are like effects everywhere in this poet. They have evidently been worked at, hard and subtly.'[90] With these judgments I am happy to concur. I would add that if, along with strictly linguistic achievements, the surest mark of great poetry is that it has a capacity deeply to move its readers and, it may be, also profoundly to change them, then I believe that, taken as a whole, Michelangelo's poetry well merits that accolade.

### Notes

1. See *The Poetry of Michelangelo: An Introduction*, pp. 12-13.

2. The 35 negative or dismissive comments accompany poems 62, 91, 130-1 (a single comment), 132, 136, 143, 145, 157, 167, 169-73, 233, 241 and 253-4; and, among those in the highly distinctive series in memory of Cecchino Bracci (179-228), 190, 192-4, 196-9, 201, 206-8, 211, 214, 218, 223 and 228. Michelangelo makes non-evaluative comments on poems 148, 156, 231, 242 and 250; and, in the Cecchino Bracci series, 186, 195, 216 and 219. All the comments may be found in Girardi; for translations, see Ryan. See also nn. 7 and 10 below.

3. In notes attached to poems 172 and 241 Michelangelo refers generically to the poems he is sending to del Riccio, which were intended for publication, as so many scribbles; poems 143 and 169 in this group he specifically dismisses with the same term. Likewise the earliest poems to del Riccio on Cecchino Bracci's death are called 'fifteen scribbles' (in comments accompanying poems 196 and 197).

4. Poems 194, 211 and 214; the same adjective is applied to the poems in comments to poems 193 and 199. All these poems are in the Cecchino Bracci series.

5. Poems 143, 145, 157, 167, 233; and in the Cecchino Bracci series, poems 190, 194, 198-9, 201, 206-7, 218 and (possibly) 223.

6. See *The Poetry of Michelangelo: An Introduction*, pp. 195 and 203.

7. To these comments of Michelangelo should be added a remark of Condivi, which may reflect something said by the subject of his biography: 'But [Michelangelo] has attended to these matters

[i.e., the writing of poetry] more to give himself pleasure than to make a profession of them, and he has always denigrated himself and alleged his ignorance in these things' (p. 68). See also n. 10 below.

8. See *The Poetry of Michelangelo: An Introduction,* n. 2.

9. The same may be said of the remarks made to Vasari quoted in n. 10 below.

10. Michelangelo more than once deprecated the value of his works of visual art. Vasari reports that 'Michelangelo's judgement was so severe that he was never content with anything [i.e., any work of art] he did'—a point on which the art historian then elaborates (p. 404). See also *Ca* CMLXXX-VII (*Let* 212); further evidence on this point is set out by Clements, pp. 140-1. Such remarks by Michelangelo regarding his art no doubt reflect both his chagrin at not being able to realize his own high ideals and a native shyness. It is basically the same spirit, I believe, that is reflected in the remark of Condivi quoted above, n. 7 (although Michelangelo's description there of himself as not being a poet by profession was certainly true). We should also remember that Condivi's remark is immediately preceded by a highly laudatory comment: '[Michelangelo] has taken delight not only in reading but also in sometimes composing verse himself, as witness some of his existing sonnets, which give a very good example of his great inventiveness and judgement'; and indeed his life of Michelangelo ends with similar praise, and the expression of a hope (never realized) of publishing some of Michelangelo's sonnets and madrigals (see n. 15 below). A note of shyness with regard to his own poetry is certainly present in Michelangelo's wry remark to Vasari: 'You will say rightly that I am old and foolish in wishing to write sonnets, but because many people say that I am in my second childhood I've tried to fulfil my part' (*Ca* MCXCVII / *Let* 390); the humour is all the more striking, and admirable, in that this comment is made in a letter accompanying poem 285, one of Michelangelo's finest sonnets, on a profoundly personal religious theme (*The Poetry of Michelangelo: An Introduction,*, pp. 205-9). Michelangelo wrote in a similar vein, also to Vasari, in a letter accompanying two other deeply felt religious poems (288-9): 'I'm sending you two sonnets and although they're simple I do so that you may see whither my thoughts are tending, and when you have reached eighty-one years, as I have, you will believe me' (*Ca* MCCVI / *Let* 399).

11. Poems 130-2, 136, 192-3 and 208; Giannotti is referred to in the notes appended to 132, 136 and 192.

12. Poem 130: see *Ca* CMXCVII (*Let* 223; I have slightly amended the translation in *Let,* which reads here 'the least lamentable'). Cp. the care Michelangelo expressed for revision by himself, *Ca* CMXCV (*Let* 220); and more generally his care for language: *Ca* CMLXXX (*Let* 210). Michelangelo's care for language is surely also reflected in two public honours which came his way: election to the Florentine Academy (on the occasion of Varchi's lectures delivered before it, in 1547), a body dedicated to the study of Italian literature and the promotion of linguistic correctness (see Bull, p. 342), and the dedication to him of Lenzoni's *Difesa della lingua fiorentina,* which he gratefully accepted (De Maio [1987], p. 450).

13. Poem 241 ('Negli anni molti e nelle molte pruove'), singled out by some critics as a fine example of the mutual illumination of art and poetry, may be an exception; to the present writer, however, the basic image of that poem seems too contrived to carry the weight that Michelangelo would have it bear.

14. Poems 62, 132, 192, 233, 241 and 254.

15. The poems Michelangelo intended to publish are, in the Girardi numbering, 62-3, 81, 88-93, 95, 97, 103-4, 106-9, 112-14, 116-50, 153-9, 162-3, 166-78, 229-33, 239-42, 246-50, 252-5, 258-9, 261 and 264. Frey lists 105 poems, but these include six poems which Girardi regards as earlier drafts of the following poems in his numbering: 91, 109, 118 (two drafts), 168 and 252: see Fedi (1990), pp. 302-5. For a summary of the MSS evidence regarding which poems Michelangelo intended to publish, see *ib.,* pp. 298-30; see also the notes in Girardi to each of the poems. The only poem about whose inclusion in the intended publication there is still some dispute is 175; Girardi's view that this poem was intended to be included seems justified: see *ib.,* p. 360. As noted above (*The Poetry of Michelangelo: An Introduction,* chapter 2, n. 6), it seems likely that Condivi's life of Michelangelo was completed with the assistance of the subject (see, e.g., Bull [1987], pp. xi-xii, and [1995], pp. 351 and 354); the biographer's final words may, therefore, also indicate a desire on Michelangelo's part to see his poetry published: 'I hope within a short while to publish some of [Michelangelo's] sonnets and madrigals, which for a long time I have collected both from him and from others'. Condivi's intention was never realized.

16. He chose to exclude all of his poetry written before 1532, despite the great merits of, e.g., poems 5, 10, 21 and 42. Particularly notable absences from the poetry composed after that date are 58-9, 83, 87, 102, 105, 151, 161, 164 and 260. It is striking that Michelangelo omitted more than

half of the poems for Cavalieri (and, in the present writer's judgment, all of the best of them), while he included all of those to the supposed 'beautiful and cruel lady', none of which is of outstanding quality.

17. Cambon (1985) constantly draws attention to the extent and importance of these revisions. See also Girardi (1974), pp. 97-110.

18. Poems 23, 25, 34, 43, 45, 47, 58, 62, 66, 72, 76-7, 79, 81, 84, 86, 88, 91, 106, 109, 118, 131, 143, 146, 148, 150, 155, 157, 159, 162, 168, 174, 178, 193, 230, 235-6, 239, 246, 248, 252, 255-6, 258-9, 262, 272, 276, 285, 288-90, 294 and 296.

19. Poems 66, 72, 76, 106, 146, 157, 159, 174, 236, 246, 256, 259, 262, 272, 285, 288-9 and 296.

20. Poems 23, 25, 34, 43, 45, 47, 58, 66, 72, 76-7, 79, 84, 86, 192, 235-6, 256, 262, 272, 276, 285, 288-90, 294 and 296.

21. Poems 23, 25, 34, 43, 45 and 47.

22. Poems 272, 276, 285, 288-90, 294 and 296.

23. Poems 285, 289 and 296.

24. See *Ca* CMLXIV (*Let* 217) and *Ca* CMLXV (*Let* 216).

25. Varchi's lecture focused on 'Non ha l'ottimo artista alcun concetto' (poem 151), but ranged widely. Michelangelo's thanks to Varchi are offered in *Ca* MLXXVI (*Let* 279); cf. also *Ca* MLXXIX, MLXXXII and MCXLIII (*Let* 281, 280 and 343).

26. See *The Poetry of Michelangelo: An Introduction*, pp. 12-13.

27. Although most critics refer to both characteristics, the predominantly negative evaluations by Parodi (1916), Cerini (1931), Bottari (1935), Fubini (1964), Toffanin (1965b) and Muscetta and Ponchiroli (1971) draw particular attention to fragmentariness, while Croce (1957) accentuates roughness (on which see also Nelson [1974]). Two English critics from very different eras have turned the thrust of the latter criticism by drawing on the classical idea that beauty is born of the 'artist's' struggle with a medium that yields to being shaped only with difficulty: Pater (1893, p. 57) quotes the dictum 'ex forti dulcedo' ('sweetness from [what is] strong'), and Clements (p. 25) similarly 'chalepta ta kala' ('beautiful things [are] difficult'); Bizzicari (1964, p. 252) argues in a like vein, as does Malagoli (see n. 54 below)

28. Poems 1, 15, 17-18, 24, 26-7, 32, 36-40, 44, 50, 52-3, 65, 69, 74-5, 100, 237, 257, 271, 273, 275, 279-81, 283-4, 286, 291-2 and 301-2. I leave aside here independent quatrains and tercets.

29. The complete sonnets are poems 3-6, 10, 23, 25, 34, 41-3, 46-7, 58-63, 66, 71-2, 76-80, 82-4, 87-90, 94-5, 97-9, 101-6, 150-1, 159-60, 166, 178, 193, 230, 233, 236, 239, 243, 248, 250-1, 259-61, 266, 272, 274, 276-7, 285, 288-90, 293-6 and 298-300.

30. The unfinished sonnets are poems 17, 40, 50, 65, 271, 273, 275, 281 and 302.

31. The partial sonnets are poems 1, 15, 18, 24, 26-7, 32, 36-9, 44, 52-3, 69, 74-5, 100, 237, 257, 279-80, 283-4, 286, 291-2 and 301.

32. It is highly instructive in this respect that only six of these poems were written during the great central period (poems 69, 74-75, 100, 237 and 257), while 14 (the poems up to 53 in the list given in the previous note) come from before then, when we may assume that Michelangelo was still working towards full poetic maturity, and eight from after 1547 (poems 279 and following in the previous note), when his powers must surely have been flagging.

33. Two other very short poems of high quality are 48 (a tercet) and 247 (a quatrain). Some indirect evidence that Michelangelo accorded value to partial sonnets is to be found in the fact that he included two quatrains in his intended anthology: in Girardi's numbering, poems 177 and 247.

34. The clearly unfinished madrigal is poem 268; the possibly incomplete or partial madrigals are 19, 28 and 115.

35. Michelangelo's undoubtedly complete madrigals are poems 7-8, 11-12, 30-1, 81, 91-3, 107, 109, 111-14, 116-49, 152-8, 161-3, 165, 167-76, 192, 229, 231-2, 234-5, 240-2, 244-6, 249, 252-6, 258, 262-5 and 269.

36. Poems 17, 33, 40, 45, 50, 54, 65, 70, 86, 268, 271, 273, 275, 281 and 302. It is noteworthy that there are only two unfinished poems (65 and 86) from the central period.

37. The partial poems are the 28 sonnets and 3 madrigals mentioned above (nn. 31 and 34) and poems 35 and 67. There are, then, in total 15 unfinished and 33 partial poems.

38. These are respectively poems 16, 29, 270 and 278; and 48, 110 and 282.

39. There are 60 quatrains: 48 in the Cecchino Bracci series (179-91, 194-228) and poems 2, 9, 49, 56-7, 64, 73, 177, 238, 247, 287 and 297.

40. As indicated above (notes 29-31), there are 79 complete sonnets, 28 partial sonnets and nine unfinished sonnets.

41. For the one unfinished, three partial and 95 complete madrigals, see nn. 34-5 above.

42. These by genres are: six *ottave* (20, 54-5, 67-8, 108), six *capitoli* (35, 45, 85-6, 96, 267), two *canzoni* (22, 51), two *sestine* (33, 70), a *barzelletta* or *frottola* (21) and a double sestet (164). Two free verses or short prose passages form a case apart (13 and 14): see *The Poetry of Michelangelo: An Introduction*, p. 37.

43. Poems 20, 22, 33, 45, 51, 54, 67-8, 70, 85-6 and 267.

44. Poems 20, 22, 51, 68, 85 and 267.

45. On parallels between Michelangelo's poetry and his drawings, see, e.g., Rivosecchi (1965), p. 94, Hirst (1988), pp. 106-7 and Girardi (1988), p. 482.

46. On such faults see Girardi, pp. 536-7, and Clements, pp. 32-3. Basic as such defects are, their extent ought not to be exaggerated: see Friedrich (1964), p. 339. Cambon (1985, p. 103) argues that these blemishes are the price Michelangelo paid for linguistic experimentation.

47. It seems reasonable to suggest that one reason why by and large Michelangelo's poetry has received if not warmer at least more widespread recognition beyond the borders of Italy than within may lie precisely in the non-native Italian's being less liable to find offensive the multiple linguistic deficiencies of that poetry. For a similar observation, see Friedrich (1964, p. 381); a connected point may be that, as Rivosecchi (1965, pp. 87-8) and Montale (1976, p. 18) surmise, Michelangelo's metre may reveal itself more to the eye than to the ear.

48. See, e.g., Parodi (1916), Fubini (1964) and Toffanin (1965b).

49. See 237:2; cf., for similar phrases, 5:20, 86:13-15 and 267:52. Michelangelo refers to sculpting (normally by way of pointing up an analogy with human life) much more than to any other visual art: see especially poems 46, 151-2, 237, 239, 240-2, 247 and 282; for further indications of the primacy of sculpting, see ch. 3, n. 9. Painting is normally mentioned only as one of a pair, with sculpture: see 84:1-4, 86:13-15, 90:1-8, 111:11-13, 164:1-3, 178:5-6, 236:1-8, 267:49-55 and 285:12-14. For one who worked so much in the medium of paint, references to painting alone are remarkably scarce and undeveloped: see 79:12-14, 173:11-16 and 202; and cf. 5, 85:31-6 and 165:5; even references to the art of metalwork are almost as frequent, and much richer: 24:5-6, 62:1-4 and 153 *passim*; cf. also 46:9-14.

50. See, e.g., *Ca* LXII, MI and MLXXXII (*Let* 45, 227 and 280); see also the references at ch. 3, n. 9, *The Poetry of Michelangelo: An Introduction*.

There seems no reason to doubt Condivi's statement that he heard Michelangelo declare that when later in life he looked at his early sculpture the Battle of the Centaurs (which he retained in his own possession) 'he realized how much wrong he had done to nature in not readily pursuing the art of sculpture, being able to judge from that work how well he could have succeeded' (pp. 15-16).

51. See n. 49 above.

52. On the sculptural qualities of Michelangelo's poetry, see especially Mariani (1941), Galassi (1942), Flora (1965) and Girardi (1988).

53. Beall (1964, p. 239) notes finely: '[Michelangelo] has a sense of the weight and mass and density of language, and of the lyrical possibilities of these physico-verbal properties.' See also Mariani (1941) *passim, id.* (1966) and Smith (1985), pp. 172-3.

54. Cambon (1985, p. 157) draws attention to Michelangelo's frequent experimentation with elliptical phrasing, although this suggests to him the artists's 'transferring to verbal language the foreshortening effects that mark his painting'; cf. also Malagoli (1968, p. 132), who sees ellipsis as reflecting Michelangelo's delight in rising to the challenge of voicing what can be expressed only with difficulty.

55. For a similar use of a phrase modelled on *Deo gratias,* see 106:12: 'né Dio, sua grazia, mi si mostra altrove [. . .]' ('but God, in his graciousness, does not show himself to me elsewhere [. . .]'.

56. For another instance of a single past participle being used where logically two are demanded, see the final line of 243: 'L'acceso amor, donde vien l'alma sciolta, / s'è calamita al suo simile ardore, / com'or purgata in foco, a Dio si torna' ('The love enkindled, by which the soul is freed, will act like a magnet to draw the ardour that is similar to itself, and so the soul, like gold, purified by fire, will return to God'): *purgata* directly governs *l'anima* of line 12, but, for the analogy to hold between gold and the soul that has suffered in love before dying, the past participle must be regarded as also governing *or,* which has been purified in physical fire as the soul has been purified in love, implicitly understood as a spiritual fire.

57. Redemption from sin by Christ is described as a new creation at *2 Corinthians* 5:17; *Galatians* 6:15; *Ephesians* 2:10 and 15, and 4:24.

58. I believe Saslow (1991, p. 162) is mistaken in taking *qual* as qualifying *militar* (which he understands, rather arbitrarily, as 'soldier'): cp. Dobelli (1931), Girardi, Barelli (1975), *ad loc.*

59. Summers (1981, p. 71) notes that the depiction of life and movement was Michelangelo's main concern in art.

60. Martino (1991, p. 79) roundly declares that in Michelangelo's early work of sculpture the Battle of the Centaurs it is the tussle (*zuffa*) between the bestial and the divine which generates movement; this view may, *mutatis mutandis,* be applied more widely to Michelangelo's art, and poetry.

61. On this point see the acute observations of Mariani (1941), pp. 16-17. Girardi (1974, p. 99) notes with admirable succinctness: 'Michelangelo ha bisogno di costringersi in poco spazio per trovare la sua forza' ('Michelangelo needs to confine himself in a small space to release his power').

62. Critics are divided regarding which of these two genres Michelangelo preferred and which most suited his talents. Those who favour the madrigal include Gilbert, De Vecchi, Beall, Fubini, Sapegno, Bonora, Girardi, Binni, Hallock, D'Angelo and most recently Fedi. To regard Michelangelo's sonnets as superior is presently a minority opinion, although it does not lack authoritative champions such as Clements, Bosco and Smith. I am firmly in the latter camp: while the madrigals as a whole undoubtedly make for easier reading, the sonnets are, in my view, much more rewarding linguistically and intellectually. The tendency in English to refer to Michelangelo's poetry as his 'sonnets' may well reveal a healthy critical bias, not just a debt to John Addington Symonds, the first major translator of Michelangelo's poetry into our language, whose volume (1878) took its name from the genre that vastly predominates in his selection: *The Complete Sonnets of Michel Angelo Buonarroti* [. . .]. Interestingly, even Condivi speaks specifically of the sonnets when he wishes to praise the quality of Michelangelo's poetry: see the passage quoted in n. 10 above. Lanster (1993) has recently suggested that the stone-like firmness of the sonnet form may be linked to the incidence of stone images in the sonnets of Michelangelo (among others).

63. This point is, of course, crucial to the argument developed here: it is only when a poet strives to express thought and feeling of some depth and complexity that these shorter forms are experienced as challengingly constrained. The sixteenth-century is replete with examples of sonnets which are loose and limp, the result in large measure of triteness of thought or shallowness of emotion.

64. In this section I am deeply indebted for material on the development of the various genres of Italian poetry to the recent work of Orlando (1994), one of whose many merits is an ample and up-to-date bibliography; Orlando often offers a fuller and more analytical treatment than that accorded by Elwert in his classic study (1973). On the sonnet, see the sections in Elwert (1973, pp. 125-34), Ramous (1984, pp. 235-40), Beltrami (1991, pp. 236-48), Orlando (1994, pp. 187-95), and the introduction by Ruschioni (1985) to his selection of sonnets from the Italian tradition.

65. The nine sonnets in question are 10, 25, 43, 47, 71, 98, 101, 248 and 299.

66. Fedi (1990) points out that fully 12 of the 13 sonnets Michelangelo intended to include in his selection for publication use the *rima ripetuta* in the octet, but he seems unaware of the almost complete dominance of the scheme in Michelangelo's sonnets as a whole. The contrast this critic helpfully draws between the pattern in Michelangelo's sonnets in the intended anthology and the patterns in the sonnets of Della Casa and Giolito holds, therefore, with respect to all of Michelangelo's sonnets: whereas Michelangelo throughout uses only three rhyme schemes, Della Casa employs 13 and Giolito 17. The difference is striking, even when due account is taken of the fact the number of sonnets composed by the other two poets was much greater.

67. Poems 10, 25, 43 and 47.

68. Poems 71, 98, 101 and 248.

69. Poem 299.

70. Even Michelangelo's partial and unfinished sonnets witness in their own way to the poet's attachment to unusually strict limits. Only four of his 28 partial sonnets (see n. 31 above) contain irregularities in their rhyme-schemes (1, 18, 75 and 283); another two have schemes unusual for Michelangelo but common in sixteenth-century sonnet practice (38 and 53); while the remaining 22 follow his preferred pattern of ABBA in the quatrain(s) and CDE in the tercet(s). All nine of Michelangelo's unfinished sonnets (see n. 30 above) as far as they go (ranging from five to twelve lines) follow his preferred pattern. It almost goes without saying that all of Michelangelo's 60 isolated quatrains (see n. 39 above) have the scheme ABBA.

71. For the poetic form of the madrigal, see the sections in Elwert (1973, pp. 134-6), Beltrami (1991, pp. 281-3 and 322-3), Orlando (1994, pp. 146-52), and the specialist studies by Ariani (1975), Capovilla (1982), Fabbri (1988) and Harrán (1988). For the musical settings of the madrigals of this period in Italy, see Einstein (1971), and Fenlon and Haar (1988).

72. '[C]iascuno sì come ad esso piace così le forma', *Prose della volgar lingua,* II.xi; on this passage, see the comment by Orlando [1994], pp. 146-7.

73. The claim that 12 is the median number of lines was made by the sixteenth-century writer G. Ruscelli; his accuracy on this point is open to doubt, however: see Harrán (1988), p. 105.

74. On the definition of a complete madrigal adopted here, see above p. 237. For a list of the 95 undoubtedly complete madrigals, see n. 35 *The Poetry of Michelangelo: An Introduction.*

75. Of the other six, two have two unrhymed line-endings (poems 11-12) and four have one (poems 7-8, 152 and 165). It is noteworthy that four of the six madrigals with unrhymed line-endings are among Michelangelo's earliest poetry.

76. Poems 8, 30, 113-14, 123, 152, 165 and 231.

77. Poem 246: this poem's penultimate line is heptasyllabic.

78. Poem 30. Of the other seven, the heptasyllable precedes the hendecasyllable in all but one (poem 8).

79. The exceptions are poems 7, 11 and 12.

80. The exceptions are poems 31, 92, 107, 109, 120, 124, 129-30, 134, 146, 148, 155, 229, 249, 253, 255 and 269.

81. Poems 31, 107, 120, 124, 129-30, 134, 146, 155, 229 and 255.

82. Poems 92, 109, 148, 249 and 269. The odd one out of the 17 poems is 253, whose penultimate couplet consists of a heptasyllable followed by a hendecasyllable.

83. The exception is poem 124, in which hendecasyllables predominate. It may be noted that poem 31 has an equal number of heptasyllables and hendecasyllables.

84. Some of the most interesting evidence of Michelangelo's desire to set himself in the madrigals to work within limits beyond the norm is, paradoxically, not at first sight clearly evident. Since (with every justification) modern editions of Michelangelo's poetry mingle the various genres according to a proposed chronological sequence, it is difficult quickly to get a sense of how Michelangelo's madrigals break down into groups according to the number of lines of which they are composed. In fact the vast majority of his complete madrigals are of between 9 and 17 lines (89 out of 95: the exceptions are poems 7 and 30 [6 lines]; 127 [eight lines], 91 [eighteen lines], and 123 and 147 [nineteen lines]), and of these the lengths Mich-

elangelo most decidedly preferred were 13 and 15 lines, of which there are 18 and 21 respectively (poems 81, 93, 109, 111, 116, 118, 126, 132-3, 136, 154, 163, 235, 240, 249, 253-4, 262; and 122, 134, 140, 143, 148, 155-8, 162, 168, 172, 174, 232, 234, 242, 244-5, 252, 256, 258; the nearest rival is the madrigal of 17 lines, of which there are 10 examples: 92, 119, 121, 128-9, 161, 175, 246, 255 and 263). When one probes these two groups of poems, one finds that within them Michelangelo worked in a majority of cases to a single pattern of rhyme: 13 of the 18 madrigals of 13 lines have the identical rhyme-scheme ABBAACDACDDEE (poems 93, 109, 111, 118, 126, 132-3, 136, 163, 235, 249, 254, 262), and the same number of the 21 madrigals of 15 lines have the scheme ABBCACCDECDEEFF (poems 143, 148, 156, 158, 162, 172, 174, 232, 234, 242, 244-5, 258). Over a quarter, then, of all Michelangelo's complete madrigals (26 out of 95) conform to two rhyme-schemes. Similar if less frequent patterns are to be found in three of the other, smaller groups of madrigals: in these three, roughly half of the madrigals have the same rhyme-scheme. This is most notably the case with the eight madrigals of nine lines: five of these eight conform to a single pattern, ABBCACCDD, and the other three to the pattern ABCABCCDD (respectively poems 137-8, 144, 171, 176; and 142, 167, 169); it may be noted that all eight poems in this group end with the double coupled rhyme CCDD. In the seven madrigals of 11 lines, three show the same rhyme-scheme, ABBCACCDDEE (poems 130, 141, 269; the other poems in this group are 107, 131, 152 and 229); this, clearly, is identical to the pattern in the main subgroup of five in the nine-line madrigals, with the addition of a further coupled rhyme. Similarly, four of the nine madrigals of 14 lines have an identical rhyme scheme, ABBCACCDEDEEFF (poems 145, 149, 192, 264; the others are 31, 112-13, 146, 170). Lest these examples of smaller groups which have a single rhyme-scheme in roughly half of the poems be dismissed as accidental, it should be noted how much they differ from the other groups of Michelangelo's madrigals with which they may reasonably be compared: the groups of 12 lines (eight examples), 16 lines (six examples) and 17 lines (ten examples): in the first two of these groups no two madrigals have the same rhyme-scheme, and in the third group only two do so.

85. On the particular importance of considering Michelangelo's thought for an evaluation of his poetry, see especially Garin (1966) *passim*; see also Ker (1888), p. 21, Friedrich (1964), p. 371, Bosco (1967), p. 78, Girardi (1967), p. xix, Smith (1985), pp. 165-66, Briosi (1991), p. 7, and Ulivi (1995).

An allied point is the argumentative quality frequently characteristic of Michelangelo's poetry, to which particular attention is drawn by May (1975, p. 35). As is made clear by Ostermark-Johansen (1995), the revival of interest in Michelangelo's poetry in the nineteenth century had much to do with an admiration for its intellectual quality; two notable early attempts to come to grips with Michelangelo's poetry primarily in terms of its thought were made by Taylor (1852) and Thomas (1892).

86. Bosco (1970a, p. 61) rightly contrasts Petrarch and Michelangelo in this respect. Spongano (1964, p. 14) notes the highly unusual direction of Michelangelo's poetic corrections, from the easy to the difficult.

87. T. S. Eliot, *Burnt Norton* I.

88. J. Keble, 'Morning Hymn'.

89. Ker (1888, p. 26) commented justly: 'With all his long and crushing labour, [Michelangelo] has still the freshness of hope.'

90. Smith (1985), p. 173.

### Bibliography of Works Cited

#### A. PRIMARY WORKS

*1. MICHELANGELO: POETRY*

*a) Major Editions*

Michelangiolo Buonarroti, *Rime* (1960), ed. E. N. Girardi, Bari: Laterza.

Michelangiolo Buonarroti, *Rime* (1967), ed. E. N. Girardi, Bari: Laterza (abridged version of 1960 edition, with new introduction and some revisions).

*b) Commentaries*

##### I) COMPLETE

Michelangelo Buonarroti, *Rime* (1975), ed. E. Barelli, Milan: Rizzoli.

*The Poetry of Michelangelo: An Annotated Translation* [with facing text] (1991), J. M. Saslow, New Haven: Yale University Press.

Michelangelo, *The Poems* (1996), ed. and tr. C. Ryan, London: Dent.

##### II) PARTIAL

Michelangelo Buonorrati, *Rime* (1931), ed. A. Dobelli, Milan: Signorelli.

*c) Major English Translations*

##### II) PARTIAL

'Selected poems of Michelangelo' (1987), tr. G. Bull and P. Porter. In Michelangelo, *Life, Letters and Poetry,* ed. G. Bull, Oxford: Oxford University Press, pp. 137-60.

*3. OTHER PRIMARY WORKS*

Condivi, A. (1964) *Vita di Michelagnolo Buonarroti,* ed. E. Spina Barelli, Milan: Rizzoli.

#### B. SECONDARY WORKS

Ariani, M. (1975) 'Giovan Battista Strozzi, il Manierismo e il madrigale del '500: strutture ideologiche e strutture formali'. In Giovan Battista Strozzi, *Rime,* ed. M. Ariani, Urbino: Argaglìa, VII-CXLVIII.

Beall, C. B. (1964), 'The literary figure of Michelangelo'. *Italica,* 41, 235-51.

Beltrami, P. G. (1991) *La metrica italiana,* Bologna: Il Mulino.

Binni, W. (1975) *Michelangelo scrittore,* 2nd edn, Turin: Einaudi.

Bizziccari, A. (1964) 'L'idea della bellezza nelle poesie di Michelangelo'. *Italica,* 41, 252-65.

Bonora, E. (1966a) 'Il classicismo dal Bembo al Guarini'. In E. Cecchi and N. Sapegno (eds) *Storia della letteratura italiana, vol. 4. Il Cinquecento,* Milan: Garzanti, pp. 151-711.

Bosco, U. (1967) 'Sulla collocazione storica di Michelangelo poeta'. In ed. anon. *Mélanges de littérature comparée et de philologie offerts a Mieczyslaw Brahmer,* Warsaw: PWN-Editions scientifiques de Pologne, pp. 73-78.

―――(1970a) 'Michelangelo poeta'. *Saggi sul Rinascimento italiano,* Florence: Le Monnier, pp. 52-76.

Bottari, S. (1935) 'Il diario poetico di Michelangelo'. *La critica figurativa e l'estetica moderna,* Bari: Laterza, pp. 119-60.

Briosi, S. (1991) *Amore e morte nelle* Rime *di Michelangelo,* Rome: Marra.

Bull, G. (1995) *Michelangelo: A Biography,* London: Viking.

Cambon, G. (1985) *Michelangelo's Poetry: Fury of Form,* Princeton: Princeton University Press.

Capovilla, G. (1982) 'Materiali per la morfologia e la storia del madrigale "antico", dal ms. Vaticano Rossi 215 al Novecento'. *Metrica,* 3, 159-252.

Cerini, M. (1931) *Michelangelo Buonarroti e i lirici minori del Cinquecento,* Turin: Paravia.

Croce, B. (1957) 'La lirica cinquecentesca'. *Poesia popolare e poesia d'arte. Studi sulla poesia italiana dal Tre al Cinquento,* 4th ed., Bari: Laterza, 341-441.

D'Angelo, P. (1978) *La poesia di Michelangelo,* Palermo: Herbita.

De Vecchi, P. L. (1963) 'Studi sulla poesia di Michelangelo'. *Giornale Storico della Letteratura Italiana,* 140, 30-66 and 364-402.

Einstein, A. (1971) *The Italian Madrigal,* 3 vols, 2nd ed., ET, Princeton: Princeton University Press.

Elwert, W. Th. (1973) *Versificazione italiana dalle origini ai nostri giorni,* Florence: Le Monnier.

Fabbri, P. (ed.) (1988) *Il madrigale tra Cinque e Seicento,* Bologna: Il Mulino.

Fedi, R. (1990) 'Il canzoniere (1546) di Michelangelo'. *La memoria della poesia. Canzonieri, lirici e libri di rime nel Rinascimento,* Rome: Salerno, pp. 264-305.

Fenlon, I. and Haar, J. (1988) *The Madrigal in Early Sixteenth-Century Italy,* Cambridge: Cambridge University Press.

Flora, F. (1965) 'Poesia di Michelangelo'. *Storia della letteratura italiana,* vol. 3, 15th ed., Milan: Mondadori, pp. 32-44.

Friedrich, H. (1964) 'Michelangelo', *Epochen der italienischen Lyrik,* Frankfurt am Main: Klostermann, 329-412.

Fubini, M. (1964) 'Michelangelo fu anche poeta?'. *La Stampa,* 27 February, 1964, p. 3 [repr. as 'Per il centenario di Michelangelo: il poeta', *Studi sulla letteratura del Rinascimento,* Florence: La Nuova Italia, 1971, pp. 289-93].

Galassi, G. (1942) 'Plasticità di Michelangiolo poeta'. *Michelangiolo Buonarroti nel IV centenario del 'Giudizio universale' (1541-1941),* ed. anon., Florence: Sansoni, 146-83.

Garin, E. (1966) '[Michelangelo as] Thinker'. In M. Salmi (ed.), *The Complete Work of Michelangelo,* vol. 2, ET, London: Macdonald, pp. 517-30.

Gilbert, C. (1945 and 1947) 'Michael Angelo's poetry in English verse', *Italica,* 22, 180-95, and 24, 46-53.

Girardi, E. N. (1988) '*La notte* di Michelangiolo. Scultura e poesia'. In id., *Letteratura italiana e arti figurative,* vol. 2, ed. A. Franceschetti, Florence: Olschki, pp. 473-83 [repr. in Girardi (1991), pp. 109-18].

Hallock, A. H. (1978) *Michelangelo the Poet: The Man behind the Myth,* Pacific Grove, Calif.: Page Ficklin.

Harrán, D. (1988) 'Tipologie metriche e formali del madrigale ai suoi esordi'. In P. Fabbri (ed.) *Il madrigale tra Cinque e Seicento,* Bologna: Il Mulino, pp. 95-122.

Hirst, M. (1988) *Michelangelo and His Drawings,* New Haven: Yale University Press.

Ker, W. P. (1888) 'The poems of Michael Angelo'. *Edinburgh Review,* 168, 1-34.

Malagoli, L. (1968) 'La nuova sensibilità e il nuovo stile: Michelangelo'. Id., *Le contraddizioni del Rinascimento,* Florence: La Nuova Italia, pp. 125-36.

Mariani, V. (1941) *Poesia di Michelangelo,* Rome: Palombi.

Martino, A. M. (1991) 'Progettualità e classicismo in Michelangelo'. In A. Toscano (ed.), *Interpreting the Italian Renaissance: Literary Perspectives,* New York: Forum Italicum, pp. 79-86.

Montale, E. (1976) 'Michelangelo poeta'. In id., A. Brissoni (ed.), *Michelangelo poeta,* Bologna: Boni, pp. 13-20.

Muscetta, C. and Ponchiroli, D. (1971) *Poesia del Quattrocento e del Cinquecento,* 4th ed., Turin: Einaudi.

Nelson, J. C. (1972) 'The poetry of Michelangelo'. In B. S. Levy (ed.) *Developments in the Early Renaissance,* Albany: State University of New York Press, pp. 15-35.

Orlando, S. (1994) *Manuale di metrica italiana,* 2nd ed., Milan: Bompiani.

Ostermark-Johansen, L. (1995) *Sweetness and Strength: The Reception of Michelangelo in Late Victorian England,* Unpublished doctoral thesis, University of Copenhagen.

Parodi, T. (1916) 'Michelangelo Buonarroti'. *Poesia e letteratura,* Bari: Laterza, pp. 184-97.

Pater, W. (1901) 'The poetry of Michelangelo'. In *The Renaissance: Studies in Art and Poetry,* 6th ed., London: Macmillan, pp. 73-97.

Ramous, M. (1984) *La metrica,* Milan: Garzanti.

Rivosecchi, M. (1965) 'La poesia'. *Michelangelo e Roma,* Rocca San Casciano: Cappelli, pp. 87-103.

Ruschioni, A. (1985) *Il sonetto italiano. Morfologia. Profilo storico,* 2nd ed., Milan: Celuc.

Sapegno, N. (1965) 'Appunti sul Michelangelo delle *Rime*'. *Rivista di Cultura Classica e Medievale,* 7 [= *Studi in onore di Alfredo Schiaffini,* 2 vols, special issue of *Rivista di Cultura Classica e Medievale,* 7], 999-1005.

Smith, A. J. (1985) 'Matter into grace: Michelangelo the love poet'. In *The Metaphysics of Love: Studies in Renaissance Love Poetry from Dante to Milton,* Cambridge: Cambridge University Press, pp. 150-76.

Spongano, R. (1964) 'Chiaramenti sulla poesia di Michelangelo'. *Il Verri,* 17, 3-15.

Summers, D. (1981) *Michelangelo and the Language of Art,* Princeton: Princeton University Press.

Taylor, J. E. (1852) *Michael Angelo Considered as a Philosophic Poet, with Translations,* 3rd ed., London: John Murray.

Thomas, G. (1892) *Michel-Ange. Étude sur l'expression de l'amour platonique dans la poésie italienne du Moyen Age et de la Renaissance,* Paris: Berget-Levrault.

Toffanin, G. (1965a) *Il Cinquecento,* 7th revised ed., Milan: Villardi.

————(1965b) 'Michelangelo: la poesia e l'epistolario'. In *Il Cinquecento,* 7th ed., Milan: Vallardi, pp. 382-5.

Ulivi, F. (1995), 'Michelangelo poeta: periplo critico'. In C. Gizzi (ed.) *Michelangelo e Dante,* Milan: Electa, pp. 155-58.

### Abbreviations

In the notes primary sources are referred to by their author, and secondary sources by their author or editor and their date of publication, with the exception of those listed below. Full publication details of each work are given in the bibliography.

Bull: G. Bull, *Michelangelo: A Biography* (1995)

*Ca: Il carteggio di Michelangelo,* 5 vols, ed. G. Poggi, P. Barocchi and R. Ristori (1965-83)

Clements: R. J. Clements, *The Poetry of Michelangelo* (1965)

Girardi: Michelangiolo Buonarroti, *Rime,* ed. E. N. Girardi (1960)

Hibbard: H. Hibbard, *Michelangelo* (1985)

*Let: The Letters of Michelangelo,* 2 vols, trans. E. H. Ramsden (1963)

Ryan: Michelangelo, *The Poems,* ed. and trans. C. Ryan (1996)

## Joseph Francese (essay date 2000)

SOURCE: Francese, Joseph. "Michelangelo's *Canzoniere*: Politics and Poetry." In *The Craft and the Fury: Essays in Memory of Glauco Cambon,* edited by Joseph Francese, pp. 138-54. West Lafayette, Ind.: Bordighera Press, 2000.

[*In the following essay, Francese discusses the public and political aspects of Michelangelo's poetry in the context of his era.*]

In 1897 the German philologist Karl Frey identified within the corpus of Michelangelo's *Rime* a distinct group of 89 compositions in verse that the poet had transcribed in 1546, in preparation for publication. The manuscripts were written with great care and accuracy, and, as Roberto Fedi points out, contain corrections and re-elaborations, many of which are in Michelangelo's own hand. The poems were serialized by Michelangelo's friend and business administrator, Luigi Del Riccio, whose contribution was, in Fedi's opinion, more than that of a friend or secretary, but that of a veritable edi-

tor.[1] The project never came to fruition, for reasons that will be mentioned later on, yet Fedi, following Frey, considers this group of poems the nucleus of an incipient *canzoniere.* He claims that because Michelangelo was well versed in the "arte del levare," we can look beyond the indecision evident in this still inchoate collection of lyrics. Then, we may examine the corrections made by the poet and consider (with the evidence at our disposal) his choices as to what to include or exclude.[2] This process of reconstruction should allow us to arrive at "the heart of the matter": the figure held captive within the corpus of Michelangelo's poetry, awaiting liberation at the hand of the poet from the superfluous. In Fedi's own words, the collection of lyrics first identified by Frey is "the fruit . . . of a highly personal need of social communication, taking place this time through the medium of the written page."[3]

In Girardi's 1960 critical edition of Michelangelo's **Rime,**[4] the poems readied for publication are indicated, but not isolated from the rest, as was the case with the Frey edition. Fedi disagrees with Girardi's strict chronological ordering, which he believes reflects the editor's conviction in the "historical becoming" of Michelangelo's poetic *oeuvre* more than Buonarroti's intentions, "even those explicitly clarified," which Fedi claims are "effectively obliterated" by Girardi. Nonetheless, while Fedi is certainly justified in considering synchronically the poems grouped in a prospected *canzoniere,* Girardi's choice to represent the diachronic growth and refinement of Michelangelo's verse is not entirely mistaken. The distinction of the use value of variants, or works *in fieri,* and the exchange value of the *factum,* the finalized, published work, is always a fundamental methodological issue. And here the question is all the more problematic because we are dealing with what Mastrocola, in her interesting introduction to her selection of Michelangelo's poems and letters, has called a *"canzoniere interminato."*[5] Michelangelo has left us with something between a work in progress and a *factum.* Therefore, in order to interrogate the hypothesis that Michelangelo, with Riccio's and Giannotti's encouragement and assistance, intended to publish the collection, it is necessary to look outside the individual poems, and consider the prospective *canzoniere,* asking ourselves why he would have set the project aside, never to pick it up again.

Lucia Ghizzoni strongly objects to Fedi's claim that within the codices preserved at the Vatican Library in Rome and the Laurentian Library in Florence "it is easy to recognize something more than a mere working collection prepared by Buonarroti for the sole purpose of personal consultation."[6] Since, in fact, a close examination of Michelangelo's correspondence reveals no extant documents that would give clear support to the existence of such a project, she believes it "highly improbable that Michelangelo communicated or submitted to another's opinion" a proposed *canzoniere,* even if one had been effectively undertaken or planned. In support of her thesis, Ghizzoni cites a letter from Michelangelo to Riccio in which the artist admonishes his friend to "guastare quella stampa e abruciare quelle che sono stampate."[7] However, we do not know the details of the incident that provoked his writing a letter that, when read, unavoidably, outside its historical context, is highly ambiguous and inconclusive evidence.[8] Ghizzoni also contends that the group of works isolated by Frey constitutes no more than a "libro-archivio d'autore" compiled by Michelangelo and his friends for strictly private reference. In her opinion, poetry was, for Michelangelo, "an absolutely private dimension" and she concludes by arguing that "we must continue to read Michelangelo's verse as so many fragments, as reflections of many completely self-contained instances."[9] Further on in these notes I will argue that Michelangelo's poetry, like his painting and sculpture, was a public art. For the moment I will limit myself to taking strong objection to Ghizzoni's last statement. Even if Ghizzoni were correct and the group of poems identified by Frey is no more than a very personal "libro-archivio," it still constitutes a very clear, "synchronic" indication of the identity of Michelangelo the poet in the mid-1540s.[10] As for Fedi's objections to Girardi's chronological ordering, this *canzoniere* project at the very least represents a highly significant watershed in Michelangelo's diachronic development as a poet.

In a second intervention Fedi reiterates his thesis, that the poems are not a "definitive but sufficiently defined" redaction, from which he extrapolates compositional nuclei whose common denominator is the image of the beloved "donna." Fedi also argues that the *canzoniere* of 1546 refutes occasionality and autobiography, eschewing even the suggestion of anything remotely "historical and verifiable." Since occasional compositions were almost completely absent from the *canzoniere* of 1546, he continues, the centrality of the exquisitely lyric nature of the collection is made evident by negation. This, in its turn, polarizes our attention on the thematic groupings focalized in the figures of the "donna bella e crudele," in the love lyrics, and, in the more spiritual compositions, la donna "santa e altera."[11] Both Fedi and Ghizzoni utilize rigorous philological methods that eschew a reading of Michelangelo's verse within a larger socio-historical context.[12] Here, I believe, lies the limit of this debate and the crux of the problem. A strict formalist reading of Michelangelo's verse does not explain the anomalous presence within the *canzoniere* or "libro-archivio d'autore," call it what you will, of the epigraph on the statue of the *Night,*[13] nor the sonnets on Dante[14] nor the madrigal dedicated to Florence.[15]

A second enigma, stressed by Gigliucci, regards the central experience of antithesis and paradox, which in his opinion characterizes Michelangelo's poetry.[16] Fedi,

too, sees extending over the whole of the macrotext (and correctly, I believe) the "basic idea of an enormous antithesis."[17] However, if the defining quality of Michelangelo's verse is its "contrastive nature" (Gigliucci), we are still left with the question of an internal coherence within the poet. On this point Mastrocola comes to our aid when she contends that

> in truth Michelangelo's *contradditorietà* has nothing to do with an interior, psychological contrast; rather it is the natural result of a process of reasoning in which the mind is left free to follow all possible developments, even the most conflicting, all united however in their dependence on a single imaginatively liberating fulcrum.

This narrative center, she writes, "reflects a mental predisposition to identify the infinite aspects of a theme, above all those based on contrast and contradiction" and examine "the infinite potentialities of an idea."[18]

The question, then, revolves around the text, but lies outside it, and centers on the ideal and affective substratum that motivated Michelangelo's compilation of a collection of lyrics, his individuation of the criteria that informed its progress, and the various biographical events that precluded its coming to fruition. Discussion of Michelangelo's *canzoniere* will unavoidably be enveloped in conjecture (unless additional documents are brought to light: Giannotti's biographer informs us, however, that Michelangelo's close friend, despondent after the death of his benefactor, burned many of his papers in 1550).[19] However, reasonable hypotheses are attainable if we bear in mind Binni's advice and consider not only "the concrete necessities and forms" of Michelangelo's long poetic experience, but also his poetic exigencies, which condition the poetry, and his suffered personal and historical situation.[20]

In this sense, Dante provides us with a good point of departure. Girardi finds in the historical and intellectual figure of the author of *La divina commedia* the unifying point of symbolic reference for Michelangelo, a model of human greatness, a stimulus for setting ever-higher goals for himself.[21] Fiorato, for his part, underscores the importance of the divine poet as an ethical and political model for Michelangelo.[22] Thus, using the figure of Dante, or better his use as an "ideological-polemical model" by the Florentine exiles,[23] we can begin to reconstruct a critical perspective that utilizes but supersedes a strictly philological reading of the *canzoniere* and seeks out an underlying consistency on which the poetic paradoxes are based. I propose that the end result will be the image of a poet who remained true to his convictions while receding from explicit manifestations of views that would have been considered heretical by the Council of Trent or subversive by Cosimo I.

As Girardi points out, Michelangelo's poetry is by no means "the fruit of a marginal and dilettantesque activity, epiphenomenon of an essential plastic vocation."

He also warns against disregarding "the fundamental unity of the mind of Michelangelo."[24] In fact, a basic coherence links the youthful Michelangelo's activity as "a sort of official artist of the [Soderini] government,"[25] and that of the man who, almost twenty years later, considered it his "duty as a citizen" to work without recompense in the defense of the second Florentine republic,[26] and then lived the rest of his life in self-imposed exile.[27] Moreover, the roots of Michelangelo's republicanism extend back to his youth, predate the first republic and are of a piece with his profound religious convictions. As Albertini has written, Savonarola's ideological stamp remained impressed on the Florentine republicans, long after the Dominican monk's execution in 1494.[28] As a youth Michelangelo too had found in Savonarola a response to many religious questions.[29] Moreover, he saw in republican government the proper expression for personal aspirations that were the direct result of the economic and social place his family occupied in the Florentine caste system.[30]

Spini reminds us that the Buonarroti were Florentine "citizens," members of a family who held the right to sit on city councils and elect magistrates,[31] a consideration which comported a very specific social, political and cultural relevance and had ethical-religious and even artistic implications which made their social status a determining influence on Michelangelo's personality and existence.[32] Spini also finds a direct continuity between "*tradizione cittadina* and humanist experience": membership in a "specific social grouping of citizens" implied "the underwriting of determinate ethos and set of social conventions," along with participation in "a great cultural network, whose apex was represented by the Florentines' domestic numen, Dante Alighieri."[33] Dante was not only their own homegrown "poeta divino" but also their "teacher of moral life and of philosophical-religious doctrine." The ethical-religious and esthetic-cultural moments of the citizens of Florence were joined in the cult of the "Poema Sacro."[34] Parenthetically, Michelangelo's belief in honest government[35] and his emotional attachment to the Florentine republic are clearly evidenced in poetry that was not included, for whatever reason, in a *canzoniere*: for example, the fragment G48 *Come fiamma più cresce più contesa,* written while the city was under siege.[36]

In the letters written in the period subsequent to the fall of the republic of 1527-1530, Binni notes the "defeat, the disappointment, the remorse, perhaps, and the retreat of [Michelangelo's] ethical-political aspirations in an intimate zone jealously defended by prudence,"[37] a prudence that I have defined elsewhere as his "Nicodemism"[38] (this clandestine spirituality parallels a covert politics that motivated the artist's self-exile in Rome: a silent, lifelong protest against the Medicean restoration and the absolutism instituted by Cosimo I). For his part, Spini discusses the way in which "political desperation

contributed to the heightening of religious tension in Michelangelo, and the sublimation of that political tension in love lyrics addressed to the "donna bella, crudele e altera," and in his explicitly religious poetry. Scaglione, writing not specifically of Michelangelo but of the pleasures of sexual frustration derived from Petrarchan love,[39] describes a behavioral pattern evinced in verse that reflects quite accurately the sublimated love of Michelangelo's poetry. In his opinion, sexual frustration becomes for the Petrarchan poets of the Cinquecento a symbolic center of human *Sehnsucht* or metaphysical unsatisfiability. The idea of "self-denial and sublimation for the sake of higher achievement," once interiorized, not only comes to define much of Michelangelo's love poetry—and is part and parcel of the Nicodemite's religious experience—but also clarifies the political stance of the would-be republican insurgent.[40]

Michelangelo's sublimation of frustrated political and sexual desires in Neoplatonic and religious verse is congruent with his political and religious "Nicodemism." Furthermore, it is highly plausible that this collection of poems, given Michelangelo's tendency to profess outwardly more orthodox views in conflict with his true sentiments, correspond to a political "parlar cifrato" necessarily in common use among those who opposed the Medici.[41] For proof of Michelangelo's political "Nicodemism," one need look no further than his letter of 22 October 1547 to his nephew Leonardo. Here the artist vehemently denied his close ties with the community of anti-Medicean Florentine exiles in Rome,[42] because the artist was well aware of the potential negative repercussions on his family and on the economic fortune he had dedicated his career to building for them in Florence.[43] That Donato Giannotti was a friend of Michelangelo is amply documented, but Giannotti, who was in his own words one of the "ribaldi di Monte Murlo,"[44] does not figure in Michelangelo's extant correspondence, particularly when the artist is pressed by his nephew to defend his association with the *fuorusciti.*[45] Parenthetically, Giannotti's intimacy with Machiavelli in the Orti Oricellari[46] and his desire to carry out in practice what the Segretario fiorentino had theorized provides another link between Michelangelo and the erstwhile Florentine republic.[47]

Therefore, the quatrain **"Caro m'è 'l sonno, e più l'esser di sasso"** (N, 17, [G247]) must be read as a testament to the political nature of certain of Michelangelo's poetry,[48] an assertion I would further clarify by arguing that it is also evidence to the public, not private, character of Michelangelo's poetic art. It was selected for inclusion in a *canzoniere,* where it was to come in immediate response to the epigram by Giovanni di Carlo Strozzi *La Notte che tu vedi in sí dolci atti,*[49] in celebration of the *Night* Michelangelo carved for the Medici tombs.[50] Thus, along with the epigram and sonnet dedicated to the death of Gandolfo Porrino's mistress,[51] it documents a very public dialogue in which Michelangelo indicates a much less lyrical reading of his statue than Strozzi's, by alluding to his aversion for the Medici restoration.[52]

Even as intimate a work of plastic art as the *Pietà del Duomo* was originally intended for public consumption. In fact, its public destination was in all likelihood the reason for the artist's damaging it. The statue has, on the face of Nicodemus (the clandestine apostle of Christ), a self-portrait of the artist. According to Tolnay, Michelangelo worked sporadically on the *Pietà del Duomo* between 1547 (the year in which his spiritual counselor, Vittoria Colonna died) and 1553, intending to have it placed on his own tomb.[53] However, after repeated insistence by his helper Urbino,[54] the artist defaced the work.

The public nature of Michelangelo's verse is further demonstrated by the publication of approximately ten poems during the poet's lifetime (several of which were madrigals the poet had set to music).[55] It is also demonstrated by the literary fellowship he enjoyed with Riccio, especially, and Giannotti, in which (in a manner similar to that of the artistic *bottega* where works were a collaborative effort), poems and critiques went back and forth (often in exchange for choice delicacies) before they were forwarded to their dedicatees. Moreover, as evidenced by Giannotti's *Dialogi,* Michelangelo was not opposed to reciting his own compositions in public.

Giannotti's *Dialogi* come to a close with Michelangelo reciting a composition he wrote a few days earlier, **"Da ciel discese, e col mortal suo, poi"** (N, 37, [G248]),[56] the sonnet in which he claims he would exchange for Dante's *virtù* the world's "happiest state," even if that meant accepting the poet's "bitter exile." Florence is also the topic of N, 48 [G249],—**"Per molti donna, anzi per mille amanti."** In this madrigal the poetic voice laments that the Heavens allowed a city that was given to many to be expropriated by one person. The voice of Florence calms the poetic interlocutor by recalling to mind the assassination of Alessandro de' Medici: the city's present ruler "col gran timor non gode il gran pecato."[57] The sonnet **"Quante dirne si de' non si può dire"** (N, 49 [G250]) deals in paradox, in this case that of the closing of Florence's city gates to the one man who, while still living, entered through those of Paradise. Interestingly, on the manuscript Michelangelo wrote, "Messer Donato, voi mi richiedete quello che io non ò." We can only speculate on what Giannotti wanted that the poet could not provide: perhaps a stronger statement than the first tercet ("Ingrata, dico, e della suo fortuna / a suo danno nutrice; ond'è ben segnio / ch'a' più perfecti abonda di più guai")?

While the criteria used by Michelangelo, Riccio, and Giannotti for the selection and revision of works for the

*canzoniere* remains shrouded in mystery, Michelangelo's motives for the compilation of a collection of his verse are entwined with his choice of editors and the inclusion of four texts that reflected his status of exile. Neither will the third question posed at the outset, which centers on why a *canzoniere* was never published,[58] be resolved unless the future brings new documents to light. Nonetheless, theories abound: Ghizzoni, as we have seen, maintains that Michelangelo never intended to publish his poems. Many believe that because of the death of Riccio, animator of the initiative, Michelangelo put the collection aside, never to take it up again. The passing of Vittoria Colonna, Michelangelo's poetic interlocutrix and inspiration, followed closely after, and this second bereavement is often mentioned as an additional reason for his abandoning the project.[59] Cambon has speculated that, in addition to the deaths of these two close associates, the concern for orthodoxy introduced by the Council of Trent, which opened in 1545,[60] might have provided Michelangelo with a strong inducement to put his *canzoniere* aside, particularly after the adverse criticism he had received for the unconventionality of the *Last Judgement.*[61] To this we must add Michelangelo's often lamented poor health, his preoccupation with advancing old age and death,[62] and the need to re-allocate energies after his designation as architect of Saint Peter's in 1547, following the death of Antonio da Sangallo the Younger.[63] An additional factor may have been the loss of Giannotti's influence. After the death of Cardinal Ridolfi Michelangelo's friend left Rome with a new benefactor and distanced himself from politics.

Giannotti's biographer postulates that the friendship between Giannotti and Michelangelo began under the second republic, when the artist was one of the *Nove della Milizia* charged with re-fortifying the city, and Giannotti occupied Machiavelli's old post as *Segretario dei Dieci.* Their camaraderie was renewed when Giannotti arrived in Rome in late 1539. Michelangelo's contacts with Riccio were more assiduous, due not only to Riccio's role as Michelangelo's administrator but also to Giannotti's frequent travels outside the city in the service of his employer, Cardinal Niccolò Ridolfi. Nonetheless, the "affectionate familiarity" that linked the artist and Giannotti continued unabated, even after Riccio's death. In fact, after the demise of Michelangelo's business manager, Giannotti became the intermediary for the members of the Florentine community in Rome with the "salvatico e terribile vegliardo di macel de' Corvi."[64] However, their literary fellowship was not as intense as the one that linked the artist and Riccio: Cambon has underscored the poetic differences separating Giannotti and Michelangelo, labelling the former a "bembista," and pointing out that, unlike Giannotti, Michelangelo placed less stock in metrical fluency and euphony than in expressive force.[65] Moreover, significant changes in Giannotti's personal situation (brought on by the demise in 1550 of his benefactor during the Conclave that elected Julius III, a death Giannotti's biographer leads one to believe was a politically motivated assassination)[66] deprived Michelangelo of an important interlocutor, the last link to the republicanism of his past,[67] and, perhaps, the catalyst he needed to overcome his political—and poetical—"Nicodemism."

### Notes

1. Roberto Fedi, "Il Canzoniere (1546) di Michelangelo," in Id., *La memoria della poesia. Canzonieri, lirici e libri di rime nel Rinascimento* (Roma: Salerno Editrice, 1990). Fedi provides a good description of the manuscripts (279-81). He credits Frey with identifying a group of sixteen additional compositions that were not serialized by Riccio, but, in Frey's opinion, were arranged by Michelangelo for inclusion in a *canzoniere* (282). However, Fedi objects to Frey's "mortifying" this discovery by "burying" such a "conspicuous group of texts in the *corpus* of Michelangelo's lyric production" (272). Walter De Gruyter & Co. of Berlin published an anastatic printing of Frey's edition, *Die Dichtungen des Michelagniolo Buonarroti* (Berlin, 1887) in 1964.

2. For example, of the four sonnets to the Night ([G101]-[G104]), only [G103] and [G104] were included. Of the texts dedicated to Riccio, two variants of [G252] were included, while [G251] was not. Only [G62] was chosen from the cycle of poems on fire [G61-G64], while G163 and G166 were selected from the quartet of sonnets on the theme of eyes [G163-G166].

3. Fedi, "Il Canzoniere di Michelangelo" 290-91.

4. Michelangelo, *Rime,* ed. Enzo Noè Girardi (Bari: Laterza, 1960). Fedi calls Girardi to task for a strictly chronological ordering of the texts, which led Girardi to include and give equal dignity to unfinished poems, drafts, and interrupted trial efforts. According to Fedi, Girardi accentuated the "rough, unfinished aspects of the verse, and the harsh, and, in the final analysis, antipetrarchan tone of the lyrics." This, in turn, created the inaccurate image of a "unique, almost a revolutionary [Cinquecento] poet" (274).

5. Paola Mastrocola, "Introduzione," *Rime e lettere di Michelangelo,* ed. P. Mastrocola (Torino: UTET, 1992) 9-43; 32.

6. Fedi, "Il Canzoniere di Michelangelo" 271.

7. *Il carteggio di Michelangelo, Volume IV, Lettere di Michelangelo e i suoi corrispondenti dal I° gennaio [1533] al [1552]* (Firenze: S.P.E.S. Editore). Sotto gli auspici dell'Istituto nazionale di Studi sul Rinascimento, 1979, Letter MLVI, "Michelangelo [in Roma] a Luigi del Riccio [in Roma], febbraio-marzo? 1546" 232.

8. Michelangelo signs this missive "Michelagniolo Buonarroti, non pictore né scultore né architectore ma quel che voi volete, ma none briaco, come vi dissi in casa," *ivi*. According to Romei, Riccio wanted Michelangelo to be, or assert, ("quel che voi volete") the other, unmentioned, aspect of his creativity, that of poet. After furnishing a good summary of the more salient points of disagreement between Fedi and Ghizzoni, Romei contradicts Ghizzoni's argument against use of extant documents in support of a *canzoniere* project by citing Condivi's biography of the Master. Condivi wrote: "Spero tra poco tempo dar fuore alcuni suoi sonetti e madrigali, quali io con lungo tempo ho raccolti sì da lui, sì da altri, e questo per dar saggio al mondo, quanto nell'invenzione vaglia, e quanti bei concetti naschino da quel divino spirito." Then, following Spini, Romei adds that Condivi was no more than a "prestanome" for the true author of Michelangelo's biography, Michelangelo himself (Danilo Romei, *Rassegna della letteratura italiana* 97.3 (1993): 288-91 (290). It should be noted in passing that Michelangelo met Condivi in Rome at the court of Cardinal Niccolò Ridolfi, a leader of the anti-Medicean faction there and Giannotti's protector, where Condivi was a guest (Ridolfi 125-26).

9. Lucia Ghizzoni, "Indagine sul canzoniere di Michelangelo," *Studi di filologia italiana* 49 (1991) 167-87; 170, 171, 187.

10. In his exegesis of the variants, Cambon has also argued that "when emendations brought to a given evolving text came to be felt by [Michelangelo] as mere alternatives to the earlier corresponding passages" the artist changed "a diachronic progression into a synchronic order," validating both versions: the "two texts accordingly became divergent yet equal variants of what had preceded them" (Glauco Cambon, *Michelangelo's Poetry. Fury of Form* [Princeton: Princeton UP, 1985] 161). See also Roberto Gigliucci, "Voci recenti su Michelangelo poeta," *Roma nel Rinascimento* (1994): 57-74: "il campione delle novanta poesie merita di essere analizzato, in relazione al resto della produzione, come testimonianza di un momento importante del gusto e della coscienza poetica dell'autore" (61).

11. Roberto Fedi, "'L'immagine vera': Vittoria Colonna, Michelangelo, e un'idea di canzoniere," *MLN* [*Modern Language Notes*] 107 (1992): 46-73; 54-55, 56, 49. In this second essay Fedi again places in relief the "complete absence" of realistic, Bernesque poems and of any sort of "autobiographical participation" in Michelangelo's poetry. In Fedi's opinion, Michelangelo set aside all contingent, political and historically verifiable

references in favor of "an imagine that was less bound to everyday life," eliminating any evident reference to occasionality (Fedi, "Il Canzoniere di Michelangelo" 286-87). Mastrocola, following Girardi, writes of a fourth thematic nucleus (in addition to those constituted by the poems dedicated to Cavalieri, Vittoria Colonna, and "la donna bella e crudele") that in her phasing is "senza agganci con alcun destinatario e con alcuna vicenda biograficamente definita: poesie legate soltanto ad uno stato interiore o ad una materia concettuale, quindi più che mai atemporali" (11). She goes on to assert that "il libro si permea di pochissimi temi portanti, che si espandono in più componimenti; per il resto ben rari sono i testi su tema isolato e per così dire 'extravagante'" (20). In her opinion everything takes place within "un processo mentale che cerca soltanto in sé le possibilità di svolgimento e non attinge nulla dall'esterno della vita e della storia" (14).

12. Fedi would "historicize" Michelangelo's poetry "stylistically." In his opinion, this is "the only non-falsified key fit for entering in a writer's laboratory" ("Il canzoniere di Michelangelo" 269); Ghizzoni prefers an "attentive analysis of Michelangelo's papers" (170).

13. N, 17, [G247], *Caro m'è 'l sonno, e più l'esser di sasso.* I will use a capital N and an Arabic numeral to indicate the place occupied by the individual compositions within the *canzoniere* manuscripts (as indicated by Fedi in the first appendix to his "Il canzoniere di Michelangelo") and a capital G surrounded by brackets to indicate its place in Girardi's chronological sequence.

14. N, 37, [G248], *Dal ciel discese, e col mortal suo, poi,* and N, 49, [G250], *Quante dirne si de' non si può dire.*

15. N, 48, [G249]—*Per molti, donna, anzi per mille amanti.* Although Ghizzoni, because of her primary concern for manuscript variants, does not address this issue, Fedi points out that [G248] is isolated within the *canzoniere* among a group of madrigals (NN, 32-39) whose theme is time and the dichotomy past/present. He also indicates that these poems are without destination or interlocutor ("'L'immagine vera'" 61), and that N, 48 and N, 49 [G249 and G250] constitute a madrigal-sonnet dyptich for the Florentine exiles; however, he stops well short of examining the consequence(s) of the thematic anomalies.

16. Gigliucci 61-62. Gigliucci provides an excellent summary of both this debate and the most salient examples of critical writings published in the 1990s on Michelangelo's poetry, although he considers the projected *canzoniere* evidence of "una volontà di scelta [. . .] documentata e inconfutabile" (61) on the one hand, and, on the other, the sonnets on the night [G101-04] emblematic of the lack of resolution and of a "finale quiete asseverativa" (66) in Michelangelo's poetry.

17. Fedi, "'L'immagine vera'" 51.

18. 22, 23, 28. Mastrocola argues that "il libro che i suoi posteri studiosi hanno con tanta meticolosa perizia approntato era già veramente un libro, il solo genere di libro che Michelangelo poteva scrivere, la cui apparente indeterminatezza ed aleatorietà è la sostanza stessa della poetica michelangiolesca" (14): Michelangelo endowed his poetry the same quality that made sculpture (which could be viewed, "a tutto tondo") in his eyes superior to painting. That is to say, by "multiplying his writings in multiple texts, variations on the same theme, [and] never arriving at a "single and definitive expression" (19, 20, 32). Thus, she postulates a *canzoniere* that shares with the *Prigioni dell'Accademia* the same formal indeterminacy, or refusal of closure, whose expressive force is to be found precisely in the unlimited potentialities of the *non-finito.* See also Creighton E. Gilbert for whom the poet would "present an argument and then [. . .] assert the opposite to see if it would stand up" ("Texts and Contexts of the Medici Chapel," in Id., *Poets Seeing Artists' Work. Instances in the Italian Renaissance* [Florence: Olschki, 1991] 227-48; 245).

19. Roberto Ridolfi, *Sommario della vita di Donato Giannotti,* in Id., *Opuscoli di storia letteraria e di erudizione* (Firenze: Bibliopolis, 1942) 55-164; 140-41.

20. Walter Binni, *Michelangelo scrittore,* 1965 (Torino: Einaudi, 1975) 3-4.

21. Girardi claims that Michelangelo moved toward a "modellazione dantesca della propria figura," an attitude consolidated around 1545, when Buonarroti wanted to "farsi presente in patria" and, to claim the nobility of his family, began to seek out his own Cacciaguida (Enzo Noè Girardi, "Michelangiolo e Dante, in Id., *Letteratura come bellezza. Studi sulla Letteratura italiana del Rinascimento* [Roma: Bulzoni, 1991] 91-108; 97, 105).

22. Adelin Fiorato, "'Fuss'io pur lui!': Michelangelo all'ascolto di Dante (11 marzo 1989)," *Letture classensi* 19 (1990): 87-104. Fiorato does well to point out Michelangelo's lack of "l'alta finalità politico-religiosa di Dante". Fiorato also places in evidence Michelangelo's "partecipazione commossa e sdegnata alla sfortuna di Dante" which corresponds to an "impegno civile comune

all'opposizione repubblicana fiorentina negli anni della restaurazione medicea giacché gli oppositori individuarono allora emblematicamente in Dante l'eroe infelice, porta vessillo delle idealità comunali fiorentine" (99-100).

23. Fiorato 99.

24. Enzo Noè Girardi, "Introduzione," Michelangelo, *Rime* (Bari: Laterza, 1967) (VII, VIII). Binni also, has stressed the drama that "impegna tutta la personalità dell'artista sicché è certamente errato risolvere l'attività delle rime in un furore di esercizio e di sperimentazione di linguaggio senza intenderne e rilevarne [. . .] la necessità e l'intrecciatissimo sgorgo interiore" (49-50).

25. Giorgio Spini, "Politicità di Michelangelo," *Rivista storica italiana* 76 (1964): 557-600; 573.

26. Albertini 120. It is well known that after the fall of popular government in Florence Michelangelo would prefer the company of Florentine exiles, and, on request of Donato Giannotti, sculpt a bust of the tyrannicide Brutus for one of the leaders of the anti-Medicean faction in Rome, Giannotti's patron, Cardinal Niccolò Ridolfi. Furthermore, in January 1946 Michelangelo fell ill and convalesced in the Strozzi residence in Rome. As a sign of his gratitude, he gave to Roberto Strozzi, another leader of the anti-Medici faction, two *Slaves* that had been intended for the tomb of Julius II. Condivi and Vasari mention this gift in passing, but do not go into detail; Steinmann postulates that they did so under instructions from Michelangelo who was well aware of Cosimo I's hatred of the rebellious Strozzi, of his covetousness of works by Michelangelo and of his desire to bring the artist back to Florence (Ernst Steinmann, "Michelangelo e Luigi Del Riccio," *Rivista storica degli archivi toscani* 3.4: 227-81; 243).

27. Albertini claims that those who continued to oppose the Medici through the first three decades of the sixteenth century and beyond held in common a belief in the necessity of banning all forms of overt tyranny from the city, of reforming public manners and morality, and of preserving the *Consiglio Grande* (in which they saw the fundamental expression of the city's liberty). In fact, in the first of Giannotti's *Dialogi,* Michelangelo explains "le ruine di Toscana nostra" by citing the factious nature of its citizens: "rade volte avviene che l'uno approvi quel che l'altro; et qualunque volta molti insieme si trovano a trattare d'alcuna cosa, sempre fanno mille divisioni." Thus, the great merit, to Michelangelo's mind, of the *Consiglio Grande* (a topic that Michelangelo enjoyed discussing, judging by Giannotti's response) was that it forged a common will, and therefore, in the words attributed to him by his friend Giannotti, was a "molto magnifica et honorata compagnia" (*Dialogi di Donato Giannotti de' giorni che Dante consumò nel cercare l'Inferno e 'Purgatorio,* Ed. Deoclecio Redig de Campos, Florence: Sansoni, 1939, 39, 40).

28. According to Albertini, the best and sincerest proponents of popular government had either experienced Savonarola's direct influence, "or they handed down his memory and spiritual world" (Rudolf von Albertini, *Firenze dalla repubblica al principato. Storia e coscienza politica,* 1955 [Turin: Einaudi, 1970] 16).

29. The influence of Savonarola on Michelangelo was duly recorded by Condivi. In Condivi's own words, "Michelangelo conservava anche da vecchio 'la memoria della . . . viva voce' del Savonarola e ne aveva studiato gli scritti, come guida alla interpretazione della Bibbia" (qtd. Spini 571).

30. According to Hollanda, Michelangelo describes republics as states "where no one is permitted to exalt himself above his neighbours" (Francisco de Hollanda, *Four Dialogues on Painting,* trans. Aubrey F. G. Bell [Westport, CT: Hyperion, 1928, 1993] 54).

31. Spini 559; see also Albertini 10. De Tolnay writes that Michelangelo's "notion of freedom did not apply to the *popolani,* the lower orders, who were, in his opinion, inferior to the free citizens, those who paid taxes (*gravezze*)" (Charles de Tolnay, *The Art and Thought of Michelangelo* [New York: Pantheon, 1964] 4).

32. Spini explains that because of their social and economic status in the city, the Buonarroti were closely linked to the Parte Guelfa and to the Arte della Lana. Therefore, they were a part of the Popolo Grasso, but not of the oligarchy, even though family members were occasionally included among the "imborsati" whose names were periodically chosen to fill the most important magistracies of the Republic (559, 560). In his own words, "il fatto veramente determinante è la discendenza da casata di "cittadini", facenti parte ereditariamente nel ceto dirigente" (563). Moreover, Spini reminds us, "a Roma, dal 1534 in avanti, le sue amicizie più strette non sono tanto con esuli di parte popolare, quanto con esuli "grandi", come gli Strozzi, il cardinale Niccolò Ridolfi e suo fratello Lorenzo, oppure con personaggi legati a costoro, come Donato Giannotti e Luigi del Riccio" (597). Spini also mentions the link between Michelangelo's plastic art production and the papacy of Paul III Farnese, who favored the representatives of the Florentine "Grandi" who were in exile in Rome and who engaged Cosimo I

in frequent controversies (598-99 [for a similar perspective on the intellectual ambience of Rome in the 1540s see Fedi, "Il canzoniere di Michelangelo," 278-79]). Albertini discusses the differences separating the Ottimati, or oligarchy of textile industrialists, bankers and owners of large merchant concerns who supported the Medici and the Popolo Grasso, the economic stratum that was threatened by the concentration of power and so sought protection in the Consiglio Grande, where decisional power was extended to include the middle bourgeoisie. In this regard, see also H. C. Butters, *Governors and Government in Early Sixteenth-Century Florence 1502-1519* (Oxford: Clarendon, 1985).

33. Spini 570.

34. In fact, on 20 October 1518, Michelangelo was one of twenty distinguished Florentines who signed a petition addressed to Leo X requesting the removal of Dante's remains from Ravenna to Florence. Appended to the petition, and written in Michelangelo's own hand, was a postscript in which the artist promised to erect a "befitting sepulchre to [Dante] and in some honorable place in this city" (Gian Roberto Sarolli, "Michelangelo: Poet of the Night," *Forum Italicum* [1967]: 133-55 [151]).

35. Cf., among the early poems, [G10], *Qua si fa elmi di calici e spade,* which denounced the corruption of the Papal court, and [G68], *Un gigante v'è ancor, d'altezza tanta.* For Cambon, the thematic nucleus of [G68] revolves around the evils of uncontrolled greed in civic matters (92). Verse 43 of this composition, "e solo a iusti fanno insidie e guerra," reflects V.99 of G47 (which contrasts the evils of life in the sixteenth century, particularly in court, to a bucolic past age of gold), "il Falso [. . .] c'a' iusti sol fa guerra," and is picked up again by the poet when he disparages Florence in *Dal ciel discese, e col mortal suo, poi,* calling it hospice of "quel popolo ingrato / che solo a' iusti manca di salute."

36. This tercet represents for Binni a "formidabile rivincita morale," and a "quasi alto emblema della sua strenua volontà eroica di offeso, di frustrato nei propri ideali" (51).

37. Binni 24. As Mastrocola indicates, with Michelangelo we are dealing with a mind characterized not only by Neoplatonic ascesis but also by a very strong attachment to the practical necessities of the quotidian (demonstrated by his letters). Michelangelo's pragmatic nature and prudence explain his overriding desire to avoid placing his own person and the well-being of his family at risk and the strict functionality of his letter writing: Michelangelo wrote to resolve practical (personal and business) matters when he could not leave his workplace. As for Michelangelo's prudence, Spini points out that Vasari, in his 1550 biography of Michelangelo, mentions how his subject "è stato nel suo dire molto coperto e ambiguo, avendo le cose sue quasi due sensi" and how another contemporary lamented a "voluta oscurità" on Michelangelo's part when asked for interpretations of his plastic creations (558).

38. Michelangelo's Nicodemism is a form of passive resistance, consisting of external obedience to the dictates of the Counter-Reformation, that allowed Michelangelo to profess intimately what he believed was the true faith, one that more closely followed the creed of the reformist movement in Italy. Cf. Joseph Francese, "Il 'nicodemismo' di Michelangelo nei 'sonetti sulla notte,'" *Quaderni d'italianistica* 14 (1993): 143-49.

39. According to Scaglione, Petrarch's "deep theme was the impossibility of satisfying our inner urges, since the satisfaction of the sexual instinct is nothing but a dangerous and unworthy delusion." Because "Petrarch's embrace of the Augustinian heritage of total introspection contributed to the establishment of the concentration on the inner experience," Petrarch could posit "pure sentimental satisfaction above the physicality of sexual implementation" (Aldo Scaglione, "Petrarchan Love and the Pleasures of Frustration," *Journal of the History of Ideas* [1997]: 557-72; 572).

40. Scaglione 558, 559. For a recent perspective on Michelangelo's use of Petrarch, see Thomas E. Mussio, "The Augustinian Conflict in the Lyrics of Michelangelo: Michelangelo Reading Petrarch," *Italica* 74 (1997): 339-59.

41. For example, as he completed work on his *Istorie fiorentine* Machiavelli wrote to Giannotti, "io non posso scrivere questa historia da che Cosimo prese lo Stato per insino alla morte di Lorenzo come io la scriverei se io fossi libero da tutti i rispetti; le azioni saranno vere e non pretermetterò cosa alchuna, solamente lascierò indrieto il discorrere le cause universali delle cose; verbi gratia, io dirò gli eventi et gli casi che successero quando Cosimo prese lo Stato; lascierò indrieto il discorrere in che modo, et con che mezzi et astuzie uno pervenga a tanta altezza; et chi vorrà ancor intendere questo, noti molto bene quello ch'io farò dire ai suoi avversarii, perché quello che non vorrò dire io, come da me, lo farò dire ai suoi avversarii" (from a letter from Giannotti to Marcantonio Micheli dated 30 June 1533 [Donato Giannotti, *Opere politiche,* Vol. 2, *Lettere italiane (1526-71),* ed. Furio Diaz (Milan: Marzorati, 1974) 35]). Similarly, Giannotti wrote to Varchi from Venice on 10

June 1538, "Io credo dare fra pochi giorni perfezione al mio libro *De Republica Veneta*; e poi cercherò d'ottenere licenzia di stamparlo. E così, poi che non possiamo ragionare de' fatti nostri, ragioneremo di quelli d'altri, e non saremo banditi da casa" (*ivi* 48).

42. On 27 November 1547 the Florentine government published a proclamation that had been under discussion at least since the beginning of October of that same year that prohibited Florentine citizens from any contact with rebels. In that context, Michelangelo wrote to his nephew acknowledging Leonardo's warnings and reassuring him that he would continue to be just as careful in the future as he had been in the past to neither talk to nor keep the company of any *fuorusciti*. He admitted that when he had fallen ill in 1546 he had recovered in the Strozzi's Roman residence, but specified that he had been lodged in Luigi Del Riccio's chambers. Del Riccio, he explained, was not only a close friend, but also a superb administrator of his business affairs. After Del Riccio passed away, Michelangelo clarified, he had not returned to the Strozzi home. He claimed that all of Rome could attest to his solitude, to the fact that he went out rarely in public, and that he spoke to hardly anyone at all, "especially Florentines." When greeted on the street he would reply courteously and quickly disengage himself. In fact, he added, if he knew exactly who the rebels were, he "would not speak to them at all." Cf. *Il carteggio di Michelangelo,* Letter MXCII, "Michelangelo in Roma al nipote Leonardo in Firenze," 22 ottobre 1547, 279-80.

43. Cf. Binni, for whom Michelangelo's "vicinanza ai fuorusciti fiorentini (che costituiva di fatto uno dei cerchi più stretti della sua socievolezza)" was "smentita assurdamente, soprattutto in relazione al danno che poteva derivare alla famiglia e alla fortuna economica costruita in Firenze" (31).

44. Donato Giannotti, lettera to Benedetto Varchi of circa 26 November 1537 (Giannotti 44). The anti-Medicean opposition was handed its definite defeat at Montemurlo on 31 July 1537 when the militia of Cosimo I triumphed over a band of Florentine rebels directed by Filippo Strozzi.

45. As Giannotti explained to Varchi in a letter dated 26 November 1537, "Guglielmo Martelli (che è qui meco), per essere ito a visitare il cardinale Salviati, è stato citato dagli Otto" (Giannotti 45).

46. Further demonstrated by Giannotti's sending to Lorenzo Strozzi, dedicatee of Machiavelli's *Arte della guerra,* a copy of Machiavelli's yet unpublished *Discorsi sulla prima Deca di Tito Livio* (Giannotti [letter to Lorenzo Strozzi dated 19 August 1532] 25).

47. De Tolnay informs us that Michelangelo knew Machiavelli personally (*The Art and Thought of Michelangelo* 4). Perhaps an additional link between Michelangelo and the Florentine rebels is to be found in the figure of Antonio Brucioli. Spini addresses the friendship between Michelangelo and Brucioli (578), while Albertini, following Cantimori, considers Brucioli's *Dialoghi della moral filosofia* a means for better understanding the spiritual and cultural world of the young men who met in the Orti Oricellari, were influenced by Machiavelli, and participated in the anti-Medicean plot of 1522 (67-85).

48. In Baratto's words, "il giudizio di M. sulla situazione di 'danno' e di 'vergogna' in cui si trovano l'Italia, e in particolare Firenze, è ellittico, ma non per questo meno eloquente" (Mario Baratto, "La poesia di Michelangelo," *Rivista di letteratura italiana* 2.3 [1984]: 405-23; 420). According to Mastrocola, "la quartina ha [. . .] un significato politico. Essendo la statua terminata nel 1531 e i versi dello Strozzi quindi posteriori a quella data, la replica di Michelangelo, di sapore antimediceo, allude presumibilmente alle condizioni di Firenze dopo la restaurazione d Alessandro de' Medici nel 1530. Seguendo invece la datazione del Frey e Girardi, che propongono il 1545 [. . .], la quartina sarebbe un attacco al governo tirannico del Duca Cosimo (contro il quale è anche il madrigale 249), e l'espressione ''l danno e la vergogna' andrebbe riferita agli eventi posteriori all'omicidio di Alessandro de' Medici per opera del Lorenzino" (Mastrocola 255).

49. Strozzi's quatrain was inserted in the *canzoniere* manuscripts at number 16. According to Fedi, it was "trascritto per giustificare la risposta di Michelangelo" ("'L'immagine vera'" 48).

50. Gilbert contends that the design of the tombs prevented the inscription of the Duke's names on them: the lack of identification left the Dukes in anonymity, a trait that was reinforced by the arrangement of the sculptures in the chapel (Gilbert 229, 242). He specifies elsewhere that the "eccentricities" of the Medici tombs "include the omission of the names of the persons buried there, as well as an unprecedented shape for the section containing the body, and the well known rejection of portrait identities, to mention only qualities about which the patron might have been expected to feel particular concern" (271).

51. N, 67 [G177] *In noi vive e qui giace la divina,* and N, 68 [G178] *La nuova alta beltà che 'n ciel terrei* (to further substantiate the dialogic nature of this collection, two sonnets by Porrino are inserted within one of the codices [Ghizzoni 186]), not to mention the compositions for Riccio (NN,

71, 72, *Perch'è troppo molesta* [G252]. I disagree with Fedi's reading of the "three directly 'dialogic' texts in the *canzoniere*," the epigram on the *Night* (N, 17) and the two compositions dedicated to the memory of Fausta Mancini Attavanti. Fedi claims that because of them "si ha *quasi* l'impressione che la scelta lirica di Michelangelo [. . .] tend[esse] a porre in secondo piano gli aspetti più vistosi, contingenti, biografici in senso politico e storicamente accertabile" censuring, "è *quasi* il caso di dirlo, ogni evidente riferimento all'occasionalità" (286, 287; my emphasis). Rather, they de-lyricize the macrotext, linking it more closely to the specifically biographical and historical and allow for a more contingent reading of the compositions to Dante and Florence.

52. This distaste is evinced, and with similar circumlocution, between the lines of Giannotti's second *Dialogo*. Michelangelo agrees with Giannotti, who contends that Brutus and Cassius were justified in killing "the tyrant of their homeland," by distinguishing between tyrants who usurped the rights of others and the hereditary *Signore* whose rule was based on the voluntary consent of his subjects. Nonetheless, Michelangelo defends the poet's placement of Caesar's assassins in the deepest pit of Hell. Michelangelo argues that Dante did well to place Brutus and Cassius in Lucifer's jaws because they betrayed the empirial majesty entrusted by God first to the Romans and later to the Emperors. Cfr. *Dialogi di Donato Giannotti de' giorni che Dante consumò nel cercare l'Inferno e 'l Purgatorio,* ed. Deoclecio Redig de Campos (Florence: Sansoni, 1939) 88 and ff.

53. Which he intended would be in an altar in Santa Maria Maggiore in Rome (Irving Lavin, "The Sculptor's 'Last Will and Testament,'" *Allen Memorial Art Museum Bulletin* 35 [1977-1978]: 4-39; 16).

54. Giorgio Vasari, *Vite scelte,* ed. Anna Maria Brizio, 1948 (Turin: UTET, 1964) 452. See also Charles de Tolnay, *Michelangelo,* 5 vol. (Princeton: Princeton UP, 1960) 5: 88. It is interesting to note that in addition to this role played in the production and destruction of the *Pietà del Duomo,* Urbino, in Michelangelo's own words, was an at times overly zealous "sollecitatore de' polizini," or drafts of his poems (cf. *Il carteggio di Michelangelo,* Letter MLVII ("Michelangelo [in Roma] a Luigi del Riccio [in Roma]," Febbraio o primi di marzo 1546, 233).

55. Michelangiolo Buonarroti, *Rime,* ed. Enzo Noè Girardi [Bari: Laterza, 1960] 499-500.

56. The version reproduced in Giannotti's *Dialogi* differs from the versions reproduced by Girardi and Mastrocola. In Giannotti the order of the quatrains is reversed (and the second is markedly different, as is the first tercet).

57. The composition closes with Florence explaining that frustrated desire is often sweeter than amorous satisfaction: "ché degli amanti è men felice stato / quello, ove 'l gran desir gran copia affrena, / ch'una miseria di speranza piena."

58. Not a "domanda oziosa," as Mastrocola claims (13), but a fundamental one.

59. For Fedi the death of the Marchioness of Pescara is the principal reason (cf. Fedi, "'L'imagine vera'" 69).

60. But whose influence was felt as early as the beginning of the decade, in the form of a censorship that antedated the installation of the Papal Indices (Fiorato 104).

61. Cambon 56-57.

62. When Michelangelo was 70 years old he drew up a will on the occasion of a near-fatal illness. It is mentioned in a letter dated January 9, 1546, from Del Riccio to the nephew Leonardo. Lavin states that it was a nearly complete document, lacking only the notary's signature. Michelangelo had previously fallen ill and been taken in by Riccio in the summer of 1544. According to Lavin the opening verse of G295, 'Di morte certo, ma non già dell'ora' follows perfectly the formulary of notarial documents of the period, particularly the introductory rationale used in wills to justify the drawing up of that document (Lavin 18).

63. Gilbert points out that of the extant poetic texts by Michelangelo, those written before he was fifty-five, comprise only one sixth of the total. The rest were written between 1530 and 1555. He cites a "biographical reason for the sudden enrichment of poetry around 1530": his friendships, most importantly that of Vittoria Colonna. He then divides Michelangelo's twenty-five years as an active poet into two main phases. The first extends from circa 1530 to 1546 (Gilbert 227, 281). "In that year," he writes, "two personal events altered Michelangelo's life," the deaths of Riccio and of San Gallo. Subsequently, the position of architect of Saint Peter's became Michelangelo's main work: "thereafter he took no commissions for painting, only finishing the pair of frescoes he had in hand, nor for sculpture, only working on the two Pietàs he made successively for himself and not finishing either of those. This was not from weakness or resignation, since he also did take on new projects to design and oversee other churches and papal building projects. The events of 1546 thus seemed to turn Michelangelo more toward

the private and personal and toward religion, relative to the range of his previous activity." (282). The final period of substantive poetic creativity, in Gilbert's opinion, lasted from 1546 until 1554-1555. In his words, these "late poems" are "more involved with religion and its institutional forms. "They are without paradox, without involution, and suggest [a] kind of achieved bare simplicity" (277). For Cambon, "one thing is clear: that after 1547 [. . .] Michelangelo's writing enters its critical last phase marked by a sharp drop in productiveness, by the much higher ratio of fragments versus finished lyrics, and by the predominantly religious inspiration" (112).

64. Ridolfi 91, 111, 120-21, 134-35.

65. Cambon 129, 134. However, Cambon writes, Michelangelo's "ingrained love for Petrarch spurred him to challenge the Petrarchists on their own ground, by exploring the formal possibilities of word, phrase, and rhythm and at times pushing that exploration to the limit" (175).

66. Ridolfi 135-38.

67. Shortly after the death of the Cardinal, the aging (born in 1492) Giannotti entered the service of a new benefactor and departed for Venice in 1551 (Ridolfi 138, 141). The death of Cardinal Ridolfi, with whom Giannotti enjoyed a great spiritual affinity, marked an important turning point in Giannotti's life, motivating, as I have already indicated, Giannotti's burning of many of his papers (Ridolfi 139-41). Giannotti's *Dialogi de' giorni che Dante consumò nel cercare l'Inferno e 'l Purgatorio*, which I have also had occasion to cite, lay unpublished in the Vatican Library until 1859 (cf. Steinmann 240).

## Joseph Francese (essay date January 2002)

SOURCE: Francese, Joseph. "On Homoerotic Tension in Michelangelo's Poetry." *MLN* 117, no. 1 (January 2002): 17-47.

[*In the following essay, Francese traces the development of Michelangelo's conflict between his love of earthly, physical beauty and his need for divine grace and inner peace as displayed in his poems.*]

The hypothesis that a latent homosexuality (or bisexuality) can be identified in Michelangelo's poetry has often been put forth, especially in the English-speaking world. Its general claim, that Michelangelo's "unorthodox sexuality" is a key to a better understanding of both his poetry and his art, is grounded mostly on psychoanalytic studies such as Robert S. Liebert's

investigation of Buonarroti's life and works.[1] Leibert's premise is "there are certain invariable laws of human behavior which operate in all individuals, irrespective of period and culture" (3). This assumption raises a fundamental methodological issue for literary readings of the *Rime* that regards the validity of utilizing this "metatemporal" framework.

Paradoxically, such philological studies attempt to read Michelangelo's verse in its historical context while using as their point of departure Leibert's metahistorical presumptions. For example, in his recent monograph (an interesting and intelligent analysis and important overview of the *Rime*), Christopher Ryan demonstrates a refined sensitivity to the nuances of difficult poetic texts. At the same time he grounds his analyses of the texts on a speculative oedipal explanation of Michelangelo's sexuality[2] that allows him to assert that "Michelangelo's sexuality was at least primarily homoerotic" (156), and then use Oedipus as a key for his reading of the *Rime*. This belief, coupled with Michelangelo's fascination with males of superior beauty and intelligence, then causes Ryan to find in the poems for the young Roman noble Tommaso Cavalieri a "rapture" that distinguishes them from the rest of the *Rime*. The poet's infatuation with Cavalieri leads Ryan to complete the circle and affirm that the "repentance" evinced in the poems Buonarroti wrote after 1547 is attributable in great measure to remorse for past homosexuality (12-13). However, it must be made clear that the original impetus for Ryan's reading (a fact he makes explicit only in an endnote) comes from "indirect and inconclusive" evidence and "fairly meagre indications in the sources" (260). James Saslow also uses Liebert to justify an "oedipal," hence homoerotic reading of Michelangelo's verse. Saslow is of the opinion that "Michelangelo's statements about love and desire leave little doubt that he conceived of intimate relationships in what would now be considered fundamentally homosexual terms" (*The Poetry of Michelangelo*, 17).[3] Robert Rodini is the author of a third highly intelligent study that seeks to link the importance of eye imagery in the poems dedicated to Cavalieri to Liebert's theses. He speculates:

> I think it can be argued that the eye, as an organ, as a corporeal orifice, and as metonymic of the body, is referential to both the intellect, the locus of apprehension and desire, and, as well, to orifices of the physical body which have highly erotic associations.
>
> (68)

Then, following Saslow, he builds on that conjecture, and writes, "we are speaking of the eye as a metonym of the "receptive body," of reception which can satisfy by illumination in bringing epiphanic moments just as it can be a metonym for the willing reception of sexual gratification which, in the case of Michelangelo, seemingly goes unfulfilled" (68-69).

Such readings take their impetus from the apparent agreement in the psychoanalytic community that "Michelangelo's deeply ambivalent relationship to his mother" not only had "a decisive influence on his creativity," but also gave vent to "a late and intense expression" in his "inflamed passion for Cavalieri" (Sterba and Sterba, 170). The same—it is claimed—can be said for the ambiguous paternalism toward other young men that can be found in Michelangelo's poetry. However, there is much that we just do not know about these relationships, and about many other aspects of Michelangelo's life. Therefore, more verifiable aspects of his personal and creative life cannot be ignored in favor of assumptions based on irretrievable aspects of his intimate biography. While art serves to reveal what is hidden, we cannot set aside obvious, conscious motivations and allow what cannot be substantiated to pre-condition exegesis. At the same time, I would like to stress that it is hardly my intention to prove or even speculate on Michelangelo's heterosexuality, especially within the historical context relative to Cinquecento Florence. Michelangelo's extant poems, variants and fragments do contain numerous gender-ambiguous references. However, we cannot draw hasty conclusions as to their significance. At the same time, the effects on his verse of his esthetic ideal, the world-view reflected in his politics, and his profound and lasting religious sentiment cannot be discounted. In sum, I would propose that, lacking more sophisticated means and methods of analysis, we proceed with much greater caution, avoiding both metatemporal explanations and tautological corroboration of as yet unproven hypotheses.

A historical reading of the **Rime** takes for granted the "necessary reciprocity" of Buonarroti's production in verse and his ideological view of the world, while placing his sexuality in a contextualized perspective. In Michelangelo's specific case, we may cite among the fundamental components of his thought the preachings of Fra' Girolamo Savonarola and the lessons of Ficino's Neo-Platonic circle on the ideal of Christian love—and their lasting effects on his intellectual formation—and the spiritual lessons he took from Vittoria Colonna in the 1530s and 1540s. The roots of Michelangelo's spirituality, particularly his youthful attentiveness to the teachings of Savonarola fed the Republicanism of his more mature years, blending with the "Nicodemistic" Reformism taken from the Marquise Vittoria Colonna.[4] Thus, his early poetry emphasized the lesson imparted by the Dominican monk regarding the transitory nature of human existence, which fused with the Neo-Platonic belief in the possibility of approaching God through identification with the beloved.

If we seek to comprehend the poet in his own time and society, and through an approximation of his own understanding of his position in both (Binni), we avoid discarding, with Leibert, important conscious motivations (such as Michelangelo's dynastic ambitions for his family in Florence, and his highly developed instincts for self-preservation). We also bring into the picture forms of male aggregation typical of the society in which Michelangelo lived. In so doing, we give more than minimal importance to cultural evolution. Instead, Leibert raises Oedipus to metahistorical category and only infrequently and fleetingly looks beyond it to the *socius* (Deleuze and Guattari). In so doing, he universalizes a particular time-bound culture by reducing and rewriting "the whole rich and random multiple realities of concrete everyday experience into the contained, strategically pre-limited terms of the family narrative" (Jameson, 22).

Leibert, as we have stated, provides the critical basis for psychoanalytic readings of Michelangelo's poetic production. When observed from historical and philological standpoints, he develops his "metatemporal" premise with excessive fervor. Rather than start with the most obvious and reasonable explanations for Michelangelo's behavior, Liebert generally ignores the formative effect of conscious ideas and reasoning. The end result is a highly ambitious narrative whose foundations creak and bend under the weight of his conclusions. He analyzes the themes of Michelangelo's paintings and sculptures while summarily ignoring the predetermining influence of the wishes of patrons on Renaissance art and the site for which the piece was intended (Paoletti, 14-16). He also fails to consider how many of Michelangelo's attitudes were typical of the Renaissance *forma mentis* (for example, how his dynastic ambitions for the Buonarroti conditioned his behavior).[5] The same negative conclusion can be drawn for Leibert's reading of Michelangelo's letters, the content of which is always taken literally, and, therefore as precise indications of unconscious motives.[6] The possibility that the content of the letters cannot always be taken at face value because the artist consciously negotiated with or purposely attempted to manipulate his interlocutors is never considered. Similarly, while the testimony of Michelangelo's "friendly" biographers (Condivi and Vasari) is viewed with suspicion, that of other contemporaries is underwritten without question: for example, events reported in works replete with hyperbole and self-justification such as Cellini's *Autobiography* are given the self-validating truth-value of a Borgesian footnote (293). When original works crucial to Leibert's theories, such as the presentation drawing of Ganymede, have been lost, the psychoanalyst applies "close readings" to copies not by the artist's hand (277). The same can be said of works whose precise historical-biographical location cannot be ascertained because the dates of their completion are not known with absolute certainty.[7] Leibert fills in the many blank spaces he finds in Michelangelo's biography with inference, speculation, and conjecture taken, in his own words, "from the realm of plausibility [and] that of probable truth" (6).

In sum, Leibert applies "the psychoanalytic method" to a "patient," Michelangelo, who is long departed, about whom there is much we cannot know with certainty, and who is—and this matters most—refractory to the crucial element of the psychoanalytic process, transference.

While Leibert's valorization of Oedipus may possibly be justifiable in a psychoanalytical context, literary critics cannot afford to ignore Timpanaro's demystification of a mode of reasoning in psychoanalysis dominated by the "anti-scientific" or non-philological interpretation of lapsus. As Vattimo has argued, the universal validity of psychoanalysis has yet to be proven.[8] Yet this is not to say that Leibert does not raise interesting issues. Since the subject exercises agency within the force-fields of contradiction characteristic of both the social and the individual psyche, art reflects the conflictual dynamic of individual desire and social constraint. This internal confrontation occurs at the critical juncture where the subject is both constructed and constructs him/herself within a condition of limited and situated freedom. The fact that certain activities were deemed unacceptable in Cinquecento Florence does not mean that people, including Michelangelo, did not feel unconscious desires. It is quite understandable that living in that environment he would have repressed homosexual tendencies if he had them. Indeed, Michelangelo's conscious suppression of possible homoerotic suggestions could well be a sign of a very real anxiety. However, while psychoanalysts may—or may not—be justified in looking for indications of a return of the repressed in Michelangelo's poetry, those of us who attempt philologically to reestablish the artistic and intellectual world of a writer must depend on documentary evidence, not on conjecture. Thus, literary studies of the *Rime* that use Leibert's study as point of departure place themselves on shaky ground. We may use psychoanalysis to support our theories, but may not over-rely on it. Hence, it is not my intent to argue against Leibert, but against certain appropriations of his theories.

Worthy of note is the fact that Leibert himself concludes that Michelangelo's love for the young Roman nobleman Tommaso Cavalieri never progressed beyond the Platonic to consummation (294, 295). Liebert adds that the same holds true for the rumored relationships with other young men (298, 302). In the final analysis, the psychoanalyst proposes at the very most a "platonic homosexual adaptation" whereby Michelangelo sublimated repressed desire in his art. For that matter, Saslow

also specifies that the homoeroticism of the verse might be due to a fascination that never reached the level of overt "genital expression," but remained "latent and intellectual."[9] And herein lies a fundamental question that needs to be answered prior to raising the issue of the presence or absence of homoerotic tension in the *Rime*: did latent homosexual desire, repressed in the unconscious, manifest itself "uncannily" in the art, or was a manifest tendency consciously suppressed? Since we know that Michelangelo was often forced actively to defend himself against gossip regarding illicit relationships with younger men, we must favor the second possibility. In fact, as we will see when we examine several of the poems further on, Michelangelo explicitly claims his Neo-Platonic intentions toward the young men in question were maliciously misconstrued. Thus, we may at most postulate that if there were manifest homosexual tendencies, they were consciously suppressed. Social constraints on the one hand, and on the other a religious faith that combined elements of the youthful Neo-Platonism (that also alimented his aesthetic ideal) and Savonarolism (prior to his embrace of Vittoria Colonna's Catholic reformism)[10] took the day. Thus, we can do no more than speculate on a return of the repressed in the *Rime,* while as philologists we are bound to adhere to what can be documented.

For that matter, the psychoanalysts Sterba and Sterba are, like Leibert, very aware that the "scarcity and limitations of the biographical material" (158) increase the difficulty of interpretation, already problematic in light of our inability to obtain conscious or unconscious confirmation of our hypotheses. Unlike Leibert, however, they proceed much more cautiously, limiting themselves to extant biographical data to support hypotheses that consider the effects of the actions of Michelangelo's mother on the artist's character formation (160). The Sterbas contend that the absent mother played a significant role in the artist's inclination toward bitterness and unhappiness, while contributing to his "negative attitude toward women"[11] and his mistrust of people in general (160). The Sterbas also propose that it is more than coincidence that the state of rapture provoked in 1532 by the friendship of Cavalieri closely followed the death of Michelangelo's father (an event that Bull [236], following Ramsden has placed in 1531).[12] They suggest that with this event an important inhibition to Michelangelo's love strivings had been lifted, triggering a behavior more characteristic of those enthralled in the first great love of their adolescent years. Concomitantly, "Michelangelo's deeply ambivalent relationship to his mother" not only had "a decisive influence on his creativity," but also gave vent to "a late and intense expression" in his "inflamed passion for Cavalieri" (170).[13] In fact, Michelangelo superseded his father as head of the family when, as an adult, he protected the older man from the other siblings, and when he reprimanded his father for acting against what

Michelangelo thought were their family's best interests. Furthermore, as Liebert himself reminds us, "for the last three decades of his eighty-seven years, [Lodovico] was almost entirely supported by Michelangelo" (29). The point is that Michelangelo's familial situation was characterized not by an absent father and dominant mother, but by an absent mother and a father who over time was deprived of symbolic power by his son. This state of affairs suggests a successful oedipal resolution. Thus, in the Sterbas' analysis of Michelangelo's art homosexual tendencies—both manifest and latent—play a much less important role than what is proposed by their colleague.

In sum, we are far from knowing with any sort of certainty the nature of Michelangelo's sexuality. We have no documentary evidence at our disposal that would indicate overt expressions of carnal desires. We do know that the dominant constellation of his ideas dictated against participation in a homosexual subculture. Nonetheless, Michelangelo's sexuality has become the focus of psychoanalytic interpretations of the *Rime.* As we will see, sexually unorthodox references to men were written out of variants, disproving hypotheses of "uncanny" returns of the repressed in his poetry. However, we will also see that unorthodox sexual references were not completely suppressed from the edition of verse prepared by Michelangelo for publication in the mid-1540s, a fact that gives purchase to Neo-Platonic readings of the poems in question. It also precludes our concluding that Michelangelo, who was well aware of what was said of him and denied all allegations, purposely "outed" himself through his poetry.

Therefore, while acknowledging the unquestionable acumen of the conclusions reached by various Anglo-American literary critics of Michelangelo's lyrics, we encounter serious methodological doubts when considering their premises. We are always well advised to use caution whenever undertaking a search for the "return of the repressed" of sublimated sexual tension in poetry. In this case, the speculative, uncorroborated nature of the hypotheses forestalls our allowing our readings of Michelangelo's production in verse to be predetermined by them.

Therefore, in the second half of this essay I will further examine the argument that an historical analysis of extant documents does not demonstrate anything more than a strong "male bonding" between Michelangelo and his friends. His relationships with youths such as Tommaso de' Cavalieri mirror his affection for older men such as Luigi Del Riccio, Donato Giannotti and his helper Urbino and for Vittoria Colonna. I will concentrate on the letter of his poetic texts, avoiding both projection onto the texts and speculation as to what might be repressed beneath the surface. I will withdraw from the sort of speculations that psychoanaly-

sis highlights, while avoiding conjecture on lacunae in his biography, particularly as regards his earliest attempts at lyric production. I will also contend that the public nature of much of his poetry indicates that his declarations of Neo-Platonic love for men did not go outside social or legal norms but fell within the limits of a sexual paradigm to a certain degree incommensurate with our own. In this context I will affirm that the gifts he made of his art to male friends are indications of the extreme emotional value he invested on the placement of products of his own hand. In other words, he would risk offending powerful patrons by refusing them his art, but would happily and spontaneously make gifts of his work to close friends and supporters of the cause of the Florentine republic. I will also argue that the remorse characteristic of the poetry of his intensely religious final years (roughly 1547-1564) reflects repentance for an enduring and excessive pride in his "divine" artistic achievements. I will also aver that the youthful Neo-Platonism that led him to place excessive value in a cult of human beauty and to seek mediators between his soul and God became a source of internal torment when, following the example of Vittoria Colonna, he came to seek a direct relationship with his Creator.

\* \* \*

Michelangelo's intellectual formation, which combined elements of Savonarolism and Neo-Platonism and informed his world-view at least until he made the acquaintance of Vittoria Colonna, would have dictated against overt homosexuality, in spite of an extensive sodomitic subculture in Florence. Sedgwick has described a heterosexual-homosocial-homosexual continuum—within the broader gender system that governs behavior between the sexes—that existed in Renaissance Florence. With the term "male homosocial desire" she designates a pattern of "male friendship, mentorship, entitlement, rivalry, and hetero- and homosexuality" (1). This particular configuration of male aggregation formed the basis of a social hierarchy that included sodomitic relationships and effectively established or created an interdependence and solidarity among males that served to reinforce dominion over females (3). She specifies that the classic Greek model on which that of the Renaissance was patterned was not endemically homophobic, as is the case with modern patriarchies, making more problematic, as stated above, an appraisal of Michelangelo's sexuality in modern terms. As Sedgwick reminds us, the homosociality of ancient Greece was "Highly structured along lines of class, and within the citizen class along lines of age, the pursuit of the adolescent boy by the older man was described by stereotypes that we associate with romantic heterosexual love (conquest, surrender, the 'cruel fair,' the absence of desire in the love object), with the passive part going to the boy" (Sedgwick, 4). Rocke informs us that male behavior in Renaissance Florence followed this classic pattern of active adult and passive adolescent.[14] Extant judicial records demonstrate that the "absolute prevalence" of the classic, pederastic model was such as to appear almost "normative" (88). He continues by saying that "only in the eighteenth century, and in northwestern Europe (England, the Netherlands, and France), did this pattern gradually begin to be replaced by a new model. After 1700 adult males are frequently found having sex with other adult males, the rigid sexual roles of the past appear to have become more fluid, homosexuality was commonly associated with effeminacy, and distinctive subcultures developed" (88).

Rocke goes on to explain that "The age structure, the rigid division of roles, the gender symbolism, and the often aggressive style of sodomy continued to express and reinforce the dominant virility expected and encouraged especially of young [adult] males" (162). Furthermore, he has demonstrated that in the Sixteenth Century it was a "highly disgraceful" event for a man over the age of twenty to assume the passive role in a homosexual relationship with a younger man (234). A situation of Michelangelo's poetry within the broader context provided by the peculiar forms of male aggregation specific to Renaissance society would indicate that a passive homoerotic relationship with Cavalieri (whom he often addresses as "Signior mie caro" in the verse) would have violated in a profound and opprobrious way the social codes reflected in the anti-sodomy laws enacted in the fifteenth century. Therefore, I propose that the use of the term "Signore" by Michelangelo to address Cavalieri in, for example, G58 and G60 [Girardi edition: Michelangelo, *Rime,* ed. Enzo Noè Girardi (Bari: Laterza, 1960)] (an appellation echoed repeatedly in the penitential works of his last years) is appears much more in keeping with his Neo-Platonism (and with rhetorical forms dictated by the caste system in place at that time, as we shall presently see).[15]

Nonetheless, the correspondence between Cavalieri and Michelangelo has been cited as evidence of Michelangelo's desire to submit to a male of superior physical and intellectual qualities. Indeed, it may be argued that Michelangelo's epistles to Cavalieri are characterized by stylistic difficulty and unease. However, if we direct our attention to the earliest extant letters exchanged between the two men in December 1532, we see that the correspondence reflects the artist's awareness of having to deal with someone of a much higher social station, a state of affairs that would dictate against a dominant homoerotic relationship. Furthermore, we note Michelangelo's awareness that his solitary nature made difficult the establishment and maintenance of friendships. As the artist wrote to his young friend:

> se io non arò l'arte del navicare per l'onde del mare del vostro valoroso ingegnio, quello mi scuserà, né si sdeg-

nierà del mio disaguagliarsigli, né desiderrà da mme quello che in me non è: perché chi è solo in ogni cosa, in cosa alcuna non può aver compagni.

> (*Il carteggio,* DCCCXCVII, late December 1532)

As Ciulich has contended, while Michelangelo's letters use "a variety of style and lexicon," they demonstrate a different physical appearance that always adapts itself to the intended recipient (*Costanza ed evoluzione,* 8). For example, the letters to Cavalieri are "distinct in their elevated style and beautiful handwriting." She adds, "the artist does not exempt himself from contemporary protocols and conventions, that in this period are governed by a complex body of formal rules: the various drafts of the same letter are justified by re-thinkings and by the use of the most opportune formulas of courtesy.[16] Thus, the letters sent by Michelangelo to Cavalieri—and to literati, princes and popes—are stylistically distinct from the quotidian, "flowing, spontaneous" form typically used in his letters to relatives or business associates, letters in which Michelangelo "does not pretend to reproduce in careful detail the phonic structure of words." In letters to friends and family he uses a "practical, often approximate style" that often trusts itself to the "good sense of the writer and the intuition of the reader." His more intimate correspondence reflects more closely than those to potentates "the degree and type" of his culture (Ciulich, *Costanza ed evoluzione,* 11), that of *omo sanza lettere.*

Furthermore, if we concentrate on the overt intentions of the poet, we see that in poems dedicated to Cavalieri and written at the outset of their relationship, Buonarroti makes reference to "immortal desio," "la casta voglia che 'l cor dentro incende / da chi sempre se stessi in altrui vede" (G58), "un casto amor," "una pietà superna" (G59), "il foco onesto / che m'arde" (G72) and "l'amor, la fede e l'onesto desio," (G83). He also explicitly denies gossip about his sexual proclivities. He tells his "signior ch'alle menzogne actende" (G58), that one must transcend earthly concerns and desires if Cavalieri's intrinsic qualities are to be understood and appreciated:

> Quel che nel tuo bel volto bramo e 'mparo,
> e mal compres'è dagli umani ingegni,
> chi 'l vuol saper convien che prima mora.
>
> (G60)

The poetic voice of these first poems to the young Roman noble also takes care to disparage the "vulgo malvagio, iscioco e rio, / di quel che sente, altrui segnia e addita" (G83). The prospect of an inadvertent admission of homoeroticism through the poetry is further weakened by the public nature of compositions such as G98: Varchi cited this same sonnet in a *Lezzione* read before the Florentine Academy, and published his talk during Michelangelo's lifetime, gaining for his efforts

Michelangelo's explicit gratitude (*Il carteggio*, MCXLIII). In his *Lezzione* Varchi specified that the poem had been dedicated to Cavalieri,

> giovane romano nobilissimo, nel quale io conobbi già in Roma (oltr'a l'incomparabile bellezza del corpo) tanta leggiadria di costumi, e così eccellente ingegno e graziosa maniera, che ben meritò, e merita ancora, che più l'amasse chi maggiormente il conosceva.

(qtd. Mastrocola, 157)

The closing tercet of G98 reads: "Se vint' e preso i' debb'esser beato, / maraviglia non è se nudo e solo / resto prigion d'un cavalier armato."[17]

Another indication of the latent homosexual tension underlying the friendship with Cavalieri are three presentation drawings of Tityus, Phaeton and Ganymede given by Michelangelo to his student.[18] Our contemporary identification of Ganymede and pederasty provides many critics with a key for interpreting these drawings. They consider them as a group of interrelated texts intended to evoke homoerotic desire: Tityus was chained, then overwhelmed by a destructive love, and finally punished by eternal damnation (Hibbert), while Phaeton died because he dared draw to close to the Sun, or the object of love. However, caution must be used when attempting univocal readings of ambiguous pictorial texts: we have no clear indication of Michelangelo's intentions. Moreover, Panofsky has contended that in the Renaissance the myth of Ganymede was connected to that of Neo-Platonic *furor divinis* (214) and "symbolize[d] the fate of every *temerarius,* presumptuous enough to overstep the bounds of his allotted 'state and situation'" (219), a state of affairs, as we have seen, that reflected the caste differences separating Michelangelo from his young student. And on the reverse of Cavalieri's fallen Phaeton Michelangelo drew its mirror image, a resurrected Christ, hardly an encouragement of an illicit relationship. And, as even Liebert admits (283), since Phaeton's flight toward the Sun constituted a challenge to the father, the drawing does not fully support the hypothesis of its use as a recondite homosexual overture.

Furthermore, the drawings for Cavalieri must also be considered in the context of other gifts purposely given and withheld by the artist. As stated in the first half of this essay, Michelangelo attached great emotional value to the destination of his work, refusing to release works to "unworthy" patrons while showing himself capable of exceptional generosity with friends. At the same time, we must note that he did not make gifts of his art only to young men, although it is true that he incurred Pietro Aretino's ire by refusing to be blackmailed into giving examples of his work. Similarly, Benvenuto Cellini sought to defame Michelangelo by accusing him of having a sodomitic relationship with Urbino after Buonarroti ignored Cellini's repeated requests to return to Florence and enter the service of Cosimo I.

Michelangelo's behavior in this latter instance is consistent with a long-standing Republicanism that also led him to evade Vasari's repeated requests that Michelangelo satisfy the Duke with something of his own hand. Vasari was finally placated by the purchase of "un'anticaglia" because Michelangelo, in complying, helped his friend Vasari ingratiate himself with the latter's patron, and forestalled possible retribution against his own heirs in Florence. In so doing Michelangelo was able to keep faith with a desire to not give anything of his own hand to those who had usurped Republican rule in his native city. In point of fact, although Vasari forwarded to the aging Michelangelo Cosimo's request that the artist "send all relevant sketches and drawings" for the sacristy of San Lorenzo, Michelangelo was not forthcoming. And soon after Michelangelo's death the Duke learned to his great vexation that Michelangelo had taken care to burn almost everything he could prior to passing away. All that remained in the house in Macel de' Corvi were "few things and still fewer drawings": Vasari then had to mollify Duke Cosimo, who wrote that this act seemed "unworthy of Michelangelo" (Bull 413-15). In contrast, Michelangelo was capable of great generosity; he provided the dowry for Urbino's daughters after his helper of many years passed away, and gave two of the Slaves intended for the tomb of Julius II to Roberto Strozzi (a leader of the anti-Medici faction in Rome) and the *Pietà del Duomo* to a friend (Vasari 482). Furthermore, other significant examples of Michelangelo's civic engagement are not lacking. At one point he offered to erect an equestrian statue in honor of Francis I at his own expense if the King of France would take up arms to restore the Florentine Republic (De Tolnay *Art and Thought,* 22, 27). In addition, the death of Francis I in March 1547 wiped out a promise to do "something in marble, something in bronze, something in painting" in recognition of the King's support of Florentine independence (Bull, 324). Michelangelo was also one of the twenty Florentine citizens who petitioned Leo X for permission to remove Dante's ashes to Florence. At the bottom of this document was appended a post-script in Michelangelo's own hand, in which the artist promised to erect a "befitting sepulchre to [Dante] and in some honorable place in this city" should their request be granted (Sarolli, 151). Buonarroti defended the Second Florentine Republic "gratis et amorevolmente" (Gaye qtd. De Tolnay, *The Art and Thought,* 16), just as he had offered to carve a Hercules—later given by the Medici to Baccio Bandinelli—free of charge to the government headed by Pier Soderini (De Tolnay, *The Art and Thought,* 13).

As for Cavalieri, Ryan affirms that the young Roman noble was the one who "opened the floodgates to Michelangelo's poetry" (11). In this context, Ryan also notes Michelangelo's late interest in writing (10), or to use his own phrasing, Buonarroti's only "sporadic interest in poetry" prior to 1520 (37). However, given Michelangelo's proclivity to consign unwanted papers to the fire, it cannot be ascertained whether or not early efforts at writing were destroyed. In fact, as was stated above, gaps in the biography cannot be filled with our suppositions. We have Condivi's remark to the effect that for a brief period of time, specifically between the completion of the Doni Tondo and the election of Julius II, Michelangelo set aside the study of the figurative arts to dedicate himself to poetry. In Condivi's own words, Michelangelo:

> Se ne stette alquanto tempo quasi senza far niuna cosa in tal arte, essendosi dato alla lezione de' poeti ed oratori volgari, ed a far sonetti per suo diletto, finché morto Alessandro papa VI, fu a Roma da papa Giulio II chiamato [. . .] Poteva esser Michelagnolo in quel tempo d'anni ventinove.
>
> (38)

Ryan also finds in the few extant youthful attempts at verse all the themes destined for development in Buonarroti's later works: the equation of love and lost freedom (G7, G8), that of lost freedom due to identification with the beloved and the desire of the soul to return to Heaven through a transcendental, genderless love (G15 [38]; G34 [244]; G49 [73]), and the fleeting nature of earthly existence (G1 [40]). In the 1520s, a quarter century after the deposition of the friar and when Michelangelo was approaching the age of fifty, he would still evoke one of the lessons imparted by Savonarola in his verse concerning the transitory nature of human life ("Chiunque nascie a morte arriva / nel fuggir del tempo" [G21]). To these themes we can add the autobiographical references of G6, G7, and G10, compositions whose occasionality reflects the implicitly autobiographical nature of G248, G249, and G250, dedicated by the Republican *fuoruscito* to Dante and to Florence.[19]

The use of the concepts correctly identified by Ryan reflect a worldview that, as proposed in the first section of this study, first grafted Savonarola's preachings onto the Neo-Platonism acquired at the Magnifico's dinner table and then grew and matured through contact with Vittoria Colonna's Reformism. For example, the asceticism advocated by Savonarola (whose enduring effects come forth in Vasari's claim that Buonarroti would get so involved in his work that he would forget to remove his boots) is to be found also among the basic tenets of Christian Neo-Platonism (Nelson, 44). Similarly, the Neo-Platonic ecstasy described in Giannotti's *Dialogi* and in verses such as "tom' a me stesso e fam' un che ti piaccia" (G161; for Colonna), reflects not only the rapture (Ryan) of the poems dedicated to Cavalieri, but poetic meditations on the Crucifix. This radical identification with the other, ("S'egli è che 'n dura pietra alcun somigli / talor l'immagin d'ogni altri a se stesso, / squalido e smorto spesso / il fo, com'i son facto da costei" [G242]) allows Michelangelo to claim

that the artist depicts always and only himself, even when representing a woman ("Che s'altri fa se stesso, / pingendo donna" [G173]), a concept that resonates throughout the *Rime*. The idea that it is possible to lose oneself in the beloved, seen as a medium between the soul and God, can be found in the early G8 ("chi m'ha tolto a me stesso"), and in G108 ("son più mie vostro, che s'i' fussi mio"). It later takes on an explicitly spiritual tone in G235, dedicated to Vittoria Colonna:

> I' credo ben, po' ch'io
> a me da·llei fu' tolto,
> fuor di me stesso aver di me pietate;
> sì sopra 'l van desio
> si sprona il suo bel volto,
> ch'i' veggio morte in ogni altra beltade.

The anagogical function of love is present throughout the *Rime*: Love is an asexual, transcendental, ennobling force because it allows contemplation of the Divine (G9, G15, G259, G260, G276), an idea that in turn reflects the Neo-Platonic identification of God and the artist-creator (G62, G84, G151, G236, G241, G279).

Parenthetically, a significant parallel between Savonarola and Ficino may be found in the common denunciation of sodomy: in *Sopra lo Amore* Ficino calls sodomy a "nefaria scelerateza" pointing out that this practice was "agramente bestemmia[ta]" by Plato, who called it a "spezie di omicidio" (qtd. Nelson, 71). Savonarola—who came to power in Florence in November 1494, when Michelangelo was nineteen and a half years old, that is to say, when the artist was still in the critical formative period, no longer a "fanciullo" but not yet an adult (see Rocke)—gave an important "programmatic" sermon in the Florentine Duomo December 14, 1494, a month after assuming the leadership of the City. On that occasion the Dominican spoke to the importance of combating both one-man rule in Florence and illicit sexual practices, especially same-sex sodomy. In the same sermon Savonarola exhorted the Florentines both to support the Consiglio grande, and to legislate ruthlessly against the "vizio abominevole" of sodomy (Savonarola, 220).

The Neo-Platonism of Michelangelo's youth comprised a cult of human beauty that was not gender-specific. Nelson writes that for the Neo-Platonists human love is a *scala coeli* that allows the lover to leave the condition of sensual love behind, to accede to a superior world, and to know God to the extent permitted to the human soul (83). Of course, this scheme of things is not without a fundamental gender chauvinism: taken for granted is the superiority of the male over the female. This attitude was typical of the culture: at the climax of Castiglione's *Cortegiano* discussion of Bembo's panegyric centers on whether women are as capable as men of a love that begins with physical attraction and ascends to contemplation of the Almighty. For his part, in G260 Michelangelo praises love between males as more capable of spiritual uplift (see 9-11 "L'amore di quel ch'i' parlo in alto aspira; / donna è dissimil troppo e mal conviensi / arder di quella al cor saggio e verile"), whence the poet's attribution of masculine properties to Colonna (see, for example G235, "Un uomo in una donna, anzi un dio / per la suo boca parla") and what has been called the radical androgyny of his poetry.

To explain, Mastrocola notes that G81 has at least twelve variants, and that although the original was dedicated to a woman, an early version was dedicated to Cavalieri. In 1546 this same madrigal was revised for publication, and rendered gender ambiguous. This sort of purging also occurred with G259 during the preparation of the *Canzoniere*. In an early variant of this sonnet, for Cavalieri, the poetic voice explains that if he loves and reveres his "signore" it is due to a "divina pace [. . .] nimica e schiva d'ogni pensier rio." The poetic voice then makes clear that "Amor non è quel ch'amor qui si crede / dal vulgo errante e dagli uomini sciochi." however, when he prepares the version for publication, perhaps dedicated to the Marquise, Michelangelo eliminates all mention of the male interlocutor. In the definitive redaction, the voice asks

> Qual più giusta cagion dell'armart'io
> è, che dar gloria a quella ecterna pace
> onde pende il divin che di te piace,
> e ch'ogni cor gentil fa casto e pio?

G230[20] and G246,[21] originally intended for a man, were also altered in the drafts intended for publication. However, when G76 was re-elaborated for publication, the gender of the poetic voice's interlocutor was changed. Although the original was dedicated to a woman, the "signior" of the final draft is presumed to be Cavalieri. The public nature of this composition (along with other "public" poems such as G98, which we have already had occasion to discuss and the "burlesque" G267, which Mastrocola includes among those prepared for publication in the *Canzoniere*) points, as already argued, toward a Neo-Platonic cult of human beauty and away from conscious suppression of homoerotic desire. Saslow, who has done interesting work with the variants, notes that Michelangelo's language "is indeed revolutionary in its ambiguity and inversion," but he too cautions that

> the degree to which it represents a self-conscious rejection of contemporary norms of masculine and feminine behavior or sexual categories needs more sophisticated scrutiny. Although Michelangelo was clearly aware of the novelty and unorthodoxy of his gender devices, one should beware of reading into them a sociopolitical agenda more characteristic of today.
>
> (*The Poetry of Michelangelo,* 51-52)

Indeed, Lucente has contributed to this discussion by addressing the lack of gender-specific adjectivization in the *Rime,* convincingly arguing that Michelangelo's

writings followed an early Tuscan system of agreement that had only one form—for both genders and numbers—of the possessive when it preceded a noun.

Moreover, it is indeed the case, as Ryan claims, that "in many significant ways love, religion and morality intertwine in Michelangelo's poetry" from the very outset (171).[22] For this reason the relevance of the androgyny must be balanced by the religious sentiment and the penitential mode of many of the poems written for the Roman nobleman, brought to the fore in one of the first poems of this series, G87. Here the ambiguity of the first quatrain (the reader is not certain if the *incipit* intends to evoke a desire to suppress homosexual attraction, or if it constitutes a direct invocation of Christ), is clarified in the second quatrain by the reference to a "grace" that absolves Michelangelo from culpability for the sin he will lament in his final compositions, his "spietato orgoglio." The poem bears citation in its entirety, because it sheds light on his pride, a source of spiritual turmoil almost until his death:

> Vorrei voler, Signior, quel ch'io non voglio:
> tra 'l foco e 'l cor di ghiaccia un vel s'asconde
> che 'l foco ammorza, onde non corrisponde
> la penna all'opre, e fa bugiardo 'l foglio.
>      I' t'amo con la lingua, e poi mi doglio
> ch'amor non giungie al cor; né so ben onde
> apra l'uscio alla grazia che s'infonde
> nel cor, che scacci ogni spietato orgoglio.
>      Squarcia 'l vel tu, Signior, rompi quel muro.
> che con la suo durezza ne ritarda
> il sol della tuo luce, al mondo spenta!
>      Manda 'l predicto lume a·nnoi venturo,
> alla tuo bella sposa, acciò ch'io arda
> il cor senz'alcun dubbio, e te sol senta.[23]

The fragments G276 and G279 are emblematic of the other source of Michelangelo's spiritual disquietude, the ongoing attempt to come to terms with a youthful Neo-Platonism that placed mediators between God and the soul, at the expense of the direct relationship between God, as imparted by Vittoria Colonna. In G276 the seventy-five year old poet makes specific reference to the ungendered nature of the object of Neo-Platonic love (when he explains how "in un momento" beauty, "d'ogni età, d'ogni sesso" passes from the eyes to the heart), to then give voice in G279 to the hope that God's grace will atone for what is too deeply ingrained:

> La forza d'un bel viso a che mi sprona?
> Ch'altro non è ch'al mondo mi dilecti:
> ascender vivo fra gli spirti electi
> per grazia tal, ch'ogni altra par men buona.
>      Se ben col factor l'opra suo consuona,
> che colpa vuol giustizia ch'io n'aspecti,
> s'i' amo, anz'ardo, e per divin concecti
> onoro e stimo ogni gentil persona?

While the earlier works reflect the Neo-Platonic identification of God and beloved, the later works, particularly those written after 1547, underscore the conflict within the poetic voice between an enduring adherence to Neo-Platonic mediation and the espousal of a direct relationship between soul and Christ of the sort advocated by his friend, the Marquise Vittoria Colonna. The Catholic Reformism characteristic of Michelangelo's later years gave preference to a direct relationship with God, outside the mediation of the Church, and placed hope for salvation in justification by faith and grace. This state of mind is reflected in poetry characterized by a penitential mode that is intimately linked to his self-image as an artist who only with great difficulty set aside the Neo-Platonic cult of human beauty.

The penitential mode of the more mature poems reflects the desire expressed in G87 to "want that which he did not want": to transcend his pride and dedicate his art and life entirely to God. It was fueled by the Nicodemistic Reformism Michelangelo took from Vittoria Colonna, a form of worship that he well knew was increasingly in danger of being branded heretical by the Counter-Reformation. The interior confusion due to "wanting that which he did not want" had come to the fore in G22, written in the mid-1520s when Michelangelo was approximately forty-nine years old (eight years prior to meeting Cavalieri). In this "autobiographical meditation on the fleeting nature of time, lost youth, and approaching death" (Mastrocola), the poetic voice reasons that he must not repeat the mistakes of his youth, but instead avoid the temptations of Love, and prepare his soul for final judgement.

Ryan has pointed out thematic similarities between the Cavalieri and Colonna poems—in both groupings love "is viewed mainly within a religious perspective: this love enhances the poet's aspiration towards friendship with God and the leading of a morally good life" (132-33). In fact, as I suggested in the methodological portion of this essay, similarities between the two friendships can and should be underscored. Both were intellectual fellowships, and moreover, in the verse both friends served as mediators between Michelangelo's soul and God. Certainly, the relationship with the Marquise produced intensely beautiful poetry. One of the first compositions dedicated to her, *Non ha l'ottimo artista alcun concetto* (G151) is striking in its equation of his very essence as an artist and the spiritual beauty of his friend. And G163, might be seen not as an example of what has been called Michelangelo's "self-loathing" (Ryan), but as the appeal of a humble sinner to a spiritual intermediary in the hope that the fear of damnation will be assuaged.

> Quante più fuggo e odio ognior me stesso,
> tanto a te, donna, con verace speme
> ricorro; e manco teme
> l'alma di me, quant'a te son più presso

A quel che 'l ciel promesso
m'ha nel tuo volto aspiro
e ne' begli occhi, pien d'ogni salute:
e ben m'acorgo spesso,
in quel ch'ogni altri miro,
che gli ochi senza 'l cor non hanno virtute.

This reflects intertextually what is asserted in both G105 ("Voglia sfrenata el senso è, non amore, / che l'ama uccide; e 'l nostro fa perfetti / gli amici qui, ma più per morte in cielo") and G106 ("né Dio, suo grazia, mi si mostra altrove / più ch 'n alcun leggiadro e mortal velo; / e quel sol amo perch'in lui si spechia"). In any event, with G161 (for Colonna, and dated 1538-41) the tone of his poems to her changes, shifting toward the more penitential and preparatory for the afterlife. This change in posture was very likely due to Colonna's bringing home to Michelangelo the realities of the Council of Trent and its implications for Catholic Reformers.[24] After Charles V visited Rome in 1536 (his stay there that ended with the complete agreement between the Emperor and Paul III concerning the establishment of the Council) preparations gained definitive and zealous impetus.

Therefore, our analysis of Michelangelo's more mature verse will be deepened by an enhanced appreciation of how his spirituality was lived on a daily basis, in an area of faith somewhere in between the Protestant Reformation and the Catholic Counter-Reformation. He believed in salvation through faith and good works. After Colonna's death (an event commemorated in G265) February 25, 1547, all references to spiritual intermediaries disappear (in spite of the fact that Cavalieri remained Buonarroti's close friend until the latter's death in 1564),

> Deh, fammiti vedere in ogni loco!
> Se da mortal bellezza arder mi sento,
> apresso al tuo mi sarà foco ispento,
> e io nel tuo sarò, com'ero, in foco.
>     Signior mei caro, i' te sol chiamo e 'nvoco
> contra' l'inutil mie cieco tormento:
> tu sol può rinnoarmi fuora e drento
> le voglie e 'l senno e 'l valor lento e poco.

(G274)

and his verse increasingly reflects a preference for a direct relationship with God, outside the mediation of the Church. His faith placed hope for salvation in justification by grace, good works and faith, a sentiment expressed quite clearly in G274, "Ogni ben senza te, Signior, mi manca; il cangiar sorte è sol poter divino." In point of fact, his *Giudizio universale* displays a highly unorthodox iconography, with respect to the Counter-Reformation: the souls must confront Jesus without the aid of the Virgin and the saints, who are powerless to intercede, while Christ's stern countenance implies that God's mercy is as *terribile* as his condemnation. De Tolnay contends that "the doctrine of justification by faith alone [. . .] probably influenced three motifs of this fresco, and pure faith, exemplified by the rosary, suffices for salvation."[25] In fact, in one of the final works, G289, we have an indirect reference to the ideology of the *Giudizio universale*: "Deh, porgi, Signior mio, quella catena / che seco annoda ogni celeste dono." This, in its turn, evokes the desire for a direct relationship between the soul and its creator through faith and prayer.

Through Vittoria Colonna Michelangelo had adopted the philanthropic spirit of Protestantism. As Vasari has told us, Michelangelo designed the Basilica of Saint Peter "per l'amor de Dio e senza alcun premio" (431),[26] outwardly serving the temporal Church while intimately circumventing its spiritual mediation. The poetry of the final years is characterized by the poetic voice's self-image,[27] that of a soul who has died but has been resurrected through Christ, in spite of the stain and predestiny of original sin that damaged almost irreparably humanity's likeness to God: "Lieti, poiché, creato il redemisti / dal primo error di suo misera sorte" (G298). At the same time, his was a forgiving God of love (who is addressed as "Amor" in G274, G276, G281, and G291), whose grace allowed hope for salvation. In this context, G292, and G296 are excellent examples of his belief that virtue is a grace that comes directly from God, outside any intercession, as is G293:

> Signior mie car, non basta che m'invogli
> ch'aspiri al ciel sol perché l'alma sia,
> non come prima, di nulla, creata.
> Anzi che del mortal la privi e spogli,
> prego m'ammezzi l'alta e erta via,
> e fie più chiara e certa la tornata.

Thus, it is very plausible that, in addition to his enduring Neo-Platonic appreciation of human beauty, a significant source of distress for the aged artist was his uneasy relationship with the Counter-Reformation. Ryan claims that the two final *Pietà* carved by Michelangelo display a "touching brilliance" yet "contain little hint of that triumphant victory which, for Christian tradition, was the essential meaning of Christ's death" (201). Yet, as we have seen, Michelangelo saw himself as a clandestine apostle of Christ who, by not coming forward as testimony to the true faith, like Simon Peter in Gethsemane, merited Christ's rebuke, not God's saving grace. Michelangelo had neither left Italy to profess what was for him the true faith, nor had he remained, spoken out and offered himself up as a martyr, as was advocated and practiced by other Italian reformers. The emotional time of the *Pietà del Duomo* is neither Good Friday—which would have allowed an opportunity for a courageous, external expression of faith—nor Easter Sunday, a day of triumph through Christ. Instead, in this piece intended for his tomb, Michelangelo portrays himself as a less-than-courageous participant in the events of Holy Saturday, the day Christ spent in the nadir of Hell, for his faithful a day even darker than the previous one.

Moreover, it is significant that in his verse the elder Michelangelo does not explicitly repent of sins of the flesh. Ryan indicates that one of the sources of Michelangelo's remorse as he readied for death was the "sensitive pride" that had gained for Michelangelo "the soubriquet 'divine'" (213). It would indeed appear that the poet's remorse is attributable to an excessive sentimental investment in a "divine" status (which in his old age may have begun to sound blasphemous) as an artist, something he desired "a mal suo grado" and descries in G285 when he speaks of his soon giving

> conto e ragion d'ogni opra triste e pia.
> Onde l'affectuosa fantasia
> che l'arte mi fece idol e monarca
> conosco or ben com'era d'error carca
> e quel ch'a mal suo grado ogn'uom desia.

In G66—probably written in the winter of 1532-33, approximately the time of his first meeting Cavalieri, but prior to his making the acquaintance of Colonna—the poet evokes his sense of sharing in the guilt of original sin. At the time of its writing, the poet was fifty-five years old. In the first quatrain Buonarroti invokes the crucified Christ ("O carne, o sangue, o legnio, o doglia strema"), and here too begs for redemption from an excessive pride that causes him to deride the misfortunes of others ("Forse perché d'altrui pietà mi vegnia, / perché dell'altrui colpe più non rida"), and lack of humility ("nel mie proprio valor, senz'altra guida, / caduta è l'alma che fu già sì degna"). Because of this, he is forced to acknowledge that he is "sì presso a morte e sì lontan da·dDio." One of Buonarroti's final compositions, G293, speaks directly to his "trist'uso radicato e forte," an intertextual allusion to the same excessive sense of self-worth lamented in G285 (a composition which in turn reflects the thoughts expressed in the 1530s in G87, a poem dedicated to Cavalieri, and which we have already had occasion to quote).

Fragments G282, G283, and G284 reflect the unresolved conflict in the aged virtuoso between the exigencies of his art, and those of his soul:

> Con tanta servitù, con tanto tedio
> e con falsi concecti e gran periglio
> dell'alma, a sculpir qui cose divine.
>
> (G282)

> Più l'alma aquista ove più 'l mondo perde;
> l'arte e la morte non va bene insieme:
> che conviene più che di me dunche speri?
>
> (G283)

S'a tuo nome ho concecto alcuno inmago,
non è senza del par seco la morte,
onde l'arte e l'ingegnio si dilegua.
　　　Ma se, quel ch'alcun crede, i' pur m'apago
che si ritorni a viver, a tal sorte
ti servirò, s'avien che l'arte segua.

(G284)

In poems composed prior to his friendship with Cavalieri the poetic I is torn between the desire to believe that Neo-Platonic rapture is not sinful ("chi dice in vechia etate esser vergognia / amar cosa divina, è gran menzogna. // L'anima che non sognia, / non peca amar le cose di natura, / usando peso, termine e misura." [G25; 1525]), and the fear his *libero arbitrio* will be the cause of his perdition:

Vivo al pecato, a·nme morendo vivo;
vita già mia non son, ma del pecato:
mie ben dal ciel, mie mal da·mme m'è dato,
dal mie sciolto voler, di ch'io son privo.
　　　Serva mie libertà, mortal mie divo
a·mme s'è facto. O infelice stato!
a che miseria, a che viver son nato!

(G32)

The same can be said for G33—of which Mastrocola writes, "he sees himself as his own double: both the passive victim of Love and the active builder of a self in danger of perdition because of excessive love" (95)—and of G70, wherein humanity's free will is the cause of original sin and the loss of Edenic grace:

Così quagiù si prende, preme e·llega
quel che lassù già 'll'alber si disciolse,
ond'a·mme tolsi la dote del cielo.
　　　Qui non mi reggie e non mi spingie il cielo,
ma potenti e terrestri e duri venti,
ché sopra me non so qual si disciolse
per [darli mano?] e·ctormi del mio arbitrio.
Così fuor di mie rete altri mi lega.
Mie colpa è, ch'ignorando a quello andai?

(G70)

As he aged, he continued to seek to distance himself from his "antico uso" of infatuation with earthly beauty: "Non è più tempo, Amor, che 'l cor m'infiammi, / né che beltà mortal più goda o tema: / giunta è già l'ora strema / che 'l tempo perso, a chi men n'ha, più duole" (G231; even though, he notes "[. . .]io / a me da·llei fu' tolto, fuor di me stesso [. . .]").

In G161 the voice declares his "invidia a' morti" in Paradise, whose metatemporal quietude is free of earthly envy (G134, 6-7). But in that same poem the voice also laments the fact that "Ch'ancor ch'i cangi 'l pelo / per gli ultim'anni e corti, / cangiar non posso il vechio mie antico uso." We can only imagine what this deeply entrenched habit toward sin is. However, we must keep in mind that this particular poem was written in 1538-41

for Colonna, as was the case with G164, a composition in which he again inveighed against the *male lingue* who misrepresented his Neo-Platonic intentions, and cited the Divine grace as a necessary condition for salvation:

Per fido esemplo alla mia vocazione
nel parto mi fu data la bellezza,
che d'ambo l'arti m'è lucerna e specchio.
S'altro si pensa, è falsa opinione.
Questo sol l'occhio porta a quella altezza
ch'a pinger e scolpir qui m'apparecchio.

　　　S'è giudizi temerari e sciocchi
al senso tiran la beltà, che muove
e porta al cielo ogni intelletto sano,
dal mortale al divin non vanno gli occhi
infermi, e fermi sempre pur là d'ove
ascender senza grazia è pensier vano.

In 1547 the spiritual, if not physical, beauty of the Marquise inspired him, but he understood that this tendency and a lack of humility were causes of perdition that deprived him of inner peace:

Più perde chi men teme
nell'ultima partita,
fidando sé nel suo propio valore
contr' a l'usato ardore:
s'a la memoria sol resta l'orechio,
non giova, senza grazia, l'esser vechio.

(G263)

After the death of Vittoria Colonna, his plea for divine grace becomes even more extreme: "Che poss'io altro che così non viva? / Ogni ben senza te, Signior, mi manca; / il cangiar sorte è sol poter divino" (G274), and is coupled with a loss of faith in his art:

Non può, Signior mie car, la fresca e verde
età sentir, quant'a l'ultimo passo
si cangia gusto, amor, voglie e pensieri.
　　　Più l'alma aquista ove più 'l mondo perde;
l'arte e la morte non va bene insieme:
che conviene più che di me dunche speri?

(G283)

And in G284 he backs away from the idea that earthly beauty can inspire "divine" art, expressing the hope that art can contribute to the well-being of the soul. Paradoxically, and indicative of the artist's enduring inner conflict, G294 contains an affectionate allusion to his past, and comes in notable contrast to the penitential mode of the final poems, and in anticipation of G300.

This, Michelangelo's last completed poem, would indicate that he did in fact achieve an inner peace prior to dying. In this composition he tells his friend, Beccadelli, that "Per croce e grazia e per diverse pene / son certo, monsignor, trovarci in cielo." Christ's death and resurrection had atoned for his sins, and God's grace, justified by the poet's faith and works and the Buonarroti's earthly sufferings had earned him a place in Heaven. Therefore, he could finally embrace death, and look forward to joining his recently departed assistant Urbino and Beccadelli in heaven:

[. . .] Sua morte poi
m'affretta e tira per altro cammino,
dove m'aspetta ad albergar con seco.

(G300)

### Notes

1. In addition, of course, to Clements' seminal study.

2. For example, he writes, "It has often been proposed that the death of Michelangelo's mother when he was six, together with a far from untroubled relationship with his father, left the artist emotionally vulnerable, and in particular susceptible to the influence of strong male figures. It may be significant in this connection that only one of the five brothers married" (27). In other words, here circumstantial evidence (the brothers' celibacy) is used to corroborate a hypothesis based on incomplete evidence.

3. While admitting the difficulties inherent in his "psychoanalytic speculation," Saslow has suggested that Michelangelo accommodated his internal "conflict as many adults do today by willfully suppressing his own feelings where they were at variance with received social constructs." He contends that Michelangelo "took refuge in, and came to believe, his own rationalizations and sublimations." According to Saslow, Michelangelo "protest[ed] too much, out of the chronic anxiety engendered by self-denial" ("'A Veil of Ice,'" [86]).

4. I have discussed elsewhere the importance of Michelangelo's self-portrait on the face of Nicodemus, one of the clandestine disciples of Christ, on the *Pietà del Duomo,* a sculpture originally intended by the artist for his tomb. His "Nicodemism" was a means of passive resistance—external obedience was observed to the dictates of the Counter-Reformation—that allowed Michelangelo to profess intimately what he believed was the true faith, one that more closely followed the creed of the reformist movement in Italy (Francese, "Il nicodemismo"). According to De Tolnay, Michelangelo worked sporadically on the *Pietà del Duomo* between 1547 and 1553. However, in response to Urbino's insistent reminders to finish the piece, Michelangelo disfigured the work (Vasari, 452, and De Tolnay, *Michelangelo,* 88). Buonarroti's clandestine spirituality parallels a covert politics that motivated the artist's self-exile in Rome: a silent, lifelong protest against the Medicean restoration and the absolutism instituted by

Cosimo I that I have discussed in "Michelangelo's *Canzoniere.*"

5. Liebert claims that Michelangelo's procrastination in completing the tomb of Julius II was not due to the artist's necessary submission to the will of the reigning pope, but to the unconscious desire to perceive himself as in a perpetual state of bondage (335). Similarly, the self-exile was not caused by Buonarroti's fear of Medicean reprisal for his role in the defense of the Second Florentine Republic, but "determined by his need to reenact" his early estrangement from the family (34, 91). On the basis of three letters Liebert is able to diagnose Michelangelo's brother Giovansimone as a manic depressive (49-50). The analyst reaches this conclusion only after discarding Michelangelo's "irrational" concern that his brother's contentment with life as a peasant would undermine Michelangelo's life-long efforts to restore the family's social and juridical status (48). After uncovering in passing the unconscious reason Lionardo da Vinci never finished his *Battle of Anghiari* fresco (he was afraid of the confrontation—throughout eternity—with the younger Michelangelo's *Battaglia di Cascina* [110]), Liebert explains that the blow to Michelangelo's cheek struck by Julius II when the artist defied the Pope was "the eruption of strong unconscious homosexual impulses" between the two men (153).

6. Liebert attributes to "distortion" the view advanced in the Condivi biography that Bramante and his circle plotted against Michelangelo, citing as evidence a letter from Piero Rosselli (*Il carteggio,* X) that the psychoanalyst, it would appear, has mistranslated (127-30). I raise this issue because to my knowledge there is no indication in the texts left by Michelangelo's contemporaries that would indicate Bramante raised suspicions of sexual nonconformity to discredit a youthful Michelangelo. Instead, Bramante, Raphael's friend and mentor, succeeded in manipulating Julius II into taking Michelangelo from the tomb project the sculptor so ardently desired to bring forward and assigning Michelangelo the Sistine ceiling instead, a project Bramante believed would be source of embarrassment for Buonarroti, who was not known as a fresco painter. According to Rosselli, Bramante told the Pope, "Pad[r] Sa[n]to, io credo che lui no' basti el animo, perché lui non à fato tropo di figure, e masimo le figure sono a[l]te e in i[s]co[r]cio ed ène atra cosa che a dipi[g]nere in tera." (*Il carteggio,* X, 10 maggio 1506). Rosselli then rose to the occasion, and defended Michelangelo's offended artistic honor by accepting the challenge for him, and promising the Pope that Buonarroti would indeed return to Rome to work on the vault.

7. Liebert's propensity to set aside consideration of conscious behavior and look directly to unconscious motivations extends to the use of dream interpretation. He not only speculates that the vision of the banishment from Florence of the son of the Magnifico in 1494 was not Cardiere's, as Michelangelo's biographer Condivi (30) reported, but was in truth Michelangelo's. He then determines that the artist manifested in this way the unconscious desire to "restore his relationship with [. . .] his first loving, adoptive father," Lorenzo the Magnificent (64). And yet, while this reenactment may very well be accurate, lacking any supporting evidence as to its veracity we would do well first to look closer to home, to the prophetic powers ascribed to dreams in a text we know Michelangelo knew by heart, Dante's *Inferno*. See XXVI, 7: "Ma se presso al mattin del ver si sogna". In their edition of the *Commedia* Grandgent and Singleton point out that for Dante "it is when the body sleeps that the soul most clearly manifests its divine nature," in other words, "Dreams that occurred shortly before dawn were thought to be prophetic."

8. Whereas Vattimo sees much contemporary psychoanalytic theory staking out claims of objectivity, he calls for a historical relativity that locates psychoanalysis and the other social sciences within Modernity. That is to say, in his view, they are fields of study that arise in response to a new complexity in social relationships (89-90).

9. In fact, Saslow distances himself from Liebert when he acknowledges "the psychological sense of shortage and scarcity" that reinforced Michelangelo's "sense of fragility," which he links to sociological factors—such as the "diminished financial circumstances" of Lodovico Buonarroti's family (*The Poetry of Michelangelo*, 28-29)—that also played an important, overt role in Michelangelo's behavior.

10. Patrizi informs us that the religious doctrine espoused by the Marquise was reminiscent of the evangelism of the "Divino Amore" group, a movement that "theorized the simplification of religious life, the abandonment of more abstract forms of philosophical speculation, and the return to an evangelical morality, and to a closer interpretation of sacred texts. It was a movement that was closer to Ficinian Humanism, than to Calvinism or Lutheranism, and echoed Savonarola's preachings" (454).

11. In this context, I would like to thank my colleague at Michigan State University, Dr. Bert Karon, for having indicated the Sterbas' essay to me, for his helpful and insightful comments, and his reading of the manuscript.

12. Bull hints that Michelangelo might have manifested an unorthodox sensuality, but proceeds very cautiously in his recent biography of Buonarroti. Much is implied between the lines, but the writer never arrives at an explicit affirmation regarding Michelangelo's homo- or bi-sexuality. Instead he circles around the topic, gradually leading his readers to draw their own conclusions, but raising enough suspicions to make those conclusions foregone.

13. They then draw a parallel between the blank, detached stares of almost all the artist's Madonnas and that of the David/Apollo in the Palazzo Vecchio, whose unbearded countenance has been identified as a portrait of Cavalieri, and conclude by with the hypothesis that the death of the father allowed for an attachment to a symbolic mothersubstitute.

14. He also argues that it was widespread, despite efforts in Italy throughout the Middle Ages and Renaissance to repress sodomy through campaigns against intellectual and sexual nonconformity, carried forth as part of a general battle against all forms of heresy (291). Rocke explains that traditional forms of social control of sodomy (the family and the neighborhood) were codified in law in Renaissance Florence in 1432 with the establishment of a magistracy whose only function was to prosecute sex crimes. The Ufficio di notte was considered "a last resort to be called on only when the efforts of loved ones and acquaintances had failed" (84).

15. Submission to a dominant male by Cavalieri, who was twenty-three years old in 1532 and therefore had exceeded the age of legal majority, would have also brought the nobleman well outside the social pale. Rocke has written that young Florentine men between the ages of eighteen and twenty passed through a critical social and sexual boundary. On one side were to be found the *fanciulli,* pubescent beardless adolescents, whose sexual subordination to older men was considered appropriate for their age and social status, even though sodomy was highly scorned. On the other side of this divide the "giovani," young men who avoided the passive role in their relations with other males and, with very few exceptions assumed the dominant role in their relations with "fanciulli" (101). This division meshed well not only with the legal boundary that established the age of majority at eighteen, but also with the hierarchy according to age and sexual role, that, in Rocke's opinion, was one of the fundamental organizational aspects of the homosexual sodomitic subculture in Renaissance Florence (97). In other words, Florentine society considered the

intermediate period (that between eighteen and twenty years of age) as a watershed in the life of male adolescents. The abandonment of sexual passivity, whether or not the individual continued to practice sodomy, signaled a symbolic and in some cases experiential rite of passage into the sexual world of adult men (101).

16. Ciulich, *Michelangelo: un percorso attraverso gli autografi,* 23. Michelangelo used perhaps even greater care when writing to Vittoria Colonna. For example, see *Il carteggio,* CMLXXXIII in which he asked his friend Giannotti to transpose his letter into a language and hand more worthy of the recipient.

17. This reflects a public statement attributed to Michelangelo by his friend Giannotti nei *Dialogi,* which, when condensed reflects a solitary character who avoids social gatherings so that he might concentrate on his work. To wit: "Qualunche volta io veggio alcuno che habbia qualche virtù, che mostri qualche destrezza d'ingegno, che sappia fare o dire qualche cosa più acconciamente che gli altri, io sono constretto ad innamorarmi di lui, et me gli do in maniera in preda, che io non sono più mio, ma tutto suo. Se io, adunque, venissi a desinare con voi, essendo tutti ornati di virtù et gentilezze, oltre a quello che ciascuno di voi tre [Giannotti, Del Riccio and Antonio Petreo] qui mi ha rubato, ciascuno di coloro che si trovasse a desinare me ne torrebbe uan parte: un'altra me ne torrebbe il sonatore, un'altra colui che ballasse, et così ciascun degli altri n'harebbe la parte sua. Talchè io, credendo per rallegrarmi con voi recuperarmi et ritrovarmi, sì come voi diceste, io tutto quanto mi smarrirei et perderei; di sorte che poi, per molti giorni, io non saprei in qual mondo mi fussi" (68-69).

18. As Perrig has pointed out, the majority of the extant drawings for Cavalieri are of the period in which the young man took drawing lessons from the Michelangelo (1533-1534), and are therefore indicative of Buonarroti's didactic method.

19. For these three poems, see Francese, "Michelangelo's *Canzoniere.*" However, unique in the *Rime,* according to Ryan, is the sensual representation of a woman, the "bella bolognese" of G4: the object of the desire of the more mature works will be more abstract and gender-ambiguous (a tendency already visible in G7). The same has been said of the writings for Cavalieri.

20. Mastrocola, in reproducing in the critical apparatus of her edition the first version of this sonnet, underscores the theme of the eternity of beauty within this poetic composition.

21. Mastrocola tells us that the fourth version of this madrigal, readied for publication in 1546, was written in 1524, and intended for a woman, as was the second. A successive redaction was intended for Febo di Poggio.

22. However, Ryan contends that those "impulses which might have led him [Michelangelo] beyond the traditional Catholic pale" (12) condition Michelangelo's religious sentiment after 1536, which he sees as increasingly characterized by self-loathing, remorse, and "pessimism" (Ryan, 214). Ryan contends that at a certain point in time Cavalieri began to constitute a moral dilemma, and cites G97 as evidence (118 [The octave reads "Al cor di zolfo, a la carne di stoppa, / a l'ossa che di seco legnio sièno; / a l'alma senza guida e senza freno, / al desir pronto, a la vaghezza troppa; / a la cieca ragion debile e zoppa / al vischio, a' lacci di che 'l mondo è pieno; / non è gran maraviglia, in un baleno / arder nel primo foco che s'intoppa."]). He writes, "much of the lyricism of the poems of the earliest stage of Michelangelo's love for Cavalieri was owed to the fact that his human love inspired him (through and with Cavalieri) to move beyond the human to the divine source of all love and being. None of the poems of the immediately succeeding years expresses this perspective, and G93 suggests that Michelangelo's human love in fact endangered his aspiration to God" (120), in spite of the fact that, in Ryan's own words, in G106 Michelangelo "asserts the exclusively religious motive of his love for human beauty" (122). Thus, he argues, the penitential spirit of the most mature poems, those composed after 1547, is to be attributed to past homosexuality, citing a consensus on the fact that Buonarroti's "difficult" Catholicism was due to "his attraction to males" (12). It is of interest that his appraisal of the verse diverges here from Liebert's who writes, "both the letters to Tommaso [Cavalieri] and the poetry, for all their searing passion, are rather impersonal in the sense that they seem to leave Tommaso bereft of any uniquely identifiable characteristics. Rather, he emerges as a tabula rasa, a blank figure whom Michelangelo could endow with the qualities that would enable him to experience the "fire" he felt he required to survive" (273).

23. Rodini sees Michelangelo positioning himself in the closing tercet, with "exquisite ambiguity, as a bride in a moment of ecstatic transport" (75). In contrast, Mastrocola, in her critical apparatus equates "sposa" with the poetic voice's soul.

24. As for the nature of Michelangelo's relationship with the Marquise, Ryan reminds us that when the correspondence between the two friends became a bit too intense, Michelangelo's 'enthusiasm' met with a "tactful rebuke." To explain, Michelangelo

wrote to Colonna in the early 1540s, telling her that rather than accept and keep gifts from the Marquise in his own house, he would prefer to enjoy them in hers. If she would grant him this favor, "mi parrà essere im paradiso." In response, the Marquise reminded the artist of his and her religious obligations (*Il carteggio,* CMLXXXIV, MCII).

25. De Tolnay then points out that the saving graces of charity are exemplified by the bearded, tonsured man in the lower left-hand corner and by those who have already found support on the clouds and lean down to help two oncoming souls to safety. Other bodies float to Heaven by virtue of God's grace (*Michelangelo,* 37).

26. In a mixture of civic and religious sentiment, Michelangelo also promised the Florentine community in Rome to participate in the redoing of S. Giovanni dei Fiorentini so that, as Vasari wrote, "tornass[e] in onore di Dio, poi per l'amore della sua nazione, qual sempre amò" (469).

27. 1547 represents a watershed year in Michelangelo's biography, the results of which are reflected in his verse. His friend and business manager, Luigi del Riccio, died shortly before the passing of Vittoria Colonna in 1547. The ensuing sense of isolation, compounded by the departure of Giannotti from Rome, could only have been aggravated by concern for orthodoxy introduced by the Council of Trent, which opened in 1545 (but whose influence was felt as early as the beginning of the decade, in the form of a censorship that antedated the installation of the Papal Indices [Fiorato 104]), which gave impetus to the adverse criticism the artist had received for the unconventionality of the *Last Judgment.* To this we must add Michelangelo's often lamented poor health, his preoccupation with advancing old age and death, and the need to re-allocate energies after his designation as architect of Saint Peter's in 1547, following the death of Antonio da Sangallo the Younger. For Cambon, "one thing is clear: that after 1547 [. . .] Michelangelo's writing enters its critical last phase marked by a sharp drop in productiveness, by the much higher ratio of fragments versus finished lyrics, and by the predominantly religious inspiration" (112).

## Works Cited

Albertini, Rudolf von. *Firenze dalla repubblica al principato. Storia e coscienza politica,* 1955, Turin: Einaudi, 1970.

Alighieri, Dante. *La divina commedia.* Edited and annotated by C. H. Grandgent, Revised by C. S. Singleton, Cambridge: Harvard UP, 1972.

Binni, Walter. *Michelangelo scrittore,* Turin: Einaudi, 1975.

Bull, George. *Michelangelo. A Biography,* New York: St. Martin's Press, 1995.

Buonarroti, Michelangelo. *Il carteggio di Michelangelo,* 5 vol., Florence: S.P.E.S. editore, Sotto gli auspici dell'Istituto nazionale di Studi sul Rinascimento, 1965-1983.

Cambon, Glauco. *Michelangelo's Poetry. Fury of Form.* Princeton: Princeton UP, 1985.

Ciulich, Lucilla Bardeschi. *Costanza ed evoluzione nella grafia di Michelangelo, Studi di grammatica italiana.* V. III, Accademia della Crusca, Firenze: Sansoni, 1973, 5-138.

———. *Michelangelo: un percorso attraverso gli autografi,* in *Michelangelo. Grafia e biografia di un genio,* Milano: Biblioteca di via Senato Edizioni, 2000, 19-27.

Clements, Robert J. *The Poetry of Michelangelo,* New York: New York University Press, 1965.

Condivi, Ascanio. *Vita di Michelangelo Buonarroti,* ed. E. S. Barelli, Milano: Rizzoli, 1964.

De Tolnay, Charles. *The Art and Thought of Michelangelo,* New York: Pantheon, 1964.

———. *Michelangelo,* 5 vol., Princeton: Princeton UP, 1960, Vol. 5.

*Dialogi di Donato Giannotti de' giorni che Dante consumò nel cercare l'Inferno e 'l Purgatorio,* ed. Deoclecio Redig de Campos, Florence: Sansoni, 1939.

Fedi, Roberto. "Il Canzoniere (1546) di Michelangelo," in Id., *La memoria della poesia. Canzonieri, lirici e libri di rime nel Rinascimento,* Roma: Salerno editrice, 1990.

———. "'L'immagine vera': Vittoria Colonna, Michelangelo, e un'idea di canzoniere," *MLN,* 107 (1992): 46-73.

Ficino, Marsilio. *Sopra lo Amore o ver' Convito di Platone. Comento di Marsilio Ficini Fiornentino sopra il Convito di Platone,* ed. G. Ottaviano, Milan: Celuc, 1973.

Fiorato, Adelin. "'Fuss'io pur lui!': Michelangelo all'ascolto di Dante, (11 marzo 1989)," *Letture classensi,* 19 (1990): 87-104.

Francese, Joseph. "Il 'nicodemismo' di Michelangelo nei 'sonetti sulla notte,'" *Quaderni d'italianistica,* 14 (1993): 143-49.

———. "Michelangelo's *Canzoniere.* Politics and Poetry," in *The Craft and the Fury. Essays in Memory of Glauco Cambon,* ed. J. Francese, West Lafayette, IN: 2000, 138-54.

Freud, Sigmund. *The standard edition of the complete psychological works of Sigmund Freud.* Trans. J. Strachey, London: Hogarth Press, 1953-74.

Ghizzoni, Lucia. "Indagine sul canzoniere di Michelangelo," *Studi di filologia italiana,* n. 49, 1991, 167-87.

Giannotti, Donato. *Dialogi di Donato Giannotti de' giorni che Dante consumò nel cercare l'Inferno e 'l Paradiso,* ed. Deoclicio Redig de' Campos, Florence: Sansoni, 1939.

Hirst, Michael. *Michelangelo and his Drawings,* New Haven, Yale UP, 1988.

Jameson, Fredric. *The Political Unconscious. Narrative as a Socially Symbolic Act,* Ithaca: Cornell UP, 1981.

Liebert, Robert S. *Michelangelo. A Psychoanalytic Study of His Life and Images,* New Haven: Yale UP, 1983.

*The Letters of Michelangelo. Translated from the original Tuscan, Edited & Annotated in Two Volumes,* Ed. E. H. Ramsden, Vol. 1. 1496-1534, Stanford: Stanford UP 1963, Appendix 23.

Lucente, Gregory L. "Absence and Desire in Michelangelo's Poetry: Literary Tradition and the Lesson(s) of the Manuscript," *Quaderni d'italianistica,* 7 (1987): 216-26.

Mastrocola, Paola ed. *Rime e lettere di Michelangelo,* Torino: UTET, 1992.

Mussio, Thomas E. "The Augustinian Conflict in the Lyrics of Michelangelo: Michelangelo Reading Petrarch," *Italica,* 74 (1997): 339-59.

Nelson, John Charles. *Renaissance Theory of Love. The Context of Giordano Bruno*'s Eroici furori, NY: Columbia UP, 1958.

Perrig, A. "Tommaso de' Cavalieri," *Dizionario biografico degli Italiani,* Ed. A. M. Ghisalberti, Roma: Istituto della Enciclopedia italiana, 1960-.

Panofsky, Erwin. *Studies in Iconology. Humanistic Themes In the Art of the Renaissance,* 1932. New York: Harper & Row, 1972.

Paoletti, John T. and Gary M. Radke. *Art in Renaissance Italy,* Upper Saddle River (NJ): Prentice Hall, 1997.

Rocke, Michael. *Forbidden Friendships: Homosexuality and Male Culture in Renaissance Florence.* New York: Oxford University Press, 1996.

Rodini, Robert. "Michelangelo's Rime and The Problematics of the Gaze," in *Italiana VI: Essays in Honor of Nicolas J. Perella,* eds. Victoria J. T. De Mara and Anthony Julian Tamburri, Lafayette, IN: Bordighera Press, 1994, 65-81.

Ryan, Christopher, *The Poetry of Michelangelo,* Madison (NJ): Fairleigh Dickinson UP, 1998.

Sarolli, Gian Roberto. "Michelangelo: Poet of the Night," *Forum Italicum,* 1967, 133-55.

Saslow, James M. *The Poetry of Michelangelo. An Annotated Translation,* New Haven: Yale UP, 1991.

————. "'A Veil of Ice between My Heart and the Fire': Michelangelo's Sexual Identity and Early Constructions of Homosexuality," *Genders,* 2 (1998): 77-90.

Savonarola, Girolamo. *Prediche sopra Aggeo,* ed. L. Firpo, Roma: Belardetti, 1965.

Sedgwick, Eve Kosofsky. *Between Men: English Literature and Male Homosocial Desire,* New York: Columbia UP, 1985.

Sterba, Richard F. and Editha. "The Personality of Michelangelo Buonarroti: Some Reflections," *American Imago. A Psychoanalytic Journal for Culture, Science, and the Arts,* V. 35, nn, 1-2, Spring-Summer 1978, 158-77.

Timpanaro, Sebastiano. *The Freudian Slip: Psychoanalysis and Textual Criticism.* Trans. Kate Soper. London: NLB; Atlantic Highlands: Humanities Press, 1976.

Vasari, Giorgio. *Vite scelte,* ed. Anna Maria Brizio, 1948. Turin: UTET, 1964.

Vattimo, Gianni. *Vocazione e responsabilità del filosofo,* Genoa: Il nuovo melangolo, 2000.

## Richard Bonanno (essay date winter-spring 2003)

SOURCE: Bonanno, Richard. "Sculptural Form and the Love Theme in Michelangelo's *Rime.*" *Italian Quarterly* 40, nos. 155-56 (winter-spring 2003): 5-16.

[*In the following essay, Bonanno asserts that, like his sculpture, Michelangelo's poems embody a "fusion of [his] formal, theoretical and thematic concerns."*]

For more than five centuries Michelangelo's life and works have been the object of the criticism of generations of scholars in various fields. Among the countless pages of commentary, the most elusive topic of interest remains the conceptions behind his art. No single critic has managed to elaborate the particularities of his ideas more cogently than Michelangelo himself, who was his own greatest critic. The central poems of his **Rime** provide revealing insights into his ideas concerning both the figurative arts and poetry. Enzo Noé Girardi's critical edition develops slowly from the coarse, often incomplete early poems that date from the first years of the sixteenth century, when the artist had not yet reached his thirtieth birthday. It is, however, likely that Michelangelo had tried his hand at poetry at a much earlier age, in particular during his formative years within the court of Lorenzo il Magnifico where he was surrounded by accomplished poets and scholars; unsuitable poems may well have been destroyed just as expeditiously as the many sculptural works that were not to the liking of their discerning creator and critic. Exhibiting a movement beyond the rough quality of the early poems, the *Rime* culminate with spiritual, prayer-like poems composed during the years immediately preceding his death in 1564. A variety of metre, theme, tone, and style characterizes the entire collection of poems, however there exists a vital high point in the *Rime.*

The central poems of the *Rime* constitute love poetry inspired by three different individuals: the young Roman Tommaso Cavalieri, the renowned noblewoman Vittoria Colonna, and the enigmatic and perhaps imaginary "donna bella e crudele," or "cruel and beautiful woman." The love poetry written for Cavalieri and the "donna bella e crudele" are rather traditional, but the poems inspired by Vittoria Colonna mark a conceptual turning point. In the poems inspired by Colonna, the theme of love and the rudiments of artistic creation merge to reveal Michelangelo's underlying neo-Platonic conception of art and beauty.

Each group of poems is inherently different and displays a sort of internal development. For example, the initial poems written for the "donna bella e crudele" counterbalance those inspired by Vittoria Colonna, and the majority of poems of the group written for the "donna bella e crudele" may be classified as more traditional examples of love poetry. Among the specific poems written for Colonna, in turn, those produced in the later years differ both thematically and stylistically from the earlier ones. In the later poems Michelangelo seems to have acquired a regenerated poetic voice that is characterized by a conceptual nature and quite different from that of the earlier poems written for Colonna. Grouped intermittently by Girardi with the poems prepared for publication, the later poems written for Colonna appear as the most original and noteworthy of the many works produced between the years 1534 and 1547. Marking the most intense period of correspondence with the Marchesa di Pescara, these years are particularly important from an artistic standpoint, and Michelangelo's biography offers a key to interpreting the poems written during this time period.

As "supremo architetto, scultore e pittore" of the church of Saint Peter,[1] Michelangelo made several significant contributions in each of his artistic fields during his period of correspondence with Vittoria Colonna, but the years in which he held this post were filled with tension resulting from a series of challenging artistic endeavors.[2] He managed to complete the frescos in the Cappella

Sistina and the Cappella Paolina, but with the onset of the Council of Trent in 1545, the orthodoxy of his Last Judgment frescos would be questioned. The unpleasant and seemingly perpetual project for the tomb of Julius II finally came to a close with the installation of the radically altered work in San Pietro in Vincoli. During these years Michelangelo also worked with his editors Luigi Del Riccio and Donato Giannotti to prepare his fast-growing collection of poems for publication, and the intense life experience of the great artist indicates the inspiration for the poems dating to this period. In particular, Michelangelo's divine skill as a painter and sculptor and his general "vocazione" as an artist come forward as a primary object of deliberation, and the works dealing with this subject tend toward a greater sense of abstraction.

The artist treads new and more fertile poetic ground during his late sixties and early seventies and manages to free himself from the conventional style and themes typical of the poems for the "donna bella e crudele." He contemplates the very essence of his approach to sculptural, figurative, and poetic creation, which will develop into the dominant topos of the later works of the *Rime.* As with the most noteworthy poems inspired earlier by Cavalieri, these poems reveal extraordinarily personal features, and the ideas themselves and, above all, the expression of these ideas are quite unique. A fairly complex grouping of two "sestine," G 164 provides not only a self-portrait but also a manifesto that offers a starting point for an analysis of the theoretical basis of his creative arts:[3]

> Per fido esemplo alla mia vocazione
> nel parto mi fu data la bellezza,
> che d'ambo l'arti m'è lucerna e specchio.
> S'altro si pensa, è falsa opinione.
> Questo sol l'occhio porta a quella altezza
> c'a pingere e scolpir qui m'apparecchio.
>
> S'e' giudizi temerari e sciocchi
> al senso tiran la beltà, che muove
> e porta al cielo ogni intelletto sano,
> dal mortale al divin non vanno gli occhi
> infermi, e fermi sempre pur là d'ove
> ascender senza grazia è pensier vano.

This madrigal is the first in a series of poems that displays a regenerated poetic vigor in which the ideal of beauty, repeated twice here as "bellezza" and "beltà," is at the very heart of Michelangelo's abstract notion of artistic refinement and Christian virtue.[4] Furthermore, the foundation of this notion marks a return to the prevailing neo-Platonic ideas found in the works for Cavalieri. By highlighting the discrepancy between the chaste nature of his divinely inspired theory and the erroneous ideas of those unable to comprehend the complexity and intensity of such mystery, the poet evokes themes found in the preceding works that were grouped together for publication.[5] However, involving the theoretical and practical groundwork of artistic creation, this morally defensive stance is more original in the works dealing with art as the central theme. The artist's understanding of the nature and force of beauty is the supreme "exemplum" or "esemplo," and he moves from the personal description in the first sestina, "alla *mia* vocazione," "*mi* fu data la bellezza," "*m*'è lucerna e specchio," to the absolute and universal ideal of beauty comprising his theory: "la beltà, che muove / e porta al cielo ogni intelletto sano." Michelangelo's inclination separates him, the divinely inspired artist, from the ignorant populace whose "giudizi temerari e sciocchi / al senso tiran la beltà." Providing additional defense of the rectitude of his ideas as expressed through his figurative and poetic creations, the poet emphatically states: "S'altro si pensa, è falsa opinione."[6] Nonetheless, Michelangelo's emphasis on contemplation and the sound intellect offers more than a simple moral defense. These notions comprise the basic neo-Platonic tenets characterizing his ideas on art.

**"Per fido esemplo alla mia vocazione"** is not simply a manifesto elaborating the theoretical basis of his art. The madrigal also accentuates the systematic moral and philosophical foundations of his ideas concerning the notion of love. Within the group of poems for Vittoria Colonna, one of the most strikingly original qualities is the correlation that the poet advances between the themes of art and love. **"Per fido esemplo alla mia vocazione"** provocatively underscores the two-fold nature of the fundamentally neo-Platonic vision guiding Michelangelo's art, which is subsequently compared to the nature of love and loving.[7] As artist, he has been granted the grace or "grazia" that will allow him to rise up (or "ascendere") to God, yet his predisposed grace and subsequent capacity to rise up are fully dependent upon inspiration that allows him to perceive beauty.[8] In this case, Vittoria Colonna advances as the figure that offers the key to this artistic and spiritual realization, and the specific poems written for her deal precisely with this neo-Platonic dialectic.

In the love poetry for Cavalieri, the poet elaborates the idea that divine ascension may be achieved through the love of an individual, which is a wholly spiritual and intellectual affection in neo-Platonic terms. Above all, the distinction of the works for Cavalieri derives precisely from the tension between these sublime ideas and the poet's sensual yearning. This tension reveals a psychological, religious, and moral impasse. However, his manifesto speaks of beauty in more universal terms and comprises not only love for individual but also love for all that is beautiful. Although the poet is clearly present within the framework of the madrigal, the more abstract and all-encompassing ideas contained in **"Per fido esemplo alla mia vocazione"** reveal a slight movement away from the sensual poems inspired by Cavalieri. This is true also in the other poems written during the Cavalieri period, which involve art as a central theme and conceptually equate artistic creation with the phenomenology of love and loving. Beauty is a divine medium, a way to God and a reflection of perfection. It is essentially "lucerna e specchio," evoking a conventionally religious and newly assimilated neo-Platonic symbolism of light. In the other central poems dealing with this particular idea and its association with art and artistic creation, Michelangelo attempts to isolate the natural and metaphysical realms that comprise the "lucerna e specchio" of God.

The correlation between love and artistic creation distinguishes the principal poems inspired by Vittoria Colonna, which involve several recurrent motifs as well as a common philosophical background. Coupled with G 165, which expounds similar neo-Platonic ideas, **"Per fido esemplo alla mia vocazione"** was presumably addressed to Vittoria Colonna while she was in retreat in a convent in Viterbo. It appears as one of the first among several poems that exemplify the association between Michelangelo's deeply spiritual exchange with Colonna and his sudden and intense deliberation on art and artistic creation. Intellectually refined, artistically impressionable, and equally interested in matters of religious import, Vittoria Colonna begins to play an important role in the development of Michelangelo's poetry dealing with the nature of artistic creation.[9] Michelangelo's contemplation of both his own art and the overall creative process is clearly a product of his exchange of ideas with Colonna, for the primary poems dealing with this topos were generally composed during the years of correspondence with the Marchesa di Pescara and often dedicated to her.

Michelangelo's most important poems dealing with the art metaphor appear in distinct groups that may be dated specifically to the initial years of his acquaintance with Vittoria Colonna as well to the years immediately following her death. However, the poems produced within this period are not the only ones in which Michelangelo elaborates the art theme. This topos may also be found in several of Michelangelo's earliest poems, such as sonnets G 5 **"I' ho già fatto un gozzo in questo stento"** and G 46 **"Se 'l mie rozzo martello i duri sassi."** Nonetheless, along with other similarly inspired poems of that particular period, the more youthful poems lack the innovative quality that distinguishes the ones written later in his lifetime and inspired by Colonna, for the references to the theme of art and artistic creation are only peripheral and do not appear among the central themes. Furthermore, the earlier works dealing with this theme do not reveal a particularly deliberate attempt at abstraction.

In the madrigals and sonnets composed both during the years of his growing correspondence with Vittoria Colonna and in the works following her death, the poet reexamines the philosophical and theoretical implications of art and artistic production.[10] The first in a series of poems written for Colonna during the early correspondence, G 151 is an extraordinary example of Michelangelo's recurrent meditations on art and the discerning capacity of the divinely inspired artist:

> Non ha l'ottimo artista alcun concetto
> c'un marmo solo in sé non circonscriva
> col suo superchio, e solo a quello arriva
> la man che ubbidisce all'intelletto.
>  Il mal ch'io fuggo, e 'l ben ch'io mi prometto,
> in te, donna leggiadra, altera e diva,
> tal si nasconde; e perch'io piú non viva,
> contraria ho l'arte al disïato effetto.
>  Amor dunque non ha, né tua beltate
> o durezza o fortuna o gran disdegno
> del mio mal colpa, o mio destino o sorte;
>  se dentro del tuo cor morte e pietate
> porti in un tempo, e che 'l mio basso ingegno
> non sappia, ardendo, trame altro che morte.

Despite its poetic refinement, this sonnet does not belong to the group of works prepared for publication. Unable to determine their precise date of composition, Girardi has catalogued this sonnet and other compositions of similar inspiration among the central works of the group of poems dealing with the meditation on art.[11] One immediately notes the return to the sonnet after a number of madrigals, but the most innovative features are the object of inspiration and the central metaphor through which the theme of love is elaborated.

For the first time the poet adopts the topic of art and artistic creation as a central metaphor in order to express his ideas on love. Although the sonnet is thematically novel, the actual rhetorical elaboration of the unique dialectic involving art and love may be of greater import. Michelangelo expresses the notion of love for a woman, Vittoria Colonna, in a fashion much different from that typical of the works for the "donna bella e crudele." Here the notion expressed in the first quatrain proves much more original than the doctrinal ideas typical of the earlier works of the *Rime.* Michelangelo speaks of the contemplative artist's skill in perceiving the figure within the block of marble, and this divinely inspired talent is likened to the lover's ability to discern "il mal" and "'l ben" within the beloved.[12] The key to artistic creation lies not in the facility of the hand itself but rather in its subordination to the "intelletto," a term found in **"Per fido esemplo alla mia vocazione"** that curiously reappears in this sonnet, revealing the essentially intellectual nature of artistic production.[13] Furthermore, the logical and rhetorical structuring of this central metaphor exhibits Michelangelo's newfound manner of elaborating ideas in verse. This orderly rhetorical arrangement of verse, or "dispositio," corresponds with meditation on the very essence of artistic creation and, more precisely, on the unique mechanics

of sculpture. The poems dealing with the art ideal therefore involve a series of topics; first and foremost among these artistic topoi is the clear parallel between the themes of love and artistic creation. The structural and stylistic qualities of these same poems are also of particular interest, for Michelangelo adopts a distinctive structuring of his ideas in verse and also a subtextual reflection of this very process within the lyric.

Verse 8 of G 151 typifies the overriding tension that has consistently characterized the love theme: "contraria ho l'arte al disïato effetto." The scope of this assertion is amplified beyond the apparently playful lexical characteristics; symbolically conjured up is the very crux of not only this particular poem but also others focusing on the art theme. Michelangelo has understood the solemnity and aesthetic importance of the presence of a supreme tension within the work of poetry. The assertion "contraria ho l'arte al disïato effetto" thus conjures up a conflict of the will in which the impetus of Michelangelo's "arte" is transgressive.[14] Still the tension of this verse is also the product of the artist's inability to translate the lofty idea into an equally worthy form, which mirrors his efforts to penetrate the very essence of artistic creation. While the ideas of these works tend toward a more abstract nature, the love poems for Cavalieri include a strong sense of realism that characterizes this tension; this is true of the most inspired works of the early period, such as G 5 and G 10, despite the fact that these poems are of a different genre altogether.

One might agree that Girardi's grouping of the poems involving meditation on art seems based more upon the references to Colonna as "donna leggiadra, altera e diva" rather than upon the poet's deliberation on the art topos, which is of primary interest. Nonetheless, G 151 effectively anticipates the concepts presented in the sestina **"Per fido esemplo alla mia vocazione,"** which is dated later and reiterates ideas that will achieve a more individual and autonomous character. The deliberation on the subject of art is more than a secondary idea. It consequently develops into a central topos, as in G 152, a madrigal that immediately follows **"Non ha l'ottimo artista alcun concetto"** according to Girardi's critical edition:

> Sí come per levar, donna, si pone
> in pietra alpestra e dura
> una viva figura,
> che là piú cresce u' piú la pietra scema;
> tal alcun'opre buone,
> per l'alma che pur trema,
> cela il superchio della propria came
> co' l'inculta sua cruda e dura scorza.
> Tu pur dalle mie streme
> parti puo' sol levarne,
> ch'in me non è di me voler né forza.

Among Michelangelo's most noteworthy works, these two previous poems are of the utmost importance not only to the art historian but also to the informal visitor to the Galleria dell'Accademia, which holds the incomplete "prigioni" sculptures that were initially intended to be included in the tomb of Julius II. These extraordinary works, though incomplete, depict in the plastic art of sculpture the tension to which Michelangelo refers in the two preceding poems.

Moving beyond the general pronouncement contained in his manifesto, Michelangelo speaks specifically of the theory governing his approach to sculpture. This brings to mind a statement that he would make some time later in a letter to the poet and historian Benedetto Varchi. Michelangelo introduces a fitting categorization of sculpture: "Io intendo scultura, quella che si fa per forza di levare: quella che si fa per via di porre, è simile alla pittura."[15] It comes as no surprise that Michelangelo's letter was in response to Varchi's "Due Lezzioni, nella prima delle quali si dichiara un sonetto di Michelangelo Buonarroti," a formal treatise offering an analysis of **"Non ha l'ottimo artista alcun concetto"** and published in 1549.[16] Examined in the light of the ideas presented in the sonnet immediately preceding it, **"Sí come per levar, donna, si pone"** once again highlights the manifold innovative qualities of the works dealing with the art metaphor.

In Michelangelo's most distinctive verse one finds an intersection of the distinct features: inspiration, style, content, and form. It is obvious that in the *Rime* a lack of inspiration often results in a typically convoluted structure and syntax, or "dispositio." In such cases the outcome is often an incomplete or an extremely hermetic expression. This is not the case with the works written for Colonna in which the art theme is of great importance. As noted above, the parallel between the theme of love and Michelangelo's ideas on art does not constitute the sole importance of the works written for Colonna; the intrinsic formal, stylistic, and theoretical attributes of these works are of added interest. In fact, in many of these poems, it appears as though Michelangelo composed them with a clear thematic groundwork in mind, and the same may be said of the rigidly formulated rhetorical structuring of their central topoi. Close attention to the formal and stylistic framework reveals what could have only been the poet's very succinct and deliberately rhetorical ordering of ideas or "dispositio."[17] The reader becomes aware of a greater profundity of expression in which the content, the formal attributes, and the general theoretical principles of the individual poems appear to merge.

**"Non ha l'ottimo artista alcun concetto"** once again serves as a fine example of the structural features of the works focusing on the art ideal. In the now famous first quatrain of this sonnet, Michelangelo elaborates the process through which the artist creates the sculptural work. The second quatrain presents the poet and his

quandary in terms typical of his poetic phraseology; the opposition is presented between the "mal" that he attempts to avoid and the "ben" that he strives to attain. After the pronouncement of the universal formula in the first quatrain and the personal depiction of the second quatrain, the poet makes a correlation, "tal si nasconde," which links the theoretical ideas concerning art with the love theme. A similar "dispositio" is noticeable in several of the poems dealing with these two principal topoi. Five such works are G 236 **"Se ben concetto ha la divina parte,"** G 239 **"Com'esser, donna, può quel c'alcun vede,"** G 240 **"Sol d'una pietra viva,"** G 241 **"Negli anni molti e nelle molte pruove,"** and G 242 **"S'egli è che 'n dura pietra alcun somigli."** Each of these poems displays in a similar manner the unique "dispositio" that characterizes the poet's elaboration of the correlation between the process of artistic creation and the love theme.

Curiously sent to Vittoria Colonna along with a painting thought to be a self-portrait, G 236 aptly displays both the thematic refinement and the unique structural quality typical of the works dealing with the art ideal. This sonnet in particular marks a return to the neo-Platonic ideas included in **"Non ha l'ottimo artista alcun concetto:"**

> Se ben concetto ha la divina parte
> il volto e gli atti d'alcun, po' di quello
> doppio valor con breve e vil modello
> dà vita a' sassi, e non è forza d'arte.
>
>   Né altrimenti in piú rustiche carte,
> anz'una pronta man prenda 'l pennello,
> fra 'dotti ingegni il piú accorto e bello
> pruova e rivede, e suo storie comparte.
>
>   Simil di me model di poca istima
> mie parto fu, per cosa alta e prefetta
> da voi rinascer po', donna alta e degna.
>
>   Se 'l poco accresce, e 'l mie superchio lima
> vostra mercé, qual penitenzia aspetta
> mie fiero ardor, se mi gastiga e 'nsegna?

Guided by the ideal of beauty, the divinely inspired artist gives life to stone, and Michelangelo displays his indebtedness to Angelo Poliziano, the great mentor who emphasized the importance of a contemplative approach to artistic creation. Both the ethereal and practical features inherent to the creative process are underscored in this case: "fra 'dotti ingegni il piú accorto e bello / pruova e rivede, e suo storie comparte" (236, 7-8). This notion is applicable to sculpture, giving "vita a' sassi," and to painting, transforming "rustiche carte." Moving beyond this statement, the poet ultimately correlates the particular notion to his own position and, in particular, to his standing with the beloved, the "donna alta e degna." As the divinely inspired artist alchemically brings the immaterial to life, so does the beloved breathe new life into the lover. Both artist and lover are ultimately inspired by the beauty of their subject.[18]

Scansion of this sonnet demonstrates the unique structure that characterizes this poem and several others dealing with artistic creation. As with a substantial number of poems, the sonnet begins with the conjunction "se" and offers a suppositional or deductive scheme that may be broken down to reveal a carefully structured pattern. The quatrains introduce the supposition while the tercets present the association between the universal ideas dealing with art and the situation befalling the poet/lover. Michelangelo presents the association in a succinct and systematic manner, as in the first tercet:

> *Simil* di me model di poca istima
> mie parto fu, per cosa alta e prefetta
> da voi rinascer po', donna alta e degna.

G 239, another sonnet, displays not only a definite thematic affinity with G 236 but also a corresponding rhetorical structure. The poem commences with a brief inquiry into the disproportion between the immortal potential of art and the ephemeral nature of the existence of both the artist and the beloved:

> Com'esser, donna, può quel c'alcun vede
> per lunga sperïenza, che piú dura
> l'immagin viva in pietra alpestra e dura
> che 'l suo fattor, che gli anni in cener riede?
> La causa a l'effetto inclina e cede,
> onde dall'arte è vinta la natura.
> I' 'l so, che 'l pruovo in la bella scultura,
> c'all'opra il tempo e morte non tien fede.
> Dunche, posso ambo noi dar lunga vita
> in qual sie modo, o di colore o sasso,
> di noi sembrando l'uno e l'altro volto;
> sí che mill'anni dopo la partita,
> quante voi bella fusti e quant'io lasso
> si veggia, e com'amarvi i' non fu' stolto.

Though slightly different from that of the other works in which the love theme is united with the art ideal, this poem advances the idea that the beauty of the beloved and the wretched condition of the artist shall endure the onslaught of time and vanquish death through the poet's rendering of her image in painting, "di colore," or in sculpture, "o sasso." In the first quatrain Michelangelo asks why the sculpted image outlasts "'l suo fattor," yet this inquiry does not yield to a resolution. Nature is vanquished by the work of art. Comprehending the death- and time-defying power of art, the artist once again projects himself as a type of divinity. Here, too, he creates a nexus between the themes of art and love, and the "dispositio" characterizing this work is once again particularly succinct and indicative of his borrowing from the theoretical basis of sculpture and its creation. The initial question posed in the first quatrain prompts the statement that the creator is outlived by his creation and also that nature is vanquished by the work of art. Bringing the second quatrain to a close, the poet and sculptor introduces himself within this scheme: "I' 'l so, che 'l pruovo in la bella scultura."[19] He subse-

quently comes to a conclusion that is introduced by the conjunction "Dunche," which denotes the parallel between the absolute qualities of art and the poet's own, personal condition. From a structural standpoint, this poem therefore presents stages of development that begin with the question mark of the initial quatrain, then move to the fixed idea and its personal relevance within the second quatrain, and finally conclude with a bonding of the theme of love and the art ideal in the final tercets.

The preceding ideas and a similar "dispositio" are once again characteristic of G 240, the madrigal that directly follows **"Com'esser, donna, può quel c'alcun vede"** according to Girardi's chronology:

> Sol d'una pietra viva
> l'arte vuol che qui viva
> al par degli anni il volto di costei.
> Che dovria il ciel di lei,
> sendo mie questa, e quella suo fattura,
> non già mortal, ma diva,
> non solo agli occhi mei?
> E pur si parte e picciol tempo dura.
> Dal lato destro è zoppa suo ventura,
> s'un sasso resta e pur lei morte affretta.
> Chi ne farà vendetta?
> Natura sol, se de' suo nati sola
> l'opra qui dura, e la suo 'l tempo invola.

Michelangelo's ideas concerning the eternal nature of sculpture recall Petrarch's elaboration of the idea that poetry has the potential to combat the onslaught of time; in essence, the poet "acknowledges that God is after all the greatest sculptor."[20] Michelangelo contemplates the pessimistic notion through a pair of questions set within a framing device. The frame begins with the principal idea stated in the first three verses; the subject of these lines has led critics to believe that he may have derived inspiration from a newly executed bust of Vittoria Colonna. The frame closes with the statement that only nature itself, through the work of its children, may avenge this offense. Within the frame the reader follows a sort of soliloquy.

In the subsequent madrigal, G 241, Michelangelo touches on many of the topics discussed thus far. From the very first lines of the madrigal one may glean the importance of the notions of contemplation and creation as they apply not only to sculptural execution but also poetic composition:

> Negli anni molti e nelle molte pruove,
> cercando, il saggio al buon concetto arriva
> d'un'immagine viva,
> vicino a morte, in pietra alpestra e dura;
> c'all'alte cose nuove
> tardi si viene, e poco poi si dura.
> Similmente natura,
> di tempo in tempo, d'uno in altro volto,

s'al sommo, errando, di bellezza è giunta
nel tuo divino, è vecchia, e de' perire:

(1-10)

Although the individual notions that characterize each of the preceding poems are quite distinct, the elaboration and presentation of the union of the art ideal and the love theme are strikingly similar. The artist or "il saggio," denoting the contemplative nature of artistic creation, attains artistic perfection through years of practice, and "*Similmente* natura" reaches the peak of beauty in the divine face of the beloved, which, to the dismay of the poet, must then die. Characteristic of Michelangelo's uniquely formulated connection between the ideals of art, love, and death, this madrigal compares "Nature's creation of Vittoria Colonna with the artist's achievement of perfect beauty, both of which, he fears, must signal impending death."[21]

The poems in which Michelangelo elaborates the love theme through a meditation on art and artistic creation are among the most noteworthy of the **Rime.** They represent the pinnacle of Michelangelo's achievements as a poet. In the poems dealing with art, Michelangelo presents an "esempro" or model that guides his poetic expression: his divine talent and vocation as a sculptor, which have granted him the capacity to discern "la bellezza." Rounding out the group written for Colonna and, once again, focusing on the art ideal as the primary metaphor for the love theme, G 242 shows how the artist himself and his profession as an artist have become principal objects of contemplation:

> S'egli è che 'n dura pietra alcun somigli
> talor l'immagin d'ogni altri a se stesso,
> squalido e smorto spesso
> il fo, com'i' son fatto da costei.
> E par ch'esempro pigli
> ognor da me, ch'i' penso di far lei.
> Ben la pietra potrei,
> per l'aspra suo durezza,
> in ch'io l'esempro, dir c'a lei s'assembra;
> del resto non saprei,
> mentre mi strugge e sprezza,
> altro sculpir che le mie afflitte membra.
> Ma se l'arte rimembra
> agli anni la beltà per durare ella,
> farà me lieto, ondi'io le' farò bella.

The examples given above display a basic rhetorical structuring. They effectively and concisely communicate abstract ideas while providing insight into the philosophical and theoretical groundwork that comprises Michelangelo's ideas on art. One notices a fusion of the formal, theoretical and thematic elements that characterize the individual art forms, namely painting, poetry and, above all, sculpture.

### Notes

1. In her critical edition of Condivi's *Vita di Michelagnolo Buonarroti* [Milano: Rizzoli, 1964], Emma Spina Barelli provides several notes chart-ing the precise years of official and unofficial appointment of the artist as head architect of "la fabbrica di San Pietro." See notes 190, 194, 224, p. 131-140.

2. In a letter to his much-loved nephew Lionardo dated January 1541, Michelangelo dissuades him from visiting and reveals the pressure of his unrelenting obligations: "Lionardo, Tu mi scrivi che vuoi venire a Roma questo settembre col Guicciardino. Io ti dico che e' non è tempo ancora, perché non sarebbe altro che acrescermi noia, oltra gli affanni che io ò. Questo dico ancora per Michele, perché sono tanto ocupato, che io non ò tempo da badare a voi, e ogni altra picola cosa m'è grandissimo fastidio, non c'altro, pure a scriver questa."

3. References to and citations of Michelangelo's poetry, unless otherwise noted, are indicated by the letter G and the corresponding number according to Girardi's critical edition: Michelangelo Buonarroti, *Rime.* Ed. Enzo Noé Girardi. Bari: Laterza, 1960.

4. In the chapter entitled "Beauty, Intellect, and Art," Robert J. Clements (*Michelangelo and the Theory of Art.* New York: NYU Press, 1961) writes that "Beauty is the artist's reason for being. He is not born to create beauty, as one might think, but to discern and reproduce pre-existing beauties in nature or, again, in Plotinian terms, to match uncorporeal with corporeal beauties. The acceptance of beauty as "at once the ultimate principle and highest aim of art (Goethe) by Michelangelo and his colleagues of similar intellectual formation was a factor in the 'arts of design' becoming known in the Romance languages as the 'beautiful arts' by the time of the Abbé Du Bos" p. 3. The critic then proceeds with a discussion of Plato's ideas as filtered down to Michelangelo.

5. Clements offers yet another cogent study of the idea of beauty and the unique relationship between eye, mind, and hand in comprehending beauty and rendering it in the work of art. It is no surprise that almost all of the poems mentioned in this study underscore Michelangelo's theoretical approach to painting and sculpture. Robert Clements. "Eye, Mind, and hand in Michelangelo's Poetry." *Publications of the Modern Language Association* 69 (1954): 324-336.

6. The importance of the idea of beauty, or "culto della bellezza," is expressed in a rather simplified manner by Condivi: "e che in lui non nascesser laidi pensieri, si può da questo anco cognoscere, ch'egli non solamente ha amata la bellezza umana, ma universalmente ogni cosa bella, un bel cavallo, un bel cane, un bel paese, una bella pianta, una

bella montagna, una bella selva, ed ogni sito e cosa bella e rara nel suo genere, ammirandole con maraviglioso affetto; così il bello dalla natura scegliendo, come l'api raccolgono il mêl da' fiori, servendosene poi nelle loro opere: il che sempre han fatto tutti quelli che nella pittura hanno avuto qualche grido" p. 82.

7. In his commentary of "Per fido esempio alla mia vocazione," Glauco Cambon (*Michelangelo's Poetry*. Princeton: Princeton University Press, 1985, p. 92) notes that "the poet talks both as lover and as a practical artist. In this capacity, to be sure, he will attain greater poetical results in other poems (for Vittoria as well a for the supposed 'fair and cruel lady')."

8. See "Scattered Beauty" in David Summers, *Michelangelo and the Language of Art.* Princeton: Princeton University Press, 1981, pp. 186-199.

9. For a discussion of Vittoria Colonna, see Roland Bainton, *Donne della Riforma in Germania, in Italia e in Francia.* Trans. Flavio Sarni. Torino: Claudiana, 1992. 247-269. See also Eva-Maria Jung, "Vittoria Colonna: Between Reformation and Counter-reformation." *Ariel* 15 (1951): 144-159, and Massimo Firpo, "Vittoria Colonna, Giovanni Morone e gli 'Spirituali'," *Rivista di Storia e Letteratura Religiosa* 24 (1988): 211-261.

10. In his now famous letter to Benedetto Varchi dealing with the superiority of either painting or sculpture, Michelangelo reveals not only a participation in this debate (one of the epoch's most important) but also a personal opinion of each of these arts as not a craft but a science: "Colui che scrisse che la pittura era piú nobile della scultura, s'egli avessi cosí bene inteso l'altre cose ch'egli ha scritte, le àrebbe meglio scritte la mia fante. Infinite cose, et non piú dette, ci sarebbe da dire di simili scienze" (Girardi 355, p. 255). Clements, however, convincingly argues that Michelangelo, despite the previous statement, could only have disapproved of the reduction of art to a mere science. Michelangelo remains faithful to the tenets of neo-Platonism that abound in the poems dealing with art and artistic creation. Art is a product of the mind, filtered through the soul. See "Eye, Mind, and Hand . . ."

11. Frey erroneously dates the work to 1536. Girardi, on the other hand, speculates that the work was written in the years 1538-41/44. In any case, Varchi's "Lezione" (delivered March 6, 1547, just two day after Colonna's death and printed in 1549 in "Due Lezzioni, nella prima delle quali si dichiara un sonetto di Michelagnolo Buonarroti") assures us that the poem was written prior to Colonna's death. This is further supported by the

reverential and high-spirited references to Vittoria Colonna, on which Varchi fails to elaborate. See Girardi, "Apparato," p. 333.

12. James Saslow (*The Poetry of Michelangelo.* Tr. James M. Saslow, New Haven: Yale U. P. 1991, p. 303) aptly summarizes the theoretical essence of the first quatrain: "These lines express Michelangelo's sculptural theory of subtraction, by which the artist physically removes excess outer mass in order to reveal the preexisting form-idea already present within; the term *concetto,* "conception," is complex and of central importance in Neoplatonic and Cinquecento art theory . . ."

13. See Clements' *Michelangelo's Theory of Art,* cit., pp. 15-20.

14. Gregory L. Lucente speaks of this tension as a general "anxiety" in Michelangelo's verse (as well as in his painting and sculpture) in his cogent study entitled "Lyric Tradition and the Desires of Absence: Rudel, Dante, and Michelangelo ('Vorrei uoler')" *Canadian Review of comparative Literature* (September 1983). He states that "By tracing such fundamental themes as absence/desire and transgression/penitence through examples of Provençal and early Italian love lyric . . . we can gauge the crucial shift that occurred in Italian Renaissance lyric in terms of the internal force of the individual poet's desire and will" p. 307. Although the article is not exhaustive, Lucente's argument is convincing and particularly relevant to any study of Michelangelo's poetry.

15. See Michelangelo Buonarroti, *Lettere.* Ed. Enzo Noé Girardi. (Arezzo: Ente Provinciale per il Turismo, 1976), p. 255.

16. Ramsden (280) amends the Milanesi edition and dates the letter to March 1547, while Girardi (355) retains Milanesi's ascription of August 1549. See Michelangelo Buonarroti,. *The Letters of Michelangelo.* Ed. Trans. E. H. Ramsden. 2 vols. Stanford: Stanford University Press, 1963. Appendix 37.

17. Lending a greater depth to the present thesis, Bernardino Daniello's treatise *Della poetica* offers a curious parallel to the structural divisions typical of Michelangelo's poems dealing with the art metaphor. In book 1 Daniello dissects the poetic process: ". . . dico tre esser le cose principali dalle quali esso suo stato e suo esser prende: l'invenzione prima delle cose, o vogliam dire ritrovamento; la disposizione poi, o ver ordine di esse; e finalmente la forma dello scrivere ornatamente le già ritrovate e disposte, che (latinamente parlando) elocuzione si chiama e che noi volgare, leggiadro et ornato parlare chiameremo"

(Bernardino Daniello, "Della poetica," *Trattati di poetica e di retorica del Cinquecento.* Ed. Bernard Weinberg. Bari: Laterza, 1970. 273. In book 2 Daniello makes a comparison between the creative components of sculpture and those of poetry which is based on the rhetorical framework consisting of invention, disposition, and elocution. See also David Summers, *Michelangelo and the Language of Art.* Princeton: Princeton University Press, 1981, pp. 207-209.

18. Clements (*The Poetry of Michelangelo,* cit. p. 65) states that this "latter sonnet to Vittoria Colonna is important in explaining the role of preliminary models in the Platonic theory of the artist. The presence of the *concetto* waiting in the rock does not obviate the necessity of practice and training, and indeed the necessity of possessing a God-given *intelletto. Intelletto* . . . is mentioned as a perceptive power, given sparingly as grace, in a number of poems . . . and in the *Diálogos* of Francisco de Hollanda."

19. The phraseology of verse 7 of "com'esser, donna, può quel c'alcun vede" recalls the theoretical foundation of Michelangelo's poetics as inspired by Poliziano: "I' 'l *so,* che 'l *pruovo* in la bella scultura" (italics are mine). The poet's knowledge of the absolute that art transcends the laws of nature is a product of contemplation and physical experience or action.

20. Robert J. Clements, *The Poetry of Michelangelo* (New York: New York University Press, 1965), p. 68.

21. See Saslow, p. 407.

---

## FURTHER READING

### Criticism

Clements, Robert J. "Michelangelo as a Baroque Poet." *PMLA* 76, no. 3 (June 1961): 182-92.

Discusses Michelangelo's Counter-Reformation leanings and what Clements terms "Baroque values" in his poetry.

Gilbert, Creighton. "Michael Angelo's Poetry in English Verse." *Italica* 22, no. 4 (December 1945): 180-95.

Catalog of English translations of Michelangelo's poetry to 1945. An addendum and cross-index to this article was published in the same periodical in March, 1947.

Moses, Gavriel. "Philosophy and Mimesis in Michelangelo's Poems." *Italianistica* 10, no. 2 (May-August 1981): 162-77.

Examines the critical suggestion that Michelangelo's verse shows the influence of Neoplatonism and concludes that it is only partially correct, pointing out that "[w]hat we find instead of a philosophically consistent poetry is a consistently professional closeness to images and concepts which Neoplatonic philosophers themselves had adopted in metaphorical terms from a realm experience which to Michelangelo was quite literal."

Nelson, John Charles. "The Poetry of Michelangelo." In *Developments in the Early Renaissance: Papers of the Second Annual conference of the Center for Medieval and Early Renaissance Studies, State University of New York at Binghamton, 4-5 May 1968,* pp. 15-35. Albany: State University of New York Press, 1972.

Overview of Michelangelo's poetry, with commentary on the themes and style of the verse, Michelangelo's homosexuality, and his "overpowering humanity." This essay was originally presented as a paper in May 1968.

Rutter, Itala. "Michelangelo's *Rime*: Form and Meaning." *Canadian Journal of Italian Studies* 8, no. 31 (1985): 160-72.

Identifies three distinct phases in Michelangelo's poetry and traces changes in imagery, theme, and emphases throughout his career.

# How to Use This Index

***CDALBS*** = *Concise Dictionary of American Literary Biography Supplement*
***CDBLB*** = *Concise Dictionary of British Literary Biography*
***CMW*** = *St. James Guide to Crime & Mystery Writers*
***CN*** = *Contemporary Novelists*
***CP*** = *Contemporary Poets*
***CPW*** = *Contemporary Popular Writers*
***CSW*** = *Contemporary Southern Writers*
***CWD*** = *Contemporary Women Dramatists*
***CWP*** = *Contemporary Women Poets*
***CWRI*** = *St. James Guide to Children's Writers*
***CWW*** = *Contemporary World Writers*
***DA*** = *DISCovering Authors*
***DA3*** = *DISCovering Authors 3.0*
***DAB*** = *DISCovering Authors: British Edition*
***DAC*** = *DISCovering Authors: Canadian Edition*
***DAM*** = *DISCovering Authors: Modules*
   ***DRAM:*** *Dramatists Module;* ***MST:*** *Most-studied Authors Module;*
   ***MULT:*** *Multicultural Authors Module;* ***NOV:*** *Novelists Module;*
   ***POET:*** *Poets Module;* ***POP:*** *Popular Fiction and Genre Authors Module*
***DFS*** = *Drama for Students*
***DLB*** = *Dictionary of Literary Biography*
***DLBD*** = *Dictionary of Literary Biography Documentary Series*
***DLBY*** = *Dictionary of Literary Biography Yearbook*
***DNFS*** = *Literature of Developing Nations for Students*
***EFS*** = *Epics for Students*
***EW*** = *European Writers*
***EWL*** = *Encyclopedia of World Literature in the 20th Century*
***EXPN*** = *Exploring Novels*
***EXPP*** = *Exploring Poetry*
***EXPS*** = *Exploring Short Stories*
***FANT*** = *St. James Guide to Fantasy Writers*
***FW*** = *Feminist Writers*
***GFL*** = *Guide to French Literature,* Beginnings to 1789, 1798 to the Present
***GLL*** = *Gay and Lesbian Literature*
***HGG*** = *St. James Guide to Horror, Ghost & Gothic Writers*
***HW*** = *Hispanic Writers*
***IDFW*** = *International Dictionary of Films and Filmmakers: Writers and Production Artists*
***IDTP*** = *International Dictionary of Theatre: Playwrights*
***LAIT*** = *Literature and Its Times*
***LAW*** = *Latin American Writers*
***JRDA*** = *Junior DISCovering Authors*
***MAICYA*** = *Major Authors and Illustrators for Children and Young Adults*
***MAICYAS*** = *Major Authors and Illustrators for Children and Young Adults Supplement*
***MAWW*** = *Modern American Women Writers*
***MJW*** = *Modern Japanese Writers*
***MTCW*** = *Major 20th-Century Writers*
***NCFS*** = *Nonfiction Classics for Students*
***NFS*** = *Novels for Students*
***PAB*** = *Poets: American and British*
***PFS*** = *Poetry for Students*
***RGAL*** = *Reference Guide to American Literature*
***RGEL*** = *Reference Guide to English Literature*
***RGSF*** = *Reference Guide to Short Fiction*
***RGWL*** = *Reference Guide to World Literature*
***RHW*** = *Twentieth-Century Romance and Historical Writers*
***SAAS*** = *Something about the Author Autobiography Series*
***SATA*** = *Something about the Author*
***SFW*** = *St. James Guide to Science Fiction Writers*
***SSFS*** = *Short Stories for Students*
***TCWW*** = *Twentieth-Century Western Writers*
***WLIT*** = *World Literature and Its Times*
***WP*** = *World Poets*
***YABC*** = *Yesterday's Authors of Books for Children*
***YAW*** = *St. James Guide to Young Adult Writers*

# Literary Criticism Series
# Cumulative Author Index

**Aleman, Mateo** 1547-1615(?) .............. **LC 81**

**Alencar, Jose de** 1829-1877 .......... **NCLC 157**
See also DLB 307; LAW; WLIT 1

**Alencon, Marguerite d'**
See de Navarre, Marguerite

**Alepoudelis, Odysseus**
See Elytis, Odysseus

**Aleshkovsky, Joseph** 1929- ............... **CLC 44**
See also CA 121; 128; DLB 317

**Aleshkovsky, Yuz**
See Aleshkovsky, Joseph

**Alexander, Barbara**
See Ehrenreich, Barbara

**Alexander, Lloyd** 1924-2007 ............. **CLC 35**
See also AAYA 1, 27; BPFB 1; BYA 5, 6,
7, 9, 10, 11; CA 1-4R; 260; CANR 1, 24,
38, 55, 113; CLR 1, 5, 48; CWRI 5; DLB
52; FANT; JRDA; MAICYA 1, 2; MAIC-
YAS 1; MTCW 1; SAAS 19; SATA 3, 49,
81, 129, 135; SATA-Obit 182; SUFW;
TUS; WYA; YAW

**Alexander, Lloyd Chudley**
See Alexander, Lloyd

**Alexander, Meena** 1951- .................. **CLC 121**
See also CA 115; CANR 38, 70, 146; CP 5,
6, 7; CWP; DLB 323; FW

**Alexander, Rae Pace**
See Alexander, Raymond Pace

**Alexander, Raymond Pace**
1898-1974 ..................................... **SSC 62**
See also CA 97-100; SATA 22; SSFS 4

**Alexander, Samuel** 1859-1938 ........ **TCLC 77**

**Alexeiev, Konstantin**
See Stanislavsky, Constantin

**Alexeyev, Constantin Sergeivich**
See Stanislavsky, Constantin

**Alexeyev, Konstantin Sergeyevich**
See Stanislavsky, Constantin

**Alexie, Sherman** 1966- ............. **CLC 96, 154;
NNAL; PC 53; SSC 107**
See also AAYA 28; BYA 15; CA 138;
CANR 65, 95, 133, 174; CN 7; DA3;
DAM MULT; DLB 175, 206, 278; LATS
1:2; MTCW 2; MTFW 2005; NFS 17;
SSFS 18

**Alexie, Sherman Joseph, Jr.**
See Alexie, Sherman

**al-Farabi** 870(?)-950 ...................... **CMLC 58**
See also DLB 115

**Alfau, Felipe** 1902-1999 .................... **CLC 66**
See also CA 137

**Alfieri, Vittorio** 1749-1803 ........... **NCLC 101**
See also EW 4; RGWL 2, 3; WLIT 7

**Alfonso X** 1221-1284 ..................... **CMLC 78**

**Alfred, Jean Gaston**
See Ponge, Francis

**Alger, Horatio, Jr.** 1832-1899 .... **NCLC 8, 83**
See also CLR 87; DLB 42; LAIT 2; RGAL
4; SATA 16; TUS

**Al-Ghazali, Muhammad ibn Muhammad**
1058-1111 ............................... **CMLC 50**
See also DLB 115

**Algren, Nelson** 1909-1981 ..... **CLC 4, 10, 33;
SSC 33**
See also AMWS 9; BPFB 1; CA 13-16R;
103; CANR 20, 61; CDALB 1941-1968;
CN 1, 2; DLB 9; DLBY 1981, 1982,
2000; EWL 3; MAL 5; MTCW 1, 2;
MTFW 2005; RGAL 4; RGSF 2

**al-Hamadhani** 967-1007 ................. **CMLC 93**
See also WLIT 6

**al-Hariri, al-Qasim ibn 'Ali Abu
Muhammad al-Basri**
1054-1122 ............................... **CMLC 63**
See also RGWL 3

**Ali, Ahmed** 1908-1998 ...................... **CLC 69**
See also CA 25-28R; CANR 15, 34; CN 1,
2, 3, 4, 5; DLB 323; EWL 3

**Ali, Tariq** 1943- ................................ **CLC 173**
See also CA 25-28R; CANR 10, 99, 161,
196

**Alighieri, Dante**
See Dante

**al-Kindi, Abu Yusuf Ya'qub ibn Ishaq** c.
801-c. 873 ................................ **CMLC 80**

**Allan, John B.**
See Westlake, Donald E.

**Allan, Sidney**
See Hartmann, Sadakichi

**Allan, Sydney**
See Hartmann, Sadakichi

**Allard, Janet CLC 59**

**Allen, Betsy**
See Harrison, Elizabeth (Allen) Cavanna

**Allen, Edward** 1948- ......................... **CLC 59**

**Allen, Fred** 1894-1956 ................... **TCLC 87**

**Allen, Paula Gunn** 1939-2008 . **CLC 84, 202,
280; NNAL**
See also AMWS 4; CA 112; 143; 272;
CANR 63, 130; CWP; DA3; DAM
MULT; DLB 175; FW; MTCW 2; MTFW
2005; RGAL 4; TCWW 2

**Allen, Roland**
See Ayckbourn, Alan

**Allen, Sarah A.**
See Hopkins, Pauline Elizabeth

**Allen, Sidney H.**
See Hartmann, Sadakichi

**Allen, Woody** 1935- ............. **CLC 16, 52, 195**
See also AAYA 10, 51; AMWS 15; CA 33-
36R; CANR 27, 38, 63, 128, 172; DAM
POP; DLB 44; MTCW 1; SSFS 21

**Allende, Isabel** 1942- ... **CLC 39, 57, 97, 170,
264; HLC 1; SSC 65; WLCS**
See also AAYA 18, 70; CA 125; 130; CANR
51, 74, 129, 165; CDWLB 3; CLR 99;
CWW 2; DA3; DAM MULT, NOV; DLB
145; DNFS 1; EWL 3; FL 1:5; FW; HW
1, 2; INT CA-130; LAIT 5; LAWS 1;
LMFS 2; MTCW 1, 2; MTFW 2005;
NCFS 1; NFS 6, 18, 29; RGSF 2; RGWL
3; SATA 163; SSFS 11, 16; WLIT 1

**Alleyn, Ellen**
See Rossetti, Christina

**Alleyne, Carla D. CLC 65**

**Allingham, Margery (Louise)**
1904-1966 ................................. **CLC 19**
See also CA 5-8R; 25-28R; CANR 4, 58;
CMW 4; DLB 77; MSW; MTCW 1, 2

**Allingham, William** 1824-1889 ...... **NCLC 25**
See also DLB 35; RGEL 2

**Allison, Dorothy E.** 1949- ......... **CLC 78, 153**
See also AAYA 53; CA 140; CANR 66, 107;
CN 7; CSW; DA3; DLB 350; FW; MTCW
2; MTFW 2005; NFS 11; RGAL 4

**Alloula, Malek CLC 65**

**Allston, Washington** 1779-1843 ....... **NCLC 2**
See also DLB 1, 235

**Almedingen, E. M.**
See Almedingen, Martha Edith von

**Almedingen, Martha Edith von**
1898-1971 ................................. **CLC 12**
See also CA 1-4R; CANR 1; SATA 3

**Almodovar, Pedro** 1949(?)- .... **CLC 114, 229;
HLCS 1**
See also CA 133; CANR 72, 151; HW 2

**Almqvist, Carl Jonas Love**
1793-1866 ............................... **NCLC 42**

**al-Mutanabbi, Ahmad ibn al-Husayn Abu
al-Tayyib al-Jufi al-Kindi**
915-965 .................................... **CMLC 66**
See also RGWL 3; WLIT 6

**Alonso, Damaso** 1898-1990 .............. **CLC 14**
See also CA 110; 131; 130; CANR 72; DLB
108; EWL 3; HW 1, 2

**Alov**
See Gogol, Nikolai (Vasilyevich)

**al'Sadaawi, Nawal**
See El Saadawi, Nawal

**al-Shaykh, Hanan** 1945- .................. **CLC 218**
See also CA 135; CANR 111; CWW 2;
DLB 346; EWL 3; WLIT 6

**Al Siddik**
See Rolfe, Frederick (William Serafino
Austin Lewis Mary)

**Alta** 1942- ........................................... **CLC 19**
See also CA 57-60

**Alter, Robert B.** 1935- ...................... **CLC 34**
See also CA 49-52; CANR 1, 47, 100, 160

**Alter, Robert Bernard**
See Alter, Robert B.

**Alther, Lisa** 1944- ........................... **CLC 7, 41**
See also BPFB 1; CA 65-68; CAAS 30;
CANR 12, 30, 51, 180; CN 4, 5, 6, 7;
CSW; GLL 2; MTCW 1

**Althusser, L.**
See Althusser, Louis

**Althusser, Louis** 1918-1990 ............. **CLC 106**
See also CA 131; 132; CANR 102; DLB
242

**Altman, Robert** 1925-2006 ....... **CLC 16, 116,
242**
See also CA 73-76; 254; CANR 43

**Alurista**
See Urista, Alberto

**Alvarez, A.** 1929- ........................... **CLC 5, 13**
See also CA 1-4R; CANR 3, 33, 63, 101,
134; CN 3, 4, 5, 6; CP 1, 2, 3, 4, 5, 6, 7;
DLB 14, 40; MTFW 2005

**Alvarez, Alejandro Rodriguez**
1903-1965 . **CLC 49; DC 32; TCLC 199**
See also CA 131; 93-96; EWL 3; HW 1

**Alvarez, Julia** 1950- .. **CLC 93, 274; HLCS 1**
See also AAYA 25; AMWS 7; CA 147;
CANR 69, 101, 133, 166; DLB 282;
LATS 1:2; LLW; MTCW 2; MTFW 2005;
NFS 5, 9; SATA 129; SSFS 27; WLIT 1

**Alvaro, Corrado** 1896-1956 ............ **TCLC 60**
See also CA 163; DLB 264; EWL 3

**Amado, Jorge** 1912-2001 ... **CLC 13, 40, 106,
232; HLC 1**
See also CA 77-80; 201; CANR 35, 74, 135;
CWW 2; DAM MULT, NOV; DLB 113,
307; EWL 3; HW 2; LAW; LAWS 1;
MTCW 1, 2; MTFW 2005; RGWL 2, 3;
TWA; WLIT 1

**Ambler, Eric** 1909-1998 .............. **CLC 4, 6, 9**
See also BRWS 4; CA 9-12R; 171; CANR
7, 38, 74; CMW 4; CN 1, 2, 3, 4, 5, 6;
DLB 77; MSW; MTCW 1, 2; TEA

**Ambrose** c. 339-c. 397 ................. **CMLC 103**

**Ambrose, Stephen E.** 1936-2002 .... **CLC 145**
See also AAYA 44; CA 1-4R; 209; CANR
3, 43, 57, 83, 105; MTFW 2005; NCFS 2;
SATA 40, 138

**Amichai, Yehuda** 1924-2000 .. **CLC 9, 22, 57,
116; PC 38**
See also CA 85-88; 189; CANR 46, 60, 99,
132; CWW 2; EWL 3; MTCW 1, 2;
MTFW 2005; PFS 24; RGHL; WLIT 6

**Amichai, Yehudah**
See Amichai, Yehuda

**Amiel, Henri Frederic** 1821-1881 .... **NCLC 4**
See also DLB 217

**Amis, Kingsley** 1922-1995 . **CLC 1, 2, 3, 5, 8,
13, 40, 44, 129**
See also AAYA 77; AITN 2; BPFB 1;
BRWS 2; CA 9-12R; 150; CANR 8, 28,
54; CDBLB 1945-1960; CN 1, 2, 3, 4, 5,
6; CP 1, 2, 3, 4; DA; DA3; DAB; DAC;
DAM MST, NOV; DLB 15, 27, 100, 139,
326, 352; DLBY 1996; EWL 3; HGG;
INT CANR-8; MTCW 1, 2; MTFW 2005;
RGEL 2; RGSF 2; SFW 4

**Amis, Martin** 1949- ... **CLC 4, 9, 38, 62, 101, 213; SSC 112**
See also BEST 90:3; BRWS 4; CA 65-68; CANR 8, 27, 54, 73, 95, 132, 166; CN 5, 6, 7; DA3; DLB 14, 194; EWL 3; INT CANR-27; MTCW 2; MTFW 2005

**Amis, Martin Louis**
See Amis, Martin

**Ammianus Marcellinus** c. 330-c. 395 .......................................... **CMLC 60**
See also AW 2; DLB 211

**Ammons, A.R.** 1926-2001 .. **CLC 2, 3, 5, 8, 9, 25, 57, 108; PC 16**
See also AITN 1; AMWS 7; CA 9-12R; 193; CANR 6, 36, 51, 73, 107, 156; CP 1, 2, 3, 4, 5, 6, 7; CSW; DAM POET; DLB 5, 165, 342; EWL 3; MAL 5; MTCW 1, 2; PFS 19; RGAL 4; TCLE 1:1

**Ammons, Archie Randolph**
See Ammons, A.R.

**Amo, Tauraatua i**
See Adams, Henry

**Amory, Thomas** 1691(?)-1788 ............. **LC 48**
See also DLB 39

**Anand, Mulk Raj** 1905-2004 ..... **CLC 23, 93, 237**
See also CA 65-68; 231; CANR 32, 64; CN 1, 2, 3, 4, 5, 6, 7; DAM NOV; DLB 323; EWL 3; MTCW 1, 2; MTFW 2005; RGSF 2

**Anatol**
See Schnitzler, Arthur

**Anaximander** c. 611B.C.-c. 546B.C. ...................................... **CMLC 22**

**Anaya, Rudolfo** 1937- ...... **CLC 23, 148, 255; HLC 1**
See also AAYA 20; BYA 13; CA 45-48; CAAS 4; CANR 1, 32, 51, 124, 169; CLR 129; CN 4, 5, 6, 7; DAM MULT, NOV; DLB 82, 206, 278; HW 1; LAIT 4; LLW; MAL 5; MTCW 1, 2; MTFW 2005; NFS 12; RGAL 4; RGSF 2; TCWW 2; WLIT 1

**Anaya, Rudolfo A.**
See Anaya, Rudolfo

**Anaya, Rudolpho Alfonso**
See Anaya, Rudolfo

**Andersen, Hans Christian** 1805-1875 ...... **NCLC 7, 79, 214; SSC 6, 56; WLC 1**
See also AAYA 57; CLR 6, 113; DA; DA3; DAB; DAC; DAM MST, POP; EW 6; MAICYA 1, 2; RGSF 2; RGWL 2, 3; SATA 100; TWA; WCH; YABC 1

**Anderson, C. Farley**
See Mencken, H. L.; Nathan, George Jean

**Anderson, Jessica (Margaret) Queale** 1916- ........................................... **CLC 37**
See also CA 9-12R; CANR 4, 62; CN 4, 5, 6, 7; DLB 325

**Anderson, Jon (Victor)** 1940- ............. **CLC 9**
See also CA 25-28R; CANR 20; CP 1, 3, 4, 5; DAM POET

**Anderson, Lindsay (Gordon)** 1923-1994 .................................. **CLC 20**
See also CA 125; 128; 146; CANR 77

**Anderson, Maxwell** 1888-1959 ........ **TCLC 2, 144**
See also CA 105; 152; DAM DRAM; DFS 16, 20; DLB 7, 228; MAL 5; MTCW 2; MTFW 2005; RGAL 4

**Anderson, Poul** 1926-2001 ................ **CLC 15**
See also AAYA 5, 34; BPFB 1; BYA 6, 8, 9; CA 1-4R, 181; 199; CAAE 181; CAAS 2; CANR 2, 15, 34, 64, 110; CLR 58; DLB 8; FANT; INT CANR-15; MTCW 1, 2; MTFW 2005; SATA 90; SATA-Brief 39; SATA-Essay 106; SCFW 1, 2; SFW 4; SUFW 1, 2

**Anderson, R. W.**
See Anderson, Robert

**Anderson, Robert** 1917-2009 ........... **CLC 23**
See also AITN 1; CA 21-24R; 283; CANR 32; CD 6; DAM DRAM; DLB 7; LAIT 5

**Anderson, Robert W.**
See Anderson, Robert

**Anderson, Robert Woodruff**
See Anderson, Robert

**Anderson, Roberta Joan**
See Mitchell, Joni

**Anderson, Sherwood** 1876-1941 ... **SSC 1, 46, 91; TCLC 1, 10, 24, 123; WLC 1**
See also AAYA 30; AMW; AMWC 2; BPFB 1; CA 104; 121; CANR 61; CDALB 1917-1929; DA; DA3; DAB; DAC; DAM MST, NOV; DLB 4, 9, 86; DLBD 1; EWL 3; EXPS; GLL 2; MAL 5; MTCW 1, 2; MTFW 2005; NFS 4; RGAL 4; RGSF 2; SSFS 4, 10, 11; TUS

**Anderson, Wes** 1969- ...................... **CLC 227**
See also CA 214

**Andier, Pierre**
See Desnos, Robert

**Andouard**
See Giraudoux, Jean(-Hippolyte)

**Andrade, Carlos Drummond de**
See Drummond de Andrade, Carlos

**Andrade, Mario de**
See de Andrade, Mario

**Andreae, Johann V(alentin)** 1586-1654 ...................................... **LC 32**
See also DLB 164

**Andreas Capellanus** fl. c. 1185- .... **CMLC 45**
See also DLB 208

**Andreas-Salome, Lou** 1861-1937 ... **TCLC 56**
See also CA 178; DLB 66

**Andreev, Leonid**
See Andreyev, Leonid

**Andress, Lesley**
See Sanders, Lawrence

**Andrew, Joseph Maree**
See Occomy, Marita (Odette) Bonner

**Andrewes, Lancelot** 1555-1626 ............. **LC 5**
See also DLB 151, 172

**Andrews, Cicily Fairfield**
See West, Rebecca

**Andrews, Elton V.**
See Pohl, Frederik

**Andrews, Peter**
See Soderbergh, Steven

**Andrews, Raymond** 1934-1991 ........ **BLC 2:1**
See also BW 2; CA 81-84; 136; CANR 15, 42

**Andreyev, Leonid** 1871-1919 ... **TCLC 3, 221**
See also CA 104; 185; DLB 295; EWL 3

**Andreyev, Leonid Nikolaevich**
See Andreyev, Leonid

**Andrezel, Pierre**
See Blixen, Karen

**Andric, Ivo** 1892-1975 ......... **CLC 8; SSC 36; TCLC 135**
See also CA 81-84; 57-60; CANR 43, 60; CDWLB 4; DLB 147, 329; EW 11; EWL 3; MTCW 1; RGSF 2; RGWL 2, 3

**Androvar**
See Prado (Calvo), Pedro

**Angela of Foligno** 1248(?)-1309 .... **CMLC 76**

**Angelique, Pierre**
See Bataille, Georges

**Angell, Judie**
See Angell, Judie

**Angell, Judie** 1937- ......................... **CLC 30**
See also AAYA 11, 71; BYA 6; CA 77-80; CANR 49; CLR 33; JRDA; SATA 22, 78; WYA; YAW

**Angell, Roger** 1920- .......................... **CLC 26**
See also CA 57-60; CANR 13, 44, 70, 144; DLB 171, 185

**Angelou, Maya** 1928- ...... **BLC 1:1; CLC 12, 35, 64, 77, 155; PC 32; WLCS**
See also AAYA 7, 20; AMWS 4; BPFB 1; BW 2, 3; BYA 2; CA 65-68; CANR 19, 42, 65, 111, 133; CDALBS; CLR 53; CP 4, 5, 6, 7; CPW; CSW; CWP; DA; DA3; DAB; DAC; DAM MST, MULT, POET, POP; DLB 38; EWL 3; EXPN; EXPP; FL 1:5; LAIT 4; MAICYA 2; MAICYAS 1; MAL 5; MBL; MTCW 1, 2; MTFW 2005; NCFS 2; NFS 2; PFS 2, 3; RGAL 4; SATA 49, 136; TCLE 1:1; WYA; YAW

**Angouleme, Marguerite d'**
See de Navarre, Marguerite

**Anna Comnena** 1083-1153 ........... **CMLC 25**

**Annensky, Innokentii Fedorovich**
See Annensky, Innokenty (Fyodorovich)

**Annensky, Innokenty (Fyodorovich)** 1856-1909 ................................. **TCLC 14**
See also CA 110; 155; DLB 295; EWL 3

**Annunzio, Gabriele d'**
See D'Annunzio, Gabriele

**Anodos**
See Coleridge, Mary E(lizabeth)

**Anon, Charles Robert**
See Pessoa, Fernando

**Anouilh, Jean** 1910-1987 ..... **CLC 1, 3, 8, 13, 40, 50; DC 8, 21; TCLC 195**
See also AAYA 67; CA 17-20R; 123; CANR 32; DAM DRAM; DFS 9, 10, 19; DLB 321; EW 13; EWL 3; GFL 1789 to the Present; MTCW 1, 2; MTFW 2005; RGWL 2, 3; TWA

**Ansa, Tina McElroy** 1949- .............. **BLC 2:1**
See also BW 2; CA 142; CANR 143; CSW

**Anselm of Canterbury** 1033(?)-1109 .......................... **CMLC 67**
See also DLB 115

**Anthony, Florence**
See Ai

**Anthony, John**
See Ciardi, John (Anthony)

**Anthony, Peter**
See Shaffer, Anthony; Shaffer, Peter

**Anthony, Piers** 1934- ........................ **CLC 35**
See also AAYA 11, 48; BYA 7; CA 200; CAAE 200; CANR 28, 56, 73, 102, 133; CLR 118; CPW; DAM POP; DLB 8; FANT; MAICYA 2; MAICYAS 1; MTCW 1, 2; MTFW 2005; SAAS 22; SATA 84, 129; SATA-Essay 129; SFW 4; SUFW 1, 2; YAW

**Anthony, Susan B(rownell)** 1820-1906 .............................. **TCLC 84**
See also CA 211; FW

**Antiphon** c. 480B.C.-c. 411B.C. .... **CMLC 55**

**Antoine, Marc**
See Proust, (Valentin-Louis-George-Eugene) Marcel

**Antoninus, Brother**
See Everson, William

**Antonioni, Michelangelo** 1912-2007 ................... **CLC 20, 144, 259**
See also CA 73-76; 262; CANR 45, 77

**Antschel, Paul** 1920-1970 .... **CLC 10, 19, 53, 82; PC 10**
See also CA 85-88; CANR 33, 61; CDWLB 2; DLB 69; EWL 3; MTCW 1; PFS 21; RGHL; RGWL 2, 3

**Anwar, Chairil** 1922-1949 .............. **TCLC 22**
See also CA 121; 219; EWL 3; RGWL 3

**Anyidoho, Kofi** 1947- ...................... **BLC 2:1**
See also BW 3; CA 178; CP 5, 6, 7; DLB 157; EWL 3

**Baumbach, Jonathan** 1933- .......... **CLC 6, 23**
See also CA 13-16R, 284; CAAE 284;
CAAS 5; CANR 12, 66, 140; CN 3, 4, 5,
6, 7; DLBY 1980; INT CANR-12; MTCW
1

**Bausch, Richard** 1945- ..................... **CLC 51**
See also AMWS 7; CA 101; CAAS 14;
CANR 43, 61, 87, 164; CN 7; CSW; DLB
130; MAL 5

**Bausch, Richard Carl**
See Bausch, Richard

**Baxter, Charles** 1947- .................. **CLC 45, 78**
See also AMWS 17; CA 57-60; CANR 40,
64, 104, 133, 188; CPW; DAM POP; DLB
130; MAL 5; MTCW 2; MTFW 2005;
TCLE 1:1

**Baxter, Charles Morley**
See Baxter, Charles

**Baxter, George Owen**
See Faust, Frederick

**Baxter, James K(eir)** 1926-1972 ....... **CLC 14**
See also CA 77-80; CP 1; EWL 3

**Baxter, John**
See Hunt, E. Howard

**Bayer, Sylvia**
See Glassco, John

**Bayle, Pierre** 1647-1706 ..................... **LC 126**
See also DLB 268, 313; GFL Beginnings to
1789

**Baynton, Barbara** 1857-1929 . **TCLC 57, 211**
See also DLB 230; RGSF 2

**Beagle, Peter S.** 1939- .................. **CLC 7, 104**
See also AAYA 47; BPFB 1; BYA 9, 10,
16; CA 9-12R; CANR 4, 51, 73, 110;
DA3; DLBY 1980; FANT; INT CANR-4;
MTCW 2; MTFW 2005; SATA 60, 130;
SUFW 1, 2; YAW

**Beagle, Peter Soyer**
See Beagle, Peter S.

**Bean, Normal**
See Burroughs, Edgar Rice

**Beard, Charles A(ustin)**
1874-1948 ................................ **TCLC 15**
See also CA 115; 189; DLB 17; SATA 18

**Beardsley, Aubrey** 1872-1898 ........... **NCLC 6**

**Beatrice of Nazareth** 1200-1268 .. **CMLC 114**

**Beattie, Ann** 1947- ..... **CLC 8, 13, 18, 40, 63,
146; SSC 11, 130**
See also AMWS 5; BEST 90:2; BPFB 1;
CA 81-84; CANR 53, 73, 128; CN 4, 5,
6, 7; CPW; DA3; DAM NOV, POP; DLB
218, 278; DLBY 1982; EWL 3; MAL 5;
MTCW 1, 2; MTFW 2005; RGAL 4;
RGSF 2; SSFS 9; TUS

**Beattie, James** 1735-1803 .............. **NCLC 25**
See also DLB 109

**Beauchamp, Kathleen Mansfield**
1888-1923 . **SSC 9, 23, 38, 81; TCLC 2,
8, 39, 164; WLC 4**
See also BPFB 2; BRW 7; CA 104; 134;
DA; DA3; DAC; DAM MST; DLB
162; EWL 3; EXPS; FW; GLL 1; MTCW
2; RGEL 2; RGSF 2; SSFS 2, 8, 10, 11;
TEA; WWE 1

**Beaumarchais, Pierre-Augustin Caron de**
1732-1799 ...................... **DC 4; LC 61**
See also DAM DRAM; DFS 14, 16; DLB
313; EW 4; GFL Beginnings to 1789;
RGWL 2, 3

**Beaumont, Francis** 1584(?)-1616 .. **DC 6; LC
33**
See also BRW 2; CDBLB Before 1660;
DLB 58; TEA

**Beauvoir, Simone de** 1908-1986 .... **CLC 1, 2,
4, 8, 14, 31, 44, 50, 71, 124; SSC 35;
TCLC 221; WLC 1**
See also BPFB 1; CA 9-12R; 118; CANR
28, 61; DA; DA3; DAB; DAC; DAM
MST, NOV; DLB 72; DLBY 1986; EW

12; EWL 3; FL 1:5; FW; GFL 1789 to the
Present; LMFS 2; MTCW 1, 2; MTFW
2005; RGSF 2; RGWL 2, 3; TWA

**Beauvoir, Simone Lucie Ernestine Marie
Bertrand de**
See Beauvoir, Simone de

**Becker, Carl (Lotus)** 1873-1945 ..... **TCLC 63**
See also CA 157; DLB 17

**Becker, Jurek** 1937-1997 ............... **CLC 7, 19**
See also CA 85-88; 157; CANR 60, 117;
CWW 2; DLB 75, 299; EWL 3; RGHL

**Becker, Walter** 1950- ......................... **CLC 26**

**Becket, Thomas a** 1118(?)-1170 .... **CMLC 83**

**Beckett, Samuel** 1906-1989 ... **CLC 1, 2, 3, 4,
6, 9, 10, 11, 14, 18, 29, 57, 59, 83; DC
22; SSC 16, 74; TCLC 145; WLC 1**
See also BRWC 2; BRWR 1; BRWS 1; CA
5-8R; 130; CANR 33, 61; CBD; CDBLB
1945-1960; CN 1, 2, 3, 4; CP 1, 2, 3, 4;
DA; DA3; DAB; DAC; DAM DRAM,
MST, NOV; DFS 2, 7, 18; DLB 13, 15,
233, 319, 321, 329; DLBY 1990; EWL 3;
GFL 1789 to the Present; LATS 1:2;
LMFS 2; MTCW 1, 2; MTFW 2005;
RGSF 2; RGWL 2, 3; SSFS 15; TEA;
WLIT 4

**Beckford, William** 1760-1844 ....... **NCLC 16,
214**
See also BRW 3; DLB 39, 213; GL 2; HGG;
LMFS 1; SUFW

**Beckham, Barry (Earl)** 1944- ......... **BLC 1:1**
See also BW 1; CA 29-32R; CANR 26, 62;
CN 1, 2, 3, 4, 5, 6; DAM MULT; DLB 33

**Beckman, Gunnel** 1910- ................... **CLC 26**
See also CA 33-36R; CANR 15, 114; CLR
25; MAICYA 1, 2; SAAS 9; SATA 6

**Becque, Henri** 1837-1899 .... **DC 21; NCLC 3**
See also DLB 192; GFL 1789 to the Present

**Becquer, Gustavo Adolfo**
1836-1870 .............. **HLCS 1; NCLC 106**
See also DAM MULT

**Beddoes, Thomas Lovell** 1803-1849 .. **DC 15;
NCLC 3, 154**
See also BRWS 11; DLB 96

**Bede** c. 673-735 ............................. **CMLC 20**
See also DLB 146; TEA

**Bedford, Denton R.** 1907-(?) .............. **NNAL**

**Bedford, Donald F.**
See Fearing, Kenneth

**Beecher, Catharine Esther**
1800-1878 ................................ **NCLC 30**
See also DLB 1, 243

**Beecher, John** 1904-1980 ..................... **CLC 6**
See also AITN 1; CA 5-8R; 105; CANR 8;
CP 1, 2, 3

**Beer, Johann** 1655-1700 ........................ **LC 5**
See also DLB 168

**Beer, Patricia** 1924- ........................... **CLC 58**
See also BRWS 14; CA 61-64; 183; CANR
13, 46; CP 1, 2, 3, 4, 5, 6; CWP; DLB
40; FW

**Beerbohm, Max**
See Beerbohm, (Henry) Max(imilian)

**Beerbohm, (Henry) Max(imilian)**
1872-1956 .......................... **TCLC 1, 24**
See also BRWS 2; CA 104; 154; CANR 79;
DLB 34, 100; FANT; MTCW 2

**Beer-Hofmann, Richard**
1866-1945 ................................ **TCLC 60**
See also CA 160; DLB 81

**Beg, Shemus**
See Stephens, James

**Begiebing, Robert J(ohn)** 1946- ....... **CLC 70**
See also CA 122; CANR 40, 88

**Begley, Louis** 1933- ........................... **CLC 197**
See also CA 140; CANR 98, 176; DLB 299;
RGHL; TCLE 1:1

**Behan, Brendan (Francis)**
1923-1964 .............. **CLC 1, 8, 11, 15, 79**
See also BRWS 2; CA 73-76; CANR 33,
121; CBD; CDBLB 1945-1960; DAM
DRAM; DFS 7; DLB 13, 233; EWL 3;
MTCW 1, 2

**Behn, Aphra** 1640(?)-1689 .. **DC 4; LC 1, 30,
42, 135; PC 13, 88; WLC 1**
See also BRWS 3; DA; DA3; DAB; DAC;
DAM DRAM, MST, NOV, POET; DFS
16, 24; DLB 39, 80, 131; FW; TEA;
WLIT 3

**Behrman, S(amuel) N(athaniel)**
1893-1973 ................................... **CLC 40**
See also CA 13-16; 45-48; CAD; CAP 1;
DLB 7, 44; IDFW 3; MAL 5; RGAL 4

**Bekederemo, J. P. Clark**
See Clark Bekederemo, J.P.

**Belasco, David** 1853-1931 ................. **TCLC 3**
See also CA 104; 168; DLB 7; MAL 5;
RGAL 4

**Belben, Rosalind** 1941- ................... **CLC 280**
See also CA 291

**Belben, Rosalind Loveday**
See Belben, Rosalind

**Belcheva, Elisaveta Lyubomirova**
1893-1991 ................................... **CLC 10**
See also CA 178; CDWLB 4; DLB 147;
EWL 3

**Beldone, Phil "Cheech"**
See Ellison, Harlan

**Beleno**
See Azuela, Mariano

**Belinski, Vissarion Grigoryevich**
1811-1848 ................................... **NCLC 5**
See also DLB 198

**Belitt, Ben** 1911- ................................. **CLC 22**
See also CA 13-16R; CAAS 4; CANR 7,
77; CP 1, 2, 3, 4, 5, 6; DLB 5

**Belknap, Jeremy** 1744-1798 .............. **LC 115**
See also DLB 30, 37

**Bell, Gertrude (Margaret Lowthian)**
1868-1926 ................................... **TCLC 67**
See also CA 167; CANR 110; DLB 174

**Bell, J. Freeman**
See Zangwill, Israel

**Bell, James Madison** 1826-1902 ..... **BLC 1:1;
TCLC 43**
See also BW 1; CA 122; 124; DAM MULT;
DLB 50

**Bell, Madison Smartt** 1957- ..... **CLC 41, 102,
223**
See also AMWS 10; BPFB 1; CA 111, 183;
CAAE 183; CANR 28, 54, 73, 134, 176;
CN 5, 6, 7; CSW; DLB 218, 278; MTCW
2; MTFW 2005

**Bell, Marvin (Hartley)** 1937- ...... **CLC 8, 31;
PC 79**
See also CA 21-24R; CAAS 14; CANR 59,
102; CP 1, 2, 3, 4, 5, 6, 7; DAM POET;
DLB 5; MAL 5; MTCW 1; PFS 25

**Bell, W. L. D.**
See Mencken, H. L.

**Bellamy, Atwood C.**
See Mencken, H. L.

**Bellamy, Edward** 1850-1898 ..... **NCLC 4, 86,
147**
See also DLB 12; NFS 15; RGAL 4; SFW
4

**Belli, Gioconda** 1948- ......................... **HLCS 1**
See also CA 152; CANR 143; CWW 2;
DLB 290; EWL 3; RGWL 3

**Bellin, Edward J.**
See Kuttner, Henry

**Bello, Andres** 1781-1865 .............. **NCLC 131**
See also LAW

**Burns, Tex**
See L'Amour, Louis

**Burnshaw, Stanley** 1906-2005 ..... **CLC 3, 13, 44**
See also CA 9-12R; 243; CP 1, 2, 3, 4, 5, 6, 7; DLB 48; DLBY 1997

**Burr, Anne** 1937- ................................. **CLC 6**
See also CA 25-28R

**Burroughs, Augusten** 1965- ........... **CLC 277**
See also AAYA 73; CA 214; CANR 168

**Burroughs, Edgar Rice** 1875-1950 . **TCLC 2, 32**
See also AAYA 11; BPFB 1; BYA 4, 9; CA 104; 132; CANR 131; DA3; DAM NOV; DLB 8; FANT; MTCW 1, 2; MTFW 2005; RGAL 4; SATA 41; SCFW 1, 2; SFW 4; TCWW 1, 2; TUS; YAW

**Burroughs, William S.** 1914-1997 . **CLC 1, 2, 5, 15, 22, 42, 75, 109; TCLC 121; WLC 1**
See also AAYA 60; AITN 2; AMWS 3; BG 1:2; BPFB 1; CA 9-12R; 160; CANR 20, 52, 104; CN 1, 2, 3, 4, 5, 6; CPW; DA; DA3; DAB; DAC; DAM MST, NOV, POP; DLB 2, 8, 16, 152, 237; DLBY 1981, 1997; EWL 3; GLL 1; HGG; LMFS 2; MAL 5; MTCW 1, 2; MTFW 2005; RGAL 4; SFW 4

**Burroughs, William Seward**
See Burroughs, William S.

**Burton, Sir Richard F(rancis)** 1821-1890 ................................. **NCLC 42**
See also DLB 55, 166, 184; SSFS 21

**Burton, Robert** 1577-1640 ................... **LC 74**
See also DLB 151; RGEL 2

**Buruma, Ian** 1951- ........................... **CLC 163**
See also CA 128; CANR 65, 141, 195

**Bury, Stephen**
See Stephenson, Neal

**Busch, Frederick** 1941-2006 .. **CLC 7, 10, 18, 47, 166**
See also CA 33-36R; 248; CAAS 1; CANR 45, 73, 92, 157; CN 1, 2, 3, 4, 5, 6, 7; DLB 6, 218

**Busch, Frederick Matthew**
See Busch, Frederick

**Bush, Barney (Furman)** 1946- ........... **NNAL**
See also CA 145

**Bush, Ronald** 1946- ........................... **CLC 34**
See also CA 136

**Busia, Abena, P. A.** 1953- ................. **BLC 2:1**

**Bustos, F(rancisco)**
See Borges, Jorge Luis

**Bustos Domecq, H(onorio)**
See Bioy Casares, Adolfo; Borges, Jorge Luis

**Butler, Octavia** 1947-2006 . **BLC 2:1; BLCS; CLC 38, 121, 230, 240**
See also AAYA 18, 48; AFAW 2; AMWS 13; BPFB 1; BW 2, 3; CA 73-76; 248; CANR 12, 24, 38, 73, 145, 240; CLR 65; CN 7; CPW; DA3; DAM MULT, POP; DLB 33; LATS 1:2; MTCW 1, 2; MTFW 2005; NFS 8, 21; SATA 84; SCFW 2; SFW 4; SSFS 6; TCLE 1:1; YAW

**Butler, Octavia E.**
See Butler, Octavia

**Butler, Octavia Estelle**
See Butler, Octavia

**Butler, Robert Olen, Jr.**
See Butler, Robert Olen

**Butler, Robert Olen** 1945- ....... **CLC 81, 162; SSC 117**
See also AMWS 12; BPFB 1; CA 112; CANR 66, 138, 194; CN 7; CSW; DAM POP; DLB 173, 335; INT CA-112; MAL 5; MTCW 2; MTFW 2005; SSFS 11, 22

**Butler, Samuel** 1612-1680 . **LC 16, 43; PC 94**
See also DLB 101, 126; RGEL 2

**Butler, Samuel** 1835-1902 ......... **TCLC 1, 33; WLC 1**
See also BRWS 2; CA 143; CDBLB 1890-1914; DA; DA3; DAB; DAC; DAM MST, NOV; DLB 18, 57, 174; RGEL 2; SFW 4; TEA

**Butler, Walter C.**
See Faust, Frederick

**Butor, Michel (Marie Francois)** 1926- ................. **CLC 1, 3, 8, 11, 15, 161**
See also CA 9-12R; CANR 33, 66; CWW 2; DLB 83; EW 13; EWL 3; GFL 1789 to the Present; MTCW 1, 2; MTFW 2005

**Butts, Mary** 1890(?)-1937 ... **SSC 124; TCLC 77**
See also CA 148; DLB 240

**Buxton, Ralph**
See Silverstein, Alvin; Silverstein, Virginia B.

**Buzo, Alex**
See Buzo, Alexander (John)

**Buzo, Alexander (John)** 1944- ......... **CLC 61**
See also CA 97-100; CANR 17, 39, 69; CD 5, 6; DLB 289

**Buzzati, Dino** 1906-1972 .................... **CLC 36**
See also CA 160; 33-36R; DLB 177; RGWL 2, 3; SFW 4

**Byars, Betsy** 1928- ............................ **CLC 35**
See also AAYA 19; BYA 3; CA 33-36R, 183; CAAE 183; CANR 18, 36, 57, 102, 148; CLR 1, 16, 72; DLB 52; INT CANR-18; JRDA; MAICYA 1, 2; MAICYAS 1; MTCW 1; SAAS 1; SATA 4, 46, 80, 163; SATA-Essay 108; WYA; YAW

**Byars, Betsy Cromer**
See Byars, Betsy

**Byatt, A. S.** 1936- ....... **CLC 19, 65, 136, 223; SSC 91**
See also BPFB 1; BRWC 2; BRWS 4; CA 13-16R; CANR 13, 33, 50, 75, 96, 133; CN 1, 2, 3, 4, 5, 6; DA3; DAM NOV, POP; DLB 14, 194, 319, 326; EWL 3; MTCW 1, 2; MTFW 2005; RGSF 2; RHW; SSFS 26; TEA

**Byatt, Antonia Susan Drabble**
See Byatt, A. S.

**Byrd, William II** 1674-1744 ............... **LC 112**
See also DLB 24, 140; RGAL 4

**Byrne, David** 1952- ........................... **CLC 26**
See also CA 127

**Byrne, John Joseph**
See Leonard, Hugh

**Byrne, John Keyes**
See Leonard, Hugh

**Byron, George Gordon (Noel)** 1788-1824 ..... **DC 24; NCLC 2, 12, 109, 149; PC 16, 95; WLC 1**
See also AAYA 64; BRW 4; BRWC 2; CD-BLB 1789-1832; DA; DA3; DAB; DAC; DAM MST, POET; DLB 96, 110; EXPP; LMFS 1; PAB; PFS 1, 14, 29; RGEL 2; TEA; WLIT 3; WP

**Byron, Robert** 1905-1941 ............... **TCLC 67**
See also CA 160; DLB 195

**C. 3. 3.**
See Wilde, Oscar

**Caballero, Fernan** 1796-1877 ......... **NCLC 10**

**Cabell, Branch**
See Cabell, James Branch

**Cabell, James Branch** 1879-1958 .... **TCLC 6**
See also CA 105; 152; DLB 9, 78; FANT; MAL 5; MTCW 2; RGAL 4; SUFW 1

**Cabeza de Vaca, Alvar Nunez** 1490-1557(?) ........................ **LC 61**

**Cable, George Washington** 1844-1925 .................... **SSC 4; TCLC 4**
See also CA 104; 155; DLB 12, 74; DLBD 13; RGAL 4; TUS

**Cabral de Melo Neto, Joao** 1920-1999 ................................. **CLC 76**
See also CA 151; CWW 2; DAM MULT; DLB 307; EWL 3; LAW; LAWS 1

**Cabrera, Lydia** 1900-1991 ............ **TCLC 223**
See also CA 178; DLB 145; EWL 3; HW 1; LAWS 1

**Cabrera Infante, G.** 1929-2005 ... **CLC 5, 25, 45, 120; HLC 1; SSC 39**
See also CA 85-88; 236; CANR 29, 65, 110; CDWLB 3; CWW 2; DA3; DAM MULT; DLB 113; EWL 3; HW 1, 2; LAW; LAWS 1; MTCW 1, 2; MTFW 2005; RGSF 2; WLIT 1

**Cabrera Infante, Guillermo**
See Cabrera Infante, G.

**Cade, Toni**
See Bambara, Toni Cade

**Cadmus and Harmonia**
See Buchan, John

**Caedmon** fl. 658-680 ........................ **CMLC 7**
See also DLB 146

**Caeiro, Alberto**
See Pessoa, Fernando

**Caesar, Julius**
See Julius Caesar

**Cage, John (Milton), (Jr.)** 1912-1992 ...................... **CLC 41; PC 58**
See also CA 13-16R; 169; CANR 9, 78; DLB 193; INT CANR-9; TCLE 1:1

**Cahan, Abraham** 1860-1951 ........... **TCLC 71**
See also CA 108; 154; DLB 9, 25, 28; MAL 5; RGAL 4

**Cain, Christopher**
See Fleming, Thomas

**Cain, G.**
See Cabrera Infante, G.

**Cain, Guillermo**
See Cabrera Infante, G.

**Cain, James M(allahan)** 1892-1977 .. **CLC 3, 11, 28**
See also AITN 1; BPFB 1; CA 17-20R; 73-76; CANR 8, 34, 61; CMW 4; CN 1, 2; DLB 226; EWL 3; MAL 5; MSW; MTCW 1; RGAL 4

**Caine, Hall** 1853-1931 .................... **TCLC 97**
See also RHW

**Caine, Mark**
See Raphael, Frederic (Michael)

**Calasso, Roberto** 1941- ..................... **CLC 81**
See also CA 143; CANR 89

**Calderon de la Barca, Pedro** 1600-1681 . **DC 3; HLCS 1; LC 23, 136**
See also DFS 23; EW 2; RGWL 2, 3; TWA

**Caldwell, Erskine** 1903-1987 ... **CLC 1, 8, 14, 50, 60; SSC 19; TCLC 117**
See also AITN 1; AMW; BPFB 1; CA 1-4R; 121; CAAS 1; CANR 2, 33; CN 1, 2, 3, 4; DA3; DAM NOV; DLB 9, 86; EWL 3; MAL 5; MTCW 1, 2; MTFW 2005; RGAL 4; RGSF 2; TUS

**Caldwell, (Janet Miriam) Taylor (Holland)** 1900-1985 ........................ **CLC 2, 28, 39**
See also BPFB 1; CA 5-8R; 116; CANR 5; DA3; DAM NOV, POP; DLBD 17; MTCW 2; RHW

**Calhoun, John Caldwell** 1782-1850 ................................. **NCLC 15**
See also DLB 3, 248

**Calisher, Hortense** 1911-2009 .... **CLC 2, 4, 8, 38, 134; SSC 15**
See also CA 1-4R; 282; CANR 1, 22, 117; CN 1, 2, 3, 4, 5, 6, 7; DA3; DAM NOV; DLB 2, 218; INT CANR-22; MAL 5; MTCW 1, 2; MTFW 2005; RGAL 4; RGSF 2

**Carr, Emily** 1871-1945 .................... **TCLC 32**
  See also CA 159; DLB 68; FW; GLL 2
**Carr, H. D.**
  See Crowley, Edward Alexander
**Carr, John Dickson** 1906-1977 .......... **CLC 3**
  See also CA 49-52; 69-72; CANR 3, 33,
  60; CMW 4; DLB 306; MSW; MTCW 1,
  2
**Carr, Philippa**
  See Hibbert, Eleanor Alice Burford
**Carr, Virginia Spencer** 1929- ........... **CLC 34**
  See also CA 61-64; CANR 175; DLB 111
**Carrere, Emmanuel** 1957- ................ **CLC 89**
  See also CA 200
**Carrier, Roch** 1937- ..................... **CLC 13, 78**
  See also CA 130; CANR 61, 152; CCA 1;
  DAC; DAM MST; DLB 53; SATA 105,
  166
**Carroll, James Dennis**
  See Carroll, Jim
**Carroll, James P.** 1943(?)- ................ **CLC 38**
  See also CA 81-84; CANR 73, 139; MTCW
  2; MTFW 2005
**Carroll, Jim** 1949-2009 ............. **CLC 35, 143**
  See also AAYA 17; CA 45-48; 290; CANR
  42, 115; NCFS 5
**Carroll, Lewis** 1832-1898 . **NCLC 2, 53, 139;**
  **PC 18, 74; WLC 1**
  See also AAYA 39; BRW 5; BYA 5, 13; CD-
  BLB 1832-1890; CLR 18, 108; DA; DA3;
  DAB; DAC; DAM MST, NOV, POET;
  DLB 18, 163, 178; DLBY 1998; EXPN;
  EXPP; FANT; JRDA; LAIT 1; MAICYA
  1, 2; NFS 27; PFS 11, 30; RGEL 2; SATA
  100; SUFW 1; TEA; WCH; YABC 2
**Carroll, Paul Vincent** 1900-1968 ...... **CLC 10**
  See also CA 9-12R; 25-28R; DLB 10; EWL
  3; RGEL 2
**Carruth, Hayden** 1921-2008 .... **CLC 4, 7, 10,**
  **18, 84; PC 10**
  See also AMWS 16; CA 9-12R; 277; CANR
  4, 38, 59, 110, 174; CP 1, 2, 3, 4, 5, 6, 7;
  DLB 5, 165; INT CANR-4; MTCW 1, 2;
  MTFW 2005; PFS 26; SATA 47; SATA-
  Obit 197
**Carson, Anne** 1950- ........... **CLC 185; PC 64**
  See also AMWS 12; CA 203; CP 7; DLB
  193; PFS 18; TCLE 1:1
**Carson, Ciaran** 1948- ..................... **CLC 201**
  See also BRWS 13; CA 112; 153; CANR
  113, 189; CP 6, 7; PFS 26
**Carson, Rachel** 1907-1964 ................ **CLC 71**
  See also AAYA 49; AMWS 9; ANW; CA
  77-80; CANR 35; DA3; DAM POP; DLB
  275; FW; LAIT 4; MAL 5; MTCW 1, 2;
  MTFW 2005; NCFS 1; SATA 23
**Carson, Rachel Louise**
  See Carson, Rachel
**Cartagena, Teresa de** 1425(?)- ........... **LC 155**
  See also DLB 286
**Carter, Angela** 1940-1992 ...... **CLC 5, 41, 76;**
  **SSC 13, 85; TCLC 139**
  See also BRWS 3; CA 53-56; 136; CANR
  12, 36, 61, 106; CN 3, 4, 5; DA3; DLB
  14, 207, 261, 319; EXPS; FANT; FW; GL
  2; MTCW 1, 2; MTFW 2005; RGSF 2;
  SATA 66; SATA-Obit 70; SFW 4; SSFS
  4, 12; SUFW 2; WLIT 4
**Carter, Angela Olive**
  See Carter, Angela
**Carter, Martin (Wylde)** 1927- ......... **BLC 2:1**
  See also BW 2; CA 102; CANR 42; CD-
  WLB 3; CP 1, 2, 3, 4, 5, 6; DLB 117;
  EWL 3
**Carter, Nick**
  See Smith, Martin Cruz
**Carter, Nick**
  See Smith, Martin Cruz

**Carver, Raymond** 1938-1988 ..... **CLC 22, 36,**
  **53, 55, 126; PC 54; SSC 8, 51, 104**
  See also AAYA 44; AMWS 3; BPFB 1; CA
  33-36R; 126; CANR 17, 34, 61, 103; CN
  4; CPW; DA3; DAM NOV; DLB 130;
  DLBY 1984, 1988; EWL 3; MAL 5;
  MTCW 1, 2; MTFW 2005; PFS 17;
  RGAL 4; RGSF 2; SSFS 3, 6, 12, 13, 23;
  TCLE 1:1; TCWW 2; TUS
**Cary, Elizabeth, Lady Falkland**
  1585-1639 ............................... **LC 30, 141**
**Cary, (Arthur) Joyce (Lunel)**
  1888-1957 ................... **TCLC 1, 29, 196**
  See also BRW 7; CA 104; 164; CDBLB
  1914-1945; DLB 15, 100; EWL 3; MTCW
  2; RGEL 2; TEA
**Casal, Julian del** 1863-1893 ......... **NCLC 131**
  See also DLB 283; LAW
**Casanova, Giacomo**
  See Casanova de Seingalt, Giovanni Jacopo
**Casanova, Giovanni Giacomo**
  See Casanova de Seingalt, Giovanni Jacopo
**Casanova de Seingalt, Giovanni Jacopo**
  1725-1798 .............................. **LC 13, 151**
  See also WLIT 7
**Casares, Adolfo Bioy**
  See Bioy Casares, Adolfo
**Casas, Bartolome de las** 1474-1566
  See Las Casas, Bartolome de
**Case, John**
  See Hougan, Carolyn
**Casely-Hayford, J(oseph) E(phraim)**
  1866-1903 ............... **BLC 1:1; TCLC 24**
  See also BW 2; CA 123; 152; DAM MULT
**Casey, John (Dudley)** 1939- .............. **CLC 59**
  See also BEST 90:2; CA 69-72; CANR 23,
  100
**Casey, Michael** 1947- ...................... **CLC 2**
  See also CA 65-68; CANR 109; CP 2, 3;
  DLB 5
**Casey, Patrick**
  See Thurman, Wallace (Henry)
**Casey, Warren** 1935-1988 ................. **CLC 12**
  See also CA 101; 127; INT CA-101
**Casey, Warren Peter**
  See Casey, Warren
**Casona, Alejandro**
  See Alvarez, Alejandro Rodriguez
**Cassavetes, John** 1929-1989 ............. **CLC 20**
  See also CA 85-88; 127; CANR 82
**Cassian, Nina** 1924- ........................ **PC 17**
  See also CWP; CWW 2
**Cassill, R(onald) V(erlin)**
  1919-2002 ............................... **CLC 4, 23**
  See also CA 9-12R; 208; CAAS 1; CANR
  7, 45; CN 1, 2, 3, 4, 5, 6, 7; DLB 6, 218;
  DLBY 2002
**Cassiodorus, Flavius Magnus** c. 490(?)-c.
  583(?) ................................... **CMLC 43**
**Cassirer, Ernst** 1874-1945 .............. **TCLC 61**
  See also CA 157
**Cassity, (Allen) Turner** 1929- ....... **CLC 6, 42**
  See also CA 17-20R; 223; CAAE 223;
  CAAS 8; CANR 11; CSW; DLB 105
**Cassius Dio** c. 155-c. 229 .............. **CMLC 99**
  See also DLB 176
**Castaneda, Carlos (Cesar Aranha)**
  1931(?)-1998 ..................... **CLC 12, 119**
  See also CA 25-28R; CANR 32, 66, 105;
  DNFS 1; HW 1; MTCW 1
**Castedo, Elena** 1937- ........................ **CLC 65**
  See also CA 132
**Castedo-Ellerman, Elena**
  See Castedo, Elena

**Castellanos, Rosario** 1925-1974 ....... **CLC 66;**
  **HLC 1; SSC 39, 68**
  See also CA 131; 53-56; CANR 58; CD-
  WLB 3; DAM MULT; DLB 113, 290;
  EWL 3; FW; HW 1; LAW; MTCW 2;
  MTFW 2005; RGSF 2; RGWL 2, 3
**Castelvetro, Lodovico** 1505-1571 ........ **LC 12**
**Castiglione, Baldassare** 1478-1529 ..... **LC 12,**
  **165**
  See also EW 2; LMFS 1; RGWL 2, 3;
  WLIT 7
**Castiglione, Baldesar**
  See Castiglione, Baldassare
**Castillo, Ana** 1953- .................. **CLC 151, 279**
  See also AAYA 42; CA 131; CANR 51, 86,
  128, 172; CWP; DLB 122, 227; DNFS 2;
  FW; HW 1; LLW; PFS 21
**Castillo, Ana Hernandez Del**
  See Castillo, Ana
**Castle, Robert**
  See Hamilton, Edmond
**Castro (Ruz), Fidel** 1926(?)- .............. **HLC 1**
  See also CA 110; 129; CANR 81; DAM
  MULT; HW 2
**Castro, Guillen de** 1569-1631 ............. **LC 19**
**Castro, Rosalia de** 1837-1885 ... **NCLC 3, 78;**
  **PC 41**
  See also DAM MULT
**Castro Alves, Antonio de**
  1847-1871 ............................... **NCLC 205**
  See also DLB 307; LAW
**Cather, Willa** 1873-1947 ....... **SSC 2, 50, 114;**
  **TCLC 1, 11, 31, 99, 132, 152; WLC 1**
  See also AAYA 24; AMW; AMWC 1;
  AMWR 1; BPFB 1; CA 104; 128; CDALB
  1865-1917; CLR 98; DA; DA3; DAB;
  DAC; DAM MST, NOV; DLB 9, 54, 78,
  256; DLBD 1; EWL 3; EXPN; EXPS; FL
  1:5; LAIT 3; LATS 1:1; MAL 5; MBL;
  MTCW 1, 2; MTFW 2005; NFS 2, 19;
  RGAL 4; RGSF 2; RHW; SATA 30; SSFS
  2, 7, 16, 27; TCWW 1, 2; TUS
**Cather, Willa Sibert**
  See Cather, Willa
**Catherine II**
  See Catherine the Great
**Catherine, Saint** 1347-1380 ... **CMLC 27, 116**
**Catherine the Great** 1729-1796 .......... **LC 69**
  See also DLB 150
**Cato, Marcus Porcius**
  234B.C.-149B.C. ..................... **CMLC 21**
  See also DLB 211
**Cato, Marcus Porcius, the Elder**
  See Cato, Marcus Porcius
**Cato the Elder**
  See Cato, Marcus Porcius
**Catton, (Charles) Bruce** 1899-1978 . **CLC 35**
  See also AITN 1; CA 5-8R; 81-84; CANR
  7, 74; DLB 17; MTCW 2; MTFW 2005;
  SATA 2; SATA-Obit 24
**Catullus** c. 84B.C.-54B.C. ............. **CMLC 18**
  See also AW 2; CDWLB 1; DLB 211;
  RGWL 2, 3; WLIT 8
**Cauldwell, Frank**
  See King, Francis (Henry)
**Caunitz, William J.** 1933-1996 ......... **CLC 34**
  See also BEST 89:3; CA 125; 130; 152;
  CANR 73; INT CA-130
**Causley, Charles (Stanley)**
  1917-2003 ............................... **CLC 7**
  See also CA 9-12R; 223; CANR 5, 35, 94;
  CLR 30; CP 1, 2, 3, 4, 5; CWRI 5; DLB
  27; MTCW 1; SATA 3, 66; SATA-Obit
  149
**Caute, (John) David** 1936- ............... **CLC 29**
  See also CA 1-4R; CAAS 4; CANR 1, 33,
  64, 120; CBD; CD 5, 6; CN 1, 2, 3, 4, 5,
  6, 7; DAM NOV; DLB 14, 231

**Chaudhuri, Nirad C(handra)**
1897-1999 ............................... **TCLC 224**
See also CA 128; 183; DLB 323

**Chavez, Denise** 1948- ............................ **HLC 1**
See also CA 131; CANR 56, 81, 137; DAM
MULT; DLB 122; FW; HW 1, 2; LLW;
MAL 5; MTCW 2; MTFW 2005

**Chaviaras, Strates** 1935- .................... **CLC 33**
See also CA 105

**Chayefsky, Paddy** 1923-1981 ............ **CLC 23**
See also CA 9-12R; 104; CAD; CANR 18;
DAM DRAM; DFS 26; DLB 23; DLBY
7, 44; RGAL 4

**Chayefsky, Sidney**
See Chayefsky, Paddy

**Chedid, Andree** 1920- ......................... **CLC 47**
See also CA 145; CANR 95; EWL 3

**Cheever, John** 1912-1982 ..... **CLC 3, 7, 8, 11,
15, 25, 64; SSC 1, 38, 57, 120; WLC 2**
See also AAYA 65; AMWS 1; BPFB 1; CA
5-8R; 106; CABS 1; CANR 5, 27, 76;
CDALB 1941-1968; CN 1, 2, 3; CPW;
DA; DA3; DAB; DAC; DAM MST, NOV,
POP; DLB 2, 102, 227; DLBY 1980,
1982; EWL 3; EXPS; INT CANR-5;
MAL 5; MTCW 1, 2; MTFW 2005;
RGAL 4; RGSF 2; SSFS 2, 14; TUS

**Cheever, Susan** 1943- .................... **CLC 18, 48**
See also CA 103; CANR 27, 51, 92, 157,
198; DLBY 1982; INT CANR-27

**Chekhonte, Antosha**
See Chekhov, Anton (Pavlovich)

**Chekhov, Anton (Pavlovich)**
1860-1904 ....... **DC 9; SSC 2, 28, 41, 51,
85, 102; TCLC 3, 10, 31, 55, 96, 163;
WLC 2**
See also AAYA 68; BYA 14; CA 104; 124;
DA; DA3; DAB; DAC; DAM DRAM,
MST; DFS 1, 5, 10, 12, 26; DLB 277;
EW 7; EWL 3; EXPS; LAIT 3; LATS 1:1;
RGSF 2; RGWL 2, 3; SATA 90; SSFS 5,
13, 14, 26; TWA

**Cheney, Lynne V.** 1941- ..................... **CLC 70**
See also CA 89-92; CANR 58, 117, 193;
SATA 152

**Cheney, Lynne Vincent**
See Cheney, Lynne V.

**Chernyshevsky, Nikolai Gavrilovich**
See Chernyshevsky, Nikolay Gavrilovich

**Chernyshevsky, Nikolay Gavrilovich**
1828-1889 .................................. **NCLC 1**
See also DLB 238

**Cherry, Carolyn Janice**
See Cherryh, C.J.

**Cherryh, C.J.** 1942- ........................... **CLC 35**
See also AAYA 24; BPFB 1; CA 65-68;
CANR 10, 147, 179; DLBY 1980; FANT;
SATA 93, 172; SCFW 2; YAW

**Chesler, Phyllis** 1940- ....................... **CLC 247**
See also CA 49-52; CANR 4, 59, 140, 189;
FW

**Chesnutt, Charles W(addell)**
1858-1932 .... **BLC 1; SSC 7, 54; TCLC
5, 39**
See also AFAW 1, 2; AMWS 14; BW 1, 3;
CA 106; 125; CANR 76; DAM MULT;
DLB 12, 50, 78; EWL 3; MAL 5; MTCW
1, 2; MTFW 2005; RGAL 4; RGSF 2;
SSFS 11, 26

**Chester, Alfred** 1929(?)-1971 ............ **CLC 49**
See also CA 196; 33-36R; DLB 130; MAL
5

**Chesterton, G(ilbert) K(eith)**
1874-1936 . **PC 28; SSC 1, 46; TCLC 1,
6, 64**
See also AAYA 57; BRW 6; CA 104; 132;
CANR 73, 131; CDBLB 1914-1945;
CMW 4; DAM NOV, POET; DLB 10, 19,

34, 70, 98, 149, 178; EWL 3; FANT;
MSW; MTCW 1, 2; MTFW 2005; RGEL
2; RGSF 2; SATA 27; SUFW 1

**Chettle, Henry** 1560-1607(?) .............. **LC 112**
See also DLB 136; RGEL 2

**Chiang, Pin-chin** 1904-1986 .............. **CLC 68**
See also CA 118; DLB 328; EWL 3; RGWL
3

**Chiang Ping-chih**
See Chiang, Pin-chin

**Chief Joseph** 1840-1904 ...................... **NNAL**
See also CA 152; DA3; DAM MULT

**Chief Seattle** 1786(?)-1866 .................. **NNAL**
See also DA3; DAM MULT

**Ch'ien, Chung-shu** 1910-1998 .......... **CLC 22**
See also CA 130; CANR 73; CWW 2; DLB
328; MTCW 1, 2

**Chikamatsu Monzaemon** 1653-1724 ... **LC 66**
See also RGWL 2, 3

**Child, Francis James** 1825-1896 . **NCLC 173**
See also DLB 1, 64, 235

**Child, L. Maria**
See Child, Lydia Maria

**Child, Lydia Maria** 1802-1880 .. **NCLC 6, 73**
See also DLB 1, 74, 243; RGAL 4; SATA
67

**Child, Mrs.**
See Child, Lydia Maria

**Child, Philip** 1898-1978 ............... **CLC 19, 68**
See also CA 13-14; CAP 1; CP 1; DLB 68;
RHW; SATA 47

**Childers, (Robert) Erskine**
1870-1922 ................................... **TCLC 65**
See also CA 113; 153; DLB 70

**Childress, Alice** 1920-1994 .... **BLC 1:1; CLC
12, 15, 86, 96; DC 4; TCLC 116**
See also AAYA 8; BW 2, 3; BYA 2; CA 45-
48; 146; CAD; CANR 3, 27, 50, 74; CLR
14; CWD; DA3; DAM DRAM, MULT,
NOV; DFS 2, 8, 14, 26; DLB 7, 38, 249;
JRDA; LAIT 5; MAICYA 1, 2; MAIC-
YAS 1; MAL 5; MTCW 1, 2; MTFW
2005; RGAL 4; SATA 7, 48, 81; TUS;
WYA; YAW

**Chin, Frank** 1940- ..... **AAL; CLC 135; DC 7**
See also CA 33-36R; CAD; CANR 71; CD
5, 6; DAM MULT; DLB 206, 312; LAIT
5; RGAL 4

**Chin, Frank Chew, Jr.**
See Chin, Frank

**Chin, Marilyn** 1955- ............................. **PC 40**
See also CA 129; CANR 70, 113; CWP;
DLB 312; PFS 28

**Chin, Marilyn Mei Ling**
See Chin, Marilyn

**Chislett, (Margaret) Anne** 1943- ...... **CLC 34**
See also CA 151

**Chitty, Thomas Willes** 1926- ........ **CLC 6, 11**
See also CA 5-8R; CN 1, 2, 3, 4, 5, 6; EWL
3

**Chivers, Thomas Holley**
1809-1858 ................................. **NCLC 49**
See also DLB 3, 248; RGAL 4

**Chlamyda, Jehudil**
See Peshkov, Alexei Maximovich

**Ch'o, Chou**
See Shu-Jen, Chou

**Choi, Susan** 1969- ............................. **CLC 119**
See also CA 223; CANR 188

**Chomette, Rene Lucien** 1898-1981 .. **CLC 20**
See also CA 103

**Chomsky, Avram Noam**
See Chomsky, Noam

**Chomsky, Noam** 1928- ..................... **CLC 132**
See also CA 17-20R; CANR 28, 62, 110,
132, 179; DA3; DLB 246; MTCW 1, 2;
MTFW 2005

**Chona, Maria** 1845(?)-1936 ............... **NNAL**
See also CA 144

**Chopin, Kate** 1851-1904 ....... **SSC 8, 68, 110;
TCLC 127; WLCS**
See also AAYA 33; AMWR 2; BYA 11, 15;
CA 104; 122; CDALB 1865-1917; DA3;
DAB; DAC; DAM MST, NOV; DLB 12,
78; EXPN; EXPS; FL 1:3; FW; LAIT 3;
MAL 5; MBL; NFS 3; RGAL 4; RGSF 2;
SSFS 2, 13, 17, 26; TUS

**Chopin, Katherine**
See Chopin, Kate

**Chretien de Troyes** c. 12th cent. - . **CMLC 10**
See also DLB 208; EW 1; RGWL 2, 3;
TWA

**Christie**
See Ichikawa, Kon

**Christie, Agatha (Mary Clarissa)**
1890-1976 .. **CLC 1, 6, 8, 12, 39, 48, 110**
See also AAYA 9; AITN 1, 2; BPFB 1;
BRWS 2; CA 17-20R; 61-64; CANR 10,
37, 108; CBD; CDBLB 1914-1945; CMW
4; CN 1, 2; CPW; CWD; DA3; DAB;
DAC; DAM NOV; DFS 2; DLB 13, 77,
245; MSW; MTCW 1, 2; MTFW 2005;
NFS 8, 30; RGEL 2; RHW; SATA 36;
TEA; YAW

**Christie, Ann Philippa**
See Pearce, Philippa

**Christie, Philippa**
See Pearce, Philippa

**Christine de Pisan**
See Christine de Pizan

**Christine de Pizan** 1365(?)-1431(?) ...... **LC 9,
130; PC 68**
See also DLB 208; FL 1:1; FW; RGWL 2,
3

**Chuang-Tzu** c. 369B.C.-c.
286B.C. ..................................... **CMLC 57**

**Chubb, Elmer**
See Masters, Edgar Lee

**Chulkov, Mikhail Dmitrievich**
1743-1792 .................................... **LC 2**
See also DLB 150

**Churchill, Caryl** 1938- ....... **CLC 31, 55, 157;
DC 5**
See also BRWS 4; CA 102; CANR 22, 46,
108; CBD; CD 5, 6; CWD; DFS 25; DLB
13, 310; EWL 3; FW; MTCW 1; RGEL 2

**Churchill, Charles** 1731-1764 ................ **LC 3**
See also DLB 109; RGEL 2

**Churchill, Chick**
See Churchill, Caryl

**Churchill, Sir Winston (Leonard Spencer)**
1874-1965 ............................... **TCLC 113**
See also BRW 6; CA 97-100; CDBLB
1890-1914; DA3; DLB 100, 329; DLBD
16; LAIT 4; MTCW 1, 2

**Chute, Carolyn** 1947- ......................... **CLC 39**
See also CA 123; CANR 135; CN 7; DLB
350

**Ciardi, John (Anthony)** 1916-1986 . **CLC 10,
40, 44, 129; PC 69**
See also CA 5-8R; 118; CAAS 2; CANR 5,
33; CLR 19; CP 1, 2, 3, 4; CWRI 5; DAM
POET; DLB 5; DLBY 1986; INT
CANR-5; MAICYA 1, 2; MAL 5; MTCW
1, 2; MTFW 2005; RGAL 4; SAAS 26;
SATA 1, 65; SATA-Obit 46

**Cibber, Colley** 1671-1757 .................... **LC 66**
See also DLB 84; RGEL 2

**Cicero, Marcus Tullius**
106B.C.-43B.C. .................. **CMLC 3, 81**
See also AW 1; CDWLB 1; DLB 211;
RGWL 2, 3; WLIT 8

**Cimino, Michael** 1943- ..................... **CLC 16**
See also CA 105

**Cioran, E(mil) M.** 1911-1995 ........... **CLC 64**
See also CA 25-28R; 149; CANR 91; DLB
220; EWL 3

**Coffin, Robert Peter Tristram**
See Coffin, Robert P. Tristram
**Cohan, George M.** 1878-1942 ........ **TCLC 60**
See also CA 157; DLB 249; RGAL 4
**Cohan, George Michael**
See Cohan, George M.
**Cohen, Arthur A(llen)** 1928-1986 ...... **CLC 7, 31**
See also CA 1-4R; 120; CANR 1, 17, 42; DLB 28; RGHL
**Cohen, Leonard** 1934- .......... **CLC 3, 38, 260**
See also CA 21-24R; CANR 14, 69; CN 1, 2, 3, 4, 5, 6; CP 1, 2, 3, 4, 5, 6, 7; DAC; DAM MST; DLB 53; EWL 3; MTCW 1
**Cohen, Leonard Norman**
See Cohen, Leonard
**Cohen, Matt(hew)** 1942-1999 ............ **CLC 19**
See also CA 61-64; 187; CAAS 18; CANR 40; CN 1, 2, 3, 4, 5, 6; DAC; DLB 53
**Cohen-Solal, Annie** 1948- ................. **CLC 50**
See also CA 239
**Colegate, Isabel** 1931- ........................ **CLC 36**
See also CA 17-20R; CANR 8, 22, 74; CN 4, 5, 6, 7; DLB 14, 231; INT CANR-22; MTCW 1
**Coleman, Emmett**
See Reed, Ishmael
**Coleridge, Hartley** 1796-1849 ........ **NCLC 90**
See also DLB 96
**Coleridge, M. E.**
See Coleridge, Mary E(lizabeth)
**Coleridge, Mary E(lizabeth)**
1861-1907 ................................. **TCLC 73**
See also CA 116; 166; DLB 19, 98
**Coleridge, Samuel Taylor**
1772-1834 ..... **NCLC 9, 54, 99, 111, 177, 197; PC 11, 39, 67, 100; WLC 2**
See also AAYA 66; BRW 4; BRWR 2; BYA 4; CDBLB 1789-1832; DA; DA3; DAB; DAC; DAM MST, POET; DLB 93, 107; EXPP; LATS 1:1; LMFS 1; PAB; PFS 4, 5; RGEL 2; TEA; WLIT 3; WP
**Coleridge, Sara** 1802-1852 ............. **NCLC 31**
See also DLB 199
**Coles, Don** 1928- ................................ **CLC 46**
See also CA 115; CANR 38; CP 5, 6, 7
**Coles, Robert (Martin)** 1929- ......... **CLC 108**
See also CA 45-48; CANR 3, 32, 66, 70; 135; INT CANR-32; SATA 23
**Colette, (Sidonie-Gabrielle)**
1873-1954 .. **SSC 10, 93; TCLC 1, 5, 16**
See also CA 104; 131; DA3; DAM NOV; DLB 65; EW 9; EWL 3; GFL 1789 to the Present; GLL 1; MTCW 1, 2; MTFW 2005; RGWL 2, 3; TWA
**Collett, (Jacobine) Camilla (Wergeland)**
1813-1895 ............................... **NCLC 22**
See also DLB 354
**Collier, Christopher** 1930- ................. **CLC 30**
See also AAYA 13; BYA 2; CA 33-36R; CANR 13, 33, 102; CLR 126; JRDA; MAICYA 1, 2; SATA 16, 70; WYA; YAW 1
**Collier, James Lincoln** 1928- ............ **CLC 30**
See also AAYA 13; BYA 2; CA 9-12R; CANR 4, 33, 60, 102; CLR 3, 126; DAM POP; JRDA; MAICYA 1, 2; SAAS 21; SATA 8, 70, 166; WYA; YAW 1
**Collier, Jeremy** 1650-1726 ............ **LC 6, 157**
See also DLB 336
**Collier, John** 1901-1980 . **SSC 19; TCLC 127**
See also CA 65-68; 97-100; CANR 10; CN 1, 2; DLB 77, 255; FANT; SUFW 1
**Collier, Mary** 1690-1762 ....................... **LC 86**
See also DLB 95
**Collingwood, R(obin) G(eorge)**
1889(?)-1943 ........................... **TCLC 67**
See also CA 117; 155; DLB 262

**Collins, Billy** 1941- ............................... **PC 68**
See also AAYA 64; CA 151; CANR 92; CP 7; MTFW 2005; PFS 18
**Collins, Hunt**
See Hunter, Evan
**Collins, Linda** 1931- .......................... **CLC 44**
See also CA 125
**Collins, Merle** 1950- ......................... **BLC 2:1**
See also BW 3; CA 175; DLB 157
**Collins, Tom**
See Furphy, Joseph
**Collins, (William) Wilkie**
1824-1889 ....... **NCLC 1, 18, 93; SSC 93**
See also BRWS 6; CDBLB 1832-1890; CMW 4; DLB 18, 70, 159; GL 2; MSW; RGEL 2; RGSF 2; SUFW 1; WLIT 4
**Collins, William** 1721-1759 ...... **LC 4, 40; PC 72**
See also BRW 3; DAM POET; DLB 109; RGEL 2
**Collodi, Carlo**
See Lorenzini, Carlo
**Colman, George**
See Glassco, John
**Colman, George, the Elder**
1732-1794 ...................................... **LC 98**
See also RGEL 2
**Colonna, Vittoria** 1492-1547 ............... **LC 71**
See also RGWL 2, 3
**Colt, Winchester Remington**
See Hubbard, L. Ron
**Colter, Cyrus J.** 1910-2002 ............... **CLC 58**
See also BW 1; CA 65-68; 205; CANR 10, 66; CN 2, 3, 4, 5, 6; DLB 33
**Colton, James**
See Hansen, Joseph
**Colum, Padraic** 1881-1972 ............... **CLC 28**
See also BYA 4; CA 73-76; 33-36R; CANR 35; CLR 36; CP 1; CWRI 5; DLB 19; MAICYA 1, 2; MTCW 1; RGEL 2; SATA 15; WCH
**Colvin, James**
See Moorcock, Michael
**Colwin, Laurie (E.)** 1944-1992 .... **CLC 5, 13, 23, 84**
See also CA 89-92; 139; CANR 20, 46; DLB 218; DLBY 1980; MTCW 1
**Comfort, Alex(ander)** 1920-2000 ........ **CLC 7**
See also CA 1-4R; 190; CANR 1, 45; CN 1, 2, 3, 4; CP 1, 2, 3, 4, 5, 6, 7; DAM POP; MTCW 2
**Comfort, Montgomery**
See Campbell, Ramsey
**Compton-Burnett, I(vy)**
1892(?)-1969 ........ **CLC 1, 3, 10, 15, 34; TCLC 180**
See also BRW 7; CA 1-4R; 25-28R; CANR 4; DAM NOV; DLB 36; EWL 3; MTCW 1, 2; RGEL 2
**Comstock, Anthony** 1844-1915 ...... **TCLC 13**
See also CA 110; 169
**Comte, Auguste** 1798-1857 ............. **NCLC 54**
**Conan Doyle, Arthur**
See Doyle, Sir Arthur Conan
**Conde (Abellan), Carmen**
1901-1996 ................................. **HLCS 1**
See also CA 177; CWW 2; DLB 108; EWL 3; HW 2
**Conde, Maryse** 1937- ......... **BLC 2:1; BLCS; CLC 52, 92, 247**
See also BW 2, 3; CA 110, 190; CAAE 190; CANR 30, 53, 76, 171; CWW 2; DAM MULT; EWL 3; MTCW 2; MTFW 2005
**Condillac, Etienne Bonnot de**
1714-1780 ...................................... **LC 26**
See also DLB 313

**Condon, Richard** 1915-1996 ...... **CLC 4, 6, 8, 10, 45, 100**
See also BEST 90:3; BPFB 1; CA 1-4R; 151; CAAS 1; CANR 2, 23, 164; CMW 4; CN 1, 2, 3, 4, 5, 6; DAM NOV; INT CANR-23; MTCW 1, 2
**Condon, Richard Thomas**
See Condon, Richard
**Condorcet**
See Condorcet, marquis de Marie-Jean-Antoine-Nicolas Caritat
**Condorcet, marquis de**
**Marie-Jean-Antoine-Nicolas Caritat**
1743-1794 .................................. **LC 104**
See also DLB 313; GFL Beginnings to 1789
**Confucius** 551B.C.-479B.C. .... **CMLC 19, 65; WLCS**
See also DA; DA3; DAB; DAC; DAM MST
**Congreve, William** 1670-1729 ... **DC 2; LC 5, 21, 170; WLC 2**
See also BRW 2; CDBLB 1660-1789; DA; DAB; DAC; DAM DRAM, MST, POET; DFS 15; DLB 39, 84; RGEL 2; WLIT 3
**Conley, Robert J.** 1940- ..................... **NNAL**
See also CA 41-44R; CANR 15, 34, 45, 96, 186; DAM MULT; TCWW 2
**Connell, Evan S.** 1924- ............. **CLC 4, 6, 45**
See also AAYA 7; AMWS 14; CA 1-4R; CAAS 2; CANR 2, 39, 76, 97, 140, 195; CN 1, 2, 3, 4, 5, 6; DAM NOV; DLB 2, 335; DLBY 1981; MAL 5; MTCW 1, 2; MTFW 2005
**Connell, Evan Shelby, Jr.**
See Connell, Evan S.
**Connelly, Marc(us Cook)** 1890-1980 . **CLC 7**
See also CA 85-88; 102; CAD; CANR 30; DFS 12; DLB 7; DLBY 1980; MAL 5; RGAL 4; SATA-Obit 25
**Connolly, Paul**
See Wicker, Tom
**Connor, Ralph**
See Gordon, Charles William
**Conrad, Joseph** 1857-1924 ..... **SSC 9, 67, 69, 71; TCLC 1, 6, 13, 25, 43, 57; WLC 2**
See also AAYA 26; BPFB 1; BRW 6; BRWC 1; BRWR 2; BYA 2; CA 104; 131; CANR 60; CDBLB 1890-1914; DA; DA3; DAB; DAC; DAM MST, NOV; DLB 10, 34, 98, 156; EWL 3; EXPN; EXPS; LAIT 2; LATS 1:1; LMFS 1; MTCW 1, 2; MTFW 2005; NFS 2, 16; RGEL 2; RGSF 2; SATA 27; SSFS 1, 12; TEA; WLIT 4
**Conrad, Robert Arnold**
See Hart, Moss
**Conroy, Donald Patrick**
See Conroy, Pat
**Conroy, Pat** 1945- ....................... **CLC 30, 74**
See also AAYA 8, 52; AITN 1; BPFB 1; CA 85-88; CANR 24, 53, 129; CN 7; CPW; CSW; DA3; DAM NOV, POP; DLB 6; LAIT 5; MAL 5; MTCW 1, 2; MTFW 2005
**Constant (de Rebecque), (Henri) Benjamin**
1767-1830 ......................... **NCLC 6, 182**
See also DLB 119; EW 4; GFL 1789 to the Present
**Conway, Jill K.** 1934- ..................... **CLC 152**
See also CA 130; CANR 94
**Conway, Jill Kathryn Ker**
See Conway, Jill K.
**Conybeare, Charles Augustus**
See Eliot, T(homas) S(tearns)
**Cook, Michael** 1933-1994 ................. **CLC 58**
See also CA 93-96; CANR 68; DLB 53

**Cook, Robin** 1940- ............................ **CLC 14**
See also AAYA 32; BEST 90:2; BPFB 1;
CA 108; 111; CANR 41, 90, 109, 181;
CPW; DA3; DAM POP; HGG; INT CA-
111

**Cook, Roy**
See Silverberg, Robert

**Cooke, Elizabeth** 1948- ....................... **CLC 55**
See also CA 129

**Cooke, John Esten** 1830-1886 .......... **NCLC 5**
See also DLB 3, 248; RGAL 4

**Cooke, John Estes**
See Baum, L. Frank

**Cooke, M. E.**
See Creasey, John

**Cooke, Margaret**
See Creasey, John

**Cooke, Rose Terry** 1827-1892 ...... **NCLC 110**
See also DLB 12, 74

**Cook-Lynn, Elizabeth** 1930- ............ **CLC 93; NNAL**
See also CA 133; DAM MULT; DLB 175

**Cooney, Ray CLC 62**
See also CBD

**Cooper, Anthony Ashley** 1671-1713 .. **LC 107**
See also DLB 101, 336

**Cooper, Dennis** 1953- ....................... **CLC 203**
See also CA 133; CANR 72, 86; GLL 1; HGG

**Cooper, Douglas** 1960- ....................... **CLC 86**

**Cooper, Henry St. John**
See Creasey, John

**Cooper, J. California** (?)- .................. **CLC 56**
See also AAYA 12; BW 1; CA 125; CANR 55; DAM MULT; DLB 212

**Cooper, James Fenimore**
1789-1851 .............. **NCLC 1, 27, 54, 203**
See also AAYA 22; AMW; BPFB 1;
CDALB 1640-1865; CLR 105; DA3;
DLB 3, 183, 250, 254; LAIT 1; NFS 25;
RGAL 4; SATA 19; TUS; WCH

**Cooper, Susan Fenimore**
1813-1894 .............................. **NCLC 129**
See also ANW; DLB 239, 254

**Coover, Robert** 1932- .. **CLC 3, 7, 15, 32, 46, 87, 161; SSC 15, 101**
See also AMWS 5; BPFB 1; CA 45-48;
CANR 3, 37, 58, 115; CN 1, 2, 3, 4, 5, 6,
7; DAM NOV; DLB 2, 227; DLBY 1981;
EWL 5; MAL 5; MTCW 1, 2; MTFW
2005; RGAL 4; RGSF 2

**Copeland, Stewart** 1952- ................... **CLC 26**

**Copeland, Stewart Armstrong**
See Copeland, Stewart

**Copernicus, Nicolaus** 1473-1543 ......... **LC 45**

**Coppard, A(lfred) E(dgar)**
1878-1957 ................... **SSC 21; TCLC 5**
See also BRWS 8; CA 114; 167; DLB 162;
EWL 3; HGG; RGEL 2; RGSF 2; SUFW
1; YABC 1

**Coppee, Francois** 1842-1908 .......... **TCLC 25**
See also CA 170; DLB 217

**Coppola, Francis Ford** 1939- ... **CLC 16, 126**
See also AAYA 39; CA 77-80; CANR 40,
78; DLB 44

**Copway, George** 1818-1869 ................ **NNAL**
See also DAM MULT; DLB 175, 183

**Corbiere, Tristan** 1845-1875 .......... **NCLC 43**
See also DLB 217; GFL 1789 to the Present

**Corcoran, Barbara (Asenath)**
1911- .......................................... **CLC 17**
See also AAYA 14; CA 21-24R, 191; CAAE
191; CAAS 2; CANR 11, 28, 48; CLR
50; JRDA; MAICYA 1; MAIC-
YAS 1; RHW; SAAS 20; SATA 3, 77;
SATA-Essay 125

**Cordelier, Maurice**
See Giraudoux, Jean(-Hippolyte)

**Cordier, Gilbert**
See Scherer, Jean-Marie Maurice

**Corelli, Marie**
See Mackay, Mary

**Corinna** c. 225B.C.-c. 305B.C. ...... **CMLC 72**

**Corman, Cid** 1924-2004 ..................... **CLC 9**
See also CA 85-88; 225; CAAS 2; CANR
44; CP 1, 2, 3, 4, 5, 6, 7; DAM POET;
DLB 5, 193

**Corman, Sidney**
See Corman, Cid

**Cormier, Robert** 1925-2000 ........ **CLC 12, 30**
See also AAYA 3, 19; BYA 1, 2, 6, 8, 9;
CA 1-4R; CANR 5, 23, 76, 93; CDALB
1968-1988; CLR 12, 55; DA; DAB; DAC;
DAM MST, NOV; DLB 52; EXPN; INT
CANR-23; JRDA; LAIT 5; MAICYA 1,
2; MTCW 1, 2; MTFW 2005; NFS 2, 18;
SATA 10, 45, 83; SATA-Obit 122; WYA;
YAW

**Cormier, Robert Edmund**
See Cormier, Robert

**Corn, Alfred (DeWitt III)** 1943- ....... **CLC 33**
See also CA 179; CAAE 179; CAAS 25;
CANR 44; CP 3, 4, 5, 6, 7; CSW; DLB
120, 282; DLBY 1980

**Corneille, Pierre** 1606-1684 .. **DC 21; LC 28, 135**
See also DAB; DAM MST; DFS 21; DLB
268; EW 3; GFL Beginnings to 1789;
RGWL 2, 3; TWA

**Cornwell, David**
See le Carre, John

**Cornwell, David John Moore**
See le Carre, John

**Cornwell, Patricia** 1956- ................. **CLC 155**
See also AAYA 16, 56; BPFB 1; CA 134;
CANR 53, 131, 195; CMW 4; CPW;
CSW; DAM POP; DLB 306; MSW;
MTCW 2; MTFW 2005

**Cornwell, Patricia Daniels**
See Cornwell, Patricia

**Cornwell, Smith**
See Smith, David (Jeddie)

**Corso, Gregory** 1930-2001 .... **CLC 1, 11; PC 33**
See also AMWS 12; BG 1:2; CA 5-8R; 193;
CANR 41, 76, 132; CP 1, 2, 3, 4, 5, 6, 7;
DA3; DLB 5, 16, 237; LMFS 2; MAL 5;
MTCW 1, 2; MTFW 2005; WP

**Cortazar, Julio** 1914-1984 ... **CLC 2, 3, 5, 10, 13, 15, 33, 34, 92; HLC 1; SSC 7, 76**
See also BPFB 1; CA 21-24R; CANR 12,
32, 81; CDWLB 3; DA3; DAM MULT,
NOV; DLB 113; EWL 3; EXPS; HW 1,
2; LAW; MTCW 1, 2; MTFW 2005;
RGSF 2; RGWL 2, 3; SSFS 3, 20; TWA;
WLIT 1

**Cortes, Hernan** 1485-1547 .................. **LC 31**

**Cortez, Jayne** 1936- ......................... **BLC 2:1**
See also BW 2, 3; CA 73-76; CANR 13,
31, 68, 126; CWP; DLB 41; EWL 3

**Corvinus, Jakob**
See Raabe, Wilhelm (Karl)

**Corwin, Cecil**
See Kornbluth, C(yril) M.

**Cosic, Dobrica** 1921- .......................... **CLC 14**
See also CA 122; 138; CDWLB 4; CWW
2; DLB 181; EWL 3

**Costain, Thomas B(ertram)**
1885-1965 ................................... **CLC 30**
See also BYA 3; CA 5-8R; 25-28R; DLB 9;
RHW

**Costantini, Humberto** 1924(?)-1987 . **CLC 49**
See also CA 131; 122; EWL 3; HW 1

**Costello, Elvis** 1954(?)- ..................... **CLC 21**
See also CA 204

**Costenoble, Philostene**
See Ghelderode, Michel de

**Cotes, Cecil V.**
See Duncan, Sara Jeannette

**Cotter, Joseph Seamon Sr.**
1861-1949 ............... **BLC 1:1; TCLC 28**
See also BW 1; CA 124; DAM MULT; DLB
50

**Couch, Arthur Thomas Quiller**
See Quiller-Couch, Sir Arthur (Thomas)

**Coulton, James**
See Hansen, Joseph

**Couperus, Louis (Marie Anne)**
1863-1923 ............................... **TCLC 15**
See also CA 115; EWL 3; RGWL 2, 3

**Coupland, Douglas** 1961- .......... **CLC 85, 133**
See also AAYA 34; CA 142; CANR 57, 90,
130, 172; CCA 1; CN 7; CPW; DAC;
DAM POP; DLB 334

**Coupland, Douglas Campbell**
See Coupland, Douglas

**Court, Wesli**
See Turco, Lewis

**Courtenay, Bryce** 1933- ..................... **CLC 59**
See also CA 138; CPW

**Courtney, Robert**
See Ellison, Harlan

**Cousteau, Jacques-Yves** 1910-1997 .. **CLC 30**
See also CA 65-68; 159; CANR 15, 67;
MTCW 1; SATA 38, 98

**Coventry, Francis** 1725-1754 ............... **LC 46**
See also DLB 39

**Coverdale, Miles** c. 1487-1569 ............. **LC 77**
See also DLB 167

**Cowan, Peter (Walkinshaw)**
1914-2002 ................................... **SSC 28**
See also CA 21-24R; CANR 9, 25, 50, 83;
CN 1, 2, 3, 4, 5, 6, 7; DLB 260; RGSF 2

**Coward, Noel** 1899-1973 .... **CLC 1, 9, 29, 51**
See also AITN 1; BRWS 2; CA 17-18; 41-
44R; CANR 35, 132, 190; CAP 2; CBD;
CDBLB 1914-1945; DA3; DAM DRAM;
DFS 3, 6; DLB 10, 245; EWL 3; IDFW
3, 4; MTCW 1, 2; MTFW 2005; RGEL 2;
TEA

**Coward, Noel Peirce**
See Coward, Noel

**Cowley, Abraham** 1618-1667 .. **LC 43; PC 90**
See also BRW 2; DLB 131, 151; PAB;
RGEL 2

**Cowley, Malcolm** 1898-1989 ............. **CLC 39**
See also AMWS 2; CA 5-8R; 128; CANR
3, 55; CP 1, 2, 3, 4; DLB 4, 48; DLBY
1981, 1989; EWL 3; MAL 5; MTCW 1,
2; MTFW 2005

**Cowper, William** 1731-1800 ..... **NCLC 8, 94; PC 40**
See also BRW 3; DA3; DAM POET; DLB
104, 109; RGEL 2

**Cox, William Trevor**
See Trevor, William

**Coyle, William**
See Keneally, Thomas

**Coyne, P. J.**
See Masters, Hilary

**Coyne, P.J.**
See Masters, Hilary

**Cozzens, James Gould** 1903-1978 . **CLC 1, 4, 11, 92**
See also AMW; BPFB 1; CA 9-12R; 81-84;
CANR 19; CDALB 1941-1968; CN 1, 2;
DLB 9, 294; DLBD 2; DLBY 1984, 1997;
EWL 3; MAL 5; MTCW 1, 2; MTFW
2005; RGAL 4

**Crabbe, George** 1754-1832 ... **NCLC 26, 121; PC 97**
See also BRW 3; DLB 93; RGEL 2

**Crace, Jim** 1946- ............... **CLC 157; SSC 61**
See also BRWS 14; CA 128; 135; CANR
55, 70, 123, 180; CN 5, 6, 7; DLB 231;
INT CA-135

**Dickey, James** 1923-1997 ....... **CLC 1, 2, 4, 7, 10, 15, 47, 109; PC 40; TCLC 151**
See also AAYA 50; AITN 1, 2; AMWS 4; BPFB 1; CA 9-12R; 156; CABS 2; CANR 10, 48, 61, 105; CDALB 1968-1988; CP 1, 2, 3, 4, 5, 6; CPW; CSW; DA3; DAM NOV, POET, POP; DLB 5, 193, 342; DLBD 7; DLBY 1982, 1993, 1996, 1997, 1998; EWL 3; INT CANR-10; MAL 5; MTCW 1, 2; NFS 9; PFS 6, 11; RGAL 4; TUS

**Dickey, James Lafayette**
See Dickey, James

**Dickey, William** 1928-1994 .......... **CLC 3, 28**
See also CA 9-12R; 145; CANR 24, 79; CP 1, 2, 3, 4; DLB 5

**Dickinson, Charles** 1951- .................. **CLC 49**
See also CA 128; CANR 141

**Dickinson, Emily** 1830-1886 ... **NCLC 21, 77, 171; PC 1; WLC 2**
See also AAYA 22; AMW; AMWR 1; CDALB 1865-1917; DA; DA3; DAB; DAC; DAM MST, POET; DLB 1, 243; EXPP; FL 1:3; MBL; PAB; PFS 1, 2, 3, 4, 5, 6, 8, 10, 11, 13, 16, 28; RGAL 4; SATA 29; TUS; WP; WYA

**Dickinson, Emily Elizabeth**
See Dickinson, Emily

**Dickinson, Mrs. Herbert Ward**
See Phelps, Elizabeth Stuart

**Dickinson, Peter** 1927- ................. **CLC 12, 35**
See also AAYA 9, 49; BYA 5; CA 41-44R; CANR 31, 58, 88, 134, 195; CLR 29, 125; CMW 4; DLB 87, 161, 276; JRDA; MAICYA 1, 2; SATA 5, 62, 95, 150; SFW 4; WYA; YAW

**Dickinson, Peter Malcolm de Brissac**
See Dickinson, Peter

**Dickson, Carr**
See Carr, John Dickson

**Dickson, Carter**
See Carr, John Dickson

**Diderot, Denis** 1713-1784 ............. **LC 26, 126**
See also DLB 313; EW 4; GFL Beginnings to 1789; LMFS 1; RGWL 2, 3

**Didion, Joan** 1934- . **CLC 1, 3, 8, 14, 32, 129**
See also AITN 1; AMWS 4; CA 5-8R; CANR 14, 52, 76, 125, 174; CDALB 1968-1988; CN 2, 3, 4, 5, 6, 7; DA3; DAM NOV; DLB 2, 173, 185; DLBY 1981, 1986; EWL 3; MAL 5; MBL; MTCW 1, 2; MTFW 2005; NFS 3; RGAL 4; TCLE 1:1; TCWW 2; TUS

**di Donato, Pietro** 1911-1992 .......... **TCLC 159**
See also CA 101; 136; DLB 9

**Dietrich, Robert**
See Hunt, E. Howard

**Difusa, Pati**
See Almodovar, Pedro

**di Lampedusa, Giuseppe Tomasi**
See Tomasi di Lampedusa, Giuseppe

**Dillard, Annie** 1945- ...... **CLC 9, 60, 115, 216**
See also AAYA 6, 43; AMWS 6; ANW; CA 49-52; CANR 3, 43, 62, 90, 125; DA3; DAM NOV; DLB 275, 278; DLBY 1980; LAIT 4, 5; MAL 5; MTCW 1, 2; MTFW 2005; NCFS 1; RGAL 4; SATA 10, 140; TCLE 1:1; TUS

**Dillard, R(ichard) H(enry) W(ilde)** 1937- .................................... **CLC 5**
See also CA 21-24R; CAAS 7; CANR 10; CP 2, 3, 4, 5, 6, 7; CSW; DLB 5, 244

**Dillon, Eilis** 1920-1994 ....................... **CLC 17**
See also CA 9-12R, 182; 147; CAAE 182; CAAS 3; CANR 4, 38, 78; CLR 26; MAICYA 1, 2; MAICYAS 1; SATA 2, 74; SATA-Essay 105; SATA-Obit 83; YAW

**Dimont, Penelope**
See Mortimer, Penelope (Ruth)

**Dinesen, Isak**
See Blixen, Karen

**Ding Ling**
See Chiang, Pin-chin

**Diodorus Siculus** c. 90B.C.-c. 31B.C. ...................................... **CMLC 88**

**Diphusa, Patty**
See Almodovar, Pedro

**Disch, Thomas M.** 1940-2008 ....... **CLC 7, 36**
See also AAYA 17; BPFB 1; CA 21-24R; 274; CAAS 4; CANR 17, 36, 54, 89; CLR 18; CP 5, 6, 7; DA3; DLB 8, 282; HGG; MAICYA 1, 2; MTCW 1, 2; MTFW 2005; SAAS 15; SATA 92; SATA-Obit 195; SCFW 1, 2; SFW 4; SUFW 2

**Disch, Thomas Michael**
See Disch, Thomas M.

**Disch, Tom**
See Disch, Thomas M.

**d'Isly, Georges**
See Simenon, Georges (Jacques Christian)

**Disraeli, Benjamin** 1804-1881 ... **NCLC 2, 39, 79**
See also BRW 4; DLB 21, 55; RGEL 2

**D'Israeli, Isaac** 1766-1848 ........... **NCLC 217**
See also DLB 107

**Ditcum, Steve**
See Crumb, R.

**Dixon, Paige**
See Corcoran, Barbara (Asenath)

**Dixon, Stephen** 1936- ......... **CLC 52; SSC 16**
See also AMWS 12; CA 89-92; CANR 17, 40, 54, 91, 175; CN 4, 5, 6, 7; DLB 130; MAL 5

**Dixon, Thomas, Jr.** 1864-1946 ..... **TCLC 163**
See also RHW

**Djebar, Assia** 1936- ....... **BLC 2:1; CLC 182; SSC 114**
See also CA 188; CANR 169; DLB 346; EWL 3; RGWL 3; WLIT 2

**Doak, Annie**
See Dillard, Annie

**Dobell, Sydney Thompson** 1824-1874 ................. **NCLC 43; PC 100**
See also DLB 32; RGEL 2

**Doblin, Alfred**
See Doeblin, Alfred

**Dobroliubov, Nikolai Aleksandrovich**
See Dobrolyubov, Nikolai Alexandrovich

**Dobrolyubov, Nikolai Alexandrovich** 1836-1861 .................................. **NCLC 5**
See also DLB 277

**Dobson, Austin** 1840-1921 .............. **TCLC 79**
See also DLB 35, 144

**Dobyns, Stephen** 1941- .............. **CLC 37, 233**
See also AMWS 13; CA 45-48; CANR 2, 18, 99; CMW 4; CP 4, 5, 6, 7; PFS 23

**Doctorow, Cory** 1971- ..................... **CLC 273**
See also CA 221

**Doctorow, E. L.** 1931- ...... **CLC 6, 11, 15, 18, 37, 44, 65, 113, 214**
See also AAYA 22; AITN 2; AMWS 4; BEST 89:3; BPFB 1; CA 45-48; CANR 2, 33, 51, 76, 97, 133, 170; CDALB 1968-1988; CN 3, 4, 5, 6, 7; CPW; DA3; DAM NOV, POP; DLB 2, 28, 173; DLBY 1980; EWL 3; LAIT 3; MAL 5; MTCW 1, 2; MTFW 2005; NFS 6; RGAL 4; RGHL; RHW; SSFS 27; TCLE 1:1; TCWW 1, 2; TUS

**Doctorow, Edgar Laurence**
See Doctorow, E. L.

**Dodgson, Charles Lutwidge**
See Carroll, Lewis

**Dodsley, Robert** 1703-1764 .................. **LC 97**
See also DLB 95; RGEL 2

**Dodson, Owen (Vincent)** 1914-1983 .................. **BLC 1:1; CLC 79**
See also BW 1; CA 65-68; 110; CANR 24; DAM MULT; DLB 76

**Doeblin, Alfred** 1878-1957 ............. **TCLC 13**
See also CA 110; 141; CDWLB 2; DLB 66; EWL 3; RGWL 2, 3

**Doerr, Harriet** 1910-2002 ................. **CLC 34**
See also CA 117; 122; 213; CANR 47; INT CA-122; LATS 1:2

**Domecq, H(onorio) Bustos**
See Bioy Casares, Adolfo; Borges, Jorge Luis

**Domini, Rey**
See Lorde, Audre

**Dominic, R. B.**
See Hennissart, Martha

**Dominique**
See Proust, (Valentin-Louis-George-Eugene) Marcel

**Don, A**
See Stephen, Sir Leslie

**Donaldson, Stephen R.** 1947- ... **CLC 46, 138**
See also AAYA 36; BPFB 1; CA 89-92; CANR 13, 55, 99; CPW; DAM POP; FANT; INT CANR-13; SATA 121; SFW 4; SUFW 1, 2

**Donleavy, J(ames) P(atrick)** 1926- .... **CLC 1, 4, 6, 10, 45**
See also AITN 2; BPFB 1; CA 9-12R; CANR 24, 49, 62, 80, 124; CBD; CD 5, 6; CN 1, 2, 3, 4, 5, 6, 7; DLB 6, 173; INT CANR-24; MAL 5; MTCW 1, 2; MTFW 2005; RGAL 4

**Donnadieu, Marguerite**
See Duras, Marguerite

**Donne, John** 1572-1631 ... **LC 10, 24, 91; PC 1, 43; WLC 2**
See also AAYA 67; BRW 1; BRWC 1; BRWR 2; CDBLB Before 1660; DA; DAB; DAC; DAM MST, POET; DLB 121, 151; EXPP; PAB; PFS 2, 11; RGEL 3; TEA; WLIT 3; WP

**Donnell, David** 1939(?)- ..................... **CLC 34**
See also CA 197

**Donoghue, Denis** 1928- ..................... **CLC 209**
See also CA 17-20R; CANR 16, 102

**Donoghue, Emma** 1969- .................. **CLC 239**
See also CA 155; CANR 103, 152, 196; DLB 267; GLL 2; SATA 101

**Donoghue, P.S.**
See Hunt, E. Howard

**Donoso (Yanez), Jose** 1924-1996 ... **CLC 4, 8, 11, 32, 99; HLC 1; SSC 34; TCLC 133**
See also CA 81-84; 155; CANR 32, 73; CDWLB 3; CWW 2; DAM MULT; DLB 113; EWL 3; HW 1, 2; LAW; LAWS 1; MTCW 1, 2; MTFW 2005; RGSF 2; WLIT 1

**Donovan, John** 1928-1992 ................. **CLC 35**
See also AAYA 20; CA 97-100; 137; CLR 3; MAICYA 1, 2; SATA 72; SATA-Brief 29; YAW

**Don Roberto**
See Cunninghame Graham, Robert Bontine

**Doolittle, Hilda** 1886-1961 . **CLC 3, 8, 14, 31, 34, 73; PC 5; WLC 3**
See also AAYA 66; AMWS 1; CA 97-100; CANR 35, 131; DA; DAC; DAM MST, POET; DLB 4, 45; EWL 3; FL 1:5; FW; GLL 1; LMFS 2; MAL 5; MBL; MTCW 1, 2; MTFW 2005; PFS 6, 28; RGAL 4

**Doppo**
See Kunikida Doppo

**Doppo, Kunikida**
See Kunikida Doppo

**Du Bois, W. E. B.** 1868-1963 .......... **BLC 1:1; CLC 1, 2, 13, 64, 96; HR 1:2; TCLC 169; WLC 2**
See also AAYA 40; AFAW 1, 2; AMWC 1; AMWS 2; BW 1, 3; CA 85-88; CANR 34, 82, 132; CDALB 1865-1917; DA; DA3; DAC; DAM MST, MULT, NOV; DLB 47, 50, 91, 246, 284; EWL 3; EXPP; LAIT 2; LMFS 2; MAL 5; MTCW 1, 2; MTFW 2005; NCFS 1; PFS 13; RGAL 4; SATA 42

**Du Bois, William Edward Burghardt**
See Du Bois, W. E. B.

**Dubus, Andre** 1936-1999 ..... **CLC 13, 36, 97; SSC 15, 118**
See also AMWS 7; CA 21-24R; 177; CANR 17; CN 5, 6; CSW; DLB 130; INT CANR-17; RGAL 4; SSFS 10; TCLE 1:1

**Duca Minimo**
See D'Annunzio, Gabriele

**Ducharme, Rejean** 1941- ................... **CLC 74**
See also CA 165; DLB 60

**du Chatelet, Emilie** 1706-1749 ........... **LC 96**
See also DLB 313

**Duchen, Claire CLC 65**

**Duck, Stephen** 1705(?)-1756 ................ **PC 89**
See also DLB 95; RGEL 2

**Duclos, Charles Pinot-** 1704-1772 ........ **LC 1**
See also GFL Beginnings to 1789

**Ducornet, Erica** 1943- ..................... **CLC 232**
See also CA 37-40R; CANR 14, 34, 54, 82; SATA 7

**Ducornet, Rikki**
See Ducornet, Erica

**Dudek, Louis** 1918-2001 .............. **CLC 11, 19**
See also CA 45-48; 215; CAAS 14; CANR 1; CP 1, 2, 3, 4, 5, 6, 7; DLB 88

**Duerrenmatt, Friedrich** 1921-1990 ... **CLC 1, 4, 8, 11, 15, 43, 102**
See also CA 17-20R; CANR 33; CDWLB 2; CMW 4; DAM DRAM; DLB 69, 124; EW 13; EWL 3; MTCW 1, 2; RGHL; RGWL 2, 3

**Duffy, Bruce** 1953(?)- ......................... **CLC 50**
See also CA 172

**Duffy, Maureen (Patricia)** 1933- ...... **CLC 37**
See also CA 25-28R; CANR 33, 68; CBD; CN 1, 2, 3, 4, 5, 6, 7; CP 5, 6, 7; CWD; CWP; DFS 15; DLB 14, 310; FW; MTCW 1

**Du Fu**
See Tu Fu

**Dugan, Alan** 1923-2003 ................... **CLC 2, 6**
See also CA 81-84; 220; CANR 119; CP 1, 2, 3, 4, 5, 6, 7; DLB 5; MAL 5; PFS 10

**du Gard, Roger Martin**
See Martin du Gard, Roger

**Duhamel, Georges** 1884-1966 ............. **CLC 8**
See also CA 81-84; 25-28R; CANR 35; DLB 65; EWL 3; GFL 1789 to the Present; MTCW 1

**du Hault, Jean**
See Grindel, Eugene

**Dujardin, Edouard (Emile Louis)**
1861-1949 .................................. **TCLC 13**
See also CA 109; DLB 123

**Duke, Raoul**
See Thompson, Hunter S.

**Dulles, John Foster** 1888-1959 ....... **TCLC 72**
See also CA 115; 149

**Dumas, Alexandre (pere)**
1802-1870 ........... **NCLC 11, 71; WLC 2**
See also AAYA 22; BYA 3; CLR 134; DA; DA3; DAB; DAC; DAM MST, NOV; DLB 119, 192; EW 6; GFL 1789 to the Present; LAIT 1, 2; NFS 14, 19; RGWL 2, 3; SATA 18; TWA; WCH

**Dumas, Alexandre (fils)** 1824-1895 ...... **DC 1; NCLC 9**
See also DLB 192; GFL 1789 to the Present; RGWL 2, 3

**Dumas, Claudine**
See Malzberg, Barry N(athaniel)

**Dumas, Henry L.** 1934-1968 . **BLC 2:1; CLC 6, 62; SSC 107**
See also BW 1; CA 85-88; DLB 41; RGAL 4

**du Maurier, Daphne** 1907-1989 .. **CLC 6, 11, 59; SSC 18, 129; TCLC 209**
See also AAYA 37; BPFB 1; BRWS 3; CA 5-8R; 128; CANR 6, 55; CMW 4; CN 1, 2, 3, 4; CPW; DA3; DAB; DAC; DAM MST, POP; DLB 191; GL 2; HGG; LAIT 3; MSW; MTCW 1, 2; NFS 12; RGEL 2; RGSF 2; RHW; SATA 27; SATA-Obit 60; SSFS 14, 16; TEA

**Du Maurier, George** 1834-1896 ..... **NCLC 86**
See also DLB 153, 178; RGEL 2

**Dunbar, Paul Laurence**
1872-1906 ........ **BLC 1:1; PC 5; SSC 8; TCLC 2, 12; WLC 2**
See also AAYA 75; AFAW 1, 2; AMWS 2; BW 1, 3; CA 104; 124; CANR 79; CDALB 1865-1917; DA; DA3; DAC; DAM MST, MULT, POET; DLB 50, 54, 78; EXPP; MAL 5; RGAL 4; SATA 34

**Dunbar, William** 1460(?)-1520(?) ....... **LC 20; PC 67**
See also BRWS 8; DLB 132, 146; RGEL 2

**Duncan, Dora Angela**
See Duncan, Isadora

**Duncan, Isadora** 1877(?)-1927 ....... **TCLC 68**
See also CA 118; 149

**Duncan, Lois** 1934- ........................... **CLC 26**
See also AAYA 4, 34; BYA 6, 8; CA 1-4R; CANR 2, 23, 36, 111; CLR 29, 129; JRDA; MAICYA 1, 2; MAICYAS 1; MTFW 2005; SAAS 2; SATA 1, 36, 75, 133, 141; SATA-Essay 141; WYA; YAW

**Duncan, Robert** 1919-1988 ... **CLC 1, 2, 4, 7, 15, 41, 55; PC 2, 75**
See also BG 1:2; CA 9-12R; 124; CANR 28, 62; CP 1, 2, 3, 4; DAM POET; DLB 5, 16, 193; EWL 3; MAL 5; MTCW 1, 2; MTFW 2005; PFS 13; RGAL 4; WP

**Duncan, Sara Jeannette**
1861-1922 ................................. **TCLC 60**
See also CA 157; DLB 92

**Dunlap, William** 1766-1839 .............. **NCLC 2**
See also DLB 30, 37, 59; RGAL 4

**Dunn, Douglas (Eaglesham)** 1942- .... **CLC 6, 40**
See also BRWS 10; CA 45-48; CANR 2, 33, 126; CP 1, 2, 3, 4, 5, 6, 7; DLB 40; MTCW 1

**Dunn, Katherine** 1945- ...................... **CLC 71**
See also CA 33-36R; CANR 72; HGG; MTCW 2; MTFW 2005

**Dunn, Stephen** 1939- ................. **CLC 36, 206**
See also AMWS 11; CA 33-36R; CANR 12, 48, 53, 105; CP 3, 4, 5, 6, 7; DLB 105; PFS 21

**Dunn, Stephen Elliott**
See Dunn, Stephen

**Dunne, Finley Peter** 1867-1936 ...... **TCLC 28**
See also CA 108; 178; DLB 11, 23; RGAL 4

**Dunne, John Gregory** 1932-2003 ..... **CLC 28**
See also CA 25-28R; 222; CANR 14, 50; CN 5, 6, 7; DLBY 1980

**Dunsany, Lord**
See Dunsany, Edward John Moreton Drax Plunkett

**Dunsany, Edward John Moreton Drax Plunkett** 1878-1957 ............ **TCLC 2, 59**
See also CA 104; 148; DLB 10, 77, 153, 156, 255; FANT; MTCW 2; RGEL 2; SFW 4; SUFW 1

**Duns Scotus, John** 1266(?)-1308 ... **CMLC 59**
See also DLB 115

**Duong, Thu Huong** 1947- ............... **CLC 273**
See also CA 152; CANR 106, 166; DLB 348; NFS 23

**Duong Thu Huong**
See Duong, Thu Huong

**du Perry, Jean**
See Simenon, Georges (Jacques Christian)

**Durang, Christopher** 1949- ........ **CLC 27, 38**
See also CA 105; CAD; CANR 50, 76, 130; CD 5, 6; MTCW 2; MTFW 2005

**Durang, Christopher Ferdinand**
See Durang, Christopher

**Duras, Claire de** 1777-1832 ......... **NCLC 154**

**Duras, Marguerite** 1914-1996 . **CLC 3, 6, 11, 20, 34, 40, 68, 100; SSC 40**
See also BPFB 1; CA 25-28R; 151; CANR 50; CWW 2; DFS 21; DLB 83, 321; EWL 3; FL 1:5; GFL 1789 to the Present; IDFW 4; MTCW 1, 2; RGWL 2, 3; TWA

**Durban, (Rosa) Pam** 1947- ............... **CLC 39**
See also CA 123; CANR 98; CSW

**Durcan, Paul** 1944- ...................... **CLC 43, 70**
See also CA 134; CANR 123; CP 1, 5, 6, 7; DAM POET; EWL 3

**d'Urfe, Honore**
See Urfe, Honore d'

**Durfey, Thomas** 1653-1723 ................. **LC 94**
See also DLB 80; RGEL 2

**Durkheim, Emile** 1858-1917 .......... **TCLC 55**
See also CA 249

**Durrell, Lawrence (George)**
1912-1990 ..... **CLC 1, 4, 6, 8, 13, 27, 41**
See also BPFB 1; BRWS 1; CA 9-12R; 132; CANR 40, 77; CDBLB 1945-1960; CN 1, 2, 3, 4; CP 1, 2, 3, 4, 5; DAM NOV; DLB 15, 27, 204; DLBY 1990; EWL 3; MTCW 1, 2; RGEL 2; SFW 4; TEA

**Durrenmatt, Friedrich**
See Duerrenmatt, Friedrich

**Dutt, Michael Madhusudan**
1824-1873 ............................. **NCLC 118**

**Dutt, Toru** 1856-1877 ..................... **NCLC 29**
See also DLB 240

**Dwight, Timothy** 1752-1817 .......... **NCLC 13**
See also DLB 37; RGAL 4

**Dworkin, Andrea** 1946-2005 ..... **CLC 43, 123**
See also CA 77-80; 238; CAAS 21; CANR 16, 39, 76, 96; FL 1:5; FW; GLL 1; INT CANR-16; MTCW 1, 2; MTFW 2005

**Dwyer, Deanna**
See Koontz, Dean

**Dwyer, K.R.**
See Koontz, Dean

**Dybek, Stuart** 1942- .......... **CLC 114; SSC 55**
See also CA 97-100; CANR 39; DLB 130; SSFS 23

**Dye, Richard**
See De Voto, Bernard (Augustine)

**Dyer, Geoff** 1958- ............................ **CLC 149**
See also CA 125; CANR 88

**Dyer, George** 1755-1841 ............... **NCLC 129**
See also DLB 93

**Dylan, Bob** 1941- .... **CLC 3, 4, 6, 12, 77; PC 37**
See also AMWS 18; CA 41-44R; CANR 108; CP 1, 2, 3, 4, 5, 6, 7; DLB 16

**Dyson, John** 1943- ............................ **CLC 70**
See also CA 144

**Dzyubin, Eduard Georgievich**
1895-1934 ................................. **TCLC 60**
See also CA 170; EWL 3

**Eliot, George** 1819-1880 ...... **NCLC 4, 13, 23, 41, 49, 89, 118, 183, 199, 209; PC 20; SSC 72; WLC 2**

See also BRW 5; BRWC 1, 2; BRWR 2; CDBLB 1832-1890; CN 7; CPW; DA; DA3; DAB; DAC; DAM MST, NOV; DLB 21, 35, 55; FL 1:3; LATS 1:1; LMFS 1; NFS 17, 20; RGEL 2; RGSF 2; SSFS 8; TEA; WLIT 3

**Eliot, John** 1604-1690 ........................... **LC 5**

See also DLB 24

**Eliot, T(homas) S(tearns)**
1888-1965 ...... **CLC 1, 2, 3, 6, 9, 10, 13, 15, 24, 34, 41, 55, 57, 113; DC 28; PC 5, 31, 90; WLC 2**

See also AAYA 28; AMW; AMWC 1; AMWR 1; BRW 7; BRWR 2; CA 5-8R; 25-28R; CANR 41; CBD; CDALB 1929-1941; DA; DA3; DAB; DAC; DAM DRAM, MST, POET; DFS 4, 13; DLB 7, 10, 45, 63, 245, 329; DLBY 1988; EWL 3; EXPP; LAIT 3; LATS 1:1; LMFS 2; MAL 5; MTCW 1, 2; MTFW 2005; NCFS 5; PAB; PFS 1, 7, 20; RGAL 4; RGEL 2; TUS; WLIT 4; WP

**Elisabeth of Schonau** c.
1129-1165 ................................ **CMLC 82**

See also MTCW 1

**Elizabeth** 1866-1941 ........................ **TCLC 41**

**Elizabeth I** 1533-1603 ......................... **LC 118**

See also DLB 136

**Elkin, Stanley L.** 1930-1995 ...... **CLC 4, 6, 9, 14, 27, 51, 91; SSC 12**

See also AMWS 6; BPFB 1; CA 9-12R; 148; CANR 8, 46; CN 1, 2, 3, 4, 5, 6; CPW; DAM NOV, POP; DLB 2, 28, 218, 278; DLBY 1980; EWL 3; INT CANR-8; MAL 5; MTCW 1, 2; MTFW 2005; RGAL 4; TCLE 1:1

**Elledge, Scott** CLC 34

**Eller, Scott**
See Shepard, Jim

**Elliott, Don**
See Silverberg, Robert

**Elliott, Ebenezer** 1781-1849 ................. **PC 96**

See also DLB 96, 190; RGEL 2

**Elliott, George P(aul)** 1918-1980 ........ **CLC 2**

See also CA 1-4R; 97-100; CANR 2; CN 1, 2; CP 3; DLB 244; MAL 5

**Elliott, Janice** 1931-1995 .................... **CLC 47**

See also CA 13-16R; CANR 8, 29, 84; CN 5, 6, 7; DLB 14; SATA 119

**Elliott, Sumner Locke** 1917-1991 ..... **CLC 38**

See also CA 5-8R; 134; CANR 2, 21; DLB 289

**Elliott, William**
See Bradbury, Ray

**Ellis, A. E.** CLC 7

**Ellis, Alice Thomas**
See Haycraft, Anna

**Ellis, Bret Easton** 1964- ..... **CLC 39, 71, 117, 229**

See also AAYA 2, 43; CA 118; 123; CANR 51, 74, 126; CN 6, 7; CPW; DA3; DAM POP; DLB 292; HGG; INT CA-123; MTCW 2; MTFW 2005; NFS 11

**Ellis, (Henry) Havelock**
1859-1939 ................................ **TCLC 14**

See also CA 109; 169; DLB 190

**Ellis, Landon**
See Ellison, Harlan

**Ellis, Trey** 1962- ................................. **CLC 55**

See also CA 146; CANR 92; CN 7

**Ellison, Harlan** 1934- .... **CLC 1, 13, 42, 139; SSC 14**

See also AAYA 29; BPFB 1; BYA 14; CA 5-8R; CANR 5, 46, 115; CPW; DAM POP; DLB 8, 335; HGG; INT CANR-5; MTCW 1, 2; MTFW 2005; SCFW 2; SFW 4; SSFS 13, 14, 15, 21; SUFW 1, 2

**Ellison, Ralph** 1914-1994 ........ **BLC 1:1, 2:2; CLC 1, 3, 11, 54, 86, 114; SSC 26, 79; WLC 2**

See also AAYA 19; AFAW 1, 2; AMWC 2; AMWR 2; AMWS 2; BPFB 1; BW 1, 3; BYA 2; CA 9-12R; 145; CANR 24, 53; CDALB 1941-1968; CN 1, 2, 3, 4, 5; CSW; DA; DA3; DAB; DAC; DAM MST, MULT, NOV; DLB 2, 76, 227; DLBY 1994; EWL 3; EXPN; EXPS; LAIT 4; MAL 5; MTCW 1, 2; MTFW 2005; NCFS 3; NFS 2, 21; RGAL 4; RGSF 2; SSFS 1, 11; YAW

**Ellison, Ralph Waldo**
See Ellison, Ralph

**Ellmann, Lucy** 1956- ......................... **CLC 61**

See also CA 128; CANR 154

**Ellmann, Lucy Elizabeth**
See Ellmann, Lucy

**Ellmann, Richard (David)**
1918-1987 ................................ **CLC 50**

See also BEST 89:2; CA 1-4R; 122; CANR 28, 61; DLB 103; DLBY 1987; MTCW 1, 2; MTFW 2005

**Ellroy, James** 1948- ......................... **CLC 215**

See also BEST 90:4; CA 138; CANR 74, 133; CMW 4; CN 6, 7; DA3; DLB 226; MTCW 2; MTFW 2005

**Elman, Richard (Martin)**
1934-1997 ................................ **CLC 19**

See also CA 17-20R; 163; CAAS 3; CANR 47; TCLE 1:1

**Elron**
See Hubbard, L. Ron

**El Saadawi, Nawal** 1931- ...... **BLC 2:2; CLC 196**

See also AFW; CA 118; CAAS 11; CANR 44, 92; CWW 2; DLB 346; EWL 3; FW; WLIT 2

**El-Shabazz, El-Hajj Malik**
See Malcolm X

**Eluard, Paul**
See Grindel, Eugene

**Eluard, Paul**
See Grindel, Eugene

**Elyot, Thomas** 1490(?)-1546 ........ **LC 11, 139**

See also DLB 136; RGEL 2

**Elytis, Odysseus** 1911-1996 ........ **CLC 15, 49, 100; PC 21**

See also CA 102; 151; CANR 94; CWW 2; DAM POET; DLB 329; EW 13; EWL 3; MTCW 1, 2; RGWL 2, 3

**Emecheta, Buchi** 1944- ... **BLC 1:2; CLC 14, 48, 128, 214**

See also AAYA 67; AFW; BW 2, 3; CA 81-84; CANR 27, 81, 126; CDWLB 3; CN 4, 5, 6, 7; CWRI 5; DA3; DAM MULT; DLB 117; EWL 3; FL 1:5; FW; MTCW 1, 2; MTFW 2005; NFS 12, 14; SATA 66; WLIT 2

**Emerson, Mary Moody**
1774-1863 ................................ **NCLC 66**

**Emerson, Ralph Waldo** 1803-1882 . **NCLC 1, 38, 98; PC 18; WLC 2**

See also AAYA 60; AMW; ANW; CDALB 1640-1865; DA; DA3; DAB; DAC; DAM MST, POET; DLB 1, 59, 73, 183, 223, 270, 351; EXPP; LAIT 2; LMFS 1; NCFS 3; PFS 4, 17; RGAL 4; TUS; WP

**Eminem** 1972- ................................. **CLC 226**

See also CA 245

**Eminescu, Mihail** 1850-1889 .. **NCLC 33, 131**

**Empedocles** 5th cent. B.C.- ........... **CMLC 50**

See also DLB 176

**Empson, William** 1906-1984 ... **CLC 3, 8, 19, 33, 34**

See also BRWS 2; CA 17-20R; 112; CANR 31, 61; CP 1, 2, 3; DLB 20; EWL 3; MTCW 1, 2; RGEL 2

**Enchi, Fumiko** 1905-1986 ................. **CLC 31**

See also CA 129; 121; DLB 182; EWL 3; FW; MJW

**Enchi, Fumiko Ueda**
See Enchi, Fumiko

**Enchi Fumiko**
See Enchi, Fumiko

**Ende, Michael (Andreas Helmuth)**
1929-1995 ................................ **CLC 31**

See also BYA 5; CA 118; 124; CANR 36, 110; CLR 14, 138; DLB 75; MAICYA 1, 2; MAICYAS 1; SATA 61, 130; SATA-Brief 42; SATA-Obit 86

**Endo, Shusaku** 1923-1996 ...... **CLC 7, 14, 19, 54, 99; SSC 48; TCLC 152**

See also CA 29-32R; 153; CANR 21, 54, 131; CWW 2; DA3; DAM NOV; DLB 182; EWL 3; MTCW 1, 2; MTFW 2005; RGSF 2; RGWL 2, 3

**Endo Shusaku**
See Endo, Shusaku

**Engel, Marian** 1933-1985 .... **CLC 36; TCLC 137**

See also CA 25-28R; CANR 12; CN 2, 3; DLB 53; FW; INT CANR-12

**Engelhardt, Frederick**
See Hubbard, L. Ron

**Engels, Friedrich** 1820-1895 .. **NCLC 85, 114**

See also DLB 129; LATS 1:1

**Enquist, Per Olov** 1934- .................. **CLC 257**

See also CA 109; 193; CANR 155; CWW 2; DLB 257; EWL 3

**Enright, D(ennis) J(oseph)**
1920-2002 .............. **CLC 4, 8, 31; PC 93**

See also CA 1-4R; 211; CANR 1, 42, 83; CN 1, 2; CP 1, 2, 3, 4, 5, 6, 7; DLB 27; EWL 3; SATA 25; SATA-Obit 140

**Ensler, Eve** 1953- ............................. **CLC 212**

See also CA 172; CANR 126, 163; DFS 23

**Enzensberger, Hans Magnus**
1929- ............................. **CLC 43; PC 28**

See also CA 116; 119; CANR 103; CWW 2; EWL 3

**Ephron, Nora** 1941- .................... **CLC 17, 31**

See also AAYA 35; AITN 2; CA 65-68; CANR 12, 39, 83, 161; DFS 22

**Epicurus** 341B.C.-270B.C. ............. **CMLC 21**

See also DLB 176

**Epinay, Louise d'** 1726-1783 ............ **LC 138**

See also DLB 313

**Epsilon**
See Betjeman, John

**Epstein, Daniel Mark** 1948- ................ **CLC 7**

See also CA 49-52; CANR 2, 53, 90, 193

**Epstein, Jacob** 1956- ......................... **CLC 19**

See also CA 114

**Epstein, Jean** 1897-1953 ................. **TCLC 92**

**Epstein, Joseph** 1937- ................ **CLC 39, 204**

See also AMWS 14; CA 112; 119; CANR 50, 65, 117, 164, 190

**Epstein, Leslie** 1938- ......................... **CLC 27**

See also AMWS 12; CA 73-76, 215; CAAE 215; CAAS 12; CANR 23, 69, 162; DLB 299; RGHL

**Equiano, Olaudah** 1745(?)-1797 ..... **BLC 1:2; LC 16, 143**

See also AFAW 1, 2; CDWLB 3; DAM MULT; DLB 37, 50; WLIT 2

**Erasmus, Desiderius** 1469(?)-1536 ..... **LC 16, 93**

See also DLB 136; EW 2; LMFS 1; RGWL 2, 3; TWA

**Erdman, Paul E.** 1932-2007 ............. **CLC 25**

See also AITN 1; CA 61-64; 259; CANR 13, 43, 84

**Erdman, Paul Emil**
See Erdman, Paul E.

**Erdrich, Karen Louise**
See Erdrich, Louise

**Gaddis, William** 1922-1998 ... **CLC 1, 3, 6, 8, 10, 19, 43, 86**
See also AMWS 4; BPFB 1; CA 17-20R; 172; CANR 21, 48, 148; CN 1, 2, 3, 4, 5, 6; DLB 2, 278; EWL 3; MAL 5; MTCW 1, 2; MTFW 2005; RGAL 4

**Gage, Walter**
See Inge, William (Motter)

**Gaiman, Neil** 1960- .......................... **CLC 195**
See also AAYA 19, 42; CA 133; CANR 81, 129, 188; CLR 109; DLB 261; HGG; MTFW 2005; SATA 85, 146, 197; SFW 4; SUFW 2

**Gaiman, Neil Richard**
See Gaiman, Neil

**Gaines, Ernest J.** 1933- .. **BLC 1:2; CLC 3, 11, 18, 86, 181; SSC 68**
See also AAYA 18; AFAW 1, 2; AITN 1; BPFB 2; BW 2, 3; BYA 6; CA 9-12R; CANR 6, 24, 42, 75, 126; CDALB 1968-1988; CLR 62; CN 1, 2, 3, 4, 5, 6, 7; CSW; DA3; DAM MULT; DLB 2, 33, 152; DLBY 1980; EWL 3; EXPN; LAIT 5; LATS 1:2; MAL 5; MTCW 1, 2; MTFW 2005; NFS 5, 7, 16; RGAL 4; RGSF 2; RHW; SATA 86; SSFS 5; YAW

**Gaines, Ernest James**
See Gaines, Ernest J.

**Gaitskill, Mary** 1954- .......................... **CLC 69**
See also CA 128; CANR 61, 152; DLB 244; TCLE 1:1

**Gaitskill, Mary Lawrence**
See Gaitskill, Mary

**Gaius Suetonius Tranquillus**
See Suetonius

**Galdos, Benito Perez**
See Perez Galdos, Benito

**Gale, Zona** 1874-1938 ......... **DC 30; TCLC 7**
See also CA 105; 153; CANR 84; DAM DRAM; DFS 17; DLB 9, 78, 228; RGAL 4

**Galeano, Eduardo** 1940- ... **CLC 72; HLCS 1**
See also CA 29-32R; CANR 13, 32, 100, 163; HW 1

**Galeano, Eduardo Hughes**
See Galeano, Eduardo

**Galiano, Juan Valera y Alcala**
See Valera y Alcala-Galiano, Juan

**Galilei, Galileo** 1564-1642 .................... **LC 45**

**Gallagher, Tess** 1943- ....... **CLC 18, 63; PC 9**
See also CA 106; CP 3, 4, 5, 6, 7; CWP; DAM POET; DLB 120, 212, 244; PFS 16

**Gallant, Mavis** 1922- ..... **CLC 7, 18, 38, 172; SSC 5, 78**
See also CA 69-72; CANR 29, 69, 117; CCA 1; CN 1, 2, 3, 4, 5, 6, 7; DAC; DAM MST; DLB 53; EWL 3; MTCW 1, 2; MTFW 2005; RGEL 2; RGSF 2

**Gallant, Roy A(rthur)** 1924- ............ **CLC 17**
See also CA 5-8R; CANR 4, 29, 54, 117; CLR 30; MAICYA 1, 2; SATA 4, 68, 110

**Gallico, Paul (William)** 1897-1976 ..... **CLC 2**
See also AITN 1; CA 5-8R; 69-72; CANR 23; CN 1, 2; DLB 9, 171; FANT; MAICYA 1, 2; SATA 13

**Gallo, Max Louis** 1932- .................... **CLC 95**
See also CA 85-88

**Gallois, Lucien**
See Desnos, Robert

**Gallup, Ralph**
See Whitemore, Hugh (John)

**Galsworthy, John** 1867-1933 ........... **SSC 22; TCLC 1, 45; WLC 2**
See also BRW 6; CA 104; 141; CANR 75; CDBLB 1890-1914; DA; DA3; DAB; DAC; DAM DRAM, MST, NOV; DLB 10, 34, 98, 162, 330; DLBD 16; EWL 3; MTCW 2; RGEL 2; SSFS 3; TEA

**Galt, John** 1779-1839 ................ **NCLC 1, 110**
See also DLB 99, 116, 159; RGEL 2; RGSF 2

**Galvin, James** 1951- .......................... **CLC 38**
See also CA 108; CANR 26

**Gamboa, Federico** 1864-1939 ........ **TCLC 36**
See also CA 167; HW 2; LAW

**Gandhi, M. K.**
See Gandhi, Mohandas Karamchand

**Gandhi, Mahatma**
See Gandhi, Mohandas Karamchand

**Gandhi, Mohandas Karamchand** 1869-1948 ................................ **TCLC 59**
See also CA 121; 132; DA3; DAM MULT; DLB 323; MTCW 1, 2

**Gann, Ernest Kellogg** 1910-1991 ..... **CLC 23**
See also AITN 1; BPFB 2; CA 1-4R; 136; CANR 1, 83; RHW

**Gao Xingjian** 1940-
See Xingjian, Gao

**Garber, Eric** 1943(?)- ...................... **CLC 38**
See also CA 144; CANR 89, 162; GLL 1

**Garber, Esther**
See Lee, Tanith

**Garcia, Cristina** 1958- ...................... **CLC 76**
See also AMWS 11; CA 141; CANR 73, 130, 172; CN 7; DLB 292; DNFS 1; EWL 3; HW 2; LLW; MTFW 2005

**Garcia Lorca, Federico** 1898-1936 ...... **DC 2; HLC 2; PC 3; TCLC 1, 7, 49, 181, 197; WLC 2**
See also AAYA 46; CA 104; 131; CANR 81; DA; DA3; DAB; DAC; DAM DRAM, MST, MULT, POET; DFS 4; DLB 108; EW 11; EWL 3; HW 1, 2; LATS 1:2; MTCW 1, 2; MTFW 2005; PFS 20, 31; RGWL 2, 3; TWA; WP

**Garcia Marquez, Gabriel** 1928- .... **CLC 2, 3, 8, 10, 15, 27, 47, 55, 68, 170, 254; HLC 1; SSC 8, 83; WLC 3**
See also AAYA 3, 33; BEST 89:1, 90:4; BPFB 2; BYA 12, 16; CA 33-36R; CANR 10, 28, 50, 75, 82, 128; CDWLB 3; CPW; CWW 2; DA; DA3; DAB; DAC; DAM MST, MULT, NOV, POP; DLB 113, 330; DNFS 1, 2; EWL 3; EXPN; EXPS; HW 1, 2; LAIT 2; LATS 1:2; LAW; LAWS 1; LMFS 2; MTCW 1, 2; MTFW 2005; NCFS 3; NFS 1, 5, 10; RGSF 2; RGWL 2, 3; SSFS 1, 6, 16, 21; TWA; WLIT 1

**Garcia Marquez, Gabriel Jose**
See Garcia Marquez, Gabriel

**Garcilaso de la Vega, El Inca** 1539-1616 .................. **HLCS 1; LC 127**
See also DLB 318; LAW

**Gard, Janice**
See Latham, Jean Lee

**Gard, Roger Martin du**
See Martin du Gard, Roger

**Gardam, Jane** 1928- .......................... **CLC 43**
See also CA 49-52; CANR 2, 18, 33, 54, 106, 167; CLR 12; DLB 14, 161, 231; MAICYA 1, 2; MTCW 1; SAAS 9; SATA 39, 76, 130; SATA-Brief 28; YAW

**Gardam, Jane Mary**
See Gardam, Jane

**Gardens, S. S.**
See Snodgrass, W. D.

**Gardner, Herb(ert George)** 1934-2003 .............................. **CLC 44**
See also CA 149; 220; CAD; CANR 119; CD 5, 6; DFS 18, 20

**Gardner, John, Jr.** 1933-1982 ... **CLC 2, 3, 5, 7, 8, 10, 18, 28, 34; SSC 7; TCLC 195**
See also AAYA 45; AITN 1; AMWS 6; BPFB 2; CA 65-68; 107; CANR 33, 73; CDALBS; CN 2, 3; CPW; DA3; DAM NOV, POP; DLB 2; DLBY 1982; EWL 3;

FANT; LATS 1:2; MAL 5; MTCW 1, 2; MTFW 2005; NFS 3; RGAL 4; RGSF 2; SATA 40; SATA-Obit 31; SSFS 8

**Gardner, John** 1926-2007 ................. **CLC 30**
See also CA 103; 263; CANR 15, 69, 127, 183; CMW 4; CPW; DAM POP; MTCW 1

**Gardner, John Champlin, Jr.**
See Gardner, John, Jr.

**Gardner, John Edmund**
See Gardner, John

**Gardner, Miriam**
See Bradley, Marion Zimmer

**Gardner, Noel**
See Kuttner, Henry

**Gardons, S.S.**
See Snodgrass, W. D.

**Garfield, Leon** 1921-1996 ................. **CLC 12**
See also AAYA 8, 69; BYA 1, 3; CA 17-20R; 152; CANR 38, 41, 78; CLR 21; DLB 161; JRDA; MAICYA 1, 2; MAIC-YAS 1; SATA 1, 32, 76; SATA-Obit 90; TEA; WYA; YAW

**Garland, (Hannibal) Hamlin** 1860-1940 ........... **SSC 18, 117; TCLC 3**
See also CA 104; DLB 12, 71, 78, 186; MAL 5; RGAL 4; RGSF 2; TCWW 1, 2

**Garneau, (Hector de) Saint-Denys** 1912-1943 ................................ **TCLC 13**
See also CA 111; DLB 88

**Garner, Alan** 1934- .......................... **CLC 17**
See also AAYA 18; BYA 3, 5; CA 73-76, 178; CAAE 178; CANR 15, 64, 134; CLR 20, 130; CPW; DAB; DAM POP; DLB 161, 261; FANT; MAICYA 1, 2; MTCW 1, 2; MTFW 2005; SATA 18, 69; SATA-Essay 108; SUFW 1, 2; YAW

**Garner, Hugh** 1913-1979 ................. **CLC 13**
See also CA 69-72; CANR 31; CCA 1; CN 1, 2; DLB 68

**Garnett, David** 1892-1981 ................. **CLC 3**
See also CA 5-8R; 103; CANR 17, 79; CN 1, 2; DLB 34; FANT; MTCW 2; RGEL 2; SFW 4; SUFW 1

**Garnier, Robert** c. 1545-1590 ............ **LC 119**
See also DLB 327; GFL Beginnings to 1789

**Garrett, George** 1929-2008 ... **CLC 3, 11, 51; SSC 30**
See also AMWS 7; BPFB 2; CA 1-4R, 202; 272; CAAE 202; CAAS 5; CANR 1, 42, 67, 109, 199; CN 1, 2, 3, 4, 5, 6, 7; CP 1, 2, 3, 4, 5, 6, 7; CSW; DLB 2, 5, 130, 152; DLBY 1983

**Garrett, George P.**
See Garrett, George

**Garrett, George Palmer**
See Garrett, George

**Garrett, George Palmer, Jr.**
See Garrett, George

**Garrick, David** 1717-1779 ........... **LC 15, 156**
See also DAM DRAM; DLB 84, 213; RGEL 2

**Garrigue, Jean** 1914-1972 ............... **CLC 2, 8**
See also CA 5-8R; 37-40R; CANR 20; CP 1; MAL 5

**Garrison, Frederick**
See Sinclair, Upton

**Garrison, William Lloyd** 1805-1879 ............................... **NCLC 149**
See also CDALB 1640-1865; DLB 1, 43, 235

**Garro, Elena** 1920(?)-1998 .. **HLCS 1; TCLC 153**
See also CA 131; 169; CWW 2; DLB 145; EWL 3; HW 1; LAWS 1; WLIT 1

**Garth, Will**
See Hamilton, Edmond; Kuttner, Henry

**Graduate of Oxford, A**
See Ruskin, John
**Grafton, Garth**
See Duncan, Sara Jeannette
**Grafton, Sue** 1940- ............................ **CLC 163**
See also AAYA 11, 49; BEST 90:3; CA 108;
CANR 31, 55, 111, 134, 195; CMW 4;
CPW; CSW; DA3; DAM POP; DLB 226;
FW; MSW; MTFW 2005
**Graham, John**
See Phillips, David Graham
**Graham, Jorie** 1950- .... **CLC 48, 118; PC 59**
See also AAYA 67; CA 111; CANR 63, 118;
CP 4, 5, 6, 7; CWP; DLB 120; EWL 3;
MTFW 2005; PFS 10, 17; TCLE 1:1
**Graham, R. B. Cunninghame**
See Cunninghame Graham, Robert Bontine
**Graham, Robert**
See Haldeman, Joe
**Graham, Robert Bontine Cunninghame**
See Cunninghame Graham, Robert Bontine
**Graham, Tom**
See Lewis, Sinclair
**Graham, W(illiam) S(ydney)**
1918-1986 ............................... **CLC 29**
See also BRWS 7; CA 73-76; 118; CP 1, 2,
3, 4; DLB 20; RGEL 2
**Graham, Winston (Mawdsley)**
1910-2003 ................................. **CLC 23**
See also CA 49-52; 218; CANR 2, 22, 45,
66; CMW 4; CN 1, 2, 3, 4, 5, 6, 7; DLB
77; RHW
**Grahame, Kenneth** 1859-1932 ...... **TCLC 64,
136**
See also BYA 5; CA 108; 136; CANR 80;
CLR 5, 135; CWRI 5; DA3; DAB; DLB
34, 141, 178; FANT; MAICYA 1, 2;
MTCW 2; NFS 20; RGEL 2; SATA 100;
TEA; WCH; YABC 1
**Granger, Darius John**
See Marlowe, Stephen
**Granin, Daniil** 1918- .......................... **CLC 59**
See also DLB 302
**Granovsky, Timofei Nikolaevich**
1813-1855 ............................... **NCLC 75**
See also DLB 198
**Grant, Skeeter**
See Spiegelman, Art
**Granville-Barker, Harley**
1877-1946 ................................. **TCLC 2**
See also CA 104; 204; DAM DRAM; DLB
10; RGEL 2
**Granzotto, Gianni**
See Granzotto, Giovanni Battista
**Granzotto, Giovanni Battista**
1914-1985 ................................. **CLC 70**
See also CA 166
**Grasemann, Ruth Barbara**
See Rendell, Ruth
**Grass, Guenter**
See Grass, Gunter
**Grass, Gunter** 1927- .. **CLC 1, 2, 4, 6, 11, 15,
22, 32, 49, 88, 207; WLC 3**
See also BPFB 2; CA 13-16R; CANR 20,
75, 93, 133, 174; CDWLB 2; CWW 2;
DA; DA3; DAB; DAC; DAM MST, NOV;
DLB 330; EW 13; EWL 3; MTCW 1, 2;
MTFW 2005; RGHL; RGWL 2, 3; TWA
**Grass, Gunter Wilhelm**
See Grass, Gunter
**Gratton, Thomas**
See Hulme, T(homas) E(rnest)
**Grau, Shirley Ann** 1929- ....... **CLC 4, 9, 146;
SSC 15**
See also CA 89-92; CANR 22, 69; CN 1, 2,
3, 4, 5, 6, 7; CSW; DLB 2, 218; INT CA-
89-92; CANR-22; MTCW 1
**Gravel, Fern**
See Hall, James Norman

**Graver, Elizabeth** 1964- ................... **CLC 70**
See also CA 135; CANR 71, 129
**Graves, Richard Perceval**
1895-1985 ................................. **CLC 44**
See also CA 65-68; CANR 9, 26, 51
**Graves, Robert** 1895-1985 ... **CLC 1, 2, 6, 11,
39, 44, 45; PC 6**
See also BPFB 2; BRW 7; BYA 4; CA 5-8R;
117; CANR 5, 36; CDBLB 1914-1945;
CN 1, 2, 3; CP 1, 2, 3, 4; DA3; DAB;
DAC; DAM MST, POET; DLB 20, 100,
191; DLBD 18; DLBY 1985; EWL 3;
LATS 1:1; MTCW 1, 2; MTFW 2005;
NCFS 2; NFS 21; RGEL 2; RHW; SATA
45; TEA
**Graves, Valerie**
See Bradley, Marion Zimmer
**Gray, Alasdair** 1934- ................. **CLC 41, 275**
See also BRWS 9; CA 126; CANR 47, 69,
106, 140; CN 4, 5, 6, 7; DLB 194, 261,
319; HGG; INT CA-126; MTCW 1, 2;
MTFW 2005; RGSF 2; SUFW 2
**Gray, Amlin** 1946- ............................. **CLC 29**
See also CA 138
**Gray, Francine du Plessix** 1930- ..... **CLC 22,
153**
See also BEST 90:3; CA 61-64; CAAS 2;
CANR 11, 33, 75, 81, 197; DAM NOV;
INT CANR-11; MTCW 1, 2; MTFW 2005
**Gray, John (Henry)** 1866-1934 ...... **TCLC 19**
See also CA 119; 162; RGEL 2
**Gray, John Lee**
See Jakes, John
**Gray, Simon** 1936-2008 ........... **CLC 9, 14, 36**
See also AITN 1; CA 21-24R; 275; CAAS
3; CANR 32, 69; CBD; CD 5, 6; CN 1, 2,
3; DLB 13; EWL 3; MTCW 1; RGEL 2
**Gray, Simon James Holliday**
See Gray, Simon
**Gray, Spalding** 1941-2004 ........ **CLC 49, 112;
DC 7**
See also AAYA 62; CA 128; 225; CAD;
CANR 74, 138; CD 5, 6; CPW; DAM
POP; MTCW 2; MTFW 2005
**Gray, Thomas** 1716-1771 ..... **LC 4, 40; PC 2,
80; WLC 3**
See also BRW 3; CDBLB 1660-1789; DA;
DA3; DAB; DAC; DAM MST; DLB 109;
EXPP; PAB; PFS 9; RGEL 2; TEA; WP
**Grayson, David**
See Baker, Ray Stannard
**Grayson, Richard (A.)** 1951- ............ **CLC 38**
See also CA 85-88, 210; CAAE 210; CANR
14, 31, 57; DLB 234
**Greeley, Andrew M.** 1928- ................ **CLC 28**
See also BPFB 2; CA 5-8R; CAAS 7;
CANR 7, 43, 69, 104, 136, 184; CMW 4;
CPW; DA3; DAM POP; MTCW 1, 2;
MTFW 2005
**Green, Anna Katharine**
1846-1935 ................................. **TCLC 63**
See also CA 112; 159; CMW 4; DLB 202,
221; MSW
**Green, Brian**
See Card, Orson Scott
**Green, Hannah**
See Greenberg, Joanne (Goldenberg)
**Green, Hannah** 1927(?)-1996 ............. **CLC 3**
See also CA 73-76; CANR 59, 93; NFS 10
**Green, Henry**
See Yorke, Henry Vincent
**Green, Julian**
See Green, Julien
**Green, Julien** 1900-1998 ......... **CLC 3, 11, 77**
See also CA 21-24R; 169; CANR 33, 87;
CWW 2; DLB 4, 72; EWL 3; GFL 1789
to the Present; MTCW 2; MTFW 2005
**Green, Julien Hartridge**
See Green, Julien

**Green, Paul (Eliot)** 1894-1981 .. **CLC 25; DC
37**
See also AITN 1; CA 5-8R; 103; CAD;
CANR 3; DAM DRAM; DLB 7, 9, 249;
DLBY 1981; MAL 5; RGAL 4
**Greenaway, Peter** 1942- ................ **CLC 159**
See also CA 127
**Greenberg, Ivan** 1908-1973 .............. **CLC 24**
See also CA 85-88; DLB 137; MAL 5
**Greenberg, Joanne (Goldenberg)**
1932- .................................... **CLC 7, 30**
See also AAYA 12, 67; CA 5-8R; CANR
14, 32, 69; CN 6, 7; DLB 335; NFS 23;
SATA 25; YAW
**Greenberg, Richard** 1959(?)- ........... **CLC 57**
See also CA 138; CAD; CD 5, 6; DFS 24
**Greenblatt, Stephen J(ay)** 1943- ...... **CLC 70**
See also CA 49-52; CANR 115
**Greene, Bette** 1934- .......................... **CLC 30**
See also AAYA 7, 69; BYA 3; CA 53-56;
CANR 4, 146; CLR 2, 140; CWRI 5;
JRDA; LAIT 4; MAICYA 1, 2; NFS 10;
SAAS 16; SATA 8, 102, 161; WYA; YAW
**Greene, Gael CLC 8**
See also CA 13-16R; CANR 10, 166
**Greene, Graham** 1904-1991 .. **CLC 1, 3, 6, 9,
14, 18, 27, 37, 70, 72, 125; SSC 29, 121;
WLC 3**
See also AAYA 61; AITN 2; BPFB 2;
BRWR 2; BRWS 1; BYA 3; CA 13-16R;
133; CANR 35, 61, 131; CBD; CDBLB
1945-1960; CMW 4; CN 1, 2, 3, 4; DA;
DA3; DAB; DAC; DAM MST, NOV;
DLB 13, 15, 77, 100, 162, 201, 204;
DLBY 1991; EWL 3; MSW; MTCW 1, 2;
MTFW 2005; NFS 16; RGEL 2; SATA
20; SSFS 14; TEA; WLIT 4
**Greene, Robert** 1558-1592 ................... **LC 41**
See also BRWS 8; DLB 62, 167; IDTP;
RGEL 2; TEA
**Greer, Germaine** 1939- .................... **CLC 131**
See also AITN 1; CA 81-84; CANR 33, 70,
115, 133, 190; FW; MTCW 1, 2; MTFW
2005
**Greer, Richard**
See Silverberg, Robert
**Gregor, Arthur** 1923- ........................... **CLC 9**
See also CA 25-28R; CAAS 10; CANR 11;
CP 1, 2, 3, 4, 5, 6, 7; SATA 36
**Gregor, Lee**
See Pohl, Frederik
**Gregory, Lady Isabella Augusta (Persse)**
1852-1932 ........................ **TCLC 1, 176**
See also BRW 6; CA 104; 184; DLB 10;
IDTP; RGEL 2
**Gregory, J. Dennis**
See Williams, John A(lfred)
**Gregory of Nazianzus, St.**
329-389 ................................. **CMLC 82**
**Gregory of Nyssa** c. 335-c. 394 ... **CMLC 118**
**Gregory of Rimini** 1300(?)-1358 . **CMLC 109**
See also DLB 115
**Grekova, I.**
See Ventsel, Elena Sergeevna
**Grekova, Irina**
See Ventsel, Elena Sergeevna
**Grendon, Stephen**
See Derleth, August (William)
**Grenville, Kate** 1950- ........................ **CLC 61**
See also CA 118; CANR 53, 93, 156; CN
7; DLB 325
**Grenville, Pelham**
See Wodehouse, P(elham) G(renville)
**Greve, Felix Paul (Berthold Friedrich)**
1879-1948 ................................. **TCLC 4**
See also CA 104; 141, 175; CANR 79;
DAC; DAM MST; DLB 92; RGEL 2;
TCWW 1, 2

**Gunter, Erich**
See Eich, Gunter

**Gurdjieff, G(eorgei) I(vanovich)**
1877(?)-1949 ............. **TCLC 71**
See also CA 157

**Gurganus, Allan** 1947- ....................... **CLC 70**
See also BEST 90:1; CA 135; CANR 114;
CN 6, 7; CPW; CSW; DAM POP; DLB
350; GLL 1

**Gurney, A. R.**
See Gurney, A(lbert) R(amsdell), Jr.

**Gurney, A(lbert) R(amsdell), Jr.**
1930- ............................ **CLC 32, 50, 54**
See also AMWS 5; CA 77-80; CAD; CANR
32, 64, 121; CD 5, 6; DAM DRAM; DLB
266; EWL 3

**Gurney, Ivor (Bertie)** 1890-1937 ... **TCLC 33**
See also BRW 6; CA 167; DLBY 2002;
PAB; RGEL 2

**Gurney, Peter**
See Gurney, A(lbert) R(amsdell), Jr.

**Guro, Elena (Genrikhovna)**
1877-1913 ................................. **TCLC 56**
See also DLB 295

**Gustafson, James M(oody)** 1925- ... **CLC 100**
See also CA 25-28R; CANR 37

**Gustafson, Ralph (Barker)**
1909-1995 ................................. **CLC 36**
See also CA 21-24R; CANR 8, 45, 84; CP
1, 2, 3, 4, 5, 6; DLB 88; RGEL 2

**Gut, Gom**
See Simenon, Georges (Jacques Christian)

**Guterson, David** 1956- ....................... **CLC 91**
See also CA 132; CANR 73, 126, 194; CN
7; DLB 292; MTCW 2; MTFW 2005;
NFS 13

**Guthrie, A(lfred) B(ertram), Jr.**
1901-1991 ................................. **CLC 23**
See also CA 57-60; 134; CANR 24; CN 1,
2, 3; DLB 6, 212; MAL 5; SATA 62;
SATA-Obit 67; TCWW 1, 2

**Guthrie, Isobel**
See Grieve, C. M.

**Gutierrez Najera, Manuel**
1859-1895 .............. **HLCS 2; NCLC 133**
See also DLB 290; LAW

**Guy, Rosa (Cuthbert)** 1925- ............. **CLC 26**
See also AAYA 4, 37; BW 2; CA 17-20R;
CANR 14, 34, 83; CLR 13, 137; DLB 33;
DNFS 1; JRDA; MAICYA 1, 2; SATA 14,
62, 122; YAW

**Gwendolyn**
See Bennett, (Enoch) Arnold

**H. D.**
See Doolittle, Hilda

**H. de V.**
See Buchan, John

**Haavikko, Paavo Juhani** 1931- .. **CLC 18, 34**
See also CA 106; CWW 2; EWL 3

**Habbema, Koos**
See Heijermans, Herman

**Habermas, Juergen** 1929- .............. **CLC 104**
See also CA 109; CANR 85, 162; DLB 242

**Habermas, Jurgen**
See Habermas, Juergen

**Hacker, Marilyn** 1942- ...... **CLC 5, 9, 23, 72,
91; PC 47**
See also CA 77-80; CANR 68, 129; CP 3,
4, 5, 6, 7; CWP; DAM POET; DLB 120,
282; FW; GLL 2; MAL 5; PFS 19

**Hadewijch of Antwerp** fl. 1250- ... **CMLC 61**
See also RGWL 3

**Hadrian** 76-138 .................................. **CMLC 52**

**Haeckel, Ernst Heinrich (Philipp August)**
1834-1919 ................................. **TCLC 83**
See also CA 157

**Hafiz** c. 1326-1389(?) ..................... **CMLC 34**
See also RGWL 2, 3; WLIT 6

**Hagedorn, Jessica T(arahata)**
1949- ...................................... **CLC 185**
See also CA 139; CANR 69; CWP; DLB
312; RGAL 4

**Haggard, H(enry) Rider**
1856-1925 .................................. **TCLC 11**
See also AAYA 81; BRWS 3; BYA 4, 5;
CA 108; 148; CANR 112; DLB 70, 156,
174, 178; FANT; LMFS 1; MTCW 2;
RGEL 2; RHW; SATA 16; SCFW 1, 2;
SFW 4; SUFW 1; WLIT 4

**Hagiosy, L.**
See Larbaud, Valery (Nicolas)

**Hagiwara, Sakutaro** 1886-1942 .......... **PC 18;
TCLC 60**
See also CA 154; EWL 3; RGWL 3

**Hagiwara Sakutaro**
See Hagiwara, Sakutaro

**Haig, Fenil**
See Ford, Ford Madox

**Haig-Brown, Roderick (Langmere)**
1908-1976 ................................. **CLC 21**
See also CA 5-8R; 69-72; CANR 4, 38, 83;
CLR 31; CWRI 5; DLB 88; MAICYA 1,
2; SATA 12; TCWW 2

**Haight, Rip**
See Carpenter, John

**Haij, Vera**
See Jansson, Tove (Marika)

**Hailey, Arthur** 1920-2004 .................... **CLC 5**
See also AITN 2; BEST 90:3; BPFB 2; CA
1-4R; 233; CANR 2, 36, 75; CCA 1; CN
1, 2, 3, 4, 5, 6, 7; CPW; DAM NOV, POP;
DLB 88; DLBY 1982; MTCW 1, 2;
MTFW 2005

**Hailey, Elizabeth Forsythe** 1938- ..... **CLC 40**
See also CA 93-96; 188; CAAE 188; CAAS
1; CANR 15, 48; INT CANR-15

**Haines, John (Meade)** 1924- ............. **CLC 58**
See also AMWS 12; CA 17-20R; CANR
13, 34; CP 1, 2, 3, 4, 5; CSW; DLB 5,
212; TCLE 1:1

**Hakluyt, Richard** 1552-1616 ................ **LC 31**
See also DLB 136; RGEL 2

**Haldeman, Joe** 1943- ........................... **CLC 61**
See also AAYA 38; CA 53-56; 179; CAAE
179; CAAS 25; CANR 6, 70, 72, 130,
171; DLB 8; INT CANR-6; SCFW 2;
SFW 4

**Haldeman, Joe William**
See Haldeman, Joe

**Hale, Janet Campbell** 1947- ............... **NNAL**
See also CA 49-52; CANR 45, 75; DAM
MULT; DLB 175; MTCW 2; MTFW 2005

**Hale, Sarah Josepha (Buell)**
1788-1879 ................................. **NCLC 75**
See also DLB 1, 42, 73, 243

**Halevy, Elie** 1870-1937 ................. **TCLC 104**

**Haley, Alex** 1921-1992 . **BLC 1:2; CLC 8, 12,
76; TCLC 147**
See also AAYA 26; BPFB 2; BW 2, 3; CA
77-80; 136; CANR 61; CDALBS; CPW;
CSW; DA; DA3; DAB; DAC; DAM MST,
MULT, POP; DLB 38; LAIT 5; MTCW
1, 2; NFS 9

**Haley, Alexander Murray Palmer**
See Haley, Alex

**Haliburton, Thomas Chandler**
1796-1865 ......................... **NCLC 15, 149**
See also DLB 11, 99; RGEL 2; RGSF 2

**Hall, Donald** 1928- ... **CLC 1, 13, 37, 59, 151,
240; PC 70**
See also AAYA 63; CA 5-8R; CAAS 7;
CANR 2, 44, 64, 106, 133, 196; CP 1, 2,
3, 4, 5, 6, 7; DAM POET; DLB 5, 342;
MAL 5; MTCW 2; MTFW 2005; RGAL
4; SATA 23, 97

**Hall, Donald Andrew, Jr.**
See Hall, Donald

**Hall, Frederic Sauser**
See Sauser-Hall, Frederic

**Hall, James**
See Kuttner, Henry

**Hall, James Norman** 1887-1951 ..... **TCLC 23**
See also CA 123; 173; LAIT 1; RHW 1;
SATA 21

**Hall, Joseph** 1574-1656 ........................ **LC 91**
See also DLB 121, 151; RGEL 2

**Hall, Marguerite Radclyffe**
See Hall, Radclyffe

**Hall, Radclyffe** 1880-1943 ...... **TCLC 12, 215**
See also BRWS 6; CA 110; 150; CANR 83;
DLB 191; MTCW 2; MTFW 2005; RGEL
2; RHW

**Hall, Rodney** 1935- ............................. **CLC 51**
See also CA 109; CANR 69; CN 6, 7; CP
1, 2, 3, 4, 5, 6, 7; DLB 289

**Hallam, Arthur Henry**
1811-1833 ............................... **NCLC 110**
See also DLB 32

**Halldor Laxness**
See Gudjonsson, Halldor Kiljan

**Halleck, Fitz-Greene** 1790-1867 .... **NCLC 47**
See also DLB 3, 250; RGAL 4

**Halliday, Michael**
See Creasey, John

**Halpern, Daniel** 1945- ....................... **CLC 14**
See also CA 33-36R; CANR 93, 174; CP 3,
4, 5, 6, 7

**Hamburger, Michael** 1924-2007 ... **CLC 5, 14**
See also CA 5-8R; 196; 261; CAAE 196;
CAAS 4; CANR 2, 47; CP 1, 2, 3, 4, 5, 6,
7; DLB 27

**Hamburger, Michael Peter Leopold**
See Hamburger, Michael

**Hamill, Pete** 1935- ..................... **CLC 10, 261**
See also CA 25-28R; CANR 18, 71, 127,
180

**Hamill, William Peter**
See Hamill, Pete

**Hamilton, Alexander** 1712-1756 ........ **LC 150**
See also DLB 31

**Hamilton, Alexander**
1755(?)-1804 ........................... **NCLC 49**
See also DLB 37

**Hamilton, Clive**
See Lewis, C.S.

**Hamilton, Edmond** 1904-1977 ........... **CLC 1**
See also CA 1-4R; CANR 3, 84; DLB 8;
SATA 118; SFW 4

**Hamilton, Elizabeth** 1758-1816 ... **NCLC 153**
See also DLB 116, 158

**Hamilton, Eugene (Jacob) Lee**
See Lee-Hamilton, Eugene (Jacob)

**Hamilton, Franklin**
See Silverberg, Robert

**Hamilton, Gail**
See Corcoran, Barbara (Asenath)

**Hamilton, (Robert) Ian** 1938-2001 . **CLC 191**
See also CA 106; 203; CANR 41, 67; CP 1,
2, 3, 4, 5, 6, 7; DLB 40, 155

**Hamilton, Jane** 1957- ...................... **CLC 179**
See also CA 147; CANR 85, 128; CN 7;
DLB 350; MTFW 2005

**Hamilton, Mollie**
See Kaye, M.M.

**Hamilton, (Anthony Walter) Patrick**
1904-1962 .................................. **CLC 51**
See also CA 176; 113; DLB 10, 191

**Hamilton, Virginia** 1936-2002 .......... **CLC 26**
See also AAYA 2, 21; BW 2, 3; BYA 1, 2,
8; CA 25-28R; 206; CANR 20, 37, 73,
126; CLR 1, 11, 40, 127; DAM MULT;
DLB 33, 52; DLBY 2001; INT CANR-
20; JRDA; LAIT 5; MAICYA 1, 2; MAI-
CYAS 1; MTCW 1, 2; MTFW 2005;
SATA 4, 56, 79, 123; SATA-Obit 132;
WYA; YAW

**Heilbrun, Carolyn G.** 1926-2003 ..... **CLC 25, 173**
See also BPFB 1; CA 45-48; 220; CANR 1, 28, 58, 94; CMW; CPW; DLB 306; FW; MSW

**Heilbrun, Carolyn Gold**
See Heilbrun, Carolyn G.

**Hein, Christoph** 1944- ..................... **CLC 154**
See also CA 158; CANR 108; CDWLB 2; CWW 2; DLB 124

**Heine, Heinrich** 1797-1856 ....... **NCLC 4, 54, 147; PC 25**
See also CDWLB 2; DLB 90; EW 5; RGWL 2, 3; TWA

**Heinemann, Larry** 1944- .................. **CLC 50**
See also CA 110; CAAS 21; CANR 31, 81, 156; DLBD 9; INT CANR-31

**Heinemann, Larry Curtiss**
See Heinemann, Larry

**Heiney, Donald (William)** 1921-1993 . **CLC 9**
See also CA 1-4R; 142; CANR 3, 58; FANT

**Heinlein, Robert A.** 1907-1988 .. **CLC 1, 3, 8, 14, 26, 55; SSC 55**
See also AAYA 17; BPFB 2; BYA 4, 13; CA 1-4R; 125; CANR 1, 20, 53; CLR 75; CN 1, 2, 3, 4; CPW; DA3; DAM POP; DLB 8; EXPS; JRDA; LAIT 5; LMFS 2; MAICYA 1, 2; MTCW 1, 2; MTFW 2005; RGAL 4; SATA 9, 69; SATA-Obit 56; SCFW 1, 2; SFW 4; SSFS 7; YAW

**Held, Peter**
See Vance, Jack

**Heldris of Cornwall** fl. 13th cent.
- ................................................. **CMLC 97**

**Helforth, John**
See Doolittle, Hilda

**Heliodorus** fl. 3rd cent. - ................ **CMLC 52**
See also WLIT 8

**Hellenhofferu, Vojtech Kapristian z**
See Hasek, Jaroslav (Matej Frantisek)

**Heller, Joseph** 1923-1999 . **CLC 1, 3, 5, 8, 11, 36, 63; TCLC 131, 151; WLC 3**
See also AAYA 24; AITN 1; AMWS 4; BPFB 2; BYA 1; CA 5-8R; 187; CABS 1; CANR 8, 42, 66, 126; CN 1, 2, 3, 4, 5, 6; CPW; DA; DA3; DAB; DAC; DAM MST, NOV, POP; DLB 2, 28, 227; DLBY 1980, 2002; EWL 3; EXPN; INT CANR-8; LAIT 4; MAL 5; MTCW 1, 2; MTFW 2005; NFS 1; RGAL 4; TUS; YAW

**Hellman, Lillian** 1905-1984 . **CLC 2, 4, 8, 14, 18, 34, 44, 52; DC 1**
See also AAYA 47; AITN 1, 2; AMWS 1; CA 13-16R; 112; CAD; CANR 33; CWD; DA3; DAM DRAM; DFS 1, 3, 14; DLB 7, 228; DLBY 1984; EWL 3; FL 1:6; FW; LAIT 3; MAL 5; MBL; MTCW 1, 2; MTFW 2005; RGAL 4; TUS

**Hellman, Lillian Florence**
See Hellman, Lillian

**Helprin, Mark** 1947- ......... **CLC 7, 10, 22, 32**
See also CA 81-84; CANR 47, 64, 124; CDALBS; CN 7; CPW; DA3; DAM NOV, POP; DLB 335; DLBY 1985; FANT; MAL 5; MTCW 1, 2; MTFW 2005; SSFS 25; SUFW 2

**Helvetius, Claude-Adrien** 1715-1771 .. **LC 26**
See also DLB 313

**Helyar, Jane Penelope Josephine**
1933- ...................................... **CLC 17**
See also CA 21-24R; CANR 10, 26; CWRI 5; SAAS 2; SATA 5; SATA-Essay 138

**Hemans, Felicia** 1793-1835 ...... **NCLC 29, 71**
See also DLB 96; RGEL 2

**Hemingway, Ernest** 1899-1961 . **CLC 1, 3, 6, 8, 10, 13, 19, 30, 34, 39, 41, 44, 50, 61, 80; SSC 1, 25, 36, 40, 63, 117; TCLC 115, 203; WLC 3**
See also AAYA 19; AMW; AMWC 1; AMWR 1; BPFB 2; BYA 2, 3, 13, 15; CA 77-80; CANR 34; CDALB 1917-1929; DA; DA3; DAB; DAC; DAM MST, NOV; DLB 4, 9, 102, 210, 308, 316, 330; DLBD 1, 15, 16; DLBY 1981, 1987, 1996, 1998; EWL 3; EXPN; EXPS; LAIT 3, 4; LATS 1:1; MAL 5; MTCW 1, 2; MTFW 2005; NFS 1, 5, 6, 14; RGAL 4; RGSF 2; SSFS 17; TUS; WYA

**Hemingway, Ernest Miller**
See Hemingway, Ernest

**Hempel, Amy** 1951- ......................... **CLC 39**
See also CA 118; 137; CANR 70, 166; DA3; DLB 218; EXPS; MTCW 2; MTFW 2005; SSFS 2

**Henderson, F. C.**
See Mencken, H. L.

**Henderson, Mary**
See Mavor, Osborne Henry

**Henderson, Sylvia**
See Ashton-Warner, Sylvia (Constance)

**Henderson, Zenna (Chlarson)**
1917-1983 ................................. **SSC 29**
See also CA 1-4R; 133; CANR 1, 84; DLB 8; SATA 5; SFW 4

**Henkin, Joshua** 1964- ..................... **CLC 119**
See also CA 161; CANR 186; DLB 350

**Henley, Beth** 1952- ... **CLC 23, 255; DC 6, 14**
See also AAYA 70; CA 107; CABS 3; CAD; CANR 32, 73, 140; CD 5, 6; CSW; CWD; DA3; DAM DRAM, MST; DFS 2, 21, 26; DLBY 1986; FW; MTCW 1, 2; MTFW 2005

**Henley, Elizabeth Becker**
See Henley, Beth

**Henley, William Ernest** 1849-1903 .. **TCLC 8**
See also CA 105; 234; DLB 19; RGEL 2

**Hennissart, Martha** 1929- ................ **CLC 2**
See also BPFB 2; CA 85-88; CANR 64; CMW 4; DLB 306

**Henry VIII** 1491-1547 ......................... **LC 10**
See also DLB 132

**Henry, O.** 1862-1910 . **SSC 5, 49, 117; TCLC 1, 19; WLC 3**
See also AAYA 41; AMWS 2; CA 104; 131; CDALB 1865-1917; DA; DA3; DAB; DAC; DAM MST; DLB 12, 78, 79; EXPS; MAL 5; MTCW 1, 2; MTFW 2005; RGAL 4; RGSF 2; SSFS 2, 18, 27; TCWW 1, 2; TUS; YABC 2

**Henry, Oliver**
See Henry, O.

**Henry, Patrick** 1736-1799 .................... **LC 25**
See also LAIT 1

**Henryson, Robert** 1430(?)-1506(?) ..... **LC 20, 110; PC 65**
See also BRWS 7; DLB 146; RGEL 2

**Henschke, Alfred**
See Klabund

**Henson, Lance** 1944- ......................... **NNAL**
See also CA 146; DLB 175

**Hentoff, Nat(han Irving)** 1925- ......... **CLC 26**
See also AAYA 4, 42; BYA 6; CA 1-4R; CAAS 6; CANR 5, 25, 77, 114; CLR 1, 52; DLB 345; INT CANR-25; JRDA; MAICYA 1, 2; SATA 42, 69, 133; SATA-Brief 27; WYA; YAW

**Heppenstall, (John) Rayner**
1911-1981 ................................. **CLC 10**
See also CA 1-4R; 103; CANR 29; CN 1, 2; CP 1, 2, 3; EWL 3

**Heraclitus** c. 540B.C.-c. 450B.C. ... **CMLC 22**
See also DLB 176

**Herbert, Frank** 1920-1986 ... **CLC 12, 23, 35, 44, 85**
See also AAYA 21; BPFB 2; BYA 4, 14; CA 53-56; 118; CANR 5, 43; CDALBS; CPW; DAM POP; DLB 8; INT CANR-5; LAIT 5; MTCW 1, 2; MTFW 2005; NFS 17; SATA 9, 37; SATA-Obit 47; SCFW 1, 2; SFW 4; YAW

**Herbert, George** 1593-1633 . **LC 24, 121; PC 4**
See also BRW 2; BRWR 2; CDBLB Before 1660; DAB; DAM POET; DLB 126; EXPP; PFS 25; RGEL 2; TEA; WP

**Herbert, Zbigniew** 1924-1998 ..... **CLC 9, 43; PC 50; TCLC 168**
See also CA 89-92; 169; CANR 36, 74, 177; CDWLB 4; CWW 2; DAM POET; DLB 232; EWL 3; MTCW 1; PFS 22

**Herbst, Josephine (Frey)**
1897-1969 ................................. **CLC 34**
See also CA 5-8R; 25-28R; DLB 9

**Herder, Johann Gottfried von**
1744-1803 ......................... **NCLC 8, 186**
See also DLB 97; EW 4; TWA

**Heredia, Jose Maria** 1803-1839 ...... **HLCS 2; NCLC 209**
See also LAW

**Hergesheimer, Joseph** 1880-1954 ... **TCLC 11**
See also CA 109; 194; DLB 102, 9; RGAL 4

**Herlihy, James Leo** 1927-1993 .......... **CLC 6**
See also CA 1-4R; 143; CAD; CANR 2; CN 1, 2, 3, 4, 5

**Herman, William**
See Bierce, Ambrose

**Hermogenes** fl. c. 175- ..................... **CMLC 6**

**Hernandez, Jose** 1834-1886 ........... **NCLC 17**
See also LAW; RGWL 2, 3; WLIT 1

**Herodotus** c. 484B.C.-c. 420B.C. .. **CMLC 17**
See also AW 1; CDWLB 1; DLB 176; RGWL 2, 3; TWA; WLIT 8

**Herr, Michael** 1940(?)- ................... **CLC 231**
See also CA 89-92; CANR 68, 142; DLB 185; MTCW 1

**Herrick, Robert** 1591-1674 .. **LC 13, 145; PC 9**
See also BRW 2; BRWC 2; DA; DAB; DAC; DAM MST, POP; DLB 126; EXPP; PFS 13, 29; RGAL 4; RGEL 2; TEA; WP

**Herring, Guilles**
See Somerville, Edith Oenone

**Herriot, James** 1916-1995
See Wight, James Alfred

**Herris, Violet**
See Hunt, Violet

**Herrmann, Dorothy** 1941- ............... **CLC 44**
See also CA 107

**Herrmann, Taffy**
See Herrmann, Dorothy

**Hersey, John** 1914-1993 .. **CLC 1, 2, 7, 9, 40, 81, 97**
See also AAYA 29; BPFB 2; CA 17-20R; 140; CANR 33; CDALBS; CN 1, 2, 3, 4, 5; CPW; DAM POP; DLB 6, 185, 278, 299; MAL 5; MTCW 1, 2; MTFW 2005; RGHL; SATA 25; SATA-Obit 76; TUS

**Hersey, John Richard**
See Hersey, John

**Hervent, Maurice**
See Grindel, Eugene

**Herzen, Aleksandr Ivanovich**
1812-1870 ......................... **NCLC 10, 61**
See also DLB 277

**Herzen, Alexander**
See Herzen, Aleksandr Ivanovich

**Herzl, Theodor** 1860-1904 ............. **TCLC 36**
See also CA 168

**Herzog, Werner** 1942- ............... **CLC 16, 236**
See also CA 89-92

**Hesiod** fl. 8th cent. B.C.- .......... **CMLC 5, 102**
See also AW 1; DLB 176; RGWL 2, 3; WLIT 8

**Horkheimer, Max** 1895-1973 ........ **TCLC 132**
See also CA 216; 41-44R; DLB 296

**Horn, Peter**
See Kuttner, Henry

**Hornby, Nicholas Peter John**
See Hornby, Nick

**Hornby, Nick** 1957(?)- .................... **CLC 243**
See also AAYA 74; CA 151; CANR 104,
151, 191; CN 7; DLB 207, 352

**Horne, Frank** 1899-1974 .................... **HR 1:2**
See also BW 1; CA 125; 53-56; DLB 51;
WP

**Horne, Richard Henry Hengist**
1802(?)-1884 ......................... **NCLC 127**
See also DLB 32; SATA 29

**Hornem, Horace Esq.**
See Byron, George Gordon (Noel)

**Horne Tooke, John** 1736-1812 ..... **NCLC 195**

**Horney, Karen (Clementine Theodore**
**Danielsen)** 1885-1952 ............. **TCLC 71**
See also CA 114; 165; DLB 246; FW

**Hornung, E(rnest) W(illiam)**
1866-1921 ............................. **TCLC 59**
See also CA 108; 160; CMW 4; DLB 70

**Horovitz, Israel** 1939- ....................... **CLC 56**
See also CA 33-36R; CAD; CANR 46, 59;
CD 5, 6; DAM DRAM; DLB 7, 341;
MAL 5

**Horton, George Moses**
1797(?)-1883(?) ........................ **NCLC 87**
See also DLB 50

**Horvath, odon von** 1901-1938
See von Horvath, Odon
See also EWL 3

**Horvath, Oedoen von** -1938
See von Horvath, Odon

**Horwitz, Julius** 1920-1986 ................ **CLC 14**
See also CA 9-12R; 119; CANR 12

**Horwitz, Ronald**
See Harwood, Ronald

**Hospital, Janette Turner** 1942- ........ **CLC 42,**
**145**
See also CA 108; CANR 48, 166; CN 5, 6,
7; DLB 325; DLBY 2002; RGSF 2

**Hosseini, Khaled** 1965- ..................... **CLC 254**
See also CA 225; SATA 156

**Hostos, E. M. de**
See Hostos (y Bonilla), Eugenio Maria de

**Hostos, Eugenio M. de**
See Hostos (y Bonilla), Eugenio Maria de

**Hostos, Eugenio Maria**
See Hostos (y Bonilla), Eugenio Maria de

**Hostos (y Bonilla), Eugenio Maria de**
1839-1903 ............................... **TCLC 24**
See also CA 123; 131; HW 1

**Houdini**
See Lovecraft, H. P.

**Houellebecq, Michel** 1958- ............. **CLC 179**
See also CA 185; CANR 140; MTFW 2005

**Hougan, Carolyn** 1943-2007 ............ **CLC 34**
See also CA 139; 257

**Household, Geoffrey (Edward West)**
1900-1988 ................................. **CLC 11**
See also CA 77-80; 126; CANR 58; CMW
4; CN 1, 2, 3, 4; DLB 87; SATA 14;
SATA-Obit 59

**Housman, A(lfred) E(dward)**
1859-1936 ......... **PC 2, 43; TCLC 1, 10;**
**WLCS**
See also AAYA 66; BRW 6; CA 104; 125;
DA; DA3; DAB; DAC; DAM MST,
POET; DLB 19, 284; EWL 3; EXPP;
MTCW 1, 2; MTFW 2005; PAB; PFS 4,
7; RGEL 2; TEA; WP

**Housman, Laurence** 1865-1959 ....... **TCLC 7**
See also CA 106; 155; DLB 10; FANT;
RGEL 2; SATA 25

**Houston, Jeanne Wakatsuki** 1934- ....... **AAL**
See also AAYA 49; CA 103, 232; CAAE
232; CAAS 16; CANR 29, 123, 167;
LAIT 4; SATA 78, 168; SATA-Essay 168

**Hove, Chenjerai** 1956- ..................... **BLC 2:2**
See also CP 7

**Howard, Elizabeth Jane** 1923- ..... **CLC 7, 29**
See also BRWS 11; CA 5-8R; CANR 8, 62,
146; CN 1, 2, 3, 4, 5, 6, 7

**Howard, Maureen** 1930- ........ **CLC 5, 14, 46,**
**151**
See also CA 53-56; CANR 31, 75, 140; CN
4, 5, 6, 7; DLBY 1983; INT CANR-31;
MTCW 1, 2; MTFW 2005

**Howard, Richard** 1929- .......... **CLC 7, 10, 47**
See also AITN 1; CA 85-88; CANR 25, 80,
154; CP 1, 2, 3, 4, 5, 6, 7; DLB 5; INT
CANR-25; MAL 5

**Howard, Robert E** 1906-1936 ......... **TCLC 8**
See also AAYA 80; BPFB 2; BYA 5; CA
105; 157; CANR 155; FANT; SUFW 1;
TCWW 1, 2

**Howard, Robert Ervin**
See Howard, Robert E

**Howard, Warren F.**
See Pohl, Frederik

**Howe, Fanny** 1940- ........................... **CLC 47**
See also CA 117, 187; CAAE 187; CAAS
27; CANR 70, 116, 184; CP 6, 7; CWP;
SATA-Brief 52

**Howe, Fanny Quincy**
See Howe, Fanny

**Howe, Irving** 1920-1993 .................... **CLC 85**
See also AMWS 6; CA 9-12R; 141; CANR
21, 50; DLB 67; EWL 3; MAL 5; MTCW
1, 2; MTFW 2005

**Howe, Julia Ward** 1819-1910 . **PC 81; TCLC**
**21**
See also CA 117; 191; DLB 1, 189, 235;
FW

**Howe, Susan** 1937- ....... **CLC 72, 152; PC 54**
See also AMWS 4; CA 160; CP 5, 6, 7;
CWP; DLB 120; FW; RGAL 4

**Howe, Tina** 1937- ............................ **CLC 48**
See also CA 109; CAD; CANR 125; CD 5,
6; CWD; DLB 341

**Howell, James** 1594(?)-1666 ................ **LC 13**
See also DLB 151

**Howells, W. D.**
See Howells, William Dean

**Howells, William D.**
See Howells, William Dean

**Howells, William Dean** 1837-1920 ... **SSC 36;**
**TCLC 7, 17, 41**
See also AMW; CA 104; 134; CDALB
1865-1917; DLB 12, 64, 74, 79, 189;
LMFS 1; MAL 5; MTCW 2; RGAL 4;
TUS

**Howes, Barbara** 1914-1996 .............. **CLC 15**
See also CA 9-12R; 151; CAAS 3; CANR
53; CP 1, 2, 3, 4, 5, 6; SATA 5; TCLE 1:1

**Hrabal, Bohumil** 1914-1997 ...... **CLC 13, 67;**
**TCLC 155**
See also CA 106; 156; CAAS 12; CANR
57; CWW 2; DLB 232; EWL 3; RGSF 2

**Hrabanus Maurus** 776(?)-856 ....... **CMLC 78**
See also DLB 148

**Hrotsvit of Gandersheim** c. 935-c.
1000 ....................................... **CMLC 29**
See also DLB 148

**Hsi, Chu** 1130-1200 ...................... **CMLC 42**

**Hsun, Lu**
See Shu-Jen, Chou

**Hubbard, L. Ron** 1911-1986 ............. **CLC 43**
See also AAYA 64; CA 77-80; 118; CANR
52; CPW; DA3; DAM POP; FANT;
MTCW 2; MTFW 2005; SFW 4

**Hubbard, Lafayette Ronald**
See Hubbard, L. Ron

**Huch, Ricarda (Octavia)**
1864-1947 ............................. **TCLC 13**
See also CA 111; 189; DLB 66; EWL 3

**Huddle, David** 1942- ......................... **CLC 49**
See also CA 57-60, 261; CAAS 20; CANR
89; DLB 130

**Hudson, Jeffery**
See Crichton, Michael

**Hudson, Jeffrey**
See Crichton, Michael

**Hudson, W(illiam) H(enry)**
1841-1922 ............................. **TCLC 29**
See also CA 115; 190; DLB 98, 153, 174;
RGEL 2; SATA 35

**Hueffer, Ford Madox**
See Ford, Ford Madox

**Hughart, Barry** 1934- ....................... **CLC 39**
See also CA 137; FANT; SFW 4; SUFW 2

**Hughes, Colin**
See Creasey, John

**Hughes, David (John)** 1930-2005 ..... **CLC 48**
See also CA 116; 129; 238; CN 4, 5, 6, 7;
DLB 14

**Hughes, Edward James**
See Hughes, Ted

**Hughes, James Langston**
See Hughes, Langston

**Hughes, Langston** 1902-1967 ........ **BLC 1:2;**
**CLC 1, 5, 10, 15, 35, 44, 108; DC 3;**
**HR 1:2; PC 1, 53; SSC 6, 90; WLC 3**
See also AAYA 12; AFAW 1, 2; AMWR 1;
AMWS 1; BW 1, 3; CA 1-4R; 25-28R;
CANR 1, 34, 82; CDALB 1929-1941;
CLR 17; DA; DA3; DAB; DAC; DAM
DRAM, MST, MULT, POET; DFS 6, 18;
DLB 4, 7, 48, 51, 86, 228, 315; EWL 3;
EXPP; EXPS; JRDA; LAIT 3; LMFS 2;
MAICYA 1, 2; MAL 5; MTCW 1, 2;
MTFW 2005; NFS 21; PAB; PFS 1, 3, 6,
10, 15, 30; RGAL 4; RGSF 2; SATA 4,
33; SSFS 4, 7; TUS; WCH; WP; YAW

**Hughes, Richard (Arthur Warren)**
1900-1976 .......... **CLC 1, 11; TCLC 204**
See also CA 5-8R; 65-68; CANR 4; CN 1,
2; DAM NOV; DLB 15, 161; EWL 3;
MTCW 1; RGEL 2; SATA 8; SATA-Obit
25

**Hughes, Ted** 1930-1998 . **CLC 2, 4, 9, 14, 37,**
**119; PC 7, 89**
See also BRWC 2; BRWR 2; BRWS 1; CA
1-4R; 171; CANR 1, 33, 66, 108; CLR 3,
131; CP 1, 2, 3, 4, 5, 6; DA3; DAB; DAC;
DAM MST, POET; DLB 40, 161; EWL
3; EXPP; MAICYA 1, 2; MTCW 1, 2;
MTFW 2005; PAB; PFS 4, 19; RGEL 2;
SATA 49; SATA-Brief 27; SATA-Obit
107; TEA; YAW

**Hughes, Thomas** 1822-1896 ......... **NCLC 207**
See also BYA 3; DLB 18, 163; LAIT 2;
RGEL 2; SATA 31

**Hugo, Richard**
See Huch, Ricarda (Octavia)

**Hugo, Richard F(ranklin)**
1923-1982 ............ **CLC 6, 18, 32; PC 68**
See also AMWS 6; CA 49-52; 108; CANR
3; CP 1, 2, 3; DAM POET; DLB 5, 206;
EWL 3; MAL 5; PFS 17; RGAL 4

**Hugo, Victor** 1802-1885 ...... **NCLC 3, 10, 21,**
**161, 189; PC 17; WLC 3**
See also AAYA 28; DA; DA3; DAB; DAC;
DAM DRAM, MST, NOV, POET; DLB
119, 192, 217; EFS 2; EW 6; EXPN; GFL
1789 to the Present; LAIT 1, 2; NFS 5,
20; RGWL 2, 3; SATA 47; TWA

**Hugo, Victor Marie**
See Hugo, Victor

**Huidobro, Vicente**
See Huidobro Fernandez, Vicente Garcia

**Inge, William (Motter)** 1913-1973 ..... **CLC 1, 8, 19; DC 37**
See also CA 9-12R; CAD; CDALB 1941-1968; DA3; DAM DRAM; DFS 1, 3, 5, 8; DLB 7, 249; EWL 3; MAL 5; MTCW 1, 2; MTFW 2005; RGAL 4; TUS

**Ingelow, Jean** 1820-1897 ........ **NCLC 39, 107**
See also DLB 35, 163; FANT; SATA 33

**Ingram, Willis J.**
See Harris, Mark

**Innaurato, Albert (F.)** 1948(?)- ... **CLC 21, 60**
See also CA 115; 122; CAD; CANR 78; CD 5, 6; INT CA-122

**Innes, Michael**
See Stewart, J(ohn) I(nnes) M(ackintosh)

**Innis, Harold Adams** 1894-1952 .... **TCLC 77**
See also CA 181; DLB 88

**Insluis, Alanus de**
See Alain de Lille

**Iola**
See Wells-Barnett, Ida B(ell)

**Ionesco, Eugene** 1912-1994 ... **CLC 1, 4, 6, 9, 11, 15, 41, 86; DC 12; WLC 3**
See also CA 9-12R; 144; CANR 55, 132; CWW 2; DA; DA3; DAB; DAC; DAM DRAM, MST; DFS 4, 9, 25; DLB 321; EW 13; EWL 3; GFL 1789 to the Present; LMFS 2; MTCW 1, 2; MTFW 2005; RGWL 2, 3; SATA 7; SATA-Obit 79; TWA

**Iqbal, Muhammad** 1877-1938 ........ **TCLC 28**
See also CA 215; EWL 3

**Ireland, Patrick**
See O'Doherty, Brian

**Irenaeus St.** 130- ............................. **CMLC 42**

**Irigaray, Luce** 1930- ........................ **CLC 164**
See also CA 154; CANR 121; FW

**Irish, William**
See Hopley-Woolrich, Cornell George

**Irland, David**
See Green, Julien

**Iron, Ralph**
See Schreiner, Olive (Emilie Albertina)

**Irving, John** 1942- . **CLC 13, 23, 38, 112, 175**
See also AAYA 8, 62; AMWS 6; BEST 89:3; BPFB 2; CA 25-28R; CANR 28, 73, 112, 133; CN 3, 4, 5, 6, 7; CPW; DA3; DAM NOV, POP; DLB 6, 278; DLBY 1982; EWL 3; MAL 5; MTCW 1, 2; MTFW 2005; NFS 12, 14; RGAL 4; TUS

**Irving, John Winslow**
See Irving, John

**Irving, Washington** 1783-1859 . **NCLC 2, 19, 95; SSC 2, 37, 104; WLC 3**
See also AAYA 56; AMW; CDALB 1640-1865; CLR 97; DA; DA3; DAB; DAC; DAM MST; DLB 3, 11, 30, 59, 73, 74, 183, 186, 250, 254; EXPS; GL 2; LAIT 1; RGAL 4; RGSF 2; SSFS 1, 8, 16; SUFW 1; TUS; WCH; YABC 2

**Irwin, P. K.**
See Page, P(atricia) K(athleen)

**Isaacs, Jorge Ricardo** 1837-1895 ... **NCLC 70**
See also LAW

**Isaacs, Susan** 1943- ........................... **CLC 32**
See also BEST 89:1; BPFB 2; CA 89-92; CANR 20, 41, 65, 112, 134, 165; CPW; DA3; DAM POP; INT CANR-20; MTCW 1, 2; MTFW 2005

**Isherwood, Christopher** 1904-1986 ... **CLC 1, 9, 11, 14, 44; SSC 56; TCLC 227**
See also AMWS 14; BRW 7; CA 13-16R; 117; CANR 35, 97, 133; CN 1, 2, 3; DA3; DAM DRAM, NOV; DLB 15, 195; DLBY 1986; EWL 3; IDTP; MTCW 1, 2; MTFW 2005; RGAL 4; RGEL 2; TUS; WLIT 4

**Ishiguro, Kazuo** 1954- . **CLC 27, 56, 59, 110, 219**
See also AAYA 58; BEST 90:2; BPFB 2; BRWS 4; CA 120; CANR 49, 95, 133; CN 5, 6, 7; DA3; DAM NOV; DLB 194, 326; EWL 3; MTCW 1, 2; MTFW 2005; NFS 13; WLIT 4; WWE 1

**Ishikawa, Hakuhin**
See Ishikawa, Takuboku

**Ishikawa, Takuboku** 1886(?)-1912 ..... **PC 10; TCLC 15**
See Ishikawa Takuboku
See also CA 113; 153; DAM POET

**Isidore of Seville** c. 560-636 ........ **CMLC 101**

**Iskander, Fazil (Abdulovich)** 1929- .. **CLC 47**
See also CA 102; DLB 302; EWL 3

**Iskander, Fazil' Abdulevich**
See Iskander, Fazil (Abdulovich)

**Isler, Alan (David)** 1934- ................... **CLC 91**
See also CA 156; CANR 105

**Ivan IV** 1530-1584 ................................ **LC 17**

**Ivanov, V.I.**
See Ivanov, Vyacheslav

**Ivanov, Vyacheslav** 1866-1949 ........ **TCLC 33**
See also CA 122; EWL 3

**Ivanov, Vyacheslav Ivanovich**
See Ivanov, Vyacheslav

**Ivask, Ivar Vidrik** 1927-1992 ............ **CLC 14**
See also CA 37-40R; 139; CANR 24

**Ives, Morgan**
See Bradley, Marion Zimmer

**Izumi Shikibu** c. 973-c. 1034 ........ **CMLC 33**

**J. R. S.**
See Gogarty, Oliver St. John

**Jabran, Kahlil**
See Gibran, Kahlil

**Jabran, Khalil**
See Gibran, Kahlil

**Jaccottet, Philippe** 1925- ..................... **PC 98**
See also CA 116; 129; CWW 2; GFL 1789 to the Present

**Jackson, Daniel**
See Wingrove, David

**Jackson, Helen Hunt** 1830-1885 .... **NCLC 90**
See also DLB 42, 47, 186, 189; RGAL 4

**Jackson, Jesse** 1908-1983 ................... **CLC 12**
See also BW 1; CA 25-28R; 109; CANR 27; CLR 28; CWRI 5; MAICYA 1, 2; SATA 2, 29; SATA-Obit 48

**Jackson, Laura** 1901-1991 . **CLC 3, 7; PC 44**
See also CA 65-68; 135; CANR 28, 89; CP 1, 2, 3, 4, 5; DLB 48; RGAL 4

**Jackson, Laura Riding**
See Jackson, Laura

**Jackson, Sam**
See Trumbo, Dalton

**Jackson, Sara**
See Wingrove, David

**Jackson, Shirley** 1919-1965 . **CLC 11, 60, 87; SSC 9, 39; TCLC 187; WLC 3**
See also AAYA 9; AMWS 9; BPFB 2; CA 1-4R; 25-28R; CANR 4, 52; CDALB 1941-1968; DA; DA3; DAC; DAM MST; DLB 6, 234; EXPS; HGG; LAIT 4; MAL 5; MTCW 2; MTFW 2005; RGAL 4; RGSF 2; SATA 2; SSFS 1, 27; SUFW 1, 2

**Jacob, (Cyprien-)Max** 1876-1944 .... **TCLC 6**
See also CA 104; 193; DLB 258; EWL 3; GFL 1789 to the Present; GLL 2; RGWL 2, 3

**Jacobs, Harriet A.** 1813(?)-1897 ... **NCLC 67, 162**
See also AFAW 1, 2; DLB 239; FL 1:3; FW; LAIT 2; RGAL 4

**Jacobs, Harriet Ann**
See Jacobs, Harriet A.

**Jacobs, Jim** 1942- ................................. **CLC 12**
See also CA 97-100; INT CA-97-100

**Jacobs, W(illiam) W(ymark)** 1863-1943 ................. **SSC 73; TCLC 22**
See also CA 121; 167; DLB 135; EXPS; HGG; RGEL 2; RGSF 2; SSFS 2; SUFW 1

**Jacobsen, Jens Peter** 1847-1885 .... **NCLC 34**

**Jacobsen, Josephine (Winder)** 1908-2003 .............. **CLC 48, 102; PC 62**
See also CA 33-36R; 218; CAAS 18; CANR 23, 48; CCA 1; CP 2, 3, 4, 5, 6, 7; DLB 244; PFS 23; TCLE 1:1

**Jacobson, Dan** 1929- ...... **CLC 4, 14; SSC 91**
See also AFW; CA 1-4R; CANR 2, 25, 66, 170; CN 1, 2, 3, 4, 5, 6, 7; DLB 14, 207, 225, 319; EWL 3; MTCW 1; RGSF 2

**Jacopone da Todi** 1236-1306 ......... **CMLC 95**

**Jacqueline**
See Carpentier (y Valmont), Alejo

**Jacques de Vitry** c. 1160-1240 ...... **CMLC 63**
See also DLB 208

**Jagger, Michael Philip**
See Jagger, Mick

**Jagger, Mick** 1943- ........................... **CLC 17**
See also CA 239

**Jahiz, al-** c. 780-c. 869 ................... **CMLC 25**
See also DLB 311

**Jakes, John** 1932- .............................. **CLC 29**
See also AAYA 32; BEST 89:4; BPFB 2; CA 57-60, 214; CAAE 214; CANR 10, 43, 66, 111, 142, 171; CPW; CSW; DA3; DAM NOV, POP; DLB 278; DLBY 1983; FANT; INT CANR-10; MTCW 1, 2; MTFW 2005; RHW; SATA 62; SFW 4; TCWW 1, 2

**Jakes, John William**
See Jakes, John

**James I** 1394-1437 ............................... **LC 20**
See also RGEL 2

**James, Alice** 1848-1892 ................. **NCLC 206**
See also DLB 221

**James, Andrew**
See Kirkup, James

**James, C(yril) L(ionel) R(obert)** 1901-1989 ..................... **BLCS; CLC 33**
See also BW 2; CA 117; 125; 128; CANR 62; CN 1, 2, 3, 4; DLB 125; MTCW 1

**James, Daniel (Lewis)** 1911-1988 ..... **CLC 33**
See also CA 174; 125; DLB 122

**James, Dynely**
See Mayne, William (James Carter)

**James, Henry Sr.** 1811-1882 .......... **NCLC 53**

**James, Henry** 1843-1916 ......... **SSC 8, 32, 47, 108; TCLC 2, 11, 24, 40, 47, 64, 171; WLC 3**
See also AMW; AMWC 1; AMWR 1; BPFB 2; BRW 6; CA 104; 132; CDALB 1865-1917; DA; DA3; DAB; DAC; DAM MST, NOV; DLB 12, 71, 74, 189; DLBD 13; EWL 3; EXPS; GL 2; HGG; LAIT 2; MAL 5; MTCW 1, 2; MTFW 2005; NFS 12, 16, 19; RGAL 4; RGEL 2; RGSF 2; SSFS 9; SUFW 1; TUS

**James, M. R.**
See James, Montague

**James, Mary**
See Meaker, Marijane

**James, Montague** 1862-1936 ...... **SSC 16, 93; TCLC 6**
See also CA 104; 203; DLB 156, 201; HGG; RGEL 2; RGSF 2; SUFW 1

**James, Montague Rhodes**
See James, Montague

**James, P. D.**
See White, Phyllis Dorothy James

**James, Philip**
See Moorcock, Michael

CWP; DA3; DAM POET; DLB 5; EWL
3; EXPP; MTCW 1, 2; MTFW 2005;
PAB; PFS 18; SATA 12

**Kumin, Maxine Winokur**
See Kumin, Maxine

**Kundera, Milan** 1929- . **CLC 4, 9, 19, 32, 68,
115, 135, 234; SSC 24**
See also AAYA 2, 62; BPFB 2; CA 85-88;
CANR 19, 52, 74, 144; CDWLB 4; CWW
2; DA3; DAM NOV; DLB 232; EW 13;
EWL 3; MTCW 1, 2; MTFW 2005; NFS
18, 27; RGSF 2; RGWL 3; SSFS 10

**Kunene, Mazisi** 1930-2006 ............... **CLC 85**
See also BW 1, 3; CA 125; 252; CANR 81;
CP 1, 6, 7; DLB 117

**Kunene, Mazisi Raymond**
See Kunene, Mazisi

**Kunene, Mazisi Raymond Fakazi Mngoni**
See Kunene, Mazisi

**Kung, Hans**
See Kung, Hans

**Kung, Hans** 1928- ........................... **CLC 130**
See also CA 53-56; CANR 66, 134; MTCW
1, 2; MTFW 2005

**Kunikida, Tetsuo**
See Kunikida Doppo

**Kunikida Doppo** 1869(?)-1908 ....... **TCLC 99**
See also DLB 180; EWL 3

**Kunikida Tetsuo**
See Kunikida Doppo

**Kunitz, Stanley** 1905-2006 ..... **CLC 6, 11, 14,
148; PC 19**
See also AMWS 3; CA 41-44R; 250; CANR
26, 57, 98; CP 1, 2, 3, 4, 5, 6, 7; DA3;
DLB 48; INT CANR-26; MAL 5; MTCW
1, 2; MTFW 2005; PFS 11; RGAL 4

**Kunitz, Stanley Jasspon**
See Kunitz, Stanley

**Kunze, Reiner** 1933- ......................... **CLC 10**
See also CA 93-96; CWW 2; DLB 75; EWL
3

**Kuprin, Aleksander Ivanovich**
1870-1938 .................................. **TCLC 5**
See also CA 104; 182; DLB 295; EWL 3

**Kuprin, Aleksandr Ivanovich**
See Kuprin, Aleksander Ivanovich

**Kuprin, Alexandr Ivanovich**
See Kuprin, Aleksander Ivanovich

**Kureishi, Hanif** 1954- .. **CLC 64, 135; DC 26**
See also BRWS 11; CA 139; CANR 113,
197; CBD; CD 5, 6; CN 6, 7; DLB 194,
245, 352; GLL 2; IDFW 4; WLIT 4;
WWE 1

**Kurosawa, Akira** 1910-1998 ..... **CLC 16, 119**
See also AAYA 11, 64; CA 101; 170; CANR
46; DAM MULT

**Kushner, Tony** 1956- .... **CLC 81, 203; DC 10**
See also AAYA 61; AMWS 9; CA 144;
CAD; CANR 74, 130; CD 5, 6; DA3;
DAM DRAM; DFS 5; DLB 228; EWL 3;
GLL 1; LAIT 5; MAL 5; MTCW 2;
MTFW 2005; RGAL 4; RGHL; SATA 160

**Kuttner, Henry** 1915-1958 ............. **TCLC 10**
See also CA 107; 157; DLB 8; FANT;
SCFW 1, 2; SFW 4

**Kutty, Madhavi**
See Das, Kamala

**Kuzma, Greg** 1944- ............................. **CLC 7**
See also CA 33-36R; CANR 70

**Kuzmin, Mikhail (Alekseevich)**
1872(?)-1936 ........................... **TCLC 40**
See also CA 170; DLB 295; EWL 3

**Kyd, Thomas** 1558-1594 .. **DC 3; LC 22, 125**
See also BRW 1; DAM DRAM; DFS 21;
DLB 62; IDTP; LMFS 1; RGEL 2; TEA;
WLIT 3

**Kyprianos, Iossif**
See Samarakis, Antonis

---

**L. S.**
See Stephen, Sir Leslie

**Labe, Louise** 1521-1566 ..................... **LC 120**
See also DLB 327

**Labrunie, Gerard**
See Nerval, Gerard de

**La Bruyere, Jean de** 1645-1696 .. **LC 17, 168**
See also DLB 268; EW 3; GFL Beginnings
to 1789

**LaBute, Neil** 1963- ......................... **CLC 225**
See also CA 240

**Lacan, Jacques (Marie Emile)**
1901-1981 .................................. **CLC 75**
See also CA 121; 104; DLB 296; EWL 3;
TWA

**Laclos, Pierre-Ambroise Francois**
1741-1803 ........................... **NCLC 4, 87**
See also DLB 313; EW 4; GFL Beginnings
to 1789; RGWL 2, 3

**Lacolere, Francois**
See Aragon, Louis

**La Colere, Francois**
See Aragon, Louis

**Lactantius** c. 250-c. 325 ............... **CMLC 118**

**La Deshabilleuse**
See Simenon, Georges (Jacques Christian)

**Lady Gregory**
See Gregory, Lady Isabella Augusta (Persse)

**Lady of Quality, A**
See Bagnold, Enid

**La Fayette, Marie-(Madelaine Pioche de la
Vergne)** 1634-1693 ................. **LC 2, 144**
See also DLB 268; GFL Beginnings to
1789; RGWL 2, 3

**Lafayette, Marie-Madeleine**
See La Fayette, Marie-(Madelaine Pioche
de la Vergne)

**Lafayette, Rene**
See Hubbard, L. Ron

**La Flesche, Francis** 1857(?)-1932 ...... **NNAL**
See also CA 144; CANR 83; DLB 175

**La Fontaine, Jean de** 1621-1695 ......... **LC 50**
See also DLB 268; EW 3; GFL Beginnings
to 1789; MAICYA 1, 2; RGWL 2, 3;
SATA 18

**LaForet, Carmen** 1921-2004 .......... **CLC 219**
See also CA 246; CWW 2; DLB 322; EWL
3

**LaForet Diaz, Carmen**
See LaForet, Carmen

**Laforgue, Jules** 1860-1887 ........ **NCLC 5, 53,
221; PC 14; SSC 20**
See also DLB 217; EW 7; GFL 1789 to the
Present; RGWL 2, 3

**Lagerkvist, Paer** 1891-1974 ... **CLC 7, 10, 13,
54; SSC 12; TCLC 144**
See also CA 85-88; 49-52; DA3; DAM
DRAM, NOV; DLB 259, 331; EW 10;
EWL 3; MTCW 1, 2; MTFW 2005; RGSF
2; RGWL 2, 3; TWA

**Lagerkvist, Paer Fabian**
See Lagerkvist, Paer

**Lagerkvist, Par**
See Lagerkvist, Paer

**Lagerloef, Selma**
See Lagerlof, Selma

**Lagerloef, Selma Ottiliana Lovisa**
See Lagerlof, Selma

**Lagerlof, Selma** 1858-1940 ........ **TCLC 4, 36**
See also CA 108; 188; CLR 7; DLB 259,
331; MTCW 2; RGWL 2, 3; SATA 15;
SSFS 18

**Lagerlof, Selma Ottiliana Lovisa**
See Lagerlof, Selma

---

**La Guma, Alex** 1925-1985 .. **BLCS; CLC 19;
TCLC 140**
See also AFW; BW 1, 3; CA 49-52; 118;
CANR 25, 81; CDWLB 3; CN 1, 2, 3;
CP 1; DAM NOV; DLB 117, 225; EWL
3; MTCW 1, 2; MTFW 2005; WLIT 2;
WWE 1

**Lahiri, Jhumpa** 1967- ......................... **SSC 96**
See also AAYA 56; CA 193; CANR 134,
184; DLB 323; MTFW 2005; SSFS 19,
27

**Laidlaw, A. K.**
See Grieve, C. M.

**Lainez, Manuel Mujica**
See Mujica Lainez, Manuel

**Laing, R(onald) D(avid)** 1927-1989 . **CLC 95**
See also CA 107; 129; CANR 34; MTCW 1

**Laishley, Alex**
See Booth, Martin

**Lamartine, Alphonse (Marie Louis Prat) de**
1790-1869 .......... **NCLC 11, 190; PC 16**
See also DAM POET; DLB 217; GFL 1789
to the Present; RGWL 2, 3

**Lamb, Charles** 1775-1834 ..... **NCLC 10, 113;
SSC 112; WLC 3**
See also BRW 4; CDBLB 1789-1832; DA;
DAB; DAC; DAM MST; DLB 93, 107,
163; RGEL 2; SATA 17; TEA

**Lamb, Lady Caroline** 1785-1828 ... **NCLC 38**
See also DLB 116

**Lamb, Mary Ann** 1764-1847 ...... **NCLC 125;
SSC 112**
See also DLB 163; SATA 17

**Lame Deer** 1903(?)-1976 .................... **NNAL**
See also CA 69-72

**Lamming, George (William)**
1927- . **BLC 1:2, 2:2; CLC 2, 4, 66, 144**
See also BW 2, 3; CA 85-88; CANR 26,
76; CDWLB 3; CN 1, 2, 3, 4, 5, 6, 7; CP
1; DAM MULT; DLB 125; EWL 3;
MTCW 1, 2; MTFW 2005; NFS 15;
RGEL 2

**L'Amour, Louis** 1908-1988 ......... **CLC 25, 55**
See also AAYA 16; AITN 2; BEST 89:2;
BPFB 2; CA 1-4R; 125; CANR 3, 25, 40;
CPW; DA3; DAM NOV, POP; DLB 206;
DLBY 1980; MTCW 1, 2; MTFW 2005;
RGAL 4; TCWW 1, 2

**Lampedusa, Giuseppe di**
See Tomasi di Lampedusa, Giuseppe

**Lampedusa, Giuseppe Tomasi di**
See Tomasi di Lampedusa, Giuseppe

**Lampman, Archibald** 1861-1899 .. **NCLC 25,
194**
See also DLB 92; RGEL 2; TWA

**Lancaster, Bruce** 1896-1963 ............. **CLC 36**
See also CA 9-10; CANR 70; CAP 1; SATA
9

**Lanchester, John** 1962- ............. **CLC 99, 280**
See also CA 194; DLB 267

**Landau, Mark Alexandrovich**
See Aldanov, Mark (Alexandrovich)

**Landau-Aldanov, Mark Alexandrovich**
See Aldanov, Mark (Alexandrovich)

**Landis, Jerry**
See Simon, Paul

**Landis, John** 1950- ........................... **CLC 26**
See also CA 112; 122; CANR 128

**Landolfi, Tommaso** 1908-1979 .... **CLC 11, 49**
See also CA 127; 117; DLB 177; EWL 3

**Landon, Letitia Elizabeth**
1802-1838 ................................. **NCLC 15**
See also DLB 96

**Landor, Walter Savage**
1775-1864 ................................. **NCLC 14**
See also BRW 4; DLB 93, 107; RGEL 2

**Landwirth, Heinz**
See Lind, Jakov

**Lane, Patrick** 1939- ............................ **CLC 25**
See also CA 97-100; CANR 54; CP 3, 4, 5, 6, 7; DAM POET; DLB 53; INT CA-97-100

**Lane, Rose Wilder** 1887-1968 ...... **TCLC 177**
See also CA 102; CANR 63; SATA 29; SATA-Brief 28; TCWW 2

**Lang, Andrew** 1844-1912 ................ **TCLC 16**
See also CA 114; 137; CANR 85; CLR 101; DLB 98, 141, 184; FANT; MAICYA 1, 2; RGEL 2; SATA 16; WCH

**Lang, Fritz** 1890-1976 ............... **CLC 20, 103**
See also AAYA 65; CA 77-80; 69-72; CANR 30

**Lange, John**
See Crichton, Michael

**Langer, Elinor** 1939- .......................... **CLC 34**
See also CA 121

**Langland, William** 1332(?)-1400(?) .... **LC 19, 120**
See also BRW 1; DA; DAB; DAC; DAM MST, POET; DLB 146; RGEL 2; TEA; WLIT 3

**Langstaff, Launcelot**
See Irving, Washington

**Lanier, Sidney** 1842-1881 . **NCLC 6, 118; PC 50**
See also AMWS 1; DAM POET; DLB 64; DLBD 13; EXPP; MAICYA 1; PFS 14; RGAL 4; SATA 18

**Lanyer, Aemilia** 1569-1645 .... **LC 10, 30, 83; PC 60**
See also DLB 121

**Lao Tzu** c. 6th cent. B.C.-3rd cent. B.C. ............................................. **CMLC 7**

**Lao-Tzu**
See Lao Tzu

**Lapine, James (Elliot)** 1949- ............. **CLC 39**
See also CA 123; 130; CANR 54, 128; DFS 25; DLB 341; INT CA-130

**Larbaud, Valery (Nicolas)** 1881-1957 .......................... **TCLC 9**
See also CA 106; 152; EWL 3; GFL 1789 to the Present

**Larcom, Lucy** 1824-1893 .............. **NCLC 179**
See also AMWS 13; DLB 221, 243

**Lardner, Ring** 1885-1933 .......... **SSC 32, 118; TCLC 2, 14**
See also AMW; BPFB 2; CA 104; 131; CDALB 1917-1929; DLB 11, 25, 86, 171; DLBD 16; MAL 5; MTCW 1, 2; MTFW 2005; RGAL 4; RGSF 2; TUS

**Lardner, Ring W., Jr.**
See Lardner, Ring

**Lardner, Ringold Wilmer**
See Lardner, Ring

**Laredo, Betty**
See Codrescu, Andrei

**Larkin, Maia**
See Wojciechowska, Maia (Teresa)

**Larkin, Philip (Arthur)** 1922-1985 ... **CLC 3, 5, 8, 9, 13, 18, 33, 39, 64; PC 21**
See also BRWS 1; CA 5-8R; 117; CANR 24, 62; CDBLB 1960 to Present; CP 1, 2, 3, 4; DA3; DAB; DAM MST, POET; DLB 27; EWL 3; MTCW 1, 2; MTFW 2005; PFS 3, 4, 12; RGEL 2

**La Roche, Sophie von** 1730-1807 ............................. **NCLC 121**
See also DLB 94

**La Rochefoucauld, Francois** 1613-1680 ........................... **LC 108, 172**
See also DLB 268; EW 3; GFL Beginnings to 1789; RGWL 2, 3

**Larra (y Sanchez de Castro), Mariano Jose de** 1809-1837 .................. **NCLC 17, 130**

**Larsen, Eric** 1941- ............................ **CLC 55**
See also CA 132

**Larsen, Nella** 1893(?)-1963 ... **BLC 1:2; CLC 37; HR 1:3; TCLC 200**
See also AFAW 1, 2; AMWS 18; BW 1; CA 125; CANR 83; DAM MULT; DLB 51; FW; LATS 1:1; LMFS 2

**Larson, Charles R(aymond)** 1938- ... **CLC 31**
See also CA 53-56; CANR 4, 121

**Larson, Jonathan** 1960-1996 ............. **CLC 99**
See also AAYA 28; CA 156; DFS 23; MTFW 2005

**La Sale, Antoine de** c. 1386-1460(?) . **LC 104**
See also DLB 208

**Las Casas, Bartolome de** 1474-1566 ......................... **HLCS; LC 31**
See also DLB 318; LAW; WLIT 1

**Lasch, Christopher** 1932-1994 ........ **CLC 102**
See also CA 73-76; 144; CANR 25, 118; DLB 246; MTCW 1, 2; MTFW 2005

**Lasker-Schueler, Else** 1869-1945 ... **TCLC 57**
See also CA 183; DLB 66, 124; EWL 3

**Lasker-Schuler, Else**
See Lasker-Schueler, Else

**Laski, Harold J(oseph)** 1893-1950 . **TCLC 79**
See also CA 188

**Latham, Jean Lee** 1902-1995 ............. **CLC 12**
See also AITN 1; BYA 1; CA 5-8R; CANR 7, 84; CLR 50; MAICYA 1, 2; SATA 2, 68; YAW

**Latham, Mavis**
See Clark, Mavis Thorpe

**Lathen, Emma**
See Hennissart, Martha

**Lathrop, Francis**
See Leiber, Fritz (Reuter, Jr.)

**Lattany, Kristin**
See Lattany, Kristin Hunter

**Lattany, Kristin Elaine Eggleston Hunter**
See Lattany, Kristin Hunter

**Lattany, Kristin Hunter** 1931- ......... **CLC 35**
See also AITN 1; BW 1; BYA 3; CA 13-16R; CANR 13, 108; CLR 3; CN 1, 2, 3, 4, 5, 6; DLB 33; INT CANR-13; MAICYA 1, 2; SAAS 10; SATA 12, 132; YAW

**Lattimore, Richmond (Alexander)** 1906-1984 ...................................... **CLC 3**
See also CA 1-4R; 112; CANR 1; CP 1, 2, 3; MAL 5

**Laughlin, James** 1914-1997 ............... **CLC 49**
See also CA 21-24R; 162; CAAS 22; CANR 9, 47; CP 1, 2, 3, 4, 5, 6; DLB 48; DLBY 1996, 1997

**Laurence, Jean Margaret Wemyss**
See Laurence, Margaret

**Laurence, Margaret** 1926-1987 ..... **CLC 3, 6, 13, 50, 62; SSC 7**
See also BYA 13; CA 5-8R; 121; CANR 33; CN 1, 2, 3, 4; DAC; DAM MST; DLB 53; EWL 3; FW; MTCW 1, 2; MTFW 2005; NFS 11; RGEL 2; RGSF 2; SATA-Obit 50; TCWW 2

**Laurent, Antoine** 1952- ..................... **CLC 50**

**Lauscher, Hermann**
See Hesse, Hermann

**Lautreamont** 1846-1870 ........ **NCLC 12, 194; SSC 14**
See also DLB 217; GFL 1789 to the Present; RGWL 2, 3

**Lautreamont, Isidore Lucien Ducasse**
See Lautreamont

**Lavater, Johann Kaspar** 1741-1801 ............................... **NCLC 142**
See also DLB 97

**Laverty, Donald**
See Blish, James

**Lavin, Mary** 1912-1996 . **CLC 4, 18, 99; SSC 4, 67**
See also CA 9-12R; 151; CANR 33; CN 1, 2, 3, 4, 5, 6; DLB 15, 319; FW; MTCW 1; RGEL 2; RGSF 2; SSFS 23

**Lavond, Paul Dennis**
See Kornbluth, C(yril) M.; Pohl, Frederik

**Lawes, Henry** 1596-1662 .................... **LC 113**
See also DLB 126

**Lawler, Ray**
See Lawler, Raymond Evenor

**Lawler, Raymond Evenor** 1922- ....... **CLC 58**
See also CA 103; CD 5, 6; DLB 289; RGEL 2

**Lawrence, D. H.** 1885-1930 ... **PC 54; SSC 4, 19, 73; TCLC 2, 9, 16, 33, 48, 61, 93; WLC 3**
See also BPFB 2; BRW 7; BRWR 2; CA 104; 121; CANR 131; CDBLB 1914-1945; DA; DA3; DAB; DAC; DAM MST, NOV, POET; DLB 10, 19, 36, 98, 162, 195; EWL 3; EXPP; EXPS; GLL 1; LAIT 2, 3; MTCW 1, 2; MTFW 2005; NFS 18, 26; PFS 6; RGEL 2; RGSF 2; SSFS 2, 6; TEA; WLIT 4; WP

**Lawrence, David Herbert Richards**
See Lawrence, D. H.

**Lawrence, T. E.** 1888-1935 ..... **TCLC 18, 204**
See also BRWS 2; CA 115; 167; DLB 195

**Lawrence, Thomas Edward**
See Lawrence, T. E.

**Lawrence of Arabia**
See Lawrence, T. E.

**Lawson, Henry (Archibald Hertzberg)** 1867-1922 ................. **SSC 18; TCLC 27**
See also CA 120; 181; DLB 230; RGEL 2; RGSF 2

**Lawton, Dennis**
See Faust, Frederick

**Laxness, Halldor (Kiljan)**
See Gudjonsson, Halldor Kiljan

**Layamon** fl. c. 1200- ............... **CMLC 10, 105**
See also DLB 146; RGEL 2

**Laye, Camara** 1928-1980 .. **BLC 1:2; CLC 4, 38**
See also AFW; BW 1; CA 85-88; 97-100; CANR 25; DAM MULT; EWL 3; MTCW 1, 2; WLIT 2

**Layton, Irving** 1912-2006 ..... **CLC 2, 15, 164**
See also CA 1-4R; 247; CANR 2, 33, 43, 66, 129; CP 1, 2, 3, 4, 5, 6, 7; DAC; DAM MST, POET; DLB 88; EWL 3; MTCW 1, 2; PFS 12; RGEL 2

**Layton, Irving Peter**
See Layton, Irving

**Lazarus, Emma** 1849-1887 ...... **NCLC 8, 109**

**Lazarus, Felix**
See Cable, George Washington

**Lazarus, Henry**
See Slavitt, David R.

**Lea, Joan**
See Neufeld, John (Arthur)

**Leacock, Stephen (Butler)** 1869-1944 ................... **SSC 39; TCLC 2**
See also CA 104; 141; CANR 80; DAC; DAM MST; DLB 92; EWL 3; MTCW 2; MTFW 2005; RGEL 2; RGSF 2

**Lead, Jane Ward** 1623-1704 ............... **LC 72**
See also DLB 131

**Leapor, Mary** 1722-1746 ........ **LC 80; PC 85**
See also DLB 109

**Lear, Edward** 1812-1888 ..... **NCLC 3; PC 65**
See also AAYA 48; BRW 5; CLR 1, 75; DLB 32, 163, 166; MAICYA 1, 2; RGEL 2; SATA 18, 100; WCH; WP

**Lear, Norman (Milton)** 1922- .......... **CLC 12**
See also CA 73-76

**Least Heat-Moon, William**
See Heat-Moon, William Least

**Leautaud, Paul** 1872-1956 ............. **TCLC 83**
See also CA 203; DLB 65; GFL 1789 to the Present

**Lenz, Jakob Michael Reinhold**
1751-1792 ................................... **LC 100**
See also DLB 94; RGWL 2, 3

**Lenz, Siegfried** 1926- .......... **CLC 27; SSC 33**
See also CA 89-92; CANR 80, 149; CWW
2; DLB 75; EWL 3; RGSF 2; RGWL 2, 3

**Leon, David**
See Jacob, (Cyprien-)Max

**Leonard, Dutch**
See Leonard, Elmore

**Leonard, Elmore** 1925- ........ **CLC 28, 34, 71,**
**120, 222**
See also AAYA 22, 59; AITN 1; BEST 89:1,
90:4; BPFB 2; CA 81-84; CANR 12, 28,
53, 76, 96, 133, 176; CMW 4; CN 5, 6, 7;
CPW; DA3; DAM POP; DLB 173, 226;
INT CANR-28; MSW; MTCW 1, 2;
MTFW 2005; RGAL 4; SATA 163;
TCWW 1, 2

**Leonard, Elmore John, Jr.**
See Leonard, Elmore

**Leonard, Hugh** 1926-2009 ................. **CLC 19**
See also CA 102; 283; CANR 78, 140;
CBD; CD 5, 6; DFS 13, 24; DLB 13; INT
CA-102

**Leonov, Leonid** 1899-1994 ................. **CLC 92**
See also CA 129; CANR 76; DAM NOV;
DLB 272; EWL 3; MTCW 1, 2; MTFW
2005

**Leonov, Leonid Maksimovich**
See Leonov, Leonid

**Leonov, Leonid Maximovich**
See Leonov, Leonid

**Leopardi, (Conte) Giacomo**
1798-1837 ........... **NCLC 22, 129; PC 37**
See also EW 5; RGWL 2, 3; WLIT 7; WP

**Le Reveler**
See Artaud, Antonin (Marie Joseph)

**Lerman, Eleanor** 1952- ....................... **CLC 9**
See also CA 85-88; CANR 69, 124, 184

**Lerman, Rhoda** 1936- ....................... **CLC 56**
See also CA 49-52; CANR 70

**Lermontov, Mikhail Iur'evich**
See Lermontov, Mikhail Yuryevich

**Lermontov, Mikhail Yuryevich**
1814-1841 ....... **NCLC 5, 47, 126; PC 18**
See also DLB 205; EW 6; RGWL 2, 3;
TWA

**Leroux, Gaston** 1868-1927 ............. **TCLC 25**
See also CA 108; 136; CANR 69; CMW 4;
MTFW 2005; NFS 20; SATA 65

**Lesage, Alain-Rene** 1668-1747 ........ **LC 2, 28**
See also DLB 313; EW 3; GFL Beginnings
to 1789; RGWL 2, 3

**Leskov, N(ikolai) S(emenovich)** 1831-1895
See Leskov, Nikolai (Semyonovich)

**Leskov, Nikolai (Semyonovich)**
1831-1895 ... **NCLC 25, 174; SSC 34, 96**
See also DLB 238

**Leskov, Nikolai Semenovich**
See Leskov, Nikolai (Semyonovich)

**Lesser, Milton**
See Marlowe, Stephen

**Lessing, Doris** 1919- .. **CLC 1, 2, 3, 6, 10, 15,**
**22, 40, 94, 170, 254; SSC 6, 61; WLCS**
See also AAYA 57; AFW; BRWS 1; CA
9-12R; CAAS 14; CANR 33, 54, 76, 122,
179; CBD; CD 5, 6; CDBLB 1960 to
Present; CN 1, 2, 3, 4, 5, 6, 7; CWD; DA;
DA3; DAB; DAC; DAM MST, NOV;
DFS 20; DLB 15, 139; DLBY 1985; EWL
3; EXPS; FL 1:6; FW; LAIT 4; MTCW 1,
2; MTFW 2005; NFS 27; RGEL 2; RGSF
2; SFW 4; SSFS 1, 12, 20, 26; TEA;
WLIT 2, 4

**Lessing, Doris May**
See Lessing, Doris

**Lessing, Gotthold Ephraim**
1729-1781 .......... **DC 26; LC 8, 124, 162**
See also CDWLB 2; DLB 97; EW 4; RGWL
2, 3

**Lester, Julius** 1939- ........................... **BLC 2:2**
See also AAYA 12, 51; BW 2; BYA 3, 9,
11, 12; CA 17-20R; CANR 8, 23, 43, 129,
174; CLR 2, 41, 143; JRDA; MAICYA 1,
2; MAICYAS 1; MTFW 2005; SATA 12,
74, 112, 157; YAW

**Lester, Richard** 1932- ........................ **CLC 20**

**Letts, Tracy** 1965- ........................... **CLC 280**
See also CA 223

**Levenson, Jay CLC 70**

**Lever, Charles (James)**
1806-1872 ................................ **NCLC 23**
See also DLB 21; RGEL 2

**Leverson, Ada Esther**
1862(?)-1933(?) ....................... **TCLC 18**
See also CA 117; 202; DLB 153; RGEL 2

**Levertov, Denise** 1923-1997 .. **CLC 1, 2, 3, 5,**
**8, 15, 28, 66; PC 11**
See also AMWS 3; CA 1-4R, 178; 163;
CAAE 178; CAAS 19; CANR 3, 29, 50,
108; CDALBS; CP 1, 2, 3, 4, 5, 6; CWP;
DAM POET; DLB 5, 165, 342; EWL 3;
EXPP; FW; INT CANR-29; MAL 5;
MTCW 1, 2; PAB; PFS 7, 17, 31; RGAL
4; RGHL; TUS; WP

**Levi, Carlo** 1902-1975 ................... **TCLC 125**
See also CA 65-68; 53-56; CANR 10; EWL
3; RGWL 2, 3

**Levi, Jonathan CLC 76**
See also CA 197

**Levi, Peter (Chad Tigar)**
1931-2000 ................................. **CLC 41**
See also CA 5-8R; 187; CANR 34, 80; CP
1, 2, 3, 4, 5, 6, 7; DLB 40

**Levi, Primo** 1919-1987 ...... **CLC 37, 50; SSC**
**12, 122; TCLC 109**
See also CA 13-16R; 122; CANR 12, 33,
61, 70, 132, 171; DLB 177, 299; EWL 3;
MTCW 1, 2; MTFW 2005; RGHL;
RGWL 2, 3; WLIT 7

**Levin, Ira** 1929-2007 ....................... **CLC 3, 6**
See also CA 21-24R; 266; CANR 17, 44,
74, 139; CMW 4; CN 1, 2, 3, 4, 5, 6, 7;
CPW; DA3; DAM POP; HGG; MTCW 1,
2; MTFW 2005; SATA 66; SATA-Obit
187; SFW 4

**Levin, Ira Marvin**
See Levin, Ira

**Levin, Ira Marvin**
See Levin, Ira

**Levin, Meyer** 1905-1981 ..................... **CLC 7**
See also AITN 1; CA 9-12R; 104; CANR
15; CN 1, 2, 3; DAM POP; DLB 9, 28;
DLBY 1981; MAL 5; RGHL; SATA 21;
SATA-Obit 27

**Levine, Albert Norman**
See Levine, Norman

**Levine, Norman** 1923-2005 ............... **CLC 54**
See also CA 73-76; 240; CAAS 23; CANR
14, 70; CN 1, 2, 3, 4, 5, 6, 7; CP 1; DLB
88

**Levine, Norman Albert**
See Levine, Norman

**Levine, Philip** 1928- .. **CLC 2, 4, 5, 9, 14, 33,**
**118; PC 22**
See also AMWS 5; CA 9-12R; CANR 9,
37, 52, 116, 156; CP 1, 2, 3, 4, 5, 6, 7;
DAM POET; DLB 5; EWL 3; MAL 5;
PFS 8

**Levinson, Deirdre** 1931- .................... **CLC 49**
See also CA 73-76; CANR 70

**Levi-Strauss, Claude** 1908-2008 ....... **CLC 38**
See also CA 1-4R; CANR 6, 32, 57; DLB
242; EWL 3; GFL 1789 to the Present;
MTCW 1, 2; TWA

**Levitin, Sonia** 1934- ........................... **CLC 17**
See also AAYA 13, 48; CA 29-32R; CANR
14, 32, 79, 182; CLR 53; JRDA; MAI-
CYA 1, 2; SAAS 2; SATA 4, 68, 119, 131,
192; SATA-Essay 131; YAW

**Levon, O. U.**
See Kesey, Ken

**Levy, Amy** 1861-1889 ............. **NCLC 59, 203**
See also DLB 156, 240

**Lewees, John**
See Stockton, Francis Richard

**Lewes, George Henry** 1817-1878 .. **NCLC 25,**
**215**
See also DLB 55, 144

**Lewis, Alun** 1915-1944 ....... **SSC 40; TCLC 3**
See also BRW 7; CA 104; 188; DLB 20,
162; PAB; RGEL 2

**Lewis, C. Day**
See Day Lewis, C.

**Lewis, Cecil Day**
See Day Lewis, C.

**Lewis, Clive Staples**
See Lewis, C.S.

**Lewis, C.S.** 1898-1963 ... **CLC 1, 3, 6, 14, 27,**
**124; WLC 4**
See also AAYA 3, 39; BPFB 2; BRWS 3;
BYA 15, 16; CA 81-84; CANR 33, 71,
132; CDBLB 1945-1960; CLR 3, 27, 109;
CWRI 5; DA; DA3; DAB; DAC; DAM
MST, NOV, POP; DLB 15, 100, 160, 255;
EWL 3; FANT; JRDA; LMFS 2; MAI-
CYA 1, 2; MTCW 1, 2; MTFW 2005;
NFS 24; RGEL 2; SATA 13, 100; SCFW
1, 2; SFW 4; SUFW 1; TEA; WCH;
WYA; YAW

**Lewis, Janet** 1899-1998 .................... **CLC 41**
See also CA 9-12R; 172; CANR 29, 63;
CAP 1; CN 1, 2, 3, 4, 5, 6; DLBY 1987;
RHW; TCWW 2

**Lewis, Matthew Gregory**
1775-1818 ........................... **NCLC 11, 62**
See also DLB 39, 158, 178; GL 3; HGG;
LMFS 1; RGEL 2; SUFW

**Lewis, Sinclair** 1885-1951 ... **TCLC 4, 13, 23,**
**39, 215; WLC 4**
See also AMW; AMWC 1; BPFB 2; CA
104; 133; CANR 132; CDALB 1917-
1929; DA; DA3; DAB; DAC; DAM MST,
NOV; DLB 9, 102, 284, 331; DLBD 1;
EWL 3; LAIT 3; MAL 5; MTCW 1, 2;
MTFW 2005; NFS 15, 19, 22; RGAL 4;
TUS

**Lewis, (Percy) Wyndham**
1884(?)-1957 . **SSC 34; TCLC 2, 9, 104,**
**216**
See also AAYA 77; BRW 7; CA 104; 157;
DLB 15; EWL 3; FANT; MTCW 2;
MTFW 2005; RGEL 2

**Lewisohn, Ludwig** 1883-1955 ......... **TCLC 19**
See also CA 107; 203; DLB 4, 9, 28, 102;
MAL 5

**Lewton, Val** 1904-1951 ................... **TCLC 76**
See also CA 199; IDFW 3, 4

**Leyner, Mark** 1956- ........................... **CLC 92**
See also CA 110; CANR 28, 53; DA3; DLB
292; MTCW 2; MTFW 2005

**Leyton, E.K.**
See Campbell, Ramsey

**Lezama Lima, Jose** 1910-1976 .... **CLC 4, 10,**
**101; HLCS 2**
See also CA 77-80; CANR 71; DAM
MULT; DLB 113, 283; EWL 3; HW 1, 2;
LAW; RGWL 2, 3

**L'Heureux, John (Clarke)** 1934- ...... **CLC 52**
See also CA 13-16R; CANR 23, 45, 88; CP
1, 2, 3, 4; DLB 244

**Li, Fei-kan**
See Jin, Ba

**MacNeice, (Frederick) Louis**
1907-1963 ....... **CLC 1, 4, 10, 53; PC 61**
See also BRW 7; CA 85-88; CANR 61; DAB; DAM POET; DLB 10, 20; EWL 3; MTCW 1, 2; MTFW 2005; RGEL 2

**MacNeill, Dand**
See Fraser, George MacDonald

**Macpherson, James** 1736-1796 .... **CMLC 28; LC 29; PC 97**
See also BRWS 8; DLB 109, 336; RGEL 2

**Macpherson, (Jean) Jay** 1931- ......... **CLC 14**
See also CA 5-8R; CANR 90; CP 1, 2, 3, 4, 6, 7; CWP; DLB 53

**Macrobius** fl. 430- ......................... **CMLC 48**

**MacShane, Frank** 1927-1999 ........... **CLC 39**
See also CA 9-12R; 186; CANR 3, 33; DLB 111

**Macumber, Mari**
See Sandoz, Mari(e Susette)

**Madach, Imre** 1823-1864 ............... **NCLC 19**

**Madden, (Jerry) David** 1933- ....... **CLC 5, 15**
See also CA 1-4R; CAAS 3; CANR 4, 45; CN 3, 4, 5, 6, 7; CSW; DLB 6; MTCW 1

**Maddern, Al(an)**
See Ellison, Harlan

**Madhubuti, Haki R.** 1942- .... **BLC 1:2; CLC 2; PC 5**
See also BW 2, 3; CA 73-76; CANR 24, 51, 73, 139; CP 2, 3, 4, 5, 6, 7; CSW; DAM MULT, POET; DLB 5, 41; DLBD 8; EWL 3; MAL 5; MTCW 2; MTFW 2005; RGAL 4

**Madison, James** 1751-1836 ......... **NCLC 126**
See also DLB 37

**Maepenn, Hugh**
See Kuttner, Henry

**Maepenn, K. H.**
See Kuttner, Henry

**Maeterlinck, Maurice** 1862-1949 ....... **DC 32; TCLC 3**
See also CA 104; 136; CANR 80; DAM DRAM; DLB 192, 331; EW 8; EWL 3; GFL 1789 to the Present; LMFS 2; RGWL 2, 3; SATA 66; TWA

**Maginn, William** 1794-1842 ............. **NCLC 8**
See also DLB 110, 159

**Mahapatra, Jayanta** 1928- ................ **CLC 33**
See also CA 73-76; CAAS 9; CANR 15, 33, 66, 87; CP 4, 5, 6, 7; DAM MULT; DLB 323

**Mahfouz, Nagib**
See Mahfouz, Naguib

**Mahfouz, Naguib** 1911(?)-2006 . **CLC 52, 55, 153; SSC 66**
See also AAYA 49; AFW; BEST 89:2; CA 128; 253; CANR 55, 101; DA3; DAM NOV; DLB 346; DLBY 1988; MTCW 1, 2; MTFW 2005; RGSF 2; RGWL 2, 3; SSFS 9; WLIT 2

**Mahfouz, Naguib Abdel Aziz Al-Sabilgi**
See Mahfouz, Naguib

**Mahfouz, Najib**
See Mahfouz, Naguib

**Mahfuz, Najib**
See Mahfouz, Naguib

**Mahon, Derek** 1941- ............. **CLC 27; PC 60**
See also BRWS 6; CA 113; 128; CANR 88; CP 1, 2, 3, 4, 5, 6, 7; DLB 40; EWL 3

**Maiakovskii, Vladimir**
See Mayakovski, Vladimir (Vladimirovich)

**Mailer, Norman** 1923-2007 ... **CLC 1, 2, 3, 4, 5, 8, 11, 14, 28, 39, 74, 111, 234**
See also AAYA 31; AITN 2; AMW; AMWC 2; AMWR 2; BPFB 2; CA 9-12R; 266; CABS 1; CANR 28, 74, 77, 130, 196; CDALB 1968-1988; CN 1, 2, 3, 4, 5, 6, 7; CPW; DA; DA3; DAB; DAC; DAM MST, NOV, POP; DLB 2, 16, 28, 185, 278; DLBD 3; DLBY 1980, 1983; EWL 3; MAL 5; MTCW 1, 2; MTFW 2005; NFS 10; RGAL 4; TUS

**Mailer, Norman Kingsley**
See Mailer, Norman

**Maillet, Antonine** 1929- ............. **CLC 54, 118**
See also CA 115; 120; CANR 46, 74, 77, 134; CCA 1; CWW 2; DAC; DLB 60; INT CA-120; MTCW 2; MTFW 2005

**Maimonides, Moses** 1135-1204 ..... **CMLC 76**
See also DLB 115

**Mais, Roger** 1905-1955 .................... **TCLC 8**
See also BW 1, 3; CA 105; 124; CANR 82; CDWLB 3; DLB 125; EWL 3; MTCW 1; RGEL 2

**Maistre, Joseph** 1753-1821 ............. **NCLC 37**
See also GFL 1789 to the Present

**Maitland, Frederic William**
1850-1906 ................................ **TCLC 65**

**Maitland, Sara (Louise)** 1950- ........ **CLC 49**
See also BRWS 11; CA 69-72; CANR 13, 59; DLB 271; FW

**Major, Clarence** 1936- ...... **BLC 1:2; CLC 3, 19, 48**
See also AFAW 2; BW 2, 3; CA 21-24R; CAAS 6; CANR 13, 25, 53, 82; CN 3, 4, 5, 6, 7; CP 2, 3, 4, 5, 6, 7; CSW; DAM MULT; DLB 33; EWL 3; MAL 5; MSW

**Major, Kevin (Gerald)** 1949- ............ **CLC 26**
See also AAYA 16; CA 97-100; CANR 21, 38, 112; CLR 11; DAC; DLB 60; INT CANR-21; JRDA; MAICYA 1, 2; MAIC-YAS 1; SATA 32, 82, 134; WYA; YAW

**Maki, James**
See Ozu, Yasujiro

**Makin, Bathsua** 1600-1675(?) ............ **LC 137**

**Makine, Andrei** 1957-
See Makine, Andrei

**Makine, Andrei** 1957- ..................... **CLC 198**
See also CA 176; CANR 103, 162; MTFW 2005

**Malabaila, Damiano**
See Levi, Primo

**Malamud, Bernard** 1914-1986 .. **CLC 1, 2, 3, 5, 8, 9, 11, 18, 27, 44, 78, 85; SSC 15; TCLC 129, 184; WLC 4**
See also AAYA 16; AMWS 1; BPFB 2; BYA 15; CA 5-8R; 118; CABS 1; CANR 28, 62, 114; CDALB 1941-1968; CN 1, 2, 3, 4; CPW; DA; DA3; DAB; DAC; DAM MST, NOV, POP; DLB 2, 28, 152; DLBY 1980, 1986; EWL 3; EXPS; LAIT 4; LATS 1:1; MAL 5; MTCW 1, 2; MTFW 2005; NFS 27; RGAL 4; RGHL; RGSF 2; SSFS 8, 13, 16; TUS

**Malan, Herman**
See Bosman, Herman Charles; Bosman, Herman Charles

**Malaparte, Curzio** 1898-1957 ........ **TCLC 52**
See also DLB 264

**Malcolm, Dan**
See Silverberg, Robert

**Malcolm, Janet** 1934- ..................... **CLC 201**
See also CA 123; CANR 89, 199; NCFS 1

**Little, Malcolm**
See Malcolm X

**Malebranche, Nicolas** 1638-1715 ....... **LC 133**
See also GFL Beginnings to 1789

**Malherbe, Francois de** 1555-1628 ......... **LC 5**
See also DLB 327; GFL Beginnings to 1789

**Mallarme, Stephane** 1842-1898 ...... **NCLC 4, 41, 210; PC 4, 102**
See also DAM POET; DLB 217; EW 7; GFL 1789 to the Present; LMFS 2; RGWL 2, 3; TWA

**Mallet-Joris, Francoise** 1930- ........... **CLC 11**
See also CA 65-68; CANR 17; CWW 2; DLB 83; EWL 3; GFL 1789 to the Present

**Malley, Ern**
See McAuley, James Phillip

**Mallon, Thomas** 1951- ..................... **CLC 172**
See also CA 110; CANR 29, 57, 92, 196; DLB 350

**Mallowan, Agatha Christie**
See Christie, Agatha (Mary Clarissa)

**Maloff, Saul** 1922- ................................ **CLC 5**
See also CA 33-36R

**Malone, Louis**
See MacNeice, (Frederick) Louis

**Malone, Michael (Christopher)**
1942- .......................................... **CLC 43**
See also CA 77-80; CANR 14, 32, 57, 114

**Malory, Sir Thomas** 1410(?)-1471(?) . **LC 11, 88; WLCS**
See also BRW 1; BRWR 2; CDBLB Before 1660; DA; DAB; DAC; DAM MST; DLB 146; EFS 2; RGEL 2; SATA 59; SATA-Brief 33; TEA; WLIT 3

**Malouf, David** 1934- ........... **CLC 28, 86, 245**
See also BRWS 12; CA 124; CANR 50, 76, 180; CN 3, 4, 5, 6, 7; CP 1, 3, 4, 5, 6, 7; DLB 289; EWL 3; MTCW 2; MTFW 2005; SSFS 24

**Malouf, George Joseph David**
See Malouf, David

**Malraux, (Georges-)Andre**
1901-1976 ........ **CLC 1, 4, 9, 13, 15, 57; TCLC 209**
See also BPFB 2; CA 21-22; 69-72; CANR 34, 58; CAP 2; DA3; DAM NOV; DLB 72; EW 12; EWL 3; GFL 1789 to the Present; MTCW 1, 2; MTFW 2005; RGWL 2, 3; TWA

**Malthus, Thomas Robert**
1766-1834 ............................... **NCLC 145**
See also DLB 107, 158; RGEL 2

**Malzberg, Barry N(athaniel)** 1939- ... **CLC 7**
See also CA 61-64; CAAS 4; CANR 16; CMW 4; DLB 8; SFW 4

**Mamet, David** 1947- .. **CLC 9, 15, 34, 46, 91, 166; DC 4, 24**
See also AAYA 3, 60; AMWS 14; CA 81-84; CABS 3; CAD; CANR 15, 41, 67, 72, 129, 172; CD 5, 6; DA3; DAM DRAM; DFS 2, 3, 6, 12, 15; DLB 7; EWL 3; IDFW 4; MAL 5; MTCW 1, 2; MTFW 2005; RGAL 4

**Mamet, David Alan**
See Mamet, David

**Mamoulian, Rouben (Zachary)**
1897-1987 .................................... **CLC 16**
See also CA 25-28R; 124; CANR 85

**Mandelshtam, Osip**
See Mandelstam, Osip (Emilievich)
See also DLB 295

**Mandelstam, Osip (Emilievich)**
1891(?)-1943(?) ....... **PC 14; TCLC 2, 6, 225**
See Mandelshtam, Osip
See also CA 104; 150; EW 10; EWL 3; MTCW 2; RGWL 2, 3; TWA

**Mander, (Mary) Jane** 1877-1949 ... **TCLC 31**
See also CA 162; RGEL 2

**Mandeville, Bernard** 1670-1733 ......... **LC 82**
See also DLB 101

**Mandeville, Sir John** fl. 1350- ...... **CMLC 19**
See also DLB 146

**Mandiargues, Andre Pieyre de**
See Pieyre de Mandiargues, Andre

**Mandrake, Ethel Belle**
See Thurman, Wallace (Henry)

**Mangan, James Clarence**
1803-1849 ............................... **NCLC 27**
See also BRWS 13; RGEL 2

**Maniere, J.-E.**
See Giraudoux, Jean(-Hippolyte)

Mankiewicz, Herman (Jacob)
1897-1953 ................................ **TCLC 85**
See also CA 120; 169; DLB 26; IDFW 3, 4
**Manley, (Mary) Delariviere**
1672(?)-1724 .............................. **LC 1, 42**
See also DLB 39, 80; RGEL 2
**Mann, Abel**
See Creasey, John
**Mann, Emily** 1952- ............................... **DC 7**
See also CA 130; CAD; CANR 55; CD 5, 6; CWD; DLB 266
**Mann, (Luiz) Heinrich** 1871-1950 ... **TCLC 9**
See also CA 106; 164, 181; DLB 66, 118; EW 8; EWL 3; RGWL 2, 3
**Mann, (Paul) Thomas** 1875-1955 . **SSC 5, 80, 82; TCLC 2, 8, 14, 21, 35, 44, 60, 168; WLC 4**
See also BPFB 2; CA 104; 128; CANR 133; CDWLB 2; DA; DA3; DAB; DAC; DAM MST, NOV; DLB 66, 331; EW 9; EWL 3; GLL 1; LATS 1:1; LMFS 1; MTCW 1, 2; MTFW 2005; NFS 17; RGSF 2; RGWL 2, 3; SSFS 4, 9; TWA
**Mannheim, Karl** 1893-1947 ........... **TCLC 65**
See also CA 204
**Manning, David**
See Faust, Frederick
**Manning, Frederic** 1882-1935 ........ **TCLC 25**
See also CA 124; 216; DLB 260
**Manning, Olivia** 1915-1980 .......... **CLC 5, 19**
See also CA 5-8R; 101; CANR 29; CN 1, 2; EWL 3; FW; MTCW 1; RGEL 2
**Mannyng, Robert** c. 1264-c.
1340 ...................................... **CMLC 83**
See also DLB 146
**Mano, D. Keith** 1942- .................... **CLC 2, 10**
See also CA 25-28R; CAAS 6; CANR 26, 57; DLB 6
**Mansfield, Katherine**
See Beauchamp, Kathleen Mansfield
**Manso, Peter** 1940- ......................... **CLC 39**
See also CA 29-32R; CANR 44, 156
**Mantecon, Juan Jimenez**
See Jimenez (Mantecon), Juan Ramon
**Mantel, Hilary** 1952- ....................... **CLC 144**
See also CA 125; CANR 54, 101, 161; CN 5, 6, 7; DLB 271; RHW
**Mantel, Hilary Mary**
See Mantel, Hilary
**Manton, Peter**
See Creasey, John
**Man Without a Spleen, A**
See Chekhov, Anton (Pavlovich)
**Manzano, Juan Franciso**
1797(?)-1854 ......................... **NCLC 155**
**Manzoni, Alessandro** 1785-1873 ... **NCLC 29, 98**
See also EW 5; RGWL 2, 3; TWA; WLIT 7
**Map, Walter** 1140-1209 ................. **CMLC 32**
**Mapu, Abraham (ben Jekutiel)**
1808-1867 ............................... **NCLC 18**
**Mara, Sally**
See Queneau, Raymond
**Maracle, Lee** 1950- ........................... **NNAL**
See also CA 149
**Marat, Jean Paul** 1743-1793 ............... **LC 10**
**Marcel, Gabriel Honore** 1889-1973 . **CLC 15**
See also CA 102; 45-48; EWL 3; MTCW 1, 2
**March, William**
See Campbell, William Edward March
**Marchbanks, Samuel**
See Davies, Robertson
**Marchi, Giacomo**
See Bassani, Giorgio
**Marcus Aurelius**
See Aurelius, Marcus

**Marcuse, Herbert** 1898-1979 ....... **TCLC 207**
See also CA 188; 89-92; DLB 242
**Marguerite**
See de Navarre, Marguerite
**Marguerite d'Angouleme**
See de Navarre, Marguerite
**Marguerite de Navarre**
See de Navarre, Marguerite
**Margulies, Donald** 1954- .................. **CLC 76**
See also AAYA 57; CA 200; CD 6; DFS 13; DLB 228
**Marias, Javier** 1951- ....................... **CLC 239**
See also CA 167; CANR 109, 139; DLB 322; HW 2; MTFW 2005
**Marie de France** c. 12th cent. - ...... **CMLC 8, 111; PC 22**
See also DLB 208; FW; RGWL 2, 3
**Marie de l'Incarnation** 1599-1672 ..... **LC 10, 168**
**Marier, Captain Victor**
See Griffith, D.W.
**Mariner, Scott**
See Pohl, Frederik
**Marinetti, Filippo Tommaso**
1876-1944 ................................ **TCLC 10**
See also CA 107; DLB 114, 264; EW 9; EWL 3; WLIT 7
**Marivaux, Pierre Carlet de Chamblain de**
1688-1763 .................... **DC 7; LC 4, 123**
See also DLB 314; GFL Beginnings to 1789; RGWL 2, 3; TWA
**Markandaya, Kamala**
See Taylor, Kamala
**Markfield, Wallace (Arthur)**
1926-2002 ................................... **CLC 8**
See also CA 69-72; 208; CAAS 3; CN 1, 2, 3, 4, 5, 6, 7; DLB 2, 28; DLBY 2002
**Markham, Edwin** 1852-1940 .......... **TCLC 47**
See also CA 160; DLB 54, 186; MAL 5; RGAL 4
**Markham, Robert**
See Amis, Kingsley
**Marks, J.**
See Highwater, Jamake (Mamake)
**Marks-Highwater, J.**
See Highwater, Jamake (Mamake)
**Markson, David M.** 1927- ................. **CLC 67**
See also AMWS 17; CA 49-52; CANR 1, 91, 158; CN 5, 6
**Markson, David Merrill**
See Markson, David M.
**Marlatt, Daphne (Buckle)** 1942- .... **CLC 168**
See also CA 25-28R; CANR 17, 39; CN 6, 7; CP 4, 5, 6, 7; CWP; DLB 60; FW
**Marley, Bob**
See Marley, Robert Nesta
**Marley, Robert Nesta** 1945-1981 ...... **CLC 17**
See also CA 107; 103
**Marlowe, Christopher** 1564-1593 . **DC 1; LC 22, 47, 117; PC 57; WLC 4**
See also BRW 1; BRWR 1; CDBLB Before 1660; DA; DA3; DAB; DAC; DAM DRAM, MST; DFS 1, 5, 13, 21; DLB 62; EXPP; LMFS 1; PFS 22; RGEL 2; TEA; WLIT 3
**Marlowe, Stephen** 1928-2008 ........... **CLC 70**
See also CA 13-16R; 269; CANR 6, 55; CMW 4; SFW 4
**Marmion, Shakerley** 1603-1639 ......... **LC 89**
See also DLB 58; RGEL 2
**Marmontel, Jean-Francois** 1723-1799 .. **LC 2**
See also DLB 314
**Maron, Monika** 1941- ..................... **CLC 165**
See also CA 201
**Marot, Clement** c. 1496-1544 ........... **LC 133**
See also DLB 327; GFL Beginnings to 1789

**Marquand, John P(hillips)**
1893-1960 ............................. **CLC 2, 10**
See also AMW; BPFB 2; CA 85-88; CANR 73; CMW 4; DLB 9, 102; EWL 3; MAL 5; MTCW 2; RGAL 4
**Marques, Rene** 1919-1979 .. **CLC 96; HLC 2**
See also CA 97-100; 85-88; CANR 78; DAM MULT; DLB 305; EWL 3; HW 1, 2; LAW; RGSF 2
**Marquez, Gabriel Garcia**
See Garcia Marquez, Gabriel
**Marquis, Don(ald Robert Perry)**
1878-1937 ................................. **TCLC 7**
See also CA 104; 166; DLB 11, 25; MAL 5; RGAL 4
**Marquis de Sade**
See Sade, Donatien Alphonse Francois
**Marric, J. J.**
See Creasey, John
**Marryat, Frederick** 1792-1848 ........ **NCLC 3**
See also DLB 21, 163; RGEL 2; WCH
**Marsden, James**
See Creasey, John
**Marsh, Edward** 1872-1953 ............. **TCLC 99**
**Marsh, (Edith) Ngaio** 1895-1982 .. **CLC 7, 53**
See also CA 9-12R; CANR 6, 58; CMW 4; CN 1, 2, 3; CPW; DAM POP; DLB 77; MSW; MTCW 1, 2; RGEL 2; TEA
**Marshall, Alan**
See Westlake, Donald E.
**Marshall, Allen**
See Westlake, Donald E.
**Marshall, Garry** 1934- ...................... **CLC 17**
See also AAYA 3; CA 111; SATA 60
**Marshall, Paule** 1929- .... **BLC 1:3, 2:3; CLC 27, 72, 253; SSC 3**
See also AFAW 1, 2; AMWS 11; BPFB 2; BW 2, 3; CA 77-80; CANR 25, 73, 129; CN 1, 2, 3, 4, 5, 6, 7; DA3; DAM MULT; DLB 33, 157, 227; EWL 3; LATS 1:2; MAL 5; MTCW 1, 2; MTFW 2005; RGAL 4; SSFS 15
**Marshallik**
See Zangwill, Israel
**Marsilius of Inghen** c.
1340-1396 .............................. **CMLC 106**
**Marsten, Richard**
See Hunter, Evan
**Marston, John** 1576-1634 ...... **DC 37; LC 33, 172**
See also BRW 2; DAM DRAM; DLB 58, 172; RGEL 2
**Martel, Yann** 1963- ......................... **CLC 192**
See also AAYA 67; CA 146; CANR 114; DLB 326, 334; MTFW 2005; NFS 27
**Martens, Adolphe-Adhemar**
See Ghelderode, Michel de
**Martha, Henry**
See Harris, Mark
**Marti, Jose** 1853-1895 ..... **HLC 2; NCLC 63; PC 76**
See also DAM MULT; DLB 290; HW 2; LAW; RGWL 2, 3; WLIT 7
**Martial** c. 40-c. 104 .......... **CMLC 35; PC 10**
See also AW 2; CDWLB 1; DLB 211; RGWL 2, 3
**Martin, Ken**
See Hubbard, L. Ron
**Martin, Richard**
See Creasey, John
**Martin, Steve** 1945- .................. **CLC 30, 217**
See also AAYA 53; CA 97-100; CANR 30, 100, 140, 195; DFS 19; MTCW 1; MTFW 2005
**Martin, Valerie** 1948- ....................... **CLC 89**
See also BEST 90:2; CA 85-88; CANR 49, 89, 165

DLB 4, 45, 51, 117; EWL 3; EXPP; GLL 2; LAIT 3; LMFS 2; MAL 5; MTCW 1, 2; MTFW 2005; PAB; PFS 4; RGAL 4; TUS; WP

**McKuen, Rod** 1933- ........................ **CLC 1, 3**
See also AITN 1; CA 41-44R; CANR 40; CP 1

**McLoughlin, R. B.**
See Mencken, H. L.

**McLuhan, (Herbert) Marshall**
1911-1980 ............................ **CLC 37, 83**
See also CA 9-12R; 102; CANR 12, 34, 61; DLB 88; INT CANR-12; MTCW 1, 2; MTFW 2005

**McMahon, Pat**
See Hoch, Edward D.

**McManus, Declan Patrick Aloysius**
See Costello, Elvis

**McMillan, Terry** 1951- .. **BLCS; CLC 50, 61, 112**
See also AAYA 21; AMWS 13; BPFB 2; BW 2, 3; CA 140; CANR 60, 104, 131; CN 7; CPW; DA3; DAM MULT, NOV, POP; MAL 5; MTCW 2; MTFW 2005; RGAL 4; YAW

**McMillan, Terry L.**
See McMillan, Terry

**McMurtry, Larry** 1936- ....... **CLC 2, 3, 7, 11, 27, 44, 127, 250**
See also AAYA 15; AITN 2; AMWS 5; BEST 89:2; BPFB 2; CA 5-8R; CANR 19, 43, 64, 103, 170; CDALB 1968-1988; CN 2, 3, 4, 5, 6, 7; CPW; CSW; DA3; DAM NOV, POP; DLB 2, 143, 256; DLBY 1980, 1987; EWL 3; MAL 5; MTCW 1, 2; MTFW 2005; RGAL 4; TCWW 1, 2

**McMurtry, Larry Jeff**
See McMurtry, Larry

**McNally, Terrence** 1939- ... **CLC 4, 7, 41, 91, 252; DC 27**
See also AAYA 62; AMWS 13; CA 45-48; CAD; CANR 2, 56, 116; CD 5, 6; DA3; DAM DRAM; DFS 16, 19; DLB 7, 249; EWL 3; GLL 1; MTCW 2; MTFW 2005

**McNally, Thomas Michael**
See McNally, T.M.

**McNally, T.M.** 1961- ........................ **CLC 82**
See also CA 246

**McNamer, Deirdre** 1950- .................. **CLC 70**
See also CA 188; CANR 163

**McNeal, Tom CLC 119**
See also CA 252; CANR 185; SATA 194

**McNeile, Herman Cyril**
1888-1937 ................................ **TCLC 44**
See also CA 184; CMW 4; DLB 77

**McNickle, D'Arcy** 1904-1977 .......... **CLC 89; NNAL**
See also CA 9-12R; 85-88; CANR 5, 45; DAM MULT; DLB 175, 212; RGAL 4; SATA-Obit 22; TCWW 1, 2

**McPhee, John** 1931- ........................ **CLC 36**
See also AAYA 61; AMWS 3; ANW; BEST 90:1; CA 65-68; CANR 20, 46, 64, 69, 121, 165; CPW; DLB 185, 275; MTCW 1, 2; MTFW 2005; TUS

**McPhee, John Angus**
See McPhee, John

**McPherson, James Alan, Jr.**
See McPherson, James Alan

**McPherson, James Alan** 1943- . **BLCS; CLC 19, 77; SSC 95**
See also BW 1, 3; CA 25-28R; 273; CAAE 273; CAAS 17; CANR 24, 74, 140; CN 3, 4, 5, 6; CSW; DLB 38, 244; EWL 3; MTCW 1, 2; MTFW 2005; RGAL 4; RGSF 2; SSFS 23

**McPherson, William (Alexander)**
1933- ........................................ **CLC 34**
See also CA 69-72; CANR 28; INT CANR-28

**McTaggart, J. McT. Ellis**
See McTaggart, John McTaggart Ellis

**McTaggart, John McTaggart Ellis**
1866-1925 ................................ **TCLC 105**
See also CA 120; DLB 262

**Mda, Zakes** 1948- .......... **BLC 2:3; CLC 262**
See also CA 205; CANR 151, 185; CD 5, 6; DLB 225

**Mda, Zanemvula**
See Mda, Zakes

**Mda, Zanemvula Kizito Gatyeni**
See Mda, Zakes

**Mead, George Herbert** 1863-1931 . **TCLC 89**
See also CA 212; DLB 270

**Mead, Margaret** 1901-1978 .............. **CLC 37**
See also AITN 1; CA 1-4R; 81-84; CANR 4; DA3; FW; MTCW 1, 2; SATA-Obit 20

**Meaker, M. J.**
See Meaker, Marijane

**Meaker, Marijane** 1927- ............. **CLC 12, 35**
See also AAYA 2, 23; BYA 1, 7, 8; CA 107; CANR 37, 63, 145, 180; CLR 29; GLL 2; INT CA-107; JRDA; MAICYA 1, 2; MAICYAS 1; MTCW 1; SAAS 1; SATA 20, 61, 99, 160; SATA-Essay 111; WYA; YAW

**Meaker, Marijane Agnes**
See Meaker, Marijane

**Mechthild von Magdeburg** c. 1207-c. 1282 ........................................ **CMLC 91**
See also DLB 138

**Medoff, Mark (Howard)** 1940- .... **CLC 6, 23**
See also AITN 1; CA 53-56; CAD; CANR 5; CD 5, 6; DAM DRAM; DFS 4; DLB 7; INT CANR-5

**Medvedev, P. N.**
See Bakhtin, Mikhail Mikhailovich

**Meged, Aharon**
See Megged, Aharon

**Meged, Aron**
See Megged, Aharon

**Megged, Aharon** 1920- ........................ **CLC 9**
See also CA 49-52; CAAS 13; CANR 1, 140; EWL 3; RGHL

**Mehta, Deepa** 1950- ........................ **CLC 208**

**Mehta, Gita** 1943- ........................... **CLC 179**
See also CA 225; CN 7; DNFS 2

**Mehta, Ved** 1934- ............................ **CLC 37**
See also CA 1-4R, 212; CAAE 212; CANR 2, 23, 69; DLB 323; MTCW 1; MTFW 2005

**Melanchthon, Philipp** 1497-1560 ......... **LC 90**
See also DLB 179

**Melanter**
See Blackmore, R(ichard) D(oddridge)

**Meleager** c. 140B.C.-c. 70B.C. ...... **CMLC 53**

**Melies, Georges** 1861-1938 ............. **TCLC 81**

**Melikow, Loris**
See Hofmannsthal, Hugo von

**Melmoth, Sebastian**
See Wilde, Oscar

**Melo Neto, Joao Cabral de**
See Cabral de Melo Neto, Joao

**Meltzer, Milton** 1915-2009 ............... **CLC 26**
See also AAYA 8, 45; BYA 2, 6; CA 13-16R; 290; CANR 38, 92, 107, 192; CLR 13; DLB 61; JRDA; MAICYA 1, 2; SAAS 1; SATA 1, 50, 80, 128, 201; SATA-Essay 124; WYA; YAW

**Melville, Herman** 1819-1891 ..... **NCLC 3, 12, 29, 45, 49, 91, 93, 123, 157, 181, 193, 221; PC 82; SSC 1, 17, 46, 95; WLC 4**
See also AAYA 25; AMW; AMWR 1; CDALB 1640-1865; DA; DA3; DAB; DAC; DAM MST, NOV; DLB 3, 74, 250, 254, 349; EXPN; EXPS; GL 3; LAIT 1, 2; NFS 7, 9; RGAL 4; RGSF 2; SATA 59; SSFS 3; TUS

**Members, Mark**
See Powell, Anthony

**Membreno, Alejandro CLC 59**

**Menand, Louis** 1952- ........................ **CLC 208**
See also CA 200

**Menander** c. 342B.C.-c. 293B.C. .... **CMLC 9, 51, 101; DC 3**
See also AW 1; CDWLB 1; DAM DRAM; DLB 176; LMFS 1; RGWL 2, 3

**Menchu, Rigoberta** 1959- .. **CLC 160; HLCS 2**
See also CA 175; CANR 135; DNFS 1; WLIT 1

**Mencken, H. L.** 1880-1956 ....... **TCLC 13, 18**
See also AMW; CA 105; 125; CDALB 1917-1929; DLB 11, 29, 63, 137, 222; EWL 3; MAL 5; MTCW 1, 2; MTFW 2005; NCFS 4; RGAL 4; TUS

**Mencken, Henry Louis**
See Mencken, H. L.

**Mendelsohn, Jane** 1965- ................... **CLC 99**
See also CA 154; CANR 94

**Mendelssohn, Moses** 1729-1786 ......... **LC 142**
See also DLB 97

**Mendoza, Inigo Lopez de**
See Santillana, Inigo Lopez de Mendoza, Marques de

**Menton, Francisco de**
See Chin, Frank

**Mercer, David** 1928-1980 ................... **CLC 5**
See also CA 9-12R; 102; CANR 23; CBD; DAM DRAM; DLB 13, 310; MTCW 1; RGEL 2

**Merchant, Paul**
See Ellison, Harlan

**Meredith, George** 1828-1909 .. **PC 60; TCLC 17, 43**
See also CA 117; 153; CANR 80; CDBLB 1832-1890; DAM POET; DLB 18, 35, 57, 159; RGEL 2; TEA

**Meredith, William** 1919-2007 ...... **CLC 4, 13, 22, 55; PC 28**
See also CA 9-12R; 260; CAAS 14; CANR 6, 40, 129; CP 1, 2, 3, 4, 5, 6, 7; DAM POET; DLB 5; MAL 5

**Meredith, William Morris**
See Meredith, William

**Merezhkovsky, Dmitrii Sergeevich**
See Merezhkovsky, Dmitry Sergeyevich

**Merezhkovsky, Dmitry Sergeevich**
See Merezhkovsky, Dmitry Sergeyevich

**Merezhkovsky, Dmitry Sergeyevich**
1865-1941 ................................ **TCLC 29**
See also CA 169; DLB 295; EWL 3

**Merezhkovsky, Zinaida**
See Gippius, Zinaida

**Merimee, Prosper** 1803-1870 . **DC 33; NCLC 6, 65; SSC 7, 77**
See also DLB 119, 192; EW 6; EXPS; GFL 1789 to the Present; RGSF 2; RGWL 2, 3; SSFS 8; SUFW

**Merkin, Daphne** 1954- ...................... **CLC 44**
See also CA 123

**Merleau-Ponty, Maurice**
1908-1961 ................................ **TCLC 156**
See also CA 114; 89-92; DLB 296; GFL 1789 to the Present

**Merlin, Arthur**
See Blish, James

**Mernissi, Fatima** 1940- .................... **CLC 171**
See also CA 152; DLB 346; FW

**Merrill, James** 1926-1995 ...... **CLC 2, 3, 6, 8, 13, 18, 34, 91; PC 28; TCLC 173**
See also AMWS 3; CA 13-16R; 147; CANR 10, 49, 63, 108; CP 1, 2, 3, 4; DA3; DAM POET; DLB 5, 165; DLBY 1985; EWL 3; INT CANR-10; MAL 5; MTCW 1, 2; MTFW 2005; PAB; PFS 23; RGAL 4

**Merrill, James Ingram**
See Merrill, James

**Merriman, Alex**
See Silverberg, Robert

**Merriman, Brian** 1747-1805 .......... **NCLC 70**

**Merritt, E. B.**
See Waddington, Miriam

**Merton, Thomas** 1915-1968 ..... **CLC 1, 3, 11, 34, 83; PC 10**
See also AAYA 61; AMWS 8; CA 5-8R; 25-28R; CANR 22, 53, 111, 131; DA3; DLB 48; DLBY 1981; MAL 5; MTCW 1, 2; MTFW 2005

**Merwin, William Stanley**
See Merwin, W.S.

**Merwin, W.S.** 1927- ..... **CLC 1, 2, 3, 5, 8, 13, 18, 45, 88; PC 45**
See also AMWS 3; CA 13-16R; CANR 15, 51, 112, 140; CP 1, 2, 3, 4, 5, 6, 7; DA3; DAM POET; DLB 5, 169, 342; EWL 3; INT CANR-15; MAL 5; MTCW 1, 2; MTFW 2005; PAB; PFS 5, 15; RGAL 4

**Metastasio, Pietro** 1698-1782 ............. **LC 115**
See also RGWL 2, 3

**Metcalf, John** 1938- ............ **CLC 37; SSC 43**
See also CA 113; CN 4, 5, 6, 7; DLB 60; RGSF 2; TWA

**Metcalf, Suzanne**
See Baum, L. Frank

**Mew, Charlotte (Mary)** 1870-1928 .. **TCLC 8**
See also CA 105; 189; DLB 19, 135; RGEL 2

**Mewshaw, Michael** 1943- .................... **CLC 9**
See also CA 53-56; CANR 7, 47, 147; DLBY 1980

**Meyer, Conrad Ferdinand** 1825-1898 .............. **NCLC 81; SSC 30**
See also DLB 129; EW; RGWL 2, 3

**Meyer, Gustav** 1868-1932 .............. **TCLC 21**
See also CA 117; 190; DLB 81; EWL 3

**Meyer, June**
See Jordan, June

**Meyer, Lynn**
See Slavitt, David R.

**Meyer, Stephenie** 1973- .................. **CLC 280**
See also AAYA 77; CA 253; CANR 192; CLR 142; SATA 193

**Meyer-Meyrink, Gustav**
See Meyer, Gustav

**Meyers, Jeffrey** 1939- ........................ **CLC 39**
See also CA 73-76; 186; CAAE 186; CANR 54, 102, 159; DLB 111

**Meynell, Alice (Christina Gertrude Thompson)** 1847-1922 .............. **TCLC 6**
See also CA 104; 177; DLB 19, 98; RGEL 2

**Meyrink, Gustav**
See Meyer, Gustav

**Mhlophe, Gcina** 1960- ...................... **BLC 2:3**

**Michaels, Leonard** 1933-2003 ..... **CLC 6, 25; SSC 16**
See also AMWS 16; CA 61-64; 216; CANR 21, 62, 119, 179; CN 3, 45, 6, 7; DLB 130; MTCW 1; TCLE 1:2

**Michaux, Henri** 1899-1984 .......... **CLC 8, 19**
See also CA 85-88; 114; DLB 258; EWL 3; GFL 1789 to the Present; RGWL 2, 3

**Micheaux, Oscar (Devereaux)** 1884-1951 ................................ **TCLC 76**
See also BW 3; CA 174; DLB 50; TCWW 2

**Michelangelo** 1475-1564 ...................... **LC 12**
See also AAYA 43

**Michelet, Jules** 1798-1874 ...... **NCLC 31, 218**
See also EW 5; GFL 1789 to the Present

**Michels, Robert** 1876-1936 ............. **TCLC 88**
See also CA 212

**Michener, James A.** 1907(?)-1997 . **CLC 1, 5, 11, 29, 60, 109**
See also AAYA 27; AITN 1; BEST 90:1; BPFB 2; CA 5-8R; 161; CANR 21, 45, 68; CN 1, 2, 3, 4, 5, 6; CPW; DA3; DAM NOV, POP; DLB 6; MAL 5; MTCW 1, 2; MTFW 2005; RHW; TCWW 1, 2

**Michener, James Albert**
See Michener, James A.

**Mickiewicz, Adam** 1798-1855 . **NCLC 3, 101; PC 38**
See also EW 5; RGWL 2, 3

**Middleton, (John) Christopher** 1926- .......................................... **CLC 13**
See also CA 13-16R; CANR 29, 54, 117; CP 1, 2, 3, 4, 5, 6, 7; DLB 40

**Middleton, Richard (Barham)** 1882-1911 ................................ **TCLC 56**
See also CA 187; DLB 156; HGG

**Middleton, Stanley** 1919-2009 ...... **CLC 7, 38**
See also CA 25-28R; 288; CAAS 23; CANR 21, 46, 81, 157; CN 1, 2, 3, 4, 5, 6, 7; DLB 14, 326

**Middleton, Thomas** 1580-1627 ...... **DC 5; LC 33, 123**
See also BRW 2; DAM DRAM, MST; DFS 18, 22; DLB 58; RGEL 2

**Mieville, China** 1972(?)- .................. **CLC 235**
See also AAYA 52; CA 196; CANR 138; MTFW 2005

**Migueis, Jose Rodrigues** 1901-1980 . **CLC 10**
See also DLB 287

**Mihura, Miguel** 1905-1977 .................. **DC 34**
See also CA 214

**Mikszath, Kalman** 1847-1910 ........ **TCLC 31**
See also CA 170

**Miles, Jack CLC 100**
See also CA 200

**Miles, John Russiano**
See Miles, Jack

**Miles, Josephine (Louise)** 1911-1985 .............. **CLC 1, 2, 14, 34, 39**
See also CA 1-4R; 116; CANR 2, 55; CP 1, 2, 3, 4; DAM POET; DLB 48; MAL 5; TCLE 1:2

**Militant**
See Sandburg, Carl (August)

**Mill, Harriet (Hardy) Taylor** 1807-1858 ............................. **NCLC 102**
See also FW

**Mill, John Stuart** 1806-1873 ... **NCLC 11, 58, 179, 223**
See also CDBLB 1832-1890; DLB 55, 190, 262; FW 1; RGEL 2; TEA

**Millar, Kenneth** 1915-1983 .. **CLC 1, 2, 3, 14, 34, 41**
See also AAYA 81; AMWS 4; BPFB 2; CA 9-12R; 110; CANR 16, 63, 107; CMW 4; CN 1, 2, 3; CPW; DA3; DAM POP; DLB 2, 226; DLBD 6; DLBY 1983; MAL 5; MSW; MTCW 1, 2; MTFW 2005; RGAL 4

**Millay, E. Vincent**
See Millay, Edna St. Vincent

**Millay, Edna St. Vincent** 1892-1950 ..... **PC 6, 61; TCLC 4, 49, 169; WLCS**
See also AMW; CA 104; 130; CDALB 1917-1929; DA; DA3; DAB; DAC; DAM MST, POET; DLB 45, 249; EWL 3; EXPP; FL 1:6; GLL 1; MAL 5; MBL; MTCW 1, 2; MTFW 2005; PAB; PFS 3, 17, 31; RGAL 4; TUS; WP

**Miller, Arthur** 1915-2005 ..... **CLC 1, 2, 6, 10, 15, 26, 47, 78, 179; DC 1, 31; WLC 4**
See also AAYA 15; AITN 1; AMW; AMWC 1; CA 1-4R; 236; CABS 3; CAD; CANR 2, 30, 54, 76, 132; CD 5, 6; CDALB 1941-1968; DA; DA3; DAB; DAC; DAM DRAM, MST; DFS 1, 3, 8; DLB 7, 266; EWL 3; LAIT 1, 4; LATS 1:2; MAL 5; MTCW 1, 2; MTFW 2005; RGAL 4; RGHL; TUS; WYAS 1

**Miller, Frank** 1957- ........................ **CLC 278**
See also AAYA 45; CA 224

**Miller, Henry (Valentine)** 1891-1980 .... **CLC 1, 2, 4, 9, 14, 43, 84; TCLC 213; WLC 4**
See also AMW; BPFB 2; CA 9-12R; 97-100; CANR 33, 64; CDALB 1929-1941; CN 1, 2; DA; DA3; DAB; DAC; DAM MST, NOV; DLB 4, 9; DLBY 1980; EWL 3; MAL 5; MTCW 1, 2; MTFW 2005; RGAL 4; TUS

**Miller, Hugh** 1802-1856 ................ **NCLC 143**
See also DLB 190

**Miller, Jason** 1939(?)-2001 .................. **CLC 2**
See also AITN 1; CA 73-76; 197; CAD; CANR 130; DFS 12; DLB 7

**Miller, Sue** 1943- ................................ **CLC 44**
See also AMWS 12; BEST 90:3; CA 139; CANR 59, 91, 128, 194; DA3; DAM POP; DLB 143

**Miller, Walter M(ichael, Jr.)** 1923-1996 ............................... **CLC 4, 30**
See also BPFB 2; CA 85-88; CANR 108; DLB 8; SCFW 1, 2; SFW 4

**Millett, Kate** 1934- ............................ **CLC 67**
See also AITN 1; CA 73-76; CANR 32, 53, 76, 110; DA3; DLB 246; FW; GLL 1; MTCW 1, 2; MTFW 2005

**Millhauser, Steven** 1943- ... **CLC 21, 54, 109; SSC 57**
See also AAYA 76; CA 110; 111; CANR 63, 114, 133, 189; CN 6, 7; DA3; DLB 2, 350; FANT; INT CA-111; MAL 5; MTCW 2; MTFW 2005

**Millhauser, Steven Lewis**
See Millhauser, Steven

**Millin, Sarah Gertrude** 1889-1968 ... **CLC 49**
See also CA 102; 93-96; DLB 225; EWL 3

**Milne, A. A.** 1882-1956 ............... **TCLC 6, 88**
See also BRWS 5; CA 104; 133; CLR 1, 26, 108; CMW 4; CWRI 5; DA3; DAB; DAC; DAM MST; DLB 10, 77, 100, 160, 352; FANT; MAICYA 1, 2; MTCW 1, 2; MTFW 2005; RGEL 2; SATA 100; WCH; YABC 1

**Milne, Alan Alexander**
See Milne, A. A.

**Milner, Ron(ald)** 1938-2004 .. **BLC 1:3; CLC 56**
See also AITN 1; BW 1; CA 73-76; 230; CAD; CANR 24, 81; CD 5, 6; DAM MULT; DLB 38; MAL 5; MTCW 1

**Milnes, Richard Monckton** 1809-1885 ............................... **NCLC 61**
See also DLB 32, 184

**Milosz, Czeslaw** 1911-2004 .... **CLC 5, 11, 22, 31, 56, 82, 253; PC 8; WLCS**
See also AAYA 62; CA 81-84; 230; CANR 23, 51, 91, 126; CDWLB 4; CWW 2; DA3; DAM MST, POET; DLB 215, 331; EW 13; EWL 3; MTCW 1, 2; MTFW 2005; PFS 16, 29; RGHL; RGWL 2, 3

**Milton, John** 1608-1674 ..... **LC 9, 43, 92; PC 19, 29; WLC 4**
See also AAYA 65; BRW 2; BRWR 2; CD-BLB 1660-1789; DA; DA3; DAB; DAC; DAM MST, POET; DLB 131, 151, 281;

**Mosher, Howard Frank** 1943- .......... **CLC 62**
  See also CA 139; CANR 65, 115, 181
**Mosley, Nicholas** 1923- ................ **CLC 43, 70**
  See also CA 69-72; CANR 41, 60, 108, 158;
  CN 1, 2, 3, 4, 5, 6, 7; DLB 14, 207
**Mosley, Walter** 1952- ... **BLCS; CLC 97, 184,
  278**
  See also AAYA 57; AMWS 13; BPFB 2;
  BW 2; CA 142; CANR 57, 92, 136, 172;
  CMW 4; CN 7; CPW; DA3; DAM MULT,
  POP; DLB 306; MSW; MTCW 2; MTFW
  2005
**Moss, Howard** 1922-1987 . **CLC 7, 14, 45, 50**
  See also CA 1-4R; 123; CANR 1, 44; CP 1,
  2, 3, 4; DAM POET; DLB 5
**Mossgiel, Rab**
  See Burns, Robert
**Motion, Andrew** 1952- ...................... **CLC 47**
  See also BRWS 7; CA 146; CANR 90, 142;
  CP 4, 5, 6, 7; DLB 40; MTFW 2005
**Motion, Andrew Peter**
  See Motion, Andrew
**Motley, Willard (Francis)**
  1909-1965 ..................................... **CLC 18**
  See also AMWS 17; BW 1; CA 117; 106;
  CANR 88; DLB 76, 143
**Motoori, Noringa** 1730-1801 ........ **NCLC 45**
**Mott, Michael (Charles Alston)**
  1930- ............................................ **CLC 15, 34**
  See also CA 5-8R; CANR 7, 29
**Moulsworth, Martha** 1577-1646 ........ **LC 168**
**Mountain Wolf Woman** 1884-1960 . **CLC 92;
  NNAL**
  See also CA 144; CANR 90
**Moure, Erin** 1955- ............................... **CLC 88**
  See also CA 113; CP 5, 6, 7; CWP; DLB
  60
**Mourning Dove** 1885(?)-1936 ............. **NNAL**
  See also CA 144; CANR 90; DAM MULT;
  DLB 175, 221
**Mowat, Farley** 1921- ............................ **CLC 26**
  See also AAYA 1, 50; BYA 2; CA 1-4R;
  CANR 4, 24, 42, 68, 108; CLR 20; CPW;
  DAC; DAM MST; DLB 68; INT CANR-
  24; JRDA; MAICYA 1, 2; MTCW 1, 2;
  MTFW 2005; SATA 3, 55; YAW
**Mowat, Farley McGill**
  See Mowat, Farley
**Mowatt, Anna Cora** 1819-1870 ..... **NCLC 74**
  See also RGAL 4
**Moye, Guan**
  See Yan, Mo
**Mo Yen**
  See Yan, Mo
**Moyers, Bill** 1934- .............................. **CLC 74**
  See also AITN 2; CA 61-64; CANR 31, 52,
  148
**Mphahlele, Es'kia** 1919-2008 ......... **BLC 1:3;
  CLC 25, 133, 280**
  See also AFW; BW 2, 3; CA 81-84; 278;
  CANR 26, 76; CDWLB 3; CN 4, 5, 6;
  DA3; DAM MULT; DLB 125, 225; EWL
  3; MTCW 2; MTFW 2005; RGSF 2;
  SATA 119; SATA-Obit 198; SSFS 11
**Mphahlele, Ezekiel**
  See Mphahlele, Es'kia
**Mphahlele, Zeke**
  See Mphahlele, Es'kia
**Mqhayi, S(amuel) E(dward) K(rune Loliwe)**
  1875-1945 .............. **BLC 1:3; TCLC 25**
  See also CA 153; CANR 87; DAM MULT
**Mrozek, Slawomir** 1930- ............... **CLC 3, 13**
  See also CA 13-16R; CAAS 10; CANR 29;
  CDWLB 4; CWW 2; DLB 232; EWL 3;
  MTCW 1
**Mrs. Belloc-Lowndes**
  See Lowndes, Marie Adelaide (Belloc)
**Mrs. Fairstar**
  See Horne, Richard Henry Hengist

**M'Taggart, John M'Taggart Ellis**
  See McTaggart, John McTaggart Ellis
**Mtwa, Percy** (?)- ................................. **CLC 47**
  See also CD 6
**Mueller, Lisel** 1924- ........ **CLC 13, 51; PC 33**
  See also CA 93-96; CP 6, 7; DLB 105; PFS
  9, 13
**Muggeridge, Malcolm (Thomas)**
  1903-1990 .............................. **TCLC 120**
  See also AITN 1; CA 101; CANR 33, 63;
  MTCW 1, 2
**Muhammad** 570-632 .......................... **WLCS**
  See also DA; DAB; DAC; DAM MST;
  DLB 311
**Muir, Edwin** 1887-1959 . **PC 49; TCLC 2, 87**
  See also BRWS 6; CA 104; 193; DLB 20,
  100, 191; EWL 3; RGEL 2
**Muir, John** 1838-1914 ..................... **TCLC 28**
  See also AMWS 9; ANW; CA 165; DLB
  186, 275
**Mujica Lainez, Manuel** 1910-1984 ... **CLC 31**
  See also CA 81-84; 112; CANR 32; EWL
  3; HW 1
**Mukherjee, Bharati** 1940- ..... **AAL; CLC 53,
  115, 235; SSC 38**
  See also AAYA 46; BEST 89:2; CA 107,
  232; CAAE 232; CANR 45, 72, 128; CN
  5, 6, 7; DAM NOV; DLB 60, 218, 323;
  DNFS 1, 2; EWL 3; FW; MAL 5; MTCW
  1, 2; MTFW 2005; RGAL 4; RGSF 2;
  SSFS 7, 24; TUS; WWE 1
**Muldoon, Paul** 1951- .......... **CLC 32, 72, 166**
  See also BRWS 4; CA 113; 129; CANR 52,
  91, 176; CP 2, 3, 4, 5, 6, 7; DAM POET;
  DLB 40; INT CA-129; PFS 7, 22; TCLE
  1:2
**Mulisch, Harry (Kurt Victor)**
  1927- ................................ **CLC 42, 270**
  See also CA 9-12R; CANR 6, 26, 56, 110;
  CWW 2; DLB 299; EWL 3
**Mull, Martin** 1943- ........................... **CLC 17**
  See also CA 105
**Muller, Wilhelm NCLC 73**
**Mulock, Dinah Maria**
  See Craik, Dinah Maria (Mulock)
**Multatuli** 1820-1881 ...................... **NCLC 165**
  See also RGWL 2, 3
**Munday, Anthony** 1560-1633 .............. **LC 87**
  See also DLB 62, 172; RGEL 2
**Munford, Robert** 1737(?)-1783 .............. **LC 5**
  See also DLB 31
**Mungo, Raymond** 1946- ................... **CLC 72**
  See also CA 49-52; CANR 2
**Munro, Alice** 1931- .... **CLC 6, 10, 19, 50, 95,
  222; SSC 3, 95; WLCS**
  See also AITN 2; BPFB 2; CA 33-36R;
  CANR 33, 53, 75, 114, 177; CCA 1; CN
  1, 2, 3, 4, 5, 6, 7; DA3; DAC; DAM MST,
  NOV; DLB 53; EWL 3; MTCW 1, 2;
  MTFW 2005; NFS 27; RGEL 2; RGSF 2;
  SATA 29; SSFS 5, 13, 19; TCLE 1:2;
  WWE 1
**Munro, H. H.** 1870-1916 .......... **SSC 12, 115;
  TCLC 3; WLC 5**
  See also AAYA 56; BRWS 6; BYA 11; CA
  104; 130; CANR 104; CDBLB 1890-
  1914; DA; DA3; DAB; DAC; DAM MST,
  NOV; DLB 34, 162; EXPS; LAIT 2;
  MTCW 1, 2; MTFW 2005; RGEL 2;
  SSFS 1, 15; SUFW
**Munro, Hector H.**
  See Munro, H. H.
**Munro, Hector Hugh**
  See Munro, H. H.
**Murakami, Haruki** 1949- ........ **CLC 150, 274**
  See also CA 165; CANR 102, 146; CWW
  2; DLB 182; EWL 3; MJW; RGWL 3;
  SFW 4; SSFS 23

**Murakami Haruki**
  See Murakami, Haruki
**Murasaki, Lady**
  See Murasaki Shikibu
**Murasaki Shikibu** 978(?)-1026(?) .. **CMLC 1,
  79**
  See also EFS 2; LATS 1:1; RGWL 2, 3
**Murdoch, Iris** 1919-1999 .. **CLC 1, 2, 3, 4, 6,
  8, 11, 15, 22, 31, 51; TCLC 171**
  See also BRWS 1; CA 13-16R; 179; CANR
  8, 43, 68, 103, 142; CBD; CDBLB 1960
  to Present; CN 1, 2, 3, 4, 5, 6; CWD;
  DA3; DAB; DAC; DAM MST, NOV;
  DLB 14, 194, 233, 326; EWL 3; INT
  CANR-8; MTCW 1, 2; MTFW 2005; NFS
  18; RGEL 2; TCLE 1:2; TEA; WLIT 4
**Murfree, Mary Noailles** 1850-1922 .. **SSC 22;
  TCLC 135**
  See also CA 122; 176; DLB 12, 74; RGAL
  4
**Murglie**
  See Murnau, F.W.
**Murnau, Friedrich Wilhelm**
  See Murnau, F.W.
**Murnau, F.W.** 1888-1931 ................ **TCLC 53**
  See also CA 112
**Murphy, Richard** 1927- ..................... **CLC 41**
  See also BRWS 5; CA 29-32R; CP 1, 2, 3,
  4, 5, 6, 7; DLB 40; EWL 3
**Murphy, Sylvia** 1937- ........................ **CLC 34**
  See also CA 121
**Murphy, Thomas** 1935- ...................... **CLC 51**
  See also CA 101; DLB 310
**Murphy, Thomas Bernard**
  See Murphy, Thomas
**Murphy, Tom**
  See Murphy, Thomas
**Murray, Albert** 1916- ....... **BLC 2:3; CLC 73**
  See also BW 2; CA 49-52; CANR 26, 52,
  78, 160; CN 7; CSW; DLB 38; MTFW
  2005
**Murray, Albert L.**
  See Murray, Albert
**Murray, Diane Lain Johnson**
  See Johnson, Diane
**Murray, James Augustus Henry**
  1837-1915 .............................. **TCLC 117**
**Murray, Judith Sargent**
  1751-1820 .............................. **NCLC 63**
  See also DLB 37, 200
**Murray, Les** 1938- ........................... **CLC 40**
  See also BRWS 7; CA 21-24R; CANR 11,
  27, 56, 103, 199; CP 1, 2, 3, 4, 5, 6, 7;
  DAM POET; DLB 289; DLBY 2001;
  EWL 3; RGEL 2
**Murray, Leslie Allan**
  See Murray, Les
**Murry, J. Middleton**
  See Murry, John Middleton
**Murry, John Middleton**
  1889-1957 .............................. **TCLC 16**
  See also CA 118; 217; DLB 149
**Musgrave, Susan** 1951- .................. **CLC 13, 54**
  See also CA 69-72; CANR 45, 84, 181;
  CCA 1; CP 2, 3, 4, 5, 6, 7; CWP
**Musil, Robert (Edler von)**
  1880-1942 ... **SSC 18; TCLC 12, 68, 213**
  See also CA 109; CANR 55, 84; CDWLB
  2; DLB 81, 124; EW 9; EWL 3; MTCW
  2; RGSF 2; RGWL 2, 3
**Muske, Carol**
  See Muske-Dukes, Carol
**Muske, Carol Anne**
  See Muske-Dukes, Carol
**Muske-Dukes, Carol** 1945- .............. **CLC 90**
  See also CA 65-68, 203; CAAE 203; CANR
  32, 70, 181; CWP; PFS 24
**Muske-Dukes, Carol Ann**
  See Muske-Dukes, Carol

**Newton, Suzanne** 1936- ..................... **CLC 35**
See also BYA 7; CA 41-44R; CANR 14;
JRDA; SATA 5, 77

**New York Dept. of Ed. CLC 70**

**Nexo, Martin Andersen**
1869-1954 ................................ **TCLC 43**
See also CA 202; DLB 214; EWL 3

**Nezval, Vitezslav** 1900-1958 ........... **TCLC 44**
See also CA 123; CDWLB 4; DLB 215;
EWL 3

**Ng, Fae Myenne** 1956- ....................... **CLC 81**
See also BYA 11; CA 146; CANR 191

**Ngcobo, Lauretta** 1931- .................... **BLC 2:3**
See also CA 165

**Ngema, Mbongeni** 1955- .................. **CLC 57**
See also BW 2; CA 143; CANR 84; CD 5,
6

**Ngugi, James T.**
See Ngugi wa Thiong'o

**Ngugi, James Thiong'o**
See Ngugi wa Thiong'o

**Ngugi wa Thiong'o** 1938- ........ **BLC 1:3, 2:3;**
**CLC 3, 7, 13, 36, 182, 275**
See also AFW; BRWS 8; BW 2; CA 81-84;
CANR 27, 58, 164; CD 3, 4, 5, 6, 7; CD-
WLB 3; CN 1, 2; DAM MULT, NOV;
DLB 125; DNFS 2; EWL 3; MTCW 1, 2;
MTFW 2005; RGEL 2; WWE 1

**Niatum, Duane** 1938- ........................ **NNAL**
See also CA 41-44R; CANR 21, 45, 83;
DLB 175

**Nichol, B(arrie) P(hillip)** 1944-1988 . **CLC 18**
See also CA 53-56; CP 1, 2, 3, 4; DLB 53;
SATA 66

**Nicholas of Autrecourt** c.
1298-1369 ............................. **CMLC 108**

**Nicholas of Cusa** 1401-1464 ................. **LC 80**
See also DLB 115

**Nichols, John** 1940- ........................... **CLC 38**
See also AMWS 13; CA 9-12R, 190; CAAE
190; CAAS 2; CANR 6, 70, 121, 185;
DLBY 1982; LATS 1:2; MTFW 2005;
TCWW 1, 2

**Nichols, Leigh**
See Koontz, Dean

**Nichols, Peter (Richard)** 1927- .... **CLC 5, 36,**
**65**
See also CA 104; CANR 33, 86; CBD; CD
5, 6; DLB 13, 245; MTCW 1

**Nicholson, Linda CLC 65**

**Ni Chuilleanain, Eilean** 1942- .............. **PC 34**
See also CA 126; CANR 53, 83; CP 5, 6, 7;
CWP; DLB 40

**Nicolas, F. R. E.**
See Freeling, Nicolas

**Niedecker, Lorine** 1903-1970 ..... **CLC 10, 42;**
**PC 42**
See also CA 25-28; CAP 2; DAM POET;
DLB 48

**Nietzsche, Friedrich (Wilhelm)**
1844-1900 ................... **TCLC 10, 18, 55**
See also CA 107; 121; CDWLB 2; DLB
129; EW 7; RGWL 2, 3; TWA

**Nievo, Ippolito** 1831-1861 ............... **NCLC 22**

**Nightingale, Anne Redmon** 1943- .... **CLC 22**
See also CA 103; DLBY 1986

**Nightingale, Florence** 1820-1910 ... **TCLC 85**
See also CA 188; DLB 166

**Nijo Yoshimoto** 1320-1388 ............. **CMLC 49**
See also DLB 203

**Nik. T. O.**
See Annensky, Innokenty (Fyodorovich)

**Nin, Anais** 1903-1977 ..... **CLC 1, 4, 8, 11, 14,**
**60, 127; SSC 10; TCLC 224**
See also AITN 2; AMWS 10; BPFB 2; CA
13-16R; 69-72; CANR 22, 53; CN 1, 2;
DAM NOV, POP; DLB 2, 4, 152; EWL
3; GLL 2; MAL 5; MBL; MTCW 1, 2;
MTFW 2005; RGAL 4; RGSF 2

**Nisbet, Robert A(lexander)**
1913-1996 ............................... **TCLC 117**
See also CA 25-28R; 153; CANR 17; INT
CANR-17

**Nishida, Kitaro** 1870-1945 ............. **TCLC 83**

**Nishiwaki, Junzaburo** 1894-1982 ........ **PC 15**
See also CA 194; 107; EWL 3; MJW;
RGWL 3

**Nissenson, Hugh** 1933- ................... **CLC 4, 9**
See also CA 17-20R; CANR 27, 108, 151;
CN 5, 6; DLB 28, 335

**Nister, Der**
See Der Nister

**Niven, Larry** 1938- ............................. **CLC 8**
See also AAYA 27; BPFB 2; BYA 10; CA
21-24R, 207; CAAE 207; CAAS 12;
CANR 14, 44, 66, 113, 155; CPW; DAM
POP; DLB 8; MTCW 1, 2; SATA 95, 171;
SCFW 1, 2; SFW 4

**Niven, Laurence VanCott**
See Niven, Larry

**Nixon, Agnes Eckhardt** 1927- ........... **CLC 21**
See also CA 110

**Nizan, Paul** 1905-1940 .................... **TCLC 40**
See also CA 161; DLB 72; EWL 3; GFL
1789 to the Present

**Nkosi, Lewis** 1936- ........... **BLC 1:3; CLC 45**
See also BW 1, 3; CA 65-68; CANR 27,
81; CBD; CD 5, 6; DAM MULT; DLB
157, 225; WWE 1

**Nodier, (Jean) Charles (Emmanuel)**
1780-1844 ................................ **NCLC 19**
See also DLB 119; GFL 1789 to the Present

**Noguchi, Yone** 1875-1947 ................ **TCLC 80**

**Nolan, Brian**
See O Nuallain, Brian

**Nolan, Christopher** 1965-2009 .......... **CLC 58**
See also CA 111; 283; CANR 88

**Nolan, Christopher John**
See Nolan, Christopher

**Noon, Jeff** 1957- ............................... **CLC 91**
See also CA 148; CANR 83; DLB 267;
SFW 4

**Norden, Charles**
See Durrell, Lawrence (George)

**Nordhoff, Charles Bernard**
1887-1947 ................................ **TCLC 23**
See also CA 108; 211; DLB 9; LAIT 1;
RHW 1; SATA 23

**Norfolk, Lawrence** 1963- ................... **CLC 76**
See also CA 144; CANR 85; CN 6, 7; DLB
267

**Norman, Marsha (Williams)** 1947- . **CLC 28,**
**186; DC 8**
See also CA 105; CABS 3; CAD; CANR
41, 131; CD 5, 6; CSW; CWD; DAM
DRAM; DFS 2; DLB 266; DLBY 1984;
FW; MAL 5

**Normyx**
See Douglas, (George) Norman

**Norris, Frank** 1870-1902 ...... **SSC 28; TCLC**
**24, 155, 211**
See also AAYA 57; AMW; AMWC 2; BPFB
2; CA 110; 160; CDALB 1865-1917; DLB
12, 71, 186; LMFS 2; MAL 5; NFS 12;
RGAL 4; TCWW 1, 2; TUS

**Norris, Kathleen** 1947- .................... **CLC 248**
See also CA 160; CANR 113, 199

**Norris, Leslie** 1921-2006 ................... **CLC 14**
See also CA 11-12; 251; CANR 14, 117;
CAP 1; CP 1, 2, 3, 4, 5, 6, 7; DLB 27,
256

**North, Andrew**
See Norton, Andre

**North, Anthony**
See Koontz, Dean

**North, Captain George**
See Stevenson, Robert Louis (Balfour)

**North, Captain George**
See Stevenson, Robert Louis (Balfour)

**North, Milou**
See Erdrich, Louise

**Northrup, B. A.**
See Hubbard, L. Ron

**North Staffs**
See Hulme, T(homas) E(rnest)

**Northup, Solomon** 1808-1863 ...... **NCLC 105**

**Norton, Alice Mary**
See Norton, Andre

**Norton, Andre** 1912-2005 ................. **CLC 12**
See also AAYA 14; BPFB 2; BYA 4, 10,
12; CA 1-4R; 237; CANR 2, 31, 68, 108,
149; CLR 50; DLB 8, 52; JRDA; MAI-
CYA 1, 2; MTCW 1; SATA 1, 43, 91;
SUFW 1, 2; YAW

**Norton, Caroline** 1808-1877 .. **NCLC 47, 205**
See also DLB 21, 159, 199

**Norway, Nevil Shute** 1899-1960 ....... **CLC 30**
See also BPFB 3; CA 102; 93-96; CANR
85; DLB 255; MTCW 2; NFS 9; RHW 4;
SFW 4

**Norwid, Cyprian Kamil**
1821-1883 ............................... **NCLC 17**
See also RGWL 3

**Nosille, Nabrah**
See Ellison, Harlan

**Nossack, Hans Erich** 1901-1977 ......... **CLC 6**
See also CA 93-96; 85-88; CANR 156;
DLB 69; EWL 3

**Nostradamus** 1503-1566 ...................... **LC 27**

**Nosu, Chuji**
See Ozu, Yasujiro

**Notenburg, Eleanora (Genrikhovna) von**
See Guro, Elena (Genrikhovna)

**Nova, Craig** 1945- ........................ **CLC 7, 31**
See also CA 45-48; CANR 2, 53, 127

**Novak, Joseph**
See Kosinski, Jerzy

**Novalis** 1772-1801 .................. **NCLC 13, 178**
See also CDWLB 2; DLB 90; EW 5; RGWL
2, 3

**Novick, Peter** 1934- .......................... **CLC 164**
See also CA 188

**Novis, Emile**
See Weil, Simone (Adolphine)

**Nowlan, Alden (Albert)** 1933-1983 ... **CLC 15**
See also CA 9-12R; CANR 5; CP 1, 2, 3;
DAC; DAM MST; DLB 53; PFS 12

**Noyes, Alfred** 1880-1958 ...... **PC 27; TCLC 7**
See also CA 104; 188; DLB 20; EXPP;
FANT; PFS 4; RGEL 2

**Nugent, Richard Bruce**
1906(?)-1987 .............................. **HR 1:3**
See also BW 1; CA 125; CANR 198; DLB
51; GLL 2

**Nunez, Elizabeth** 1944- ..................... **BLC 2:3**
See also CA 223

**Nunn, Kem CLC 34**
See also CA 159

**Nussbaum, Martha Craven** 1947- .. **CLC 203**
See also CA 134; CANR 102, 176

**Nwapa, Flora (Nwanzuruaha)**
1931-1993 ................... **BLCS; CLC 133**
See also BW 2; CA 143; CANR 83; CD-
WLB 3; CWRI 5; DLB 125; EWL 3;
WLIT 2

**Nye, Robert** 1939- ........................ **CLC 13, 42**
See also BRWS 10; CA 33-36R; CANR 29,
67, 107; CN 1, 2, 3, 4, 5, 6, 7; CP 1, 2, 3,
4, 5, 6, 7; CWRI 5; DAM NOV; DLB 14,
271; FANT; HGG; MTCW 1; RHW;
SATA 6

**Nyro, Laura** 1947-1997 .................... **CLC 17**
See also CA 194

**O. Henry**
See Henry, O.

**Oates, Joyce Carol** 1938- .. **CLC 1, 2, 3, 6, 9, 11, 15, 19, 33, 52, 108, 134, 228; SSC 6, 70, 121; WLC 4**
See also AAYA 15, 52; AITN 1; AMWS 2; BEST 89:2; BPFB 2; BYA 11; CA 5-8R; CANR 25, 45, 74, 113, 129, 165; CDALB 1968-1988; CN 1, 2, 3, 4, 5, 6, 7; CP 5, 6, 7; CPW; CWP; DA; DA3; DAB; DAC; DAM MST, NOV, POP; DLB 2, 5, 130; DLBY 1981; EWL 3; EXPS; FL 1:6; FW; GL 3; HGG; INT CANR-25; LAIT 4; MAL 5; MBL; MTCW 1, 2; MTFW 2005; NFS 8, 24; RGAL 4; RGSF 2; SATA 159; SSFS 1, 8, 17; SUFW 2; TUS

**O'Brian, E.G.**
See Clarke, Arthur C.

**O'Brian, Patrick** 1914-2000 ............ **CLC 152**
See also AAYA 55; BRWS 12; CA 144; 187; CANR 74; CPW; MTCW 2; MTFW 2005; RHW

**O'Brien, Darcy** 1939-1998 ................. **CLC 11**
See also CA 21-24R; 167; CANR 8, 59

**O'Brien, Edna** 1932- ..... **CLC 3, 5, 8, 13, 36, 65, 116, 237; SSC 10, 77**
See also BRWS 5; CA 1-4R; CANR 6, 41, 65, 102, 169; CDBLB 1960 to Present; CN 1, 2, 3, 4, 5, 6, 7; DA3; DAM NOV; DLB 14, 231, 319; EWL 3; FW; MTCW 1, 2; MTFW 2005; RGSF 2; WLIT 4

**O'Brien, E.G.**
See Clarke, Arthur C.

**O'Brien, Fitz-James** 1828-1862 ..... **NCLC 21**
See also DLB 74; RGAL 4; SUFW

**O'Brien, Flann**
See O Nuallain, Brian

**O'Brien, Richard** 1942- .................... **CLC 17**
See also CA 124

**O'Brien, Tim** 1946- ........ **CLC 7, 19, 40, 103, 211; SSC 74, 123**
See also AAYA 16; AMWS 5; CA 85-88; CANR 40, 58, 133; CDALBS; CN 5, 6, 7; CPW; DA3; DAM POP; DLB 152; DLBD 9; DLBY 1980; LATS 1:2; MAL 5; MTCW 2; MTFW 2005; RGAL 4; SSFS 5, 15; TCLE 1:2

**O'Brien, William Timothy**
See O'Brien, Tim

**Obstfelder, Sigbjorn** 1866-1900 ..... **TCLC 23**
See also CA 123; DLB 354

**O'Casey, Brenda**
See Haycraft, Anna

**O'Casey, Sean** 1880-1964 .... **CLC 1, 5, 9, 11, 15, 88; DC 12; WLCS**
See also BRW 7; CA 89-92; CANR 62; CBD; CDBLB 1914-1945; DA3; DAB; DAC; DAM DRAM, MST; DFS 19; DLB 10; EWL 3; MTCW 1, 2; MTFW 2005; RGEL 2; TEA; WLIT 4

**O'Cathasaigh, Sean**
See O'Casey, Sean

**Occom, Samson** 1723-1792 .... **LC 60; NNAL**
See also DLB 175

**Occomy, Marita (Odette) Bonner** 1899(?)-1971 ..... **HR 1:2; PC 72; TCLC 179**
See also BW 2; CA 142; DFS 13; DLB 51, 228

**Ochs, Phil(ip David)** 1940-1976 ........ **CLC 17**
See also CA 185; 65-68

**O'Connor, Edwin (Greene)** 1918-1968 ................................. **CLC 14**
See also CA 93-96; 25-28R; MAL 5

**O'Connor, Flannery** 1925-1964 ..... **CLC 1, 2, 3, 6, 10, 13, 15, 21, 66, 104; SSC 1, 23, 61, 82, 111; TCLC 132; WLC 4**
See also AAYA 7; AMW; AMWR 2; BPFB 3; BYA 16; CA 1-4R; CANR 3, 41; CDALB 1941-1968; DA; DA3; DAB; DAC; DAM MST, NOV; DLB 2, 152; DLBD 12; DLBY 1980; EWL 3; EXPS;

LAIT 5; MAL 5; MBL; MTCW 1, 2; MTFW 2005; NFS 3, 21; RGAL 4; RGSF 2; SSFS 2, 7, 10, 19; TUS

**O'Connor, Frank** 1903-1966
See O'Donovan, Michael Francis

**O'Dell, Scott** 1898-1989 .................... **CLC 30**
See also AAYA 3, 44; BPFB 3; BYA 1, 2, 3, 5; CA 61-64; 129; CANR 12, 30, 112; CLR 1, 16, 126; DLB 52; JRDA; MAICYA 1, 2; SATA 12, 60, 134; WYA; YAW

**Odets, Clifford** 1906-1963 ..... **CLC 2, 28, 98; DC 6**
See also AMWS 2; CA 85-88; CAD; CANR 62; DAM DRAM; DFS 3, 17, 20; DLB 7, 26, 341; EWL 3; MAL 5; MTCW 1, 2; MTFW 2005; RGAL 4; TUS

**O'Doherty, Brian** 1928- ..................... **CLC 76**
See also CA 105; CANR 108

**O'Donnell, K. M.**
See Malzberg, Barry N(athaniel)

**O'Donnell, Lawrence**
See Kuttner, Henry

**O'Donovan, Michael Francis** 1903-1966 ....... **CLC 14, 23; SSC 5, 109**
See also BRWS 14; CA 93-96; CANR 84; DLB 162; EWL 3; RGSF 2; SSFS 5

**Oe, Kenzaburo** 1935- .. **CLC 10, 36, 86, 187; SSC 20**
See also CA 97-100; CANR 36, 50, 74, 126; CWW 2; DA3; DAM NOV; DLB 182, 331; DLBY 1994; EWL 3; LATS 1:2; MJW; MTCW 1, 2; MTFW 2005; RGSF 2; RGWL 2, 3

**Oe Kenzaburo**
See Oe, Kenzaburo

**O'Faolain, Julia** 1932- .... **CLC 6, 19, 47, 108**
See also CA 81-84; CAAS 2; CANR 12, 61; CN 2, 3, 4, 5, 6, 7; DLB 14, 231, 319; FW; MTCW 1; RHW

**O'Faolain, Sean** 1900-1991 ...... **CLC 1, 7, 14, 32, 70; SSC 13; TCLC 143**
See also CA 61-64; 134; CANR 12, 66; CN 1, 2, 3, 4; DLB 15, 162; MTCW 1, 2; MTFW 2005; RGEL 2; RGSF 2

**O'Flaherty, Liam** 1896-1984 ....... **CLC 5, 34; SSC 6, 116**
See also CA 101; 113; CANR 35; CN 1, 2, 3; DLB 36, 162; DLBY 1984; MTCW 1, 2; MTFW 2005; RGEL 2; RGSF 2; SSFS 5, 20

**Ogai**
See Mori Ogai

**Ogilvy, Gavin**
See Barrie, J(ames) M(atthew)

**O'Grady, Standish (James)** 1846-1928 .................................. **TCLC 5**
See also CA 104; 157

**O'Grady, Timothy** 1951- ................... **CLC 59**
See also CA 138

**O'Hara, Frank** 1926-1966 ....... **CLC 2, 5, 13, 78; PC 45**
See also CA 9-12R; 25-28R; CANR 33; DA3; DAM POET; DLB 5, 16, 193; EWL 3; MAL 5; MTCW 1, 2; MTFW 2005; PFS 8, 12; RGAL 4; WP

**O'Hara, John** 1905-1970 . **CLC 1, 2, 3, 6, 11, 42; SSC 15**
See also AMW; BPFB 3; CA 5-8R; 25-28R; CANR 31, 60; CDALB 1929-1941; DAM NOV; DLB 9, 86, 324; DLBD 2; EWL 3; MAL 5; MTCW 1, 2; MTFW 2005; NFS 11; RGAL 4; RGSF 2

**O'Hehir, Diana** 1929- ........................ **CLC 41**
See also CA 245; CANR 177

**O'Hehir, Diana F.**
See O'Hehir, Diana

**Ohiyesa**
See Eastman, Charles A(lexander)

**Okada, John** 1923-1971 ......................... **AAL**
See also BYA 14; CA 212; DLB 312; NFS 25

**Okigbo, Christopher** 1930-1967 ..... **BLC 1:3; CLC 25, 84; PC 7; TCLC 171**
See also AFW; BW 1, 3; CA 77-80; CANR 74; CDWLB 3; DAM MULT, POET; DLB 125; EWL 3; MTCW 1, 2; MTFW 2005; RGEL 2

**Okigbo, Christopher Ifenayichukwu**
See Okigbo, Christopher

**Okri, Ben** 1959- ....... **BLC 2:3; CLC 87, 223; SSC 127**
See also AFW; BRWS 5; BW 2, 3; CA 130; 138; CANR 65, 128; CN 5, 6, 7; DLB 157, 231, 319, 326; EWL 3; INT CA-138; MTCW 2; MTFW 2005; RGSF 2; SSFS 20; WLIT 2; WWE 1

**Old Boy**
See Hughes, Thomas

**Olds, Sharon** 1942- ...... **CLC 32, 39, 85; PC 22**
See also AMWS 10; CA 101; CANR 18, 41, 66, 98, 135; CP 5, 6, 7; CPW; CWP; DAM POET; DLB 120; MAL 5; MTCW 2; MTFW 2005; PFS 17

**Oldstyle, Jonathan**
See Irving, Washington

**Olesha, Iurii**
See Olesha, Yuri (Karlovich)

**Olesha, Iurii Karlovich**
See Olesha, Yuri (Karlovich)

**Olesha, Yuri (Karlovich)** 1899-1960 . **CLC 8; SSC 69; TCLC 136**
See also CA 85-88; DLB 272; EW 11; EWL 3; RGWL 2, 3

**Olesha, Yury Karlovich**
See Olesha, Yuri (Karlovich)

**Oliphant, Mrs.**
See Oliphant, Margaret (Oliphant Wilson)

**Oliphant, Laurence** 1829(?)-1888 .. **NCLC 47**
See also DLB 18, 166

**Oliphant, Margaret (Oliphant Wilson)** 1828-1897 ... **NCLC 11, 61, 221; SSC 25**
See also BRWS 10; DLB 18, 159, 190; HGG; RGEL 2; RGSF 2; SUFW

**Oliver, Mary** 1935- ... **CLC 19, 34, 98; PC 75**
See also AMWS 7; CA 21-24R; CANR 9, 43, 84, 92, 138; CP 4, 5, 6, 7; CWP; DLB 5, 193, 342; EWL 3; MTFW 2005; PFS 15, 31

**Olivi, Peter** 1248-1298 ................. **CMLC 114**

**Olivier, Laurence (Kerr)** 1907-1989 . **CLC 20**
See also CA 111; 150; 129

**O.L.S.**
See Russell, George William

**Olsen, Tillie** 1912-2007 ........ **CLC 4, 13, 114; SSC 11, 103**
See also AAYA 51; AMWS 13; BYA 11; CA 1-4R; 256; CANR 1, 43, 74, 132; CDALBS; CN 2, 3, 4, 5, 6, 7; DA3; DAB; DAC; DAM MST; DLB 28, 206; DLBY 1980; EWL 3; EXPS; FW; MAL 5; MTCW 1, 2; MTFW 2005; RGAL 4; RGSF 2; SSFS 1; TCLE 1:2; TCWW 2; TUS

**Olson, Charles (John)** 1910-1970 .. **CLC 1, 2, 5, 6, 9, 11, 29; PC 19**
See also AMWS 2; CA 13-16; 25-28R; CABS 2; CANR 35; CAP 1; CP 1; DAM POET; DLB 5, 16, 193; EWL 3; MAL 5; MTCW 1, 2; RGAL 4; WP

**Olson, Merle Theodore**
See Olson, Toby

**Olson, Toby** 1937- ............................. **CLC 28**
See also CA 65-68; CAAS 11; CANR 9, 31, 84, 175; CP 3, 4, 5, 6, 7

**Olyesha, Yuri**
See Olesha, Yuri (Karlovich)

Olympiodorus of Thebes c. 375-c.
430 ............................................. **CMLC 59**
Omar Khayyam
See Khayyam, Omar
Ondaatje, Michael 1943- ..... **CLC 14, 29, 51,
76, 180, 258; PC 28**
See also AAYA 66; CA 77-80; CANR 42,
74, 109, 133, 172; CN 5, 6, 7; CP 1, 2, 3,
4, 5, 6, 7; DA3; DAB; DAC; DAM MST;
DLB 60, 323, 326; EWL 3; LATS 1:2;
LMFS 2; MTCW 2; MTFW 2005; NFS
23; PFS 8, 19; TCLE 1:2; TWA; WWE 1
Ondaatje, Philip Michael
See Ondaatje, Michael
Oneal, Elizabeth 1934- ...................... **CLC 30**
See also AAYA 5, 41; BYA 13; CA 106;
CANR 28, 84; CLR 13; JRDA; MAICYA
1, 2; SATA 30, 82; WYA; YAW
Oneal, Zibby
See Oneal, Elizabeth
O'Neill, Eugene (Gladstone)
1888-1953 ... **DC 20; TCLC 1, 6, 27, 49,
225; WLC 4**
See also AAYA 54; AITN 1; AMW; AMWC
1; CA 110; 132; CAD; CANR 131;
CDALB 1929-1941; DA; DA3; DAB;
DAC; DAM DRAM, MST; DFS 2, 4, 5,
6, 9, 11, 12, 16, 20, 26; DLB 7, 331; EWL
3; LAIT 3; LMFS 2; MAL 5; MTCW 1,
2; MTFW 2005; RGAL 4; TUS
Onetti, Juan Carlos 1909-1994 ... **CLC 7, 10;
HLCS 2; SSC 23; TCLC 131**
See also CA 85-88; 145; CANR 32, 63; CD-
WLB 3; CWW 2; DAM MULT, NOV;
DLB 113; EWL 3; HW 1, 2; LAW;
MTCW 1, 2; MTFW 2005; RGSF 2
O'Nolan, Brian
See O Nuallain, Brian
O Nuallain, Brian 1911-1966 .... **CLC 1, 4, 5,
7, 10, 47**
See also BRWS 2; CA 21-22; 25-28R; CAP
2; DLB 231; EWL 3; FANT; RGEL 2;
TEA
Ophuls, Max
See Ophuls, Max
Ophuls, Max 1902-1957 .................. **TCLC 79**
See also CA 113
Opie, Amelia 1769-1853 .................. **NCLC 65**
See also DLB 116, 159; RGEL 2
Oppen, George 1908-1984 ..... **CLC 7, 13, 34;
PC 35; TCLC 107**
See also CA 13-16R; 113; CANR 8, 82; CP
1, 2, 3; DLB 5, 165
Oppenheim, E(dward) Phillips
1866-1946 ............................... **TCLC 45**
See also CA 111; 202; CMW 4; DLB 70
Oppenheimer, Max
See Ophuls, Max
Opuls, Max
See Ophuls, Max
Orage, A(lfred) R(ichard)
1873-1934 ............................... **TCLC 157**
See also CA 122
Origen c. 185-c. 254 ....................... **CMLC 19**
Orlovitz, Gil 1918-1973 .................... **CLC 22**
See also CA 77-80; 45-48; CN 1; CP 1, 2;
DLB 2, 5
Orosius c. 385-c. 420 .................... **CMLC 100**
O'Rourke, Patrick Jake
See O'Rourke, P.J.
O'Rourke, P.J. 1947- ....................... **CLC 209**
See also CA 77-80; CANR 13, 41, 67, 111,
155; CPW; DAM POP; DLB 185
Orris
See Ingelow, Jean

Ortega y Gasset, Jose 1883-1955 ...... **HLC 2;
TCLC 9**
See also CA 106; 130; DAM MULT; EW 9;
EWL 3; HW 1, 2; MTCW 1, 2; MTFW
2005
Ortese, Anna Maria 1914-1998 ........ **CLC 89**
See also DLB 177; EWL 3
Ortiz, Simon
See Ortiz, Simon J.
Ortiz, Simon J. 1941- . **CLC 45, 208; NNAL;
PC 17**
See also AMWS 4; CA 134; CANR 69, 118,
164; CP 3, 4, 5, 6, 7; DAM MULT, POET;
DLB 120, 175, 256, 342; EXPP; MAL 5;
PFS 4, 16; RGAL 4; SSFS 22; TCWW 2
Ortiz, Simon Joseph
See Ortiz, Simon J.
Orton, Joe
See Orton, John Kingsley
Orton, John Kingsley 1933-1967 ....... **CLC 4,
13, 43; DC 3; TCLC 157**
See also BRWS 5; CA 85-88; CANR 35,
66; CBD; CDBLB 1960 to Present; DAM
DRAM; DFS 3, 6; DLB 13, 310; GLL 1;
MTCW 1, 2; MTFW 2005; RGEL 2;
TEA; WLIT 4
Orwell, George
See Blair, Eric
Osborne, David
See Silverberg, Robert
Osborne, Dorothy 1627-1695 ............. **LC 141**
Osborne, George
See Silverberg, Robert
Osborne, John 1929-1994 .... **CLC 1, 2, 5, 11,
45; TCLC 153; WLC 4**
See also BRWS 1; CA 13-16R; 147; CANR
21, 56; CBD; CDBLB 1945-1960; DA;
DAB; DAC; DAM DRAM, MST; DFS 4,
19, 24; DLB 13; EWL 3; MTCW 1, 2;
MTFW 2005; RGEL 2
Osborne, Lawrence 1958- ................. **CLC 50**
See also CA 189; CANR 152
Osbourne, Lloyd 1868-1947 ........... **TCLC 93**
Osceola
See Blixen, Karen
Osgood, Frances Sargent
1811-1850 ............................... **NCLC 141**
See also DLB 250
Oshima, Nagisa 1932- ...................... **CLC 20**
See also CA 116; 121; CANR 78
Oskison, John Milton
1874-1947 ................... **NNAL; TCLC 35**
See also CA 144; CANR 84; DAM MULT;
DLB 175
Ossoli, Sarah Margaret
See Fuller, Margaret
Ossoli, Sarah Margaret Fuller
See Fuller, Margaret
Ostriker, Alicia 1937- ..................... **CLC 132**
See also CA 25-28R; CAAS 24; CANR 10,
30, 62, 99, 167; CWP; DLB 120; EXPP;
PFS 19, 26
Ostriker, Alicia Suskin
See Ostriker, Alicia
Ostrovsky, Aleksandr Nikolaevich
See Ostrovsky, Alexander
Ostrovsky, Alexander 1823-1886 .. **NCLC 30,
57**
See also DLB 277
Osundare, Niyi 1947- ....................... **BLC 2:3**
See also AFW; BW 3; CA 176; CDWLB 3;
CP 7; DLB 157
Otero, Blas de 1916-1979 ................. **CLC 11**
See also CA 89-92; DLB 134; EWL 3
O'Trigger, Sir Lucius
See Horne, Richard Henry Hengist
Otto, Rudolf 1869-1937 .................. **TCLC 85**
Otto, Whitney 1955- ......................... **CLC 70**
See also CA 140; CANR 120

Otway, Thomas 1652-1685 .. **DC 24; LC 106,
170**
See also DAM DRAM; DLB 80; RGEL 2
Ouida
See De La Ramee, Marie Louise
Ouologuem, Yambo 1940- ............... **CLC 146**
See also CA 111; 176
Ousmane, Sembene 1923-2007 ....... **BLC 1:3,
2:3; CLC 66**
See also AFW; BW 1, 3; CA 117; 125; 261;
CANR 81; CWW 2; EWL 3; MTCW 1;
WLIT 2
Ovid 43B.C.-17 ............. **CMLC 7, 108; PC 2**
See also AW 2; CDWLB 1; DA3; DAM
POET; DLB 211; PFS 22; RGWL 2, 3;
WLIT 8; WP
Owen, Hugh
See Faust, Frederick
Owen, Wilfred (Edward Salter)
1893-1918 ..... **PC 19, 102; TCLC 5, 27;
WLC 4**
See also BRW 6; CA 104; 141; CDBLB
1914-1945; DA; DAB; DAC; DAM MST,
POET; DLB 20; EWL 3; EXPP; MTCW
2; MTFW 2005; PFS 10; RGEL 2; WLIT
4
Owens, Louis (Dean) 1948-2002 ........ **NNAL**
See also CA 137, 179; 207; CAAE 179;
CAAS 24; CANR 71
Owens, Rochelle 1936- ........................ **CLC 8**
See also CA 17-20R; CAAS 2; CAD;
CANR 39; CD 5, 6; CP 1, 2, 3, 4, 5, 6, 7;
CWD; CWP
Oz, Amos 1939- ...... **CLC 5, 8, 11, 27, 33, 54;
SSC 66**
See also CA 53-56; CANR 27, 47, 65, 113,
138, 175; CWW 2; DAM NOV; EWL 3;
MTCW 1, 2; MTFW 2005; RGHL; RGSF
2; RGWL 3; WLIT 6
Ozick, Cynthia 1928- . **CLC 3, 7, 28, 62, 155,
262; SSC 15, 60, 123**
See also AMWS 5; BEST 90:1; CA 17-20R;
CANR 23, 58, 116, 160, 187; CN 3, 4, 5,
6, 7; CPW; DA3; DAM NOV, POP; DLB
28, 152, 299; DLBY 1982; EWL 3; EXPS;
INT CANR-23; MAL 5; MTCW 1, 2;
MTFW 2005; RGAL 4; RGHL; RGSF 2;
SSFS 3, 12, 22
Ozu, Yasujiro 1903-1963 .................. **CLC 16**
See also CA 112
Pabst, G. W. 1885-1967 ................. **TCLC 127**
Pacheco, C.
See Pessoa, Fernando
Pacheco, Jose Emilio 1939- ................. **HLC 2**
See also CA 111; 131; CANR 65; CWW 2;
DAM MULT; DLB 290; EWL 3; HW 1,
2; RGSF 2
Pa Chin
See Jin, Ba
Pack, Robert 1929- ........................... **CLC 13**
See also CA 1-4R; CANR 3, 44, 82; CP 1,
2, 3, 4, 5, 6, 7; DLB 5; SATA 118
Packer, Vin
See Meaker, Marijane
Padgett, Lewis
See Kuttner, Henry
Padilla (Lorenzo), Heberto
1932-2000 ............................... **CLC 38**
See also AITN 1; CA 123; 131; 189; CWW
2; EWL 3; HW 1
Paerdurabo, Frater
See Crowley, Edward Alexander
Page, James Patrick 1944- ............... **CLC 12**
See also CA 204
Page, Jimmy 1944-
See Page, James Patrick
Page, Louise 1955- ........................... **CLC 40**
See also CA 140; CANR 76; CBD; CD 5,
6; CWD; DLB 233

**Rojas, Fernando de** 1475-1541 ... **HLCS 1, 2;
LC 23, 169**
See also DLB 286; RGWL 2, 3
**Rojas, Gonzalo** 1917- ........................ **HLCS 2**
See also CA 178; HW 2; LAWS 1
**Rolaag, Ole Edvart**
See Rolvaag, O.E.
**Roland (de la Platiere), Marie-Jeanne**
1754-1793 ....................................... **LC 98**
See also DLB 314
**Rolfe, Frederick (William Serafino Austin
Lewis Mary)** 1860-1913 ......... **TCLC 12**
See also CA 107; 210; DLB 34, 156; GLL
1; RGEL 2
**Rolland, Romain** 1866-1944 .......... **TCLC 23**
See also CA 118; 197; DLB 65, 284, 332;
EWL 3; GFL 1789 to the Present; RGWL
2, 3
**Rolle, Richard** c. 1300-c. 1349 ...... **CMLC 21**
See also DLB 146; LMFS 1; RGEL 2
**Rolvaag, O.E.**
See Rolvaag, O.E.
**Rolvaag, O.E.**
See Rolvaag, O.E.
**Rolvaag, O.E.** 1876-1931 ........ **TCLC 17, 207**
See also AAYA 75; CA 117; 171; DLB 9,
212; MAL 5; NFS 5; RGAL 4; TCWW 1,
2
**Romain Arnaud, Saint**
See Aragon, Louis
**Romains, Jules** 1885-1972 ................... **CLC 7**
See also CA 85-88; CANR 34; DLB 65,
321; EWL 3; GFL 1789 to the Present;
MTCW 1
**Romero, Jose Ruben** 1890-1952 .... **TCLC 14**
See also CA 114; 131; EWL 3; HW 1; LAW
**Ronsard, Pierre de** 1524-1585 . **LC 6, 54; PC
11**
See also DLB 327; EW 2; GFL Beginnings
to 1789; RGWL 2, 3; TWA
**Rooke, Leon** 1934- ........................ **CLC 25, 34**
See also CA 25-28R; CANR 23, 53; CCA
1; CPW; DAM POP
**Roosevelt, Franklin Delano**
1882-1945 ................................. **TCLC 93**
See also CA 116; 173; LAIT 3
**Roosevelt, Theodore** 1858-1919 ..... **TCLC 69**
See also CA 115; 170; DLB 47, 186, 275
**Roper, Margaret** c. 1505-1544 ........... **LC 147**
**Roper, William** 1498-1578 .................... **LC 10**
**Roquelaure, A. N.**
See Rice, Anne
**Rosa, Joao Guimaraes** 1908-1967
See Guimaraes Rosa, Joao
**Rose, Wendy** 1948- . **CLC 85; NNAL; PC 13**
See also CA 53-56; CANR 5, 51; CWP;
DAM MULT; DLB 175; PFS 13; RGAL
4; SATA 12
**Rosen, R.D.** 1949- .............................. **CLC 39**
See also CA 77-80; CANR 62, 120, 175;
CMW 4; INT CANR-30
**Rosen, Richard**
See Rosen, R.D.
**Rosen, Richard Dean**
See Rosen, R.D.
**Rosenberg, Isaac** 1890-1918 .......... **TCLC 12**
See also BRW 6; CA 107; 188; DLB 20,
216; EWL 3; PAB; RGEL 2
**Rosenblatt, Joe**
See Rosenblatt, Joseph
**Rosenblatt, Joseph** 1933- ................... **CLC 15**
See also CA 89-92; CP 3, 4, 5, 6, 7; INT
CA-89-92
**Rosenfeld, Samuel**
See Tzara, Tristan
**Rosenstock, Sami**
See Tzara, Tristan

**Rosenstock, Samuel**
See Tzara, Tristan
**Rosenthal, M(acha) L(ouis)**
1917-1996 .................................. **CLC 28**
See also CA 1-4R; 152; CAAS 6; CANR 4,
51; CP 1, 2, 3, 4, 5, 6; DLB 5; SATA 59
**Ross, Barnaby**
See Dannay, Frederic; Lee, Manfred B.
**Ross, Bernard L.**
See Follett, Ken
**Ross, J. H.**
See Lawrence, T. E.
**Ross, John Hume**
See Lawrence, T. E.
**Ross, Martin** 1862-1915
See Martin, Violet Florence
See also DLB 135; GLL 2; RGEL 2; RGSF
2
**Ross, (James) Sinclair** 1908-1996 ... **CLC 13;
SSC 24**
See also CA 73-76; CANR 81; CN 1, 2, 3,
4, 5, 6; DAC; DAM MST; DLB 88;
RGEL 2; RGSF 2; TCWW 1, 2
**Rossetti, Christina** 1830-1894 ... **NCLC 2, 50,
66, 186; PC 7; WLC 5**
See also AAYA 51; BRW 5; BYA 4; CLR
115; DA; DA3; DAB; DAC; DAM MST,
POET; DLB 35, 163, 240; EXPP; FL 1:3;
LATS 1:1; MAICYA 1, 2; PFS 10, 14, 27;
RGEL 2; SATA 20; TEA; WCH
**Rossetti, Christina Georgina**
See Rossetti, Christina
**Rossetti, Dante Gabriel** 1828-1882 . **NCLC 4,
77; PC 44; WLC 5**
See also AAYA 51; BRW 5; CDBLB 1832-
1890; DA; DAB; DAC; DAM MST,
POET; DLB 35; EXPP; RGEL 2; TEA
**Rossi, Cristina Peri**
See Peri Rossi, Cristina
**Rossi, Jean-Baptiste** 1931-2003 ........ **CLC 90**
See also CA 201; 215; CMW 4; NFS 18
**Rossner, Judith** 1935-2005 ........ **CLC 6, 9, 29**
See also AITN 2; BEST 90:3; BPFB 3; CA
17-20R; 242; CANR 18, 51, 73; CN 4, 5,
6, 7; DLB 6; INT CANR-18; MAL 5;
MTCW 1, 2; MTFW 2005
**Rossner, Judith Perelman**
See Rossner, Judith
**Rostand, Edmond (Eugene Alexis)**
1868-1918 ............... **DC 10; TCLC 6, 37**
See also CA 104; 126; DA; DA3; DAB;
DAC; DAM DRAM, MST; DFS 1; DLB
192; LAIT 1; MTCW 1; RGWL 2, 3;
TWA
**Roth, Henry** 1906-1995 ..... **CLC 2, 6, 11, 104**
See also AMWS 9; CA 11-12; 149; CANR
38, 63; CAP 1; CN 1, 2, 3, 4, 5, 6; DA3;
DLB 28; EWL 3; MAL 5; MTCW 1, 2;
MTFW 2005; RGAL 4
**Roth, (Moses) Joseph** 1894-1939 ... **TCLC 33**
See also CA 160; DLB 85; EWL 3; RGWL
2, 3
**Roth, Philip** 1933- ... **CLC 1, 2, 3, 4, 6, 9, 15,
22, 31, 47, 66, 86, 119, 201; SSC 26,
102; WLC 5**
See also AAYA 67; AMWR 2; AMWS 3;
BEST 90:3; BPFB 3; CA 1-4R; CANR 1,
22, 36, 55, 89, 132, 170; CDALB 1968-
1988; CN 3, 4, 5, 6, 7; CPW 1; DA; DA3;
DAB; DAC; DAM MST, NOV, POP;
DLB 2, 28, 173; DLBY 1982; EWL 3;
MAL 5; MTCW 1, 2; MTFW 2005; NFS
25; RGAL 4; RGHL; RGSF 2; SSFS 12,
18; TUS
**Roth, Philip Milton**
See Roth, Philip

**Rothenberg, Jerome** 1931- ............ **CLC 6, 57**
See also CA 45-48; CANR 1, 106; CP 1, 2,
3, 4, 5, 6, 7; DLB 5, 193
**Rotter, Pat** **CLC 65**
**Roumain, Jacques (Jean Baptiste)**
1907-1944 ............... **BLC 1:3; TCLC 19**
See also BW 1; CA 117; 125; DAM MULT;
EWL 3
**Rourke, Constance Mayfield**
1885-1941 .................................. **TCLC 12**
See also CA 107; 200; MAL 5; YABC 1
**Rousseau, Jean-Baptiste** 1671-1741 ...... **LC 9**
**Rousseau, Jean-Jacques** 1712-1778 .... **LC 14,
36, 122; WLC 5**
See also DA; DA3; DAB; DAC; DAM
MST; DLB 314; EW 4; GFL Beginnings
to 1789; LMFS 1; RGWL 2, 3; TWA
**Roussel, Raymond** 1877-1933 ........ **TCLC 20**
See also CA 117; 201; EWL 3; GFL 1789
to the Present
**Rovit, Earl (Herbert)** 1927- ................ **CLC 7**
See also CA 5-8R; CANR 12
**Rowe, Elizabeth Singer** 1674-1737 ..... **LC 44**
See also DLB 39, 95
**Rowe, Nicholas** 1674-1718 .................... **LC 8**
See also DLB 84; RGEL 2
**Rowlandson, Mary** 1637(?)-1678 ........ **LC 66**
See also DLB 24, 200; RGAL 4
**Rowley, Ames Dorrance**
See Lovecraft, H. P.
**Rowley, William** 1585(?)-1626 ... **LC 100, 123**
See also DFS 22; DLB 58; RGEL 2
**Rowling, J.K.** 1965- ................ **CLC 137, 217**
See also AAYA 34; BYA 11, 13, 14; CA
173; CANR 128, 157; CLR 66, 80, 112;
MAICYA 2; MTFW 2005; SATA 109,
174; SUFW 2
**Rowling, Joanne Kathleen**
See Rowling, J.K.
**Rowson, Susanna Haswell**
1762(?)-1824 ............... **NCLC 5, 69, 182**
See also AMWS 15; DLB 37, 200; RGAL 4
**Roy, Arundhati** 1960(?)- .......... **CLC 109, 210**
See also CA 163; CANR 90, 126; CN 7;
DLB 323, 326; DLBY 1997; EWL 3;
LATS 1:2; MTFW 2005; NFS 22; WWE
1
**Roy, Gabrielle** 1909-1983 ............ **CLC 10, 14**
See also CA 53-56; 110; CANR 5, 61; CCA
1; DAB; DAC; DAM MST; DLB 68;
EWL 3; MTCW 1; RGWL 2, 3; SATA
104; TCLE 1:2
**Royko, Mike** 1932-1997 ................... **CLC 109**
See also CA 89-92; 157; CANR 26, 111;
CPW
**Rozanov, Vasilii Vasil'evich**
See Rozanov, Vassili
**Rozanov, Vasily Vasilyevich**
See Rozanov, Vassili
**Rozanov, Vassili** 1856-1919 .......... **TCLC 104**
See also DLB 295; EWL 3
**Rozewicz, Tadeusz** 1921- ...... **CLC 9, 23, 139**
See also CA 108; CANR 36, 66; CWW 2;
DA3; DAM POET; DLB 232; EWL 3;
MTCW 1, 2; MTFW 2005; RGHL;
RGWL 3
**Ruark, Gibbons** 1941- ........................ **CLC 3**
See also CA 33-36R; CAAS 23; CANR 14,
31, 57; DLB 120
**Rubens, Bernice (Ruth)** 1923-2004 . **CLC 19,
31**
See also CA 25-28R; 232; CANR 33, 65,
128; CN 1, 2, 3, 4, 5, 6, 7; DLB 14, 207,
326; MTCW 1
**Rubin, Harold**
See Robbins, Harold
**Rudkin, (James) David** 1936- .......... **CLC 14**
See also CA 89-92; CBD; CD 5, 6; DLB 13

**Saintsbury, George (Edward Bateman)**
  1845-1933 ................................. **TCLC 31**
    See also CA 160; DLB 57, 149
**Sait Faik**
    See Abasiyanik, Sait Faik
**Saki**
    See Munro, H. H.
**Sala, George Augustus** 1828-1895 . **NCLC 46**
**Saladin** 1138-1193 ........................... **CMLC 38**
**Salama, Hannu** 1936- ...................... **CLC 18**
    See also CA 244; EWL 3
**Salamanca, J(ack) R(ichard)** 1922- .. **CLC 4,
  15**
    See also CA 25-28R, 193; CAAE 193
**Salas, Floyd Francis** 1931- .................. **HLC 2**
    See also CA 119; CAAS 27; CANR 44, 75,
    93; DAM MULT; DLB 82; HW 1, 2;
    MTCW 2; MTFW 2005
**Sale, J. Kirkpatrick**
    See Sale, Kirkpatrick
**Sale, John Kirkpatrick**
    See Sale, Kirkpatrick
**Sale, Kirkpatrick** 1937- ..................... **CLC 68**
    See also CA 13-16R; CANR 10, 147
**Salinas, Luis Omar** 1937- ... **CLC 90; HLC 2**
    See also AMWS 13; CA 131; CANR 81,
    153; DAM MULT; DLB 82; HW 1, 2
**Salinas (y Serrano), Pedro**
  1891(?)-1951 .................... **TCLC 17, 212**
    See also CA 117; DLB 134; EWL 3
**Salinger, J.D.** 1919- . **CLC 1, 3, 8, 12, 55, 56,
  138, 243; SSC 2, 28, 65; WLC 5**
    See also AAYA 2, 36; AMW; AMWC 1;
    BPFB 3; CA 5-8R; CANR 39, 129;
    CDALB 1941-1968; CLR 18; CN 1, 2, 3,
    4, 5, 6, 7; CPW 1; DA; DA3; DAB; DAC;
    DAM MST, NOV, POP; DLB 2, 102, 173;
    EWL 3; EXPN; LAIT 4; MAICYA 1, 2;
    MAL 5; MTCW 1, 2; MTFW 2005; NFS
    1, 30; RGAL 4; RGSF 2; SATA 67; SSFS
    17; TUS; WYA; YAW
**Salisbury, John**
    See Caute, (John) David
**Sallust** c. 86B.C.-35B.C. ................. **CMLC 68**
    See also AW 2; CDWLB 1; DLB 211;
    RGWL 2, 3
**Salter, James** 1925- ........ **CLC 7, 52, 59, 275;
  SSC 58**
    See also AMWS 9; CA 73-76; CANR 107,
    160; DLB 130; SSFS 25
**Saltus, Edgar (Everton)** 1855-1921 . **TCLC 8**
    See also CA 105; DLB 202; RGAL 4
**Saltykov, Mikhail Evgrafovich**
  1826-1889 ................................. **NCLC 16**
    See also DLB 238:
**Saltykov-Shchedrin, N.**
    See Saltykov, Mikhail Evgrafovich
**Samarakis, Andonis**
    See Samarakis, Antonis
**Samarakis, Antonis** 1919-2003 ........... **CLC 5**
    See also CA 25-28R; 224; CAAS 16; CANR
    36; EWL 3
**Samigli, E.**
    See Schmitz, Aron Hector
**Sanchez, Florencio** 1875-1910 ........ **TCLC 37**
    See also CA 153; DLB 305; EWL 3; HW 1;
    LAW
**Sanchez, Luis Rafael** 1936- ............... **CLC 23**
    See also CA 128; DLB 305; EWL 3; HW 1;
    WLIT 1
**Sanchez, Sonia** 1934- . **BLC 1:3, 2:3; CLC 5,
  116, 215; PC 9**
    See also BW 2, 3; CA 33-36R; CANR 24,
    49, 74, 115; CLR 18; CSW; CWP; DA3; DAM MULT; DLB 41;
    DLBD 8; EWL 3; MAICYA 1, 2; MAL 5;
    MTCW 1, 2; MTFW 2005; PFS 26; SATA
    22, 136; WP

**Sancho, Ignatius** 1729-1780 ................. **LC 84**
**Sand, George** 1804-1876 .... **DC 29; NCLC 2,
  42, 57, 174; WLC 5**
    See also DA; DA3; DAB; DAC; DAM
    MST, NOV; DLB 119, 192; EW 6; FL 1:3;
    FW; GFL 1789 to the Present; RGWL 2,
    3; TWA
**Sandburg, Carl (August)** 1878-1967 . **CLC 1,
  4, 10, 15, 35; PC 2, 41; WLC 5**
    See also AAYA 24; AMW; BYA 1, 3; CA
    5-8R; 25-28R; CANR 35; CDALB 1865-
    1917; CLR 67; DA; DA3; DAB; DAC;
    DAM MST, POET; DLB 17, 54, 284;
    EWL 3; EXPP; LAIT 2; MAICYA 1, 2;
    MAL 5; MTCW 1, 2; MTFW 2005; PAB;
    PFS 3, 6, 12; RGAL 4; SATA 8; TUS;
    WCH; WP; WYA
**Sandburg, Charles**
    See Sandburg, Carl (August)
**Sandburg, Charles A.**
    See Sandburg, Carl (August)
**Sanders, Ed** 1939- ............................. **CLC 53**
    See also BG 1:3; CA 13-16R; CAAS 21;
    CANR 13, 44, 78; CP 1, 2, 3, 4, 5, 6, 7;
    DAM POET; DLB 16, 244
**Sanders, Edward**
    See Sanders, Ed
**Sanders, James Edward**
    See Sanders, Ed
**Sanders, Lawrence** 1920-1998 .......... **CLC 41**
    See also BEST 89:4; BPFB 3; CA 81-84;
    165; CANR 33, 62; CMW 4; CPW; DA3;
    DAM POP; MTCW 1
**Sanders, Noah**
    See Blount, Roy, Jr.
**Sanders, Winston P.**
    See Anderson, Poul
**Sandoz, Mari(e Susette)** 1900-1966 .. **CLC 28**
    See also CA 1-4R; 25-28R; CANR 17, 64;
    DLB 9, 212; LAIT 2; MTCW 1, 2; SATA
    5; TCWW 1, 2
**Sandys, George** 1578-1644 ................... **LC 80**
    See also DLB 24, 121
**Saner, Reg(inald Anthony)** 1931- ....... **CLC 9**
    See also CA 65-68; CP 3, 4, 5, 6, 7
**Sankara** 788-820 ........................... **CMLC 32**
**Sannazaro, Jacopo** 1456(?)-1530 ........... **LC 8**
    See also RGWL 2, 3; WLIT 7
**Sansom, William** 1912-1976 . **CLC 2, 6; SSC
  21**
    See also CA 5-8R; 65-68; CANR 42; CN 1,
    2; DAM NOV; DLB 139; EWL 3; MTCW
    1; RGEL 2; RGSF 2
**Santayana, George** 1863-1952 ........ **TCLC 40**
    See also AMW; CA 115; 194; DLB 54, 71,
    246, 270; DLBD 13; EWL 3; MAL 5;
    RGAL 4; TUS
**Santiago, Danny**
    See James, Daniel (Lewis)
**Santillana, Inigo Lopez de Mendoza,
  Marques de** 1398-1458 ............... **LC 111**
    See also DLB 286
**Santmyer, Helen Hooven**
  1895-1986 ............. **CLC 33; TCLC 133**
    See also CA 1-4R; 118; CANR 15, 33;
    DLBY 1984; MTCW 1; RHW
**Santoka, Taneda** 1882-1940 ............ **TCLC 72**
**Santos, Bienvenido N(uqui)**
  1911-1996 ... **AAL; CLC 22; TCLC 156**
    See also CA 101; 151; CANR 19, 46; CP 1;
    DAM MULT; DLB 312, 348; EWL;
    RGAL 4; SSFS 19
**Santos, Miguel**
    See Mihura, Miguel
**Sapir, Edward** 1884-1939 ............. **TCLC 108**
    See also CA 211; DLB 92
**Sapper**
    See McNeile, Herman Cyril

**Sapphire** 1950- ................................... **CLC 99**
    See also CA 262
**Sapphire, Brenda**
    See Sapphire
**Sappho** fl. 6th cent. B.C.- ... **CMLC 3, 67; PC
  5**
    See also CDWLB 1; DA3; DAM POET;
    DLB 176; FL 1:1; PFS 20, 31; RGWL 2,
    3; WLIT 8; WP
**Saramago, Jose** 1922- ............. **CLC 119, 275;
  HLCS 1**
    See also CA 153; CANR 96, 164; CWW 2;
    DLB 287, 332; EWL 3; LATS 1:2; NFS
    27; SSFS 23
**Sarduy, Severo** 1937-1993 ........... **CLC 6, 97;
  HLCS 2; TCLC 167**
    See also CA 89-92; 142; CANR 58, 81;
    CWW 2; DLB 113; EWL 3; HW 1, 2;
    LAW
**Sargeson, Frank** 1903-1982 ..... **CLC 31; SSC
  99**
    See also CA 25-28R; 106; CANR 38, 79;
    CN 1, 2, 3; EWL 3; GLL 2; RGEL 2;
    RGSF 2; SSFS 20
**Sarmiento, Domingo Faustino**
  1811-1888 .............. **HLCS 2; NCLC 123**
    See also LAW; WLIT 1
**Sarmiento, Felix Ruben Garcia**
    See Dario, Ruben
**Saro-Wiwa, Ken(ule Beeson)**
  1941-1995 ............. **CLC 114; TCLC 200**
    See also BW 2; CA 142; 150; CANR 60;
    DLB 157
**Saroyan, William** 1908-1981 ... **CLC 1, 8, 10,
  29, 34, 56; DC 28; SSC 21; TCLC 137;
  WLC 5**
    See also AAYA 66; CA 5-8R; 103; CAD;
    CANR 30; CDALBS; CN 1, 2; DA; DA3;
    DAB; DAC; DAM DRAM, MST, NOV;
    DFS 17; DLB 7, 9, 86; DLBY 1981; EWL
    3; LAIT 4; MAL 5; MTCW 1, 2; MTFW
    2005; RGAL 4; RGSF 2; SATA 23; SATA-
    Obit 24; SSFS 14; TUS
**Sarraute, Nathalie** 1900-1999 .... **CLC 1, 2, 4,
  8, 10, 31, 80; TCLC 145**
    See also BPFB 3; CA 9-12R; 187; CANR
    23, 66, 134; CWW 2; DLB 83; 321; EW
    12; EWL 3; GFL 1789 to the Present;
    MTCW 1, 2; MTFW 2005; RGWL 2, 3
**Sarton, May** 1912-1995 ... **CLC 4, 14, 49, 91;
  PC 39; TCLC 120**
    See also AMWS 8; CA 1-4R; 149; CANR
    1, 34, 55, 116; CN 1, 2, 3, 4, 5, 6; CP 1,
    2, 3, 4, 5, 6; DAM POET; DLB 48; DLBY
    1981; EWL 3; FW; INT CANR-34; MAL
    5; MTCW 1, 2; MTFW 2005; RGAL 4;
    SATA 36; SATA-Obit 86; TUS
**Sartre, Jean-Paul** 1905-1980 . **CLC 1, 4, 7, 9,
  13, 18, 24, 44, 50, 52; DC 3; SSC 32;
  WLC 5**
    See also AAYA 62; CA 9-12R; 97-100;
    CANR 21; DA; DA3; DAB; DAC; DAM
    DRAM, MST, NOV; DFS 5, 26; DLB 72,
    296, 321, 332; EW 12; EWL 3; GFL 1789
    to the Present; LMFS 2; MTCW 1, 2;
    MTFW 2005; NFS 21; RGHL; RGSF 2;
    RGWL 2, 3; SSFS 9; TWA
**Sassoon, Siegfried (Lorraine)**
  1886-1967 ............. **CLC 36, 130; PC 12**
    See also BRW 6; CA 104; 25-28R; CANR
    36; DAB; DAM MST, NOV, POET; DLB
    20, 191; DLBD 18; EWL 3; MTCW 1, 2;
    MTFW 2005; PAB; PFS 28; RGEL 2;
    TEA
**Satterfield, Charles**
    See Pohl, Frederik
**Satyremont**
    See Peret, Benjamin
**Saul, John III**
    See Saul, John

**Sholokhov, Mikhail (Aleksandrovich)**
1905-1984 .............................. **CLC 7, 15**
See also CA 101; 112; DLB 272, 332; EWL
3; MTCW 1, 2; MTFW 2005; RGWL 2,
3; SATA-Obit 36

**Sholom Aleichem** 1859-1916
See Rabinovitch, Sholem

**Shone, Patric**
See Hanley, James

**Showalter, Elaine** 1941- .................. **CLC 169**
See also CA 57-60; CANR 58, 106; DLB
67; FW; GLL 2

**Shreve, Susan**
See Shreve, Susan Richards

**Shreve, Susan Richards** 1939- .......... **CLC 23**
See also CA 49-52; CAAS 5; CANR 5, 38,
69, 100, 159, 199; MAICYA 1, 2; SATA
46, 95, 152; SATA-Brief 41

**Shue, Larry** 1946-1985 ..................... **CLC 52**
See also CA 145; 117; DAM DRAM; DFS
7

**Shu-Jen, Chou** 1881-1936 . **SSC 20; TCLC 3**
See also CA 104; EWL 3

**Shulman, Alix Kates** 1932- ........... **CLC 2, 10**
See also CA 29-32R; CANR 43, 199; FW;
SATA 7

**Shuster, Joe** 1914-1992 ..................... **CLC 21**
See also AAYA 50

**Shute, Nevil**
See Norway, Nevil Shute

**Shuttle, Penelope (Diane)** 1947- ......... **CLC 7**
See also CA 93-96; CANR 39, 84, 92, 108;
CP 3, 4, 5, 6, 7; CWP; DLB 14, 40

**Shvarts, Elena** 1948- ........................... **PC 50**
See also CA 147

**Sidhwa, Bapsi**
See Sidhwa, Bapsy (N.)

**Sidhwa, Bapsy (N.)** 1938- ............... **CLC 168**
See also CA 108; CANR 25, 57; CN 6, 7;
DLB 323; FW

**Sidney, Mary** 1561-1621 ............... **LC 19, 39**
See also DLB 167

**Sidney, Sir Philip** 1554-1586 ........ **LC 19, 39,
131; PC 32**
See also BRW 1; BRWR 2; CDBLB Before
1660; DA; DA3; DAB; DAC; DAM MST,
POET; DLB 167; EXPP; PAB; PFS 30;
RGEL 2; TEA; WP

**Sidney Herbert, Mary**
See Sidney, Mary

**Siegel, Jerome** 1914-1996 .................. **CLC 21**
See also AAYA 50; CA 116; 169; 151

**Siegel, Jerry**
See Siegel, Jerome

**Sienkiewicz, Henryk (Adam Alexander Pius)**
1846-1916 .................................. **TCLC 3**
See also CA 104; 134; CANR 84; DLB 332;
EWL 3; RGSF 2; RGWL 2, 3

**Sierra, Gregorio Martinez**
See Martinez Sierra, Gregorio

**Sierra, Maria de la O'LeJarraga Martinez**
See Martinez Sierra, Maria

**Sigal, Clancy** 1926- ........................... **CLC 7**
See also CA 1-4R; CANR 85, 184; CN 1,
2, 3, 4, 5, 6, 7

**Siger of Brabant** 1240(?)-1284(?) . **CMLC 69**
See also DLB 115

**Sigourney, Lydia H.**
See Sigourney, Lydia Howard
See also DLB 73, 183

**Sigourney, Lydia Howard**
1791-1865 ........................... **NCLC 21, 87**
See Sigourney, Lydia H.
See also DLB 1, 42, 239, 243

**Sigourney, Lydia Howard Huntley**
See Sigourney, Lydia Howard

**Sigourney, Lydia Huntley**
See Sigourney, Lydia Howard

**Siguenza y Gongora, Carlos de**
1645-1700 ...................... **HLCS 2; LC 8**
See also LAW

**Sigurjonsson, Johann**
See Sigurjonsson, Johann

**Sigurjonsson, Johann** 1880-1919 ... **TCLC 27**
See also CA 170; DLB 293; EWL 3

**Sikelianos, Angelos** 1884-1951 ............ **PC 29;
TCLC 39**
See also EWL 3; RGWL 2, 3

**Silkin, Jon** 1930-1997 ................ **CLC 2, 6, 43**
See also CA 5-8R; CAAS 5; CANR 89; CP
1, 2, 3, 4, 5, 6; DLB 27

**Silko, Leslie** 1948- ...... **CLC 23, 74, 114, 211;
NNAL; SSC 37, 66; WLCS**
See also AAYA 14; AMWS 4; ANW; BYA
12; CA 115; 122; CANR 45, 65, 118; CN
4, 5, 6, 7; CP 4, 5, 6, 7; CPW 1; CWP;
DA; DA3; DAC; DAM MST, MULT,
POP; DLB 143, 175, 256, 275; EWL 3;
EXPP; EXPS; LAIT 4; MAL 5; MTCW
2; MTFW 2005; NFS 4; PFS 9, 16; RGAL
4; RGSF 2; SSFS 4, 8, 10, 11; TCWW 1,
2

**Sillanpaa, Frans Eemil** 1888-1964 ... **CLC 19**
See also CA 129; 93-96; DLB 332; EWL 3;
MTCW 1

**Sillitoe, Alan** 1928- .. **CLC 1, 3, 6, 10, 19, 57,
148**
See also AITN 1; BRWS 5; CA 9-12R, 191;
CAAE 191; CAAS 2; CANR 8, 26, 55,
139; CDBLB 1960 to Present; CN 1, 2, 3,
4, 5, 6; CP 1, 2, 3, 4, 5; DLB 14, 139;
EWL 3; MTCW 1, 2; MTFW 2005; RGEL
2; RGSF 2; SATA 61

**Silone, Ignazio** 1900-1978 ................... **CLC 4**
See also CA 25-28; 81-84; CANR 34; CAP
2; DLB 264; EW 12; EWL 3; MTCW 1;
RGSF 2; RGWL 2, 3

**Silone, Ignazione**
See Silone, Ignazio

**Siluriensis, Leolinus**
See Jones, Arthur Llewellyn

**Silver, Joan Micklin** 1935- ............... **CLC 20**
See also CA 114; 121; INT CA-121

**Silver, Nicholas**
See Faust, Frederick

**Silverberg, Robert** 1935- ............. **CLC 7, 140**
See also AAYA 24; BPFB 3; BYA 7, 9; CA
1-4R, 186; CAAE 186; CAAS 3; CANR
1, 20, 36, 85, 140, 175; CLR 59; CN 6, 7;
CPW; DAM POP; DLB 8; INT CANR-
20; MAICYA 1, 2; MTCW 1, 2; MTFW
2005; SATA 13, 91; SATA-Essay 104;
SCFW 1, 2; SFW 4; SUFW 2

**Silverstein, Alvin** 1933- ..................... **CLC 17**
See also CA 49-52; CANR 2; CLR 25;
JRDA; MAICYA 1, 2; SATA 8, 69, 124

**Silverstein, Shel** 1932-1999 ................... **PC 49**
See also AAYA 40; BW 3; CA 107; 179;
CANR 47, 74, 81; CLR 5, 96; CWRI 5;
JRDA; MAICYA 1, 2; MTCW 2; MTFW
2005; SATA 33, 92; SATA-Brief 27;
SATA-Obit 116

**Silverstein, Virginia B.** 1937- ............ **CLC 17**
See also CA 49-52; CANR 2; CLR 25;
JRDA; MAICYA 1, 2; SATA 8, 69, 124

**Silverstein, Virginia Barbara Opshelor**
See Silverstein, Virginia B.

**Sim, Georges**
See Simenon, Georges (Jacques Christian)

**Simak, Clifford D(onald)** 1904-1988 . **CLC 1,
55**
See also CA 1-4R; 125; CANR 1, 35; DLB
8; MTCW 1; SATA-Obit 56; SCFW 1, 2;
SFW 4

**Simenon, Georges (Jacques Christian)**
1903-1989 ............ **CLC 1, 2, 3, 8, 18, 47**
See also BPFB 3; CA 85-88; 129; CANR
35; CMW 4; DA3; DAM POP; DLB 72;
DLBY 1989; EW 12; EWL 3; GFL 1789
to the Present; MSW; MTCW 1, 2; MTFW
2005; RGWL 2, 3

**Simic, Charles** 1938- .... **CLC 6, 9, 22, 49, 68,
130, 256; PC 69**
See also AAYA 78; AMWS 8; CA 29-32R;
CAAS 4; CANR 12, 33, 52, 61, 96, 140;
CP 2, 3, 4, 5, 6, 7; DA3; DAM POET;
DLB 105; MAL 5; MTCW 2; MTFW
2005; PFS 7; RGAL 4; WP

**Simmel, Georg** 1858-1918 ............... **TCLC 64**
See also CA 157; DLB 296

**Simmons, Charles (Paul)** 1924- ........ **CLC 57**
See also CA 89-92; INT CA-89-92

**Simmons, Dan** 1948- ......................... **CLC 44**
See also AAYA 16, 54; CA 138; CANR 53,
81, 126, 174; CPW; DAM POP; HGG;
SUFW 2

**Simmons, James (Stewart Alexander)**
1933- ........................................... **CLC 43**
See also CA 105; CAAS 21; CP 1, 2, 3, 4,
5, 6, 7; DLB 40

**Simmons, Richard**
See Simmons, Dan

**Simms, William Gilmore**
1806-1870 ................................... **NCLC 3**
See also DLB 3, 30, 59, 73, 248, 254;
RGAL 4

**Simon, Carly** 1945- ........................... **CLC 26**
See also CA 105

**Simon, Claude** 1913-2005 ... **CLC 4, 9, 15, 39**
See also CA 89-92; 241; CANR 33, 117;
CWW 2; DAM NOV; DLB 83, 332; EW
13; EWL 3; GFL 1789 to the Present;
MTCW 1

**Simon, Claude Eugene Henri**
See Simon, Claude

**Simon, Claude Henri Eugene**
See Simon, Claude

**Simon, Marvin Neil**
See Simon, Neil

**Simon, Myles**
See Follett, Ken

**Simon, Neil** 1927- ....... **CLC 6, 11, 31, 39, 70,
233; DC 14**
See also AAYA 32; AITN 1; AMWS 4; CA
21-24R; CAD; CANR 26, 54, 87, 126;
CD 5, 6; DA3; DAM DRAM; DFS 2, 6,
12, 18,, 24; DLB 7, 266; LAIT 4; MAL 5;
MTCW 1, 2; MTFW 2005; RGAL 4; TUS

**Simon, Paul** 1941(?)- ........................ **CLC 17**
See also CA 116; 153; CANR 152

**Simon, Paul Frederick**
See Simon, Paul

**Simonon, Paul** 1956(?)- ..................... **CLC 30**

**Simonson, Rick CLC 70**

**Simpson, Harriette**
See Arnow, Harriette (Louisa) Simpson

**Simpson, Louis** 1923- ... **CLC 4, 7, 9, 32, 149**
See also AMWS 9; CA 1-4R; CAAS 4;
CANR 1, 61, 140; CP 1, 2, 3, 4, 5, 6, 7;
DAM POET; DLB 5; MAL 5; MTCW 1,
2; MTFW 2005; PFS 7, 11, 14; RGAL 4

**Simpson, Mona** 1957- ................. **CLC 44, 146**
See also CA 122; 135; CANR 68, 103; CN
6, 7; EWL 3

**Simpson, Mona Elizabeth**
See Simpson, Mona

**Simpson, N(orman) F(rederick)**
1919- ........................................... **CLC 29**
See also CA 13-16R; CBD; DLB 13; RGEL
2

**Smith, William Jay** 1918- ................... **CLC 6**
    See also AMWS 13; CA 5-8R; CANR 44,
    106; CP 1, 2, 3, 4, 5, 6, 7; CSW; CWRI
    5; DLB 5; MAICYA 1, 2; SAAS 22;
    SATA 2, 68, 154; SATA-Essay 154; TCLE
    1:2

**Smith, Woodrow Wilson**
    See Kuttner, Henry

**Smith, Zadie** 1975- ......................... **CLC 158**
    See also AAYA 50; CA 193; DLB 347;
    MTFW 2005

**Smolenskin, Peretz** 1842-1885 ....... **NCLC 30**

**Smollett, Tobias (George)** 1721-1771 ... **LC 2,
    46**
    See also BRW 3; CDBLB 1660-1789; DLB
    39, 104; RGEL 2; TEA

**Snodgrass, Quentin Curtius**
    See Twain, Mark

**Snodgrass, Thomas Jefferson**
    See Twain, Mark

**Snodgrass, W. D.** 1926-2009 .... **CLC 2, 6, 10,
    18, 68; PC 74**
    See also AMWS 6; CA 1-4R; 282; CANR
    6, 36, 65, 85, 185; CP 1, 2, 3, 4, 5, 6, 7;
    DAM POET; DLB 5; MAL 5; MTCW 1,
    2; MTFW 2005; PFS 29; RGAL 4; TCLE
    1:2

**Snodgrass, W. de Witt**
    See Snodgrass, W. D.

**Snodgrass, William de Witt**
    See Snodgrass, W. D.

**Snodgrass, William De Witt**
    See Snodgrass, W. D.

**Snorri Sturluson** 1179-1241 ......... **CMLC 56**
    See also RGWL 2, 3

**Snow, C(harles) P(ercy)** 1905-1980 ... **CLC 1,
    4, 6, 9, 13, 19**
    See also BRW 7; CA 5-8R; 101; CANR 28;
    CDBLB 1945-1960; CN 1, 2; DAM NOV;
    DLB 15, 77; DLBD 17; EWL 3; MTCW
    1, 2; MTFW 2005; RGEL 2; TEA

**Snow, Frances Compton**
    See Adams, Henry

**Snyder, Gary** 1930- . **CLC 1, 2, 5, 9, 32, 120;
    PC 21**
    See also AAYA 72; AMWS 8; ANW; BG
    1:3; CA 17-20R; CANR 30, 60, 125; CP
    1, 2, 3, 4, 5, 6, 7; DAM POET; DLB
    5, 16, 165, 212, 237, 275, 342; EWL 3;
    MAL 5; MTCW 2; MTFW 2005; PFS 9,
    19; RGAL 4; WP

**Snyder, Zilpha Keatley** 1927- .......... **CLC 17**
    See also AAYA 15; BYA 1; CA 9-12R, 252;
    CAAE 252; CANR 38; CLR 31, 121;
    JRDA; MAICYA 1, 2; SAAS 2; SATA 1,
    28, 75, 110, 163; SATA-Essay 112, 163;
    YAW

**Soares, Bernardo**
    See Pessoa, Fernando

**Sobh, A.**
    See Shamlu, Ahmad

**Sobh, Alef**
    See Shamlu, Ahmad

**Sobol, Joshua** 1939- ......................... **CLC 60**
    See also CA 200; CWW 2; RGHL

**Sobol, Yehoshua** 1939-
    See Sobol, Joshua

**Socrates** 470B.C.-399B.C. .............. **CMLC 27**

**Soderberg, Hjalmar** 1869-1941 ...... **TCLC 39**
    See also DLB 259; EWL 3; RGSF 2

**Soderbergh, Steven** 1963- .............. **CLC 154**
    See also AAYA 43; CA 243

**Soderbergh, Steven Andrew**
    See Soderbergh, Steven

**Sodergran, Edith** 1892-1923 .......... **TCLC 31**
    See also CA 202; DLB 259; EW 11; EWL
    3; RGWL 2, 3

**Soedergran, Edith Irene**
    See Sodergran, Edith

**Softly, Edgar**
    See Lovecraft, H. P.

**Softly, Edward**
    See Lovecraft, H. P.

**Sokolov, Alexander V.** 1943- ............. **CLC 59**
    See also CA 73-76; CWW 2; DLB 285;
    EWL 3; RGWL 2, 3

**Sokolov, Alexander Vsevolodovich**
    See Sokolov, Alexander V.

**Sokolov, Raymond** 1941- ..................... **CLC 7**
    See also CA 85-88

**Sokolov, Sasha**
    See Sokolov, Alexander V.

**Solo, Jay**
    See Ellison, Harlan

**Sologub, Fedor**
    See Teternikov, Fyodor Kuzmich

**Sologub, Feodor**
    See Teternikov, Fyodor Kuzmich

**Sologub, Fyodor**
    See Teternikov, Fyodor Kuzmich

**Solomons, Ikey Esquir**
    See Thackeray, William Makepeace

**Solomos, Dionysios** 1798-1857 ....... **NCLC 15**

**Solwoska, Mara**
    See French, Marilyn

**Solzhenitsyn, Aleksandr** 1918-2008 ... **CLC 1,
    2, 4, 7, 9, 10, 18, 26, 34, 78, 134, 235;
    SSC 32, 105; WLC 5**
    See also AAYA 49; AITN 1; BPFB 3; CA
    69-72; CANR 40, 65, 116; CWW 2; DA;
    DA3; DAB; DAC; DAM MST, NOV;
    DLB 302, 332; EW 13; EWL 3; EXPS;
    LAIT 4; MTCW 1, 2; MTFW 2005; NFS
    6; RGSF 2; RGWL 2, 3; SSFS 9; TWA

**Solzhenitsyn, Aleksandr I.**
    See Solzhenitsyn, Aleksandr

**Solzhenitsyn, Aleksandr Isayevich**
    See Solzhenitsyn, Aleksandr

**Somers, Jane**
    See Lessing, Doris

**Somerville, Edith Oenone**
    1858-1949 ................. **SSC 56; TCLC 51**
    See also CA 196; DLB 135; RGEL 2; RGSF
    2

**Somerville & Ross**
    See Martin, Violet Florence; Somerville,
    Edith Oenone

**Sommer, Scott** 1951- ......................... **CLC 25**
    See also CA 106

**Sommers, Christina Hoff** 1950- ...... **CLC 197**
    See also CA 153; CANR 95

**Sondheim, Stephen** 1930- .. **CLC 30, 39, 147;
    DC 22**
    See also AAYA 11, 66; CA 103; CANR 47,
    67, 125; DAM DRAM; DFS 25; LAIT 4

**Sondheim, Stephen Joshua**
    See Sondheim, Stephen

**Sone, Monica** 1919- ............................... **AAL**
    See also DLB 312

**Song, Cathy** 1955- ..................... **AAL; PC 21**
    See also CA 154; CANR 118; CWP; DLB
    169, 312; EXPP; FW; PFS 5

**Sontag, Susan** 1933-2004 ... **CLC 1, 2, 10, 13,
    31, 105, 195, 277**
    See also AMWS 3; CA 17-20R; 234; CANR
    25, 51, 74, 97, 184; CN 1, 2, 3, 4, 5, 6, 7;
    CPW; DA3; DAM POP; DLB 2, 67; EWL
    3; MAL 5; MBL; MTCW 1, 2; MTFW
    2005; RGAL 4; RHW; SSFS 10

**Sophocles** 496(?)B.C.-406(?)B.C. .... **CMLC 2,
    47, 51, 86; DC 1; WLCS**
    See also AW 1; CDWLB 1; DA; DA3;
    DAB; DAC; DAM DRAM, MST; DFS 1,
    4, 8, 24; DLB 176; LAIT 1; LATS 1:1;
    LMFS 1; RGWL 2, 3; TWA; WLIT 8

**Sordello** 1189-1269 ......................... **CMLC 15**

**Sorel, Georges** 1847-1922 ............... **TCLC 91**
    See also CA 118; 188

**Sorel, Julia**
    See Drexler, Rosalyn

**Sorokin, Vladimir** **CLC 59**
    See also CA 258; DLB 285

**Sorokin, Vladimir Georgievich**
    See Sorokin, Vladimir

**Sorrentino, Gilbert** 1929-2006 ....... **CLC 3, 7,
    14, 22, 40, 247**
    See also CA 77-80; 250; CANR 14, 33, 115,
    157; CN 3, 4, 5, 6, 7; CP 1, 2, 3, 4, 5, 6,
    7; DLB 5, 173; DLBY 1980; INT
    CANR-14

**Soseki**
    See Natsume, Soseki

**Soto, Gary** 1952- ... **CLC 32, 80; HLC 2; PC
    28**
    See also AAYA 10, 37; BYA 11; CA 119;
    125; CANR 50, 74, 107, 157; CLR 38;
    CP 4, 5, 6, 7; DAM MULT; DFS 26; DLB
    82; EWL 3; EXPP; HW 1, 2; INT CA-
    125; JRDA; LLW; MAICYA 2; MAIC-
    YAS 1; MAL 5; MTCW 2; MTFW 2005;
    PFS 7, 30; RGAL 4; SATA 80, 120, 174;
    WYA; YAW

**Soupault, Philippe** 1897-1990 ........... **CLC 68**
    See also CA 116; 147; 131; EWL 3; GFL
    1789 to the Present; LMFS 2

**Souster, (Holmes) Raymond** 1921- .... **CLC 5,
    14**
    See also CA 13-16R; CAAS 14; CANR 13,
    29, 53; CP 1, 2, 3, 4, 5, 6, 7; DA3; DAC;
    DAM POET; DLB 88; RGEL 2; SATA 63

**Southern, Terry** 1924(?)-1995 ............. **CLC 7**
    See also AMWS 11; BPFB 3; CA 1-4R;
    150; CANR 1, 55, 107; CN 1, 2, 3, 4, 5,
    6; DLB 2; IDFW 3, 4

**Southerne, Thomas** 1660-1746 ........... **LC 99**
    See also DLB 80; RGEL 2

**Southey, Robert** 1774-1843 ........ **NCLC 8, 97**
    See also BRW 4; DLB 93, 107, 142; RGEL
    2; SATA 54

**Southwell, Robert** 1561(?)-1595 ........ **LC 108**
    See also DLB 167; RGEL 2; TEA

**Southworth, Emma Dorothy Eliza Nevitte**
    1819-1899 ................................. **NCLC 26**
    See also DLB 239

**Souza, Ernest**
    See Scott, Evelyn

**Soyinka, Wole** 1934- .. **BLC 1:3, 2:3; CLC 3,
    5, 14, 36, 44, 179; DC 2; WLC 5**
    See also AFW; BW 2, 3; CA 13-16R;
    CANR 27, 39, 82, 136; CD 5, 6; CDWLB
    3; CN 6, 7; CP 1, 2, 3, 4, 5, 6 ,7; DA;
    DA3; DAB; DAC; DAM DRAM, MST,
    MULT; DFS 10, 26; DLB 125, 332; EWL
    3; MTCW 1, 2; MTFW 2005; PFS 27;
    RGEL 2; TWA; WLIT 2; WWE 1

**Spackman, W(illiam) M(ode)**
    1905-1990 ................................. **CLC 46**
    See also CA 81-84; 132

**Spacks, Barry (Bernard)** 1931- ........ **CLC 14**
    See also CA 154; CANR 33, 109; CP 3, 4,
    5, 6, 7; DLB 105

**Spanidou, Irini** 1946- ........................ **CLC 44**
    See also CA 185; CANR 179

**Spark, Muriel** 1918-2006 ....... **CLC 2, 3, 5, 8,
    13, 18, 40, 94, 242; PC 72; SSC 10, 115**
    See also BRWS 1; CA 5-8R; 251; CANR
    12, 36, 76, 89, 131; CDBLB 1945-1960;
    CN 1, 2, 3, 4, 5, 6, 7; CP 1, 2, 3, 4, 5, 6,
    7; DA3; DAB; DAC; DAM MST, NOV;
    DLB 15, 139; EWL 3; FW; INT CANR-
    12; LAIT 4; MTCW 1, 2; MTFW 2005;
    NFS 22; RGEL 2; TEA; WLIT 4; YAW

**Spark, Muriel Sarah**
    See Spark, Muriel

**Spaulding, Douglas**
    See Bradbury, Ray

**Thoreau, Henry David** 1817-1862 .. **NCLC 7, 21, 61, 138, 207; PC 30; WLC 6**
See also AAYA 42; AMW; ANW; BYA 3; CDALB 1640-1865; DA; DA3; DAB; DAC; DAM MST; DLB 1, 183, 223, 270, 298; LAIT 2; LMFS 1; NCFS 3; RGAL 4; TUS

**Thorndike, E. L.**
See Thorndike, Edward L(ee)

**Thorndike, Edward L(ee)**
1874-1949 ............................ **TCLC 107**
See also CA 121

**Thornton, Hall**
See Silverberg, Robert

**Thorpe, Adam** 1956- ........................ **CLC 176**
See also CA 129; CANR 92, 160; DLB 231

**Thorpe, Thomas Bangs**
1815-1878 ............................. **NCLC 183**
See also DLB 3, 11, 248; RGAL 4

**Thubron, Colin** 1939- ...................... **CLC 163**
See also CA 25-28R; CANR 12, 29, 59, 95, 171; CN 5, 6, 7; DLB 204, 231

**Thubron, Colin Gerald Dryden**
See Thubron, Colin

**Thucydides** c. 455B.C.-c.
399B.C. ........................... **CMLC 17, 117**
See also AW 1; DLB 176; RGWL 2, 3; WLIT 8

**Thumboo, Edwin Nadason** 1933- ........ **PC 30**
See also CA 194; CP 1

**Thurber, James (Grover)**
1894-1961 .. **CLC 5, 11, 25, 125; SSC 1, 47**
See also AAYA 56; AMWS 1; BPFB 3; BYA 5; CA 73-76; CANR 17, 39; CDALB 1929-1941; CWRI 5; DA; DA3; DAB; DAC; DAM DRAM, MST, NOV; DLB 4, 11, 22, 102; EWL 3; EXPS; FANT; LAIT 3; MAICYA 1, 2; MAL 5; MTCW 1, 2; MTFW 2005; RGAL 4; RGSF 2; SATA 13; SSFS 1, 10, 19; SUFW; TUS

**Thurman, Wallace (Henry)**
1902-1934 .. **BLC 1:3; HR 1:3; TCLC 6**
See also BW 1, 3; CA 104; 124; CANR 81; DAM MULT; DLB 51

**Tibullus** c. 54B.C.-c. 18B.C. .......... **CMLC 36**
See also AW 2; DLB 211; RGWL 2, 3; WLIT 8

**Ticheburn, Cheviot**
See Ainsworth, William Harrison

**Tieck, (Johann) Ludwig**
1773-1853 ..... **NCLC 5, 46; SSC 31, 100**
See also CDWLB 2; DLB 90; EW 5; IDTP; RGSF 2; RGWL 2, 3; SUFW

**Tiger, Derry**
See Ellison, Harlan

**Tilghman, Christopher** 1946- .......... **CLC 65**
See also CA 159; CANR 135, 151; CSW; DLB 244

**Tillich, Paul (Johannes)**
1886-1965 ............................. **CLC 131**
See also CA 5-8R; 25-28R; CANR 33; MTCW 1, 2

**Tillinghast, Richard (Williford)**
1940- .......................................... **CLC 29**
See also CA 29-32R; CAAS 23; CANR 26, 51, 96; CP 2, 3, 4, 5, 6, 7; CSW

**Tillman, Lynne** (?)- ......................... **CLC 231**
See also CA 173; CANR 144, 172

**Timrod, Henry** 1828-1867 .............. **NCLC 25**
See also DLB 3, 248; RGAL 4

**Tindall, Gillian (Elizabeth)** 1938- ...... **CLC 7**
See also CA 21-24R; CANR 11, 65, 107; CN 1, 2, 3, 4, 5, 6, 7

**Ting Ling**
See Chiang, Pin-chin

**Tiptree, James, Jr.**
See Sheldon, Alice Hastings Bradley

**Tirone Smith, Mary-Ann** 1944- ........ **CLC 39**
See also CA 118; 136; CANR 113; SATA 143

**Tirso de Molina** 1580(?)-1648 ............ **DC 13; HLCS 2; LC 73**
See also RGWL 2, 3

**Titmarsh, Michael Angelo**
See Thackeray, William Makepeace

**Tocqueville, Alexis (Charles Henri Maurice Clerel Comte) de** 1805-1859 .. **NCLC 7, 63**
See also EW 6; GFL 1789 to the Present; TWA

**Toe, Tucker**
See Westlake, Donald E.

**Toer, Pramoedya Ananta**
1925-2006 ............................... **CLC 186**
See also CA 197; 251; CANR 170; DLB 348; RGWL 3

**Toffler, Alvin** 1928- ........................ **CLC 168**
See also CA 13-16R; CANR 15, 46, 67, 183; CPW; DAM POP; MTCW 1, 2

**Toibin, Colm** 1955- ......................... **CLC 162**
See also CA 142; CANR 81, 149; CN 7; DLB 271

**Tolkien, John Ronald Reuel**
See Tolkien, J.R.R

**Tolkien, J.R.R** 1892-1973 ...... **CLC 1, 2, 3, 8, 12, 38; TCLC 137; WLC 6**
See also AAYA 10; AITN 1; BPFB 3; BRWC 2; BRWS 2; CA 17-18; 45-48; CANR 36, 134; CAP 2; CDBLB 1914-1945; CLR 56; CN 1; CPW 1; CWRI 5; DA; DA3; DAB; DAC; DAM MST, NOV, POP; DLB 15, 160, 255; EFS 2; EWL 3; FANT; JRDA; LAIT 1; LATS 1:2; LMFS 2; MAICYA 1, 2; MTCW 1, 2; MTFW 2005; NFS 8, 26; RGEL 2; SATA 2, 32, 100; SATA-Obit 24; SFW 4; SUFW; TEA; WCH; WYA; YAW

**Toller, Ernst** 1893-1939 ................... **TCLC 10**
See also CA 107; 186; DLB 124; EWL 3; RGWL 2, 3

**Tolson, M. B.**
See Tolson, Melvin B(eaunorus)

**Tolson, Melvin B(eaunorus)**
1898(?)-1966 .... **BLC 1:3; CLC 36, 105; PC 88**
See also AFAW 1, 2; BW 1, 3; CA 124; 89-92; CANR 80; DAM MULT, POET; DLB 48, 76; MAL 5; RGAL 4

**Tolstoi, Aleksei Nikolaevich**
See Tolstoy, Alexey Nikolaevich

**Tolstoi, Lev**
See Tolstoy, Leo (Nikolaevich)

**Tolstoy, Aleksei Nikolaevich**
See Tolstoy, Alexey Nikolaevich

**Tolstoy, Alexey Nikolaevich**
1882-1945 ............................... **TCLC 18**
See also CA 107; 158; DLB 272; EWL 3; SFW 4

**Tolstoy, Leo (Nikolaevich)**
1828-1910 .......... **SSC 9, 30, 45, 54, 131; TCLC 4, 11, 17, 28, 44, 79, 173; WLC 6**
See also AAYA 56; CA 104; 123; DA; DA3; DAB; DAC; DAM MST, NOV; DLB 238; EFS 2; EW 7; EXPS; IDTP; LAIT 2; LATS 1:1; LMFS 1; NFS 10, 28; RGSF 2; RGWL 2, 3; SATA 26; SSFS 5; TWA

**Tolstoy, Count Leo**
See Tolstoy, Leo (Nikolaevich)

**Tomalin, Claire** 1933- ..................... **CLC 166**
See also CA 89-92; CANR 52, 88, 165; DLB 155

**Tomasi di Lampedusa, Giuseppe**
1896-1957 ............................... **TCLC 13**
See also CA 111; 164; DLB 177; EW 11; EWL 3; MTCW 2; MTFW 2005; RGWL 2, 3; WLIT 7

**Tomlin, Lily** 1939(?)- ....................... **CLC 17**
See also CA 117

**Tomlin, Mary Jane**
See Tomlin, Lily

**Tomlin, Mary Jean**
See Tomlin, Lily

**Tomline, F. Latour**
See Gilbert, W(illiam) S(chwenck)

**Tomlinson, (Alfred) Charles** 1927- .... **CLC 2, 4, 6, 13, 45; PC 17**
See also CA 5-8R; CANR 33; CP 1, 2, 3, 4, 5, 6, 7; DAM POET; DLB 40; TCLE 1:2

**Tomlinson, H(enry) M(ajor)**
1873-1958 ............................... **TCLC 71**
See also CA 118; 161; DLB 36, 100, 195

**Tomlinson, Mary Jane**
See Tomlin, Lily

**Tonna, Charlotte Elizabeth**
1790-1846 ............................. **NCLC 135**
See also DLB 163

**Tonson, Jacob** fl. 1655(?)-1736 ........... **LC 86**
See also DLB 170

**Toole, John Kennedy** 1937-1969 ..... **CLC 19, 64**
See also BPFB 3; CA 104; DLBY 1981; MTCW 2; MTFW 2005

**Toomer, Eugene**
See Toomer, Jean

**Toomer, Eugene Pinchback**
See Toomer, Jean

**Toomer, Jean** 1894-1967 ... **BLC 1:3; CLC 1, 4, 13, 22; HR 1:3; PC 7; SSC 1, 45; TCLC 172; WLCS**
See also AFAW 1, 2; AMWS 3, 9; BW 1; CA 85-88; CDALB 1917-1929; DA3; DAM MULT; DLB 45, 51; EWL 3; EXPP; EXPS; LMFS 2; MAL 5; MTCW 1, 2; MTFW 2005; NFS 11; PFS 31; RGAL 4; RGSF 2; SSFS 5

**Toomer, Nathan Jean**
See Toomer, Jean

**Toomer, Nathan Pinchback**
See Toomer, Jean

**Torley, Luke**
See Blish, James

**Tornimparte, Alessandra**
See Ginzburg, Natalia

**Torre, Raoul della**
See Mencken, H. L.

**Torrence, Ridgely** 1874-1950 .......... **TCLC 97**
See also DLB 54, 249; MAL 5

**Torrey, E. Fuller** 1937- ..................... **CLC 34**
See also CA 119; CANR 71, 158

**Torrey, Edwin Fuller**
See Torrey, E. Fuller

**Torsvan, Ben Traven**
See Traven, B.

**Torsvan, Benno Traven**
See Traven, B.

**Torsvan, Berick Traven**
See Traven, B.

**Torsvan, Berwick Traven**
See Traven, B.

**Torsvan, Bruno Traven**
See Traven, B.

**Torsvan, Traven**
See Traven, B.

**Toson**
See Shimazaki, Haruki

**Tourneur, Cyril** 1575(?)-1626 ............. **LC 66**
See also BRW 2; DAM DRAM; DLB 58; RGEL 2

**Tournier, Michel** 1924- .... **CLC 6, 23, 36, 95, 249; SSC 88**
See also CA 49-52; CANR 3, 36, 74, 149; CWW 2; DLB 83; EWL 3; GFL 1789 to the Present; MTCW 1, 2; SATA 23

23, 64, 74, 186, 189, 11, 343; EXPN; EXPS; JRDA; LAIT 2; LMFS 1; MAI-CYA 1, 2; MAL 5; NCFS 4; NFS 1, 6; RGAL 4; RGSF 2; SATA 100; SFW 4; SSFS 1, 7, 16, 21, 27; SUFW; TUS; WCH; WYA; YABC 2; YAW

**Twohill, Maggie**
See Angell, Judie

**Tyler, Anne** 1941- . CLC **7, 11, 18, 28, 44, 59, 103, 205, 265**
See also AAYA 18, 60; AMWS 4; BEST 89:1; BPFB 3; BYA 12; CA 9-12R; CANR 11, 33, 53, 109, 132, 168; CDALBS; CN 1, 2, 3, 4, 5, 6, 7; CPW; CSW; DAM NOV, POP; DLB 6, 143; DLBY 1982; EWL 3; EXPN; LATS 1:2; MAL 5; MBL; MTCW 1, 2; MTFW 2005; NFS 2, 7, 10; RGAL 4; SATA 7, 90, 173; SSFS 17; TCLE 1:2; TUS; YAW

**Tyler, Royall** 1757-1826 .................... NCLC **3**
See also DLB 37; RGAL 4

**Tynan, Katharine** 1861-1931 ... TCLC **3, 217**
See also CA 104; 167; DLB 153, 240; FW

**Tyndale, William** c. 1484-1536 ......... LC **103**
See also DLB 132

**Tyutchev, Fyodor** 1803-1873 ......... NCLC **34**

**Tzara, Tristan** 1896-1963 .... CLC **47**; PC **27**; TCLC **168**
See also CA 153; 89-92; DAM POET; EWL 3; MTCW 2

**Uc de Saint Circ** c. 1190B.C.-13th cent. B.C. ...................................... CMLC **102**

**Uchida, Yoshiko** 1921-1992 .................. AAL
See also AAYA 16; BYA 2, 3; CA 13-16R; 139; CANR 6, 22, 47, 61; CDALBS; CLR 6, 56; CWRI 5; DLB 312; JRDA; MAI-CYA 1, 2; MTCW 1, 2; MTFW 2005; NFS 26; SAAS 1; SATA 1, 53; SATA-Obit 72

**Udall, Nicholas** 1504-1556 ................... LC **84**
See also DLB 62; RGEL 2

**Ueda Akinari** 1734-1809 ............... NCLC **131**

**Uhry, Alfred** 1936- ............... CLC **55**; DC **28**
See also CA 127; 133; CAD; CANR 112; CD 5, 6; CSW; DA3; DAM DRAM, POP; DFS 11, 15; INT CA-133; MTFW 2005

**Ulf, Haerved**
See Strindberg, (Johan) August

**Ulf, Harved**
See Strindberg, (Johan) August

**Ulibarri, Sabine R(eyes)**
1919-2003 ................... CLC **83**; HLCS **2**
See also CA 131; 214; CANR 81; DAM MULT; DLB 82; HW 1, 2; RGSF 2

**Ulyanov, V. I.**
See Lenin

**Ulyanov, Vladimir Ilyich**
See Lenin

**Ulyanov-Lenin**
See Lenin

**Unamuno (y Jugo), Miguel de**
1864-1936 .. HLC **2**; SSC **11, 69**; TCLC **2, 9, 148**
See also CA 104; 131; CANR 81; DAM MULT, NOV; DLB 108, 322; EW 8; EWL 3; HW 1, 2; MTCW 1, 2; MTFW 2005; RGSF 2; RGWL 2, 3; SSFS 20; TWA

**Uncle Shelby**
See Silverstein, Shel

**Undercliffe, Errol**
See Campbell, Ramsey

**Underwood, Miles**
See Glassco, John

**Undset, Sigrid** 1882-1949 ....... TCLC **3, 197**; WLC **6**
See also AAYA 77; CA 104; 129; DA; DA3; DAB; DAC; DAM MST, NOV; DLB 293, 332; EW 9; EWL 3; FW; MTCW 1, 2; MTFW 2005; RGWL 2, 3

**Ungaretti, Giuseppe** 1888-1970 ... CLC **7, 11, 15**; PC **57**; TCLC **200**
See also CA 19-20; 25-28R; CAP 2; DLB 114; EW 10; EWL 3; PFS 20; RGWL 2, 3; WLIT 7

**Unger, Douglas** 1952- .................... CLC **34**
See also CA 130; CANR 94, 155

**Unsworth, Barry** 1930- ............ CLC **76, 127**
See also BRWS 7; CA 25-28R; CANR 30, 54, 125, 171; CN 6, 7; DLB 194, 326

**Unsworth, Barry Forster**
See Unsworth, Barry

**Updike, John** 1932-2009 .... CLC **1, 2, 3, 5, 7, 9, 13, 15, 23, 34, 43, 70, 139, 214, 278**; PC **90**; SSC **13, 27, 103**; WLC **6**
See also AAYA 36; AMW; AMWC 1; AMWR 1; BPFB 3; BYA 12; CA 1-4R; 282; CABS 1; CANR 4, 33, 51, 94, 133, 197; CDALB 1968-1988; CN 1, 2, 3, 4, 5, 6, 7; CP 1, 2, 3, 4, 5, 6, 7; CPW 1; DA; DA3; DAB; DAC; DAM MST, NOV, POET, POP; DLB 2, 5, 143, 218, 227; DLBD 3; DLBY 1980, 1982, 1997; EWL 3; EXPP; HGG; MAL 5; MTCW 1, 2; MTFW 2005; NFS 12, 24; RGAL 4; RGSF 2; SSFS 3, 19; TUS

**Updike, John Hoyer**
See Updike, John

**Upshaw, Margaret Mitchell**
See Mitchell, Margaret

**Upton, Mark**
See Sanders, Lawrence

**Upward, Allen** 1863-1926 ............... TCLC **85**
See also CA 117; 187; DLB 36

**Urdang, Constance (Henriette)**
1922-1996 ................................. CLC **47**
See also CA 21-24R; CANR 9, 24; CP 1, 2, 3, 4, 5, 6; CWP

**Urfe, Honore d'** 1567(?)-1625 ............ LC **132**
See also DLB 268; GFL Beginnings to 1789; RGWL 2, 3

**Uriel, Henry**
See Faust, Frederick

**Uris, Leon** 1924-2003 .................... CLC **7, 32**
See also AITN 1, 2; BEST 89:2; BPFB 3; CA 1-4R; 217; CANR 1, 40, 65, 123; CN 1, 2, 3, 4, 5, 6; CPW 1; DA3; DAM NOV, POP; MTCW 1, 2; MTFW 2005; RGHL; SATA 49; SATA-Obit 146

**Urista, Alberto** 1947- ........... HLCS **1**; PC **34**
See also CA 45-48R; CANR 2, 32; DLB 82; HW 1; LLW

**Urista Heredia, Alberto Baltazar**
See Urista, Alberto

**Urmuz**
See Codrescu, Andrei

**Urquhart, Guy**
See McAlmon, Robert (Menzies)

**Urquhart, Jane** 1949- ............... CLC **90, 242**
See also CA 113; CANR 32, 68, 116, 157; CCA 1; DAC; DLB 334

**Usigli, Rodolfo** 1905-1979 ................ HLCS **1**
See also CA 131; DLB 305; EWL 3; HW 1; LAW

**Usk, Thomas** (?)-1388 .................... CMLC **76**
See also DLB 146

**Ustinov, Peter (Alexander)**
1921-2004 .................................... CLC **1**
See also AITN 1; CA 13-16R; 225; CANR 25, 51; CBD; CD 5, 6; DLB 13; MTCW 2

**U Tam'si, Gerald Felix Tchicaya**
See Tchicaya, Gerald Felix

**U Tam'si, Tchicaya**
See Tchicaya, Gerald Felix

**Vachss, Andrew** 1942- ...................... CLC **106**
See also CA 118, 214; CAAE 214; CANR 44, 95, 153, 197; CMW 4

**Vachss, Andrew H.**
See Vachss, Andrew

**Vachss, Andrew Henry**
See Vachss, Andrew

**Vaculik, Ludvik** 1926- ....................... CLC **7**
See also CA 53-56; CANR 72; CWW 2; DLB 232; EWL 3

**Vaihinger, Hans** 1852-1933 ............. TCLC **71**
See also CA 116; 166

**Valdez, Luis (Miguel)** 1940- ..... CLC **84**; DC **10**; HLC **2**
See also CA 101; CAD; CANR 32, 81; CD 5, 6; DAM MULT; DFS 5; DLB 122; EWL 3; HW 1; LAIT 4; LLW

**Valenzuela, Luisa** 1938- ........... CLC **31, 104**; HLCS **2**; SSC **14, 82**
See also CA 101; CANR 32, 65, 123; CD-WLB 3; CWW 2; DAM MULT; DLB 113; EWL 3; FW; HW 1, 2; LAW; RGSF 2; RGWL 3

**Valera y Alcala-Galiano, Juan**
1824-1905 ............................... TCLC **10**
See also CA 106

**Valerius Maximus** CMLC **64**
See also DLB 211

**Valery, (Ambroise) Paul (Toussaint Jules)**
1871-1945 ........... PC **9**; TCLC **4, 15, 231**
See also CA 104; 122; DA3; DAM POET; DLB 258; EW 8; EWL 3; GFL 1789 to the Present; MTCW 1, 2; MTFW 2005; RGWL 2, 3; TWA

**Valle-Inclan, Ramon (Maria) del**
1866-1936 ........... HLC **2**; TCLC **5, 228**
See also CA 106; 153; CANR 80; DAM MULT; DLB 134, 322; EW 8; EWL 3; HW 2; RGSF 2; RGWL 2, 3

**Vallejo, Antonio Buero**
See Buero Vallejo, Antonio

**Vallejo, Cesar (Abraham)**
1892-1938 .............. HLC **2**; TCLC **3, 56**
See also CA 105; 153; DAM MULT; DLB 290; EWL 3; HW 1; LAW; PFS 26; RGWL 2, 3

**Valles, Jules** 1832-1885 ................... NCLC **71**
See also DLB 123; GFL 1789 to the Present

**Vallette, Marguerite Eymery**
1860-1953 ................................. TCLC **67**
See also CA 182; DLB 123, 192; EWL 3

**Valle Y Pena, Ramon del**
See Valle-Inclan, Ramon (Maria) del

**Van Ash, Cay** 1918-1994 .................. CLC **34**
See also CA 220

**Vanbrugh, Sir John** 1664-1726 ............ LC **21**
See also BRW 2; DAM DRAM; DLB 80; IDTP; RGEL 2

**Van Campen, Karl**
See Campbell, John W(ood, Jr.)

**Vance, Gerald**
See Silverberg, Robert

**Vance, Jack** 1916- ............................ CLC **35**
See also CA 29-32R; CANR 17, 65, 154; CMW 4; DLB 8; FANT; MTCW 1; SCFW 1, 2; SFW 4; SUFW 1, 2

**Vance, John Holbrook**
See Vance, Jack

**Van Den Bogarde, Derek Jules Gaspard Ulric Niven** 1921-1999 ........... CLC **14**
See also CA 77-80; 179; DLB 14

**Vandenburgh, Jane** CLC **59**
See also CA 168

**Vanderhaeghe, Guy** 1951- ................ CLC **41**
See also BPFB 3; CA 113; CANR 72, 145; CN 7; DLB 334

**van der Post, Laurens (Jan)**
1906-1996 ................................... CLC **5**
See also AFW; CA 5-8R; 155; CANR 35; CN 1, 2, 3, 4, 5, 6; DLB 204; RGEL 2

**Violis, G.**
See Simenon, Georges (Jacques Christian)

**Viramontes, Helena Maria** 1954- .... **HLCS 2**
See also CA 159; CANR 182; DLB 122, 350; HW 2; LLW

**Virgil**
See Vergil

**Visconti, Luchino** 1906-1976 ............ **CLC 16**
See also CA 81-84; 65-68; CANR 39

**Vitry, Jacques de**
See Jacques de Vitry

**Vittorini, Elio** 1908-1966 .......... **CLC 6, 9, 14**
See also CA 133; 25-28R; DLB 264; EW 12; EWL 3; RGWL 2, 3

**Vivekananda, Swami** 1863-1902 .... **TCLC 88**

**Vives, Juan Luis** 1493-1540 ............. **LC 170**
See also DLB 318

**Vizenor, Gerald Robert** 1934- ....... **CLC 103, 263; NNAL**
See also CA 13-16R, 205; CAAE 205; CAAS 22; CANR 5, 21, 44, 67; DAM MULT; DLB 175, 227; MTCW 2; MTFW 2005; TCWW 2

**Vizinczey, Stephen** 1933- ................... **CLC 40**
See also CA 128; CCA 1; INT CA-128

**Vliet, R(ussell) G(ordon)**
1929-1984 ................................ **CLC 22**
See also CA 37-40R; 112; CANR 18; CP 2, 3

**Vogau, Boris Andreevich**
See Vogau, Boris Andreyevich

**Vogau, Boris Andreyevich**
1894-1938 ................. **SSC 48; TCLC 23**
See also CA 123; 218; DLB 272; EWL 3; RGSF 2; RGWL 2, 3

**Vogel, Paula A.** 1951- ........... **CLC 76; DC 19**
See also CA 108; CAD; CANR 119, 140; CD 5, 6; CWD; DFS 14; DLB 341; MTFW 2005; RGAL 4

**Voigt, Cynthia** 1942- .......................... **CLC 30**
See also AAYA 3, 30; BYA 1, 3, 6, 7, 8; CA 106; CANR 18, 37, 40, 94, 145; CLR 13, 48, 141; INT CANR-18; JRDA; LAIT 5; MAICYA 1, 2; MAICYAS 1; MTFW 2005; SATA 48, 79, 116, 160; SATA-Brief 33; WYA; YAW

**Voigt, Ellen Bryant** 1943- ................... **CLC 54**
See also CA 69-72; CANR 11, 29, 55, 115, 171; CP 5, 6, 7; CSW; CWP; DLB 120; PFS 23

**Voinovich, Vladimir** 1932- .. **CLC 10, 49, 147**
See also CA 81-84; CAAS 12; CANR 33, 67, 150; CWW 2; DLB 302; MTCW 1

**Voinovich, Vladimir Nikolaevich**
See Voinovich, Vladimir

**Vollmann, William T.** 1959- ...... **CLC 89, 227**
See also AMWS 17; CA 134; CANR 67, 116, 185; CN 7; CPW; DA3; DAM NOV, POP; DLB 350; MTCW 2; MTFW 2005

**Voloshinov, V. N.**
See Bakhtin, Mikhail Mikhailovich

**Voltaire** 1694-1778 .. **LC 14, 79, 110; SSC 12, 112; WLC 6**
See also BYA 13; DA; DA3; DAB; DAC; DAM DRAM, MST; DLB 314; EW 4; GFL Beginnings to 1789; LATS 1:1; LMFS 1; NFS 7; RGWL 2, 3; TWA

**von Aschendrof, Baron Ignatz**
See Ford, Ford Madox

**von Chamisso, Adelbert**
See Chamisso, Adelbert von

**von Daeniken, Erich** 1935- ............... **CLC 30**
See also AITN 1; CA 37-40R; CANR 17, 44

**von Daniken, Erich**
See von Daeniken, Erich

**von Eschenbach, Wolfram** c. 1170-c. 1220 ......................................... **CMLC 5**
See also CDWLB 2; DLB 138; EW 1; RGWL 2, 3

**von Hartmann, Eduard**
1842-1906 ................................. **TCLC 96**

**von Hayek, Friedrich August**
See Hayek, F(riedrich) A(ugust von)

**von Heidenstam, (Carl Gustaf) Verner**
See Heidenstam, (Carl Gustaf) Verner von

**von Heyse, Paul (Johann Ludwig)**
See Heyse, Paul (Johann Ludwig von)

**von Hofmannsthal, Hugo**
See Hofmannsthal, Hugo von

**von Horvath, Odon**
See von Horvath, Odon

**von Horvath, Odon**
See von Horvath, Odon

**von Horvath, Odon** 1901-1938 ....... **TCLC 45**
See also CA 118; 184, 194; DLB 85, 124; RGWL 2, 3

**von Horvath, Oedoen**
See von Horvath, Odon

**von Kleist, Heinrich**
See Kleist, Heinrich von

**Vonnegut, Kurt, Jr.**
See Vonnegut, Kurt

**Vonnegut, Kurt** 1922-2007 .... **CLC 1, 2, 3, 4, 5, 8, 12, 22, 40, 60, 111, 212, 254; SSC 8; WLC 6**
See also AAYA 6, 44; AITN 1; AMWS 2; BEST 90:4; BPFB 3; BYA 3, 14; CA 1-4R; 259; CANR 1, 25, 49, 75, 92; CDALB 1968-1988; CN 1, 2, 3, 4, 5, 6, 7; CPW 1; DA; DA3; DAB; DAC; DAM MST, NOV, POP; DLB 2, 8, 152; DLBD 3; DLBY 1980; EWL 3; EXPN; EXPS; LAIT 4; LMFS 2; MAL 5; MTCW 1, 2; MTFW 2005; NFS 3, 28; RGAL 4; SCFW; SFW 4; SSFS 5; TUS; YAW

**Von Rachen, Kurt**
See Hubbard, L. Ron

**von Sternberg, Josef**
See Sternberg, Josef von

**Vorster, Gordon** 1924- ...................... **CLC 34**
See also CA 133

**Vosce, Trudie**
See Ozick, Cynthia

**Voznesensky, Andrei (Andreievich)**
1933- ...................................... **CLC 1, 15, 57**
See also CA 89-92; CANR 37; CWW 2; DAM POET; EWL 3; MTCW 1

**Voznesensky, Andrey**
See Voznesensky, Andrei (Andreievich)

**Wace, Robert** c. 1100-c. 1175 ........ **CMLC 55**
See also DLB 146

**Waddington, Miriam** 1917-2004 ....... **CLC 28**
See also CA 21-24R; 225; CANR 12, 30; CCA 1; CP 1, 2, 3, 4, 5, 6, 7; DLB 68

**Wade, Alan**
See Vance, Jack

**Wagman, Fredrica** 1937- .................... **CLC 7**
See also CA 97-100; CANR 166; INT CA-97-100

**Wagner, Linda W.**
See Wagner-Martin, Linda (C.)

**Wagner, Linda Welshimer**
See Wagner-Martin, Linda (C.)

**Wagner, Richard** 1813-1883 ..... **NCLC 9, 119**
See also DLB 129; EW 6

**Wagner-Martin, Linda (C.)** 1936- .... **CLC 50**
See also CA 159; CANR 135

**Wagoner, David (Russell)** 1926- .... **CLC 3, 5, 15; PC 33**
See also AMWS 9; CA 1-4R; CAAS 3; CANR 2, 71; CN 1, 2, 3, 4, 5, 6, 7; CP 1, 2, 3, 4, 5, 6, 7; DLB 5, 256; SATA 14; TCWW 1, 2

**Wah, Fred(erick James)** 1939- ......... **CLC 44**
See also CA 107; 141; CP 1, 6, 7; DLB 60

**Wahloo, Per** 1926-1975 ...................... **CLC 7**
See also BPFB 3; CA 61-64; CANR 73; CMW 4; MSW

**Wahloo, Peter**
See Wahloo, Per

**Wain, John (Barrington)** 1925-1994 . **CLC 2, 11, 15, 46**
See also CA 5-8R; 145; CAAS 4; CANR 23, 54; CDBLB 1960 to Present; CN 1, 2, 3, 4, 5; CP 1, 2, 3, 4, 5; DLB 15, 27, 139, 155; EWL 3; MTCW 1, 2; MTFW 2005

**Wajda, Andrzej** 1926- .............. **CLC 16, 219**
See also CA 102

**Wakefield, Dan** 1932- ......................... **CLC 7**
See also CA 21-24R, 211; CAAE 211; CAAS 7; CN 4, 5, 6, 7

**Wakefield, Herbert Russell**
1888-1965 ................................ **TCLC 120**
See also CA 5-8R; CANR 77; HGG; SUFW

**Wakoski, Diane** 1937- ...... **CLC 2, 4, 7, 9, 11, 40; PC 15**
See also CA 13-16R, 216; CAAE 216; CAAS 1; CANR 9, 60, 106; CP 1, 2, 3, 4, 5, 6, 7; CWP; DAM POET; DLB 5; INT CANR-9; MAL 5; MTCW 2; MTFW 2005

**Wakoski-Sherbell, Diane**
See Wakoski, Diane

**Walcott, Derek** 1930- . **BLC 1:3, 2:3; CLC 2, 4, 9, 14, 25, 42, 67, 76, 160; DC 7; PC 46**
See also BW 2; CA 89-92; CANR 26, 47, 75, 80, 130; CBD; CD 5, 6; CDWLB 3; CP 1, 2, 3, 4, 5, 6, 7; DA3; DAB; DAC; DAM MST, MULT, POET; DLB 117, 332; DLBY 1981; DNFS 1; EFS 1; EWL 3; LMFS 2; MTCW 1, 2; MTFW 2005; PFS 6; RGEL 2; TWA; WWE 1

**Waldman, Anne (Lesley)** 1945- .......... **CLC 7**
See also BG 1:3; CA 37-40R; CAAS 17; CANR 34, 69, 116; CP 1, 2, 3, 4, 5, 6, 7; CWP; DLB 16

**Waldo, E. Hunter**
See Sturgeon, Theodore (Hamilton)

**Waldo, Edward Hamilton**
See Sturgeon, Theodore (Hamilton)

**Walker, Alice** 1944- .... **BLC 1:3, 2:3; CLC 5, 6, 9, 19, 27, 46, 58, 103, 167; PC 30; SSC 5; WLCS**
See also AAYA 3, 33; AFAW 1, 2; AMWS 3; BEST 89:4; BPFB 3; BW 2, 3; CA 37-40R; CANR 9, 27, 49, 66, 82, 131, 191; CDALB 1968-1988; CN 4, 5, 6, 7; CPW; CSW; DA; DA3; DAB; DAC; DAM MST, MULT, NOV, POET, POP; DLB 6, 33, 143; EWL 3; EXPN; EXPS; FL 1:6; FW; INT CANR-27; LAIT 3; MAL 5; MBL; MTCW 1, 2; MTFW 2005; NFS 5; PFS 30; RGAL 4; RGSF 2; SATA 31; SSFS 2, 11; TUS; YAW

**Walker, Alice Malsenior**
See Walker, Alice

**Walker, David Harry** 1911-1992 ...... **CLC 14**
See also CA 1-4R; 137; CANR 1; CN 1, 2; CWRI 5; SATA 8; SATA-Obit 71

**Walker, Edward Joseph** 1934-2004 .. **CLC 13**
See also CA 21-24R; 226; CANR 12, 28, 53; CP 1, 2, 3, 4, 5, 6, 7; DLB 40

**Walker, George F(rederick)** 1947- .. **CLC 44, 61**
See also CA 103; CANR 21, 43, 59; CD 5, 6; DAB; DAC; DAM MST; DLB 60

**Walker, Joseph A.** 1935-2003 ............ **CLC 19**
See also BW 1, 3; CA 89-92; CAD; CANR 26, 143; CD 5, 6; DAM DRAM, MST; DFS 12; DLB 38

Webb, Beatrice 1858-1943 ............. **TCLC 22**
See also CA 117; 162; DLB 190; FW
Webb, Beatrice Martha Potter
See Webb, Beatrice
Webb, Charles 1939- ........................ **CLC 7**
See also CA 25-28R; CANR 114, 188
Webb, Charles Richard
See Webb, Charles
Webb, Frank J. **NCLC 143**
See also DLB 50
Webb, James, Jr.
See Webb, James
Webb, James 1946- ........................... **CLC 22**
See also CA 81-84; CANR 156
Webb, James H.
See Webb, James
Webb, James Henry
See Webb, James
Webb, Mary Gladys (Meredith)
1881-1927 ................................. **TCLC 24**
See also CA 182; 123; DLB 34; FW; RGEL
2
Webb, Mrs. Sidney
See Webb, Beatrice
Webb, Phyllis 1927- .......................... **CLC 18**
See also CA 104; CANR 23; CCA 1; CP 1,
2, 3, 4, 5, 6, 7; CWP; DLB 53
Webb, Sidney 1859-1947 ................. **TCLC 22**
See also CA 117; 163; DLB 190
Webb, Sidney James
See Webb, Sidney
Webber, Andrew Lloyd
See Lloyd Webber, Andrew
Weber, Lenora Mattingly
1895-1971 ................................. **CLC 12**
See also CA 19-20; 29-32R; CAP 1; SATA
2; SATA-Obit 26
Weber, Max 1864-1920 ................... **TCLC 69**
See also CA 109; 189; DLB 296
Webster, John 1580(?)-1634(?) ...... **DC 2; LC
33, 84, 124; WLC 6**
See also BRW 2; CDBLB Before 1660; DA;
DAB; DAC; DAM DRAM, MST; DFS
17, 19; DLB 58; IDTP; RGEL 2; WLIT 3
Webster, Noah 1758-1843 ............... **NCLC 30**
See also DLB 1, 37, 42, 43, 73, 243
Wedekind, Benjamin Franklin
See Wedekind, Frank
Wedekind, Frank 1864-1918 ............ **TCLC 7**
See also CA 104; 153; CANR 121, 122;
CDWLB 2; DAM DRAM; DLB 118; EW
8; EWL 3; LMFS 2; RGWL 2, 3
Wehr, Demaris **CLC 65**
Weidman, Jerome 1913-1998 ............ **CLC 7**
See also AITN 2; CA 1-4R; 171; CAD;
CANR 1; CD 1, 2, 3, 4, 5; DLB 28
Weil, Simone (Adolphine)
1909-1943 ................................. **TCLC 23**
See also CA 117; 159; EW 12; EWL 3; FW;
GFL 1789 to the Present; MTCW 2
Weininger, Otto 1880-1903 ............. **TCLC 84**
Weinstein, Nathan
See West, Nathanael
Weinstein, Nathan von Wallenstein
See West, Nathanael
Weir, Peter (Lindsay) 1944- .............. **CLC 20**
See also CA 113; 123
Weiss, Peter (Ulrich) 1916-1982 .. **CLC 3, 15,
51; DC 36; TCLC 152**
See also CA 45-48; 106; CANR 3; DAM
DRAM; DFS 3; DLB 69, 124; EWL 3;
RGHL; RGWL 2, 3
Weiss, Theodore (Russell)
1916-2003 ................................. **CLC 3, 8, 14**
See also CA 9-12R; 189; 216; CAAE 189;
CAAS 2; CANR 46, 94; CP 1, 2, 3, 4, 5,
6, 7; DLB 5; TCLE 1:2

Welch, (Maurice) Denton
1915-1948 ................................. **TCLC 22**
See also BRWS 8; CA 121; 148; RGEL 2
Welch, James (Phillip) 1940-2003 ..... **CLC 6,
14, 52, 249; NNAL; PC 62**
See also CA 85-88; 219; CANR 42, 66, 107;
CN 5, 6, 7; CP 2, 3, 4, 5, 6, 7; CPW;
DAM MULT, POP; DLB 175, 256; LATS
1:1; NFS 23; RGAL 4; TCWW 1, 2
Weldon, Fay 1931- . **CLC 6, 9, 11, 19, 36, 59,
122**
See also BRWS 4; CA 21-24R; CANR 16,
46, 63, 97, 137; CDBLB 1960 to Present;
CN 3, 4, 5, 6, 7; CPW; DAM POP; DLB
14, 194, 319; EWL 3; FW; HGG; INT
CANR-16; MTCW 1, 2; MTFW 2005;
RGEL 2; RGSF 2
Wellek, Rene 1903-1995 .................... **CLC 28**
See also CA 5-8R; 150; CAAS 7; CANR 8;
DLB 63; EWL 3; INT CANR-8
Weller, Michael 1942- .................... **CLC 10, 53**
See also CA 85-88; CAD; CD 5, 6
Weller, Paul 1958- ............................. **CLC 26**
Wellershoff, Dieter 1925- ................... **CLC 46**
See also CA 89-92; CANR 16, 37
Welles, (George) Orson 1915-1985 .. **CLC 20,
80**
See also AAYA 40; CA 93-96; 117
Wellman, John McDowell 1945- ...... **CLC 65**
See also CA 166; CAD; CD 5, 6; RGAL 4
Wellman, Mac
See Wellman, John McDowell; Wellman,
John McDowell
Wellman, Manly Wade 1903-1986 ... **CLC 49**
See also CA 1-4R; 118; CANR 6, 16, 44;
FANT; SATA 6; SATA-Obit 47; SFW 4;
SUFW
Wells, Carolyn 1869(?)-1942 .......... **TCLC 35**
See also CA 113; 185; CMW 4; DLB 11
Wells, H(erbert) G(eorge) 1866-1946 . **SSC 6,
70; TCLC 6, 12, 19, 133; WLC 6**
See also AAYA 18; BPFB 3; BRW 6; CA
110; 121; CDBLB 1914-1945; CLR 64,
133; DA; DA3; DAB; DAC; DAM MST,
NOV; DLB 34, 70, 156, 178; EWL 3;
EXPS; HGG; LAIT 3; LMFS 2; MTCW
1, 2; MTFW 2005; NFS 17, 20; RGEL 2;
RGSF 2; SATA 20; SCFW 1, 2; SFW 4;
SSFS 3; SUFW; TEA; WCH; WLIT 4;
YAW
Wells, Rosemary 1943- ...................... **CLC 12**
See also AAYA 13; BYA 7, 8; CA 85-88;
CANR 48, 120, 179; CLR 16, 69; CWRI
5; MAICYA 1, 2; SAAS 1; SATA 18, 69,
114, 156; YAW
Wells-Barnett, Ida B(ell)
1862-1931 ................................. **TCLC 125**
See also CA 182; DLB 23, 221
Welsh, Irvine 1958- .................... **CLC 144, 276**
See also CA 173; CANR 146, 196; CN 7;
DLB 271
Welty, Eudora 1909-2001 .... **CLC 1, 2, 5, 14,
22, 33, 105, 220; SSC 1, 27, 51, 111;
WLC 6**
See also AAYA 48; AMW; AMWR 1; BPFB
3; CA 9-12R; 199; CABS 1; CANR 32,
65, 128; CDALB 1941-1968; CN 1, 2, 3,
4, 5, 6, 7; CSW; DA; DA3; DAB; DAC;
DAM MST, NOV; DFS 26; DLB 2, 102,
143; DLBD 12; DLBY 1987, 2001; EWL
3; EXPS; HGG; LAIT 3; MAL 5; MBL;
MTCW 1, 2; MTFW 2005; NFS 13, 15;
RGAL 4; RGSF 2; RHW; SSFS 2, 10, 26;
TUS
Welty, Eudora Alice
See Welty, Eudora
Wen I-to 1899-1946 ........................ **TCLC 28**
See also EWL 3
Wentworth, Robert
See Hamilton, Edmond

Werewere Liking 1950- .................... **BLC 2:2**
See also EWL 3
Werfel, Franz (Viktor) 1890-1945 .... **PC 101;
TCLC 8**
See also CA 104; 161; DLB 81, 124; EWL
3; RGWL 2, 3
Wergeland, Henrik Arnold
1808-1845 ................................. **NCLC 5**
See also DLB 354
Werner, Friedrich Ludwig Zacharias
1768-1823 ................................. **NCLC 189**
See also DLB 94
Werner, Zacharias
See Werner, Friedrich Ludwig Zacharias
Wersba, Barbara 1932- ...................... **CLC 30**
See also AAYA 2, 30; BYA 6, 12, 13; CA
29-32R, 182; CAAE 182; CANR 16, 38;
CLR 3, 78; DLB 52; JRDA; MAICYA 1,
2; SAAS 2; SATA 1, 58; SATA-Essay 103;
WYA; YAW
Wertmueller, Lina 1928- ................... **CLC 16**
See also CA 97-100; CANR 39, 78
Wescott, Glenway 1901-1987 .. **CLC 13; SSC
35**
See also CA 13-16R; 121; CANR 23, 70;
CN 1, 2, 3, 4; DLB 4, 9, 102; MAL 5;
RGAL 4
Wesker, Arnold 1932- ................ **CLC 3, 5, 42**
See also CA 1-4R; CAAS 7; CANR 1, 33;
CBD; CD 5, 6; CDBLB 1960 to Present;
DAB; DAM DRAM; DLB 13, 310, 319;
EWL 3; MTCW 1; RGEL 2; TEA
Wesley, Charles 1707-1788 ................ **LC 128**
See also DLB 95; RGEL 2
Wesley, John 1703-1791 ...................... **LC 88**
See also DLB 104
Wesley, Richard (Errol) 1945- ............ **CLC 7**
See also BW 1; CA 57-60; CAD; CANR
27; CD 5, 6; DLB 38
Wessel, Johan Herman 1742-1785 ....... **LC 7**
See also DLB 300
West, Anthony (Panther)
1914-1987 ................................. **CLC 50**
See also CA 45-48; 124; CANR 3, 19; CN
1, 2, 3, 4; DLB 15
West, C. P.
See Wodehouse, P(elham) G(renville)
West, Cornel 1953- ............. **BLCS; CLC 134**
See also CA 144; CANR 91, 159; DLB 246
West, Cornel Ronald
See West, Cornel
West, Delno C(loyde), Jr. 1936- ........ **CLC 70**
See also CA 57-60
West, Dorothy 1907-1998 ...... **HR 1:3; TCLC
108**
See also AMWS 18; BW 2; CA 143; 169;
DLB 76
West, Edwin
See Westlake, Donald E.
West, (Mary) Jessamyn 1902-1984 ... **CLC 7,
17**
See also CA 9-12R; 112; CANR 27; CN 1,
2, 3; DLB 6; DLBY 1984; MTCW 1, 2;
RGAL 4; RHW; SATA-Obit 37; TCWW
2; TUS; YAW
West, Morris L(anglo) 1916-1999 ..... **CLC 6,
33**
See also BPFB 3; CA 5-8R; 187; CANR
24, 49, 64; CN 1, 2, 3, 4, 5, 6; CPW; DLB
289; MTCW 1, 2; MTFW 2005
West, Nathanael 1903-1940 ...... **SSC 16, 116;
TCLC 1, 14, 44**
See also AAYA 77; AMW; AMWR 2; BPFB
3; CA 104; 125; CDALB 1929-1941;
DA3; DLB 4, 9, 28; EWL 3; MAL 5;
MTCW 1, 2; MTFW 2005; NFS 16;
RGAL 4; TUS
West, Owen
See Koontz, Dean

# *PC* Cumulative Nationality Index

Stryk, Lucien **27**
Swenson, May **14**
Tapahonso, Luci **65**
Tate, Allen **50**
Taylor, Edward **63**
Teasdale, Sara **31**
Thoreau, Henry David **30**
Tolson, Melvin B. **88**
Toomer, Jean **7**
Tuckerman, Frederick Goddard **85**
Updike, John **90**
Urista, Alberto H. **34**
Very, Jones **86**
Viereck, Peter (Robert Edwin) **27**
Wagoner, David (Russell) **33**
Wakoski, Diane **15**
Walker, Alice (Malsenior) **30**
Walker, Margaret (Abigail) **20**
Warren, Robert Penn **37**
Welch, James **62**
Wheatley (Peters), Phillis **3**
Whitman, Walt(er) **3, 91**
Whittier, John Greenleaf **93**
Wilbur, Richard **51**
Williams, William Carlos **7**
Wright, James (Arlington) **36**
Wylie, Elinor (Morton Hoyt) **23**
Yamada, Mitsuye **44**
Yau, John **61**
Zukofsky, Louis **11**

### ARGENTINIAN

Borges, Jorge Luis **22, 32**
Storni, Alfonsina **33**

### AUSTRALIAN

Gilmore, Mary **87**
Hope, A. D. **56**
Wright, Judith (Arundell) **14**

### AUSTRIAN

Trakl, Georg **20**

### BARBADIAN

Brathwaite, Edward Kamau **56**

### CANADIAN

Atwood, Margaret (Eleanor) **8**
Birney, (Alfred) Earle **52**
Bissett, Bill **14**
Carman, (William) Bliss **34**
Carson, Anne **64**
Ondaatje, (Philip) Michael **28**
Page, P(atricia) K(athleen) **12**
Service, Robert **70**

### CHILEAN

Godoy Alcayaga, Lucila **32**
Neruda, Pablo **4, 64**
Parra, Nicanor **39**

### CHINESE

Li Ho **13**
Li Po **29**
Tu Fu **9**
Wang Wei **18**

### CUBAN

Guillén, Nicolás (Cristobal) **23**
Martí, José **76**

### CZECH

Seifert, Jaroslav **47**
Werfel, Franz **101**

### ENGLISH

Arnold, Matthew **5, 94**
Auden, W(ystan) H(ugh) **1**
Barker, George **77**
Barker, Jane **91**
Barrett Browning, Elizabeth **6, 62**
Behn, Aphra **13, 88**
Belloc, (Joseph) Hilaire (Pierre Sebastien Rene Swanton) **24**
Betjeman, John **75**
Blake, William **12, 63**
Blunden, Edmund **66**
Bradstreet, Anne **10**
Bridges, Robert (Seymour) **28**
Brontë, Emily (Jane) **8**
Brooke, Rupert (Chawner) **24**
Browning, Robert **2, 61, 97**
Butler, Samuel **94**
Byron, George Gordon (Noel) **16, 95**
Campion, Thomas **87**
Carroll, Lewis **18, 74**
Carew, Thomas **29**
Chapman, George **96**
Chaucer, Geoffrey **19, 58**
Chesterton, G(ilbert) K(eith) **28**
Clare, John **23**
Clough, Arthur Hugh **103**
Coleridge, Samuel Taylor **11, 39, 67, 100**
Collins, William **72**
Cowley, Abraham **90**
Cowper, William **40**
Crabbe, George **97**
Crashaw, Richard **84**
Davenant, William **99**
Davie, Donald (Alfred) **29**
Day Lewis, C(ecil) **11**
de La Mare, Walter **77**
Dobell, Sydney **100**
Donne, John **1, 43**
Drayton, Michael **98**
Dryden, John **25**
Duck, Stephen **89**
Eliot, George **20**
Eliot, T(homas) S(tearns) **5, 31, 90**
Elliott, Ebenezer **96**
Enright, D. J. **93**
Finch, Anne **21**
Gower, John **59**
Graves, Robert (von Ranke) **6**
Gray, Thomas **2**
Gunn, Thom(son William) **26**
Hardy, Thomas **8, 92**
Herbert, George **4**
Herrick, Robert **9**
Hood, Thomas **93**
Hopkins, Gerard Manley **15**
Housman, A(lfred) E(dward) **2, 43**
Howard, Henry (Earl of Surrey) **59**
Hughes, Ted **7, 89**
Hunt, Leigh **73**
Jonson, Ben(jamin) **17**
Keats, John **1, 96**
Kipling, (Joseph) Rudyard **3, 91**
Lanyer, Aemilia **60**
Larkin, Philip (Arthur) **21**
Lawrence, D(avid) (H)erbert **54**
Leapor, Mary **85**
Lear, Edward **65**
Levertov, Denise **11**

Lovelace, Richard **69**
Loy, Mina **16**
Marlowe, Christopher **57**
Marvell, Andrew **10, 86**
Masefield, John **78**
Meredith, George **60**
Milton, John **19, 29**
Montagu, Mary (Pierrepont) Wortley **16**
Morris, William **55**
Noyes, Alfred **27**
Owen, Wilfred (Edward Salter) **19, 102**
Page, P(atricia) K(athleen) **12**
Patmore, Coventry **59**
Peacock, Thomas Love **87**
Philips, Katherine **40**
Pope, Alexander **26**
Prior, Matthew **102**
Raleigh, Walter **31**
Rossetti, Christina (Georgina) **7**
Rossetti, Dante Gabriel **44**
Sassoon, Siegfried (Lorraine) **12**
Shakespeare, William **84, 89, 98, 101**
Shelley, Percy Bysshe **14, 67**
Sidney, Philip **32**
Sitwell, Edith **3**
Skelton, John **25**
Smart, Christopher **13**
Smith, Stevie **12**
Spender, Stephen **71**
Spenser, Edmund **8, 42**
Suckling, John **30**
Swift, Jonathan **9**
Swinburne, Algernon Charles **24**
Tennyson, Alfred **6, 101**
Thomas, (Philip) Edward **53**
Tomlinson, (Alfred) Charles **17**
Traherne, Thomas **70**
Waller, Edmund **72**
Wilmot, John (Earl of Rochester) **66**
Wordsworth, William **4, 67**
Wroth, Mary **38**
Wyatt, Thomas **27**

### FILIPINO

Villa, José García **22**

### FRENCH

Apollinaire, Guillaume **7**
Baudelaire, Charles **1**
Bonnefoy, Yves **58**
Breton, André **15**
Char, René **56**
Christine de Pizan **68**
Éluard, Paul **38**
Gautier, Théophile **18**
Hugo, Victor (Marie) **17**
Laforgue, Jules **14**
Lamartine, Alphonse (Marie Louis Prat) de **16**
Leger, (Marie-Rene Auguste) Alexis Saint-Leger **23**
Mallarmé, Stéphane **4, 102**
Marie de France **22**
Merton, Thomas **10**
Nerval, Gérard de **13**
Péret, Benjamin **33**
Rimbaud, (Jean Nicolas) Arthur **3, 57**
Ronsard, Pierre de **11**
Tzara, Tristan **27**
Valéry, (Ambroise) Paul (Toussaint Jules) **9**
Verlaine, Paul (Marie) **2, 32**
Vigny, Alfred (Victor) de **26**
Villon, François **13**

Nationality Index

ISBN-13: 978-1-4144-4758-2
ISBN-10: 1-4144-4758-2

90000